# THE DICTIONARY OF
# COMPOSERS
## AND THEIR MUSIC

# THE DICTIONARY OF
# COMPOSERS
# AND THEIR MUSIC

*A Listener's Companion*

—— ERIC GILDER——

**WINGS BOOKS**
NEW YORK

This 1993 edition is published by Wings Books,
distributed by Random House Value Publishing, Inc.,
201 East 50th Street, New York, New York 10022,

http://www.randomhouse.com/
Random House
New York • Toronto • London • Sydney • Auckland

Printed and bound in the United States of America

Library of Congress Cataloging-in-Publication Data
Gilder, Eric.
  The dictionary of composers and their music : a listener's
companion / Eric Gilder.
   p.     cm.
   Originally published: New York : Holt, Rinehart, and Winston,
1986. With new introd.
   ISBN 0-517-09295-6
   1. Music—Bibliography.  2. Music—Chronology.  I. Title.
II. Title: Composers and their music.
[ML113.G4    1993]
780'.92'2—dc20                           93-14824
                                           CIP
                                           MN

ISBN 0-517-09295-6

10  9  8  7  6  5  4

# PREFACE

To school children, history means learning the dates of kings. The real historian, however, may know the dates engraved on historic milestones, but is unlikely to remember the dates of the thousands of little incidents occurring during his journey through time; he is more interested in the scenery.

Having spent a large part of my life teaching musical appreciation and history, I know that 1685 was a good year for composers, bringing forth Bach, Handel and the younger Scarlatti; but if you asked me when Liadov wrote *Kukalki* I really could not tell you off-hand. In order to be equipped for all the questions thrown at me by students I needed to go to the lecture room carrying a dozen bulky volumes. (Grove's *Dictionary of Music and Musicians* has lengthened my left arm considerably.) What I required was certain factual ungarnished information contained snugly between the covers of one book. I combed the libraries for such a book, but could not find one; so I wrote my own, and the present volume is the result. Research of a different nature has shown that this could be of lasting value as a permanent reference work, not only to the academic student, but also to the vast numbers of interested laymen – the music-lovers, concert-goers, record collectors, and listeners.

The original intention has become Part One of this book – an alphabetical list of composers with their music arranged chronologically. To have called it 'A Complete List of Everything Ever Composed by Anybody' would have been an absurd boast; call it rather 'A List of Everything That Mattered Composed by Anyone Who Mattered'. All composers must have their jottings, tentative pieces, trifling things that have been discarded as unworthy, mere exercises. Some of these have been preserved, and may be seen in museums in the composer's own handwriting; but their contribution to the world's musical treasury is too inconsiderable to make them worthy of special mention. There are some works that composers themselves would not wish to be immortalised. Dukas, for example, who was his own severest critic, burned all his unpublished compositions when in his early forties and, although still composing, published no more.

Omissions and exceptions are therefore inevitable. One of my source-books lists *6,000 Contemporary American Composers!* My apologies for not including all of them, but I had to bear in mind the intended size of this book. Of the countless people who have written music, the 426 represented here are those whose works may be heard today in the concert hall, the opera or ballet house and the church. Many of these composers have also written incidental music and music for the theatre which is included here; but a complete list of works for the theatre could fill a large book by itself and, in general, composers who have written for that medium alone have been omitted. The lists of works are reasonably comprehensive, but the student requiring more definitive lists is recommended to the great number of much bulkier volumes.

One can suppose that the history of music truly began when our cave-dwelling mothers chose certain words in their limited language and intoned them, while our fathers were banging on hollow tree-trunks. The development of the art, bearing in mind the frailty of the human voice and the poverty of ancient instruments, was slow and seemingly casual. My contention is that the flowering of music, modern music as we know it today, has occurred in Europe only in the last 600 years. It is therefore a very young art, which explains why during our own lifetimes there have been such impressive steps forward.

Using this as a milestone, the earliest composer mentioned in this book is Guillaume de Machaut, born around 1300, and the lists go up to 1984. In later editions this could be updated. For each composer there is a short biography, then a chronological list of works. Beside each date is the composer's age, for the sake of the student who is not also a profound mathematician. As far as possible the dates given are those when the work was first conceived – there was sometimes a long gestation period before the work was finally born into the world.

It was during the compiling of Part One that the ideas for Parts Two and Three emerged, and for me these became the most fascinating sections in some respects.

Part Two is a chronological survey, enabling the reader to turn to any year from 1300 to 1984 and see exactly what music was written, which composers were born and which died. Such a historical overview can perhaps best be appreciated if one sticks a pin somewhere in the calendar.

Take the year 1847. That was the year Mendelssohn died. Spontini who had been so prolific writing operas in the classical mould, was still alive; Balakirev, Brahms, Bizet, Dvořák, Fauré, Grieg, Mussorgsky, Rimsky-Korsakov, Saint-Saëns, Sullivan and Tchaikovsky were children; Donizetti, whose operas were well rooted in tradition, still had a year to live; and in that year Verdi wrote *Macbeth* and Wagner was already working on *Lohengrin*, to be produced four years later. It was a good year for opera, contributions coming from Balfe, Dargomizhsky, Flotow and Schumann. Berwald, Meybeer and Rossini were all writing with middle-aged maturity, while the fourteen-year-old Borodin produced his Flute Concerto; Glinka, called the father of Russian music, wrote *Greeting to the Fatherland*, Berlioz was in his forties, Liszt his thirties, and Chopin was an ailing man of thirty-seven with only two years to live. Offenbach and Franck were both in their twenties and already established as powers in the musical world. Lalo, the elegant Frenchman of Spanish descent, was already writing music of Spanish flavour which was to influence Falla, Debussy and Ravel. Smetana was twenty-three and was later to establish the great nationalist school of Czech music and to conduct the Czech Opera in which Dvořák played the viola.

When Spontini was born, Boyce was still alive; when Boyce was born, Corelli was still alive; and Corelli was born a mere ten years after Monteverdi died. In this year of 1847 Spontini still had four more years to live; by the time he died, d'Indy was born, and *he* lived until 1931, by which time Boulez was very much alive. So, with the names of five men – Corelli, Boyce, Spontini, d'Indy and Boulez – who could just have met each other, we span the whole of musical composition from the glees, madrigals and motets to the music of today, a matter of something over 300 years.

Part Three is a timeline, enabling one to see at a glance which composers were contemporaries, when each was born and died. It is a visual aid to gaining a clear perspective of musical history.

Research for this book brought up copious anomalies. Standard books on the subject have often been at variance with each other in the matter of dates. This is something quite understandable. Certain modern composers, for example, were only accepted by publishers or performing or copyright organisations quite late in their composing careers, and a large collection of early works bears only the date of such acceptance. Not all manuscripts bear a date in the composer's handwriting. I am a very minor composer myself, and if I were asked the date of a certain composition I might easily say, 'Oh, about twenty years ago,' unable to be any more accurate. With the more ancient composers there was often little or no documentation at all, and in some cases we do not even know exactly when they were born. Many composers did not give their works opus numbers, and some who did appeared to be unable to count! Such catalogues as Kochel's of Mozart must be accepted as definitive; but for the rest, I have been ruled by the greatest consensus of opinion.

There has been a great variety of spellings of the names and works of Russian composers. The only accurate way to spell them, of course, is in the original Russian; any other spelling must be purely phonetic. We must almost be grateful that there are no Chinese or Japanese in our lists! This book incorporates spellings that are generally accepted in the Western world. In a similar way, the titles of works given are the titles by which they are best known, be they translated or in the original language: thus, *L'Après-midi d'un faune* and *Night on the Bare Mountain*.

Special mention must be made of the list of works by Johann Sebastian Bach, which can generally only be dated according to the years he spent in various appointments; ie during the nine years between 1708 and 1717 while at Weimar, as court organist, chamber musician and finally *Kapellmeister*, he composed most of his great organ works. Then at Cöthen, between 1717 and 1722 as *Kapellmeister* and conductor of the court orchestra, he wrote the Brandenburg Concerti, the suites for orchestra, the violin concerti and much chamber music. From 1722 until his death in 1750 he was Cantor of the Leipzig Thomasschule, and there he composed approximately 265 church cantatas as well as compositions for one of the Leipzig musical societies of which he was conductor.

# ACKNOWLEDGEMENTS

In making acknowledgements, I must mention first June G. Coombs, without whose dedicated research on my behalf and whose typing, retyping, editing and proof-reading this book might never have appeared at all. I must thank a large number of modern composers who have written to me personally with lists of their works – I have one from Shostakovitch in fractured French – and the many publishers, notably Messrs Boosey and Novello, who have been so cooperative in helping me fill the gaps. My sincere thanks, too, to Sir Adrian Boult, Sir David Willcocks and Sir Anthony Lewis, among many others, for their encouragement.

Among the many source-books were such standard works as Grove's *Dictionary of Music and Musicians*, the Oxford Histories, Scholes's *Oxford Companion to Music*, the *International Cyclopaedia of Music and Musicians*, Osborne's *Dictionary of Composers* and Anderson's *Contemporary American Composers*. The British Performing Right Society and the American ASCAP contributed much information on the contemporary scene; for the rest, the reference books in French, German and Italian, and the biographies of composers, have been too numerous for me to be able to remember all of them.

To all these, who furnished me with such great excitement over years of research, I give my grateful thanks.

*Eric Gilder*

# PART ONE

In this alphabetical listing of composers, their music is arranged in chronological order. The dates, next to which appear the composers' ages, are those when the music is first mentioned. It is not always possible to ascertain whether these dates refer to the commencement or to the completion of a piece of music. Where possible, both dates are given, as Stravinsky: *Les Noces* (1917–1923). In some cases, the first information available is a mention of a first performance, in which case the name of the work is prefaced with the letters *fp*; in others, the first information may refer to the date of publication, when the letter *p* is used. For some works, the letter *c* for *circa* prefaces the nearest approximation. *Posthumous* in the age column indicates that the work was published, or first performed, after the composer's death. When dates of some of a composer's music cannot be traced, those works are listed at the end of the entry and undated.

Collections of short works are sometimes not listed individually. Consider the five hundred chamber cantatas of Alessandro Scarlatti, or the two hundred songs of Charles Ives: to list all such music would require many volumes. Instead, in such cases, works are referred to as so many 'songs', 'piano pieces', 'cantatas', etc.

Key signatures are generally given in full, such as *Rhapsody* in C♯ minor. However, if a number of works of the same kind were written in any one year, keys are abbreviated: for example, Four string quartets in Dm: C: A: F♯m, indicating works in D minor, C major, A major and F♯ minor.

In the section for Bach, a number of works bear the suffix (*& continuo*). This indicates that the continuo is not generally used in modern performance.

A few composers, although generally considered as being of a particular nationality, were born in another country. In these instances both countries are listed: for example, USA (b Germany). In cases where the country of a composer's birth no longer exists, the modern equivalent is also included: Bohemia (Czechoslovakia).

As explained in the preface, works are given the names by which they are best known to English-speaking people.

## ABBREVIATIONS

| | |
|---|---|
| *fp* | First performance |
| *p* | Date of publication |
| SATB | Soprano, alto, tenor and bass |
| SPNM | Society for the Promotion of New Music |
| SSA | Soprano, soprano and alto |
| vv | Voices |

## ADAM, Adolphe
b Paris, 24 July 1803
d Paris, 3 May 1856, aged fifty-two

Discouraged by his father, who was a pianist, teacher and composer, Adam had to study music secretly. When he was fourteen his father relented and allowed him to enter the Paris Conservatory – on condition that he would never compose for the theatre. He studied under Boïeldieu, who persuaded him to write *opéra comique*. In 1847 he founded the Théâtre National. In 1848 he lost all his money in the Revolution, and was poor for the rest of his life. In 1849 he became professor of composition at the Paris Conservatory.

| | | |
|---|---|---|
| 1832 | (29) | *Faust*, ballet |
| 1834 | (31) | *Le Châlet*, opera |
| 1836 | (33) | *Le Postillon de Longjumeau*, opera |
| 1839 | (36) | *La Jolie fille de Gand*, ballet |
| 1841 | (38) | *Giselle*, ballet |
| 1849 | (46) | *Le Toréador*, opera |
| 1852 | (49) | *Si j'etais roi*, opera |
| 1856 | (52) | *Le Corsaire*, ballet |

Adam composed a total of thirty-nine operas, as well as many ballets, choruses, songs and much church music.


## ALBÉNIZ, Isaac
b Campródon, Gerona, Spain, 29 May 1860
d Cambo-les-Bains, France, 18 May 1909, aged forty-eight

He appeared as a pianist in Barcelona at the age of four. At seven he passed the entrance examination for piano at the Paris Conservatory, but was refused admission because of unruly behaviour. He went to the Madrid Conservatory, but ran away, becoming a vagabond, and making a living by playing. By the age of fifteen he had given concerts around the world. He studied with Liszt, d'Indy and Dukas, but could never accept musical discipline; Fauré, with whom he associated when he went to live in Paris in 1893, most helped his development. An English banker paid him well to turn his verse-dramas into operas; but fundamentally he was a composer for piano, though some of his works are extremely difficult to play.

| | | |
|---|---|---|
| 1886 | (26) | *Recuerdof de Viaje*, for piano |
| | | *Torre Bermeja*, for piano |
| 1887 | (27) | Piano Concerto |
| | | *Rhapsodia Española*, for orchestra |
| 1889 | (29) | *Suite Española*, for piano |
| 1893 | (33) | *The Magic Opal*, opera |
| 1894 | (34) | *San Antonio de la Florida*, opera |
| 1895 | (35) | *Enrico Clifford*, opera |
| 1896 | (36) | *Pepita Jiménez*, opera |
| | | *Cantos de España*, for piano |
| | | *España*, for piano |
| 1899 | (39) | p *Catalonia*, orchestral rhapsody |
| 1906 | (46) | *Merlin*, opera |
| 1906–9 | | *Iberia*, piano cycle |
| 1908 | (48) | *Navarra*, for piano |

He also left a great mass of piano music, much of it extremely difficult to play.

## ALBINONI, Tomaso Giovanni
*b Venice, 14 June 1671*
*d Venice, 17 January 1751, aged seventy-nine*

The son of a wealthy paper merchant, he studied the violin and singing. Despite an exceptional talent he did not attempt to seek a post at church or court, but preferred to remain a man of independent means who made music for the love of it. His main concern was in writing and directing his own operas, and he married an operatic soprano, Margherita Rimondi, by whom he had six children. His career reached its climax in 1722, when the Elector of Bavaria, Maximilian Emanual II, to whom he had just dedicated a set of twelve concertos, invited him to Munich to direct his own operas. After that he began to compose less, and appears to have retired in 1741, spending the last two years of his life confined to bed. His musical output was, however, immense.

| | | |
|---|---|---|
| 1694 | (23) | *Zenobia, regina di Palmireni*, opera |
| 1707 | (36) | Sinfonie e Concerti a cinque |
| 1710 | (39) | Concerti a cinque |
| c1716 | (c45) | Twelve Concerti a cinque |
| c1722 | (c51) | Twelve Concerti a cinque |

Albinoni composed many works of concerto grosso type, as well as more than fifty operas.


## ALFVÉN, Hugo
*b Stockholm, 1 May 1872*
*d Falún, Sweden, 8 May 1960, aged eighty-eight*

A violinist, he went to Stockholm Conservatory from 1887 to 1891, and played in an opera orchestra from 1890 to 1892. He then toured Europe as a conductor, specialising in choral works. From 1910 to 1939 he was musical director at Uppsala University.

| | | |
|---|---|---|
| 1896 | (24) | Sonata and Romance for violin and piano |
| 1897 | (25) | Symphony No 1 in F minor |
| 1898–9 | (26) | Symphony No 2 in D major |
| | | *Elegy*, for horn and organ |
| 1904 | (32) | Swedish Rhapsody No 1, *Midsommervaka* |
| 1905 | (33) | Symphony No 3 in E major |
| | | *En Skargardssagen*, symphonic poem |
| 1907 | (35) | Swedish Rhapsody No 2, *Uppsalarapsodi* |
| 1912 | (40) | *Sten Sture*, cantata for male voices |
| 1918–19 | (46) | Symphony No 4 in C minor |
| 1923 | (51) | *Bergakungen*, pantomime drama |
| 1928 | (56) | *Manhem*, cantata for male voices |
| 1932 | (60) | *Spamannen*, incidental music |
| | | *Vi*, incidental music |
| 1937 | (65) | Swedish Rhapsody No 3, *Dalarapsodi* |
| 1942 | (70) | Symphony No 5 in A minor |

Between 1898 and 1937 Alfvén wrote a number of piano pieces, and between 1900 and 1928 he wrote ten cantatas, for solo voices, chorus and orchestra.


## ALKAN, Charles Henri Valentin
*b Paris, 30 November 1813*
*d Paris, 29 March 1888, aged seventy-four*

The Jewish family name was Morhange, but he, with his four brothers and his sister, who were all musicians, assumed the name of Alkan. He studied at the

11

Paris Conservatory, taking first prize in piano at age ten, in harmony age thirteen and in organ age twenty. In 1831 he received honourable mention in the Prix de Rome competition. He devoted himself to composition and teaching, visiting London and settling in Paris in 1833. He was a shy, rather misanthropic man, who held no official appointments and made very few concert appearances.

| | | |
|---|---|---|
| 1832 (19) | *Hermann et Ketty*, vocal work | |
| | Chamber Concerto No 1 | |
| 1834 (21) | Chamber Concerto No 2 | |
| | *L'Entrée en Loge*, vocal | |
| 1840 (27) | *Pas redoublé*, for wind band | |
| | *Grand duo concertante*, for violin and piano | |
| 1841 (28) | Piano Trio | |
| 1844 (31) | Symphony (lost) | |
| 1845 (31) | *Romance du phare d'Eddystone*, vocal (lost) | |
| 1847 (33) | *Etz chajjim hi*, vocal | |
| 1857 (43) | *Sonata de concert*, cello and piano | |
| | *Halelouyoh*, vocal | |
| 1859 (45) | *Marcia Funèbre*, for piano | |
| | *Stances de Millevoye*, for piano | |

Alkan also wrote a large number of works for piano.

## ALWYN, William
*b Northampton, 1905*

He was educated at the Royal Academy of Music, gaining scholarships in flute and composition. Later he also studied piano, introducing to England many new works of Ravel, Roussel and Goossens. He was professor of composition at the Royal Academy from 1926 to 1956 and is a fellow there. Many works have been commissioned from him and he has written much film music. He was chairman of the Composers' Guild and is a member of the Council of the Performing Right Society.

| | |
|---|---|
| 1927 (22) | Five Preludes for orchestra |
| 1930 (25) | Piano Concerto |
| 1936 (31) | *Marriage of Heaven and Hell*, choral work |
| 1939 (34) | Violin Concerto |
| | *Rhapsody*, for piano quartet |
| | *Sonata-Impromptu*, for violin and viola |
| 1940 (35) | *Masquerade*, overture |
| | Divertimento for solo flute |
| 1942 (37) | Concerto Grosso No 1 |
| 1943 (38) | *Pastoral Fantasia*, for viola and strings |
| 1945 (40) | Concerto for oboe, harp and strings |
| 1946 (41) | Suite of Scottish Dances |
| 1947 (42) | *Manchester Suite*, for orchestra |
| | Three Songs (Louis MacNeice) |
| | Piano Sonata |
| 1948 (43) | *Three Winter Poems*, for string quartet |
| 1949 (44) | Symphony No 1 |
| 1951 (46) | Festival March |
| | Concerto Grosso No 2 |
| 1953 (48) | Symphony No 2 |
| | *The Magic Island*, symphonic prelude |

| 1954 (49) | *Lyra Angelica*, for harp and strings |
|---|---|
| 1955 (50) | *Autumn Legend*, for English horn and strings |
| 1956 (51) | Symphony No 3 |
| 1957 (52) | *Elizabethan Dances*, for orchestra |
| 1959 (54) | Symphony No 4 |
| 1964 (59) | Concerto Grosso No 3 |
| 1966 (61) | *Derby Day*, overture |
| 1970 (65) | Sinfonietta for strings |
| 1973 (68) | Symphony No 5, *Hydriotaphia* |
| 1974 (69) | *Mirages*, song cycle |
| 1976 (71) | Six Nocturnes, for baritone and orchestra |
| | String Quartette No 2 'Spring Waters' |
| | *Moto Perpetuo*, for recorders |
| 1977 (72) | *Miss Julie*, opera |
| | *What Shall We Do With a Drunken Sailor*, vocal |
| 1979 (74) | *Green Hills*, piano solo |
| 1980 (75) | *Leave Taking*, song cycle |
| | Rhapsody for piano, violin, viola and cello |
| | String Quartet No 3 |

## ANTHEIL, George
*b Trenton, New Jersey, 8 July 1900*
*d New York, 12 February 1959, aged fifty-eight*

He was of German descent. He studied piano from the age of six, and from age thirteen commuted to Philadelphia for lessons in theory and composition. During 1920 he studied with Bloch and in 1922 moved to Berlin to pursue a career as a concert pianist, but abandoned the idea. In 1923 he lived and wrote in Paris, and from 1924 onwards began writing for films. In 1930 he published a mystery novel and in 1945 his autobiography, *Bad Boy of Music*.

| 1922 (22) | *Airplane Sonata*, for piano |
|---|---|
| | *Sonata Sauvage*, for piano |
| | Symphony No 1 |
| 1923 (23) | *Ballet Mécanique* (1923–4, revised 1953) |
| | Violin Sonata No 1 |
| 1926 (26) | *Jazz Symphonietta*, for twenty-two instruments |
| 1928–9 (28–9) | *Transatlantic*, opera |
| 1931 (31) | *Helen Retires*, opera |
| 1935 (35) | *Dreams*, ballet |
| 1936 (36) | *Course*, dance score |
| 1942 (42) | Symphony No 4 |
| 1947–8 (47–8) | Symphony No 5 |
| 1948 (48) | Symphony No 6 |
| | *McKonkey's Ferry*, overture for orchestra |
| | *Serenade*, for string orchestra |
| | Piano Sonata No 4 |
| | *Songs of Experience* (Blake poems), for voice and piano |
| 1950 (50) | *Volpone*, opera |
| 1951 (51) | *Eight Fragments from Shelley*, for chorus |
| 1953 (53) | *Capital of the World*, ballet |
| 1955–6 (55–6) | *Cabezza de Vacca*, cantata |

## ARENSKY, Anton Stepanovitch
b Novgorod, Russia, 12 July 1861
d Terioki, Finland, 25 February 1906, aged forty-four

His father was a doctor and a keen cellist, his mother an excellent pianist. In 1879 he entered the St Petersburg Conservatory, studying composition with Rimsky-Korsakov, and after graduation became professor of harmony and counterpoint at the Moscow Conservatory, where among his pupils were Rachmaninov, Skriabin and Glière. His friends included Tchaikovsky and Taneyev. From 1888 to 1895 he directed concerts of the Russian Choral Society, then moved from Moscow to St Petersburg.

1890 (29)   fp A Dream on the Volga, opera
1894 (33)   fp Raphael, opera
1899 (38)   Nal and Damayanti, opera (completed)
Arensky also composed:
Egyptian Night, ballet
The Wolf, for bass voice and orchestra
Two symphonies, in B minor and A minor
Nearly 100 piano pieces, including three suites for two pianos and six pieces for four hands
Many string quartets, songs, vocal duets and cantatas, as well as music for unaccompanied chorus
Fantasia on Russian Folk Songs, for piano and orchestra


## ARNE, Thomas
b London, 12 March 1710
d London, 5 March 1778, aged sixty-seven

His father was an upholsterer and coffin-maker, though, surprisingly, he produced a Handel opera. Thomas went to Eton College, played flute and violin and taught himself composition. His sister and brother were both singers, as was his wife, Cecilia, whom he married in 1737, and they all performed in his operas and masques. In 1742 he went to Dublin, where his music was very popular, and on returning to London in 1744 he was appointed resident composer at the Drury Lane Theatre. Henceforth he worked closely with Garrick, who was actor-manager there. In 1759 the University of Oxford conferred on him the degree of doctor of music.

1733 (23)   Rosamund, opera
            Opera of Operas, opera
            Dido and Aeneas, opera
1736 (26)   Zara, incidental music
1738 (28)   Comus, a masque
1740 (30)   Alfred, a masque (in which occurs 'Rule Britannia')
            The Judgment of Paris, opera
1743 (33)   Eliza, opera
            Britannia, a masque
1744 (34)   Abel, oratorio
1750 (40)   p Seven trio sonatas for two violins with figured bass
1762 (52)   Artaxerxes, opera
            Love in a Village, pasticcio
1764 (54)   Judith, oratorio (possibly 1761)
            Olimpiade, opera
1775 (65)   Caractacus, oratorio

14

**ARNELL, Richard**
*b London, 15 September 1917*

He studied at the Royal College of Music with John Ireland from 1936 to 1939. From 1943 to 1945 he was music consultant for the British Broadcasting Corporation, and in 1948 he began teaching at Trinity College of Music, London. From 1969 to 1970 he was Fulbright exchange professor at Bowdain College, Maine, and from 1970 to 1972 visiting professor at Hofstra University in the USA. In 1972 he was made music consultant to the London Film School.

| | | |
|---|---|---|
| 1939 | (22) | String Quartet No 1 |
| 1940 | (23) | Violin Concerto |
| 1941 | (24) | String Quartet No 2 |
| 1942 | (25) | Symphony No 2 |
| 1943 | (26) | Symphony No 1 |
| 1944 | (27) | Symphony No 3 |
| 1945 | (28) | String Quartet No 3 |
| 1946 | (29) | Piano Trio |
| | | Piano Concerto |
| 1947 | (30) | *Punch and the Child*, ballet |
| | | Harpsichord Concerto |
| 1948 | (31) | Symphony No 4 |
| 1950 | (33) | Symphony No 5 |
| | | String Quintet |
| 1951 | (34) | *Harlequin in April*, ballet |
| | | String Quartet No 4 |
| 1953 | (36) | *The Great Detective*, ballet |
| | | *Lord Byron*, a symphonic portrait |
| 1955 | (38) | *Love in Transit*, opera |
| 1956 | (39) | *Landscape and Figures*, for orchestra |
| 1957 | (40) | *The Angels*, ballet |
| 1958 | (41) | *Moonflowers*, opera |
| 1959 | (42) | *Paralyzed Princess*, operetta |
| 1961 | (44) | Brass Quintet |
| 1962 | (45) | String Quartet No 5 |
| 1963 | (46) | *Musica Pacifica*, for orchestra |
| 1966 | (49) | *Robert Flaherty*, a symphonic portrait |
| 1967 | (50) | *Sections*, for piano and orchestra |
| 1968 | (51) | *The Food of Love*, overture |
| | | *Nocturne: Prague 1968*, for mixed media |
| 1971 | (54) | *I Think of All Soft Limbs*, for mixed media |
| 1973 | (56) | *Astronaut One*, for mixed media |
| 1975 | (58) | *Jennifer plus Robert equals Wedding*, piano, four hands |
| 1977 | (60) | *Ring Bells*, electronic church bells and chorus |

**ARNOLD, Malcolm**
*b Northampton, 21 October 1921*

He won a scholarship in 1938 to the Royal College of Music, to study composition and trumpet. In 1941 he won the Cobbett Prize, and in 1942 joined the London Philharmonic Orchestra as First Trumpet. After war service from 1944 to 1945 he rejoined the LPO in 1946. In 1948 he won the Mendelssohn Scholarship and spent a year in Italy. He was awarded the title of honorary doctor of music at Exeter University in 1969, and in 1970 was made a CBE.

| | | |
|---|---|---|
| 1943 | (22) | *Beckus the Dandipratt*, overture |
| | | *Larch Trees*, symphonic poem |

| | |
|---|---|
| 1944 (23) | Horn Concerto |
| | *Variations on a Ukrainian Folksong*, for piano |
| 1946 (25) | Symphony for strings |
| 1947 (26) | Violin Sonata No 1 |
| | Viola Sonata |
| | *Children's Suite*, for piano |
| 1948 (27) | *The Smoke*, overture |
| | Festival Overture |
| | Symphonic Suite |
| | Sonatina for flute and piano |
| 1949 (28) | Clarinet Concerto |
| 1950 (29) | Symphony No 1 |
| | Serenade for small orchestra |
| | Eight English Dances |
| | String Quartet No 1 (possibly 1946) |
| 1951 (30) | *Sussex*, overture |
| | Concerto for piano duet and strings |
| | Sonatina in three movements for clarinet and piano |
| | Sonatina in three movements for oboe and piano |
| 1952 (31) | *Curtain Up*, overture |
| | Three Shanties for wind quintet |
| 1953 (32) | Symphony No 2 |
| | Oboe Concerto |
| | *Homage to the Queen*, ballet |
| | Violin Sonata No 2 |
| | Sonatina for recorder and piano |
| 1954 (33) | Harmonica Concerto |
| | Concerto for organ and orchestra |
| | Concerto for flute and strings |
| | Sinfonietta No 1, for two oboes, two horns and strings |
| | *The Tempest*, incidental music |
| 1955 (34) | *Tam o'Shanter*, overture |
| | Little Suite for Orchestra No 1 |
| | *John Clare* Cantata, for voices and piano duet |
| | Serenade for guitar and strings |
| 1956 (35) | *The Dancing Master*, opera |
| | *The Open Window*, opera |
| | *Solitaire*, ballet suite |
| | *A Grand Overture*, for orchestra |
| 1957 (36) | *Toy Symphony* |
| | *Four Scottish Dances*, for orchestra |
| | Symphony No 3 |
| 1958 (37) | Sinfonietta No 2, for flutes, horns and strings |
| 1959 (38) | Guitar Concerto |
| | Oboe Quartet |
| | *Five Songs of William Blake*, for voice and strings |
| 1960 (39) | Symphony No 4 |
| | *Rinaldo and Armida*, ballet |
| | *Song of Simeon*, nativity play, with chorus, brass, harp, percussion, celesta and strings |
| 1961 (40) | Symphony No 5 |
| | Divertimento No 2 for full orchestra |
| 1962 (41) | Concerto for two violins and strings |
| 1963 (42) | Little Suite for Orchestra No 2 |
| 1964 (43) | Sinfonietta No 3 for strings and wind |
| | *Water Music* |

| 1965 (44) | Fantasy for bassoon |
| | Fantasy for clarinet |
| | Fantasy for horn |
| | Fantasy for flute |
| | Fantasy for oboe |
| 1967 (46) | Symphony No 6 |
| | *Peterloo*, for orchestra |
| | *Trevelyan Suite*, for wind band |
| | *Concert Piece*, for piano and percussion |
| 1973 (52) | Symphony No 7 |
| 1974 (53) | Clarinet Concerto |
| | Fantasy for brass band |
| 1975 (54) | *Fantasy on a theme of John Field*, for orchestra |
| | String Quartet No 2 |
| | Fantasy for harp |
| 1976 (55) | Philharmonic Concerto |
| 1976–7 (55–6) | *The Return of Odysseus*, for chorus and orchestra |
| 1977 (56) | Sonata for flute and piano |
| 1979 (58) | Symphony No 8 |
| 1982 (61) | Trumpet Concerto |

**ARRIAGA, Juan Cristóstomo**
*b Bilbao, 27 January 1806*
*d Paris, 17 January 1826, aged nineteen*

He played violin and composed from a very early age. Before he was fifteen his only opera, *Los esclavos felices*, was performed in Bilbao. In 1821 he entered the Paris Conservatory, studying violin, harmony and counterpoint, and winning the *second prix* in 1823. In 1824 he was appointed répétiteur in a *classe de répétition* in harmony and counterpoint and issued the only work he published, the three string quartets on which his reputation mainly rests. In Bilbao a theatre has been named after him and a statue erected.

| 1817 (11) | Octet |
| 1818 (12) | Two Overtures |
| | Symphony in D |
| 1820 (14) | *Los esclavos felices*, opera |
| | Theme and Variations for string quartet |
| 1822 (16) | *La Húngara*, variations for string quartet |
| 1824 (18) | Three String Quartets |
| Undated | Three Character Studies, for piano |
| | *Agar*, for soprano and orchestra |
| | *Ermina*, for soprano and orchestra |
| | *Où vais-je malheureuse?*, for tenor and piano |
| | *Hymen*, for soprano and piano |
| | *All'aurora*, for bass, tenor and orchestra |
| | *O Salutaris*, for three voices and string quintet |
| | *Stabat Mater*, for three voices and small orchestra |
| | Mass for four voices (lost) |
| | *Salva regina* (lost) |
| | *Et vitam venturi*, fugue for eight voices (lost) |

## AUBER, Daniel

*b Caen, Normandy, 29 January 1782*
*d Paris, 12 May 1871, aged eighty-nine*

Born to an artistic and aristocratic family, he was sent to London in 1802 to learn the trade of art dealing. Whilst there he gave some public performances of his songs, and decided on a career in music. He returned to Paris in 1804 and studied with Cherubini. His operas had little success, not receiving acclaim until *La Bergère châtelaine* opened two days before his thirty-eighth birthday. He was very modest and retiring, despite his enormous success. He became a member of the Académie Française in 1829 and was appointed director of the Conservatory in 1842, remaining in that post until his death. In 1871 Napoleon III named him *maître de chapelle*. With his contemporaries Adam and Herold, he made the link between the comic opera of Mozart, Rossini and Donizetti and the operettas of Offenbach and Messager.

| | |
|---|---|
| 1828 (46) | *La muette de Portici* (also called *Masaniello*), opera |
| 1830 (48) | *Fra Diavolo*, opera |
| 1835 (53) | *The Bronze Horse*, opera (revised 1857) |
| 1837 (55) | *Le Domino noir*, opera |
| 1841 (59) | *Les Diamants de la couronne*, opera |
| 1846 (64) | *fp Manon Lescaut*, opera |
| 1858 (76) | *p* Piano Trio in D major, Op 1 |

## AUBERT, Louis

*b Paramé, Ille-et-Vilaine, 19 February 1877*
*d 1969, aged ninety-two*

He was a pupil of his father, and of Fauré at the Paris Conservatory. He intended to make a career as piano virtuoso, but returned to composition. He was made a member of the Légion d'honneur.

| | |
|---|---|
| 1892 (15) | 'Sous bois', song |
| 1894 (17) | 'Vielle chanson Espagnole' |
| 1896 (19) | *Rimes tendres*, song cycle |
| 1897 (20) | *Les Noces d'Apollon et d'Urainie*, cantata |
| 1899 (22) | Fantaisie, for piano and orchestra |
| 1900 (23) | *Suite brève*, for two pianos (orchestrated and revised 1913) |
| | *Trois esquisses*, for piano |
| | *La Lettre*, vocal work |
| 1902 (25) | *La Légende du Sang* |
| 1903 (26) | *La Momie*, ballet |
| 1904 (27) | *Chrysothemis*, ballet |
| | *The Blue Forest*, opera (1904–10) |
| 1908 (31) | *Crépuscules d'Automne*, song cycle |
| 1911 (34) | *Nuit Mauresque* (possibly 1907) |
| 1913 (36) | *Sillages*, three pieces for piano |
| 1917 (40) | *Six poèmes Arabes* (possibly 1907) |
| | *Tu es Patrus*, for chorus and organ |
| 1919 (42) | *La Habanera*, symphonic poem |
| 1921 (44) | *Dryade*, symphonic poem |
| 1923 (46) | *La nuit ensorcelée*, ballet |
| 1925 (48) | *Capriccio*, for violin and orchestra |
| 1927 (50) | *p Noël pastoral*, for piano and orchestra |
| | *p* Violin Sonata in D minor and D major |
| 1930 (53) | *Feuilles d'images*, for orchestra |
| 1937 (60) | *Les fêtes d'été*, for orchestra |

| 1947 | (70) | *Offrande*, for orchestra |
| 1948 | (71) | *Le Tombeau de Chateaubriande*, for orchestra |
| 1952 | (76) | *Cinéma*, for orchestra |

## AURIC, Georges
*b Lodève, Hérault, France, 15 February 1899*

After studying at the Montpellier Conservatory, he moved to Montmartre and became a pupil of d'Indy at the Schola Cantorum and of Gédalge at the Paris Conservatory, like Milhaud, Honegger and his exact contemporary Poulenc. In 1913 he met Satie, who influenced him greatly. He became leader of 'Les Six', the group of lively Paris-based musicians who, in the 1920s, were much helped and inspired by Cocteau. Auric was president of Lamoureux Concerts, and general administrator of the Paris Opéra for six years. He has been elected to the Académie des Beaux-Arts, and now works as a critic.

| 1920 | (21) | *Les Mariés de la Tour Eiffel*, ballet |
| 1923 | (24) | *Les Fâcheux*, ballet |
| 1924 | (25) | Chamber Suite |
|      |      | *Les Matelots*, ballet |
| 1925 | (26) | *Pastorale*, ballet |
| 1927 | (28) | *Sous le Masque*, opera |
| 1928 | (29) | *Les Enchantements de la Fée Alcine*, ballet |
|      |      | *Rondeau*, ballet |
| 1931 | (32) | *La Concurrence*, ballet |
| 1933 | (34) | *Les Imaginaires*, ballet |
| 1936 | (37) | Sonata in G, for violin and piano |
| 1937 | (38) | *La Seine au Matin*, for orchestra |
| 1938 | (39) | *Ouverture*, for orchestra |
|      |      | Trio in D, for oboe, clarinet and bassoon |
| 1940 | (41) | Five *Chansons Françaises*, for chorus |
| 1944 | (45) | *Quadrille*, ballet |
| 1946 | (47) | *La Fontaine de Jouvenance*, ballet |
|      |      | *Impromptu*, for oboe and piano |
| 1948 | (49) | *Le Peintre et son Modèle*, ballet |
| 1949 | (50) | *Phèdre*, ballet |
| 1951 | (52) | *Chemin de Lumière*, ballet |
| 1952 | (53) | *Ecossaise*, for orchestra |
| 1954 | (55) | *La Chambre*, ballet |
| 1956 | (57) | *Hommage à Marguerite Long*, for orchestra |
| 1960 | (61) | *Le Bal de Voleurs*, ballet |
| 1968 | (69) | *Imaginées I*, for flute and piano |
| 1969 | (70) | *Imaginées II*, for cello and piano |
| 1971 | (72) | *Imaginées III*, for clarinet and piano |
| 1973 | (74) | *Imaginées IV*, for viola and piano |

Auric has also written incidental music and film scores, piano works and songs.

## BABBITT, Milton Byron
*b Philadelphia, 10 May 1916*

He played violin at the age of four and later learned clarinet and saxophone. In 1931 he entered Pennsylvania University to study mathematics, but transferred to New York University to study music, graduating in 1935. In 1938 he joined the Princeton music faculty, working with Sessions, and became professor of music there in 1960. He has held many other posts and received many awards.

| 1935 | (19) | *Generatrix*, for orchestra |
| 1939 | (23) | String Trio |
| 1941 | (25) | Composition for orchestra |
| | | *Music for the Mass I*, for chorus |
| 1942 | (26) | *Music for the Mass II*, for chorus |
| 1946 | (30) | *Fabulous Voyage*, musical |
| 1948 | (32) | Composition for flute, clarinet, violin and cello |
| | | Composition for twelve instruments |
| | | String Quartet No 1 |
| 1949 | (33) | *Into the Good Ground*, film score |
| 1950 | (34) | Composition for viola and piano |
| 1953 | (37) | Woodwind Quartet |
| 1954 | (38) | String Quartet No 2 |
| 1957 | (41) | *All Set*, for ensemble |
| 1965 | (49) | *Relata I*, for orchestra |
| 1966 | (50) | Sextets for violin and piano |
| 1968 | (52) | *Relata II*, for orchestra |
| 1969 | (53) | String Quartet No 3 |
| | | Four Canons for female chorus |
| 1970 | (54) | String Quartet No 4 |
| 1973–4 | (57–8) | *Arie da Capo*, for flute, clarinet, piano, violin and cello |
| 1975 | (59) | *Kräfte*, opera |

Babbitt has also written for piano, solo voice, works with tape, and many critical articles.

## BACH, Carl Philipp Emanuel
*b Weimar, 8 March 1714*
*d Hamburg, 15 December 1788, aged seventy-four*

He was the second surviving son of Johann Sebastian by his first wife. Telemann was one of his godparents. He was educated at Thomasschule, Leipzig, then at the University of Frankfurt-on-Oder. In 1740 he was appointed cembalist in the *Kapelle* of Frederick the Great, himself a flautist. While at court he wrote two volumes on the art of piano technique, and he may be regarded as the founder of modern piano-playing, as well as one of the originators of the sonata-symphony form. In 1767 he succeeded Telemann as director of the five principal churches in Hamburg.

| 1731 | (17) | Trio in B minor |
| 1742 | (28) | Prussian Sonata |
| 1743 | (29) | Sonata for clavier, *Wurtemburgian* |
| 1747 | (33) | Sonata in D major |
| 1762 | (48) | Harp Sonata in B minor |
| 1770 | (56) | *Passion Cantata* |
| | | Solfeggio in C minor |
| | | Duo in E minor |
| 1773 | (59) | Fantasia in C minor |
| 1775 | (61) | *The Israelites in the Wilderness*, oratorio |
| 1780 | (66) | Symphony in F major |
| 1787 | (73) | *The Resurrection and Ascension of Jesus*, oratorio |
| 1788 | (74) | Concerto in E♭ , for harpsichord, fortepiano and strings |
| | | Quartet in G major |

C. P. E. Bach's works include 210 solo clavier pieces, fifty-two concertos with orchestral accompaniment, twenty-two passions, many cantatas, sonatas for violin and piano, and trios.

## BACH, Johann Christian
*b Leipzig, 5 September 1735*
*d London, 1 January 1782, aged forty-six*

The youngest son of Johann Sebastian by his second wife, Johann Christian studied with his father until 1750, then with his half-brother Carl Philipp Emanuel in Berlin. In 1754 he went to Italy, abandoned Protestantism for Roman Catholicism, and became organist in Milan Cathedral. He went to London in 1762 and was appointed music master to Queen Charlotte Sophia, wife of George III; and since then he has been called the 'English Bach'. He introduced Mozart to English musical society. In the early 1770s he was at the height of his career as performer and composer; then his popularity waned, his health and income deteriorated, and when he died he was £4,000 in debt. He is buried in St Pancras' Churchyard.

| 1761 | (26) | fp Artaserse, opera |
|------|------|---------------------|
| | | fp Catone in Utica, opera |
| 1762 | (27) | fp Allessandro nell'Indie, opera |
| 1763 | (28) | Orione, opera |
| | | Zanaida, opera |
| 1765 | (30) | Adriano in Siria, opera |
| 1767 | (32) | Carattaco, opera |
| 1770 | (35) | Gioas, Re di Giuda, oratorio |
| 1772 | (37) | Endimione, cantata |
| | | Temistocle, opera |
| 1776 | (41) | Lucio Silla, opera |
| 1779 | (44) | Amadis des Gaules, opera |

J. C. Bach also composed symphonies, opera overtures, concertos, sextets, quintets, quartets, trios, piano and violin sonatas, violin duets, piano sonatas, military marches, etc.


## BACH, Johann Sebastian
*b Eisenach, 21 March 1685*
*d Leipzig, 28 July 1750, aged sixty-five*

Musicians in Bach's family go back to the early sixteenth century, but their fame was purely local. Although Bach's education was irregular he studied music, organ and violin. Possessing a fine voice, in 1700 he was appointed boy soprano at Lüneberg, from where he once walked thirty miles to Hamburg to hear Reinken play the organ. At this time his first compositions were produced. In 1703 he became, briefly, violinist in the court orchestra at Weimar, but weeks later he was appointed organist in the Bonifacius-Kirche at Arnstadt. In October 1705 he obtained a month's leave and again took a long walk, this time to Lübeck to hear Buxtehude, who had enormous influence on him, though it is doubtful if the two men ever met. On returning to Arnstadt after four months he found his job gone. In 1707, aged twenty-two, he became organist at Muhlhausen, where he married his cousin Maria Barbara. Dissension in the Lutheran Church there interfered with his composing, and in 1708 he returned to Weimar as court organist, remaining there for nine years and becoming conductor of the court orchestra. In 1716 he applied for the vacant position of *Kapellmeister*, but was refused. A similar position at Prince Leopold's court at Cöthen was offered to him, but his Weimar employer refused to release him and had him arrested and confined for some weeks. On his release he joined Prince Leopold's court, becoming very friendly with his master. In 1719 he travelled to Halle to meet Handel; but Handel had already returned to England, so the two greatest composers of the age never met. In 1720 his wife died, and eighteen months later he married again; Anna Magdalena, daughter of a musician, was twenty. Bach, a staunch Lutheran, was unhappy about the Calvinist schools for his children, and the Prince's new wife was opposed to the arts; so in 1722 Bach applied for and received the position of cantor at the Thomasschule in Leipzig, in which town he remained for the rest of his life. The four children of his first marriage were joined by seven more; in all Bach had twenty children, but many did not survive childhood. In 1749 his sight began to fail and he was soon totally blind. He died of a stroke. His grave was unmarked and lost, and was rediscovered during excavations in 1894.

| | |
|---|---|
| 1700–08 (15–23) | Five Fantasies in Bm: C: Cm: G: G for organ |
| | Fantasy and Fugue in A minor for organ |
| | Three Fugues in Cm: D: G for organ |
| | Four Preludes in Am: C: C: G for organ |
| | Four Preludes and Fugues in Am: C: Cm: Em (Short) for organ |
| | Toccata and Fugue in E for organ |
| | Variations on Chorales (Partitas) for organ: |
| |    (1) 'Christ, der du bist der helle Tag' |
| |    (2) 'O Gott, du frommer Gott' |
| |    (3) 'Sei gegrüsset, Jesu gütig' |
| | Fantasy in C minor for clavier |
| | Fantasy (on a Rondo) in C minor for clavier |
| | Fughetta in C minor for clavier |
| | Five Fugues in C: Cm: Dm: Dm: Em for clavier |
| | Two Preludes (Fantasies) in Am: Cm for clavier |
| | Four Preludes and Fughettas in Dm: Em: F: G for clavier |
| | Prelude and Fugue in A minor for clavier |
| | Sonata in A minor (one movement) for clavier |
| | Five Toccatas in D: Dm: Em: G: Gm for clavier |
| c1704 (c19) | Sonata in D for clavier |
| c1705 (c20) | Quodlibet, for four voices and continuo |
| 1708–17 (23–32) | 'Alla breve pro organo pleno' in D for organ |
| | Four organ concertos (after Vivaldi and others) in Am: C: C: G |
| | Two Fantasies and Fugues in Cm: Gm for organ |
| | Fantasy in C minor for organ |
| | Four Fugues in Bm: Cm: G 'Jig': Gm for organ |
| | 'Passacaglia' in C minor for organ |
| | 'Pastorale' in F for organ |
| | Eight Preludes and Fugues in A: Am (Great): C: Cm (Great): D: Fm: G (Great): Gm for organ |
| | Eight Short Preludes and Fugues in C: Dm: Em: F: G: Gm: Am: B♭ for organ |
| | Four Toccatas and Fugues in C: Dm (Dorian): Dm: F for organ |
| | Three Trios in Cm: Dm: F (Aria) for organ |
| | Fantasy in G minor for clavier |
| | Fantasy (Prelude) in A minor for clavier |
| | Five Fugues in A: A: A (on a theme by Albinoni): Am: Bm for clavier |
| | Suite in A minor for clavier |
| | Suite in E♭ for clavier |
| | Suite ('Ouverture') in F for clavier |
| c1714 (c29) | 'Canzona' in D minor for organ |
| 1717 (32) | Orgelbüchlein, for organ |
| 1717–23 (32–8) | Violin Concerto in A minor with strings (& continuo) |
| | Violin Concerto in D with strings (& continuo) |
| | Concerto in D minor for two violins with strings (& continuo) |

Fugue in G minor for violin and continuo
Sonata in E minor for violin and continuo
Sonata in G for violin and continuo
Three sonatas for flute and continuo:
    No 1 in C: No 2 in E minor: No 3 in E
Sonata in C for two violins and continuo
Sonata in C minor for flute, violin and continuo (?1717–23)
Sonata in G for flute, violin and continuo
Sonata in G for two flutes and continuo
Three Sonatas for clavier and flute:
    No 1 in B minor: No 2 in E♭ : No 3 in A minor
Three Sonatas for clavier and viola da gamba:
    No 1 in G: No 2 in D: No 3 in G minor
Six Sonatas for clavier and violin:
    No 1 in B minor: No 2 in A: No 3 in E: No 4 in C minor: No 5 in
    F minor: No 6 in G
Suite in A for clavier and violin
Fantasy and Fugue in A minor for clavier
Twelve Little Preludes, for clavier
Prelude and Fugue in A minor for clavier
Six Preludes for Beginners, for clavier
Suite in D for clavier (possibly not by Bach)
Two Toccatas in Cm: F♯m for clavier

c1720 (c35)    Six Sonatas (Partitas) for solo violin:
    No 1 in G minor: No 2 in A minor: No 3 in C: No 4 in B minor:
    No 5 in D minor: No 6 in E
    Six Suites (Sonatas) for solo cello:
    No 1 in G: No 2 in D minor: No 3 in C: No 4 in E♭ : No 5 in C
    minor: No 6 in D

1720 (35)    'Clavierbüchlein vor Wilhelm Friedemann Bach'

1720–3 (35–8) Chromatic Fantasy and Fugue in D minor for clavier

1721 (36)    The 'Brandenburg' Concerti:
    No 1 in F for violino piccolo, three oboes, two horns, bassoon,
    strings (& continuo)
    No 2 in F for violin, flute, oboe, trumpet, strings (& continuo)
    No 3 in G for strings (& continuo)
    No 4 in G for violin, two flutes, strings (& continuo)
    No 5 in D for clavier, violin, flute, strings (& continuo)
    No 6 in B♭ for strings (without violins and continuo)

1722 (37)    'Clavierbüchlein vor Anna Magdalena Bachin'
    Six Suites ('French'), in Dm: Cm: Bm: E♭ : G: E for clavier (c1722)
    *The Well-Tempered Clavier*, Book I

1723 (38)    Magnificat in D, for solo voices, chorus, orchestra and continuo
    (?1723)
    Motet: 'Jesu, meine Freunde', for five-part chorus
    Passion according to St John, for soprano, contralto, tenor and bass
    soli, chorus, organ and continuo
    'Sanctus' in D, for eight-part chorus, orchestra and organ (c1723)
    Five Preludes and Fugues, in Bm (Great): C (Great): Dm: E♭ (St
    Anne): Em (Great or 'The Wedge') (1723–39)
    Variations on Chorale (Partita) 'Vom Himmel hoch da Komm' ich
    her' (1723–50)

1725 (40)    'Notenbuch vor Anna Magdalena Bachin', for clavier
    Five songs from Anna Magdalena Bach's 'Notenbuch'
    Six Suites ('English'), in A: Am: Gm: F: Em: Dm for clavier

c1726 (c41)    Motet: 'Fürchte dich nicht', for eight-part chorus

1727–36 (42–51) Concerto in C for two claviers with strings
Concerto in C minor for two claviers with strings (identical to the Concerto for two violins in D minor, 1717–23)
Concerto in C minor for two claviers with strings
1729 (44) Motet: 'Der Geist hilft unsrer Schwachheit auf', for eight-part chorus with accompaniment
Passion according to St Matthew, for soprano, contralto, tenor and bass soli, double chorus, double orchestra and continuo
1729–33 (44–8) Six Sonatas (Trios) in Eb : Cm: Dm: Em: C: G for organ
1729–36 (44–51) Clavier Concerto in A with strings (& continuo)
Clavier Concerto in D with strings (& continuo) (identical to Violin Concerto in E)
Clavier Concerto in D minor with strings (& continuo) (probably originally a violin concerto)
Clavier Concerto in E with strings (& continuo)
Clavier Concerto in F with two flutes, strings (& continuo) (identical to Brandenburg Concerto No 4 in G)
Clavier Concerto in F minor with strings (& continuo)
Clavier Concerto in G minor with strings (& continuo) (identical to Violin Concerto in A minor)
c1730 (c45) Concerto in A minor for clavier, flute and violin with strings
1731 (46) Six Partitas for clavier, in Bb : Cm: Am: D: G: Em
c1733 (c48) Concerto in C for three claviers with strings
Concerto in D minor for three claviers with strings
Concerto in A minor for four claviers with strings (transcription of Concerto for four violins by Vivaldi)
1733–?8 (48–?53) Mass in B minor for two sopranos, contralto, tenor, bass, chorus, orchestra and continuo
1734 (49) Christmas Oratorio (six cantatas) for solo voices, chorus, orchestra and organ
1735 (50) Concerto in the Italian Style, for clavier, in F
Ascension Oratorio (Cantata No 11 'Lobet Gott in seinen Reichen') (1735–6)
Partita (Ouverture) in B minor for clavier
1736 (51) Easter Oratorio for solo voices, chorus, orchestra and organ
c1737–40 (c52–5) Lutheran Masses for solo voices, chorus, orchestra and organ: No 1 in F: No 2 in Gm: No 3 in Am: No 4 in G
c1738 (c53) Fantasy (with unfinished Fugue) in C minor for clavier
1739 (54) Catechism Preludes (Clavierübung, Vol. III):
(1) Kyrie: Christie: Kyrie
(2) ditto ('alio modo')
(3) Allein Gott in der Höh' sei Ehr'
(4) ditto
(5) ditto (fughetta)
(6) Dies sind die heil'gen zehn Gebot'
(7) ditto (fughetta)
(8) Wir glauben all' an einem Gott
(9) ditto (fughetta 'Giant' fugue)
(10) Vater unser in Himmelreich
(11) ditto
(12) Christ unser Herr zum Jordan kam
(13) ditto
(14) Aus tiefer Not schrei ich zu dir
(15) ditto
(16) Jesus Christ unser Heiland
(17) ditto (fugue)

Clavier Duets (two-part pieces for one player)

1742 (57)  Aria with thirty variations, 'Goldberg Variations' for double-keyboard harpsichord
1744 (59)  *The Well-Tempered Clavier*, Book II
1747 (62)  *A Musical Offering*, for flute and violin, with continuo:
        'Ricercare a tre voci'
        'Canon perpetuus super thema regium'
        'Canones diversi 1–5'
        'Fuga canonica in Epidiapente'
        'Ricercare a sei voci'
        Two canons
c1747–50 (c62–5)  *Schübler's Book*, for organ
1748–50 (63–5)  *The Art of Fugue*, for unspecified instruments:
        (1–14) Contrapunctus I–XIV
        (15–18) Four Canons
        (19–20) Two Fugues for two keyboards
        (21) Unfinished Fugue on three subjects
Dates unknown: Overtures (Suites):
        (1) in C for woodwind, strings (& continuo)
        (2) in B minor for flute, strings (& continuo)
        (3) in D for oboes, bassoons, trumpets, timpani, strings (& continuo)
        (4) in D for oboes, bassoons, trumpets, timpani, strings (& continuo)

J. S. Bach also composed:
Two psalms:
  'Lobet den Herrn, alle Heiden', for four-part chorus
  'Singet dem Herrm ein neues Lied', for eight-part chorus
Fantasy and Fugue in A minor for clavier, after 1717
Prelude and Fugue in E♭ for clavier, after 1723
198 church cantatas
Twenty-three secular cantatas
Shorter keyboard works, including fifteen two-part inventions and fifteen 'symphonies', known today as three-part inventions.


## BALAKIREV, Mily
*b Nizhny-Novgorod, 2 January 1837*
*d St Petersburg, 29 May 1910, aged seventy-three*

Largely self-taught in music, he entered the University of Kazan as a mathematics student. In 1855 he went to St Petersburg and met Glinka, whose spiritual heir he became. In 1862 he organised the founding of the Russian Free School of Music, becoming the father-figure of the 'Mighty Handful' otherwise known as 'The Five' – Mussorgsky, Rimsky-Korsakov, Borodin, Glazounov and Cui. In 1867 he became principal conductor of the Russian Music Society, and in 1883 director of music at the Imperial Chapel. In 1894 he resigned from this post and spent the rest of his life composing.

1852 (15)  *Grand Fantaisie on Russian Folksongs*, for piano and orchestra
        Septet for flute, clarinet, strings and piano
1854 (17)  String Quartet, *Quatour original russe* (1854–5)
c1855 (c18)  Piano Concerto No 1 in F♯ minor
        'Three Forgotten Songs'
1855–6 (18–19) Octet for flute, oboe, horn, strings and piano
1858 (21)  Overture on Russian Themes
1858–65 (21–8) Twenty songs

1861 (24)    Piano Concerto No 2 begun: resumed 1909; completed by Liadov
1866–98 (29–61) Symphony No 1 in C major
1867 (30)    Overture on Czech themes
             *Thamar*, symphonic poem (1867–82)
1869 (32)    *fp Islamey*, piano fantasy
1884 (47)    *Russia*, symphonic poem
1895–6 (58–9) Ten songs
1903–4 (66–7) Ten songs
1905 (68)    Piano Sonata in B minor
1907–08 (70–1) Symphony No 2 in D minor
1910 (73)    Suite on pieces by Chopin


**BALFE, Michael William**
*b Dublin, 15 May 1808*
*d Rowney Abbey, Hertfordshire, 20 October 1870, aged sixty-two*

Both sides of his family had connections with music and the stage. He was
taught violin and piano by his father. In 1823 he left Dublin for London and
played violin in the Drury Lane Theatre orchestra. In 1824, aged sixteen, he was
taken up by an Italian nobleman and sent to Rome to study. Travelling via Paris,
he met Cherubini, who later introduced him to Rossini. He studied singing and
had a successful operatic career in Italy from 1830 to 1834, then returned to
London. He wrote operas there for the rest of his life, his *Bohemian Girl* (Drury
Lane 1843) being an enormous popular success.

1829 (21)    *I rivali de se stesso*, opera
1830 (22)    *Un avvertimento ai gelosi*, opera
1833 (25)    *Enrico IV al Passo della Marna*, opera
1835 (27)    *The Siege of Rochelle*, opera
1836 (28)    *The Maid of Artois*, opera (based on *Manon Lescaut*)
1837 (29)    *Catherine Grey*, opera
             *Joan of Arc*, opera
1838 (30)    *Falstaff*, opera
             *Diadeste*, opera
1841 (33)    *Keolanthe*, opera
1843 (35)    *The Bohemian Girl*, opera
             *Geraldine*, opera
1844 (36)    *The Castle of Aymon*, opera
             *Daughter of St Mark*, opera
1845 (37)    *The Enchantress*, opera
1846 (38)    *The Bondman*, opera
1847 (39)    *The Maid of Honour*, opera
1852 (44)    *The Devil's in it*, opera
             *The Sicilian Bride*, opera
1857 (49)    *The Rose of Castille*, opera
1860 (52)    *Bianca*, opera
1861 (53)    *The Puritan's Daughter*, opera
1863 (55)    *The Armourer of Nantes*, opera
             *Blanche de Nevers*, opera
1864 (56)    *The Sleeping Queen*, opera
Performed posthumously:
1874         *Il Talismano*, opera

## BANKS, Don

*b Melbourne, 25 October 1923*
*d Sydney, 1 October 1980, aged fifty-six*

His father was a professional jazz musician, and Don learned five instruments, including piano. In 1948, after war service in the Australian Army Medical Corps, he studied composition at the University of Melbourne Conservatorium. In 1950 he went to London to study under Seiber, won a scholarship that took him to Salzburg, then went to Florence to study with Dallapiccola and later with Nono. During the 1950s he published little, living in London as a copyist and arranger and writing for commercials and documentary films. He became chairman of the SPNM, and from 1969 to 1971 was music director at Goldsmiths' College. After leaving England he became chairman of the Australian Council for the Arts' Music Board, and head of composition and electronic music studies at the Canberra School of Music; he also formed the Composers' Guild of Australia. In 1978 he became head of the School of Composition Studies at Sydney Conservatorium.

| | |
|---|---|
| 1951 (28) | Divertimento for flute and string trio |
| | Duo for violin and cello |
| 1953 (30) | Sonata for violin and piano |
| | Four Pieces for orchestra |
| 1954 (31) | Five North Country Folk Songs for soprano or tenor, piano and string orchestra |
| | *Psalm LXX*, for soprano and chamber orchestra |
| 1955 (32) | Three North Country Folk Songs for soprano or tenor and piano |
| | Three Studies for cello and piano |
| 1956 (33) | *Pezzo Dramatico*, for piano |
| 1958 (35) | *Episode*, for chamber orchestra |
| 1961 (38) | *Sonata da camera*, for ensemble |
| 1962 (39) | Trio for horn, violin and piano |
| 1963–4 (40–1) | *Equation 1*, for jazz group and ensemble |
| 1964 (41) | *Three Episodes*, for flute and piano |
| 1964–5 (41–2) | *Divisions*, for orchestra |
| 1965 (42) | Horn Concerto |
| 1966 (43) | *Assemblies*, for orchestra |
| | *Settings from Roget*, for jazz singer and ensemble |
| 1967 (44) | *Sequence*, for cello |
| 1968 (45) | Violin Concerto |
| | *Tirade*, for mezzo or baritone, piano, harp and three percussion instruments |
| | *Findings Keepings*, for chorus, drums and double-bass |
| 1969 (46) | *Dramatic Music*, for youth orchestra |
| | *Fanfare*, for orchestra |
| | *Intersections*, for orchestra and tape |
| | *Equation II*, for jazz group and ensemble |
| 1970 (47) | *Meeting Place*, for jazz group, ensemble and electronics |
| 1971 (48) | Three Short Songs for voice and jazz quartet |
| | *Limbo*, for three solo voices, eight instruments and two-track tape |
| | Music for wind band |
| | *Nexus*, for orchestra and jazz band |
| | Four Pieces for string quartet |
| 1972 (49) | *Walkabout*, for children's voices and instruments |
| | *Equation III*, for jazz group, ensemble and electronics |
| | String Quartet |
| | *Shadows of Space*, for four-track tape |
| 1973 (50) | *Prospects*, for orchestra |

**BANTOCK, Granville**
*b London, 7 August 1868*
*d London, 11 October 1946, aged seventy-eight*

The son of a doctor, Bantock was educated for a post in the Indian Civil Service. He studied at the Royal Academy of Music from 1889 to 1893, and from 1894 to 1895 travelled the world as a conductor. In 1897 he was appointed musical director of the Tower, New Brighton, and in 1900 principal of the Birmingham School of Music. In 1908 he succeeded Elgar as Peyton professor at Birmingham University, remaining in that post until 1934. He then became chairman of the Corporation of Trinity College of Music. He was a great friend of Sibelius; was made an honorary MA and a doctor of music at Edinburgh University; and was knighted in 1930.

| | | |
|---|---|---|
| 1892 | (24) | *Aegypt*, ballet |
| | | *Fire Worshippers*, for soli, chorus and orchestra |
| 1899 | (31) | String Quartet in C minor |
| 1900 | (32) | Tone Poem No 1, *Thalaba the Destroyer* |
| 1901 | (33) | Tone Poem No 2, *Dante* |
| | | Tone Poem No 3, *Fifine at the Fair* |
| 1902 | (34) | Tone Poem No 4, *Hudibras* |
| | | Tone Poem No 5, *Witch of Atlas* |
| | | Tone Poem No 6, *Lalla Rookh* |
| | | *The Time Spirit*, for chorus and orchestra |
| 1903 | (35) | Serenade for four horns |
| 1906 | (38) | *Omar Khayyam*, for soli, chorus and orchestra |
| 1915 | (47) | *Hebridean Symphony* |
| 1918 | (50) | *Pibroch*, for cello and piano or harp |
| 1919 | (51) | *Colleen*, Viola sonata in F major |
| 1922 | (54) | *Song of Songs*, for soli, chorus and orchestra |
| 1923 | (55) | *Pagan Symphony* |
| 1924 | (56) | *The Seal-woman*, opera |
| 1928 | (60) | *Pilgrim's Progress*, for soli, chorus and orchestra |
| 1937 | (69) | *King Solomon*, for narrator, chorus and orchestra |
| 1938 | (70) | *Aphrodite in Cyprus*, symphonic ode |

Bantock also composed a setting of Swinburne's 'Atalanta in Calydon'; 'Fantastic Poem' and 'Celtic Poem', for cello and piano; 'Hamabdil', for cello and harp (or piano).


**BARBER, Samuel**
*b Westchester, Pennsylvania, 9 March 1910*

He studied piano and conducting, and singing with his aunt who was a famous contralto; he later developed a good baritone voice. He began composing when still a child, and studied at the Curtis Institute, Philadelphia, graduating in 1932. He won the Pulitzer Prize twice and the Prix de Rome. He was a great friend of Menotti. In 1945 he was awarded a Guggenheim Fellowship and became a doctor of music.

| | | |
|---|---|---|
| 1929 | (19) | Serenade for string orchestra or string quartet |
| 1931 | (21) | *School for Scandal*, overture |
| | | *Dover Beach*, for voice and string quartet |
| 1932 | (22) | Cello Sonata |
| 1933 | (23) | *Music for a Scene from Shelley*, for orchestra |
| 1936 | (26) | Symphony No 1, in one movement |
| | | String Quartet No 1 |
| | | *Adagio for Strings*, arranged from String Quartet No 1 |

| 1937 | (27) | *First Essay for Orchestra* |
|------|------|------|
| 1939 | (29) | Violin Concerto |
| 1940 | (30) | *A Stop-watch and an Ordnance Map*, for male chorus and orchestra |
| 1942 | (32) | *Second Essay for Orchestra* |
| 1944 | (34) | Symphony No 2 (revised 1947) |
| | | *Capricorn Concerto*, for flute, oboe, trumpet and strings |
| | | *Excursions*, for piano |
| 1945 | (35) | Cello Concerto |
| 1946 | (36) | *Medea: the Cave of the Heart*, ballet |
| 1947 | (37) | *Knoxville: Summer of 1915*, ballet suite for voice and orchestra |
| 1948 | (38) | Piano Sonata |
| | | String Quartet No 2 |
| 1953 | (43) | *Souvenirs*, ballet suite |
| 1954 | (44) | *Prayers of Kierkegaard*, for soprano, chorus and orchestra |
| 1956 | (46) | *Summer Music*, for woodwind quintet |
| 1958 | (48) | *Vanessa*, opera (libretto by Gian-Carlo Menotti, *qv*) |
| 1959 | (49) | *A Hand of Bridge*, opera, for four solo voices and chamber orchestra |
| 1960 | (50) | *Toccata Festiva*, for organ and orchestra |
| 1961 | (51) | *Dies Natalis*, choral preludes for Christmas on 'Silent Night' |
| 1962 | (52) | Piano Concerto |
| | | *Andromache's Farewell*, for soprano and orchestra |
| 1966 | (56) | *Antony and Cleopatra*, opera |
| 1969 | (59) | *Despite and Still*, song cycle |
| 1971 | (61) | *The Lovers*, for baritone, chorus and orchestra |
| 1973 | [63] | *fp* String Quartet |

## BARTÓK, Béla

*b Nagyszentmiklós, Hungary (now Romania), 25 March 1881*
*d New York, 26 September 1945, aged sixty-four*

His father, director of an agricultural college and a good amateur pianist, died when Bartók was seven. His mother, a schoolteacher, guided his early career. In 1892 the family moved to Pozsony, and there Bartók met Dohnányi, succeeding him as organist in the Gymnasium Chapel. In 1898 he went to the Budapest Academy of Music, taking a teaching post there from 1907 to 1934. From 1922 he appeared as a concert pianist with great success in Salzburg and London, and paid his first visit to the USA in 1927. He married twice, each time to a young pupil. In 1940 he returned to the USA and stayed there for the rest of his life. He was dogged by ill-health, and the disintegration of his homeland from World War I onwards affected him mentally and physically.

| 1902 | (21) | Scherzo for orchestra |
|------|------|------|
| 1903 | (22) | *Kossuth*, tone poem |
| | | Violin Sonata |
| 1904 | (23) | *Rhapsody*, for piano and orchestra |
| | | *Burlesca*, for orchestra |
| | | Piano Quintet |
| 1905 | (24) | Suite No 1, for orchestra |
| | | Suite No 2, for orchestra (1905–7, revised 1943) |
| 1907 | (26) | Hungarian Folksongs for piano |
| 1908 | (27) | *Portraits*, for orchestra (1907–8) |
| | | Violin Concerto No 1 |
| | | String Quartet No 1 in A minor |
| 1909 | (28) | *For Children*, for piano |
| 1910 | (29) | *Four Dirges*, for piano |
| | | *Deux Images*, for orchestra |

| 1911 (30) | *Duke Bluebeard's Castle*, opera |
| | *Allegro barbaro*, for piano |
| | Three Burlesques for piano |
| 1912 (31) | Four Pieces for Orchestra |
| 1914 (33) | Fifteen Hungarian Peasant Songs (1914–17) |
| | *The Wooden Prince*, ballet (1914–16) |
| 1915 (34) | Roumanian Folk Dances for Piano |
| | Twenty Roumanian Christmas Songs for Piano |
| | String Quartet No 2 in A minor (1915–17) |
| 1916 (35) | Suite for piano |
| 1918–19 (37) | *The Miraculous Mandarin*, ballet |
| 1920 (39) | Eight Improvisations on Peasant Songs |
| 1921 (40) | Violin Sonata No 1 (Atonal) |
| 1922 (41) | Violin Sonata No 2 |
| 1923 (42) | Dance Suite for Orchestra |
| 1924 (43) | *Five Village Scenes* (Slovak folk songs), for female voices and piano |
| 1926 (45) | Piano Concerto No 1 |
| | *Cantata Profana*, for tenor and baritone soli, mixed chorus and orchestra |
| | Piano Sonata |
| | Nine Little Pieces for piano |
| | *Out of Doors*, suite for piano |
| | *Three Village Scenes*, for chorus and orchestra |
| | *Mikrokosmos*, Books I–VI, 150 small pieces for piano, arranged in order of technical difficulty (1926–37) |
| 1927 (46) | String Quartet No 3 |
| 1928 (47) | *Rhapsody* No 1 and No 2, for violin and orchestra |
| | *Rhapsody* No 1, for cello and piano |
| | String Quartet No 4 |
| 1930–1 (49) | Piano Concerto No 2 |
| 1931 (50) | Forty-four Duos for two violins |
| 1934 (53) | String Quartet No 5 |
| 1936 (55) | *Music for Strings, Percussion and Celesta* |
| | *Petite Suite*, for piano |
| 1938 (57) | Violin Concerto No 2 |
| | Sonata for two pianos and percussion |
| | *Contrasts*, trio for clarinet, violin and piano, the violinist using two instruments, one of normal tuning, the other tuned: G♯, D, A, E♭ |
| 1939 (58) | Divertimento for Strings |
| | String Quartet No 6 |
| 1941 (60) | Concerto for two pianos and percussion (also orchestra) |
| 1943 (62) | Concerto for Orchestra |
| 1944 (63) | Sonata for unaccompanied violin |
| 1945 (64) | Piano Concerto No 3 |
| | Viola Concerto |

**BAX, Arnold Edward Trevor**
*b London, 8 November 1883*
*d Cork, 3 October 1953, aged sixty-nine*

He trained at the Royal Academy of Music, then travelled widely, particularly to Ireland, whose folklore and culture greatly influenced him. He became an honorary doctor of music at Oxford in 1934, at Durham in 1935, and at the National University of Eire in 1947. He was knighted in 1937, became Master of the King's Musick in 1942, and received the KCVO. He was also an excellent poet, under the pseudonym of Dermot O'Byrne. His brother was Clifford Bax, the playwright.

| | |
|---|---|
| 1906 (23) | Piano Trio in E major, in one movement |
| 1907 (24) | *Fatherland*, for two sopranos, chorus and orchestra |
| 1908 (25) | *Lyrical Interlude*, for string quintet |
| 1909 (26) | Christmas Carol |
| | *Enchanted Summer*, for tenor, chorus and orchestra |
| 1910 (27) | *In the Faery Hills*, symphonic poem |
| | Violin Sonata No 1 (1910–15) |
| 1912 (29) | *Christmas Eve on the Mountains*, for orchestra |
| | *Nympholept*, for orchestra |
| 1913 (30) | Scherzo for orchestra |
| 1914–15 (31–2) | Piano Quintet in G minor |
| 1915 (32) | *Légende*, for violin and piano |
| | Violin Sonata No 2 |
| | *The Maiden with the Daffodils*, for piano |
| | *Winter Waters*, for piano |
| 1916 (33) | *Ballade*, for violin and piano |
| | *Dream in Exile*, for piano |
| | *Elegy*, trio for flute, viola and harp |
| 1917 (34) | Symphonic Variations for piano and orchestra |
| | *Tintagel*, symphonic poem |
| | *November Woods*, symphonic poem |
| | *An Irish Elegy*, for English horn, harp and strings |
| | *Moy Well (An Irish Tone Poem)*, for two pianos |
| | *Between Dusk and Dawn*, ballet |
| 1918 (35) | String Quartet No 1 in G major |
| | *Folk Tale*, for cello and piano |
| 1919 (36) | Piano Sonata No 1 in F♯ minor |
| | Piano Sonata No 2 in G major |
| | Harp Quintet in F minor |
| | *What the Minstrel Told Us*, for piano |
| 1920 (37) | *The Truth About Russian Dancers*, ballet |
| | *The Garden of Fand*, symphonic poem |
| | *Summer Music*, for orchestra |
| | *Phantasy*, for viola and orchestra |
| | Four Pieces for piano: 'Country Tune', 'Hill Tune', 'Lullaby' and 'Mediterranean' |
| 1921 (38) | *Mater Ora Filium*, for unaccompanied chorus |
| | *Of a Rose I Sing*, for small chorus, harp, cello and double-bass |
| | Viola Sonata |
| | Symphony No 1 in E♭ major and minor (1921–2) |
| 1922 (39) | *The Happy Forest*, symphonic poem |
| 1923 (40) | *Romantic Overture*, for small orchestra |
| | *Saga Fragment*, for piano, strings, trumpet and cymbals |
| | Piano Quartet |
| | Oboe Quintet in G |
| | Cello Sonata in E minor |
| 1924 (41) | *Cortège*, for orchestra |
| | Symphony No 2 in E minor and C major (1924–5) |
| | String Quartet No 2 in E minor (1924–5) |
| 1927 (44) | Violin Sonata No 3 in G minor |
| 1928 (45) | Sonata for viola and harp |
| | Sonata for two pianos |

|            | Symphony No 3 in C major (1928–9)                                    |
|------------|----------------------------------------------------------------------|
| 1929 (46)  | *Legend*, for viola and piano                                        |
|            | Overture, Elegy and Rondo for orchestra                              |
| 1930 (47)  | Symphony No 4 in E♭ (1930–1)                                          |
|            | *Winter Legends*, for piano and orchestra                            |
|            | *Overture to a Picaresque Comedy*, for orchestra                     |
| 1931 (48)  | *The Tale the Pine Trees Knew*, symphonic poem                       |
|            | Nonet for flute, oboe, clarinet, harp and strings                    |
|            | String Quintet in one movement                                       |
|            | Symphony No 5 in C♯ minor (1931–2)                                   |
| 1932 (49)  | *A Northern Ballad*, for orchestra (1932–3)                          |
|            | Sinfonietta                                                          |
|            | Cello Concerto in G minor                                            |
|            | Piano Sonata No 4 in G major                                         |
| 1933 (50)  | Sonatina in D for cello and piano                                    |
| 1934 (51)  | Symphony No 6 in C major                                             |
|            | Concerto for flute, oboe, harp and string quartet                    |
|            | Octet for horn, strings and piano                                    |
|            | Clarinet Sonata in D major                                           |
| 1935 (52)  | *The Morning Watch*, for chorus and orchestra                       |
|            | *Overture to Adventure*, for orchestra                               |
| 1936 (53)  | Concerto for bassoon (or viola), harp and string sextet              |
|            | String Quartet No 3 in F major                                       |
| 1937 (54)  | Violin Concerto                                                      |
|            | *A London Pageant*, for orchestra                                    |
|            | *Northern Ballad No 2* for orchestra                                 |
| 1939 (56)  | Symphony No 7 in A♭                                                  |
| 1943 (60)  | *Work in Progress*, overture                                         |
| 1944 (61)  | *Legend*, for orchestra                                              |
| 1945 (62)  | *Legend-Sonata*, for cello and piano in F♯ minor                    |
| 1946 (63)  | *Te Deum*, for chorus and organ                                      |
|            | *Gloria*, for chorus and organ                                       |
| 1947 (64)  | *Epithalamium*, for chorus and organ                                 |
|            | Two Fanfares for the wedding of Princess Elizabeth and Prince Philip |
|            | *Morning Song*, for piano and small orchestra                        |
| 1950 (67)  | Concertante for orchestra with piano (left hand), written for Harriet Cohen |
| 1953 (70)  | *Coronation March*                                                   |

## BEACH, Amy Marcy Cheney
*b Henniker, New Hampshire, 5 September 1867*
*d New York, 27 December 1944, aged seventy-seven*

She made her début as a pianist with the Boston Symphony Orchestra in 1885. Her 'Gaelic' Symphony was the first symphony composed by an American woman. She concentrated on composition from her marriage in 1885 until her husband's death in 1910, then resumed her concert career.

| 1891 (24)  | Mass for chorus and orchestra                        |
|------------|------------------------------------------------------|
| 1892 (25)  | *Festival Jubilate*, for chorus and orchestra        |
| 1896 (29)  | Symphony 'Gaelic'                                     |
|            | Sonata for violin and piano                          |
| 1899 (32)  | Piano Concerto                                        |
| 1907 (40)  | *The Chambered Nautilus*, for chorus and orchestra   |
| 1908 (41)  | Piano Quintet                                         |

1920 (53)    Variations for flute and string quartet
1925 (58)    *The Canticle of the Sun*, for chorus and orchestra
1931 (64)    *Christ in the Universe*, for chorus and orchestra
1932 (65)    *Cabildo*, opera
1938 (71)    Piano Trio

Amy Beach wrote four other choral works, three other works for violin and piano, piano pieces and songs, and fifty unaccompanied choral pieces.


## BEDFORD, David
*b London, 1937*

He began composing at an early age and studied with Lennox Berkeley at the Royal Academy of Music, where he was much influenced by the music of Schoenberg. In 1961 he was awarded a grant by the Italian government enabling him to study with Nono in Venice, and during the following year he worked at the Electronic Music Studio in Milan. He has been extensively involved with pop and rock music, and has written much educational work for young players.

1963 (26)    *Two Poems*, for chorus
             *Piece for Mo*, for percussion, vibraphone, accordion, three violins, cello and double-bass
1964–5 (27–8) *A Dream of the Seven Lost Stars*, for mixed chorus and chamber ensemble
1965 (28)    *This One for You*, for orchestra
             *Music for Albion Moonlight*, for soprano and instruments
             'O Now the Drenched Land Awakes', for baritone and piano duet
1966 (29)    *That White and Radiant Legend*, for soprano, speaker and instruments
             *Piano Piece I*
1967 (30)    *Five*, for two violins, viola and two cellos
             *Trona for Twelve*, for instrumental ensemble
             *18 Bricks Left on April 21st*, for two electric guitars
1968 (31)    *Gastrula*, for orchestra
             *Pentomino*, for wind quintet
             *Piano Piece II*
             'Come In Here Child', for soprano and amplified piano
1969 (32)    *The Tentacles of the Dark Nebula*, for tenor and instruments
1970 (33)    *The Garden of Love*, for instrumental ensemble
             *The Sword of Orion*, for instrumental ensemble
1971 (34)    *Star Clusters, Nebulae and Places in Devon*, for mixed double chorus and brass
             *Nurse's Song with Elephants*, for ten acoustic guitars and singer
             *With 100 Kazoos*, for instrumental ensemble and one hundred kazoos played by the public
             'Some Stars Above Magnitude 2.9', for soprano and piano
1972 (35)    *Holy Thursday with Squeakers*, for soprano and instruments
             *When I Heard the Learned Astronomer*, for tenor and instruments
             *An Easy Decision*, for soprano and piano
             *Spillihpnerak*, for viola
1973 (36)    *A Horse, His Name Was Hunry Fencewaver Walkins*, for instrumental ensemble
             *Jack of Shadows*, for solo viola and instruments
             *Pancakes, with Butter, Maple Syrup and Bacon and the TV Weatherman*, for wind quintet
             *Variations on a Rhythm by Mike Oldfield*, for percussion (three players, eighty-four instruments and conductor)

33

| 1974 (37) | *Star's End*, for rock instruments and orchestra |
| | *Twelve Hours of Sunset*, for mixed choir and orchestra |
| | *The Golden Wine is Drunk*, for sixteen solo voices |
| | *Because He Liked to be at Home*, for tenor (doubling recorder) and harp |
| 1976 (39) | *Alleluia Timpanis*, for orchestra |
| | *The Odyssey*, for chorus and orchestra |
| | *Circe Variations*, for instrumental ensemble |
| | *The Ones Who Walked Away from Omelas*, for instrumental ensemble |
| 1977 (40) | *The Song of the White Horse*, for chorus and orchestra |
| | *On the Beach at Night*, for voices and instruments |
| 1977–8 (40–1) | *The Way of Truth*, for chorus and electronics |
| 1978 (41) | *The Rime of the Ancient Mariner*, school opera |
| 1979 (42) | *The Death of Baldur*, school opera |
| | *Of Beares, Foxes and Many, Many Wonders*, for chorus and orchestra |
| 1980 (43) | *Fridiof's Saga*, school opera |
| | *Requiem*, for soprano solo, chorus and orchestra |
| | *Fridiof Kennings*, for saxophone quartet |
| 1981 (44) | *Alleluia Timpanis* (revised) |
| | *Prelude for a Maritime Nation*, orchestra |
| | *Ocean Star a Dreaming Song*, for youth orchestra |
| | Symphony for twelve musicians |
| | Wind Sextet |
| | String Quartet |
| | *Vocoder Sextet* |
| | *Elegy and Caprice*, for oboe and piano |
| | Toccata for piano |
| | *Sonata in One Movement*, for piano |
| 1982 (45) | *The Juniper Tree*, for soprano, recorder and harpsichord |
| 1983 (46) | *The Valley Sleeper, the Children, the Snakes and the Giant*, for orchestra |
| | *Five Diversions*, for two flutes |
| 1984 (47) | $\mathrel{\lower 2pt\hbox{$\downharpoonright$}}\!=120$, for bass clarinet and tape |

**BEETHOVEN, Ludwig van**
*b Bonn, 15/16 December 1770*
*d Vienna, 25 March 1827, aged fifty-six*

His father and grandfather were musicians. His parents were both alcoholics, and the family was very poor. As a result he had little general education, and found difficulty in expressing himself, which probably explains his subsequent boorishness in aristocratic company. He did, however, study piano, organ, violin and viola, and in 1784, aged fourteen, he was made assistant to his teacher as the court organist at Hanover. In 1787 he was sent to Vienna where he had some tuition from Mozart. He returned home after a short time because of his mother's death, and at nineteen was solely responsible for his drunken father and his two younger brothers. To make a living he taught, and played viola in the opera orchestra. In 1792 he returned to Vienna, studying with Haydn. Despite his manner he had a great number of aristocratic patrons, which eased his financial situation. After the age of thirty he suffered from a progressive loss of hearing, and by his mid-forties he was almost stone-deaf, and subject to various other ailments.

| 1780 (10) | Nine Variations on a March by Dressler, in C minor for piano, Op 176 |

1781 (11)    'Schilderung eines Mädchen', song, Op 229
1782–1802 (12–32) Seven Bagatelles for piano, in E♭ : C: F: A: C: D: A♭ , Op 33
1783 (13)    Minuet in E♭ for piano, Op 165
             p Three Piano Sonatas, in E♭ : Fm: D. Op 161 (composed very
             early)
1784 (14)    p 'An einem Säugling', song, Op 230
             p Rondo, allegretto in A major for piano, Op 164
1785 (15)    Piano Quartets No 1–3 in E♭ : D: C, Op 152
             Piano Trio No 9 in E♭ , Op 153
             Prelude in F minor for piano, Op 166
1786 (16)    Trio in G major for piano, flute and bassoon, Op 259
1789 (19)    Two preludes through all twelve major keys, for piano or organ,
             Op 39
1790 (20)    'Musik zu einem Ritterballet', for orchestra, Op 149
             Twenty-four Variations on Righini's air 'Venni amore', for piano,
             Op 177
             Cantata on the death of Emperor Joseph II, Op 196a
             Cantata on the ascension of Leopold II 'Er schlummert', Op 196b
1791 (21)    Thirteen Variations on Dittersdorf's air 'Es war einmal', for piano,
             Op 178
1792 (22)    Allegro and Menuetto in G major for two flutes, Op 258
1793 (23)    p Twelve Variations in F major on 'Se vuol ballare', for violin and
             piano, Op 156
1794 (24)    Trio for two oboes and English horn, Op 87
             Rondo Allegro in G major for violin and piano, Op 155
             p Variations in G major on a theme by Count von Waldenstein for
             piano (four hands), Op 159
1795 (25)    p Three Piano Trios, in E♭ : G: Cm, Op 1
             Piano Concerto No 2 in B♭ , Op 19
             'Adelaide', song, Op 46
             p Twelve *Deutsche Tänze*, for orchestra, Op 140
             Six Minuets for piano, Op 167
             Six Allemandes for violin and piano, Op 171
             p Nine Variations on Paisello's air 'Quant è più bello', for piano,
             Op 179
             Twelve Variations on Minuet from ballet *Le nozze disturbate*, Op
             181
             'Der Freie Mann', song, Op 233
             'Die Flamme lodert', opferlied, Op 234
             'Seufer eines Ungeliebten' and 'Gegenliebe', songs, Op 254
1796 (26)    Twelve Variations on a Russian Dance from Wianizky's 'Wald-
             machen', Op 182
             'Ah, perfido', scena and aria for soprano and orchestra, Op 65
             p Six Variations on Paisello's duet 'Nel cor più', for piano, Op 180
             'Farewell to Vienna's citizens', song, Op 231
1797 (27)    p Piano Sonatas No 1–3 in Fm: A: C, Op 2
             p String Trio in E♭ , Op 3
             p String Quintet in E♭ , Op 4
             p Cello Sonatas No 1 and 2, Op 5
             p Sonata in D for piano (four hands), Op 6
             p Piano Sonata No 4 in E♭ , Op 7
             p Serenade in D for string trio, Op 8
             Quintet for piano, oboe, clarinet, bassoon and horn, Op 16
             p Rondo for piano, Op 51
             p Twelve Variations in G on 'See, the conquering hero comes', for
             cello and piano, Op 157

|  |  |
|---|---|
|  | War Song of the Austrians, for voices and piano, Op 232 |
|  | Symphony in C, *Jena* (authenticity doubtful), Op 257 |
| 1798 (28) | *p* Three String Trios, in G: D: Cm, Op 9 |
|  | *p* Piano Sonatas No 5–7, in Cm: F: D, Op 10 |
|  | *p* Trio in E♭ for piano, clarinet (or violin) and cello, Op 11 |
|  | *p* Twelve Variations on 'Ein Mädchen' for piano and cello, Op 66 |
|  | *p* Twelve Minuets, Op 139 |
|  | *p* Six Easy Variations in F on a Swiss air, for piano or harp, Op 183 |
|  | *p* Eight Variations in C on Grétry's air 'Une fièvre brûlante', Op 184 |
| 1799 (29) | *p* Violin Sonatas No 1–3, Op 12 |
|  | *p* Piano Sonata No 8 in Cm, *Pathétique*, Op 13 |
|  | *p* Piano Sonatas No 9–10 in E: G, Op 14 |
|  | *p* Seven Ländler Dances for piano in D, Op 168 |
|  | Ten Variations on Salieri's air 'La stessa, la stessissima', for piano, Op 185 |
|  | *p* Seven Variations on Wonter's 'Kind, willst du', for piano, Op 186 |
|  | Eight Variations on Sussmayer's Trio 'Tandeln und Scherzen', Op 187 |
|  | 'Der Wachtelschlag', song, Op 237 |
| 1800 (30) | Sonata for piano and horn (or violin), Op 17 |
|  | String Quartets No 1–6 in F: G: D: Cm: A: B♭ , Op 18 |
|  | Septet in E♭ , for violin, viola, horn, clarinet, bassoon, cello and double-bass, Op 20 |
|  | Symphony No 1 in C major |
|  | Piano Sonata No 11 in B♭ , Op 22 |
|  | Sonata for piano, violin and viola, Op 23 |
|  | *Mount of Olives*, oratorio, Op 85 |
|  | Piano Concerto No 3 in C minor, Op 37 |
|  | Air with Six Variations on 'Ich denke dein', for piano (four hands), Op 160 |
|  | Six Very Easy Variations on an original theme for piano, Op 188 |
| 1801 (31) | *p* Piano Concerto No 1 in C, Op 15 |
|  | *p* Violin Sonata No 5 in F, *Spring*, Op 24 |
|  | String Quintet in C, Op 29 |
|  | *fp The Creatures of Prometheus* (No 1–16) ballet, Op 43 |
| 1802 (32) | *p* Serenade for flute, violin and viola, Op 25 |
|  | *p* Piano Sonata No 12 in A♭ , Op 26 |
|  | *p* Piano Sonata No 13 in E♭ , *Sonata quasi una fantasia*, Op 27 |
|  | *p* Piano Sonata No 14 in C♯ minor, *Moonlight*, Op 27 |
|  | *p* Piano Sonata No 15 in D, *Pastoral*, Op 28 |
|  | Violin Sonatas No 6–8 in A: Cm: G, Op 30 |
|  | Six Variations in F on an original theme for piano, Op 32 |
|  | Fifteen Variations with a fugue on a theme from 'Prometheus' for piano, Op 35 |
|  | Symphony No 2 in D, Op 36 |
|  | Violin Sonata No 9, *Kreutzer*, Op 47 |
|  | Piano Sonatas No 16–18 in C: D: E♭ , Op 31 (1802–4) |
|  | Two Easy Sonatas (No 19–20) in Gm: C for piano, Op 49 |
|  | *p* Rondo for piano, Op 51 |
|  | Terzetto, *Tremate*, for soprano, tenor and bass, Op 116 |
|  | Opferlied, Op 121b |
|  | *p* Seven Variations on 'Bei Mannern' for cello and piano, Op 158 |
|  | *p* Six Ländler Dances in D (No 4 in D minor), Op 169 |
| 1803 (33) | Romance in G for violin and orchestra, Op 40 |
|  | *p* Six Songs for soprano, Op 48 |

*Fidelio*, opera (commenced 1803, last revision 1814), Op 72
*p* 'Das Glück der Freundschaft', song, Op 88
*p* Twelve Kontretänze for orchestra, Op 141
*p* 'Zärtliche Liebe', song, Op 235
*p* 'La Partenza', song, Op 236
Six Songs, Op 75 (1803–10)

1804 (34)    *p* Fourteen Variations in E♭ for piano trio, Op 44
*p* Three Grand Marches, for piano (four hands), Op 45
Piano Sonata No 21, *Waldstein*, Op 53
Symphony No 3, *Eroica*, Op 55
Triple Concerto in C major for piano, violin, cello and orchestra, Op 56
Piano Sonata No 23 in F minor, *Appassionata*, Op 57
Andante favori in F, for piano, Op 170
*p* Seven Variations on 'God save the King', for piano, Op 189
*p* Five Variations on 'Rule, Britannia' for piano, Op 190

1805 (35)    *p* 'An die Hoffnung', song, Op 32
*p* Romance in F for violin and orchestra, Op 5
*p* Eight Songs, Op 52
Piano Concerto No 4 in G, Op 58
Symphony No 5 in C minor, Op 67

1806 (36)    *p* Piano Sonata No 22 in F, Op 54
Symphony No 4 in B♭ , Op 60
Violin Concerto in D major (also same arranged for piano and orchestra), Op 61
Thirty-two Variations in C minor for piano, Op 191 (1806–7)

1807 (37)    *Coriolanus*, overture, Op 62
Mass in C major, Op 86
*Leonore No 1* overture, Op 138
'In questa tomba oscura', arietta, Op 239
String Quartets No 7–9, *Rassumovsky* in F: Em: C, Op 59

1808 (38)    *p* 'Sehnsucht', songs with piano, Op 241

1809 (39)    *p* Symphony No 6 in F, *Pastoral*, Op 68
*p* Cello Sonata No 3 in A, Op 69
*p* Trios No 4–5, for piano, violin and cello, Op 70
Piano Concerto No 5 in E♭ , *Emperor*, Op 73
String Quartet No 10 in E♭ , *Harp*, Op 74
Military March in F, Op 145
*p* 'Als die Geleibt sich trennan wollt', song, Op 238
'Als mir hoch', song, Op 242
'Turteltaube', song, Op 255

1810 (40)    *p* Wind Sextet, Op 71 (early work)
*p* Six Variations in D for piano, Op 76
*p* Fantasy in G minor for piano, Op 77
*p* Piano Sonata No 24 in F♯ , Op 78
*p* Piano Sonata No 25 in G, Op 79
*p* Sextet in E♭ for two violins, viola, cello and two horns, Op 81b
*p* Three Songs for soprano and piano, Op 83
*Egmont*, incidental music, Op 84
String Quartet No 11 in Fm, *Quartett serioso*, Op 95
*p* 'Andenken', song, Op 240
*p* 'Welch ein wunderbares Leben', song, Op 243
*p* 'Der Frühling entbluhet', song, Op 244
'Gedenke mein! Ich denke dein', song, Op 256

1811 (41)    *p* Choral Fantasia in C minor for piano, orchestra and chorus (theme Beethoven's song 'Gegenliebe'), Op 80

|            |                                                                                                      |
|------------|------------------------------------------------------------------------------------------------------|
|            | *p* Piano Sonata No 26 in E♭ , *Les Adieux*, Op 81a                                                  |
|            | *p* Four Ariettas and Duet for soprano and tenor with piano, Op 82                                   |
|            | Piano Trio No 6 in B♭ , *The Archduke*, Op 97                                                        |
|            | *The Ruins of Athens*, overture and eight numbers, Op 113                                            |
|            | *King Stephen*, overture and nine numbers, Op 117                                                    |
|            | 'O dass ich dir', song, Op 247                                                                       |
| 1812 (42)  | Symphony No 7 in A, Op 92                                                                             |
|            | Symphony No 8 in F, Op 93                                                                             |
|            | Violin Sonata No 10 in G, Op 96                                                                       |
|            | Piano Trio No 10 in B♭ , Op 154                                                                       |
| 1813 (43)  | *Wellington's Victory* (or *Battle of Vittoria*), for orchestra, Op 91                               |
|            | Triumphal March in C for orchestra, Op 143                                                           |
|            | 'Dort auf dem hohen Felsen', song, Op 248                                                            |
| 1814 (44)  | Polonaise in C, for piano, Op 89                                                                     |
|            | Piano Sonata No 27 in E minor, Op 90                                                                 |
|            | 'Merkenstein', duet, Op 100                                                                          |
|            | Overture in C, *Namensfeier*, Op 115                                                                 |
|            | Elegiac Song, Op 118                                                                                 |
|            | *Der glorreiche Augenblick*, cantata, Op 136                                                         |
|            | *p* 'Germania', bass solo, Op 193                                                                    |
|            | *Leonore Prohaska*, incidental music, Op 245                                                         |
|            | *p* Twenty-five Irish Songs, Op 223 (1814–16)                                                        |
|            | *p* Twenty Irish Songs, Op 224 (1814–16)                                                             |
|            | *p* Twelve Irish Songs, Op 225 (1814–16)                                                             |
| 1815 (45)  | Cello Sonatas No 4–5 in C: D, Op 102                                                                 |
|            | *Calm Sea and Prosperous Voyage*, for chorus and orchestra, Op 112                                   |
|            | Three Duos for clarinet and bassoon, Op 147                                                          |
|            | *p* 'Es ist vollbracht', bass solo, Op 194                                                           |
|            | Twelve Songs of varied nationality, Op 228                                                           |
|            | 'Wo bluht das Blümchen', song, Op 250                                                                |
|            | Twenty-five Scottish Songs for one and sometimes two voices and small orchestra, Op 108 (1815–16)    |
|            | 'Der stille Nacht', song, Op 246 (1815–16)                                                           |
| 1816 (46)  | 'An die Hoffnung', song, Op 94                                                                        |
|            | 'Wenn ich ein Vöglein war', song, Op 249                                                             |
|            | *An die ferne Geliebe*, song cycle, Op 98                                                            |
|            | *p* 'Der Mann von Wort', song, Op 99                                                                 |
|            | Military March in D, Op 144                                                                           |
| 1817 (47)  | *p* Piano Sonata No 28 in A, Op 101                                                                  |
|            | String Quintet in Cm. (arranged from Op 1, No 3), Op 104                                             |
|            | Fugue in D, Op 137                                                                                    |
|            | *Song of the Monks*, from 'William Tell', Op 197                                                     |
|            | *p* Twenty-six Welsh Songs, Op 226                                                                   |
|            | 'Nord oder Süd', song, Op 251                                                                        |
|            | 'Lisch aus, mein Licht', song, Op 252                                                                |
|            | Symphony No 9, *Choral*, Op 125 (1817–23)                                                            |
| 1818 (48)  | *Missa Solemnis* in D major, Op 123                                                                 |
|            | 'Ziemlich Lebhaft' in B♭ for piano, Op 172                                                           |
|            | Six Very Easy Themes varied, for piano, flute or violin, Op 105 (1818–19)                            |
|            | Piano Sonata No 29 in B♭ . *Hammerklavier*, Op 106 (1818–19)                                         |
|            | Ten National Themes with Variations, for flute or violin and piano, Op 107 (1818–20)                 |
| 1820 (50)  | Piano Sonata No 30 in E, Op 109                                                                       |
|            | Allegro con brio in C, for violin and orchestra, Op 148                                              |
|            | 'Wenn die Sonne nieder sinket', song, Op 253                                                         |

| 1821 (51) | Piano Sonata No 31 in A♭, Op 110 |
|---|---|
| | Bagatelles for piano, Op 119 |
| 1822 (52) | *Consecration of the House*, overture, Op 124 |
| | 'The Kiss', arietta, Op 128 |
| | 'Bundeslied', Op 122 (1822–3) |
| 1823 (53) | Piano Sonata No 32 in C minor, Op 111 |
| | Bagatelles for piano, Op 126 |
| | Variations on a Waltz by Diabelli, Op 120 |
| | 'Minuet of Congratulations', Op 142 |
| | Cantata in E♭, Op 199 |
| 1824 (54) | p *The Ruins of Athens*, march and chorus, Op 114 |
| | p Variations on 'Ich bin der Schneider Kakadu', Op 121a |
| | String Quartet No 12 in E♭, Op 127 |
| 1825 (55) | Great Fugue in B♭ for violins, viola and cello, Op 133 |
| | Rondo a capriccio in G, for piano, Op 129 (1825–6) |
| | String Quartet No 13 in B♭, *Scherzoso*, Op 130 (1825–6) |
| 1826 (56) | String Quartet No 14 in C♯ minor, Op 131 |
| | String Quartet No 15 in A minor, Op 132 |
| | String Quartet No 16 in F, Op 135 |
| | Andante maestoso in C major for piano, Op 174 |

Other works:

Op 38 Trio, arranged from Op 25
Op 41 Revision of Op 25
Op 42 Notturno in D, arranged from Op 8
Op 63 Arrangement of Op 4 for piano trio
Op 64 Arrangement of Op 3 for cello and piano
Op 134 Great Fugue in B♭ for piano (four hands), arrangement of Op 133
Op 150 (MS) Sonatina and Adagio in C minor, for mandolin and cembalo
Op 163 Two Sonatinas for piano (doubtful authenticity)
Op 173 *Für Elise* in A minor, for piano
Op 195 (no details)
Op 198 'O Hoffnung', chorus (four bars), c1818
Op 201 (no details)
Ops 203–22 Canons and small incidental pieces
Op 247a Another setting of Op 247

Published posthumously:

1828 Op 119 Bagatelles for piano
1829 Op 151 Rondo in B♭ for piano and orchestra
    Op 146 Rondino in E♭ (composed very early)
1830 Op 162 Piano Sonata in C, called 'Easy'
1831 Op 192 Eight Variations in E♭ on 'Ich habe ein kleines Huttchen nur'
1834 Op 103 Octet in E♭, for two oboes, two clarinets, two horns, two bassoons
        (original of Op 4)
1836 Op 175 Ten Cadenzas to the piano concertos
1841 Op 227 Twelve Scottish Songs
1865 Op 200 Cantata in E♭, 'Graf, graf, lieber graf'


## BELLINI, Vincenzo
*b Catania, Sicily, 3 November 1801*
*d Puteaux, near Paris, 23 September 1835, aged thirty-three*

He was born of a musical family. From an early age he studied piano under his father, who was himself a composer. A priest gave him the rudiments of schooling, and at the age of seven he studied Latin, modern languages, rhetoric and philosophy. He went to Naples in 1819 to study at the Real Conservatorio di

Musica at the expense of a Sicilian nobleman. The Conservatorio arranged for their student to stage his first opera, *Adelson e Salvina*, in 1825, as a result of which he was given the libretto for an opera for La Scala, Milan, where he mainly lived from 1827 to 1833. In 1830 he had the first attack of gastro-enteritis which was to kill him five years later, and he spent the summer of that year convalescing on Lake Como. 1833 saw him in London to rehearse three of his operas; then to Paris, where he was made a Chevalier of the Légion d'honneur. He was planning to marry at the time of his death.

| | |
|---|---|
| 1825 (24) | *Adelson e Salvina*, opera |
| | *Bianca e Fernando*, opera |
| 1827 (26) | *Il Pirata*, opera |
| 1829 (28) | *La Straniera*, opera |
| | *Zaira*, opera |
| 1830 (29) | *I Capuleti ed i Montecchi*, opera |
| 1831 (30) | *La Sonnambula*, opera |
| | *Norma*, opera |
| 1833 (32) | *Beatrice di Tenda*, opera |
| 1835 (34) | *I Puritani*, opera |

## BENJAMIN, Arthur
*b Sydney, 18 September 1893*
*d London, 10 April 1960, aged sixty-six*

After a general education at Brisbane Grammar School, he entered the Royal College of Music at the age of eighteen and stayed there until the outbreak of war in 1914. After the war he taught piano at the Sydney Conservatorium, returning to London in 1921. In 1924 he won the Carnegie Award, in 1926 he joined the staff of the Royal College of Music, and in 1956 was awarded the Cobbett Medal.

| | |
|---|---|
| 1920 (27) | *Three Impressions*, for voice and string quartet |
| 1924 (31) | *Pastoral Fantasy*, for string quartet |
| | Sonatina for violin and piano |
| 1925 (32) | *Three Mystical Songs*, for unaccompanied chorus |
| 1928 (35) | *Concerto quasi una fantasia*, for piano and orchestra |
| 1931 (38) | *The Devil Take Her*, comic opera |
| 1932 (39) | Violin Concerto |
| 1933 (40) | *Prima Donna*, comic opera |
| 1935 (42) | *Heritage*, for orchestra |
| | *Romantic Fantasy*, for violin, viola and orchestra |
| 1937 (44) | *Nightingale Lane*, for two voices and piano |
| | *Overture to an Italian Comedy*, for orchestra |
| 1938 (45) | Two Jamaican Pieces for orchestra, 'Jamaican Song' and 'Jamaican Rumba' |
| | Sonatina for cello and piano |
| | *Cotillon Suite of English Dance Tunes*, for orchestra |
| 1940 (47) | Sonatina for chamber orchestra |
| 1942 (49) | Concerto for oboe and strings |
| 1944–5 (51–2) | Symphony No 1 |
| 1945 (52) | *From San Domingo*, for orchestra |
| | *Red River Jig*, for orchestra |
| | *Elegy, Waltz and Toccata*, for viola and orchestra |
| 1946 (53) | *Caribbean Dance*, for orchestra |
| 1947 (54) | Ballade for strings |
| 1949 (56) | *The Tale of Two Cities*, opera (1949–50) |

         *Valses Caprices*, for clarinet (or viola) and piano
1951 (58)   *Orlando's Silver Wedding*, ballet
         *North American Square Dance*, for orchestra
1952 (59)   *Divertimento on themes by Glück*, for orchestra
1953 (60)   Three Fanfares
1956 (63)   *Mañana*, opera
1958 (65)   *Le Tombeau de Ravel*, for viola, cello and piano
1959 (66)   String Quartet No 2
1959–60 (66–7) *Tartuffe*, opera
Benjamin also wrote many works for piano.


## BENNETT, Richard Rodney
*b Broadstairs, Kent, 29 March 1936*

His mother was a pupil of Holst. In 1953 he won a scholarship to the Royal Academy of Music, studying with Lennox Berkeley. In 1958 he was awarded a French government scholarship and went to Paris for two years, studying with Boulez. He was awarded the Arnold Bax Society Prize in 1964 and the Ralph Vaughan Williams Award for Composer of the Year in 1965. In 1970/1 he was composer-in-residence at the Peabody Institute, Baltimore.

1954 (18)   Piano Sonata
         Sonatina for flute
1957 (21)   Five Pieces for orchestra
         String Quartet No 3
         Violin Sonata
         Sonata for solo violin
         Sonata for solo cello
         *Four Improvisations*, for violin
1959 (23)   *The Approaches of Sleep*, for soli, chorus and orchestra
1960 (24)   *Journal*, for orchestra
         *Calendar*, for chamber ensemble
         *Winter Music*, for flute and piano (also for orchestra)
1961 (25)   *The Ledges*, one-act opera
         *Suite Française*, for small orchestra
         Oboe Sonata
1962 (26)   *London Pastoral Fantasy*, for tenor and chamber orchestra
         *Three Elegies*, for chorus
         *Fantasy*, for piano
         Sonata No 2 for solo violin
1964 (28)   *The Mines of Sulphur*, opera
         *Jazz Calendar*, ballet in seven scenes
         *Aubade*, for orchestra
         String Quartet No 4
         *Nocturnes*, for piano
1965 (29)   Symphony No 1
         Trio for oboe, flute and clarinet
         *Diversions*, for piano
1966 (30)   *Epithalamion*, for voices and orchestra
         *Childe Rolande*, for voice and piano
1967 (31)   *A Penny for a Song*, opera
         Symphony No 2
         Wind Quintet
         *The Music That Her Echo Is*, song cycle
1968 (32)   Piano Concerto
         *All the King's Men*, children's opera

|          | *Crazy Jane,* for soprano, clarinet, cello and piano |
| 1969 (33) | *A Garland for Marjory Fleming,* for soprano and piano |
| 1970 (34) | Guitar Concerto |
| 1972 (36) | *Commedia II,* for flute, cello and piano |
| 1973 (37) | Concerto for Orchestra |
|          | Viola Concerto for viola and chamber orchestra |
|          | *Commedia III,* for flute/piccolo, oboe/English horn, bass clarinet, horn, trumpet, two percussion, piano/celesta, violin and cello |
|          | *Commedia IV,* for two trumpets, horn, trombone and tuba |
|          | *Alba,* for organ |
|          | *Scena I,* for piano |
|          | *Scena II,* for cello |
| 1974 (38) | *Spells,* for soprano, chorus and orchestra |
|          | *Love Spells,* for soprano and orchestra |
|          | *Sonnet Sequence,* for tenor and strings |
|          | *Four-piece Suite,* divertimento for two pianos |
|          | *Time's Whiter Series,* for counter-tenor and lute |
| 1975 (39) | Violin Concerto in two movements |
|          | Oboe Quartet |
|          | *Travel Notes, Book I,* for string quartet |
| 1976 (40) | *Zodiac,* for orchestra |
|          | *Serenade,* for orchestra |
|          | *The Little Ghost who Died for Love,* for soprano and piano |
|          | *Travel Notes, Book II,* for flute, oboe, clarinet and bassoon |
| 1977 (41) | *Actaeon (Metamorphosis I),* for horn and orchestra |
|          | Music for Strings |
|          | *Kandinsky Variations,* for two pianos |
|          | *Scena III,* for solo clarinet |
|          | *Eustace and Hilda,* for piano |
|          | *Eustace and Hilda,* TV incidental music |
|          | *The Christians,* TV incidental music |
| 1978 (42) | Double-bass Concerto |
|          | Horn Sonata, with piano |
|          | Violin Sonata, with piano |
| 1979 (43) | *Sonnets to Orpheus,* for cello and orchestra |
|          | *Just Friends in Print,* for voice and piano |
|          | *Nonsense,* for youth choir and orchestra |
| 1980 (44) | Harpsichord Concerto |
|          | *Metamorphoses,* octet |
|          | *Puer Nobis,* for chorus |
| 1981 (45) | *Six Tunes for the Instruction of Singing-birds,* for flute solo |
|          | Music for string quartet |
|          | Impromptu on the name of Haydn, for piano |
|          | Sonatina for clarinet solo |
|          | *Noctuary,* ballet, for piano |
|          | *Vocalise,* for soprano and piano |
|          | *Isadore,* ballet |
| 1982 (46) | *Anniversaries,* for ensemble |
|          | *Freda's Fandango,* for ensemble |
|          | *After Syrinx,* for oboe and piano |
|          | *Summer Music,* for flute and piano |
| 1983 (47) | *Memento,* for flute and string orchestra |
|          | Concerto for wind quintet |
|          | Guitar Sonata |
|          | *Letters to Lindbergh,* for female voices and piano duet |
|          | *Seachange,* for unaccompanied chorus |

1984 (48)    *After Syrinx II*, for marimba
             *Nonsense*, for chorus and piano duet
             *Five Sonnets of Louise Labé*, for soprano and eleven players
             *Lullay Mine Liking*, for unaccompanied chorus


## BERG, Alban
*b Vienna, 9 February 1885*
*d Vienna, 24 December 1935, aged fifty*

He was born of a wealthy and artistic family. He trained for and entered the Civil Service, and before he met Schoenberg in 1904 his musical education was negligible. Schoenberg taught him and Webern at the same time, but Schoenberg's championship of Berg brought the latter no great acclaim. He was in the Austrian Army during World War I, though his health was precarious – bronchial asthma plagued him for the rest of his life. During leave in 1917 he started work on *Wozzeck*, and published some other works at his own expense. Devaluation of Austrian currency after 1918 brought him financial problems, and he was often in difficulties; but though he was made a member of the Prussian Academy of Arts in 1930, Nazi Germany made performances of his work impossible. He died from blood-poisoning after an insect bite.

1905–8 (20–3) Seven 'Frühe Lieder' for soprano and piano or orchestra
1906–8 (21–3) Piano Sonata
1908 (23)    *An Leukon*, for voice and piano
1909–10 (24) Four Songs for medium voice and piano
1910 (25)    String Quartet
1912 (27)    Five Orchestral Songs to picture postcard texts by Peter Altenberg
1913 (28)    Four pieces for clarinet and piano
             Three Orchestral Pieces (1913–14)
1917–21 (32–6) *Wozzeck*, opera
1923–5 (38–40) Chamber Concerto for piano, violin and thirteen wind instruments
1925–6 (40)  *Lyric Suite*, for string quartet
1928–34 (43–9) *Lulu*, opera
1929 (44)    Three Pieces for Orchestra
             *Der Wein*, concert aria for soprano and orchestra (possibly 1920)
1935 (50)    Violin Concerto, 'in memory of an angel' (ie Manon Gropius, eighteen-year-old daughter of Mahler's widow by her second husband)


## BERIO, Luciano
*b Oneglia, Italy, 24 October 1925*

He started his studies very early with his father and grandfather, who were both musicians, then continued at the Milan Conservatory with Paribeni and Ghedini. He taught at the Berkshire Music Festival (Tanglewood), at Darmstadt, at Mulls College (California), at Harvard University, the Northwestern University and the Juilliard School of Music in New York. In 1955 he founded the Milan Electronic Studio.

1936 (11)    Pastorale
1946–7 (21)  Four Popular Songs for female voice and piano
1947 (22)    *Petite Suite*, for piano
1949 (24)    *Magnificat*, for two sopranos, mixed chorus and instruments
1950 (25)    Concertino for solo clarinet, solo violin, harp, celeste and strings
             *Opus Number Zoo*, for woodwind quintet and narrator (revised 1970)

43

| 1951 (26) | Two Pieces for Violin and Piano |
|---|---|
| 1952 (27) | *Allez Hop – story for voice, mime and dance,* for mezzo-soprano, eight mimes, ballet and orchestra |
| | Five Variations for piano (1952–3) |
| 1953 (28) | *Chamber Music,* for female voice, clarinet, cello and harp |
| 1954 (29) | *Nones,* for orchestra |
| | Variations for chamber orchestra |
| | *Mutations,* electronic music |
| 1956 (31) | *Allelujah I,* for orchestra |
| | *Allelujah II,* for orchestra |
| | String Quartet |
| | *Perspectives,* electronic music |
| 1957 (32) | Divertimento for orchestra (with Bruno Maderna) |
| | *Serenata,* for flute and fourteen instruments |
| | *El Mar la Mar,* for soprano, mezzo-soprano and seven instruments |
| | *Momenti,* for electronic sound |
| 1958 (33) | *Tempi Concertati,* for flute, violin, two pianos and other instruments (1958–9) |
| | *Differences,* for five instruments and tape |
| | *Sequence I,* for flute |
| | *Theme (Homage to Joyce),* electronic music |
| 1959 (34) | *Quaderni I, II and III from 'Epifanie',* for orchestra (1959–63) |
| 1960 (35) | *Circles,* for female voice, harp and two percussion |
| 1961 (36) | *Visage,* electronic music with voice |
| 1962 (37) | *Passaggio,* messa in scena for soprano, two choirs and instruments |
| 1963 (38) | *Sequence II,* for harp |
| | *Sincronie,* for string quartet (1963–4) |
| 1965 (40) | *Laborintus II,* for voices, instruments and tape |
| | *Rounds,* for cembalo |
| | *Sequence III,* for solo voice |
| 1966 (41) | *Il cambattimento di Tancredi e Clorinda,* for soprano, baritone, tenor, three violins and continuo |
| | *Sequence IV,* for piano |
| | *Sequence V,* for trombone |
| 1967 (42) | *Rounds,* for piano |
| | *Sequence VI,* for viola |
| | *O King,* for voice and five players |
| 1968 (43) | Sinfonia |
| | *Questo vuol dire che,* for three female voices, small choir and tape |
| 1969 (44) | *Opera,* opera in four acts |
| | *Sequence VII,* for oboe |
| | *The Modification and Instrumentation of a Famous Hornpipe as a Merry and Altogether Sincere Homage to Uncle Alfred,* for five instruments |
| 1970 (45) | *Memory,* for electric piano and electric cembalo |
| 1971 (46) | *Bewegung,* for orchestra |
| | *Bewegung II,* for baritone and orchestra |
| | *Ora,* for soprano, mezzo-soprano, flute, English horn, small chorus and orchestra |
| | *Amores,* for sixteen vocalists and fourteen instrumentalists |
| | *Agnus,* for two sopranos and three clarinets |
| | *Autre fois – berceuse canonique pour Igor Stravinsky,* for flute, clarinet and harp |
| 1972 (47) | *E Vó – Sicilian Lullaby,* for soprano and instruments |
| | Concerto for two pianos and orchestra (1972–3) |
| | *Recital I (for Cathy),* for mezzo-soprano and seventeen instruments |

1973 (48)    *Still*, for orchestra
             *Eindrücke*, for orchestra (1973–4)
             *. . . Points on the Curve to Find . . .*, for piano and twenty-two
                instruments
             *Linea*, for two pianos, vibraphone and marimbaphone
1974 (49)    *Per la dolce memoria di quel giorno*, ballet
             *Après visage*, for orchestra and tape
             *Chorus*, for voices and instruments
             *Calmo*, for soprano and instruments
1975 (50)    *Il malato immaginario*, incidental music
             *La ritirata notturna di Madrid*, for orchestra
             *Sequence VIII*, for percussion
             *Sequence IX*, for violin
1976–7 (51–2) *Il Ritorno degli Snovidenia*, for cello and orchestra
1978 (53)    *Encore*, for orchestra
1979–82 (54–7) Duet for two violins
1979–83 (54–8) *Un Re in Ascolto*, opera
1980 (55)    *Entrata*, for orchestra
             *Sequence IXa*, for clarinet
1981 (56)    *La Vera Storia*, suite for orchestra
             *Accordo*, for four groups of musicians
             *Chorale on Sequence VIII*, ensemble
             *Sequence IXb*, for alto saxophone
1982 (57)    *Duo*, for baritone, two violins, choir and orchestra
             *Fanfare*, for orchestra
1983 (58)    *Song*, for clarinet solo


**BERKELEY, Lennox**
*b Boars Hill, near Oxford, 12 May 1903*

He was educated at Gresham's School, Holt, in Norfolk, then at Merton College, Oxford. Through meeting Ravel he studied in Paris with Nadia Boulanger from 1927 to 1932, becoming friendly with Poulenc, Stravinsky, Milhaud, Honegger and Roussel. From 1942 to 1945 he was on the staff of the BBC Music Department. He became president of the Performing Right Society, was awarded the CBE in 1957 and was knighted in 1974. He was professor of composition at the Royal Academy from 1946 to 1968, his pupils including Nicholas Maw, Richard Rodney Bennett, David Bedford and John Tavener. His honours and awards include: Collard Fellowship, 1946; Cobbett Medal, 1962; Ordre de Merite Cultural, Monaco, 1967; Composers' Guild Composer of the Year, 1973, and the Papal Knighthood of St Gregory in the same year; Hon Fellow of Merton College, 1974; and Hon Professor, University of Keele and Hon Fellowship of the Royal Northern College of Music, 1975.

1925 (22)    'The Thresher', for medium voice and piano
c1933 (c30)  Violin Sonata No 2
1934 (31)    Polka for piano
             Three pieces for two pianos (Polka, Nocturne, Capriccio) (1934–8)
1935 (32)    *Jonah*, oratorio
             Overture for orchestra
             String Quartet No 1
             'How Love Came In', for medium voice and piano
             *Etude, Berceuse and Capriccio*, for piano
1936 (33)    Five Short Pieces for piano
1937 (34)    *Domini est terra*, for chorus and orchestra
             *Mont Juic* – suite of Catalan Dances, for orchestra (with Britten *qv*)

| 1938 (35) | *The Judgement of Paris*, ballet |
| | Introduction and Allegro for two pianos and orchestra |
| 1939 (36) | Serenade for string orchestra |
| | Five Songs for solo voice and piano (1939–40) |
| 1940 (37) | Symphony No 1 |
| | Sonatina for recorder (flute) and piano |
| | Four Concert Studies, Set I, for piano |
| | Five Housman Songs for tenor and piano |
| 1942 (39) | String Quartet No 2 |
| | Sonatina for violin and piano |
| 1943 (40) | Divertimento for orchestra |
| | String Trio |
| 1944 (41) | 'Lord, when the Sense of Thy sweet Grace', for mixed choir and organ |
| 1945 (42) | Piano Sonata |
| | Violin Sonata |
| | Six Preludes for piano |
| | *Festival Anthem*, for mixed choir and organ |
| 1946 (43) | Introduction and Allegro for solo violin |
| | Nocturne for orchestra |
| | Five Songs (de la Mare) for high voice and piano |
| 1947 (44) | Piano Concerto |
| | *Four Poems of St Teresa of Avila* for contralto and strings |
| | *Stabat Mater*, for six solo voices and twelve instruments |
| | 'The Lowlands of Holland', for low voice and piano |
| 1948 (45) | Concerto for two pianos and orchestra |
| 1949 (46) | *Colonus' Praise*, for chorus and orchestra |
| | Three Mazurkas for piano |
| | Scherzo for piano |
| 1950 (47) | Sinfonietta for orchestra |
| | Elegy for violin and piano |
| | Toccata for violin and piano |
| | Theme and Variations for solo violin |
| 1951 (48) | *Gibbons Variations*, for tenor, chorus, strings and organ |
| | Three Greek Songs for medium voice and piano |
| 1952 (49) | Flute Concerto |
| | *Four Ronsard Sonnets, Set 1*, for two tenors and piano |
| 1953 (50) | Suite for orchestra |
| c1954 (c51) | *A Dinner Engagement*, opera in one act |
| | *Nelson*, opera in three acts |
| | Trio for violin, horn and piano |
| | Sonatina for piano duet |
| 1955 (52) | Concerto for flute, violin, cello and harpsichord (or piano) |
| | Suite from *Nelson*, for orchestra |
| | Sextet for clarinet, horn and string quartet |
| | *Crux fidelis*, for tenor and mixed choir |
| | *Salve regina*, for unison voices and organ |
| | *Look up Sweet Babe*, for soprano and mixed choir |
| | Concert Study in E♭ for piano |
| 1956 (53) | *Ruth*, opera in three scenes |
| 1957 (54) | Sonatina for guitar |
| | 'Sweet was the Song', for mixed choir and organ |
| 1958 (55) | Concerto for piano and double string orchestra |
| | *Five Poems of W. H. Auden*, for medium voice and piano |
| 1959 (56) | Overture for light orchestra |
| | Sonatina for two pianos |

|          | 'So Sweet Love Seemed', for medium voice and piano |
|----------|-----------------------------------------------------|
| 1960 (57) | *A Winter's Tale*, suite for orchestra |
|          | *Improvisation on a Theme of Falla*, for piano |
|          | Prelude and Fugue for clavichord |
|          | *Missa Brevis*, for mixed choir and organ |
|          | 'Thou hast made me', for mixed choir and organ |
| 1961 (58) | Concerto for violin and chamber orchestra |
|          | Five Pieces for violin and orchestra |
| 1962 (59) | Sonatina for oboe and piano |
|          | *Batter my Heart*, for soprano, mixed choir, organ and chamber orchestra |
|          | 'Autumn's Legacy', for high voice and piano |
| 1963 (60) | *Four Ronsard Sonnets – Set 2*, for tenor and orchestra |
|          | *Justorum Animae*, for mixed choir |
|          | 'Counting the Beats', for high voice and piano |
|          | 'Automne', for medium voice and piano |
| 1964 (61) | *Diversions*, for eight instruments |
|          | 'Songs of the Half-light', for high voice and guitar |
|          | Mass for five voices |
| 1965 (62) | Partita for chamber orchestra |
|          | Three Songs for four male voices |
| 1966–8 (63–5) | Three Pieces for organ |
| 1967 (64) | *Castaway*, opera in one act |
|          | *Signs in the Dark*, for mixed choir and strings |
|          | Oboe Quartet |
|          | Nocturne for harp |
| 1968 (65) | 'The Windhover', for mixed choir |
|          | Theme and Variations for piano duet |
| 1969 (66) | Symphony No 3 |
|          | *Windsor Variations*, for piano duet |
| 1970 (67) | *Dialogues*, for cello and chamber orchestra |
|          | String Quartet No 3 |
|          | Theme and Variations for guitar |
| 1971 (68) | *Palm Court Waltz*, for orchestra/piano duet |
|          | *In Memoriam Igor Stravinsky*, for string quartet |
|          | 'Duo', for cello and piano |
|          | Introduction and Allegro for double-bass and piano |
|          | 'Chinese Songs', for medium voice and piano |
| 1972 (69) | *Four Concert Studies, Set II*, for piano |
|          | Three Latin Motets for five-part choir |
|          | 'Hymn for Shakespeare's Birthday', for mixed choir and organ |
| 1973 (70) | Sinfonia Concertante for oboe and orchestra |
|          | *Antiphon*, for string orchestra |
|          | *Voices of the Night*, for orchestra |
| 1974 (71) | Suite for strings |
|          | Guitar Concerto |
|          | 'Herrick Songs' for high voices and harp |
| 1975 (72) | Quintet for piano and wind |
|          | *The Lord is my Shepherd*, choral |
|          | *The Hill of the Graces*, choral |
| 1976 (73) | Fantaisie for organ |
| 1981 (78) | Bagatelles for two pianos |
| 1982 (79) | Mazurka for piano |
|          | Sonnet for high voice and piano |
|          | *Faldon Park*, opera |

**BERKELEY, Michael**
*b London, 29 May 1948*

He is the son of Lennox Berkeley. He received his early musical training at Westminster Cathedral Choir School and then went on to the Royal Academy of Music; he continued his later studies with his father and Richard Rodney Bennett.

| | |
|---|---|
| 1975 (27) | *Meditations*, for string orchestra |
| 1977 (29) | Concerto for oboe |
| 1978 (30) | Fantasia Concertante |
| | *The Wild Winds*, for soprano and small orchestra |
| | String Trio |
| | *Strange Meeting*, for piano |
| 1979 (31) | *Étude des fleurs*, for cello and piano |
| | Sonata for violin and piano |
| | *Rain*, for tenor, violin and cello |
| | Organ Sonata |
| | *Primavera*, for orchestra |
| | *Fanfare and National Anthem*, for chorus and orchestra |
| 1980 (32) | *American Suite*, for flute/recorder and cello/bassoon |
| | Chamber Symphony |
| | *Uprising*, symphony in one movement |
| 1981 (33) | String Quartet No 1 |
| | String Quartet No 2 |
| | *Wessex Graves*, for voice and harp |
| 1981–2 | *Flames*, for orchestra |
| 1982 (34) | Nocturne for flute, harp, violin, viola and cello |
| | Piano Trio |
| | *Sonata in One Movement*, for guitar |
| | *Gregorian Variations*, for orchestra |
| | *The Romance of the Rose*, for orchestra |
| | *Easter*, anthem for choir, organ and brass |
| | *The Crocodile & Father William*, for girls' choir |
| 1983 (35) | Cello Concerto |
| | *Or Shall We Die?*, oratorio, for soli, chorus and orchestra |
| 1984 (36) | *Funerals & Fandangos*, for solo violin |
| | *Music from Chaucer*, for brass quintet |
| | Horn Concerto |

**BERLIOZ, Hector**
*b La-Côté-St-André, near Grenoble, 11 December 1803*
*d Paris, 8 March 1869, aged sixty-five*

He was the son of a doctor. He was taught piano locally, but preferred guitar and flute, which he mastered. In 1821 he went to Paris to study medicine, but disliked it and went instead to the Paris Conservatory. In 1830 he won the Grand Prix de Rome, after five attempts. In 1835, because of financial difficulties, he became a critic, and remained so for twenty-five years. In the 1840s he travelled widely, conducting his own music. In 1844 he wrote a treatise on instrumentation and orchestration. His music was always neglected in his native France; and in his last years, when his health was poor, he lived the life of a solitary eccentric.

| | |
|---|---|
| 1827 (24) | *Waverley*, overture |
| | *Les francs-juges*, overture |
| | *La Mort d'Orphée*, cantata |

48

| 1828 | (25) | *Herminie*, cantata |
|------|------|------|
| 1829 | (26) | *Cléopâtra*, cantata |
| | | *Huit scènes de Faust*, cantata |
| | | *Irlande*, five songs with piano (1829–30) |
| 1830 | (27) | *Symphonie fantastique* (revised 1831) |
| | | *Sardanapale*, cantata |
| 1831 | (28) | *Le Corsaire*, overture (revised 1855) |
| | | *King Lear*, overture |
| 1832 | (29) | *Le Cinq Mai*, cantata (1830–2) |
| 1834 | (31) | *Harold in Italy*, symphony with solo viola |
| | | *Sara la baigneuse*, for three choirs, with orchestra |
| | | *Les nuits d'été*, song cycle for soprano and orchestra |
| 1837 | (34) | *Grande messe des morts*, requiem |
| 1838 | (35) | *Benvenuto Cellini*, opera (1834–8) |
| | | *Roméo et Juliette*, dramatic symphony for solo voices and chorus (1838–9) |
| 1839 | (36) | *Rêverie et Caprice*, for violin and orchestra |
| 1840 | (37) | *Symphonie funèbre et triomphale*, for chorus, strings and military band |
| 1844 | (41) | *Roman Carnival*, overture (from material from *Benvenuto Cellini*) |
| 1846 | (43) | *The Damnation of Faust*, dramatic cantata (in which occurs Berlioz's arrangement of the Rákóczy March) |
| 1848 | (45) | *La Mort d'Ophelie*, for two-part female chorus (also for voice and piano) |
| 1854 | (51) | *L'Enfance du Christ*, oratorio (1850–4) |
| 1856–9 | (53–6) | *The Trojans*, opera (Part II produced 1863; Part I produced 1890) |
| 1862 | (59) | *Béatrice et Bénédict*, opera (1860–2) |

## BERNERS, Gerald Hugh Tyrwhitt-Wilson (Lord Berners)
*b Bridgnorth, Shropshire, 18 September 1883*
*d London, 19 April 1950, aged sixty-six*

He was educated at Eton. As a composer he was mainly self-taught, though he received encouragement from Stravinsky and Casella. He joined the diplomatic service and became honorary attaché to Constantinople (1909–11) and Rome (1911–19). He wrote under the name of Gerald Tyrwhitt until succeeding his uncle as the 14th Baron and 5th Baronet in 1919. Though virtually an amateur, he had many literary and musical friends – Walton dedicated *Belshazzar's Feast* to him. He also wrote two volumes of autobiography and some novels, and was a talented painter.

| 1919 | (36) | Three Pieces for orchestra – *Chinoiserie, Valse sentimentale, Kasatchok* |
|------|------|------|
| 1920 | (37) | *Fantaisie Espagnole*, for orchestra |
| 1924 | (41) | *Le Carrosse du Saint Sacrement*, opera |
| 1926 | (43) | *The Triumph of Neptune*, ballet |
| 1928 | (45) | Fugue for orchestra |
| 1930 | (47) | *Luna Park*, ballet |
| 1936 | (53) | *A Wedding Bouquet*, ballet |
| 1939 | (56) | *Cupid and Psyche*, ballet |
| 1946 | (63) | *Les Sirènes*, ballet (unpublished) |

He also wrote works for piano, songs, and scores for the films *Halfway House* (1944) and *Nicholas Nickleby* (1947).

**BERNSTEIN, Leonard**
*b Lawrence, Massachusetts, 25 August 1918*

He studied music and piano privately before going to Harvard, where he studied under Piston and soon displayed extraordinary musical abilities. He graduated in 1939 and went on to the Curtis Institute, studying conducting, orchestration and piano. Scholarships then enabled him to attend the Berkshire Music Center at Tanglewood in 1940 and 1941, where he became Koussevitsky's special protégé. He was made Koussevitsky's assistant at Tanglewood in 1942 and the following year was appointed assistant conductor to Rodzinski with the New York Philharmonic Orchestra. In 1943 he was a sensational success when he substituted for Bruno Walter at short notice. In 1945 he began a three-year directorship of the New York City Symphony Orchestra; from 1951 to 1955 he was head of orchestra and conducting departments at Tanglewood, and in 1958 he became musical director of the New York Philharmonic Orchestra, holding this post for eleven years, and being given the honour by that orchestra in 1969 of Laureate Conductor for life.

| | |
|---|---|
| 1937 (19) | Pianoforte Trio |
| | Music for two pianos |
| 1938 (20) | Piano Sonata |
| | *Music for the Dance, No 1* |
| | *Music for the Dance, No 2* |
| | *The Birds*, incidental music |
| 1939 (21) | *Scenes from the City of Sin*, for piano (four hands) |
| 1940 (22) | *The Peace*, incidental music |
| | Sonata for violin and piano |
| | Four Studies for two clarinets, three bassoons and piano |
| 1942 (24) | Sonata for clarinet and piano |
| | Symphony No 1, *Jeremiah* |
| 1943 (25) | *Seven Anniversaries*, for piano |
| | 'I Hate Music', a cycle of five kid songs for soprano and piano |
| 1944 (26) | *Fancy Free*, ballet and suite |
| | *On the Town*, musical comedy and three dance episodes |
| 1945 (27) | *Hashkivenu*, for cantorial solo (tenor), SATB choir and organ |
| | *Afterthought*, for voice and piano |
| 1946 (28) | *Facsimile*, ballet and choreographic essay |
| 1947 (29) | *La Bonne Cuisine*, four recipes for voice and piano |
| | *Simchu na*, for chorus and orchestra/piano |
| | *Reena*, for chorus and orchestra |
| 1948 (30) | Brass Music |
| | *Four Anniversaries*, for piano |
| 1949 (31) | Two Love Songs (Rilke), for voice and piano |
| | Symphony No 2, for piano and orchestra, *The Age of Anxiety* |
| | *Prelude, Fugue and Riffs*, for solo clarinet and jazz ensemble |
| 1950 (32) | *Peter Pan*, incidental music |
| | *Yigdal*, for chorus and piano |
| | *Trouble in Tahiti*, opera in one act |
| 1951 (33) | *Five Anniversaries*, for piano |
| | *Silhouette (Galilee)*, for voice and piano |
| 1953 (35) | *Wonderful Town*, musical comedy |
| 1954 (36) | *Serenade* (after Plato's 'Symposium'), for solo violin, string orchestra, harp and percussion |
| | *On the Waterfront*, film score and suite |
| 1955 (37) | *The Lark*, French and Latin choruses |
| | 'Get Help!', marching song |
| | *Salome*, incidental music |

| 1956 | (38) | *Candide*, comic operetta and overture |
| 1957 | (39) | *Harvard Choruses* |
| | | *West Side Story*, musical and symphonic dances |
| 1958 | (40) | *The Firstborn*, incidental music |
| 1961 | (43) | *Fanfares*, for orchestral ensembles |
| 1963 | (45) | Symphony No 3, for orchestra, mixed chorus, boys' choir, speaker and soprano solo, *Kaddish* |
| 1965 | (47) | *Chichester Psalms*, for mixed choir, boy soloist and orchestra |
| 1968 | (50) | *So Pretty*, for voice and piano |
| 1969 | (51) | *Shivaree*, for double brass ensemble and percussion |
| 1970 | (52) | *Warm-up*, a round for mixed chorus |
| 1971 | (53) | *Mass*, a theatre piece for singers, players and dancers |
| | | *Two Meditations from Mass*, for violoncello and piano |
| 1973 | (55) | *A Little Norton Lecture*, for male chorus |
| 1974 | (56) | *Dybbuk*, ballet and suites |
| 1975 | (57) | *By Bernstein*, a revue |
| 1976 | (58) | *600 Pennsylvania Avenue*, a musical about the problems of housekeeping |
| 1977 | (59) | *Three Meditations from Mass*, for violoncello and orchestra |
| | | *Songfest*, a cycle of American poems for six singers and orchestra |
| | | *Slava!*, overture for orchestra band |
| | | CBS Music |
| 1980 | (62) | Divertimento for orchestra |
| | | *A Musical Toast*, for orchestra |
| | | *Touches*, for piano |
| 1981 | (63) | *Halil*, for flute and orchestra |
| 1982–4 | (64) | *A Quiet Place and Trouble in Tahiti*, opera |

**BERWALD, Franz**
*b Stockholm, 23 July 1796*
*d Stockholm, 3 April 1868, aged seventy-one*

He had no formal education, but studied violin with his father. An astute business man, he set up an orthopaedic institute in Vienna, managed and part-owned a glass works and launched a saw-mill. Most of his musical output was written in the ten years after he sold the orthopaedic institute in 1841. He had some success as a composer in Vienna, but his native Sweden would not accept his rather advanced musical thinking, and few of his works were performed there – though he was made a fellow of the Royal Academy of Music in Stockholm in 1864 and professor of composition in 1867. Many of his works were unperformed in his lifetime and some are now lost. Only in the twentieth century has his work been rediscovered and his worth accepted.

| 1816 | (20) | Theme and Variations for violin and orchestra |
| 1817 | (21) | Double Concerto for two violins and orchestra (now lost) |
| | | Septet for violin, viola, cello, clarinet, bassoon, horn and double-bass |
| 1819 | (23) | Quartet for piano, clarinet, bassoon and horn |
| 1820 | (24) | Symphony No 1 |
| | | Violin Concerto in C♯ minor |
| 1825 | (29) | Serenade for tenor and six instruments |
| 1827 | (31) | *Gustav Wasa*, opera |
| | | Concertstücke for bassoon and orchestra |
| 1842 | (46) | Symphony No 2, *Sérieuse* |
| | | Symphony No 3 |
| | | (Symphony No 4 is lost) |

1844 (48)    *A Country Wedding*, for organ (four hands)
1845 (49)    Symphony No 5, *Singulière*
                 Symphony No 6
                 Five Piano Trios
1852–4 (56–8) Three Piano Trios
1855 (59)    Piano Concerto in D major
1856–8 (60–2) Two Piano Quintets (possibly 1853–4)
1859 (63)    *p* Cello Sonata
1862 (66)    *Estrella de Soria*, opera
Berwald also composed Violin Sonata in E♭. His String Quartet in E♭ major and String Quartet in A minor were performed posthumously in 1887 and 1905 respectively.

## BIRTWISTLE, Harrison
*b Accrington, Lancashire, 15 July 1934*

He studied clarinet and won a scholarship to the Royal Manchester College of Music, later going on to the Royal Academy of Music. From 1962 to 1965 he was on the staff of Cranborne Chase School. In 1966 he was awarded a Harkness International Fellowship and became a visiting fellow of Princeton University in the USA. In 1973 he was Cornell visiting professor at Swarthmore College in Pennsylvania.

1957 (23)    *Refrains and Choruses*, for flute, oboe, clarinet, bassoon and horn
1959 (25)    *Monody for Corpus Christi*, for soprano, flute, horn and violin
                 *Preçis*, for piano
1960 (26)    *The World is Discovered*, for instrumental ensemble
1962–3 (28–9) Chorales for orchestra
1964 (30)    Three Movements with Fanfares for orchestra
                 *Entr'actes and Sappho Fragments*, for soprano and instruments
                 *Description of the Passing of a Year*, narration for mixed choir à
                    cappella
1965 (31)    *Tragoedia*, for instrumental ensemble
                 *Ring a Dumb Carillon*, for soprano, clarinet and percussion
                 *Carmen Paschale*, Motet for mixed choir and organ
1966 (32)    *Verses*, for clarinet and piano
                 *Punch and Judy*, opera (1966–7)
1968 (34)    *Nomos*, for four amplified wind instruments and orchestra
                 *Linoi*, for clarinet and piano
1969 (35)    *Down by the Greenwood Side*, dramatic pastoral
                 *Verses for Ensembles*. for instrumental ensemble
                 *Ut Heremita Solus*, arrangement of instrumental motet
                 *Hoquetus David (Double Hoquet)*, arrangement of instrumental
                    motet
                 *Medusa*, for instrumental ensemble (1969–70)
                 *Cantata*, for soprano and instrumental ensemble
1970 (36)    *Prologue*, for tenor and instruments
                 *Nenia on the Death of Orpheus*, for soprano and instruments
                 *Four Interludes from a Tragedy*, for clarinet and tape
1971 (37)    *An Imaginary Landscape*, for orchestra
                 *Meridian*, for mezzo-soprano, six-part choir and ensemble
                 *The Fields of Sorrow*, for two sopranos, eight-part mixed choir and
                    instruments
                 *Chronometer*, for eight-track electronic tape
1972 (38)    *The Triumph of Time*, for orchestra
                 *Tombeau – in memoriam Igor Stravinsky*, for flute, clarinet, harp and
                    string quartet

*Dinah and Nick's Love Song*, for three soprano saxophones and harp
(or three English horns and harp)
*La Plage – Eight Arias of Remembrance*, for soprano, three clarinets,
piano and marimba
*Epilogue – 'Full Fathom Five'*, for baritone and instruments

1973 (39)    *Grimethorpe Aria*, for brass band
*Chanson de geste*, for solo sustaining instrument and tape
*Five Choral Preludes arranged from Bach*, for soprano and instrumental ensemble

1974 (40)    *Chorales from a Toyshop*, in five parts with variable orchestration
1976 (42)    *Melencolia I*, for orchestra
1977 (43)    *Silbury Air*, for orchestra
*For O, For O, the Hobby Horse is Forgot*, for instrumental ensemble
*Bow Down*, improvised music-theatre
*Frames, Pulse and Interruptions*, ballet

1977–8 (43–4) *Carmen Arcadiae Mechanicae Perpetuum*, for orchestra
1979 (45)    *agm*, choral
*Some Petals from the Garland*, instrumental ensemble
1980 (46)    *On the Sheer Threshold of the Night*, choral
*Clarinet Quintet*
1981 (47)    *Pulse Sampler*, for oboe and claves
1983 (49)    *Deowa*, for soprano and clarinet
*Duets for Storab*, for two flutes

**BIZET, Georges**
*b Paris, 25 October 1838*
*d Bougival, 3 June 1875, aged thirty-six*

His father taught singing and his mother was a gifted pianist. He was admitted to the Paris Conservatory just before his eleventh birthday, studying with Gounod – the greatest influence on his musical life – and Halévy. In 1857 he won the Grand Prix de Rome. In Paris, for a living, he taught piano and did hackwork for publishers. He married Halévy's daughter in 1869. After the early promise of his Symphony in C, written before he was seventeen, his other works were patchy and only moderately received, until with his *Jeux d'enfants* in 1871 he received world acclaim. He died of a throat infection.

1854 (16)    *La Prêtresse*, one-act opera
1855 (17)    Symphony in C major (not performed until 1935)
1857 (19)    *Le Docteur Miracle*, operetta
*Clovis et Clothilde*, cantata
1859 (21)    *Don Procopio*, opera
1863 (25)    *The Pearl Fishers*, opera
1865 (27)    *Chasse fantastique*, for piano
*Ivan the Terrible*, opera (withdrawn, thought lost, recovered
1944, produced 1946 in Würtemburg)
1866 (28)    *Trois esquisses musicales*, for piano or harmonium
1867 (29)    *The Fair Maid of Perth*, opera
1868 (30)    Symphony in C major, *Roma*
*Marche funèbre*, for orchestra
*Variations chromatiques*, for piano
*Marine*, for piano
1869 (31)    *Vasco da Gama*, symphonic ode with chorus
1871 (33)    *Petite Suite d'Orchestre*
*Jeux d'enfants*, twelve pieces for piano duet (later five were made
into an orchestral suite)

| 1872 (34) | *L'Arlésienne*, incidental music |
| | *Djarmileh*, opera |
| 1873 (35) | *Patrie*, overture |
| 1875 (37) | *fp Carmen*, opera |

## BLACHER, Boris
*b Niu-chang, China, 19 January 1903*
*d Berlin, 30 January 1975, aged seventy-two*

He went to Berlin in 1922 to study architecture and mathematics. He studied composition with Koch from 1924 to 1926, and then at Berlin University until 1931. In 1938 he was made director of a composition class at Dresden Conservatory, but in 1939 he relinquished the post because of disagreement with the Nazis. He returned to teaching in Berlin after the war, becoming professor at the Berlin Hochschule in 1948 and director there from 1953 to 1970. He lectured in Salzburg and in the USA, and received many awards; many of his composition pupils have achieved fame.

| 1929 (26) | *Habemeajaja*, chamber opera (lost) |
| | Symphony (unpublished, destroyed) |
| 1931 (28) | Concerto for two trumpets and strings (destroyed) |
| 1932 (29) | *Kleine Marschmusik*, orchestra |
| 1933 (30) | *Capriccio*, for orchestra |
| | *Kurmusik*, for small orchestra |
| 1935 (32) | *Fest im Süden*, dance drama |
| | *Divertimente*, for strings |
| | Piano Concerto (unpublished, lost) |
| 1936 (33) | Three Orchestral Studies (unpublished, destroyed) |
| | *Divertimento*, for wind |
| | *Geigenmusik*, for violin and orchestra |
| 1937 (34) | *Lustspiel-Ouvertüre* (unpublished, destroyed) |
| | *Concertante Musiche*, for orchestra |
| 1938 (35) | Symphony |
| 1939 (36) | *Harlekinade*, ballet |
| | *Concerto da camera* |
| 1940 (37) | *Fürstin Tarakanowa*, opera |
| | *Hamlet*, symphonic poem |
| | Concerto for strings |
| 1941 (38) | *Das Zauberbuch von Erzerum*, ballet |
| 1943 (40) | *Romeo und Julia*, chamber opera |
| 1945 (42) | *Partita*, for strings and percussion |
| 1946 (43) | Concerto for jazz orchestra (unpublished) |
| | *Die Flut*, chamber opera |
| | *Chiarima*, ballet |
| 1947 (44) | *Die Nachtschwalbe*, nocturne |
| | Variations on a theme of Paganini for orchestra |
| | Piano Concerto No 1 |
| 1948 (45) | Violin Concerto |
| 1949 (46) | *Preussisches Märchen*, ballet-opera |
| | *Hamlet*, ballet |
| 1950 (47) | *Lysistrata*, ballet |
| | Concerto for clarinet, bassoon, horn, trumpet, harp and strings |
| | *Dialogue*, for flute, violin, piano and strings |
| 1952 (49) | Piano Concerto No 2 |
| 1953 (50) | *Abstrakte Oper No 1*, opera |
| | *Orchester-Ornament* |

|          | *Studie in Pianissimo*, for orchestra |
| 1954 (51) | *Two Inventions*, for orchestra |
|          | Viola Concerto |
| 1955 (52) | *Der Mohr von Venedig*, ballet |
|          | *Orchester-Fantasie* |
| 1956 (53) | *Hommage à Mozart*, for orchestra |
| 1957 (54) | *Music for Cleveland*, for orchestra |
| 1959 (56) | *Musica Giocosa*, for orchestra |
| 1960 (57) | *Rosamunde Floris*, opera |
| 1961 (58) | Variations on a Theme of Clementi for piano and orchestra |
| 1963 (60) | *Demeter*, ballet |
|          | *Konzertstück*, for wind quintet and strings |
| 1964 (61) | Cello Concerto |
| 1965 (62) | *Tristan*, ballet |
| 1966 (63) | *Virtuose Musik*, for violin, ten wind instruments, timpani, percussion and harp |
|          | *Plus Minus One*, for string quartet and jazz ensemble (unpublished) |
| 1968 (65) | *Collage*, for orchestra |
| 1969 (66) | *Zweihunderttausend Taler*, opera |
| 1970 (67) | Concerto for high trumpet and strings |
|          | *Triga I*, for small orchestra |
| 1971 (68) | Concerto for clarinet and chamber orchestra |
|          | Sonata for two cellos and eleven instruments *ad lib* |
| 1972 (69) | *Yvonne, Prinzessin von Burgund*, opera |
|          | *Stars and Strings*, for jazz ensemble and strings |
| 1974 (71) | *Poème*, for orchestra |
|          | *Pentagramm*, for strings |
| 1975 (72) | *Das Geheimnis des entwendeten Briefs*, chamber opera |

Blacher also wrote incidental music, film scores, five string quartets and other chamber works, works for piano and electronics, choral and solo vocal works.

## BLAKE, David
*b London, 2 September 1936*

He was educated at Latymer Upper School, Hammersmith. After National Service in Hong Kong, where he learned Chinese, he read music at Gonville and Caius College, Cambridge, from 1957 to 1960. He studied in East Berlin in 1960–1, then returned to England to teach for two years before going to the University of York as Granada arts fellow (1963–4). In 1964 he was appointed lecturer there and promoted to professor in 1976.

| 1961–2 (25) | String Quartet No 1 |
| 1964 (28) | *Three Choruses to poems by Robert Frost*, for mixed chorus |
| 1966 (30) | *Beata L'Alma*, for soprano and piano |
|          | Chamber Symphony |
| 1967 (31) | *What is the Cause?* for six unaccompanied voices |
|          | *Sequence*, for two flutes |
| 1968 (32) | *The Almanack*, for mixed chorus |
| 1971 (35) | *Metamorphoses*, for orchestra |
|          | Nonet for wind |
| 1972 (36) | *Scenes*, for solo cello |
|          | *The Bones of Chuang Tzu*, for baritone and piano |
| 1973 (37) | String Quartet No 2 |
|          | *In Praise of Krishna*, for soprano and nine players |
| 1974–6 (38–40) | *Toussaint*, opera |

| 1976 | (40) | Violin Concerto |
|---|---|---|

1976 (40)    Violin Concerto
1978 (42)    *Sonata à la Marcia,* for chamber orchestra
             *Arias,* for solo clarinet
             *From the Mattress Grave,* for high voice and eleven players
             *Nine Poems of Heine,* for high voice and orchestra
1979 (43)    *Cassation,* for wind octet
             Clarinet Quintet
1980 (44)    *Capriccio,* for seven players
1982 (46)    String Quartet No 3
             *Change is Going to Come,* for mezzo, baritone, chorus and four
                 players
1983 (47)    *Rise, Dove,* for baritone and orchestra


**BLISS, Arthur**
b *London, 2 August 1891*
d *London, 27 March 1975, aged eighty-three*

His father was American. He was educated at Rugby and at Pembroke College, Cambridge. In 1914 he attended the Royal College of Music for one term, studying under Stanford, Vaughan Williams and Holst. He obtained an Army commission, served in France, was wounded on the Somme in 1916, gassed at Cambrai in 1918, and mentioned in dispatches. In 1923 he went to Santa Barbara, California, where he lived for two years and married; he made his second visit to America in 1939. In 1941 he worked in the Overseas Music Service of the BBC, and was director of music there from 1942 to 1944. He received a knighthood in 1950, and in 1953 was appointed Master of the Queen's Musick in succession to Sir Arnold Bax. He was an honorary MusD of Edinburgh, London, Cambridge and Bristol universities, an honorary LLD of Glasgow, an honorary fellow of Pembroke College, honorary Freeman of the Worshipful Company of Musicians and gold medallist of the Royal Philharmonic Society.

*c*1915 (*c*24) Piano Quartet in A minor
             String Quartet in A major
1916 (25)    Two Pieces for clarinet and piano
1918 (27)    *Madam Noy,* for soprano, flute, clarinet, bassoon, harp, viola and
                 double-bass
1919 (28)    *As You Like It,* incidental music for two solo violins, viola, cello and
                 singers
             *Rhapsody,* (wordless) for mezzo-soprano, tenor, flute, English
                 horn, string quartet and double-bass
             Piano Quintet (unpublished, MS lost)
1920 (29)    *Rout,* for soprano and chamber orchestra (revised version for full
                 orchestra written at the invitation of Diaghilev, *fp* 1921)
             *Conversations,* for chamber orchestra
             Two Studies for orchestra
             Concerto for piano and tenor voice, strings and percussion
                 (revised 1923; revised as Concerto for two pianos and orchestra,
                 1924)
1920–1 (29–30) *The Tempest,* overture and interludes
1921 (30)    *Mêlée fantasque,* for orchestra (revised 1965)
             *A Colour Symphony* (1921–2, revised 1932). Movements are headed
                 Purple, Red, Blue and Green, and are interpreted in the light of
                 their heraldic associations
1923 (32)    *Ballads of the Four Seasons* (Li-Po), for medium voice and piano
             String Quartet (1923–4) (MS lost)

|          |                                                                                                    |
|----------|----------------------------------------------------------------------------------------------------|
|          | *The Women of Yueh* (Li-Po), song cycle for voice and chamber ensemble                             |
| 1924 (33) | *Masks I–IV*, for piano                                                                           |
| 1926 (35) | Introduction and Allegro for orchestra (revised 1937)                                            |
|          | *Hymn to Apollo*, for orchestra (revised 1965)                                                     |
| 1927 (36) | Four Songs for high voice and violin                                                             |
|          | Oboe Quintet                                                                                       |
| 1928 (37) | *Pastoral: Lie Strewn the White Flocks*, for mezzo-soprano, chorus, flute, drums and string orchestra |
| 1929 (38) | *Serenade*, for baritone and orchestra                                                           |
| 1930 (39) | *Morning Heroes*, symphony for orator, chorus and orchestra                                      |
|          | *Fanfares for Heroes*, for three trumpets, three trombones, timpani and cymbals                    |
| 1931 (40) | Clarinet Quintet                                                                                 |
| 1933 (42) | Viola Sonata                                                                                      |
| 1934–5 (43–4) | *Things to Come*, suite for orchestra from music for the film                                |
| 1935 (44) | *Music for Strings*                                                                              |
| 1936 (45) | *Kenilworth Suite*, for brass                                                                    |
| 1937 (46) | *Checkmate*, ballet                                                                              |
| 1938 (47) | Piano Concerto                                                                                    |
| 1940 (49) | *Seven American Poems*, for low voice and piano                                                  |
| 1941 (50) | String Quartet in B♭ major                                                                        |
| 1943 (52) | *Three Jubilant and Three Solemn Fanfares* for three trumpets, three trombones and tuba, or full military band |
| 1944 (53) | *Miracle in the Gorbals*, ballet                                                                 |
|          | *The Phoenix, Homage to France – August 1944*, orchestral march                                    |
|          | 'Auvergnat', for high voice and piano                                                              |
| 1945 (54) | *Baraza*, concert piece for piano and orchestra with men's voices ad lib                         |
| 1946 (55) | *Adam Zero*, ballet                                                                              |
| 1948–9 (57–8) | *The Olympians*, opera                                                                        |
| 1950 (59) | String Quartet No 2                                                                              |
| 1952 (61) | *The Enchantress*, scena for contralto and orchestra                                             |
|          | Piano Sonata                                                                                        |
| 1953 (62) | *Processional* for full orchestra and organ (composed for performance in Westminster Abbey at the Coronation of Her Majesty Queen Elizabeth II) |
| 1954 (63) | *A Song of Welcome*, for soprano, baritone, chorus and orchestra                                 |
| 1955 (64) | Violin Concerto                                                                                   |
|          | *Meditations on a Theme of John Blow*, for orchestra                                               |
|          | *Elegiac Sonnet*, for tenor, string quartet and piano                                              |
| 1956 (65) | *Edinburgh Overture*, for full orchestra                                                         |
| 1957 (66) | *Discourse*, for orchestra (recomposed 1965)                                                     |
| 1958 (67) | *The Lady of Shalott* ballet                                                                     |
| 1960 (69) | *Tobias and the Angel*, opera in two acts                                                        |
| 1962 (71) | *The Beatitudes*, cantata for soprano, tenor, chorus, orchestra and organ                        |
| 1963 (72) | *Mary of Magdala*, cantata for contralto, bass, chorus and orchestra                             |
|          | *Belmont Variations*, for brass band                                                               |
|          | *A Knot of Riddles*, for baritone and eleven instruments                                           |
| 1964 (73) | *Homage to a Great Man (Winston Churchill)*, march for orchestra                                 |
|          | *The Golden Cantata*, for tenor, mixed chorus and orchestra                                        |
| 1966 (75) | *Fanfare Prelude* for orchestra                                                                  |
| 1967 (76) | *River Music*, for unaccompanied choir                                                           |
| 1969 (78) | *The World is Charged with the Grandeur of God*, for chorus and wind instruments                |

*Angels of the Mind*, song cycle for soprano and piano
Miniature Scherzo for piano

1970 (79)    Cello Concerto
1971 (80)    Two Ballads for women's chorus and small orchestra
            *Triptych*, for piano
1972 (81)    Three Songs for voice and piano
            *Metamorphic Variations*, for orchestra
1974 (83)    *Prelude 'Lancaster'*, for orchestra
1975 (84)    *Shield of Faith*, cantata for soprano, baritone, chorus and organ


## BLITZSTEIN, Marc
*b Philadelphia, 2 March 1905*
*d Martinique, 22 January 1964, aged fifty-eight*

He began to study music at the age of three, made his first public appearance as a pianist at the age of five and began composing aged seven. At sixteen he entered Pennsylvania University, then studied with Boulanger in Paris and Schoenberg in Berlin. He became music critic in *Modern Music*, his particular interest being in the sociological aspects of music. In 1940 and again in 1941 he received Guggenheim Fellowships, and from 1942 to 1945 he was in the US Air Force in England. As a composer he worked chiefly for the theatre. He was killed while on holiday after what appeared to be a political argument.

1926 (21)    *Sarabande*, for orchestra
1928 (23)    *Triple Sec*, opera-farce
1929 (24)    *Parabola and Circula*, opera-ballet
1930 (25)    *Cain*, ballet
            *Romantic Piece*, for orchestra
1931 (26)    *The Harpies*, opera
            Piano Concerto
1932 (27)    *The Condemned*, choral opera
1933 (28)    *Surf and Seaweed*, orchestral suite
1934 (29)    Variations for orchestra
1935 (30)    *Send for the Militia*, theatre sketch
1936–7 (31–2)  *The Cradle Will Rock*, play in music
1937 (32)    *I've Got a Tune*, radio song-play
            *Plowed Under*, theatre sketch
1938–40 (33–35) *No for an Answer*, opera
1942 (37)    *Labor for Victory*, radio series
1943 (38)    *Freedom Morning*, symphonic poem
1944–6 (39–41) *The Airborne*, for tenor, bass, narrator, male chorus and orchestra
1945 (40)    *Galoopchik*, musical play
1946 (41)    *Show*, ballet
            *Native Land*, orchestral suite
            *Regina*, opera
1948 (43)    *The Guests*, ballet
1955 (50)    *Reuben, Reuben*, musical play
1957 (52)    *This is the Garden*, for chorus and orchestra
1957–9 (52–4) *Juno*, musical play
1958 (53)    *Lear*, orchestral study
1959–64 (54–9) *Sacco and Vanzetti*, opera
1963 (58)    *The Magic Barrel*, opera
            *Idiots First*, opera

Blitzstein also wrote incidental music to plays of Shakespeare, Shaw and Hellman; film scores; other choral and vocal works; two string quartets and works for piano.

**BLOCH, Ernest**
*b Geneva, 24 July 1880*
*d Oregon, 15 July 1959, aged seventy-eight*

He was of a Swiss-Jewish family and much of his work is strongly Jewish. He studied in Geneva and other European capitals between the ages of fourteen and twenty-two and was later much in demand as a teacher of composition. He took American citizenship in 1924. In 1930 an endowment enabled him to return to Europe and to full-time composing for eight years; he then returned to America in 1938 and spent the rest of his life composing.

| | |
|---|---|
| 1900–29 (20–49) | *Helvetia*, a symphonic fresco for orchestra |
| 1901–2 (21–2) | Symphony in C♯ minor |
| 1904–5 (24–5) | *Hiver*, symphonic poem |
| | *Printemps*, symphonic poem |
| 1906 (26) | *Poèmes d'Automne*, for voice and orchestra |
| 1910 (30) | fp *Macbeth*, opera (written possibly 1903–9) |
| 1912–4 (32–3) | Prelude and Two Psalms for high voice |
| | *Israel Symphony*, with two sopranos, two altos and bass (1912–16) |
| 1913 (33) | *Trois poèmes Juifs*, for orchestra |
| 1915–16 (35–6) | *Schelomo – Hebrew Rhapsody*, for cello and orchestra |
| 1916 (36) | String Quartet No 1 in B minor |
| 1918–19 (38–9) | Suite for viola |
| | Suite for viola and piano |
| 1920 (40) | Violin Sonata No 1 |
| 1921–3 (41–3) | Piano Quintet |
| 1922–4 (42–4) | *In the Night*, for piano |
| | *Poems of the Sea*, for piano |
| 1923 (43) | *Baal Shem*, for violin and piano |
| | *Melody*, for violin and piano |
| | *Enfantines*, for piano |
| | *Five Sketches in Sepia*, for piano |
| | *Nirvana*, for piano |
| 1924–5 (44–5) | Concerto Grosso for strings with piano obbligato |
| | *In the Mountains (Haute Savoie)*, for string quartet |
| | *Night*, for string quartet |
| | *Three Landscapes*, for string quartet |
| | Three Nocturnes for piano trio |
| | Violin Sonata No 2, *Poème mystique* |
| | *Exotic Night*, for violin and piano |
| | *From Jewish Life*, for cello and piano |
| | *Méditation Hébraïque*, for cello and piano |
| 1925 (45) | *Prélude (Recueillement)*, for string quartet |
| 1926 (46) | *America: an Epic Rhapsody*, for orchestra |
| | Four Episodes for chamber orchestra |
| 1929 (49) | *Abodah*, for violin and piano |
| 1933 (53) | *Avodath Hakodesh*, sacred service for baritone, chorus and orchestra |
| 1934–6 (54–6) | *A Voice in the Wilderness*, symphonic poem for cello and orchestra |
| 1935 (55) | Piano Sonata |
| 1937 (57) | *Evocations*, symphonic suite |
| | Violin Concerto (1937–8) |
| 1938 (58) | Piece for string quartet |
| 1944 (64) | *Suite Symphonique* |
| 1945 (65) | String Quartet No 2 |
| 1946–8 (66–8) | *Concerto Symphonique*, for piano |
| 1949 (69) | *Scherzo fantasque*, for piano |

| 1950 | (70) | Concertino for viola, flute and strings |
| | | Piece for string quartet |
| 1951 | (71) | *Cinq pièces Hébraïques*, for viola and piano |
| | | String Quartet No 3 (1951–2) |
| 1952 | (72) | *Sinfonia Brève* |
| | | Concerto Grosso for string quartet and string orchestra |
| 1953 | (73) | String Quartets No 4 and 5 |

## BLOW, John
*b Newark, Nottinghamshire, baptized 23 February 1649*
*d Westminster, 1708, aged fifty-nine*

His early education was at the Magnus Song School, Newark. At the Restoration he became a chorister in the Chapel Royal, until his voice broke in 1664. In 1668 he became organist at Westminster Abbey, and in 1674 became Master of the Children of the Chapel Royal – a post he kept for the rest of his life. In 1676 he was organist at the Chapel Royal, and in 1677 the degree of doctor of music was conferred on him by the Dean and Chapter of Canterbury. In 1700 he was appointed composer of the Chapel Royal.

| c1684 | (c35) | *Venus and Adonis*, a masque |
| | | Ode for St Cecilia's Day – 'Begin the Song' |
| 1697 | (48) | 'My God, my God, look upon me', anthem |
| 1700 | (51) | *Amphion Anglicus*, collection of songs and vocal chamber music |

Blow also composed many harpsichord pieces, odes for state occasions, secular songs and catches, 110 anthems, thirteen services, etc.

## BOCCHERINI, Luigi
*b Lucca, Italy, 19 February 1743*
*d Madrid, 28 May 1805, aged sixty-two*

He came from an artistic family; his father was a cellist and bass-player. Luigi became a concert cellist, and in 1757 went with his father to play in the Court theatre orchestra in Vienna. In 1766 he made an extensive concert tour, mainly to Paris and in 1768 he went to Madrid where, in 1770, he was appointed to the service of the Infante.

| 1765 | (22) | *La confederazione*, opera |
| 1786 | (43) | *La Clementina*, opera |
| 1801 | (58) | *Stabat Mater* |

Boccherini also composed:
Four cello concerti
Twenty symphonies, including eight concertantes
Twenty-one sonatas for piano and violin
Six sonatas for violin and bass
Six sonatas for cello and bass
Six duets for two violins
Forty-eight trios for two violins and cello
Twelve trios for violin, viola and cello
Eighteen quintets for flute or oboe, violins, viola and cello
Twelve quintets for piano, two violins, viola and cello
Over a hundred quintets for two violins, viola and two cellos
Twelve quintets for two violins, two violas and cello
Sixteen sextets for various instruments
Two octets for various instruments
Vocal works, totalling 467 in all, including a mass for four voices and

instruments; a Christmas cantata; and fourteen concert arias and duets with orchestra
One suite for full orchestra
Over a hundred string quartets


## BOËLLMANN, Leon

*b Ensisheim, Haut-Rohin (now in Alsace), 25 September 1862*
*d Paris, 11 October 1897, aged thirty-five*

In 1871 he went to Paris to enter the École Niedermeyer, graduating from there in 1881, and becoming organist of St Vincent-de-Paul in Paris.

1877 (15)    Piano Quartet
Boëllmann wrote many works for organ, including:
*Fantaisée dialogue*, for organ and orchestra
*Gothic Suite* for organ
Fantasia in A major, for organ
*Heures mystiques*, for organ
Boëllmann also composed:
Symphony in F major
Symphonic Variations for cello and orchestra
Piano Trio
Cello Sonata


## BOÏELDIEU, François Adrien

*b Rouen, 16 December 1775*
*d Jarcy, near Paris, 8 October 1834, aged fifty-eight*

He studied music locally. The libretti of his first two operas were written by his father. At the age of twenty he went to Paris, where he soon received commissions for other operas. In 1798 he became professor of piano at the Paris Conservatory, and studied counterpoint with Cherubini. In 1803 he was appointed conductor of the Imperial Opera in St Petersburg, staying there for eight years. He returned to Paris in 1817 as professor of composition at the Conservatory.

1793 (18)    *La fille coupable*, opera
1795 (20)    Harp Concerto in G major
1800 (25)    *Le calife de Bagdad*, opera
1803 (28)    *Ma Tante Aurore*, opera
1812 (37)    *Jean de Paris*, opera
1825 (50)    *La dame blanche*, opera


## BOITO, Arrigo

*b Padua, 24 February 1842*
*d Milan, 10 June 1918, aged seventy-six*

His mother was a Polish countess. He studied music at the Milan Conservatory, but developed a talent for literature, becoming a music critic and journalist. His first opera, *Mefistofele*, written in 1868, resulted in a riot between progressives and traditionalists at its first performance. He worked on his other opera, *Nerone*, for the rest of his life, never completing it; it was first performed in 1924, six years after his death. Otherwise, his musical output was extremely small. His chief claim to fame is as librettist for other opera composers; notable are his *La Giaconda* for Ponchielli and *Otello* and *Falstaff* for Verdi. His later life was uneventful; he was interested in politics and became a senator in 1912.

1860 (18)    Il Quattro Giugno, cantata
1861 (19)    Le Sorelle d'Italia, opera
1868 (26)    Mefistofele, opera
1875 (33)    La Notte Difonde, for four voices and piano
1877–1915 (35–73) Nerone, operatic tragedy


## BORODIN, Alexander
b St Petersburg, 12 November 1833
d St Petersburg, 27 February 1887, aged fifty-three

The illegitimate son of a prince, he was given the name of one of his father's servants. He had a mediocre upbringing, and initially neglected music in favour of chemistry. He entered the Academy of Physicians at age seventeen, graduated, and practised medicine. Meeting Mussorgsky stimulated his interest in music, and in 1862 he met Balakirev, who persuaded him that his destiny was to compose; but his duties as professor of the Academy of Physicians, his public status as scientist and research chemist, and constant financial difficulties, reduced his musical output. He died of a burst artery in the heart. The musical Kismet is based on his themes.

1847 (14)    Concerto for Flute in D major and minor, with piano
1862–7 (29–34) Symphony No 1 in E♭ major
1867 (34)    The Bogatirs, opera-farce
1869–76 (36–43) Symphony No 2 in B minor
1869–87 (36–54) Prince Igor, opera (left unfinished and completed by Rimsky-
               Korsakov and Glazunov, qv)
1875–9 (42–6) String Quartet No 1 in A major
1880 (47)    In the Steppes of Central Asia, orchestral 'picture'
1881 (48)    String Quartet No 2 in D major
1885 (52)    Petite Suite for piano
             Scherzo in A♭ for piano
1886 (53)    Serenata alla Spagnola, a movement for the string quartet 'B-la-F'
             (the other movements were by Rimsky-Korsakov, Liadov and
             Glazunov, qv)


## BOULEZ, Pierre
b Montbrison, France, 26 March 1925

His early interests were mathematics and science, but in 1943 he began to study composition with Messiaen. On the recommendation of Honegger he was made musical director of the new Compagnie Renaud-Barrault in 1946. In 1954 he founded the Domaine Musicale series of concerts; in 1955 he was a lecturer at Darmstadt and in 1963 lectured at Harvard University and gave courses for conductor at Basle. In 1967 he became guest conductor for the Cleveland Orchestra, and in 1971 he became musical director of the BBC Symphony and the New York Philharmonic orchestras, relinquishing the former post in 1974 and the latter in 1978. In 1974 he took up the direction of the Institut de Recherche et de Coordination Acoustique/Musique in Paris, in which post he has been able to expand himself as one of the great experimenters with serial techniques and with electronics.

1946 (21)    Le visage nuptial, for soprano, alto and chamber orchestra (first
             version)
             Piano Sonata No 1

Sonatina for flute and piano
1947–8 (22–3) *Le soleil des eaux*, for voices and orchestra
Piano Sonata No 2
1949 (24)    *Livre pour cordes*, for string orchestra
*Livre pour quatour*, for string quartet
1951 (26)    *fp Polyphonie X*, for eighteen instruments
Second version of *Le visage nuptial*, for soprano, alto, choir and orchestra
1952 (27)    *fp Structures, Book I*, for two pianos
1954 (29)    *Le marteau sans maître*, for alto voice and six instruments
1955 (30)    *Symphonie mécanique*, music for the film
1957 (32)    *Doubles* for three orchestral groups divisi
*Poésie pour pouvoir*, for reciter, orchestra and tape
*Deux improvisations sur Mallarmé*, for soprano and instrumental ensemble
Piano Sonata No 3
1959 (34)    *fp Tombeau*, for orchestra
1960 (35)    *fp Pli selon pli, Portrait de Mallarmé (Don; Improvisations I, II, III; Tombeau)*, for soprano and orchestra
1961 (36)    *Structures, Book II*, for two pianos
1964 (39)    *fp Figures-Doubles-Prismes*, for orchestra
*Eclat*, for fifteen instruments
1968 (43)    *fp Domaines*, for clarinet and twenty-one instruments
1970 (45)    *Multiples*, for orchestra
*fp Cummings ist der Dichter*, for sixteen mixed voices and instruments
1972–4 (47–9) *. . . Explosante-fixe . . .* , for ensemble and live electronics
1974–5 (49–50) *Rituel, in memoriam Maderna*, for orchestra in eight groups
1981 (56)    *Répons*, for soloists, tape and ensemble
1982–3 (57)  *Poésie Pour Pouvoir* (revision)


**BOYCE, William**
*b London, 1710*
*d London, 7 February 1779, aged sixty-eight*

As a boy he sang in the choir at St Paul's Cathedral. Although he became hard of hearing at an early age, he became composer of the Chapel Royal, director of the Three Choirs Festival and Master of the King's Musick, and was awarded the degree of doctor of music at Cambridge in 1747. Garrick commissioned him and Arne to write musical 'entertainments' for Drury Lane Theatre. He was granted the sole right of publishing his own works – an early instance of musical copyright. He is buried beneath the dome of St Paul's.

*c*1750 (*c*40)  *p* Eight Symphonies in Eight Parts . . . Opera Seconda
1758 (48)    Ode to the New Year
1769 (59)    Ode to the King's Birthday
1772 (62)    Ode to the New Year
1775 (65)    Ode to the King's Birthday
Performed posthumously:
*c*1785        Ten voluntaries for organ or harpsichord
1786          Ode to the King's Birthday
1790          'Oh where shall wisdom be found?', anthem
Boyce also composed church and stage music and songs.

**BRAHMS, Johannes**
*b Hamburg, 7 May 1833*
*d Vienna, 3 April 1897, aged sixty-three*

He studied piano and composition under local teachers. His father played horn and double-bass in local orchestras. A series of introductions culminated in his meeting the Schumann family, and his long friendship with them had an immense influence on him. Schumann was so impressed with Brahms' early compositions that he wrote a critical article about him, and this first brought Brahms to the notice of the world. He became popular as pianist and conductor, holding a position at the court of Detmold for four years. He lived for a year or two in Switzerland, then went to Vienna where he spent the remainder of his life. He died there of cancer of the liver, the same disease that killed his father. Though living in the days of the romantic composers, his own work was always in the classical mould.

| | |
|---|---|
| 1851 (18) | Scherzo in E♭ minor for piano, Op 4 |
| | Six Songs for tenor or soprano, Op 7 (1851–3) |
| 1852 (19) | Piano Sonata No 1 in C major, Op 1 (1852–3) |
| | Piano Sonata No 2 in F♯ minor, Op 2 |
| | Six Songs for tenor or soprano, Op 3 (1852–3) |
| | Six Songs for tenor or soprano, Op 6 (1852–3) |
| 1853 (20) | Piano Sonata No 3 in F minor, Op 5 |
| | Piano Trio No 1 in B major, Op 8 (1853–4) |
| 1854 (21) | Variations on a Theme by Schumann for piano, Op 9 |
| | Four Ballades for piano, in Dm: D: B: Bm, Op 10 |
| | Piano Concerto No 1 in D minor, Op 15 (1854–8) |
| 1855–68 (22–35) | Seven Songs, Op 48 |
| 1855–75 (22–42) | Piano Quartet No 3 in C minor, Op 60 |
| 1855–76 (22–43) | Symphony No 1 in C minor, Op 68 |
| 1856 (23) | 'Lass dich nur nichts dauern', sacred song, Op 30 |
| | Variations on an original theme, for piano, Op 21/1 |
| | Variations on a Hungarian theme, for piano, Op 21/2 |
| 1857–8 (24) | Serenade for orchestra in D major, Op 11 |
| 1857–60 (24–7) | Serenade for orchestra in A major, Op 16 |
| 1857–68 (24–35) | Four Songs, Op 43 |
| | *German Requiem*, Op 45 |
| 1858 (25) | 'Ave Maria', for women's chorus, orchestra and organ, Op 12 |
| | 'Funeral Hymn', for mixed chorus and wind orchestra, Op 13 |
| | Eight Songs and Romances, Op 14 |
| 1858–9 (25–6) | Five Songs, Op 19 |
| 1858–60 (25–7) | Three Duets for soprano and alto, Op 20 |
| 1858–68 (25–35) | Five Songs, Op 47 |
| 1859 (26) | *Marienlieder*, for four-part mixed choir, Op 22 |
| | The 13th Psalm, for three-part women's chorus and organ, Op 27 |
| 1859–60 (26–7) | Three Quartets for solo voices with piano, Op 31 |
| 1859–61 (26–8) | Three Songs, Op 42 |
| 1859–63 (26–30) | Three Sacred Choruses, Op 37 |
| | Twelve Songs and Romances, Op 44 |
| 1859–73 (26–40) | String Quartet No 1 in C minor, Op 51 |
| | String Quartet No 2 in A minor |
| 1860 (27) | Part-Songs for women's chorus, two horns and harp, Op 17 |
| | String Sextet No 1 in B♭ major, Op 18 |
| | Two Motets for five-part mixed choir a cappella, Op 29 |
| 1860–2 (27–9) | Four Duets for alto and baritone, Op 28 |
| 1861 (28) | Variations and Fugue on a Theme by Handel, for piano, Op 24 |
| | Piano Quartet No 1 in G minor, Op 25 |

Piano Quartet No 2 in A major, Op 26
1861–2 (28–9) 'Soldaten Lieder', five songs, Op 41
1861–8 (28–35) Fifteen Romances from 'Magelone', Op 33
1862–3 (29) Piano Studies (Variations on a Theme by Paganini) Books I and II,
Op 35
1862–5 (29–32) Cello Sonata No 1 in Em, Op 38
1862–74 (29–41) Three Quartets for solo voices, Op 63
1863 (30) Song for alto, viola and piano, Op 91
1863–8 (30–5) *Rinaldo*, cantata, Op 50
1863–77 (30–44) Two Motets, Op 74
1863–90 (30–57) Thirteen Canons, Op 113
1864 (31) Fourteen German Folk Songs for four-part choir
Piano Quintet in F minor, Op 34
Four Songs, Op 46
1864–5 (31–2) String Sextet No 2 in G major, Op 36
1864–8 (31–5) Five Songs, Op 49
1865 (32) Trio for piano, violin and horn, in E♭ major, Op 40
1869 (36) *Liebslieder Walzers* (words, Daumer), Op 52
*p* Piano Studies in five books, Books I–II
1870 (37) Alto Rhapsody for alto, male chorus and orchestra, Op 53
1870–1 (37–8) *Triumphlied*, for chorus and orchestra, Op 55
1871 (38) *Schicksallied (Song of Destiny)*, Op 54
Eight Songs, Op 57
Eight Songs, Op 58
1871–3 (38–40) Eight Songs, Op 59
1871–8 (38–45) Eight Piano Pieces in two books: No 1, 2, 5 and 8 are Capriccios;
No 3, 4, 6 and 7 are Intermezzi, Op 76
1873 (40) Variations on a Theme by Haydn, *St Anthony*, for orchestra,
Op 56a
1873–4 (40–1) Nine Songs, Op 63
1874 (41) Four Duets for soprano and alto, Op 61
Seven Songs, Op 62
1875 (42) String Quartet No 3 in B♭ major, Op 67
Fifteen *Neues Liebeslieder* for piano duet, Op 65
1875–7 (42–4) Four Songs, Op 70
1876 (43) Symphony No 1 (completed)
1876–7 (43–4) Five Songs, Op 72
1877 (44) Nine Songs, Op 69
Five Songs, Op 71
Symphony No 2 in D major, Op 73
1877–8 (44–5) Four Ballads and Romances for two voices, Op 75
Six Songs, Op 86
1877–9 (44–6) Six Songs, Op 85
1877–84 (44–51) Four Vocal Quartets, Op 92
1878 (45) Violin Concerto in D major, Op 77
1878–9 (45–6) Violin Sonata No 1 in G major, *Regen Sonate*
1878–81 (45–48) Piano Concerto No 2 in B♭ major, Op 83
Five Songs and Romances for one or two voices, Op 84
1879 (46) Two Rhapsodies for piano, No 1 in Bm: No 2 in Gm, Op 79
*p* Piano Studies in five books, Books III–V
1880 (47) *Academic Festival Overture*, Op 80
1880–1 (47–8) *Tragic Overture*, Op 81
1880–2 (47–9) Piano Trio No 2 in C, Op 87
1882 (49) *Nanie*, Op 82
String Quintet No 1 in F major, Op 88
'Gesang de Parzen', Op 89

1883 (50)    Symphony No 3 in F major, Op 90
1883–4 (50–1) Six Songs and Romances, Op 93a
1884 (51)    'Tagelied (Dank der Damen)', Op 93b
             Five Songs, Op 94
             Seven Songs, Op 95
             Four Songs, Op 96
             Six Songs, Op 97
1884–5 (51–2) Symphony No 4 in E minor, Op 98
1886 (53)    Cello Sonata No 2 in F major, Op 99
             Violin Sonata No 2 in A major, *Meistersinger*, Op 100
             Five Songs, Op 105
             Five Songs, Op 106
             Five Songs, Op 107
1886–8 (53–5) Violin Sonata No 3 in D minor, *Thuner-Sonate*, Op 108
             *Deutsche Fest- und Gedenkspruche*, Op 109
1887 (54)    Double Concerto for violin, cello and orchestra in A minor, Op 102
             *Zigeunerliede*, Op 103
1888 (55)    Five Songs, Op 104
1888–91 (55–8) Six Vocal Quartets, Op 112
1889 (56)    Three Motets, Op 110
1890 (57)    String Quintet No 2 in G major, Op 111
1891 (58)    Trio for piano, violin and clarinet in A minor, Op 114
             Clarinet Quintet in B minor, Op 115
1892 (59)    *Fantasien*, for piano, in two books, Op 116
             Three Intermezzi for piano, Op 117
             Six Piano Pieces (intermezzi, ballade, romance), Op 118
             Four Piano Pieces (three intermezzi, one rhapsody), Op 119
1894 (61)    Sonata No 1 in F minor for piano and clarinet, or viola, Op 120
             Sonata No 2 in E♭ major for piano and clarinet, or viola, Op 120
1896 (63)    Four Serious Songs, Op 121


**BRIAN, Havergal**
*b Dreadan, Staffordshire, 29 January 1876*
*d Shoreham, Sussex, 28 November 1972, aged ninety-six*

At the age of fifteen he was organist at the local church. He became apprenticed to a joiner, and then a representative for timber merchants. He was self-taught in composition, and befriended Elgar and Bantock. In 1912 he moved to London, but was very unsuccessful and destitute. In 1918 he became assistant editor of the *Musical Opinion*, staying in this post until 1939 and writing magazine articles.

1895–6 (19)  *Requiem*, for baritone, chorus and orchestra (discarded)
1899 (23)    *Pantalon and Columbine*, romance for small orchestra (discarded)
1900 (24)    *Tragic Prelude*, for large orchestra (discarded)
1903 (27)    *Burlesque*, variations and overture on an original theme for large
                orchestra
             *Legende*, for large orchestra (lost)
1903 or 1905 (27 or 29) 'Shall I Compare Thee to a Summer's Day?', partsong
1904 (28)    *For Valour*, concert overture
             *Hero and Leander*, symphonic poem (lost)
1904–5 (28–9) Psalm 23 for tenor, chorus and orchestra
1905 (29)    Psalm 137 for baritone, chorus and orchestra
1906 (30)    *First English Suite*
             *Carmilham*, for contralto, chorus and orchestra
1906–7 (30–1) Psalm 68 for soprano, double chorus and orchestra

1907 (31)    *The Vision of Cleopatra*, for soloists, chorus and orchestra
1907–8 (31–2) *Fantastic Symphony* (revised 1912)
1911 (35)    *In Memoriam*, symphonic poem
             *Doctor Merryheart*, comedy overture for orchestra
1912 (36)    'Three Herrick Songs'
             'The Pilgrimage to Kevlaar', ballad for chorus and orchestra (lost)
1914 (38)    *Red May*, march for brass band (lost)
             *English Rhapsody*, tone poem for orchestra (lost)
             Children's Operetta (lost)
1915 (39)    English Suite No 2 (lost)
             *Legend*, for orchestra (lost)
1916 (40)    Three Comic Dances for orchestra (lost)
             *Razamoff*, symphonic drama (lost)
1917–20 (41–4) Comic Opera (revised 1925–32)
1919 (43)    *Tales of Olden Times*, three preludes for small orchestra (lost)
1919–20 (43–4) English Suite No 3
1919–27 (43–51) Symphony No 1, *Gothic*
1920 (44)    Five Symphonic Dances
             *Legend*, for violin and piano
1921 (45)    English Suite No 4
1930–1 (54–5) Symphony No 2
1931–2 (55–6) Symphony No 3
1932–3 (56–7) Symphony No 4
1934 (58)    Violin Concerto No 1 (lost)
1934–5 (58–9) Violin Concerto No 2 (lost)
1937 (61)    Symphony No 5, *Wine of Summer*
1938–44 (62–8) *Prometheus Unbound*, cantata
1947–8 (71–2) Symphony No 6, *Sinfonia Tragica*
1948 (72)    *The Tinker's Wedding*, comedy overture
             Symphony No 7
1949 (73)    Symphony No 8
1950–1 (74–5) *Turandot*, opera
1951 (75)    Symphony No 9
1952 (76)    *The Cenci*, opera
1953 (77)    English Suite No 5
1953–4 (77–8) Symphony No 10
1954 (78)    Symphony No 11
             *Elegy*, symphonic poem for orchestra
1955–6 (79–80) *Faust*, opera
1957 (81)    Symphony No 12
             *Agamemnon*, opera
1959 (83)    Symphony No 13
1959–60 (83–4) Symphony No 14
1960 (84)    Symphony No 15
             Symphony No 16
1960–1 (84–5) Symphony No 17
1961 (85)    Symphony No 18
             Symphony No 19
1962 (86)    *The Jolly Miller*, comedy overture
             Symphony No 20
1963 (87)    Symphony No 21
1964 (88)    Cello Concerto
             Concerto for orchestra
1964–5 (88–9) Symphony No 22, *Symphonia Brevis*
1965 (89)    Symphony No 23
             Symphony No 24

1965–6 (89–90) Symphony No 25
1966 (90)      Symphony No 26
1967 (91)      Symphony No 27
               Symphony No 28
               Symphony No 29
               Symphony No 30
               Fanfare for orchestral brass
1967–8 (91–2) Symphony No 31
1968 (92)      *Legend – Ave atque vale*, for orchestra
               Symphony No 32


**BRIDGE, Frank**
*b Brighton, 26 February 1879*
*d Eastbourne, 10 January 1941, aged sixty-one*

He obtained a scholarship to the Royal College of Music, London, in 1899. In 1906 he joined the Joachim String Quartet as violinist, then the English String Quartet, remaining with them until 1915. Over this period he also did much conducting. In 1923 he visited the USA, as a conductor of his own music.

1902 (23)   *Berceuse*, for violin and small orchestra
1904 (25)   *Novelleten*, for string quartet
            Violin Sonata
1905 (26)   Piano Quintet
            *Phantasie Quartet* in F♯ minor
            *Norse Legend*, for violin and piano
1906 (27)   Three Idylls for string orchestra
            String Quartet in E minor
            Nine Miniatures for cello and piano
1907 (28)   *Isabella*, symphonic poem
            Trio No 1 in C minor, *Phantasie*
1908 (29)   *Dance Rhapsody*, for orchestra
            Suite for strings
1909 (30)   *Dance Poem*, for orchestra
1911 (32)   *The Sea*, suite for orchestra
1912 (33)   String Sextet
1914 (35)   *Summer*, tone poem
1915 (36)   *The Open Air*, poem for orchestra
            *The Story of My Heart*, poem for orchestra
            *Lament*, for strings
            String Quartet in G minor
1916 (37)   'A Prayer', for chorus
1917 (38)   Cello Sonata in D minor and D major
1919–29 (40–50) *The Christmas Rose*, opera
1922 (43)   *Sir Roger de Coverley*, for string quartet or orchestra
            Piano Sonata (1922–5)
1926 (47)   String Quartet No 3
1927 (48)   *Enter Spring*, for orchestra
1928 (49)   *Rhapsody*, for two violins and viola
1929 (50)   Trio No 2
1930 (51)   *Oration 'concert elegiaco'*, for cello and orchestra
1931 (52)   *Phantasm*, rhapsody for piano and orchestra
1937 (58)   String Quartet No 4
1940 (61)   *Rebus*, for orchestra
            *Vignettes de danse*, for small orchestra
            Divertimento for flute, oboe, clarinet and bassoon

## BRITTEN, Benjamin
b Lowestoft, 22 November 1913
d Aldeburgh, 4 December 1976, aged sixty-three

His father was a dental surgeon, his mother a singer. He composed from the age of five and was taught piano, viola and composition, winning a scholarship to the Royal College of Music in 1930 and studying under Ireland and Benjamin. In 1935 he joined the GPO Film Unit and spent four years writing incidental music for films, which led to commissions for theatre and radio work. He met and collaborated with W. H. Auden, who had a great influence on him. In 1939, being a conscientious objector, he went to Canada and America, staying there for two and a half years, and returning to the UK in 1942. He returned to his old home at Snape, and in 1947 moved to Aldeburgh. At the suggestion of his friend Peter Pears the first Aldeburgh Festival was held there in 1948. At the end of 1955 he and Pears made an extended tour of the Far East. For Britten's operas and other large works the Snape Maltings was converted into a concert and opera theatre in 1967; though it was burned down in 1969 it was immediately rebuilt. In 1973 he was admitted to hospital with a heart lesion; and although he continued writing he never fully recovered.

| | |
|---|---|
| 1930 (17) | 'Hymn to the Virgin' |
| 1932 (19) | Sinfonietta for chamber orchestra |
| | Phantasy Quartet for oboe and string trio |
| 1933 (20) | A Boy was Born, choral variations for men's, women's and boys' voices unaccompanied with organ ad lib |
| | Two Part-songs for chorus and piano |
| | Friday Afternoons, twelve children's songs with piano (1933–5) |
| 1934 (21) | Simple Symphony, for string orchestra (based entirely on material which the composer wrote between the ages of nine and twelve) |
| | Suite for violin and piano (1934–5) |
| | Holiday Diary, suite for piano |
| | Te Deum in C major |
| 1936 (23) | Our Hunting Fathers, song cycle |
| | Soirées musicales, suite |
| 1937 (24) | Mont Juic, suite of Catalan Dances for orchestra (with Berkeley, L. qv) |
| | Variations on a Theme of Frank Bridge, for strings |
| | On This Island, song cycle |
| 1938 (25) | Piano Concerto No 1 in D major (revised 1945) |
| 1939 (26) | Violin Concerto in D minor (revised 1958) |
| | Canadian Carnival, for orchestra (1939–40) |
| | Ballad of Heroes, for high voice, choir and orchestra |
| | Les Illuminations, song cycle |
| 1940 (27) | Diversions on a Theme, for piano (left hand) and orchestra |
| | Paul Bunyan, operetta (c1940–1, revised 1974) |
| | Sinfonia da Requiem, for orchestra |
| | Seven Sonnets of Michelangelo, for tenor and piano |
| 1941 (28) | Scottish Ballad, for two pianos and orchestra |
| | Matinées musicales, for orchestra |
| | String Quartet No 1 |
| 1942 (29) | Hymn to St Cecilia, for five-part chorus with solos unaccompanied |
| | A Ceremony of Carols, for treble voices and harp |
| 1943 (30) | Rejoice in the Lamb, a festival cantata |
| | Prelude and Fugue for strings |
| | Serenade, song cycle for tenor, horn and strings |
| 1944 (31) | Festival Te Deum, for chorus and organ |
| 1945 (32) | Peter Grimes, opera |

|           | *The Holy Sonnets of John Donne*, for high voice and piano |
|-----------|------------------------------------------------------------|
|           | String Quartet No 2 |
| 1946 (33) | Variations and Fugue on a Theme of Purcell (*Young Person's Guide to the Orchestra*), for speaker and orchestra |
|           | *The Rape of Lucretia*, opera |
| 1947 (34) | *Albert Herring*, opera |
|           | Canticle No 1, 'My Beloved is Mine' |
|           | Prelude and Fugue on a Theme of Vittoria for organ |
| 1948 (35) | *St Nicholas*, for tenor, choir, strings, piano and percussion |
|           | *The Beggar's Opera*, by John Gay realised from original airs |
| 1949 (36) | *The Little Sweep (Let's Make an Opera)* |
|           | *Spring Symphony*, for three solo singers, mixed choir, boys' choir and orchestra |
|           | A Wedding Anthem for soprano, tenor, chorus and organ |
| 1950 (37) | *Lachrymae*, for viola and piano |
|           | *Five Flower Songs*, for unaccompanied chorus |
| 1951 (38) | *Billy Budd*, opera |
|           | *Six Metamorphoses after Ovid*, for solo oboe |
| 1952 (39) | Canticle No 2, 'Abraham and Isaac', for contralto, tenor and piano |
| 1953 (40) | *Gloriana*, opera |
|           | *Winter Words*, songs |
| 1954 (41) | *The Turn of the Screw*, opera |
|           | Canticle No 3, 'Still Falls the Rain', for tenor, chorus and piano |
| 1955 (42) | *Alpine Suite*, for recorder trio |
|           | Hymn to St Peter, for choir and organ |
| 1956 (43) | *The Prince of the Pagodas*, ballet |
|           | *Antiphon*, for mixed choir and organ |
| 1957 (44) | *Noye's Fludde*, mystery play with music |
|           | Songs from the Chinese, for high voice and guitar |
| 1958 (45) | *Nocturne*, song cycle for tenor, seven obbligato instruments and strings |
|           | *Sechs Hölderlin-Fragmente*, song cycle |
| 1959 (46) | *Missa Brevis* |
|           | *Cantata Academica, Carmen Basiliense*, for soprano, alto, tenor and bass soli, chorus and orchestra |
| 1960 (47) | *A Midsummer Night's Dream*, opera |
| 1961 (48) | *War Requiem*, for soprano, tenor and baritone soli, chorus, orchestra, chamber orchestra, boys' choir, and organ |
|           | Cello Sonata in C major |
| 1963 (50) | Symphony for cello and orchestra |
|           | *Cantata misericordium*, for tenor, baritone, string quartet, string orchestra, piano, harp and timpani |
|           | *Nocturnal*, after John Dowland, for guitar |
| 1964 (51) | *Curlew River*, parable for church performance |
|           | Cello Suite No 1 |
| 1965 (52) | *Gemini Variations*, for flute, violin and piano (four hands) |
|           | *Songs and Proverbs of William Blake*, for voice and piano |
|           | *Voices for Today*, anthem for chorus |
|           | *The Poet's Echo*, for high voice and piano |
| 1966 (53) | *The Burning Fiery Furnace*, parable for church performance |
|           | *The Golden Vanity*, for boys and piano |
| 1967 (54) | Cello Suite No 2 |
|           | *The Building of the House*, overture, with or without chorus |
| 1968 (55) | *The Children's Crusade*, for children's voices and orchestra |
|           | *The Prodigal Son*, parable for church performance |
| 1969 (56) | Suite for harp |

'Who are these children?', for tenor and piano
1970 (57)   *Owen Wingrave*, opera
1971 (58)   Cello Suite No 3
            Canticle No 4, 'Journey of the Magi'
1973 (60)   *Death in Venice*, opera
1974 (61)   Canticle No 5, 'The Death of St Narcissus', for tenor and harp
            Suite on English Folk Tunes for orchestra
            *A Birthday Hansel*, for voice and harp
1975 (62)   *Phaedra*, dramatic cantata for mezzo-soprano and small orchestra
            String Quartet No 3
            *Sacred and Profane*, eight medieval lyrics for unaccompanied
            voices
1976 (63)   Eight Folk Song Arrangements with harp and piano
            *Welcome Ode*, for young people's chorus and orchestra


## BROWN, Earle
*b Luneberg, Massachusetts, 26 December 1926*

He studied engineering and mathematics at the North-eastern University at Boston, before taking a course in composition and theory at the Schillinger School from 1946 to 1950, then teaching there from 1950 to 1952. He became an editor and recording engineer for Capitol Records. From 1968 to 1972 he was composer-in-residence at the Peabody Conservatory in Baltimore, where he received an honorary doctorate of music in 1970. In 1972 he received an award from the National Institute of Arts and Letters and was commissioned by the Koussevitzky Foundation. In 1974 he received a commission from the New York State Council for the Arts and a grant from the National Endowment for the Arts. He was composer-in-residence at the Conservatories of Rotterdam (1974) and Basle (1975).

1952 (26)      *Folio and Four Systems*, for piano and orchestra
               Music for violin, cello and piano
1953 (27)      *Twenty-five Pages — from one to twenty-five pianos*
1961 (35)      *Available Forms II*, for ninety-eight players and two conductors
1962 (36)      *Novara*, for instrumental ensemble
1963 (37)      *From Here*, for chorus and twenty instruments (chorus optional)
               *Times Five*, for flute, trombone, harp, violin, cello and four-channel
                  tape
1964 (38)      *Corroborree*, for two or three pianos
1965 (39)      *Nine Rarebits*, for one or two harpsichords
               String Quartet
1966 (40)      *Modules 1 and 2*, for orchestra
1967–8 (41–2)  *Event-Synergy II*, for instrumental ensemble
1969 (42)      *Modules 3*, for orchestra
1970 (43)      *Syntagm III*, for instrumental ensemble
1972 (45)      *Time Spans*, for orchestra
               *New Piece: Loops*, for choir and/or orchestra
               *Sign Sounds*, for instrumental ensemble
1973 (46)      *Centering*, for solo violin and ten instruments


## BRUCH, Max
*b Cologne, 6 January 1838*
*d Friedenau, near Vienna, 2 October 1920, aged eighty-two*

His mother's family was musical. At the age of fourteen he won the Frankfurt Mozart scholarship. He made a leisurely tour of Germany and Austria, under various teachers, and composed much choral work. In 1867 he became director of the Court Orchestra at Schwartzburg-Sondershausen, after which he toured extensively as a conductor, visiting the USA and spending the years 1880 to 1883 in Liverpool. By the mid-1890s he was generally rated as one of the major composers of the century; then his popularity waned, and when he died he was a much embittered man. Despite his setting of *Kol Nidrei*, the great Hebrew prayer, he was not Jewish.

| 1856 (18) | String Quartet in C minor |
| 1857 (19) | Piano Trio in C minor |
| 1858 (20) | *Scherz, List und Rache*, opera |
| 1860 (22) | String Quartet in E major |
| 1863 (25) | *Die Lorely*, opera |
| c1864 (c26) | *Frithjof-Scenen*, for solo voices, chorus and orchestra |
| 1868 (30) | Violin Concerto No 1 in G minor |
| 1870 (32) | Symphony No 1 in E♭ major |
| | Symphony No 2 in F minor |
| 1872 (34) | *Hermione*, opera |
| | *Odysseus*, Cantata |
| 1878 (40) | Violin Concerto No 2 in D minor |
| 1881 (43) | *p Kol Nidrei*, for cello and piano, or orchestra |
| 1887 (49) | Symphony No 3 in E major |
| 1891 (53) | Violin Concerto No 3 in E major |
| 1905 (67) | Suite on a popular Russian melody |
| 1911 (73) | Konzertstücke for violin, in F♯ minor |

## BRUCKNER, Anton
*b Ansfelden, Upper Austria, 4 September 1824*
*d Vienna, 11 October 1896, aged seventy-two*

He was born into a family of schoolteachers and educated as a chorister at St Florian monastery, where he learned violin, piano, organ and theory. He became a teacher in the same school, an occupation that restricted his development as a composer. In 1856 he became organist at Linz, travelling to Vienna for further study. Unsure of his capacity, he did not commence mature writing until he was well into his thirties. He taught counterpoint and organ at Vienna Conservatory in 1868, becoming professor there in 1871. He made pilgrimages to Bayreuth and became an ardent Wagnerian; this showed in his work and alienated the followers of Brahms, who tended to be critical of Wagner. As a result his compositions received a mixed reception. In 1891 he resigned from the Conservatory, which gave him an honorary doctor of philosophy degree. He retired from public life and continued working on his Ninth Symphony, which he never finished, until the day of his death.

| 1849 (25) | Requiem in D minor |
| 1854 (30) | Solemn Mass in B♭ major |
| 1863 (39) | Symphony in F minor (unnumbered, known as No 00) |
| | Overture in G minor |
| | *Germanenzug*, for chorus and brass |
| 1864 (40) | Symphony in D minor (known as No 0, revised 1869) |
| | Mass No 1 in D minor |
| | *Um Mitternacht*, for male-voice chorus |
| 1866 (42) | Symphony No 1 in C minor (revised 1891) |
| | Mass No 2 in E minor |
| 1868 (44) | Mass No 3 in F minor, *Grosse Messe* (revised 1871 and 1890) |
| 1869 (45) | 'Locus iste', motet |
| 1871 (47) | 'Os uisti', motet |

| 1872 (48) | Symphony No 2 in C minor (revised 1891) |
| 1873 (49) | Symphony No 3 in D minor, *Wagner* (revised 1877 and 1888) |
| 1874 (50) | Symphony No 4 in Eb major, *Romantic* (revised 1880) |
| 1877 (53) | Symphony No 5 in Bb major (revised 1878) |
| 1878 (54) | *Abendzauber*, for baritone and male chorus |
| 1879 (55) | String Quartet |
| 1881 (57) | Symphony No 6 in A major |
| 1883 (59) | Symphony No 7 in E major |
| 1884 (60) | Symphony No 8 in C minor, *Apocalyptic* (possibly 1887, revised 1890) |
|  | *Te Deum* |
| 1894 (70) | Symphony No 9 in D minor (unfinished, *fp* 1903) |

## BULL, John
*b England, c1562*
*d Antwerp, 1628, aged csixty-six*

He was a choirboy in the Chapel Royal of Elizabeth I, became organist at Hereford Cathedral and then at the Chapel Royal. He was a doctor of music at both Oxford and Cambridge, and the first professor of music at Gresham College, London. Falling into trouble with the court, he went to Belgium, becoming organist at the royal chapel at Brussels, and then on to Antwerp, where he was cathedral organist for the last eleven years of his life. He was one of the founders of the keyboard repertoire, standing with Sweelinck at the beginning of the development of contrapuntal keyboard music which culminated with Bach. He is reputedly the originator of the melody 'God Save the Queen', but this is questionable. His works are represented in the Fitzwilliam Virginal Book; he wrote a 'Star' Anthem, which was a geometrical puzzle canon, for voices and viola, one of many musical tricks he liked to play; 120 canons, much sacred vocal music and keyboard works on sacred and secular models, dances and fantasies. No chronological list of his works is available.

## BUSH, Alan
*b London, 22 December 1900*

He studied at the Royal Academy of Music from 1918 to 1922. In 1921 he met Ireland, and was his pupil from 1922 to 1927. In 1925 he was appointed professor at the Royal Academy. He went to Berlin in 1929, studying philosophy and musicology at the university. In 1935 he became a member of the Communist Party, and the following year he formed the Workers' Music Association. He served in the Army from 1941 to 1950, and afterwards toured as conductor, mainly in East European countries.

| 1923 (23) | String Quartet |
| 1924 (24) | Piano Quartet |
| 1924–5 (24–5) | Five Pieces for clarinet, horn and string quartet |
| 1925 (25) | Two Songs for soprano, chorus and orchestra |
| 1927 (27) | *Symphonic Impressions* |
|  | Prelude and Fugue for piano |
| 1928 (28) | *Relinquishment*, for piano |
| 1929 (29) | *Dialectic*, for string quartet |
|  | *Songs of the Doomed*, for tenor, female chorus and piano |
| 1930–5 (30–5) | Dance Overture |
| 1936 (36) | Concert Piece for cello and piano |
| 1937 (37) | Piano Concerto for baritone, piano, chorus and orchestra |
| 1940 (40) | Symphony No 1 |

| 1941 (41) | *Meditation on a German Song*, for violin, piano and strings |
|---|---|
| 1942 (42) | *A Birthday Overture* |
| 1943 (43) | *Esquisse: 1e 14 juillet*, for piano |
| | *Britain's Part*, for speaker, chorus, percussion and piano |
| 1944 (44) | *Lyric Interlude*, for violin and piano |
| 1945 (45) | *Resolution*, overture |
| | English Folk Songs for chorus |
| 1946 (46) | *The Press-Gang*, children's opera |
| | *Homage to William Sterndale Bennett*, for strings |
| | *English Suite*, for strings |
| | *Winter Journey*, for soprano, baritone, chorus, strings and harp |
| 1947 (47) | *Piers Plowman's Day*, suite |
| | Three Concert Studies for piano trio |
| 1948 (48) | Violin Concerto |
| 1948–51 (48–51) | *Wat Tyler*, opera |
| 1949 (49) | Symphony No 2, 'Nottingham' |
| | *Song of Fellowship*, for baritone, chorus and orchestra |
| 1950 (50) | *The Dream of Llewelyn ap Gruffydd*, for male chorus and piano |
| | *Times of Day*, three children's pieces for piano |
| 1951 (51) | *Trent's Broad Reaches*, for horn and piano |
| | *Outdoors and Indoors*, for cello and piano |
| 1952 (52) | Concert Suite for cello and orchestra |
| | *Defender of Peace*, for orchestra |
| | Three English Song Preludes for organ |
| | Ten English Folk Songs for chorus |
| | *Voices of the Prophets*, for voices and piano |
| 1953 (53) | *The Spell Unbound*, children's opera |
| | *Pavane for the Castleton Queen*, for brass band |
| | *Northumbrian Impressions*, for oboe and piano |
| | *The Ballad of Freedom's Soldier*, for tenor, baritone, chorus and orchestra |
| 1954 (54) | *Autumn Poem*, for horn and piano |
| 1954–5 (54–5) | *Men of Blackmoor*, opera |
| 1957 (57) | Nocturne for piano |
| | Melodies for viola and piano |
| 1957–8 (57–8) | *Two Ballads of the Sea*, for piano |
| 1958 (58) | *Ballad of Aldermaston*, for speaker, chorus and orchestra |
| | *The World is His Song*, for baritone, chorus and orchestra |
| 1959 (59) | *Dorian Passacaglia and Fugue* |
| 1959–60 (59–60) | *Byron Symphony*, for baritone, chorus and orchestra |
| 1960 (60) | Suite for harpsichord/piano |
| 1961 (61) | *The Ferryman's Daughter*, children's opera |
| | *Three Raga Melodies*, for violin |
| | *The Tide That Will Never Turn*, for two speakers, baritone, chorus and orchestra |
| 1962 (62) | *The Sugar Reapers*, opera |
| | *Variations, Nocturne and Finale on an English Sea Song*, for piano and orchestra |
| 1963–4 (63–4) | Prelude, Air and Dance for violin, string quartet and percussion |
| 1965 (65) | Partita Concertante |
| | Two Dances for cimbalon |
| 1966–8 (66–8) | *Joe Hill: The Man Who Never Died*, opera |
| 1967 (67) | Suite for two pianos |
| 1968 (68) | *The Alps and Andes of the Living World*, for speaker, tenor, chorus and orchestra |
| 1968–9 (68–9) | *Five Songs of the Asian Struggle*, for chorus and piano |

               *Time Remembered*, for chamber orchestra
1969 (69)      Scherzo for wind and percussion
               Serenade for string quartet
               *The Freight of Harvest*, for tenor and piano
1969–70 (69–70) Sonata for piano
1971–2 (71–2) *Africa*, symphonic movement for piano and orchestra
1972 (72)      *The Liverpool Overture*
               *Corenty ne Kwe-Kwe*, for piano
               *Song for Angela Davis*, for chorus and piano
1973 (73)      *Festival March of British Youth*, for brass band
               Four Songs for mezzo and piano
1974 (74)      Two Songs for baritone and piano
               *Letter Galliard*, for piano
1975 (75)      *Suite of Six*, for string quartet
               Sonatina for recorders and piano
1976 (76)      *Compass Points*, for pipes
1977 (77)      Twenty-four Preludes for piano


## BUSH, Geoffrey
b London, 23 March 1920

He was educated at Salisbury Cathedral Choir School, Lancing College, and
Balliol College, Oxford, where he read classics and music. He has been a lecturer
at both Oxford and London universities. In 1957 he became chairman of the
Composers' Guild, and in 1969 the visiting professor in music at King's College,
London.

1939 (19)      Sonata for two pianos
1940 (20)      Rhapsody for clarinet and string quartet
1941 (21)      *The Spanish Rivals*, opera
               *La belle dame sans merci*, choral
               Piano Concerto
               Sinfonietta Concertante for cello
1943 (23)      Divertimento for strings
               Sonatina for piano
               Nocturne for strings
               *The Rehearsal*, overture
1944 (24)      Sonata for trumpet and piano
1945 (25)      Sonata for violin and piano
1946 (26)      Four Pieces for piano
1947 (27)      Christmas Cantata
1948 (28)      Concerto for oboe and strings
               *A Summer Serenade*, choral
1949 (29)      *Yorick*, overture
               Four Songs of Herrick
1951 (31)      *Twelfth Night, an Entertainment*, choral
1952 (32)      Trio for oboe, bassoon and piano
1954 (34)      Symphony No 1
1955 (35)      *In Praise of Mary*, choral
1956 (36)      *If the Cap Fits*, opera
1957 (37)      Symphony No 2, 'The Guildford'
1959 (39)      *Songs of Wonder*
1960 (40)      *Dialogue*, for oboe and piano
1961 (41)      *Whydah Variations*, for two pianos
               *A Lover's Progress*, songs
1963 (43)      Wind Quintet

1964 (44)    Greek Love Songs
1967 (47)    *The Equation*, opera
               Music for orchestra
1971 (51)    *A Nice Derangement of Epitaphs*, choral
1972 (52)    *Lord Arthur Saville's Crime*, opera
1974 (54)    *The Cat Who Went to Heaven*, opera
               *Dafydd in Love*, choral
1976 (56)    *Magnificat and Nunc Dimittis*, choral
               *A Little Love-Music*, songs
               Concertino No 2 for piano and orchestra
               Six Song Cycles
               *The Blind Beggar's Daughter*, opera
               *The Miller and his Men*, overture
               Concerto for trumpet, piano and strings
               Concerto for light orchestra

Geoffrey Bush has also written many other songs.

## BUSONI, Ferruccio
*b Empoli, near Florence, 1 April 1866*
*d Berlin, 27 July 1924, aged fifty-eight*

He was of Italian/Austrian parentage. His father was a clarinettist and his mother a pianist. He studied piano, attaining concert standard by his mid-teens. He stayed in Leipzig for some years, then travelled to teach in Helsinki, Moscow and the USA. After giving up teaching he worked as a virtuoso pianist, based in Berlin, until 1914. During the war he refused to perform in any of the warring countries, retiring to Switzerland to compose. After the war he returned to Berlin and to concert-giving, but his health failed and he died of a kidney disease.

1880–1 (14–15) String Quartet No 1 in C major
1882 (16)    *Spring, Summer, Autumn, Winter*, for male voice and orchestra
               *Il Sabato del villagio*, for solo voices, chorus and orchestra
               *Serenata*, for cello and piano
1883 (17)    Piano Sonata in F minor
1886 (20)    String Quartet in C minor
               Little Suite for cello and piano
1888 (22)    Symphonic Suite
               *Konzert-Fantasie*, for piano and orchestra; later (1892) called 'Symphonisches Tongedicht'
1889 (23)    String Quartet No 2 in D minor
1890 (24)    *Konzertstücke*, for piano
               Violin Sonata No 1
1895 (29)    Orchestral Suite No 2
1896–7 (30–1) Violin Concerto in D major
1897 (31)    *Comedy Overture*
1898 (32)    Violin Sonata No 2
1903–4 (37–8) Piano Concerto (using male choir)
1907 (41)    *Elégien*, for piano
1908–11 (42–5) *The Bridal Choice*, for orchestra
1909 (43)    *Berceuse élégiaque*, for orchestra
1912 (46)    *Nocturne Symphonique*, for orchestra
1913 (47)    *Indian Fantasy*, for piano and orchestra
1914–16 (48–50) *Arlecchino*, opera
1916–24 (50–8) *Doktor Faust*, opera (completed by Jarnach after Busoni's death and produced in Dresden in 1925)

| 1917 (51) | *Turandot*, opera |
| | *Die Brautwahl*, orchestral suite |
| 1919 (53) | Concertino for clarinet and small orchestra |
| 1920 (54) | Divertimento for flute and orchestra |
| | Sonatina No 6 for piano (chamber fantasy on Bizet's *Carmen*) |
| 1921 (55) | Romance and Scherzo for piano |
| | Elegy for clarinet and piano |
| 1923 (57) | Ten Variations on a Chopin prelude |

Busoni also composed many piano solos and a *Fantasia Contrappuntista* for two pianos, based on Bach's *Art of Fugue*.


## BUTTERWORTH, George
*b London, 12 July 1885*
*d Pozieres, France, 5 August 1916, aged thirty-one*

He spent his boyhood in York, and was educated at Eton. In 1904 he went to Oxford to read Greats. He met Cecil Sharp and Vaughan Williams and worked with them in the English Folk Dance and Song Society. He then spent a year at the Royal College of Music, and wrote critical articles for *The Times*. He destroyed many of his earlier manuscripts in 1914, when he enlisted in the Army; he gained a commission, won the Military Cross, and was killed in action.

| 1909 (24) | 'I Fear Thy Kisses', song |
| 1911 (26) | Six Songs from Housman's *A Shropshire Lad* |
| | Two English Idylls for small orchestra |
| | 'Requiescat', song |
| 1912 (27) | *A Shropshire Lad*, rhapsody for orchestra |
| | *On Christmas Night*, for chorus |
| | *We Get Up In The Morn*, arranged for male chorus |
| | *In the Highlands*, arranged for female voices and piano |
| | 'Bredon Hill' and other songs |
| | Eleven Folk Songs from Sussex |
| | p 'Love Blows as the Wind Blows', for baritone and string quartet |
| 1913 (28) | *Banks of Green Willow*, idyll for orchestra |


## BUXTEHUDE, Diderik
*b Helsingør, Denmark, 1637*
*d Lübeck, 9 May 1707, aged seventy*

He studied organ with his father. In 1660 he was appointed organist at Helsingør, and in 1688 at the Marienkirche in Lübeck, a very lucrative post. It was to hear him play here that J. S. Bach made his famous 200-mile journey. He instigated a series of concerts in Lübeck, the tradition of which extended into the early nineteenth century. One condition of the appointment to the Marienkirche was that the newcomer should marry his predecessor's daughter; this Buxtehude did, and when he retired in 1703 he enforced the same conditions on his successors. One of the applicants was Handel – who refused.

| 1671 (34) | Wedding Arias |
| 1678 (41) | Wedding Arias |
| 1692 (55) | Sonata in D major for viola da gamba, cello and harpsichord |
| 1696 (59) | Seven Trio Sonatas for violin, gamba and basso continuo, Op 1 |
| | Seven Trio Sonatas for violin, gamba and basso continuo, Op 2 |
| 1705 (68) | Wedding Arias |

## BYRD, William
b Lincolnshire, 1543
d Stondon Massey, Essex, 4 July 1623, aged eighty

He was organist at Lincoln Cathedral in 1563. In 1570 he was appointed Gentleman of the Chapel Royal, and at the end of 1572 he moved to London to become joint organist with Tallis at the Chapel Royal. In 1577 he moved to Middlesex, where his wife died. In 1593 he moved to Stondon Massey and remarried, his second wife dying in 1605.

| | |
|---|---|
| 1575 (32) | p Seventeen Motets |
| c1586 (c43) | p A Printed Broadside, for six voices |
| 1588 (45) | p Psalmes, Sonnets and Songs |
| 1589 (46) | p Cantiones sacrae, Book I, twenty-nine motets for five voices |
| | p Songs of Sundrie Natures |
| 1591 (48) | p Cantiones sacrae, Book II, twenty motets for five voices; twelve motets for six voices |
| 1605 (62) | p Gradualia, Book I, thirty-two motets for five voices; twenty motets for four voices; eleven motets for three voices |
| 1607 (64) | p Gradualia, Book II, nineteen motets for four voices; seventeen motets for five voices; nine motets for six voices |
| 1611 (68) | p Psalmes, Songs and Sonnets |

Undated:
Latin Mass to three voices
Latin Mass to four voices
Latin Mass to five voices


## CAGE, John
b Los Angeles, 5 September 1912

He was the son of an inventor. After leaving Pomono College in Claremont in 1930 he went to Paris, Berlin and Madrid to study music, art and architecture. On returning to California he studied with Weiss, Cowell and Schoenberg, and took courses in theory at the University of California in Los Angeles. In 1937 he moved to Seattle, becoming composer-accompanist at the Cornish School. He organised a percussion orchestra in Seattle in 1938, and in 1939 moved to San Francisco. In 1941 he went to Chicago to give courses in New Music.

| | |
|---|---|
| 1933 (21) | Sonata for solo clarinet |
| 1934 (22) | Six Short Inventions for seven instruments |
| 1938 (26) | Metamorphosis, for piano |
| 1939 (27) | First Construction (In Metal), for percussion sextet |
| | Imaginary Landscape No 1, for two variable-speed phonoturntables, frequency recordings, muted piano and cymbal |
| 1941 (29) | Double Music, for percussion |
| 1942 (30) | Wonderful Widow of 18 Springs, for voice and closed piano |
| 1943 (31) | She is Asleep, for twelve tom-toms, voice and prepared piano |
| | Amores, for prepared piano and percussion |
| | Perilous Night, suite for prepared piano (1943-4) |
| 1944 (32) | A Book of Music, for two prepared pianos |
| | Three Dances for two amplified prepared pianos (1944-5) |
| 1946-8 (34-6) | Sonatas and Interludes for prepared pianos |
| 1950 (38) | String Quartet in Four Parts |
| 1951 (39) | Concerto for prepared piano and chamber orchestra |
| | Music of Changes, for piano |
| | Imaginary Landscape No 4, for twelve radios, twenty-four players and conductor |

| | |
|---|---|
| 1952 (40) | *Water Music*, for pianist with accessory instruments |
| | *Williams Mix*, for eight-track tape |
| | *4' 33" (tacet)*, for piano, in four movements |
| 1953–6 (41–4) | *Music for piano '4–84 for 1–84 pianists'* |
| 1954 (42) | *34' 46.776" for a pianist*, for prepared piano |
| 1955 (43) | *26' 1.1499" for a string player* |
| 1957–8 (45–6) | *Winter Music*, for one to twenty pianists |
| | Concerto for piano and orchestra (one to thirteen instrumental parts) |
| 1958 (46) | *Variations I*, for any kind and number of instruments |
| | *Fontana Mix*, (a) a score for the production of one or more tape tracks or for any kind and number of instruments |
| | (b) prerecorded tape material to be performed in any way |
| 1960 (48) | *Cartridge Music* |
| | *Theater Piece*, for one to eight performers |
| 1961 (49) | *Music for Carillon, No 4* |
| | *Variations II* |
| | *Atlas eclipticalis*, for orchestra (1961–2) |
| 1963 (51) | *Variations III* |
| | *Variations IV* |
| 1965 (53) | *Variations V* |
| 1966 (54) | *Variations VI* |
| 1967–9 (55–7) | *H P S C H D*, for seven harpsichords and fifty-two computer-generated tapes (with Lejaren Hiller) |
| 1969 (57) | *Cheap Imitation*, for piano |
| 1970 (58) | *Song Books* |
| 1971 (59) | *Les Chants de Maldoror*, for French-speaking audience of not more than 200 |
| | *62 Mesostics*, for amplified voice |
| | *WGBH-TV*, for composer and technicians |
| 1972 (60) | *Bird Cage*, for twelve tapes |
| 1973 (61) | *Etcetera*, for small orchestra and tape |
| 1974 (62) | *Score and twenty-three parts* |
| | Two Pieces for piano |
| 1974–5 (62–3) | *Etudes Australe*, thirty-two pieces for piano |
| 1975 (63) | *Child of Tree*, for percussion using amplified plant material |
| | *Lecture on the Weather*, for twelve instruments/voices, tapes and film |
| 1976 (64) | *Apartment House*, mixed media event |
| | *Branches*, for percussion solo and amplified plant material |
| | Quartet for twelve amplified voices and concert band |
| | Quartets I–VIII |
| | *Renga*, for seventy-eight instruments and voices |
| 1977 (65) | *Freeman Etudes*, for violin |
| | *Telephones and Birds*, for three performers |
| | *Inlets*, for four performers with couch shells |
| | *49 Waltzes for Five Boroughs* |
| 1978 (66) | *A Dip in the Lake*, for undetermined forces |
| | Chorals for violin |
| 1980 (68) | *Litany for the Whale*, vocal work for two voices |
| 1981 (69) | Thirty Pieces for five orchestras |

**CAMPION (or CAMPIAN), Thomas**
*b probably 1562*
*Baptised London, 12 February 1567*
*Buried London, 1 March 1620, aged fifty-three*

In 1581 he entered Peterhouse, Cambridge, staying there until 1584 but taking no degree. In 1586 he was admitted to Gray's Inn, where the company was literary as well as legal. He qualified as a doctor of medicine at Caen University in 1605. His fame rests as much on his poetry as his music. He composed more than a hundred songs with lute accompaniment.

1601 (39)    *p* A Book of Airs to be Sung to the Lute
1607 (45)    *p* Songs for a Masque to Celebrate the Marriage of Sir James Hay
1613 (51)    *p* Songs for a Masque to Celebrate the Marriage of Princess Elizabeth

**CANTELOUBE (de Calaret), Marie Joseph**
*b Annonay, 21 October 1879*
*d Gridney, 4 November 1957, aged seventy-eight*

He was a pupil of d'Indy at the Schola Cantorum in Paris, and spent most of his life composing, collecting and arranging folk songs of France.

1903 (24)    *Colloque sentimentale,* for voices and string quartet
1904 (25)    *Dans la montagne,* suite for violin and piano
1909 (30)    *Eglogue d'automne,* for voice and orchestra
1910–11 (31) *Vers la princesse lointaine,* symphonic poem
1910–13 (31–4) *Le Mas,* opera
1913 (34)    *Au printemps,* for voice and orchestra
1914 (35)    *Triptyque,* for voice and orchestra
1918–22 (39–43) *L'Arade,* six songs with piano
1929 (50)    *Lauriers,* three pieces for orchestra
1930–2 (51–3) *Vercingétorix,* opera
1934–5 (55)  *Pièces françaises,* for piano and orchestra
1937 (58)    *Poème,* violin and orchestra
1946 (67)    *Rustiques,* for oboe, clarinet and bassoon
Canteloube wrote many folk-song arrangements for chorus or soloists, including the popular *Songs of the Auvergne* (4 vols, 1923–30).

**CARISSIMI, Giacomo**
*b Marini, near Rome, baptised 18 April 1605*
*d Rome, 12 January 1674, aged sixty-eight*

He was the youngest son of an artisan. He became a member of the choir of Tivoli Cathedral from 1623 to 1625, then remained there as organist until 1627. He worked at Assisi from 1628 to 1629, when he was appointed to the Collegio Germanico in Rome as *maestro di cappella,* becoming a priest there in 1637. Despite attractive offers of work elsewhere he remained at the Collegio until his death. He was one of the most influential of seventeenth-century composers, and the first important composer of oratorios. His colossal output, chiefly undated, comprised masses and many motets, oratorios and cantatas.

**CARPENTER, John Alden**
*b Park Ridge, Illinois, 28 February 1876*
*d Chicago, 26 April 1951, aged seventy-five*

His father was a wealthy industrialist and his mother a church singer. He graduated from Harvard in 1897, and was a pupil of Elgar in Rome for several months in 1906. From 1909 to 1936 he was vice-president of his father's firm, but managed to combine business with composing.

| | |
|---|---|
| 1904 (28) | 'Improving Songs for Anxious Children' |
| 1912 (36) | Violin Sonata |
| 1913 (37) | *Gitanjali*, song cycle on poems of Tagore |
| 1915 (39) | *Adventures in a Perambulator*, for orchestra |
| | Concertino for piano and orchestra (revised 1947) |
| 1917 (41) | Symphony No 1 |
| 1918 (42) | Four Negro Songs |
| 1919 (43) | *Birthday of the Infanta*, ballet |
| 1920 (44) | *A Pilgrim Vision*, for orchestra |
| 1921 (45) | *Krazy Kat*, ballet |
| 1925 (49) | *Skyscrapers*, ballet |
| 1928 (52) | String Quartet |
| 1932 (56) | *Patterns*, for piano and orchestra |
| | *Song of Faith*, for chorus and orchestra |
| 1933 (57) | *Sea Drift*, symphonic poem |
| 1934 (58) | Piano Quintet |
| 1935 (59) | *Danza*, for orchestra |
| 1936 (60) | Violin Concerto |
| 1940 (64) | Symphony No 2 |
| 1941 (65) | *Song of Freedom*, for chorus and orchestra |
| 1942 (66) | Symphony No 3 |
| 1943 (67) | *The Anxious Bugler*, for orchestra |
| 1945 (69) | *The Seven Ages*, symphonic suite |
| 1948 (72) | *Carmel Concerto* |

**CARTER, Elliott**
*b New York, 11 December 1908*

He was educated at Harvard from 1926 to 1932, and then from 1932 to 1935 he studied in Paris at the École Normale de Musique and with Boulanger. On returning to the USA he became musical director of the Ballet Caravan until 1940; until 1942 he was on the teaching staff of St John's College, Annapolis. From 1943 to 1944 he worked as a consultant in the Office of War Information, and in 1945 won a Guggenheim Fellowship. He was professor of composition at the Peabody Conservatory from 1946 to 1948, and at Columbia University until 1950. He then retired to the seclusion of Arizona to compose. In 1955/6 he was professor of composition at Queens College, New York; in 1958 he taught at the Salzburg Seminars; and from 1960 to 1962 was professor of composition at Yale. In 1963 he was elected a member of the American Academy of Arts and Sciences, and was appointed composer-in-residence at the American Academy in Rome, taking a similar appointment in Berlin in 1964. In 1972 he was appointed to teach composition at the Juilliard School. He holds many honorary doctorates.

| | |
|---|---|
| 1934 (25) | Flute Sonata (withdrawn) |
| | *Tom and Lily*, oratorio (incomplete) |
| 1936 (27) | Incidental Music to *Sophocles* (unpublished) |

*Mostellaria*, for tenor, baritone, male chorus and chamber orchestra (unpublished)

*Pocahontas*, ballet

1937 (28)  *The Ball Room Guide*, for orchestra
English Horn Concerto (incomplete)
*The Bridge*, oratorio (incomplete)
*Let's Go Gay*, for female voices and two pianos (unpublished)
*Harvest Home*, for unaccompanied voices (unpublished)
*To Music*, for unaccompanied voices (unpublished)

1938 (29)  Prelude, Fanfare and Polka for small orchestra (unpublished)
*Heart not so Heavy as Mine*, for unaccompanied voices (unpublished)
Musical Studies (withdrawn)
*Tell Me, Where is Fancy Bred?* for alto and guitar

1939 (30)  *Canonic Suite* for four saxophones

1940 (31)  Pastorale for cor anglais, horn, viola, cello and piano

1942 (33)  Symphony No 1 (revised 1954)
*The Defense of Corinth*, for speaker, male voices and piano

1943 (34)  *Three Poems of Robert Frost*, for voice and piano
*Warble for Lilac Time*, for voice and piano or small orchestra
*Voyage*, for mezzo or baritone and piano

1944 (35)  *Holiday Overture* (revised 1961)
*The Harmony of Morning*, for female voices and small orchestra

1945 (36)  *Musicians Wrestle Everywhere*, for voices and strings

1945–6 (36–7) Piano Sonata

1947 (38)  *The Minotaur*, ballet
*Emblems*, for male voices and piano

1948 (39)  Wind Quintet
Sonata for cello and piano

1950 (41)  Eight Etudes and a Fantasy for flute, oboe, clarinet and bassoon

1950–1 (41–2) String Quartet No 1

1950–6 (41–7) Eight Pieces for four timpani (one player)

1952 (43)  Sonata for flute, oboe, cello and harpsichord
Elegy for strings

1954 (45)  Symphony No 1, Revised version

1954–5 (45–6) Variations for orchestra

1959 (50)  String Quartet No 2

1961 (52)  Double concerto for harpsichord and piano
*Holiday Overture*, Revised version

1964–5 (55–6) Piano Concerto

1969 (60)  Concerto for orchestra

1971 (62)  String Quartet No 3
Canon for Three

1973–4 (64–5) Duo for violin and piano

1974 (65)  Brass Quintet
*Fantasy on Purcell's Fantasy on One Note*, for brass quintet

1975 (66)  *A Mirror on Which to Dwell*, for soprano and ensemble

1976–7 (67–8) A Symphony of Three Orchestras

1978 (69)  *Syringa*, for mezzo or baritone and eleven instruments

1981 (72)  *In Sleep, In Thunder*, for tenor and fourteen instruments

1983 (74)  *Triple Duo*
*Changes*, for guitar

1984 (75)  *Canon For 4, 'Homage to William'*, for flute, bass clarinet, violin and cello
*Riconoscenza*, for solo violin

## CASELLA, Alfredo
b Turin, 25 July 1883
d Rome, 5 March 1947, aged sixty-three

He learnt piano with his mother from the age of four, and entered the Paris Conservatory in 1896, studying with Fauré. After a term as professor of composition there, in 1915 he returned to Italy. A champion of all that was new in the arts, he founded the Societá Nazionale di Musica in 1917. He wrote many essays and treatises on music, and was a great pianist.

1901 (18)  *Pavana*, for piano
1903 (20)  *Variations sur une chaconne*, for piano
1904 (21)  Toccata for piano
1905–6 (22–3) Symphony No 1
1907 (24)  Cello Sonata No 1
1908 (25)  Sarabande for piano, or harp
           Symphony No 2 (1908–9)
1909 (26)  *Italia*, orchestral rhapsody
           *Notturnino*, for piano or harp
           *Berceuse triste*, for piano
           Orchestral Suite in C major (1909–10)
1910 (27)  *Barcarola*, for piano
1912–13 (29–30) *Le Couvent sur l'eau*, ballet
1913 (30)  *Notte di Maggio*, for voice and orchestra
1914–17 (31–4) *Siciliana* and *Burlesca*, for piano trio
1916 (33)  *Pupazzetti*, for nine instruments
           *Pagine di Guerra*, for orchestra
           *Elegia eroica*, for orchestra
1920 (37)  Five Pieces for string quartet
1921 (38)  *A Notte alta*, for orchestra
1923–4 (40–1) Concerto for string quartet
1924 (41)  *La Giara*, ballet
           Partita for piano (1924–5)
1926 (43)  *Concerto Romano*, for organ and orchestra
           *Introduction, Aria and Toccata*, for orchestra
           *Adieu à la vie*, for voice and orchestra
           *Scarlattiana*, for small orchestra
1927 (44)  Cello Sonata No 2
           Concerto for strings
1928 (45)  Violin Concerto in A minor
           *La Donna Serpente*, opera (1928–31)
1930 (47)  Serenade for small orchestra
1931–5 (48–52) *Introduction, corale e marcia*, for woodwind
1932 (49)  *La Favolo d'Orfeo*, opera
           Sinfonia for clarinet, trumpet and piano
1933 (50)  Concerto for violin, cello, piano and orchestra
1934 (51)  *Notturno e Tarantella*, for cello
           Cello Concerto (1934–5)
1937 (54)  Concerto for orchestra
           *Il deserto tentato*, oratorio
1939–40 (56–7) Sinfonia
1942 (59)  *Paganiniana*, for orchestra
1943 (60)  Concerto for strings, piano and percussion
           Harp Sonata
1944 (61)  *Missa Solemnis 'Pro Pace'*

## CASTELNUOVO-TEDESCO, Mario
b Florence, 3 April 1895
d Hollywood, 15 March 1968, aged seventy-two

He was a pupil of Pizzetti. During and after World War I he was associated with Casella's Societá Italiano di Musica Moderna. He made musical settings of all the songs from Shakespeare's plays – sometimes misunderstanding the text, and once even setting a stage direction! He was at his best in his early work, but later he wrote some excellent guitar music.

| | |
|---|---|
| 1915 (20) | *Copias*, for guitar (orchestra version 1967) |
| 1920 (25) | *Cipressi*, for guitar |
| | *La Mandragola*, opera (1920–3) |
| 1921–5 (26–30) | Thirty-three Shakespeare Songs |
| 1925 (30) | *Le danze del re David*, for piano |
| 1927 (32) | Piano Concerto No 1 |
| 1933 (38) | *Homage to Boccherini*, Sonata for guitar |
| 1936 (41) | Tarantella |
| | Concerto for two guitars and orchestra |
| | Concertino for harp and chamber orchestra |
| 1938 (43) | *Aucassin et Nicolette*, for voice, instruments and marionettes |
| 1939 (44) | Guitar Concerto |
| | Violin Concerto No 2, *The Prophets* |
| 1956 (61) | *All's Well that Ends Well*, opera |
| 1958 (63) | *The Merchant of Venice*, opera |
| | *Saul*, oratorio |
| 1963 (68) | *Song of Songs* |
| 1966 (71) | Sonata for cello and harp |

Castelnuovo-Tedesco also composed:
Violin Concerti No 1 and 3
Piano Concerto No 2
*Concerto Italiano*
Symphonic Variations for violin and orchestra
*An American Rhapsody*
*In Toscana*, opera
Many oratorios


## CATALANI, Alfredo
b Lucca, 19 June 1854
d Milan, 7 August 1893, aged thirty-nine

In his youth he was closely associated with Boito. From 1871 he studied in Paris, where he was much influenced by Gounod and Bizet. His misfortune as an opera writer was in his bad librettists.

| | |
|---|---|
| 1883 (29) | *Dejanire*, opera |
| 1886 (32) | *Edmea*, opera |
| 1890 (36) | *Lorely*, opera |
| 1892 (36) | *La Wally*, opera |


## CAVALLI, Pietro Francesco
b Crema, Italy, 14 February 1602
d Venice, 17 January 1676, aged seventy-three

He was taught music by his father. He became organist at St Mark's, Venice, and spent two years working in Paris. He was a pupil and follower of Monteverdi. His operas are remarkable for their beautiful arias.

1650 (48)   *Magnificat*
1675 (73)   *Vespers*
He wrote more than thirty operas and many sacred works.


## CHABRIER, Emmanuel
*b Ambert, France, 18 January 1841*
*d Paris, 13 September 1894, aged fifty-three*

His father, a successful barrister, determined that Emmanuel should study law, with music as a hobby. He learnt piano from the age of six; two of his early teachers were Spanish, exciting his interest in Spanish music. He studied law in Paris and entered the Ministry of the Interior. He remained a civil servant for eighteen years, but found the leisure to pursue his musical studies. He was over thirty when his first work was published, and nearly forty before he resigned from the Civil Service to devote himself to music and to dabble in painting. He was a great friend of musicians and writers and a patron of artists, including Manet. After ten years of composing he fell into a state of melancholia, and died on the verge of insanity.

1860 (19)   Impromptu in C for piano
1877 (36)   *L'Etoile*, opera
1879 (38)   *Une Education manquée*, operetta
1880 (39)   *Dix Pièces pittoresques*, for piano
1883 (42)   *fp España*, orchestral rhapsody
            *Trois valses romantiques*, for piano duo
1885 (44)   *Habanèra*, for piano
1886 (45)   *Gwendoline*, opera
1887 (46)   *Le Roi malgré lui*, opera
1888 (47)   *Marche joyeuse*, for orchestra


## CHAMINADE, Cécile
*b Paris, 8 August 1857*
*d Monte Carlo, 18 April 1944, aged eighty-six*

A pupil of Godard, she began composing at the age of eight, and from the age of eighteen was appearing frequently in concerts, often playing her own works.

1888 (31)   *Callirhoe*, ballet
Chaminade also composed:
Konzertstücke for piano and orchestra
Two orchestral suites
*Le Sevillane*, opera-comique
Two piano trios
Many songs and piano pieces


## CHARPENTIER, Gustave
*b Dieuze, near Nancy, 25 June 1860*
*d Paris, 18 February 1956, aged ninety-five*

His father was a baker. At the age of fifteen he began work in a spinning mill, where he taught violin to his employer – who was so impressed with Charpentier's talent that he sponsored his entry into the Lille Conservatory. In 1881 he went to the Paris Conservatory, studying with Massenet from 1885 and winning the Prix de Rome in 1887. In 1902 he founded the Conservatoire Populaire Mimi Pinson, to give working girls greater opportunities to enjoy and perform music. He succeeded Massenet as a member of the Académie des Beaux Arts in 1912. After World War II he became a recluse.

| 1890 (30) | *Impressions d'Italie*, orchestral suite |
| 1892 (32) | *La vie du poète*, cantata |
| 1894 (34) | *Poèmes chantées*, for voice and piano or orchestra |
| 1895 (35) | *Impressions fausses*, for voice and orchestra |
| 1896 (36) | *Sérénade à Watteau*, for voice and orchestra |
| 1900 (40) | *Louise*, opera |
| 1913 (53) | *Julien*, opera |

## CHARPENTIER, Marc-Antoine
*b Paris, ?1645–50*
*d Paris, 24 February 1704*

He studied with Carissimi in Rome from 1662 to 1667, when he took up his first employment with the Duchesse de Guise. After Molière's collaboration with Lully ended in 1672 Charpentier worked with Molière in his theatre, composing music for plays and ballets. By 1680 he was employed by the Grand Dauphin as musical director, and in 1680 he became composer to the principal Jesuit church in Paris. In 1698 he was made *maître de musique* of the Sainte-Chapelle, holding that position until his death.

Marc-Antoine Charpentier wrote: eleven masses; eighty-four psalms and much other church music; thirty-five oratorios; eight cantatas; fifteen pastorals and operas; many sacred and secular instrumental works

## CHAUSSON, Ernest
*b Paris, 20 January 1855*
*d Limay, near Mantes, Yvelines, 10 June 1899, aged forty-four*

He studied law at the University of Paris and then entered the Conservatory, as a pupil of Massenet, for composition, and Franck, for organ; after a few months he withdrew from the Conservatory and became a private pupil of Franck. His house became a rendezvous for the well-known musicians, writers and painters of the day. His great friend was Debussy, whom he often helped financially. He was killed in a bicycling accident while on holiday.

| 1880 (25) | *Les Caprices de Marianne*, opera |
| | *Joan of Arc*, for chorus |
| 1882 (27) | *Viviane*, symphonic poem |
| | Piano Trio in G minor |
| | *Poème de l'amour et de la mer*, for voice and piano (1882–92) |
| 1884–5 (29–30) | *Hélène*, opera |
| 1886 (31) | *Hymne Védique*, for chorus and orchestra |
| | *Solitude dans les bois*, for orchestra |
| 1887 (32) | *Chant Nuptial* |
| 1890 (35) | Symphony in B♭ major |
| 1891 (36) | Concerto for piano, violin and string quartet |
| 1895 (40) | *Le Roi Arthus*, opera, *fp* 1903 |
| 1896 (41) | *Poème*, for violin and orchestra |
| 1897 (42) | *Chant funèbre* |
| | *Ballata* |
| | Piano Quartet in A major |
| 1898 (43) | *Soir de fête*, symphonic poem |
| 1899 (44) | String Quartet in C minor, unfinished |

## CHÁVEZ, Carlos
b Mexico City, 13 June 1899
d Mexico City, 2 August 1978, aged seventy-nine

His grandfather was Indian, and his father a government official. He first studied music under his elder brother, then from 1910 to 1914 with Ponce. His training was as a pianist; he took no lessons in composition. In 1921 he made his début as a composer with a concert of his works. In 1923 he went to the USA, where he formed strong musical associations and friendships. In 1928 he became director of the new Mexico Symphony Orchestra, a position he held for twenty years. Also in 1928 he became director of the National Conservatory. He was director-general of the National Institute of Fine Arts from 1947 to 1952. He gained many international honours.

| | |
|---|---|
| 1920 (21) | Symphony |
| | Piano Sonata No 1 |
| 1921 (22) | *El Fuego Nuevo*, ballet |
| | String Quartet No 1 |
| 1923 (24) | Piano Sonata No 2 |
| 1924 (25) | Sonatina for violin and piano |
| | Sonatina for cello and piano |
| 1925 (26) | *Energia*, for nine instruments |
| 1926 (27) | *Los cuatro soles*, ballet |
| 1927 (28) | *HP* (ie, Horsepower), ballet |
| 1930 (31) | Sonata for horns |
| 1932 (33) | String Quartet No 2 |
| 1933 (34) | Symphony No 1, *Sinfonia di Antigona* |
| | Cantos de Mexico |
| | *Soli No 1*, for oboe, clarinet, trumpet and bassoon |
| 1935 (36) | Symphony No 2, *Sinfonia India* |
| | *Obertura Republicana* |
| 1938 (39) | Concerto for four horns |
| 1939 (40) | Four Nocturnes for voice and orchestra |
| 1940 (41) | Piano Concerto |
| | *Antigona*, ballet |
| | *Xochipili-Macuilxochitl* (the Aztec God of Music), for Mexican orchestra |
| 1942 (43) | Toccata for percussion instruments |
| 1944 (45) | *Hija de Colquide* (Daughter of Colchis), ballet |
| 1945 (46) | String Quartet No 3 |
| | *Piramide*, ballet |
| 1948–50 (49–51) | Violin Concerto, in eight sections played without a break (revised 1962) |
| 1951 (52) | Symphony No 3 |
| 1953 (54) | Symphony No 4, *Sinfonia Romantica* |
| | Symphony No 5, *Symphony for Strings* |
| 1958 (59) | *Inventions No 1*, for piano |
| 1960 (61) | *Love Propitiated*, opera |
| 1961 (62) | Symphony No 6 |
| | *Soli No 2*, for wind quintet |
| 1964 (65) | *Resonancias*, for orchestra |
| | *Tambuco*, for six percussion |
| 1965 (66) | *Soli No 3*, for bassoon, trumpet, viola, timpani and orchestra |
| | Violin Concerto No 2 |
| | *Inventions No 2*, for violin, viola and cello |
| 1966 (67) | *Soli No 4*, for brass trio |
| 1967 (68) | *Inventions No 3*, for harp |

| 1969 | (70) | *Clio*, symphonic ode |
| | | *Discovery*, for orchestra |
| | | *Fuego Olimpico*, suite for orchestra |
| | | Variations for violin and piano |
| 1974 | (75) | *Estudio a Rubinstein*, for piano |
| 1975–6 | (76–7) | Five Caprichos for piano |

## CHERUBINI, Luigi
*b Florence, 14 September 1760*
*d Paris, 15 March 1842, aged eighty-one*

He was the son of a musician. By the age of seventeen he had written many works for the church, including three masses. The then Grand Duke of Tuscany was so impressed that he sent Cherubini to study in Venice. In 1784 he went to London and stayed for two years, holding the post of Composer to the King (George III). In 1788 he settled in Paris, where he remained for the rest of his life. He was appointed one of the inspectors when the Conservatory was founded in 1795. He was unpopular with Napoleon, which caused him some hardship. After a visit to Vienna in 1805 he wrote little for the next ten years; but under Louis XVIII he became a member of the Institut Français and, in 1822, the director of the Conservatory.

| 1778 | (18) | *Demophon*, opera |
| 1788 | (28) | *Ifigenia in Aulide*, opera |
| 1797 | (37) | *Médée*, opera |
| 1800 | (40) | *Les Deux Journées*, opera |
| 1803 | (43) | *Anacreon*, opera |
| 1814 | (54) | String Quartet No 1 in E♭ major |
| 1815–29 | (55–69) | String Quartet No 2 in C major |
| | | String Quartet No 3 in D minor |
| 1833 | (73) | *Ali Baba*, opera |
| 1835 | (75) | String Quartet No 4 in E major |
| | | String Quartet No 5 in F major |
| | | String Quartet No 6 in A minor |
| 1836 | (76) | *Requiem Mass*, in D minor |
| 1837 | (77) | String Quartet in E minor |

## CHOPIN, Frédéric
*b Zelazowa Wola (Poland), 1 March 1810*
*d Paris, 17 October 1849, aged thirty-nine*

His father was a teacher. Chopin studied at home until the age of thirteen, before entering the Warsaw Lyceum, and, at sixteen, the newly founded Warsaw Conservatory, where he became interested in the national music of Poland. In 1829 he went to Vienna, but an unrequited love affair and political unrest made him leave for Paris in 1831. At first he had acute financial problems, and his concerts were received with some reservations; but a meeting with the Rothschild family, and consequent playing and teaching in the great houses of Paris, restored him. He paid a nostalgic visit to Poland in 1835, where he fell in love again; but the girl's parents refused consent to marriage because of Chopin's ill-health. He returned to Paris, where he met George Sand. They went to Majorca together in 1838, but returned abruptly to Marseilles when Chopin fell seriously ill. In 1839 he was well enough to return to Paris, and now commanded high fees as pianist and teacher. He and George Sand separated in 1847, and early in 1848 he went to Scotland with a pupil who was in love with him; but he could not compose there, and returned to Paris in November. Eleven months later he died.

| | |
|---|---|
| 1817 (7) | Polonaises No 13 in G minor, and No 14 in B♭ major |
| 1821 (11) | Polonaise No 15 in A♭ major |
| 1822 (12) | Polonaise No 16 in G minor |
| 1825 (15) | Polonaise No 8, Op 71/1 |
| 1826 (16) | Three Écossaises |
| | Polonaise No 11 in B♭ minor |
| | Introduction and Variations in E minor, on *Der Schweizerbub* |
| 1827 (17) | Nocturne No 19, Op 72 |
| 1828 (18) | *Krakowiak*, concerto rondo for orchestra |
| | *Fantasia on Polish Airs*, in A major, for piano and orchestra |
| | Rondo in C major for two pianos |
| | Piano Sonata No 1 in C minor |
| | Polonaises No 9 and 10, Op 71 |
| 1829 (19) | Piano Concerto No 2 in F minor |
| | Introduction and Polonaise in C major for cello and piano |
| | Twelve Grand Studies for piano (No 5 'Black Keys', No 12 'Revolutionary') |
| | Polonaise No 12 in G♭ major |
| | *Variations on a theme by Paganini* in A major |
| | Waltz No 10, Op 69/2 |
| | Waltz No 13, Op 70/3 |
| 1830 (20) | Piano Concerto No 1 in E minor |
| 1830–1 (20–1) | Nocturnes No 1–3, Op 9 |
| | Nine Mazurkas for piano |
| 1830–3 (20–3) | Nocturnes No 4–6, Op 15 |
| 1831 (21) | Waltz No 1 in E♭ major |
| | Waltz No 3 |
| 1831–4 (21–4) | *Andante Spianoto*, and *Grand Polonaise Brillant*, in E♭ |
| 1832 (22) | Allegro de Concert in A major (sketched, completed 1841) |
| | Scherzo No 1 |
| 1833 (23) | Bolero in C major |
| | *Introduction and Variations on a Theme by Hérold*, in B♭ major |
| 1834 (24) | Fantaisie Impromptu in C♯ minor |
| | Prelude No 26 in A♭ major |
| 1834–5 (24–5) | Polonaises No 1–2 |
| 1834–6 (24–6) | Etudes No 13–24 |
| 1835 (25) | Nocturnes No 7–8 |
| | Waltz No 2 |
| | Waltz No 9 |
| | Waltz No 11 |
| | Ballade, Op 23 |
| 1836–7 (26–7) | Nocturnes No 9–10 |
| 1836–9 (26–9) | Ballade, Op 38 |
| | Preludes No 1–24 |
| 1837 (27) | Impromptu, Op 29 |
| | Scherzo No 2 |
| | Nocturne in C minor (*p* posthumous) |
| 1838 (28) | Waltz No 4 |
| 1838–9 (28–9) | Nocturnes No 11–12 |
| | Polonaises No 3–4 |
| 1839 (29) | Etudes No 25–7 in Fm: A♭ : D♭ |
| | Impromptu, Op 36 |
| | Scherzo No 3 |
| | Piano Sonata No 2 in B♭ minor |
| 1840 (30) | Waltz No 5 |
| 1840–1 (30–1) | Ballade, Op 47 |

|          |      | Fantasia in F minor |
|----------|------|---------------------|
| 1841 | (31) | Nocturnes No 13–14 |
|          |      | Polonaise No 5 |
|          |      | Prelude No 25 |
|          |      | Waltz No 12 |
| 1842 | (32) | Impromptu, Op 51 |
|          |      | Polonaise No 6 |
|          |      | Scherzo No 6 |
|          |      | Ballade, Op 52 |
| 1843 | (33) | Berceuse in D♭ major (revised 1844), Op 57 |
|          |      | Nocturnes No 15–16 |
| 1844 | (34) | Piano Sonata No 3 in B minor |
| 1845–6 | (35–6) | Cello Sonata in G minor, Op 65 |
|          |      | Barcarolle in F♯ minor, Op 60 |
|          |      | Polonaise No 7 |
| 1846 | (36) | Nocturnes No 17–18 |
| 1846–7 | (36–7) | Waltzes No 6–8, Op 64 |

## CILEA, Francesco
*b Palmi, Italy, 26 July 1866*
*d Varezza, 20 November 1950, aged eighty-four*

He studied piano at the Naples Conservatory and became professor of composition at the Reale Instituto Musicale in Florence. He wrote little after his most popular opera *Adriana Lecouvreur*, spending most of his time in a succession of professorial appointments.

| 1886 | (20) | Piano Trio |
|------|------|------------|
| 1887 | (21) | Suite for orchestra |
| 1889 | (23) | *Gina*, opera |
| 1892 | (26) | *La Tilda*, opera |
| 1894 | (28) | Cello Sonata |
| 1897 | (31) | *L'Arlesiania*, opera |
| 1902 | (36) | *Adriana Lecouvreur*, opera |
| 1907 | (41) | *Gloria*, opera |
| 1913 | (47) | *Il Canto della vita*, for voice, chorus and orchestra |
| 1931 | (65) | Suite for orchestra |

## CIMAROSA, Domenico
*b Aversa, Italy, 17 December 1749*
*d Venice, 11 January 1801, aged fifty-one*

He was born of a poor family and studied in Naples. He came to the fore in 1772 with his first opera, and for the next fifteen years divided his time between Naples and Rome. From 1787 to 1791 he was court composer to Catherine II of Russia in St Petersburg. In 1792 Leopold II offered him the position of *Kapellmeister* to the Austrian court in Vienna; and when Leopold died later that year Cimarosa returned to Naples to become *maestro di cappella* to King Ferdinand of Naples and music teacher of the princesses. When the French republican army marched into Naples and overthrew Ferdinand. Cimarosa embraced its cause; and when Ferdinand, helped by Lord Nelson, was reinstated, Cimarosa was thrown into prison. On release he left for St Petersburg, but died near Venice on the first leg of his journey.

| 1772 | (23) | *Le stravaganze del conte*, opera |
|------|------|-----------------------------------|
| 1778 | (29) | *L'Italiana in Londra*, opera |

90

| 1780 | (31) | *Giuditta*, oratorio |
| 1781 | (32) | *Il pittore parigino*, opera |
| | | *Il convito*, opera |
| 1782 | (33) | *La ballerina amante*, opera |
| | | *Absalon*, oratorio |
| 1784 | (35) | *L'Olimpiade*, opera |
| | | *Artaserse*, opera |
| 1786 | (37) | *L'impresario in Angustie*, opera |
| 1789 | (40) | *Cleopatra*, opera |
| 1792 | (43) | *Il matrimonio segreto*, opera (this won wide fame for its combination of dramatic and musical values, in a style near Mozart's) |
| 1793 | (44) | *I Traci amanti*, opera |
| | | Concerto for two flutes and orchestra |
| 1794 | (45) | *Penelope*, opera |
| 1796 | (47) | *Gli Orazi e Curiazi*, opera |

## CLEMENTI, Muzio
*b Rome, 23 January 1752*
*d Evesham, Worcestershire, 10 March 1832, aged eighty*

His father was a musician who had him trained in music from an early age. From 1766 to 1770 he studied in England, where he created a sensation as pianist and composer. He made London his home, touring from there to Paris, Strasbourg, Munich, Vienna and Russia. He has been called the father of the modern style of piano-playing; Beethoven, whom he met in 1807, esteemed him highly. He established the London firm of Clementi and Co, which traded in pianos and other stringed instruments, and published music. He is buried in Westminster Abbey.

1773–1832 (21–80) One hundred sonatas, including sixty for piano

## COATES, Eric
*b Hucknall, Nottinghamshire, 27 August 1886*
*d Chichester, 23 December 1957, aged seventy-one*

He began violin lessons at the age of six and then took up the viola, playing in amateur orchestras. In 1906 he entered the Royal Academy of Music and studied viola under Tertis. After gaining experience in theatre orchestras, he played viola in the major British symphony orchestras. As a composer, he concentrated on writing light music.

| 1911 | (25) | Miniature Suite for orchestra |
| 1915 | (29) | *From the Countryside*, suite |
| 1919 | (33) | *Summer Days*, suite |
| 1922 | (36) | *Joyous Youth*, suite |
| | | *The Merrymakers*, overture |
| 1925 | (39) | *The Selfish Giant*, fantasy |
| 1926 | (40) | *The Three Bears*, fantasy |
| 1927 | (41) | *Four Ways*, suite |
| 1929 | (43) | *Cinderella*, fantasy |
| 1932 | (46) | *The Jester at the Wedding*, ballet |
| | | *From Meadow to Mayfair*, suite |
| 1933 | (47) | Two Symphonic Rhapsodies |
| | | *London Every Day*, suite |
| 1935 | (49) | *The Three Men*, suite |
| 1936 | (50) | *London Again*, suite |

| 1937 (51) | *Springtime*, suite |
| 1938 (52) | *The Enchanted Garden*, ballet |
| 1942 (56) | *Four Centuries*, suite |
| 1944 (58) | *The Three Elizabeths*, suite |
| 1955 (69) | *The Dam Busters*, film score |

Coates also wrote about 100 songs, many marches, etc.


## COLERIDGE-TAYLOR, Samuel
*b London, 15 August 1875*
*d Croydon, 1 September 1912, aged thirty-seven*

His father, a physician, was a native of Sierra Leone, his mother was English. He entered the Royal Academy of Music in 1890 as a violin student, winning a scholarship in composition in 1893. He studied with Stanford until 1897, and in 1898 was appointed violin teacher at the Academy. He was chosen as conductor of the Handel Society in 1904, and made three successful tours of the USA conducting his own works.

| 1896 (21) | Symphony in A minor |
| 1898 (23) | *Hiawatha's Wedding Feast*, cantata (words by Longfellow) |
| | Ballade in A minor for orchestra |
| 1899 (24) | *Death of Minnehaha*, cantata (Longfellow) |
| | Solemn Prelude |
| 1900 (25) | *Hiawatha's Departure*, cantata (Longfellow) |
| 1901 (26) | *The Blind Girl of Castel-Cuille*, cantata |
| | *Toussaint l'ouverture*, concert overture |
| | *Idyll*, for orchestra |
| 1902 (27) | *Meg Blane*, rhapsody for mezzo and chorus |
| 1903 (28) | *The Atonement*, oratorio |
| 1905 (30) | Five Choral Ballads |
| 1906 (31) | *Kubla Khan*, rhapsody for mezzo and chorus |
| 1909 (34) | *Bon-Bon*, suite |
| 1910 (35) | *Endymion's Dream*, for chorus |
| 1911 (36) | *A Tale of Old Japan*, cantata |
| | *Bamboula*, rhapsodic dance |
| | Violin Concerto in G minor |

Coleridge-Taylor also composed chamber music and many piano solos


## COOKE, Arnold
*b near Leeds, 4 November 1906*

He was educated at Repton School, and Cambridge. From 1929 until 1932 he was a pupil of Hindemith at the Hochschule für Musik in Berlin. He then became director of music at the Festival Theatre, Cambridge, and was appointed professor of harmony and composition at the Royal Manchester College from 1933 to 1938. He served with the Royal Navy during World War II. He was appointed professor of harmony and composition at Trinity College of Music in 1947 and received his doctorate in music at Cambridge in 1948.

| 1941 (35) | Cello Sonata |
| 1947 (41) | Symphony No 1 |
| 1948 (42) | Oboe Quartet |
| 1950 (44) | String Trio |
| 1951 (45) | Violin Sonata No 2 |
| 1954 (48) | Oboe Concerto |
| 1955 (49) | Clarinet Concerto |

| 1957 (51) | Oboe Sonata for oboe and piano |
| | Scherzo for piano |
| 1958 (52) | Violin Concerto |
| 1959 (53) | Five Part-songs for unaccompanied chorus |
| 1961 (55) | *O Sing unto the Lord*, for chorus and organ |
| 1963 (57) | *The Lord at First did Adam Make*, for chorus |
| 1966 (60) | *Song on May Morning*, for unaccompanied chorus |
| 1974 (68) | Cello Concerto |

## COPLAND, Aaron
*b Brooklyn, New York, 14 November 1900*

His parents were Russian-Jewish emigrés, who had little interest in music. From 1917 he studied for four years with Rubin Goldmark, then in 1921 he went to Paris to study for three years with Nadia Boulanger, returning to the USA in 1924. In 1925 he won a Guggenheim Fellowship, which was renewed in 1926. Since then he has led an extremely active life as a lecturer, pianist and conductor. He has written four books on musical subjects, and the highest international honours have been showered on him.

| 1923 (23) | *As It Fell Upon a Day*, for soprano, flute and clarinet |
| 1924 (24) | Symphony for organ and orchestra |
| 1925 (25) | *Grogh*, ballet |
| | *Dance Symphony* (1922–5) |
| | *Music for the Theater*, suite for small orchestra |
| 1926 (26) | Piano Concerto |
| 1928 (28) | Symphony No 1 (an orchestral version of the Symphony for organ, minus organ) |
| 1929 (29) | *Symphonic Ode* (revised 1955) |
| | *Vitebsk*, study on a Jewish theme, for piano trio |
| 1930 (30) | Piano Variations |
| 1933 (33) | Symphony No 2, *Short Symphony* |
| 1934 (34) | *Statements*, for orchestra |
| | *Hear Ye! Hear Ye!*, ballet |
| 1936 (36) | *El salon Mexico*, for orchestra |
| 1938 (38) | *An Outdoor Overture* |
| | *Billy the Kid*, ballet and orchestral suite |
| 1940 (40) | *Quiet City*, orchestral suite for trumpet, English horn and strings |
| 1941 (41) | Piano Sonata |
| 1942 (42) | *Danzon Cubano* |
| | *Rodeo*, ballet |
| | fp *A Lincoln Portrait*, for narrator and orchestra |
| 1943 (43) | Violin Sonata |
| 1944 (44) | *Appalachian Spring*, ballet and orchestral suite |
| 1946 (46) | Symphony No 3 |
| 1948 (48) | Concerto for clarinet and strings, with harp and piano |
| 1950 (50) | Piano Quartet |
| | *Twelve Poems of Emily Dickinson*, for voice and piano |
| 1951 (51) | *Pied Piper*, ballet |
| 1954 (54) | *The Tender Land*, opera in three acts |
| 1955 (55) | *Symphonic Ode* |
| | *A Canticle of Freedom*, for mixed chorus and orchestra (revised 1965) |
| 1957 (57) | Orchestral Variations |
| | Piano Fantasy |
| 1959 (59) | *Dance Panels*, ballet in seven sections (revised 1962) |

| 1960 (60) | Nonet for strings |
| 1962 (62) | *Connotations*, for orchestra |
| | *Down a Country Lane*, for orchestra |
| 1964 (64) | *Music for a Great City*, for orchestra |
| | *Emblems for a Symphonic Band* |
| 1967 (67) | *Inscape*, for orchestra |
| 1969 (69) | *Inaugural Fanfare*, for wind |
| | *An Evening Air*, for piano |
| 1971 (71) | Duo for flute and piano |
| 1972 (72) | Three Latin-American Sketches |
| | *Threnody I*, for flute and string trio |
| | *Night Thoughts*, for piano |
| | *Vocalise*, for flute and piano |
| 1973 (73) | *Threnody II*, for string trio |
| 1982 (82) | *Midday Thoughts*, for piano |
| | *Proclamation*, for piano |

## CORELLI, Arcangelo
*b Fusignano, Italy, 17 February 1653*
*d Rome, 8 January 1713, aged fifty-nine*

He started his studies at a very early age, and was admitted to the Accademia Filarmonica in Bologna in 1670. In 1675 he went to Rome, playing as a theatre violinist, and by 1679 was directing the orchestra at the Teatro Capranica, earning very high fees. In 1687 he became music master to Cardinal Panfili, and in 1689 director of music of the household of Cardinal Ottobini. He was admitted to the exclusive Accademia dei Arcadi. As a violinist his influence over the succeeding generation of players was enormous.

| 1681 (28) | p Sonatas in three parts (Twelve sonatas da chiesa) |
| 1685 (32) | p Sonatas in three parts (Twelve sonatas da camera) |
| 1689 (36) | p Sonatas in three parts (Twelve sonatas da chiesa) |
| 1694 (41) | p Sonatas in three parts (Twelve sonatas da camera) |
| 1700 (47) | p Sonatas for violin and violone or harpsichord. The first six of these are 'da chiesa'; the next five, 'da camera'; and the last, the famous set of variations on *La Folia* |
| c1714 (c54) | p Concerti Grossi |

## COUPERIN, François
*b Paris, 10 November 1668*
*d Paris, 12 September 1733, aged sixty-four*

He was one of a famous musical family. His early study was with his father and uncles. In 1693, aged twenty-five, he was chosen as organist at the Chapel Royal at Versailles by Louis XIV. In 1694 he was appointed Maître de Clavecin des Enfants de France, and a Lateran Order made him Chevalier. He wrote a book on the art of the clavecin. In 1717 he became Ordinaire de la Musique.

| 1690 (22) | Pièces d'orgue en deux messes: |
| | *Messe pour les paroisses*, twenty-one organ pieces |
| | *Messe pour les couvents*, twenty-one organ pieces |
| | *Messe solenelle* |
| 1692 (24) | Trio Sonata, *La Steinkerque* |
| 1709 (41) | *Messe à l'usage des couvents* |
| 1713 (45) | Harpsichord Works, Book I |
| 1715 (47) | *Leçons de ténèbres*, for one and two voices |

| 1717 (49) | Harpsichord Works, Book II |
| 1722 (54) | Harpsichord Works, Book III |
| | Four *Concerts royeaux* for harpsichord, strings and wind instruments |
| 1724 (56) | *Les goûts-réunis*, ten concerts for various instruments |
| 1730 (62) | *p* Harpsichord Works, Book IV |

## COUPERIN, Louis
*b Chaumes, near Paris, c1626*
*d Paris, 29 August 1661, aged cthirty-five*

Little is known of his early life, but by 1651 he was a member of the establishment of a diplomat and statesman who lived at Meudon, a suburb of Paris. He then held the post of organist at St Gervais, where he lived with his two brothers in the organist's lodging. He was given the post of treble viol player at the Royal court.

Louis Couperin composed: about eighteen preludes for harpsichord; seventeen allemandes; thirty-two courantes; thirty-one sarabandes; five gigues; about fourteen chaconnes and passacailes; three galliards, and other works for harpsichord; two preludes for organ; thirty-three fugues; two duos; six division basses; twenty-seven plainsong verstes; two psaumes; other organ works, and fantasies and sinfonias for various ensemble combinations.

## COWELL, Henry
*b Menlo Park, California, 11 March 1897*
*d Shady, New York, 10 December 1965, aged sixty-eight*

He began studying the violin at the age of three and gave it up because of ill-health at the age of eight. As a composer he was largely self-taught until he went to the University of California in 1913. In 1919 he wrote a book called *New Musical Resources*. From 1931 to 1932 he worked on oriental music at the University of Berlin, and from 1956 to 1957 he went to Asia under a Rockefeller grant to study Indian music at the Academy of Music, Madras. He also studied Japanese and Iranian music, and wrote books and articles promoting the works of other composers.

| 1914–20 (17–23) | *Vestiges*, for orchestra |
| 1918 (21) | Symphony No 1 |
| 1920 (23) | *Communication*, for orchestra |
| 1922 (25) | *The Building of Banba*, ballet |
| 1924 (27) | *Ensemble*, for chamber orchestra |
| 1926 (29) | *Atlantis*, ballet |
| | *Seven Paragraphs*, for chamber ensemble |
| 1927 (30) | *Some Music*, for orchestra |
| | Suite for violin and piano |
| 1928 (31) | Sinfonietta for chamber orchestra |
| 1929 (32) | *Irish Suite*, for chamber orchestra |
| 1930 (33) | *Polyphonica*, for twelve instruments |
| | *Exultation*, for ten stringed instruments |
| | *Reel No 1*, for orchestra |
| | Suite for woodwind quintet |
| 1931 (34) | *Synchrony*, for orchestra |
| | *Rhythmicana*, for orchestra |
| | *Havana Hornpipe*, for orchestra |
| | *Competitive Sport*, for chamber orchestra |

|           |                                                                       |
|-----------|-----------------------------------------------------------------------|
|           | *Steel and Stone*, for chamber orchestra                              |
|           | *Heroic Dance*, for chamber orchestra                                 |
| 1932 (35) | *Jig*, for orchestra                                                  |
|           | *Reel No 2*, for orchestra                                            |
| 1933 (36) | *Four Casual Developments*, ballet                                    |
|           | Scherzo for orchestra                                                 |
|           | *Four Continuations*, for chamber orchestra                           |
|           | String Quartet No 2, 'Mosaic'                                         |
| 1934 (37) | Movement for instruments                                              |
| 1935 (38) | *Six Casual Developments*, for chamber orchestra                      |
| 1936 (39) | String Quartet No 4, 'United'                                         |
| 1937 (40) | *Immediate Tragedy*, ballet                                           |
|           | *Deep Song*, ballet                                                   |
|           | *Old American Country Set*, for orchestra                             |
|           | *Chrysanthemums*, for soprano, two saxes and four strings             |
|           | *Sarabande*, for oboe, clarinet and percussion                        |
|           | Three Ostinati with Chorales for oboe or clarinet and piano           |
| 1939 (42) | Symphony No 2, *Anthropos*                                            |
|           | *Shipshape*, overture                                                 |
|           | *Symphonic Set*, for orchestra                                        |
|           | *American Melting Pot*, for orchestra                                 |
|           | *Celtic Set*, for orchestra                                           |
| 1940 (43) | *Pastorale and Fiddler's Delight*, for orchestra                      |
|           | *Voxhumana*, for orchestra                                            |
|           | *Ancient Desert Drone*, for orchestra                                 |
|           | *Concerto Piccolo*, for piano and orchestra                           |
| 1941 (44) | *Schoonthree*, for orchestra                                          |
|           | *Tales of our Countryside*, for orchestra                             |
|           | *Two Bits*, for flute and piano                                       |
|           | *Grinnell Fanfare*, for organ and brass                               |
| 1942 (45) | Symphony No 3, *Gaelic*                                               |
|           | *Trickster Coyote*, for flute and percussion                          |
| 1943 (46) | *American Pipers*, for orchestra                                      |
|           | Little Concerto for piano and orchestra                               |
|           | *Action in Brass*, for horn, two trumpets and two trombones           |
|           | *This is America*, for brass ensemble                                 |
|           | *Improvisation on a Persian Mode*, for orchestra                      |
| 1944 (47) | *United Music*, for orchestra                                         |
|           | *Animal Magic*, for wind band                                         |
| 1945 (48) | *Philippine Return*, for orchestra                                    |
|           | *Big Sing*, for orchestra                                             |
|           | *Fanfare*, for wind band                                              |
|           | *Two Appositions*, for wind band                                      |
|           | *Grandma's Rumba*, for wind band                                      |
|           | *Triad*, for trumpet and piano                                        |
|           | Violin Sonata No 1                                                    |
|           | *Hymn*, for string orchestra                                          |
| 1946 (49) | Symphony No 4, *Short Symphony*                                       |
|           | Festival Overture for two orchestras                                  |
|           | Saxophone Quartet                                                     |
| 1947 (50) | *Tune Takes a Trip*, for five clarinets                               |
| 1948 (51) | Symphony No 5                                                         |
|           | *Festive Occasion*, for orchestra                                     |
|           | *Tall Tale*, for brass ensemble                                       |
|           | *Saturday Night at the Firehouse*, for orchestra                      |
| 1949 (52) | *O'Higgins of Chile*, opera                                           |

|          |                                                                                    |
|----------|------------------------------------------------------------------------------------|
|          | *Four Declamations with Return*, for cello and piano                               |
|          | *The Sax-happy Quartet*                                                             |
|          | *Congratulations*, for strings                                                     |
|          | *A Curse and a Blessing*, for wind band                                            |
|          | Overture for orchestra                                                             |
| 1951 (54) | Symphony No 6                                                                     |
| 1952 (55) | Symphony No 7                                                                     |
|          | *Fiddler's Jig*, for violin and string orchestra                                   |
|          | *Fantasie*, for wind band                                                          |
|          | *Four Trumpets for Alan*, for four trumpets and piano                              |
| 1953 (56) | Symphony No 8 for chorus and orchestra                                            |
|          | Symphony No 9                                                                      |
|          | Symphony No 10 for chamber orchestra                                              |
|          | Symphony No 11, *Seven Rituals of Music*                                          |
|          | Rondo for orchestra                                                               |
|          | *Towards a Bright Day*, for orchestra                                            |
|          | *Singing Band*, for brass                                                        |
| 1955 (58) | Ballad for strings                                                               |
| 1955–6 (58–9) | Symphony No 12                                                               |
|          | *Set of Two*, for violin and piano                                               |
|          | *Set of Four*, for harpsichord                                                   |
|          | *Set of Five*, for violin, piano and percussion                                  |
|          | String Quartet No 5                                                               |
|          | Septet, for five wordless voices, clarinet and keyboard                           |
| 1956 (59) | Variations for orchestra                                                         |
|          | *A Thanksgiving Psalm*, for male chorus                                          |
| 1956–7 (59–60) | *Persian Set*, for orchestra                                                |
| 1957 (60) | Music for orchestra                                                              |
|          | *Ongaku*, for orchestra                                                          |
| 1957–8 (60–1) | Symphony No 13, *Madras*                                                     |
| 1958–9 (61–2) | *Antiphony*, for divided orchestra                                          |
| 1959 (62) | Concerto for percussion                                                          |
|          | *Mela Fair*, for orchestra                                                       |
|          | *Characters*, for orchestra                                                      |
|          | *Homage to Iran*, for violin and piano                                          |
| 1960 (63) | Symphony No 14                                                                   |
|          | *Concerto Brevis*, for accordion and orchestra                                  |
|          | *Thesis*, for orchestra                                                          |
|          | *Variations on thirds* for orchestra                                            |
|          | Introduction and Allegro for viola and harpsichord                              |
|          | Prelude and Allegro for violin and harpsichord                                  |
| 1961 (64) | *Chiaroscuro*, for orchestra                                                     |
| 1962 (65) | Symphony No 15, *Thesis*                                                         |
|          | Quartet for flute, oboe, cello and harp                                         |
| 1963 (66) | Symphony No 16, *Icelandic*                                                      |
|          | Symphony No 17, *Lancaster*                                                      |
|          | Symphony No 18                                                                   |
| 1964 (67) | Concerto for koto and orchestra                                                 |
| 1965 (68) | Symphony No 19                                                                   |

Cowell also wrote sixteen hymn-and-fuguing-tunes for various combinations, many choral works, songs and piano works.

## COWIE, Edward
*b Birmingham, 17 August 1943*

Studied first at the Trinity College of Music and later with Fricker, Goehr and Lutoslawski. In 1973 he was appointed lecturer and composer-in-residence at Lancaster University; visited the USA for the first time in 1977; in 1979 was guest professor at the University of Kassel, West Germany; was made professor of creative arts at the University of Wollongong, New South Wales, in 1983, and for 1983–6 the composer-in-residence for the Royal Liverpool Philharmonic Orchestra.

1969 (26)    Concerto for bass clarinet and tape
1970 (27)    *Dungeness Choruses*
1972 (29)    *Shinkokinshu*, for high voice and ensemble
1973 (30)    String Quartet No 1
              *Endymion Nocturnes*, tenor and string quartet
              *Somnus ei inductus*, for four trombones
1974–5 (31–2) *Leighton Moss*, cantata, chorus and chamber orchestra
1975 (32)    *Leviathan*, symphonic poem for orchestra
              Clarinet Concerto No 2
1976 (33)    *Gesangbuch*, for twenty-four voices and twelve instruments
              Piano Variations
              Piano Concerto (1976–7)
              *Commedia*, opera (1976–8)
1977 (34)    *L'or de la trompette d'été*, for eighteen strings
              *Cathedral Music*, Sonata for symphonic brass
              String Quartet No 2
1979 (36)    *Columbine*, for soprano and chamber orchestra
              *Brighella's World*, for baritone and piano
1980 (37)    *Harlequin*, for solo harp
              *The Falls of Clyde*, for two pianos
              *Commedia Lazzis*, for guitar
              Concerto for orchestra
1980–1 (37–8) *Madrigals*, for twelve voices
              *Leonardo*, for chamber orchestra
              Symphony No 1 ('The American')
              *Kelly-Nolan-Kelly*, for clarinet in A
              *Kelly Variations*, for piano
              *Kelly*, opera
1981 (38)    *Kelly Choruses*, for voices and harp
1981–2 (38–9) *Choral Symphony (Symphonies of Rain, Sea and Speed)*
1982 (39)    *Kelly Ballet*
              Harp Concerto
              *Kate Kelly's Roadshow*, music-theatre
              Symphony No 2 ('The Australian')
1983 (40)    *Missa Brevis* (Mass for Peace)
              *Ancient Voices*, for four voices
              String Quartet No 3 ('Creative Arts Quartet')
              String Quartet No 4 ('Australian II')

## CROSSE, Gordon
*b Bury, Lancashire, 1 December 1937*

He was educated at Oxford and the Accademia di St Cecilia, Rome. From 1964 to 1966 he was on the extra-mural staff of Birmingham University; he was a Haywood Fellow from 1966 to 1969, and a Gulbenkian Fellow of Essex University in 1969.

| | | |
|---|---|---|
| 1962 | (24) | *Concerto da Camera*, for violin, wind and percussion |
| | | *Changes*, for soli voices, chorus and orchestra |
| 1963 | (25) | *Meet My Folk*, for children's chorus and instrumental ensemble |
| | | *Ceremony*, for cello and orchestra |
| | | Violin Concerto |
| 1964 | (26) | Symphony No 1 for chamber orchestra |
| | | Symphony No 2 |
| 1966 | (28) | *Purgatory*, opera |
| 1967 | (29) | *The Grace of Todd*, opera |
| 1970 | (32) | *The Story of Vasco*, opera |
| 1980 | (43) | *A Year and a Day*, for solo clarinet |
| | | String Quartet |
| | | *Harvest Songs*, for choir and orchestra |
| | | *Voice from the Tomb*, for medium voice and piano |
| 1981 | (44) | *Elegy & Scherzo Alla Marcia*, for string orchestra |
| | | *Wildboy*, ballet score |
| | | *Fear No More*, for oboe, oboe d'amore and cor anglais |
| | | *Peace*, for Brass |
| | | Dreascanon 1, for choir, piano and percussion |
| 1982 | (45) | *A Wake*, for flute, clarinet, cello and piano |
| | | *Trio: Rhymes & Reasons*, for clarinet, cello and piano |
| 1983 | (46) | *Wave Songs*, for cello and piano |

## CRUMB, George
*b Charleston, West Virginia, 24 October 1929*

He was educated at the universities of Illinois (1953) and Michigan (1959). He was awarded the Fulbright Fellowship, the Koussevitzky Foundation, the Guggenheim Foundation, and the Pulitzer Prize of 1968. He was on the faculty of the University of Colorado from 1959 to 1964, professor at the University of Pennsylvania from 1965, and visiting professor at Harvard in 1968 and at Tanglewood in 1970.

| | | |
|---|---|---|
| 1954 | (25) | String Quartet |
| 1955 | (26) | Sonatina for unaccompanied cello |
| 1959 | (30) | *Variazioni*, for orchestra |
| 1962 | (33) | Five Pieces for piano |
| 1963 | (34) | *Night Music I*, for soprano, celeste, piano and percussion |
| | | *Night Music II*, for violin and piano |
| 1964 | (35) | Four Nocturnes for violin and piano |
| 1965 | (36) | *Madrigals, Book I*, for soprano, vibraphone and double-bass |
| | | *Madrigals, Book II*, for soprano, alto flute and percussion |
| 1966 | (37) | *Eleven Echoes of Autumn*, for violin, flute, clarinet and piano |
| 1967 | (38) | *Echoes of Time and the River*, for orchestra |
| 1968 | (39) | *Songs, Drones and Refrains of Death*, for baritone and instruments |
| 1969 | (40) | *Night of the Four Moons*, for ensemble |
| | | *Madrigals, Book III*, for soprano, harp and percussion |
| | | *Madrigals, Book IV*, for soprano and instruments |
| 1970 | (41) | *Ancient Voices of Children*, for soprano, boy soprano and seven instruments |
| | | *Black Angels*, for electric string quartet |
| 1971 | (42) | *Voice of the Whale*, for flute, cello and piano |
| 1973 | (44) | *Makrokosmos I*, for piano |
| 1974 | (45) | *Makrokosmos II*, for amplified piano |

**CUI, César**
*b Vilna, 18 January 1835*
*d St Petersburg, 14 March 1918, aged eighty-three*

His father was a French army officer. He studied military engineering, and on graduation in 1857 was appointed sub-professor and held the rank of Lieutenant-General of Engineers. A meeting with Balakirev started him on serious composition. In 1864 he began writing articles on music, and his witty and literary criticisms were an important part of his life's work.

| | | |
|---|---|---|
| 1857 | (22) | Scherzo for orchestra, No 1 and 2 |
| 1858 | (23) | *The Caucasian Prisoner*, opera |
| 1859 | (24) | Tarantella |
| | | *The Mandarin's Song*, opera |
| 1869 | (34) | *William Ratcliffe*, opera |
| 1875 | (40) | *Angelo*, opera |
| 1881 | (46) | *Marche solenelle* |
| 1883 | (48) | *Suite Concertante*, for violin and orchestra |
| 1886 | (51) | *Deux Morceaux*, for cello and orchestra |
| 1888–9 | (53–4) | *Le Filibustier*, opera |
| 1890–1913 | (55–78) | String Quartet in C minor |
| | | String Quartet in D major |
| | | String Quartet in E♭ major |
| 1897 | (62) | p Five Little Duets for flute and violin with piano |
| 1899 | (64) | *The Saracen*, opera |
| 1903 | (68) | *Mlle Fifi*, opera |
| 1907 | (72) | *Matteo Falcone*, opera |
| 1911 | (76) | *The Captain's Daughter*, opera |
| | | p Violin Sonata in D major |

Cui also composed:
*Petite Suite* for violin and piano
Twelve miniatures for violin and piano

**d'ALBERT, Eugene Francis Charles**
*b Glasgow, 10 April 1864*
*d Riga, 3 March 1932, aged sixty-seven*

The son of a ballet-master at Covent Garden, he studied music at the National Training School, London – predecessor of the Royal College – and was elected Mendelssohn Scholar there in 1881. He went to Vienna, then to Weimar as a pupil of Liszt, and became a piano virtuoso. He lived mainly in Germany but toured widely. He was court conductor at Weimar for a short time in 1885, and became director of the Berlin Hochschule in 1907. He married and divorced six times.

| | | |
|---|---|---|
| 1883 | (19) | Suite for piano |
| 1884 | (20) | Piano Concerto in B♭ |
| 1886 | (22) | Symphony in F |
| 1887 | (23) | String Quartet No 1 |
| 1888 | (24) | Overture to *Grillparzer* |
| 1893 | (29) | Piano Concerto in E |
| | | Piano Sonata |
| | | String Quartet No 2 |
| | | *Der Rubin*, opera |
| | | *Der Mensch und das Leben*, for chorus |
| 1895 | (31) | *Ghismonda*, opera |
| 1897 | (33) | *Gernot*, opera |

|  | *Seejungfräulein*, for voice and orchestra |
| 1898 (34) | *Die Abreise*, opera |
| 1899 (35) | Cello Concerto |
| 1900 (36) | *Kain*, opera |
| 1902 (38) | *Der Improvisator*, opera |
| 1903 (39) | *Tiefland*, music drama |
|  | *Wie wir die Natur erleben*, for voice and orchestra |
| 1904 (40) | Two Songs with orchestra |
|  | *Mittelalterliche Venushymne*, for tenor, male chorus and orchestra |
|  | *An den Genius von Deutschland*, for solo voices and chorus |
| 1905 (41) | *Flauto Solo*, musical comedy |
| 1907 (43) | *Tragaldabas*, comic opera |
| 1909 (45) | *Izeÿl*, music drama |
| 1912 (48) | *Die verschenkte Frau*, comic opera |
| 1916 (52) | *Die toten Augen*, opera |
| 1918 (54) | *Der Stier von Olivera*, opera |
| 1919 (55) | *Revolutionshochzeit*, opera |
| 1921 (57) | *Sirocco*, opera |
| 1923 (59) | *Mareike von Nymwegen*, opera |
| 1924 (60) | *Aschenputtel*, orchestral suite |
|  | Symphonic Prelude to *Tiefland* |
| 1926 (62) | *Der Golem*, music drama |
| 1928 (64) | *The Black Orchid*, burlesque opera |
| 1932 (68) | *Mister Wu*, opera |

d'Albert also wrote fifty-eight songs and four volumes of piano pieces.


## DALLAPICCOLA, Luigi
*b Pisino d'Istria (then Austria), 3 February 1904*
*d Florence, 19 February 1975, aged seventy-one*

His father was a schoolmaster. From 1912 to 1916 he learned piano, and in 1922 he went to the Conservatorio Cherubini in Florence, where he won a diploma as a pianist and began teaching and giving recitals. In 1934 he was made professor at the Conservatorio Cherubini, a post he held until he retired in 1967. The fact that he had a Jewish wife made him hate Fascism, and this impeded his development in pre-war Italy. After a brief health crisis in 1972 he gave up composing.

| 1937–8 (33–4) | *Volo di Notte*, opera |
| 1938–41 (34–7) | *Canti di prigionia*, for chorus and instruments |
| 1942 (38) | *Cinque Frammente di Saffo*, for soprano and chamber orchestra |
|  | *Marsia*, ballet (1942–3) |
| 1943 (39) | *Sex carmina Alcaei*, for soprano and instruments |
| 1944–5 (40–1) | *Due liriche di Anacreonte*, for soprano and instruments |
| 1944–8 (40–4) | *Il Prigioniero*, opera |
| 1945 (41) | Ciaccona, Intermezzo e Adagio for cello |
| 1946–7 (42–3) | Two Pieces for orchestra |
| 1948 (44) | *Quattro liriche di Antonio Machado*, for soprano and piano |
| 1949 (45) | *Tre poemi*, for soprano and chamber orchestra |
| 1949–50 (45–6) | *Job*, mystery play, for narrator, solo voices, chorus and orchestra |
| 1951–5 (47–51) | *Canti di Liberazione*, for chorus and orchestra |
| 1952 (48) | *Quaderno musicale di Annalibera*, for piano |
|  | Goethe-Lieder for mezzo-soprano and three clarinets (1952–3) |
| 1954 (50) | *Piccola musica notturna*, for orchestra |
| 1955 (51) | *An Mathilde*, cantata |
| 1956 (52) | *Cinque canti*, for baritone and eight instruments |

*Concerto per la notte di natale dell'anno*, for soprano and chamber orchestra

1957–8 (53–4) *Requiescat*, for chorus and orchestra
1959–60 (55–6) *Dialoghi*, for cello and orchestra
1960–8 (56–64) *Ulisse*, opera
1962 (58)     *Preghiere*, for baritone and chamber orchestra
1964 (60)     *Parole di San Paolo*, for voice and instruments
                  *Quattro liriche di Antonio Machado*, version for soprano and orchestra
1970 (66)     *Sicut umbra*, for mezzo-soprano and twelve instruments
                  *Tempus aedificandi*, for chorus
1971 (67)     *Tempus destruendi*, for chorus


## DARGOMITZHSKY, Alexander Sergeivitch
*b Troitskoye, Tula district, 14 February 1813*
*d St Petersburg, 17 January 1869, aged fifty-five*

The son of a government official, he was educated at St Petersburg, studying violin and piano. He worked in the Civil Service from 1831 to 1843, while teaching himself musical theory from books. A meeting with Glinka in 1844 made him decide to devote his time to composition, and he became a pioneer of the Russian Nationalist School. His travels took him all over Europe until 1864, when he retired to St Petersburg to write.

1847 (34)     *Esmeralda*, opera (possibly *c*1839)
1856 (43)     *fp Rusalka*, opera
1861–3 (48–50) *Baba-Yaga*, fantasy for orchestra
1867 (54)     *The Triumph of Bacchus*, opera-ballet
Performed posthumously: 1872 *The Stone Guest*, opera (completed by Cui, orchestrated by Rimsky-Korsakov, *qv*)
Dargomitzhsky also composed:
About ninety songs
Fifteen vocal duets
*Tarentelle Slav.* for piano, four hands
*Finnish Fantasy*
*Kosachok*, Ukrainian dance
*The Dance of the Mummers*


## DARKE, Harold Edwin
*b London, 29 October 1888*
*d Cambridge, 28 November 1976, aged eighty-eight*

He studied organ with Parratt and composition with Stanford. He spent his life as an organist and working for choral festivals, and composed much music. His best-known works are his 'Meditation on Brother James's Air' and his setting of the carol, 'In the Bleak Mid-winter'.


## DAVIES, (Sir) Henry Walford
*b Oswestry, Shropshire, 6 September 1869*
*d Wrington, Somerset, 11 March 1941, aged seventy-one*

For five years he was pupil-assistant to Parratt, organist of St George's Chapel, Windsor, and in 1890 won a composition scholarship to the Royal College of Music, studying under Parry and Stanford. In 1895 he joined the staff there, teaching counterpoint. He became well known as an organist and choir-master, lecturer and adjudicator. He conducted the Bach Choir from 1903 to 1907, was director of music for the RAF in 1917, and from 1919 to 1926 was professor of music at the University of Wales. In 1924 he became Gresham Professor of Music, was organist at St George's Chapel from 1927 to 1932, and adviser to the BBC from 1927 to 1939. He was knighted in 1922, and on Elgar's death in 1934 he became Master of the King's Musick. His busy life did not allow much time for composition, but he wrote a book, *The Pursuit of Music*, which was published in 1935.

1904 (35)   *Everyman*, oratorio
1908 (39)   *Solemn Melody*, for organ and strings


## DAVIES, Peter Maxwell
*b Manchester, 8 September 1934*

He was educated at Leigh Grammar School, Royal Manchester College of Music and Manchester University. In 1957 he won an Italian government scholarship to study in Rome. From 1959 to 1962 he was director of music at Cirencester Grammar School. In 1962 he was awarded a Harkness Fellowship and went to Princeton University Graduate Music School; he gave a series of lectures in Austria, Switzerland, Australia and New Zealand in 1965; and in 1966 was composer-in-residence at the University of Adelaide, South Australia. In May 1967 he formed,with Harrison Birtwistle, the Pierrot Players. He lived in a remote Dorset village until 1970, and since then he has made his home in the Orkneys. In 1979 the University of Edinburgh awarded him an honorary doctorate of music.

1952 (18)   *Quartet Movement*, for string quartet
1955 (21)   Sonata for trumpet and piano
1956 (22)   Five Pieces for piano, Op 2
            *Stedman Doubles*, for clarinet and percussion (revised 1968)
            Clarinet Sonata (1956–7)
1957 (23)   *Alma redemptoris mater*, for instrumental ensemble
            *St Michael*, sonata for seventeen wind instruments
1958 (24)   Sextet
            *Stedman Caters* (revised 1968)
            *Prolation*, for orchestra
1959 (25)   *Ricercar and doubles on 'To Many a Well'*, for instrumental ensemble
            Five Motets, for SATB soloists, double choir and instrumental
                ensemble
            *Five Klee Pictures*, for school, amateur or professional orchestra
                (revised 1976)
            *William Byrd: Three Dances*, arranged for school or amateur
                orchestra
1960 (26)   *O Magnum Mysterium*, for unaccompanied SATB, with two
                instrumental sonatas and organ fantasia
            Five Voluntaries, arranged for school or amateur orchestra
            Organ Fantasia from *O Magnum Mysterium*
1961 (27)   String Quartet
            *Ave Maria, Hail Blessed Flower*, carol for SATB
            *Te lucis ante terminum*, for SATB and instrumental ensemble
1962 (28)   First Fantasia on *In Nomine* of John Taverner, for orchestra
            Four Carols, for SATB unaccompanied
            *Leopardi Fragments*, for soprano, contralto, and instrumental
                ensemble
            *The Lord's Prayer*, for SATB unaccompanied
            Sinfonia for chamber orchestra

103

| 1963 (29) | *Veni Sancte Spiritus*, for SATB soloists, SATB and small orchestra |
|---|---|
| 1964 (30) | Seven *In Nomine*, for instrumental ensemble (1964–5) |
| | Second Fantasia on John Taverner's *In Nomine*, for orchestra |
| | *Shakespeare Music*, for instrumental ensemble |
| | *Ave, Plena Gracia*, for SATB with optional organ |
| 1965 (31) | *Ecce manus tradentis*, for SATB soloists, SATB chorus and instrumental ensemble |
| | *Revelation and Fall*, for soprano and sixteen instruments (revised 1980) |
| | *Shall I Die for Mannis Sake?*, carol for SA with piano |
| | *The Shepherd's Calendar*, for young singers (SATB) and instrumentalists |
| 1966 (32) | *Notre dame des fleurs*, for soprano, mezzo-soprano, counter tenor and instrumental ensemble |
| | *Five Carols*, for SA unaccompanied |
| | *Solita*, for flute with musical box |
| 1967 (33) | *Antechrist*, for instrumental ensemble |
| | *Five Little Pieces for piano* |
| | *Hymnos*, for clarinet and piano |
| 1968 (34) | *Missa Super L'Homme Armé*, for speaker or singer (male or female) and instrumental ensemble (revised 1971) |
| | *Stedman Caters*, for instrumental ensemble |
| | *Purcell: Fantasia on a Ground and two Pavans*, realisation for instrumental ensemble |
| 1969 (35) | *St Thomas Wake*, foxtrot for orchestra on a pavan by John Bull |
| | *Worldes Bliss*, for orchestra |
| | *Eight Songs for a Mad King*, for male voice and instrumental ensemble |
| | *Eram Quasi Agnus*, instrumental motet |
| | *Gabrielli: Canzona*, realisation for chamber ensemble |
| | *Vesalii Icones*, for dancer, solo cello and instrumental ensemble |
| 1970 (36) | *Taverner*, opera in two acts |
| | Points and Dances from *Taverner*, instrumental dances and keyboard pieces from the opera |
| | *Sub Tuam Protectionem*, for piano |
| | *Ut Re Mi*, for piano |
| 1971 (37) | *From Stone to Thorn*, for mezzo-soprano and instrumental ensemble |
| | *Bell Tower (Turris campanarum sonantium)*, for percussion |
| | *Buxtehude: Also hat Gott die Welt Geliebet*, cantata for soprano and instrumental ensemble; realisation including 'original' interpretation |
| | Suite from *The Devils* for instrumental ensemble with soprano obligato drawn from the sound track of Ken Russell's film |
| | Suite from *The Boyfriend* for small orchestra; drawn from the sound track of Ken Russell's film, based on the musical by Sandy Wilson |
| 1972 (38) | *Blind Man's Buff*, masque for soprano (or treble), mezzo-soprano, mime and small orchestra |
| | *Fool's Fanfare*, for speaker and instrumental ensemble |
| | *Hymn to St Magnus*, for instrumental ensemble with mezzo-soprano obligato |
| | *Tenebrae super Gesualdo*, for mezzo-soprano, guitar and instrumental ensemble |
| | *Canon in memoriam Igor Stravinsky*, puzzle canon for instrumental ensemble |

*Lullabye for Ilian Rainbow*, for guitar

*J. S. Bach: Prelude and Fugue in C# minor, 'The 48', Book I*, realisation for instrumental ensemble

*Dunstable: Veni sancte spiritus – veni creator spiritus*, realisation plus original work, for instrumental ensemble

1973 (39)    *Stone Litany – Runes from a House of the Dead*, for mezzo-soprano and orchestra

*Renaissance Scottish Dances*, for instrumental ensemble (anon arranged by Maxwell Davies)

*Si quis diligit me*, motet for instrumental ensemble (Peebles and Heagy, arranged by Maxwell Davies)

*Purcell: Fantasia on One Note*, realisation for instrumental ensemble

1973–4 (39–40)  *Fiddlers at the Wedding*, for mezzo-soprano and instrumental ensemble

1974 (40)    *Dark Angels*, for voice and guitar

*Miss Donnithorne's Maggot*, for mezzo-soprano and instrumental ensemble

*All Sons of Adam*, motet for instrumental ensemble (anon Scottish sixteenth century, arranged by Maxwell Davies)

*Psalm 124*, motet for instrumental ensemble (Peebles, Fethy, anon arranged by Maxwell Davies)

*J. S. Bach: Prelude and Fugue in C# major, 'The 48', Book I*, realisation for instrumental ensemble

1975 (41)    *Ave maris Stella*, for instrumental ensemble

*The Door of the Sun*, for viola

*The Kestrel Paced Round the Sun*, for flute

*The Seven Brightnesses*, for clarinet in B♭

*Three Studies for percussion*, for eleven percussionists

*My Lady Lothian's Lilte*, for instrumental ensemble with mezzo-soprano obligato (realisation)

*Stevie's Ferry to Hoy*, for piano (beginners)

1976 (42)    Three Organ Voluntaries, (formerly Three Preludes for Organ)

*Kinloche His Fantassie*, realisation for instrumental ensemble

*Anakreontika*, Greek songs for mezzo-soprano and instrumental ensemble

*The Blind Fiddler*, song cycle for soprano and instrumental ensemble

Symphony No 1

*The Martyrdom of Saint Magnus*, chamber opera in nine scenes without interval for mezzo-soprano, tenor, two baritones, bass and instrumental ensemble

1977 (43)    *Norn pater noster*, prayer for SATB and organ

*Westerlings*, for unaccompanied SATB

*Runes from a Holy Island*, for instrumental ensemble

*A Mirror of Whitening Light*, for instrumental ensemble

*Ave rex angelorum*, for SATB unaccompanied or with organ

*Our Father Whiche in Heaven Art*, motet for instrumental ensemble (Angus arranged by Maxwell Davies)

1978 (44)    *The Two Fiddlers*, opera in two acts for young people to perform

*Le Jongleur de Notre Dame*, masque for baritone, mime/juggler, instrumental ensemble and children's band

*Salome*, ballet in two acts and nine scenes for full orchestra

*Four Lessons*, for two clavichords

Dances from *The Two Fiddlers* for instrumental ensemble

1979 (45)    *Black Pentecost*, for mezzo-soprano, baritone and orchestra

*Solstice of Light,* for tenor solo, SATB chorus and organ
Nocturne for alto flute
*Kirkwall Shopping Songs,* for children's voices, recorders, percussion and piano
*The Lighthouse,* chamber opera in one act with prologue for tenor, baritone, bass, and instrumental ensemble

1980 (46)  *Cinderella,* pantomime opera in two acts for children to play and sing
*The Yellow Cake Revue,* comment in words and music on the threat of uranium mining in Orkney for voice and piano
*Farewell to Stromness,* piano interlude from *The Yellow Cake Revue,* arranged for guitar by Timothy Walker
*Yesnaby Ground,* piano interlude from *The Yellow Cake Revue*
*A Welcome to Orkney,* for instrumental ensemble
*Little Quartet,* string quartet for young musicians
Symphony No 2

1981 (47)  *The Medium,* monodrama for mezzo-soprano
Piano Sonata
*The Rainbow,* short music theatre work for young children to sing and play
*Hill Runes,* for guitar
*The Bairns of Brugh,* for chamber ensemble
*Little Quartet No 2,* string quartet for young musicians
Tenor arias from *The Martyrdom of Saint Magnus,* for solo tenor, piano or organ
*Lullabye for Lucy.* for SATB
*Salome,* reduction for theatre orchestra of ballet score (1978) for thirty-eight instruments
*Brass Quintet,* unconducted
*Seven Songs Home,* for unaccompanied children's voices SAA

1982 (48)  *Songs of Hoy,* masque for children's voices and instruments
*Sea Eagle,* for horn
*Image, Reflection, Shadow,* for instrumental ensemble
Sinfonia Concertante for chamber orchestra
Organ Sonata
*Tallis: Four Voluntaries,* arranged for brass quintet
*Tallis: Four Voluntaries,* arranged for brass band
*Gesualdo: Two Motets,* arranged for brass quintet
*Gesualdo: Two Motets,* arranged for brass band
*March – The Pole Star,* for brass quintet
*March – The Pole Star,* for brass band

1983 (49)  *Birthday Music for John,* trio for flute, viola and cello
*Into the Labyrinth,* cantata for solo tenor and chamber orchestra
*Sinfonietta Accademica,* for chamber orchestra

1984 (50)  *Agnus Dei,* for two solo sopranos, viola and cello
Sonatine for violin and cimbalom
*Unbroken Circle,* for instrumental ensemble
*The Number 11 Bus,* music theatre work for tenor, mezzo-soprano, baritone, two dancers, mime and instrumental ensemble
Guitar Sonata
*One Star, At Last,* carol for SATB
Symphony No 3

## DEBUSSY, Claude
*b St Germain-en-Laye, 22 August 1862*
*d Paris, 25 March 1918, aged fifty-five*

He had his first piano lesson when he visited an aunt in Cannes in 1871. The following year he entered the Paris Conservatory. He was fortunate in finding wealthy patronesses, and in 1882 he first appeared as a composer in a concert of his songs and violin pieces. In 1884 he won the Prix de Rome, which required him to stay in that city. He returned to Paris in 1887. For a time he was very short of money and and gave a piano lesson on his wedding morning in 1899 in order to pay for the reception. Then his works gradually became more accepted; he was given the Légion d'honneur and was appointed to the advisory board of the Conservatory. Financially more secure, it was ironic that when he divorced and remarried in 1908 his new wife was wealthy. His health began to deteriorate in 1909 and progressively worsened until his death.

1876–9 (14–17) Trio in G minor
1880 (18)     *Danse bohémienne*, for piano
             Andante for piano
             'La belle au bois dormant', song (1880–3)
1881 (19)     Fugue for piano
1882 (20)     Two Four-part Fugues for piano
             *Triomphe de Bacchus*, for piano duet
             *Intermezzo*, for orchestra
             *Printemps*, for women's choir and orchestra
1883 (21)     *Invocation*, for male voice choir and orchestra
             *Le Gladiateur*, cantata
1884 (22)     *L'enfant prodigue*, cantata
             *Diane au bois*, for chorus
             *Divertissement No 1*, for orchestra
             Suite for orchestra, No 1
1885 (23)     *Almanzor*, for chorus
1887–8 (25–6) *The Blessed Damozel* (*La Damoiselle élue*), cantata (on a French
             translation of Rossetti's poem)
1887–9 (25–7) *Cinq poèmes de Baudelaire*, songs
1888 (26)     *Petite Suite*, for piano (four hands):
                'En bateau'; 'Cortège'; 'Menuet'; 'Ballet'
             *Arabesques I* and *II*, for piano
             *Ariettes oubliées*, songs
1889–90 (27–8) *Fantaisie*, for piano and orchestra
1890 (28)     *Suite Bergamasque*, for piano:
                'Prélude'
                'Menuet'
                'Clair de lune'
                'Passepied' (1890–1905)
             *Tarentelle Styrienne (Danse)*, for piano
             *Ballade*, for piano
             *Rêverie*, for piano
             *Valse romantique*, for piano
1891 (29)     *Mazurka*, for piano
             *Marche écossaise*
             *Trois mélodies de Verlaine*, songs
             *Deux romances*, songs
             *Rodrigue et Chimène*, opera in three acts (unfinished) (1891–2)
1892 (30)     *Fêtes galantes*, songs (first series)
1893 (31)     String Quartet in G minor
             *Proses lyriques*, songs

| 1894 (32) | *Prélude à l'après-midi d'un faune*, for orchestra |
|---|---|
| 1897 (35) | *Chansons de Bilitis*, songs |
| 1900 (38) | *Nocturnes*, for orchestra |
| | 'Nuages' |
| | 'Fêtes' |
| | 'Sirènes', with wordless female chorus |
| 1901 (39) | *Pour le piano*: (possibly 1896) |
| | 'Prélude' |
| | 'Sarabande' |
| | 'Toccata' |
| 1902 (40) | *Pelléas et Mélisande*, opera |
| 1903 (41) | *Estampes*, for piano: |
| | 'Pagodas' |
| | 'Soirée dans Grenade' |
| | 'Jardins sous la pluie' |
| | *Danse sacrée et danse profane*, for harp and strings |
| | *D'un cahier d'esquisses*, for piano |
| | *Le Diable dans le beffroi*, libretto and musical sketches |
| 1903–5 (41–3) | *Rhapsodie*, for saxophone, contralto and orchestra |
| 1904 (42) | *L'isle joyeuse*, for piano |
| | *Trois chansons de France* |
| | *Masques*, for piano |
| | *La Mer*, three symphonic sketches |
| | *Fêtes galantes*, songs (second series) |
| 1905 (43) | *Images*, for piano, Book I: |
| | 'Reflets dans l'eau' |
| | 'Hommage à Rameau' |
| | 'Mouvement' |
| 1907 (45) | *Images*, for piano, Book II: |
| | 'Cloches à travers les feuilles' |
| | 'Et la lune descend sur la temple qui fut' |
| | 'Poissons d'or' |
| 1908 (46) | *Children's Corner*, for piano: |
| | 'Doctor Gradus ad Parnassum' |
| | 'Jumbo's Lullaby' |
| | 'Doll's Serenade' |
| | 'Snow is Dancing' |
| | 'Little Shepherd' |
| | 'Golliwog's Cake-walk' |
| | *Ibéria*, (No 2 of *Images* for orchestra) |
| | *Trois chansons de Charles d'Orléans*, for unaccompanied chorus |
| | *The Fall of the House of Usher* (sketches for libretto and vocal score, unfinished, 1908–10) |
| 1909 (47) | *Rondes de Printemps* (No 3 of *Images* for orchestra) |
| | *Homage à Haydn*, for piano |
| 1909–10 (47–8) | Preludes for piano, Book I (twelve preludes) |
| | *Trois ballades de François Villon*, songs |
| | *Petite pièce en Bb major*, for clarinet and piano |
| | *La plus que lente*, for piano |
| | *Le Promenoir des deux amants*, three songs |
| | Rhapsody for clarinet and orchestra, No 1 |
| 1911 (49) | *The Martyrdom of St Sebastian*, incidental music to d'Annunzio's mystery-play |
| 1912 (50) | *Gigues* (No 1 of *Images* for orchestra) |
| | *Jeux*, poème dansé, for orchestra |
| | *Khamma*, ballet |

|          |      | *Syrinx*, for solo flute                                      |
|----------|------|----------------------------------------------------------------|
| 1913     | (51) | *La Boîte à Joujoux*, ballet music for piano                   |
|          |      | Preludes for piano, Book II (twelve preludes)                  |
|          |      | *Trois poèmes de Stéphane Mallarmé*, songs                     |
| 1914     | (52) | *Berceuse héroïque*, for piano                                 |
| 1915     | (53) | Cello Sonata in D minor                                        |
|          |      | *En blanc et noir*, piano duet                                 |
|          |      | *Douze Etudes*, for piano                                      |
|          |      | *Six epigraphes antiques*, for piano                           |
|          |      | *Noël des enfants*, for chorus                                 |
| 1916     | (54) | Sonata for flute, viola and harp, in G minor                   |
|          |      | *Ode à la France*, for chorus (1916–17)                        |
| 1917     | (55) | Violin Sonata in G minor and G major                           |

## DELIBES, Léo
*b St Germain-du-Val, 21 February 1836*
*d Paris, 16 January 1891, aged fifty-four*

He entered the Paris Conservatory at the age of twelve and, studying under Adam, obtained a first prize two years later. In 1853, at the age of seventeen, he became organist of St Pierre de Cahillot, and held many organist appointments subsequently. Also in 1853 he became accompanist at the Théâtre Lyrique, holding that post for ten years. In 1863 he became accompanist at the Opéra, rising to second chorus-master in 1865. By 1866 he could afford to spend the rest of his life composing.

| 1866 | (30) | *La Source (Nalla)*, ballet          |
|------|------|--------------------------------------|
| 1870 | (34) | *Coppélia*, ballet                   |
| 1876 | (40) | *Sylvia*, ballet                     |
| 1882 | (46) | *Le Roi s'amuse*, incidental music   |
| 1883 | (47) | *Lakmé*, opera                       |

## DELIUS, Frederick
*b Bradford, 29 January 1862*
*d Grez-sur-Loing, France, 10 June 1934, aged seventy-two*

He was the son of a wealthy Prussian industrialist who had settled in Bradford. In 1882 he left home to take control of an orange plantation in Florida, where negro music suddenly gave him inspiration. He went to Leipzig to study for three years, then lived in Paris from 1888 to 1897. He married a painter and settled permanently in Grez-sur-Loing, though still travelling widely in Europe and Scandinavia. He was nearly forty before he discovered his musical maturity. From the early 1920s he slowly became blind and paralytic, the result of syphilis contracted in 1890. In 1928 he was able to resume work through the services of Eric Fenby as his amanuensis.

| 1886 | (24) | *Florida Suite*, for orchestra                                                        |
|------|------|---------------------------------------------------------------------------------------|
| 1888 | (26) | *Marche caprice*, for orchestra                                                       |
|      |      | *Sleigh Ride*, for orchestra                                                          |
| 1892 | (30) | *Irmelin*, opera                                                                      |
| 1895 | (33) | *Over the Hills and Far Away*, tone poem                                              |
| 1899 | (37) | *Paris – The Song of a Great City*, nocturne for orchestra                            |
| 1902 | (40) | *Appalachia*, for orchestra, with final chorus                                        |
| 1903 | (41) | *Sea Drift*, for baritone, chorus and orchestra                                       |
| 1904 | (42) | *Koanga*, opera                                                                       |
| 1905 | (43) | *A Mass of Life*, for soloists, chorus and orchestra, text from Nietzsche's *Thus Spake Zarathustra* |

| 1906 (44) | Piano Concerto in C minor |
| 1907 (45) | *Brigg Fair – An English Rhapsody*, for orchestra |
| | *Songs of Sunset* |
| | *A Village Romeo and Juliet*, opera (from which comes the 'Walk to the Paradise Garden') |
| 1908 (46) | Dance Rhapsody No 1 for orchestra |
| | *In a Summer Garden*, rhapsody for orchestra |
| 1912 (50) | *On Hearing the First Cuckoo in Spring*, for orchestra |
| | *Summer Night on the River*, for orchestra |
| | *Song of the High Hills*, for wordless chorus and orchestra |
| 1914 (52) | *North Country Sketches*, for orchestra |
| 1916 (54) | Violin Concerto |
| | Dance Rhapsody No 2 for orchestra |
| 1917 (55) | *Eventyr*, for chorus and orchestra |
| 1918 (56) | *A Song Before Sunrise*, for small orchestra |
| 1919 (57) | *Fennimore and Gerda*, opera |
| 1920 (58) | *Hassan*, incidental music |
| 1922 (60) | *A Pagan Requiem* (possibly 1914–16) |
| 1925 (63) | *Caprice and Elegy*, for cello and orchestra |
| 1930 (68) | *A Song of Summer*, for orchestra |
| 1932 (70) | *Prelude to Irmelin* (based on themes from the earlier opera) |
| 1934 (72) | *Songs of Farewell*, for choir and orchestra |

## DIAMOND, David
*b Rochester, New York, 9 July 1915*

He first trained at the Cleveland Institute of Music from 1927 to 1929, then at the Eastman School of Music from 1930 to 1934. He later went to New York to study with Sessions and to Paris to study with Boulanger. In 1937 he won the Juillard Award, in 1938 and 1941 a Guggenheim Fellowship, in 1942 the Prix de Rome, and in 1943 the Paderewski Prize. He received many commissions, and in 1951 he went to Europe as a Fulbright professor and settled in Florence, remaining there until 1965. He then joined the faculty of the Manhattan School of Music, but since 1967 has devoted his time exclusively to composition.

| 1935 (20) | Partita for oboe, bassoon and piano |
| 1936 (21) | *Psalm*, for orchestra |
| | Sinfonietta |
| | *TOM*, ballet |
| | Concerto for string quartet |
| | Violin Concerto No 1 |
| | Cello Sonata |
| 1937 (22) | Variations for small orchestra |
| | Quintet for flute, string trio and piano |
| 1938 (23) | *Heroic Piece*, for small orchestra |
| | *Elegy in memory of Ravel*, for brass, harps and percussion |
| | *Music* for double string orchestra, brass and timpani |
| | Cello Concerto |
| | Piano Quartet |
| 1940 (25) | Concerto for small orchestra |
| | Symphony No 1 |
| | Quartet No 1 |
| 1941 (26) | *The Dream of Audubon*, ballet |
| 1942 (27) | Symphony No 2 |
| | Concerto for two solo pianos |
| 1943 (28) | Quartet No 2 |

| 1944 (29) | The Tempest, incidental music |
| | Rounds, for string orchestra |
| 1945 (30) | Symphonies No 3 and 4 |
| 1946 (31) | Quartet No 3 |
| | Violin Sonata |
| 1947 (32) | Violin Concerto No 2 |
| | Romeo and Juliet, incidental music |
| | Piano Sonata |
| 1948 (33) | Chaconne, for violin and piano |
| 1949 (34) | L'âme de Debussy, song cycle |
| | Timon of Athens, symphonic portrait |
| 1950 (35) | Piano Concerto |
| | Chorale for chorus |
| | Quintet for two violas, two cellos and clarinet |
| 1951 (36) | Quartet No 4 |
| | Symphony No 6 |
| | Mizmor l'David, sacred service for tenor, chorus, orchestra and organ |
| | The Midnight Meditation, song cycle |
| | Piano Trio |
| 1954 (39) | Sinfonia Concertante |
| | Sonata for solo violin |
| 1956 (41) | Sonata for solo cello |
| 1957 (42) | The World of Paul Klee, for orchestra |
| 1958 (43) | Woodwind Quintet |
| 1959 (44) | Symphony No 7 |
| 1960 (45) | Symphony No 8 |
| | Quartet No 5 |
| 1961 (46) | Nonet for three violins, three violas and three cellos |
| 1962 (47) | This Sacred Ground, for baritone, chorus, children's chorus and orchestra |
| | Quartet No 6 |
| 1963 (48) | Quartet No 7 |
| 1964 (49) | Quartet No 8 |
| | We Two, song cycle |
| 1966 (51) | Quartets No 9 and 10 |
| 1967 (52) | To Music, choral symphony for tenor, bass-baritone, chorus and orchestra |
| | Hebrew Melodies, song cycle |
| | Violin Concerto No 3 |
| 1969 (54) | Music for chamber orchestra |
| 1974 (59) | fp Quartet No 10 |

## DICKINSON, Peter
b Lytham St Annes, Lancashire, 15 November 1934

He was an organ scholar at Queens' College, Cambridge and in 1958 was given a scholarship to the Juilliard School. He worked as a pianist with the New York City Ballet, and as a critic and lecturer. From 1962 to 1970 he held various lectureships in London and Birmingham, finally resigning to work freelance. In 1974 he was made the first professor of music at Keele University.

| 1958 (25) | String Quartet No 1 (revised 1974) |
| 1959 (26) | Three Juilliard Dances, for instrumental ensemble |
| | Variations, ballet |
| | Vitalitas, ballet |

|  |  | Monologue for strings |
| --- | --- | --- |
| 1963 | (30) | Motets |
| 1965 | (32) | *The Judas Tree*, for actors, singers and ensemble |
| 1966 | (33) | *Martin of Tours*, for chorus, soloists and organ |
|  |  | *Elegy*, for counter-tenor, harpsichord and cellos |
| 1967 | (34) | *The Dry Heart*, for chorus |
|  |  | *Fanfares and Elegies*, for six brass and organ |
|  |  | *Paraphrase I*, for organ |
|  |  | *Paraphrase II*, for piano |
| 1968 | (35) | *Outcry*, for alto, chorus and strings |
| 1969 | (36) | *Five Diversions*, for orchestra |
| 1970 | (37) | *Transformations*, for orchestra |
| 1971 | (38) | *Winter Afternoons*, for six solo voices and double-bass |
|  |  | Organ Concerto |
|  |  | Concerto for strings, percussion and electric organ |
|  |  | *Translations*, for recorder, viola da gamba and harpsichord |
| 1972–83 | (39–50) | *Suite for the Centenary of Lord Berners*, for clavichord |
| 1973 | (40) | *Hymns, Blues and Improvisations*, for piano quintet and tape |
| 1974 | (41) | *Lust*, for six solo voices |
| 1975 | (42) | *Late Afternoon in November*, for sixteen solo voices |
|  |  | String Quartet No 2 with tape and piano |
| 1976 | (43) | *Solo*, for baryton, tape and viola da gamba |
|  |  | *Surrealist Landscape*, for mezzo |
| 1977 | (44) | Aria for horn, oboe, clarinet and bassoon |
|  |  | *Four Auden Songs*, for soprano or tenor and piano |
|  |  | *A Memory of David Munrow*, for two counter-tenors, two recorders, viola da gamba and harpsichord |
|  |  | *Schubert in Blue*, for mezzo and piano |
| 1978 | (45) | Four Duos for flute or oboe and cello |
|  |  | *Reminiscences*, for mezzo, sax and piano |
| 1979 | (46) | *A Brithday Surprise*, for orchestra |
| 1982 | (49) | *The Unicorns*, for soprano and brass band |
| 1984 | (51) | Piano Concerto |

Peter Dickinson has also written many songs.


### d'INDY, Vincent
*b Paris, 27 March 1851*
*d Paris, 2 December 1931, aged eighty*

He was born into a noble family, and had a very strict upbringing. He studied piano with his paternal grandmother, and soon became a prodigy. He began studying harmony at the age of fourteen. After distinguished service during the Franco-Prussian War of 1870/71, he studied with Franck at the Paris Conservatory. His association with Saint-Saëns, Massenet, Bizet, Brahms, Liszt and Wagner gave him a wide horizon of musical ideas. He formed the Schola Cantorum, and was its principal and chief lecturer. He was a teacher of great influence.

| 1874 | (23) | *Max et Thecla*, symphonic overture (Part 2 of *Wallenstein Trilogy*) |
| --- | --- | --- |
|  |  | *Jean Hunyade*, symphony (1874–5) |
| 1876 | (25) | *Anthony and Cleopatra*, overture |
|  |  | *Attendez-moi sous l'Orme*, opera (1876–8) |
| 1878 | (27) | *The Enchanted Forest*, ballad-symphony |
|  |  | Piano Quartet in A major (1878–88) |
| 1879–83 | (28–32) | *Le Chant de la Cloche*, opera |

1880 (29)   *Le Camp de Wallenstein*, symphonic overture (Part 1 of *Wallenstein Trilogy*)

1882 (31)   *La Mort de Wallenstein*, symphonic overture (Part 3 of *Wallenstein Trilogy*)

1884 (33)   *Saugefleure*, orchestral legend
            Lied for cello (or viola) and orchestra

1886 (35)   *Symphony on a French Mountain Air*
            Suite in D major for trumpet, two flutes and string quartet

1887 (36)   *Serenade and Valse*, for small orchestra
            Trio for clarinet, cello and piano

1888 (37)   *Fantasie*, for oboe and orchestra

1890 (39)   *Karadec*, incidental music
            String Quartet No 1 in Bb

1891 (41)   *Tableaux de Voyage*, for orchestra

1896 (45)   *Istar*, symphonic variations for orchestra

1897 (46)   *Fervaal*, lyric drama
            String Quartet No 2 in E

1898 (47)   *Medée*, incidental music
            *Chansons et danses*, for seven wind instruments in Bb
            *L'Etranger*, lyric drama (1898–1901)

1902–3 (51–2) Symphony No 2 in Bb

1903 (52)   *Choral Varié*, for saxophone and orchestra

1904 (53)   Violin Sonata in C

1905 (54)   *Jour d'été à la montagne*, symphonic triptych

1906 (55)   *Souvenirs*, tone poem

1916–18 (65–7) *Sinfonia brève de ballo Gallico*

1918 (67)   *Sarabande et Minuet*, for piano, flute, oboe, clarinet, horn and bassoon

1920 (69)   *Légende de St Christophe*, opera
            *Le Poème des Rivages*, symphonic suite (1920–1)

1922–3 (71–2) *Le Rêve de Cynias*, lyric comedy

1924 (73)   Piano Quintet in G minor

1925 (74)   Cello Sonata in D major
            *Diptyque méditerranéen* (1925–6)

1927 (76)   Concerto for piano, flute, cello and string quartet
            *Suites en parties*, for harp, flute, viola, and cello

1929 (78)   String Sextet in Bb

1930 (79)   String Quartet No 4 in Db
            Piano Trio No 2 in the form of a suite
            Suite for flute obbligato, violin, viola, cello and harp

**DITTERSDORF, Carl Ditters von**
*b Vienna, 2 November 1739*
*d Neuhof, Pilgram, Bohemia, 24 October 1799, aged sixty*

His father was costumier to the court and theatre in Danzig. He was given a good education, and engaged to play in the orchestra of Prince Joseph Friedrich; but in 1765 he tried to leave the service of the Prince, was arrested and brought back, then dismissed. Gluck and Haydn were his friends. He entered the service of Emperor Joseph II but left soon after when he was refused a rise in salary. He then became *Kapellmeister* to a bishop, who fell from favour and had to dismiss his orchestra. Next he entered the service of the Prince Bishop of Breslau, who allowed him to restore a theatre on his estate and collect a company of singers, one of whom he married. His last years were spent in poverty and ill-health.

| 1767 | (28) | *Amore in musica*, opera |
|---|---|---|
| 1770 | (31) | *Il viaggiatore americano*, opera |
| 1771 | (32) | *L'amore disprezzato*, opera |
| 1773 | (34) | *Il tutore e la pupilla*, opera |
| 1774 | (35) | *Il tribunale de Giove*, opera |
| 1775 | (36) | *Il finto pazzo per amore*, opera |
| | | *Il maniscalco,* opera |
| | | *Lo sposo burlato*, opera |
| 1776 | (37) | *La contadina felice*, opera |
| | | *La moda*, opera |
| | | *Il barone di Rocca Antica*, opera |
| 1777 | (38) | *L'Arcifanfano, re de' matti*, opera |
| 1786 | (47) | *Doktor und Apotheker*, opera |
| | | *Betrug durch Aberglauben*, opera |
| 1787 | (48) | *Democrito corretto*, opera |
| | | *Die Liebe in Narrenhaus*, opera |
| 1789 | (50) | *Hieronimus Knicker*, opera |
| 1790 | (51) | *Das rote Käppchen*, opera |
| 1791 | (52) | *Hokus Pokus*, opera |
| 1794 | (55) | *Das Gespeust mit der Trommel*, opera |
| 1795 | (56) | *Don Quixote der Zeite*, opera |
| | | *Gott Mars*, opera |
| | | *Schach vom Schiras*, opera |
| 1796 | (57) | *Ugolino*, opera |
| | | *Die Lustigen Weiber von Windsor*, opera |
| | | *Der Durchmarsch*, opera |
| 1797 | (58) | *Der Terno secco*, opera |
| | | *Der Mädchenmarkt*, opera |

Dittersdorf also composed church music, symphonies, and string quartets.


## DODGSON, Stephen
*b London, 17 March 1924*

He was educated at the Royal College of Music, and has taught there since 1965.

He has written: four concertos; symphony for wind instruments; two suites for clavichord; vocal and chamber music; music for harpsichord and piano.


## DOHNÁNYI, Ernst von
*b Bratislava, 27 July 1877*
*d New York, 11 February 1960, aged eighty-two*

His father was a professor of mathematics and a good amateur cellist. At the age of seventeen Dohnányi enrolled at the Budapest Royal Academy of Music, leaving to become a successful concert pianist, a career he later abandoned to become a teacher and composer. For ten years he taught at the Berlin Hochschule, then became director of the Budapest Academy, and conductor of the Budapest Philharmonic Orchestra. In 1927 he was awarded a grant from the State. He became director of the Hungarian Broadcasting Service. From 1947 he settled in the USA.

| 1895 | (18) | *fp* Piano Quintet in C minor (Op 1, published 1902) |
|---|---|---|
| 1896 | (19) | *Zrinyi*, overture |
| 1897 | (20) | Symphony No 1 in F major |
| 1903 | (26) | *p* String Quartet in A major |
| | | *p* Cello Sonata in B♭ minor |

| 1904 | (27) | p Serenade in C major for string trio |
|------|------|---------------------------------------|
| 1907 | (30) | p String Quartet in D major |
| 1910 | (33) | *Der Schlier der Pierette*, ballet |
|      |      | p Piano Quintet in E♭ major |
| 1913 | (36) | p Violin Sonata in C♯ minor |
|      |      | *Tante Simona*, opera |
| 1915 | (38) | Violin Concerto No 1 |
| 1916 | (39) | *Variations on a Nursery Song*, for piano and orchestra |
| 1919 | (42) | Suite in F♯ minor |
| 1920 | (43) | *Hitvallas*, for tenor, choir and orchestra |
| 1922 | (45) | *The Tower of the Voivod*, romantic opera |
| 1929 | (52) | *A Tenor*, opera |
| 1930 | (53) | *Szeged Mass*, for twelve voices, orchestra and organ |
| 1933 | (56) | *Symphonic Minutes*, for orchestra |
| 1935 | (58) | Sextet in C |
| 1939–41 | (62–4) | *Cantus Vitae*, symphonic cantata (unpublished) |
| 1942–3 | (65–6) | *Suite en Valse*, for orchestra |
| 1943–4 | (66–7) | Symphony No 2 in D minor, Op 9 |
| 1945 | (68) | Six Pieces for piano |
| 1946 | (69) | Piano Concerto No 2 |
| 1950 | (73) | Twelve Studies for piano |
| 1952 | (75) | Violin Concerto No 2 |
|      |      | Harp Concerto |
| 1953 | (76) | *Stabat Mater* |
| 1954 | (77) | *American Rhapsody* |

Dohnányi also composed:
Konzertstücke for cello, Op 12
*Ruralia Hungarica*, for piano (later orchestrated), Op 33
Symphony No 3 in E major

## DONIZETTI, Gaetano
*b Bergamo, 29 November 1797*
*d Bergamo, 8 April 1848, aged fifty*

He studied music locally, advancing so quickly that he was sent to the Liceo Filarmonica in Bologna. Returning home by the time he was twenty, uncertain what he should do next, he began composing for local amateur societies. In 1818 he received his first operatic commission, and subsequently wrote up to four or five operas a year. Honours were heaped upon him, and he was appointed *Kapellmeister* to the Austrian Emperor. From 1843 recurrent bouts of fever slowed his work; his condition deteriorated until he finally collapsed into paralysis and insanity, the last stages of a venereal disease. His last two years were spent in a coma.

| 1830 | (33) | *Anna Bolena*, opera |
|------|------|----------------------|
| 1832 | (35) | *L'Elisir d'Amore*, opera |
| 1833 | (36) | *Lucrezia Borgia*, opera |
| 1834 | (37) | *Rosmonda d'Inghilterra*, opera |
| 1835 | (38) | *Lucia di Lammermoor*, opera |
| 1840 | (43) | *La Favorita*, opera |
|      |      | *La Fille du Régiment*, opera |
| 1842 | (45) | *Linda de Chamounix*, opera |
| 1843 | (46) | *Maria de Rohan*, opera |
|      |      | *Don Pasquale*, opera |
|      |      | *Don Sébastien*, opera |

Donizetti composed more than sixty operas, some in French.

## DOWLAND, John
*b London?, 1563*
*d London, 20/21 January 1626, aged sixty-three*

Nothing is known of his early years. In 1580 he went to Paris as a servant of the English Ambassador, and while there he converted to Catholicism. In 1588 he became a bachelor of music at Christ Church, Oxford, and then began to travel all over Europe. In 1598 he was appointed lutenist to King Christian IV of Denmark, but was dismissed in 1606 after a financial battle. In 1612, back in England, he was appointed one of the King's (James 1) Musicians for the Lute.

| | | |
|---|---|---|
| 1597 | (34) | *p* First Book of Songes or Ayres |
| 1600 | (37) | *p* Second Book of Songes |
| 1603 | (40) | *p* Third Book of Songes or Ayres |
| 1604 | (41) | *p Lachrymae* |
| 1612 | (49) | *p* Fourth Book of Songes, *A Pilgrimes Solace* |

## DUFAY, Guillaume
*b Cambrai, c1400*
*d Cambrai, 27 November 1474, aged c seventy-four*

He had no formal musical training, but learned by working for and copying the music of older musicians and composers. It is thought he worked in Italy from before 1420 until 1426, then returned to Cambrai and held two benefices in the Laon diocese. From 1428 to 1433 he was a singer in the papal choir, and from then on became one of the most famous musicians in Europe, holding many posts, benefices and connections with several courts, though always keeping residence in Cambrai. During the 1450s he spent seven years in Savoy; his name occurs in the archives of Turin and Besançon. He was friend and host to some of the greatest musicians and churchmen of the day. He left a great quantity of church music and secular works, mostly undated.

## DUKAS, Paul
*b Paris, 1 October 1865*
*d Paris, 17 May 1935, aged sixty-nine*

He studied at the Paris Conservatory from 1882 to 1889, and won second prize in the Prix de Rome. He became music inspector of the Administration des Beaux-Arts and an officer of the Légion d'honneur. He contributed many articles to musical papers. From 1909 until his death he taught composition at the Paris Conservatory. A large number of his compositions were unpublished, and all of these he destroyed shortly before his death.

| | | |
|---|---|---|
| 1883 | (18) | *King Lear*, overture |
| 1884 | (19) | *Götz von Berlichingen*, overture |
| 1888 | (23) | *Velléda*, cantata |
| 1892 | (27) | *Polyeucte*, overture |
| 1896 | (31) | Symphony in C major |
| 1897 | (32) | *The Sorcerer's Apprentice*, symphonic poem |
| 1901 | (36) | Piano Sonata in E♭ minor |
| 1903 | (38) | *Variations, Interlude and Finale on a theme by Rameau*, for piano |
| 1906 | (41) | *Villanelle*, for horn and piano |
| 1907 | (42) | *Ariadne and Bluebeard*, opera |
| 1909 | (44) | *Prélude élégiaque*, for piano |
| | | *Vocalise* |
| 1912 | (47) | *La Péri – poème dansé*, for orchestra (possibly 1921) |
| 1921 | (56) | *La Plainte, au loin, du faune*, for piano |
| 1924 | (59) | *Sonnet de Ronsard*, for voice and piano |

**DUPARC, Marie Eugène Henri Fouques**
*b Paris, 21 January 1848*
*d Mont-de-Marsan, 12 February 1933, aged eighty-five*

He was educated at the Jesuit College of Vaugirard, where the music master was Franck, whose group of young composers he joined. One of them, Chausson, became his life-long friend. In 1869 he went to Weimar where, in Liszt's house, he met Wagner, whose music influenced him greatly. He also painted very well, but in this and his music he was self-critical to a morbid degree, destroying a great deal of his work. In 1885, at the age of thirty-seven, he abandoned composition altogether and left Paris for Switzerland and the south of France, living there for the rest of his life. For nearly the next fifty years he was tortured by neurasthenia and rheumatism, and at the end was almost completely blind.

| | | |
|---|---|---|
| 1864 | (16) | *Six Rêveries*, for piano |
| 1867 | (19) | Sonata for piano and cello (destroyed) |
| | | *Feuilles volantes*, for piano |
| 1869 | (21) | *Beaulieu*, for piano |
| 1874 | (26) | *Suite des Valses*, for orchestra |
| | | *Poème*, nocturne for orchestra (parts 2 and 3 lost) |
| 1875 | (27) | *Lénore*, symphonic poem |
| 1879–85 | (31–7) | *Roussalka*, opera, destroyed |
| 1882 | (34) | *Danse lente*, for orchestra |
| 1883 | (35) | *Aux étoiles*. nocturne |
| | | *Benedicat vobis Dominus*, motet for three voices |

Duparc also wrote fourteen splendid songs.


**DUPRÉ, Marcel**
*b Rouen, 3 May 1886*
*d Meudon, 30 May 1971, aged eighty-five*

He began his studies with his father at the age of seven; at twelve he became organist at St Vivien in Rouen, and at fifteen had his first choral piece performed. From 1902 to 1914, at the Paris Conservatory, he studied organ, with Widor among others, winning the Prix de Rome in 1914. He learned all Bach's organ works and performed them at the Conservatory in 1920, the first time such a performance had been given. In that same year he made his first appearance outside France, with a capacity audience at the Albert Hall in London. In 1921 he gave a series of concerts in Philadelphia and New York, and thereafter visited the USA regularly. He toured the world; but after his 1,900th concert in 1953 he gave up recitals. However, he kept until the end of his life his post as organist to St Sulpice.

Apart from a great number of organ and sacred choral works, he also wrote:

| | | |
|---|---|---|
| 1909 | (23) | Sonata for violin and piano |
| 1912 | (26) | *Fantaisie* for piano and orchestra |
| 1914 | (28) | *Psyché*, cantata |
| 1916 | (30) | Four Motets for chorus |
| | | Six Preludes for piano |
| | | Three Pieces for cello and piano |
| 1917 | (31) | *De Profundis*, for soli, chorus, organ and orchestra |
| 1921 | (35) | Four Pieces for piano |
| 1924 | (38) | Variations for piano |
| 1928 | (42) | Symphony with organ |
| 1932 | (46) | Concerto for organ and orchestra |
| 1936 | (50) | *Poème héroïque*, for organ and brass |
| 1938 | (52) | Variations for piano and organ |

1946 (60)    Sinfonia for piano and organ
1952 (66)    Quartet for organ and string trio
1952–3 (66–7) *La France au Calvaire*, oratorio
1960 (74)    Trio for organ, violin and cello


## DURUFLÉ, Maurice
*b Louviers, 11 January 1902*

He was taught piano and organ privately. In 1920 he went to the Paris Conservatory, gaining several first prizes. In 1930 he was appointed organist of St Etienne-du-Mont. He became professor of harmony at the Paris Conservatory in 1943, remaining there until 1969.

1926 (24)    Scherzo for organ
1927 (25)    *Triptyque*, for piano
1928 (26)    *Prélude, récitatif et variations*, for flute, viola and piano
1929 (27)    Prélude, Adagio and Chorale Variations on 'Veni, Creator', for organ
1930 (28)    Suite (Prélude, Sicilienne and Toccata) for organ
1935 (33)    Three Dances for orchestra
1940 (38)    Andante and Scherzo for orchestra
1942 (40)    *Prélude et fugue sur le nom Alain*, for organ
1947 (45)    *Requiem*, for mezzo-soprano, bass, choir, orchestra and organ
1960 (58)    Four Motets on Gregorian themes for choir a cappella
1967 (65)    *Cum Jubilo*, Mass for baritone solo, choir, orchestra and organ


## DVOŘÁK, Antonin
*b Nelahozeves, Bohemia, 8 September 1841*
*d Prague, 1 May 1904, aged sixty-two*

His father, a village butcher and publican, had an interest in music and played the zither. Dvořák studied singing, violin, piano and organ. When he was sixteen he went to Prague to study, and in order to earn money he played viola in cafés and the organ in a mental asylum. In 1862 Smetana started to establish the National Theatre of Prague, and Dvořák joined it as a viola player and stayed for about ten years. He left to take a position as a church organist, which gave him more time for composition. He was much encouraged by Brahms. From 1892 to 1895 he was in New York as head of the National Conservatory; then he returned to Prague where, a few years later, he became head of the Conservatory there.

1857–9 (16–18) Mass in Bb major
1861 (20)    String Quintet in A minor
1862 (21)    String Quartet No 1 in A major
1865 (24)    Symphony No 1 in C minor
             Symphony No 2 in Bb major
             Cello Concerto in A major
             Clarinet Quintet
             *The Cypresses*, ten love songs for string quartet, later for voice and piano
1870 (29)    *Alfred*, song with piano
             *Dramatic (Tragic) Overture*
             *Notturno*, in B major, for strings
             String Quartet in Bb major
             String Quartet in D major
             String Quartet in E minor

| 1871 (30) | King and Charcoal Burner, opera (1st version) |
| | Rosmarine, songs with piano |
| | Overture in F major |
| | Piano Trios, No 1 and 2 |
| | Cello Sonata |
| 1872 (31) | Patriotic Hymn |
| | May Night, nocturne for orchestra |
| | Piano Quintet in A major |
| 1873 (32) | Symphony No 3 in E♭ major |
| | Romance, for violin and orchestra |
| | String Quartet in F minor |
| | String Quartet in A minor |
| | Octet, Serenade |
| | Violin Sonata in A minor |
| 1874 (33) | Symphony No 4 in D minor |
| | Rhapsody for Orchestra, in A minor |
| | String Quartet in A minor |
| 1875 (34) | Symphony No 5 in F major (old numbering: No 3) |
| | Serenade for Strings, in E major |
| | String Quintet, with double-bass, in G major |
| | Piano Quartet in D major |
| | Piano Trio in B♭ major |
| | Moravian Vocal Duets |
| 1876 (35) | Piano Concerto in G minor |
| | Stabat Mater |
| | String Quartet in E major |
| | Piano Trio in G minor |
| | Four Songs for mixed choir |
| 1877 (36) | The Cunning Peasant, opera |
| | Symphonic Variations for orchestra |
| | String Quartet in D minor |
| 1878 (37) | Slavonic Dances, for orchestra (first series) |
| | Slavonic Rhapsodies, for orchestra |
| | Serenade in D minor, for orchestra |
| | String Sextet in A major |
| | Bagatelles for two violins, cello and harmonium (or piano) |
| 1879 (38) | Violin Concerto in A minor (1879–80) |
| | Festival March |
| | Czech Suite, in D major |
| | Mazurka for violin and orchestra |
| | String Quartet in E♭ major |
| | Polonaise in E♭ major |
| 1880 (39) | Symphony No 6 in D major (old numbering: No 1) |
| | Violin Sonata in F major |
| | Seven Gipsy Songs |
| 1881 (40) | Legends, for orchestra |
| | String Quartet in C major |
| 1882 (41) | My Home, overture |
| 1883 (42) | Husitská, overture |
| | Scherzo Capriccioso for orchestra |
| | Piano Trio in F minor |
| 1885 (44) | Symphony No 7 in D minor (old numbering: No 2) |
| | The Spectre's Bride, cantata |
| 1886 (45) | Slavonic Dances, for orchestra (second series) |
| | St Ludmila, oratorio |
| 1887 (46) | Piano Quintet in A major |

|      |      | Piano Quartet in E♭ major |
|------|------|---------------------------|
|      |      | Terzetto for two violins and viola |
| 1889 | (48) | Symphony No 8 in G major (old numbering: No 4) |
| 1890 | (49) | Gavotte for three violins |
|      |      | *Dumka*, for piano trio (1890–1) |
| 1891 | (50) | *Nature, Life and Love*, cycle of overtures: |
|      |      | 'Amid Nature' |
|      |      | 'Carnival' |
|      |      | 'Othello' (1891–2) |
|      |      | Rondo for cello and orchestra |
|      |      | *Forest Calm*, for cello and orchestra |
| 1892 | (51) | *Te Deum* |
| 1893 | (52) | Symphony No 9 in E minor, *From the New World* (old numbering: No 5) |
|      |      | String Quartet in F major, *American* |
|      |      | String Quintet in E♭ major |
| 1895 | (54) | Suite for orchestra |
|      |      | Cello Concerto in B minor |
|      |      | String Quartet in A♭ major |
|      |      | String Quartet in G major |
| 1896 | (55) | Four Symphonic Poems: |
|      |      | 'The Watersprite' |
|      |      | 'The Noonday Witch' |
|      |      | 'The Wood Dove' |
|      |      | 'The Golden Spinning-wheel' |
| 1897 | (56) | 'Heroic Song' |
| 1901 | (60) | *fp Rusalka*, opera |

## ELGAR, (Sir) Edward

*b Broadheath, near Worcester, 2 June 1857*
*d Worcester, 23 February 1934, aged seventy-six*

He lived most of his life in the area of Worcester, near where he was born. His father was an organist and music-seller, and he himself played piano, violin, cello, double-bass, bassoon and trombone. He became a bandmaster in a mental home, and his first compositions, for local music festivals, were works of great variety, for wind instruments, strings and for voices. It was not until the age of forty-two, with the first performance of his *Enigma Variations* in 1899, that he suddenly came to the front rank as a composer. He was knighted in 1904.

| 1878 | (21) | *Romance*, for violin and piano (also arrangement for violin and orchestra) |
|------|------|------|
|      |      | *Promenades*, six pieces for wind instruments |
| 1879 | (22) | *Harmony Music*, seven pieces for wind instruments (No 7 1881) |
|      |      | *Intermezzos for Wind*, five pieces |
| 1883 | (26) | *Une Idyll*, for violin and piano (*c*1883) |
|      |      | Fugue in D minor for oboe and violin |
| 1890 | (33) | *Froissart*, concert overture |
| 1891 | (34) | *La Capriceuse*, for violin and piano |
| 1892 | (35) | *Serenade for Strings* |
|      |      | *The Black Knight*, cantata |
| 1894–5 | (37–8) | *Scenes from the Saga of King Olaf*, cantata |
| 1895 | (38) | Organ Sonata in G major |
| 1896 | (39) | *The Light of Life (Lux Christi)*, oratorio |
| 1897 | (40) | Imperial March |
|      |      | *The Banner of St George*, a ballad for soprano, chorus and orchestra |

|  |  |
|---|---|
|  | *Sea Pictures*, five songs for contralto and orchestra |
| 1898 (41) | *Caractacus*, cantata for soprano, tenor, baritone and bass soli, chorus and orchestra |
|  | *Variations on an Original Theme ('Enigma')*, for orchestra (1898–9) |
| 1899–1904 (42–7) | *Sérénade Lyrique*, for orchestra |
|  | *In the South (Alassio)*, concert overture |
| 1900 (43) | *The Dream of Gerontius*, oratorio |
| 1901 (44) | *Cockaigne*, overture (*In London Town*) |
|  | Concerto Allegro for piano |
|  | *Introduction and Allegro for strings* (1901–5) |
|  | *Pomp and Circumstance Marches 1–4* (1901–7) |
| 1902 (45) | Coronation Ode |
|  | *Dream Children*, two pieces for piano or small orchestra |
|  | *Falstaff*, symphonic study in C minor (1902–13) |
| 1903 (46) | *The Apostles*, oratorio |
| c1903–10 (c46–53) | Symphony No 2 in E♭ major |
| 1906 (49) | *The Kingdom*, oratorio |
|  | *The Wand of Youth*, Suites 1 and 2, for orchestra – final version 1906–7 (begun in 1867, 1869, or 1871; revised 1879–81; revised again c1902) |
| 1907 (50) | Symphony No 1 in A♭ major (1907–8) |
| 1909 (52) | Violin Concerto (c1909–10) |
|  | *Elegy*, for string orchestra |
| 1910 (53) | *Romance*, for bassoon and orchestra |
| 1912 (55) | *The Music Makers*, for contralto, chorus and orchestra |
| 1914 (57) | *Carillon*, recitation with orchestra |
|  | p *Sospiri*, for orchestra |
| 1915 (58) | *Polonia*, symphonic prelude |
|  | *Une voix dans le desert*, recitation with orchestra |
| 1917 (60) | fp *The Spirit of England*, three pieces for voices and orchestra: |
|  | No 1 *The Fourth of August* (finished 1917) |
|  | No 2 *To Women* (1915) |
|  | No 3 *For the Fallen* (1915) |
|  | *Le Drapeau Belge*, recitation with orchestra |
|  | *Fringes of the Fleet*, song cycle |
| 1918 (61) | Violin Sonata in E minor |
|  | String Quartet in E minor |
|  | Piano Quintet in A minor (1918–19) |
| 1919 (62) | Cello Concerto in E minor |
| 1923 (66) | fp *King Arthur*, incidental music |
| 1924 (67) | fp *Pageant of Empire*, for chorus and orchestra |
| 1928 (71) | fp *Beau Brummel*, incidental music |
| 1930 (73) | *Severn Suite*, for brass band, also arranged for orchestra |
|  | *Pomp and Circumstance, March No 5* for orchestra |
| 1931 (74) | p *Nursery Suite*, for orchestra (dedicated to TRH Princesses Elizabeth and Margaret Rose) |

## ENESCO, Georges
*b Liveni, Moldavia, 19 August 1881*
*d Paris, 4 May 1955, aged seventy-three*

He began studying violin at the age of four, and at seven went to the Vienna Conservatory. At thirteen he entered the Paris Conservatory, studying with Massenet and Fauré. He made his début as a composer at the age of sixteen, and won a first prize for violin in 1899. He was much in demand as a teacher, and one of his pupils was Yehudi Menuhin. He was made a member of the Romanian Academy in 1912. He resided in the USA for a time from 1946, returning to France not long before his death. He is generally known as the father of Romanian national music.

| 1895 (14) | *Ouverture tragica e ouverture trionfale* |
| | Four *Sinfonie scolastiche* (1895–6) |
| 1897 (16) | *Romanian Poem* |
| 1898 (17) | p Violin Sonata No 1 |
| 1899 (18) | *Fantaisie Pastorale* |
| 1901 (20) | *Romanian Rhapsody*, No 1 |
| | *Symphonie Concertante*, for cello and orchestra |
| | p Violin Sonata No 2 |
| 1902 (21) | *Romanian Rhapsody*, No 2 |
| 1903 (22) | Suite for orchestra |
| 1905 (24) | Symphony No 1 in E♭ major |
| | p String Octet in C major |
| 1911 (30) | Symphony No 2 in A major |
| 1915 (34) | Suite for orchestra |
| 1919 (38) | Symphony No 3 with organ and chorus |
| 1921 (40) | Violin Concerto |
| | *Oedipus*, opera (begun *c*1921) |
| 1937 (56) | *Suite Villageoise*, for orchestra |
| 1950 (69) | *Vox Maris*, symphonic poem |

## FALLA, Manuel de
*b Cadiz, 23 November 1876*
*d Alta Gracïa, Argentina, 14 November 1946, aged sixty-nine*

He was the son of a wealthy merchant. At the age of twenty he passed all the piano examinations of the Madrid Conservatory as an external candidate. He won a first prize in 1905 in an opera-writing competition, but the opera, *La Vida brève*, was not performed at the time. In 1907 he took this work to Paris with him, and befriended Debussy, Ravel, Dukas, Stravinsky and Albéniz. He earned a living by teaching and translating. By the 1930s he was a sick man, and when in 1939 he was invited to Buenos Aires for a concert tour his ill-health made him stay on in Argentina.

| 1908 (32) | *Pièces espagnoles*, for piano |
| 1909 (33) | *Trois mélodies*, songs |
| | *Nights in the Gardens of Spain*, for piano and orchestra (1909–15) |
| 1913 (37) | fp *La Vida Brève*, opera |
| 1915 (39) | fp *El Amor Brujo*, ballet |
| 1919 (43) | fp *The Three-cornered Hat*, ballet |
| | *Fantasia bética*, piano solo |
| 1921 (45) | *Homage pour le tombeau de Debussy*, for guitar |
| 1922 (46) | *El Retablo de Maese Pedro*, opera |
| | Seven Spanish Popular Songs |
| 1923–6 (47–50) | Concerto for harpsichord, flute, oboe, clarinet, violin and cello |
| 1934 (58) | Fanfare for wind and percussion |
| 1935 (59) | *Pour le tombeau de Paul Dukas*, for piano |
| 1940 (67) | *Homenajes*, orchestral version of *Homage pour le tombeau de Debussy* |

**FARNABY, Giles**
*b c1563*
*Buried London, 25 November 1640, aged c seventy-seven*

Like his father he was a joiner by trade. Since his father worked in London it is likely that Giles was born there, and it is certain he worked there at his trade. What little instruction he had in music was intermittent, yet he was able to graduate as Bachelor of Music at Oxford in 1592. Two years later he moved into the country, as teacher to the children of Sir Nicholas Saunderson in Lincolnshire. By 1614, however, he was back in London, pursuing the life of a composer.

1598 (*c*38)    *p* Canzonets to Foure Voyces
Farnaby also composed over fifty pieces in the Fitzwilliam Virginal Book.


**FAURÉ, Gabriel**
*b Pamiers, Ariège, 12 May 1845*
*d Paris, 4 November 1924, aged seventy-nine*

He was the son of a village schoolmaster. At the age of nine he was sent to the school of Louis Niedermeyer, who made no charge for the boy's education. He remained there until 1865, forming a friendship with another teacher, Saint-Saëns. In 1866 he became organist at Rennes. In 1870 he joined a light infantry regiment for the Franco-Prussian War. From 1871 to 1873 he was an organist in Paris and taught at the École Niedermeyer. In 1877 he became assistant organist and choirmaster at the Madeleine, and in 1896 chief organist at the Madeleine and professor of composition at the Paris Conservatory. He was appointed director of the Conservatory in 1905, and retired from that post in 1920. From 1910, however, he became increasingly deaf, and this handicapped him seriously for the rest of his life.

| | |
|---|---|
| 1870 (25) | 'Puisqu'ici-bas', duet for two sopranos |
| | 'Tarentella', duet for two sopranos |
| 1873 (28) | *Cantique de Jean Racine* |
| 1875 (30) | *Les Djinns*, for chorus and orchestra |
| | Suite for orchestra |
| | *Allegro Symphonique*, for orchestra |
| 1876 (31) | Violin Sonata in A major |
| 1878 (33) | Violin Concerto |
| 1879 (34) | Piano Quartet No 1 in C minor |
| 1880 (35) | *Berceuse*, for violin and piano |
| 1881 (36) | Ballade for piano and orchestra |
| | *Le Ruisseau*, for two female voices and piano |
| 1882 (37) | *Romance*, for violin and orchestra |
| | *La Naissance de Vénus*, for soli, chorus and orchestra |
| 1883 (38) | *Élégie*, in C minor |
| | Four Valse-caprices for piano (1883–94) |
| | Five Impromptus (1883–1910) |
| | Thirteen Nocturnes (1883–1922) |
| | Thirteen Barcarolles (1883–1921) |
| 1884 (39) | Symphony in D minor (unpublished) |
| 1886 (41) | Piano Quartet No 2 in G minor |
| 1887 (42) | *Requiem* |
| | *Pavane*, with chorus *ad lib* |
| 1888 (43) | *Caligula*, incidental music |
| 1889 (44) | *Shylock*, incidental music |
| | *Petite pièce*, for cello and piano |

1890 (45)   *Cinq Mélodies de Verlaine*, songs
1891–2 (46–7) *La bonne chanson*, nine songs
1893 (48)   *Dolly Suite*, for piano duet
1895 (50)   *Romance*, for cello and piano
1897 (52)   Theme and Variations for piano
1898 (53)   *Pelléas et Mélisande*, incidental music
            Andante for violin and piano
            *Papillon*, for cello and piano
            *Sicilienne*, for cello and piano
            *Fantaisie*, for flute and piano
1900 (55)   *Promethée*, lyric tragedy
1901 (56)   *La voile du bonheur*, incidental music
1904 (59)   Impromptu for harp
1906 (61)   Piano Quintet in D minor
            *Le chanson d'Eve*, song cycle (1906–10)
1908 (63)   *Sérénade*, for cello and piano
1910 (65)   Nine Préludes
1913 (68)   *Pénélope*, opera
1915–18 (70–3) *Le jardin clos*, eight songs
1917 (72)   Violin Sonata No 2 in E minor and E major
1918 (73)   Cello Sonata No 1 in D minor
            *Une Châtelaine et sa tour*, for harp
1919 (74)   *Fantaisie*, for piano and orchestra
            *Mirages*, four songs
1920 (75)   *Masques et Bergamasques*, suite for orchestra
1921 (76)   Piano Quintet No 2 in C minor
1922 (77)   Cello Sonata No 2 in G minor
            *L'horizon chimérique*, songs
1923 (78)   Piano Trio in D minor
1924 (79)   String Quartet


## FELDMAN, Morton
*b New York, 12 January 1926*

He studied piano and composition. He was a friend of the avant-garde composer John Cage, and of many abstract expressionist painters, the results being reflected in his music. He was made Edgar Varèse Professor at the State University of New York at Buffalo and also the director of the Center for Creative and Performing Arts.

1951 (25)   *Projections 1 and 2*, for flute, trumpet, violin and cello
            *Intersection I*, for orchestra, piano and cello
1957 (31)   Pieces for four pianos
1959 (33)   *Atlantis*, for chamber orchestra
1960 (34)   *Durations I & II*, for various combinations
1961 (35)   *Durations III & V*, for various combinations
1962 (36)   *Durations IV*, for various combinations
            *Last Pieces*, for piano
            *The Swallows of Salangan*, for chorus and sixteen instruments
1963 (37)   *Christian Wolff in Cambridge*, for chorus
1965 (39)   *Journey to the End of Night*, for soprano and four wind instruments
            *De Kooning*, for piano trio, horn and percussion
            *Four Instruments*
1966–7 (40–1) *First Principles*, for chamber orchestra
1967 (41)   *Chorus and Instruments*
            *In Search of an Orchestration*, for orchestra

1968 (42)    *Vertical Thoughts 2*, for orchestra
              *False Relationships and the Extended Ending*, for two chamber
                  groups
1969 (43)    *On Time and the Instrumental Factor*, for orchestra
1970 (44)    *Madame Press Died Last Week at 90*, for instrumental ensemble
              *The Viola in My Life I and II*, for solo viola and instruments
              *The Viola in My Life III*, for viola and piano
1971 (45)    *The Viola in My Life IV*, for viola and orchestra
              *Chorus and Orchestra I*
              *Three Clarinets, Cello and Piano*
              *Rothko Chapel*, for solo viola, soprano, alto, chorus, percussion and
                  celeste
              *I Met Heine on the Rue Fürstenberg*, for voice and chamber
                  ensemble
1972 (46)    *Cello and Orchestra*
              *Voice and Instruments*
              *Chorus and Orchestra II*
              *Voices and Instruments*
              *Piano and Voices*, for five pianos (pianists also hum)
              *Pianos and Voices II*, for five pianos and five voices
1973 (47)    *String Quartet and Orchestra*
              *For Frank O'Hara*, for instrumental ensemble
              *Voices and Cello*
1974 (48)    *Instruments I*
              *Voice and Instruments II*
1975 (49)    *Piano and Orchestra*
              *Instruments II*
              *Four Instruments II*, for piano, violin, viola and cello
1976 (50)    *Orchestra*
              *Oboe and Orchestra*
              *Routine Investigations*, for instrumental ensemble
              *Voice, Violin and Piano*
1977 (51)    *Neither*, opera in one act
              *Instruments III*, for flute, oboe and percussion
              *Piano*
              *Only*, for single voice
1977–8 (51–2) *Flute and Orchestra*
1978 (52)    *Why Patterns*, for flute, alto flute, piano and percussion
              *Spring of Chosroes*, for violin and piano
1979 (53)    *Violin and Orchestra*
              *String Quartet*
1980 (54)    *The Turfan Fragments*, for orchestra
              *Trio*, for violin, cello and piano
              *Principal Sound for Organ*
              *Repertoire*, for violin, cello and piano
1981 (55)    *Bass Clarinet and Percussion*
1982 (56)    *For John Cage*, for violin and piano
              *Three Voices*, for sopranos and tape
1983 (57)    *Crippled Symmetry*, for flute, piano and percussion
              *Clarinet and String Quartet*
              *String Quartet No 2*

**FERNEYHOUGH, Brian**
*b Coventry, 16 January 1943*

He studied at the Birmingham School of Music and the Royal Academy in London. In 1968 he won a Mendelssohn Scholarship and worked at the Amsterdam Conservatory. From 1969 until 1971 he studied at Basle, and from 1973 worked and taught in Germany.

| | | |
|---|---|---|
| 1963 (20) | | Sonatina for three clarinets and bassoon |
| 1965 (22) | | *Four Miniatures*, for flute and piano |
| 1966 (23) | | *Coloratura*, for oboe and piano |
| | | *Epigrams*, for piano |
| | | Sonata for two pianos |
| | | Three Pieces for piano |
| 1967 (24) | | *Prometheus*, for woodwind ensemble |
| 1968 (25) | | Sonatas for string quartet |
| | | *Epicycle*, for twenty strings |
| 1969 (26) | | *Missa Brevis*, for twelve solo voices |
| 1969–71 (26–8) | | *Firecycle Beta*, for orchestra |
| 1969–74 (26–31) | | *Funérailles*, for string ensemble and harp |
| 1971 (28) | | *Cassandra's Dream Song*, for flute |
| | | *Sieben Sterne*, for organ |
| 1971–7 (28–34) | | *Time and Motion Study I*, for bass clarinet |
| 1972–5 (29–32) | | *Transit*, for six solo voices, chamber orchestra and electronics |
| 1973–6 (30–3) | | *Time and Motion Study II*, for cello, tape and electronics |
| 1974 (31) | | *Time and Motion Study III*, for sixteen solo voices, chamber orchestra and electronics |
| 1975 (32) | | *Unity Capsule*, for flute |
| 1976–9 (33–6) | | *La terre est un homme*, for instruments |
| 1980 (37) | | *Funérailles Version II*, for harp and strings |
| | | String Quartet No 2 |
| 1981 (38) | | *Lemma-Icon-Epigram*, for piano |
| | | *Superscripto*, for solo piccolo |
| 1982 (39) | | *Carceri d'Invenzione I*, for chamber orchestra |
| 1983 (40) | | *Adagissimo*, for string quartet |

**FIELD, John**
*b Dublin, July 1782*
*d Moscow, 23 January 1837, aged fifty-four*

One of several children of a musical family, he was compelled to take up music in order to supplement their income. In 1793 the family left Dublin, stayed briefly in Bath, then moved to London. Already a fine pianist, he was apprenticed to Clementi as a demonstrator of pianos. He began serious composition when he was fourteen. In 1802 Clementi took him to Paris, Vienna and St Petersburg, and in 1806 he first appeared in Moscow as a concert pianist. He became very popular, and wealthy, as a teacher; but by 1830 his health had deteriorated, due to drink and other indulgences. In 1831 he left Russia for a concert tour of Europe, even though cancer was slowly killing him, and he returned to Moscow in 1835, hardly able to play or teach. His great contribution to music was his invention of the nocturne.

| | |
|---|---|
| 1814 (22) | Three Nocturnes for piano |
| 1832 (50) | *fp* Piano Concerto No 1 in E♭ major |

Field also composed: seven concertos; four sonatas; twenty nocturnes; six rondos; two divertissements; two fantasias; two piano quintets; four romances, etc.

**FINE, Irving**
*b Boston, Massachusetts, 3 December 1914*
*d Boston, 23 August 1962, aged forty-seven*

He studied with Piston at Harvard, and with Boulanger in Cambridge and Paris. He won two Guggenheim grants and many other awards; he was on the faculty of Harvard from 1939 to 1950, of the Berkshire Music Center from 1946 to 1950, and at Brandeis University from 1950 until he died.

| | |
|---|---|
| 1942 (28) | *Alice in Wonderland*, incidental music |
| 1944 (30) | *The Choral New Yorker*, cantata |
| 1946 (32) | *Fantasia*, for string trio |
| | Violin Sonata |
| 1948 (34) | *Toccata Concertante*, for orchestra |
| | Partita for wind quintet |
| 1949 (35) | *The Hour-glass*, choral cycle |
| 1952 (38) | String Quartet |
| | *Mutability*, song cycle |
| 1955 (41) | *Serious Song and Lament*, for string orchestra |
| 1960 (46) | *Diversion*, for orchestra |
| 1961 (47) | *Romanza*, for wind quintet |
| 1962 (48) | Symphony No 2 |

**FINNISSY, Michael**
*b London, 7 March 1946*

He studied composition and piano at the Royal College of Music, London, and in Italy. He then formed a music department at the London School of Contemporary Dance, where he taught from 1969 to 1974. He has also lectured and taught at the Chelsea School of Art and at Dartington Summer School, and received several commissions.

| | |
|---|---|
| 1963–5 (17–19) | *Song 5*, for piano |
| 1963–7 (17–21) | *Song 8*, for piano |
| 1963–8 (17–22) | *Le Dormeur du Val*, for mezzo and ensemble |
| 1964–5 (18–19) | *Song 6*, for ensemble |
| 1965–6 (19–20) | *Song 7*, for piano |
| 1965–70 (19–24) | *From the Revelations of Saint John the Divine*, for soprano and ensemble |
| 1966 (20) | *Song 1*, for soprano |
| 1966–7 (20–1) | *Afar*, for ensemble |
| 1966–8 (20–2) | *As When upon a Tranced Summer Night*, for ensemble |
| 1966–71 (20–5) | *Horrorzone*, for soprano and ensemble |
| 1967 (21) | *Untitled Piece to honour Igor Stravinsky*, for flute |
| 1967–8 (21–2) | *Song 2*, for ensemble |
| | *Song 4*, for ensemble |
| 1967–71 (21–5) | *Jeanne d'Arc*, for soprano and ensemble |
| 1968 (22) | *Song 10*, for ensemble |
| | *Song 9*, for piano |
| 1968–71 (22–5) | *Transformations of the Vampire*, for ensemble |
| | *Autumnal*, for piano |
| 1968–74 (22–8) | *World*, for soli, chorus and orchestra |
| 1969 (23) | *n*, for ensemble |
| 1969–70 (23–4) | *Folk-song Set*, for voice and ensemble |
| 1969–71 (23–5) | *Song 11*, for soprano and clarinet |
| 1970 (24) | *Alice I*, for instruments |
| 1970–5 (24–9) | *Alice II*, for cello |

|  | *Alice III*, for double-bass |
| 1971 (25) | *Babylon*, for mezzo and ensemble |
|  | *Untitled Piece to honour Igor Stravinsky II*, for flute, viola and harp |
| 1971–3 (25–7) | *Tsuru-Kame*, for soprano or alto, small female chorus, three dancers, flute, viola and two percussion |
| 1972 (26) | *Snowdrift*, for piano |
| 1972–3 (26–7) | *Song 3*, for soprano and ensemble |
|  | *Song 12*, for soprano and ensemble |
| 1972–9 (26–33) | *Mysteries*, music-theatre: |

*The Parting of Darkness from Light*
*The Earthly Paradise*
*Noah and the Great Flood*
*The Prophecy of Daniel*
*The Parliament of Heaven*
*The Annunciation*
*The Betrayal and Crucifixion of Jesus of Nazareth*
*The Deliverance of Souls*

| 1973 (27) | *Song 13*, for violin |
|  | *Circle, Chorus and Formal Act*, music-theatre |
| 1973–5 (27–9) | *Commedia dell'Incompresibile Potere che alcune Donne hanno sugli Uomini*, music-theatre |
| 1973–6 (27–30) | *Medea*, music-theatre |
| 1974 (28) | *Wild Flowers*, for two pianos |
|  | *Evening*, for alto saxophone, horn, trumpet, percussion, harp, cello and double-bass |
|  | *Cipriano*, for ten solo voices |
|  | *Ives*, for voices |
| 1974–5 (28–9) | *Orfeo*, music-theatre |
| 1975 (29) | Piano Concerto No 1 |
|  | *Bouffe*, music-theatre |
|  | *Ru Tchou – The Ascent of the Sun*, for drummer |
| 1975–6 (29–30) | Piano Concerto No 2 |
|  | *Offshore*, for orchestra |
| 1975–8 (29–32) | *Tom Fool's Wooing*, music-theatre |
| 1976 (30) | *Jazz*, for piano |
|  | *Song 17*, for guitar |
|  | *Song 18*, for double-bass |
|  | *Song 16*, for soprano |
|  | *Pathways of Sun and Stars*, for orchestra |
| 1976–7 (30–1) | *Mr Punch*, music-theatre |
| 1977 (31) | *Mine Eyes Awake*, for soprano and piano interior |
|  | *English Country Tunes*, for piano |
|  | *all.fall.down*, for piano |
|  | *All the Trees they are so High*, for violin |
|  | *Lost Lands*, for ensemble |
| 1977–78 (31–2) | *Long Distance*, for piano and ensemble |
| 1978 (32) | *Sir Tristran*, for soprano and ensemble |
|  | *Corō*, for tenor and ensemble |
|  | Piano Concerto No 3 |
|  | *Runnin' Wild*, for saxophone |
|  | *Mountainfall*, for mezzo |
|  | *Ohi! Ohi! Ohi!*, for solo voice |
| 1978–9 (32–3) | Piano Concerto No 4 |
|  | *Fast Dances, Slow Dances*, for piano |
|  | Piano Studies |
| 1979 (33) | *Talawva*, for mezzo and ensemble |

... *fairest noonday* . . ., for tenor and piano
*Alongside*, for ensemble
*Kagami-Jishi*, for flute and harp
*Grainger*, for piano
*Sikangnuga*, for flute
*Hinomi*, for percussion
1979–80 (33–4) *Sea and Sky.* for orchestra
1980 (34)    *Lord Melbourne*, for soprano, clarinet and piano
*Green Bushes*, for contralto and piano
Piano Concerto No 5
*Boogie-Woogie*, for piano
*Nancarrow*, for piano
*Moon's Goin' Down*, for solo voice or instrument
1980–1 (34–5) Piano Concerto No 6
*Nobody's Jig*, for string quartet
1980–3 (34–7) *Whitman*, for voice and instruments
1981 (35)    Piano Concerto No 7
*Kelir*, for six voices
*Tree Setting*, for piano
*Jisei*, for ensemble
*Reels*, for piano
*White Rain*, for piano or clavichord
*Duru-duru*, for mezzo, flute, percussion and piano
*Stomp*, for accordion
*Andimironnai*, for solo cello
*Keroiylu*, for oboe, bassoon and piano
*Yalli*, for solo cello
*Terekkeme*, for solo cembalo
*Rushes*, for piano
1982 (36)    *Warara*, for tenor, flute, clarinet and two percussion
*Aijal*, for flute, oboe and percussion
*Banumbirr*, for ensemble
*Tya*, for ensemble
*Mississippi Hornpipe*, for violin and piano
*Dilok*, for oboe and percussion
*Gerhana*, for solo percussion
*Anninnia*, for soprano and piano
1982–3 (36–7) *Ouraa*, for ensemble
1982–4 (36–8) *Lyrics and Limericks*, for voice and piano
1983 (37)    *Vaudeville*, for mezzo, baritone and ensemble
*Australian Sea Shanties*, for voices, recorders and piano
*Soda Fountain*, for voices and cymbals
1983–4 (37–8) *Ngano*, for soli, chorus, flute and percussion
1984 (38)    *Câtana*, for ensemble
*Delal*, for trumpet and piano


**FINZI, Gerald**
*b London, 14 July 1901*
*d Oxford, 28 September 1956, aged fifty-five*

He studied in Harrogate from 1914 to 1916, then in York with Bairstow from 1917 to 1922. In 1925 he took a course in counterpoint with R. O. Morris. From 1930 to 1933 he taught at the Royal Academy of Music. From 1941 to 1945 he was in the Ministry of War Transport. In 1951 he learned that he was suffering from a form of leukaemia and had less than ten years to live.

| 1924 | (23) | *Severn Rhapsody* |
|---|---|---|

1924 (23)    *Severn Rhapsody*
1933 (32)    *A Young Man's Exhortation*, song cycle
1934–37 (33–6) Seven Part-songs (Bridges) for unaccompanied chorus
1935 (34)    *Introit*, for violin and orchestra, revised 1945
1936 (35)    *Earth, Air and Rain*, song cycle
             Three Short Elegies for unaccompanied chorus
             Five Two-part Songs (Christina Rossetti) and Five Unison Songs
             Two Sonnets by John Milton for high voice and small orchestra
             *Interlude*, for oboe and string quartet
1940 (39)    *Dies Natalis*, cantata
1942 (41)    *Let us Garlands Bring*, five songs
             Prelude and Fugue for violin, viola and cello
1945 (44)    *Farewell to Arms*, for tenor and small orchestra
             Five Bagatelles for clarinet and piano
1946 (45)    'Lo, the full and final sacrifice', festival anthem
1947 (46)    *Ode for St Cecilia's Day* (possibly 1950)
1948 (47)    *Love's Labours Lost*, incidental music
1949 (48)    Clarinet Concerto
             *Before and After Summer*, song cycle
1950 (49)    *Intimations of Immortality*, for tenor, chorus and orchestra
1952 (51)    *Love's Labours Lost*, orchestral suite
1954 (53)    *Grand Fantasia and Toccata*, for piano and orchestra
1955 (54)    Cello Concerto
1956 (55)    *In Terra Pax*, for chorus and orchestra
             *Eclogue*, for piano and string orchestra
Performed posthumously:
1958         *The Fall of the Leaf*, for orchestra
1959         *To a Poet*, song cycle


## FLOTOW, Friedrich von
*b Tuetendorf, near Nev-Sanitz, Mechlenburg-Schwerin, 26 April 1812*
*d Darmstadt, 24 January 1883, aged seventy*

Nobly born, he was intended for a diplomatic life, and was sent to Paris for training at the age of fifteen. However, he found artistic circles more congenial, and soon became aware of his musical potential. He studied music seriously for a time and, sometimes in partnership with Offenbach, gained a hearing at the aristocratic soirées. From 1856 to 1863 he was the intendant of the court theatre at Schwerin. He spent his later years in Paris and Vienna, and saw his operas performed as far afield as St Petersburg and Turin. He composed a great many operas, but the only one to survive is *Martha*, written in 1847 when he was thirty-five.


## FOSS, Lukas
*b Berlin, 15 August 1922*

He learned piano and flute in Paris, then went to the USA in 1937 to study at the Curtis Institute. He was made a US citizen in 1942. He spent several summers at Tanglewood and took special courses at Yale. He has received many awards, and has had many professorial appointments and conductorships.

1938 (16)    Four Two-part Inventions for piano
             *Drei Goethe-Lieder*
1940 (18)    Music for *The Tempest*
             Two Symphonic Pieces
             Four Preludes for flute, clarinet and bassoon

| 1941 (19) | *Allegro Concertante*, for orchestra |
| | *Dance Sketch*, for orchestra |
| | Duo for cello and piano |
| 1942 (20) | *The Prairie*, for chorus with soloists and orchestra |
| | Clarinet Concerto (later revised as Piano Concerto No 1) |
| 1943 (21) | *Paradigm*, for percussion |
| 1944 (22) | *The Heart Remembers*, ballet |
| | *Within These Walls*, ballet |
| | Symphony |
| | *Ode*, for orchestra (revised 1958) |
| 1945 (23) | *Song of Anguish*, for voice and piano, or orchestra |
| 1946 (24) | *Song of Songs*, for voice and orchestra |
| | *Composer's Holiday*, for violin and piano |
| 1947 (25) | String Quartet |
| 1948 (26) | Oboe Concerto |
| | *Ricordare*, for orchestra |
| | *Capriccio*, for cello and piano |
| 1949 (27) | *The Jumping Frog of Calaveras County*, opera |
| | Piano Concerto No 2 |
| 1952 (30) | *Parable of Death*, for tenor, narrator and orchestra |
| 1955 (33) | *Griffelkin*, opera |
| | *The Gift of the Magi*, ballet |
| 1956 (34) | Psalms for chorus and orchestra |
| 1957 (35) | *Behold! I Build an House*, for chorus |
| 1958 (36) | *Symphony of Chorales* |
| 1959 (37) | *Introductions and Goodbyes*, opera |
| 1960 (38) | *Time Cycle*, four songs with orchestra |
| 1963 (41) | *Echoi*, for clarinet, cello, piano and percussion |
| 1964 (42) | *Elytres*, for orchestra |
| 1965 (43) | *Fragments of Archilochos*, for chorus, speaker, soloists and chamber ensemble |
| 1966 (44) | *Discrepancy*, for twenty-four wind instruments |
| 1967 (45) | Cello Concerto |
| | *Phorion*, for orchestra, electric organ, harpsichord and guitar |
| | *Baroque Variations*, for orchestra |
| 1969 (47) | *Geod*, for orchestra with optional voices |
| 1972 (50) | *Ni bruit, ni vitesse*, for two pianos, two percussion and inside piano |
| | *Cave of the Winds*, for wind quintet |
| 1973 (51) | *MAP*, a musical game for an entire evening, any four musicians can play |
| 1974 (52) | *fp Orpheus*, for viola, cello or guitar and orchestra |
| 1980 (58) | *Measure for Measure*, for tenor and chamber orchestra |
| | *Curriculum Vitae With Time Bomb*, for accordion and percussion |
| | *Night Music for John Lennon*, for brass quintet and orchestra |
| 1981 (59) | *Solo*, for piano solo |
| | *Solo Observed*, for piano and three instruments or for orchestra |

## FRANÇAIX, Jean
*b Le Mans, 23 May 1912*

He studied first with his father, who was director of the Le Mans Conservatory; then he went to Paris, where he was a pupil of Boulanger at the Conservatory. He took first prize there for piano in 1930, and has made many tours as a piano virtuoso.

| 1931 (19) | Eight Bagatelles, for piano |

| 1932 (20) | Concertino for piano and orchestra |
| | Scherzo for piano |
| 1933 (21) | *Scuola di Ballo*, ballet |
| | *Divertissement*, for string trio, wind, harp and double-bass |
| | *A trois*, for string trio |
| | *A quatre*, for flute, oboe, clarinet and bassoon |
| 1934 (22) | Suite for violin and orchestra |
| | *Serenade 1*, for orchestra |
| | String Quartet |
| | *A cinq*, for flute, string trio and harp |
| | *A deux*, sonatina for violin and piano |
| 1935 (23) | *Les Malheures de Sophie*, ballet |
| | *Le Roi nu*, ballet |
| | Quadruple Concerto for flute, oboe, clarinet and bassoon |
| | Saxophone Quartet |
| 1936 (24) | *Le jeu sentimental*, ballet |
| | *La Lutherie enchantée*, ballet |
| | *Au Musée Grévin*, for orchestra |
| | Piano Concerto |
| | *Cinq portraits de jeunes filles*, for piano |
| 1937 (25) | *Le diable boiteux*, chamber opera |
| | *Musique de Cour*, for flute, violin and orchestra |
| 1938 (26) | *Le jugement d'un fou*, ballet |
| | *Verrières de Venise*, ballet |
| 1940 (28) | *L'apostrophe*, opera |
| 1944 (32) | *Mouvement perpetuel*, for cello and piano |
| 1945 (33) | *La main de gloire*, opera |
| 1946 (34) | *Rhapsodie*, for viola and wind |
| | *Les bosquets de Cythère*, for orchestra |
| | *La douce France*, for orchestra |
| 1947 (35) | *L'heure du Berger*, for orchestra |
| | *Eloge de la danse*, for piano |
| | *Divertissement*, for oboe, clarinet and bassoon |
| 1948 (36) | *Les demoiselles de la nuit*, ballet |
| | *Symphonie d'archets* |
| | Quintet for wind instruments |
| 1950 (38) | *Les camélias*, ballet |
| | *Les zigues de Mars*, ballet |
| | Two Pieces for guitar |
| | *Variations de Concert*, for cello and strings |
| 1952 (40) | *Le Roi Midas*, ballet |
| | Sonatina for trumpet and piano |
| | *Serenade BEA*, for strings |
| 1953 (41) | *Canon at the octave*, for horn and piano |
| | *Divertimento*, for flute and keyboard |
| | *L'insectarium*, for harpsichord |
| | Symphony |
| 1954 (42) | *Paris à nous deux*, opera |
| | Violin Concerto |
| 1955 (43) | Fantaisie, for cello and orchestra |
| 1956 (44) | *Hymne Solonelle*, for orchestra |
| 1957 (45) | *Eight Exotic Dances* for two pianos |
| | *Marche Solonelle*, for organ |
| | *Six Grandes Marches*, for orchestra |
| 1958 (46) | *La dame dans la lune*, ballet |
| | Divertimento for horn and orchestra |

| 1959 (47) | *Danse des trois Arlequins*, for piano |
| | *L'horloge de Flore*, for oboe and orchestra |
| | Concerto for harpsichord, flute and strings |
| 1960 (48) | Piano Sonata |
| | *Le Dialogue des Carmélites*, suite for orchestra |
| 1962 (50) | Suite for flute |
| 1963 (51) | Six Preludes for strings |
| 1965 (53) | *Bis*, for piano |
| | *La Princesse de Clèves*, opera |
| | Double Piano Concerto |
| 1967 (55) | Flute Concerto |
| 1968 (56) | Clarinet Concerto |
| | *Divertissement*, for bassoon and strings |
| 1970 (58) | Violin Concerto |
| | *Jeu poétique*, for harp and orchestra |
| 1971 (59) | Theme and Variations for orchestra |
| | Quartet for cor anglais and string trio |
| 1972 (60) | Trio for flute, cello and harp |
| | *A nuit*, for clarinet, bassoon, horn and string quartet |
| 1973 (61) | *La ville mystérieuse*, for orchestra |
| | *Cassazione*, for three orchestras |
| | *Neuf pièces caractéristiques*, for ensemble |
| 1974 (62) | Double-bass Concerto |
| 1975 (63) | *Quasi Improvisando*, for eleven wind instruments |
| 1976 (64) | Concerto Grosso for wind quintet, string quintet and orchestra |
| 1977 (65) | Quintet for clarinet and string quartet |

Françaix has also written many choral works, songs and film scores.


**FRANCK, César**
*b Liège, 10 December 1822*
*d Paris, 8 November 1890, aged sixty-seven*

He and his brother showed marked musical gifts at an early age and were sent to the Liège Conservatory. When he was twelve he had already completed his first tour as a pianist with his violinist brother. In 1837 he entered the Paris Conservatory, and did concert tours in 1842 to 1843. He settled down to teaching, which was an unceasing round of drudgery for the rest of his life – travelling to pupils on weekdays, and working as an organist and choirmaster at weekends. In 1872 he was made professor of organ at the Conservatory where his pupils included d'Indy, Chausson and Pierné. He died as a result of being knocked down by a horse omnibus.

| 1840 (18) | Three Piano Trios in F♯m: B♭ : Bm, Op 1 |
| 1842 (20) | Piano Trio No 4 in B major |
| 1843 (21) | Andante quietoso for violin and piano in A major |
| 1846 (24) | *Ruth*, cantata |
| | *Ce qu'on entend sur la montagne*, symphonic poem (*c*1846) |
| 1851–2 (29–30) | *Le valet de ferme*, opera |
| 1858 (36) | *Ave Maria*, motet |
| 1865 (43) | *The Tower of Babel*, oratorio |
| 1872 (50) | *Panis Angelicus*, for voice, organ, harp, cello and double-bass |
| 1874 (52) | *Redemption*, cantata with symphonic interlude |
| 1876 (54) | *Les Éolides*, symphonic poem |
| 1878 (56) | Cantabile for organ |
| | *Fantaisie* in A major for organ |
| | *Pièce héroïque*, for organ |

| 1879 | (57) | *Béatitudes*, cantata |
| | | Piano Quintet in F minor |
| 1880 | (58) | *L'Organiste*, fifty-five pieces for harmonium |
| 1881 | (59) | *Rebecca*, for soli, chorus and orchestra |
| 1882 | (60) | *Le chasseur maudit*, symphonic poem |
| | | *Hulda*, opera (1882–5) |
| 1884 | (62) | *Les djinns*, symphonic poem for piano and orchestra |
| | | *Prélude, Chorale et Fugue* for piano |
| | | 'Nocturne' song |
| 1885 | (63) | *Symphonic Variations*, for piano and orchestra |
| 1886 | (64) | Violin Sonata in A major |
| 1887 | (65) | *Prélude, Chorale et Finale* for piano |
| 1888 | (66) | Symphony in D minor (1886–8) |
| | | *Psyche*, symphonic poem |
| | | *Ghisele*, opera (1888–90) |
| 1889 | (67) | String Quartet in D major |
| 1890 | (68) | Chorales for organ |

## FRANKEL, Benjamin
*b London, 31 January 1906*
*d London, 12 February 1973, aged sixty-seven*

He took up the violin at an early age. He was apprenticed as a watchmaker, but between the wars played jazz fiddle in clubs, worked on arrangements and wrote film music. He became prominent after World War II.

| 1939 | (33) | *Elégie Juivre*, for cello and piano |
| 1942 | (36) | *Youth Music*, for string orchestra |
| 1944 | (38) | String Trio No 1 |
| | | Trio for clarinet, cello and piano |
| | | Sonata No 1 for solo violin |
| | | String Quartet No 1 |
| 1945 | (39) | String Quartet No 2 |
| 1946 | (40) | *Novelette*, for violin and piano |
| | | *Pieces for Geraldine*, for piano |
| 1947 | (41) | String Quartet No 3 |
| | | *The Aftermath*, for tenor, trumpet, timpani and strings |
| | | *Sonatina Leggiera*, for piano |
| 1948 | (42) | *Early Morning Music*, for oboe, clarinet and bassoon |
| | | String Quartet No 4 |
| 1949 | (43) | *May Day*, overture |
| 1950 | (44) | *Three Poems*, for cello and piano |
| 1951 | (45) | Concerto for violin and orchestra |
| | | *Mephistopheles' Serenade and Dance*, for orchestra |
| 1953 | (47) | *Concertante Lirico*, for string orchestra |
| | | Piano Quartet |
| 1959 | (53) | Bagatelles for eleven instruments |
| | | Eight Songs for medium voice and piano |
| 1960 | (54) | *Messa Stromentale*, orchestral mass without words |
| 1961 | (55) | *Serenata Concertante*, for piano trio and orchestra |
| 1962 | (56) | Symphony No 2 |
| | | Sonata No 2 for solo violin |
| 1964 | (58) | Symphony No 3 |
| | | *Pezzi Pianissimi*, for clarinet, cello and piano |
| 1965 | (59) | String Quartet No 5 |
| | | *Catalogue of Incidents from Romeo and Juliet*, for orchestra |

| 1966 | (60) | Symphony No 4 |
| 1967 | (61) | Concerto for viola and orchestra |
|      |      | Symphony No 5 |
| 1968 | (62) | *Konzert für Jungendpublikum*, for orchestra |
| 1969 | (63) | Symphony No 6 |
|      |      | Symphony No 7 |
| 1970 | (64) | *Overture to a Ceremony*, for orchestra |
| 1972 | (66) | Symphony No 8 |
|      |      | *Pezzi Melodici*, for orchestra |
| 1972–3 | (67) | *Marching Song*, opera |

## FRESCOBALDI, Girolamo
*b Ferrara, September 1583*
*d Rome, 1 March 1643, aged fifty-nine*

He was a singer, organist and lutenist. In 1607 he was organist in a church in Rome, went to the Netherlands for a short time, and returned to Rome in 1608 to become organist at St Peter's. In 1628 he was appointed organist to the Grand Duke of Tuscany in Florence; but in 1634 he returned again to St Peter's, where he stayed until his death.

| 1615 | (32) | *p Toccate d'involatura* |
|      |      | *p Ricercare e canzone francesi* |
| 1624 | (41) | *p Capricci sopra diversi soggetti* |
| 1627 | (44) | *p* Second Book of Toccate |
| 1628 | (45) | *p Libro delle canzoni* |
| 1630 | (47) | *Arie musicali* |
| 1635 | (52) | *p Fiori musicali* |

Frescobaldi composed many toccatas, fugues, ricercari, etc, for organ and harpsichord; also madrigals and motets.

## FRICKER, Peter Racine
*b London, 5 September 1920*

He was educated at St Paul's School and intended to join the Navy, but was rejected because of poor eyesight. He went to the Royal College of Music in 1937. In 1941 he joined the Royal Air Force as a radio operator. When he was demobilised in 1945 he went to Morley College, where the director, Tippett, suggested he studied with Seiber. In 1952 he became director of Morley College, and from 1955 taught composition at the Royal College. From 1964 to 1965 he was visiting professor of music at the University of California; he became a full-time professor there, and in 1970 was made chairman of the music department.

| 1941–4 | (21–4) | Three Preludes for piano |
| 1946 | (26) | Four Fughettas for two pianos |
| 1947 | (27) | Sonata for organ |
|      |      | Two Madrigals |
|      |      | Wind Quintet |
|      |      | *Three Sonnets of Cecco Angiolieri*, for tenor and seven instruments |
|      |      | String Quartet in one movement |
| 1948 | (28) | Symphony No 1 (1948–9) |
|      |      | *Rondo Scherzoso*, for orchestra |
| 1949 | (29) | *Prelude, Elegy and Finale*, for string orchestra |
|      |      | Concerto for violin and small orchestra, No 1 (1949–50) |
| 1950 | (30) | Violin Sonata |
|      |      | Concertante No 1 for English horn and strings |

|            | Symphony No 2 (1950–1) |
|            | Four Impromptus for piano (1950–2) |
| 1951 (31)  | Concertante No 2 for three pianos, strings and timpani |
|            | *Canterbury Prologue*, ballet |
|            | Viola Concerto (1951–3) |
| 1952 (32)  | String Quartet No 2 (1952–3) |
|            | Concerto for piano and small orchestra (1952–4) |
| 1953–4 (33–4) | Violin Concerto No 2, *Rapsodie Concertante* |
| 1954 (34)  | *Dance Scene*, for orchestra |
|            | Nocturne and Scherzo for piano (four hands) |
| 1955 (35)  | Horn Sonata |
|            | *The Tomb of St Eulalia*, elegy for counter-tenor, gamba and harpsichord |
|            | *Litany*, for double string orchestra |
|            | *Musick's Empire*, for chorus and small orchestra |
| 1956 (36)  | Cello Sonata |
|            | Suite for harpsichord |
| 1957–8 (37–8) | *The Vision of Judgment*, oratorio |
|            | Octet for flute, clarinet, bassoon, horn, violin, viola, cello and double-bass |
|            | Variations for piano |
| 1958 (38)  | *Comedy Overture*, for orchestra |
|            | Toccata for piano and orchestra (1958–9) |
| 1959 (39)  | Serenade No 1 for flute, clarinet, bass-clarinet, viola, cello and harp |
|            | Serenade No 2 for flute, oboe and piano |
| 1960 (40)  | Symphony No 3 |
| 1961 (41)  | Cantata for tenor and chamber ensemble (1961–2) |
|            | Twelve Studies for piano |
| 1963 (43)  | *O longs désirs*, five songs for soprano and orchestra |
| 1964–6 (44–6) | Symphony No 4 |
| 1965 (45)  | Ricercare for organ |
|            | Four *Dialogues*, for oboe and piano |
|            | Four Songs for soprano and piano (also orchestrated) |
| 1966 (46)  | Fantasy for viola and piano |
|            | *Three Scenes*, for orchestra |
|            | *The Day and the Spirits*, for soprano and harp (1966–7) |
| 1967 (47)  | Seven Counterpoints for orchestra |
|            | *Ave Maris Stella*, for male voices and piano |
|            | *Episodes I*, for piano (1967–8) |
|            | *Cantilena and Cabaletta*, for solo soprano (1967–8) |
| 1968 (48)  | *Refrains*, for solo oboe |
|            | *Magnificat*, for solo voices, choir and orchestra |
|            | Concertante No 4, for flute, oboe, violin and strings |
|            | *Gladius Domini*, toccata for organ |
|            | *Some Serious Nonsense*, for tenor, flute, oboe, cello and harpsichord |
|            | Six Pieces for organ |
| 1969 (49)  | Saxophone Quartet |
|            | Praeludium for organ |
| 1970 (50)  | *Paseo*, for guitar |
|            | *The Roofs*, for coloratura soprano and percussion |
| 1971 (51)  | *Sarabande in memoriam Igor Stravinsky* |
|            | *Nocturne* for chamber orchestra |
|            | Intrada for organ |
|            | *A Bourrée for Sir Arthur Bliss*, for cello |
|            | Concertante No 5 for piano and string quartet |
| 1972 (52)  | *Introitus*, for orchestra |

|             |                                                        |
|-------------|--------------------------------------------------------|
|             | *Come Sleep*, for contralto, alto flute and bass clarinet |
|             | *Fanfare for Europe*, for trumpet                      |
|             | *Ballade*, for flute and piano                         |
|             | Seven Little Songs for chorus                          |
| 1973 (53)   | Gigue for cello                                        |
|             | *The Groves of Dodona*, for six flutes                 |
| 1974 (54)   | *Spirit Puck*, for clarinet and percussion             |
|             | Two Petrarch Madrigals                                 |
|             | Trio sonata for organ                                  |
| 1975 (55)   | String Quartet No 3                                    |
|             | Symphony No 5                                          |
| 1976 (56)   | String Quartet No 4                                    |
|             | *Seachant*, for flute and double-bass                  |
|             | Invention and Little Toccata for organ                 |
| 1976–7 (56–7) | Sinfonia for seventeen wind instruments              |
| 1977 (57)   | *A Wish for a Party*, for male voices                  |
|             | *Anniversary*, for organ                               |
|             | Two Songs for baritone and piano                       |

## FROBERGER, Johann Jacob
*b Stuttgart, 18 May 1616*
*d Héricourt, Haute-Saône, 7 May 1667, aged fifty*

He was appointed court organist at Vienna in 1637, then spent four years in Italy studying with Frescobaldi, under whose influence he was converted to Catholicism. He left the service of the Austrian emperor in 1657 and in 1662 went to London where, becoming destitute, he earned money as an organ-blower at Westminster Abbey. A former pupil presented him to King Charles II, and as a result he became court organist.

Froberger composed: thirty harpsichord suites; a great number of works for keyboard; two works for voices.

## FUX, Johann Joseph
*b Hirtenfeld, Styria, 1660*
*d Vienna, 13 February 1741, aged eighty-one*

He was born into a peasant family, but his early life is uncertain. In 1680 he entered the Jesuit University in Graz and in 1681 was admitted to a Jesuit residential school for musically gifted students. He later became employed by the Primate of Hungary, who also had a residence in Vienna. He enjoyed increasing imperial favour after Leopold I heard some of his masses, and held the post of organist at the Schottenkirche in Vienna from 1696 until 1702. He went to Rome in 1700 to study at the emperor's expense, and after the emperor's death he continued as court composer under Joseph I. In 1713 he became vice *Kapellmeister* to the court and *Kapellmeister* to Joseph's widow. Charles VI appointed him chief *Kapellmeister* in 1715, a post he occupied until his death. His career reached its summit in 1723 with the performance of his coronation opera, *Costanza Fortezza*.

He wrote nineteen operas, many large and small sacred works, some instrumental works, and books on music such as his *Gradus ad Parnassum* (1725).

## GABRIELI, Andrea
*b Venice, c1510*
*d Venice 1586, aged seventy-six*

Nothing is known of his early life. He may have been a singer in St Marks, and was organist of the church of St Geremia in 1558. From 1562 he travelled in southern Germany, returning to Venice in 1566 to become organist at St Marks. His nephew Giovanni collected and edited his compositions.

| | | |
|---|---|---|
| 1562–5 (52–5) | *p Sacrae cantiones*, a 5 vv motets | |
| 1576 (66) | *p Cantiones ecclesiasticae*, a 4 vv motets | |
| 1578 (68) | *p Cantiones sacrae* | |

Performed posthumously:

| | |
|---|---|
| 1589 | *Madrigali e ricercare a 4* |
| 1605 | *Canzoni all francese et ricercare Arlosi* |

## GABRIELI, Giovanni
*b Venice, c1557*
*d Venice, 12 August 1612, aged c fifty-five*

After studying with his uncle, Andrea Gabrieli, he went to Munich in 1575 and served as a musician at the Bavarian court for several years. He returned to Venice in 1584, became organist at St Marks in 1584 and remained there until his death. Many pupils came to him from Germany, among whom was Schütz.

| | |
|---|---|
| 1587 (30) | *p* Concerti for six to sixteen voices |
| | *p Madrigali e ricercare* |
| 1597 (40) | *p Sacrae symphoniae*, Book I |
| 1608 (51) | *p* Canzona (*La Spiritosa*) |

Performed posthumously:

| | |
|---|---|
| 1615 | *p Canzoni e sonate* |
| | *p Sacrae symphoniae*, Book II |

## GADE, Niels Wilhelm
*b Copenhagen, 22 February 1817*
*d Copenhagen, 21 December 1890, aged seventy-three*

He was the son of an instrument maker, and entered the Royal Danish orchestra as a violinist. In 1841 he won a prize that enabled him to travel in Germany and Italy. He befriended Mendelssohn in Leipzig. From 1861 he was the court *Kapellmeister*, and from 1867 one of the directors of the Copenhagen Conservatory. He received his PhD in 1879, and in 1886 was made Commander of the Order of Daneborg. He visited England in 1876.

| | |
|---|---|
| 1840 (23) | *Faedrelandets Muser*, ballet |
| | *Echoes from Ossian*, overture |
| | Piano Sonata |
| 1841 (24) | Symphony No 1 in C minor |
| 1842 (25) | *Napoli*, ballet |
| | Violin Sonata No 1 in A major |
| 1844 (27) | *In the Highlands*, overture |
| 1846 (29) | *p* String Quartet in E minor |
| 1847 (30) | Symphony No 3 in A minor |
| 1849 (32) | *p* String Octet in F major |
| 1850 (33) | *Mariotta*, incidental music |
| | Symphony No 4 in B♭ major |
| | *p* Violin Sonata No 2 in D minor |
| 1852 (35) | Symphony No 5 in D minor |

|            |      | *Spring Fantasy*, for voices and orchestra |
|------------|------|--------------------------------------------|
| 1855 | (38) | *p Novelleten*, for piano trio |
| c1856 | (c39) | Symphony No 6 in G minor |
| 1861 | (44) | *Hamlet*, concerto overture |
|       |      | *Michelangelo*, overture |
| 1864 | (47) | Symphony No 2 in E major |
|       |      | Symphony No 7 in F major |
|       |      | Fantasies for clarinet |
|       |      | *p* Piano Trio in F major |
|       |      | *p Fantasiestücke*, for cello and piano |
| 1865 | (48) | *p* String Sextet in D minor |
| 1871 | (54) | Symphony No 8 in B minor |
| 1874 | (57) | *Novelleten*, for string orchestra |
| 1879 | (62) | *En Sommertag paa Landet*, five pieces for orchestra |
| 1880 | (63) | Violin Concerto |
| 1884 | (67) | *Holbergiana Suite* |
| 1887 | (70) | *p* Violin Sonata No 3 in B♭ major |
| 1888–90 | (71–3) | *Ulysses*, march |
| 1890 | (73) | *p* String Quartet in D major |

## GEMINIANI, Francesco (Xaviero)
*b Lucca, c1680*
*d Dublin, 17 September 1762, aged eighty-two*

He studied first with his father and later with A. Scarlatti and with Corelli, who was the most powerful influence on him. In 1707 he joined the Signoria theatre orchestra in Lucca, and in 1711 became leader of the opera orchestra in Naples. In 1714 he left Italy for London, where he spent most of the rest of his life, moving finally to Ireland. His greatness was as a virtuoso violinist and writer of treatises, though during his lifetime he was overshadowed as a composer by his teacher Corelli and his contemporaries Vivaldi and Handel.

He wrote many solo works for violin, eight concerti grossi, numerous other works, six important treatises on violin and harmony and one on playing guitar or cittra.

## GERHARD, Roberto
*b Catalonia, Spain, 25 September 1896*
*d Cambridge, 5 January 1970, aged seventy-three*

He studied piano with Granados and composition with Pedrell. He worked with Schoenberg in Vienna and Berlin from 1923 to 1928, then held a brief professorship at the Excola Normal de la Generalitat in Barcelona and served as head of the music department of the Catalan Library. After the Civil War he settled in Cambridge, England. He was visiting professor of composition at the University of Michigan and the Berkshire Music Center during 1960.

| 1918 | (22) | *L'Infantament Meravellos de Shahrazade*, for voice and piano |
|------|------|----------------------------------------------------------------|
|      |      | Piano Trio |
| 1922 | (26) | *Seven Haï-Ku* for voice and five instruments |
| 1928 | (32) | Wind Quintet |
| 1934 | (38) | *Ariel*, ballet |
| 1940–1 | (44–5) | *Don Quixote*, ballet |
| 1941 | (45) | *Hommaje a Pedrell*, symphony |
| 1942–5 | (46–9) | Violin Concerto |
| 1944 | (48) | *Alegrias*, ballet suite |
|      |      | *Pandora*, ballet (1944–5) |

1945–7 (49–51) *The Duenna*, opera
1950 (54)      Impromptus for piano
1951 (55)      Concerto for piano and strings
1952–3 (56)    Symphony No 1
1955–6 (59)    Concerto for harpsichord, strings and percussion
               String Quartet No 1
1956 (60)      Nonet for eight wind instruments and accordion
1957 (61)      *Don Quixote*, ballet suite
1959 (63)      Symphony No 2
1960 (64)      Symphony No 3, *Collages*, for tape and orchestra
               String Quartet No 2 (1960–2)
1962 (66)      *Concert for Eight*, for flute, clarinet, guitar, mandolin, double-bass,
                  accordion, piano and percussion
1963 (67)      *Hymnody*, for eleven players
               *The Plague*, for speaker, chorus and orchestra (1963–4)
1965 (69)      Concerto for orchestra
1966 (70)      *Epithalium*, for orchestra
               *Gemini*, for violin and piano
1967 (71)      Symphony No 4, *New York*
1968 (72)      *Libra*, for flute, clarinet, violin, guitar, piano and percussion
1969 (73)      *Leo*, chamber symphony for ten players


**GERMAN, (Sir) Edward (Edward German JONES)**
*b Whitchurch, Shropshire, 17 February 1862*
*d London, 11 November 1936, aged seventy-four*

His father was a church organist, and he himself was sent to study at the Royal
Academy of Music. In 1888 he became the musical director of the Globe Theatre,
and much of his interest was in theatre music. He was made a fellow of the
Royal Academy in 1895, a member of the Philharmonic Society in 1901, and was
knighted in 1928.

1886 (24)      *The Rival Poets*, operetta
1889 (27)      *Richard III*, incidental music
1890 (28)      Symphony No 1 in E minor
1891 (29)      Funeral March
1892 (30)      *Gipsy Suite*
               *Henry VIII*, incidental music
1893 (31)      *The Tempter*, incidental music
               *Romeo and Juliet*, incidental music
               Symphony No 2 in A minor
1895 (33)      Symphonic Suite in D minor
1896 (34)      *As You Like It*, incidental music
1897 (35)      *In Commemoration*, fantasia
               *Hamlet*, symphonic poem
1899 (37)      *The Seasons*, symphonic suite
1900 (38)      *Nell Gwynne*, incidental music
1901 (39)      *The Emerald Isle*, operetta (completion of unfinished operetta by
                  Sullivan, *qv*)
1902 (40)      *Merrie England*, operetta
1903 (41)      *A Princess of Kensington*, operetta
1904 (42)      *Welsh Rhapsody*, for orchestra
1907 (45)      *Tom Jones*, operetta
1909 (47)      *Fallen Fairies*, comic opera
1911 (49)      Coronation March and Hymn (for the coronation of George V)
1919 (57)      Theme and Six Variations for orchestra

140

**GERSHWIN, George**
b New York, 26 September 1898
d Hollywood, 11 July 1937, aged thirty-eight

He was the second of three children of Russian immigrants; the eldest, Ira, was a great lyric-writer with whom George collaborated all his life. From an early age he listened to all the music he could, particularly ragtime and jazz; he had piano lessons, intending to become a concert pianist – an ambition that was never fulfilled. He left school at the age of fifteen and joined the staff of Remick's, a Tin Pan Alley publisher. There, influenced by such popular composers as Jerome Kern and Irving Berlin, he began writing for the theatre. He wrote his first song in 1916, and his first big success was with the song 'Swannee' in 1919. Since he had only a limited knowledge of music technique – and, indeed, never became very proficient at reading music – the actual writing and arranging was largely done by other people, notably Fernand Grofé. Paul Whiteman encouraged him to compose a jazz concerto, and the result, in 1924, was the *Rhapsody in Blue*, orchestrated by Grofé who was Whiteman's arranger. His reputation as a master of serious music brought a commission from Walter Damrosch for the Concerto in F (1925) and *An American in Paris* (1928). Their success led to other large-scale orchestral pieces and ultimately to his masterpiece, the opera *Porgy and Bess* (1934–5). Otherwise his fame lies with his songs and the great number of musicals and films he wrote with his brother Ira. He died of a brain tumour.

| | |
|---|---|
| 1919 (21) | *Lullabye*, for string quartet |
| | *La La Lucille*, musical |
| | *Morris Gest Midnight Whirl*, musical |
| 1920 (22) | *George White's Scandals of 1920*, musical |
| | *Broadway Brevities of 1920* (including song 'Swannee') |
| 1921 (23) | *A Dangerous Maid*, musical |
| | *George White's Scandals of 1921*, musical |
| 1922 (24) | *George White's Scandals of 1922*, musical |
| | *Blue Monday Blues* (also called *135th Street*), opera |
| | *Our Nell*, musical |
| 1923 (25) | *The Rainbow*, musical |
| | *George White's Scandals of 1923*, musical |
| 1924 (26) | *Rhapsody in Blue* (arr Grofé), for piano and orchestra |
| | *Sweet Little Devil*, musical |
| | *George White's Scandals of 1924*, musical |
| | *Primrose*, musical |
| | *Lady, Be Good*, musical (including song 'Fascinating Rhythm') |
| 1925 (27) | *Novelettes*, for violin and piano |
| | Concerto in F for piano and orchestra |
| | *Tell Me More*, musical |
| | *Tip-Toes*, musical |
| | *Song of the Flame*, musical |
| | *Oh, Kay!*, musical (including songs 'Do, Do, Do' and 'Someone to Watch Over Me') |
| 1926 (28) | Preludes for piano |
| 1927 (29) | *Strike Up The Band*, musical |
| | *Funny Face*, musical (including songs 'He Loves and She Loves' and 'Swonderful') |
| 1928 (30) | *An American In Paris*, for orchestra |
| | *Rosalie*, musical |
| | *Treasure Girl*, musical |
| 1929 (31) | *Show Girl*, musical |
| 1930 (32) | *Girl Crazy*, musical (including songs 'Bidin' My Time', |

'Embraceable You' and 'I Got Rhythm')
1931 (33)    *Of Thee I Sing*, musical
             *2nd Rhapsody*, for piano and orchestra
             *Delicious*, film score
1932 (34)    *Cuban Overture*, for orchestra
             *George Gershwin Song-Book*, piano arrangement of eighteen songs
1933 (35)    *Pardon My English*, musical
             *Let Them Eat Cake*, musical
             Two Waltzes for piano
1934 (36)    'I Got Rhythm', variations for piano and orchestra
1935 (37)    *Porgy and Bess*, opera
1936–7 (38–9) *Shall We Dance*, film score (including songs 'Let's Call the Whole
             Thing Off', 'Shall We Dance', 'They Can't Take That Away from
             Me')
1937 (38)    *A Damsel in Distress*, film score (including song 'Nice Work if You
             Can Get It')
Performed posthumously:
1938         *The Goldwyn Follies*, film score (including song 'Love Walked In')
Gershwin also wrote film music based on his musicals and songs, and many
other individual songs.


## GESUALDO, Carlo, Prince of Venosa
*b Naples, c1560*
*d Naples, 8 September 1613, aged c fifty-three*

Of noble lineage, he married his cousin in 1586, and in 1590 arranged for her
murder and that of her lover, the Duke of Andrea. The scandal of this brought to
the fore both his name and his music, which he had previously kept in semi-
secrecy. A second marriage took him to Ferrara in 1594, and there his music was
given the greatest encouragement. Much of his life was occupied with politics,
from which he eventually withdrew completely, renouncing his princely
powers and taking refuge in his music.

1594–6 (*c*34–6) First four books of madrigals
1611 (*c*51)    Madrigals, books 5 and 6
Many sacred vocal works


## GIBBONS, Orlando
*b Oxford, 1583*
*d Canterbury, 5 June 1625, aged forty-two*

He entered the choir of King's College, Cambridge, where his brother Edward
was Master of the Choristers, in 1596, and matriculated in 1598. From 1602 to
1603 he earned his living by composing music for special occasions, and in 1605,
aged 21, he was appointed organist of the Chapel Royal, a post he held for the
rest of his life. He was awarded a degree in music at Cambridge in 1606, and a
doctorate at Oxford in 1622. He enjoyed considerable Royal patronage, and in
1623 became organist at Westminster Abbey. He died of an apoplectic fit.

1612 (29)    *p* Madrigals and Motets of Five Parts: Apt for Viols and Voyces
Gibbons' other works include about forty anthems and other church music,
music for viols, keyboard pieces, and expressive madrigals, such as 'The Silver
Swan'.

## GILDER, Eric
*b London, 25 December 1911*

He first studied mathematics and physics, and was then granted a scholarship to the Royal College of Music from 1936 until he went into war service. Since the war, he has worked variously as a pianist, conductor and broadcaster, and as principal of his own school of music.

1939 (28)   *Seascape*, for piano and orchestra
1945 (34)   *The Tide*, for soprano, baritone, chorus, organ and orchestra
1950 (39)   *Christmas Sounds*, for soli, chorus and orchestra
1953 (42)   *Nursery Suite*, for orchestra
1954 (43)   *A Sea Suite*, for orchestra
1975 (64)   *A Processional Overture*
1979 (68)   Sonata, for violin and piano
1981 (70)   *Three Pastorals*, for orchestra

Gilder has written other orchestral, choral and piano works; songs, some with orchestra; song-cycles; music for the theatre; plays, poetry and fiction; and has contributed to music periodicals.


## GILLIS, Don
*b Cameron, Missouri, 17 June 1912*
*d Columbia, South Carolina, 10 January 1978, aged sixty-five*

He played trumpet and trombone in school bands. He graduated from Texas Christian University in 1936. From 1944 he was programme arranger for the NBC in New York; from 1967 to 1968, chairman of the music department at the Southern Methodist University; and from 1968 to 1972, chairman of fine arts at Dallas Baptist College. He was a radio scriptwriter as well as a composer.

1936 (24)   *Four Moods in Three Keys*, for chamber orchestra
1937 (25)   *The Woolyworm*, symphonic satire
            *The Panhandle*, suite for orchestra
            *Thoughts Provoked on Becoming a Prospective Papa*, suite for orchestra
            *The Crucifixion*, for solo voices, narrator, chorus and orchestra
1938 (26)   *The Raven*, for narrator and orchestra
1939–40 (27–8) Symphony No 1, *An American Symphony*
1940 (28)   *Portrait of a Frontier Town*, suite for orchestra
            Symphony No 2, *Symphony of Faith*
            Symphony No 3, *A Symphony of Free Men* (1940–1)
1941 (29)   *The Night Before Christmas*, for narrator and orchestra
1942 (30)   Three Sketches for strings
1943 (31)   *Prairie Poem*, for orchestra
            Symphony No 4
1944 (32)   *A Short Overture to an Unwritten Opera*, for orchestra
            *The Alamo*, symphonic poem
            Symphony No 5 (1944–5)
1945 (33)   *To an Unknown Soldier*, symphonic poem
1946–7 (34–5) Symphony No 5½, *A Symphony for Fun*
1947 (35)   Symphony No 6
            *Dude Ranch*, for orchestra
            Three Short Pieces for strings
1948 (36)   Symphony No 7, *Saga of a Prairie School*
1950 (38)   Symphony No 8, *The Man Who Invented Music*, for narrator and orchestra
1957 (45)   *Tulsa*, for orchestra

| 1966 (54) | Piano Concerto No 2 |
| 1970 (58) | *The Nazarene*, opera |
| 1973 (61) | *Behold the Man*, opera |
| | *Let Us Pray*, choral |

Gillis also composed:
Symphonies No 9–12
*A short, short symphony*
Six string quartets
Two sonatinas for four trumpets
*Shindig*, ballet
*The Park Avenue Kids*, opera
*The Gift of the Magi*, opera
*Pep Rally*, opera
*The Legend of Star Valley Junction*, opera
*Atlanta*, orchestral suite
*Twinkletoes*, orchestral suite
*Four Scenes from Yesterday*, orchestral suite
*Amarillo*, for orchestra
*Alice in Orchestralia*, for narrator and orchestra
*Thomas Wolfe, American*, for narrator and orchestra
*Toscanini, a Portrait of a Century*, for narrator and orchestra
*A Ceremony of Allegiance*, for narrator and orchestra
*His Name was John*, for narrator and orchestra
*The Answer*, for narrator and orchestra
Other choral and piano works


## GINASTERA, Alberto
*b Buenos Aires, 11 April 1916*
*d Geneva, 25 June 1983, aged sixty-seven*

He started piano lessons at the age of seven, and at age twelve he went to Williams Conservatory, graduating in 1935. From 1936 to 1938 he was at the National Conservatory, graduating with the highest honours, and in 1941 became professor of composition there. In 1945 he was dismissed from his chair at the National Military Academy because of Peron's rise to power, and he went to the USA, staying until 1947. He then journeyed widely in America and Europe, returning to Argentina in 1955 when Peron was overthrown. In 1958 he was made dean of the Faculty of Arts and Science at the Argentine Catholic University. In 1968 he went again to live in the USA and in 1970 went to Europe, settling in Geneva. He has had many commissions, been granted many honours, and held many administrative posts. He destroyed most of his very early works.

| 1934–6 (18–20) | *Panambi*, ballet |
| 1937 (21) | *Danzas Argentinas*, for piano |
| 1938 (22) | Two Songs with piano |
| | *Songs of Tucumán*, for voice, flute, harp, violin and drums |
| | *Psalm*, for clarinet, chorus, boys' chorus and orchestra |
| 1940 (24) | Three Pieces for piano |
| | *Malambo*, for piano |
| 1941 (25) | *Estancia*, ballet |
| 1943 (27) | Overture to *Faust* |
| | *Five Popular Argentine Songs*, for voice and piano |
| | *Las Horas de una Estancia*, for voice and piano |
| 1944 (28) | *Twelve American Preludes*, for piano |
| 1945 (29) | Duo for flute and oboe |

| 1946 (30) | *Lamentation of the Prophet Jeremiah*, for chorus |
| | *Suite of Criole Dances*, for piano |
| 1947 (31) | *Pampeana No 1*, for violin and piano |
| | *Ollantay*, three symphonic movements |
| | Toccata, Villancico and Fugue for organ |
| | *Rondo on Argentine Children's Songs*, for piano |
| 1948 (32) | String Quartet No 1 |
| 1950 (34) | *Pampeana No 2*, for cello and piano |
| 1952 (36) | Piano Sonata No 1 |
| 1953 (37) | Variations Concertante for chamber orchestra |
| 1954 (38) | *Pampeana No 3*, pastoral symphony |
| 1956 (40) | Harp Concerto |
| 1958 (42) | String Quartet No 2 |
| 1960 (44) | *Cantata Drammatico No 1* |
| 1961 (45) | Piano Concerto No 1 |
| 1963 (47) | Piano Quintet |
| | Violin Concerto |
| 1963–4 (47–8) | *Don Rodrigo*, opera |
| 1964 (48) | *Cantata Drammatico No 2, Bomarzo* |
| 1965 (49) | Concerto for strings |
| 1966–7 (50–1) | *Bomarzo*, opera |
| 1967 (51) | Symphonic Studies for orchestra |
| 1968 (52) | Cello Concerto No 1 |
| 1971 (55) | *Cantata Drammatico No 3, Milena* |
| | *Beatrix Cenci*, opera |
| 1972 (56) | Piano Concerto No 2 |
| 1973 (57) | String Quartet No 3 |
| | *Puneña No 1*, for flute |
| | Toccata for piano |
| | Serenata for baritone, cello and nine instruments |
| 1974 (58) | *Turbai ad Passionem Gregorianum*, for soli, chorus and orchestra |
| 1975 (59) | *Popol Vuh*, for orchestra |
| 1976 (60) | *Puneña No 2*, for cello |
| | *On a Theme of Pau Casals*, for string quintet and strings |
| | Guitar Sonata |
| 1977 (61) | *Barabbas*, opera |
| 1980 (64) | *Iubilum, 'Celebracion Sinfonica'*, for orchestra |
| | Fanfare for four trumpets |
| | Variations and Toccata on *Aurora lucis rutilat*, for organ |
| 1980–1 (64–5) | Cello Concerto No 2 |
| 1981 (65) | Piano Sonata No 2 |
| 1982 (66) | Piano Sonata No 3 |

Ginastera also wrote eleven film scores, and six incidental scores.


**GIORDANO, Umberto**
*b Foggia, 27 August 1867*
*d Milan, 12 November 1948, aged eighty-one*

The son of a chemist, he was destined for the same profession, but his father allowed him to study music. In 1881 he went to the Naples Conservatory. He wrote his first opera in competition with Mascagni's *Cavalleria Rusticana* – and lost the competition! Nevertheless, he befriended Mascagni, and also Illica, the librettist, who he once threatened to shoot (with a toy pistol). When La Scala refused to stage *Andrea Chénier*, Giordano hurried to Mascagni for advice at the moment when Mascagni should have been riding on a tram with other dignitaries to celebrate the opening of Milan's new transport system. The tram crashed, killing and injuring several people; Mascagni maintained that Giordano had saved his life, and helped his career from then on. Giordano was a simple, retiring man with a warm sense of humour.

| 1889 (22) | *Marina*, opera |
| 1892 (25) | *Mala Vita*, opera |
| 1894 (27) | *Regina Diaz*, opera |
| 1896 (29) | *Andrea Chénier*, opera |
| 1898 (31) | *Fedora*, opera |
| 1904 (37) | *Siberia*, opera |
| 1907 (40) | *Marcella*, opera |
| 1910 (43) | *Mese Mariano*, opera |
| 1915 (48) | *Madame Sans-Gêne*, opera |
| 1921 (54) | *Giove a Pompeii*, opera |
| 1924 (57) | *La Cena delle Beffe*, opera |
| 1929 (62) | *Il re*, opera |

## GIULIANI, Mauro
*b near Bari, 27 July 1781*
*d Naples, 8 May 1829, aged forty-seven*

He studied cello and counterpoint, and became a brilliant guitarist. Italy being full of guitarists at that time, he moved to Vienna in 1796 in order to make a living. He wrote nearly 150 works with opus numbers and seventy without. He was made *virtuoso onorario di camera* for Napoleon's second wife in about 1814. In 1819, heavily in debt, he returned to Italy.

His output included: three guitar concertos with orchestra; chamber music, which always included the guitar; solo guitar works and songs with guitar accompaniment.

## GLASS, Philip
*b Chicago, 31 January 1937*

He studied at the University of Chicago and the Juillard School, then in Paris with Nadia Boulanger from 1964 to 1966. He withdrew all the works he had written prior to 1966 when he worked with Ravi Shankar, became interested in Indian music, and changed his style fundamentally.

| 1968 (31) | *1 plus 1*, for solo and table-top |
| 1969 (32) | *Two Pages* |
| | *Music in 5ths* |
| | *Music in Similar Motion* |
| 1970 (33) | *Music with Changing Parts* |
| 1971–4 (34–7) | *Music in 12 Parts* |
| 1974 (37) | *Another Look at Harmony*, for ensemble |
| 1975 (38) | *Einstein on the Beach*, opera |
| 1976 (39) | *Paris*, opéra-comique |

## GLAZOUNOV, Alexander
*b St Petersburg, 29 July 1865*
*d Paris, 21 March 1936, aged seventy*

He was the son of a successful publisher; his mother was a good amateur pianist who had studied with Balakirev. He became a pupil of Rimsky-Korsakov. At his opening concert he was befriended by a wealthy timber merchant, Belayev, who started a publishing house to bring young Russian composers to the fore. In 1899 he was appointed professor at the St Petersburg Conservatory, and in 1905 he became director there. He travelled much in Europe and the USA, conducting his own works; but his home remained in Leningrad until 1928, when he went to live in Paris.

| | |
|---|---|
| 1881 (16) | Symphony No 1 (first performed under the baton of Balakirev, *qv*) |
| | *Overture on Greek Themes*, No 1 (1881–4) |
| 1882 (17) | String Quartet in D major |
| | *Overture on Greek Themes*, No 2 (1882–5) |
| 1883 (18) | Serenade No 1 |
| | String Quartet in F major |
| 1884 (19) | Serenade No 2 |
| 1885 (20) | *Stenka Razin*, tone poem |
| 1886 (21) | Symphony No 2 |
| 1887 (22) | *Suite Caractéristique* (possibly 1884) |
| | *Lyric Poem*, for orchestra |
| 1889 (24) | *The Forest*, fantasia (possibly 1887) |
| 1890 (25) | *Wedding March* |
| | *Une Fête Slave*, for orchestra |
| | *The Sea*, fantasy for orchestra |
| 1891 (26) | *Oriental Rhapsody* |
| 1892 (27) | Symphony No 3 (possibly 1890) |
| | *The Kremlin*, symphonic picture (possibly 1890) |
| | *Le Printemps*, tone poem |
| | String Quartet in A major |
| 1893 (28) | Symphony No 4 |
| 1894 (29) | *Carnival*, overture |
| | *Chopiniana Suite* |
| | String Quartet in A minor |
| 1895 (30) | Symphony No 5 |
| | *Cortège Solennel* |
| 1896 (31) | Symphony No 6 |
| 1899 (34) | String Quartet in D minor |
| 1900 (35) | *Ouverture Solennelle* |
| 1901 (36) | *The Seasons*, ballet (possibly earlier) |
| 1902 (37) | Symphony No 7 |
| | *Ballade* |
| 1904 (39) | Violin Concerto |
| 1905 (40) | *Scène Dansante* |
| | Symphony No 8 |
| 1907 (42) | *Canto di destino*, overture |
| 1909 (44) | Symphony No 9 (left unfinished, first performed 1948) |
| 1911 (46) | Piano Concerto |
| 1933 (68) | *Epic Poem* |
| 1936 (71) | Saxophone Concerto |

## GLIÈRE, Reinhold Moritzovitch
*b Kiev, 11 January 1875*
*d Moscow, 26 June 1956, aged eighty-one*

He studied at the Moscow Conservatory. In 1913 he was a professor of composition at the Kiev Conservatory and in 1914 became its director. In 1920 he returned to the Moscow Conservatory as professor of composition.

1899–1900 (24–5) Symphony No 1

| 1900 (25) | String Octet in D major |
| | String Sextet No 1 |
| | String Quartet No 1 in A major |
| 1902 (27) | String Sextet No 2 |
| 1904 (29) | String Sextet No 3 in C major |
| 1905 (30) | String Quartet No 2 in G minor |
| 1907 (32) | Symphony No 2 |
| 1908 (33) | *The Sirens*, symphonic poem |
| 1909–11 (34–6) | Symphony No 3, *Ilya Murometz* |
| 1912 (37) | *Chrysis*, ballet |
| 1915 (40) | *Trizna*, symphonic poem |
| 1919 (44) | *Imitation of Jezekiel*, symphonic poem for narrator and orchestra |
| 1921 (46) | *Cossacks of Zaporozh*, symphonic poem |
| 1922, 1930 (47, 55) | *Comedians*, ballet |
| 1923–5 (48–50) | *Shakh-Senem*, opera |
| 1924 (49) | Two Poems for soprano and orchestra |
| | *For the Festival of the Comintern*, fantasy for wind orchestra |
| | *March of the Red Army*, for wind orchestra |
| 1925 (50) | *Cleopatra*, ballet |
| 1926–7 (51–2) | *Red Poppy*, ballet |
| 1928 (53) | String Quartet No 3 |
| 1938 (63) | Harp Concerto in E♭ major |
| 1942 (67) | Concerto for coloratura soprano |

Glière also composed many songs and piano pieces.


## GLINKA, Mikhail
*b Novospasskoye, 1 June 1804*
*d Berlin, 15 February 1857, aged fifty-two*

He is known as the father of Russian music. Brought up in comfortable circumstances, he was always financially secure, though his health was poor. He had little formal musical training, but delighted in the company of other musicians. On leaving school in 1822 he resisted his father's pressure to enter the foreign service, preferring to be a musical dilettante in the drawing-rooms of St Petersburg. He travelled a lot, worked from 1824 to 1828 in the Ministry of Communications, which was no onerous task, but otherwise enjoyed a frivolous life. His interest in exotic places and their folk-music infected his writings, which became something of a model for future Russian composers.

| 1822 (18) | *Variations on a Theme of Mozart* for piano |
| 1826 (22) | Memorial Cantata |
| | *Pathétique* Trio, for piano, clarinet and bassoon, or piano, violin and cello (1826–7) |
| 1830 (26) | String Quartet in F major |
| 1833–4 (29–30) | Sextet for piano and strings |
| 1836 (32) | *A Life for the Tsar*, opera (called *Ivan Susanin* in Russia) |
| | *The Moldavian Gipsy*, incidental music |
| 1839 (35) | *Valse-fantaisie*, for orchestra (revised 1856) |
| 1840 (36) | *Farewell to Petersburg*, song cycle |
| 1842 (38) | *Russlan and Ludmilla*, opera |
| 1845 (41) | Spanish Overture No 1, *Jota Aragonesa* |
| 1847 (43) | *Greeting to the Fatherland*, for piano |
| 1848 (44) | *Wedding Song (Kamarinskaya)*, fantasia for orchestra |

Glinka also composed many piano pieces and songs.

## GLUCK, Christoph Willibald
*b Erasbach, Bavaria, 2 July 1714*
*d Vienna, 15 November 1787, aged seventy-three*

He was the son of a huntsman. It is believed that from 1726 to 1728 he was at a Jesuit school and that he entered Prague University in 1732. From then until 1736 he earned a living by teaching and by performing on violin, cello and keyboard instruments, and as assistant church organist. In 1736 he became chamber musician in the household of Prince Lobkowitz in Vienna. From 1737 to 1740 he studied music in Milan. By 1745 his operas were so successful that he was invited to London, where he met Arne and Handel. He returned to Vienna in 1749, and married a wealthy wife there in 1750. For a year or two he travelled widely, and in 1754 he was made musical director to the court of Francis I in Vienna, retiring from that post in 1764. He continued to work both in Vienna and Paris, but in 1781 he had a stroke which limited his activities in his remaining years.

| | | |
|---|---|---|
| 1741 | (27) | *Artaserse*, opera |
| 1742 | (28) | *Demetrio*, opera |
| 1743 | (29) | *Il Tigrane*, opera |
| 1745 | (31) | *Ippolito*, opera |
| 1746 | (32) | *Artmene*, opera |
| | | p Six Sonatas for two violins and continuo |
| 1747 | (33) | *Le nozze d'Ercole e d'Ebe*, opera |
| 1750 | (36) | *Ezio*, opera |
| 1752 | (38) | *Issipile*, opera |
| 1753 | (39) | Nine Symphonies |
| 1755 | (41) | *Les Amours champêtres*, opera |
| | | *Alessandro*, ballet |
| 1756 | (42) | *Antigono*, opera |
| | | *Le Chinois poli en France*, opera |
| 1758 | (44) | *L'Isle de Merlin, ou, le Monde renversé*, opera |
| 1759 | (45) | *L'Arbre enchanté*, opera |
| 1761 | (47) | *La Cadi dupé*, opera |
| | | *Don Juan*, ballet |
| 1762 | (48) | *Orfeo ed Euridice*, opera |
| 1764 | (50) | *Poro*, opera |
| | | *La Rencontre imprévue*, opera |
| 1765 | (51) | *Semiramide*, ballet |
| 1766 | (52) | *L'Orfano della China*, ballet |
| 1767 | (53) | *Alceste*, opera |
| 1770 | (56) | *Paride ed Elena*, opera |
| 1774 | (60) | *Iphigénie en Aulide*, opera |
| 1777 | (63) | *Armide*, opera |
| 1779 | (65) | *Iphigénie en Tauride*, opera |

Gluck also wrote seven sonatas for two violins and bass.


## GODARD, Benjamin Louis Paul
*b Paris, 18 August 1849*
*d Cannes, 10 January 1895, aged forty-five*

He entered the Paris Conservatory in 1863, and became a fine violinist; in 1887 he was made professor of the ensemble class. He was named Chevalier of the Légion d'honneur in 1889.

| | | |
|---|---|---|
| 1876 | (27) | Violin Concerto No 2, *Concerto romantique* |
| 1878 | (29) | Piano Concerto |

> *La Tasse*, dramatic symphony for solo voices, chorus and orchestra
> *Les Bijoux de Jeanette*, one-act opera

1879 (30)    *Scènes poétiques*
1880 (31)    Symphony
              *Diane: poème dramatique*
1882 (33)    *Symphonie*, ballet
1883 (34)    *Symphonie Gothique*
1884 (35)    *Symphonie Orientale*
              *Pedro de Zalamea*, four-act opera
1886 (37)    *Symphonie Légendaire*
1888 (39)    *Jocelyn*, opera
1890 (41)    *Dante*, opera

Godard also composed: three string quartets; three violin sonatas; one piano trio; *Suite de trois morceaux*, for flute; over a hundred songs.


## GOEHR, Alexander
*b Berlin, 10 August 1932*

He studied composition at the Royal Manchester College, and went to the Paris Conservatory on a French government scholarship. From 1960 to 1968 he worked at the BBC, and was then awarded a Churchill Fellowship that enabled him to go to Tokyo. From 1968 to 1969 he was composer-in-residence at the New England Conservatory of Music in Boston, and in 1970 became assistant professor of music at Yale University. He was appointed professor of music at Cambridge University in 1976.

1951 (19)    *Songs of Babel*
              Piano Sonata (1951–2)
1954 (22)    Fantasias for clarinet and piano
              Fantasia for orchestra (revised 1958)
1956–7 (24–5) String Quartet No 1
1957 (25)    Capriccio for piano
              *The Deluge*, cantata for soprano, contralto, flute, horn, trumpet, harp, violin, viola, cello and double-bass
1958 (26)    *La Belle Dame sans merci*, ballet
1959 (27)    Variations for flute and piano
              Four Songs from the Japanese, for high voice with orchestra or piano
              *Sutter's Gold*, cantata for bass solo, chorus and orchestra (1959–60)
              *Hecuba's Lament*, for orchestra (1959–61)
1961 (29)    Suite for flute, clarinet, horn, harp, violin (doubling viola) and cello
              Violin Concerto (1961–2)
1962 (30)    *A Little Cantata of Proverbs*
              Two Choruses for mixed chorus a cappella
1963 (31)    *Virtutes*, cycle of songs and melodramas for chorus, piano duet and percussion
              *Little Symphony* (In memory of Walter Goehr), for small orchestra
              *Little Music for Strings*
1964 (32)    *Five Poems and an Epigram of William Blake*, for mixed chorus
              Three Pieces for piano
1965 (33)    *Pastorals*, for orchestra
1966 (34)    *Arden muss sterben (Arden Must Die)*, opera
1967 (35)    *Warngedichte*, for low voice and piano
              String Quartet No 2
1968 (36)    *Romanza*, for cello and orchestra

                   *Naboth's Vineyard*, a dramatic madrigal
1969 (37)    *Konzertstücke*, for piano and small orchestra
                   *Nonomiya*, for piano
                   Paraphrase on the madrigal 'Il combattimento de Tancredi e
                      Clorinda' by Monteverdi, for solo clarinet
1970 (38)    Symphony in one movement
                   *Shadowplay-2*, music theater for tenor, alto flute, alto saxophone,
                      horn, cello and piano
                   *Sonata about Jerusalem*
                   Concerto for eleven instruments
1972 (40)    Concerto for piano and orchestra
1973–4 (41–2) *Metamorphosis*, dance for orchestra
1974 (42)    Chaconne for wind instruments
                   Lyric Pieces
1975–6 (43–4) String Quartet No 3
1976 (44)    *Psalm IV*, for soloists, female chorus and organ
                   *Fugue on the notes of Psalm IV*, for string orchestra
1977 (45)    *Romanza on the notes of Psalm IV*, for string orchestra
1980 (48)    *Sinfonia*, for orchestra
1981 (49)    *Deux Études*, for orchestra
                   *Behold the Sun*, for soprano, vibraphone and chamber ensemble
1982–4 (50–2) *Behold the Sun*, opera


## GOLDMARK, Carl
*b Keszthely, Hungary, 18 May 1830*
*d Vienna, 2 January 1915, aged eighty-four*

His father was a cantor in a synagogue, and he himself was taught music by a
local schoolmaster, becoming a gifted violinist. He went to the Vienna
Conservatory at the age of fourteen. In 1848 he joined a theatre orchestra in
Györ, in Hungary, but during the revolution he was arrested as a rebel and
nearly shot, the mistake being discovered just in time. He returned to Vienna to
compose in 1850; studied in Budapest for a while and then in 1860 was back
again in Vienna teaching piano. For several years he played in the orchestra of
the Carl Theatre in Vienna, which inspired him to write operas.

1875 (45)    *The Queen of Sheba*, opera
1876 (46)    *Rustic Wedding*, symphony
1886 (56)    *Merlin*, opera
1896 (66)    *The Cricket on the Hearth*, opera
1908 (78)    *A Winter's Tale*, opera


## GOSSEC, François Joseph
*b Vergnies, Hainault, 17 January 1734*
*d Passy, 16 February 1829, aged ninety-five*

The son of a Belgian farmer, he was a chorister at Antwerp Cathedral until the
age of fifteen. He went to Paris in 1751 to conduct a private orchestra, and in
1762 he entered the service of the Prince of Condé. He was subsequently in
demand to conduct many orchestras, and was professor of composition at the
Paris Conservatory from 1795 to 1815. In 1802 he was given the Légion
d'honneur.

1760 (26)    Requiem Mass
1761 (27)    *Le Tonnelier*, opera
1765 (31)    *Le Faux Lord*, opera

151

| 1766 | (32) | *Les Pêcheurs*, opera |
|------|------|------------------------|
| 1767 | (33) | *Toinon et Toinette*, opera |
|      |      | *Le Double déguisemente*, opera |
| 1774 | (40) | *Sabinus*, opera |
|      |      | *La Nativité*, oratorio |
| 1775 | (41) | *Alexis et Daphné*, opera |
| 1776 | (42) | *Hylas et Sylvie*, incidental music |
| 1778 | (44) | *La Fête du Village*, opera |
| 1779 | (45) | *Les Scythes enchaînes*, ballet |
|      |      | *Mirsa*, ballet |
| 1781 | (47) | *L'Arche d'Alliance*, oratorio |
| 1782 | (48) | *Thésée*, opera |
| 1786 | (52) | *Rosine*, opera |
| 1796 | (62) | *La Reprise de Toulon*, opera |
| 1803 | (69) | *Les Sabots et le Cerisier*, opera |
| 1813 | (79) | *Dernière Messe des vivants* |

## GOTTSCHALK, Louis Moreau
*b New Orleans, 8 May 1829*
*d Tijuca, Brazil, 18 December 1869, aged forty*

He was the son of a London-born merchant. Showing musical aptitude before the age of four, he was sent to Paris to study in 1842. He gave his first piano recital at fifteen and soon became a virtuoso; his piano compositions became extremely popular. His father's death in 1853 compelled him to work fiercely to support his six younger brothers and sisters, and he gave an enormous number of concerts. A scandal in 1867 with a girl student forced him to flee to South America, and he never returned to the USA. His strenuous concert tours eventually killed him.

His output included: two symphonies; a piano concerto and other works for piano and orchestra; eight chamber works (all lost); six operas (five of them lost); some songs with piano, and a great deal of piano music, much of it lost, and the rest at present unfashionable.

## GOULD, Morton
*b New York, 10 December 1913*

He studied at the Institute of Musical Art, New York. He was on the staff of the NBC, has been guest conductor of most major American orchestras, and has received many commissions.

| 1932 | (19) | Chorale and Fugue in jazz |
|------|------|----------------------------|
| 1936 | (23) | Little Symphony |
|      |      | Symphonette No 2 |
| 1937 | (24) | Piano Concerto |
|      |      | Spirituals for orchestra |
| 1939 | (26) | Symphonette No 3 |
|      |      | *Jericho*, for concert band |
| 1940 | (27) | *A Foster Gallery*, for orchestra |
|      |      | Latin-American Symphonette |
| 1941 | (28) | *Lincoln Legend*, for orchestra |
| 1943 | (30) | Symphony No 1 |
|      |      | Symphony No 2 (on marching tunes) |
|      |      | Concertette for viola and orchestra |
|      |      | Viola Concerto |

|          |                                                                    |
|----------|--------------------------------------------------------------------|
|          | *Interplay*, for piano and orchestra                               |
| 1944 (31) | Concerto for orchestra                                            |
| 1945 (32) | *Harvest*, for vibraphone, harp and strings                      |
|          | Ballade for band                                                   |
| 1946 (33) | *Minstrel Show*, for orchestra                                     |
|          | Symphony No 3                                                      |
| 1947 (34) | *Fall River Legend*, ballet                                       |
| 1948 (35) | Serenade of carols                                                |
| 1950 (37) | *Family Album*, for orchestra                                      |
| 1951 (38) | *The Battle Hymn of the Republic*                                 |
| 1952 (39) | *Dance Variations*, for two pianos and orchestra                  |
| 1953 (40) | Inventions for four pianos and orchestra                          |
| 1955 (42) | *Jekyll and Hyde Variations*, for orchestra                       |
|          | *Derivations*, for clarinet and band                               |
| 1956 (43) | *Dialogue*, for piano and strings                                 |
|          | *Santa Fé Saga*, for band                                          |
| 1957 (44) | *Declaration Suite*                                               |
| 1958 (45) | *Rhythm Gallery*, for narrator and orchestra                      |
|          | *St Lawrence Suite*, for band                                      |
| 1964 (51) | *Festive Music*, for off-stage trumpet and orchestra              |
|          | *Marches: Formations*, for band                                    |
|          | *World War I: Revolutionary Prelude, Prologue* (1964–5)            |
| 1966 (53) | *Venice*, audiograph for two orchestras                           |
|          | *Columbia*, for orchestra                                          |
| 1967 (54) | *Vivaldi Gallery*, for string quartet and divided orchestra       |
| 1968 (55) | *Troubador Music*, for four guitars and orchestra                 |
| 1969 (56) | *Soundings*, for orchestra                                        |
| 1971 (58) | Suite for tuba and three horns                                    |
| 1976 (63) | American Ballads                                                  |
|          | Symphony of Spirituals                                            |

## GOUNOD, Charles
*b Paris, 18 June 1818*
*d St Cloud, 18 October 1893, aged seventy-five*

His father was a painter. He had early piano lessons from his mother, who was the daughter of a professor of piano at the Paris Conservatory. After a classical education he entered the Conservatory in 1836. He won the Grand Prix de Rome in 1839, and in Rome and Vienna he made many musical friends. While organist and choirmaster in a church in Paris he became interested in the priesthood and in 1846 he was accepted as an external student at the seminary of St Sulpice. However, this phase passed. He married in 1864. From 1870 to 1875 he was in England, conducting, and forming what has now been named the Royal Choral Society. Most of the rest of his life he spent in writing.

|                    |                                              |
|--------------------|----------------------------------------------|
| 1837 (19)          | Scherzo for orchestra                        |
| 1840 (22)          | *Marche militaire suisse*, for orchestra     |
| 1851 (33)          | *Sapho*, opera                               |
| 1852–4 (34–6)      | *La nonne sanglante*, opera                  |
| 1852–9 (34–41)     | *Faust*, opera                               |
| 1855 (37)          | Symphony No 1 in D minor                     |
|                    | Symphony No 2 in E♭ major                    |
|                    | *Messe Solennelle de St Cécile*              |
| 1857 (39)          | *Le médecin malgré lui*, opera               |
| 1860 (42)          | *Philémon et Baucis*, opera                  |
| 1862 (44)          | *La Reine de Saba*, opera                    |

| 1864 (46) | *Mireille*, opera |
|---|---|
| 1865 (47) | 'Chant des compagnons' |
| 1867 (49) | *Roméo et Juliette*, opera |
| 1871 (53) | Saltarello for orchestra |
| 1873 (55) | *Funeral March of a Marionette*, for orchestra |
| 1876–7 (58) | *Cinq-Mars*, opera |
| 1878 (60) | *Marche Religieuse*, for orchestra |
| 1879 (61) | *The Redemption*, oratorio |
| 1881 (63) | *Le Tribut de Zamora*, opera |
| 1884 (66) | fp *Mors et Vita*, oratorio |
| 1888 (70) | Petite Symphonie for ten wind instruments |

## GRAINGER, Percy Aldridge
b *Melbourne, Australia, 8 July 1882*
d *New York, 20 February 1961, aged seventy-eight*

He studied in Melbourne, in Frankfurt, and with Busoni in Berlin, making his first concert appearance as a pianist in England in 1900. There followed tours of South Africa and Australia, and he made his American début in New York in 1915. From 1917 to 1919 he served with the US Army as bandsman and music instructor, and became a US citizen in 1918. From 1919 to 1931 he taught piano at the Chicago Musical College, and was made chairman of the music department of New York University in 1932. Among his close friends were Grieg and Delius.

| 1910 (28) | *Mock Morris*, for piano |
|---|---|
| 1911 (29) | *Handel in the Strand*, for piano trio |
| 1916 (34) | *In a Nutshell*, suite for piano and orchestra |
| 1918 (36) | *Children's March*, for piano |
| 1921 (39) | *Molly on the Shore*, for orchestra/solo piano/wind band |
| 1922 (40) | *Shepherd's Hey*, for orchestra/solo piano/wind band |
| 1925 (43) | *Country Gardens*, for piano duet |
| 1927 (45) | *Shallow Brown*, for chorus and orchestra |
| | *Irish Tune from County Derry (Londonderry Air)* |
| 1928 (46) | Colonial Songs |
| | *Over the Hills and Far Away*, for orchestra |
| 1929 (47) | *English Dance*, for orchestra |
| 1930 (48) | *Lord Peter's Stable Boy*, for chorus and orchestra |
| | *Spoon River*, for piano duet |
| | *To a Nordic Princess*, for orchestra |
| 1931 (49) | *The Nightingale and the Two Sisters*, for orchestra |
| 1932 (50) | *Blithe Bells*, for orchestra |

## GRANADOS, Enrique
b *Lérida, Catalonia, 27 July 1867*
d *at sea, 24 March 1916, aged forty-eight*

His father was a Cuban serving in the Spanish Army. He won a scholarship at the age of sixteen while living in Barcelona, supporting himself as a café pianist. Private patronage sent him to Paris, but ill-health prevented his entering the Conservatory. He studied privately for two years, then returned to Barcelona, where he settled and married. In 1901 he founded his own piano school. He and his wife attended the first performance of his opera *Goyescas* in New York, but on the return journey his ship, the *Sussex*, was torpedoed by a German submarine on the Folkestone-Dieppe crossing, and he was drowned while trying to save his wife.

| 1898 | (31) | *Maria del Carmen*, opera |
|---|---|---|
| 1911 | (43) | *Goyescas*, for piano |
| 1916 | (48) | *Goyescas*, opera |

Granados also composed:
*Elisenda*, suite
*Navidad*, suite
*Suite Arabe*
*Suite Gallega*
*Marcha de los Vencidos*
*La Nit del Mort*, symphonic poem
*Serenata*, for orchestra
*Tres Danzas Espagnoles*, for orchestra
*Serenata*, for two violins and piano
*Trova*, for cello and piano
Trio for piano, violin and cello
*Oriental*, for oboe and strings
*Cant de las Estrelled*, for chorus, organ and piano
Many songs and piano works


## GRANDJANY, Marcel
*b Paris, 3 September 1891*
*d New York, 24 February 1975, aged eighty-three*

He studied harp at the Paris Conservatory, winning the Premier Prix at the age of thirteen. He made his Paris début as a harpist at the age of seventeen, giving recitals until World War I, when he served in the French Army. After the war he continued to give recitals, and taught at the Fontainebleau Summer School from 1921 to 1936, after which he went to the USA. He became head of the Juillard harp department in 1938 and at the Conservatoire de Musique in Quebec from 1938 to 1958. He was made a US citizen in 1945. From 1956 to 1966 he taught at the Manhattan School of Music.

(dates unknown) *Poème*, for harp, horn and orchestra
Aria in Classic Style for harp and strings
*Children's Hour Suite*, for harp
*Colorado Trail*, for harp
*Divertissement*, for harp
*Rhapsody*, for harp
Fantasia on a theme of Haydn
*The Erie Canal*


## GRÉTRY, André
*b Liège, 11 February 1741*
*d Montmorency, near Paris, 29 September 1813, aged seventy-two*

His early training was as a chorister. From 1760 to 1766 he was attached to the Liège College in Rome. In 1767 he moved to Geneva, then to Paris. He wrote operas memorable for their tenderness and humour, achieving his peak in 1780; his more tragic works were less well received. In later years he wrote less music and more literature. He lost his wife and three daughters and spent his last years in isolation, dying in comparative obscurity.

| 1769 | (28) | *Le tableau parlant*, opéra-comique |
|---|---|---|
| 1771 | (30) | *Zemire et Azor*, opéra-comique |
| 1778 | (37) | *L'amant jaloux*, opéra-comique |
| 1784 | (43) | *L'épreuve villageoise*, opéra-comique |
| | | *Richard Coeur-de-Lion*, opéra-comique |

**GRIEG, Edvard Hagerup**
*b Bergen, 15 June 1843*
*d Bergen, 4 September 1907, aged sixty-four*

His family, three generations of whom were British consuls in Bergen, had Scottish antecedents. He studied piano with his mother, who was an accomplished concert pianist, and he married his cousin Nina Hagerup, who was a fine singer. Not surprisingly, his greatness rests on his piano works and his songs. His first work, a set of variations, was composed when he was nine. At fifteen he was sent to the Leipzig Conservatory, where he was influenced by Schumann, and later he was greatly encouraged by Liszt. He lived for a while in Copenhagen in 1863, then settled for the rest of his life in a villa near Bergen, where he associated with such nationalist writers as Ibsen and Bjornson. An attack of pleurisy in his youth left him a sick man for the rest of his life, but he still made annual concert tours to promote not only his own music but that of Norwegian composers generally. He is buried in the wall of a cliff over a fiord near his home.

| | |
|---|---|
| 1865 (22) | *In Autumn*, concert overture |
| | Violin Sonata No 1 |
| 1867 (24) | Lyric Pieces for piano, Book I |
| | Violin Sonata No 2 |
| 1869 (26) | Piano Concerto in A minor |
| 1872 (29) | *Sigurd Jorsalfar*, incidental music |
| 1875 (32) | *Peer Gynt*, incidental music |
| 1880 (37) | Two Elegiac Melodies |
| 1881 (38) | Norwegian Dances |
| 1883 (40) | Lyric Pieces for piano, Book II |
| 1884 (41) | Lyric Pieces for piano, Book III |
| 1885 (42) | *Holberg Suite*, for strings or piano |
| 1887 (44) | Violin Sonata No 3 |
| 1888 (45) | Lyric Pieces for piano, Book IV |
| 1891 (48) | Lyric Pieces for piano, Book V |
| 1893 (50) | Lyric Pieces for piano, Book VI |
| 1895 (52) | Lyric Pieces for piano, Book VII |
| 1896 (53) | Lyric Pieces for piano, Book VIII |
| 1898 (55) | Lyric Pieces for piano, Book IX |
| | *Symphonic Dances*, for orchestra |
| 1901 (58) | Lyric Pieces for piano, Book X |
| 1906 (63) | *Moods*, for piano |

Grieg also composed other piano works and many songs.


**GRIFFES, Charles Tomlinson**
*b New York, 17 September 1884*
*d New York, 8 April 1920, aged thirty-five*

In 1899 he began studying piano with a local teacher, who financed his moving to Berlin to study at the Stern Conservatory, where he worked under Humperdinck, among others. He remained in Berlin until 1907, teaching and appearing as piano soloist and accompanist. On his return to the USA he became director of music at the Hockley School in Tarrytown, NY, holding the post till 1920, the year in which he died.

| | |
|---|---|
| 1912 (28) | *Tone Images*, for mezzo and piano |
| | *The Pleasure Dome of Kubla Khan*, symphonic poem (1912–16) |
| 1915 (31) | *Three Tone Pictures*, for piano: |
| | *The Lake at Evening* |

                    *The Vale of Dreams*
                    *The Night Wind*
                    *Fantasy Pieces* for piano:
                        *Barcarolle*
                        *Notturno*
                        *Scherzo*
1916 (32)           *The Kairn of Koridwen*, dance drama for woodwinds, harp, celesta
                        and piano
                    *Two Sketches on Indian Themes*, for string quartet
                    *Roman Sketches*, for orchestra:
                        *The White Peacock*
                        *Nightfall*
                        *The Fountain of Acqua Paolo*
                        *Clouds*
1917 (33)           *Sho-Jo*, pantomimic drama for four woodwinds, four strings, harp
                        and percussion
1918 (34)           *Poem*, for flute and orchestra
                    Piano Sonata
1919 (35)           Nocturnes for orchestra

Griffes also composed many choral works and songs.


## GROFÉ, Ferde
*b New York, 27 March 1892*
*d Santa Monica, California, 3 April 1972, aged eighty*

He studied in New York, and received honorary doctorates from Illinois
Wesleyan University and the Western State College of Colorado. He was a
violinist in the Los Angeles Symphony Orchestra from 1909 to 1919, then
pianist and arranger with Paul Whiteman's band from 1919 to 1933. In 1924 he
orchestrated Gershwin's *Rhapsody in Blue*.

1931 (39)           *Grand Canyon Suite*, for orchestra
1937 (45)           *Broadway at Night*, for orchestra
                    *Symphony in Steel* (uses four pairs of shoes, two brooms, locomo-
                        tive bell, pneumatic drill and compressed air tank)
1964 (72)           *World's Fair Suite*

Grofé also wrote: *Tabloid, Death Valley Suite, Mississippi Suite, Mark Twain Suite,
Hollywood Suite, Milk, Wheels, Three Shades of Blue, New England Suite,
Metropolis, Aviation Suite*.


## GRUENBERG, Louis
*b near Brest-Litovsk (then Poland), 3 August 1884*
*d Beverly Hills, 10 June 1964, aged seventy-nine*

He was taken to the USA at the age of two. At nineteen he went to Berlin to
study with Busoni and Koch, and in 1912 was appointed teacher at the Vienna
Conservatory. In 1919 he abandoned performing as a pianist and concentrated
on composition. He was head of the composition department at the Chicago
Musical College from 1933 to 1936.

1912 (28)           Sonata for violin and piano
                    *The Witch of the Brocken*, children's opera
1913 (29)           *The Bride of the Gods*, opera
1914 (30)           Suite for violin and piano
                    *Puppet Suite*, for orchestra
                    Piano Concerto No 1

| 1919 (35) | Sonata for violin and piano |
| | *The Hill of Dreams*, for orchestra |
| | Symphony No 1 |
| 1920 (36) | *Vagabondia*, for orchestra |
| 1922 (38) | *Four Indiscretions*, for string quartet |
| | *Four Bagatelles*, for cello and piano |
| | *The Sleeping Beauty*, children's opera |
| 1925 (41) | *Four Whimsicalities*, for string quartet |
| | *Poem in the Form of a Sonata*, for cello and piano |
| | *Jazz Suite* |
| 1926 (42) | *Jazzettes*, for violin and piano |
| 1929 (45) | *Jack and the Beanstalk*, children's opera |
| | *The Enchanted Isle*, symphonic poem |
| | *Nine Moods*, for orchestra |
| | *Music for an Imaginary Ballet* |
| 1930 (46) | *Four Diversions*, for string quartet |
| 1931 (47) | *The Emperor Jones*, opera |
| | *The Dumb Wife*, opera |
| 1934 (50) | *Serenade to a Beauteous Lady*, for orchestra |
| 1936 (52) | *Helena of Troy*, opera |
| 1937 (53) | *Green Mansions*, radio opera |
| | Piano Quintet |
| 1938 (54) | String Quartet |
| | Piano Concerto No 2 |
| 1942 (58) | Symphonies No 2 and 3 |
| 1944 (60) | Violin Concerto |
| 1945 (61) | *American Suite*, for orchestra |
| | *Volpone*, opera |
| | *One Night of Cleopatra*, opera |
| | *The Miracle of Flanders*, mystery play |
| 1946 (62) | *Dance Rhapsody*, for violin and orchestra |
| | Symphony No 4 |
| 1948 (64) | Variations for orchestra |
| 1949 (65) | Cello Concerto |
| 1959–62 (75–8) | *A Song of Faith*, oratorio |

Gruenberg also wrote other vocal and piano works.

## GURNEY, Ivor (Bertie)
*b Gloucester, 28 August 1890*
*d Dartford, 26 December 1937, aged forty-seven*

He was a chorister at Gloucester Cathedral in 1900, then an articled pupil to the organist there. He went to the Royal College of Music to study under Stanford. After World War I, in which he was wounded, gassed and shell-shocked, he returned to the Royal College to study under Vaughan Williams. He left in 1921 and returned to Gloucester, but became mentally unstable; he died of tuberculosis in a mental hospital. He published one volume of poetry during the war and another in 1919, both enjoying some success; but his greatness lies in his eighty-two published songs, most of which were written between 1919 and 1922. Two hundred more songs remain in MS.

| 1919 (29) | *The Apple Orchard*, for violin and piano |
| 1919–20 (29–30) | Five Preludes for piano |
| | Scherzo for violin and piano |
| 1920 (30) | *Five Western Watercolours*, for piano |

Gurney also wrote: Six sonatas for violin and piano; five string quartets; *A Gloucester Rhapsody*, for orchestra.

158

## HAHN, Reynaldo
*b Caracas, 9 October 1875*
*d Paris, 28 January 1947, aged seventy-one*

His family moved from Venezuela to Paris when Hahn was three, and took French nationality. At the Paris Conservatory he studied harmony with Dubois and composition with Massenet. His song 'Si mes vers avaint des ailes' was composed when he was thirteen. A pianist, conductor and pleasing singer, he composed mainly for the theatre. In 1945 he was appointed director of the Paris Opéra.

| | | |
|---|---|---|
| 1892 (17) | *Fin d'amour*, ballet-pantomime | |
| 1897 (22) | *Nuit d'amour bergamasque*, symphonic poem | |
| 1898 (23) | *L'île du rêve*, opera | |
| 1902 (27) | *La Carmélite*, opéra-comique | |
| 1908 (33) | *Promethée triomphant*, for soli, chorus and orchestra | |
| | *La Pastorale de Noël*, a Christmas mystery | |
| 1909 (34) | *Le Bal de Béatrice d'Este*, ballet | |
| 1910 (35) | *La Fête chez Thérèse*, ballet | |
| 1912 (37) | *Le Bois sacré*, ballet-pantomime | |
| | *Le Dieu bleu*, ballet | |
| 1919 (44) | *Fête triomphale*, opera | |
| | *Nausicaa*, opéra-comique | |
| 1921 (46) | *La Colombe de Bouddha*, conte lyrique | |
| 1923 (48) | *Ciboulette*, operetta | |
| 1925 (50) | *Mozart*, musical comedy | |
| 1926 (51) | *La Reine de Sheba*, scène lyrique | |
| | *Une Revue* | |
| | *Le Temps d'aimer*, musical comedy | |
| 1927 (52) | Violin Concerto | |
| 1931 (56) | Piano Concerto | |
| | *Brummel*, operetta | |
| 1933 (58) | *O mon bel inconnu!* musical comedy | |
| 1935 (60) | *Malvina*, operetta | |
| | *Le Marchand de Vénise*, opera | |
| 1936 (61) | *Beaucoup de bruit pour rien*, musical comedy | |
| 1937–8 (62–3) | *Aux bosquets d'Idalie*, ballet | |
| | *Le Oui des jeunes filles*, opera | |

Hahn also wrote incidental music to seven plays; song cycles and other songs; some chamber work and pieces for piano; and wrote four books.

## HALÉVY, (original name Elias Lévy) Jacques François Fromental
*b Paris, 27 May 1799*
*d Nice, 17 March 1862, aged sixty-two*

He studied with Cherubini at the Paris Conservatory from 1809. In 1819 he won the Grand Prix de Rome, and while in Rome wrote an opera and some church music. He taught at the Paris Conservatory from 1827, becoming professor of composition in 1840; his pupils included Gounod and Bizet. From 1830 to 1845 he was chorus-master at the Opéra. He was elected to the Institut Français in 1836, and from 1854 was the permanent secretary to the Académie des Beaux-Arts, in which post he wrote many eulogical essays.

| | | |
|---|---|---|
| 1816 (17) | *Les derniers moments du Tasso*, cantata | |
| 1817 (18) | *La mort d'Adonis*, cantata | |
| 1819 (20) | *Herminie*, cantata | |
| 1820 (21) | *De Profundis*, for three voices and orchestra | |

| 1827 | (28) | L'artisan, opera |
| --- | --- | --- |
| 1828 | (29) | Le roi et le batelier, opera |
| | | Clari, opera |
| 1829 | (30) | Le dilettante d'Avignon, opera |
| 1830 | (31) | Manon Lescaut, ballet |
| 1831 | (32) | La langue musicale, opera |
| 1832 | (33) | La tentation, ballet-opera |
| 1833 | (34) | Les souvenirs de Lafleur, opera |
| | | Ludovic, opera (completion of Hérold's work) |
| 1835 | (36) | La juive, opera |
| | | L'éclair, opera |
| 1838 | (39) | Guido et Ginevra, opera |
| 1839 | (40) | Les treize, opera |
| | | Le shérif, opera |
| 1840 | (41) | Le drapier, opera |
| 1841 | (42) | Le Guitarrero, opera |
| | | La reine de Chypre, opera |
| 1843 | (44) | Charles VI, opera |
| 1844 | (45) | Le Lazzarone, opera |
| 1846 | (47) | Les mousquetaires de la reine, opera |
| 1847 | (48) | Les premiers pas, opera |
| 1848 | (49) | Le val d'Andorre, opera |
| 1849 | (50) | La fée aux roses, opera |
| | | Prométhée Enchaîné, incidental music |
| | | Italic, cantata |
| 1850 | (51) | La tempesta, opera |
| | | La dame de Picque, opera |
| 1852 | (53) | Le juif errant, opera |
| 1853 | (54) | Le nabab, opera |
| 1855 | (56) | Jaguarita l'Indienne, opera |
| 1856 | (57) | Valentine d'Aubigny, opera |
| 1858 | (59) | La Magicienne, opera |
| | | Vanina d'Ornano, opera (unfinished) |
| | | Noé or Le déluge, opera (unfinished, completed by Bizet) |
| 1859 | (60) | Les plages du Nil, cantata |

Halévy also wrote piano pieces and songs.


**HAMILTON, Iain**
b Glasgow, 6 June 1922

He moved to London at the age of seven, attending Mill Hill School, and first worked in engineering for seven years. In 1947 he won a scholarship at the Royal Academy of Music, gaining there the Koussevitsky Foundation award and the Royal Philharmonic Society, Edwin Evans Memorial and Dove prizes. He became a lecturer at Morley College and London University. In 1961 he lectured at Duke University, North Carolina, and in 1962 became the Mary Duke Biddle professor there; he was also chairman of the music department from 1966 to 1967. In 1970 he received an honorary doctorate of music from Glasgow University.

| 1948 | (26) | Quintet for clarinet and string quartet |
| --- | --- | --- |
| | | Symphonic Variations for string orchestra |
| 1949 | (27) | Symphony No 1 |
| | | String Quartet No 1 |
| 1950 | (28) | Clarinet Concerto |
| 1951 | (29) | Symphony No 2 |

|              |                                                                                         |
|--------------|-----------------------------------------------------------------------------------------|
|              | *Clerk Saunders*, ballet                                                                |
|              | Flute Quartet                                                                           |
|              | Piano Sonata (revised 1971)                                                             |
| 1952 (30)    | Violin Concerto                                                                         |
|              | *Bartholomew Fair*, overture                                                            |
| 1954 (32)    | String Octet                                                                            |
|              | *Four Border Songs and the Fray of Suport*                                              |
|              | *Songs of Summer*, for soprano and piano                                                |
| 1956 (34)    | Scottish Dances                                                                         |
|              | Sonata for chamber orchestra                                                            |
| 1957 (35)    | Cantata for tenor and piano                                                             |
|              | Five Love Songs for tenor and orchestra                                                 |
| 1958 (36)    | *Overture 1912*                                                                         |
|              | Concerto for jazz trumpet and orchestra                                                 |
|              | Sonata for solo cello                                                                   |
| 1959 (37)    | Sinfonia for two orchestras                                                             |
|              | *Ecossaise*, for orchestra                                                              |
| 1960 (38)    | Piano Concerto (revised 1967)                                                           |
| 1962 (40)    | Arias for small orchestra                                                               |
|              | Sextet for strings                                                                      |
| 1963 (41)    | *Sonatas and Variants*, for ten wind instruments                                        |
|              | *Nocturnes with Cadenza*, for piano                                                     |
| 1964 (42)    | Organ Concerto                                                                          |
|              | *Cantos*, for orchestra                                                                 |
|              | *Jubilee*, for orchestra                                                                |
| 1965 (43)    | *Dialogues*, for soprano and five instruments                                           |
|              | *Aubade*, for solo organ                                                                |
|              | String Quartet No 2                                                                     |
| 1966 (44)    | *Threnos – In Time of War*, for solo organ                                              |
|              | *Five Scenes*, for trumpet and piano                                                    |
|              | Flute Sonata                                                                            |
| 1967–9 (45–7)| *Agamemnon*, opera                                                                      |
|              | *The Royal Hunt of the Sun*, opera                                                      |
| 1968 (46)    | *Pharsalia*, opera                                                                      |
| 1969 (47)    | *Circus*, for two trumpets and orchestra                                                |
| 1970 (48)    | *Epitaph for This World and Time*, for three choruses and three organs                  |
|              | *Alastor*, for orchestra                                                                |
|              | *Voyage*, for horn and chamber orchestra                                                |
| 1971 (49)    | Violin Concerto No 2, *Amphion*                                                         |
| 1972 (50)    | *Commedia*, concerto for orchestra                                                      |
|              | *Descent of the Celestial City*, for chorus and organ                                   |
|              | *Palinodes*, for solo piano                                                             |
| 1974 (52)    | *The Cataline Conspiracy*, opera                                                        |
|              | Piano Sonata No 2                                                                       |
| 1975 (53)    | *Te Deum*                                                                               |
|              | Violin Sonata No 1                                                                      |
|              | Cello Sonata No 2                                                                       |
|              | *Sea Music*, for chorus and string quartet                                              |
|              | *Aurora*, for orchestra                                                                 |
|              | *A Vision of Canopus*, for organ                                                        |
|              | *To Columbus*, for chorus, brass and percussion                                         |
| 1976 (54)    | *Tamburlaine*, lyric drama                                                              |
|              | *The Alexandrian Sequence*, for chamber orchestra                                       |
| 1977 (55)    | *Cleopatra*, dramatic scene for soprano and orchestra                                   |
|              | *Hyperion*, for clarinet, horn, violin, cello and piano                                 |

|        |      | *Spirits of the Air*, for solo bass trombone |
|--------|------|-----|
| 1978   | (56) | *Anna Karenina*, opera |
|        |      | Piano Sonata No 3 |
| 1980   | (58) | *Mass in A*, for chorus a capella |
|        |      | *Vespers*, for mixed chorus, two pianos, harp and percussion |
|        |      | *Dick Whittington*, lyric comedy (1980–1) |
| 1981   | (59) | Symphony No 3, *Spring* |
|        |      | Symphony No 4 |
|        |      | *La Ricordanza*, for tenor and orchestra |
|        |      | *The Morning Watch*, for mixed chorus and ten wind instruments |
| 1982   | (60) | *Love is Life's Spring*, for soprano and piano |
|        |      | *The Passion According to St Mark*, for soli and chorus |
|        |      | *Lancelot*, opera (1982–3) |

## HANDEL, George Frideric
b Halle, Saxony, 23 February 1685
d London, 14 April 1759, aged seventy-four

His father was an elderly barber-surgeon who opposed his son's wish for a musical career. In spite of this, Handel managed to learn composition, oboe, violin, organ and harpsichord. In 1702 he entered the University of Halle to study law; but music had a stronger appeal. He moved to Hamburg, finding employment as a violinist and harpsichordist; then he went to Lübeck, where the organist, Buxtehude, was contemplating retirement. One condition of taking Buxtehude's post was to marry Buxtehude's daughter, and Handel retreated rapidly. In 1705 he went to Italy, where he astonished the Italians with his playing of organ and harpsichord. While he was there he wrote several church works, though still remaining a Protestant. In Venice he met Prince Ernst of Hanover, younger brother of the Elector, and returned with him to Germany as *Kapellmeister* to the court of Hanover. Shortly after he was invited to England, was given leave of absence, and arrived in London in 1710. His Italian-style operas were an immense success, and he was reluctant to leave London and resume his responsibilities in Hanover; but in 1714 the Elector of Hanover became George I of England, and Handel and his employer were reconciled. He became composer-in-residence to the Duke of Chandos, leaving in 1719 to find singers for a new Italian opera company to be based at the King's Theatre, Haymarket. The company opened most successfully in 1720. In 1727 he became a naturalised British subject. In 1728 John Gay's *The Beggar's Opera* opened to immediate popular acclaim and spelt doom for Italian opera; within six months Handel's company went bankrupt. He formed a new Italian company which opened in 1729, but competition from the new-style works decimated his audiences. His health suffered, and in 1737 he went to Aix-la-Chapelle to take the waters. Restored, he concentrated on writing oratorios, and in 1741 he went to Ireland for the first performance of *Messiah*. The success of his oratorios reimbursed him for his losses over opera, and he died a wealthy man. His sight slowly failed, and eventually he became totally blind. He is buried in Westminster Abbey.

| 1707 | (22) | 'Laudate pueri Dominum', aria |
|------|------|-----|
|      |      | *Rodrigo*, opera (c1707) |
| 1708 | (23) | *La Resurrezione*, Easter oratorio |
| 1711 | (26) | *Rinaldo*, opera |
| 1712 | (27) | *Il pastor fido*, opera (first version) |
| 1713 | (28) | *Teseo*, opera |
|      |      | *Te Deum and Jubilate*, for the Peace of Utrecht |
| 1715 | (30) | *Amadigi de Gaula*, opera |

|             | The *Water Music* (1715–17)                                                 |
| ----------- | --------------------------------------------------------------------------- |
| c1720 (c35) | The *Chandos Anthems*                                                        |
|             | *Acis and Galatea*, secular cantata                                         |
|             | *Radamisto*, opera                                                          |
|             | *Huit Suites de pièces*, for harpsichord                                    |
| 1721 (36)   | *Floridante*, opera                                                         |
| 1723 (38)   | *Ottone*, opera                                                             |
| 1724 (39)   | *Giulio Cesare*, opera                                                      |
|             | Fifteen Chamber Sonatas                                                      |
| 1725 (40)   | *Rodelinda*, opera                                                         |
|             | Trio Sonata in D minor                                                       |
| 1727 (42)   | *Zadok the Priest*, coronation anthem                                       |
|             | *Admeto*, opera                                                             |
| 1728 (43)   | *Tolomeo*, opera                                                           |
| c1731 (c46) | Nine Sonatas for two violins and continuo                                   |
| 1732 (47)   | *Esther*, English biblical oratorio                                        |
|             | *Sosarme*, opera                                                           |
|             | *Ezio*, opera                                                              |
| 1733 (48)   | *Orlando*, opera                                                           |
|             | *Huit Suites de pièces*, for harpsichord                                    |
| 1734 (49)   | *Persichore*, ballet                                                       |
|             | *Il pastor fido* (second and third versions)                               |
|             | *Arianna*, opera                                                          |
|             | p Six Concerti Grossi                                                        |
| 1735 (50)   | *Alcina*, opera                                                            |
| 1736 (51)   | *Atalanta*, opera                                                          |
|             | *Alexander's Feast*, secular cantata                                       |
|             | Six Fugues for harpsichord                                                   |
| 1737 (52)   | *Berenice*, opera                                                          |
|             | Concerto grosso in C major                                                   |
| 1738 (53)   | *Xerxes*, opera (which includes 'Ombra mai fu', known as 'Handel's Largo') |
|             | Six organ concerti                                                          |
| 1739 (54)   | *Israel in Egypt*, oratorio                                                |
|             | *Saul*, oratorio (which includes the 'Dead March')                         |
|             | Ode for St Cecilia's Day                                                     |
|             | Twelve Concerti Grossi                                                       |
|             | Seven Trio Sonatas                                                           |
| 1740 (55)   | p Concerti for oboe and strings                                             |
|             | p Six Organ Concerti                                                         |
|             | Three Double Concerti (1740–50)                                             |
| 1741 (56)   | *Messiah*, oratorio (composed in under four weeks)                         |
|             | Five Concerti Grossi                                                         |
| 1742 (57)   | *Forest Music*                                                             |
| 1743 (58)   | *Samson*, oratorio                                                         |
|             | The *Dettingen Te Deum*                                                     |
| 1744 (59)   | *Semele*, secular oratorio                                                 |
| 1745 (60)   | *Belshazzar*, oratorio                                                     |
| 1746 (61)   | *Occasional Oratorio*                                                      |
| 1747 (62)   | *Judas Maccabaeus*, oratorio                                               |
| 1748 (63)   | *Joshua*, oratorio                                                         |
| 1749 (64)   | *Music for the Royal Fireworks*                                            |
|             | *Solomon*, oratorio                                                        |
|             | *Susanna*, oratorio                                                        |
| 1750 (65)   | *Theodora*, oratorio                                                       |

1752 (67)   *Jephtha*, oratorio
Performed posthumously:
1760         Six Organ Concerti


## HANSON, Howard
*b Wahoo, Nebraska, 28 October 1896*

His initial musical education was with his mother, he then went to Luther College, the Institute of Musical Art of New York, and graduated from the Northwestern University. At age twenty he joined the faculty of the College of the Pacific, becoming dean of their Conservatory of Fine Arts three years later. In 1921 he won the Prix de Rome, then accepted the position of director of the Eastman School of Music of the University of Rochester. He has received no less than thirty-five honorary degrees and countless commissions and honours, including, in 1944, the Pulitzer Prize.

1915 (19)   Prelude and Double Fugue for two pianos
1916 (20)   Symphonic Prelude
            Piano Quintet
1917 (21)   *Symphonic Legend*
            Concerto de Camera for piano and string quartet
1919 (23)   Symphonic Rhapsody
1920 (24)   *Before the Dawn*, symphonic poem
            *Exaltation*, symphonic poem with piano obbligato
1921 (25)   Concerto for organ, strings and harp
1922 (26)   Symphony No 1 in E minor, *Nordic*
1923 (27)   *North and West*, symphonic poem
            *Lux Aeterna*, symphonic poem with viola obbligato
            String Quartet
1925 (29)   *The Lament of Beowulf*, for chorus
1926 (30)   Organ Concerto
            *Pan and the Priest*, symphonic poem
1927 (31)   *Heroic Elegy*, for chorus and orchestra
1930 (34)   Symphony No 2, *Romantic*
1933 (37)   *The Merry Mount*, opera
1935 (39)   *Drum Taps*, for baritone, chorus and orchestra
1938 (42)   Symphony No 3
1943 (47)   Symphony No 4, *Requiem* (in memory of his father)
1945 (49)   Serenade for flute, strings, harp and orchestra
1948 (52)   Piano Concerto
1951 (55)   *Fantasia on a Theme of Youth*, for piano and strings
1955 (59)   Symphony No 5, *Sinfonia sacrae*
1956 (60)   *Elegy in memory of Serge Koussevitsky*, for orchestra
1958 (62)   *Mosaics*, for orchestra
1959 (63)   *Summer Seascapes*, for orchestra
1961 (65)   *Bold Island Suite*, for orchestra
1963 (67)   *For the First Time*, for orchestra
1967 (71)   *Dies Natalis*, for orchestra
1968 (72)   Symphony No 6
            *Psalm CXXI*, for chorus and orchestra
1969 (73)   *Streams in the Desert*, for chorus and orchestra
1970 (74)   *The Mystic Trumpeter*, for narrator, chorus and orchestra
1976 (80)   *New Land, New Covenant*, oratorio
1977 (81)   Symphony No 7, *Sea*, with chorus

164

**HARRIS, Roy**
*b Lincoln County, Oklahoma, 12 February 1898*
*d Santa Monica, California, 1 October 1979, aged eight-one*

In 1919 he entered the University of California at Berkeley, and in 1926 went to Paris to study with Boulanger. He won the Guggenheim Fellowship in 1927/8, the Creative Fellowship from Pasadena Music and Arts Association, and was awarded honorary musical doctorates from Rutgers and the University of Rochester. He held many teaching posts.

| | |
|---|---|
| 1926 (28) | *Impressions of a Rainy Day*, for string quartet |
| 1927 (29) | Concerto for clarinet and string quartet |
| 1928 (30) | Piano Sonata |
| 1929 (31) | *American Portraits*, for orchestra |
| 1930 (32) | String Quartet No 1 |
| 1931 (33) | *Toccata*, for orchestra |
| 1932 (34) | Chorale for strings |
| | Fantasy for piano and woodwind quintet |
| | String Sextet |
| 1933 (35) | Symphony No 1 |
| | String Quartet No 2 |
| 1934 (36) | Symphony No 2 |
| | *When Johnny Comes Marching Home*, overture |
| | *Songs for Occupations*, for chorus |
| | Piano Trio |
| 1936 (38) | *Symphony for Voices* |
| | *Time Suite*, for orchestra |
| | Prelude and Fugue for string orchestra |
| | Piano Quintet |
| 1937 (39) | Symphony No 3 |
| | String Quartet No 3 |
| 1938 (40) | *Soliloquy and Dance*, for viola and piano |
| 1939 (41) | Symphony No 4 |
| | String Quartet No 4 |
| 1940 (42) | *Western Landscape*, ballet |
| | *Challenge*, for baritone, chorus and orchestra |
| | *American Creed*, for orchestra |
| | *Evening Piece*, for orchestra |
| | *Ode to Truth*, for orchestra |
| | String Quintet |
| 1941 (43) | *From This Earth*, ballet |
| | *Acceleration*, for orchestra |
| | Violin Sonata |
| 1942 (44) | Piano Concerto with band |
| | Symphony No 5 |
| | *What so proudly we hail*, ballet |
| 1943 (45) | Cantata for chorus, organ and brass |
| | Mass for male chorus and organ |
| 1944 (46) | Symphony No 6 |
| 1945 (47) | Piano Concerto No 1 |
| 1946 (48) | Concerto for two pianos |
| | Accordion Concerto |
| 1947 (49) | *Quest*, for orchestra |
| 1948 (50) | *Elegy and Pæan*, for viola and orchestra |
| 1949 (51) | *Kentucky Spring*, for orchestra |
| 1951 (53) | *Cumberland Concerto*, for orchestra |
| | Symphony No 7 |

| 1953 (55) | Piano Concerto No 2 |
| | *Abraham Lincoln Walks at Midnight*, chamber cantata |
| 1954 (56) | Fantasy for piano and orchestra |
| 1956 (58) | *Folk Fantasy for Festivals*, for piano and choir |
| 1959 (61) | *Give Me the Splendid Silent Sun*, cantata for baritone and orchestra |
| 1961 (63) | *Canticle to the Sun*, cantata for soprano and chamber orchestra |
| 1962 (64) | Symphony No 8 |
| | Symphony No 9 |
| 1963 (65) | *Epilogue to Profiles in Courage: J.F.K.*, for orchestra |
| | *Salute to Death*, for voices and orchestra |
| 1964 (66) | Duo for cello and piano |
| | *Horn of Plenty*, for orchestra |
| 1965 (67) | Symphony No 10 |
| | *Rhythm and Spaces*, for string orchestra |
| 1967 (69) | Symphony No 11 |
| 1968 (70) | Concerto for amplified piano, brass and percussion |
| | Piano Sextet |
| 1969 (71) | Symphony No 12 |
| | Symphony No 13 (possibly 1969) |
| 1975 (77) | Symphony No 14 |

## HARTY, Sir (Herbert) Hamilton
*b Hillsborough, Co Down, 4 December 1879*
*d Brighton, 19 February 1941, aged sixty-one*

He was taught viola, piano and counterpoint by his father, and at the age of twelve was organist at a local church. In 1900 he went to London, where he soon became known as a composer and accompanist, and as conductor of the London Symphony Orchestra. He was appointed conductor of the Hallé Orchestra in Manchester in 1920, making it into one of the best orchestras in England. He was knighted in 1925 and received the Gold Medal of the Royal Philharmonic Society in 1934.

| 1901 (22) | Trio |
| 1904 (25) | Piano Quartet |
| 1907 (28) | *Comedy Overture* |
| | *Ode to a Nightingale*, for soprano and orchestra |
| 1909 (30) | Violin Concerto |
| 1910 (31) | *With the Wild Geese*, tone poem |
| 1913 (34) | *The Mystic Trumpeter*, cantata |
| 1924 (45) | *Irish Symphony* |

## HAYDN, (Franz) Joseph
*b Rohrau, Austria, 31 March 1732*
*d Vienna, 31 May 1809, aged seventy-seven*

He was the son of a wheelwright; there was no tradition of music in the family. He was admitted aged eight as a chorister at St Stephen's Cathedral in Vienna, staying until 1748, when his voice broke. Though in great poverty for a time, he continued to teach himself music. From 1759 to 1961 he was *Musikdirektor* to Count Morzin at Lucaveč for a small salary. He made an unsuccessful marriage in 1760. In 1761 Prince Esterházy employed Haydn as second *Kapellmeister*; he became sole *Kapellmeister* in 1766, remaining until 1790 in full employment with the wealthy Esterházy family. He met Mozart in 1781/2, and each held the other in high esteem. In 1790 the Prince died, leaving Haydn a handsome pension;

but Esterházy's son dismissed the whole musical establishment, and Haydn moved to Vienna. There he was persuaded to visit England, which he did in 1791 with great success. Oxford University conferred on him an honorary doctorate of music. In 1792 he returned to Vienna via Bonn, where he met Beethoven, who from then until 1794 was his pupil. In 1794 he returned to England and continued to have remunerative success; but he was becoming infirm, and in 1798 he went back to Vienna, where he remained until he died. His great musical contributions were in the development of the symphony, and he was directly responsible for the establishment of the string quartet.

| | |
|---|---|
| 1755 (23) | String Quartets No 1–13 |
| 1756 (24) | Organ Concerto No 1 in C major |
| | Piano Concerto in C major |
| 1759 (27) | Symphony No 1 in D major |
| 1760 (28) | Organ Concerto No 2 in C major |
| | Symphony No 2 in C major (c1760) |
| c1761 (c29) | Symphony No 3 in G major |
| | Symphony No 4 in D major |
| | Symphony No 5 in A major |
| | Symphony No 6 in D major, *Le matin* |
| | Symphony No 7 in C major, *Le midi* |
| | Symphony No 8 in G major, *Le soir, ou la tempête* |
| | Symphony No 19 in D major |
| 1762 (30) | Symphony No 9 in C major |
| before 1763 | Symphony No 10 in D major |
| | Symphony No 11 in Eb major |
| | Piano Sonata No 3 in A major |
| 1763 (31) | Symphony No 12 in E major |
| | Symphony No 13 in D major |
| before 1764 | Symphonies No 14 and 15 |
| c1764 (c32) | Symphonies No 16–18 |
| 1764 (32) | Symphony No 22 in Eb major, *Der Philosoph* |
| 1765 (33) | Symphony No 26 in D minor, *Lamentations* (c1765) |
| | Symphony No 30 in C major, *Alleluia* |
| | Symphony No 31 in D major, *Horn Signal* |
| | String Quartets No 14–19 |
| 1766 (34) | Mass No 4 in Eb, *Great Organ* |
| | Piano Sonatas No 4–7 |
| | Piano Sonatas No 8–12 (1766–7) |
| c1767 (c35) | Piano Sonatas No 13–16 |
| 1767 (35) | Piano Sonata No 17 |
| before 1769 | Violin Concerto in C major |
| | Violin Concerto in G major |
| 1769 (37) | String Quartets No 20–5 |
| before 1770 | Violin Concerto in D major |
| 1770 (38) | Mass No 5 in Bb, *Little Organ* or *St John* |
| after 1770 | Piano Concerto in G major |
| before 1771 | Piano Concerto in F major |
| | Violin Concerto in A major |
| 1771 (39) | String Quartets No 26–31 |
| | Piano Sonata No 18 in C minor |
| before 1772 | Symphony No 43 in Eb major, *Mercury* |
| | Symphony No 44 in E minor, *Trauersymphonie* |
| 1772 (40) | Symphony No 45 in F# minor, *Farewell* |
| | Symphony No 46 in B major |
| | Symphony No 48 in C major, *Maria Teresa* |
| | Mass No 3, *St Cecilia* |

|  | String Quartets No 32–7, *Sun* or *Great* |
|  | Symphony No 52 in C minor (1772–4) |
| before 1773 | Symphony No 49 in F minor, *The Passion* |
| 1773 (41) | Violin Sonatas No 2–4 (without violin, Piano Sonatas No 22–4) |
|  | Piano Sonatas No 19–24 |
| before 1774 | Symphony No 53 in D major, *The Imperial* |
| 1774 (42) | Symphony No 55 in E♭ major, *The Schoolmaster* |
| before 1776 | Symphony No 59 in A major, *Feuersymphonie* |
| 1776 (44) | Symphony No 60 in C major, *Il distratto* |
|  | Piano Sonatas No 25–30 |
| 1777 (45) | Symphony No 63 in C major, *La Roxolane* |
|  | Piano Sonatas No 31 and 32 (1777–8) |
| 1779 (47) | Symphony No 69 in C major, *Laudon* |
|  | Piano Sonatas No 33–7 (1779–80) |
| 1781 (49) | Symphony No 73 in D major, *La Chasse* |
|  | Concerto No 2 for horn and strings |
|  | String Quartets No 38–43, *Russian* or *Jungfern* |
| 1783 (51) | Cello Concerto in D major |
| before 1784 | Piano Sonatas No 38–40 |
| 1784 (52) | *Armida*, opera |
|  | String Quartets No 44–50, dedicated to the King of Prussia (1784–7) |
| c1785 (c53) | Piano Sonata No 41 in A♭ major |
| 1785 (53) | Piano Sonata No 42 in G minor (1785–6) |
|  | Piano Sonata No 44 in A♭ major (1785–6) |
|  | Symphony No 87 in A major (with Symphonies No 82–6 comprise the *Paris* symphonies) |
| 1786 (54) | Symphony No 82 in C major, *The Bear* |
|  | Symphony No 83 in G minor, *La Poule* |
|  | Symphony No 84 in E♭ major |
| c1786 (c54) | Symphony No 85 in B♭ major, *La Reine* |
|  | Symphony No 86 in D major, *The Miracle* |
| 1787 (55) | Symphony No 88 in G major |
|  | Symphony No 89 in F major |
|  | String Quartets No 51–7. *The Seven Words*, arranged for quartet |
|  | Piano Sonata No 45 in F major (1787–8) |
| 1788 (56) | Symphony No 90 in C major |
|  | Symphony No 91 in E♭ major |
|  | Symphony No 92 in G major, *Oxford* |
|  | *Toy Symphony* in C major, for two violins, double-bass, keyboard and toy trumpet, drum, rattle, triangle and bird-warblers |
| 1789 (57) | String Quartets No 58 and 59 |
|  | Piano Sonata No 46 in C major |
|  | Piano Sonata No 47 in E♭ major (1789–90) |
| before 1790 | Violin Sonata No 1 |
| 1790 (58) | Piano Sonata No 48 in C major (c1790) |
|  | Seven Nocturnes for the King of Naples |
| 1791 (59) | Symphony No 93 in D major |
|  | Symphony No 94 in G major, *Surprise* |
|  | Symphony No 95 in C minor |
|  | Symphony No 96 in D major, *Miracle* |
| 1792 (60) | Symphony No 97 in C major |
|  | Symphony No 98 in B♭ major |
|  | *The Storm*, oratorio |
| before 1793 | String Quartets No 60–9 |
| 1793 (61) | Symphony No 99 in E♭ major |
|  | String Quartets No 70–5, dedicated to Count Apponyi |

| 1794 (62) | Symphony No 100 in G major, *Military* |
| | Symphony No 101 in D major, *Clock* |
| before 1795 | Piano Sonata No 49 in D major |
| 1795 (63) | Symphony No 102 in B♭ major |
| | Symphony No 103 in E♭ major, *Drum Roll* |
| | Symphony No 104 in D major |
| 1796 (64) | Trumpet Concerto in E♭ major |
| | Mass No 9 in B♭, *Heiligenmesse* |
| | Mass No 10 in C major, *Paukenmesse* |
| 1797–8 (65) | *The Creation*, oratorio |
| | String Quartets No 76–81 |
| 1798 (66) | Mass No 11 in D minor, *Nelson* or *Imperial* |
| | Piano Sonata No 50 in E♭ major |
| | *The Seasons*, oratorio (1798–1801) |
| 1799 (67) | String Quartets No 82–3 |
| | Mass No 12 in B♭ major, *Theresienmesse* |
| 1800 (68) | *Te Deum* |
| 1803 (71) | String Quartet No 84 |

Haydn's last twelve symphonies are known as the *Salomon* symphonies. He also composed: 125 trios with barytone, more than twenty Italian and German operas, many songs, some in English.

## HAYDN, (Johann) Michael
*b Rohrau, Austria, 14 September 1737*
*d Salzburg, 10 August 1806, aged sixty-eight*

The younger brother of Joseph Haydn, he was a chorister at St Stephen's Cathedral, Vienna, from 1745 to 1754, succeeding his brother as principal soloist. He became a violinist, organist and academic, teaching himself composition. In 1757 he was appointed *Kapellmeister* to the Bishop of Grosswardien; in 1762 he became conductor of the Salzburg court orchestra; and in 1777 was appointed organist of the churches of Holy Trinity and St Peter. In 1768 he married the singer Maria Magdalene, who took principal soprano parts in several of Mozart's early operas. When Salzburg was taken by the French in 1800 Michael's property was seized, but his brother sent money and he also received valuable commissions from such influential people as the Empress Maria Theresa and Prince Esterházy. He had much influence on Mozart, with whom he collaborated in some of his works.

He left a large number of masses and other sacred works; fourteen secular cantatas; about fifty songs and well over a hundred unaccompanied vocal works; forty-three symphonies; twelve concertos; thirty divertimenti; thirteen other works for orchestra; many minuets and marches; twelve string quartets and other chamber works.

## HENZE, Hans Werner
*b Gütersloh, Westphalia, 1 July 1926*

His father was a schoolteacher. In 1942 he went to the State Music School in Brunswick; in 1944 he was conscripted into the Army and was taken prisoner by the British. He became *repetiteur* with the Bielefeld Municipal Theatre in 1945, and from 1946 continued his musical studies in Heidelberg. In 1950 he was made artistic director and conductor of the ballet of the Wiesbaden State Theatre. Disenchanted with Germany, he moved to Italy; he became a Marxist, and was much preoccupied with Cuban politics. From 1962 to 1966 he gave master-classes at the Salzburg Mozarteum, and from 1969–1970 was teaching and researching in Havana, Cuba; but Rome remained his permanent home. In 1971 he was awarded an honorary doctorate of music at Edinburgh University.

| | |
|---|---|
| 1946 (20) | Chamber Concerto for solo piano, solo flute and strings |
| | Sonata for violin and piano |
| 1947 (21) | Symphony No 1, first version |
| | Violin Concerto No 1 |
| | Concertino for piano and wind orchestra, with percussion |
| | Five Madrigals for small mixed choir and eleven solo instruments |
| | String Quartet No 1 |
| 1948 (22) | *Chorus of the Captured Trojans*, for mixed choir and large orchestra |
| | *The Reproach*, concert aria for baritone, trumpet, trombone and string orchestra |
| | *Lullaby of the Blessed Virgin*, for boys' choir and nine solo instruments |
| | *Whispers from Heavenly Death*, cantata for high voice and eight solo instruments |
| | *The Magic Theater*, one-act opera for actors (new version for singers, 1964) |
| | Chamber Sonata for piano, violin and cello (revised 1963) |
| 1949 (23) | *Jack Pudding*, ballet |
| | *Ballet Variations* |
| | Symphony No 2 |
| | Symphony No 3 (1949–50) |
| | *Apollo et Hyazinthus*, improvisations for harpsichord, contralto and eight solo instruments |
| | Varirations for piano |
| | Serenade for solo cello |
| 1950 (24) | *Symphonic Variations*, for piano and orchestra |
| | Piano Concerto No 1 |
| | *Rosa Silber*, ballet |
| 1951 (25) | *Labyrinth*, choreographic fantasy |
| | *The Sleeping Princess*, ballet |
| | *Boulevard Solitude*, lyric drama |
| | *A Country Doctor*, radio opera (stage version 1964) |
| 1952 (26) | *The Idiot*, ballet-pantomime |
| | *King Stag*, opera (1952–5) |
| | Quintet for wind instruments |
| | String Quartet No 2 |
| 1953 (27) | *Ode to the Westwind*, for cello and orchestra |
| | *The End of a World*, radio opera |
| 1955 (29) | Symphony No 4 (in one movement) |
| | Three Symphonic Studies for orchestra (revised 1964) |
| | *Quattro Poemi*, for orchestra |
| 1956 (30) | *Maratona*, ballet |
| | *Ondine*, ballet (1956–7) |
| | *Concerto per il Marigny*, for piano and seven instruments |
| | Five Neapolitan Songs for medium voice and chamber orchestra |
| 1957 (31) | *Nocturnes and Arias*, for soprano and orchestra |
| | *Sonata per archi* (1957–8) |
| 1958 (32) | *Three Dithyrambs*, for chamber orchestra |
| | Chamber Music |
| | *Der Prinz von Homburg*, opera |
| | *Three Tentos*, for guitar |
| 1959 (33) | *The Emperor's Nightingale*, ballet |
| | *Elegy for Young Lovers*, opera (1959–61) |
| | Piano Sonata |

170

| 1960 (34) | Antifone, for orchestra |
| 1961 (35) | Six absences pour le clavecin, for harpsichord |
| 1962 (36) | Symphony No 5 |
| | Les Caprices de Marianne, incidental music |
| | In re cervo (or The Errantries of Truth), opera |
| | Novae de infinito laudes, cantata |
| 1963 (37) | Los Caprichos, fantasia for orchestra |
| | Ariosi, for soprano, violin and orchestra |
| | Adagio, for clarinet, horn, bassoon and string quintet |
| | Lucy Escott Variations, for piano (also for harpsichord) |
| | Being Beauteous, cantata |
| | Cantata della fiaba estrema |
| 1964 (38) | Tancredi, ballet |
| | The Young Lord, comic opera |
| | Choral Fantasy |
| | Divertimenti for two pianos |
| 1965 (39) | The Bassarids, opera |
| | In Memoriam: The White Rose, for chamber orchestra |
| 1966 (40) | Double Concerto for oboe, harp and strings |
| | Fantasia for strings |
| | Muses of Sicily, concerto for choir, two pianos, wind instruments and timpani |
| 1967 (41) | Piano Concerto No 2 |
| | Telemanniana, for orchestra |
| | Moralities, three scenic cantatas for soli, speaker, choir and small orchestra |
| 1968 (42) | Essay on Pigs, for voice and orchestra |
| | The Raft of the 'Medusa', oratorio vulgare e militare in due parti – per Che Guevara, for soprano, baritone, speaker, mixed choir with nine boys' voices and orchestra |
| 1969 (43) | Symphony No 6 for two chamber orchestras |
| | Compases (viola concerto) for viola and twenty-two players (1969–70) |
| | El Cimarrón, recital for four musicians (1969–70) |
| 1971 (45) | Violin Concerto No 2 |
| | Heliogabalus imperator, for orchestra (1971–2) |
| | Der langwierige Weg in die Wohnung, for orchestra |
| 1973 (47) | La Cubana, a vaudeville |
| | Voices, for two voices and instruments |
| | Tristan, preludes for piano and orchestra |
| 1974–6 (48–50) | We Come to a River, for chorus and orchestra |
| 1975 (49) | Katharina Blum, film score |
| | Ragtimes and Habaneras, for brass band |
| 1975–6 (49–50) | Royal Winter Music, for guitar |
| | String Quartet No 3 |
| 1976 (50) | Don Chisciotte, opera |
| | Jephte, oratorio |
| | Violin Sonata |
| | String Quartet No 4 |
| | Amicizia, for clarinet, trombone, cello, piano and percussion |
| 1976–7 (50–1) | String Quartet No 5 |
| 1977 (51) | Aria de la Folia Española, for chamber orchestra |
| | Il Vitalino Raddoppiato, for violin and chamber orchestra |
| 1980 (54) | Pollicino, opera for children |
| | El Rey de Harlem, Imaginary Theatre I, for solo voice and eight instruments |

*Barcarola*, for orchestra
*The Return of Ulysses*, after Monteverdi
1981 (55)   *The Miracle of the Rose, Imaginary Theatre II.* for clarinet and thirteen players
1983 (57)   *Three Auden Songs*, for tenor and piano


## HÉROLD, Louis Joseph Ferdinand
*b Paris, 28 January 1791*
*d Les Ternes, 19 January 1833, aged forty-one*

He studied piano with Louis Adam, his godfather, and entered the Paris Conservatory in 1806. In 1812 he won the Grand Prix de Rome, then went to Naples as pianist to Queen Caroline. From 1820 to 1827 he was accompanist at the Theâtre des Italiens. In 1827, he became choirmaster at the Académie de Musique (Opéra). Consumption, from which he had suffered for a long time, killed him.

1812 (21)   *Mlle de la Vallière*, cantata
1813 (22)   *Hymne sur la Transfiguration*, for voices and orchestra
1815 (24)   *La Gioventù di Enrico Quinto*, opera
1816 (25)   *Charles de France*, opera (with Boïeldieu)
1817 (26)   *Les Rosières*, opera
            *La Clochette*, opera
1818 (27)   *Le Premier Venu*, opera
1819 (28)   *Les Troqueurs*, opera
            *L'Amour Platonique*, opera (rehearsal only)
1820 (29)   *L'Auteur Mort et Vivant*, opera
1823 (32)   *Le Muletier*, opera
            *Lasthénie*, opera
            *Vendôme en Espagne*, opera (with Auber)
1824 (33)   *Le Roi René*, opera
1825 (34)   *Le Lapin Blanc*, opera
1826 (35)   *Marie*, opera
1827 (36)   *Astolph et Joconde*, ballet
            *La Somnambule*, ballet
1828 (37)   *Lydie*, ballet
            *La fille mal gardée*, ballet
1829 (38)   *La Belle au bois dormant*, ballet
            *L'Illusion*, opera
            *Emmeline*, opera
1830 (39)   *L'Auberge d'Aurey*, opera (with Carafa)
1831 (40)   *Zampa*, opera
1832 (41)   *La Médicine sans médicin*, opera
            *Le Pré aux Clercs*, opera
1833 (42)   *Ludovic*, opera (completed by Halévy)

Hérold also composed incidental music for *Missolonghi*, two symphonies, three string quartets and piano pieces.


## HINDEMITH, Paul
*b Hanau, 16 November 1895*
*d Frankfurt, 28 December 1963, aged sixty-eight*

He was one of three gifted children who appeared in public very young as a trio. At the age of thirteen he entered the Hoch Conservatory in Frankfurt-am-Main. He was conscripted into the Army in 1917 and served for eighteen months. He then became principal violinist in the Frankfurt Opera Orchestra until 1923, and continued his career as performer and teacher. In 1927 he moved to Berlin to become professor of composition at the Hochschule, but after 1933 he fell foul of Nazi propaganda. He left Germany in 1935, not returning until after the war. He went to Turkey for a year, then to the USA, where in 1940 he joined the musical staff of Yale and in 1946 became an American citizen. He toured Europe, was appointed to the music faculty at Zurich University in 1948, and settled in Switzerland in 1953. His health declined rapidly in the 1960s, and he died of a stroke.

| | |
|---|---|
| 1916 (21) | Cello Concerto No 1 (unpublished) |
| 1917 (22) | Three Pieces for cello and piano |
| 1918 (23) | Violin Sonata No 1 in E♭ major |
| | Violin Sonata No 2 in D major |
| | String Quartet No 1 in F minor |
| 1919 (24) | Viola Sonata in F major |
| | Sonata for solo viola |
| | Cello Sonata |
| 1921–2 (26) | *Chamber Music* No 1 |
| 1922 (27) | String Quartet No 2 in C major |
| | String Quartet No 3 |
| | Suite for klavier |
| | Sonata for solo viola |
| | *Die Junge Magd*, six songs |
| 1923 (28) | String Quartet No 4 |
| | *Kleine Sonata für Viola d'amore und Klavier* |
| | Sonata for solo cello |
| 1924 (29) | Piano Concerto |
| | *Chamber Music* No 2 |
| | Sonata for solo violin |
| | *Das Marienleben*, song cycle |
| 1925 (30) | Concerto for orchestra |
| | *Chamber Music* No 3 and 4 |
| 1926 (31) | *Cardillac*, opera |
| 1927 (32) | *Chamber Music* No 5 |
| 1928 (33) | Concerto for organ and chamber orchestra |
| | *Chamber Music* No 6 |
| 1930 (35) | *Concert Music*, for piano, harps and brass |
| 1931 (36) | *The Unceasing*, oratorio |
| 1932 (37) | *Philharmonic Concerto* |
| 1934 (39) | *Mathis der Maler*, opera, also symphony |
| 1935 (40) | Viola Concerto, *Der Schwanendreher* |
| | Concerto for orchestra |
| 1937 (42) | *Symphonic Dances*, for orchestra |
| | Organ Sonatas No 1 and 2 |
| 1938 (43) | *Nobilissima visione*, ballet |
| 1939 (44) | Violin Concerto |
| 1940 (45) | Symphony in E♭ major |
| | Cello Concerto No 2 |
| | Theme and Variations for piano and strings, *The four Temperaments* |
| | Harp Sonata |
| 1943 (48) | *Symphonic Metamorphoses on a theme by Weber*, for orchestra |
| | *Cupid and Psyche*, overture |
| | *Ludus Tonalis*, for piano |
| 1944 (49) | *Hérodiade*, for speaker and chamber orchestra |
| 1945 (50) | Piano Concerto |

| 1946 (51) | *When Lilacs in the Dooryard Bloomed – an American Requiem* (for Walt Whitman) |
| 1947 (52) | *Symphonia Serena* (possibly 1946) |
| | Clarinet Concerto |
| 1948 (53) | Concerto for trumpet, bassoon and strings |
| | Septet for wind instruments |
| 1949 (54) | Horn Concerto |
| | Concerto for woodwind, harp and orchestra |
| | Organ Sonata No 3 |
| 1950 (55) | Sinfonietta |
| | *Requiem for Those We Love* (possibly 1946) |
| 1951 (56) | *Der Harmonie der Welt*, symphony |
| 1952 (57) | Symphony In Bb for military band |
| | Sonata for four horns |
| 1958 (63) | Octet |

## HODDINOTT, Alun
*b Bargoed, Glamorgan, 11 August 1929*

He was educated at Gowerton Grammar School and the University College of South Wales, graduating in 1949. He then studied for some years with Arthur Benjamin. He was awarded the Walford Davies prize for composition at the age of twenty-four. In 1951 he was appointed lecturer in music at Cardiff College of Music and Drama; he became lecturer in music at the University College of South Wales in 1959, reader in music in 1965, and professor of music in 1967. He was awarded the Arnold Bax Medal for composers in 1957 and was made an Hon RAM in 1971.

| 1953 (24) | fp *Fugal Overture*, for orchestra |
| | fp *Nocturne*, for orchestra |
| 1954 (25) | fp Concerto for clarinet and string orchestra |
| 1955 (26) | fp Symphony No 1 |
| 1956 (27) | fp Septet for wind, strings and piano |
| 1957 (28) | *Rondo Scherzoso*, for trumpet and piano |
| 1958 (29) | fp Harp Concerto |
| | fp Serenade for string orchestra |
| | fp Concertino for viola and small orchestra |
| | fp Four Welsh Dances for orchestra |
| 1959 (30) | fp *Nocturne and Dance*, for harp and orchestra |
| | fp Piano Sonata No 1 |
| 1960 (31) | fp Concerto No 1 for piano, wind and percussion |
| | fp Sextet for flute, clarinet, bassoon, violin, viola and cello |
| 1961 (32) | fp Concerto No 2 for piano and orchestra |
| | fp Violin Concerto |
| 1962 (33) | fp *Rebecca*, ballad for unaccompanied mixed voices |
| | fp Variations for flute, clarinet, harp and string quartet |
| | fp Symphony No 2 |
| 1963 (34) | fp Divertimento for oboe, clarinet, horn and bassoon |
| | fp Sinfonia for string orchestra |
| 1964 (35) | fp *Danegeld*, six episodes for unaccompanied mixed voices |
| | fp *Jack Straw*, overture |
| | fp Harp Sonata |
| | fp *Toccata all Giga*, for organ |
| | fp *Intrada*, for organ |
| | fp *Sarum Fanfare*, for organ |
| 1965 (36) | fp *Dives and Lazarus*, cantata |

|            |                                                                                      |
|------------|--------------------------------------------------------------------------------------|
|            | *fp* Concerto Grosso No 1                                                            |
|            | *fp* *Aubade and Scherzo*, for horn and strings                                     |
| 1966 (37)  | *fp* String Quartet No 1                                                            |
|            | *fp* Concerto No 3 for piano and orchestra                                          |
|            | *fp* *Pantomime*, overture                                                          |
|            | *fp* Concerto Grosso No 2                                                           |
|            | *fp* *Variants*, for orchestra                                                     |
|            | *fp* Piano Sonata No 4                                                             |
| 1967 (38)  | *fp* *Night Music*, for orchestra                                                  |
|            | *fp* Clarinet Sonata                                                               |
|            | *fp* Organ Concerto                                                                |
|            | *fp* Suite for harp                                                                |
| 1968 (39)  | *fp* Symphony No 3                                                                 |
|            | *fp* *Nocturnes and Cadenzas*, for clarinet, violin and piano                      |
|            | *fp* *Roman Dream*, scena for solo soprano and instrumental ensemble               |
|            | *fp* *An Apple Tree and a Pig*, scena for unaccompanied mixed voices               |
|            | *fp* Sinfonietta 1                                                                 |
|            | *fp* Piano Sonata No 5                                                             |
|            | *fp* Divertimenti for eight instruments                                            |
|            | *fp* *Fioriture*, for orchestra                                                    |
| 1969 (40)  | *fp* *Black Bart*, ballade for mixed voices and orchestra                          |
|            | *fp* *Nocturnes and Cadenzas*, for cello and orchestra                             |
|            | *fp* Violin Sonata No 1                                                            |
|            | *fp* Horn Concerto                                                                 |
|            | *fp* *Investiture Dances*, for orchestra                                           |
|            | *fp* Sinfonietta 2                                                                 |
|            | *fp* Divertimento for orchestra                                                    |
|            | *fp* Symphony No 4                                                                 |
| 1970 (41)  | *fp* Fantasy for harp                                                              |
|            | *fp* Sinfonietta 3                                                                 |
|            | *fp* Violin Sonata No 2                                                            |
|            | *fp* Cello Sonata                                                                  |
|            | *fp* *The Sun, the Great Luminary of the Universe*, for orchestra                  |
| 1971 (42)  | *fp* Concerto for oboe and strings                                                 |
|            | *fp* Concertino for trumpet, horn and orchestra                                    |
|            | *fp* *Out of the Deep*, motet for unaccompanied mixed voices                       |
|            | *fp* Violin Sonata No 3                                                            |
|            | *fp* Horn Sonata                                                                   |
|            | *fp* *The Tree of Life*, for soprano and tenor, chorus, organ and orchestra        |
| 1972 (43)  | *fp* *Aubade*, for small orchestra                                                 |
|            | *fp* *The Hawk is Set Free*, for orchestra                                         |
|            | *fp* Piano Sonata No 6                                                             |
| 1973 (44)  | *fp* *The Floore of Heav'n*, for orchestra                                         |
|            | *fp* Symphony No 5                                                                 |
| 1974 (45)  | *fp* *The Beach of Falesa*, opera                                                  |
|            | *fp* *Ritornelli*, for solo trombone, wind instruments and percussion             |
| 1975 (46)  | *fp* *Landscapes*, for orchestra                                                   |
|            | *The Magician*, one-act opera                                                      |
|            | *Five Landscapes*, for tenor and piano                                            |
| 1976 (47)  | Violin Sonata No 4                                                                 |
|            | *A Contemplation upon Flowers*, for soprano and orchestra                         |
| 1977 (48)  | *What the Old Man Does is Always Right*, one-act opera                            |
|            | *French Suite*, for orchestra                                                      |
|            | *Passaggio*, for orchestra                                                         |

                    *Sinfonia Fidei*, for soprano, tenor, chorus and orchestra
                    *Italian Suite*, for recorder and guitar
                    Cello Sonata No 2
1978 (49)           *Dulcia Iuventutis*, for chorus and piano duet
                    Sonata for guitar
1979 (50)           *The Rajah's Diamond*, one-act opera
                    Sonatina for two pianos
                    *Scena*, for string quartet
                    Ritornelli for brass
(possibly 1979) *Welsh Dances*, Suite No 2, for orchestra
Since 1980          *French Suite*, for small orchestra
                    *Passaggio*, for orchestra
                    *The Heaventree of Stars*, for violin and orchestra
                    *Italian Suite*, for recorder or flute and guitar
                    *Ritornelli 2*, for brass quintet
                    Scena for String Quartet
                    Sonata No 2 for cello and piano
                    Sonatina for Guitar
                    Sonata for Organ
                    *Dulcia Iuventutis*, 3 songs for mixed voices and piano duet
                    *The Trumpet Major*, opera
                    *Nocturnes & Cadenzas*, for solo flute
                    *Doubles*, for oboe, harpsichord and strings
                    Five Studies for Orchestra
                    *Lanterne Des Morts*, for orchestra
                    *Great Is The Lord*, for choir and organ

## HOLBORNE, Anthony
*d c1602*

The first recorded date for him is that of his marriage at St Margaret's, Westminster on 14 June 1584. His name occurs in various letters by other people, showing that his reputation was high, but there is little exact documentation available. About three-quarters of his output consists of dances that made him widely popular in his life-time, but he was not a major composer.

## HOLBROOKE, Joseph
*b Croydon, 5 July 1878*
*d London, 5 August 1958, aged eighty*

He studied at the Royal Academy of Music. He made his piano début at the age of twelve, playing in music hall, and later supported himself by playing piano and conducting. He spent all his life as a composer, creating works for large orchestras.

1886–90 (18–22) Piano Concerto
1900 (22)           *The Raven*, symphonic poem
                    Variations on 'Three Blind Mice', for orchestra
                    Variations on 'The Girl I Left Behind Me', for orchestra
1901 (23)           *Ode to Victory*, for chorus and orchestra
1901–3 (23–5) *Ulalume*, symphonic poem
1902 (24)           *Queen Mab*, for chorus and orchestra
1903 (25)           *The New Renaissance*, overture
                    *The Bells*, for chorus and orchestra
1904 (26)           *The Vikings*, symphonic poem

| 1905 (27) | *Les Hommages*, for orchestra |
| 1906 (28) | *Byron*, for chorus and orchestra |
| | Variations on 'Auld Lang Syne', for orchestra |
| 1907 (29) | *Apollo and the Seaman*, for orchestra |
| | Piano Concerto No 1 |
| 1908 (30) | Dramatic Choral Symphony |
| 1909 (31) | *Pierrot and Pierrette*, opera |
| 1912 (34) | *The Children of Don*, opera |
| 1914 (36) | *Dylan*, opera |
| 1915 (37) | *The Enchanter*, opera |
| 1917 (39) | Violin Concerto |
| 1925 (47) | *The Birds of Rheannon*, symphonic poem |
| | Symphony No 3, *Ships* |
| 1927 (49) | *Columba*, for orchestra |
| 1928 (50) | Piano Concerto No 2 |
| 1929 (51) | *Bronwen*, opera |
| | Symphony No 4 |
| 1936 (58) | Cello Concerto |
| | *Aucassin et Nicolette*, ballet |
| 1939 (61) | *Tamerlaine*, concerto for clarinet or saxophone, bassoon and orchestra |
| Undated | *The Red Mask*, ballet |
| | *The Moth and the Flame*, ballet |
| | *Coromanthe*, ballet |
| | *The Sailor's Arms*, opera |
| | *The Snob*, opera |
| | *Tamlane*, opera |
| | Two late ballets in MS |
| | Four symphonies in MS |
| | Suite for chorus and orchestra |
| | Sinfonietta for chamber orchestra |

Holbrooke also wrote twenty-four works for brass band, a large number of chamber works, some works for piano and many songs with piano or instrumental accompaniment.


## HOLLOWAY, Robin
*b Leamington Spa, 19 October 1943*

From 1952 to 1957 he was a chorister at St Paul's Cathedral, and also attended Dartington Summer School. From 1959 to 1963 he was a pupil of Alexander Goehr, and from 1961 to 1964 was at King's College, Cambridge. He studied from 1965 to 1967 at New College, Oxford, then returned to Cambridge as a research student at Gonville and Caius College, gaining a fellowship there in 1969.

| 1962 (19) | *Garden Music*, Op 1, for eight players |
| 1964 (21) | Concertino No 1, Op 2, for small orchestra (new finale 1968–9) |
| 1964–5 (21–2) | *Three Poems of William Empson*, Op 3, for mezzo-soprano and ensemble |
| 1965 (22) | Music for Eliot's *Sweeney Agonistes*, Op 4 |
| 1965–6 (22–3) | *In Chymick Art*, Op 5, cantata for soprano, baritone and nine players |
| | Concerto for organ and wind, Op 6 |
| | *Four Housman Fragments*, Op 7, for soprano and piano |
| 1966–9 (23–6) | Concerto for orchestra, Op 8 |
| 1967 (24) | *Melodrama*, Op 9, for speaker, small male chorus and ensemble |

177

Concertino No 2, Op 10, for small orchestra (menuetto added 1974)
1968 (25)    Divertimento No 1, Op 11, for amateur orchestra
1968–9 (25–6) *Four Poems of Stevie Smith*, Op 12, for unaccompanied soprano
1969–70 (26–7) *Scenes from Schumann*, Op 13, for orchestra
1970 (27)    *The Wind Shifts*, Op 14, for high voice and strings
1971 (28)    *Banal Sojourn*, Op 15, for high voice and piano
             *Fantasy-Pieces*, Op 16, on the Heine 'Liederkreis' of Schumann, for
             thirteen players
1972 (29)    *Evening with Angels*, Op 17, for sixteen players
             Divertimento No 2, Op 18, for wind nonet
             Georgian Songs, Op 19, for baritone and piano
1972–3 (29–30) *Cantata on the Death of God*, Op 20
             *Five Little Songs about Death*, Op 21, for unaccompanied soprano
1973 (30)    Five Madrigals, Op 22, for unaccompanied mixed voices
1973–4 (30–1) *Domination of Black*, Op 23, symphonic poem for large orchestra
1974 (31)    *Lights Out*, Op 24, four poems of Edward Thomas for baritone and
             piano
             *In the Thirtieth Year*, Op 25, for tenor and piano
             *Author of Light*, Op 26, four Jacobean songs for contralto and piano
             *The Leaves Cry*, Op 27, two songs for soprano and piano
1974–5 (31–2) *Sea Surface Full of Clouds*, Op 28, cantata
1975 (32)    Concertino No 3, *Homage to Weill*, Op 29, for eleven players
             *Clarissa*, Op 30, opera
1976 (33)    *Romanzá*, Op 31, for violin and small orchestra
1977 (34)    *This Is Just to Say*, Op 32, song cycle for tenor and piano
             Divertimento No 3, *Nursery Rhymes*, Op 33, for soprano and wind
             quintet
             *The Rivers of Hell*, Op 34, for chamber ensemble
             *The Blue Doom of Summer*, Op 35 No 1, cantata for voice and harp
             *Willow Cycle*, Op 35 No 2, for tenor and harp
             *Hymn for Voices*, Op 36, for unaccompanied chorus
             *From High Windows*, Op 37, song cycle for baritone and piano
             *The Consolation of Music*, Op 38 No 1, for chorus
1978 (35)    *He-She-Together*, Op 38 No 2, for chorus
             *Killing Time*, for unaccompanied soprano (texts by Auden, Stevie
             Smith, and Raleigh)
             *Three Slithy Toves*, for two clarinets
1978–9 (35–6) *The Noon's Repose*, Op 39, three songs for tenor and harp
             Second Concerto for orchestra, Op 40
1979 (36)    Serenade in C, Op 41
             *Conundrums*, for soprano and wind quintet
1979–80 (36–7) Idyll for small orchestra
             Sonata for horn and orchestra
             Adagio and Rondo for horn and orchestra
             Aria for chamber orchestra
1980 (37)    Ode for four winds and strings
1980–1 (37–8) *Wherever We May Be*, five songs for soprano and piano
1981 (38)    *Clarissa Symphony*, for soprano, tenor and orchestra
             Sonata for solo violin
             *Brand*, dramatic ballad for soli, chorus, organ and orchestra
             *The Lovers' Well*, for bass-baritone and piano
1981–2 (38–9) *Men Marching*, for brass band
             *From Hills and Valleys*, for brass band
1982 (39)    Suite for Saxophone
             *Anthem*, for unaccompanied chorus
             *Women in War*, review for four female soloists and piano

          *Serenata Notturna,* for four horns and small orchestra
1982–3 (39–40) *Showpiece* (Concertino No 4) for fourteen players
1983 (40)     Second Idyll for small orchestra
1983–4 (40–1) Viola Concerto
          Serenade in E flat for wind quintet and string quintet
1984 (41)     *Moments of Vision,* cycle for speaker and four players
          Romanza for oboe and strings
          *On Hope,* cantata for soprano, mezzo and string quartet


## HOLMBOE, Vagn
*b Horsens, Denmark, 20 December 1909*

He first trained in Copenhagen and then in 1933 embarked on a tour to study Romanian folk music, returning to Denmark in 1934. He taught at the Danish Institute for the Blind in the 1940s, and was music critic of a Copenhagen daily newspaper from 1947 to 1950. In the early 1950s he joined the staff of the Copenhagen Conservatory, where he was appointed professor of composition in 1955.

1927 (18)     Symphony in F
1928 (19)     Symphony in D
          Quintet for viola and string quartet
1929 (20)     Concerto for orchestra
1930–1 (21–2) Three String Trios
1931 (22)     Concerto for chamber orchestra
          *Requiem,* for boys' voices and chamber orchestra
1932 (23)     Overture
          Concerto for strings
          Trio for oboe, bassoon and horn
          Duets for flute and viola
          Duo for flute and violin
          Duo for flute and cello
1933 (24)     Wind Quintet
1935 (26)     Suite No 1 for chamber orchestra
          Overture
          Symphony No 1 for chamber orchestra
          Violin Sonata No 1
1936 (27)     Suite No 2 for chamber orchestra
          Suite No 3 for chamber orchestra
          Serenade for clarinet and piano quartet
          Quartet for flute and piano trio
          Quintet for flute, oboe, clarinet, violin and viola
1937 (28)     *Psalm LXII,* for boys' voices
1938 (29)     Violin Concerto
          *Rapsodisk Interludium,* for clarinet, violin and piano
1939 (30)     Symphony No 2
          Concerto for piano and chamber orchestra
          Violin Sonata No 2
1940 (31)     Chamber Concerto No 2 for flute, violin and strings
          Chamber Concerto No 3 for clarinet, two trumpets, two horns and
            strings
          Concertino for violin, viola and strings
          Concertino No 2 for violin and strings
          *The Devil, the Mayor,* opera
          Serenade for flute and piano trio
          Notturno for wind quintet

| | |
|---|---|
| 1941 (32) | Symphony No 3, *Sinfonia Rustica* |
| | Symphony No 4, *Sinfonia Sacra*, for chorus and orchestra |
| | Symphonic Overture |
| 1942 (33) | Chamber Concerto No 4 for violin, cello and orchestra |
| | *Sonatina capricciosa*, for flute and piano |
| 1943 (34) | Chamber Concerto No 5 for viola and orchestra |
| | *Den Galsindede Tyk*, ballet |
| | Chamber Concerto No 6 for violin and orchestra |
| | Four Songs |
| 1944 (35) | Symphony No 5 |
| | Chamber Concerto No 7 for oboe and orchestra |
| | *Jeg Ved En Urt*, for chorus |
| 1945 (36) | Chamber Concerto No 8 (Sinfonia concertante) |
| 1946 (37) | Chamber Concerto No 9 for violin, viola and orchestra |
| | Chamber Concerto No 10 for woodwind, brass and strings |
| | Cantata No 5 (Cantatas 1–4 and 6–13, 1940–72, unpublished) |
| | *Lave og Jon*, opera |
| 1947 (38) | Symphony No 6 |
| 1948 (39) | Chamber Concerto No 11 for trumpet, horns and strings |
| 1949 (40) | String Quartet No 1 |
| | String Quartet No 2 |
| | String Quartet No 3 |
| 1950 (41) | Symphony No 7 |
| | Chamber Concerto No 12 for trombone and orchestra |
| | *Isomeric*, for two violins and piano |
| 1951 (42) | Chamber Symphony No 1 |
| | *Primavera*, for flute and piano trio |
| 1951–2 (42–3) | Symphony No 8, *Sinfonia Boreale* |
| 1953 (44) | *Traet*, for four voices and chamber orchestra |
| 1954 (45) | Sinfonia in memoriam |
| | String Quartet No 4 |
| | Piano Trio |
| 1955 (46) | String Quartet No 5 |
| 1955–6 (46–7) | Chamber Concerto No 13 for oboe, viola and orchestra |
| 1956 (47) | *Epitaph*, symphonic metamorphoses |
| | *Quartetto medico*, for flute, oboe, clarinet and percussion |
| 1957 (48) | Flute Sonata |
| | Concertino for recorder and string trio |
| | *Aspekte*, for wind quintet |
| 1957–62 (48–53) | *Kairos* (Sinfonias No 1–4), for strings |
| 1959–60 (50–1) | *The Knife*, for chamber opera |
| 1960 (51) | *Monolith*, symphonic metamorphoses |
| | *The Forest*, for solo voices, chorus and orchestra |
| | *Solhymne*, for chorus |
| | *Tropos*, for viola and string quartet |
| 1961 (52) | String Quartet No 6 |
| 1961–2 (52–3) | *Epilogue*, symphonic metamorphoses |
| | Quintet for two trumpets, horn, trombone and tuba |
| 1962 (53) | Double-bass Sonata |
| 1962–4 (53–5) | *Hevjid i homrum*, for four voices |
| 1963 (54) | Sonata for violin and viola |
| 1963–4 (54–5) | *Requiem for Nietzsche*, for solo voices, chorus and orchestra |
| 1964 (55) | String Quartet No 7 |
| 1965 (56) | String Quartet No 8 |
| | Violin Sonata No 3 |
| 1966 (57) | String Quartet No 9 |

                    Quartet for flute and string trio
                    Sonatina for oboe and piano
1966–8 (57–9) Three Jaeger-sänge
1967–8 (58–9) Symphony No 9
1968 (59)     Chamber Symphony No 2
              Trio for flute, cello and piano
1969 (60)     String Quartet No 10
              Cello Sonata
1970 (61)     Chamber Symphony No 3, *Frise*
1970–1 (61–2) Symphony No 10
1971 (62)     *Tempo Variabile*, for orchestra
1972 (63)     *A Lyke Wake Dirge*, for four voices
              *The Wee Wee Man*, for four voices
              String Quartet No 11
1973 (64)     String Quartet No 12
              *Diafora*, for strings
              Sextet for flute, clarinet, bassoon and string trio
              *Ondata*, for six percussion
1974 (65)     Violin Concerto
              Recorder Concerto
              *Fanfare*, for three trumpets and timpani
1975 (66)     String Quartet No 13
              String Quartet No 14
              Flute Concerto
              *Triade*, for trumpet and organ
1976 (67)     Tuba Concerto
              *Nuigen*, for piano trio
1976–7 (67–8) *Firefir*, for four flutes
Holmboe has also composed pieces for piano.


**HOLST, Gustav**
*b Cheltenham, 21 September 1874*
*d London, 25 May 1934, aged fifty-nine*

He was of Swedish descent; his father taught music and his mother was a
pianist. He studied at the Royal College of Music and became a lifelong friend of
fellow-pupil Vaughan Williams. After leaving college he earned his living
mainly as an orchestral trombonist. In 1903 he became a teacher, remaining so
for the rest of his life, and worked at St Paul's Girls' School, Morley College, and
at the Royal College from 1919 to 1923. A fall in 1923 permanently weakened his
health. He visited the USA twice to conduct his own music. He refused to accept
honorary degrees, but did accept the Gold Medal of the Royal Philharmonic
Society in 1930.

1895 (21)     *The Revoke*, one-act opera
1896 (22)     *Fantasiestücke*, for oboe and string quartet
              Quintet for wind and piano
              Four Songs
1897 (23)     *A Winter Idyll*, for orchestra
              *Clear and Cool*, for choir and orchestra
1898 (24)     *Ornulf's Drapa*, for baritone and orchestra
1899 (25)     *Walt Whitman*, overture
              Five Part-songs for mixed voices (1899–1900)
              *Sita*, opera (1899–1906)
1900 (26)     *Cotswolds Symphony*
              *Suite de Ballet*, in E♭

|            | *Ave Maria*, for eight-part female choir |
| 1902 (28)  | *The Youth's Choice*, opera |
|            | Four Part-songs for mixed voices |
|            | Six Songs for baritone |
|            | Six Songs for soprano |
| 1903 (29)  | *Indra*, symphonic poem |
|            | *King Estmere*, for choir and orchestra |
|            | Quintet for wind |
| 1904 (30)  | *The Mystic Trumpeter*, for soprano and orchestra |
| 1905 (31)  | *Song of the Night*, for violin and orchestra |
|            | Four Carols for mixed voices |
|            | Song from 'The Princess' |
| 1906 (32)  | *Songs of the West*, for orchestra |
|            | *Two Songs Without Words*, dedicated to Vaughan Williams (*qv*) |
| 1907 (33)  | *Somerset Rhapsody*, for orchestra |
|            | Nine Hymns from the Rig-Veda (1907–08) |
| 1908 (34)  | *Savitri*, opera |
|            | Choral Hymns from the Rig-Veda, Group 1 |
| 1909 (35)  | *A Vision of Dame Christian*, incidental music |
|            | First Suite for Military Band, in E♭ major |
|            | Choral Hymns from the Rig-Veda, Group 2 |
| 1910 (36)  | *Beni Mora*, oriental suite |
|            | *The Cloud Messenger*, ode |
|            | Choral Hymns from the Rig-Veda, Group 3 |
| 1911 (37)  | *Invocations*, for cello and orchestra |
|            | *Oh England My Country*, for choir and orchestra |
|            | *Hecuba's Lament*, for choir and orchestra |
|            | Second Suite for Military Band, in F major |
| 1912 (38)  | Choral Hymns from the Rig-Veda, Group 4 |
| 1913 (39)  | *St Paul's Suite*, for strings |
|            | *Hymn to Dionysus*, for choir and orchestra |
| 1914–16 (40–2) | *The Planets*, orchestral suite in seven movements |
| 1915 (41)  | *Japanese Suite*, for orchestra |
| 1916 (42)  | Five Part-songs |
|            | Four Songs for voice and violin |
|            | Three Festival Choruses |
| 1917 (43)  | *Hymn of Jesus*, for two choruses, semi-chorus and orchestra |
|            | *A Dream of Christmas,* for female chorus, piano and strings |
| 1919 (45)  | Festival Te Deum |
|            | Ode to Death |
| 1921 (47)  | *The Perfect Fool*, opera |
|            | *The Lure*, ballet |
| 1922 (48)  | Fugal Overture No 1 |
| 1923 (49)  | Fugal Overture No 2 |
|            | Choral Symphony (1923–4) |
| 1924 (50)  | *At the Boar's Head*, opera |
|            | *Terzetto*, for flute, oboe and viola |
|            | Two Motets for mixed voices |
| 1925–6 (51) | Seven Part-songs (Bridges) |
| 1926 (52)  | *The Golden Goose*, choral ballet |
|            | *Chrissemas Day in the Morning*, for piano |
| 1927 (53)  | *Egdon Heath*, symphonic poem |
|            | *The Morning of the Year*, choral ballet |
|            | *The Coming of Christ*, mystery play |
|            | Two Folk Song arrangements for piano |
| 1928 (54)  | *Moorside Suite*, for brass band |

1929 (55)    Concerto for two violins
               *The Tale of the Wandering Scholar*, opera
               Twelve Songs
1930 (56)    Choral Fantasia
               *Hammersmith*, Prelude and Scherzo, for orchestra
1933 (59)    *Lyric Movement*, for viola and strings
               *Brook Green Suite*, for strings

## HONEGGER, Arthur
*b Le Havre, 10 March 1892*
*d Paris, 27 November 1955, aged sixty-three*

Though he was born in France and spent most of his life there he retained his Swiss citizenship. At the age of eighteen he went to the Zurich Conservatory for two years, his studies being interrupted by military service in 1914. In the 1920s he came under the influence of the group of Paris musicians known as 'Les Six', led by Satie, but soon rejected it. Until World War II he spent his time writing, living during the war in occupied Paris. He died of a heart disease.

1916–17 (24) String Quartet No 1
1916–18 (24–6) Violin Sonata No 1
1919 (27)    Violin Sonata No 2
               *Dance of the Goat*, for flute
1920 (28)    *Pastorale d'été*, for orchestra
               Viola Sonata
               Cello Sonata
1921 (29)    *King David*, oratorio with spoken narration
               *Horace Victorieux*, 'mimed symphony'
               Sonatina for clarinet and piano (1921–2)
1923 (31)    *Chant de joie*
1924 (32)    *Pacific 231*, Mouvement Symphonique No 1, for orchestra
1925 (33)    *Judith*, opera
               Concertino for piano and orchestra
1927 (35)    *Antigone*, lyric drama
1928 (36)    *Rugby*, Mouvement Symphonique No 2, for orchestra
1930 (38)    Symphony No 1
               *Les aventures du roi pausole*, light opera
1931 (39)    *Cries of the World*, for chorus and orchestra
               *Amphion*, ballet-melodrama
1932 (40)    Mouvement Symphonique No 3, for orchestra (1932–3)
               Sonatina for violin and cello
1934 (42)    Cello Concerto
               *Sémiramis*, ballet, using voice and Ondes Martenot
               String Quartet No 2 (1934–6)
1936 (44)    Nocturne
               String Quartet No 3
1937 (45)    *L'Aiglon*, opera (with Ibert, *qv*)
               *1001 Nights*, a musical spectacle
1938 (46)    *La Famille Cardinal*, opera (with Ibert)
               *Joan of Arc at the Stake*, incidental music
               *La danse des morts*, for solo voices, chorus and orchestra
1941 (49)    Symphony No 2, for strings and trumpet
1943 (51)    *Jour de fête suisse*, suite
1946 (54)    Symphony No 3, *Liturgique*
               Symphony No 4, *Deliciae basiliensis*
1949 (57)    Concerto da camera

| 1951 (59) | Symphony No 5, *Di Tre Re* |
| | *Monopartita*, for orchestra; a suite whose movements are linked and intended to form a single musical structure |
| 1952 (60) | *Suite archaïque* |
| 1953 (61) | *Christmas Cantata* |


## HOPKINSON, Francis
*b Philadelphia, 21 September 1737*
*d Philadelphia, 9 May 1791, aged fifty-three*

He was, in his own words, 'the first Native of the United States who has produced a Musical Composition'. His work was entirely vocal, with organ or harpsichord accompaniment. He was a judge from 1779 until his death. He wrote essays, poetry and pamphlets; drew and designed well; invented a shaded candlestick, a new method of quilling a harpsichord, and a metronome. As a statesman he was one of the signers of the Declaration of Independence.

| 1759 (22) | *My Days Have Been So Wondrous Free*, for voice and harpsichord |
| 1763 (26) | *Collection of Psalm Tunes* |
| 1767 (30) | *The Psalms of David*, for voices and organ |
| 1788 (51) | Seven Songs |


## HOWELLS, Herbert (Norman)
*b Lydney, Gloucestershire, 17 October 1892*
*d London, February 1983, aged ninety*

In 1912 he won an open scholarship to the Royal College of Music. Ill-health cut short his first appointment as sub-organist at Salisbury Cathedral, but in 1920 he started teaching composition at the Royal College of Music and continued until the age of eighty. From 1936 to 1962 he was director of music at St Paul's Girls' School, succeeding Holst. In 1950 he was appointed King Edward VII professor of music at London University. He was made a CBE in 1953 and a Companion of Honour in 1972.

| 1913 (21) | Piano Concerto No 1 |
| 1914 (22) | *The Tinker's Song*, for two voices and piano |
| | Variations for eleven instruments |
| 1915 (23) | Three Dances for violin and orchestra |
| 1916 (24) | Suite, 'The B's', for orchestra |
| | *Lady Audrey's Suite*, for string quartet |
| | Piano Quartet |
| 1917 (25) | Elegy for viola and string quartet |
| | *Rhapsodic Quintet*, for clarinet and string quartet |
| | Suite for clarinet and piano |
| 1917–20 (25–8) | *Puck's Minuet and Merry-Eye*, for orchestra |
| 1918 (26) | *Sir Patrick Spens*, for chorus and orchestra |
| | *Phantasy*, for string quartet |
| 1918–20 (26–8) | Three Carol-anthems |
| 1918–23 (26–31) | Three Sonatas for violin and piano |
| 1922 (30) | *Sine Nomine*, for two voices, chorus and orchestra |
| | *Procession*, for orchestra |
| 1923 (31) | *Pastoral Rhapsody*, for orchestra |
| | String Quartet, *In Gloucestershire* |
| 1923–5 (31–3) | Six Choral Songs |
| 1924 (32) | Piano Concerto No 2 |
| 1925 (33) | *My Eyes for Beauty Pine*, for chorus and organ |

|  |  | *Paradise Rondel*, for orchestra |
| 1933 | (41) | *A Kent Yeoman's Wooing Song*, for voices, chorus and orchestra |
| 1934 | (42) | *Pageantry*, for brass band |
| 1938 | (46) | *Hymnus Paradisi*, for voices, chorus and orchestra |
| 1939 | (47) | Concerto for strings |
| 1941 | (49) | Four Anthems |
| 1943 | (51) | Sonata for oboe and piano |
| 1944 | (52) | *Collegium Regale*, canticles for chorus |
|  |  | Suite for strings |
| 1946 | (54) | *Gloucester Canticles*, for chorus |
| 1949 | (57) | *Music for a Prince*, suite for orchestra |
|  |  | Sonata for clarinet and piano |
|  |  | *A Maid Peerless*, for four voices, female chorus, strings and piano |
| 1949–58 | (57–66) | Three Motets |
| 1951 | (59) | Cello Concerto (unfinished) |
| 1954 | (62) | *Missa Sabrinensis*, for voices, chorus and orchestra |
|  |  | *St Paul's Canticles*, for chorus |
| 1956 | (64) | *An English Mass*, for chorus |
| 1958 | (66) | *St John's Canticles*, for chorus |
|  |  | *Missa Aedis Christi*, for chorus |
| 1960 | (68) | *Triptych*, for brass band |
| 1961 | (69) | *A Hymn for St Cecilia*, for chorus and orchestra |
|  |  | *A Sequence for St Michael*, for chorus |
| 1963 | (71) | *Stabat Mater*, cantata |
| 1964 | (72) | *Motet on the Death of President Kennedy*, for chorus |
| 1968 | (76) | *The Coventry Mass*, for chorus and organ |
|  |  | *Sarum Canticles*, for chorus |
|  |  | *Winchester Canticles*, for chorus |
| 1974 | (82) | *Exultate Deo*, for chorus and organ |
| 1976 | (84) | *The Fear of the Lord*, for chorus and organ |
|  |  | *Let All the World*, antiphon for chorus |
|  |  | *Come My Soul*, anthem for chorus |
|  |  | *Sweetest of Sweetes*, anthem for chorus |

Howells also wrote other choral works, about forty songs, and keyboard works.


## HUMMEL, Johann Nepomuk
*b Pressburg, Bratislava, 14 November 1778*
*d Weimar, 17 October 1837, aged fifty-eight*

He was the son of the director of the Imperial School of Military Music. Unsuccessful with the violin, he began to study piano, and in 1785 he went to Vienna, where he was a pupil of Mozart for two years. From 1804 to 1811 he was *Kapellmeister* to Prince Esterházy; from 1816 to 1820 he worked in Stuttgart, and then moved to Weimar. He gave many concert tours, visiting St Petersburg, Paris and London.

He composed about one hundred and thirty works, including sonatas, variations, rondos, waltzes, fantasias, seven concertos and other piano works. He also wrote some church music, ballets, nine operas, cantatas and masses; but he is best known for his book, *Piano School*, published in 1828.

## HUMPERDINCK, Engelbert
*b Sieburg, near Bonn, 1 September 1854*
*d Neustrelitz, 27 September 1921, aged sixty-seven*

He studied in Cologne and Munich, and in 1879 won the Mendelssohn Prize which enabled him to travel to Italy. There he met Wagner, who invited him to Bayreuth to assist in the preparation of *Parsifal*. He then won further scholarships to Italy, France, and to Spain where he became professor at the Barcelona Conservatory in 1885. Two years later he returned to Germany, teaching in Frankfurt. His *Hänsel und Gretel* eclipsed all his other works in international popularity.

| | | |
|---|---|---|
| 1880 | (26) | *Humoreske* |
| 1893 | (39) | *Hänsel und Gretel*, opera |
| 1895 | (41) | *Die Sieben Geislein*, opera |
| 1898 | (44) | *Moorish Rhapsody*, for orchestra |
| 1902 | (48) | *Dornröschen*, opera |
| 1905 | (51) | *Die Heirat wieder Willen*, comic opera |
| 1910 | (56) | *Königskinder*, opera |
| 1911 | (57) | *The Miracle*, a pantomime |
| 1914 | (60) | *Die Marketenderin*, light opera |
| 1919 | (65) | *Gaudeamus*, musical scenes |

## IBERT, Jacques
*b Paris, 15 August 1890*
*d Paris, 5 February 1962, aged seventy-one*

He trained at the Paris Conservatory, winning the Prix de Rome in 1919. He was the director of the French Academy in Rome from 1937 to 1955, then until 1957 was director of the Paris Opéra and Opéra-Comique.

| | | |
|---|---|---|
| 1922 | (32) | *Ports of Call (Escales)*, orchestral suite |
| | | *Ballad of Reading Gaol*, ballet |
| 1925 | (35) | *Scherzo féerique* |
| | | Concerto for cello and wind instruments |
| 1926 | (36) | *Jeux*, for orchestra |
| 1927 | (37) | *Angélique*, opera |
| 1929 | (39) | *Persée et Andromédée*, opera |
| 1930 | (40) | *Le Roi d'Yvetot*, opera |
| | | *Divertissement*, for chamber orchestra |
| 1932 | (42) | *Donogoo*, for orchestra |
| | | *Paris*, symphonic suite |
| 1934 | (44) | *Diane de Poitiers*, ballet |
| | | *Concertino da camera*, for alto saxophone and small orchestra |
| 1935 | (45) | *Gonzaque*, opera |
| 1937 | (47) | *L'Aiglon*, opera (with Honegger, *qv*) |
| 1938 | (48) | *La Famille Cardinal*, opera (with Honegger) |
| | | Capriccio for ten instruments |
| 1943 | (53) | String Quartet in C major |
| 1944 | (54) | Trio for violin, cello and harp |
| | | *Suite Elisabethaine*, for orchestra |
| 1949 | (59) | *Etude-Caprice, pour un tombeau de Chopin*, for solo cello |
| 1951 | (61) | Sinfonia Concertante |

## IPPOLITOF-IVANOF, Michail Michailovitch
*b Gatchina, near St Petersburg, 19 November 1859*
*d Moscow, 28 January 1935, aged seventy-five*

He was a pupil of Rimsky-Korsakov in St Petersburg. He made his début in St Petersburg as composer and conductor in 1883, then spent the next ten years as head of the Conservatory in Tiflis. After the revolution he became director of the Moscow Conservatory, and in 1935 was appointed conductor of the Moscow Opera.

| | | |
|---|---|---|
| 1882 | (23) | *Yar-Khmel*, for orchestra |
| 1887 | (28) | *Ruth*, opera |
| | | *p* Violin Sonata |
| 1890 | (31) | *Asra*, opera |
| 1894–5 | (35–6) | *Armenian Rhapsody* |
| 1895 | (36) | *Caucasian Sketches*, suite for orchestra |
| 1897 | (38) | *p* String Quartet in A minor |
| 1898 | (39) | *p* Piano Quartet in A♭ major |
| 1900 | (41) | *Assia*, lyric scenes |
| 1907 | (48) | Symphony |
| 1909 | (50) | *Treachery*, opera |
| 1912 | (53) | *The Spy*, opera |
| 1916 | (57) | *Ole the Norseman*, opera |
| 1923–4 | (64–5) | *Mtzyry*, symphonic poem |
| 1928 | (69) | *Episodes from Schubert's Life*, for orchestra |
| 1933–4 | (74–5) | *The Last Barricade*, opera (unpublished and unperformed) |
| 1934 | (75) | *Catalan Suite*, for orchestra |


## IRELAND, John
*b Bowden, Cheshire, 13 August 1879*
*d Rock Mill, Washington, Sussex, 12 June 1962, aged eighty-two*

His parents were writers, friends of Carlyle and Emerson. His mother was interested in music and his sisters were pianists. He went to the Royal College of Music in 1893, earning his living as an organist, and then to Durham University. From 1904 to 1926 he was organist at St Luke's Church, Chelsea. As a composer, he discarded all that he had written before 1908. He taught composition at the Royal College, his pupils including Moeran, Alan Bush, Britten, Arnell and the present writer. He was in the Channel Islands when World War II broke out, but escaped the German occupation in 1940.

| | | |
|---|---|---|
| 1895 | (16) | Two Pieces for piano |
| 1905 | (26) | *Songs of a Wayfarer* |
| 1906 | (27) | Piano Trio No 1, *Phantasy Trio* |
| 1909 | (30) | Violin Sonata No 1 |
| 1912 | (33) | *Greater Love Hath No Man*, motet |
| 1913 | (34) | *The Forgotten Rite*, for orchestra |
| | | *Decorations*, for piano: |
| | | 'The Island Spell' |
| | | 'Moonglade' |
| | | 'Scarlet Ceremonies' |
| | | Three Dances for piano |
| | | 'Sea Fever', song (words Masefield) |
| | | 'Marigold', song |
| | | 'Impressions', song |
| 1915 | (36) | Preludes for piano |
| 1917 | (38) | Piano Trio No 2 |

                    Violin Sonata No 2
                    *The Cost*, songs
1918 (39)           *Leaves from a Child's Sketchbook*, for piano
1919 (40)           *Summer Evening*, for piano
                    *The Holy Boy*, prelude for piano
1920 (41)           *Three London Pieces*, for piano
                    Piano Sonata
1921 (42)           *Mai-Dun*, symphonic rhapsody
                    *Land of Lost Content*, song cycle
1923 (44)           Cello Sonata
1927 (48)           *Sonatina*, for piano
1929 (50)           *Ballade*, for piano
1930 (51)           Piano Concerto in E♭ major
1931 (52)           *Songs Sacred and Profane*
1932 (53)           *A Downland Suite*, for brass band
1933 (54)           *Legend*, for piano and orchestra
1934 (55)           *A Comedy Overture*, for brass band
1936 (57)           *London Overture*, for orchestra
1937 (58)           *These Things Shall Be*, for baritone, choir and orchestra
                    *Green Ways*, for piano
1938 (59)           Piano Trio No 3
1939 (60)           *Concertino Pastorale*, for strings
1941 (62)           *Sarnia*, for piano
                    *Three Pastels*, for piano
                    'O Happy Land', song
1942 (63)           Epic March
1943 (64)           *Fantasy Sonata*, for clarinet and piano
1944 (65)           *A Maritime Overture*, for military band
1946 (67)           fp *Satyricon Overture*
Ireland also composed:
*Minuet and Elegy*, for string orchestra
*Equinox*, for piano
Many songs and piano compositions


**IVES, Charles**
*b Danbury, Connecticut, 20 October 1874*
*d New York, 19 May 1954, aged seventy-nine*

His father was a well-known bandmaster who much influenced his son, a cornet-player in the town band. He went to Yale in 1894 but failed to absorb academic training and left in his first year there. He sold insurance in New York and in 1906 he co-founded an insurance company that gave him a comfortable income for the rest of his life. In 1928 ill-health forced him to stop composing, and in 1930 he retired from business to his farm in Connecticut. He became diabetic and suffered from a heart disease. His music is completely individual and uniquely American.

1891 (17)           Variations on 'America', for organ
1896 (22)           Quartet No 1, *Revival Service*
                    Symphony No 1 in D minor (1896–8)
1897–1902 (23–8) Symphony No 2
1898–1907 (24–33) *Calcium Light Night*, for chamber orchestra
                    *Central Park in the Dark*, for orchestra
1900–6 (26–32) and 1914–15 (40–1) *Children's Day at the Camp Meeting*, three
                    pieces for violin and piano
1901–4 (27–30) Symphony No 3

1902–10 (28–36) Violin Sonata No 2
1903–8 (29–34) Violin Sonata No 1
1903–14 (29–40) *Three Places in New England*, for orchestra
1904 (30)    *Thanksgiving, and/or Father's Day* (Part 4 of *Holidays Symphony*)
1904–11 (30–7) Theater Orchestra Set No 1:
       *In the Cage*
       *In the Inn*
       *In the Night*
1906 (32)    *The Pond*, for small orchestra
1908 (34)    *The Unanswered Question*, for small orchestra
1910–16 (36–42) Symphony No 4
1911 (37)    *Browning Overture*
       *Hallowe'en*, for piano and strings
       *The Gong on the Hook and Ladder*, for small orchestra
       *Tone-Roads*, No 1 for chamber orchestra (1911–15)
1912 (38)    *Decoration Day* (Part 2 of *Holidays Symphony*)
       *Lincoln, the Great Commoner*, for chorus and orchestra
1913 (39)    *Washington's Birthday* (Part 1 of *Holidays Symphony*)
       *Fourth of July* (Part 3 of *Holidays Symphony*)
       *Over the Pavements*, for chamber orchestra
1914 (40)    *Protests*, piano sonata
1915 (41)    *Concord*, piano sonata (1909–15)
       Orchestral Set No 2
       *Tone-Roads*, No 3 for chamber orchestra
1919–27 (45–33) Orchestral Set No 3
Ives also composed:
Eleven volumes of chamber music
*The Celestial Country*, for chorus
Three *Harvest Home Chorales*
*General Booth's Entrance into Heaven*, with brass band and chorus
Many psalm settings and other choral works
About 200 songs
Many piano pieces


**JACOB, Gordon**
*b London, 5 July 1895*
*d Saffron Walden, 8 June 1984, aged eighty-eight*

He was educated at Dulwich College, then the Royal College of Music, studying under Stanford and Howells immediately after World War I. After teaching theory and composition at Birkbeck and Morley colleges he joined the staff of the Royal College in 1926 and continued there until he retired in 1966. He was made a CBE in 1968.

Up to and including
1936 (41)    *The Jar in the Bush*, ballet
       *Uncle Remus*, ballet
       Symphony in C
       Oboe Concerto
       Piano Concerto
       Viola Concerto
       Violin Concerto
       *The Piper at the Gates of Dawn*, tone poem
       Variations on an original theme for orchestra
       Variations on an air by Purcell for string orchestra
       *Denbigh Suite*, for strings

|          | *Donald Caird*, for chorus and orchestra |
|----------|------------------------------------------|
|          | *William Byrd Suite*, for military band |
|          | *Serenade*, for five wind instruments |
|          | Quartets No 1 and 2 |
| 1945 (50) | Symphony No 2 |
|          | Clarinet Concerto |
| 1950 (55) | Sinfonietta in D major |
|          | *A Goodly Heritage*, cantata |
| 1951 (56) | Concerto for flute |
|          | *Fantasia on Songs of the British Isles* |
| 1956 (61) | Piano Concerto No 2 |
|          | Sextet for strings |
|          | Piano Trio |
| 1958 (63) | Suite for recorder and string quartet |
|          | *Diversions*, for woodwind and strings |
|          | Miniature String Quartet |
|          | *Old Wine in New Bottles*, for wind instruments |
| 1961 (66) | *Fantasia on Scottish Tunes* |
|          | Improvisations on a Scottish tune, for orchestra |
|          | Trombone Concerto |
| 1962 (67) | *News from Newtown*, cantata |
| 1963 (68) | Suite for brass band |
| 1965 (70) | *Festival Te Deum*, for chorus and orchestra |
| 1966 (71) | Oboe Sonata |
|          | *Variations on a Theme of Schubert* |
| 1967 (72) | Concerto for band |
|          | *Animal Magic*, cantata for children |
|          | Six Miniatures |
| 1968 (73) | Suite for bassoon and string quartet |
|          | Divertimento in E♭ |
| 1969 (74) | *Redbridge Variations* |
|          | Piano Quartet |
| 1970 (75) | *A York Symphony*, for orchestra |
|          | *The Pride of Youth*, for brass band |
|          | *A Joyful Noise*, for brass band |
| 1971 (76) | *Rhapsody for Three Hands*, for piano |
| 1972 (77) | Double-bass Concerto |
|          | *Tuba Suite*, for orchestra or piano |
|          | Psalm 103 for chorus |
| 1973 (78) | Saxophone Quartet |
| 1974 (79) | Quartet for clarinets |
|          | Sinfonia Brevis |
|          | *Havant Suite*, for chamber orchestra |
| 1975 (80) | Concerto for organ, strings and percussion |
|          | *Fantasy Sonata*, for organ |
|          | *Rhapsody*, for piano |
| 1978 (83) | Sonata for viola and piano |
| 1979 (84) | Viola Concerto No 2 |
| 1982 (87) | Flute Concerto No 2, for flute and strings |

Jacob also wrote the following undated works:

*Six Shakespearian Sketches*

*Swedish Rhapsody*, for brass band

Symphony for strings

Two Choral Preludes for brass band

*Two Sketches*, for string orchestra

*Victorian Rhapsody*, for brass band

*Sospan Fach*, march for brass band
*Nun's Priest's Tale*, cantata
Quartet for oboe and string trio
Quintet for clarinet and string quartet

## JANÁČEK, Leoš
*b Hukvaldy, Moravia, 3 July 1854*
*d Prague, 12 August 1928, aged seventy-four*

The ninth of fourteen children of a poor schoolmaster, he attended a monastery school in Brno and then at fourteen entered the Imperial and Royal Teachers' Training Institute on a state scholarship, staying there for three years. He passed his examinations with honours, and returned to the monastery to teach. Music was becoming more important to him, so he obtained a year's leave, borrowed some money, went to Prague and completed a three-year course at the Organ School in one year. He returned to Brno and the teachers' training school, this time as a music teacher, and he also became director of the Philharmonic Society. Later he spent a short time at the Conservatories of Leipzig and Vienna, studying composition. All his greatest compositions were written during the last twenty-four years of his life. He died of bronchial pneumonia.

| | | |
|---|---|---|
| 1877 | (23) | Suite for strings |
| 1880 | (26) | *Dumka*, for violin and piano |
| 1887 | (33) | *Sarka*, opera |
| 1889 | (35) | Six Lach Dances |
| 1891 | (37) | *The Beginning of a Romance*, opera |
| | | *Rákos Rákóczy*, ballet |
| 1894–1903 | (40–9) | *Jenůfa*, opera |
| 1904 | (50) | *Osud (Fate)*, opera |
| 1908–17 | (54–63) | *Mr Brouček's Excursion to the Moon*, opera |
| 1915–18 | (61–4) | *Taras Bulba*, rhapsody for orchestra |
| 1919 | (65) | *Katya Kabanova*, opera (1919–21) |
| | | *Diary of a Young Man who Disappeared*, song cycle |
| 1920 | (66) | *Ballad of Blanik*, symphonic poem |
| 1921 | (67) | Violin Sonata |
| 1923 | (69) | String Quartet No 1 in E minor |
| 1924 | (70) | *The Cunning Little Vixen*, opera |
| | | *The Makropoulos Affair*, opera (1924–6) |
| | | *Miade (Youth)*, suite for wind |
| 1925 | (71) | Sinfonietta (1925–6) |
| | | Concertino for piano, two violins, viola, cello, bassoon and horn |
| 1926 | (72) | *Capriccio*, for piano and wind instruments |
| | | *Festliche Messe* |
| 1927 | (73) | *From the House of the Dead*, opera (1927–8) |
| | | *Glagolitic Mass* |
| 1928 | (74) | String Quartet No 2, *Intimate Pages* |

## JOHNSON, Robert
*b London, c1583*
*d London, 1633, aged c fifty*

He was the son of John Johnson, a composer. He was indentured from 1596 to 1603 as servant to the Lord Chamberlain, who had him taught music. In 1604 he was appointed lutenist to James I and later to Charles I, holding the post until he died. He wrote a few sacred and many secular vocal works, some dances and masques, and works for lute and other instruments.

**JONES, Daniel Jenkyn**
*b Pembroke, 7 December 1912*

He began composing when still a child. He read English at Swansea University, and studied conducting, composition, viola and horn at the Royal Academy of Music from 1935 to 1938. A friend of Dylan Thomas, he wrote the music for a radio version of *Under Milk Wood* in 1954. He has gained many commissions and awards.

| | | |
|---|---|---|
| 1938 | (26) | Symphonic Prologue |
| 1939 | (27) | Five Pieces for orchestra |
| 1943 | (31) | *Comedy Overture* |
| 1944 | (32) | *Cloud Messenger*, for orchestra |
| 1945 | (33) | Symphony No 1 |
| 1947 | (35) | *The Flute Player*, for orchestra |
| | | *Miscellany*, twenty pieces for small orchestra |
| 1950 | (38) | Symphony No 2 |
| 1951 | (39) | Symphony No 3 |
| | | Concert Overture |
| 1954 | (42) | Symphony No 4 |
| 1956 | (44) | *Ieuenctid*, overture |
| 1958 | (46) | Symphony No 5 |
| | | *The Country Beyond the Stars*, for chorus and orchestra |
| 1960 | (48) | *O Lord, have Thou Respect*, anthem for chorus |
| 1961 | (49) | *The Knife*, opera |
| 1962 | (50) | *St Peter*, oratorio |
| 1964 | (52) | Symphony No 6 |
| 1965 | (53) | Capriccio for flute, harp and strings |
| 1966 | (55) | Violin Concerto |
| 1967 | (56) | *Orestes*, opera |
| 1969 | (58) | Investiture Processional Music |
| | | *The Three Hermits*, for chorus and organ |
| | | *The Ballad of the Standard Bearer*, for tenor and piano |
| | | *Triptych*, for chorus and piano |
| 1971 | (60) | *The Witnesses*, for male chorus and orchestra |
| | | *Môr*, for chorus and piano |
| 1972 | (61) | Sinfonietta |
| | | Symphony No 7 |
| | | Symphony No 8 |
| 1974 | (63) | Symphony No 9 |

Jones has also written some chamber and instrumental works.


**JONGEN, Joseph**
*b Liège, 14 December 1873*
*d Sart-Lez Spa, Liège, 12 July 1953, aged seventy-nine*

He studied at the Liège Conservatory, winning the Prix de Rome in 1897. From 1891 to 1898 he was assistant professor of counterpoint at Liège, becoming professor of harmony in 1903. He lived in England during World War I, and in 1919 resumed his teaching post in Liège. In 1920 he became professor of counterpoint and fugue at the Brussels Conservatory, and was director there until 1939.

| | | |
|---|---|---|
| 1893–1905 | (20–32) | Piano Trio in B minor |
| | | Violin Sonata No 1 in D major |
| 1894 | (21) | *p* String Quartet No 1 in C minor |
| 1898 | (25) | *Fantaisie*, for violin and orchestra |

| 1899 (26) | Symphony |
| | Violin Concerto |
| 1902 (29) | *Fantaisie sur deux Noëls wallons*, for orchestra |
| | Piano Quartet in E♭ major |
| 1904 (31) | *Lalla Rookh*, symphonic poem |
| 1907 (34) | *Félyane*, opera (unfinished) |
| after 1905 and | |
| before 1909 | Piano Trio in F♯ minor |
| 1909 (36) | Violin Sonata No 2 in E major |
| 1911 (38) | *S'Arka*, ballet |
| | Cello Sonata (1911–12) |
| 1912 (39) | *Deux rondes wallons*, for orchestra |
| 1913 (40) | *Impressions d'Ardennes*, for orchestra |
| 1915 (42) | *Suites en deux parties*, for viola and orchestra |
| 1916 (43) | String Quartet No 2 in A major |
| 1917 (44) | *Tableaux pittoresques*, for orchestra |
| 1918 (45) | p *Sérénade Tendre* and *Sérénade Triste*, for string quartet |
| 1919 (46) | *Poème héroïque*, for violin and orchestra |
| 1922 (49) | *Rhapsody*, for piano, flute, oboe, clarinet, horn and bassoon |
| 1928 (55) | *Pièce symphonique*, for piano and orchestra |
| 1929 (56) | *Passacaille et Gigue*, for orchestra |
| | Suite for viola and orchestra |
| 1930 (57) | *Sonata Eroica* |
| 1933 (60) | *La Légende de Saint-Nicholas*, for children's choir and orchestra |
| | *Symphonie Concertante*, for organ and orchestra |
| 1936 (63) | *Triptyque*, three suites for orchestra |
| 1938 (65) | *Hymne à la Meuse*, for chorus and orchestra |
| 1939 (66) | *Ouverture-Fanfare*, for orchestra |
| 1941 (68) | *La-cigale et le fourmi*, for children's chorus |
| | *Ouverture de fête*, for orchestra |
| 1943 (70) | Piano Concerto |
| 1944 (71) | *Bourrée*, for orchestra |

Jongen also composed:
Concerto for harp
Concerto for wind quintet

## JOSEPHS, Wilfred
*b Newcastle, 24 July 1927*

He studied medicine and then trained as a dentist. He found time for composing and won a Gaudamus Prize with a piano trio. After studying at the Guildhall School of Music he was awarded a Leverhulme Scholarship which took him to Paris for a year as a pupil of Max Deutsch. He has won first prize at the International Composition Competition in Milan and the Harriet Cohen Commonwealth Medal.

| 1950 (23) | *Machine Made*, for theatre orchestra |
| 1955 (28) | *The Ants*, comedy overture |
| | Symphony No 1 |
| | *Siesta*, for violin and piano |
| 1957 (30) | *Elegy*, for strings |
| | *Wry Rumba*, for wind quintet |
| | *Twelve Letters*, for speaker, clarinet, piano and string trio |
| 1959 (32) | *Little Venice Serenade*, for small orchestra |
| | *Pièces pour ma belle-mère*, for piano |
| | *Concerto a Dodici*, for wind ensemble |

| 1960 (33) | Concerto da camera, for violin, harpsichord and strings |
|---|---|
| 1961 (34) | *The Magical Being*, ballet |
| | *Meditatio de Beornmundo*, for viola, two oboes, two horns and strings |
| | *Aeolian Dances*, for orchestra |
| | *Monkchester Dances*, for orchestra |
| | *An Old English Suite*, for clarinet sextet |
| | String Quintet, incorporated in *Requiem* |
| 1962 (35) | *The Nottingham Captain*, music-theatre |
| | Cello Concerto |
| | *Five Fictitious Folk Songs*, for woodwind quartet |
| 1962–8 (35–41) | *King of the Coast*, musical for children |
| 1963 (36) | *Pathelin*, opera-entertainment |
| | Chacony, for violin and piano |
| | Piano Sonata |
| | *Requiem*, for baritone, double chorus, string quintet and orchestra |
| | *Four Chinese Lyrics*, for two voices and piano/guitar |
| 1964 (37) | Symphony No 2 |
| | Octet, for clarinet, bassoon, horn, string quartet and double-bass |
| | *Protégez-moi*, for children's chorus and instruments |
| 1964–5 (37–8) | *La Répétition de Phèdre*, ballet |
| 1965 (38) | Piano Concerto No 1 |
| | *Canzonas on a Theme of Rameau*, for strings |
| | Sonata for violin and piano |
| | *So She Went into the Garden*, for chorus and piano |
| | *Four Japanese Lyrics*, for voice, clarinet and piano |
| 1966 (39) | Concerto for light orchestra |
| | Trio for flute, violin and piano |
| | Fourteen Studies for piano |
| | String Trio |
| | *This is the Key to the Kingdom*, for children's chorus |
| | *Two Cat Songs*, for chorus |
| 1967 (40) | *Adam and Eve*, for speaker and ensemble |
| | *Polemic*, for strings |
| | *Rail*, symphonic picture |
| | Concerto for oboe, percussion and small orchestra |
| | Symphony No 3, *Philadelphia*, for chamber orchestra |
| 1967–9 (40–2) | *Mortales*, for solo voices, chorus, children's chorus and orchestra |
| 1968 (41) | *The Appointment*, television opera |
| | Serenade for small orchestra |
| | Toccata for guitar |
| | *Three Medieval Lyrics*, for chorus and wind quintet |
| 1969 (42) | *Variations on a Theme of Beethoven* for orchestra |
| | Concerto for two violins and chamber orchestra |
| | Twenty-nine Preludes for piano |
| 1969–70 (42–3) | Symphony No 4 for alto, baritone and orchestra |
| 1970 (43) | Sonata for cello and piano |
| | *Nightmusic*, for alto and orchestra |
| | *Death of a Young Man*, for baritone and orchestra |
| 1971 (44) | Symphony No 5, *Pastoral* |
| | Piano Concerto No 2 with chamber orchestra |
| | *The Last Post*, for orchestra |
| | Horn Trio for horn, violin and piano |
| | String Quartet |
| | *Happytaphs*, for children's chorus and piano |
| | *A Child of the Universe*, music-theatre |

| 1972 (45) | *Saratoga Concerto*, for guitar, harp, harpsichord and chamber orchestra |
| | *Encore on a Theme of Scott Joplin*, for guitar, harp and harpsichord |
| | *Songs of Innocence*, for chorus and orchestra |
| 1972–4 (45–7) | Symphony No 6 for soprano, baritone, chorus and orchestra |
| 1973 (46) | Five Pieces for unaccompanied voices |
| | Solo Oboe Pieces |
| 1974 (47) | *The Four Horsemen of the Apocalypse*, overture |
| | Concerto for brass band |
| | Concerto for school orchestra |
| | *A Trio of Trios*, for piano and violins |
| | Sonata for two trumpets, horn, trombone and tuba |
| 1975 (46) | Concerto for clarinet and chamber orchestra |
| | Sonata No 2 for violin and piano |
| | Waltz and Song for harp and strings |
| 1976 (49) | Symphony No 7 for small orchestra |
| 1977 (50) | Symphony No 8 for wind |
| | Piano Quintet |
| | Sonata Duo for piano (four hands) |
| | Sonata for flute and piano |
| 1980 (53) | Consort Music for brass |
| | Double-bass Concerto |
| | Double-bass Sonata |
| | *Tombeaux*, for organ |
| | *Equus*, ballet |
| 1981 (54) | *The Brontës*, overture |
| | *Eight Aphorisms*, for trombone octet |
| | Quartet Prelude in honour of Joseph Haydn |
| | String Quartet No 4 |
| | *Testimony*, toccata for organ |
| | *Blessings*, for chorus and organ |
| | *Spring Songs*, for chorus |
| 1982 (55) | *High Spirits*, overture |
| | Percussion Concerto with brass |
| | Two Flute Studies |
| | *The Montgolfiers' Famous Flying Globe*, operetta for schools |
| | Viola Concerto |

## JOSQUIN des Prez
*b ?Picardy, c1440*
*d Condé-sur-l'Escaut, near Valenciennes, 27 August 1521, aged c eighty-one*

He was one of the greatest and most prolific composers of the Renaissance. Northern French by birth, he spent some of his life resident in Italy. Little is known of his background and his early days; but from 1459 to 1472 he was a singer at Milan Cathedral, and then went into the service of Galeazzo Maria Sforza.

His music was both sacred – motets and masses – and secular, and he wrote many chansons.

## JOUBERT, John
*b Cape Town, 20 March 1927*

He received his early musical education in Cape Town, and in 1946 was awarded a Performing Right Society Scholarship to the Royal Academy of

Music, London. In 1950 he was appointed to a lectureship in music at the University of Hull, and since 1962 has lived in Birmingham, where he holds the post of reader in music at the University. In 1979 he was visiting professor at the University of Otago, New Zealand.

1950 (23)   String Quartet No 1
Divertimento, piano duet
1951 (24)   Overture for orchestra
Sonata for viola and piano
Five Songs for tenor and piano
1952 (25)   *O Lorde, the Maker of Al Thing*, for chorus and organ
*Torches*, carols for chorus and organ or orchestra
1953 (26)   Miniature String Quartet
*The Burghers of Calais*, cantata for soloists, chorus and chamber orchestra
1954 (27)   *Antigone*, a radio opera
Symphonic Prelude for orchestra
Concerto for violin
'There is no Rose', for unaccompanied chorus
1955 (28)   *Great Lord of Lords*, for chorus and organ
*In the Drought*, one-act opera
Symphony No 1
1956 (29)   Dance Suite for piano
*The God Pan*, for female voices and piano
*Incantation*, for unaccompanied chorus
1957 (30)   Piano Concerto
*A North Country Overture*
Sonata No 1, in one movement, for piano
*Two Invocations*, for tenor and piano
*Welcome Yule*, for unaccompanied chorus
1958 (31)   String Trio
1960 (33)   *Pro Pace*, three unaccompanied choral motets
1961 (34)   *Silas Marner*, opera
Octet for clarinet, bassoon, horn, string quartet and double-bass
Passacaglia and Fugue for organ
*Christ is Risen*, for chorus and organ
*Missa Beata Ioannis*, for chorus and orchestra
1962 (35)   'Sweet Content', for unaccompanied chorus
Sinfonietta for orchestra
*In Memoriam 1820*, for orchestra
1963 (36)   *Sonata a Cinque*, for flute, two violins, cello and harpsichord
*Leaves of Life*, ballad cantata for soli, chorus and piano
*Urbs Beata*, cantata for soli, chorus and orchestra
*O Lord Our Lord*, for chorus and organ
1964 (37)   *The Holy Mountain*, canticle for chorus and two pianos
*The Beatitudes*, for unaccompanied chorus
*The Quarry*, one-act opera
Communion Service in D for chorus and organ
1966 (39)   *Te Deum*, for chorus and organ
1968 (41)   *The Choir Invisible*, choral symphony
'Let There Be Light', unaccompanied choral motet
'O Praise God in His Holiness', for chorus and organ
'Lord Thou Hast Been Our Refuge', for chorus and organ
'Nowell', for chorus and organ
*Under Western Eyes*, opera
*Six Poems of Emily Brontë*, for soprano and piano
*Magnificat and Nunc Dimittis*, for chorus and organ

1969 (42)   *The Martyrdom of St Alban*, cantata for speaker, soli, chorus and chamber orchestra
'How Are My foes Increased, Lord', for unaccompanied chorus
'All Wisdom Cometh from the Lord', for female voices and organ
'I Will Lift up Mine Eyes unto the Hills', for female voices and piano
1970 (43)   Symphony No 2
*Dialogue*, for soprano, counter-tenor, cello and harpsichord
Duo for violin and cello
*African Sketchbook*, for vocal quartet and wind quintet
*Kontakion*, for cello and piano
1971 (44)   *The Raising of Lazarus*, oratorio with orchestra
*Behold, the Tabernacles of God*, for chorus and organ
1972 (45)   *Three Hymns to St Oswald*, for chorus and organ
'Four Stations on the Road to Freedom', for unaccompanied chorus
Piano Sonata No 2
1973 (46)   *The Prisoner*, opera
Concerto for bassoon and chamber orchestra
*Coverdale's Carol*, for unaccompanied chorus
*Threnos*, for harpsichord and twelve solo strings
1974 (47)   *The Magus*, for soli, chorus and orchestra
*Sleep Canticle*, for unaccompanied chorus
*Crabbed Age and Youth*, for counter-tenor, recorder, viola de gamba and harpsichord
1977 (50)   'Lines from the Youth of Man', a capella choir
1978 (51)   *Déploration*, for harp, percussion and strings
1979 (52)   *Herefordshire Canticles*, for soli, chorus and orchestra
*The Turning Wheel*, for soprano and piano
Joubert has also written other choral works.


## KABALEVSKY, Dmitry
*b St Petersburg, 30 December 1904*

His family moved to Moscow in 1918 and he entered the Skriabin Music College, subsequently studying at the Moscow Conservatory. He graduated in composition in 1929 and in piano a year later. He has always been very active in the political life of the USSR, and for his labours has received many honours and awards. He is the honorary president of the International Society for Music Education of UNESCO.

1929 (25)   Piano Concerto No 1 in A minor
String Quartet in A minor
1930 (26)   *Poem of Struggle*, for chorus and orchestra
1932 (28)   Symphony No 1, *Proletarians Unite!*, for chorus and orchestra
Symphony No 2 in E minor
March for wind band
1933 (29)   Symphony No 3, *Requiem for Lenin*, for chorus and orchestra
1936 (32)   Piano Concerto No 2 in G minor
1937 (33)   *The Testament*, for chorus and orchestra
1938 (34)   *Colas Breugnon*, opera, revised 1968–9
*Vasilek*, ballet
1939 (35)   Symphony No 4, *Shchors*, for chorus and orchestra
1940 (36)   *The Golden Spikes*, ballet
*The Comedians*, suite for small orchestra
Suite for jazz
1941 (37)   *Youth Parade*, for children's chorus and orchestra

| 1942 (38) | *People's Avengers*, suite for chorus and orchestra |
| | *Before Moscow*, opera |
| | *Our Great Fatherland*, cantata |
| c1944 (c40) | *The Family of Taras*, opera |
| 1945 (41) | String Quartet No 2 |
| 1948 (44) | Violin Concerto |
| 1949 (45) | Cello Concerto |
| 1952 (48) | Piano Concerto No 3 |
| | Cello Sonata |
| 1955 (51) | *Nikita Vershinin*, opera |
| 1956 (52) | Symphony No 5 |
| | *Romeo and Juliet*, symphonic suite |
| | *Song of the Party Membership Card*, for chorus and orchestra |
| 1957 (53) | *Spring Sings*, operetta |
| 1957–8 (53–4) | *Songs of Morning, Spring and Peace*, cantata for children's chorus and orchestra |
| 1958–9 (54–5) | *Leninists*, cantata |
| 1960 (56) | *Overture Pathétique*, for orchestra |
| | *The Spring*, symphonic poem |
| | *Camp of Friendship*, six children's songs (begun 1935) |
| | *Gasts in the Kitchen-garden*, play for children |
| | Major-minor études for solo cello |
| | Three Dancing Songs for children |
| 1961 (57) | Rondo for violin and piano |
| 1962 (58) | *Requiem*, for two soloists, children's and mixed choirs and orchestra (1962–3) |
| | Cello Sonata |
| 1963 (59) | Three Songs of Revolutionary Cuba |
| | Three Songs |
| | Five Songs (1963–4) |
| 1964 (60) | Rhapsody for piano and orchestra, *School Years* |
| | Cello Concerto No 2 |
| 1965 (61) | *Symphonic Prelude in Memory of Heroes of Gorlovka* |
| | Rondo for cello and piano |
| | Twenty Easy Pieces for violin and piano |
| | Spring Plays and Dances for piano |
| 1966 (62) | *The Motherland*, cantata for children's choir and orchestra |
| 1967 (63) | *Recitative and Rondo*, for piano |
| 1968 (64) | *Music for the Memorial in Bryansk*, for orchestra |
| | *Colas Breughnen*, (revised version) |
| 1968–9 (64–5) | *Sisters*, lyric opera |
| 1974 (70) | *To the Heroes of the 1905 Revolution*, for wind band |
| 1975 (71) | *Prague Concerto*, for piano and string orchestra |

Kabalevsky has also written incidental music, many piano and choral works, the latter especially for children.


## KHACHATURIAN, Aram
*b Tiflis, 6 June 1903*
*d Moscow, 1 May 1978, aged seventy-four*

The son of an Armenian bookbinder, he had no particular interest in music until he was nineteen, when he approached Gnesin, a pupil of Rimsky-Korsakov, because he wanted to compose but knew nothing about music. In 1929 he entered the Moscow Conservatory, staying there for five years. His Violin Concerto of 1940 won for him the Stalin Prize.

| 1927 (24) | *Poème*, for piano |
| 1932 (29) | Violin Sonata |
| | String Quartet in C major |
| | Trio in G minor, for clarinet, violin and piano |
| 1933 (30) | Symphony No 1 (1933–4) |
| | *Dance Suite* |
| 1936 (33) | Piano Concerto |
| 1937 (34) | *Song of Stalin*, for chorus and orchestra |
| 1939 (36) | *Happiness*, ballet |
| | *Masquerade*, incidental music |
| 1940 (37) | Violin Concerto |
| 1942 (39) | *Gayane*, ballet |
| | Symphony No 2 |
| 1944 (41) | Concerto for violin and cello |
| | *Masquerade Suite* |
| 1945 (42) | Solemn Overture, *To the End of the War* |
| 1947 (44) | *Symphonie-Poème* |
| 1950 (47) | Cello Concerto |
| 1954 (51) | *Spartacus*, ballet |
| 1955 (52) | Three Suites for orchestra |
| 1956 (53) | *Ode of Joy*, for soloist, chorus and orchestra |
| 1957 (54) | *Lermontov Suite* |
| 1958 (55) | Sonatina for piano |
| 1960 (57) | Rhapsody for violin and orchestra |
| | *Ballade*, for bass with orchestra |
| 1961 (58) | Piano Sonata |
| 1962 (59) | Cello Sonata |
| 1965 (62) | *Concerto-Rhapsody*, for cello and orchestra |
| 1966 (63) | Suite for Orchestra No 4 |

## KNUSSEN, Oliver
*b Glasgow, 12 June 1952*

The son of a double-bass player, he began composing at the age of six. From 1964 to 1967 he attended the Central Tutorial School for Young Musicians, and he studied at Tanglewood in the USA from 1970 to 1973.

| 1966–7 (14–15) | Symphony No 1 |
| 1968 (16) | Concerto for orchestra (revised 1976) |
| | *Pantomime*, for wind quintet and string quartet (revised 1978) |
| 1969 (17) | *Masks*, for flute |
| | *Fire*, capriccio for flute and string trio |
| 1970 (18) | *Little Fantasies*, for wind quintet (revised 1976) |
| 1970–1 (18–19) | Symphony No 2 for soprano and chamber orchestra |
| 1970–2 (18–20) | *Choral*, for wind orchestra |
| 1971 (19) | *Turba*, for double-bass |
| 1972 (20) | *Rosary Songs* |
| 1972–3 (20–1) | *Océan de Terre*, for ensemble |
| | *Puzzle Music*, for ensemble |
| 1973–9 (21–7) | Symphony No 3 |
| 1975 (23) | *Trumpets*, for violin and three clarinets |
| | *Ophelia Dances*, for ensemble |
| 1976–7 (24–5) | *Autumnal*, for violin and piano |
| 1977 (25) | *Cantata*, for oboe and string trio |
| 1977–8 (25–6) | *Sonya's Lullaby*, for piano |
| | *Where the Wild Things Are*, fantasy in two acts |

1979 (27)    *Coursing*, for chamber orchestra
1979–80 (27–28) *Songs and a Sea Interlude*, for soprano and orchestra
1979–81 (27–29) *Where the Wild Things Are*, opera
1984 (32)    *Higglety Pigglety Pop!*, opera


## KODÁLY, Zoltán
*b Kecskemét, Hungary, 16 December 1882*
*d Budapest, 6 March 1967, aged eighty-four*

His father was a violinist and his mother a pianist. He took up the cello in order
to help his father make a quartet. He went to Budapest in 1900 to study at the
Academy of Music. In 1905, with Bartók, he began research into Hungarian folk
music, using a recording cylinder. In 1906 he went to Berlin and in 1907 to Paris,
but returned to Budapest that year to take up a teaching post at the Academy.
He was suspended from the Academy by the bureaucratic regime in 1919 but
was reinstated in 1922, resigning in 1941. He travelled a good deal, especially to
the USA.

1897 (15)    Overture for orchestra
1901 (19)    Adagio for violin (or viola) and piano
1906 (24)    *Summer Evening*, for orchestra
1908 (26)    String Quartet No 1 in C minor
1909–10 (27–8) Cello Sonata (Atonal)
1914 (32)    Duo for violin and cello (Atonal)
1915 (33)    Sonata for unaccompanied cello
1916–17 (34–5) String Quartet No 2 in D major
1917–18 (35–6) Seven Piano Pieces
1919–20 (37–8) *Serenade*, for two violins and viola
1923 (41)    *Psalmus Hungaricus*, for tenor, chorus and orchestra
1925 (43)    *Meditation on a Theme of Debussy*, for piano
1926 (44)    *Háry János*, opera
1930 (48)    *Dances of Marosszeck*, for piano (afterwards orchestrated)
1931 (49)    *Theater Overture*
             *The Spinning Room*, lyric scenes (1931–2)
             *Pange lingua*, for mixed choir and organ
1933 (51)    *Dances of Galanta*, orchestral suite
1934 (52)    *Jesus and the Merchants*, for chorus and orchestra
1936 (54)    *Te Deum*, for chorus and orchestra
1938–9 (56–7) *Variations on a Hungarian Folk Song*, for orchestra
1939 (57)    Concerto for orchestra
             *The Peacock Variations*, for orchestra
1945 (63)    *Missa Brevis*
1947 (65)    Viola Concerto
             String Quartet
1948 (66)    *Czinka Panna*, opera
1954 (72)    *Spartacus*, ballet
1960 (78)    Symphony in C major
1965 (83)    Variations for piano
1967 (85)    *Laudes Organi*, fantasia on twelfth-century sequence, for mixed
             choir and organ

**KOECHLIN, Charles**
*b Paris, 27 November 1867*
*d Le Canadel, Var, 31 December 1950, aged eighty-three*

He came from a rich industrial family and was intended for a military career, but ill-health prevented it. He entered the Paris Conservatory in 1890, studying with Massenet, then with Fauré, whose influence was the strongest in his musical life. He founded the Societé Musicale Indépendante in 1909, and from 1915 began a long career as a writer on musical theory. He lectured in America in 1918, 1928 and 1937, and is best remembered as a teacher.

His output as a composer extends to 226 Opus numbers, including stage works, two symphonies and other symphonic works, choral works and songs, and chamber and instrumental works. He also wrote a great deal of music for films.

**KORNGOLD, Erich Wolfgang**
*b Brno, 29 May 1897*
*d Hollywood, 29 November 1957, aged sixty*

He studied in Vienna and was a child prodigy in piano and composition, publishing a piano trio at the age of twelve. In 1924 he received the Art Prize of the City of Vienna. He became a US citizen in 1943.

| | |
|---|---|
| 1910–13 (13–16) | Piano Trio |
| 1916 (19) | *Der Ring des Polykrates*, opéra bouffe |
| 1919 (22) | *Much Ado About Nothing*, incidental music |
| 1920 (23) | *The Dead City*, opera |
| 1939 (42) | *Die Kathrin*, opera |
| 1940 (43) | *Songs of the Clown* |
| | Four Shakespeare Songs |
| 1941 (44) | *Psalm*, for solo, chorus and orchestra |
| 1942 (45) | *Prayer*, for tenor, chorus and orchestra |
| | 'Tomorrow', song |
| 1945 (48) | Violin Concerto |
| | String Quartet No 3 |
| 1946 (49) | *The Silent Serenade*, comedy with music |
| | Cello Concerto |
| 1947 (50) | *Symphonic Serenade*, for strings |
| | Five Songs for middle voice |
| 1951 (54) | Symphony in F♯ major |
| 1952 (55) | 'Sonnet to Vienna', song |
| 1953 (56) | Theme and Variations for orchestra |
| | *Straussiana*, for orchestra |

**KORTE, Karl**
*b Ossining, New York, 25 August 1928*

He studied at the Juillard School and with Copland. He received a Fulbright grant to Italy, two Guggenheim Fellowships, the Ford Foundation, and many other awards. He has been composer-in-residence at Oklahoma City and Albuquerque Schools, and was professor at the State University of New York from 1964 to 1971. Since then he has been professor at the University of Texas.

| | |
|---|---|
| 1948 (20) | String Quartet No 1 |
| 1955 (27) | *Concertato on a Choral Theme*, for orchestra |
| 1958 (30) | *Story of the Flutes*, symphonic poem |
| 1959 (31) | *For a Young Audience*, for orchestra |

|         |      | *Fantasy*, for violin and piano |
|---------|------|--------------------------------|
| 1960 | (32) | Quintet for oboe and strings |
| 1961 | (33) | Symphony No 2 |
|      |      | *Four Blake Songs*, for women's voices and piano |
| 1962 | (34) | Nocturne and March, for band |
|      |      | *Ceremonial Prelude and Passacaglia*, for band |
| 1963 | (35) | *Southwest*, a dance overture |
|      |      | *Prairie Song*, for trumpet and band |
|      |      | *Introductions*, for brass quintet |
|      |      | *Mass for Youth*, with orchestra or keyboard |
| 1964 | (36) | *Diablerie*, for woodwind quintet |
| 1965 | (37) | *Aspects of Love*, seven songs on various texts |
|      |      | String Quartet No 2 |
| 1968 | (40) | Symphony No 3 |
|      |      | *Matrix*, for woodwind quartet, piano, percussion and saxophone |
|      |      | *May the Sun Bless Us*, four settings of texts of Tagore, for male voices, brass and percussion |
| 1969 | (41) | *Facets*, for saxophone quartet |
|      |      | *Dialogue*, for saxophone and tape |
| 1970 | (42) | *Gestures*, for electric brass, percussion, piano and band |
|      |      | *Psalm XIII*, for chorus and tape |
| 1971 | (43) | *I Think You Would Have Understood*, for stage band, solo trumpet and two-channel tape |
|      |      | *Remembrances*, for flute and tape |
| 1974 | (46) | *Libera me*, four songs |

## KŘENEK, Ernst
*b Vienna, 23 August 1900*

He studied with Schreker at the Vienna Academy of Music and at Berlin. He married Mahler's daughter, Anna, in 1922. The success of his opera *Jonny spielt auf*, first produced in 1927, enabled him to live in comfortable independence – though it offended Nazi ideals. He stayed in Vienna until the outbreak of war in 1939, then emigrated to America.

| 1919 | (19) | Serenade for piano, violin, viola and cello |
|------|------|---------------------------------------------|
|      |      | Piano Sonata No 1 |
| 1921 | (21) | Symphony No 1 |
|      |      | String Quartet No 1 |
|      |      | String Quartet No 2 |
| 1922 | (22) | *Die Zwingburg*, opera |
|      |      | Symphonic Music for nine instruments |
|      |      | Symphony No 2 |
|      |      | Symphony No 3 |
| 1923 | (23) | *Der Sprung über den Schatten*, opera |
|      |      | *Orpheus und Eurydike*, opera |
|      |      | Piano Concerto No 1 |
|      |      | String Quartet No 3 |
|      |      | String Quartet No 4 |
| 1924 | (24) | Concerto Grosso |
|      |      | Concertino for flute, violin, cembalon and strings |
|      |      | Violin Concerto No 1 |
|      |      | Seven Orchestral Pieces |
|      |      | Symphony for wind and percussion |
|      |      | Violin Sonata No 1 |
| 1925 | (25) | *Jonny spielt auf*, opera |

| | |
|---|---|
| | *Mammon*, ballet |
| | *Der vertauschte Cupido*, ballet, after Rameau |
| 1926 (26) | *Der Diktator*, opera |
| | *Drei Lustige Märsche*, for orchestra |
| 1926–7 (26–7) | *Das Geheime Königreich*, opera |
| 1927 (27) | *Schwergewicht*, or *Die Ehre der Nation*, opera |
| | *Triumph der Empfindsamkeit*, orchestral suite |
| | *Potpourri*, for orchestra |
| 1928 (28) | Piano Sonata No 2 |
| | Little Symphony |
| 1928–9 (28–9) | *Leben des Orest*, opera |
| 1930 (30) | String Quartet No 5 |
| 1930–3 (30–3) | *Karl V*, opera |
| 1931 (31) | Theme and Thirteen Variations for orchestra |
| | *A Little Wind-music* |
| 1932 (32) | *Cantata on the Transitoriness of Earthly Things* |
| 1933–4 (33–4) | *Cefalo e Procri*, opera |
| 1934 (34) | Piano Sonata No 3 |
| 1935–6 (35–6) | *The Coronation of Poppea*, opera, after Monteverdi |
| 1936 (36) | Adagio and Fugue for string orchestra |
| | String Quartet No 6 |
| 1937 (37) | Piano Concerto No 2 |
| 1939 (39) | *Eight Column Line*, ballet |
| | Symphonic Piece for string orchestra |
| | Suite for cello |
| 1940 (40) | *Tarquin*, opera |
| | Little Concerto for organ, cembalo and chamber orchestra |
| 1941 (41) | *Lamentations of Jeremiah*, for chorus |
| 1942 (42) | Viola Sonata |
| 1943 (43) | String Quartet No 7 |
| 1944 (44) | *Cantata for Wartime*, for female choir and orchestra |
| 1944–5 (44–5) | Sonata for violin and piano |
| 1945 (45) | *Vertrauenssache*, opera |
| 1946 (46) | *Symphonic Elegy*, for string orchestra |
| | Piano Concerto No 3 |
| 1947 (47) | Symphony No 4 |
| 1947–9 (47–9) | Symphony No 5 |
| 1948 (48) | Violin Sonata No 2 |
| | Piano Sonata No 4 |
| | Sonata for viola and piano |
| 1950 (50) | *Dark Waters*, one-act opera |
| | Piano Concerto No 4 |
| | Double Concerto for violin, piano and chamber orchestra |
| | Piano Sonata No 5 |
| 1951 (51) | Concerto for harp and chamber orchestra |
| | Concerto for two pianos and orchestra |
| | Piano Sonata No 6 |
| 1952 (52) | Sinfonietta for string orchestra, *La Brasiliera* |
| 1952–5 (52–5) | *Pallas Athene weint*, opera |
| 1953 (53) | Concerto for cello and orchestra |
| 1954 (54) | Symphony, *Pallas Athene* |
| | Violin Concerto No 2 |
| | *Elf Transparente*, for orchestra |
| 1955 (55) | Capriccio for cello and chamber orchestra |
| | Harp Sonata |
| 1955–6 (55–6) | *The Belltower*, one-act opera |

|        |        | *Spiritus Intelligentiae, Sanctus,* for voices and electronics |
| 1956 | (56) | *Monologue,* for clarinet |
|        |        | Sonatina for oboe |
| 1957 | (57) | *Jest of Cards,* ballet |
|        |        | *Sestina,* for soprano, violin, guitar, flute, clarinet, trumpet and percussion |
|        |        | Suite for guitar |
| 1957–8 | (57–8) | *Missa Duodecim Tonorum,* for choir and organ |
| 1959 | (59) | Six Motets from Kafka |
| 1961 | (61) | *Ausgerechnet und Verspielt,* opera |
| 1962 | (62) | *5+1,* ballet |
|        |        | *Alpbach Quintet,* for wind |
| 1963 | (63) | *Der Goldene Bock,* opera |
|        |        | *San Fernando Sequence,* for electronics |
| 1964 | (64) | *O Holy Ghost,* choral |
| 1966 | (66) | *Glauben und wissen,* choral |
|        |        | *Proprium Missae,* choral |
|        |        | *Der Zauberspiel,* television opera |
| 1967 | (67) | Five Pieces for trombone and piano |
|        |        | *Exercises of a Late Hour,* for small orchestra and tape |
|        |        | *Horizons Circled,* for orchestra |
|        |        | *Perspectives,* for orchestra |
| 1967–9 | (67–9) | *Sardakai,* opera |
| 1968 | (68) | German Mass |
|        |        | *Six Profiles,* for orchestra |
| 1969 | (69) | *Fivefold Enfoldment,* for orchestra |
| 1970 | (70) | *Gib uns dem Frieden,* choral mass |
|        |        | Duo for flute and double-bass |
| 1971 | (71) | *Orga-nastro,* for organ and tape |
| 1971–2 | (71–2) | *Kitharaulos,* for oboe, harp and small orchestra |
| 1972 | (72) | *Statisch und Ekstatisch,* for orchestra |
| 1973 | (73) | *Choralvorspiel,* for organ |
|        |        | *Flaschenpost vom Paradies,* for electronics |
| 1974 | (74) | *Von Vorn Herein,* for small orchestra, piano and cello |
| 1974–5 | (74–5) | *Feierstag,* cantata |
| 1975 | (75) | *Dream Sequence,* for wind band |
| 1978 | (78) | *The Dissembler,* for orchestra |
| 1979 | (79) | Concerto for organ and strings |
|        |        | *Die Vierwinde,* for organ |
|        |        | *Opus 231,* for violin and organ |

Křenek has written many articles and books on musical subjects; works for electronics, songs, instrumental duos and trios, film and piano music.

## KURTÁG, György
*b Lugoj, Romania, 19 February 1926*

A Hungarian of Romanian birth, he entered Budapest Academy of Music in 1946, taking diplomas in composition, piano and chamber music in 1955. In 1957 he studied with Milhaud and Messiaen at the Paris Conservatory. He became coach and tutor at the Bartók Secondary Music School from 1958 to 1963, and was with the National Philharmonia from 1960 to 1968. In 1967 he was appointed to the staff of Budapest Academy.

| 1943 | (17) | Suite for piano |
| 1949 | (23) | *Klárisok,* for chorus |
| 1950 | (24) | Suite for piano duet |

1953 (27)   *Koreai Kantáta*
1954 (28)   Viola Concerto

Kurtág has also written numerous instrumental and chamber works and incidental music.


## LALO, Édouard
*b Lille, 27 January 1823*
*d Paris, 22 April 1892, aged sixty-nine*

He trained as a string player at the Lille and Paris Conservatories, making a living by teaching and playing in a string quartet. In 1865 he married a singer who encouraged him to write for the stage, but the advent of the Franco-Prussian war made production impossible. His works had a mixed reception until his opera *Le Roi d'Ys* became a popular success in 1888.

1855 (32)   String Quartet in E♭
1872 (49)   *Deux Aubades*, for small orchestra
            Violin Concerto in F major
            *Divertissement*, for small orchestra
1873 (50)   *Symphonie espagnole*, for violin and orchestra, in five movements
1875 (52)   *Allegro Symphonique*
1876 (53)   Cello Concerto
1881 (58)   *Rhapsodie norvégienne*
1882 (59)   Ballet Suites No 1 and 2, *Namouna*
1884 (61)   Scherzo
1886 (63)   Symphony in G minor
1888 (65)   *Le Roi d'Ys*, opera
1889 (66)   Piano Concerto in G minor


## LAMBERT, Constant
*b London, 23 August 1905*
*d London, 21 August 1951, aged forty-five*

He was the son of an Australian painter. He was educated at Christ's College from 1915 to 1922, then won a scholarship to the Royal College of Music. From 1931 to 1947 he was musical director of Sadler's Wells Ballet (later called the Royal Ballet), and in 1948 became its artistic director.

1925–6 (20–1) *Romeo and Juliet*, ballet
1926 (21)   *Pomona*, ballet
            *Poems by Li-Po*
1927 (22)   Music for orchestra
            *Elegiac Blues*
1928–9 (23–4) Piano Sonata
1929 (24)   *The Rio Grande*, for chorus, orchestra and piano solo
1931 (26)   Concerto for piano and nine instruments
1936 (31)   *Summer's Last Will and Testament*, for chorus and orchestra
1937 (32)   *Horoscope*, ballet
1940 (35)   *Dirge*, for male voices and strings
1942 (37)   *Aubade héroïque*, for orchestra
1950 (45)   *Tiresias*, ballet

## LASSUS, Orlando de
b *Mons, Hainault, 1532*
d *Munich, 14 June 1594, aged sixty-two*

At the age of twelve he entered the service of the house of Mantua. He began composing while in Naples, then went to Rome to become *maestro di cappella* in 1553 at St John Lateran. In 1555 he was in Antwerp, where his first compositions were printed. He went to Munich in 1556 to join the court of the Duke of Bavaria, singing in the chapel, and in 1563 he became head of the chapel, holding that position for thirty years, until his death.

He had a vast output of compositions, including: madrigals, masses, magnificat settings, offices, lessons, lamentations, litanies, nunc dimittis, falsibordoni, hymns, responsories, motets, chansons and lieder.

## LAWES, William
b *Salisbury, 1602*
d *Chester, 24 September 1645, aged forty-three*

His father was a lay vicar at Salisbury Cathedral, and William was probably a chorister there. He studied music with his father and then, under John Coprario, met fellow-pupil Prince Charles who later became Charles I. He became one of the private musicians to the court, and in 1635 was appointed 'musician in ordinary for the lutes and voices'. He followed King Charles to the wars, rode into Chester with him and was shot and killed.

He wrote many suites for consorts and other groups of instruments, about 126 aires and dances, a great number of secular songs and some sacred vocal works.

## LECLAIR, Jean-Marie
b *Lyons, 10 May 1697*
d *Paris, 22 October 1764, aged sixty-seven*

By the age of nineteen he had mastered violin playing, dancing and lace-making! At the same age, in 1716, he married, while working as a dancer at the Lyons Opera. Under wealthy patronage he went in 1723 to Paris. His wife died and he remarried in 1730, to Louise Roussel, who engraved all his subsequent works. From 1733 to 1737 he was appointed by Louis XV as Ordinaire de la Musique du Roi; then he went to the court of Orange in the Netherlands, spending three months there in every year from 1738 to 1743. On returning permanently to Paris he remained for a few years in semi-retirement, teaching and composing. In 1748 he was called into the service of the Duke of Gramont, holding this position until, for reasons unknown, he was murdered.

| | | |
|---|---|---|
| 1723 (26) | p | Sonatas for Violin Alone, with a Bass, Book I |
| 1728 (31) | p | Sonatas for Violin Alone, with a Bass, Book II |
| 1734 (37) | p | Sonatas for Violin Alone, with a Bass, Book III |
| 1737 (40) | p | Six Concertos for violin |
| 1746 (49) | | *Scylla et Glaucus*, opera |

## LEHÁR, Franz
b *Komáron, then Hungary, 30 April 1870*
d *Bad Ischl, 24 October 1948, aged seventy-eight*

He was the son of an Army bandmaster, whose continual moving compelled Franz junior to study as best he could. At the age of twelve he won a scholarship to the Music Academy in Prague, where he stayed for six years, and became a proficient violinist. Dvořák and Brahms both encouraged him to concentrate on composition. He, too, became a bandmaster, the youngest ever appointed by the Austrian Army, at the age of twenty. The interest shown in him by a Viennese publisher made him give up the Army and become a full-time composer. After initial popularity – with *The Merry Widow*, for example – came a less successful period coinciding with the World War I years; then came renewed success, particularly from the time that he met Tauber, for whom all his subsequent operettas were written.

| | |
|---|---|
| 1905 (35) | *The Merry Widow*, operetta |
| 1909 (39) | *Count of Luxembourg*, operetta |
| 1928 (58) | *Frederica*, operetta |
| 1929 (59) | *The Land of Smiles*, operetta |

Lehár also composed many other operettas and a violin concerto.


## LEIGHTON, Kenneth
*b Wakefield, 2 October 1929*

He studied classics and composition at Queen's College, Oxford, and in 1951 won the Mendelssohn Scholarship which took him to Rome. In 1968 he was appointed lecturer and fellow of Worcester College, Oxford, and in 1970 the Reid professor of music at Edinburgh University.

| | |
|---|---|
| 1949 (20) | Symphony for strings |
| 1950 (21) | *Veris gratia*, for oboe, cello and strings |
| 1951 (22) | *Primavera romana*, overture |
| | Piano Concerto No 1 |
| 1952 (23) | Concerto for violin and small orchestra |
| | Concerto for viola, harp, timpani and strings |
| 1953 (24) | Concerto for oboe and strings |
| | *A Christmas Caroll*, for baritone, chorus, piano/organ and strings |
| 1954 (25) | *The Birds*, for soli, chorus, piano and strings |
| | Concerto for two pianos, timpani and strings |
| 1956 (27) | Cello Concerto |
| 1957 (28) | Passacaglia, Chorale and Fugue for orchestra |
| | *Burlesque*, for orchestra |
| 1958 (29) | *The Light Invisible*, sinfonia sacra |
| 1960 (31) | Piano Concerto No 2 |
| 1961 (32) | Concerto for strings |
| | *Crucifixus pro nobis*, for tenor, chorus and organ |
| 1962 (33) | *Festive Overture* |
| | *Missa Sancti Thomæ*, for chorus and organ |
| 1964 (35) | Symphony |
| | Mass for chorus and organ |
| 1965 (36) | *Communion Service*, for chorus and organ |
| 1967 (38) | *Missa brevis*, for chorus |
| 1968 (39) | Dance Suite for orchestra |
| | *An Easter Sequence*, for female voices, organ and trumpet |
| 1969 (40) | Piano Concerto No 3, *Estivo* |
| 1970 (41) | Concerto for organ, timpani and strings |
| | Dance Suite No 2 |
| 1971 (42) | *Dance Overture* |
| | *Laudes animantium*, for soli and chorus |
| | *The Second Service*, for chorus and organ |
| 1972 (43) | *Elizabethan Lyrics*, for female voices |
| | *Sarum Mass*, for soli, chorus and organ |

| 1973 | (44) | *Laudate pueri*, for three choirs |
| 1974 | (45) | Symphony No 2, *Sinfonia mistica* |
| 1975 | (46) | *Laudes montium*, for baritone, chorus and orchestra |
| 1976 | (47) | *Hymn to Matter*, for baritone, chorus, strings and percussion |
| 1978 | (49) | *Columba mea*, for soli, strings, celeste and harpsichord |
| 1979 | (50) | Mass for treble voices and organ |
| 1980 | (51) | Fantasy on a Chorale for violin and organ |
| | | *Missa de Gloria*, organ solo |
| | | *Columba*, opera |
| | | *Animal Heaven*, for soprano, recorder, cello and harpsichord |
| | | *Missa Cornelia*, for treble voices and organ |
| 1981 | (52) | *Household Pets*, for piano |
| | | *These are Thy Wonders*, for high voice and organ |
| 1982 | (53) | Fantasy-Octet, *Homage to Percy Grainger* |

Leighton has also written works for various chamber combinations, and for piano and organ.

## LEONCAVALLO, Ruggiero
*b Naples, 8 March 1858*
*d Montecatani, 9 August 1919, aged sixty-one*

His father was a judge, on one of whose cases the libretto of *I Pagliacci* was based. He studied at the Naples Conservatory, leaving at the age of eighteen with the diploma of *maestro*. He lived by teaching singing and piano, and accompanying soloists in café concerts in France, Holland, Germany, England and Cairo. His later operas achieved only moderate success.

| 1892 | (34) | *I Pagliacci*, opera |
| 1894 | (36) | *Serafita*, symphonic poem |
| 1897 | (39) | *La Bohème*, opera (this failed whereas Puccini's on the same subject succeeded) |
| 1900 | (42) | *Zaza*, opera |

## LIADOV, Anatol
*b St Petersburg, 11 May 1855*
*d Polinovka, Novgorod, 28 August 1914, aged fifty-nine*

He first studied with his father, who was the conductor at the Mariinsky Theatre. In 1870 he entered the St Petersburg Conservatory and attended Rimsky-Korsakov's composition classes. In 1878 he became a teacher of elementary theory at the Conservatory, of advanced counterpoint in 1901, and of composition in 1906. His marriage in 1884 brought him financial independence. He was a very indolent man, which accounted for his comparatively small output. He made numerous appearances as a conductor, and collected and published several volumes of folk-song arrangements.

| 1876 | (21) | *Birulki*, for piano |
| 1879 | (24) | *Arabesque*, for piano |
| 1887 | (32) | *Scherzo*, for orchestra |
| 1888 | (33) | *Mazurka*, for orchestra |
| 1890 | (35) | *Dal tempo antico*, for piano |
| 1892 | (37) | *Kukalki*, for piano |
| 1893 | (38) | *Une tabatière à musique*, for piano |
| 1899 | (44) | *Slava*, for women's chorus, two harps and two pianos |
| 1900 | (45) | *Polonaise*, for orchestra |
| 1904 | (49) | *Baba Yaga*, symphonic poem |

| 1906 (51) | *Eight Popular Russian Songs*, for orchestra |
| 1909 (54) | *The Enchanted Lake*, symphonic poem |
| 1910 (55) | *Kikimora*, symphonic poem |
| | *Dance of the Amazons*, for orchestra |
| 1914 (59) | *Naenia (Dirge)* |

## LIGETI, György
*b Dicsöszentmárton, Siebenbürgen, Romania, 28 May 1923*

He studied at the Budapest Academy of Music, and taught there from 1950 to 1956, before moving to Vienna. From 1957 to 1958 he worked at the Cologne Studio for Electronic Music, and in 1959 became a lecturer at Darmstadt. He was visiting professor in Stockholm, Bilthoven, Essen and the USA, becoming professor at the College of Music in Stockholm in 1961.

| 1953 (30) | String Quartet |
| 1958 (35) | *Artikulation*, for tape |
| | *Apparitions*, for large orchestra (1958–9) |
| 1960 (37) | *Atmospheres*, for large orchestra |
| 1961 (38) | *Fragment*, for eleven instruments |
| | *Volumina*, for organ (1961–2) |
| 1962 (39) | *Poème Symphonique*, for one hundred metronomes |
| | *Aventures*, for three singers and seven instruments |
| | *Nouvelles aventures*, for three singers and seven instruments (1962–5) |
| 1963–5 (40–2) | *Requiem* |
| 1966 (43) | Cello Concerto |
| | *Lux aeterna* |
| 1967 (44) | *Lontana*, for large orchestra |
| | Two Studies for organ (1967–9) |
| 1968 (45) | *Ramifications*, for string orchestra (1968–9) |
| | Ten Pieces for wind quintet |
| | String Quartet No 2 |
| | *Continuum*, for harpsichord |
| 1969–70 (46–7) | Chamber Concertante for thirteen instruments |
| 1971 (48) | *Melodien*, for orchestra |
| | *Horizont*, for recorder |
| 1972 (49) | *Kylwiria*, opera |
| | Double Concerto for flute, oboe and orchestra |
| 1972–3 (49–50) | *Clocks and Clouds*, for twelve female voices and orchestra |
| 1973–4 (50–1) | *San Francisco Polyphony*, for orchestra |
| 1976 (53) | *Monument, Self-Portrait*, for two pianos |
| | *Three Objects*, for two pianos |
| 1978 (55) | *Le Grand Macabre*, music-theatre |
| 1982 (59) | Trio for violin, horn and piano |
| | *Three Fantasies*, for choir a capella |
| | *Magyar Studies*, for choir a capella |

## LISZT, Franz (Ferencz)
*b Raiding, Hungary, 22 October 1811*
*d Bayreuth, 31 July 1886, aged seventy-four*

He took his first piano lessons from his father, who was an official at the Esterházy court, which many prominent musicians – including Haydn, Cherubini and Hummel – visited. He appeared in concerts at the age of nine.

Some magnates set up a fund for his education, and in 1821 the family moved to Vienna, where Liszt met Beethoven and Schubert. In 1823 they moved to Paris, where Cherubini refused to have Liszt in the Conservatory because he was a foreigner. He gave many concerts, but touring affected his health. He earned his living by teaching piano, fell in love with a pupil, became ill when the attachment was broken off, and went through a period of religious doubt. In 1830 he threw off his lethargy, began studying intensively, and met Berlioz, Paganini and Chopin. In 1834 he began an affair with Comtesse Marie d'Agoult, resulting in three children – one of whom, Cosima, later married Wagner. To raise money he went back to being a travelling virtuoso, until 1847; then in 1848 he settled in Weimar, where he had been director of music extraordinary since 1842. This was his most productive period – composing, and conducting the operas of Wagner, Donizetti and Verdi. He remained in Weimar until 1861, living with a princess whom he hoped to marry in Rome; but the Pope revoked his sanction of her divorce. Liszt took four minor orders of the Catholic Church in 1868 but never became a priest. In 1869 he gave master-classes in Weimar, and from 1871 did the same in Budapest. He continued teaching, playing and conducting until dropsy developed into the pneumonia from which he died.

1830–49 (19–38) Piano Concerto No 1 in E♭ major
1831 (20)     *Harmonies poétiques et religieuses*, for piano and orchestra
1835–83 (24–72) *Anneés de pèlerinage*, for piano
1839 (28)     Piano Concerto No 2 in A minor
c1840 (c29)   *Malediction*, for piano and strings
1843 (32)     *Valse Impromptu*, in A♭ major
1849–50 (38–9) *Héroïde funèbre*, for orchestra
1850 (39)     *Consolations*, for piano
              *Prometheus*, symphonic poem
              *Liebestraüme*, nocturnes for piano
1852 (41)     *Hungarian Rhapsodies*, No 1–15
1854 (43)     *Orpheus*, tone poem
              *Les préludes*, symphonic poem
              *Hungaria*, symphonic poem
c1855 (c44)   *Totentanz*, for piano and orchestra
1856 (45)     *Tasso*, symphonic poem
              *Die Hunnenschlacht*, symphonic poem
1857 (46)     *Mazeppa*, symphonic poem
              *Faust*, symphony (possibly 1854–7)
              *Dante*, symphony (possibly 1855–6)
1859 (48)     *Hamlet*, symphonic poem
              *Die Ideale*, for orchestra
c1860 (c49)   *Fantasy on Hungarian Folktunes*, for piano and orchestra
1863 (52)     Two Concert Studies for piano
1866 (55)     *Deux Légendes*, for piano
1867 (56)     *Legend of St Elizabeth* (possibly 1857–62)
1879 (68)     *Via Crucis*
c1880 (c69)   *Hungarian Rhapsodies*, No 16–20
1881 (70)     *Mephisto Waltz*


**LITOLFF, Henry Charles**
*b London, 7 August 1818*
*d Bois-Colombes, 5 August 1891, aged seventy-two*

He was the son of an Alsatian dance violinist who had settled in London. He studied music under his father until the age of twelve, and from 1830 to 1835 under Moscheles. At the age of seventeen he eloped to Gretna Green, and moved to France, where he became a concert pianist. In 1844 he went to Germany, where he taught Hans von Bülow and befriended his family. He returned to England hoping for a divorce, but he failed in this and spent a short time in prison, from which he escaped with the help of the gaoler's daughter. He then went to Holland, where he became very popular. In 1846 he made a friend of Gottfried Meyer, the music publisher. After Meyer's death in 1849 Litolff became a citizen of Brunswick; he succeeded in divorcing his wife, married Meyer's widow and took control of Meyer's publishing firm, changing its name to his own. He divorced his second wife in 1858 and went to Paris, where he settled for the rest of his life. He married twice more, but still found time to perform and conduct throughout Europe.

He wrote vocal scores for stage works:
c1847 (c29)    *Die Braut von Kynast*, vocal score
1871 (53)      *La Boîte de Pandora*, vocal score
1872 (54)      *Héloïse et Abelard*, vocal score
1874 (56)      *La Fiancée du Roi de Garbe*, vocal score
1886 (68)      *Les Templiers*, vocal score
1888 (70)      *L'Escadron volant de la reine*, vocal score
c1890 (c72)    *König Lear*, vocal score
Five other stage works
Litolff also composed:
Four overtures and three other orchestral works
Five concertos symphoniques for piano and orchestra (No 1 lost), of which the popular *Scherzo* comes from No 4
Four works for violin and orchestra
A string quartet
Three piano trios
Over a hundred pieces for piano
Nineteen songs with piano

## LLOYD, George
*b St Ives, Cornwall, 28 June 1913*

He studied at the Royal Academy of Music and at Trinity College of Music. War injuries prevented his being a full-time composer. He was awarded the OBE in 1970.

1933 (20)      Canon for orchestra
1933–4 (20–1) *Iernin*, opera
1936–8 (23–5) *The Serf*, opera
1941 (28)      *Trinidad March*, for military band
                *Charade*, suite for orchestra
1951 (38)      *John Socman*, opera
1980 (67)      *The Vigil of Venus*, for soprano, tenor, chorus and orchestra
Lloyd has also written nine symphonies, four piano concertos and two violin concertos.

## LOCKE, Matthew
*b Devon, c1621–2*
*d London, August 1677, aged c fifty-six*

His musical training was as a chorister and secondary at Exeter Cathedral, where he met both Charles I and the future Charles II. In 1648 he served Prince Charles in the Netherlands, becoming converted to Catholicism there, and receiving great favour from the future Charles II when he returned to England in 1651. He probably married in the mid-1650s, when he lived in Herefordshire.

From 1656 to 1663 he wrote much incidental music for plays. He was a friend of Purcell, on whom he had a strong influence, and is mentioned several times by Pepys. He was given many posts at court, and when the court moved to Oxford in 1665 to 1666 Locke went with them. He wrote many pamphlets, often vitriolic in nature.

He left a great amount of music for the stage, some instrumental works, sacred works in both English and Latin, and secular songs.

## LOEFFLER, Charles
*b Mulhouse, Alsace, 30 January 1861*
*d Medfield, Massachusetts, 19 May 1935, aged seventy-four*

His father was a German writer and teacher. His studies in music were with private teachers in Switzerland and Germany. He emigrated to the USA in 1881, playing violin in orchestras, and becoming assistant leader of the Boston Symphony Orchestra until 1903. Then he decided to devote himself to teaching and composing. He became Officier de l'Academie in 1906 and Chevalier de Légion d'honneur in 1919. He was awarded an honorary doctorate in music from Yale University in 1926.

| | | |
|---|---|---|
| 1891 | (30) | *The Nights in the Ukraine,* for violin and orchestra |
| 1894 | (33) | *Fantasy Concerto,* for cello and orchestra |
| 1895 | (34) | *Divertimento,* for violin and orchestra |
| 1901 | (40) | *Divertissement Espagnol,* for saxophone and orchestra |
| 1902 | (41) | *Poème,* for orchestra |
| 1905 | (44) | *La Mort de Tintagiles,* symphonic poem for two viola d'amore and orchestra |
| | | *La Villanelle du Diable,* symphonic fantasy for organ and orchestra |
| | | *A Pagan Poem,* for piano, English horn and three trumpets |
| 1916 | (55) | *Hora Mystica,* symphony with men's chorus |
| 1923 | (62) | 'Avant que tu ne t'en ailles', poem |
| 1925 | (64) | *Memories of My Childhood,* for orchestra |
| 1928 | (67) | *Clowns,* intermezzo |

## LULLY, Jean-Baptiste
*b Florence, 29 November 1632*
*d Paris, 22 March 1687, aged fifty-four*

He was the son of a Florentine miller. At fourteen he became *valet de chambre* to Mlle de Montpensier, cousin of the Chevalier de Guise. Between his arrival in France and 1652 he studied composition; then he left de Montpensier for the court, where he made his mark not only as a musician but also as a dancer. He became a favourite of Louis XIV, producing for him a stream of ballets – usually in collaboration with Molière – until 1671. He became a naturalised Frenchman in 1661 and married in 1662. His association with Molière ended when Lully pressed the king to award him a series of patents which gave him complete monopoly and domination of the Parisian theatre. While conducting a *Te Deum* to celebrate the king's recovery from a serious illness,he stabbed a cane into his foot, and died from the subsequent infection.

| | | |
|---|---|---|
| 1658 | (26) | *fp Ballets d'Alcidiane* |
| 1659 | (27) | *fp Ballets de la raillerie* |
| 1660 | (28) | *fp Ballet de Xerxes* |
| 1661 | (29) | *fp Ballet de l'impatience* |
| | | *fp Ballet des saisons* |
| | | *fp Ballet de l'Ercole amante* |

| 1663 (31) | fp *Ballets des arts* |
| | fp *Ballets des noces de village* |
| 1664 (32) | fp *Ballet des amours déguisés* |
| | fp *Le mariage forcé*, comedy ballet |
| | fp *La Princesse d'Elide*, comedy ballet |
| | fp Entr'actes for Corneille's *Oedipe* |
| | *Miserere*, concert setting of 'Miserere mei Deus', psalm |
| 1665 (33) | fp *La Naissance de Venus*, ballet |
| | fp *Ballet des gardes* |
| | fp *L'amour médecin*, comedy ballet |
| 1666 (34) | fp *Ballet des Muses* |
| | fp *Le triomphe de Bacchus dans les Indes*, ballet |
| 1667 (35) | fp *Le Sicilien*, comedy ballet |
| 1668 (36) | fp *Le Carnaval, ou Mascarade de Versailles*, ballet |
| | fp *Georges Dandin*, comedy ballet |
| | fp *Plaude Laetare*, motet |
| 1669 (37) | fp *Ballet de Flore* |
| | fp *Monsieur de Pourceaugnac*, comedy ballet |
| 1670 (38) | fp *Les amants magnifiques*, comedy ballet |
| | fp *Le bourgeois gentilhomme*, comedy ballet |
| 1671 (39) | fp *Ballet des ballets* |
| | fp *Psyche*, tragi-comedy |
| 1673 (41) | fp *Cadmus et Hermione*, opera |
| 1674 (42) | fp *Alceste, ou le triomphe d'Alcide*, opera |
| 1675 (43) | fp *Thésée*, opera |
| 1676 (44) | fp *Atys*, opera |
| 1677 (45) | fp *Isis*, opera |
| | fp *Te Deum* |
| 1678 (46) | fp *Psyche*, opera |
| 1679 (47) | fp *Bellérophon*, opera |
| 1680 (48) | fp *Prosperine*, opera |
| 1681 (49) | fp *Le triomphe de l'amour*, ballet |
| 1682 (50) | fp *Persée*, opera |
| 1683 (51) | fp *Phaéton*, opera |
| | fp *De Profundis* |
| 1684 (52) | fp *Amadis de Gaule*, opera |
| | fp *Motets for two choirs* |
| 1685 (53) | fp *Roland*, opera |
| | fp *Le temple de la paix*, ballet |
| 1686 (54) | fp *Armide et Renaud*, opera |
| | fp *Acis et Galathée*, opera |

## LUTOSLAWSKI, Witold
*b Warsaw, 25 January 1913*

His first piece, a prelude for piano, dates from 1922, when he was nine years old. Much of his early work has been lost because of the Nazi occupation and the later Stalinist era. He studied privately from 1924 to 1925, then was at the Warsaw Conservatory from 1932 to 1936, receiving diplomas in piano and composition. From 1932 to 1955 he appeared as a pianist, and since 1953 has been a conductor. He has lectured in the USA, Denmark, England, Sweden and Germany, and has won many international awards and honours.

| 1934 (21) | Piano Sonata |
| 1938 (25) | Symphonic Variations for orchestra |
| 1941 (28) | *Variations on a Theme of Paginini* for two pianos |

Symphony No 1 (1941–7)
1949 (36)     Overture for strings
1950–4 (37–41) Concerto for orchestra
1951 (38)     *Little Suite*, for orchestra
              *Silesian Triptych*, for soprano and orchestra
1954 (41)     *Dance Preludes*, first version for clarinet and piano
1955 (42)     *Dance Preludes*, second version for clarinet and instruments
1957 (44)     Five Songs
1958 (45)     *Funeral Music*, for strings
              Three Postludes for orchestra (1958–63)
1959 (46)     *Dance Preludes*, third version, for instruments
1961 (48)     *Jeux Vénitiens*, for chamber orchestra
1962–3 (49–50) *Trois poèmes d'Henri Michaux*, for mixed chorus of twenty voices,
              wind instruments, two pianos, harp and percussion
1964 (51)     String Quartet
1965 (52)     *Paroles tissées*, for voice and instruments
1967 (54)     Symphony No 2
1968 (55)     *Livre pour orchestre*
1969–70 (56–7) Cello Concerto
1972 (59)     Preludes and Fugue for thirteen solo strings
1975 (62)     *Les espaces du sommeil*, for baritone and orchestra
              *Sacher Variation*, for cello
1976 (63)     *Mi-parti*, for orchestra
1978–9 (65–6) *Novelette*, for orchestra
1979 (66)     *Epitaph*, for oboe and piano
1981 (68)     *Grave*, for cello and piano
1982 (69)     *Mini Overture*
1983 (70)     fp Symphony No 3
              *Chain I*, for small orchestra
Lutoslawski has also written vocal and instrumental music for children, and
music for radio.


## LUTYENS, Elisabeth
*b London, 6 July 1906*
*d London, 14 April 1983, aged seventy-six*

She was the daughter of architect Sir Edwin Lutyens. She studied at the École
Normale in Paris in 1922, then went to the Royal College of Music. After World
War II she survived by writing for films and radio while bringing up four
children. She formed the Composers' Concourse in the 1950s and her own
publishing company, Olivan Press, in the mid-1960s. In 1969 she was awarded
the CBE.

1938 (32)     String Quartets No 1 and 2
              Partita for two violins
              Sonata for solo viola
1939 (33)     Three Pieces for orchestra
              String Trio
1940 (34)     Chamber Concerto No 1, for nine instruments
              Chamber Concerto No 2, for clarinet, tenor saxophone, piano,
              concertante and string orchestra (1940–1)
              *Midas*, ballet for string quartet and piano
1941 (35)     Five Intermezzi for piano
1942 (36)     Three Symphonic Preludes
              Nine Bagatelles for cello and piano
              Two Songs (Auden) for voice and piano

| 1944 (38) | *Suite Gauloise*, for small orchestra |
|---|---|
| 1945 (39) | Chamber Concerto No 3, for bassoon, string orchestra and percussion |
| | Five Little Pieces for clarinet and piano |
| 1947 (41) | Viola Concerto |
| | Chamber Concerto No 4, for horn and small orchestra |
| | Chamber Concerto No 5, for string quartet and small orchestra |
| | *The Pit*, dramatic scene for tenor and bass soli, women's chorus and orchestra |
| 1948 (42) | Chamber Concerto No 6, for oboe, harp and string orchestra |
| | *Aptote*, for solo violin |
| | Three Improvisations for piano |
| | Nine Songs for voice and piano |
| 1949 (43) | String Quartet No 3 |
| 1950 (44) | *Concertante*, for five players |
| 1951 (45) | *Requiem for the Living* |
| | *Penelope*, music drama for violin, cello and piano soli, choir and orchestra |
| | *Nativity*, for soprano and strings or organ |
| 1952 (46) | String Quartets No 4–6 |
| 1953 (47) | Three Songs and Incidental Music, for Group Theater's *Homage to Dylan Thomas* |
| 1954 (48) | *Infidelio*, seven scenes for soprano and tenor soli and seven instruments |
| | *Valediction*, for clarinet and piano |
| 1955 (49) | Music for Orchestra I |
| | *Capriccii*, for two harps and percussion |
| | *Nocturnes*, for violin, guitar and cello |
| | Sinfonia for organ |
| 1956 (50) | Chorale for orchestra, *Hommage à Stravinsky* |
| | *In the Temple of a Bird's Wing*, for baritone and piano (also 1965) |
| 1956–7 (50–1) | Three Duos: |
| | (1) Horn and piano |
| | (2) Cello and piano |
| | (3) Violin and piano |
| 1957 (51) | *Six Tempi for Ten Instruments*, for flute, oboe, clarinet, bassoon, horn, trumpet, violin, viola, cello and piano |
| | *De Amore*, cantata for soprano and tenor soli, choir and orchestra |
| | Variations, for solo flute |
| 1958 (52) | *Piano e Forte*, for solo piano |
| 1959–60 (53–4) | *Quincunx*, for soprano and baritone soli and orchestra |
| 1960 (54) | Wind Quintet |
| 1961 (55) | Symphonies for solo piano, wind, harps and percussion |
| | *Catena*, cantata for soprano and tenor soli and twenty-one instruments |
| 1962 (56) | Music for Orchestra II |
| | Five Bagatelles for piano |
| 1963 (57) | Music for Orchestra III |
| | *Encomion* 'Let us now praise famous men . . .', for chorus, brass and percussion |
| | String Quintet |
| | Wind Trio for flute, clarinet and bassoon |
| | *Fantasie Trio*, for flute, clarinet and piano |
| | *Présages*, for solo oboe |
| | *The Country of the Stars*, motet |
| 1964 (58) | Music for Piano and Orchestra |

Music for Wind for double wind quintet
*Scena*, for violin, cello and percussion

1965 (59) *The Numbered*, opera in prologue and two acts (1965–7)
*The Valley of Hatsu-Se*, for soprano solo, flute, clarinet, cello and piano
*Magnificat* and *Nunc Dimittis*, for unaccompanied chorus
*The Hymn of Man*, motet for unaccompanied male chorus (revised for mixed chorus 1970)

1966 (60) *And Suddenly It's Evening*, for solo tenor and eleven instruments
*Akapotik Rose*, for solo soprano, flute, two clarinets, string trio and piano
*The Fall of the Leafe*, for solo oboe and string quartet
*Music for Three*, for flute, oboe and piano

1967 (61) *Novenaria*, for orchestra
*Time Off? Not a Ghost of a Chance*, charade in four scenes and three interruptions, for baritone, actor, vocal quartet, two mixed choruses and instruments
*Scroll for Li-Ho*, for violin and piano
*Helix*, for piano (four hands)

1968 (62) *Essence of Our Happiness*, for solo tenor, chorus and orchestra
*Horai*, for violin, horn and piano
*Epithalamium*, for organ (soprano solo optional)
*A Phœnix*, for solo soprano, violin, clarinet and piano
*The Egocentric*, for tenor or baritone and piano
*The Tyme Doth Flete*, for unaccompanied chorus, prelude and postlude for two trumpets and two trombones optional

1969 (63) *Isis and Osiris*, lyric drama for eight voices and small orchestra (1969–70)
*Temenos*, for organ
*The Dying of the Sun*, for solo guitar
*Trois pièces brèves*, for chamber organ
*The Tides of Time*, for double-bass and piano
String Trio

1970 (64) *Anerca* (Eskimo poetry), for speaker/actress, ten guitars and percussion
*Vision of Youth*, for soprano, three clarinets, piano and percussion
*Oda a la Tormenta*, for mezzo-soprano and piano
*In the Direction of the Beginning*, for bass and piano
*Verses of Love*, for mixed choir unaccompanied

1971 (65) *Islands*, for soprano, tenor, narrator and instrumental ensemble
*The Tears of Night*, for counter-tenor, six sopranos and three instrumental ensembles
*Dirge for the Proud World*, for soprano, counter-tenor, harpsichord and cello
*Requiescat (Igor Stravinsky 1971)*, for soprano and string trio
*Driving Out the Death*, for oboe and string trio

1972 (66) *The Linnet from the Leaf*, music-theatre for five singers and two instrumental groups
*Voice of Quiet Waters*, for chorus and orchestra
*Counting Your Steps*, for chorus, four flutes and four percussion
*Chimes and Cantos*, for baritone solo, two trumpets, two trombones, four violins, two double-basses and percussion
*Plenum I*, for solo piano
*Dialogo*, for tenor and lute

1973 (67) *One and the Same*, scena for soprano, speaker, two female mimes, male mime and instrumental ensemble

216

|          |                                                                          |
|----------|--------------------------------------------------------------------------|
|          | *The Waiting Game*, three scenes for mezzo-soprano, baritone and small orchestra |
|          | *Roads*, for two sopranos, counter-tenor, baritone and bass              |
|          | *Rape of the Moone*, for wind octet                                      |
|          | *Laudi*, for soprano, three clarinets, piano and percussion              |
|          | *Tre*, for solo clarinet                                                 |
|          | *Plenum II*, for solo oboe                                               |
|          | *Plenum III*, for string quartet                                         |
| 1974 (68)| *The Winter of the World*, for orchestras                                |
|          | *Kareniana (for Karen Phillips)*, for instrumental ensemble              |
|          | *Sloth, One of the Seven Deadly Sins*, for male voices                   |
| 1975 (69)| *Eos*, for small orchestra                                               |
|          | *Fanfare for a Festival*, for three trumpets and three trombones         |
|          | *Pietá*, for harpsichord                                                 |
|          | *Ring of Bone*, for solo piano                                           |
| 1976 (70)| *Mare et Minutiae*, for string quartet                                   |
|          | *Constants*, for cello and piano                                         |
| 1977 (71)| *Rondel*, for chamber ensemble                                           |
| 1978 (72)| *Doubles*, for string quartet                                            |
|          | Seven Preludes for piano                                                 |
|          | *Elegy of the Flowers*, for three instrumental groups                    |
|          | *Footfalls*, for flute and piano                                         |
| 1979 (73)| *Echoi*, for mezzo and orchestra                                         |
|          | Cantata for soprano and ensemble                                         |
|          | 'She Tells Her Love While Half Asleep', for unaccompanied voice          |
|          | *The Great Seas*, for piano                                              |
|          | Prelude for solo violin                                                  |
|          | Cantata for soprano, alto, baritone and ensemble                         |
|          | Trio for clarinet, cello and piano                                       |
|          | *The Roots of the World*, for chorus and cello                           |
|          | *That Sun*, for contralto and piano                                      |

## McCABE, John
*b Huyton, Liverpool, 21 April 1930*

He studied at Manchester University and the Royal Manchester College of Music, continuing at the Hochschule für Musik in Munich. From 1965 to 1968 he was pianist-in-residence at University College, Cardiff, and subsequently has lived and worked in London.

|          |                                                                          |
|----------|--------------------------------------------------------------------------|
| 1959 (29)| Violin Concerto No 1                                                     |
| 1960 (30)| Partita for string quartet                                              |
| 1961 (31)| Sinfonia for organ                                                      |
| 1962 (32)| *Concerto Funèbre*, for viola and chamber orchestra                      |
| 1963 (33)| Variations for piano                                                    |
|          | Three Folk Songs for high voice and piano                               |
| 1964 (34)| *Variations on a Theme of Hartmann*, for orchestra                       |
|          | Symphony for ten wind instruments                                       |
|          | *Musica Notturna*, for violin, viola and piano                           |
|          | Three Pieces for clarinet and piano                                     |
|          | Movement for clarinet, violin and cello (revised 1966)                  |
|          | Five Bagatelles for piano                                               |
|          | Prelude for organ                                                       |
|          | *Johannis-Partita*, for organ                                            |
|          | *Mary Laid Her Child*, for unaccompanied chorus                          |
| 1965 (35)| Chamber Concerto for viola, cello and orchestra                         |

|  | Concertante for harpsichord and chamber ensemble |
|---|---|
|  | Symphony No 1, *Elegy* |
|  | String Trio |
|  | Fantasy for brass quartet |
|  | Bagatelles for two clarinets |
|  | Elegy for organ |
| 1966 (36) | Piano Concerto No 1 |
|  | Concerto for chamber orchestra (revised 1968) |
|  | Partita for solo cello |
|  | *Nocturnal*, for piano and string quartet |
|  | Miniconcerto for organ, percussion and audience |
|  | *Rain Songs*, for soprano, counter-tenor or alto, cello and harpsichord |
|  | *Great Lord of Lords*, for chorus and organ |
|  | *A Hymne to God the Father*, for unaccompanied chorus |
|  | *Canticles for Salisbury*, for chorus and organ |
| 1967 (37) | Dance-Movements for horn, violin and piano |
|  | Rounds for brass quintet |
|  | *Fantasy on a Theme of Liszt*, for piano |
|  | *Aspects of Whiteness*, for chorus and piano (revised 1969) |
| 1968 (38) | *The Morning Watch*, for chorus and organ |
|  | Concertino for piano duet and orchestra |
|  | Concertante Music for orchestra |
|  | *Metamorphoses*, for harpsichord and orchestra |
|  | Canto for guitar |
|  | Oboe Quartet |
|  | Intermezzi for piano |
|  | *The Lion, the Witch and the Wardrobe*, children's opera |
| 1969 (39) | Sonata for clarinet, cello and piano |
|  | Concerto for piano and wind quintet |
|  | *The Greensleeves Round*, for harpsichord |
|  | *Capriccio* (Study No 1), for piano |
|  | *Sostenuto* (Study No 2), for piano |
|  | *To Us in Bethlem City*, for unaccompanied chorus |
|  | *This Town's a Corporation Full of Crooked Streets*, an entertainment for speaker, tenor, children's chorus, mixed chorus and ensemble |
| 1970 (40) | *Notturni ed Alba*, for soprano and orchestra |
|  | Piano Concerto No 2, *Sinfonia Concertante* |
|  | *Concertante Variations on a Theme of Nicholas Maw*, for strings |
|  | Canzona for wind and percussion |
|  | *Gaudi* (Study No 3), for piano |
|  | *Aubade* (Study No 4), for piano |
|  | *Basse Danse*, for two pianos |
|  | *Norwich Canticles*, for unaccompanied chorus |
| 1971 (41) | Symphony No 2 |
|  | Dance-Prelude for oboe d'amore and piano |
|  | *Requiem Sequence*, for soprano and piano |
| 1972 (42) | Oboe d'amore Concerto |
|  | String Quartet No 2 |
|  | *Voyage*, for soli, chorus and orchestra |
| 1973 (43) | *Maze Dances*, for solo violin |
|  | Madrigal for chamber orchestra |
|  | *The Castle of Arianrhod*, for horn and piano |
|  | *Das Letzte Gerichte*, for voice, guitar and percussion |
|  | *Time Remembered*, for soprano and ensemble |

Upon the High Midnight, three carols for unaccompanied chorus
The Teachings of Don Juan, ballet
Arabesque, for ensemble
1973–5 (43–5) The Goddess Trilogy, for horn and piano
1974 (44) The Chagall Windows, for orchestra
The Play of Mother Courage, chamber opera
Sam, for orchestra
1975 (45) Behold the Silly Tender Babe, for chorus and organ
Mary Queen of Scots, ballet
1976 (46) Sonata on a motet for string orchestra
Piano Concerto No 3, Dialogues
Couples, theme music for piano
Stabat Mater, for soprano, chorus and orchestra
Five Folk Songs for high voice, horn and piano
1977 (47) Jubilee Suite, for orchestra
Clarinet Concerto
Reflections of a Summer Night, for chorus and orchestra
A Lute-book Lullaby, for SSA and flute
1978 (48) Images, for brass band
Symphony No 3, Hommages
Star Preludes, for violin and piano
String Quartet No 3
1979 (49) The Shadow of Light, for orchestra
Motet for chorus
Les Soirs bleus, for soprano, recorder, cello and harpsichord
1980 (50) Siberia, for unaccompanied chorus
Violin Concerto No 2
Portraits, for flute and piano
Dances for trumpet and piano
Mosaic (Study No 6), for piano
1981 (51) Desert I: Lizard, for woodwind and percussion
Desert II: Horizon, for ten brass instruments
Afternoons and Afterwards, for piano
Music's Empire, for soli, chorus and orchestra
1982 (52) Concerto for orchestra
Desert III: Landscape, for violin, cello and piano
String Quartet No 4
Lamentation Rag, for piano


## MacDOWELL, Edward Alexander
b New York, 18 December 1860
d New York, 23 January 1908, aged forty-seven

His father was of Scottish descent and his mother Irish. At the age of fifteen he went to Paris to study, and in 1877 won a scholarship to the Paris Conservatory, where Debussy was a fellow student. He then moved to Frankfurt to study composition with Raff. He was appointed chief piano teacher at Darmstadt, and from the age of twenty-one began to achieve recognition as a composer. At the age of twenty-six he returned to America and settled in Boston, and at thirty-five he moved to New York as professor of music at Columbia University. He resigned after eight years of excessive work and developed brain trouble, from which he died.

1882 (21) Piano Concerto No 1 in A minor
1883 (22) Modern Suite No 1, for piano
1884 (23) Forest Idylls, four pieces for piano

| 1885 (24) | p Hamlet and Ophelia, symphonic poem |
| 1887 (26) | Six Idylls after Goethe for piano |
| | Six Poems after Heine for piano |
| 1888 (27) | Lancelot and Elaine, symphonic poem |
| | Marionettes, eight pieces for piano |
| | Romance, for cello |
| 1889 (28) | Les Orientales, after Hugo, for piano |
| | Lamia, symphonic poem |
| 1890 (29) | Piano Concerto No 2 in D minor |
| | Twelve Studies for piano, Books I and II |
| 1891 (30) | Suite No 1 for orchestra |
| | The Saracens, symphonic poem |
| | The Lovely Alda, symphonic poem |
| 1893 (32) | Piano Sonata No 1, Tragica |
| 1894 (33) | Twelve Virtuoso Studies for piano |
| 1895 (34) | Piano Sonata No 2, Eroica |
| 1896 (35) | Indian Suite (Suite No 2), for orchestra |
| | Woodland Sketches, for piano |
| 1898 (37) | Sea Pieces, for piano |
| 1900 (39) | Piano Sonata No 3, Norse (dedicated to Grieg, qv) |
| 1901 (40) | Piano Sonata No 4, Keltic |
| 1902 (41) | Fireside Tales, for piano |
| | New England Idylls |

## MACHAUT, Guillaume de
b Rheims, c1300
d Rheims, April 1377, aged seventy-seven

He was in the service of the King of Bohemia from about 1323 until the king's death in 1346. Pope John XXII granted him canonries in 1330, 1332 and 1333. He settled in Rheims in about 1340, and for the rest of his life enjoyed the friendship and patronage of the highest nobility in France. He had a larger output of compositions than any other composer in the fourteenth century.

His work was almost entirely vocal, and included: a mass; twenty-three motets; forty-two ballades; twenty-two rondeaux; thirty-three virelais; nineteen lais.

## MACONCHY, Elizabeth
b Broxbourne, Hertfordshire, 19 March 1907

Though born in England she is Irish. She studied at the Royal College of Music under Charles Wood and Vaughan Williams. She was awarded the Octavia Travelling Scholarship and went to Prague, where her first major work, the 1930 Concertino for piano and orchestra, was performed. She became the first woman chairman of the Composers' Guild in 1959, and was chairman of the SPNM from 1972 to 1975. She received the Cobbett Medal, and in 1977 was awarded the CBE.

| 1930 (23) | Concertino for piano and orchestra |
| | The Land, for ochestra |
| 1933 (26) | String Quartet No 1 |
| 1937 (30) | String Quartet No 2 |
| 1938 (31) | String Quartet No 3 |
| 1948 (41) | String Quartet No 5 |
| 1953 (46) | Proud Thames, overture |
| 1956–7 (49–50) | The Sofa, one-act opera |

1958 (51)    *The Three Strangers*, one-act opera
1960–1 (53–4) *The Departure*, one-act opera
1963 (56)    Serenata Concertante for violin and orchestra
1963–4 (56–7) *Samson and the Gates of Gaza*, cantata
1964–70 (57–63) *Three Settings of Poems by Gerard Manley Hopkins*, for high voice
                and chamber orchestra
1965 (58)    Variazioni Concertante for orchestra
1965–6 (58–9) Notebook for Harpsichord
1968–9 (61–2) String Quartet No 9
1969 (62)    *And Death Shall Have No Dominion*, choral
1970 (63)    *Ariadne*, for soprano and orchestra
             *The Jesse Tree*, opera
1971 (64)    String Quartet No 10
1974 (67)    Three Songs for tenor and harp
             *Siren's Song*, for chorus
1974–5 (67–8) *King of the Golden River*, opera
1975 (68)    *Two Epitaphs*, for female chorus
             *Epyllion*, for solo cello and fifteen strings
1975–6 (68–9) Sinfonietta for orchestra
1976 (69)    Three Pieces for harp
             String Quartet No 11
             *Hopkins Motets*
1977 (70)    *Héloïse and Abelard*, choral
1978 (71)    *Sun, Moon and Stars*, for soprano and piano
             *Contemplation*, for cello and piano
1979 (72)    *Romanza*, for viola and piano
1981 (74)    *Piccola Musica*, for violin, viola and cello
             *Trittico*, for two oboes, bassoon and harpsichord
             *Little Symphony*
1982 (75)    *My Dark Heart*, for soprano and ensemble
             Wind Quintet
1983 (76)    *Tribute*, for violin and woodwinds
             *L'Horloge*, for soprano, clarinet and piano
             Music for strings

## MAHLER, Gustav
*b Kaliste, Bohemia, 7 July 1860*
*d Vienna, 18 May 1911, aged fifty*

Complicated family matters gave him a traumatic childhood, and the effects of
this remained with him for the rest of his life. He gave a piano recital at the age
of ten, and in 1875 went to the Vienna Conservatory, ending his studies there
one year later, laden with honours. In the 1880s he became an opera conductor,
working mainly in Leipzig and later in Budapest and Hamburg. In 1897 he went
to Vienna to conduct *Lohengrin*, and became the artistic director of the Vienna
Court Opera and of the Vienna Philharmonic. He married Alma Schindler,
herself a fine musician, in 1902. In 1907 he left Vienna for the USA, lost his elder
daughter, and discovered that he had a chronic heart condition. Nevertheless,
in 1909 he conducted two opera productions for the Metropolitan and three
concerts by the New York Symphony Orchestra, and followed this by taking
over the conductorship of the New York Philharmonic Orchestra. While
conducting he was taken ill; he returned to Europe, and shortly afterwards died
in Vienna. He had already made a draft and some notes about his tenth
symphony, and since then there have been some inspired completions of it,
notably by Deryk Cooke. His music fell into disfavour after his death, but in the
1950s came a much-deserved revival.

| 1880 | (20) | *Klagende Lieder* |
|------|------|------|
| 1882 | (22) | *Lieder und Gesänge aus der Jugendzeit* |
| 1883 | (23) | *Lieder eines fahrenden Gesellen*, for voice and orchestra |
| 1888 | (28) | *Lieder aus des Knaben Wunderhorn*, song cycle for voice and orchestra |
|      |      | Symphony No 1 in D major |
| 1894 | (34) | Symphony No 2 in C minor, *Resurrection*, with final movement for soprano and contralto soloists, choir and orchestra |
| 1895 | (35) | Symphony No 3 in D minor, with final movement for contralto, boys' and female choruses and orchestra |
| 1900 | (40) | Symphony No 4 in G major, with final movement for soprano and orchestra |
| 1902 | (42) | Symphony No 5 in C♯ minor |
|      |      | Five Rückert Songs |
| 1904 | (44) | Symphony No 6 in A minor |
| 1905 | (45) | Symphony No 7 in E minor |
|      |      | *Kindertotenlieder*, song cycle for voice and orchestra |
| 1907 | (47) | Symphony No 8 in E♭ major, *Symphony of a Thousand*, with eight vocal soloists, two choruses, boys' chorus, organ and orchestra |
| 1908 | (48) | *Das Lied von der Erde* (The Song of the Earth), song cycle of symphonic dimensions |
| 1909 | (49) | Symphony No 9 in D major |
| 1910 | (50) | Symphony No 10 begun, unfinished at Mahler's death (A completion was made in 1964 by Deryk Cooke which is now used as the performing version) |

## MALIPIERO, Gian Francesco
b Venice, 18 March 1882
d Treviso, 1 August 1973, aged ninety-one

Though both his father and his grandfather were musicians he showed no early interest in music. At the age of fourteen he attended classes in harmony at the Vienna Conservatory, and became engrossed in the subject. He married the daughter of a Venetian artist in 1910 and settled down to a life of composition. An authority on early Italian music, his horizons suddenly broadened on hearing Stravinsky's *Rite of Spring* in Paris in 1913. He wrote most of the libretti for his own operas. The traumas caused by World War II inhibited his work, and he took a considerable time to recover. His last years were spent privately, studying old music.

| 1906 | (24) | *Sinfonia del Mare* |
|------|------|------|
| 1908 | (26) | Cello Sonata |
| 1910 | (28) | *Sinfonia del Silenzio e della Morte* |
|      |      | *Impressioni dal Vero, I* (1910–11) |
| 1914–15 | (32–3) | *Impressioni dal Vero, II* |
| 1917 | (35) | *Ditirambo Tragico* |
|      |      | *Armenia*, for orchestra |
| 1918 | (36) | *Grottesco*, for small orchestra |
|      |      | *Pantea*, ballet |
|      |      | *L'Orfeide*, opera (1918–21) |
| 1919–21 | (37–9) | *Tre Commedie Goldiane*, opera |
| 1920 | (38) | *Oriente immaginario* |
| 1921–2 | (39–40) | *Impressioni dal Vero, III* |
| 1925 | (43) | *Filomela e l'infatuato*, opera |
|      |      | *Merlino maestro d'organi*, opera (1925–8) |
|      |      | *Il Mistero di Venezia*, opera (1925–8) |

| 1926 (44) | L'Esilio dell'Eroe, five symphonic impressions |
| 1929 (47) | Torneo notturno, opera |
| 1930 (48) | La bella e il mostro, opera |
| 1931 (49) | Concerto for orchestra |
| 1932 (50) | Violin Concerto |
| | Sette Invenzione, for orchestra |
| | Inni, for orchestra |
| 1933 (51) | La favola del figlio cambiato, opera |
| 1934 (52) | Symphony No 1 |
| | Piano Concerto No 1 |
| 1936 (54) | Julius Caesar, opera |
| | Symphony No 2, Elegiaca |
| 1937 (55) | Piano Concerto No 2 |
| | Cello Concerto |
| 1938 (56) | Anthony and Cleopatra, opera |
| | Triple Concerto for violin, cello and piano |
| 1939 (57) | Ecuba, opera |
| 1940 (58) | La vita e'sogno, opera |
| 1941–2 (59–60) | I Capriccio di Callot, opera |
| 1942 (60) | Minnie la candida, opera |
| 1943 (61) | L'allegra brigata, opera |
| 1944 (62) | Symphony No 3, Delle Campane |
| 1946 (64) | Symphony No 4, In Memoriam |
| 1947 (65) | Symphony No 5, Concertante in eco, with two pianos |
| | Symphony No 6, Degli Archi, for strings |
| 1948 (66) | Symphony No 7, Delle Canzoni |
| | Piano Concerto No 3 |
| | Mondi celeste e infernali, opera (1948–9) |
| 1950 (68) | Symphony in one movement |
| | Piano Concerto No 4 |
| 1951 (69) | Sinfonia del zodiaco |
| 1952 (70) | Violin Concerto |
| 1957 (75) | Quintet for piano and strings |
| 1959 (77) | Musica da Camera, for wind quintet |
| | Sei poesie di Dylan Thomas, for soprano and ten instruments |
| 1960 (78) | String Quartet No 3 |
| 1964 (82) | In Time of Daffodils, for soprano, baritone, flute, clarinet, bass-clarinet, viola, double-bass, guitar and percussion |
| | Symphony No 8 |
| 1965 (83) | Costellazioni, for piano |
| 1966 (84) | Symphony No 9 |
| 1967 (85) | Carnet de Notes, for chamber orchestra |
| | Cassazione, for string sextet |
| | Symphony No 10 |
| 1968 (86) | Gli Eroi di Bonaventura, for orchestra |
| | Flute Concerto |
| 1970 (88) | Symphony No 11 |

## MARENZIO, Luca

b Coccaglia, near Brescia, 1553
d Rome, 22 August 1599, aged forty-six

He studied the organ, and became *maestro* to two courts in Rome. He was in the service of the King of Poland, either from 1588 to 1590 or 1591 to 1593, and was appointed to the Papal Chapel in 1595. He wrote much church music and was particularly famous for his madrigals, of which he left: sixteen books; one book of five-part spiritual madrigals; three books of motets; one book of Sacri Concerti; six books of villanelles.


## MARTIN, Frank
b Geneva, 15 September 1890
d Naarden, Holland, 21 November 1974, aged eighty-four

He was the tenth child of a Calvinist minister. He began composing at the age of eight, though his parents allowed him to have only one private teacher in music. He lectured on chamber music at Geneva Conservatory, and became the director of a private music school. From 1943 to 1946 he was president of the Swiss Musicians' Union. In 1946 he moved to the Netherlands, travelling from his home to hold composition classes in Cologne from 1950 to 1957. Composition did not come easily to him, and he was lucky to have the help and influence of the conductor Ansermet. He toured the world as a piano performer, and won many prizes and honours.

| | | |
|---|---|---|
| 1926 | (36) | *Rythmes*, three symphonic movements |
| 1931 | (41) | Violin Sonata |
| | | *Chaconne*, for cello and piano |
| 1933 | (43) | Four Short Pieces for guitar |
| 1934 | (44) | Piano Concerto No 1 |
| 1935 | (45) | *Rhapsody*, for two violins, two violas and double-bass, or string orchestra |
| 1936 | (46) | Symphony for full orchestra (1936–7) |
| | | *Danse de la peur*, for two pianos and small orchestra |
| | | String Trio |
| 1938 | (48) | *Ballade*, for alto saxophone, string orchestra, piano, timpani and percussion |
| | | *Le Vin herbe*, opera (Der Zaubertrank) (1938–41) |
| | | Sonata da Chiesa for viola d'amore and organ |
| 1939 | (49) | *Ballade*, for piano and orchestra |
| | | *Ballade*, for flute, string orchestra and piano |
| | | *Ballade*, for flute and piano |
| 1941 | (51) | Sonata da Chiesa for flute and string orchestra |
| 1942–3 | (52–3) | *Die Weise von Liebe und Tod des Cornets Christoph Rilke*, for high voice and orchestra |
| 1943 | (53) | *Sechs Monologe aus Jedermann*, for baritone and piano |
| 1944 | (54) | *Petite symphonie concertante* (1944–5) |
| | | *In terra pax*, oratorio |
| | | Passacaglia for organ |
| 1945–8 | (55–8) | *Golgotha*, oratorio |
| 1946 | (56) | Overture to Racine's *Athalie*, for orchestra |
| 1947 | (57) | *Trois chants de Noël*, for high voice, flute and piano |
| 1948 | (58) | *Ballade*, for cello and piano |
| | | Eight Piano Preludes |
| 1949 | (59) | Concerto for seven wind instruments |
| 1950 | (60) | Violin Concerto (1950–1) |
| | | *Five Ariel Songs*, for mixed chamber choir |
| 1951 | (61) | Concerto for cembalo and small orchestra (1951–2) |
| 1952–5 | (62–5) | *La Tempête*, opera |
| 1955–6 | (65) | *Études*, for string orchestra |
| 1956 | (66) | *Overture in Homage to Mozart*, for orchestra |
| 1957–9 | (67–9) | *La Mystère de la Nativité*, oratorio |
| 1958 | (68) | *Overture in Rondo*, for orchestra |

|  | *Pseaumes de Genève*, for mixed choir, children's voices, organ and orchestra |
|---|---|
| 1960 (70) | *Drey Minnelieder*, for soprano and piano |
| 1961–2 (71–2) | *Monsieur de Pourceaugnac*, opera |
| 1963–4 (73–4) | *Les quatre éléments*, symphonic studies: Earth, Water, Air, Fire |
| 1964 (74) | *Pilate*, cantata |
| 1965–6 (75–6) | Cello Concerto |
| 1967 (77) | String Quartet |
| 1968 (78) | *Maria-Triptychon (Ave Maria – Magnificat – Stabat Mater)*, for soprano, solo violin and orchestra |
|  | Piano Concerto No 2 |
| 1969 (79) | *Erasmi Monumentum*, for orchestra and organ |
|  | *Poèmes de la mort*, for tenor, baritone, bass and three electric guitars (1969–71) |
| 1970 (80) | Three Dances, for oboe, harp, string quintet and string orchestra |
| 1971–2 (81–2) | *Requiem*, for soprano, contralto, tenor and bass soli, mixed choir, orchestra and organ |
| 1972 (82) | *Ballade*, for viola, wind orchestra, cembalo, harp and timpani |
| 1973 (83) | *Polyptyque*, for violin and two small string orchestras |
|  | *Fantasy on Flamenco Rhythms*, for piano |
| 1974 (84) | *Et la vie l'emporta*, chamber cantata |

## MARTINŮ , Bohuslav
*b Polička, Czechoslovakia, 8 December 1890*
*d Liestal, Switzerland, 28 August 1959, aged sixty-nine*

He was the son of a cobbler who was also keeper of the church tower in which he was born and lived for his first eleven years. He showed early signs of musical talent and became involved with local festivals. His prowess as a violinist impelled local citizens to send him to the Prague Conservatory. He passed his teaching examinations and became a violin teacher in his home town in 1916; after World War I he played in the Czech Philharmonic orchestra. He went to Paris in 1923, remaining there composing until the Nazis drove him to America in 1940. After the war he refused the offer of a professorship at Prague Conservatory. He died of stomach cancer.

| 1918 (28) | *Czech Rhapsody*, for chorus |
|---|---|
| 1921 (31) | *Istar*, ballet |
| 1922 (32) | *The Grove of the Satyrs*, symphonic poem |
|  | *Shadows*, symphonic poem |
|  | *Vanishing Midnight*, symphonic poem |
| 1925 (35) | *Half Time*, symphonic poem |
|  | Piano Concerto No 1 |
|  | *On tourne*, ballet |
| 1927 (37) | *La bagarre*, symphonic poem |
|  | *La revue de cuisine*, ballet |
|  | *Le raid merveilleux*, ballet (1927–8) |
| 1928 (38) | *The Soldier and the Dancer*, opera |
|  | *Les Lames du Couteau*, opera |
|  | *Echéc au roi*, ballet |
|  | *La Rapsodie* |
|  | *Entr'acte*, for orchestra |
|  | Concertino for piano (left hand) and chamber orchestra |
| 1929 (39) | *Journée de bonté*, opera |
|  | *The Butterfly that Stamped*, ballet |
| 1930 (40) | *Serenade*, for chamber orchestra |

|          | Violin Sonata No 1 |
| 1931 (41) | Cello Concerto |
|          | Partita (Suite No 1) |
|          | *Spaliček*, ballet |
| 1932 (42) | *Les Rondes*, for orchestra |
|          | Sinfonia for two orchestras |
|          | Overture for the Sokol Festival |
| 1933 (43) | *The Miracle of Our Lady*, opera |
| 1934 (44) | *Inventions*, for orchestra |
| 1935 (45) | *The Suburban Theatre*, opera |
|          | *Le Jugement de Paris*, ballet |
|          | Concertino No 2 for piano |
| 1936–7 (46–7) | *Juliette, or The Key to Dreams*, opera |
| 1937 (47) | *Alexandre bis*, opera |
|          | *Comedy on the Bridge*, opera |
| 1938 (48) | Concerto for two string orchestras, piano and timpani |
|          | Concerto Grosso for orchestra |
|          | *Tre Ricercare* for orchestra |
|          | Quartet No 5 |
|          | Madrigals for women's voices |
| 1939 (49) | Field Mass |
| 1940 (50) | Military March |
| 1942 (52) | Symphony No 1 |
| 1943 (53) | Symphony No 2 |
|          | Concerto for two pianos |
|          | Violin Concerto |
|          | *In Memory of Lidice*, for orchestra |
| 1944 (54) | Symphony No 3 |
|          | Cello Concerto (1944–5) |
| 1945 (55) | Symphony No 4 |
|          | *Thunderbolt P-47*, for orchestra |
| 1946 (56) | Symphony No 5 |
| 1947 (57) | Quartet No 7 |
| 1948 (58) | Piano Concerto No 3 |
|          | *The Strangler*, ballet |
| 1949 (59) | Sinfonia Concertante |
|          | *Mazurka-Nokturne* for string quartet |
| 1950 (60) | Double Violin Concerto No 2 |
|          | Intermezzo for orchestra |
|          | Sinfonietta, *La Jolla*, for piano and orchestra |
|          | Piano Trio No 2 |
| 1951 (61) | Piano Trio No 3 |
|          | *Stowe Pastorals*, for chamber ensemble |
|          | *Serenade*, for two clarinets and string trio |
| 1951–3 (61–3) | Symphony No 6, *Fantasies Symphoniques* |
| 1952 (62) | *What Men Live By*, TV opera |
|          | *Rhapsodie*, for viola and orchestra |
| 1953 (63) | *The Marriage*, opera |
|          | *Accusation against the Unknown*, TV opera |
|          | Concerto for violin, piano and orchestra |
|          | Overture |
|          | *Fresky Piero della Francesco*, for orchestra |
| 1954 (64) | *Mirandolina*, opera |
|          | *Hymn to Jacob*, for soli, chorus, horn, strings and organ |
|          | *Mount of Three Lights*, cantata |
| 1954–5 (64–5) | *The Epic of Gilgamesh*, oratorio |

| 1955 (65) | Three Frescoes, for orchestra |
| | Oboe Concerto |
| | The Opening of the Wells, chamber cantata |
| 1955–6 (65–6) | Piano Concerto No 4, Incantations |
| 1956 (66) | Legend of the Smoke, chamber cantata |
| 1956–9 (66–9) | The Greek Passion, opera |
| 1957 (67) | Piano Concerto No 5, Fantasia Concertante |
| 1957–8 (67–8) | The Parables, for orchestra |
| 1958 (68) | Ariadne, opera |
| | Three Estampie for orchestra |
| 1959 (68) | Mikeš of the Mountains, chamber cantata |
| | Festival of Birds, for children's voices and trumpet |
| | The Prophecy of Isaiah, for voices and ensemble |
| | The Burden of Moab, for male voices and piano |
| | Chamber Music for clarinet, harp and piano quartet |
| | Nonet for wind quintet, string trio and double-bass |

## MASCAGNI, Pietro
b Leghorn, 7 December 1863
d Rome, 2 August 1945, aged eighty-one

His father forbade him to study music, intending him for the law, so he took lessons secretly. When his father found out an uncle came to the rescue and adopted him, and he made such rapid progress that the first performances of his works were given when he was only sixteen. He was able later to go to the Milan Conservatory to study under Ponchielli, who was also Puccini's teacher. He travelled as conductor with a touring opera company, then married, and settled down in a small town to manage the municipal school and give piano lessons. He rose to instant fame with *Cavalleria Rusticana*, but nothing he wrote subsequently made a comparable mark. He once said: 'It is a pity I wrote *Cavalleria Rusticana* first; I was crowned before I was king!' He supported Italy's fascist regime, but with Mussolini's overthrow Mascagni was stripped of his property and honours, and spent his last years in poverty and disgrace in a small hotel room in Rome.

| 1879 (16) | Symphony in C minor |
| 1881 (18) | Symphony in F major |
| | In Filanda, for voices and orchestra |
| 1890 (27) | Cavalleria Rusticana, opera |
| 1891 (28) | L'Amico Fritz, opera |
| | Solemn Mass |
| 1892 (29) | I Rantzau, opera |
| 1895 (32) | Guglielmo Ratcliff, opera |
| | Silvano, opera |
| 1896 (33) | Zanetto, opera |
| 1898 (35) | Iris, opera |
| 1901 (38) | Le Maschera, opera |
| 1905 (42) | Amica, opera |
| 1911 (48) | Isabeau, opera |
| 1913 (50) | Parisina, opera |
| 1917 (54) | Lodoletta, opera |
| | Satanic Rhapsody |
| 1919 (56) | Si, opera |
| 1921 (58) | Il Piccolo Marat, opera |
| 1932 (69) | Pinotta, opera |
| 1935 (72) | Nero, opera |

## MASSENET, Jules
b Montaud, 12 May 1842
d Paris, 13 August 1912, aged seventy

He was the son of an ironmaster. He took piano lessons from his mother, and at the age of eleven was able to enter the Paris Conservatory. As a student he earned pocket-money by playing in the percussion section of orchestras in various theatres. He won a first prize for piano, and in 1863 he won the Prix de Rome, which took him to the Villa Medici. In Rome he met Liszt, through whom Massenet was to meet his future wife. His teacher, Ambroise Thomas, used his influence to obtain performances of Massenet's early work, and from then on there was no looking back – his success as an opera writer was unbroken until his death. From 1878 onward he was professor of composition at the Paris Conservatory.

| | | |
|---|---|---|
| 1863 | (21) | Ouverture de Concert |
| | | David Rizzio, cantata |
| 1865 | (23) | Suite for orchestra, No 1 |
| 1871 | (29) | Suite for orchestra, No 2, Scènes hongroises |
| 1873 | (31) | Suite for orchestra, No 3, Scènes dramatiques |
| | | Phèdre, concert overture |
| 1874 | (32) | Suite for orchestra, No 4, Scènes pittoresques |
| 1875 | (33) | Eve, oratorio |
| 1876 | (34) | Suite for orchestra, No 5, Scènes napolitaines |
| 1877 | (35) | Le Roi de Lahore, opera |
| | | Narcisse, cantata |
| 1879 | (37) | Suite for orchestra, No 6, Scènes de féerie |
| 1880 | (38) | La Vierge, oratorio |
| 1881 | (39) | Suite for orchestra, No 7, Scènes alsaciennes |
| | | Hérodiade, opera |
| 1884 | (42) | Manon, opera |
| 1885 | (43) | Le Cid, opera |
| 1887 | (45) | Parade Militaire |
| 1890 | (48) | Visions, symphonic poem |
| 1892 | (50) | Werther, opera |
| 1894 | (52) | Thaïs, opera |
| | | La Navarraise, opera |
| 1897 | (55) | Marche solennelle |
| | | Fantaisie, for cello and orchestra |
| | | Sappho, lyric play |
| | | Devant la Madone, opera |
| 1899 | (57) | Brumaire, overture |
| | | Cendrillon, opera |
| 1900 | (58) | La Terre promisée, oratorio |
| 1902 | (60) | Piano Concerto |
| | | Le Jongleur de Notre Dame, opera |
| 1910 | (68) | Don Quixote, opera |

## MATHIAS, William
b Whitland, Dyfed, 1 November 1934

He graduated from the University College of Wales in 1956, and was awarded an open scholarship to the Royal Academy of Music to study composition with Lennox Berkeley and piano with Peter Katin. He became a lecturer in music at the University College in 1959, was elected a fellow of the Royal Academy in 1965, and gained a doctorate in music from the University of Wales in 1966. In

1968 he was awarded the Bax Society Prize and became senior lecturer in composition at Edinburgh University; in 1970 he became professor and head of the department of music at the University College of North Wales in Bangor.

| | |
|---|---|
| 1958 (24) | Divertimento for string orchestra |
| 1959 (25) | Improvisations for solo harp |
| 1961 (27) | Piano Concerto No 2 |
| | Music for strings |
| 1962 (28) | Sonata for violin and piano |
| | Dance Overture |
| | Invocation and Dance for orchestra |
| | Serenade for small orchestra |
| | Partita for organ |
| | *All Thy Works Shall Praise Thee*, for mixed voices and organ |
| | Variations on a hymn tune for organ |
| 1963 (29) | Quintet for flute, oboe, clarinet, horn and bassoon |
| 1964 (30) | Piano Sonata |
| | Divertimento for flute, oboe and piano |
| | Prelude, Aria and Finale for strings |
| | *Make a Joyful Noise Unto the Lord*, for mixed voices and organ |
| 1965 (31) | *Festival Te Deum*, for mixed voices and organ |
| | *Wassail Carol*, for mixed voices and organ or orchestra |
| | *O Sing Unto the Lord*, for mixed voices and organ |
| 1966 (32) | Concerto for orchestra |
| | Symphony No 1 |
| | *Three Medieval Lyrics*, for chorus and instruments |
| 1967 (33) | Sinfonietta for orchestra |
| | Invocations for organ |
| | Toccata Giocosa for organ |
| | Communion Service in C |
| | *Litanies*, concertante music for orchestra |
| 1968 (34) | String Quartet |
| | Piano Concerto No 3 |
| | *Lift Up Your Heads O Ye Gates*, for mixed voices and organ |
| 1969 (35) | *Ave Rex*, for chorus and organ or orchestra |
| | *Psalm 150*, for chorus, organ and orchestra |
| 1970 (36) | *Festival Overture* |
| | Capriccio for flute and piano |
| | Concerto for harp |
| | *O Salutaris Hostia*, for unaccompanied male voices |
| | *Bless the Lord*, for mixed voices and organ |
| | *Gloria*, for male voices and organ |
| 1971 (37) | *Holiday Overture* |
| | Concerto for harpsichord, strings and percussion |
| 1972 (38) | *Elegy for a Prince*, for baritone and orchestra |
| | *Alleluya Psallat*, for mixed voices and organ |
| | Celtic Dances for orchestra |
| | *A Vision of Time and Eternity*, for contralto and piano |
| | *The Law for the Lord*, for unaccompanied mixed voices |
| 1973 (39) | *Magnificat* and *Nunc Dimittis*, for mixed voices and organ |
| | *Missa Brevis*, for mixed voices |
| | Intrada for orchestra |
| | Laudi for orchestra |
| | *Ceremony after a Fire Raid*, for mixed voices, piano and percussion |
| 1974 (40) | Concertino in F for oboe, bassoon and piano |
| | *This Worldes Joie*, for chorus and orchestra |
| 1975 (41) | *Vistas*, for orchestra |

```
                    Clarinet Concerto
                    Jubilate, for organ
                    Zodiac Trio, for flute, viola and harp
1976 (42)           Carmen Paschale, for chorus
                    Communion, for voices and organ
1977 (43)           Dance Variations for orchestra
                    Vivat Regina, for brass
                    Helios, for orchestra
                    Requiescat, for orchestra
                    Melos, for flute, harp, strings and percussion
                    A Royal Garland, for chorus and orchestra
                    The Fields of Praise, for tenor and piano
1978 (44)           Shine, for Your Light Has Come, for chorus and organ
                    Nativity Carol, for chorus
                    A May Magnificat, for chorus and organ
                    Eight Shakespeare Songs for chorus and piano
                    Fantasy, for organ
1979 (45)           Songs of William Blake for mezzo, cello, harp, piano and strings
1981 (47)           Rex Gloriæ, for unaccompanied voices
1982 (48)           Lux Aeterna, for soli, chorus, organ and orchestra
                    Salvator Mundi, for female choir, piano duet, percussion and
                        strings
                    Antiphonies, for organ
1983 (49)           Symphony No 2
                    Tantum Ergo, for choir and organ
                    Angelus, for women's voices
                    Alleluja! Christ is risen!, anthem
                    Horn Concerto
                    Missa Brevis
                    Let Us Now Praise Famous Men, for chorus and orchestra
                    Organ Concerto
                    Violin Sonata No 2
Since 1980          Reflections on a Theme of Tomkins, for flute, organ, oboe, harpsi-
                        chord and strings
                    String Quartet No 2
                    Trio for piano, violin and cello
                    Let the People Praise Thee O Lord, for choir and organ or orchestra
                    Investiture Anniversary Fanfare, for brass and percussion
                    Several anthems
```

## MAW, Nicholas
b Grantham, Lincolnshire, 5 November 1935

He studied harmony, counterpoint and composition at the Royal Academy of
Music and won a French government scholarship to study with Boulanger for a
year in Paris. He also won the 1959 Lili Boulanger Prize. He has lectured for the
Workers' Educational Association and for the universities of London and
Oxford. From 1966 to 1970 he was composer-in-residence at Trinity College,
Cambridge. He has written much music for films and radio, and has had many
commissions.

```
1956 (21)      Eight Chinese Lyrics, for solo mezzo-soprano
1956–7 (21–2)  Requiem, for soli, chorus and orchestra
1957 (22)      Sonatina for flute and piano
1957–8 (22–3)  Nocturne for mezzo-soprano and chamber orchestra
1959 (24)      Six Chinese Songs, for contralto and piano
```

| 1960 (25) | Five Epigrams, for unaccompanied mixed voices |
| 1961 (26) | Our Lady's Song, carol for unaccompanied mixed voices |
| | Essay, for organ (revised 1963) |
| 1962 (27) | Chamber Music for oboe, clarinet, horn, bassoon and piano |
| | Scenes and Arias for soprano, mezzo-soprano, contralto and orchestra (revised 1966) |
| 1963 (28) | Round for children's voices, mixed chorus and piano |
| | The Angel Gabriel, carol for mixed chorus unaccompanied |
| 1964 (29) | Balulalow, carol for unaccompanied mixed voices |
| | One Man Show, comic opera in two acts (revised 1966, 1970) |
| | Corpus Christi Carol, arranged for sopranos and descant with piano |
| 1965 (30) | String Quartet |
| 1966 (31) | Sinfonia for small orchestra |
| | The Voice of Love, song-cycle for mezzo-soprano and piano |
| | Six Interiors, for tenor and guitar |
| 1967 (32) | Double Canon for Igor Stravinsky on his 85th birthday, for various instruments |
| | Severn Bridge Variations for orchestra (in collaboration with Malcolm Arnold, Michael Tippett, Alun Hoddinott, Grace Williams and Daniel Jones) |
| | Sonata for strings and two horns |
| 1967–70 (32–5) | The Rising of the Moon, opera in three acts |
| 1971 (36) | Epitaph – Canon in Memory of Igor Stravinsky, for flute, clarinet and harp |
| 1972 (37) | Concert Music for orchestra (derived from The Rising of the Moon) |
| 1973 (38) | Five Irish Songs for mixed chorus |
| | Serenade for small orchestra (revised 1977) |
| | Life Studies, for fifteen solo strings |
| | Personae, for piano |
| 1975 (40) | Te Deum, for treble, tenor, mixed chorus, congregation and organ |
| | Reverdie, five songs for male voices |
| 1976 (41) | Annes!, for mixed chorus |
| | Nonsense Rhymes for Children, twenty songs with piano accompaniment |
| | Life Study No 2 |
| 1979 (44) | La Vita Nuova, for soprano and chamber ensemble |
| 1980 (45) | The Ruin, for chorus and solo horn |
| 1981 (46) | Flute Quartet |
| | Summer Dances, for youth orchestra |
| 1982 (47) | Night Thoughts, for solo flute |
| | String Quartet No 2 |
| 1982–3 (47–8) | Spring Music, for orchestra |

## MEALE, Richard Graham
b Sydney, 24 August 1932

He entered the New South Wales Conservatorium at the age of twelve to study piano, though as a composer he is largely self-taught. He worked in the gramophone industry while gaining experience as a pianist and conductor. In 1960 a Ford Foundation grant took him to the University of California for a year. He worked for the Australian Broadcasting Corporation from 1962 to 1969, then became a lecturer at the University of Adelaide. In 1971 he was appointed to the Adelaide Festival Centre Trust.

| 1961 (29) | Songs for Sheridan plays |
| 1962–3 (30–1) | Homage to Garcia Lorca, for two string orchestras |

| 1965 | (33) | *The Maids*, incidental music |
| | | *Images*, for orchestra |
| 1965–7 | (33–5) | Nocturnes for orchestra |
| 1968 | (36) | *King Lear*, incidental music |
| | | *Very High Kings*, for orchestra |
| 1969 | (37) | *Clouds Now and Then*, for orchestra |
| | | *Soon It Will Die*, for orchestra |
| | | Variations for orchestra |
| 1971 | (39) | *Incredible Floridas*, for chamber ensemble |
| 1972 | (40) | *Evocation*, for oboe, violin and chamber orchestra |
| 1974–5 | (42–3) | *Juliet's Memoirs*, opera |
| 1978 | (46) | *Viridian*, for string orchestra |
| 1980 | (48) | String Quartet |
| 1983 | (51) | Aria from *Voss*, for soprano, baritone and orchestra |

Meale has also written various chamber and instrumental works.


## MEDTNER, Nikolay Karlovich
*b Moscow, 5 January 1880*
*d London, 13 November 1951, aged seventy-one*

He studied first with his mother and an uncle, and at the age of twelve entered the Moscow Conservatory. He left in 1900 with a gold medal for piano, but decided to concentrate on composition. He returned to the Conservatory in 1909 to teach piano, but pressure of other work made him leave in 1910. He resumed teaching in 1914, but in 1921 he followed his friend Rachmaninov and others into exile, and, apart from a concert tour in 1927, did not see Russia again. In 1928 the Royal Academy of Music made him an honorary member. He had settled near Paris in 1925, but English friends persuaded him to live in England, which he did from 1935 until his death. Apart from songs, his output was almost exclusively for piano.

| 1904 | (24) | Nine Songs (Goethe) |
| 1907 | (27) | Three Songs (Heine) |
| 1908 | (28) | Twelve Songs (Goethe) |
| 1910 | (30) | Three Songs (Nietzsche, etc) |
| | | Violin Sonata |
| 1912 | (32) | Three Nocturnes for violin and piano |
| 1916–18 | (36–8) | Piano Concerto No 1 in C minor |
| 1921 | (41) | Sonata-Vocalise No 1 |
| 1924 | (44) | Violin Sonata |
| 1926–7 | (46–7) | Piano Concerto No 2 in C minor |
| 1936 | (56) | Violin Sonata, *Sonata Epica* |
| 1942–3 | (62–3) | Piano Concerto No 3 in E minor, *Ballade* |


## MELLERS, Wilfrid Howard
*b Leamington Spa, 26 April 1914*

He was educated at Cambridge University, but studied composition at the same time with Rubbra in Oxford. He held appointments at Dartington Hall from 1938 to 1940 and at Downing College, Cambridge, from 1945 to 1948. He later taught in Birmingham University and was professor of music at the universities of Pittsburgh, in the USA, and York. Apart from his music, he is known for the vast number of musical articles he wrote for leading periodicals.

| 1945 | (31) | String Trio |
| 1946 | (32) | Sonata for viola and piano |

|        |      | Serenade for oboe, clarinet and bassoon |
|--------|------|------------------------------------------|
| 1947 | (33) | *Prometheus*, incidental music |
| 1948 | (34) | *Lysistrata*, play in music |
| 1950–2 | (36–8) | *The Tragicall History of Christopher Marlowe*, opera |
| 1951 | (37) | *Festival Galliard*, for orchestra |
| 1952 | (38) | *Galliard*, for trombone and piano |
| 1953 | (39) | Symphony |
| 1956 | (42) | Sonatina for recorder and piano |
| 1960 | (46) | *Eclogue*, for recorder, harpsichord, percussion, violin and cello |
| 1961 | (47) | Cello Sonata |
|      |      | *Alba in Nine Metamorphoses*, for flute and orchestra |
| 1962 | (48) | Trio for flute, cello and piano |
|      |      | *Cantilena e ciacone*, for viola |
|      |      | *Noctambule and Sun-Dance*, for wind band |
| 1964 | (50) | *Laus Amoris*, for strings |
| 1965 | (51) | *Cat Charms*, nine pieces for piano |
| 1968 | (54) | *Natalis Invicti Solis*, for piano |
| 1969 | (55) | *Opus Alchymicum*, for organ |
| 1970 | (56) | *The Ancient Wound*, monodrama |
| 1973 | (59) | *A Blue Epiphany*, for guitar |
| 1975 | (61) | *Threnody*, for eleven stringed instruments |

Mellers has also written a great deal of accompanied and unaccompanied choral work, and songs.


## MENDELSSOHN, (-Bartholdy), Felix
*b Hamburg, 3 February 1809*
*d Leipzig, 4 November 1847, aged thirty-eight*

He was the son of a Jewish banker, though he himself converted to Christianity later. His mother gave him the rudiments of music, and then he had various private teachers. His brother and two sisters were also accomplished musicians. He made his début as a pianist in Berlin in 1818, at the age of nine, and from 1824 he also studied violin. In Paris in 1825 he won a wide circle of musical and poetic friends, and with his Octet and the *Midsummer Night's Dream* Overture the following year he established himself as a major composer. He also studied philosophy and geography. In 1829 he first visited Britain, going to Scotland and the Hebrides and meeting Sir Walter Scott. Afterwards he made a Grand Tour, taking in Austria, Switzerland, Italy, Germany and France before returning to England in 1832. He next became conductor of the Lower Rhine Festival, reviving many neglected works, and in 1835 became musical director at the Leipzig Gewandhaus. He made further journeys to England in 1837 and 1840, playing and conducting, and becoming a favourite of Queen Victoria; his *Scotch* Symphony is dedicated to her. He became *Kapellmeister* in Berlin at the behest of Frederick William IV in 1841, and founded the Leipzig Conservatory in 1843. His many commitments affected his health, and after the first performance of *Elijah* in Birmingham he returned exhausted to Leipzig. He still continued to work, but a series of severe fits killed him.

| 1821 | (12) | Piano Sonata No 2 in G minor |
|------|------|------------------------------|
| 1822 | (13) | Piano Quartet No 1 in C minor, Op 1 |
| 1823 | (14) | Piano Quartet No 2 in F minor |
|      |      | Violin Sonata in F minor |
| 1824 | (15) | Piano Quartet No 3 in B minor |
|      |      | Symphony No 1 in C minor |
| 1825 | (16) | *Wedding of the Camacho*, comic opera |
|      |      | *Trumpet Overture*, for orchestra |

|          |                                                                                          |
|----------|------------------------------------------------------------------------------------------|
|          | String Octet in E♭ major                                                                 |
|          | Capriccio in F♯ minor for piano                                                          |
| 1826 (17) | *A Midsummer Night's Dream*, overture                                                    |
|          | String Quintet in A major                                                                 |
|          | Piano Sonata No 1 in E major                                                              |
|          | Six Songs (1826–7)                                                                        |
| 1827 (18) | String Quartet No 2 in A minor                                                            |
|          | Fugue in E♭ major for string quartet                                                     |
|          | Piano Sonata No 3 in B♭ major                                                             |
|          | p Seven Pieces for piano                                                                  |
| 1829 (20) | *Die Heimkehr aus der Fremde*, operetta                                                  |
|          | String Quartet No 1 in E♭ major                                                          |
|          | *Variations concertantes*, for cello and piano, in D major                               |
|          | Three Fantasies for piano                                                                 |
|          | Twelve Songs                                                                              |
| 1830 (21) | Symphony No 5, *Reformation*                                                             |
|          | *Hebrides*, concert overture                                                             |
|          | Twelve Songs                                                                              |
|          | Six Songs                                                                                 |
| 1831 (22) | Piano Concerto No 1 in G minor                                                           |
|          | *Die erste Walpurgisnacht*, for solo voices, chorus and orchestra                       |
|          | Song                                                                                      |
| 1832 (23) | *Meerstille (Calm Sea and Prosperous Voyage)*, concert overture                         |
|          | *Capriccio Brillant*, in B minor, for piano and orchestra                               |
|          | Six Preludes and Fugues for piano (1832–7)                                               |
| 1833 (24) | Symphony No 4, *Italian*                                                                 |
|          | *Die schöne Melusine*, overture                                                          |
|          | Fantasy in F♯ minor, for piano                                                           |
|          | Three Capriccios for piano (1833–4)                                                       |
| 1834 (25) | *Rondo Brillant* in E♭ for piano and orchestra                                          |
|          | p *Songs Without Words*, Book I for piano                                                |
|          | Piano Sextet in D major                                                                   |
|          | Three Studies for piano (1834–6)                                                          |
|          | *Two Romances of Byron*                                                                  |
|          | Six Songs (1834–7)                                                                        |
|          | Song                                                                                      |
| 1835 (26) | p *Songs Without Words*, Book II for piano                                               |
|          | Two Sacred Songs                                                                          |
|          | Two Songs after Eichendorff                                                               |
| 1836 (27) | *St Paul*, oratorio                                                                      |
|          | Étude in F minor for piano                                                                |
| 1837 (28) | Piano Concerto No 2 in D minor                                                           |
|          | Three Organ Preludes and Fugues                                                           |
|          | Capriccio in E major for piano                                                            |
|          | Gondellied in A major, for piano                                                          |
|          | String Quartets No 3–5 in D: Em: E♭ (1837–8)                                             |
|          | Six Songs (1837–42)                                                                       |
| 1838 (29) | Serenade and Allegro Gioioso in B minor for piano and orchestra                         |
|          | Cello Sonata No 1 in B♭ major                                                            |
|          | Piano Trio No 1 in D minor                                                                |
|          | Andante Cantabile, and Presto Agitato, in B major, for piano                            |
| 1839 (30) | *Ruy Blas*, overture                                                                     |
|          | *Songs Without Words*, Book III for piano                                                |
|          | Six Songs                                                                                 |
|          | Song                                                                                      |
| 1840 (31) | *Lobegesang (Hymn of Praise)*, symphony-cantata (Symphony No 2)                         |

                    *Festgesang*, for male chorus and orchestra
1841 (32)    *Cornelius March*
                    *Songs Without Words*, Books IV and VII for piano
                    *Allegro Brillant*, in A major for piano
                    Variations in B♭ major
                    Variations in E♭ major
                    *Variations sérieuses*
                    Six Songs (1841–5)
1842 (33)    Symphony No 3, *Scottish*
                    Cello Sonata in D major (1842–3)
                    *Songs Without Words*, Book VIII, for piano (1842–5)
                    *Kinderstücke (Children's Pieces)*, for piano
1843 (34)    *Athalie*, incidental music
                    Andante in E major for string quartet
                    Scherzo in A minor for string quartet
                    Capriccio in E minor for string quartet
                    *Songs Without Words*, Books V and VI, for piano
1844 (35)    Violin Concerto in E minor
                    *Hear My Prayer*, for soprano, chorus and organ
                    p Six Organ Sonatas (1844–5)
1845 (36)    Piano Trio No 2 in C minor
                    String Quintet in B♭ major
                    *Songs Without Words*, for cello and piano
1846 (37)    String Quartet No 6 in F minor
                    fp *Elijah*, oratorio
                    *Lauda Sion*, cantata
1847 (38)    *Lorely*, opera (unfinished)
Mendelssohn also composed:
1827–41 (18–32) Prelude and Fugue in E minor, for piano
1827–47 (18–38) Four Pieces for string quartet
Performed posthumously:
1852            *Christus*, oratorio (unfinished)


**MENNIN, Peter**
*b Erie, Pennsylvania, 17 May 1923*

He is of Italian parentage. He studied at the Oberlin Conservatory, then served
in the US Army Air Force. After demobilisation he resumed his music studies at
the Eastman School, under Howard Hanson and took a summer course in
conducting with Koussevitzky at Tanglewood. From 1947 to 1958 he taught at
the Juillard School, then served as director of the Peabody Conservatory in
Baltimore from 1958 to 1962. In 1962 he was appointed president of the Juillard
School.

1945 (22)    Concertino for flute, strings and percussion
1946 (23)    Symphony No 3
1947 (24)    Fantasia for string orchestra
1949 (26)    Symphony No 4, *The Cycle*, for choir and orchestra
                    *The Christmas Story*, cantata
1950 (27)    Symphony No 5
                    Violin Concerto
                    *Canto and Toccata*, for piano
                    Five Pieces for piano
1951 (28)    *Canzona*, for band
1952 (29)    Concertato for orchestra, *Moby Dick*
                    Quartet No 2

| 1953 | (30) | Symphony No 6 |
| 1956 | (33) | Cello Concerto |
| | | Sonata Concertante for violin and piano |
| 1958 | (35) | Piano Concerto |
| 1963 | (40) | Symphony No 7 (1963–4) |
| | | *Canto*, for orchestra |
| 1967 | (44) | Piano Sonata |
| 1968–9 | (45–6) | *Cantata de virtute*, for chorus and orchestra, children's chorus, soloists and narrator |
| 1971 | (48) | Sinfonia for orchestra |
| 1973 | (50) | *fp* Symphony No 8 |
| 1976 | (53) | *Voices*, for violin, piano, harp, harpsichord and percussion |

## MENOTTI, Gian-Carlo
*b Cadigliano, Italy, 7 July 1911*

He began his musical studies at the age of twelve at the Verdi Conservatory in Milan, and continued at the Curtis Institute of Music in Philadelphia. Since then he has been permanently resident in the USA. From his first success with the opera *Amelia al Ballo* at the age of twenty-five he has spent his life composing. He founded the Festival of Two Worlds in 1958 in Spoleto. He has written all the libretti for his own operas, and the libretto for Barber's *Vanessa*.

| 1931 | (20) | *Variations on a Theme of Schumann*, for piano |
| 1936 | (25) | *Trio for a Housewarming Party*, for flute, cello and piano |
| 1937 | (26) | *Amelia al Ballo*, opera (the only one Menotti wrote in Italian) |
| 1939 | (28) | *The Old Maid and the Thief*, opera |
| 1942 | (31) | *The Island God*, opera |
| 1944 | (33) | *Sebastian*, ballet |
| 1945 | (34) | Piano Concerto in A minor |
| 1946 | (35) | *The Medium*, opera |
| 1947 | (36) | *The Telephone*, opera |
| | | *Errand into the Maze*, ballet |
| 1950 | (39) | *The Consul*, opera |
| 1951 | (40) | *Amahl and the Night Visitors*, opera |
| | | *Apocalypse*, for orchestra |
| 1952 | (41) | Violin Concerto |
| 1954 | (43) | *The Saint of Bleecker Street*, opera |
| 1956 | (45) | *The Unicorn, the Gorgon and the Manticore*, ballet |
| 1958 | (47) | *Maria Golovin*, opera |
| 1963 | (52) | *Labyrinth*, opera |
| | | *The Last Savage*, opera |
| | | *Death of the Bishop of Brindisi*, cantata |
| 1964 | (53) | *Martin's Lie*, opera |
| 1967 | (56) | *Canti della lontananza*, song cycle |
| 1968 | (57) | *Help, Help, the Globolinks*, children's opera |
| 1970 | (59) | *The Leper*, drama |
| | | *Triplo concerto a tre*, symphonic piece |
| 1971 | (60) | *fp The Most Important Man in the World*, opera |
| 1973 | (62) | *fp* Suite for two cellos and piano |
| | | *Tamu-Tamu*, opera |
| 1976 | (65) | *The Hero*, comic opera |
| | | *The Egg*, church opera |
| | | *Landscapes and Remembrances*, cantata |
| | | Symphony, *The Halcyon* |
| 1978 | (67) | *The Trial of the Gypsy*, for voices and piano |

## MESSAGER, André Charles Prosper
*b Montluçon, Allier, 30 December 1853*
*d Paris, 24 February 1929, aged seventy-five*

He was admitted to the École Niedermeyer in Paris in 1869, and was taught by Fauré and Saint-Saëns, who were to remain his close friends. In 1874 he became organist at St Sulpice, and in 1876 won first prize with a symphony in a competition. He conducted at the *Folies Bergère* and in theatres in Brussels. In 1881 he became organist at St Paul-St Louis and from 1882 to 1884 was *maître de chapelle* at Ste Marie-des-Batignolles. From 1883 his popularity as a composer grew, until 1899, when other commitments became pressing and he had less time to write. He was also an opera administrator, pianist, orchestrator and critic.

| | | |
|---|---|---|
| 1875 | (22) | Symphony |
| 1877 | (24) | *Don Juan et Haydée*, cantata |
| 1878 | (25) | *Fleur d'Oranger, ballet* |
| 1885 | (32) | *La Béarnasie*, operetta |
| 1886 | (33) | *Les deux pigeons*, ballet |
| 1888 | (35) | *Isoline, opera* |
| 1890 | (37) | *La Basoche*, operetta |
| 1893 | (40) | *Madame Chrysanthème*, operetta |
| 1894 | (41) | *Mirette*, operetta |
| 1896 | (43) | *Le Chavalier d'Harmenthal*, operetta |
| 1897 | (44) | *Les P'tites Michu*, operetta |
| 1898 | (45) | *Véronique*, operetta |
| 1907 | (54) | *Fortuno*, operetta |
| 1914 | (61) | *Béatrice*, operetta |
| 1919 | (66) | *Monsieur Beaucaire*, operetta |

## MESSIAEN, Oliver
*b Avignon, 10 December 1908*

His father was a professor of literature, his mother a poetess. He began to teach himself piano and composition at the age of eight, and at eleven entered the Paris Conservatory, staying there for eleven years and winning many prizes. In 1931 he became organist at the Trinité, Paris, and held that post for twenty years. In 1936 he helped to found the Jeune France group of young French avant-garde composers, and also became professor at the École Normale. He served with the French forces during World War II and was made a prisoner-of-war. After repatriation in 1942 he became professor of harmony at the Paris Conservatory. His work is much influenced by his strong Catholic beliefs.

| | | |
|---|---|---|
| 1928 | (20) | Fugue in D minor for orchestra |
| | | *Le Banquet eucharistique*, for orchestra (unpublished) |
| | | *Le Banquet céleste*, for organ |
| 1929 | (21) | *Préludes*, for piano |
| 1930 | (22) | *Simple chant d'une âme* |
| | | *Les Offrandes oubliées*, for orchestra |
| | | *Diptyque*, for organ |
| 1931 | (23) | *Le Tombeau resplendissant*, for orchestra |
| 1932 | (24) | *Hymne au Saint Sacrement*, for orchestra |
| | | *Fantaisie burlesque*, for piano |
| | | *Apparition de l'Eglise éternelle*, for organ |
| 1933 | (25) | *L'Ascension*, for organ |
| | | Mass for eight sopranos and four violins |
| 1935 | (27) | *La nativité du Seigneur*, nine meditations for organ |

| 1937 (29) | *Poèmes pour mi*, for voice and orchestra |
| 1939 (31) | *Les corps glorieux*, for organ |
| 1941 (33) | *Quatour pour la fin du temps*, for violin, clarinet, cello and piano |
| 1943 (35) | *Visions de l'Amen*, for two pianos |
| | *Rondeau*, for piano |
| 1944 (36) | *Vingt regards sur l'enfant Jésus*, for piano |
| 1947 (39) | *Turangalila*, symphony for orchestra, piano and Ondes Martenot |
| 1950 (42) | *Le merle noir*, for piano and flute |
| | *Messe de la Pentecôte* |
| 1953 (45) | *Reveil des oiseaux*, for piano and orchestra |
| 1956 (48) | *Oiseaux exotiques*, for piano, wind instruments and percussion |
| 1960 (52) | *Chronochromie*, for orchestra |
| 1963 (55) | *Sept Haï-Kaï*, for orchestra |
| 1964 (56) | *Couleurs de la cité céleste*, for orchestra |
| 1965 (57) | *La Transfiguration de notre Seigneur Jésus-Christ*, for chorus and orchestra (1965–9) |
| | *Méditations sur le mystère de la Sainte Trinité*, for ogan |
| 1970–4 (62–6) | *Des canyons aux étoiles*, for piano, horn and orchestra |
| 1971 (63) | *Le tombeau de Jean-Pierre Guezec*, for horn and tape |
| 1972 (64) | *La fauvette des jardins*, for piano |
| 1974–83 (66–75) | *Saint François d'Assise*, opera |

## MEYERBEER, Giacomo
*b Berlin, 5 September 1791*
*d Paris, 2 May 1864, aged seventy-two*

He was the eldest son of a successful Jewish banker. He spent three years from 1810 to 1813 studying at Darmstadt, making a close friendship with fellow student Weber. A period of composition in Vienna met with only a mixed success, but a move to Italy and the writing of operas in imitation of Rossini brought him fame. In 1826 his father, Weber, and his two children died in Berlin and this checked his career; he did not leave Berlin until 1830. His great wealth made it easy for him to stage lavish productions and he was fortunate, too, in having Scribe as his librettist. The enormous popularity of his operas and the influence of his family earned him the post of *General-musikdirektor* in Berlin from 1842 to 1849. However, anti-Semitic criticism by such people as Wagner and Heine proved damaging to his health.

| 1831 (40) | *Robert le diable*, opera |
| 1836 (45) | *Les Huguenots*, opera |
| 1849 (58) | *Le prophète*, opera |
| 1854 (63) | *L'étoile du nord*, opera |
| 1859 (68) | *Dinorah*, opera |
| Performed posthumously: | |
| 1865 | *L'Africaine*, opera |

## MIASKOVSKY, Nikolai
*b Novogeorgievsky, 20 April 1881*
*d Moscow, 9 August 1950, aged sixty-nine*

He was born into a military family, and fought for the Russian Army from 1914 to 1916. In 1908 he won a scholarship to the Conservatory of St Petersburg, where he studied under Rimsky-Korsakov and Liadov. After World War I he became professor of composition at the Conservatory of Moscow.

1907–9 (26–8) Sonata No 1, for piano

| 1908 | (27) | Symphony No 1 |
| 1910 | (29) | *Silence*, symphonic poem |
| 1911 | (30) | Sonata for cello and piano |
| | | Sinfonietta for small orchestra |
| | | Symphony No 2 |
| 1912 | (31) | Sonata No 2 for piano |
| 1913 | (32) | *Alastor*, symphonic poem |
| 1914 | (33) | Symphony No 3 |
| 1918 | (37) | Symphonies No 4 and 5 |
| 1920 | (39) | Sonata No 3 for piano |
| 1922 | (41) | *Fancies*, six pieces for piano |
| 1923 | (42) | Symphonies No 6 and 7 |
| 1925 | (44) | Symphony No 8 |
| | | Sonata No 4 for piano |
| 1927 | (46) | Symphonies No 9 and 10 |
| | | *Souvenirs*, six pieces for piano |
| 1928 | (47) | *The Yellowed Pages*, seven pieces for piano |
| 1929 | (48) | Serenade for small orchestra |
| | | Sinfonietta for string orchestra |
| | | *Lyric Concerto*, for string orchestra |
| 1932 | (51) | Symphonies No 11 and 12 |
| 1933 | (52) | Symphonies No 13 and 14 |
| 1934 | (53) | Symphony No 15 |
| 1936 | (55) | Symphony No 16 |
| 1937 | (56) | Symphonies No 17 and 18 |
| 1938 | (57) | Children's Pieces for piano, in three books |
| 1939 | (58) | Symphony No 19 |
| 1940 | (59) | Symphonies No 20 and 21 |
| 1941 | (60) | Symphonies No 22 and 23 |
| 1943 | (62) | Symphony No 24 |

Miaskovsky also wrote nine string quartets and many songs.


## MILHAUD, Darius
*b Aix-en-Provence, 4 September 1892*
*d Geneva, 22 June 1974, aged eighty-one*

By the time he entered the Paris Conservatory at the age of seventeen he was already an accomplished violinist and organist, and a developing composer. He went to Brazil from 1917 to 1918, and afterwards made two visits to the USA. In 1940 he took up an appointment at Mills College, Oakland, California, but after World War II returned to France, becoming professor of composition at the Paris Conservatory in 1947. Despite severe arthritis he remained active for the rest of his life.

| 1910–15 | (18–23) | *La brèbis égarée*, opera |
| 1911 | (19) | Violin Sonata |
| 1912 | (20) | String Quartet No 1 in A minor |
| 1913–14 | (21–2) | Suite Symphonique No 1 |
| 1914 | (22) | Sonata for two violins and piano |
| | | *Printemps*, for violin and piano |
| | | String Quartet No 2, (atonal) (1914–15) |
| 1916 | (24) | String Quartet No 3 |
| 1917 | (25) | Symphony No 1 for small orchestra, *Le Printemps* |
| 1918 | (26) | Symphony No 2 for small orchestra, *Pastorale* |
| | | Sonata for flute, oboe, clarinet and piano |
| | | *L'homme et son désir*, ballet |

|                | String Quartet No 4 |
| -------------- | ------------------- |
| 1919 (27)      | Suite Symphonique No 2, *Protée* |
|                | *Machines agricoles*, six pastoral songs for middle voice and instruments |
| 1920 (28)      | *Le boeuf sur le toit*, ballet |
|                | *Ballade*, for piano and orchestra |
|                | Five Studies for piano and orchestra |
|                | *Sérénade* (1920–1) |
|                | *Printemps*, six piano pieces |
|                | String Quartet No 5 |
| 1921 (29)      | *Saudades de Brasil*, dance suite |
|                | Symphony No 3 for small orchestra, *Sérénade* |
|                | Symphony No 4 for strings, *Ouverture, Choral, Étude* |
| 1922 (30)      | Symphony No 5 for small wind orchestra |
|                | *La création du monde*, ballet, using jazz idiom (1922–3) |
|                | Three *Rag-Caprices* |
|                | String Quartet No 6 |
| 1923 (31)      | Symphony No 6 for soprano, contralto, tenor, bass, oboe and cello |
| 1924 (32)      | *Les malheurs d'Orphée*, opera |
|                | *Esther de Carpentras*, comic opera (1924–5) |
|                | *Le Train Bleu*, ballet |
| 1925 (33)      | String Quartet No 7 |
|                | *Deux Hymnes* |
| 1926 (34)      | *Le pauvre matelot*, opera |
| 1927 (35)      | Violin Concerto No 1 |
|                | *Carnival of Aix*, for piano and orchestra |
| 1928 (36)      | *Christophe Columb*, opera (revised 1956) |
|                | *Cantate pour louer le Seigneur* |
| 1929 (37)      | Viola Concerto |
|                | Concerto for percussion and small orchestra |
| 1930 (38)      | *Maximilien*, opera |
| 1932 (40)      | String Quartet No 8 |
| 1933 (41)      | Piano Concerto No 1 |
| 1935 (43)      | Cello Concerto No 1 |
|                | String Quartet No 9 |
| 1936 (44)      | *Suite provençale* |
| 1937 (45)      | *Cantate de la paix* |
| 1938 (46)      | *Medée*, opera |
| 1939 (47)      | Symphony No 1 for full orchestra |
|                | *King René's Chimney*, for wind quartet |
| 1940 (48)      | String Quartet No 10, *Birthday Quartet* |
| 1941 (49)      | Piano Concerto No 2 |
|                | Clarinet Concerto |
|                | Concerto for two pianos |
|                | Four Sketches |
| 1942 (50)      | String Quartet No 11 |
| 1943 (51)      | *Bolivar*, opera |
| 1944 (52)      | Symphony No 2 for full orchestra |
|                | *Jeux de printemps* |
|                | *Suite française* |
| 1945 (53)      | *The Bells*, ballet |
|                | Cello Concerto No 2 |
|                | String Quartet No 12, *In Memory of Fauré* |
| 1946 (54)      | Symphony No 3 for full orchestra and chorus, *Hymnus Ambrosianus* |
|                | Piano Concerto No 3 |
|                | Violin Concerto No 2 |

|            | String Quartet No 13 |
| 1947 (55) | Symphony, *1848* |
|            | Concerto for marimba and vibraphone |
| 1949 (57) | Piano Concerto No 4 |
|            | String Quartets No 14 and 15, to be played together as octet, or separately |
| 1951 (59) | *The Seven-branched Candelabra*, for piano |
| 1953 (61) | *David*, opera |
| 1954 (62) | Harp Concerto |
| 1955 (63) | Symphonies No 5 and 6 |
| 1956 (64) | Symphony No 7 |
| 1957 (65) | Symphony No 8, *Rhodanienne* |
|            | Oboe Concerto |
|            | *Aspen Serenade* |
| 1958 (66) | Violin Concerto No 3, *Concerto royal* |
| 1960 (68) | Symphony No 10 |
| (possibly 1960) | Symphony No 11 |
| 1962 (70) | Symphony No 12 |
| 1963 (71) | *Pacem in terris*, for chorus and orchestra |
| 1964 (72) | *La mère coupable*, opera (1964–5) |
|            | String Septet |
|            | Harpsichord concerto |
| 1965 (73) | *Music for Boston*, for orchestra |
|            | *Music for Prague*, for orchestra |
|            | *Elégie pour Pierre*, for viola and percussion |
|            | *Cantate de Job*, for chorus and organ |
| 1966 (74) | *Jerusalem à Carpentras*, incidental music |
|            | *Music for Indiana*, for orchestra |
|            | *Music for Lisbon*, for orchestra |
|            | *Music for New Orleans*, for orchestra |
|            | Piano Quintet |
| 1967 (75) | Promenade Concert for orchestra |
| 1968 (76) | *Tobie et Sarah*, incidental music |
|            | *Musique pour l'univers Claudélien*, for orchestra |
|            | Piano Trio |
| 1968–9 (76–7) | *Music for Graz*, for orchestra |
| 1969 (77) | Suite in G for orchestra |
|            | *Music for Ars Nova*, for orchestra |
|            | *Stanford Serenade*, for chamber orchestra |
| 1970 (78) | *St Louis, roi de France*, opera |
| 1971 (79) | *Music for San Francisco*, for orchestra |
|            | *Hommage à Stravinsky* |
|            | Harp Sonata |
| 1971–2 (79–80) | *Promesse de Dieu*, for unaccompanied chorus |
| 1972 (80) | *Ode pour Jerusalem*, for orchestra |
|            | *Les Momies d'Egypte*, for unaccompanied chorus |
|            | *Ani Maamin*, for chorus and orchestra |

**MOERAN, Ernest John**
*b London, 31 December 1894*
*d Kenmare, Co Kerry, 1 December 1950, aged fifty-five*

The son of a Norfolk clergyman, he was educated at Uppingham School, where he learned violin and played in a string quartet. He entered the Royal College of Music in 1913, then served in the Army and was wounded. In 1919 he returned to his old school as music master, and thereafter devoted his life to composing.

| 1919 | (25) | Three Piano Pieces |
| 1920 | (26) | Theme and Variations for piano |
| | | Piano Trio in E minor |
| | | *Ludlow Town*, song cycle |
| 1921 | (27) | *In the Mountain Country*, symphonic impression |
| | | *On a May Morning*, for piano |
| 1922 | (28) | Rhapsody No 1 in F major |
| | | *Three Fancies*, for piano |
| 1924 | (30) | Rhapsody No 2 in E major |
| 1925 | (31) | *Summer Valley*, for piano |
| 1926 | (32) | *Irish Love Song*, for piano |
| 1932 | (38) | *Farrago*, suite for orchestra |
| 1934 | (40) | *Nocturne*, for baritone, chorus and orchestra |
| 1937 | (43) | Symphony in G minor |
| 1942 | (48) | Violin Concerto |
| 1943 | (49) | Rhapsody No 3 in F♯ major for piano and orchestra |
| 1944 | (50) | Sinfonietta |
| | | *Overture for a Masque* |
| 1945 | (51) | Cello Concerto |
| 1946 | (52) | *Fantasy Quartet*, for oboe and strings |
| 1948 | (54) | Serenade in G major |

## MONTEVERDI, Claudio
*b Cremona, May 1567*
*d Venice, 29 November 1643, aged seventy-six*

He was the son of a barber-surgeon-cum-chemist. He had no musical antecedents, though his brother also became a professional musician. He studied with the *maestro di cappella* at the local cathedral, and by the age of fifteen had written and published a group of religious pieces; before he was out of his teens he was already an accomplished composer. At the age of twenty-three he was a string player in the court at Mantua, and soon afterwards he produced a revolutionary book of madrigals. Journeys to Hungary and Flanders broadened his outlook. In 1599 he married a singer in the Duke of Mantua's court, and had three children. In 1602 he was promoted to *maestro di cappella*; his wife continued her work as a singer. By the age of forty he was one of the most famous composers in Europe. His wife died in 1607, and his subsequent depression lasted for several years. In 1610 the Duke of Mantua died and Monteverdi was suddenly unemployed; but in 1611 he was invited to become *maestro di cappella* at St Mark's in Venice. The outbreak of the plague in 1630 totally disrupted what had hitherto been a calm and productive life; he became a priest, and wrote little for a few years. Then came a period of great productivity – particularly in his writing of operas – which lasted until his death.

| 1584 | (17) | *p* Canzonettes for three voices |
| 1587 | (20) | *p* Madrigals for five voices, Book I |
| 1590 | (23) | *p* Madrigals for five voices, Book II |
| 1592 | (25) | *p* Madrigals for five voices, Book III |
| 1603 | (36) | *p* Madrigals for five voices, Book IV |
| 1605 | (38) | *p* Madrigals for five voices, Book V |
| 1607 | (40) | *p* Scherzi Musicali for three voices |
| | | *fp Orfeo*, opera |
| 1608 | (41) | *Il ballo delle ingrate* |
| | | *fp L'Arianna*, opera |
| 1610 | (43) | Vespers |
| | | *p* Masses |

| 1614 | (47) | *p* Madrigals for five voices, Book VI |
| 1615 | (48) | *fp Tirsi e Clori*, ballet |
| 1617 | (50) | *La Maddalena*, opera |
| 1619 | (52) | *p* Madrigals, for one, two, three, four and six voices, Book VII |
| 1627 | (60) | *Armida*, opera |
| 1628 | (61) | *fp Mercurio e Marte*, opera |
| 1632 | (65) | *p* Scherzi Musicali for one or two voices |
| 1638 | (71) | *p* Madrigals, of war and love (*Madrigali guerrieri e amorosi*) Book VIII |
| 1640 | (73) | *Selve morale e spirituale* |
| 1641 | (74) | *Il ritorno d'Ulisse in patria*, opera |
| 1642 | (75) | *L'incoronazione di Poppea*, opera |

Performed posthumously:

| 1650 | | Masses for four voices and psalms |
| 1651 | | Madrigals and Canzonettes for two or three voices, Book IX |

## MOORE, Douglas Stuart
*b Cutchogue, New York, 10 August 1893*
*d Greenport, New York, 25 July 1969, aged seventy-five*

He was educated at Yale, then served in the Navy. In 1919 he went to Paris, studying with d'Indy and Boulanger. In 1921 he accepted a position with the Cleveland Museum, and in 1926 was appointed to teach at Columbia University, remaining there until his retirement in 1962. He was president of the National Institute and the American Academy of Arts and Letters. He received many honorary degrees.

| 1924 | (31) | *The Pageant of P.T. Barnum*, suite for orchestra |
| 1928 | (35) | *A Symphony of Autumn* |
| | | *Moby Dick*, for orchestra |
| 1929 | (36) | Violin Sonata |
| 1930 | (37) | *Overture on an American Theme* |
| 1933 | (40) | String Quartet |
| 1935 | (42) | *White Wings*, opera (possibly 1948) |
| 1936 | (43) | *The Headless Horseman*, opera |
| 1938 | (45) | *Dedication*, for chorus |
| 1939 | (46) | *The Devil and Daniel Webster*, opera |
| 1941 | (48) | *Village Music*, suite for small orchestra |
| 1942 | (49) | Quintet for woodwinds and horn |
| 1943 | (50) | *In Memoriam*, symphonic poem |
| 1944 | (51) | *Down East Suite*, for violin with piano or orchestra |
| 1945 | (52) | Symphony in A major |
| 1946 | (53) | Quintet for clarinet and strings |
| 1947 | (54) | *Farm Journal*, suite for chamber orchestra |
| 1948 | (55) | *The Emperor's New Clothes*, opera for children |
| 1950 | (57) | *Giants in the Earth*, opera |
| 1952 | (59) | *Cotillion*, suite for string orchestra |
| 1953 | (60) | Piano Trio |
| 1956 | (63) | *The Ballad of Baby Doe*, opera |
| 1957 | (64) | *Gallantry*, a soap opera |
| 1961 | (68) | *Wings of the Dove*, opera |
| 1962 | (69) | *The Greenfield Christmas Tree*, a Christmas entertainment |
| 1966 | (73) | *Carry Nation*, opera |

**MORLEY, Thomas**
*b London?, 1557*
*d London, October 1602, aged forty-five*

He was a chorister in St Paul's Cathedral, and then became a pupil of Byrd. He was choirmaster at Norwich Cathedral from 1583 to 1587. He graduated from Oxford in 1588. In 1589 he became organist at St Paul's, and in 1592 was sworn as a Gentleman of the Chapel Royal. Between 1596 and 1601 he lived in the same parish in London as Shakespeare, and there is little doubt that they knew each other.

| | |
|---|---|
| 1593 (36) | *p* Canzonets, or Little Short Songs to Three Voyces |
| 1594 (37) | *p* Madrigalls to Foure Voyces |
| 1595 (38) | *p* The First Booke of Balletts to Fiue Voyces |
| | *p* The First Booke of Canzonets to Two Voyces |
| 1597 (40) | *p* Two songs in 'Canzonets or Little Short Songs to Foure Voyces. Celected out of the best and approved Italian Authors' |
| | *p* Canzonets or Little Short Aers to Fiue and Sixe Voyces |
| | *p* A Plaine and Easie Introduction to Practicall Musicke |
| 1598 (41) | *p* Madrigalls to Fiue Voyces. Celected out of the best approved Italian Authors |
| 1599 (42) | *p* The First Booke of Consort Lessons, made by diuerse exquisite Authors for six Instruments |
| 1600 (43) | *p* The First Booke of Ayres or Little Short Songs: to sing and play to the Lute with the Base Viole |
| 1601 (44) | *p* Two madrigals in '*The Triumphs of Oriana*, to five and six voyces, composed by diuverse seuerall authors' |

**MOSZKOWSKY, Moritz**
*b Breslau, 23 August 1854*
*d Paris, 4 March 1925, aged seventy*

He studied first at Dresden, then in Berlin, where he later taught piano. He toured extensively as a pianist, retired to Paris in 1897, and was elected a member of the Berlin Academy in 1899.

| | |
|---|---|
| 1892 (38) | *Boabdil*, opera |
| 1896 (42) | *Laurin*, ballet |

Moszkowsky also wrote:
*Don Juan and Faust*, incidental music
Serenata for orchestra
*Jeanne d'Arc*, symphonic poem
*Aus aller Herren Ländern*, orchestral suite
Violin Concerto
Piano Concerto
Two other orchestral suites
Chamber and piano works

**MOZART, Wolfgang Amadeus**
*b Salzburg, 27 January 1756*
*d Vienna, 5 December 1791, aged thirty-five*

His father, Leopold, was a violinist and composer. Wolfgang was composing by the age of five, and Leopold used his gifted son to his own commercial advantage, introducing him to various courts throughout Europe. In 1769, father and son travelled together to Italy, where Wolfgang had an audience with the Pope, wrote an opera, and was fêted wherever he went. In 1777 he journeyed to Paris, this time with his mother, but the months spent there were unfruitful, and his mother died, so he returned to Salzburg. The Archbishop of Salzburg took him into his entourage; but Mozart hated his almost menial position and resigned. Moving to Vienna, he married, and lived frugally by teaching. Despite the success of his operas there were no lucrative commissions. Having become a Freemason, he borrowed money from his fellows, in order to live. He was appointed court composer to the Emperor, but the salary was nominal. He refused the lucrative post of *Kapellmeister* in Berlin in 1789, because he loved Vienna. For all his success he died in poverty, of uraemia, and was buried in an unmarked grave.

| | |
|---|---|
| 1762–4 (6–8) | Sonata in C major for violin and piano, K6 |
| 1763–4 (7–8) | Sonata in D major for violin and piano, K7 |
| | Sonata in Bb major for violin and piano, K8 |
| 1764 (8) | Sonata in G major for violin and piano, K9 |
| | Sonata in Bb major for violin and piano, K10 |
| | Sonata in G major for violin and piano, K11 |
| | Sonata in A major for violin and piano, K12 |
| | Sonata in F major for violin and piano, K13 |
| | Sonata in C major for violin and piano, K14 |
| | Sonata in Bb major for violin and piano, K15 |
| | Symphony No 1 in Eb major, K16 |
| | Symphony No 4 in D major, K19 |
| 1765 (9) | Piano Sonatas (four hands) in C major, K19d (unpublished) |
| | Three Sonatas by J. C. Bach arranged as concertos with string orchestra, K107 |
| | Symphony No 5 in Bb major, K22 |
| 1766 (10) | Sonata in Eb major for violin and piano, K26 |
| | Sonata in G major for violin and piano, K27 |
| | Sonata in C major for violin and piano, K28 |
| | Sonata in D major for violin and piano, K29 |
| | Sonata in F major for violin and piano, K30 |
| | Sonata in Bb major for violin and piano, K31 |
| 1767 (11) | Piano Concerto in F major, K37 |
| | Piano Concerto in Bb major, K39 |
| | Piano Concerto in D major, K40 |
| | Piano Concerto in G major, K41 |
| | Symphony No 6 in F major, K43 |
| | Sonata for organ and strings in Eb major, K62 |
| | Sonata for organ and strings in Bb major, K68 |
| | Sonata for organ and strings in D major, K69 |
| | Symphony No 43 in F major, K76 |
| 1768 (12) | *Bastien und Bastienne*, operetta |
| | Symphony No 7 in D major, K45 |
| | Symphony No 8 in D major, K48 |
| 1769 (13) | Mass in C major, K66 |
| | Symphony No 9 in C major, K73 |
| | Symphony No 42 in F major, K75 |
| 1770 (14) | String Quartet in G major, K80 |
| | Symphony No 10 in G major, K74 |
| | Symphony No 11 in D major, K81 |
| | Symphony No 45 in D major, K95 |
| | Symphony No 47 in D major, K97 |
| | Symphony No 12 in G major, K110 |
| 1771 (15) | Symphony No 46 in C major, K96 |
| | Symphony No 13 in F major, K112 |

Symphony No 14 in A major, K114
Symphony No 50 in D (finale only, to the overture of *Asanio in Alba*), K120
Symphony in D, finale only to the overture of *La finta giardinera*, K121
1772 (16)    Piano Sonata (four hands) in D major, K381
String Quartet in D major, K155
String Quartet in G major, K156
String Quartet in C major, K157
String Quartet in F major, K158
String Quartet in B♭ major, K159
String Quartet in E♭ major, K160
Sonata for organ and strings in D major, K144
Sonata for organ and strings in F major, K145
Mass in C minor and C major, K139
Symphony No 15 in G major, K124
Symphony No 16 in C major, K128
Symphony No 17 in G major, K129
Symphony No 19 in E♭ major, K132
Symphony No 20 in D major, K133
Symphony No 21 in A major, K134
Symphony in D major (first two movements identical with the overture *Il sogno di Scipiona*, K126), K161
Symphony No 22 in C major, K162
Symphony No 51 in D major (finale only, to the overture of *Il sogno di Scipiona*), K163
*Lucio Silla*, opera
1773 (17)    Piano Concerto in D major, K175
Concertone in C major for two violins, K190
String Quartet in F major, K168
String Quartet in A major, K169
String Quartet in C major, K170
String Quartet in E♭ major, K171
String Quartet in B♭ major, K172
String Quartet in D minor, K173
String Quintet in B♭ major, K174
Symphony No 23 in D major, K181
Symphony No 24 in B♭ major, K182
Symphony No 25 in G minor, K183
Symphony No 26 in E♭ major, K184
1774 (18)    Bassoon Concerto in B♭ major, K191
Symphony No 27 in G major, K199
Symphony No 28 in C major, K200
Symphony No 29 in A major, K201
Symphony No 30 in D major, K202
Piano Sonata in C major, K279
Piano Sonata in F major, K280
Piano Sonata in B♭ major, K281
Piano Sonata in E♭ major, K282
Piano Sonata in G major, K283
Piano sonata in D major, K284
Piano Sonata (four hands) in B♭ major, K358
1775 (19)    *La finta giardiniera*, opera
*Il re pastore*, opera
Symphony No 49 in C major (finale only, to the overture of *Il re pastore*), K102

|      |                                                                                         |
|------|-----------------------------------------------------------------------------------------|
|      | Violin Concerto in B♭ major, K207                                                       |
|      | Violin Concerto in D major, K211                                                        |
|      | Violin Concerto in G major, K216                                                        |
|      | Violin Concerto in D major, K218                                                        |
|      | Violin Concerto in A major, K219                                                        |
|      | Sonata for organ and strings in B♭ major, K212                                          |
| 1776 (20) | Piano Concerto in B♭ major, K238                                                   |
|      | Piano Concerto in F major for three pianos, K242                                        |
|      | Piano Concerto in C major, K246                                                         |
|      | Adagio to K219, Violin Concerto, K261                                                   |
|      | Rondo Concertante to K207, Violin Concerto, K269                                        |
|      | Piano Trio in B♭ major, K254                                                            |
|      | Sonata for organ and strings in F major, K224                                           |
|      | Sonata for organ and strings in A major, K225                                           |
|      | Sonata for organ and strings in G major, K241                                           |
|      | Sonata for organ and strings in F major, K244                                           |
|      | Sonata for organ and strings in D major, K245                                           |
|      | Mass in C major, K257                                                                   |
| 1777 (21) | Piano Concerto in E♭ major, K271                                                   |
|      | Violin Concerto in D major, K271a                                                       |
|      | Piano Sonata in C major, K309                                                           |
|      | Sonata for organ and strings in G major, K274                                           |
| 1778 (22) | Concerto in C major for flute and harp, K299                                       |
|      | Concerto in G major for flute, K313                                                     |
|      | Concerto in D major for flute, K314                                                     |
|      | Andante in C major for flute, K315                                                      |
|      | Sinfonia Concertante in E♭ for flute, oboe, horn and bassoon (app K9)                   |
|      | Piano Sonata in A minor, K310                                                           |
|      | Piano Sonata in D major, K311                                                           |
|      | Piano Sonata in C major, K330                                                           |
|      | Piano Sonata in A major, K331                                                           |
|      | Piano Sonata in F major, K332                                                           |
|      | Piano Sonata in B♭ major, K333                                                          |
|      | Violin Sonata in C major, K296                                                          |
|      | Violin Sonata in G major, K301                                                          |
|      | Violin Sonata in B♭ major, K302                                                         |
|      | Violin Sonata in C major, K303                                                          |
|      | Violin Sonata in E minor, K304                                                          |
|      | Violin Sonata in A major, K305                                                          |
|      | Violin Sonata in D major, K306                                                          |
|      | Symphony No 31 in D major, *Paris*, K297                                                |
| 1779 (23) | Sinfonia Concertante in E♭ for violin and viola, K364                              |
|      | Concerto for two pianos, K365                                                           |
|      | Sonata for organ and strings in C major, K328                                           |
|      | Mass in C major, K317                                                                   |
|      | Symphony No 32 in G major, K318                                                         |
|      | Symphony No 33 in B♭ major, K319                                                        |
| 1780 (24) | Violin Concerto in E♭ major, K268 (1780–1) (authenticity doubtful)                 |
|      | Sonata for organ and strings in C major, K336                                           |
|      | String Quartet in B♭, K46 (arrangement of K361 Serenade, may be spurious)               |
|      | Symphony No 34 in C major, K338                                                         |
|      | Six Variations for violin and piano on *Hélas, j'ai perdu mon amant*, K360              |

| 1781 (25) | *Idomeneo*, opera |
| | Rondo in C major for violin and orchestra, K373 |
| | Concerto Rondo in E♭ for horn, K371 |
| | Twelve Variations on *La bergère Célimène*, for violin and piano, K359 |
| | Violin Sonata in F major, K376 |
| | Violin Sonata in F major, K377 |
| | Violin Sonata in B♭ major, K378 |
| | Violin Sonata in G minor and G major, K379 |
| | Violin Sonata in E♭ major, K380 |
| | Sonata for two pianos in D major, K448 |
| 1782 (26) | *Il Seraglio*, opera |
| | Concerto Rondo in D minor to K175 Piano Concerto, K382 |
| | Concerto Rondo in A major, (discarded from K414 Piano Concerto), K386 |
| | Piano Concerto in F major, K413 |
| | Piano Concerto in A major, K414 |
| | Piano Concerto in C major, K415 |
| | Horn Concerto in D major, K412 |
| | Violin Sonata in A major and A minor (finished by Stadler), K402 |
| | Violin Sonata in C major, unfinished, K403 |
| | Violin Sonata in C major, unfinished, K404 |
| | String Quartet in G major (Haydn Set, No 1), K387 |
| | Five Fugues from Bach's *Well-Tempered Clavier*, for string quartet, K405 |
| | Symphony No 35 in D major, *Haffner*, K385 |
| 1783 (27) | Oboe Concerto in F major, fragment, K293 |
| | Votive Mass |
| | Horn Concerto in E♭ major, K417 |
| | Horn Concerto in E♭ major, K447 |
| | String Quartet in D minor (Haydn Set, No 2), K421 |
| | String Quartet in E♭ major (Haydn Set, No 3), K428 |
| | Piano Trio in D minor and D major (completed by Stadler), K442 |
| | Symphony No 36 in C major, *Linz*, K425 |
| | Symphony No 37 in G major, K444 (introduction only, the rest by M. Haydn) |
| 1784 (28) | Piano Concerto in E♭ major, K449 |
| | Piano Concerto in B♭ major, K450 |
| | Piano Concerto in D major, K451 |
| | Piano Concerto in G major, K453 |
| | Piano Concerto in B♭ major, K456 |
| | Piano Concerto in F major, K459 |
| | Violin Sonata in B♭ major, K454 |
| | Piano Sonata in C minor, K457 |
| | String Quartet in B♭ major (Haydn Set, No 4), K458 |
| 1785 (29) | Piano Concerto in D minor, K466 |
| | Piano Concerto in C major, K467 |
| | Piano Concerto in E♭ major, K482 |
| | Andante for a Violin Concerto, in A major, K470 |
| | Violin Sonata in E♭ major, K481 |
| | String Quartet in A major (Haydn Set, No 5), K464 |
| | String Quartet in C major (Haydn Set, No 6), K465 |
| | Piano Quartet in G minor, K478 |
| 1786 (30) | *The Impresario*, opera |
| | *Le nozze di Figaro*, opera |
| | Piano Concerto in A major, K488 |

Piano Concerto in C minor, K491
Piano Concerto in C major, K503
Horn Concerto in E♭ major, K495
Piano Sonata (four hands) in G major, K357
Piano Sonata (four hands) in F major, K497
String Quartet in D major, K499
Piano Quartet in E♭ major, K493
Piano Trio in G major, K496
Piano Trio in B♭ major, for piano, clarinet and viola, K498
Piano Trio in B♭ major, K502
Symphony No 38 in D major, *Prague*, K504

1787 (31)    *Don Giovanni*, opera
Piano Sonata (four hands) in C major, K521
Violin Sonata in A major, K526
String Quintet in C minor, K406 (arrangement of *Serenade*, K388)
String Quintet in C major, K515
String Quintet in G minor, K516
*Eine Kleine Nachtmusik*, for strings

1788 (32)    Piano Concerto in D major, *Coronation*, K537
Piano Sonata (Sonatina) in C major, K545
Violin Sonata in F major, K547
String Quartet in D minor, Adagio and Fugue (fugue identical with K426 for two pianos), K546
Piano Trio in E major, K542
Piano Trio in C major, K548
Piano Trio in G major, K564
Symphony No 39 in E♭ major, K543
Symphony No 40 in G minor, K550
Symphony No 41 in C major, *Jupiter*, K551

1789 (33)    Piano Sonata in B♭ major (better known as a violin sonata, but the violin part is not by Mozart), K570
Piano Sonata in D major, K576
String Quartet in D major (King of Prussia Set, No 1), K575

1790 (34)    *Così fan tutte*, opera
String Quartet in B♭ major (King of Prussia Set, No 2), K589
String Quartet in F major (King of Prussia Set, No 3), K590
String Quintet in D major, K593

1791 (35)    *La clemenza di Tito*, opera
*Die Zauberflöte*, opera
Piano Concerto in B♭ major, K595
Clarinet Concerto in A major, K622
String Quintet in E♭ major, K614
Requiem in D minor, K626 (unfinished, completed by Sussmeyr)
One early symphony, recently discovered


**MULDOWNEY, Dominic**
*b Southampton, 19 July 1952*

He studied with Birtwistle and at York University. From 1974 to 1976 he was composer-in-residence to the Southern Arts Association, and since 1976 has been musical director of the National Theatre.

1970 (18)    *Bitter Lemons*, for unaccompanied female chorus
1971 (19)    *A Heavyweight Dirge*, for soli and ensemble
1972 (20)    *Driftwood to the Flow*, for eighteen solo strings
1973 (21)    String Quartet No 1

1974 (22)  *Music at Chartres*, for orchestra
           *Solo/Ensemble*, for orchestra
1975 (23)  *Perspectives*, for orchestra
           Cantata for chorus, soli, two cellos and percussion
           *Da Capo al Fine*, tape for ballet
1976 (24)  Three-part Motet for eleven instruments
           Twelve Shorter Chorale Preludes of Bach for eight wind-players
           Ten Longer Chorale Preludes of Bach for eight wind-players
           *One from Arcady*, for unaccompanied violin
           *Three from Arcady*, for cor anglais, viola and cello
           *The Earl of Essex's Galliard*, for actors, dancer and seven players
1976–9 (24–7) *Changes*, ballet
1977 (25)  *Four from Arcady*, for four oboes
           *Variations on 'Mein Junges Leben'*, for eight players
           *Double Helix*, for eight players
           *Entr'acte*, for eight players
           *Procurans Odium*, for soprano and eight players
1978 (26)  *Warrior Queen*, for eight saxophones and percussion
           Five Melodies for four saxophones
           *A Garland of Chansons*, for six oboes and three bassoons
           *Two from Arcady*, for basset horn and tuba
           *Three Hymns to Agape*, for oboe player
           *A First Show*, for percussion and tape
1979 (27)  *Macbeth*, ballet music for orchestra
           *Six Psalms*, for soli, choir, ensemble and tape
           *A Little Piano Book*, twenty-four pieces
           *. . . In a Hall of Mirrors . . .*, for alto sax and piano
1980 (28)  String Quartet No 2
           *From Little Gidding*, for baritone, treble and piano
           *Theatre Poems*, for mezzo and ensemble
           Piano Trio
           *Five Theatre Poems*, for baritone and piano
1981 (29)  *In Dark Times*, for soli and ensemble
           *Sports et Divertissements*, for reciter and ensemble
1983 (31)  Piano Concerto
           *The Duration of Exile*, for mezzo and ensemble
           *A Second Show*, for contralto and ensemble
1984 (32)  Saxophone Concerto


## MUSGRAVE, Thea
*b Edinburgh, 27 May 1928*

After graduating from Edinburgh University, she went to Paris to study under
Nadia Boulanger, and while still a student she won the Donald Francis Tovey
Prize and the Lili Boulanger Memorial Prize. She taught at London University
and has been visiting professor at the University of California. She now lives in
the USA, where she has received the Koussevitsky Award and a Guggenheim
Fellowship. In 1973 she was invited to become an honorary fellow of New Hall,
Cambridge.

1953 (25)  *A Tale for Thieves*, ballet in one act
           *A Suite of Bairnsangs*, for voice and piano
1954 (26)  *Cantata for a Summer's Day*
1955 (27)  *The Abbot of Drimock*, chamber opera in one act
           Five Love Songs for soprano and guitar
1958 (30)  *Obliques*, for orchestra
           String Quartet

                        *A Song for Christmas*, for high voice and piano
1959 (31)    *Triptych*, for tenor and orchestra
1960 (32)    *Colloquy*, for violin and piano
                        Trio for flute, oboe and piano
                        *Monologue*, for piano
1961 (33)    Serenade for flute, clarinet, harp, viola and cello
                        *Sir Patrick Spens*, for tenor and guitar
1962 (34)    Chamber Concerto No 1
                        *The Phoenix and the Turtle*, for small choir and orchestra
1963 (35)    *The Five Ages of Man*, for chorus and orchestra
1964–5 (36–7) *The Decision*, opera in three acts
1965 (37)    *Festival Overture*, for orchestra
                        *Excursions*, for piano (four hands)
1966 (38)    Nocturnes and Arias for orchestra
                        Chamber Concerto No 2, *In Homage to Charles Ives*
                        Chamber Concerto No 3
1967 (39)    Concerto for orchestra
                        Impromptu for flute and oboe
                        Music for horn and piano
1968 (40)    Clarinet Concerto
                        *Beauty and the Beast*, ballet in two acts for chamber orchestra and
                            tape (1968–9)
1969 (41)    *Night Music*, for chamber orchestra
                        *Soliloquy*, for guitar and tape
                        *Memento vitae (Concerto in Homage to Beethoven)*, for orchestra
1970 (42)    *Elegy*, for viola and cello
                        Impromptu No 2, for flute, oboe and clarinet
                        *From One to Another*, for viola and tape
1971 (43)    Horn Concerto
                        *Primavera*, for soprano and flute
1972–3 (44–5) *The Voice of Ariadne*, chamber opera in three acts
1973 (45)    Viola Concerto
1974 (46)    *Space Play*, a concerto for nine instruments
1975 (47)    *Orfeo I*, an improvisation on a theme for flute and tape
                        *Orfeo II*, for solo flute and fifteen strings
1977 (49)    *Mary, Queen of Scots*. opera
1978 (50)    *O Caro m'e il Sonno*, for unaccompanied chorus
1979 (51)    *A Christmas Carol*, opera
1980 (52)    *The Last Twilight*, for chorus, brass and percussion
                        *From One to Another*, for viola and fifteen strings
1981 (53)    *Preipeteia*, for orchestra
                        *An Occurrence at Owl Creek Bridge*, radio opera
1982 (54)    *Fanfare*, for brass quintet


## MUSSORGSKY, Modeste
*b Karesk, 21 March 1839*
*d St Petersburg, 28 March 1881, aged forty-two*

His father was a landowner. As a child he studied piano, but he rebelled against
his teachers. He was intended for a military career, and at the age of ten entered
the military academy at St Petersburg. At the age of seventeen he joined a
Guards Regiment and began drinking heavily – a habit that eventually killed
him. He met a number of great composers, including Balakirev, under whose
influence he, too, began to compose. However, his originality and his
innovations did not appeal to his contemporaries. He left the Army, and in
1863, when he was twenty-five, the Russian liberation of the serfs so

251

impoverished his family that he took the job of a government clerk. Rimsky-Korsakov, whom he had met in 1861, shared a room with him. His operas were not well received, and his drinking increased. He toured southern Russia for a time as an accompanist, but in 1881 was thrown out of his lodgings and had an epileptic fit. He survived, in a military hospital, for only one more month.

| | |
|---|---|
| 1857 (18) | *Souvenir d'enfance*, for piano |
| 1858 (19) | Scherzo for orchestra |
| | *Edipo*, for mixed chorus (1858–60) |
| 1859 (20) | *Marcia di Sciamie*, for soloists, choir and orchestra |
| | *Impromptu passione*, for piano |
| 1861 (22) | *Alla marcia notturna*, for orchestra |
| | Scherzo and Finale for a symphony in D major (1861–2) |
| 1867 (28) | *St John's Night on the Bare Mountain*, for piano |
| | *La disfatta di Sennacherib*, first version for choir and orchestra |
| | Symphonic Intermezzo 'in modo classico' |
| 1868 (29) | fp *Zenitha* (The Marriage), opera (private performance) |
| | *The Nursery*, song cycle (1868–72) |
| 1869 (30) | *Boris Godunov*, opera, first version with piano (rewritten 1872) |
| 1872 (33) | *Khovantschina*, opera |
| 1874 (35) | *Pictures from an Exhibition*, for piano |
| | *Sunless*, song cycle |
| | *Sorochinsky Fair*, opera (a passage from this work was freely arranged and orchestrated as *Night on the Bare Mountain* by Rimsky-Korsakov, qv) |
| | *Jesus Navin*, for contralto, bass, choir and piano (1874–7) |
| 1875–7 (36–8) | *Songs and Dances of Death*, song cycle |
| 1879 (40) | 'Song of the Flea', setting of Mephistophiles' song in Goethe's *Faust* |
| 1880 (41) | Five Popular Russian Songs, for male chorus |
| | *Turkish March*, for orchestra |
| | *Meditation*, for piano |
| | *Une larme*, for piano |
| | *Au village*, for piano |

## NICOLAI, Carl Otto
*b Königsberg, 9 June 1810*
*d Königsberg, 11 May 1849, aged thirty-eight*

He first learned piano with his father, but ran away from home at the age of sixteen to study in Berlin. In 1833 he was appointed organist in the chapel of the Prussian Embassy in Rome, and in 1837 was *Kapellmeister* and singing master in Vienna. From 1841 to 1847 he was *Kapellmeister* of the court opera in Vienna, and he founded the Philharmonic concerts there in 1842. In 1847 he was appointed director of the Berlin opera. He died of apoplexy.

| | |
|---|---|
| 1831 (21) | Symphony |
| 1832 (22) | Mass |
| 1835 (25) | Symphony |
| | *Funeral March* (for the death of Bellini) |
| 1838 (28) | *Von Himmel Hoch*, overture |
| 1839 (29) | *Henry II*, opera |
| 1840 (30) | *Il Templario*, opera |
| | *Gildippe ed Odoardo*, opera |
| 1841 (31) | *Il Proscritto*, opera |
| 1844 (34) | *Ein Feste Burg*, overture with chorus |
| 1849 (39) | fp *The Merry Wives of Windsor*, opera |

## NIELSEN, Carl
*b Nørre Lyndelse, Denmark, 9 June 1865*
*d Copenhagen, 3 October 1931, aged sixty-six*

He was born into a peasant family; his father played violin and cornet. At the age of fourteen he became a military bandsman in Odense, and soon began to compose chamber music. In 1884 he entered the Copenhagen Conservatory, and from 1889 to 1905 played second violin in the Royal Theatre Orchestra, of which he was later conductor from 1908 to 1914. He was appointed to the governing body of the Conservatory in 1915, remaining there until 1927, and teaching theory there from 1916 to 1919. Heart trouble affected him increasingly from 1922. He became director of the Conservatory in 1931 and died of a heart attack later that same year. In his first symphony he showed the influence of the orchestral style of Brahms, but though his form and harmony were classical he was showing contemporary developments in chromaticism and tone colour. By his fifth symphony he was using progressive tonality, and was demonstrating the reformulation of traditional symphonic form.

1881–2 (16–17) Sonata No 1 in G for violin and piano (unpublished)
1882–3 (17–18) Two Character Pieces for piano (unpublished)
String Quartet in Dm (unpublished)
*Duet in A*, for two violins (unpublished)
1883 (18) Piano Trio in G (unpublished)
1883–7 (18–22) Various string quartet movements (unpublished)
1887–8 (22–3) String Quartet in Gm
1888 (23) String Quintet in G
Little Suite for strings
Symphonic Rhapsody (unpublished)
1889 (24) *Fantasistykker*, for oboe and piano
1890 (25) String Quartet in Fm
Five Pieces for piano
1890–92 (25–7) Symphony No 1
1893 (28) *Snefrid*, melodrama (unpublished)
1894 (29) Symphonic Suite for piano
1894–7 (29–32) *Humoreske-bagateller*, for piano
1895 (30) Sonata in A for violin and piano
1896–7 (31–2) *Hymnus amoris*, for baritone, bass, chorus and orchestra
1897–8 (32–3) String Quartet in E♭
1900 (35) *Fest-praeludium*, for piano
Cantata for the Lorens Frelich Festival (unpublished)
1901 (36) Cantata for the Students' Association (unpublished)
1901–2 (36–7) Symphony No 2, *The Four Temperaments*
1902 (37) *Saul and David*, opera
1903 (38) *Helios*, overture
1903–4 (38–9) *Søvnen*, for chorus and orchestra
1905 (40) *Drømmen om 'Glade Jul'*, for piano
1906 (41) fp *Maskarade*, opera
String Quartet in F
1907–8 (42–3) *Saga-drøm*, for orchestra
1908 (43) Cantata for the Anniversary of Copenhagen University
1909 (44) Cantata for a Commemoration (unpublished)
Cantata for the National Exhibition at Århus (unpublished)
1910 (45) *At the Young Artist's Bier*, for string quartet
1910–11 (45–6) Symphony No 3, *Espansiva*
1911 (46) Violin Concerto
1912 (47) Sonata No 2 for violin and piano
Paraphrase on 'Nearer My God to Thee', for wind (unpublished)

| 1913 (48) | *Canto Serioso*, for horn and piano |
| 1914 (49) | *Serenata in vano*, for clarinet, bassoon, horn, cello and double-bass |
| 1914-16 (49-51) | Symphony No 4, *The Inextinguishable* |
| 1916 (51) | Chaconne for piano |
| 1917 (52) | Theme and Variations for piano |
| | Cantata for the Centenary of the Merchants' Committee |
| 1917-18 (52-3) | *Pan and Syrinx*, for orchestra |
| 1918 (53) | Three Compositions for piano |
| 1919-20 (54-5) | Suite, *Den Luciferiske*, for piano |
| 1921 (56) | *Springtime in Fyn*, for soprano, tenor, bass, chorus and orchestra |
| 1921-2 (56-7) | Symphony No 5 |
| 1922 (57) | *Hyldest til Holberg*, for solo voices, chorus and orchestra (unpublished) |
| | Wind Quintet |
| 1923 (58) | Prelude and Theme with Variations for violin |
| 1924-5 (59-60) | Symphony No 6, *The Simple* |
| 1926 (61) | Flute Concerto |
| 1927 (62) | *En Fantasirejse til Faerøerne*, rhapsodic overture |
| 1927-8 (62-3) | Prelude and Presto for violin |
| 1928 (63) | Clarinet Concerto |
| | *Bøhmisk-dansk folketom*, for strings |
| | Three Pieces for piano |
| 1929 (64) | Cantata for the Centenary of the Polytechnic High School (unpublished) |
| | *Hymne til Kunsten*, for soprano, tenor, chorus and wind (unpublished) |
| | Twenty-nine Little Preludes for organ |
| 1930 (65) | Cantata for the 50th Anniversary of the Danish Cremation Union (unpublished) |
| | Cantata for the 50th Anniversary of the Young Merchants' Educational Association (unpublished) |
| | *Klaviermusick for Smaa og Store*, two volumes |
| | Two Preludes for organ |
| 1931 (66) | Allegretto in F, for two recorders |
| | *Commotio*, for organ |

Nielsen also wrote much incidental music, unaccompanied choral works, and many songs.


**NILSSON, Bo**
*b Skelleftehamm, Sweden, 1 May 1937*

His elementary musical training was with local teachers. He studied counterpoint and instrumentation with Pedersen and acoustics with Dr Clair Renard from 1954 to 1955. He lives in Sweden.

| c1956 (c19) | *Frequenzen*, for eight players |
| 1957 (20) | *Kreutzungen*, for instrumental ensemble |
| | *Buch der Veränderungen*, for chamber orchestra |
| | *Mädchentotenlieder* (1957-8) |
| 1958 (21) | *Quantitaten*, for piano |
| | *Zwanzig Gruppen für Blaser*, for piccolo, oboe and clarinet (1958-9) |
| | *Stunde eines Blocks*, for soprano and six players |
| 1959 (22) | *Und die Zeiger seiner Augen wurden langsam zurückgedreht*, for solo voices, chorus and mixed media |
| | *Ein irrender Sohn*, for high voice and instruments |
| 1960 (23) | *Szene I*, for chamber orchestra |

|           | *Reaktionen*, for four percussionists |
|-----------|---------------------------------------|
| 1961 (24) | *Szene II*, for chamber orchestra |
| 1962 (25) | *Szene III*, for chamber orchestra |
|           | *Entrée*, for large orchestra and tape |
| 1963 (26) | *Versuchungen*, for large orchestra |
| 1964 (27) | *La Bran*, for mixed choir and orchestra |
| 1965 (28) | *Litanei über das verlorene Schlagzeug* |
| 1967 (30) | *Revue*, for orchestra |
| 1970 (33) | *Attraktionen*, for string quartet |
|           | *Exit*, for orchestra |
|           | *Om Kanalerna på Mars*, for mezzo, tenor and eight instruments |
| 1973 (36) | *Nazm*, for soli, chorus and orchestra |
|           | *Tesbih*, for orchestra |
|           | *Déjà-connu*, for wind quintet |
| 1974 (37) | *Taqsim-Caprice-Maqam*, for ensemble |
| 1975 (38) | *Szene IV*, for jazz sax and chorus |
| 1976 (39) | *Flöten aus der Einsamkeit*, for soprano and nine players |
| 1977 (40) | *Mez*, for ensemble |

Nilsson has also written choral works, songs and music for films and television.


## NONO, Luigi
*b Venice, 29 January 1924*

In 1941 he entered the Venice Conservatory, and attended Malipiero's composition classes from 1943 to 1945. He graduated in law from Padua University and became a member of the Italian Communist Party. In 1955 he married Schoenberg's daughter, Nuria. From 1954 to 1960 he explored electronics and taught at Darmstadt; and from 1959 onwards he has been in great demand as a teacher, lecturer, debater and writer.

| | |
|---|---|
| 1950 (26) | *Variazioni di Schoenberg*, for chamber orchestra |
| 1951 (27) | Composizione No 1, for orchestra |
|           | *Polifonica-monodia-ritmica*, for instrumental ensemble |
| 1951–3 (27–9) | *Epitaph for Lorca*, for speaker, chorus and orchestra |
| 1953 (29) | *Due Espressioni*, for orchestra |
| 1954 (30) | *The Red Mantle*, ballet |
|           | *Liebeslied*, for chorus and instruments |
|           | *La Victoire de Guernica*, for chorus and orchestra |
| 1954–5 (30–1) | *Canti per 13*, for thirteen instruments |
| 1955 (31) | *Incontri*, for twenty-four instruments |
| 1955–6 (31–2) | *Il Canto Sospeso*, for soli, chorus and orchestra |
| 1957 (33) | *Virianti*, for violin, woodwind and strings |
| 1957–8 (33–4) | *La Terra e la Compagna*, for soli, chorus and instruments |
| 1958 (34) | *Cori di Didone*, for chorus and percussion |
| 1958–9 (34–5) | Composizione No 2 for orchestra |
| 1960 (36) | *Homage to Emilio Vedova*, for tape |
|           | *Ha Venido*, for female voices |
|           | *Sara Dolce Tacere*, for eight solo voices |
| 1961 (37) | *Intolleranza 1960*, scenic action |
| 1962 (38) | *Canti di Hiroshima*, for orchestra |
| 1962–3 (38–9) | *Canciones a Guiomar*, for six female voices and instruments |
| 1964 (40) | *La Fabbrica Illuminata*, for voice and tape |
| 1965 (41) | *Die Ermittlung*, incidental music on tape |
| 1966 (42) | *Ricorda cosa ti hanno fatto in Auschwitz*, for tape |
| 1967 (43) | *À Floresta*, for speaker, instruments and tape |
|           | *Per Bastiana Tai-Yang Cheng*, for orchestra and tape |

1967–8 (43–4) *Contrappunto Dialettico*, for tape
1968–9 (44–5) *Musica-manifesto No 1*, for tape
1969 (45)   *Musiche per Manzù*, for tape
1969–70 (45–6) *Y Entonces Comprendió*, for six female voices, chorus, tape and
          electronics
1970 (46)   *Voci . . .*, for soli, speakers, chorus and orchestra
1971 (47)   *Ein Gespenst*, for soprano, chorus and orchestra
1971–2 (47–8) *Como una ola de fuerza y luz*, for piano, orchestra and tape
1972–5 (48–51) *Al gran sole carico d'amore*, scenic action
1973 (49)   *Siamo la Gioventù del Vietnam*, for unison voices
1974 (50)   *Für Paul Dessau*, for tape
          *Notturni-Albe*, for piano and tape
1976 (52)   *Safferte onde Serene*, for piano and tape
1980 (56)   *Fragmente-Stille*, for string quartet
1981 (57)   *Das Atmende Klarsein*, for bass flute and small chorus
          *Fragment from Prometheus*, for three sopranos, small chorus, bass
          flute, bass clarinet and tape
1982 (58)   *Donde Estas Hermano?*, for female voices
          *Quando Stanno Morendo*, for female vocal quartet, flute, cello and
          electronics
1983 (59)   *Guai Ai Gelidi Mostri*, for two contraltos, ensemble and electronics
          *Homage to György Kürtag*, for contralto, bass tuba, flute and
          electronics


**NOVÁK, Vitězslav**
*b Kamenice nad Lipou, Bohemia, 5 December 1870*
*d Skutec, near Prague, 18 July 1949, aged seventy-eight*

His potential was not apparent until his teens, when in 1889 he went to Prague
University to study law and instead devoted his time and money to music. He
became a remarkable pianist and started to compose, studying under Dvořák.
He lacked confidence in himself and made his living by teaching. A holiday in
the Czech countryside and his discovery of its folk idiom revitalised him,
however, and by 1900 he was at the height of his creative powers, becoming the
outstanding Czech composer of the day. In 1909 he was made professor of the
composition master-class at the Prague Conservatory, and was elected to the
Czech Academy. His popularity became overshadowed by Janáček, but he
continued teaching, his association with the Conservatory lasting over thirty
years.

1892 (22)   *Korzár*, overture
1894–5 (24–5) Serenade in F for small orchestra
1895 (25)   Piano Concerto
1898 (28)   Two Ballads for chorus and piano duet
          *Maryša*, dramatic overture
1900 (30)   Two Ballads for chorus and piano duet
1901 (31)   Two Choruses for female chorus and piano
1902 (32)   *In the Tatra Mountains*, symphonic poem
1903 (33)   *Slovak Suite*, for small orchestra
          *Eternal Longing*, for orchestra
1905 (35)   Serenade in D for small orchestra
1906 (36)   *Toman and the Wood-nymph*, symphonic poem
          Six male choruses
1907 (37)   *Lady Godiva*, overture
1908–10 (38–40) *The Storm*, for soli, chorus and orchestra
1911 (41)   *On Native Soil*, for eight male choruses

1912 (42)    Four Poems for chorus
             *The Wedding Shift*, for soli, chorus and orchestra
1913–14 (43–4) *The Zvikov Imp*, comic opera
1914–15 (44–5) *Karlštejn*, opera
1916–17 (46–7) *Strength and Defiance*, for six male choruses
1918 (48)    Three Czech Songs for male chorus and orchestra
1919–22 (49–52) *Lucerna*, musical fairy-tale
1922–5 (52–5) *Grandfather's Legacy*, opera
1926–8 (56–8) *Signorina Gioventu*, ballet-pantomime
1929 (59)    *Nikotina*, ballet-pantomime
1931 (61)    Twelve Lullabies for female chorus
             *Autumn Symphony*, for mixed chorus and orchestra
1932 (62)    *From Life*, for twelve male choruses
1936 (66)    *South Bohemian Suite*, for orchestra
1941 (71)    *De Profundis*, symphonic poem
             *St Wenceslas Triptych*, for organ and orchestra
             *Home*, for six male choruses
1942 (72)    Five mixed choruses
             Ten children's choruses
1943 (73)    *May Symphony*, for soli, chorus and orchestra
1948 (78)    *Žižka*, incidental music
             *Song of the Zlin Workers*, small cantata
1949 (79)    *Stars*, for female chorus and orchestra

Novák also wrote chamber and instrumental works and songs, and some folk-song arrangements.


**OFFENBACH, Jacques**
*b Cologne, 20 June 1819*
*d Paris, 4 October 1880, aged sixty-one*

He was the son of a Jewish cantor, musician, author and book-binder, from whom he learned violin. He started composing at the age of six, and in 1833 was accepted by the Paris Conservatory, where he studied cello. He then played cello in the orchestra of the Opéra-Comique, later making very successful tours as a fashionable salon cellist. From 1850 to 1855 he was conductor of the Comédie Française; then he began to lease his own theatres, for performances both of his own works and of others. He visited London to conduct his own operettas in 1857, 1866 and 1870, but in 1875 his trip to America was a disaster, and the bad sea-voyage nearly killed him. He died when the gout from which he had suffered attacked his heart.

1853 (34)    *Le mariage aux lanternes*, operetta
1858 (39)    *Orpheus in the Underworld*, operetta
1864 (45)    *La Belle Hélène*, operetta
1866 (47)    *Bluebeard*, operetta
             *La vie parisienne*, opera
1867 (48)    *La Grande Duchesse de Gérolstein*, operetta
1868 (49)    *La Périchole*, operetta
1878 (59)    *Madame Favart*, operetta

Performed posthumously:
1881         *The Tales of Hoffman*, operetta

**OLIVER, Stephen**
*b Liverpool, 1950*

He made a special study of electronic music at Oxford, and then taught composition at the Huddersfield School of Music for two years. He now works full time as a composer.

| | |
|---|---|
| 1969 (19) | *Slippery Souls, a Christmas Drama*, for chorus, violin, percussion, organ and piano |
| 1972 (22) | *Music for the Wreck of the Deutschland*, for piano quintet |
| | *Sirens*, song-cycle for baritone and piano |
| | *Overheard on a Saltmarsh*, for six male voices |
| | *The Three Wise Monkeys*, one-act opera for children |
| 1973 (23) | *Ricercare* for clarinet, violin, cello and piano |
| | *A Fur Coat for Summer*, one-act opera |
| | *Sufficient Beauty*, for baritone, actor and orchestra |
| | *The Donkey*, children's opera |
| 1973–4 (23–4) | *Perseverance*, religious opera |
| 1974 (24) | *Past Tense*, for voices and instruments |
| | *Cadenus Observed*, baritone solo |
| | *The Boy and the Dolphin*, for orchestra |
| 1974–5 (24–5) | *Tom Jones*, opera |
| 1975 (25) | *Luv*, for orchestra |
| | *Bad Times*, for baritone and string quartet |
| 1976 (26) | Symphony |
| | *O No*, comedy for brass band |
| | *Many Happy Returns*, for brass band |
| | *Magnificat and Nunc Dimittis*, for boys' voices, recorders and organ |
| | *The Elixir*, for soloists and chorus |
| | *The Waiter's Revenge*, for six voices |
| | *Three Instant Operas*, for children |
| | *The Great McPorridge Disaster*, for voices and instruments |
| 1977 (27) | *Kyoto*, organ duet |
| | *The Garden*, for voices and instruments |
| | *The Duchess of Malfi*, opera |
| | *A Stable Home*, dramatic cantata |
| 1978 (28) | Sonata for guitar |
| | *Exchange*, for three male voices and piano |
| | *Canzonet*, for five male voices |
| | *The Girl and the Unicorn*, opera |
| 1979 (29) | Study for piano |
| | *A Dialogue between Mary and Her Child*, for soprano, baritone and chorus |
| | *Ballad of the Breadman*, carol for unison voices and piano or guitar |
| | *The Dreaming of the Bones*, one-act opera |
| 1980 (30) | *The Key to the Zoo*, for narrator and instruments |
| | *The Child from the Sea*, for solo, chorus and orchestra |
| | *Wedding Anthem*, for treble voices and organ |
| | *A String of Beads*, for chorus and orchestra |
| | *Jacko's Play*, children's operetta |
| | *A Man of Feeling*, for soprano, baritone and piano |
| 1981 (31) | Wind Octet |
| | Mass for unaccompanied chorus |

**ORFF, Carl**
b Munich, 10 July 1895
d Germany, 29 March 1982, aged eighty-seven

He came from a musical family, and as a boy studied piano, organ and cello. His first works, all vocal, were published when he was sixteen, before he had any proper academic training. From 1913 to 1915 he was *répétiteur* and conductor at the Munich Kammerspiele. A turning point in his life came when he founded in 1924, with Dorothee Günther, the Günther Schule of Gymnastic Dancing; he became interested in musical education, and obsessed with primitive and evocative rhythms, and with renaissance music. His appointment as conductor of the Bach Society of Munich led to imaginative staging of Schütz and Bach, and these influences led to *Carmina Burana*.

| 1925 | (30) | Prelude for orchestra |
| 1927 | (32) | Concertino for wind |
| 1928 | (33) | *Entrata* (revised 1940) |
| 1930 | (35) | *Catulli Carmina*, choral setting of poems of Catullus (revised 1943) |
| 1934 | (39) | *Bayerische Musik* |
| 1935–6 | (40–1) | *Carmina Burana*, scenic cantata on Latin texts |
| 1936 | (41) | *Olympischer Reigen*, for chorus and orchestra |
| 1937–8 | (42–3) | *Der Mond*, opera |
| 1941–2 | (46–7) | *Die Kluge*, opera |
| 1944 | (49) | *Die Bernauerin*, opera (1944–5) |
| 1945–6 | (50–1) | *Astutuli*, opera |
| 1947–8 | (52–3) | *Antigone*, opera |
| 1950–1 | (55–6) | *Trionfo di Afrodite*, opera |
| 1955 | (60) | *Der Sänger der Vorwelt*, opera |
| | | *Comoedia de Christi resurrectione*, for chorus and orchestra |
| 1956 | (61) | *Nanie und Dithyrambe*, choral work |
| 1958 | (63) | *Oedipus, der Tyrann*, opera |
| 1960 | (65) | *Ludus de nato Infante mirificus*, opera |
| 1962 | (67) | *Ein Sommernachtstraum*, opera |
| 1969–71 | (74–6) | *De Temporum fine comoedia*, dramatic cantata |
| 1973 | (78) | *Rota*, for chorus and instruments |

**PACHELBEL, Johann**
b Nuremberg, August 1653
d Nuremburg, March 1706, aged fifty-two

Prior to 1669 he studied music locally, then entered the University of Altdorf, also serving as organist. His father could not afford to support him at university for more than a year; but in 1670 he was given a special scholarship to the Gymnasium Poeticum in Regensburg. He went to Vienna in 1673 to become deputy organist at St Stephen's Cathedral, and in 1677 became court organist at Eisenach for a year. In 1678 he became organist at the Protestant Church at Erfurt, serving there for twelve years. He was much in demand as an organist and teacher. Four of his children became well known in their own right.

His output included a great many organ works, chamber works, arias, motets, sacred concertos, music for vespers, and masses.

**PADEREWSKI, Ignace Jan**
b Kurylówka, Poland, 18 November 1860
d New York, 29 July 1941, aged eighty

He composed his first piece at the age of six, and at twelve entered the Warsaw Musical Institute, studying piano and theory, and graduating as a pianist in

1878. In 1881 he went to Germany to study counterpoint and orchestration, and from 1884 to 1887 he stayed in Vienna, studying piano and earning a living by teaching. In Paris in 1888 and in London in 1890 he was acclaimed as a great master of the piano; he travelled widely, and visited America. In 1899 he settled in Switzerland. From 1910 he took an interest in politics, becoming in time the epitome of Polish patriotism, and prime minister of Poland in 1919. He resigned a year later. He was a great philanthropist and was decorated by Poland, Great Britain, Belgium, France and Italy, and received a great number of honorary degrees.

| 1880 | (20) | Violin Sonata |
| 1884 | (24) | Polish Dances for piano, Books I and II |
| 1888 | (28) | Piano Concerto in A minor |
| 1893 | (33) | *Polish Fantasy on Original Themes*, for piano and orchestra |
| 1901 | (41) | *Manru*, opera |
| 1903–7 | (43–7) | Symphony in B minor |

## PAGANINI, Niccolò
*b Genoa, 17 October 1782*
*d Nice, 27 May 1840, aged fifty-seven*

The son of a dockyard worker, he was a violin virtuoso by the time he was eleven, and received tuition from famous teachers. In his mid-teens a number of concerts in Italy ensured that he was no longer povery-stricken, but success made him gamble and drink so heavily that it nearly killed him. Nursed back to health by a noblewoman who befriended him, he resumed giving concerts at the age of twenty-three, but in 1824 his indulgences caused another breakdown. After his recovery in 1827 he made triumphant tours of Austria, Germany, France, and Westphalia where he was made a baron. He also visited Britain. In the late 1830s his health and his luck began to fail, and he died of a disease of the larynx. His legendary pact with the Devil ensured that he could not be buried in consecrated ground, and his body continued to be moved around until 1926.

| 1795 | (13) | Variations on 'La Carmagnole' |
| 1807 | (25) | Sonata, *Napoleone* |
| 1810 | (28) | *Polacca con Variazione*, for violin and orchestra |
| 1813 | (31) | *Le Streghe*, variations on theme of Sussmeyer, for violin and orchestra |
| 1815 | (33) | Concerto for violin |
| 1816 | (34) | Sonata, *Maria Luisa* |
| 1817 | (35) | Concerto No 1 |
| 1819 | (37) | *Inno all'armonia*, cantata (lost) |
| | | Introduction and Variations on 'Non più mesta' |
| | | Introduction and Variations on 'Di tanti palpiti' |
| | | Introduction and Variations on 'Dal tuo stellato soglio' |
| 1825 | (43) | Sonata, *Militaire* |
| 1826 | (44) | Concerto No 2 |
| | | Concerto No 3 |
| 1828 | (46) | *È Pur Amabile*, canzonetta for voice and piano |
| | | *La Tempesta*, for chorus and orchestra |
| | | *Maestoso sonata sentimentale* |
| | | Sonata and Variations on 'Pria ch'io l'impegno' |
| 1828–30 | (46–8) | *Le Couvent du St Bernard*, for male voices and orchestra |
| 1829 | (47) | Variations on 'God Save the King' |
| | | Variations on 'O mamma, mamma cara' |

                    Sonata, *Varsaria*
                    Sonata, *Appassionata*
1830 (48)    *Quel jours heureux*, for solo, chorus and piano
                    Concerto No 4
                    Concerto No 5
                    *Moto Perpetuo*, for violin and orchestra
1831 (49)    Sonata amorosa galante
                    *Potpourri*, for violin and orchestra (violin part lost)
                    *St Patrick's Day*, variations on an Irish song
                    Sonatina e Polacchetta
                    Concertino for bassoon, horn and orchestra
1834 (52)    Sonata for viola and orchestra
1838 (56)    Sonata, *La Primavera*
Paganini also wrote chamber music and works for solo violin and guitar.


## PAISIELLO, Giovanni
*b Roccaforsata, near Taranto, 8 May 1740*
*d Naples, 5 June 1816, aged seventy-six*

From 1754 to 1763 he studied at the Naples Conservatory, then composed his
first operas. In 1776 he was invited to be *maestro di cappella* for Catherine II of
Russia for several years. He later returned to Naples under the patronage of
Ferdinand IV. He was much admired by Napoleon Buonaparte, who in 1802
made him his director of chapel music. He was made a member of the Légion
d'honneur in 1806, and a member of the French Institute in 1809.

He wrote ninety operas, as well as cantatas, sacred oratorios, masses and other
liturgical works, chamber and orchestral works.


## PALESTRINA, Giovanni Pierluigi da
*b Palestrina, c1525*
*d Rome, 2 February 1594, aged c sixty-nine*

He was a chorister at the Cathedral of Sant' Agapit, and in 1537 joined the choir
school of Santa Maria Maggiore in Rome. He became organist and choirmaster
of Sant' Agapit in 1544, remaining there until 1551. He was appointed master of
the choir which sang the services at St Peter's in Rome, and then went to St John
Lateran as *maestro di cappella* for the next five years. In 1561 he returned to Santa
Maria Maggiore, and from 1565 to 1571 taught at the Jesuit seminary in Rome.
He was ordained as a priest, but renounced his religious vows. Two marriages
had brought him substantial wealth, and when he contemplated retirement to
Palestrina he was both prosperous and famous. However, he was taken ill as he
prepared to leave Rome, and died some days later.

1554 (*c*29)    *p* First Book of Masses
1563 (*c*38)    *p* First Book of Motets
1567 (*c*42)    *Missa Papae Marcelli*
1569 (*c*44)    *p* Second Book of Masses
1570 (*c*45)    *p* Third Book of Masses
                        *Missa Brevis*
1584 (*c*59)    *p* Settings of *The Song of Solomon*
1590 (*c*65)    *p* Aeterna Christi Munera*, mass
                        *Stabat Mater* (*c*1590)
Palestrina also composed many motets and madrigals.

**PANUFNIK, Andrzej**
*b Warsaw, 24 September 1914*

He studied theory and composition at the Warsaw State Conservatory from 1932
to 1936, then conducted at the Vienna State Academy from 1937 to 1938, and
continued his studies in Paris and London until 1939. He was in Warsaw during
World War II, and his pre-1944 compositions were destroyed by fire. From 1945
to 1947 he was conductor of the Cracow and Warsaw Philharmonic orchestra.
He served on various cultural committees in Poland and with UNESCO. In 1954
he decided to leave Poland and settle in England where, apart from occasional
conducting, he spends his life composing.

| | | |
|---|---|---|
| 1934 | (20) | Piano Trio |
| 1940 | (26) | Five Polish Peasant Songs |
| 1942 | (28) | Tragic Overture |
| 1947 | (33) | Twelve Miniature Studies for piano |
| | | Nocturne for orchestra |
| | | Lullaby for strings and two harps |
| | | Divertimento for strings on trios by Janiewicz |
| 1948 | (34) | *Sinfonia Rustica* |
| 1949 | (35) | *Hommage à Chopin*, for soprano and piano |
| 1950 | (36) | *Old Polish Suite*, for string orchestra |
| 1951 | (37) | Concerto in modo antico for trumpet and orchestra |
| 1952 | (38) | *Heroic Overture* |
| 1956 | (42) | Rhapsody for orchestra |
| 1957 | (43) | *Sinfonia Elegiaca* |
| 1959 | (45) | *Polonia*, for orchestra |
| 1962 | (48) | Piano Concerto |
| | | *Landscape*, for string orchestra |
| | | *Autumn Music*, for orchestra |
| 1963 | (49) | Two Lyric Pieces for young players |
| | | *Sinfonia Sacra* |
| 1964 | (50) | 'Song to the Virgin Mary' |
| 1966 | (52) | *Hommage à Chopin*, arranged for flute and string orchestra |
| | | *Jagiellonian Triptych*, for string orchestra |
| 1967 | (53) | *Katyń Epitaph*, for orchestra |
| 1968 | (54) | *Reflections*, for piano |
| 1968–9 | (54–5) | *Universal Prayer* |
| 1969 | (55) | *Thames Pageant*, for young singers and players |
| 1971 | (57) | Violin Concerto |
| 1972 | (58) | *Triangles*, for three flutes and three cellos |
| | | *Winter Solstice*, for solo voices, chorus and instruments |
| | | *Invocation for Peace*, for treble voices, two trumpets and two trombones |
| 1973 | (59) | Sinfonia Concertante for flute, harp and strings |
| 1975 | (61) | *Sinfonia di Sfere* |
| 1976 | (62) | String Quartet No 1 |
| 1977 | (63) | *Dreamscape*, for mezzo-soprano and piano |
| | | *Sinfonia Mistica* |
| 1978 | (64) | *Metasinfonia*, for organ, strings and timpani |
| 1979 | (65) | *Concerto Festivo*, for orchestra |
| 1980 | (66) | Concertino for timpani, percussion and strings |
| | | String Quartet No 2, *Messages* |
| 1981 | (67) | *Sinfonia Votiva* |
| 1982–3 | (68–9) | *A Procession for Peace*, for orchestra |
| 1983 | (69) | *Arbor Cosmica*, for twelve solo strings |

**PARKER, Horatio**
*b Auburndale, Massachusetts, 15 September 1863*
*d Cedarhurst, Long Island, 18 December 1919, aged fifty-six*

From the age of fourteen he learned piano and organ with his mother, then studied theory and composition in Boston. From 1882 to 1885 he attended the Munich Hochschule für Musick, and spent the rest of his life as a teacher, organist, composer and conductor. He died of pneumonia.

| | |
|---|---|
| 1884 (21) | Concert Overture |
| | *Regulus*, overture héroique |
| | Venetian Overture |
| | Scherzo for orchestra |
| 1885 (22) | Symphony |
| | String Quartet |
| 1890 (27) | *Count Robert of Paris*, overture |
| 1893 (30) | Suite for piano, violin and cello |
| 1894 (31) | String Quintet |
| | Suite for piano and violin |
| 1899 (36) | *A Northern Ballad*, symphonic poem |
| 1902 (39) | Organ Concerto |
| 1903 (40) | *Vathek*, symphonic poem |
| | *The Eternal Feminine*, incidental music (lost) |
| 1906 (43) | *The Prince of India*, incidental music |
| 1910 (47) | *Mona*, opera |
| 1911 (48) | *Collegiate Overture*, with male chorus |
| 1914 (51) | *Fairyland*, opera |
| 1916 (53) | *Cupid and Psyche*, a masque |
| | *An Allegory of War and Peace*, for chorus and band |

Parker also composed many sacred and secular choral works, songs, anthems and services, and some keyboard works.


**PARRY, Charles Hubert Hastings (Sir)**
*b Bournemouth, 27 February 1848*
*d Rustington, Sussex, 7 October 1918, aged seventy*

He obtained his MusB degree while still at Eton, and then went to Exeter College, Oxford. He joined the staff of the Royal College of Music in 1883, becoming director in 1894. He succeeded Stainer as professor of music at Oxford in 1900. He remained at the Royal College until his death, but resigned the Oxford chair in 1908. He was awarded several honorary doctorates, was knighted in 1898 and made a baronet five years later.

| | |
|---|---|
| 1878–9 (30–1) | Piano Concerto |
| 1878–82 (30–4) | Symphony No 1 |
| 1883 (35) | Symphony No 2, *Cambridge* |
| | *The Birds*, incidental music |
| 1885–6 (37–8) | *Guinevere*, opera |
| 1886 (38) | *Suite moderne*, for orchestra |
| 1889 (41) | Symphony No 3, *English* |
| | Symphony No 4 |
| 1892 (44) | *The Frogs*, incidental music |
| 1893 (45) | *Hypatia*, incidental music |
| 1894 (46) | *Lady Radnor's Suite*, for orchestra |
| 1897 (49) | Symphonic Variations |
| 1899 (51) | *A Repentance*, incidental music |
| 1900 (52) | *Agamemnon*, incidental music |

| 1905 | (57) | *The Clouds*, incidental music |
| 1912 | (64) | *Proserpina*, incidental music |
| | | Symphonic Fantasia |
| 1914 | (66) | Symphonic Poem |
| | | *The Acharnions*, incidental music |
| 1915 | (67) | *An English Suite*, for orchestra |

Parry also wrote sacred and secular choral works, songs, chamber and keyboard music, as well as much literary work.

## PATTERSON, Paul
*b Chesterfield, 1947*

From 1964 he studied trombone and composition at the Royal Academy of Music. On leaving he won a scholarship to study with Richard Rodney Bennett. He became director of contemporary music at Warwick University in 1974, and professor of composition at the Royal Academy. In 1980 he took up a two-year post as composer-in-residence at King's School, Canterbury. He has made lecture tours for the British Council and is visiting lecturer to various American universities.

| 1967 | (20) | Wind Quintet |
| 1968 | (21) | Wind Trio |
| 1969 | (22) | Trumpet Concerto |
| 1970 | (23) | Concertante for orchestra |
| | | Partita for orchestra |
| | | Monologue for solo oboe |
| 1971 | (24) | Horn Concerto |
| | | Piccola Sinfonia |
| | | Symphonic Study |
| 1972 | (25) | *Fiesta Sinfonica* |
| | | *Comedy for Five Winds* |
| | | *Kyrie*, for chorus and piano |
| 1973 | (26) | *Sonors*, for orchestra |
| | | *Intersections*, for instrumental ensemble |
| | | *Gloria*, for chorus and piano |
| | | *Time-Piece*, for six male voices |
| | | *The Abode of the Dead*, for voices and ensemble |
| | | *You'll Never Be Alone*, for voices and ensemble |
| | | *Fluorescence*, for organ |
| 1974 | (27) | *Fusions*, for orchestra |
| | | *Floating Music*, for ensemble |
| | | *Conversations*, for clarinet and piano |
| | | *Chromascope*, for brass band |
| 1975 | (28) | *The Circular Ruins*, for orchestra |
| | | *Strange Meeting*, for orchestra |
| | | *Count Down*, for brass band |
| | | *Cataclysm*, for brass band |
| | | *Requiem*, for chorus and orchestra |
| | | *Shadows*, for clarinet and tape |
| 1976 | (29) | Clarinet Concerto |
| | | *Wildfire*, for orchestra |
| | | *Diversions*, for saxophone ensemble |
| 1977 | (30) | *Spare Parts*, for six male voices |
| | | *Games*, for organ |
| 1978 | (31) | *Brain Storm*, for four voices and live electronics |
| 1979 | (32) | *Voices of Sleep*, for soprano, chorus and orchestra |

| 1980 (33) | Sing Praises! for chorus and orchestra |
| | At the Still Point of the Turning World, for ensemble |
| | Deception Pass, for brass ensemble |
| 1981 (34) | The Canterbury Psalms, for chorus and orchestra |
| | Concerto for orchestra |
| 1982 (35) | Sinfonia for strings |
| 1983 (36) | Mass of the Sea, for soli, chorus and orchestra |

Patterson also composed:
Luslawice Variations, for violin
Spiders, for harp
Duologue, for oboe and piano
Three Portraits, for piano
Christ is the King, for choir

## PENDERECKI, Krzysztof
*b Dębica, near Cracow, 23 November 1933*

He first studied privately, then from 1955 to 1958 was a pupil at the Cracow Conservatory, where he later taught and was appointed rector in 1972. He has appeared widely as a lecturer and has received many commissions in Europe and the USA, and many awards, including an honorary doctorate from the University of Rochester, New York. He is also an honorary member of the Royal Academy of Music in London.

| 1958 (25) | Epitaphium on the Death of Artur Malawski, for string orchestra and timpani |
| | Emanations, for two string orchestras |
| | The Psalms of David, for mixed choir and instruments |
| 1959 (26) | Strophes, for soprano, narrator and ten instruments |
| 1960 (27) | Anaklasis, for strings and percussion groups |
| | String Quartet No 1 |
| 1961 (28) | Fluorescences, for orchestra |
| | Dimensions of Time and Silence, for choir and orchestra |
| | Threnody, for fifty-two stringed instruments |
| | Kanon, for strings and electronic tape |
| 1962 (29) | Polymorphia, for forty-eight strings |
| | Stabat Mater, for three sixteen-part choirs |
| 1963 (30) | Violin Concerto |
| 1964 (31) | Sonata for cello and orchestra |
| 1965 (32) | Capriccio for oboe and strings |
| 1967 (34) | Dies Irae, oratorio for soprano, tenor and bass soli, chorus and orchestra |
| | Pittsburgh Overture, for wind and percussion |
| | Capriccio for violin and orchestra |
| 1968 (35) | The Devils of Loudon, opera (1968–9) |
| | String Quartet No 2 |
| | Capriccio for Siegfried Palm, for solo cello |
| 1969–71 (36–8) | Utrenja, for soprano, contralto, tenor, bass and basso profundo soli, two mixed choirs and orchestra |
| 1970 (37) | Kosmogonia, for soprano, tenor and bass soli, chorus and orchestra |
| 1971 (38) | De Natura Sonoris II, for wind, percussion and strings |
| | Prélude (1971), for wind, percussion and contrabasses |
| | Actions, for jazz ensemble |
| 1972 (39) | Canticum Canticorum Salomonis (Song of Songs), for sixteen-voice chorus, chamber orchestra and dance pair |

Partita, concerto for harpsichord, five solo instruments electronically amplified and orchestra
Cello Concerto

1973 (40)   Symphony No 1
1974 (41)   *The Dream of Jacob*, for orchestra
1978 (45)   *Paradise Lost*, opera
1979 (46)   *Ubu Roi*, opera
            *Te Deum*, for soli, chorus and orchestra
1980 (47)   Symphony No 2
1983–4 (50–51) *Requiem*, for soli, chorus and orchestra


## PERGOLESI, Giovanni Battista
*b Jesi, Italy, 4 January 1710*
*d Pazzuola, 16 March 1736, aged twenty-six*

He entered the Conservatorium dei Poveri di Gesù Cristo in Naples in 1725. He taught at the Conservatorium of the Madonna of Loreto from 1725 to 1728. His compositions earned him the patronage of the Prince of Stigliano. His secular music was a failure; this undermined his health, and he died of tuberculosis.

1731 (21)   *Salustia*, opera
1732 (22)   *Lo frate innamorato*, opera
            *La serva padrona*, opera
1733 (23)   *Il prigionier superbo*, opera
1734 (24)   *Adriano in Siria*, opera
            *La contadina astuta*, opera
1735 (25)   *L'Olimpiade*, opera
            *Flamincio*, opera
1736 (26)   *Stabat Mater*, for female voices

Pergolesi also composed eight other operas, twelve cantatas, over thirty sonatas, symphonies, concertos.


## PETTERSSEN, Gustaf Allan
*b Västra Ryd, 19 September 1911*
*d Stockholm, 20 June 1980, aged sixty-eight*

He was brought up in poverty. He studied at Stockholm University from 1930 to 1939. A Jenny Lind Scholarship in 1939 took him to Paris, but the German invasion forced him to return home. Until 1951 he was a violist in the Stockholm Philharmonic Orchestra; then he returned to Paris, as a pupil of Honegger at the Conservatory. After 1964 arthritis prevented him from playing the viola.

1936 (25)   Four Improvisations for string trio
1943–5 (32–4) *Barefoot Songs*
1948 (37)   Fugue for woodwind
1949 (38)   Concerto for violin and string quartet
1973 (62)   Symphonic Movement
1979 (68)   Violin Concerto

Petterssen also wrote fifteen symphonies, three concertos for strings, and other instrumental works and songs.

## PIERNÉ, Henri Constant Gabriel
b Metz, 16 August 1863
d Morlaix, 17 July 1937, aged seventy-three

He became a pupil at the Paris Conservatory at the age of eight, studying under Franck and Massenet. In 1882 he won the Prix de Rome. He succeeded Franck as organist at Ste Cécile from 1890 to 1898. In 1903 he became assistant conductor of the Concerts Colonne, then first conductor from 1910 to 1932. In 1925 he was elected a member of the Institut Français.

| | |
|---|---|
| 1882 (19) | *Edith*, cantata |
| 1883 (20) | *Le chemin de l'amour*, opera-comique |
| | *Trois pièces formant suite de concert*, for orchestra |
| 1885 (22) | Symphonic Overture |
| | *Fantaisie-Ballet*, for piano and orchestra |
| 1886 (23) | *Don Luis*, opera-comique |
| 1887 (24) | Piano Concerto in C minor |
| 1889 (26) | *Marche Solennelle* |
| | *Pantomime*, for orchestra |
| 1890 (27) | *Scherzo Caprice*, for piano and orchestra |
| 1891 (28) | *Le Collier de saphire*, ballet |
| 1892 (29) | *Les joyeuses commères de Paris*, ballet |
| 1893 (30) | *Lizarda*, opera-comique (1893–4) |
| | *Bouton d'or*, ballet |
| | *Le docteur blanc*, ballet |
| 1895 (32) | *La coupe enchantée*, opera-comique |
| | *Salomé*, ballet |
| 1897 (34) | *Vendée*, opera-comique |
| | *L'an mil*, symphonic poem with chorus |
| 1900 (37) | Violin Sonata |
| 1901 (38) | *La Fille de Tabarin*, opera-comique |
| | *Poème symphonique*, for piano and orchestra |
| | *Konzertstücke*, for harp |
| 1902 (39) | *The Children's Crusade*, oratorio |
| 1907 (44) | *Canzonetta*, for clarinet |
| 1908 (45) | *The Children of Bethlehem*, oratorio |
| 1919 (56) | Piano Quintet |
| | Cello Sonata |
| 1920 (57) | *Paysages franciscains*, for orchestra |
| 1923 (60) | *Cydalise and the Satyr*, ballet |
| 1927 (64) | *Sophie Arnould*, opera-comique |
| 1931 (68) | *Divertissement sur un thème pastorale*, for orchestra |
| | *Fantaisie basque*, for violin |
| 1934 (71) | *Giration*, ballet |
| | *Fragonard*, ballet |
| 1935 (72) | *Images*, ballet |
| 1937 (74) | *Gulliver in Lilliput*, ballet |

## PISTON, Walter
b Rocklands, Maine, 20 January 1894
d Belmont, Massachusetts, 12 November 1976, aged eighty-two

He taught himself violin and piano and played in theatre orchestras and dance bands. His main studies were in draughtsmanship and architecture. During World War I he played saxophone in a Navy band. He entered Harvard University in 1920 and after graduating in 1924 he went to Paris to study with

Boulanger and Dukas. In 1926 he returned to the USA and a position at Harvard, teaching there until 1960. He won many prizes and honours, and his books on harmony, counterpoint and orchestration have received international acclaim.

| | |
|---|---|
| 1926 (32) | Three Pieces for flute, clarinet and bassoon |
| | Piano Sonata |
| 1927 (33) | Symphonic Piece |
| 1929 (35) | Suite No 1 for orchestra |
| 1930 (36) | Flute Sonata |
| 1931 (37) | Suite for oboe and piano |
| 1933 (39) | Concerto for orchestra |
| | String Quartet No 1 |
| 1934 (40) | Prelude and Fugue for orchestra |
| 1935 (41) | String Quartet No 2 |
| | Piano Trio No 1 |
| 1937 (43) | Symphony No 1 |
| | *Concertino*, for piano and chamber orchestra |
| 1938 (44) | *The Incredible Flutist*, ballet |
| 1939 (45) | Violin Concerto No 1 |
| | Violin Sonata |
| 1940 (46) | Chromatic Study for organ |
| 1941 (47) | Sinfonietta for orchestra |
| 1942 (48) | *Fanfare for the Fighting French* |
| | Flute Quintet |
| | *Interlude*, for viola and piano |
| 1943 (49) | Symphony No 2 |
| | Prelude and Allegro for organ and strings |
| | Passacaglia for piano |
| 1944 (50) | *Fugue on a Victory Tune* |
| | Partita for violin, viola and organ |
| 1945 (51) | Sonata for violin and harpsichord |
| 1946 (52) | Divertimento for nine instruments |
| 1947 (53) | Symphony No 3 |
| | String Quartet No 3 |
| 1948 (54) | Suite No 2 for orchestra |
| | Toccata for orchestra |
| 1949 (55) | Piano Quintet |
| | Duo for violin and cello |
| 1950 (56) | Symphony No 4 |
| 1951 (57) | String Quartet No 4 |
| 1952 (58) | *Fantasy*, for English horn, harp and strings |
| 1954 (60) | Symphony No 5 |
| 1955 (61) | Symphony No 6 |
| 1956 (62) | *Serenata*, for orchestra |
| | Quintet for wind |
| 1957 (63) | Viola Concerto |
| 1958 (64) | *Psalm and Prayer of David*, for chorus and seven instruments |
| 1959 (65) | *Three New England Sketches*, for orchestra |
| | Concerto for two pianos and orchestra |
| 1960 (66) | Violin Concerto No 2 |
| | Symphony No 7 |
| 1961 (67) | Symphonic Prelude |
| 1962 (68) | *Lincoln Center*, festival overture |
| | String Quartet No 5 |
| 1963 (69) | *Variations on a theme by Edward Burlingame Hill*, for orchestra |
| | *Capriccio*, for harp and string orchestra |
| 1964 (70) | Sextet for stringed instruments |

|              | Piano Quartet |
| 1965 (71)    | Symphony No 8 |
|              | *Pine Tree Fantasy*, for orchestra |
| 1966 (72)    | Variations for cello and orchestra |
|              | Piano Trio No 2 |
| 1967 (73)    | Clarinet Concerto |
|              | *Ricercare*, for orchestra |
| 1969 (75)    | *Ceremonial Fanfare*, for wind |
| 1970 (76)    | *Fantasia*, for violin and orchestra |
| 1971 (77)    | Flute Concerto |
| 1973 (79)    | Duo for cello and piano |
| 1976 (82)    | Concerto for string quartet, woodwind and percussion |

## PIZZETTI, Ildebrando
*b Parma, 20 September 1880*
*d Rome, 13 February 1968, aged eighty-seven*

His father was a piano teacher. Pizzetti attended the Reggio Emilia Gymnasium and in 1895 was enrolled at Parma University, remaining there for six years. His life was spent chiefly in educational posts; after teaching in Parma he moved in 1908 to Florence, becoming director at the Instituto Musicale Cherubini from 1917 to 1924. In 1924 he was appointed director of the Milan Conservatory, then he moved to Rome, to take the chair of composition at the Academia Sta Cecilia from 1936 until his retirement in 1960.

| 1904 (24)        | Three Symphonic Preludes to *Oedipus Rex* |
| 1906 (26)        | String Quartet in A major |
| 1909–12 (29–32)  | *Phaedra*, opera |
| 1914 (34)        | *Sinfonia del Fuoco* |
| 1915–21 (35–41)  | *Deborah and Jael*, opera |
| 1918 (38)        | Violin Sonata in A minor and A major |
| 1921 (41)        | Cello Sonata in F major |
| 1922 (42)        | *Lo straniero*, opera |
|                  | Requiem |
| 1925–7 (45–7)    | *Fra Gherardo*, opera |
| 1928 (48)        | *Concerto dell'estate* |
| 1929 (49)        | *Rondo veneziano*, for orchestra |
| 1930 (50)        | Piano Concerto |
| 1931–5 (51–5)    | *Orseolo*, opera |
| 1933–4 (53–5)    | Cello Concerto |
| 1938–42 (58–62)  | *L'Oro*, opera |
| 1940 (60)        | Symphony in A major |
| 1942 (62)        | Piano Sonata |
| 1944 (64)        | Violin Concerto |
| 1949 (69)        | *Vanna Lupa*, opera |
| 1950 (70)        | *Ifigenia*, opera |
| 1953 (73)        | *Cagliostro*, opera |
| 1958 (78)        | *Murder in the Cathedral*, opera (on T. S. Eliot's play) |

## PONCE, Manuel
*b Fresnillo, Mexico, 2 December 1882*
*d Mexico City, 24 April 1948, aged sixty-five*

He studied piano in Berlin and composition in Bologna. He taught at the National Conservatory in Mexico, and conducted the National Symphony Orchestra there for two years. From 1915 to 1918 he taught in Havana, Cuba, and from 1933 again in Mexico.

| 1911 (29) | *Trio Romantico*, for piano trio |
| 1912 (30) | Piano Concerto |
| 1914 (32) | *Balada Mexicana*, for piano and orchestra |
| 1923 (41) | *Estampas Nocturnas*, for orchestra |
| 1929 (47) | Three *Bocetos Sinfónicos*, for orchestra |
| | Sonata for cello and piano |
| | Miniature String Quartet |
| 1933 (51) | *Canto y Danza de los Antiguos Mexicana* (Songs and Dances of Old Mexico), for orchestra |
| | *Three Songs of Tagore*, for low voice and orchestra |
| | Sonata for violin and piano |
| | String Trio |
| 1935 (53) | *Elegiac Poem*, for chamber orchestra |
| | *Suite en Estilo Antiguo (Suite in Olden Style)*, for orchestra |
| | Sonata for violin and viola |
| 1938 (56) | *Instantáneas Mexicanas*, for orchestra |
| 1940 (57) | *Ferial*, divertimento sinfónico |
| 1941 (58) | *Conciérto del sur*, for guitar and orchestra |
| 1943 (60) | Viola Concerto |

Ponce also wrote works for solo guitar and piano, and many songs.


## PONCHIELLI, Amilcare
*b Cremona, 1 September 1834*
*d Milan, 17 January 1886, aged fifty-one*

He was the son of a shopkeeper. He went to the Milan Conservatory at the age of nine, and became a bandmaster in Piacenze. Success did not really arrive until 1872, when he was commissioned to write an opera for the Teatro dal Verme in Milan. During his last ten years he was *maestro di cappella* of Bergamo Cathedral and professor of composition at the Milan Conservatory.

| 1861 (27) | *La Savoiarda*, opera |
| 1863 (29) | *Roderico*, opera |
| 1872 (38) | *I Promessi Sposi*, opera |
| 1873 (39) | *Il Parlatore Eterno*, opera |
| | *Le Due Gemelle*, ballet |
| 1874 (40) | *I Lituani*, opera (revised as *Aldona*) |
| 1875 (41) | *A Gaetano Donizetti*, cantata |
| 1876 (42) | *La Giaconda*, opera (from which comes the *Dance of the Hours*) |
| 1880 (46) | *Il Figliuol Prodigo*, opera |
| 1882 (48) | *In Memoria di Garibaldi*, cantata |
| 1885 (51) | *Marion Delorme*, opera |


## PORPORA, Niccolò Antonio
*b Naples, 17 August 1686*
*d Naples, 3 March 1768, aged eighty-one*

He studied at the Conservatory of San Loreto in Naples. He was appointed musical director to the Portuguese Ambassador in Naples, was chamber virtuoso to the Prince of Hesse-Darmstadt, and later conductor to the King of Poland in Vienna. In 1712 he established a school of singing in Naples; he taught singing at the Conservatory of San Onofrio in Naples in 1719, and in Venice in 1725, and was in demand for his services in many other cities. He also travelled to London and Dresden, and his final appointment was in Naples as director at San Onofrio. Despite his popularity he died, as he was born, in poverty.

| 1708 (22) | *Agrippina*, opera |
| 1711 (25) | *Flavio Anicio Olibrio*, opera |
| | *Il martirio di S Giovanni Nepomuceno*, oratorio |
| 1713 (27) | *Basilio, re d'Oriente*, opera |
| 1714 (28) | *Arianna e Teseo*, opera |
| 1718 (32) | *Temistocle*, opera |
| 1719 (33) | *Faramondo*, opera |
| 1721 (35) | *Il martirio di Santa Eugenia*, oratorio |
| 1723 (37) | *Adelaide*, opera |
| 1724 (38) | *Griselda*, opera |
| 1726 (40) | *Imeneo in Atene*, opera |
| 1727 (41) | *Ezio*, opera |
| 1729 (43) | *Semiramide riconosciuta*, opera |
| 1730 (44) | *Mitridate*, opera |
| 1731 (45) | *Poro*, opera |
| 1732 (46) | *Germanico in Germania*, opera |
| 1733 (47) | *Arianna in Nasso*, opera |
| 1734 (48) | *Enea nel Lazio*, opera |
| | *Davide e Bersabea*, oratorio |
| 1735 (49) | *Polifemo*, opera |
| | *Ifigenia in Aulide*, opera |
| 1737 (51) | *Lucio Papirio*, opera |
| 1738 (52) | *Carlo il Calvo*, opera |
| 1739 (53) | *Il Barone di Zampano*, opera |
| 1740 (54) | *Il trionfo di Camilla*, opera |
| 1742 (56) | *Statira*, opera |
| 1747 (61) | *Filandro*, opera |

Porpora also wrote songs, chamber music, harpsichord music, etc.


## POULENC, Francis
*b Paris, 7 January 1899*
*d Paris, 30 January 1963, aged sixty-four*

His mother gave him his first piano lessons, but afterwards he had little formal musical education. However, his friendships with other composers, particularly Milhaud, Honegger, Satie, Schoenberg, Berg and Webern, were influential. He inherited a strong religious feeling from his father, which is apparent in his works. He was high-spirited and witty, and very popular. Apart from time spent in the Army during World War I, he devoted his life to composing.

| 1917 (18) | *Rapsodie nègre*, for cello, piano, flute and string quartet |
| 1918 (19) | Sonata for two clarinets |
| | Sonata for piano (four hands) |
| | *Trois mouvements perpetuelles*, for piano |
| | *Toréador*, songs (1918–32) |
| 1919 (20) | *Valse*, for piano |
| | *Le Bestaire au cortège d'Orphée*, songs |
| | *Cocardes*, songs |
| 1920 (21) | *Cinq impromptus*, for piano |
| | Suite in C major for piano |
| 1921 (22) | *La Baigneuse de Trouville* and *Discours du General*, for orchestra: two numbers of a group work composed by all members of 'les Six' (except Louis Durey) for a play by Jean Cocteau |
| 1922 (23) | Sonata for trumpet, horn and trombone |
| | Sonata for clarinet and bassoon |
| | *Chanson à boire*, for a cappella male choir |

| 1923 (24) | *Les Biches,* ballet |
|---|---|
| 1924 (25) | *Promenade,* for piano |
| | *Poèmes de Ronsard* (1924–5) |
| 1925 (26) | *Napoli Suite,* for piano |
| 1926 (27) | Trio for oboe, bassoon and piano |
| | *Chansons gaillardes* |
| 1927–8 (28–9) | *Concert champêtre,* for harpsichord and orchestra |
| | *Deux novelettes,* for piano |
| | *Airs chantés* |
| 1928 (29) | *Trois pièces,* for piano |
| 1929 (30) | *Aubade,* for piano and eighteen instruments |
| | *Hommage à Roussel,* for piano |
| | *Huit nocturnes,* for piano (1929–38) |
| 1930 (31) | *Epitaphe,* song |
| 1931 (32) | *Bagatelle,* for violin and piano |
| | *Trois poèmes de Louise Lalanne,* songs |
| | Four Songs |
| | Five Songs |
| 1932 (33) | Concerto in D major, for two pianos and orchestra |
| | Sextet for piano and wind quintet (1932–40) |
| | Improvisations for piano (1932–43) |
| | *Intermezzo,* in D minor, for piano |
| | *La bal masqué,* cantata |
| 1933 (34) | *Feuillets d'album,* for piano (*Ariette, Rêve, Gigue*) |
| | *Villageoises,* children's piano pieces |
| 1934 (35) | *Intermezzo,* in D♭ major, for piano |
| | *Intermezzo,* in C major, for piano |
| | *Presto, Badinage* and *Humoresque,* for piano |
| | *Huit chansons polonaises* |
| | *Quatre chansons pour enfants* (1934–5) |
| 1935 (36) | *Suite française,* for chamber orchestra |
| | *Cinq poèmes* (Paul Eluard) |
| | 'A sa guitare' (Ronsard), song |
| | *Margot,* incidental music (in collaboration with Auric) |
| 1936 (37) | *Sept chansons,* for a cappella mixed choir |
| | *Litanies à la Vierge noire,* for women's or children's voices and organ |
| | *Petites voix,* five choruses for three-part a cappella children's choir |
| | *Les soirées de Nazelles,* for piano |
| 1937 (38) | *Deux marches et un intermède,* for chamber orchestra |
| | Mass in G major |
| | *Sécheresses,* cantata |
| | *Bourée d'Auvergne,* for piano |
| | *Tel jour telle nuit,* songs |
| 1938 (39) | Concerto in G major, for organ, strings and timpani |
| | Four Penitential Motets (1938–9) |
| 1939 (40) | *Fiançailles pour rire,* songs |
| 1940 (41) | *Mélancolie,* for piano |
| | *Banalities,* songs |
| | *Histoire de Babar le petit éléphant,* for piano and narrator (1940–5) |
| | Cello Sonata (1940–8) |
| 1941 (42) | *Salve regina,* for four-part a cappella mixed choir |
| | *Exultate Deo,* for four-part a cappella mixed choir |
| | *Les animaux modèles,* ballet |
| | *La fille du jardinier,* incidental music |
| 1942 (43) | Violin Sonata (1942–3) |

|            | *Chansons villageoises*, songs |
|------------|---|
| 1943 (44)  | *Figure humaine*, cantata |
|            | *Metamorphoses*, songs |
|            | *Deux poèmes*, songs |
|            | 'Montparnasse', song |
| 1944 (45)  | *Les mamelles de Tiresias*, opera bouffe |
|            | *Le Voyageur sans bagage*, incidental music |
|            | *La nuit de la Saint-Jean*, incidental music |
|            | *Un soir de neige*, cantata |
| 1945 (46)  | *Chansons françaises*, for a cappella mixed choir |
|            | *Le soldat et la sorcière*, incidental music |
| 1946 (47)  | Two Songs |
| 1947 (48)  | Flute Sonata |
| 1948 (49)  | *Quatre petites prières (St Francis)*, for a cappella male choir |
| 1949 (50)  | Piano Concerto |
| 1950 (51)  | *Stabat Mater*, for soprano, mixed choir and orchestra |
| 1953 (54)  | Sonata for two pianos |
|            | *Dialogues des Carmelites*, opera (1953–6) |
| 1954 (55)  | *La Guirlande de Compra (Matelote provençale)*, for orchestra, in collaboration with other composers |
|            | *Variations sur le nom de Marguerite Long (Bucolique)*, for orchestra, in collaboration with other composers |
| 1956 (57)  | *Le travail du peintre*, song cycle |
|            | *Deux mélodies*, songs |
| 1957 (58)  | *Elegy*, for horn and piano |
| 1958 (59)  | *La voix humaine*, lyric tragedy, monodrama for soprano |
| 1959 (60)  | *Gloria*, for soprano, mixed choir and orchestra |
| 1960 (61)  | *Elegy*, for two pianos |
| 1961 (62)  | *La dame de Monte Carlo*, monologue for soprano and orchestra |
| 1962 (63)  | *Sept répons des ténèbres*, for soprano, choir and orchestra |
|            | Oboe Sonata |
|            | Clarinet Sonata |

## PRAETORIUS, Michael
*b near Eisenach, 15 February 1571*
*d Wolfenbüttel, 15 February 1621, aged fifty*

In 1582 he matriculated at the University of Frankfurt, and in 1587 he was appointed as organist of St Marien in Frankfurt, remaining until 1590, his name becoming famous among the Lutherans there. In 1604 he became *Kapellmeister*. Most of his collections of music appeared between 1605 and 1613. From 1613 to 1616 he was *Kapellmeister* at Dresden, thereafter receiving an honorarium from Dresden for the rest of his life. As an organiser of musical events he travelled widely, mainly in Germany. He became a rich man, but died of ill-health due to over-work. He was a devout Christian and most of his works were sacred vocal ones.

## PREVIN, André
*b Berlin, 6 April 1929*

He studied piano as a child at the Berlin Hochschule and at the Paris Conservatory. His family, who were of Russian-Jewish origin, emigrated to the USA in 1939, where he studied with Castelnuovo-Tedesco and Toch. He became a naturalised American in 1943. To begin with he was extremely successful as a jazz pianist, but in 1951, during Army service, he began to learn conducting with Monteux. His conducting début was with the St Louis Symphony

Orchestra in 1963; he was conductor-in-chief of the Houston Symphony Orchestra from 1967 to 1970, and from 1969 to 1979 was principal conductor of the London Symphony Orchestra, who then honoured him with the title 'Conductor Emeritus'. He has also worked with the Pittsburgh Symphony Orchestra, and has been a guest conductor all over the world.

1949 (20)    *The Sun Comes Up*, film score
1960 (31)    *Overture to a Comedy*, for orchestra
1962 (33)    Symphony for strings
1968 (39)    Cello Concerto
1969 (40)    *Coco*, film score
1971 (42)    Guitar Concerto
1974 (45)    *The Good Companions*, film score
             *Four Outings*, for brass quintet
1977 (48)    *E, G, B, D, F*, for piano
1980 (51)    *Principals*, for orchestra
             *Reflections*, for orchestra

Dates unknown:
*Little Drummer*, piano pieces
*Invitation to the Dance*, film score
*The Subterraneans*, film score
*Bells and Ringing*, film score
*Who Was That Lady?*, film score
*Portrait*, for strings
String Quartet
Flute Quintet
Cello Sonata
*Impressions*, for piano
Other chamber and piano works, and songs


**PROKOFIEV, Sergei**
*b Sontsovka, Ukraine, 23 April 1891*
*d Moscow, 7 March 1953, aged sixty-one*

He wrote his first music at the age of five and his first opera at nine. He was a pupil of Glière before entering the St Petersburg Conservatory at the age of thirteen, where he studied harmony and counterpoint with Liadov, orchestration with Rimsky-Korsakov and conducting with Tcherepnin, as well as piano. He graduated with the Rubinstein Prize in 1914. He travelled extensively over the next twenty years, visiting America and touring Western Europe as a pianist and conductor of his own works. By 1936 he had settled permanently back in Russia but his work fell foul of the Soviet authorities in 1948, and it was not until 1959 that his music was officially reinstated and approved in Russia. He died of a brain haemorrhage.

1907–09 (16–20) Piano Sonata No 1 in F minor
1907–11 (16–18) Four Pieces for piano
1908–12 (17–21) Four Pieces for piano
1909 (18)    Four Etudes for piano
             Sinfonietta in A major (final version 1929) (1909–14)
             Two Poems for female voices and orchestra (1909–10)
1910 (19)   · *Dreams*, symphonic poem
             *Autumnal Sketch*, for orchestra (revised 1934)
             *Deux poèmes*, for voice and piano (1910–11)
1911–12 (20) Piano Concerto No 1 in D♭ major
1911–13 (20–2) *Magdalene*, opera
1912 (21)    Piano Concerto No 2 in D minor

|          |                                                                                           |
|----------|-------------------------------------------------------------------------------------------|
|          | *Ballade*, for cello and piano                                                            |
|          | Piano Sonata No 2 in D minor                                                              |
|          | *Toccata*, in C major, for piano                                                          |
|          | *Sarcasms*, for piano (1912–14)                                                           |
| 1914 (23) | Violin Concerto No 1                                                                      |
|          | *Scythian Suite (Ala et Lolly)*, for orchestra (1914–15)                                  |
|          | *The Ugly Duckling*, for voice and piano                                                  |
| 1915 (24) | *The Gambler*, opera (revised 1928)                                                       |
|          | *Chout*, ballet (revised 1920)                                                            |
|          | *Visions fugitives*, for piano                                                            |
|          | *Cinq poésies*, for voice and piano                                                       |
| 1916 (25) | Symphony No 1, *Classical* (1916–17)                                                      |
|          | *Cinq poésies d'Anna Akhmatova*, for voice and piano                                      |
| 1917 (26) | Piano Sonata No 3 in A minor (begun in 1907)                                              |
|          | Piano Sonata No 4 in C minor (begun in 1908)                                              |
|          | *Seven, they are seven*, Akhadian incantation for tenor, chorus and orchestra             |
|          | Piano Concerto No 3 in C major (1917–21)                                                  |
| 1919 (28) | *The Love of Three Oranges*, opera (Symphonic Suite of the same name composed 1919–24)    |
|          | *The Fiery Angel*, opera (1919–27)                                                        |
|          | *Overture on Hebrew Themes*, for piano, clarinet and string quartet                       |
| 1920 (29) | *Five Songs Without Words*, for voice and piano                                           |
| 1921 (30) | Five Songs                                                                                |
| 1923 (32) | Piano Sonata No 5 in C major                                                              |
| 1924 (33) | Symphony No 2 in D minor (1924–5)                                                         |
|          | Quintet in G minor, for oboe, clarinet, violin, viola and double-bass                     |
| 1925 (34) | *Pas d'acier*, ballet (1925–6)                                                            |
|          | Divertimento for orchestra (1925–9)                                                      |
| 1928 (37) | *The Prodigal Son*, ballet                                                                |
|          | Symphony No 3 in C minor                                                                  |
| 1929–30 (38–9) | Symphony No 4 in C major (second version 1947)                                       |
| 1930 (39) | *Sur le Borysthène (On the Dnieper)*, ballet                                              |
|          | *Four Portraits*, symphonic suite from the opera *The Gambler* (1930–1)                   |
|          | String Quartet No 1                                                                       |
| 1931 (40) | Piano Concerto No 4 in B♭ major, for the left hand                                        |
| 1932 (41) | Piano Concerto No 5 in G major                                                            |
|          | Sonata in C for two violins                                                               |
| 1933 (42) | *Chant symphonique*, for orchestra                                                        |
|          | Cello Concerto in E minor (1933–8)                                                       |
| 1934 (43) | *Egyptian Night*, symphonic suite                                                         |
|          | *Lieutenant Kijé*, symphonic suite for orchestra and baritone voice ad lib               |
| 1935 (44) | *Romeo and Juliet*, ballet (1935–6)                                                      |
|          | Violin Concerto No 2 in G minor                                                          |
|          | *Musique d'enfants*, for piano                                                            |
| 1936 (45) | *Peter and the Wolf*, for orchestra and narrator                                          |
|          | *Russian Overture*                                                                        |
|          | Cantata for the Twentieth Anniversary of the October Revolution, for double chorus, military band, accordions and orchestra (1936–7) |
| 1938 (47) | Sonata No 1, for violin and piano                                                         |
| 1938–9 (47–8) | *Alexander Nevsky*, cantata for mezzo-soprano, chorus and orchestra                   |

1939 (48)    *Simeon Kotko*, opera
             *Zdravitsa*, cantata for chorus and orchestra
             Piano Sonata No 6 in A major (1939–40)
             Piano Sonata No 7 in B♭ major (1939–42)
             Piano Sonata No 8 in B♭ major (1939–44)
1940 (49)    *The Duenna*, opera (1940–1)
             *Cinderella*, ballet (1940–4)
1941 (50)    Symphonic March
             Suite for orchestra, *1941*
             *A Summer's Day*, suite for small orchestra (transcribed from the
                *Musique d'enfants* of 1935)
             String Quartet No 2 in E major
1941–3 (50–2) *War and Peace*, opera (revised 1946–52)
1942 (51)    *Ivan the Terrible*, film score
1942–3 (51–2)Flute Sonata in D major
             *Ballad of an Unknown Boy*, cantata
1943–4 (52–3) Sonata No 2 in D for violin and piano
1944 (53)    Symphony No 5 in B♭ major
1945–7 (54–6) Piano Sonata No 9 in C major
             Symphony No 6 in E♭ minor
1947 (56)    *Flourish, Mightly Homeland*, cantata
             Sonata in D, for violin
1947–48 (56–7) *The Story of a Real Man*, opera
1948–53 (57–62) *The Stone Flower*, ballet
1949 (58)    Cello Sonata in C major
             *Winter Bonfire*, suite for narrator, boys' chorus and orchestra
                (1949–50)
1950 (59)    *On Guard for Peace*, choral
1950–2 (59–61) Sinfonia Concertante in E minor, for cello and orchestra (this is a
             reworking of the 1933–8 cello concerto)
1951–2 (60–1) Symphony No 7 in C♯ minor
1952 (61)    Cello Concertino in G minor
Prokofiev left unfinished a Concerto for two pianos and strings; a Cello Sonata
in C♯ minor; a second version of the Symphony No 2; and sketches for a 10th
and 11th piano sonata.


**PUCCINI, Giacomo**
*b Lucca, 22 December 1858*
*d Brussels, 29 November 1924, aged sixty-five*

He came from a musical family. A visit to Pisa to see *Aida* when he was eighteen
was the beginning of his interest in opera. He studied first at the Pacini
Conservatory in Lucca, then in Milan at the Reale Conservatory, under
Ponchielli. The publisher Ricordi became his mentor, and the success of *Manon
Lescaut* in 1893 established him. In 1891 he acquired a house in Torre del Lago,
where he lived nearly all the rest of his life. He died of cancer of the throat.

1884 (26)    *Le Villi*, opera
1889 (31)    *Edgar*, opera
1893 (35)    *Manon Lescaut*, opera
1896 (38)    *La Bohème*, opera
1900 (42)    *Tosca*, opera
1904 (46)    *Madam Butterfly*, opera
1910 (52)    *Girl of the Golden West (La Fanciulla del West)*, opera
1917 (59)    *La Rondine*, opera

1918 (60)   *Il Trittico*, three contrasted one-act operas to be produced in a
            single evening:
            *Suor Angelica*
            *Il Tabarro*
            *Gianni Schicchi*
Performed posthumously:
1926        *Turandot*, opera


## PUJOL, Juan Pablo
*b Barcelona, c1573*
*d Barcelona, May 1626, aged c fifty-three*

In 1593 he became *maestro de canto* at Tarragona Cathedral, and in 1596 organist
at El Pilar, Saragossa. He received minor orders and in 1600 became a priest.
From 1612 until his death he was choirmaster at Barcelona Cathedral.

*Sacred works*: thirteen masses, eight Magnificats, six Nunc Dimittis, twelve
antiphons, twelve responsories, two litanies, one sequence, seventy-four
psalms, nine motets, eleven hymns, three lamentations, nine Passion settings,
nineteen songs.
*Secular works*: twelve romances, two letrillas, one lira, one folia, one novena, one
tono, sixteen other works.


## PURCELL, Henry
*b London, 1659*
*d London, 21 November 1695, aged thirty-six*

He came from a musical family. He was a chorister in the Chapel Royal and in
1677 was appointed composer-in-ordinary for the violins there. Two years later
he became organist at Westminster Abbey. His life was spent in writing, and
his operas foreshadowed the later operatic advances made by Handel. The
music he had composed for the funeral of Queen Mary in 1694 was performed at
his own funeral a year later.

1680 (21)    Nine Fantasias of four parts
c1682 (c23)  'Hear my prayer' Anthem
1683 (24)    Twelve Sonatas of three parts
1688 (29)    *How Pleasant is this Flowery Plain*, secular cantata
1689 (30)    fp *Dido and Aeneas*, opera
             *Musick's Handmaid*, for harpsichord
1690 (31)    *The Prophetess* or *The History of Dioclesian*, opera
1691 (32)    *King Arthur* or *The British Worthy*, opera
             *The Wives' Excuse*, incidental music
1692 (33)    *The Faery Queen*, opera
             *The Libertine*, incidental music
             *Oedipus*, incidental music
1693 (34)    *Epsom Wells*, incidental music
1694 (35)    *The Married Beau*, incidental music
1695 (36)    *The Indian Queen*, opera
             *The Tempest* or *The Enchanted Island*, opera
             *Bonduca*, incidental music
Performed posthumously:
1696         A choice collection of Lessons for the Harpsichord or Spinet
             Harpsichord Suites No 1–8
Purcell also composed much church music, stage music, chamber music,
complimentary odes to royalty, harpsichord pieces, etc.

**QUILTER, Roger**
b Brighton, 1 November 1877
d London, 21 September 1953, aged seventy-five

He was educated at Eton, and then studied for five years at the Hoch
Conservatory in Frankfurt, together with Grainger, Scott, Balfour Gardiner and
O'Neill. He first became known in 1900 as a composer of songs. He was a
founder member of the Musicians' Benevolent Fund.

| | | |
|---|---|---|
| 1906 | (29) | *To Julia*, song cycle |
| 1907 | (30) | *Serenade*, for orchestra |
| 1908 | (31) | *Songs of Sorrow* |
| 1909 | (32) | Seven Elizabethan Lyrics |
| 1910 | (33) | Three English Dances |
| | | Four Songs |
| 1911 | (34) | *Where the Rainbow Ends*, incidental music |
| | | Three Songs of the Sea |
| 1914 | (37) | *A Children's Overture* |
| | | Four Child Songs |
| 1916 | (39) | Three Songs of William Blake |
| 1921 | (44) | Five Shakespeare Songs |
| | | Three Pastoral Songs |
| 1922 | (45) | *As You Like It*, incidental music |
| 1925 | (48) | *The Rake*, ballet suite |
| | | Five Jacobean Lyrics |
| 1936 | (59) | *Julia*, opera |
| 1946 | (69) | *Tulips*, for chorus and orchestra |
| 1948 | (71) | *The Sailor and His Lass*, for soloist, choir and orchestra |
| 1949 | (72) | *Love at the Inn*, opera |

**RACHMANINOV, Sergei**
b Oneg, near Novgorod, 1 April 1873
d Beverly Hills, 28 March 1943, aged sixty-nine

He came from an aristocratic family whose fortunes were steadily declining. He
studied piano at the Conservatories of St Petersburg and Moscow. Lack of
satisfaction with his work, and a bad bout of malaria, started the depression
that haunted most of the rest of his life; but by 1892 he was being accepted both
as a pianist and a composer. He earned very little and was forced to play as an
accompanist and to teach, neither of which suited his taste. In 1897 he was
offered a second conductorship in the Moscow opera house, and the experience,
followed by an invitation to London to compose, play and conduct, restored his
finances and his will to continue writing. A return to Russia in 1900 brought
back his depression, but a pyschologist recommended that the best treatment
was to continue writing; and financial help from a friend and a happy marriage
in 1902 helped the treatment. After conducting at the Bolshoi from 1904 to 1906
he moved with his family to Dresden; he then went back to Moscow – where his
music was now highly esteemed – en route to America for a concert tour in 1909.
He returned to Russia in 1910, conducting the Moscow Philharmonic concerts
from 1911 to 1914, but left after the 1917 revolution, because his music was now
labelled 'bourgeois'. He played in Scandinavia and America, and eventually
settled by Lake Lucerne in 1931. It was a great happiness to him when, in 1939,
Russia accepted that his music was no longer decadent. During 1942 and 1943
he toured America, the proceeds of the concerts going to war relief; but in 1943
he died of cancer, and he is buried in the Kensico cemetery near New York.

1890–1 (17–18) Piano Concert No 1 in F♯ minor
1890–3 (17–20) Six Songs

| 1891 (18) | Scherzo for strings |
|---|---|
| 1892 (19) | *Prélude* and *Danse orientale*, for cello and piano |
| | Five *Morceaux de Fantaisie*, for piano (includes the C♯ minor prélude) |
| | *Intermezzo* |
| 1893 (20) | *Aleko*, opera |
| | *The Rock*, fantasy for orchestra |
| | *Trio élégiaque*, in D minor |
| | *Romance* and *Danse hongroise*, for violin and piano |
| | Suite No 1, *Fantasy*, for two pianos |
| | Six Songs |
| 1894 (21) | *Caprice bohémien*, for orchestra |
| | Seven Piano Pieces |
| | Six Piano Duets |
| 1895 (22) | Symphony No 1 in D minor |
| 1896 (23) | Six *Moments musicaux*, for piano |
| | Twelve Songs |
| | Six Songs for female, or boys' voices |
| 1900–06 (27–33) | Twelve Songs |
| 1901 (28) | Piano Concerto No 2 in C minor |
| | Suite No 2 for two pianos |
| | Cello Sonata in G minor |
| 1902 (29) | *The Spring*, cantata |
| 1903 (30) | *Variations on a theme by Chopin*, for piano |
| | Ten Preludes for piano |
| 1906 (33) | *Francesca da Rimini*, opera |
| | *The Miserly Knight*, opera |
| | Fifteen Songs |
| 1907 (34) | Symphony No 2 in E minor |
| | *The Isle of the Dead*, symphonic poem |
| | Piano Sonata No 1 in D minor |
| 1909 (36) | Piano Concerto No 3 in D minor |
| 1910 (37) | *The Bells*, choral symphony (after Poe) |
| | Thirteen Piano Preludes |
| | *Liturgy of St John Chrystostum* |
| 1911 (38) | Six *Études-Tableaux*, for piano |
| 1912 (39) | Fourteen Songs |
| 1913 (40) | Piano Sonata No 2 in B♭ minor |
| 1915 (42) | Vesper Mass |
| 1916 (43) | Six Songs |
| | *Neuf Études-Tableaux*, for piano (1916–17) |
| 1927 (54) | Piano Concerto No 4 in G minor |
| 1930 (57) | Three Russian Folk Songs for chorus and orchestra (possibly 1927) |
| 1932 (59) | *Variations on a Theme by Corelli*, for piano |
| 1934 (61) | *Rhapsody on a Theme by Paganini*, variations for piano and orchestra |
| 1936 (63) | Symphony No 3 in A minor |
| 1941 (68) | *Three Symphonic Dances*, for orchestra |

## RAFF, Joachim

*b Lachen, near Zurich, 27 May 1822*
*d Frankfurt, 25 June 1882, aged sixty*

His father was a teacher and organist, and he himself took a teacher-training course in Switzerland and taught from 1840 to 1844 in Rapperswil. It was Mendelssohn who recommended his early piano pieces for publication. In 1845

Liszt found him a job in a music shop, and later with a publisher in Hamburg. In 1850 he went to live with Liszt. In 1856 he gave up his job and went to Wiesbaden to teach piano and write; and in 1877 he was appointed director of the Hoch Conservatory in Frankfurt.

1848 (26)    *Psalm CXXI*, for soli and chorus
1848–50 (26–8) *König Alfred*, opera
1853 (31)    *Te Deum*, for chorus and orchestra
1853–7 (31–5) *Samson*, opera (unperformed)
1854 (32)    Grosse Symphonie (lost)
             Suite No 1 for orchestra
1855 (33)    *Dornröschen*, for soli, chorus and orchestra
1858 (36)    *Wachet auf!*, for soli and orchestra
1859–61 (37–9) Symphony No 1
1862–3 (40–1) *Deutschland Auferstchung*, for male voices and orchestra
1867 (45)    *De Profundis*, for mixed voices and orchestra
1868 (46)    *Die Parole*, opera (unperformed)
1869 (47)    *Dame Kobold*, comic opera
             Symphony No 2
1871 (49)    Two Songs for chorus and orchestra
             Symphony No 3
             *Italian Suite*
1872 (50)    Symphony No 4
1873 (51)    Symphony No 5
             *Morgenlied*, for chorus and orchestra
1874 (52)    Symphony No 6
             Suite No 2 for orchestra
1876 (54)    Symphony No 7
1877 (55)    Symphony No 8
             *Thuringer Suite*, for orchestra
1877–8 (55–6) *Benedetto Marcello*, opera (unperformed)
             *Die Tageszeiten*, for chorus, piano and orchestra
1879 (57)    Symphony No 9
1879–81 (57–9) *Weltende*, oratorio
1880 (58)    *Die Sterne*, for chorus and orchestra
1881–2 (59–60) *Die Eifersüchtigen*, opera (unperformed)
1882 (60)    Symphony No 10
             Symphony No 11

Raff also composed many other orchestral, choral, vocal, instrumental and chamber works.


**RAINIER, Priaulx**
*b Howick, Natal, South Africa, 3 February 1903*

She was born in a remote area near Zululand. At the age of ten she went as a violin student to the South African College of Music. In 1920 a scholarship brought her to the Royal Academy of Music in London, where she settled permanently. A grant in 1935 enabled her to concentrate on composition. Before the outbreak of World War II she studied briefly with Boulanger in Paris. In 1942 she was appointed professor of composition at the Royal Academy and she was elected a fellow in 1953. Also in 1953 she was made a Collard fellow of the Worshipful Company of the City of London. She has received many commissions.

1937 (34)    *Three Greek Epigrams*, for soprano and piano
1939 (36)    String Quartet
1943 (40)    Suite for clarinet and piano

| 1945 | (42) | Sonata for viola and piano |
| 1947 | (44) | *Sinfonia da Camera* |
| 1948 | (45) | *Dance of the Rain*, for tenor and guitar |
| | | *Ubunzima*, for high voice and guitar |
| 1949 | (46) | *Barbaric Dance Suite*, for piano |
| 1950 | (47) | *Ballet Suite*, for orchestra |
| 1951 | (48) | Five Pieces for keyboard |
| 1953 | (50) | *Cycle for Declamation*, for solo soprano, tenor or baritone |
| 1954 | (51) | Six Pieces for five woodwind instruments |
| 1955–6 | (52–3) | *Requiem*, for solo tenor and chorus |
| 1959 | (56) | Trio-suite for violin, cello and piano |
| 1960 | (57) | *Pastoral Triptych*, for solo oboe |
| 1960–1 | (57–8) | *Phala-Phala*, dance concerto for orchestra |
| 1961–2 | (58–9) | *Quanta*, for oboe and string trio |
| 1963–5 | (60–2) | Cello Suite |
| 1964 | (61) | Concerto for cello and orchestra |
| 1965–6 | (62–3) | String Trio |
| 1966–7 | (63–4) | *Aequora Lunae*, for orchestra |
| 1969–73 | (66–70) | Trios and Triads for ten trios and percussion |
| 1970 | (67) | *The Bee Oracles*, for tenor or baritone and ensemble |
| 1971 | (68) | *Quinque*, for harpsichord |
| 1972 | (69) | *Organ Gloriana*, for organ |
| 1973 | (70) | *Duo-Vision and Prayer*, for tenor and piano |
| | | *Ploërmel*, for winds and percussion |
| 1974 | (71) | *Primordial Canticles*, for organ |
| 1974–5 | (71–2) | *Prayers from the Ark*, for harp |
| 1974–7 | (71–4) | Violin Concerto |
| 1977 | (74) | Concertante Duo for oboe, clarinet and small orchestra |
| 1981 | (78) | *Concertante for Two Winds*, for oboe, clarinet and orchestra |
| 1983 | (80) | *Grand Duo*, for cello and piano |

## RAMEAU, Jean-Philippe
*b Dijon, 25 September 1683*
*d Paris, 12 September 1764, aged eighty*

His father was a church organist. Jean-Philippe was meant to be a lawyer, but he showed such promise in music that he was allowed to leave the Jesuit College of Dijon and find his own musical education in Italy. In 1702 he was organist at Avignon Cathedral, then similarly at Clermont-Ferrand. In 1706 he was in Paris making a further study of the organ, and in 1709 he took over his father's post as organist at Dijon. In 1713 he went to Lyons to organise the musical celebrations of the Treaty of Utrecht, returning to Paris in 1722. After 1749 he wrote nothing of importance.

| 1706 | (23) | *p* Harpsichord Works, Book I |
| 1728 | (45) | *p* Harpsichord Works, Book II |
| 1733 | (50) | *Hippolyte et Aricie*, opera |
| 1735 | (52) | *Les Indes galantes*, opera-ballet |
| 1737 | (54) | *Castor et Pollux*, opera-ballet |
| 1739 | (56) | *Dardanus*, opera |
| | | *Les Fêtes d'Hebe*, ballet |
| 1741 | (57) | *p* Harpsichord Works, Book III |
| 1745 | (62) | *Platée*, ballet |
| 1748 | (65) | *Pigmalion*, ballet |
| | | *Zais*, ballet |
| 1754 | (71) | *Zephyre*, ballet |

1760 (78)    *Les Paladins*, opera-ballet
Rameau composed more than twenty operas and opera-ballets, church music, chamber music, cantatas, etc.


**RAVEL, Maurice**
*b Ciboure, 7 March 1875*
*d Paris, 28 December 1937, aged sixty-two*

He was the son of a railway engineer. He began piano lessons at the age of seven, and in 1889 enrolled at the Paris Conservatory, remaining there as a student for 10 years, but failing to gain the Prix de Rome. He volunteered for service in the 1914–18 war, but was rejected as medically unfit – though he went to the front in 1916 as a driver. After the war he suffered from insomnia and nervous debility, but his career went well; he travelled to Vienna, Stockholm and London between 1920 and 1922 and to Italy, Scandinavia and the USA from 1923 to 1928. In 1928 he received an honorary doctorate from Oxford University. From 1933 his recurring insomnia made him increasingly ill. It was thought he had a brain tumour, but an operation in December 1937 showed no sign of one. He lingered on unconscious for a few days before he died.

| | |
|---|---|
| 1893 (18) | *Sérénade grotesque*, for piano |
| 1895 (20) | *Menuet antique* |
| 1896 (21) | 'Sainte', song |
| 1899 (24) | *Pavane pour une Infante défunte*, for piano |
| 1901 (26) | *Jeux d'eau*, for piano |
| | *Myrrha*, cantata |
| 1902 (27) | *Alcyone*, cantata |
| 1903 (28) | *Schéhérezade*, three songs with orchestra |
| | String Quartet in F major |
| | *Alyssa*, cantata |
| 1905 (30) | *Miroirs*, for piano |
| | Sonatina for piano |
| 1906 (31) | Introduction and Allegro for harp, flute, clarinet and string quartet |
| 1907 (32) | *Rhapsodie espagnole*, for orchestra |
| | *Cinq mélodies populaires greques*, for voice and piano |
| | *Pièce en forme de Habanera* |
| | 'Sur l'herbe', song |
| 1908 (33) | *Ma mère l'oye*, suite for piano |
| | *Gaspard de la nuit*, for piano |
| 1909 (34) | *Menuet sur le nom d'Haydn*, for piano |
| 1911 (36) | *L'heure espagnole*, opera |
| | *Valses nobles et sentimentales*, for piano or orchestra |
| 1912 (37) | *Daphnis et Chloé*, ballet with chorus |
| 1914 (39) | *Two Hebrew Songs*, for soprano and orchestra |
| | Piano Trio in A minor |
| 1915 (40) | Three Songs for unaccompanied choir |
| 1917 (42) | *Le Tombeau de Couperin*, for piano |
| 1920 (45) | *La Valse*, choreographic poem for orchestra |
| | Sonata for violin and cello (1920–2) |
| 1922 (47) | *Berceuse sur le nom Fauré* |
| 1924 (49) | *Tzigane*, for violin and piano |
| 1925 (50) | *L'enfant et les sortilèges*, opera |
| 1926 (51) | *Chansons madécasses*, for voice, flute, cello and piano |
| 1928 (53) | *Bolero*, for orchestra |
| 1931 (56) | Piano Concerto in G major |
| | Piano Concerto for the left hand |

## RAWSTHORNE, Alan
b Haslingden, Lancashire, 2 May 1905
d Cambridge, 24 July 1971, aged sixty-six

Though trained as a dentist, he entered the Royal Manchester College of Music in his early twenties, studying piano, cello and composition. In 1930 he went abroad to continue his studies, and from 1932 to 1934 he taught at Dartington Hall, composing there for the School of Dance-Mime. He settled in London in 1935, and served in the Army during World War II. He was awarded the CBE in 1961, and was made honorary doctor of music of Liverpool, Essex and Belfast universities.

| | |
|---|---|
| 1935 (30) | Viola Sonata (revised 1954) |
| 1936 (31) | Concerto for clarinet and string orchestra |
| 1937 (32) | Theme and variations for two violins |
| 1938 (33) | Symphonic Studies for orchestra |
| 1939 (34) | String Quartet No 1, *Theme and Variations* |
| 1941 (36) | *The Creel*, suite for piano duet |
| 1942 (37) | Piano Concerto No 1 |
| 1944 (39) | *Street Corner Overture* |
| 1945 (40) | *Cortèges*, fantasy overture |
| 1946 (41) | *Prisoner's March*, for orchestra |
| 1947 (42) | Concerto for oboe and string orchestra |
| 1948 (43) | Violin Concerto No 1 |
| | Clarinet Quartet |
| 1949 (44) | Concerto for string orchestra |
| | Cello Sonata |
| 1950 (45) | Symphony No 1 |
| 1951 (46) | Piano Concerto No 2 |
| | Concertante Pastorale, for flute, horn and strings |
| 1952 (47) | *Canticle of Man*, chamber cantata for baritone, mixed chorus, flute and strings |
| 1954 (49) | *Practical Cats*, for speaker and orchestra |
| | String Quartet No 2 |
| 1955 (50) | *Madame Chrysanthème*, ballet |
| 1956 (51) | Violin Concerto No 2 |
| 1957 (52) | Violin Sonata |
| 1958 (53) | *Halle Overture* |
| 1959 (54) | Symphony No 2, *A Pastoral Symphony* |
| 1961 (56) | *Improvisations on a Theme by Constant Lambert*, for orchestra |
| | Concerto for ten instruments |
| 1962 (57) | *Medieval Diptych*, for baritone and orchestra |
| | Divertimento for chamber orchestra |
| | Quintet for piano and wind |
| | Piano Trio |
| 1963 (58) | *Carmen Vitale*, for soprano solo, mixed chorus and orchestra |
| 1964 (59) | Symphony No 3 |
| | *Elegiac Rhapsody*, for strings |
| 1965 (60) | *Tankas of the Four Seasons*, for tenor and chamber ensemble |
| | Concertante for violin and piano |
| 1966 (61) | Cello Concerto |
| | Sonatine, for flute, oboe and piano |
| | String Quartet No 3 |
| 1967 (62) | *Overture for Farnham* |
| | Theme, Variations and Finale for orchestra |
| | *The God in the Cave*, cantata for mixed chorus and orchestra |
| | *Scena rustica*, for soprano and harp |

| 1968 (63) | Concerto for two pianos and orchestra |
| | Trio for flute, viola and harp |
| 1969 (64) | *Triptych*, for orchestra |
| 1970 (65) | Oboe Quartet |
| 1971 (66) | Quintet for piano, clarinet, horn, violin and cello |

## REGER, Max
*b Brand, Bavaria, 19 March 1873*
*d Leipzig, 11 May 1916, aged forty-three*

He was the son of a teacher. He studied music privately, and in 1901 went to Munich as a pianist, teacher and an already established composer. In 1907 he became a professor at the Leipzig Conservatory, staying there for the rest of his life. In 1911 he was appointed director of the court orchestra at Meiningen, but in 1914 he relinquished the post and retired to Jena to write. Excessive indulgence in food and drink resulted in the heart attack that killed him.

| 1891 (18) | Piano Trio in B minor |
| | Violin Sonata in D major |
| 1892 (19) | Cello Sonata in F minor |
| 1897–8 (24–5) | Piano Quintet in C minor |
| | Cello Sonata in G minor |
| | Violin Sonata in A major |
| 1900 (27) | Two *Romances*, for solo instruments and orchestra |
| | Clarinet Sonata in A♭ major |
| | Clarinet Sonata in F♯ minor |
| | String Quartet in G minor (1900–01) |
| | String Quartet in A major (1900–01) |
| 1902 (29) | Piano Quintet in C minor |
| | Violin Sonata in C major |
| 1903 (30) | *Gesang der Verklarten*, for voice and orchestra |
| 1904 (31) | String Quartet in D minor |
| | *Serenade*, for flute, violin and viola, or two violins and viola |
| | String Trio in A minor |
| | Cello Sonata in F major |
| | *Variations and Fugue on a Theme of Beethoven*, for two pianos |
| | Violin Sonata in F♯ minor |
| 1905 (32) | Sinfonietta, for orchestra |
| | *Suite in the Old Style*, for violin and piano, in F major |
| 1906 (33) | *Serenade* |
| 1907 (34) | *Variations and Fugue on a Theme of Hiller* |
| 1908 (35) | *Symphonic Prologue to a Tragedy* |
| | Violin Concerto |
| | Sonata for clarinet (or viola) and piano |
| | Piano Trio |
| 1909 (36) | *The 100th Psalm*, for voice and orchestra |
| | *Die Nonnen*, for voice and orchestra |
| | String Quartet in E♭ major |
| 1910 (37) | Piano Concerto |
| | String Sextet in F major |
| | Piano Quartet in D minor |
| | Cello Sonata in A minor |
| 1911 (38) | *Die Weihe der Nacht*, for chorus and orchestra |
| | *Eine Lustspielouverture* |
| | String Quartet in F♯ minor |
| | Violin Sonata in E minor |

| 1912 (39) | *Konzert im Alten Stil* |
| | *Romischer Triumphgesang*, for voice and orchestra |
| | *A Romantic Suite* |
| 1913 (40) | *Vier Tondichtunger nach A. Böcklin* |
| | *Eine Ballettsuite* |
| 1914 (41) | *Eine Vaterländische Ouverture* |
| | Three Canons, Duets and Fugues in Ancient Style for two violins |
| | *Variations and Fugue on a Theme of Mozart* |
| | Piano Quartet in A minor |
| | Piano Sonata in C minor |
| | Cello Sonata in C minor |
| 1915 (42) | *Serenade*, for flute, violin and viola (or two violins and viola) in G major |
| | String Trio in D minor |
| | *Der Einsiedler*, for chorus and orchestra |
| 1916 (43) | Quintet in A major |

## REICH, Steve Michael
*b New York, 3 October 1936*

He studied at Cornell University from 1953 to 1957, graduating with honours in Philosophy; then studied music at the Juillard School from 1958 to 1961, moving on to Mills College in 1963 where he worked with Milhaud and Berio and received his MA in music. In 1966 he formed his own group of keyboard and percussion instrumentalists. He spent the summer of 1970 studying African drumming and the summer of 1973 in Balinese music. From 1976–7 he studied ancient Hebrew chanting. In 1978 he was awarded a Guggenheim Fellowship.

| 1963 (27) | *The Plastic Haircut*, film music |
| 1964 (28) | Music for three or more pianos or piano and tape |
| 1965 (29) | *Oh Dem Watermelons*, film music |
| | *It's Gonna Rain*, for tape |
| 1966 (30) | *Come Out*, for tape |
| | *Melodica*, for tape |
| | *Reed Phase*, for soprano saxophone and tape |
| 1967 (31) | *Piano Phase*, for two pianos or two marimbas |
| | *Slow Motion Sound*, for tape |
| | *My Name Is*, for three or more tape recorders, performers, and audience |
| | *Violin Phase*, for violin and pre-recorded tape or four violins |
| 1968 (32) | *Pendulum Music*, for three or more microphones, amplifiers, and loud speakers |
| 1969 (33) | *Pulse Music*, for phase-shifting pulse gate |
| | *Four Log Drums*, for phase-shifting pulse gate and log drums |
| 1970 (34) | *Four Organs*, for four electric organs and maracas |
| | *Phase Patterns*, for four electric organs |
| 1971 (35) | *Drumming*, for eight small tuned drums, three marimbas, three glockenspiels, two female voices, whistling, and piccolo |
| 1972 (36) | *Clapping Music*, for two performers |
| 1973 (37) | *Six Pianos*, for six pianos |
| | *Music for Mallet Instruments, Voices and Organ*, for four marimbas, two glockenspiels, metallophone, three female voices, and electric organ |
| | *Music for Pieces of Wood*, for five pairs of tuned claves |
| 1976 (40) | *Music for Eighteen Musicians* |
| 1978 (42) | *Music for a Large Ensemble* |

1979 (43)   *Octet*, for two pianos, string quartet, two clarinets/bass clarinet/
            flute/piccolo
            *Variations for Winds, Strings and Keyboards*, for chamber orchestra
            or orchestra
1980 (44)   *My Name is – Ensemble Portrait (Octet)*, for tape
1981 (45)   *Tehillim*, for voices and ensemble or voices and full orchestra
1982 (46)   *Vermont Counterpoint*, for flute and tape, or eleven flutes, or violin
            and tape
1983 (47)   *Eight Lines*, arrangement of *Octet* for chamber orchestra
            *The Desert Music*, for chorus and orchestra


## RESPIGHI, Ottorino
*b Bologna, 9 July 1879*
*d Rome, 18 April 1936, aged fifty-six*

He studied at the Liceo Musicale in Bologna. In 1900 he went to St Petersburg as
first violinist in the opera orchestra and while there he took lessons from
Rimsky-Korsakov. Up until 1908 his career was that of a violinist; but then he
was appointed professor of composition and, in 1923, director, at the Santa
Cecilia Conservatory in Rome. He resigned in 1926 in order to write, and died
after a long illness.

1902 (23)   Piano Concerto
1905 (26)   *Re Enzo*, comic opera
            *Notturno*, for orchestra
            *Burlesca*
            Suite in G major for string orchestra and organ
1907 (28)   *Fantasy*, for piano and orchestra
            String Quartet in D major
            String Quartet in D minor
1908 (29)   *Concerto in the Old Style*, for violin and orchestra
1909 (30)   *Chaconne* by Vitali, transcribed for violin, strings and organ
1910 (31)   *Semirama*, lyric tragedy
1913 (34)   *Carnival*, overture
1914 (35)   Suite for strings and organ
1915 (36)   *Sinfonia drammatica*
1917 (38)   *The Fountains of Rome*, symphonic poem
            *Old Airs and Dances for Lute*, transcribed for orchestra, Series I
            Violin Sonata in B minor
1918 (39)   *Il Tramonto*, for mezzo-soprano and string quartet
1919 (40)   *La boutique fantasque*, ballet music arranged from pieces by Rossini
1920 (41)   *Scherzo Veneziano*, choreographic comedy
            *Dance of the Gnomes*, for orchestra
1921 (42)   *Adagio with Variations*, for cello and orchestra
1922 (43)   *The Sleeping Beauty*, musical fable in three acts
            *Concerto Gregoriano*, for violin and orchestra
1923 (44)   *Belfagor*, lyric comedy
            *La Primavera*, lyric poem for soloists, chorus and orchestra
1924 (45)   *Concerto in the Mixo-Lydian Mode*, for orchestra
            *The Pines of Rome*, symphonic poem
            *Old Airs and Dances for Lute*, Series II
            String Quartet, *Doric*
1927 (48)   *The Sunken Bell*, opera
            *Three Botticelli Pictures*, for orchestra:
                *Spring (Primavera)*
                *The Adoration of the Magi*

The Birth of Venus

The Birds, suite for small orchestra based on seventeenth- and eighteenth-century bird-pieces for lute and for harpsichord:
Prelude
Dove
Hen
Nightingale
Cuckoo

Church Windows, four symphonic impressions for orchestra

Brazilian Impressions, for orchestra

| | | |
|---|---|---|
| 1928 | (49) | Toccata, for piano and orchestra |
| 1929 | (50) | The Festivals of Rome, orchestral suite |
| 1930 | (51) | Metamorphosen modi XII, theme and variations for orchestra |
| | | Bach's Prelude and Fugue in D major, transcribed for orchestra |
| 1932 | (53) | Belkis, Queen of Sheba, ballet |
| | | Mary of Egypt, mystery in one act and three episodes |
| | | Old Airs and Dances for Lute, Series III |
| 1934 | (55) | La Fiamma, melodrama in three acts |
| | | Concerto for oboe, horn, violin, double-bass, piano and string orchestra |
| | | Passacaglia in C minor (Bach), orchestral interpretation |

Performed posthumously:

| | |
|---|---|
| 1937 | Lucrezia |

## RIEGGER, Wallingford
b Albany, Georgia, 29 April 1885
d New York, 2 April 1961, aged seventy-five

His mother was a pianist and his father a violinist, and he began his early studies at home. In 1900 he studied cello and theory in New York, and in 1907 went to Berlin to the Hochschule. He returned to the USA in 1917 to teach theory and cello.

| | | |
|---|---|---|
| 1919 | (34) | Piano Trio |
| 1926 | (41) | Rhapsody for orchestra |
| | | Study in Sonority, for ten instruments |
| 1929 | (44) | Suite for flute |
| 1930 | (45) | Fantasy and Fugue for organ and orchestra |
| 1931 | (46) | Dichotomy, for chamber orchestra |
| | | Canons for woodwind |
| 1932 | (47) | Scherzo for orchestra |
| 1933 | (48) | Divertissement, for flute, harp and cello |
| 1935 | (50) | New Dance, for orchestra |
| 1936 | (51) | Music for voice and flute |
| 1938–9 | (53–4) | String Quartet No 1 |
| 1941 | (56) | Canon and Fugue for strings or orchestra |
| 1942 | (57) | Passacaglia and Fugue for band or orchestra |
| 1943 | (58) | Duos for three woodwind |
| 1946–7 | (61–2) | Symphony No 2 |
| 1947 | (62) | Sonatina for violin and piano |
| 1948 | (63) | String Quartet No 2 |
| | | Music for brass choir |
| 1951 | (66) | In Certainty of Song, cantata |
| | | Nonet for brass |
| | | Piano Quintet |
| 1952 | (67) | Woodwind Quintet |

Concerto for piano and wind quintet
1953 (68)    Variations for piano and orchestra
1954 (69)    *Suite for Younger Orchestra*
1955 (70)    *Dance Rhythms*, orchestra
1956 (71)    Variations for violin and viola
1957 (72)    *Movement*, for two trumpets, trombone and piano
             Symphony No 3
             *Festival Overture*
1959 (74)    Variations for violin and orchestra
             *Quintuple Jazz*, for ensemble
             Sinfonietta for orchestra
1960 (75)    Introduction and Fugue for cello and wind
             Duo for piano and orchestra
Riegger composed other choral and piano works, songs and dance pieces


## RIMSKY-KORSAKOV, Nicolai
*b Tikhvin, 6 March 1844*
*d St Petersburg, 21 June 1908, aged sixty-four*

His father was a retired civil governor and landowner, and the whole family
was fond of music. Destined for a naval career he entered the Naval College in
St Petersburg at the age of twelve, studying piano solely as a hobby. His teacher
introduced him to Balakirev, with whom Rimsky-Korsakov, Cui, Borodin and
Mussorgsky formed the group of composers known as 'The Five'. After three
years in the Navy he came back to St Petersburg at the age of twenty-one and
tinkered with composition, in which he was showing a growing interest. At
twenty-seven, to his amazement, he was offered the post of professor of
composition and instrumentation at the St Petersburg Conservatory. At this
time he shared lodgings with Mussorgsky. He was still officially in the Navy,
and in 1873 he was appointed inspector of military bands, which furthered his
interest in orchestration; and eventually the self-taught amateur became one of
the great masters. Overwork caused him to have a nervous breakdown when he
was in his forties, but he recovered to enter another period of creative activity.
He was very much concerned with the political upheavals in Russia in 1905. He
died of angina pectoris.

1861–5 (17–21) Symphony No 1 in E♭ major
1866 (22)    Overture on Russian Themes
             Symphony No 3 in C major (1866–73)
1867 (23)    *Sadko*, tone poem (later developed into a ballet-opera)
             *Fantasia on Serbian Themes*, for orchestra
1868–72 (24–8) *The Maid of Pskov (Ivan the Terrible)*, opera
1869 (25)    *Antar*, symphonic suite (originally Symphony No 2)
1875 (31)    Quartet No 1
             Three Pieces for piano
             Six Fugues
1876 (32)    Sextet for strings
             Quintet for piano and wind
1878 (34)    *May Night*, opera
             *Variations on BACH*, for piano
             Four Pieces for piano
1879 (35)    *Sinfonietta on Russian Themes*
             *Legend*, for orchestra (1879–80)
1880–1 (36–7) *The Snow Maiden*, opera
1882–3 (38–9) Piano Concerto in C♯ minor
1886 (42)    *Fantasia Concertante on Russian Themes*, for violin and orchestra

| 1887 (43) | *Capriccio espagnol*, for orchestra |
| 1888 (44) | *Russian Easter Festival Overture* |
| | *Schéhérezade*, symphonic suite |
| 1892 (48) | fp *Mlada*, opera |
| 1895 (51) | *Christmas Eve*, opera |
| 1897 (53) | Three Song Cycles: |
| |    *In Spring* |
| |    *To the Poet* |
| |    *By the Sea* |
| | Piano Trio |
| 1898 (54) | *Mozart and Salieri*, opera |
| 1899 (55) | *The Tsar's Bride*, opera |
| 1900 (56) | *The Legend of Tsar Sultan*, opera |
| 1902 (58) | fp *Kaschey the Immortal*, opera |
| 1903 (59) | *Souvenir de trois chants polonais*, for violin and orchestra |
| | *Serenade*, for cello and piano |
| | *The Invisible City of Kitezh*, opera (1903–5) |
| 1905 (61) | fp Orchestral Variations on a Russian people's song |
| 1906–7 (62–3) | *Le coq d'or*, opera |

Rimsky-Korsakov also wrote a cantata, *Ballad of the Doom of Oleg*.


## ROBERTSON, Leroy
*b Fountain Green, Utah, 21 December 1896*
*d Salt Lake City, 25 July 1971, aged seventy-four*

He was a pupil at the New England Conservatory, received his diploma in 1923, then studied in Europe. He received an MA from the University of Utah in 1932, and a PhD from the University of Southern California in 1954. He was professor and chairman of the music department of the Brigham Young University from 1925 to 1948, and held a similar post at the University of Utah from 1948 to 1962.

| 1923 (27) | *Endicott Overture* |
| 1938 (42) | Piano Quintet |
| 1940 (44) | Prelude, Scherzo and Ricercare for orchestra |
| | String Quartet |
| 1944 (48) | Rhapsody for piano and orchestra |
| | *American Serenade*, for string quartet |
| 1945 (49) | *Punch and Judy Overture* |
| 1947 (51) | *Trilogy*, for orchestra |
| 1948 (52) | Violin Concerto |
| 1953 (57) | *The Book of Mormon*, oratorio |
| 1966 (70) | Piano Concerto |

Robertson also composed:
Cello Concerto
Fantasia for organ
*Come, Come, Ye Saints*, for chorus
*Hatikva*, for chorus
*From the Crossroads*, for chorus
*The Lord's Prayer*, for chorus
Passacaglia for orchestra

**ROCHBERG, George**
*b Paterson, New Jersey, 5 July 1918*

After graduating from Montclair State Teachers' College, he studied composition at the Mannes School of Music in New York from 1939 to 1942. He continued his studies at the Curtis Institute of Music in Philadelphia, and the University of Pennsylvania. From 1948 to 1954 he was a member of the faculty of the Curtis Institute, and from 1951 to 1960 was director of publications for a publisher. He became acting chairman of the music department at the University of Pennsylvania, and chairman from 1961 to 1968, and then continued there as professor of composition.

| | |
|---|---|
| 1949 (31) | *Night Music*, for chamber orchestra |
| | Symphony No 1 |
| 1952 (34) | Twelve Bagatelles for piano |
| | String Quartet No 1 |
| 1953 (35) | Chamber Symphony for nine instruments |
| 1954 (36) | Three Psalms for chorus |
| | *David the Psalmist*, cantata |
| 1955 (37) | Duo Concertante for violin and cello |
| 1956 (38) | Sinfonia Fantasia |
| 1958 (40) | Symphony No 2 |
| | *Dialogues*, for clarinet and piano |
| | *Cheltenham Concerto*, for chamber orchestra |
| 1959 (41) | *La Bocca della verita*, for oboe and piano |
| | String Quartet No 2 |
| 1960 (42) | *Time-Span*, for orchestra (revised 1962) |
| 1961 (43) | *Songs of Innocence and Experience*, for soprano and chamber orchestra |
| 1963 (45) | Piano Trio |
| 1965 (47) | *Music for the Magic Theater* |
| | *Zodiac*, orchestral version of the Twelve Bagatelles |
| | *Contra mortem et tempus*, for violin, flute, clarinet and piano |
| | *Black Sounds*, for winds and percussion |
| 1968 (50) | *Tableaux*, for soprano and eleven players |
| | Symphony No 3, *A Twentieth-century Passion*, for orchestra, four solo voices, eight-part chamber choir and double chorus |
| 1970 (52) | *Songs of Krishna*, for soprano and piano |
| | *Mizmor L'Piyus*, for bass-baritone and small orchestra |
| 1972 (54) | *Electrikaleidoscope*, for violin, cello, flute, clarinet and electric piano |
| | *Ricordanza*, for cello and piano |
| | String Quartet No 3 |
| 1974 (56) | *Imago Mundi*, for orchestra |
| 1975 (57) | Violin Concerto |
| | Piano Quintet |
| 1980 (62) | *Octet, A Grand Fantasia* |
| | *Trio*, for clarinet, horn and piano |
| 1982 (64) | String Quintet |
| | *The Confidence Man*, opera |
| 1983 (65) | Oboe Concerto |

Rochberg also composed a Book of Songs (1937–69).


**RODRIGO, Joaquin**
*b Sagunto, Spain, 22 November 1901*

He was blind from the age of three. He took composition lessons in Valencia, and in 1927 entered the Schola Cantonum in Paris, as a pupil of Dukas and with

290

encouragement from Falla. He lived in Paris and Germany during the Spanish Civil War, returning to Madrid in 1939. He has travelled widely, and has been awarded his country's highest honours.

| | |
|---|---|
| 1934 (32) | *Cantico de la Esposa*, for voice and piano |
| 1939 (37) | *Concierto de Aranjuez*, for guitar and orchestra |
| 1942 (40) | *Concierto Heroico*, for piano and orchestra |
| 1943 (41) | *Concierto de Estio*, for violin and orchestra |
| 1947 (45) | Four *Madrigales Amatorias*, for voice and piano (with orchestra, 1948) |
| 1948 (46) | *Ausencias de Dulcinea*, for bass, four sopranos and orchestra |
| 1949 (47) | *Concierto Galante*, for cello and orchestra |
| 1952 (50) | Four *Villancicos*, for voice and piano |
| | Four *Villancicos*, for chorus (*Canciones de Navidad*) |
| 1954 (52) | *Concert-Serenade*, for harp and orchestra |
| c1955 (c53) | *Fantasia para un gentilhombre*, for guitar |
| 1965 (63) | *Sonata Pimpante*, for violin and piano (1965–6) |
| 1967 (65) | *Concierto Andaluz*, for four guitars and orchestra |
| 1968 (66) | *Concierto Madrigal*, for two guitars and orchestra |
| 1969 (67) | *Sonata a la Española*, for guitar |
| 1970 (68) | *Con Antonio Machado*, for voice and piano |

Rodrigo has also composed:
*Sones en la Giralda* (Fantasia Sevillana), for harp and orchestra
*Triptic de Mosen Cinto*


## ROGERS, Bernard
*b New York, 4 February 1893*
*d Rochester, New York, 24 May 1968, aged seventy-five*

He learned piano from the age of twelve, then studied composition with Bloch, and in 1921 went to the Institute of Musical Art. He taught, and worked as a music critic, and held Guggenheim Fellowships which enabled him to work with Bridge in England and Boulanger in Paris. He taught at the Eastman School until his retirement in 1967, and received honorary degrees from Valparaiso and Wayne State universities.

| | |
|---|---|
| 1918 (25) | String Quartet No 1 |
| | Free Variations and Fugue for string quartet |
| 1922 (29) | *Deidre*, opera |
| 1925 (32) | String Quartet No 2 |
| 1926 (33) | Symphony No 1, *Adonais* |
| 1928 (35) | Symphony No 2 |
| 1929 (36) | *The Raising of Lazarus*, for chorus and orchestra |
| 1931 (38) | *The Marriage of Aude*, opera |
| | *The Exodus*, for chorus and orchestra |
| 1936 (43) | Symphony No 3, *On a Thanksgiving Song* |
| 1940 (47) | Symphony No 4 |
| 1942 (49) | *The Passion*, oratorio |
| 1944 (51) | *The Warrior*, opera |
| 1947 (54) | *A Letter from Pete*, cantata |
| 1950 (57) | *The Veil*, opera |
| | *The Prophet Isaiah*, cantata |
| 1953 (60) | String Trio |
| 1954 (61) | *The Nightingale*, opera |
| 1959 (66) | Symphony No 5, *Africa* |
| 1962 (69) | Sonata for violin and piano |
| 1964 (71) | *The Light of Man*, for chorus and orchestra |

Rogers also composed other choral and vocal works with orchestra, works for large and small orchestras, chamber works, twelve songs, four solo instrumental pieces, and eight transcriptions.


## ROPARTZ, Joseph Guy
*b Guingamp, Côtes-du-Nord, 15 June 1864*
*d Lanloup, 22 November 1955, aged ninety-one*

At the Jesuit College in Vannes he played bugle, horn and double-bass. He read law at Rennes and graduated in 1885, but decided on a musical career and went to the Paris Conservatory, later studying with Franck. In 1894 he became director of the Nancy Conservatory, leaving in 1919 to go to Strasbourg. He retired to Brittany in 1929 but continued to compose. He was made a member of the Institut Français in 1949.

| | | |
|---|---|---|
| 1887 | (23) | *La cloche des morts*, for orchestra |
| 1888 | (24) | *Les Landes*, for orchestra |
| | | *Marche de fête* |
| 1889 | (25) | *Cinq pièces brèves*, for orchestra |
| | | *Carnaval*, for orchestra |
| 1892 | (28) | *Serenade* |
| 1893 | (29) | *Le diable couturier*, opera |
| | | *Dimanche breton*, for orchestra |
| | | String Quartet No 1 in G minor |
| 1900 | (36) | Five Motets |
| 1904 | (40) | Cello Sonata No 1 in E major |
| 1907 | (43) | Violin Sonata No 1 in D minor |
| | | *Pastorale and Dance*, for oboe and orchestra |
| 1911–12 | (47–8) | String Quartet No 2 in D minor |
| | | *Serenade*, for string quartet |
| 1912 | (48) | *Le Pays*, opera |
| | | *A Marie endormie*, for orchestra |
| | | *La Chasse du Prince Arthur*, for orchestra |
| 1913 | (49) | *Soir sur les Chaumes*, for orchestra |
| | | *Dans l'ombre de la montagne*, for orchestra |
| 1915 | (51) | *Divertissement No 1* |
| 1917 | (53) | Violin Sonata No 2 in E major |
| | | *Musiques au jardin*, for orchestra |
| 1918 | (54) | Piano Trio in A minor |
| | | Cello Sonata No 2 in A minor (1918–19) |
| 1924–5 | (60–1) | String Quartet No 3 in G major |
| 1926 | (62) | Romance and Scherzino for violin and orchestra |
| 1928 | (64) | *Rhapsody*, for cello and orchestra |
| 1933 | (69) | *Sérénade champêtre* |
| 1937 | (73) | *Requiem*, with orchestra |
| 1942 | (78) | *De profundis*, with orchestra |
| 1943 | (79) | *Indiscret*, ballet |
| | | *Petite Symphonie* |
| 1947 | (83) | *Divertissement No 2* |

Ropartz also composed five symphonies (1895–1945), No 3 with soloists and chorus.

## ROSSINI, Gioacchino Antonio
*b Pesaro, Italy, 29 February 1792*
*d Passy, near Paris, 13 November 1868, aged seventy-six*

His father was a town trumpeter and inspector of slaughter-houses; his mother later became leading lady in comic opera: At the Conservatory of Bologna he studied cello and composition, and was composing chamber works at the age of sixteen. He wrote his first opera at eighteen, and by his early twenties he was director of the San Carlo Theatre in Naples. Between 1810 and 1829 he wrote sixteen operas, then never wrote another for the remaining forty years of his life.

| | |
|---|---|
| 1808 (16) | Sonatas for two violins, cello and double-bass |
| 1809 (17) | Variations for clarinet and orchestra, in C major |
| 1810 (18) | *La cambiale di matrimonio*, opera |
| 1812 (20) | *La Scala di seta (The Silken Ladder)*, opera |
| 1813 (21) | *L'Italiana in Algeri*, opera |
| | *Tancredi*, opera |
| 1815 (23) | *Elisabetta, Regina d'Inghilterra*, opera |
| 1816 (24) | *Otello*, opera |
| | *The Barber of Seville*, opera |
| 1817 (25) | *La Cenerentola*, opera |
| | *La Gazza ladra (The Thieving Magpie)*, opera |
| 1818 (26) | *Mosè*, opera |
| 1820 (28) | *Maometto II*, opera |
| | Solemn Mass |
| 1822 (30) | *Zelmira*, opera |
| 1823 (31) | *Semiramide*, opera |
| 1825 (33) | *Il viaggio a Reims*, opera |
| 1826 (34) | *Le Siège de Corinthe*, opera (French-language version of *Maometto II*) |
| 1827 (35) | *Moïse*, opera (French-language version of *Mosè*) |
| 1828 (36) | fp *Comte Ory*, comedy-opera |
| 1829 (37) | *William Tell*, opera |
| 1863 (71) | Petite Messe Solennelle |

Rossini also composed:
*Stabat Mater* (1832–41)
Soirées musicales
Piano pieces etc


## ROUSSEL, Albert
*b Tourcoing, 5 April 1869*
*d Royan, 23 August 1937, aged sixty-eight*

He was born into a family of wealthy industrialists. He trained for a naval career, but resigned in 1894 and went to Paris to study music. In 1898 he enrolled at the Schola Cantorum, completing the course ten years later. He was professor of counterpoint from 1902 to 1914. In 1909 he began an extended tour of India and south-east Asia. In 1922 he moved to Normandy, where he stayed for the rest of his life, continuing to write in spite of indifferent health.

| | |
|---|---|
| 1902 (33) | Piano Trio |
| 1903 (34) | *Resurrection*, for orchestra |
| | Violin Sonata |
| 1904–6 (35–6) | Symphony No 1, *La poème de la forêt* |
| 1905 (36) | *Divertissement*, for piano, flute, oboe, clarinet, horn and bassoon |
| 1910–11 (41–2) | *Evocations*, for orchestra |

| 1912 (43) | *The Spider's Feast*, ballet |
| 1919 (50) | *Impromptu*, for harp |
| | Symphony No 2 in B♭ major (1919–21) |
| 1925 (56) | *Pour une Fête de printemps*, tone poem |
| | *Sérénade*, for harp, flute, violin, viola and cello |
| | Violin Sonata |
| | *Joueurs de flûte*, four pieces for flute and piano |
| | *Segovia*, for guitar |
| 1927 (58) | Piano Concerto in G major |
| 1929–30 (60–1) | Symphony No 3 in G minor |
| 1931 (62) | *Bacchus and Ariadne*, ballet |
| 1932 (63) | Quartet |
| 1934 (65) | Symphony No 4 in A major |
| | Sinfonietta for strings |
| 1936 (67) | Concertino for cello |
| | *Rhapsodie flamande* |
| 1937 (68) | String Trio |

## RUBBRA, Edmund
*b Northampton, 23 May 1901*

He studied privately under Cyril Scott, and won composition scholarships to Reading University (1920) and the Royal College of Music (1921). From 1947 to 1968 he was lecturer in music at Oxford University and from 1961 professor of composition at the Guildhall School. Among his awards are a Collard Fellowship in 1948; the Cobbett Medal (1955); an honorary LLD at Leicester University (1959); the CBE (1960); and Fellowship of Worcester College, Oxford (1963). He is also a fellow of the Guildhall School of Music and a member of the Royal Academy of Music. He holds degrees of MA (Oxford) and honorary DMus (Durham).

| 1921 (20) | *The Secret Hymnody*, for mixed choir and orchestra |
| 1924 (23) | Double Fugue for orchestra |
| 1925 (24) | *La belle dame sans merci*, for mixed chorus and small orchestra |
| | Violin Sonata No 1 |
| 1929 (28) | Triple Fugue for orchestra |
| 1931 (30) | Piano Concerto |
| | Violin Sonata No 2 |
| 1933 (32) | *Bee-Bee-Bei*, one-act opera |
| 1934 (33) | Sinfonia Concertante for piano and orchestra |
| | *Rhapsody*, for violin and orchestra |
| 1936 (35) | Symphony No 1 |
| 1937 (36) | Symphony No 2 |
| | String Quartet in F minor |
| 1938 (37) | *Prism*, ballet music |
| 1939 (38) | Symphony No 3 |
| 1941 (40) | Symphony No 4 |
| | *The Morning Watch*, for choir and orchestra |
| 1944 (43) | *Soliloquy*, for cello and orchestra |
| 1946 (45) | *Missa Cantuariensis*, for double choir unaccompanied except for organ in the Credo |
| 1947 (46) | *Festival Overture*, for orchestra |
| | Cello Sonata in G minor |
| | Symphony No 5 in B♭ major (1947–8) |
| 1948 (47) | *The Buddha*, suite for flute, oboe, violin, viola and cello |
| 1951 (50) | *Festival Te Deum*, for soprano, chorus and orchestra |

|  | String Quartet No 2 in E♭ major |
|---|---|
| 1952 (51) | Viola Concerto in A major |
| 1954 (53) | Symphony No 6 |
| 1955 (54) | Piano Concerto in G major |
| 1956 (55) | Symphony No 7 in C major |
| 1957 (56) | *In Honorem Mariae matris Dei*, cantata |
| 1958 (57) | Oboe Sonata in C major |
|  | *Pezzo Ostinato*, for harp |
| 1959 (58) | Violin Concerto |
| 1961 (60) | *Cantata da Camera* (Crucifixus pro nobis) |
| 1964 (63) | String Quartet No 3 |
|  | Improvisation for solo cello |
| 1965 (64) | *Inscape*, suite for chorus, strings and harp |
| 1966 (65) | Eight Preludes for piano |
| 1968 (67) | Symphony No 8 |
|  | *Advent Cantata* (Natum Maria Virgine), for baritone, chorus and small orchestra |
|  | Violin Sonata No 3 |
| 1969 (68) | *Missa brevis*, for treble voices and organ |
| 1970 (69) | Piano Trio No 2 |
|  | Four Studies for piano |
| 1971 (70) | *Sinfonia Sacra*, for soli, chorus and orchestra, Op 140 |
|  | Transformations for solo harp, Op 141 |
|  | *Fanfare for Europe*, for six trumpets, Op 142 |
|  | *Agnus Dei*, for unaccompanied chorus, Op 143 |
|  | Examination Piece for violin, Op 144 |
|  | Chamber Symphony No 10, Op 145 |
|  | *This Spiritual House*, for unaccompanied chorus, Op 146 |
|  | *Blessed is He*, for unaccompanied chorus, Op 147 |
|  | *Fly, Envious Time*, for tenor and piano, Op 148 |
|  | *Resurgam*, overture, Op 149 |
|  | String Quartet No 4, Op 150 |
|  | Three Greek Folk Songs for unaccompanied chorus, Op 151 |
|  | *Prayer for the Queen*, for unaccompanied chorus, Op 152 |
|  | Symphony No 11, Op 153 |
|  | *Fantasia on a Chord*, for recorder and harpsichord, Op 154 |
| 1980 (79) | *How Shall My Tongue Express?*, for unaccompanied chorus |
|  | Duo for cor anglais and piano |
|  | *Mass in Honour of St Teresa of Avila*, for unaccompanied chorus |
|  | Canzona for brass in honour of Ste Cecilia |
| Undated: | |
|  | *St Teresa's Bookmark*, for chorus and organ |
|  | *Invention on the name Haydn*, for piano |
|  | Fantasy Fugue for piano |
|  | *Introit*, for unaccompanied chorus |

Rubbra has also composed music for unaccompanied choir; anthems; part-songs; and liturgical works.


## RUBINSTEIN, Anton
*b Vikhvatinets, Russia, 28 November 1829*
*d Peterhof, 20 November 1894, aged sixty-four*

His early piano lessons were from his mother. His first public concert was in 1839, when he was ten years old, and from 1840 to 1843 he toured Europe as a child virtuoso – to Paris (where he met Chopin and Liszt), the Netherlands, London (where he was received by Queen Victoria), Norway, Sweden,

Germany and Russia. He spent two years in poverty in Vienna from 1846 to 1848; then he was adopted by a Russian Grand Duchess. His professional concert career started in 1854, and he became one of the world's greatest pianists. In 1859 he and the Duchess founded the Russian Musical Society and, in 1862, the St Petersburg Conservatory, of which he was director until 1867. He made another world tour as a pianist, returning in 1887 to direct the Conservatory again.

He wrote: twenty operas; choral and chamber works; six symphonies; five piano concertos; two cello concertos, one violin concerto; other orchestra works and a great many piano works and songs, few of which have survived.

## RUGGLES, Carl Sprague
b East Marion, Massachusetts, 11 March 1876
d Bennington, Vermont, 24 October 1971, aged ninety-five

He studied as a violinist, worked as an engraver for a Boston music publisher, and was a critic. He held various teaching posts, gained many awards and honours, and also spent much of his time painting.

c1912–23 (23–47) The Sunken Bell, opera (destroyed)
c1918 (42)    Mood, for violin and piano
1920 (44)     Men and Angels, for orchestra
1923 (47)     Vox clamans in deserto, for small orchestra
1924 (48)     Men and Mountains, for orchestra
1925 (49)     Portals, for thirteen strings or string orchestra
1926–31 (50–5) Sun-treader, for orchestra
1944–7 (68–71) Organum, for orchestra

## SAINT-SAËNS, Camille
b Paris, 9 October 1835
d Algiers, 16 December 1921, aged eighty-six

His family was of peasant origin. He started piano lessons at the age of seven and played in public at the age of ten. He went to the Paris Conservatory in 1848 and entered Halévy's composition class in 1851. In 1852 he failed to win the Prix de Rome. He became organist at Saint-Merry in 1853 and at the Madeleine in 1857. His only period of teaching was from 1861 to 1865 at the École Niedermeyer, where his pupils included Fauré and Messager. He failed the Prix de Rome again in 1864; but his friendship with Liszt helped to establish him as a composer. In 1868, at the age of thirty-three, he was decorated with the Légion d'honneur. In 1875 he began the first of many triumphant foreign concert tours. Cambridge awarded him an honorary doctorate. After 1890 he wrote little of musical consequence, but was able to indulge his literary gifts.

1855 (20)    Symphony No 1 in E♭ major
             Piano Quintet in A major, with double-bass ad lib
1857 (22)    Organ Fantasia No 1
1858 (23)    Piano Concerto No 1 in D major
1859 (24)    Violin Concerto No 1 in A minor
1863 (28)    Piano Trio No 1 in F major
1866 (31)    Suite in D minor for piano, cello (violin or viola)
1868 (33)    Piano Concerto No 2 in G minor
1869 (34)    Piano Concerto No 3 in E♭ major
1870 (35)    Introduction and Rondo Capriccioso, for violin and orchestra
             Mélodies persanes, six songs
1871 (36)    Omphale's Spinning-wheel, symphonic poem

|            |        | *Marche héroïque*, for orchestra |
|------------|--------|----------------------------------|
| 1872 | (37) | *La Princesse jaune*, opera |
| 1873 | (38) | Cello Concerto No 1 in A minor |
|      |      | *Phaeton*, symphonic poem |
| 1874 | (39) | *Danse macabre*, symphonic poem |
| 1875 | (40) | Piano Concerto No 4 in C minor |
| 1876 | (41) | *The Deluge*, oratorio |
| 1877 | (42) | *Samson and Delilah*, opera |
|      |      | *La Jeunesse d'Hercule*, symphonic poem |
|      |      | Suite for orchestra |
| 1878 | (43) | Symphony No 2 in A minor |
| 1879 | (44) | Violin Concerto No 2 in C major |
|      |      | *Suite Algérienne* |
| 1880 | (45) | Violin Concerto No 3 in B minor |
| 1885 | (50) | Violin Sonata No 1 in D minor |
| 1886 | (51) | *Le Carnaval des animaux*, for piano and orchestra |
|      |      | Symphony No 3 in C minor, with organ and two pianos |
| 1892 | (57) | Piano Trio No 2 in E minor |
| 1894 | (59) | Preludes and Fugues for organ |
| 1895 | (60) | Piano Concerto No 5 in F major |
| 1896 | (61) | Violin Sonata No 2 in E♭ major |
| 1897 | (62) | Seven Improvisations for grand organ |
| 1898 | (63) | Preludes and Fugues for organ |
| 1900 | (65) | String Quartet in E minor |
| 1902 | (67) | Cello Concerto No 2 in D minor |
|      |      | Coronation March |
| 1913 | (78) | fp *The Promised Land*, oratorio |
| 1915 | (80) | *La cendre rouge*, ten songs |
| 1918 | (83) | *Fantasia No 3*, for organ |

Saint-Saëns also composed:
Serenade for piano, organ, violin, and viola (or cello)
Cello Sonata No 1 in C minor
Piano Quartet in B♭ major
Septet in E♭ major for piano, trumpet, oboe and string quartet
Caprice on Danish and Russian Airs
Cello Sonata No 2 in F major
*Fantaisie*, for harp and violin
*Le Muse et le poète*, for piano trio
String Quartet in G major
Clarinet Sonata in E♭ major
Bassoon Sonata in G major

**SALLINEN, Aulis**
*b Salmi, Finland, 9 April 1935*

He entered the Sibelius Academy, Helsinki, in 1955, and from the age of thirty was on the staff there, dividing his time between teaching and composing. He has been awarded a number of scholarships and professorships.

| 1962 | (27) | *Mauermusik*, for orchestra |
|------|------|------------------------------|
| 1964 | (29) | *Elegy for Sebastian Knight*, for solo cello |
| 1965 | (30) | *Cadenze*, for solo violin |
| 1966 | (31) | *Notturno*, for piano |
| 1968 | (33) | Violin Concerto |
| 1969 | (34) | String Quartet No 3 |

| 1970 (35) | Chorali for orchestra |
| | Chaconne for organ |
| | *Four Études*, for violin and piano |
| 1971 (36) | String Quartet No 4 |
| | Solo Cello Sonata |
| | *Suita Grammaticale*, for children's choir and school orchestra |
| | Symphony No 1 |
| 1972 (37) | *Four Dream Songs*, for soprano and piano or orchestra |
| | Symphony No 2, *Symphonic Dialogue* |
| 1974 (39) | *Metamorfora*, for cello and piano |
| 1975 (40) | *Canto e Ritornello*, for solo violin |
| | Symphony No 3 |
| | *Chamber Music I*, for string orchestra |
| 1976 (41) | *Chamber Music II*, for alto flute and strings |
| | Cello Concerto |
| 1976–8 (41–3) | *The Red Line*, opera |
| 1978 (43) | *Dies Irae*, for soli, male chorus and orchestra |
| 1979 (44) | Symphony No 4 |
| 1980 (45) | *Song Around a Song*, for children's choir |
| 1982 (47) | *Shadows*, prelude for orchestra |
| 1983 (48) | *The Iron Age*, suite for soprano, choir and orchestra |
| | *The King Goes Forth to France*, opera |


## SAMMARTINI, Giuseppe
*b Milan, 6 January 1695*
*d London, November 1750, aged fifty-five*

The son of a French oboist, he was himself an oboist, reputedly the finest in Europe. He gave his first performance in 1711. In 1728 he left Italy for London, where he stayed for the rest of his life, giving concerts and playing in orchestras. He became music-master to the household of Frederick, Prince of Wales, in 1736. It was only after his death that his compositions became well-known.

| 1728–47 (33–52) | 112 Concerti Grossi |
Performed posthumously:
| 1752 | Overtures |
| 1754 | Four *Giuseppe St Martinis* Concertos |
| 1756 | Eight overtures |
| | Six concertos |

Sammartini also composed seventeen other concertos, three ballets, minuets and marches, many sonatas for various instruments, other solo pieces, nine cantatas and other vocal works.


## SARASATE, Fabio de
*b Pamplona, 10 March 1844*
*d Biarritz, 20 September 1908, aged sixty-four*

The son of a military bandmaster, he played violin at the age of five and gave his first public concert when he was eight. In 1856 he was sent to Paris to study at the Conservatory. After his training he gave concert tours for the rest of his life.

| 1878 (34) | *Zigeunerweisen*, orchestral fantasy |
Sarasate also composed:
Danses espagnoles, *Malaguena*
Danses espagnoles, *Habanera*

*Romanza Andaluza*
*Jota Navarra*
*Playera*
*Zapateado*
*Caprice basque*
*Introduction and Tarantella*, for violin and orchestra
Many works for violin


## SATIE, Erik
*b Honfleur, 17 May 1866*
*d Paris, 1 July 1925, aged fifty-nine*

He entered the Paris Conservatory in 1879, staying for only a year because of his distaste for academic routine. He received much inspiration from religious mysticism, and disliked romanticism. He had a great deal of influence on Debussy, though Satie was the younger, and became the standard bearer of 'Les Six' (Honegger, Auric, Milhaud, Tailleferre, Durey and Poulenc); Satie was with them, though not of them. Aware of his technical shortcomings, in 1905 he enrolled in the Schola Cantorum to study with d'Indy and Roussel.

| | | |
|---|---|---|
| 1886 (20) | *Ogives*, for piano | |
| 1887 (21) | *Trois sarabandes*, for piano | |
| 1888 (22) | *Trois gymnopédies*, for piano | |
| 1890 (24) | *Trois gnossiènnes*, for piano | |
| 1891 (25) | *Trois préludes* from *Les fils des étoiles*, for piano | |
| 1892 (26) | *Uspud*, ballet | |
| | *Sonneries de la Rose-Croix*, for piano | |
| 1893 (27) | *Danses gothiques*, for piano | |
| | *Quatre préludes*, for piano | |
| 1894 (28) | *Préludes de la porte héroïque du ciel*, for piano | |
| 1895 (29) | *Messe des pauvres* | |
| 1897 (31) | *Deux pièces froides*, for piano | |
| 1899 (33) | *Généviève de Brabant*, puppet opera | |
| | *Jack-in-the-Box*, ballet | |
| 1903 (37) | *Trois morceaux en forme de poire*, for piano duet | |
| 1905 (39) | *Pousse l'amour*, operetta | |
| 1906 (40) | *Prélude en tapisserie*, for piano | |
| | *Passacaille*, for piano | |
| 1908 (42) | *Aperçus désagréables*, for piano duet | |
| 1911 (45) | *En habit de cheval*, two chorales and two fugues for orchestra | |
| 1912 (46) | *Choses vues à droite et à gauche (sans lunette)*, for violin and piano | |
| 1913 (47) | *Le piège de Medusa*, operetta | |
| | *Descriptions automatiques*, for piano | |
| | *Embryons desséchés*, for piano | |
| | *Croquis et agarceries d'un gros bonhomme en bois*, for piano | |
| | *Chapitres tournés en tous sens*, for piano | |
| | *Enfantines*, three sets of children's pieces for piano | |
| 1914 (48) | *Cinq grimaces pour le Songe d'une nuit d'été*, for orchestra | |
| | *Vieux sequins et vielles cuirasses*, for piano | |
| | *Heures séculaires et instantées*, for piano | |
| | *Trois valses du précieux dégoûte*, for piano | |
| | *Sports et divertissements*, for piano | |
| | *Les Pantins dansent*, for piano | |
| | *Trois poèmes d'amour*, songs | |
| 1915 (49) | *Avant-dernières pensées*, for piano | |
| 1916 (50) | *Parade*, ballet | |

|           | *Trois mélodies*, songs                                                   |
| 1918 (52) | *Socrates*, symphonic drama for four sopranos and chamber orchestra       |
| 1919 (53) | *Quatre petites pièces montées*, for small orchestra                      |
|           | *Nocturnes*, for piano                                                    |
| 1920 (54) | *La belle excentrique*, for orchestra                                     |
|           | *Premier minuet*, for piano                                               |
|           | *Trois petites mélodies*, songs                                           |
| 1923 (57) | *Ludions*, songs                                                          |
| 1924 (58) | *Mercure*, ballet                                                         |
|           | *Relâche*, ballet                                                         |

## SCARLATTI, Alessandro
*b Palermo, 2 May 1660*
*d Naples, 25 October 1725, aged sixty-five*

Very little is known of his early life. He married in 1678 and had ten children, of whom Domenico, also a composer of importance, was the sixth. Queen Christina of Sweden was his first patron. In 1684 he was appointed *maestro di cappella* of the royal chapel in Naples and, with leave of absence, he went in 1702 to Florence with Domenico, to enjoy the patronage of the Medicis; then, after a few years in Rome as *maestro* at Santa Maria Maggiore, he returned in 1709 to his old position in Naples. He was made a 'Cavalier', a secular church honour.

| 1679 (19)    | *fp Gli equivoci nel sembiante*, opera                                |
| 1683 (23)    | *fp Pompeo*, opera                                                    |
|              | *fp Psiche*, opera                                                    |
| 1690 (30)    | *fp Gli equivoci in amore*, opera                                     |
| 1694 (34)    | *fp Pirro e Demetrio*, opera                                          |
| 1698 (38)    | *fp Flavio cuniberto*, opera                                          |
|              | *fp La donna ancora e'fedele*, opera                                  |
| 1699 (39)    | Two Sonatas for flute and continuo                                    |
| 1706 (46)    | *Il sedecia, re di Gerusalemme*, oratorio                             |
| 1707 (47)    | *fp Mitridate eupatore*, opera                                        |
|              | *fp Il trionfo della libertà*, opera                                  |
| c1710 (c50)  | *Est dies tropael*, Motet                                             |
|              | *Informata vulnerate*, cantata                                        |
| 1715 (55)    | *fp Tigrone*, opera                                                   |
|              | Twelve Sinfonias                                                      |
|              | Four quartets for two violins, viola and cello, without harpsichord   |
| 1718 (58)    | *fp Telemaco*, opera                                                  |
| 1719 (59)    | *fp Marco Attilo Regolo*, opera                                       |
| 1720 (60)    | *fp Tito o sempronio gracco*, opera                                   |
| 1721 (61)    | *fp Griselda*, opera                                                  |

Scarlatti also composed over a hundred other operas, five hundred chamber cantatas, two hundred masses, and fourteen oratorios.

## SCARLATTI, Domenico
*b Naples, 26 October 1685*
*d Madrid, 23 July 1757, aged seventy-one*

He studied first with his father Alessandro, then in 1701 became organist and composer at the royal chapel in Naples. In 1708 he went to Venice for further study and became a firm friend of Handel there. In 1709 he entered the service of the Queen of Poland in Rome. In 1714 he became *maestro di cappella* to the Portuguese Ambassador and, in 1715, was also *maestro* of the Cappella Giuliana in the Vatican. He resigned in 1719, and in 1720 or 1721 became *maestro* at the royal chapel in Lisbon. He returned to Italy in 1724, then moved to Madrid in 1729, where he spent his remaining years as music-master to the Queen of Spain. For his long services to the Spanish royal family he received a Spanish knighthood in 1738. More than half of his numerous harpsichord sonatas were composed during the last six years of his life.

| | | |
|---|---|---|
| 1703 | (18) | *fp Ottavia ristituta al trono*, opera |
| | | *fp Giustina*, opera |
| 1704 | (19) | *fp Irene*, opera |
| 1710 | (25) | *fp La Sylvia*, opera |
| 1711 | (26) | *fp Orlando*, opera |
| | | *fp Tolomeo e Alessandro*, opera |
| 1712 | (27) | *fp Tetide in sciro*, opera |
| 1713 | (28) | *fp Ifigenia in Aulide*, opera |
| | | *fp Ifigenia in Tauride*, opera |
| 1714 | (29) | *fp Amor d'un ombra*, opera |
| 1715 | (30) | *fp Ambleto*, opera |
| 1718 | (33) | *fp Berenice*, opera |
| 1738 | (53) | *p* Essercizi per Gravicembalo |
| 1739 | (54) | *p* XLII Suites de pièces pour le clavecin |

Scarlatti also wrote over 550 single-movement harpsichord sonatas.


## SCHEIDT, Samuel
*b Halle, baptised 3 November 1587*
*d Halle, 24 March 1654, aged sixty-six*

He was the son of the wine and beer steward and superintendent of water for the City of Halle. He first attended the local Gymnasium, then from 1603 to 1608 was organist at the Moritzkirche. He studied in Amsterdam with Sweelinck, and returned to Halle in 1609 as court organist to Prince Christian Wilhelm of Brandenburg. In 1619 he was appointed *Kapellmeister* there. His court life ended abruptly in 1625 when Christian Wilhelm went to battle in the Thirty Years War, but was resumed in 1638 with the return of peace.

| | |
|---|---|
| 1620–40 (33–53) | Seven collections of vocal music, all sacred |
| 1621 (34) | *Ludi musici* (4 volumes), for instrumental ensemble |
| 1624 (37) | *Tabulatura nova* (3 volumes), keyboard music |


## SCHMIDT, Franz
*b Pressburg, 22 December 1874*
*d near Vienna, 11 February 1939, aged sixty-four*

He was a fine pianist by the age of fourteen, but family financial problems compelled him to earn a living by playing in dancing schools. He entered the Vienna Conservatory in 1890; from 1896 to 1911 he was cellist in the Vienna Court Opera Orchestra, and also taught cello at the Conservatory from 1901 to 1908. In 1914 he was appointed professor of piano at the Vienna Staatsakademie, and became professor of counterpoint and composition in 1922. He was the director of the Staatsakademie from 1925 to 1927, and director of the Musikhochschule from 1927 to 1931. On his sixtieth birthday he received an honorary doctorate from Vienna University.

| | |
|---|---|
| 1896–9 (22–5) | Symphony No 1 |
| 1902–4 (28–30) | *Notre Dame*, opera |

1911–13 (37–9) Symphony No 2
1916–21 (42–7) *Fredigundis*, opera
1922 (48)    Romance for piano
1923 (49)    Piano Concerto No 1
1924 (50)    Fantasy and Fugue for organ
             Toccata for organ
             Prelude and Fugue for organ
1925 (51)    Chaconne for organ
             String Quartet in A
1926 (52)    Piano Quintet in G
1927 (53)    Fugue in F for organ
1928 (54)    Symphony No 3
             Four Little Preludes and Fugues for organ
1929 (55)    String Quartet in G
1930–1 (56–7) *Variationen über ein Husarenlied*, for orchestra
1931 (57)    Chaconne for orchestra
1932 (58)    Piano Quintet in B
1933 (59)    Symphony No 4
1934 (60)    Piano Concerto No 2
             Prelude and Fugue in A for organ
1935 (61)    Toccata and Fugue in A♭ for organ
1935–7 (61–3) *Das Buch mit sieben Siegeln*, oratorio
1937 (63)    *Fuga Solemnis*, for organ
1938 (64)    Toccata for piano
             Piano Quintet in A

Schmidt also composed two clarinet quintets and many organ pieces.

## SCHMITT, Florent

*b Blâmont, Meurthe-et-Moselle, 28 September 1870*
*d Neuilly-sur-Seine, 17 August 1958, aged eighty-seven*

At the age of seventeen he was admitted to the Nancy Conservatory to study piano and harmony, and at nineteen entered the Paris Conservatory. He won the Prix de Rome in 1900 at his fifth attempt. He was director of the Lyons Conservatory from 1922 to 1924, and music critic of *Le Temps* from 1929 to 1939. He was a member of the Institut Français and commander of the Légion d'honneur.

1894 (24)    *En été*, for orchestra
1897–9 (27–9) *Musique de plein air*, for orchestra
1900–4 (30–4) *Le palais hanté*, for orchestra
1903–10 (33–40) *Scherzo vif*, for violin and orchestra
1906 (36)    *Sélamlik*, for orchestra
1907 (37)    *La Tragédie de Salomé*, ballet
1912–13 (42–3) *Le petit elfe ferme-l'oeil*, ballet
1913–15 (43–5) *Rêves*, for orchestra
1914–25 (44–55) *Dionysiaques*, for band
1918 (48)    *Légende*, for viola, violin, sax and orchestra
1920 (50)    *Antoine et Cléopatre*, incidental music
1923–4 (53–4) *Kermesse*, waltz for orchestra
1924 (54)    *Fonctionnaire M.C.XII*, for orchestra
1925 (55)    *Salammbô*, film score
             *Danse d'Abisag*, for orchestra
1926 (56)    *Final*, for cello and orchestra
1927 (57)    *Ronde burlesque*, for orchestra
1928–31 (58–61) Symphonie Concertante for piano and orchestra

1929 (59)    *Cancunik,* for orchestra
1938 (68)    *Oriane et le prince d'amour,* ballet
             *Enfants,* for small orchestra
1941 (71)    *Janian,* for strings
1943 (73)    *Essais de locomotives,* film score
1950–2 (80–2) *Scènes de la vie moyenne,* for orchestra
1951–2 (81–2) *Introit, récit et congé,* for cello and orchestra
1958 (87)    Symphony No 2
Schmitt also composed many choral works, with orchestra, with instruments or
unaccompanied; chamber works; solo vocal works; and works for keyboard.


**SCHNITTKE, Alfred**
*b Engels, Volga, 1934*

He studied until 1958 at the Moscow Conservatory, and then taught instrumentation and composition there. He resigned in order to devote his time to
composing.

1964 (30)    Music for piano and chamber orchestra
1965 (31)    *Dialog,* for cello and seven instruments
1966 (32)    String Quartet
1968 (34)    *. . . Pianissimo . . .,* for large orchestra
             Concerto for oboe, harp and string orchestra
             Serenade for clarinet, violin, double-bass, percussion and piano
             *Quasi una Sonata,* for violin and piano
1978 (44)    Violin Concerto No 3
             Sonata for cello and piano
1979 (45)    Symphony, *St Florian*
1979–80 (45–6) *Passacaglia,* for orchestra
1980–1 (46–7) *Minnesang,* for chorus
1981 (47)    *Two Little Pieces for Organ*
             String Quartet
             Symphony No 3
1981–2 (47–8) Violin Concerto No 4
1982 (48)    Septet
             *Seid Nüchtern und Wachet . . .,* cantata
1983 (49)    *Schall und Hall,* for trombone and organ


**SCHOECK, Othmar**
*b Brunnen, Switzerland, 1 September 1886*
*d Zurich, 8 March 1957, aged seventy*

His father was a painter. In 1905 he entered the Zurich Conservatory, then went
to Leipzig to study with Reger from 1907 to 1908. He spent his life composing
and conducting in Zurich until a heart complaint forced him to retire in 1944.
He gained many honours.

1906–7 (20–1) *Serenade,* for small orchestra
1911 (25)    *Dithyrambe,* for small orchestra
             Violin Concerto (1911–12)
             *Erwin und Elmire,* incidental music (1911–16)
1915 (29)    *Trommelschlage,* for chorus and orchestra
1917–18 (31–2) *Don Ranudo de Colibrados,* comic opera
1918 (32)    *Das Wandbild,* scene and pantomime
1919–20 (33–4) *Venus,* opera
1922–3 (36–7) *Élégie,* song cycle for voice and chamber orchestra

1924–5 (38–9) *Penthesiles*, opera
1928–30 (42–4) *Vom Fischer und syner Fru*, dramatic cantata
1932 (46)     *Praeludium*, for orchestra
1937 (51)     *Massimilla Doni*, opera
1938–9 (52–3) *Das Schloss Durande*, opera
1945 (59)     *Sommernacht*, for strings
              Suite in A major for strings
1947 (61)     Cello Concerto
1951 (65)     Horn Concerto
              *Festlichen Hymnus*
1952 (66)     *Befreite Sehnsucht*, song cycle for voice and orchestra
Schoeck also composed many songs.


## SCHOENBERG, Arnold
*b Vienna, 13 September 1874*
*d Los Angeles, 13 July 1951, aged seventy-six*

His father ran a shoe shop, and both parents were interested in music. As a child he learned violin, viola and cello. When his father died in 1890 he took a job in a bank in order to support his mother and sister, but he did not enjoy his work and left in 1895, obtaining work as a chorus-master. His friend Zemlinsky gave him the only formal music training he ever had and introduced him to the music of Wagner, which greatly influenced him from then onward. In 1898 he left his father's Jewish faith and became a Protestant. To make a living he conducted theatre orchestras. In 1901 he married Zemlinsky's sister, and in that year obtained the Liszt Scholarship with the help of Richard Strauss. In 1903 he began his long career as a teacher, his many pupils including Webern and Berg. Marital problems brought Schoenberg a period of depression and, furthermore, opposition to his work made for a difficult financial period. In 1911 he left Vienna to teach at the Stern Conservatory in Berlin. After World War I came his most successful period as a' composer; but his health deteriorated and he became victim of Nazi anti-Semitism. After going to France and retaking the Jewish faith, he went to America, becoming an American citizen in 1941. He held various teaching posts, and wrote numerous books and articles.

1899 (25)     *Verklärte Nacht*, for string sextet (arranged for string orchestra
              1917; revised 1943)
1900–13 (26–39) *Gurre-Lieder*, for four solo singers, three male choruses, one
              mixed chorus, large orchestra including eight flutes and a set of
              iron chains
1903 (29)     *Pelleas und Melisande*, suite for orchestra
1905 (31)     String Quartet No 1 in D minor
1906 (32)     Chamber Symphonies No 1 and 2
1907 (33)     String Quartet No 2 (transcribed for string orchestra 1917)
              *Friede auf Erden*, for choir
1908 (34)     *Buch der hängenden Gärten*, setting of fifteen poems by Stefan
              George for solo voice and piano
1909 (35)     *Erwartung*, monodrama for soprano and orchestra
              Five Pieces for orchestra (revised 1949)
1910–13 (36–9) *Die Glückliche Hand*, music drama
1911 (37)     *Herzgewächse*, for coloratura soprano, celesta, harmonium and
              harp
1912 (38)     *Pierrot Lunaire*, song cycle of twenty-one poems
1923 (49)     Serenade, for septet and baritone
1924 (50)     Quintet for wind instruments
1927 (53)     String Quartet No 3

| 1928 (54) | Variations for orchestra |
| 1929 (55) | *Von Heute auf Morgen*, opera |
| 1932 (58) | *Moses und Aron*, two-act opera |
| 1934 (60) | Suite in G major for strings |
| 1936 (62) | Violin Concerto |
| 1937 (63) | String Quartet No 4 |
| 1939 (65) | *Kol Nidrei*, for speaker, chorus and orchestra |
| 1941 (67) | Variations and Recitative for organ |
| 1942 (68) | Piano Concerto |
| 1943 (69) | *Ode to Napoleon*, for speaker, strings and piano |
| 1945 (71) | Prelude to a *Genesis* Suite |
| 1947 (73) | *A Survivor from Warsaw*, cantata, for speaker, men's chorus and orchestra |
| 1949 (75) | *Fantasia*, for violin and piano |
| 1951 (77) | *De profundis*, for a cappella choir |

## SCHREKER, Franz
*b Monaco, 23 March 1878*
*d Berlin, 21 March 1934, aged fifty-five*

He studied violin and composition from 1892 to 1900 at the Vienna Conservatory. He achieved his first success in 1908 with a ballet, and in that same year founded the Philharmonic Choir, which he conducted until 1920. In 1912 he was appointed to teach composition at the Vienna Akademie für Musik, and in 1920 was made director of the Berlin Hochschule, staying there until 1932. He was dismissed from this post in 1932 and took over a master-class in composition at the Prussian Academy of Arts, from which he was also dismissed in 1933. The shock caused a fatal heart attack.

| 1895 (17) | *Love Song*, for strings and harp (lost) |
| 1900 (22) | *Flammen*, opera |
| | *Psalm CXVI*, for three female voices, organ and orchestra |
| 1901–10 (23–32) | *Der Ferne Klang*, opera |
| 1902 (24) | *Romantische Suite* (unpublished) |
| | *Ekkehard*, symphonic overture |
| | *Phantastische Ouverture* (unpublished) |
| | *Schwanengesang*, for chorus and orchestra |
| 1908 (30) | *Der Geburtstag der Infantin*, a pantomime |
| | *Der Wind*, for clarinet and piano quartet (unpublished) |
| | *Rokoko*, ballet |
| 1913 (35) | *Das Spielwerk und die Prinzessin*, opera |
| 1913–15 (35–7) | *Die Gezeichneten*, opera |
| 1916 (38) | Chamber Symphony |
| 1918 (40) | *Der Schatzgräber*, opera |
| 1919–23 (41–5) | *Irrelohe*, opera |
| 1924–7 (46–9) | *Christophorus*, opera |
| | *Der Singende Teufel*, opera |
| 1927 (49) | *Vom Ewigen Leben*, for voice and orchestra |
| 1928 (50) | Little Suite for chamber orchestra |
| 1929–32 (51–4) | *Der Schmied von Gent*, opera |
| 1930 (52) | Four Little Pieces for orchestra |
| | *Das Welb des Intaphernes*, for speaker and orchestra |

Schreker composed other choral works and songs, and a few unpublished solo instrumental works.

## SCHUBERT, Franz
*b Vienna, 31 January 1797*
*d Vienna, 19 November 1828, aged thirty-one*

His father was a schoolmaster and a keen amateur musician; Franz learned violin from him and piano from his elder brother. In 1808 he was accepted as a choirboy in the court chapel; then he became a schoolteacher, composing in his spare time. His songs attracted immediate attention, and in 1816 he temporarily gave up teaching in order to compose. In 1818 he had the opportunity to teach music to the children of Count Esterházy, and so he moved to Hungary. However, he soon missed his beloved Vienna and his great circle of friends, and went back home. In 1822 he became ill with syphilis, but it was typhoid that ultimately killed him.

| | |
|---|---|
| 1811 (14) | Quintet-overture |
| 1812 (15) | *Eine Kleine Trauermusik*, nonet |
| | Quartet-overture |
| | String Quartets No 1–3 in Bb : C: Bb |
| | Sonata movement for piano trio in Bb major |
| 1813 (16) | Symphony No 1 in D major |
| | Minuet and Finale of a wind octet in F major |
| | String Quartets No 4–6, in C: Bb : D |
| | Three Sonatinas for violin and piano in D: Am: Gm |
| | Five German Dances, with coda and seven trios |
| | Five Minuets with six trios |
| | *Des Teufels Lustschloss*, opera (1813–14) |
| 1814 (17) | Quartet for flute, guitar, viola and cello, in G major |
| | String Quartets No 7 and 8, in D: Bb |
| | 'Gretchen am Spinnade' (Gretchen at the Spinning-wheel), song |
| 1815 (18) | Symphony No 2 in Eb major |
| | Symphony No 3 in D major |
| | String Quartet No 9 in G minor |
| | Piano Sonatas No 1 and 2, in E: C |
| | 'Der Erlkönig', song |
| 1816 (19) | Symphony No 4 in C minor, *Tragic* |
| | Symphony No 5 in Bb major |
| | *Konzertstücke*, for violin and orchestra |
| | Rondo for violin and string quartet |
| | String Trio (one movement) in Bb major |
| | Piano Sonata No 3 in E major, five movements |
| | *Adagio and Rondo Concertante*, for piano quartet |
| 1817 (20) | String Quartet No 10 in Eb major (possibly 1813) |
| | String Quartet No 11 in E major |
| | Violin Sonata in A major |
| | Piano Sonata No 4 in Ab , with finale in Eb |
| | Piano Sonata No 5 in E minor, two movements |
| | Piano Sonata No 6 in Eb major |
| | Piano Sonata No 7 in F# minor |
| | Piano Sonata No 8 in B major |
| | Piano Sonata No 9 in E minor |
| | 'An die Musik', and 'Tod und das Mädchen', songs |
| 1818 (21) | Symphony No 6 in C major |
| | Piano Sonatas No 10 and 11, in C: Fm (unfinished) |
| 1819 (22) | Piano Quintet in A major, *The Trout* |
| | Piano Sonata No 12 in C# minor (fragmentary) |
| | Piano Sonata No 13 in A major |
| 1820 (23) | *Die Zauberharfe*, melodrama |

|  | String Quartet No 12 in C minor |
|---|---|
| 1821 (24) | *Variation on a Theme by Diabelli* |
|  | Symphony No 7 in E major (sketched only) |
|  | *Alfonso und Estrella*, opera (1821–2) |
| 1822 (25) | Symphony No 8 in B minor, *Unfinished* |
| 1823 (26) | *Fierrabras*, opera |
|  | *Die häusliche Krieg*, opera |
|  | *Rosamunde*, incidental music |
|  | Piano Sonata No 14 in A minor |
|  | *Die Schöne Mullerin*, song cycle |
| 1824 (27) | Octet in F major for strings and wind instruments |
|  | String Quartet No 13 in A minor |
|  | String Quartet No 14 in D minor, *Death and the Maiden* |
|  | Cello Sonata in A minor, *Arpeggione* |
|  | Introduction and Variations for flute and piano, in E minor |
| 1825 (28) | Piano Sonata No 15 in C major |
|  | Piano Sonata No 16 in A minor |
|  | Piano Sonata No 17 in D major |
| 1826 (29) | String Quartet No 15 |
|  | Piano Trio in Bb major |
|  | *Rondo Brilliant*, for violin and piano, in B minor |
|  | Piano Sonata No 18 in G major |
| 1827 (30) | Piano Trio in Eb major |
|  | *Phantasie*, for violin and piano, in C major |
|  | *Die Winterreise*, song cycle |
| 1828 (31) | Symphony No 9 in C major, *The Great* |
|  | Symphony No 10 (unfinished, recently discovered) |
|  | String Quintet in C major |
|  | Piano Sonata No 19 in C minor |
|  | Piano Sonata No 20 in A major |
|  | Piano Sonata No 21 in Bb major |
|  | *Schwanengesang*, song cycle |

Schubert also composed more than 600 songs. Two unfinished symphonies, written between his 6th and 7th, have recently been discovered.


## SCHÜLLER, Gunther
*b New York, 22 November 1925*

He was the son of an orchestral violinist. He studied composition, flute and horn at St Thomas' Choir School from 1938 to 1942, and became a professional horn-player. In 1959 he gave up playing in order to concentrate on composing. He taught at Manhattan School of Music from 1950 to 1962, Yale School of Music from 1964 to 1967, and the New England Conservatory, of which he was president, from 1967 to 1977; he also worked at Tanglewood.

| 1943–4 (18–19) | Six Early Songs |
|---|---|
| 1944 (19) | Horn Concerto |
| 1945 (20) | *Vertige d'Eros*, for orchestra |
| 1947–8 (22–3) | Symphonic Study |
| 1950 (25) | Symphony for brass and percussion |
| 1951 (26) | *Dramatic Overture* |
| 1953 (28) | Recitative and Rondo for violin and orchestra |
| 1955 (30) | *Symphonic Tribute to Duke Ellington* |
| 1957 (32) | *Little Fantasy*, for orchestra |
| 1958 (33) | *Contours*, for orchestra |
|  | *Spectra*, for orchestra |

| 1959 (34) | Concertino for jazz quartet |
| | *Seven Studies on Themes of Paul Klee*, for orchestra |
| 1960 (35) | Capriccio for tuba and orchestra |
| | *Contrasts*, for wind quintet and orchestra |
| | *Variants*, for jazz quartet and orchestra |
| | *Meditations*, for voices |
| 1962 (37) | *Journey to the Stars*, film score |
| | *Journey into Jazz*, for narrator, jazz quintet and orchestra |
| | *Movements*, for flute and strings |
| | Piano Concerto |
| | Six Renaissance Lyrics for tenor and seven instruments |
| 1963 (38) | *Yesterday in Fact*, film score for jazz quintet and five instruments |
| | *Composition in Three Parts*, for orchestra |
| | *Diptych*, for brass quintet and band |
| | *Meditation*, for band |
| | *Threnos*, for oboe and orchestra |
| 1964 (39) | Five Bagatelles for orchestra |
| | Shakespearean Songs for baritone and orchestra |
| 1965 (40) | *American Triptych*, for orchestra |
| | Symphony |
| 1965–6 (40–1) | Concerto for orchestra, *Gala Music* |
| 1966 (41) | *The Visitation*, opera |
| | *Study in Textures*, for band |
| | Five Études for orchestra |
| | Sacred Cantata |
| 1967 (42) | *The Five Senses*, TV ballet |
| | *Triplum*, for orchestra |
| 1968 (43) | *Colloquy*, for two pianos and orchestra |
| | Double-bass Concerto |
| | *Fanfare for St Louis*, for orchestra |
| 1969 (44) | *Shapes and Designs*, for orchestra |
| 1970 (45) | *The Fisherman and his Wife*, children's opera |
| | *Consequents*, for orchestra |
| | *Museum Piece*, for ensemble |
| 1971 (46) | *The Power Within Us*, oratorio |
| 1972 (47) | *Poems of Time and Eternity*, for chorus and nine instruments |
| | *Capriccio Stravagante*, for orchestra |
| 1973 (48) | Three Nocturnes for orchestra |
| 1975 (50) | *Four Soundscapes*, for orchestra |
| | *Triplum II*, for orchestra |
| 1975–6 (50–1) | Violin Concerto |
| 1977 (52) | Horn Concerto |
| | Symphony No 7 |
| | String Quartet No 7 |
| 1978 (53) | *Deai*, for two orchestras |

Schüller has also composed a great deal of music for ensembles.


## SCHUMAN, William
*b New York, 4 August 1910*

He played violin, banjo and double-bass, and also studied harmony and counterpoint. He graduated from the Teachers' College of Columbia University in 1935, and since then has devoted his time to composition. He has received many awards, and holds honorary doctorates from twenty American colleges and universities.

| 1934 (24) | *Choreographic Poem*, for seven instruments |
| 1935 (25) | Symphony No 1, for eighteen instruments |
| 1936 (26) | String Quartet No 1 |
| 1937 (27) | Symphony No 2 |
| | String Quartet No 2 |
| | Choral Étude |
| 1939 (29) | *American Festival Overture* |
| | *Quartettino*, for four bassoons |
| | String Quartet No 3 |
| | *Prelude for Voices* |
| 1940 (30) | Secular Cantata No 1, 'This is Our Time' |
| 1941 (31) | Symphony No 3 |
| | Symphony No 4 |
| | *Newsreel* suite for orchestra |
| 1942 (32) | Piano Concerto |
| | Secular Cantata No 2, 'A Free Song' |
| | *Requiescat* |
| 1943 (33) | *William Billings*, overture |
| | Symphony No 5 for strings |
| | *A Prayer in Time of War*, for orchestra |
| 1944 (34) | *Circus Overture* |
| | *Te Deum* |
| 1945 (35) | *Undertow*, ballet |
| 1947 (37) | *Night Journey*, ballet |
| | Violin Concerto |
| 1948 (38) | Symphony No 6 |
| 1949 (39) | *Judith*, ballet |
| 1950 (40) | String Quartet No 4 |
| 1953 (43) | *The Mighty Casey*, baseball opera |
| | *Voyage*, for piano |
| 1955 (45) | *Credendum*, for orchestra |
| 1956 (46) | *New England Triptych*, for orchestra |
| 1957 (47) | *Prologues*, for chorus and orchestra |
| 1959 (49) | *Three Moods*, for piano |
| 1960 (50) | Symphony No 7 |
| 1962 (52) | *Song of Orpheus*, fantasy for cello and orchestra |
| 1963 (53) | Symphony No 8 |
| 1964 (54) | Symphony No 9 |
| | String Trio |
| 1969 (59) | *In Praise of Shahn*, canticle for orchestra |
| 1973 (63) | *Concerto on Old English rounds*, for solo viola, women's chorus and orchestra |
| | *To Thy Love*, choral fantasy |
| 1974 (64) | *Prelude for a Great Occasion*, for brass and percussion |
| 1976 (66) | Symphony No 10 |
| | *Casey at the Bak*, cantata |
| | *The Young Dead Soldiers*, for soprano, horn, woodwind and strings |

## SCHUMANN, Robert
*b Zwickau, 6 June 1810*
*d Endenich, 29 July 1856, aged forty-six*

The son of a well-to-do bookseller and publisher, he had a wide literary education. Though his parents were not musical he was allowed piano lessons at school, and soon showed outstanding ability. When his father, who had encouraged him, died, his mother directed him towards law, which he studied from 1828 at Leipzig University. His heart was in music, however, and in 1830 he found board and lodging with his piano teacher, Wieck. In 1832 his right hand became permanently crippled, so he concentrated on composing, and also embarked on his secondary career as a writer and critic. He married Wieck's younger daughter, Clara, a concert pianist, in 1840. She encouraged him to develop his gifts, from writing songs and piano pieces to symphonies and chamber works. But marital friction seriously affected his health, and his near nervous breakdown may have been caused by this or by an earlier attack of syphilis. He resigned from a post Mendelssohn had created for him in the new Leipzig Conservatory in 1843, and in 1844 the couple moved to the quiet of Dresden. In 1850 he accepted the post of director of music in Düsseldorf, but he was forced to resign in 1853 because he was rapidly declining mentally. He threw himself into the Rhine in 1854, was rescued and taken to an asylum near Bonn, where he died two and a half years later.

| 1829–31 (19–21) | *Papillons*, twelve pieces for piano |
| 1830 (20) | *Theme and Variations on the name 'Abegg'*, for piano |
| 1832 (22) | Six Concert Studies on Caprices by Paganini, Set I |
| 1833 (23) | Six Concert Studies on Caprices by Paganini, Set II |
| 1834–5 (24–5) | *Carnaval (Scènes mignonnes)*, twenty-one piano pieces |
| 1836 (26) | *Phantasie* in C major, for piano |
| 1837 (27) | *Fantasiestücke*, for piano, Books I and II |
| | p *Études symphoniques*, twelve symphonic studies for piano |
| | *Davidsbündler-Tänze*, eighteen piano pieces (revised 1850) |
| 1838 (28) | *Kinderscenen*, thirteen short piano pieces |
| | *Kriesleriana*, for piano (dedicated to Chopin) |
| | *Novelleten*, eight piano pieces |
| 1839 (29) | *Nachtstücke*, for piano |
| 1840 (30) | *Dichterliebe (Poet's Love)*, song cycle |
| | *Frauenliebe und -leben*, song cycle |
| | *Liederkreise*, nine songs (Heine) |
| 1841 (31) | Symphony No 1, *Spring*, in B♭ major |
| | Symphony No 4 in D minor (withdrawn and revised in 1851) |
| | *Overture, Scherzo and Finale*, for orchestra (*Finale* revised 1845) |
| | Piano Concerto in A minor (1841–5) |
| 1842 (32) | Piano Quintet in E♭ major |
| | Piano Quartet in E♭ major |
| | Four *Fantasiestücke* for piano trio, in Am: F: Fm: Am |
| | Andante and Variations for two pianos, two cellos and horn (best known as duet for two pianos) (1842?) |
| | Three String Quartets, in Am: F: A |
| | *Liederkreise*, twelve songs (Eichendorff) |
| 1843 (33) | *Das Paradies und die Peri*, cantata |
| 1845–6 (35–6) | Symphony No 2 in C major |
| 1847 (37) | *Genoveva*, opera (1847–8) |
| | Piano Trio No 1 in D minor and D major |
| | Piano Trio No 2 in F major |
| 1849 (39) | *Manfred*, dramatic poem |
| | Three *Fantasiestücke* for piano and clarinet with violin or cello *ad lib*, in Am: A: A |
| | *Adagio and Allegro*, for piano and horn, in A♭ major |
| 1850 (40) | Symphony No 3 in E♭ major, *Rhenish* |
| | Cello Concerto in A minor |
| 1851 (41) | Piano Trio No 3 in G minor and G major |
| | Violin Sonata in A minor |
| | Violin Sonata in D minor |
| | Four *Marchenbilder*, for piano and viola (or violin) |

| 1853 | (43) | Violin Concerto |
|---|---|---|

1853 (43)    Violin Concerto
*Märchenerzählungen*, four pieces for piano, clarinet (or violin), and viola
*Introduction and Allegro*, for piano
*Fantasy*, for violin

1854 (44)    *p Albumblätter*, twenty pieces for piano

## SCHÜTZ, Heinrich
*b Köstritz, 8 October 1585*
*d Dresden, 6 November 1672, aged eighty-seven*

In 1599 he became a chorister at the chapel of the Landgrave of Hesse-Kassel, and received a thorough general and musical education. In 1608 he entered the University of Marburg to study law, but the Landgrave paid for him to go to Venice as a pupil of G. Gabrielli, and he remained there from 1609 to 1612. He then went to Leipzig to resume his law studies, but finally abandoned them when he was appointed organist to the Landgrave. In 1613 he visited Dresden and in 1615 was appointed to the Electoral chapel there. He went to Italy in 1628 to study the music of Monteverdi; but on his return home he found that Saxony had begun to take part in the Thirty Years War in 1628, and economic pressures were being felt at the Court. This determined him to go to Copenhagen, to become *Kapellmeister* at the Danish court from 1633 to 1635. He continued afterwards to make occasional visits to Denmark, but the Elector of Saxony compelled him to continue working in Dresden from 1641. His hearing failed in his later years.

1611 (26)    *p* Italian Madrigals
1619 (34)    *p* Psalms and Motets
            *p* Psalmen Davids for two, three or four choirs of voices and instruments
1623 (38)    *Resurrection Oratorio*
            *Easter Oratorio*
            *p Historia der Auferstehung Jesu Christi*, for voices and instruments
1625 (40)    *p Cantiones sacrae*, for four voices
1627 (42)    *fp Dafne*, opera
1629 (44)    *p Symphoniae sacrae*, Part I
1636 (51)    *Musicalische exequien* (Funeral music)
            *Kleine Geistliche Concerte*, Book I
1638 (53)    *fp Orpheus and Euridice*, ballet
1639 (54)    *Kleine Geistliche Concerte*, Book II
1645 (60)    *The Seven Words from the Cross*, choral
1647 (62)    *p Symphoniae sacrae*, Part II
1648 (63)    *p Musicali ad chorum sacrum*
1650 (65)    *p Symphoniae sacrae*, Part III
1664 (79)    *Christmas Oratorio*
1665–6 (80–1) Four Passions (*Matthew, Mark, Luke* and *John*)
1671 (86)    *Deutsches Magnificat*

## SCOTT, Cyril Meir
*b Oxton, Cheshire, 27 September 1879*
*d Eastbourne, 31 December 1970, aged ninety-one*

He was sent to the Hoch Conservatory in Frankfurt at the age of twelve, remaining there for eighteen months. He went back to Frankfurt in 1895, and became a member of the 'Frankfurt Group' with Grainger, Gardiner, O'Neill and Quilter. He finally returned to England in 1898, and from 1900 onward spent his life teaching, composing and writing. Unfortunately, many of his original MSS were destroyed during World War II. He wrote books on occultism, naturopathy, osteopathy and homoeopathy, as well as several volumes of poetry, many unpublished plays and an autobiography (1924). He received honours from the International Academy, the Chicago Conservatory and the Royal Academy of Music.

| | | |
|---|---|---|
| 1900 (21) | Symphony No 1 | |
| 1903 (24) | Symphony No 2 (three symphonic dances) | |
| 1913 (34) | *Nativity Hymn*, for chorus and orchestra | |
| 1915 (36) | Piano Concerto No 1 | |
| 1916 (37) | *La Belle Dame sans merci*, for baritone, chorus and orchestra | |
| 1917 (38) | *The Alchemist*, opera | |
| 1923 (44) | *The Incompetent Apothecary*, ballet | |
| 1925 (46) | *The Saint of the Mountain*, opera | |
| | *The Ballad of Fair Helen of Kirkconnel*, for baritone and orchestra | |
| 1926 (47) | *Karma*, ballet | |
| 1927 (48) | Violin Concerto | |
| 1931 (52) | Cello Concerto | |
| 1932 (53) | *The Masque of the Red Death*, ballet | |
| 1933 (54) | *Rima's Call to the Birds*, for soprano and orchestra | |
| | *Mystic Ode*, for chorus and orchestra | |
| 1935 (56) | Concerto for two violins | |
| | *Let Us Now Praise Famous Men*, for chorus and orchestra | |
| 1936 (57) | *Ode to Great Men*, for tenor and orchestra | |
| 1937 (58) | Harpsichord Concerto | |
| 1939 (60) | Symphony No 3, *The Muses* | |
| 1946 (67) | *Maureen O'Mara*, opera | |
| | Oboe Concerto | |
| 1947 (68) | *Hymn of Unity*, for soli, chorus and orchestra | |
| 1954 (75) | Sinfonietta for strings, organ and harp | |
| 1958 (79) | Piano Concerto No 2 | |
| 1962 (83) | Sinfonietta for strings | |

Scott also wrote many overtures and suites, over a hundred songs and a quantity of chamber works.


## SEIBER, Mátyás
*b Budapest, 4 May 1905*
*d Kruger National Park, S Africa, 24 September 1960, aged fifty-five*

He was born into a musical family, and began studying cello at the age of ten. From 1919 to 1924 he studied at the Budapest Academy of Music with Kodály; then he taught in Frankfurt. In 1927 he joined a ship's orchestra as a cellist, and came back to Frankfurt in 1928 to join the staff of the Hoch Conservatory, and to conduct at theatres in the city. He went to England in 1935 and stayed there for the rest of his life. He taught at Morley College from 1942 to 1957; founded, with Chagrin, the SPNM in 1943; and founded the Dorian Singers in 1945. He frequently went abroad to festivals and to lecture, and it was while he was lecturing at South African universities that he was killed in a car crash.

| | |
|---|---|
| 1924 (19) | String Quartet No 1 |
| | *Sarabande and Gigue*, for cello and piano |
| | *Missa Brevis*, for unaccompanied chorus |
| 1925 (20) | *Serenade*, for six wind instruments |
| | *Sonata da Camera*, for cello and violin |
| 1926–8 (21–3) | Divertimento for clarinet and string quartet |
| 1934 (29) | *Eva spielt mit Puppen*, opera |
| | String Quartet No 2 (1934–5) |

| 1940 | (35) | *Besardo Suite* No 1 |
| 1941 | (36) | *Besardo Suite* No 2, for strings |
| | | *Transylvanian Rhapsody* |
| | | *Fantasy*, for cello and piano |
| | | *Pastorale and Burlesque*, for flute and strings (1941–2) |
| 1942 | (37) | *Balaton*, opera |
| | | *La Blanchisseuse*, ballet music |
| 1943–4 | (38–9) | *Fantasia Concertante*, for violin and strings |
| 1944 | (39) | *Notturno*, for horn and strings |
| 1945 | (40) | *Phantasy*, for flute, horn and strings |
| 1948 | (43) | *Johnny Miner*, radio opera |
| | | String Quartet No 3, *Quartetto lyrico* (1948–51) |
| 1949 | (44) | *Ulysses*, cantata (possibly 1946–7) |
| | | *Andantino and Pastorale*, for clarinet and piano |
| 1951 | (46) | *The Seasons*, for orchestra |
| | | *Concertino*, for clarinet and strings |
| 1953 | (48) | Three Pieces for cello and orchestra |
| 1954 | (49) | *Elegy*, for violin and small orchestra |
| | | *To Poetry*, song cycle |
| 1958 | (53) | *Permutazione a cinque*, for flute, oboe, clarinet, horn and bassoon |
| | | *Portrait of the Artist as a Young Man*, chamber cantata |
| 1959 | (54) | *Improvisation for Jazz Band and Symphony Orchestra* (with Dankworth) |
| 1960 | (55) | *Invitation*, ballet |
| | | *A Three-cornered Fanfare* |

Performed posthumously:
| 1962 | | Violin Sonata |

## SESSIONS, Roger
*b Brooklyn, New York, 28 December 1896*

He entered Harvard at the age of fourteen and, after graduating, went on to Yale. He taught theory at Smith College from 1917 to 1921, then became Bloch's assistant at Cleveland Conservatory. From 1925 to 1933 he lived mainly in Europe, and returned to the USA to teach at Princeton from 1935 to 1944. He was professor of music at the University of California at Berkeley from 1944 to 1952, and at Princeton from 1953 to 1965. From 1966 to 1967 he was Bloch Professor at Berkeley, was Norton Professor at Harvard from 1968 to 1969, and taught at the Juillard School. He has received a great number of honours.

| 1923 | (27) | *The Black Maskers*, incidental music |
| 1927 | (31) | Symphony No 1 |
| 1930 | (34) | Piano Sonata No 1 |
| 1935 | (39) | Violin Concerto with orchestra which includes five clarinets but no violins |
| 1936 | (40) | String Quartet No 1 |
| 1938 | (42) | *Scherzino and March*, for orchestra |
| 1939 | (43) | *Pages from a Diary* (From My Diary), for piano |
| 1941–63 | (45–67) | *Montezuma*, opera |
| 1942 | (46) | Duo for violin and piano |
| 1944–6 | (48–50) | Symphony No 2 |
| 1946 | (50) | Piano Sonata No 2 |
| 1947 | (51) | *fp The Trial of Lucullus*, opera |
| 1951 | (55) | String Quartet No 2 |
| 1953 | (57) | Sonata for solo violin |
| 1954 | (58) | *The Idyll of Theocritus*, for soprano and orchestra |

| 1955 | (59) | Mass for unison male voices and organ |
|------|------|---------------------------------------|
| 1956 | (60) | Piano Concerto |
| 1957 | (61) | Symphony No 3 |
| 1958 | (62) | Symphony No 4 |
|      |      | String Quintet |
| 1960 | (64) | Divertimento for orchestra |
| 1963 | (67) | *Psalm 140*, for soprano with organ or orchestra |
| 1964 | (68) | Symphony No 5 |
| 1965 | (69) | Piano Sonata No 3 |
| 1966 | (70) | Symphony no 6 |
|      |      | Six Pieces for cello |
| 1967 | (71) | Symphony No 7 |
| 1968 | (72) | Symphony No 8 |
| 1970 | (74) | *Rhapsody*, for orchestra |
|      |      | *When Lilacs Last in the Dooryard Bloom'd*, cantata |
| 1971 | (75) | Concerto for viola and cello |
| 1971–2 | (75–6) | Three Choruses on Biblical Texts |
| 1972 | (76) | Concertino for chamber orchestra |
| 1975 | (79) | Five Pieces for chamber orchestra |
| 1982 | (86) | Concerto for orchestra |
| Undated |   | Symphony No 9 |
|      |      | Concertino for chamber orchestra |
|      |      | *Turn, O Libertad*, for chorus and orchestra |
|      |      | *Idyll of Theocritus*, for soprano and orchestra |

## SHAPERO, Harold
*b Lynn, Massachusetts, 29 April 1920*

He first studied at Malkin Conservatory in Boston, then under Piston and Křenek, at Harvard, and with Hindemith and Boulanger. He was professor at Brandeis University, and from 1970 to 1971 was composer-in-residence at the American Academy in Rome.

| 1938 | (18) | *Three Pieces for Three Pieces*, for woodwind trio |
|------|------|---------------------------------------------------|
| 1939 | (19) | Trumpet Sonata |
| 1940 | (20) | String Quartet |
| 1941 | (21) | *Nine-minute Overture* |
|      |      | Piano Sonata (four hands) |
| 1942 | (22) | Violin Sonata |
| 1944 | (24) | *Three Amateur Sonatas*, for piano |
| 1945 | (25) | Serenade in D major for string orchestra |
| 1947 | (27) | Piano Sonata No 1 |
| 1948 | (28) | Symphony for classical orchestra |
|      |      | *The Travellers*, for orchestra |
| 1951–8 | (31–8) | Concerto for orchestra |
| 1954 | (34) | *Poems of Halevi*, cantata |
| 1955 | (35) | *Credo*, for orchestra |
| 1958 | (38) | *On Green Mountain*, for jazz combo |
| 1960 | (40) | Partita, for piano and orchestra |
| 1968 | (48) | Three Improvisations for piano and synthesizer |
| 1969 | (49) | Three Studies for piano and synthesizer |

Shapero has also composed:
*Pocahontas*, ballet
*The Minotaurs*, ballet
*The Defence of Corinth*, for men's voices and piano (four hands)
*Emblems*, for men's voices

*Hebrew Cantata*
Sinfonia in C major
Variations in C major, for piano


## SHAPEY, Ralph
*b Philadelphia, 12 March 1921*

He began his violin studies at the age of seven. His work has been mainly as a conductor and as professor of music at the University of Chicago.

| | |
|---|---|
| 1946 (25) | String Quartet No 1 |
| | Piano Sonata |
| 1947 (26) | Piano Quintet |
| 1949 (28) | String Quartet No 2 |
| | *Three Essays on Thomas Wolfe*, for piano |
| 1950 (29) | Violin Sonata |
| 1951 (30) | *Fantasy*, for orchestra |
| | String Quartet No 3 |
| | Cantata, for soprano, tenor, bass, narrator, chamber orchestra and percussion |
| 1952 (31) | Symphony No 1 |
| | Quartet for oboe and string trio |
| | Oboe Sonata |
| | Suite for piano |
| 1953 (32) | String Quartet No 4 |
| | Cello Sonata |
| 1954 (33) | Concerto for clarinet, with violin, cello, piano, horn, tom-tom and bass drum |
| | *Sonata Variations*, for piano |
| 1955 (34) | *Challenge – The Family of Man*, for orchestra |
| | Piano Trio |
| 1956 (35) | *Mutations No 1* for piano |
| 1957 (36) | String Quartet No 5, with female voices (1957–8) |
| | *Rhapsodie*, for oboe and piano |
| | Duo for viola and piano |
| 1958 (37) | *Ontogeny*, for orchestra |
| | *Walking Upright*, eight songs for female voice and violin |
| 1959 (38) | Violin Concerto |
| | *Rituals*, for orchestra |
| | *Soliloquy*, for narrator, string quartet and percussion |
| | *Evocation*, for violin, piano and percussion |
| | *Form*, for piano |
| 1960 (39) | *Dimensions*, for soprano and twenty-three instruments |
| | *De Profundis*, for solo double-bass and instruments |
| | *Movements*, for woodwind quartet |
| | *Five*, for violin and piano |
| | *This Day*, for female voice and piano |
| 1961 (40) | *Incantations*, for soprano and ten instruments |
| | *Discourse*, for flute, clarinet, violin and piano |
| 1962 (41) | *Chamber Symphony*, for ten solo players |
| | *Convocation*, for chamber group |
| | *Piece*, for violin and instruments |
| | *Birthday Piece*, for piano |
| 1963 (42) | Brass Quintet |
| | String Quartet No 6 |
| | *Seven*, for piano (four hands) |

| 1965 (44) | String Trio |
| | *Configurations*, for flute and piano |
| 1966 (45) | Partita for violin and thirteen players |
| | *Poème*, for violin and piano |
| | *Mutations* No 2 for piano |
| | Partita for solo violin |
| 1967 (46) | *Partita-Fantasy*, for cello and sixteen players |
| | *Reyem*, for flute, violin and piano |
| | *Deux*, for two pianos |
| | *For Solo Trumpet* |
| | *Songs of Ecstasy*, for soprano, piano, percussion and tape |
| 1971 (50) | *Praise*, for baritone, double chorus and ensemble |
| 1972 (51) | Violin Sonata |
| 1973 (52) | Thirty-one Variations for piano |
| 1975 (54) | *Songs of Eros*, for soprano and orchestra |
| | *Oh Jerusalem*, for soprano and flute |
| 1980 (59) | *Song of Songs II*, for baritone, ensemble and tape |
| | *Song of Songs III*, for soprano, baritone, ensemble and tape |
| | Four Etudes for violin |
| 1981 (60) | Fanfare for brass quintet |

## SHCHEDRIN, Rodion Konstantinovich
*b Moscow, 16 December 1932*

He is the son of a music theorist and writer. In 1948 he enrolled in the Moscow Choral School and began to compose, and in 1951 went to the Moscow Conservatory, graduating in 1955 with honours. He is one of the most prominent Soviet composers, though his work is rarely heard in the West.

| 1951 (19) | *The Story of a Real Man*, symphonic poem |
| 1952 (20) | Piano Quintet |
| 1953 (21) | *The Twenty-Eight*, cantata |
| 1954 (22) | Piano Concerto No 1 |
| 1956 (24) | *The Little Humpbacked Horse*, ballet |
| 1956–8 (24–6) | Symphony No 1 |
| 1961 (29) | *Not Love Alone*, opera |
| | Chamber Suite |
| 1963 (31) | Concerto for orchestra, No 1 |
| | *Bureaucratadia*, cantata |
| 1965 (33) | *Solfeggi*, song cycle |
| | Symphony No 2 |
| 1966 (34) | Piano Concerto No 2 |
| 1967 (35) | Concerto for orchestra, No 2 |
| 1968 (36) | *Carmen*, ballet |
| | *Poetoria*, for soli, chorus and orchestra |
| 1972 (40) | *Anna Karenina*, ballet |
| | *Lenin Lives*, cantata |
| 1973 (41) | Symphonic Fanfares |
| 1981 (49) | *Supplice de Pougatchev*, for choir a cappella |
| | *Stanzas from Eugene Onegin*, for choir a cappella |
| | *The Frescoes of Dionysys*, for nine instruments |
| | *Notebook for Youth*, fifteen pieces for piano |
| 1982 (50) | Solemn Overture |
| | Concertino for chorus a cappella |

Shchedrin has also composed incidental music and film scores, three string quartets, and works for piano.

## SHOSTAKOVICH, Dmitri
b St Petersburg, 25 September 1906
d Moscow, 9 August 1975, aged sixty-eight

His parents were both musical and intellectual. His mother taught him piano from the age of nine; he entered the St Petersburg Conservatory in 1916 and became an outstanding pianist. His compositions received good reception from audiences, but from 1927 they were criticised by the Soviet authorities as not being sufficiently idealistic. *Pravda* bitterly attacked his opera *Lady Macbeth of the Mtsensk District* in 1936, and as one result he withdrew his Fourth Symphony, written in that year; it was not performed until 1961. However, with his Fifth Symphony he returned to the forefront of Soviet music. He taught at the Moscow Conservatory from 1942; but in 1948 he again displeased the authorities with so-called non-Soviet works. From then on he wrote on two levels; a private one, and one acceptable to Soviet ideology. He received the Stalin Prize and the Lenin Prize, travelled abroad a good deal, and was given an honorary doctorate by Oxford University. In the 1960s his health began to give serious cause for anxiety. Heart trouble was diagnosed, but nevertheless he continued writing until the end.

| | |
|---|---|
| 1919 (13) | Scherzo in F♯ minor for orchestra |
| | Eight Preludes for piano |
| 1920–1 (14–15) | Five Preludes for piano |
| 1921–2 (15–16) | Theme with Variations, in B major for orchestra |
| 1922 (16) | *Two Fables of Krilov*, for mezzo-soprano and orchestra |
| | *Three Fantastic Dances*, for piano |
| | Suite in F♯ minor for two pianos |
| 1923 (17) | Piano Trio No 1 |
| 1924 (18) | Symphony No 1 in F minor (1924–5) |
| | Scherzo in E♭ for orchestra |
| | Prelude and Scherzo for string octet (double string quartet) or string orchestra (1924–5) |
| 1926 (20) | Piano Sonata No 1 |
| 1927 (21) | *The Nose*, opera (1927–8) |
| | *The Age of Gold*, ballet (1927–30) |
| | Symphony No 2 in B major, *October*, with chorus |
| | *Aphorisms*, ten pieces for piano |
| 1928 (22) | *New Babylon*, for orchestra (film music) |
| | *Six Romances on Words by Japanese poets*, for tenor and orchestra (1928–32) |
| 1929 (23) | Symphony No 3 in E♭ major, *The First of May*, with chorus |
| 1930 (24) | *The Bolt*, choreographic spectacle (1930–1) |
| | *Alone*, film music (1930–1) |
| | *Lady Macbeth of the Mtsensk District*, opera (1930–2) |
| 1931–2 (25–6) | *Hamlet*, incidental music |
| 1932 (26) | *From Karl Marx to Our Own Days*, symphonic poem for solo voices, chorus and orchestra |
| | *Encounter*, film music |
| | Twenty-four Preludes for piano (1932–3) |
| 1933 (27) | Piano Concerto No 1 in C minor, for piano, string orchestra and trumpet |
| | *The Human Comedy*, incidental music (1933–4) |
| 1934 (28) | *Bright Stream*, comedy ballet (1934–5) |
| | Suite for jazz orchestra, No 1 |
| | Cello Sonata in D minor |
| | *Girl Companions*, film music (1934–5) |
| | *Love and Hate*, film music |

|  |  |
|---|---|
|  | *Maxim's Youth (The Bolshevik)*, film music (1934–5) |
| 1935 (29) | Symphony No 4 in C minor (1935–6) |
|  | Five Fragments for small orchestra |
| 1936 (30) | *Salute to Spain*, incidental music |
|  | *Four Romances on Verses of Pushkin*, for bass and piano |
|  | *Maxim's Return*, film music |
|  | *Volochayevka Days*, film music |
| 1937 (31) | Symphony No 5 in D minor |
| 1938 (32) | Suite for jazz orchestra, No 2 |
|  | String Quartet No 1 in C major |
|  | *Friends*, film music |
|  | *The Great Citizen*, film music |
|  | *Man at Arms*, film music |
|  | *Vyborg District*, film music |
| 1939 (33) | Symphony No 6 in B minor |
|  | *The Great Citizen*, Part II, film music |
| 1940 (34) | Piano Quintet in G minor |
|  | Three Pieces for solo violin |
|  | *King Lear*, incidental music |
| 1941 (35) | Symphony No 7 in C major, *Leningrad* |
|  | *The Gamblers*, opera |
| 1942 (36) | *Native Leningrad*, suite included in the theatre show *Motherland* |
|  | Piano Sonata No 2 |
|  | *Six Romances on Verses of English poets*, for bass and piano |
| 1943 (37) | Symphony No 8 in C minor |
| 1944 (38) | *Russian River*, suite |
|  | String Quartet No 2 in A major |
|  | Piano Trio No 2 |
|  | *Children's Notebook*, six pieces for piano |
|  | *Eight English and American Folk Songs*, for low voice and orchestra |
|  | *Zoya*, film music |
| 1945 (39) | Symphony No 9 in E♭ major |
|  | Two Songs |
|  | *Simple Folk*, film music |
| 1946 (40) | String Quartet No 3 in F major |
| 1947 (41) | Violin Concerto No 1 (1947–8) |
|  | *Poem of the Motherland*, cantata |
|  | *Pirogov*, film music |
|  | *Young Guards*, film music |
| 1948 (42) | *From Jewish Folk Poetry*, song cycle for soprano, contralto, tenor and piano |
|  | *Meeting on the Elbe*, film music |
|  | *Michurin*, film music |
| 1949 (43) | Ballet Suite No 1 for orchestra |
|  | String Quartet No 4 in D major |
|  | *The Song of the Forests*, oratorio |
|  | *The Fall of Berlin*, film score |
| 1950 (44) | Twenty-four Preludes and Fugues for piano (1950–1) |
|  | *Two Romances on Verses by Mikhail Lermontov*, for male voice and piano |
|  | *Byelinski*, film music |
| 1951 (45) | Ballet Suite No 2 for orchestra |
|  | *Ten Poems on Texts by Revolutionary poets*, for chorus a cappella |
|  | *The Memorable Year 1919*, film music |
| 1952 (46) | Ballet Suite No 3 for orchestra |
|  | String Quartet No 5 in B♭ major |

|  | *Four Monologues on Verses of Pushkin*, for bass and piano |
|  | *The Sun Shines over Our Motherland*, cantata |
| 1953 (47) | Symphony No 10 in E minor |
|  | Ballet suite No 4 for orchestra |
|  | Concertino for two pianos |
| 1954 (48) | *Festival Overture*, for orchestra |
|  | *Five Romances (Songs of our Days)*, for bass and piano |
| 1955 (49) | *The Gadfly*, film music |
| 1956 (50) | *Katerina Ismailova*, opera (new version of *Lady Macbeth of the Mtsensk District*) |
|  | String Quartet No 6 in G major |
|  | *Spanish Songs*, for soprano and piano |
|  | *The First Echelon*, film music |
| 1957 (51) | Piano Concerto No 2 in F major |
|  | Symphony No 11 in G minor, *The Year 1905* |
| 1958 (52) | *Moscow, Cheremushki*, musical comedy |
| 1959 (53) | Cello Concerto No 1 in E♭ major |
| 1960 (54) | *Novorossiysk Chimes (The Fire of Eternal Glory)*, for orchestra |
|  | String Quartet No 7 in F♯ minor |
|  | String Quartet No 8 in C minor |
|  | *Satires (Pictures of the Past)*, for soprano and piano |
|  | *Five Days – Five Nights*, film music |
| 1961 (55) | Symphony No 12 in D minor, *1917* |
| 1962 (56) | Symphony No 13 in B♭ minor, *Babi-Yar*, for bass solo, bass choir and orchestra |
| 1963 (57) | Overture on Russian and Kirghiz Folk Themes for orchestra |
|  | *Hamlet*, film music |
| 1964 (58) | String Quartet No 9 in E♭ major |
|  | String Quartet No 10 in A♭ major |
|  | *The Execution of Stepan Razin*, cantata |
| 1965 (59) | *Five Romances on Texts from 'Krokodil' magazine*, for bass and piano |
| 1966 (60) | Cello Concerto No 2 in G major |
|  | String Quartet No 11 in F minor |
|  | *Preface to the Complete Collection of my Works, and Brief Reflections apropos this Preface*, for bass and grand piano |
| 1967 (61) | Violin Concerto No 2 in C♯ minor |
|  | *Funeral-Triumphal Prelude*, for orchestra |
|  | *October*, symphonic poem |
|  | *Spring, Spring*, for bass and grand piano |
|  | *Sofya Perovoskaya*, film music |
|  | *Seven Romances on Poems of Alexander Blok*, for soprano and piano trio |
| 1968 (62) | String Quartet No 12 in D♭ major |
|  | Sonata for violin and grand piano |
| 1969 (63) | Symphony No 14, for soprano, bass, string orchestra and percussion |
| 1970 (64) | *March of the Soviet Militia*, for wind orchestra |
|  | String Quartet No 13 in B♭ minor |
|  | *Loyalty*, eight ballads for male chorus |
|  | *King Lear*, film music |
| 1971 (65) | Symphony No 15 in A major |
| 1972–3 (66–7) | String Quartet No 14 in F♯ major |
| 1973 (67) | *Six Poems of Marina Tsvetaeva*, suite for contralto and piano |
| 1974 (68) | String Quartet No 15 in E♭ minor |
|  | *Suite on Verses of Michelangelo Buonarroti*, for bass and piano |
|  | *Four Verses of Capitan Lebjadkin*, for bass and piano |

1975 (69)     Sonata for viola and grand piano
              *The Dreamers*, ballet (largely drawn from *The Age of Gold* and *The Bolt*, with some new material)

It is believed that Shostakovich had completed two movements of Symphony No 16 just before his death, but this has not so far been confirmed by the Soviet authorities.


## SIBELIUS, Jean
*b Hämeenlinna, Finland, 8 December 1865*
*d Järvenpää, 20 September 1957, aged ninety-one*

His father was a doctor who died of cholera when Jean was two. As a child he studied violin. Later he went to Helsinki to study law, and there met Busoni with whom he made a life-long friendship. He graduated in 1889, went to Berlin and Vienna for further musical studies, and finally returned to Finland in 1891. His acceptance as Finland's leading composer was immediate, and his music showed the powerful impact that Finnish mythology made upon him. His fame spread and he toured Germany and England, conducting his own music. He was seriously ill with suspected throat cancer in 1908 and had a series of operations. On his recovery he travelled as a conductor again. In 1912 he was offered the chair of composition at the Vienna Imperial Academy of Music; and in 1914 he was given an honorary doctorate at Yale as a climax of his visit to the USA. In the mid-1920s he retired from active composition, apart from writing his Eighth Symphony, which he completed in 1929 and subsequently destroyed. He died of a cerebral haemorrhage.

1881–2 (16–17) Piano Trio in F minor
              Piano Quartet in E minor
1885 (20)     String Quartet in E♭ major
1888 (23)     Theme and Variations for quartet in C♯ minor
1889 (24)     Piano Quintet
              Quartet in B♭ major
              Suite for violin, viola and cello
              Violin Sonata in F major
1890–1 (25–6) Overture in A minor
              Overture in E major
1891 (26)     *Scène de ballet*
              Piano Quartet in C major
1892 (27)     *En Saga*, symphonic poem (revised 1901)
              *Kullervo*, symphonic poem
1893 (28)     *Karelia*, overture
              *Karelia*, suite, for orchestra
              *The Swan of Tuonela*, for orchestra (No 3 of the *Four Legends from Kalevala*)
1894 (29)     *Spring Song*, symphonic poem
1895 (30)     *Cassazione*, for orchestra (unpublished)
              *Lemminkäinen and the Maidens* (No 1 of the *Four Legends from Kalevala*)
              *Lemminkäinen in Tuonela* (No 2 of the *Four Legends from Kalevala*)
              *Lemminkäinen's Homecoming* (No 4 of the *Four Legends from Kalevala*)
1896 (31)     *The Girl in the Tower*, opera (unpublished)
1898 (33)     *King Christian II*, incidental music
              Symphony No 1 in E minor (1898–9)
1899 (34)     *Scènes historiques*, Suite No 1, three orchestral pieces
1900 (35)     *Finlandia*, symphonic poem

| 1901 (36) | Symphony No 2 in D major |
| | *Cortège*, for orchestra (unpublished) |
| | *Portraits*, for strings |
| 1902 (37) | *The Origin of Fire*, for baritone, male voices and orchestra (revised 1910) |
| 1903 (38) | Violin Concerto in D minor (revised 1905) |
| | *Romance*, for strings |
| 1904 (39) | *Kuolema*, incidental music, includes 'Valse Triste' |
| | Symphony No 3 in C major (1904–07) |
| 1905 (40) | *Pelléas et Mélisande*, incidental music |
| | *Not With Lamentations*, for mixed voices |
| 1906 (41) | *Pohjola's Daughter*, symphonic fantasy |
| | *The Liberated Queen*, cantata for mixed voices and orchestra |
| 1907 (42) | *Balshazzar's Feast*, suite for orchestra |
| | *Night-ride and Sunrise*, tone poem |
| 1908 (43) | String Quartet in five movements, *Voces Intimae* |
| 1911 (46) | Symphony No 4 in A minor |
| | *Rakastava Suite*, for orchestra |
| | *Valse romantique*, for orchestra |
| | *Canzonetta*, for strings |
| 1912 (47) | *Scènes historiques*, Suite No 2, three orchestral pieces |
| | Two Serenades for violin (1912–13) |
| 1913 (48) | *Scaramouche*, pantomime |
| | *Il Bardo*, symphonic poem |
| 1914 (49) | *Oceanides*, symphonic poem |
| | Symphony No 5 in E♭ major (1914–15) |
| 1916 (51) | *Everyman*, incidental music |
| 1917 (52) | *Humoresques*, for violin and orchestra |
| 1918 (53) | *Our Native Land*, cantata for mixed voices and orchestra |
| 1919 (54) | *Song of the Earth*, cantata for mixed voices and orchestra |
| | *Scène pastorale*, for orchestra |
| 1920 (55) | *Hymn of the Earth*, cantata for mixed voices and orchestra |
| | *Valse lyrique*, for orchestra |
| | *Valse chevaleresque*, for orchestra |
| 1921 (56) | *Suite mignonne*, for flute and strings |
| | *Suite champêtre*, for strings |
| 1922 (57) | *Suite caractéristique* (Vivo, Lento, Commodo) |
| 1923 (58) | Symphony No 6 in D minor |
| 1924 (59) | Symphony No 7 in C major, in one movement |
| 1925 (60) | *Tapiola*, symphonic poem |
| 1926 (61) | *The Tempest*, incidental music |
| 1929 (64) | Symphony No 8 (destroyed) |

Sibelius also wrote other incidental music, songs, vocal works, chamber, instrumental and piano works.


### SIEGMEISTER, Elie
*b New York, 15 January 1909*

He studied at Columbia College, and with Boulanger in Paris. He has appeared as a conductor and lecturer, and taught at Hofstra University.

| 1932 (23) | Theme and Variations for piano |
| 1933 (24) | *American Holiday*, for orchestra |
| | *Strange Funeral in Braddock*, for orchestra |
| 1935 (26) | String Quartet No 1 |
| 1937 (28) | *Abraham Lincoln Walks at Midnight*, for orchestra |

| 1940 (31) | *Johnny Appleseed*, choral |
|---|---|
| 1943 (34) | *Ozark Set*, for orchestra |
| 1944 (35) | *Sing Out, Sweet Land*, musical |
| | *Prairie Legend*, for orchestra |
| | *As I Was Going Along*, choral |
| 1945 (36) | *Western Suite*, for orchestra |
| | *A Tooth for Paul Revere*, choral |
| 1946 (37) | *Lonesome Hollow*, for orchestra |
| | *Lazy Afternoon*, choral |
| | *Summer Day*, for band |
| 1947 (38) | *Summer Night*, for orchestra |
| | Symphony No 1 |
| 1949 (40) | *From My Window*, for orchestra |
| | *The New Colossus*, choral |
| 1950 (41) | Symphony No 2 |
| 1951 (42) | *Pastoral*, for band |
| 1952 (43) | *Darling Corrie*, opera |
| 1953 (44) | Divertimento for orchestra |
| 1955 (46) | *Miranda and the Dark Young Man*, opera |
| | *Hootenanny*, for band |
| 1956 (47) | Clarinet Concerto |
| 1957 (48) | Symphony No 3 |
| 1958 (49) | *The Mermaid in Lock No 7*, opera |
| 1959 (50) | *They Came to Cordura*, film score |
| 1960 (51) | Flute Concerto |
| | *Theater Set*, for orchestra |
| | String Quartet No 2 |
| 1963–9 (54–60) | *The Plough and the Stars*, opera |
| 1965 (56) | *In Our Time*, choral |
| | Sextet for brass and percussion |
| 1966 (57) | *Dick Whittington and his Cat*, orchestra |
| 1967 (58) | *I Have a Dream*, cantata |
| 1967–70 (58–61) | Symphony No 4 |
| 1968 (59) | Ballad for brass |
| 1971 (62) | Symphony No 5, *Visions of Time* |
| | *On This Ground*, for piano |
| 1973 (64) | String Quartet No 3 |
| 1974 (65) | Piano Concerto |
| | *A Cycle of Cities*, for soli, chorus, orchestra and dancers |
| 1974–6 (65–7) | *Night of the Moonspell*, opera |
| 1975 (66) | *Shadows and Light*, for orchestra |
| | String Quartet No 4 |
| 1975–6 (66–7) | *Fables from the Dark Wood*, ballet |
| 1976 (67) | *An Entertainment*, for violin, piano and orchestra |
| 1977–8 (68–9) | Violin Concerto |
| 1980 (71) | *Julietta*, opera |

Siegmeister has also written film scores and incidental music, several song cycles, and five sonata for violin and piano.


## SIMPSON, Robert
*b Leamington, Warwickshire, 2 March 1921*

He intended to become a doctor but gave up medicine after two years and studied music under Howells from 1942 to 1946. He joined the BBC music staff in 1951, staying until 1980. In 1951 he also received his DMus from Durham University.

1946 (25)   Piano Sonata
1948 (27)   *Variations and Finale on a Theme of Haydn*, for piano
1951 (30)   Symphony No 1
1951–2 (30–1) String Quartet No 1
1953 (32)   String Quartet No 2
1953–4 (32–3) String Quartet No 3
1956 (35)   Symphony No 2
1957–9 (36–8) Violin Concerto
1958 (37)   Canzona for brass
1959 (38)   Variations and Fugue for recorder and string quartet
1962 (41)   Symphony No 3
1967 (46)   Piano Concerto
            Trio for clarinet, cello and piano
1968 (47)   Clarinet Quintet
1971 (50)   *Energy*, symphonic study for brass band
1971–2 (50–1) Symphony No 4
1972 (51)   Symphony No 5
1973 (52)   String Quartet No 4
1974 (53)   String Quartet No 5
1975 (54)   String Quartet No 6
            *Media Morte* . . . motet for voices, brass and timpani
1976 (55)   Symphony No 6
            Quartet for horn and piano trio
1977 (56)   Symphony No 7
            String Quartet No 7
1979 (58)   String Quartet No 8
Simpson has also written books on the symphonies of various composers.


**SINDING, Christian August**
*b Konigsberg, Norway, 11 January 1856*
*d Oslo, 3 December 1941, aged eighty-five*

He trained as a violinist, but in 1874, when he went to Leipzig University, he abandoned violin for composition. He spent forty years in Germany, and from 1920 to 1921 was in the USA teaching theory and composition at the Eastman School.

1880 (24)   *Carmen nuptiale*, for voices and orchestra
1882–4 (26–8) Piano Quintet
1889 (33)   *Til molde*, for baritone, voices and piano
            *Konzertouverture*, for orchestra
            Piano Concerto
1900 (44)   *Sange*, for female voices and piano
            *Legende*, for violin and orchestra
1882–4 (26–8) Piano Quintet
1902 (46)   *Kantate ved abeljubilaeet*, for soli, chorus and orchestra
1904 (48)   *Mannamaal*, for male voices and orchestra
1909 (53)   *Kantate ved hundreaarsfesten*, for soli, chorus and orchestra
1910 (54)   *Romanze*, for violin and orchestra
1912 (56)   *Der heilige Berg*, opera
1914 (58)   *Jubilaeumskantate*, for soli, chorus and orchestra
1915 (59)   *Abendstimmung*, for violin and orchestra
Sinding also wrote other orchestral and piano works, much chamber music, and about 250 songs.

**SKALKOTTAS, Nickolaos**
*b Halkis, Evia, Greece, 21 March 1904*
*d Athens, 20 September 1949, aged forty-five*

He began studying violin at the age of five and entered the Athens Conservatory at ten, graduating in 1920. In 1921 a scholarship took him to the Hochschule für Musik in Berlin. In 1925 he gave up a promising career as a violinist to concentrate on composition, and studied privately until 1931, financially aided by a wealthy patron. But hard times followed, and he returned to Athens in 1933, poor and ill. He played back-desk violin in an orchestra and wrote in his spare time. He died of a strangulated hernia.

| | |
|---|---|
| 1924 (20) | String Trio (lost) |
| | String Quartet (lost) |
| 1925 (21) | Violin Sonata |
| 1927 (23) | Piano Sonatina |
| | Fifteen Little Variations for piano |
| 1928 (24) | String Quartet No 1 |
| | Sonata No 1 for violin and piano (lost) |
| | Symphonic Suite (lost) |
| 1929 (25) | Concerto for wind (lost) |
| | Little Suite for violin and chamber orchestra (lost) |
| | String Quartet No 2 (lost) |
| | *Easy Music*, for string quartet (lost) |
| | Sonatina No 1 for violin and piano |
| | Octet for flute, clarinet, bassoon, trumpet, trombone and piano trio (lost) |
| | Sonatina No 2 for violin and piano |
| 1930 (26) | Concerto for piano, violin and chamber orchestra (lost) |
| 1931 (27) | Piano Concerto No 1 |
| | Octet for woodwind quartet and string quartet |
| 1931–6 (27–32) | Thirty-six Greek Dances for orchestra |
| 1935 (31) | Concertino for two pianos and orchestra |
| | Symphonic Suite No 1 |
| | String Quartet No 3 |
| | String Trio |
| | Sonatina No 3 for violin and piano |
| | Sonatina No 4 for violin and piano |
| 1936 (32) | Piano Trio |
| | Piano Suite No 1 |
| 1937–8 (33–4) | Piano Concerto No 2 |
| | Violin Concerto |
| | Five Pieces for violin and piano |
| | Suite for cello and piano (lost) |
| 1938 (34) | Cello Concerto (lost) |
| | *The Maiden and Death*, ballet |
| | Duo for violin and viola |
| | Eight Variations on a Greek Folk Song, for piano trio |
| 1938–9 (34–5) | Piano Concerto No 3 |
| 1939 (35) | Three Pieces for violin and piano |
| | Concertino for oboe and piano |
| 1939–40 (35–6) | Concerto for violin, viola, wind and double-bass |
| | Scherzo for piano quartet |
| 1940 (36) | Ten Musical Sketches for string quartet |
| | Piano Suites No 2, 3 and 4 |
| | Sonata No 2 for violin and piano |
| | String Quartet No 4 |

1940–1 (36–7) Thirty-two Piano Pieces
              Four Piano Studies
1940–2 (36–8) Two Quartets for oboe, bassoon, trumpet and piano
              Concertino for trumpet and piano
1941–2 (37–8) *Largo*, for cello and piano
1942 (38)     Little Suite for strings
1942–3 (38–9) *The Return of Ulysses*, overture
              Double-bass Concerto
1943 (39)     Sonata Concertante for bassoon and piano
1944 (40)     Symphonic Suite No 2
1944–5 (40–1) Concerto for two violins (piano arrangement only)
1945 (41)     *Mikri Serenata*, for cello and piano
              *Bolero*, for cello and piano
1946 (42)     Little Suite No 2 for violin and piano
1947 (43)     *Four Parties*, for violin and cello
              *Classic Symphony*
1947–8 (43–4) *Henry V*, incidental music (lost)
1948 (44)     Sinfonietta
              Piano Concertino
1948–9 (44–5) Little Dance Suite for orchestra
1949 (45)     *Nocturne-Divertimento*, for xylophone and orchestra
              *The Sea*, for orchestra
              Sonatina for cello and piano
              *Zarte Melodie*, for cello and piano
Skalkottas also wrote some choral works and songs.


## SKRIABIN, Alexander
*b Moscow, 6 January 1872*
*d Moscow, 27 April 1915, aged forty-three*

He spent nine years in the Moscow Army Cadet Corps, where music was one of
the subjects studied. He entered the Moscow Conservatory in 1888, but left
without a diploma. He then made a concert tour as a pianist from 1895–1896,
and in 1898 became professor of piano at the Moscow Conservatory, resigning
in 1903 in order to live in Switzerland and compose. He went back to Russia in
1909 and in 1910 toured extensively. He died suddenly of a tumour on the lip.

1894 (22)     Piano Concerto
              *Rêverie*, for orchestra
1895 (23)     Symphony No 1 in E major
1901 (29)     Symphony No 2 in C minor
1903 (31)     Symphony No 3 in C major, *The Divine Poem*
1908 (36)     *Poem of Ecstasy*, for orchestra
1909–10 (37–8) *Poem of Fire – Prometheus*, for orchestra, piano, chorus *ad lib*,
              organ and colour keyboard
Skriabin also composed: ten piano sonatas (1892–1913); eighty-four preludes for
piano; twenty-one mazurkas for piano; eight impromptus for piano; twenty-
three studies for piano; fifteen 'poems' for piano.


## SMETANA, Bedřich
*b Litomyšl, Bohemia, 2 March 1824*
*d Prague, 12 May 1884, aged sixty*

The son of a keen amateur musician, at the age of five he played first violin in a
Haydn quartet and gave a public piano recital when he was six. He studied
composition and theory in Prague, and was appointed resident piano teacher to

325

the family of Count Leopold Thun. During that time he met Berlioz and the Schumanns. In 1847, unable to establish himself as a piano virtuoso, he decided to open his own music school; he wrote to Liszt for advice and a loan, but Liszt sent only advice. The school opened in 1848, and in that year political upheavals sparked off his nationalistic fervour. For the next eight years he made little progress; his wife showed symptoms of tuberculosis and in 1855 three of his four daughters died. He moved to Göteborg in Sweden, where he found immediate success as a conductor, pianist and teacher. His wife died in 1859, and he married again in 1860. The political situation in Prague suddenly changed for the better, so he returned there in 1861. Despite further political unrest and official hostility, and the deafness that overtook him in 1874, he continued writing. He died of syphilis.

1848–9 (24–5) *Festive Overture*, in D major
1853–4 (29–30) *Festive Symphony*, in E major
1855 (31)     Piano Trio in G minor
1858 (34)     *Richard III*, symphonic poem
              *Wallenstein's Camp*, symphonic poem (1858–9)
1860–1 (36–7) *Haakon Jarl*, symphonic poem
1862 (38)     *On the Sea-shore*, for piano
1863 (39)     *The Brandenburgers in Bohemia*, opera
1866 (42)     *The Bartered Bride*, opera
1868 (44)     fp *Dalibor*, opera
              Solemn Prelude in C major for orchestra
1874 (50)     *The Two Widows*, opera
              *Má Vlast*, six symphonic poems:
                  *Vyšehrad (The High Castle)*
                  *Vltava*
                  *Sàrka*
                  *From Bohemia's Woods and Fields*
                  *Tabor*
                  *Blanik*
1876 (52)     *The Kiss*, opera
              String Quartet No 1, *From My Life*, in E minor
1878 (54)     *The Secret*, opera
              *Czech Dances*
1881 (57)     fp *Libuse*, opera
1882 (58)     String Quartet No 2 in D minor
1883 (59)     *The Prague Carnival*
              String Quartet No 3

## SMYTH, (Dame) Ethel
*b London, 22 April 1858*
*d Woking, Surrey, 9 May 1944, aged eighty-six*

She was born into a prosperous musical family. In 1877 she entered the Leipzig Conservatory, then had private tuition. Her worth as a composer was recognised quite early. Around 1909 she became involved with the suffragette movement. She wrote little music in her later years, partly due to increasing deafness, but continued to write excellent prose. She was given an honorary DMus from Durham University in 1910 and her DBE in 1922.

1887 (29)     Violin Sonata in A minor
1890 (32)     *Anthony and Cleopatra*, overture
              Serenade in D major for orchestra
1891 (33)     Suite for strings
1893 (35)     Mass in D major

| 1898 | (40) | Fantastic, opera |
| 1901 | (43) | The Forest, opera |
| 1902 | (44) | String Quartet in E minor (completed c1912) |
| 1906 | (48) | The Wreckers, opera |
| 1911 | (53) | March of the Women, for orchestra |
| | | Three Songs of Sunrise, for unaccompanied chorus |
| 1916 | (58) | The Boatswain's Mate, opera |
| 1920 | (62) | Dreamings, for chorus |
| 1923 | (65) | Fête galante, opera |
| | | Soul's Joy, for unaccompanied chorus |
| 1926 | (68) | Entente Cordiale, opera |
| | | A Spring Canticle, for chorus and orchestra |
| | | Sleepless Dreams, for chorus and orchestra |
| 1927 | (69) | Concerto for violin and horn (also known as Horn Concerto) |
| 1930 | (72) | The Prison, for soprano, baritone, chorus, and orchestra |

## SOR, Fernando
*b Barcelona, baptised 14 February 1778*
*d Paris, 10 July 1839, aged sixty-one*

He was educated at the Choir School of the monastery of Montserrat, then attended the military academy in Barcelona. In 1799 he moved to Madrid, holding administrative posts until 1808. In 1815 he moved to London, and in 1823 he went to Russia to see the performance of his ballet *Cendrillon*. In 1826 he moved finally to Paris. He taught and played guitar until his death.

| 1797 | (19) | Telemaco, opera |
| | | Don Trastillo, opera (lost) |
| 1821 | (43) | Le Foire de Smyrne, ballet (lost) |
| | | Le Seigneur généreux, ballet (lost) |
| 1822 | (44) | Cendrillon, ballet |
| 1823 | (45) | L'Amant Peintre, ballet |
| 1826 | (48) | Hercule et Omphale, ballet |
| 1827 | (49) | Le Sicilien, ballet |
| 1828 | (50) | Hassan et le Calife, ballet (lost) |

Sor also wrote incidental music, many songs and pieces for guitar, two symphonies, three string quartets and other works.

## SOWERBY, Leo
*b Grand Rapids, Michigan, 1 May 1895*
*d Port Clinton, Ohio, 7 July 1968, aged seventy-three*

He studied piano, theory and organ in Chicago. During World War I he served in the Army as a bandmaster. In 1921 he received the Prix de Rome, which enabled him to spend three years in Italy. He returned to Chicago to teach composition at the American Conservatory from 1925 to 1962, and was also organist and choirmaster at St James' Cathedral from 1927 to 1962. In 1946 he won the Pulitzer Prize.

| 1916 | (21) | Woodwind Quintet |
| 1917 | (22) | Piano Concerto No 1 (revised 1919) |
| | | Serenade for string quartet |
| | | Comes Autumn Time, for organ |
| 1919 | (24) | Trio for flute, viola and piano |
| 1920 | (25) | Cello Sonata |
| | | The Edge of Dreams, song cycle |

| 1921 | (26) | Symphony No 1 |
| | | Violin Sonata No 1 |
| 1922 | (27) | *From the Northland*, for piano |
| | | *Ballad of King Estmere*, for two pianos and orchestra |
| 1924 | (29) | *Synconata*, for jazz orchestra |
| 1925 | (30) | *From the Northland*, for orchestra |
| | | *The Vision of Sir Launfal*, for chorus and orchestra |
| | | *Monotony*, for jazz orchestra |
| 1926 | (31) | *Mediaeval Poem*, for organ and orchestra |
| 1928 | (33) | Symphony No 2 |
| 1929 | (34) | Cello Concerto (1929–34) |
| | | *Prairie*, symphonic poem |
| | | *Florida Suite*, for piano |
| 1930 | (35) | Organ Symphony |
| 1931 | (36) | Passacaglia, Interlude and Fugue, for orchestra |
| 1932 | (37) | Piano Concerto No 2 |
| 1936 | (41) | Organ Concerto No 1 |
| 1938 | (43) | *Theme in Yellow*, for orchestra |
| | | Clarinet Sonata |
| 1939 | (44) | *Forsaken of Man*, cantata |
| 1940 | (45) | Symphony No 3 |
| 1941 | (46) | *Poem*, for viola with organ or orchestra |
| 1944 | (49) | *Classic Concerto*, for organ and strings |
| | | Violin Sonata No 2 |
| | | *Canticle of the Sun*, cantata |
| 1945 | (50) | Trumpet Sonata |
| 1947 | (52) | Symphony No 4 |
| 1949 | (54) | *Ballade*, for English horn and strings |
| 1950 | (55) | *Christ Reborn*, cantata |
| 1951 | (56) | *Concert Piece*, for organ and orchestra |
| 1952 | (57) | String Trio |
| 1954 | (59) | *All on a Summer's Day*, for orchestra |
| | | *Fantasy*, for trumpet and organ |
| 1957 | (62) | *The Throne of God*, for chorus and orchestra |
| 1959 | (64) | *Ark of the Covenant*, cantata |
| 1964 | (69) | Symphony No 5 |
| | | Piano Sonata |
| 1965 | (70) | *Solomon's Garden*, for chorus and orchestra |
| 1966 | (71) | *Symphonia brevis*, for organ |
| 1967 | (72) | *Dialogue*, for organ and piano |
| | | Organ Concerto No 2 |
| | | *Organ Passacaglia* |

Sowerby also composed over 300 songs.


**SPOHR, Ludwig (Louis)**
*b Brunswick, 5 April 1784*
*d Cassel, 22 October 1859, aged seventy-five*

While still in his teens he was employed as a violinist at the court of the Duke of Brunswick, who paid for his private tuition; and after a concert tour with his teacher, Eck, from 1802 to 1803, he returned to Brunswick a complete virtuoso. Most of his life was spent touring, playing his own works among others, save for the years 1805 to 1812 when he was appointed to the court of Gotha; 1812 to 1814, when he was musical director of the Theater an der Wien; 1817 to 1819, when he directed the opera at Frankfurt-am-Main; and from 1822 when he became musical director at the court of Cassel.

He wrote eleven operas; incidental music; nine symphonies and other orchestral works; fifteen violin concertos; four clarinet and six other concertos; thirty-six string quartets; much other chamber music and virtuoso solo work; sacred and secular choral works, oratorios and cantatas, and songs.


## SPONTINI, Gasparo
b Majolati, Italy, 14 November 1774
d Majolati, 24 January 1851, aged seventy-six

He studied at a music school in Naples and with Piccini. His operas were a success from the time he was twenty-two. In 1802 he left Italy for Paris, living there until 1819, taking French nationality and marrying a French wife. At first he received hostility from his critics, then acceptance, and the favours of Empress Josephine and Frederick William III of Prussia. The latter made him Kapellmeister at his court in 1820, where he met much opposition and where his output dwindled until he was pensioned off in 1842. He returned to his birthplace in Italy, his final years troubled by deafness.

| | | |
|---|---|---|
| 1807 | (33) | La Vestale, opera |
| 1809 | (35) | Ferdinand Cortez, opera |
| 1819 | (45) | Olympie, opera |
| 1821 | (47) | Nurmahal, opera |
| 1829 | (55) | Agnes von Hohenstaufen, opera |


## STAINER, (Sir) John
b London, 6 June 1840
d Verona, 31 March 1901, aged sixty

He was the son of a parish schoolmaster who taught him organ from an early age. He lost the sight of his left eye in an accident at the age of five. In 1848 he became a chorister at St Paul's Cathedral, and in 1854 an organist, first in London then in Tenbury. He entered Christ Church, Oxford, in 1859, where he obtained both music and arts degrees. In 1860 he was appointed organist of Magdalen College and in 1861 organist to the University. He returned to St Paul's as organist in 1872, but had to resign in 1888 because of failing eyesight. He was knighted in that year. In 1889 he returned to Oxford as professor of music, and held high office in many music societies and associations. He died suddenly while visiting Italy.

| | | |
|---|---|---|
| 1865 | (25) | Gideon, oratorio |
| 1878 | (38) | The Daughter of Jairus, cantata |
| 1887 | (47) | St Mary Magdalen, cantata |
| | | Jubilee, cantata |
| | | The Crucifixion, oratorio |
| 1893 | (53) | The Story of the Cross, cantata |

Stainer also wrote eight services and other church works, music for organ, madrigals, partsongs and songs.


## STAMITZ, Johann
b Německý Brod, baptised 19 June 1717
d Mannheim, 27 March 1757, aged thirty-nine

His early instruction was from his father. From 1728 to 1734 he attended the Jesuit Gymnasium in Jahlava, and from 1734 to 1735 he was at Prague University. He was appointed to the Mannheim court in 1741 as violin virtuoso, also playing viola d'amore, cello and double-bass. He advanced rapidly at court and by 1750 was created director of instrumental music. He married in 1744 and had five children, including the composers Karl and Anton. In 1754 he undertook a year-long journey to Paris, where his work was immensely successful.

He wrote: twenty-nine symphonies, ten orchestral trios, seventeen violin concertos and many concertos for other instruments, and other orchestral works; many chamber works and sacred choral works and songs. A great deal of his output has been lost.


## STAMITZ, Karl
*b Mannheim, baptised 8 May 1745*
*b Jena, 9 November 1801, aged fifty-six*

He was the son of Johann Stamitz, who was his first teacher. He was second violinist with the electoral orchestra at Mannheim from 1762 to 1770 and became a brilliant technician. In 1770 he went to Paris, gaining great success both as violinist and as composer, and from 1777 led the life of a travelling virtuoso. Despite his success he became completely impoverished, and his debts were so great that on his death his possessions had to be auctioned off.

He wrote: over fifty symphonies, thirty-eight symphonies concertantes, more than sixty concerti, a huge output of chamber music for which he is chiefly remembered, and some vocal works.


## STANFORD, (Sir) Charles Villiers
*b Dublin, 30 September 1852*
*d London, 29 March 1924, aged seventy-one*

He was the son of a lawyer who was also a keen amateur musician. Though intended for the legal profession, he was permitted to study music, and in 1870 he entered Queens' College, Cambridge, as a choral scholar. In 1873 he was appointed organist of Trinity College. After graduating in 1874 he spent two years studying abroad, coming home to the offer of leading appointments. At the opening of the Royal College of Music in 1883 he was made professor of composition, and from 1885 until 1902 he was conductor of the London Bach Choir. He was elected professor of music at Cambridge in 1887. He received many honours, including honorary degrees, and was knighted in 1902.

| | | |
|---|---|---|
| 1876 | (24) | Symphony in B♭ major |
| 1877 | (25) | *Festival Overture* |
| 1881 | (29) | *The Veiled Prophet*, opera |
| 1882 | (30) | *Elegiac Symphony*, in D minor |
| | | Serenade, in G major, for orchestra |
| 1884 | (32) | *Canterbury Pilgrims*, opera |
| | | *Savonarola*, opera |
| 1886 | (34) | *The Revenge*, choral-ballad |
| 1887 | (35) | *Queen of the Seas*, overture |
| | | *Irish Symphony* in F minor |
| | | Prelude *Oedipus Rex* |
| 1888 | (36) | Symphony in F major |
| 1891 | (39) | *Eden*, oratorio |
| 1894 | (42) | Symphony in D major, *L'Allegro ed il pensiero* |
| 1895 | (43) | Piano Concerto No 1 in G major |
| | | Suite of Ancient Dances |
| 1896 | (44) | *Shamus O'Brien*, opera |
| 1898 | (46) | *Te Deum* |

| 1899 (47) | Evening Service in C major |
|---|---|
| 1901 (49) | *Much Ado About Nothing*, opera |
| | *Irish Rhapsody* No 1 in D minor |
| 1904 (52) | Violin Concerto No 1 in D major |
| | Evening Service in G major |
| 1907 (55) | *Stabat Mater* |
| 1911 (59) | Symphony No 7 in D minor |
| 1914 (62) | *Irish Rhapsody* No 4 in A minor |
| 1915 (63) | Piano Concerto No 2 in C minor |
| 1916 (64) | *The Critic*, opera |

Performed posthumously:

| 1925 | *The Travelling Companion*, opera |
|---|---|

## STILL, Robert
*b London, 10 June 1910*
*d Bucklebury, Berkshire, 13 January 1971, aged sixty*

He was educated at Eton, at Trinity College, Oxford, from 1929 to 1932, and the Royal College of Music from 1932 to 1934. He did not start serious composing until after World War II. In 1963 he was given the Oxford DMus.

| 1954 (44) | Symphony No 1 |
|---|---|
| 1954–6 (44–6) | *Oedipus*, opera |
| 1956 (46) | *Ballad of the Bladebone Inn*, overture |
| | Symphony No 2 |
| 1960 (50) | Symphony No 3 |
| 1963 (53) | *Elegie*, for baritone, voices and small orchestra |
| 1964 (54) | Concerto for strings |
| | Symphony No 4 |
| 1969 (59) | Violin Concerto |
| 1970 (60) | Piano Concerto |

Still also composed:
Clarinet Quintet
Five string quartets
Oboe Quartet
Trio for flute, oboe and piano
Trio for clarinet, violin and piano
Three piano sonatas
Piano suite, *Other People*
Many songs and partsongs

## STOCKHAUSEN, Karlheinz
*b Cologne, 22 August 1928*

He studied from 1947 to 1951 at the State Hochschule für Musik in Cologne and then at the University of Cologne. He spent some years experimenting with electronic music, phonetics and communication, and in 1958 made his first tour of concert lectures in America and Canada. Since then he has made extended tours every year as conductor, performer and lecturer. He has held many professorial posts.

| 1950 (22) | *Chöre Für Doris*, three movements for mixed choir a cappella |
|---|---|
| | Three Lieder, for voice and chamber orchestra: 1) 'Der Rebell', 2) 'Frei', 3) 'Der Saitenmann' |
| | *Choral*, for mixed choir a cappella |
| 1951 (23) | Sonatine, for violin and piano |

|          | *Kreuzspiel*, for oboe, bass-clarinet, piano and percussion |
|          | *Formel*, for orchestra |
| 1952 (24) | *Étude*, musique concrète |
|          | *Spiel*, for orchestra |
|          | *Schlagtrio*, for piano and timpani |
|          | *Punkte*, for orchestra (1952–3) |
|          | *Kontrapunkte*, for ten instruments (1952–3) |
|          | *Klavierstücke* I–IV (1952–3) |
| 1953 (25) | *Elektronische Studie I*, electronic music |
| 1954 (26) | *Elektronische Studie II*, electronic music |
|          | *Klavierstücke* V–VIII (1954–5) |
|          | *Klavierstücke* IX–X (revised 1961) |
| 1955–6 (27–8) | *Gruppen*, for three orchestras (1955–7) |
|          | *Zeitmasze*, for oboe, flute, English horn, clarinet and bassoon |
|          | *Gesang der Jünglinge*, electronic music |
| 1956 (28) | *Klavierstücke* XI |
| 1959 (31) | *Carré*, for four orchestras and four choirs (1959–60) |
|          | *Refrain*, for piano, celesta and percussion |
|          | *Zyklus*, for one percussionist |
|          | *Kontakte*, for electronic sound (1959–60) |
| 1962–4 (34–6) | *Momente*, for soprano solo, four choral groups and thirteen instrumentalists |
| 1963 (35) | *Plus Minus*, 2 × 7 pages 'for working out' |
| 1964 (36) | *Mikrophonie I*, for mixed media |
|          | *Mixtur*, for five orchestral groups and electronics |
| 1965 (37) | *Mikrophonie II*, for choir, Hammond organ, electronic instruments and tape |
|          | *Stop*, for orchestra |
|          | *Solo*, for a melody instrument and tape (1965–6) |
| 1966 (38) | *Telemusik*, electronic music |
|          | *Adieu*, for flute, oboe, clarinet, horn and bassoon |
|          | *Hymnen*, for electronics and musique concrète (four-channel tape) |
| 1967 (39) | *Prozession*, for tam-tam, viola, elektronium, piano and electronics |
| 1968 (40) | *Stimmung*, for six vocalists |
|          | *Kurzwellen*, for piano, amplified instruments and electronics |
|          | *Aus den Sieben Tagen*, fifteen compositions for ensemble |
|          | *Spiral*, for one soloist with short-wave receiver |
|          | *Für Kommende Zeiten*, seventeen texts for intuitive music |
| 1969 (41) | *For Dr K.*, for flute, bass clarinet, percussion, piano, viola and cello |
|          | *Fresco*, for four orchestral groups |
|          | *Pole für 2* (1969–70) |
|          | *Expo für 3* (1969–70) |
| 1970 (42) | *Mantra*, for two pianists |
|          | *Sternklang*, for five groups |
|          | *Trans*, for orchestra |
| 1972 (44) | *Alphabet für Liège*, for soloists and duos |
|          | *Am Himmel Wandre Ich . . .*, Indianerlieder |
|          | *Ylem*, for nineteen players/singers |
| 1973–4 (45–6) | *Inori*, for soloist and orchestra |
| 1974 (46) | *Atmen gibt das Leben . . .*, for mixed choir |
|          | *Herbstmusik*, for four players |
|          | *Vortrag über Hu*, for solo voice |
| 1975 (47) | *Musik im Bauch*, for six percussionists |
|          | *Tierkreis (Zodiac)*, for various vocal and instrumental combinations |
| 1976 (48) | *Amour*, five pieces for clarinet |
|          | *Tierkreis*, for instruments |

| 1977 (49) | *Tierkreis*, for chamber orchestra |
| | *Jubiläum*, for orchestra |
| | *In Freundschaft*, for six instruments |
| | *Der Jahreslauf*, for dancers and orchestra |
| 1978 (50) | *Michaels Reise um die Erde*, for trumpet and orchestra |
| 1979 (51) | *Michaels Heimkehr*, for dancers, chorus and orchestra |

## STRAUSS, Johann (II)
*b Vienna, 25 October 1825*
*d Vienna, 3 June 1899, aged seventy-three*

His father, a great composer of waltzes, refused to allow him to enter the music profession; he worked first as a bank clerk, but studied violin and theory privately. At the age of nineteen he formed his own orchestra, and his fame quickly rivalled that of his father; he toured Europe and Russia, composing and playing his own dance music. A meeting with Offenbach in 1863 encouraged him to try his hand at operetta, and in that year too he was appointed director of the Imperial Court Balls in Vienna. His music was much loved by Brahms and Wagner, and his brothers Josef and Eduard and his nephew Johann all became great musicians.

| 1867 (42) | *Blue Danube Waltz* |
| 1868 (43) | *Tales from the Vienna Woods*, for orchestra |
| 1871 (46) | *Indigo und die verzig Räuber*, operetta |
| 1874 (49) | *Die Fledermaus*, operetta |
| 1883 (58) | *Eine Nacht in Venedig*, operetta |
| 1885 (60) | *Zigeunerbaron*, operetta |
| 1887 (62) | *Simplizius*, operetta |
| 1895 (70) | *Waldmeister*, operetta |

## STRAUSS, Richard
*b Munich, 11 June 1864*
*d Garmisch, 8 September 1949, aged eighty-five*

He was the son of a brilliant horn-player, and he himself took piano lessons from the age of four. He entered the University of Munich in 1882, studying philosophy and aesthetics while still continuing his music studies privately. He graduated in 1883, and in 1884 was made assistant musical director of the Meiningen Court Orchestra. He rose to become leading conductor, and soon was conductor of the Court Opera and Orchestra in Berlin, remaining so until 1908, when he was promoted to general musical director, a post he held until 1924. A meeting with the poet Hofmannsthal in 1900 resulted in a great operatic collaboration. From 1919 to 1924 he was director of the State Opera in Vienna; from then onward he had no permanent post but travelled extensively as a conductor. After Hofmannsthal's death in 1933 he wrote the libretti for his own operas. He fell foul of the Nazi regime, which disgraced him in 1935.

| 1876 (12) | *Festmarch*, for orchestra, Op 1 |
| 1879 (15) | Overture in A minor |
| 1880 (16) | Symphony in D minor |
| | String Quartet in A major |
| 1881–2 (17–18) | Violin Concerto in D minor |
| 1882–3 (18–19) | Horn Concerto No 1 in E♭ major |
| 1883 (19) | *Concert Overture* in C minor |
| | Piano Quartet in C minor (1883–4) |
| 1884 (20) | Symphony in F minor |

p *Serenade for Wind*
p Cello Sonata in F major
1886 (22)   *Aus Italien*, symphonic fantasia
            *Macbeth*, symphonic poem (1886–90)
1888 (24)   *Don Juan*, symphonic poem
            p Violin Sonata in Eb major
1889 (25)   *Tod und Verklärung*, symphonic poem
1892–3 (28–9) *Guntram*, opera (new version 1940)
1894 (30)   *Also sprach Zarathustra*, symphonic poem
1895 (31)   *Till Eulenspiegel*, symphonic poem
1896 (32)   *Don Quixote*, fantasy variations for cello and orchestra
1898 (34)   *Ein Heldenleben*, symphonic poem
1901 (37)   *Feuersnot*, opera
1904 (40)   *Symphonia Domestica*
1905 (41)   *Salome*, opera
1906–8 (42–4) *Elektra*, opera
1909–10 (45–6) *Der Rosenkavalier*, opera
1912 (48)   *Ariadne auf Naxos*, opera (first version)
1913 (49)   *Alpine Symphony*
1914 (50)   *Josephs-Legend*, ballet
            *Die Frau ohne Schatten*, opera (1914–17)
1921 (57)   *Schlagobers*, ballet
1922–3 (58–9) *Intermezzo*, opera
1924–7 (60–3) *The Egyptian Helen*, opera
1930–2 (66–8) *Arabella*, opera
1934 (70)   Symphony for wind instruments
1935 (71)   *The Silent Woman*, opera
            *Der Friedenstag*, opera (1935–6)
1936–7 (72–3) *Daphne*, opera
1938–40 (74–6) *The Love of Danae*, opera (*fp* 1952)
1940–1 (76–7) *Capriccio*, opera
1942 (78)   Horn Concerto No 2 in Eb major
1945 (81)   *Metamorphoses*, for twnety-three solo instruments
            Oboe Concerto
1948 (84)   Duet Concertino, for clarinet, bassoon and strings
Performed posthumously:
1950        Four Last Songs
Strauss also composed many songs.


**STRAVINSKY, Igor**
*b Oranienbaum, near St Petersburg, 17 June 1882*
*d New York, 6 April 1971, aged eighty-eight*

His father was a singer in the St Petersburg Imperial Opera. He learnt music as a child, but his parents refused to allow him a musical career. Instead, he went to St Petersburg University to study criminal law and legal philosophy; but he was discontented, and in 1902 asked the advice of Rimsky-Korsakov. Through him Stravinsky's work came to the attention of Diaghilev, who commissioned *Firebird*, and other ballets soon followed. He married in 1906, and at the beginning of World War I moved his family to Switzerland for health reasons; but the October Revolution in Russia meant the drying up of his finances and the confiscation of his property in Russia, so he remained in exile. He settled in France in 1920, conducting and playing piano for his livelihood, and in 1934 became a French citizen. He toured all over Europe and America until 1937. The years 1935 to 1939 were a period of ill-health, in which he lost his wife, his

334

mother and a daughter. He then left Europe for the USA, re-married there in 1940, and shortly after the end of the war became an American citizen. He resumed touring in his later years, visiting Russia for the first time since he left it forty-eight years earlier.

| | |
|---|---|
| 1898 (16) | Tarantella for piano |
| 1902 (20) | *Storm Cloud*, for voice and piano |
| | Scherzo for piano |
| 1904 (22) | Sonata in F# minor for piano |
| | Cantata for mixed choir and piano (lost) |
| | *The Mushrooms going to War*, for bass and piano |
| 1906 (24) | *Conductor and Tarantula*, for voice and piano (lost) |
| 1907 (25) | Symphony in Eb |
| | *Faun and Shepherdess*, for mezzo-soprano and orchestra |
| | Pastorale for soprano and piano |
| 1907–8 (25–6) | Two Songs for mezzo-soprano and piano |
| 1908 (26) | *Scherzo Fantastique*, for orchestra |
| | *Lament*, for orchestra |
| | *Fireworks*, for orchestra |
| | *Chant Funèbre*, for wind instruments (lost) |
| | Four Studies for piano |
| 1908–14 (26–32) | *Le Rossignol*, opera |
| 1909 (27) | Orchestration of Grieg's *Kobold* |
| | Orchestration of Chopin's Nocturne in Ab and Valse brillante in Eb (lost) |
| | *Mephistopheles Lied vom Floh*, Beethoven arrangement |
| 1910 (28) | *Chanson de Méphistophélès*, Mussorgsky arrangement |
| | *L'Oiseau de feu (The Firebird)*, ballet |
| | *Two Poems of Verlaine*, for voice and piano |
| 1911 (29) | *Petrushka*, ballet |
| | *Two Poems of Balmont*, for high voice and piano |
| 1911–12 (29–30) | *Zvezdoliki*, for male chorus and orchestra |
| 1913 (31) | Three Japanese Lyrics |
| | *Le sacre du printemps (The Rite of Spring)*, ballet |
| | Orchestration (with Ravel) of parts of Mussorgsky's *Pictures from an Exhibition* |
| | Trois petites chansons for voice and piano |
| 1914 (32) | Three Pieces for string quartet (revised 1918) |
| | *Pribaoutki*, for voice and eight instruments |
| | *Valse des fleurs*, for two pianos |
| 1914–15 (32–3) | Three Easy Pieces for piano duet |
| 1914–23 (32–41) | *Les Noces*, dance scenes (three versions) |
| 1914–17 (32–5) | *Podblyudnya (Saucers)*, for female voices a capella |
| 1915 (33) | *Souvenir d'une Marche Boche*, for piano |
| 1915–16 (33–4) | *Berceuses du chat* for voice and three clarinets |
| 1915–17 (33–5) | *Trois histoires pour enfants*, for voice and piano |
| 1916 (34) | *Renard*, a burlesque |
| 1916–17 (34–5) | *Valse pour les enfants*, for piano |
| 1917 )35) | Five Easy Pieces for piano duet |
| | *Chant du rossignol*, symphonic poem |
| | *Chant des bateliers du Volga*, arrangement for wind and percussion |
| | Canons for two horns (lost) |
| | Étude for pianola |
| | Berceuse for voice and piano |
| 1918 (36) | *L'histoire du soldat*, for speakers, dancer, and ensemble |
| | *Ragtime*, for eleven instruments |

Three Pieces for clarinet solo
*Lied ohne Name*, for two bassoons
1918–19 (36–7) Four Russian Songs for voice and piano
1919 (37)     *La Marseillaise*, arranged for solo violin
    *Piano-Rag-Music*, for piano
1920 (38)     *Pulcinella*, ballet with songs
    Concertino for string quartet
    Symphonies for wind instruments
1921 (39)     *Les cinq doigts*, for piano
    Orchestration of two pieces from Tchaikovsky's *The Sleeping Beauty*
    Suite No 2 for chamber orchestra
1922 (40)     *Mavra*, opera bouffe
1923 (41)     Octet for wind instruments
1924 (42)     Concerto for piano and wind instruments
    Piano Sonata
    Serenade in A for piano
1925 (43)     Suite No 1 for small orchestra
1926 (44)     *Otche Nash' (Pater Noster)*, for chorus a cappella
1926–7 (44–5) *Oedipus Rex*, opera-oratorio
1928 (46)     *Apollon musagète*, ballet for string orchestra
    *Le baiser de la fée*, ballet
1929 (47)     Quatre Études for orchestra
    Capriccio for piano and orchestra
1930 (48)     *Symphony of Psalms*, for chorus and orchestra
1931 (49)     Violin Concerto
1932 (50)     Duo Concertante for violin and piano
    *Suite Italienne*, from *Pulcinella*
    *Simbol' Vyeri (Credo)*, for chorus a cappella
1933–4 (51–2) *Perséphone*, melodrama
1934 (52)     *Bogoroditse D'vo (Ave Maria)*, for chorus a cappella
    Divertimento from *Le baiser de la fée*
1935 (53)     Concerto for two solo pianos
1936 (54)     *Jeu de cartes*, ballet
1936–53 (54–71) *Praeludium*, for jazz ensemble
1937 (55)     *Petit Ramusianum Harmonique*, for unaccompanied voices (in *Hommage à C.-F. Ramuz*, Lausanne, 1938)
1938 (56)     *Dumbarton Oaks*, Concerto in E♭, for chamber orchestra
1940 (56)     Symphony in C
    Tango for piano
1941 (59)     Orchestration of 'The Star-spangled Banner'
    Arrangement of Tchaikovsky's *Bluebird pas de deux*
1942 (60)     Danses concertantes for chamber orchestra
    *Circus Polka*, for orchestra
    *Four Norwegian Moods*, for orchestra
1943 (61)     *Ode: Elegiacal Chant*, for orchestra
1944 (62)     *Babel*, cantata
    Sonata for two pianos
    *Scherzo à la Russe*, for jazz ensemble
    *Scènes de ballet*, for orchestra
    Elegy for unaccompanied viola
1945 (63)     Symphony in three movements
    *Ebony Concerto*, for clarinet and jazz ensemble
1946 (64)     Concerto in D for string orchestra
1947 (65)     *Petit Canon pour la fête de Nadia Boulanger*, for two voices
    *Orpheus*, ballet

| 1948 (66) | Mass for mixed chorus and double wind quintet |
| 1948–51 (66–9) | *The Rake's Progress*, opera |
| 1952 (70) | Cantata |
| | Concertino for twelve instruments |
| 1953 (71) | Septet |
| | *Three Songs from William Shakespeare*, for mezzo and piano |
| 1954 (72) | *In Memoriam Dylan Thomas*, for voice, trombones and string quartet |
| | Four Songs for voice, flute, harp and guitar |
| | *Two Poems of Balmont* (orchestral version) |
| 1955 (73) | *Greeting Prelude*, for orchestra |
| | *Canticum Sacrum ad Honorem Sancti Marci Nominis* |
| 1956 (74) | Chorale Variations on *Vom Himmel hoch* for chorus and orchestra |
| 1957 (75) | *Agon*, ballet |
| 1958 (76) | *Threni: id est Lamentationes Jeremiae Prophetae*, for soloists, chorus and orchestra |
| 1959 (77) | Movements for piano and orchestra |
| | *Epitaphium*, for flute, clarinet and harp |
| | *Tres sacrae cantiones*, completion of *Gesualdo* |
| | Double Canon for string quartet |
| 1960 (78) | *Monumentum pro Gesualdo di Venosa ad CD Annum*, for orchestra |
| 1961 (79) | *A Sermon, a Narrative, and a Prayer*, cantata |
| 1962 (80) | Anthem 'The Dove descending breaks the air' |
| | Eight Instrumental Miniatures for fifteen players |
| | *The Flood*, musical play |
| 1963 (81) | *Abraham and Isaac*, for baritone and chamber orchestra |
| | Orchestration of Sibelius's *Canzonetta* |
| 1964 (82) | *Elegy for JFK*, for voice and three clarinets |
| | *Fanfare for a New Theatre*, for two trumpets |
| | Variations for Orchestra |
| 1965 (83) | *Introitus*, for male chorus and ensemble |
| | Canon for concert introduction or encore |
| 1966 (84) | Requiem Canticles for soli, chorus and orchestra |
| | *The Owl and the Pussy-cat*, for voice and piano |
| 1968 (85) | Two Sacred Songs arranged from Hugo Wolf |
| 1969 (86) | Instrumentation of four Preludes and Fugues from J. S. Bach's *Das wohltemperirte Klavier* |

## SUK, Josef
*b Křečovice, (then Austria), 4 January 1874*
*d Benesov, near Prague, 29 May 1935, aged sixty-one*

He learnt piano, violin and organ from his choirmaster father. In 1885 he entered the Prague Conservatory graduating in 1891, and staying on for an extra year to study under Dvořák. He joined the Czech Quartet as second violin and stayed until his retirement in 1933. In 1898 he married Dvořák's daughter, Otilie. In 1922 he was appointed professor of composition for the advanced classes of the Prague Conservatory, and was rector there in 1924, 1926, 1933 and 1935.

| 1888 (14) | Mass in Bb major |
| 1889 (15) | *Fantasy*, for strings |
| | Piano Trio in C minor (1889–90) |
| 1891 (17) | *Dramatic Overture* |
| | Piano Quartet in A minor |
| 1892 (18) | Serenade for strings |

| 1893 (19) | Piano Quintet in B minor |
| 1896 (22) | String Quartet No 1 in B♭ major |
| 1899 (25) | Symphony No 1 in E major |
| 1903 (29) | *Fantasy*, for violin and orchestra |
| 1904 (30) | *Prague*, symphonic poem |
| | Symphony No 2 in C minor, *Asrael* (1904–6) |
| 1907 (33) | *A Summer Tale*, symphonic poem |
| 1910–11 (36–7) | String Quartet No 2 |
| 1914 (40) | *Meditation on a Theme of an old Bohemian Chorale*, for string quartet |
| 1917 (43) | *Harvestide*, symphonic poem |
| 1919 (45) | *Legend of Dead Victors*, for orchestra |
| | *Towards a New Life*, for orchestra |
| 1931 (57) | Mass in B♭ major |

## SULLIVAN, (Sir) Arthur
*b London, 13 May 1842*
*d London, 22 November 1900, aged fifty-eight*

His father was a bandmaster at the Royal Military College at Sandhurst, and by the age of eight Arthur could play every instrument in the band. At twelve he was admitted to the Chapel Royal as a chorister. He went to Leipzig in 1858 under the Mendelssohn Scholarship he won at the Royal Academy of Music. In 1875 he was commissioned to set to music *Trial By Jury*, by W. S. Gilbert. The great success of this compelled the impresario Richard d'Oyly Carte to lease the Opéra Comique Theatre in Paris expressly to perform the works of Gilbert and Sullivan, and in 1881 the company transferred to the new Savoy Theatre in London. In 1883 Sullivan was knighted. The relationship between Gilbert and Sullivan was professional rather than social, and it often became strained.

| 1862 (20) | *The Tempest*, incidental music |
| 1864 (22) | *L'île enchantée*, ballet music |
| | *Kenilworth*, cantata |
| 1866 (23) | Cello Concerto |
| | *Irish Symphony* |
| | *In Memoriam Overture* |
| 1867 (25) | *Cox and Box*, operetta (libretto, Burnand) |
| 1869 (27) | *The Prodigal Son*, oratorio |
| 1870 (28) | *Overture di Ballo*, concert overture |
| 1873 (31) | *The Light of the World*, oratorio |
| 1875 (33) | *The Zoo*, operetta (libretto, Stephenson) |
| | *Trial by Jury*, operetta (libretto, Gilbert) |
| 1877 (35) | *The Sorcerer*, operetta (libretto, Gilbert) |
| | 'The Lost Chord', song |
| 1878 (36) | *HMS Pinafore*, operetta (libretto, Gilbert) |
| | *Henry VIII*, incidental music |
| | *The Martyr of Antioch*, oratorio |
| 1880 (38) | *The Pirates of Penzance*, operetta (libretto, Gilbert) |
| 1881 (39) | *Patience*, operetta (libretto, Gilbert) |
| 1882 (40) | *Iolanthe*, operetta (libretto, Gilbert) |
| 1884 (42) | *Princess Ida*, operetta (libretto, Gilbert) |
| 1885 (43) | *The Mikado*, operetta (libretto, Gilbert) |
| 1886 (44) | *The Golden Legend*, cantata |
| 1887 (45) | *Ruddigore*, operetta (libretto, Gilbert) |
| 1888 (46) | *The Yeoman of the Guard*, operetta (libretto, Gilbert) |
| 1889 (47) | *The Gondoliers*, operetta (libretto, Gilbert) |
| 1891 (49) | *Ivanhoe*, opera (libretto, Sturgis) |

| 1892 | (50) | *Haddon Hall*, opera (libretto, Grundy) |
|------|------|------|
| 1893 | (51) | *Utopia, Ltd.*, operetta (libretto, Gilbert) |
| 1895 | (53) | *The Chieftain*, operetta (libretto, Burnand) |
| 1896 | (54) | *The Grand Duke*, operetta (libretto, Gilbert) |
| 1897 | (55) | *Te Deum* |
| 1898 | (56) | *The Beauty Stone*, opera (libretto, Pinero and Conyers Carr) |
| 1899 | (57) | *The Rose of Persia*, operetta (libretto, Hood) |

Performed posthumously:

| 1901 | | *The Emerald Isle*, operetta (libretto, Hood), completed by German |
|------|--|------|

## SUPPÉ, Franz von

*b Spalato (Split), 18 April 1819*
*d Vienna, 21 May 1895, aged seventy-six*

He studied at the University of Padua, and became conductor at the Josephstadt Theatre in Vienna. He wrote incidental music for plays at the Theater an der Wien and the theatre at Baden.

| 1855 | (36) | Requiem |
|------|------|------|

Suppé also composed: masses and other church music; secular choral works; songs; symphonies; overtures; dances; string quartets and about 250 stage works described variously as operas, farces with music, comedies with songs, vaudevilles, operettas, comic operas, etc.

## SWEELINCK, Jan

*b Deventer, c May 1562*
*d Amsterdam, 16 October 1621, aged fifty-nine*

He studied with his father, who was organist at the Oude Kerk in Amsterdam, succeeding his father in this post in 1577 and holding it for the rest of his life. He was never away from Amsterdam for more than a few days in his whole life, travelling no further than Rotterdam, Antwerp and Deventer to advise on the construction and purchase of musical instruments. His income from the Oude Kerk, who permitted him to live in his house rent-free, should have enabled him to take other posts; but the church restricted such activities in order that he should have sufficient free time to teach and compose.

| 1592–4 | (30–2) | *p Chansons françaises*, in three parts |
|--------|--------|------|
| 1612 | (50) | *p Rimes françaises et italiennes* |
| 1619 | (57) | *p Cantiones sacrae* |

Sweelinck also composed:
*Psaeumes mis en musique*
Many organ, harpsichord and choral (sacred and secular) works.

## SZYMANOWSKI, Karol

*b Tymoszówka, Ukraine, 6 October 1882*
*d Lausanne, 29 March 1937, aged fifty-four*

He was the son of wealthy landowners. Both his parents played piano, and he himself studied privately from an early age, entering the Warsaw Conservatory in 1901. He was much influenced by Beethoven, Wagner, Chopin, R. Strauss and later Stravinsky, and he achieved early fame as a composer. After World War I, the Russian revolution brought financial hardship from which he never recovered. In 1926 he accepted the directorship of the Warsaw Conservatory for two years. In his last years he was seriously affected by tuberculosis.

| 1905 | (22) | *Concert Overture* |
| 1907 | (24) | Symphony No 1 in F minor |
| 1909 | (26) | Symphony No 2 in B♭ major |
| 1912–13 | (29–30) | *Hagith*, opera |
| 1915–16 | (32–3) | Symphony No 3, *Song of the Night*, with tenor and chorus |
| 1917 | (34) | Violin Concerto No 1 |
| | | String Quartet in C major |
| 1920–4 | (37–41) | *King Roger*, opera |
| 1924 | (41) | *Prince Potemkin*, incidental music |
| 1926 | (43) | *Harnasie*, ballet |
| | | *Stabat Mater* |
| 1931–2 | (48–9) | Symphonie Concertante for piano |
| 1932–3 | (49–50) | Violin Concerto No 2 |

Szymanowski also composed symphonic poems, piano music, choral music and songs.

## TAKEMITSU, Tôru
b Tokyo, 8 October 1930

Largely self-taught, he has a very individual style with unorthodox structures. In 1964 he lectured with Cage in Hawaii. He was made director of the Space Theatre in the Steel Pavilion at Expo '70 in Osaka. In 1975 he taught composition at Yale University. Travels widely as lecturer and guest composer.

| 1951 | (21) | *The Joy to Live*, ballet |
| 1955 | (25) | Chamber Concerto |
| 1957 | (27) | Requiem for strings |
| 1958 | (28) | *Solitude sonore*, for orchestra |
| | | *Black Painting*, for reciter and small orchestra |
| 1961 | (31) | *Tree Music*, for orchestra |
| 1961–6 | (31–6) | *Arc*, for piano and orchestra |
| 1962 | (32) | *Coral Island*, for soprano and orchestra |
| 1966 | (36) | *Dorian Horizon*, for strings |
| 1967 | (37) | *November Steps*, double concerto for Japanese instruments |
| 1968 | (38) | *Asterism*, for piano and orchestra |
| 1969 | (39) | *Stanza I*, for ensemble |
| | | *Crossing*, for orchestra |
| 1971 | (41) | *Cassiopea*, for percussion and orchestra |
| 1972 | (42) | *Gemeaux*, for oboe, trombone and two orchestras |
| 1973 | (43) | *Autumn*, for two Japanese instruments and orchestra |
| 1975 | (45) | *Gitimalya*, for orchestra |
| | | *Quatraine*, for clarinet, violin, cello, piano and orchestra |
| 1976 | (46) | *Marginalia*, for orchestra |
| | | *Mar Concerto* |
| | | *Green*, for harp, cello and strings |
| 1977 | (47) | *A Flock Descends into the Pentagonal Garden*, for orchestra |
| 1980 | (50) | *Far Calls Coming, Far*, for violin and orchestra |
| 1981 | (51) | *Rain Tree*, for three keyboards |
| | | *Towards the Sea*, for alto flute and guitar |
| | | *A Way Alone*, for string quartet |
| 1982 | (52) | *Grass*, for male chorus |
| | | *Rain Tree Sketch*, for piano |
| | | *Rain Spell*, for flute, clarinet, harp, piano and vibraphone |
| | | *Rain Coming*, for chamber orchestra |
| 1983 | (53) | *From far beyond Chrysanthemums and November fog*, for violin and piano |

Rocking Mirror Daybreak, for violin duo
Star Isle, for orchestra
Orion, for cello and orchestra
1983–4    Towards the edge of dream, for guitar and orchestra
1984 (54)   Vers l'arc en ciel, Palma, for guitar, oboe d'amore and orchestra


## TALLIS, Thomas
b London?, c1505
d Greenwich, 23 November 1585, aged c eighty

He held various small appointments and then in 1543 was made a Gentleman of the Chapel Royal, remaining so for the rest of his life. Both Queen Mary and Queen Elizabeth granted him leases and money. In 1572 he and Byrd were granted a royal licence giving them the sole rights for printing music and music paper in England.

1567 (c62)    p Psalm tunes printed in 'Archbishop Parker's Psalter'
Tallis composed many Latin masses, lamentations, motets (including Spem in alium, for forty-part choir), pieces for keyboard, viols, etc.


## TANSMAN, Alexandre
b Lódz, 12 June 1897

He studied music at the Lódz Conservatory from 1912 to 1914, and also law and philosophy at Warsaw University. In 1919 he went to Paris and befriended Ravel, Milhaud and Honegger. He made his first tour as a pianist in 1927 with the Boston Symphony Orchestra under Koussevitzky, later touring extensively in Europe, Canada and Palestine. He began to conduct his own works, and from 1932 to 1933 travelled to the Far East. During World War II he lived in the USA, writing film music and giving concerts. He was awarded the Coolidge Medal in 1941, and returned to France in 1946.

1916 (19)    Symphony No 1
1922 (25)    Sextuor, ballet
1924 (27)    Sinfonietta
1925 (28)    Symphony No 2
             La Nuit Kurde, opera (1925–7)
1926 (29)    Piano Concerto No 1
1927 (30)    Piano Concerto No 2
1928 (31)    Lumières, ballet
1929 (32)    Le cercle éternel, ballet
1930 (33)    Triptych, for string orchestra
1931 (34)    Symphony No 3, Symphony Concertante (1931–2)
             Concertino, for piano
1932 (35)    La Grande Ville, ballet
             Two Symphonic Movements
1933 (36)    Partita for string orchestra
1936 (39)    Viola Concerto
             Two Intermezzi
1937 (40)    Bric-à-Brac, ballet
             Fantasy for violin
             Fantasy for cello
1938 (41)    Le toison d'or, opera
             Symphony No 4
1942 (45)    Symphony No 5
1943 (46)    Symphony No 6, In Memoriam

|              |                                                              |
|--------------|--------------------------------------------------------------|
|              | *Symphonic études*                                           |
| 1944 (47)    | Symphony No 7                                                |
|              | *Le roi qui jouait le fou*, ballet                           |
|              | Partita for piano and orchestra                              |
| 1945 (48)    | Concertino, for guitar and orchestra                         |
| 1947 (50)    | *Isiah the Prophet*, for tenor, chorus and orchestra         |
|              | Music for orchestra                                          |
| 1948 (51)    | Music for strings                                            |
| 1949 (52)    | *Ricercari*, for orchestra                                   |
|              | *Tombeau de Chopin*, for strings                             |
| 1950 (53)    | *Phèdre*, ballet                                             |
| 1951 (54)    | Symphony No 8                                                |
| 1955 (58)    | *Le Sermant*, opera                                          |
|              | Capriccio, for orchestra                                     |
|              | Concerto for orchestra                                       |
| 1961 (64)    | *Psalms*, for tenor, chorus and orchestra                    |
| 1962 (65)    | *Resurrection*, for orchestra                                |
|              | Six Symphonic Studies for orchestra                          |
| 1963 (66)    | Six Movements for string orchestra                           |
| 1964 (67)    | *Il usignolo di Boboli*, opera                               |
| 1966 (69)    | Concertino, for oboe and chamber orchestra                   |
| 1968 (71)    | Four Movements for orchestra                                 |
| 1969 (72)    | Concertino, for flute and chamber orchestra                  |
|              | *Hommage à Erasme de Rotherdam*, for orchestra               |
|              | *Diptyque*, for orchestra                                    |
|              | *Hommage à Chopin*, for guitar                               |
| 1972 (75)    | *Stèle (in memoriam Stravinsky)*, for voice and instruments  |
|              | *Variations on a theme of Skriabin*, for guitar              |
| 1974 (77)    | *Georges Dandin*, comic opera                                |
| 1976 (79)    | *Élégie in memory of Darius Milhaud*, for orchestra          |
| 1977 (80)    | *Musique à six*, for clarinet, string quartet and piano      |

Tansman has also written many songs, chamber and piano works, and incidental music for theatre, cinema and radio.


**TÁRREGA, Francisco**
*b Villareal, Castellón, 21 November 1852*
*d Barcelona, 15 December 1909, aged fifty-seven*

He began to study classical guitar at the age of ten, and was to pave the way for the rebirth of the instrument in the twentieth century. He entered the Madrid Conservatory in 1874, studying theory, harmony and piano. By 1877 he was earning his living as a music teacher and concert guitarist. He settled in Barcelona in 1885, and made many concert tours. In 1903 he became paralysed in his right side, but continued playing.

His output is largely for guitar, including seventy-eight original works, and over a hundred transcriptions, some of which are for two guitars.


**TARTINI, Giuseppe**
*b Pirano, 8 April 1692*
*d Padua, 26 February 1770, aged seventy-seven*

His father wanted him to study theology, but instead he studied law at Padua University, where he also developed his love of music and became a most proficient fencer. Leaving university in 1713, he eloped with and married the ward of Cardinal Giorgio Carnario who ordered Tartini's arrest. He fled disguised as a monk and entered the monastery at Assisi, staying there for two years and studying the violin. The differences with the cardinal being resolved, he and his wife settled in Venice for some time. His fame as a violinist spread, and in 1721 he was appointed first violin at the Capella del Santo in Padua. From 1723 to 1725 he directed Count Kimsky's orchestra in Prague. He returned to Padua in 1726, founded his school of violin playing and wrote a number of treatises on theoretical aspects of music. Despite lucrative offers to go abroad he remained in Italy playing, composing and teaching until he died after years of suffering from a malignant growth of the foot.

He left some sacred vocal music, about a hundred and fifty violin concertos, over two hundred sonatas and other instrumental works.

## TAVENER, John
b London, 28 January 1944

He was educated at Highgate School, and the Royal College of Music from 1961 to 1965. He won the Prince Rainier of Monaco Prize in 1965. His work shows the great influence upon him of his Catholic faith.

1962 (18)    Piano Concerto (1962–3)
        *Three Holy Sonnets*, for voice and orchestra
1963–4 (19–20) *Three Sections*, from T. S. Eliot's *The Four Quartets*, for tenor and piano
1964 (20)    *The Cappemakers*, for two narrators, two soloists, male chorus and instruments
1965 (21)    Chamber Concerto (revised 1968)
        *Cain and Abel*, dramatic cantata
        *The Whale*, for choir and orchestra (1965–6)
1967–8 (23–4) *Grandma's Footsteps*, for chamber orchestra
        *Three Surrealist Songs*, for mezzo-soprano, tape and piano doubling bongoes
1968 (24)    *In Alium*, for high soprano and orchestra
1969 (25)    *Celtic Requiem*, for voices and orchestra
1970 (26)    *Nomine Jesu*, for voices and orchestra
        *Coplas*, for voices and tape
1971 (27)    *In Memoriam Igor Stravinsky*, for two alto flutes, organ and bells
        *Responsorium in Memory of Annon Lee Silver*, for two soprano soli, mixed chorus and two flutes
1972 (28)    *Variations on 'Three Blind Mice'*, for orchestra
        *Ma fin est mon commencement*, for voices and instruments
        *Little Requiem for Father Malachy Lynch*, for voices and instruments
        *Ultimos ritos*, for voices and orchestra, including amplified instruments
        *Canciones espanolas*, for voices and instruments
1973 (29)    *Requiem for Father Malachy*, for choir and instruments
        *Thérèse*, opera (1973–6)
1976 (32)    *A Gentle Spirit*, for soprano, tenor and ensemble
        *Canticle of the Mother of God*, for soprano and chorus
1977 (33)    *Kyklike Kinesis*, for soprano, chorus, cello and orchestra
        *Lamentation, Lost Prayer and Exaltation*, for soprano with handbells or piano
        *Palin*, for piano
        *Palintropos*, for piano and orchestra
        *The Last Prayer of Mary Queen of Scots*, for soprano and handbells
1978 (34)    Six Russian Folk Songs for soprano and ensemble
        *The Instrument of Antigone*, for soprano and orchestra

1979 (35)   *Greek Interlude*, for flute and piano
            *Six Abbasid Songs* for four flutes and percussion
1979–80 (35–6) *Akhmatova: Requiem*, for soprano and baritone soli, brass, percussion and strings
1980 (36)   *Risen!*, for chorus and orchestra
            *Sappho: Lyrical Fragments*, for two sopranos and strings
1981 (37)   *Prayer for the World*, for sixteen solo voices
            *Funeral Ikos*, for chorus
            *Mandelion*, for organ
            *Trisagion*, for brass quintet
            *The Great Canon of the Ode to Saint Andrew of Crete*, for chorus
1982 (38)   *Towards The Son: Ritual Procession*, for chamber orchestra
            *Doxa*, for chorus
            *Lord's Prayer*, for chorus
            *Mandoodles*, for a young pianist
            *The Lamb*, for unaccompanied chorus
1983 (39)   *He Hath Entered The Heven*, for unaccompanied trebles
            *To a Child Dancing in the Wind*, for soprano, flute, harp and viola
1984 (40)   *Sixteen Haiku of Seferis*, for soprano, tenor and ensemble
            *Ikon of Light*, for chorus and string trio
            *Little Missenden Calm*, for oboe, clarinet, bassoon and horn
            *Vigil Service*, for a capella choir, four violins and organ
            *Chant*, for solo guitar
            *Mini Song Cycle for Gina*, for voice and piano


**TAYLOR, Deems**
b New York, 22 December 1885
d New York, 3 July 1966, aged eighty

He began to study piano in 1895. In 1906 he graduated from New York University. He worked in publishing and journalism, and became a music critic, broadcaster and author. He received four honorary doctorates.

1912 (27)   *The Siren Song*, for orchestra
1914 (29)   *The Highwayman*, for baritone, women's voices and orchestra
            *The Chambered Nautilus*, for chorus and orchestra
1918 (33)   *The Portrait of a Lady*, for eleven instruments
1919 (34)   *Through the Looking-glass*, suite for chamber orchestra (version for full orchestra, 1922)
1923 (38)   *A Kiss in Xanadu*, pantomime in two scenes, for two pianos
1925 (40)   *Jurgen*, for orchestra
            *Fantasy on Two Themes*, for orchestra
            *Circus Days*, for jazz orchestra (version for full orchestra, 1933)
1926 (41)   *The King's Henchman*, opera
1930 (45)   *Peter Ibbetson*, opera
1936 (51)   *Lucrece*, for string quartet
1937 (52)   *Ramuntcho*, opera
            *Casanova*, ballet
1941 (56)   *Processional*, for orchestra
1943 (58)   *Christmas Overture*, for orchestra
1945 (60)   *Elegy*, for orchestra
1950 (65)   *Restoration Suite*, for orchestra
1954 (69)   *The Dragon*, opera

## TCHAIKOVSKY, Peter Ilych
b Kamsko-Votkinsk, 7 May 1840
d St Petersburg, 6 November 1893, aged fifty-three

The first eight years of his life, in which he learnt piano, were comparatively settled; but in 1848 his father, a mining engineer, resigned from his government post and the family began a difficult migratory period. In 1850 he went to the St Petersburg School of Jurisprudence, becoming an indifferent lawyer, and a clerk in the Ministry of Justice in 1859. In 1862 he entered the new St Petersburg Conservatory, and in 1863 resigned his secure government post. Two years later he was teaching harmony at the Moscow Conservatory, and plunged into composition, to the detriment of his nervous health. In 1868 he met the group of young composers known as 'The Five' – Balakirev, Cui, Borodin, Mussorgsky and Rimsky-Korsakov – but never joined them, though Balakirev helped and advised him with his early works. The next four years were comparatively untroubled; then the failure of some of his works to find immediate success, coupled with his guilt about his homosexuality, brought renewed depression. His marriage in 1877 was a disaster; he tried to drown himself, and nearly lost his reason. He moved to Switzerland and was aided in his recovery by Mme von Meck, a woman he had scarcely met but who gave him friendship and financial assistance. But his inspiration failed and did not re-emerge until 1888, after which some of his finest works were written. He made some exhausting tours and suffered a new nervous collapse. He died of cholera, probably as a result of drinking unboiled tap-water.

| | |
|---|---|
| 1866 (26) | Symphony No 1 in G minor, *Winter Daydreams* |
| 1868 (28) | *Fate*, symphonic poem |
| 1869 (29) | *Romeo and Juliet*, fantasy overture (final version 1880) |
| 1871 (31) | String Quartet in D major |
| 1872 (32) | Symphony No 2 in C minor, *Little Russian* |
| 1874–5 (34–5) | Piano Concerto No 1 in B♭ minor |
| | String Quartet in F major |
| 1875 (35) | *Swan Lake*, ballet (*fp* 1895) |
| | Symphony No 3 in D major, *Polish* |
| | String Quartet in E♭ minor |
| 1876 (36) | *Variations on a Rococo Theme*, for cello and orchestra |
| | *Slavonic March*, for orchestra |
| 1877 (37) | Symphony No 4 in F minor |
| | *Francesca da Rimini*, symphonic fantasy |
| | *Waltz-Scherzo*, for violin and orchestra |
| 1878 (38) | Violin Concerto in D major |
| 1879 (39) | *Eugene Onegin*, opera |
| | *Capriccio Italien*, for orchestra |
| | Piano Concerto No 2 in G major (1879–80) |
| 1880 (40) | Serenade for strings |
| | *Romeo and Juliet*, overture (final revision) |
| 1881 (41) | *Joan of Arc*, opera |
| 1882 (42) | *1812*, overture |
| | Piano Trio in A minor |
| 1884 (44) | *Mazeppa*, opera |
| | *Concert-fantasy*, for piano and orchestra |
| 1885 (45) | *Manfred Symphony* |
| 1888 (48) | *The Sleeping Beauty*, ballet |
| | *Hamlet*, overture |
| | Symphony No 5 in E minor |
| 1890 (50) | *The Queen of Spades*, opera |
| 1892 (52) | *Iolanthe*, opera |

Casse Noisette (The Nutcracker), ballet
p String Sextet in D minor
1893 (53)   Symphony No 6 in B minor, *Pathétique*
Piano Concerto No 3


## TELEMANN, Georg Philipp
b Magdeburg, 14 March 1681
d Hamburg, 25 June 1767, aged eighty-six

His father was a clergyman. He was largely self-taught in music, though he studied languages and science at the University of Leipzig. He composed operas for Leipzig theatres, became a church organist and later was *Kapellmeister* for various small courts. Eventually he returned to the church, and was musical director of five principal churches in Hamburg from 1721 until his death.

1708–12 (27–31) Trio Sonata in E♭ major
1715–20 (34–39) Concerto in A major
Suite in D minor
1716 (35)   *Die Kleine Kammermusik*
Six Suites for violin, querflute and piano
1718 (37)   Six Trios for two violins and cello, with bass continuo
1723 (42)   *Hamburger Ebb und Fluht*, overture in C major
1725 (44)   *Pimpinone*, opera
1728 (47)   *Der getreuer Musikmeister*, cantata
1759 (78)   *St Mark Passion*

Telemann also composed forty operas; six hundred overtures; over forty liturgical passions; several oratorios; innumerable cantatas and psalms.


## THEODORAKIS, Mikis
b Khios, Greece, 29 July 1925

He entered the Paris Conservatory in 1954. On his return to Greece in 1959, he issued revolutionary criticism of the contemporary Greek arts, and as a result he was imprisoned in 1967 and his music banned. He was released in 1970.

His large output includes many oratorios, ballets, film scores and song cycles with pop orchestras, nearly all of them on Greek subjects.


## THOMAS, Ambroise
b Metz, 5 August 1811
d Paris, 12 February 1896, aged eighty-four

The son of a composer, he played piano and violin at a very early age. He entered the Paris Conservatory at seventeen and won the Grand Prix de Rome in 1832. In 1868 he became director of the Conservatory.

1832 (21)   *Hermann et Ketty*, cantata
1837 (26)   *La double échelle*, opera
1838 (27)   *Ke Perruquier de la régence*, opera
1839 (28)   *Le panier fleuri*, opera
*La Gipsy*, ballet
1840 (29)   *Carlino*, opera
1841 (30)   *Le Comte de Carmagnola*, opera
1842 (31)   *Le Guerillero*, opera
1843 (32)   *Angélique et Médor*, opera

|            |      | *Mina*, opera                            |
| ---------- | ---- | ---------------------------------------- |
| 1846       | (35) | *Betty*, ballet                          |
| 1849       | (38) | *Le Caïd*, opera                         |
| 1850       | (39) | *Le songe d'une nuit d'été*, opera       |
| 1851       | (40) | *Raymond*, opera                         |
| 1853       | (42) | *La Tonelli*, opera                      |
| 1855       | (44) | *La cour de Célimène*, opera             |
| 1857       | (46) | *Psyché*, opera                          |
|            |      | *Le carnaval de Venise*, opera           |
|            |      | Messe Solennelle                         |
| 1860       | (49) | *Le roman d'Elvire*, opera               |
| 1865       | (54) | *Marche religieuse*, for orchestra       |
| 1866       | (55) | *Mignon*, opera                          |
| 1868       | (57) | *Hamlet*, grand opera                    |
| 1874       | (63) | *Gille et Gillotin*, opera               |
| 1882       | (71) | *Françoise de Rimini*, opera             |
| 1889       | (78) | *La tempête*, ballet                     |

## THOMPSON, Randall
*b New York, 21 April 1899*
*d Boston, 9 July 1984, aged eighty-five*

He graduated in 1920 from Harvard and received Guggenheim Fellowships in 1929 and 1930. From 1937 to 1939 he was professor of music at the University of California at Berkeley; and from then until 1941 he was director of the Curtis Institute in Philadelphia. Between 1941 and his retirement in 1965 he held positions at the universities of Virginia, Princeton and Harvard. He has gained many degrees and honours.

| 1922 | (23) | *Pierrot and Cathurnis*, orchestral prelude |
| ---- | ---- | ---------------------------------------- |
| 1924 | (25) | *The Piper at the Gates of Dawn*, orchestral prelude |
|      |      | *The Wind in the Willows*, for string quartet |
| 1928 | (29) | *Jazz Poem*, for piano and orchestra    |
| 1929 | (30) | Symphony No 1                            |
| 1931 | (32) | Symphony No 2                            |
| 1940 | (41) | Suite for oboe, violin and viola         |
| 1941 | (42) | String Quartet No 1                      |
| 1942 | (43) | *Solomon and Balkis*, opera              |
| 1947–9 | (48–50) | Symphony No 3                      |
| 1953–4 | (54–5) | *A Trip to Nahant*, symphonic fantasy |
| 1961 | (62) | *The Nativity*, church opera             |
| 1967 | (68) | String Quartet No 2                      |
| 1971 | (72) | *Wedding Music*, for string quartet      |

Thompson has also written twenty chorale preludes, four inventions and fugues for keyboard, and many sacred and secular vocal and choral works.

## THOMSON, Virgil
*b Kansas City, 25 November 1896*

He first became known as a music critic. After World War I he went to Harvard, and to Paris as a pupil of Boulanger. He became organist and choirmaster of King's Chapel, Boston. He then studied piano and spent from 1925 to 1932 at the École Normale de Musique in Paris on a scholarship, becoming closely associated with the influential composers known as 'Les Six'.

| 1923 (27) | Two Sentimental Tangos |
| 1926 (30) | Sonata da Chiesa, for five instruments |
| 1928 (32) | Symphony on a Hymn Tune |
| 1929 (33) | Five Portraits, for four clarinets |
| 1930 (34) | Violin Sonata |
| 1931 (35) | Quartet No 1 |
| | Serenade for flute and violin |
| | Four Portraits, for violin and piano |
| | Stabat Mater |
| 1932 (36) | Quartet No 2 |
| 1934 (38) | Four Saints in Three Acts, opera |
| 1937 (41) | Filling Station, ballet |
| 1941 (45) | Symphony No 2 |
| 1942 (46) | Canon for Dorothy Thomson |
| | The Mayor La Guardia Waltzes |
| 1943 (47) | Flute Sonata |
| 1944 (48) | Suite No 1, Portraits |
| | Suite No 2 |
| 1947 (51) | The Mother of Us All, opera |
| | The Seine at Night, for orchestra |
| 1948 (52) | Wheatfield at Noon, for orchestra |
| | Arcadian Songs and Dances |
| 1949 (53) | Cello Concerto |
| 1951 (55) | Five Songs of William Blake, for baritone and orchestra |
| 1952 (56) | Sea Piece with Birds, for orchestra |
| 1954 (58) | Concerto for flute, strings and percussion |
| 1957 (61) | The Lively Arts, fugue |
| 1959 (63) | Fugues and Cantilenas, for orchestra |
| | Collected Poems, for soprano, baritone and orchestra |
| 1960 (64) | Mass for solo voice and piano (version with orchestra, 1962) |
| | Missa pro defunctis (Requiem Mass), for men's chorus, women's chorus and orchestra |
| 1961 (65) | A Solemn Music, for orchestra (transcribed from original band score) |
| 1962 (66) | A Joyful Fugue, to follow A Solemn Music |
| | Pange lingua, for organ |
| 1964 (68) | The Feast of Love, for baritone and orchestra |
| | Autumn Concertino, for harp, strings and percussion |
| 1966 (70) | Lord Byron, opera (1966–8) |
| | Fantasy in Homage to an Earlier England, for orchestra |
| | The Nativity, for mixed chorus, soloists and orchestra (1966–7) |
| | Étude, for cello and piano |
| 1967 (71) | Shipwreck and Love Scene, from Byron's 'Don Juan', for orchestra and tenor soloist |
| 1973 (77) | Cantata based on Nonsense Rhymes |
| 1981 (85) | Nineteen Piano Portraits |
| 1982 (86) | Ten Études for piano |

Thomson has also composed four piano sonatas.


## TIPPETT, (Sir) Michael
b London, 2 January 1905

He studied composition at the Royal College of Music. After a few years as a school teacher he retreated to a small village in Surrey to compose. In 1940 he was appointed director of music at Morley College. He withdrew or destroyed all his compositions written before 1935, deeming them unworthy. His pacifist

348

convictions resulted in his being imprisoned for three months in 1943. In 1951 he left Morley College, and apart from lecturing and broadcasting has since devoted himself solely to writing. He is a CBE and has been honoured with doctorates by several universities. He was knighted in 1966 and made a Companion of Honour in 1979.

1934–5 (29–30) String Quartet No 1 in A major (revised 1943)
1936–7 (31–2) Piano Sonata (revised 1942)
1937 (32)     *A Song of Liberty*
1938–9 (33–4) Concerto for double string orchestra
1939–41 (34–6) *A Child of Our Time*, oratorio
              *Fantasia on a Theme by Handel*, for piano and orchestra
1941–2 (36–7) String Quartet No 2
1942 (37)     *The Source* and *The Windhover*, madrigals
1943 (38)     *Boyhood's End*, song cycle
              *Plebs angelica*, motet for double chorus
1944 (39)     Symphony No 1 (1944–5)
              *The Weeping Babe*, motet for soprano solo and chorus
1945–6 (40–1) String Quartet No 3
1946 (41)     *Little Music*, for strings
1947–52 (42–8) *The Midsummer Marriage*, opera
1948 (43)     Suite in D major
1950–1 (45–6) *Heart's Assurance*, song cycle for high voice and piano
1952 (47)     *Dance Clarion Air*, madrigal
1953 (48)     *Fantasia Concertante on a Theme by Corelli*, for strings
              Divertimento for chamber orchestra, *Sellingers Round* (1953–4)
              Piano Concerto (1953–5)
1955 (50)     Sonata for four horns
1956–7 (51–2) Symphony No 2
1958 (53)     *King Priam*, opera (1958–61)
              *Crown of the Year*, for chorus and orchestra
              *Prelude, Recitative and Aria*, for flute, oboe and harpsichord
1961 (56)     *Three Songs for Achilles*, for voice and guitar
              *Magnificat* and *Nunc Dimittis*
1962 (57)     Concerto for orchestra (1962–3)
              *Praeludium*, for brass, bells and percussion
              Piano Sonata No 2, in one movement
              *Songs for Ariel*
1965 (60)     *Vision of St Augustine*, for baritone, choir and orchestra
              *The Shires Suite*, for choir and orchestra (1965–70)
1966–70 (61–5) *The Knot Garden*, opera
1970 (65)     Symphony No 3, with soprano soloist (1970–2)
              *Songs for Dov*, for tenor solo and small orchestra
1972–3 (67–8) Piano Sonata No 3
1973–6 (68–71) *The Ice Break*, opera
1976–7 (71–2) Symphony No 4
1977–8 (72–3) String Quartet No 4
1978–9 (73–4) Triple Concerto, for violin, viola, cello and orchestra
1980 (75)     *Wolf Trap Fanfare*, for three trumpets, two trombones and tuba
1980–3 (75–8) *The Mask of Time*, for soli, chorus and orchestra
1983 (78)     *Festal Brass with Blues*, for brass ensemble

**TOCH, Ernst**
*b Vienna, 7 December 1887*
*d Santa Monica, California, 1 October 1964, aged seventy-six*

He began his career in medicine, but soon turned to music, in which he was
entirely self-taught. In 1909 he won the Mozart Prize of the City of Frankfurt and
moved to Germany. In 1913 he was appointed teacher of composition at the
Mannheim Musikhochschule, where he remained for some years. Political
pressure made him move to London in 1933, and in 1934 he went to the USA,
becoming an American citizen in 1940. He held several lectureships in the US,
and visited Europe in the 1950s. In 1956 he won the Pulitzer and the
Huntington-Hartford Prizes and was elected to the American National Institute
of Arts and Letters. In 1960 he won the American Grammy Award and in 1964
received an honorary doctorate from the Hebrew College of Cincinnati.

| | |
|---|---|
| 1904 (17) | Scherzo for orchestra |
| | Piano Concerto (lost) |
| 1913 (26) | *From My Fatherland*, for orchestra |
| 1920 (33) | *Phantastische Nachtmusik*, for orchestra |
| 1926 (39) | Piano Concerto |
| | *Spiel*, for wind |
| 1927 (40) | *Die Prinzessin auf der Erbse*, opera |
| | *Narziss*, for orchestra (lost) |
| | *Gewitter*, for orchestra (lost) |
| | *Komödie*, for orchestra |
| 1928 (41) | *Fanal*, for organ and orchestra |
| | *Bunte Suite* |
| 1929 (42) | *Kleine Ouvertüre zu Der Fächer* |
| 1930 (43) | *Der Fächer*, opera |
| | *Kleine Theater-suite* |
| 1931 (44) | *Tragische Musik*, for orchestra (lost) |
| | *Zwei Kultische Stücke*, for orchestra (lost) |
| 1933 (46) | Symphony for piano and orchestra |
| | *Variations on a Mozart Theme*, for orchestra |
| 1934 (47) | *Big Ben*, for orchestra |
| 1935 (48) | *Pinocchio*, for orchestra |
| 1936 (49) | *Musical Short Story*, for orchestra (lost) |
| | *Orchids*, for orchestra (lost) |
| 1938 (51) | *The Idle Stroller*, suite for orchestra |
| 1945 (58) | *The Covenant*, for orchestra (lost) |
| 1947 (60) | *Hyperion*, for orchestra |
| 1950 (63) | Symphony No 1 |
| 1951 (64) | Symphony No 2 |
| 1953 (66) | *Circus Overture* |
| | *Notturno*, for orchestra |
| 1955 (68) | Symphony No 3 |
| 1956 (69) | *Peter Pan*, for orchestra |
| 1957 (70) | Symphony No 4 |
| 1959 (72) | *Epilogue*, for orchestra |
| | *Intermezzo*, for orchestra |
| 1961 (74) | *Short Story*, for orchestra |
| 1962 (75) | *The Last Tale*, opera |
| 1963 (76) | *Jephta*, rhapsodic poem (Symphony No 5) |
| | Capriccio for orchestra |
| | *Puppetshow*, for orchestra |
| | Symphony No 6 |
| | *The Enamoured Harlequin*, for orchestra |

1964 (76)    Symphony No 7
               Sinfonietta for strings
               Theme and Variations for orchestra

Toch also wrote thirteen string quartets and other chamber works (early ones lost); many songs and choral works with orchestra; literary works.


**TOMKINS, Thomas**
*b St David's, Pembrokeshire, 1572*
*d Martin Hussingtree, Worcestershire, 1656, aged eighty-four*

The son of a churchman, he became vocal instructor at Worcester Cathedral in 1596. He was later appointed Gentleman in Ordinary at the Chapel Royal, and organist there in 1621. He was well connected with all the great names of his day, being especially active in Worcester. When the parliamentary forces dismantled the cathedral organ in 1646 he continued to live in the cathedral precincts until 1654.

He left some liturgical works, a great number of anthems, madrigals, keyboard works and consort music.


**TORELLI, Giuseppe**
*b Verona, 22 April 1658*
*d Bologna, 8 February 1709, aged fifty*

His early musical training was in Verona, but he moved to Bologna between 1681 and 1684, being admitted to the Accademia Filarmonica there in 1684. He studied violin and viola there, playing regularly in the orchestra at S Petronio until 1695, the year before the orchestra was disbanded. He then travelled to Germany with his friend Pistocchi and became *maestro di concerto* for the Margrave of Brandenburg in Ansbach, remaining there till the end of 1699. In 1700 the two friends were in Vienna, grew tired of it and travelled until 1701, when he was again violinist in the reformed S. Petronio orchestra in Bologna.

He wrote a large quantity of chamber works, most of it still in manuscript, and is chiefly remarkable for his development of the instrumental concerto, both the concerto grosso and the solo concerto, the pattern taken up by subsequent composers.


**TURINA, Joaquin**
*b Seville, 9 December 1882*
*d Madrid, 14 January 1949, aged sixty-six*

He made his début as a pianist in 1897. He went to Madrid, where he befriended Falla, and studied at the Madrid Conservatory. He moved to Paris in 1905. Though influenced by d'Indy and Debussy, he was advised by Albéniz to look for material in Spanish folk music. He graduated from the Scola Cantorum in Paris in 1913, and became choirmaster of the Teatro Real in Madrid until its closure in 1925. He was professor of composition at Madrid Conservatory in 1930. Though persecuted by republicans during the Civil War he found favour again afterwards and was awarded the Spanish Grand Cross. He was for a number of years the music critic for a newspaper.

1907 (25)    Piano Quintet
1911 (29)    Quartet
1912 (30)    *La Procesion del Rocio*, symphonic poem
1914 (32)    *Margot*, lyric comedy

| 1915 (33) | *Evangelio*, symphonic poem |
| 1916 (34) | *Navidad*, incidental music |
| 1917 (35) | *La Adultera penitente*, incidental music |
| 1918 (36) | *Poema en forma de canciones*, for voice and piano |
| 1920 (38) | *Sinfonia Sevillana* |
| | *Danzas fantasticas* |
| 1921 (39) | *Canto a Sevillana*, song cycle |
| 1923 (41) | *Jardin de Oriente*, opera |
| 1926 (44) | *La oracion del torero*, for string quartet |
| | Piano Trio |
| 1928 (46) | *Ritmos*, choreographic fantasy |
| 1929 (47) | *Triptico*, songs |
| 1931 (49) | *Rapsodia sinfonica*, for piano and strings |
| | Piano Quartet |
| 1933 (51) | Piano Trio |
| 1935 (53) | Serenade for quartet |

## VARÈSE, Edgard
b Paris, 22 December 1885
d New York, 6 November 1965, aged seventy-nine

He studied mathematics and natural history at the École Polytechnique, but at the age of nineteen decided on a musical career against his father's wishes. He went to the Schola Cantorum from 1904 to 1906 and entered the Paris Conservatory in 1907. From 1909 to 1914 he lived in Berlin, where he became friends with Busoni. He was guest conductor for the Prague Philharmonic Orchestra in 1914, then returned to France and went into the Army, from which he was discharged after an illness in 1915. He went to America in 1916 and stayed there the rest of his life.

| 1905 onwards (works lost or destroyed) | |
| | *La Chanson des jeunes hommes* |
| | *Le Prélude à la fin d'un jour* |
| | *Rhapsodie romance* |
| | *Bourgoyne* |
| | *Gargantua* |
| | *Mehr Licht* |
| | *Les Cycles du Nord* |
| | *Oedipus and the Sphynx*, opera |
| 1921 (36) | *Offrandes*, for soprano, chorus and orchestra |
| 1923 (38) | *Hyperprism*, for small orchestra and percussion |
| | *Octandre*, for small orchestra and percussion |
| | *Intégrales*, for chamber orchestra and percussion |
| 1926 (41) | *Amériques*, for orchestra |
| 1927 (42) | *Arcana*, for orchestra |
| 1931 (46) | *Ionisation*, for forty-one percussion and two sirens |
| 1932 (47) | *Metal* (unfinished or lost) |
| 1936 (51) | *Density 21.5*, for flute solo |
| 1937 (52) | *Espace*, for orchestra |
| 1943 (58) | *Ecuatorial*, for bass voice and orchestra |
| 1947 (62) | *Étude pour espace*, for two pianos and percussion |
| 1953–4 (68–9) | *Déserts*, for orchestra |
| 1955–6 (70–1) | *Good Friday Procession in Verges*, electronic composition for film |
| 1957–8 (72–3) | *Poème electronique* |
| 1961 (76) | *Nocturnal*, for soprano and orchestra |

# VAUGHAN WILLIAMS, Ralph
*b Down Ampney, Gloucestershire, 12 October 1872*
*d London, 26 August 1958, aged eighty-five*

He was the son of a clergyman. He studied theory, piano and violin before the age of nine, and was educated at Charterhouse, the Royal College of Music, and Trinity College, Cambridge. After graduating from Cambridge he returned to the Royal College as a pupil of Stanford, and whilst there made a life-long friendship with Holst. He later went to Berlin to study under Bruch and Ravel. His private income allowed him to spend a great deal of time researching into English folk melody. After serving in World War I he taught at the Royal College. His last thirty years were spent mainly in creative work, and he achieved both fame and honours.

| | | |
|---|---|---|
| 1888 | (16) | Piano Trio |
| 1900 | (28) | *Bucolic Suite*, for orchestra |
| 1903 | (31) | *The House of Life*, song cycle (No 2 is 'Silent Noon') |
| 1904 | (32) | *Songs of Travel* |
| 1906 | (34) | *Norfolk Rhapsodies* No 1 to 3, for orchestra (No 2 and 3 are lost) |
| 1907 | (35) | *In the Fen Country*, symphonic impression |
| | | *Towards the Unknown Region*, song for chorus and orchestra |
| 1908 | (36) | String Quartet in G minor |
| 1909 | (37) | *A Sea Symphony* (Symphony No 1), words by Walt Whitman, for soprano, baritone, chorus and orchestra |
| | | *The Wasps*, incidental music |
| | | *On Wenlock Edge*, song cycle |
| 1910 | (38) | *Fantasia on a Theme by Thomas Tallis*, for strings (No 9 in Archbishop Parker's Psalter, *p* 1567) |
| 1911 | (39) | *Five Mystical Songs*, for baritone, mixed chorus and orchestra |
| 1912 | (40) | Fantasia on Christmas Carols |
| | | *Phantasy Quintet*, for strings |
| 1913 | (41) | *A London Symphony* (Symphony No 2) |
| 1920 | (48) | *Shepherd of the Delectable Mountains*, one-act opera (now also forms Act IV of *The Pilgrim's Progress*) (1920–1) |
| | | *The Lark Ascending*, for violin and small orchestra |
| | | *Suite de Ballet*, for flute and piano |
| | | Mass in G minor (1920–1) |
| | | Three Preludes for organ |
| 1921 | (49) | *A Pastoral Symphony* (Symphony No 3) |
| 1923 | (51) | *Old King Cole*, ballet |
| 1924 | (52) | *Hugh the Drover*, opera |
| 1925 | (53) | *Concerto accademico*, for violin and string orchestra |
| | | *Flos Campi*, suite for viola, small wordless choir and small orchestra |
| | | *Sancta civitas*, oratorio |
| 1927 | (55) | *Along the Field*, eight songs (Housman) for voice and violin |
| 1928 | (56) | *Sir John in Love*, opera |
| | | *Te Deum*, in G major |
| 1929 | (57) | *Benedicte*, for soprano, mixed choir and orchestra |
| 1930 | (58) | *Job, a Masque for Dancing*, for orchestra |
| | | Prelude and Fugue in C minor for orchestra |
| 1931 | (59) | Symphony No 4 in F minor (1931–4) |
| | | Piano Concerto in C major |
| | | *In Windsor Forest*, cantata |
| 1932 | (60) | *Magnificat*, for contralto, women's chorus, solo flute and orchestra |
| 1933 | (61) | *The Running Set*, for medium orchestra |
| 1934 | (62) | *Fantasia on Greensleeves*, for orchestra |

|          |                                                                                   |
|----------|-----------------------------------------------------------------------------------|
|          | Suite for viola and small orchestra                                               |
| 1935 (63) | *Five Tudor Portraits*, choral suite in five movements                            |
| 1936 (64) | *Riders to the Sea*, opera in one act                                             |
|          | *The Poisoned Kiss*, romantic extravaganza with spoken dialogue, for thirteen soloists, mixed chorus and orchestra |
|          | *Dona nobis pacem*, cantata                                                        |
| 1937 (65) | *Festival Te Deum*, in F major                                                    |
| 1938 (66) | *The Bridal Day*, masque                                                          |
|          | *Serenade to Music*, for sixteen solo voices and orchestra                        |
| 1939 (67) | *Five Variants of Dives and Lazarus*, for strings and harp                       |
| 1940 (68) | *Six Choral Songs – to be sung in time of war*                                   |
|          | *Valiant for Truth*, motet                                                        |
| 1941 (69) | *England, My England*, for baritone, double chorus, unison voices and orchestra  |
| 1942 (70) | *Coastal Command*, orchestral suite from the film                                |
| 1943 (71) | Symphony No 5 in D major                                                          |
| 1944 (72) | Symphony No 6 in E minor (1944–7)                                                 |
|          | Concerto for oboe and strings                                                     |
|          | *A Song of Thanksgiving*, for soprano, speaker, mixed choir and orchestra        |
|          | String Quartet No 2 in A minor                                                    |
| 1945 (73) | *Story of a Flemish Farm*, orchestral suite from the film                        |
| 1946–8 (74–6) | Partita for double string orchestra                                          |
|          | Introduction and Fugue for two pianos                                             |
| 1949 (77) | *Fantasia (quasi variazione) on the 'Old 104th' Psalm Tune*, for piano, chorus, organ (optional) and orchestra |
|          | *An Oxford Elegy*, for speaker, chorus and small orchestra                        |
|          | *Folk Songs of the Four Seasons*, cantata                                         |
| 1950 (78) | Concerto Grosso for string orchestra                                             |
|          | *The Sons of Light*, cantata                                                      |
|          | *Sun, Moon, Stars and Man*, song cycle                                            |
| 1951 (79) | *The Pilgrim's Progress*, a Morality in a Prologue, Four Acts, and an Epilogue, for thirty-four soloists, chorus and orchestra |
|          | *Romance*, in D♭ major, for harmonica, strings and piano                          |
| 1952 (80) | *Sinfonia Antarctica* (Symphony No 7), in five movements                         |
| 1954 (82) | Concerto for bass tuba and orchestra in F minor                                  |
|          | *This Day (Hodie)*, a Christmas cantata                                           |
|          | Violin Sonata in A minor                                                          |
| 1955 (83) | Symphony No 8 in D minor (this was the first of the symphonies which Vaughan Williams allowed to be given a number) |
| 1956 (84) | *A Vision of Aeroplanes*, motet                                                  |
|          | Symphony No 9 in E minor (revised 1958)                                          |
|          | Two Organ Preludes, *Romanza* and *Toccata*                                      |
|          | *Epithalamium*, cantata (1956–7)                                                 |
|          | *Ten Blake Songs*, for tenor and oboe                                            |
| 1958 (86) | *The First Nowell*, nativity play for soloist, mixed chorus and small orchestra  |
|          | *Vocalises*, for soprano and B♭ clarinet                                         |
|          | *Four Last Songs*, for voice and piano                                           |
|          | *Thomas the Rhymer*, opera in three acts (uncompleted at Vaughan Williams' death; exists in short score only) |

**VERDI, Giuseppe**
*b Le Roncole, 10 October 1813*
*d Milan, 21 January 1901, aged eighty-seven*

He was the son of an innkeeper. He studied music from an early age, but was refused admittance to the Milan Conservatory at the age of eighteen because he was considered too old. He moved to Milan when La Scala accepted his first opera, *Oberto*. The deaths of his two children and his wife brought him to the edge of a nervous collapse; but the success of his third opera, *Nabucco*, restored him. In 1860 he was elected, rather reluctantly, to the new Italian parliament, and he stayed in politics for five years. His writing continued, and he was fortunate in having Boito as his main librettist. He died of a stroke.

| | | |
|---|---|---|
| 1839 | (26) | *fp Oberto*, opera |
| 1842 | (29) | *fp Nabucco*, opera |
| 1843 | (30) | *fp I Lombardi*, opera |
| 1844 | (31) | *fp Ernani*, opera |
| | | *fp I due Foscari*, opera |
| 1845 | (32) | *fp Alzira*, opera |
| | | *fp Giovanna d'Arco*, opera |
| 1846 | (33) | *fp Attila*, opera |
| 1847 | (34) | *fp Macbeth*, opera |
| | | *fp I masnadieri*, opera |
| 1849 | (36) | *fp Luisa Miller*, opera |
| 1851 | (38) | *fp Rigoletto*, opera |
| 1853 | (40) | *fp La Traviata*, opera |
| | | *fp Il Trovatore*, opera |
| 1855 | (42) | *fp I Vespri Siciliani*, opera |
| 1857 | (44) | *fp Araldo*, opera |
| | | *fp Simon Boccanegra*, opera |
| 1859 | (46) | *fp Un ballo in Maschera*, opera |
| 1862 | (49) | *fp La Forza del destino*, opera |
| | | *fp Inno delle nazioni*, for chorus |
| 1867 | (54) | *fp Don Carlos*, opera |
| 1871 | (58) | *fp Aida*, opera |
| 1873 | (60) | String Quartet in E minor |
| 1874 | (61) | Requiem Mass |
| 1887 | (74) | *fp Otello*, opera |
| 1889–98 | (76–85) | Four Sacred Pieces |
| 1893 | (80) | *fp Falstaff*, opera |

**VICTORIA (Vittoria), Tomás Luis de**
*b Avila, c1548*
*d Madrid, 27 August 1611, aged sixty-three*

Little is known of his early years. He was probably a chorister in Avila Cathedral from 1558 to 1565, then he went to the Collegium Germanicum in Rome to study for the priesthood. He left there in 1569 to become an organist and choirmaster. In 1571 he succeeded Palestrina as *maestro di cappella* at the Collegium Romanum, two years later assuming a similar post at the Collegium Germanicum and remaining there until 1575. In that year he was ordained a priest. From 1578 until 1585 he was chaplain of S Girolamo della Carità, and he did not return to Spain until 1596. From then until his death he was organist and choirmaster at the convent of the Descalzas Reales in Madrid.

His compositions comprise forty-four motets; twenty masses; eighteen magnificats; a Nunc Dimittis; thirty-four hymns; ten psalms; and various other religious works.

**VIEUXTEMPS, Henry**
*b Verviers, Belgium, 17 February 1820*
*d Mustapha, Algeria, 6 June 1881, aged sixty-one*

He studied violin with his father and made his first public appearance at the age of six. He became famous as a violinist, receiving a royal stipend in 1831 and playing his own works with enormous success all over the world. In 1871 he accepted a professorship at Brussels University. He suffered a paralytic stroke in 1873, which eventually forced him to give up work.

He wrote seven violin concertos; works for solo violin and other instruments, and for orchestra; a large amount of chamber music.

**VILLA-LOBOS, Heitor**
*b Rio de Janeiro, 5 March 1887*
*d Rio de Janeiro, 17 June 1959, aged seventy-two*

He was taught viola, clarinet and piano as a child, but when his father died his mother forbade him to continue his music studies. He ran away from home at the age of sixteen, helped by an uncle, and travelled all over Brazil, listening to folk music. In 1923 he went to Europe for the first time, chiefly to Paris where he fell under the influence of Debussy and Ravel. He returned to Brazil in 1930, and rose to become superintendent of musical education in Rio de Janeiro.

| | |
|---|---|
| 1908 (21) | *Recouli*, for small orchestra |
| 1910 (23) | *Suite dos canticos sertanejos*, for small orchestra |
| 1912 (25) | *Aglaia*, opera |
| 1913 (26) | *Suite da terra*, for small orchestra |
| | Suite for piano |
| 1914 (27) | *Izaht*, opera |
| | *Suite popular, Brasiliera*, for guitar |
| | *Ibericarabé*, symphonic poem |
| | *Dansas dos Indios Mesticos*, for orchestra |
| | Suite for strings |
| 1915 (28) | String Quartets No 1 and 2 |
| 1916 (29) | Symphony No 1, *The Unforeseen* |
| | *Centauro de Ouro*, symphonic poem |
| | *Miremis*, symphonic poem |
| | *Naufragio de Kleonica*, symphonic poem |
| | *Marcha religiosa No 1*, for orchestra |
| | *Sinfonietta on a Theme by Mozart* |
| | Cello Concerto |
| | String Quartet No 3 |
| 1917 (30) | *Uirapurú*, ballet |
| | *Amazonas*, ballet for orchestra |
| | Symphony No 2, *The Ascension* |
| | *Fantasia*, symphonic poem |
| | *Iara*, symphonic poem |
| | *Lobishome*, symphonic poem |
| | *Saci Perêrê*, symphonic poem |
| | *Tédio de alvorado*, symphonic poem |
| | *Sexteto mistico*, for flute, clarinet, saxophone, harp, celesta and double-bass |
| | String Quartet No 4 |
| 1918 (31) | *Jesus*, opera |
| | *Marcha religiosa No 3*, for orchestra |
| | *Marcha religiosa No 7*, for orchestra |

|           | *Vidapura*, oratorio |
|-----------|----------------------|
| 1919 (32) | *Zoé*, opera |
|           | Symphony No 3, *The War* |
|           | Symphony No 4, *The Victory* |
|           | *Dansa frenetica*, for orchestra |
| 1920 (33) | Symphony No 5, *The Peace* |
|           | *Dansa diabolica*, for orchestra |
|           | *Chôros No 1*, for guitar |
| 1921 (34) | *Malazarte*, opera |
|           | Quartet for harp, celesta, flute and saxophone, with women's voices |
| 1923 (36) | Suite for voice and viola |
| 1924 (37) | *Chôros No 2*, for flute and clarinet |
|           | *Chôros No 7*, for flute, oboe, clarinet, saxophone, bassoon, violin and cello |
| 1925 (38) | *Chôros No 3*, for clarinet, saxophone, bassoon, three horns and trombones, with male voice choir |
|           | *Chôros No 8*, for two pianos and orchestra |
|           | *Chôros No 10*, for choir and orchestra |
| 1926 (39) | *Chôros No 4*, for three horns and trombones |
|           | *Chôros No 5*, for piano |
|           | *Chôros No 6*, for orchestra |
|           | *Chôros No 6 bis*, for violin and cello |
| 1928 (41) | *Chôros No 11*, for piano and orchestra |
|           | *Chôros No 14*, for orchestra, band and choir |
| 1929 (42) | *Suite sugestiva*, for voice and orchestra |
|           | *Chôros No 9*, for orchestra |
|           | *Chôros No 12*, for orchestra |
|           | *Chôros No 13*, for two orchestras and band |
|           | *Introdução aos Chôros*, for orchestra |
|           | Twelve Studies for guitar |
| 1930 (43) | *Bachianas Brasilieras No 1*, for orchestra: Preludio, Aria, Fuga |
|           | *Bachianas Brasilieras No 2*, for orchestra: Preludio, Aria, Dansa, Tocata |
| 1931 (44) | String Quartet No 5 |
| 1932 (45) | *Caixinha de Bôas Festas*, ballet (also an orchestral suite) |
| 1933 (46) | *Pedra Bonita*, ballet |
| 1936 (49) | *Bachianas Brasilieras No 4*, for piano: Preludio, Aria, Coral Dansa (1930–6) |
| 1937 (50) | *Currupira*, ballet |
|           | *Sebastiao*, for three voices |
|           | *Descobrimento do Brasil*, four suites for chorus and orchestra |
| 1938 (51) | *Bachianas Brasilieras No 3*, for piano and orchestra: Preludio, Aria, Tocata |
|           | *Bachianas Brasilieras No 6*, for flute and bassoon: Aria, Fantasia |
|           | String Quartet No 6 |
| 1939 (52) | *New York Skyline*, for orchestra (Villa-Lobos 'drew' the melody by following the outline of skyscrapers on graph paper. He then harmonized the resultant melodic line and scored it for orchestra.) |
| 1940 (53) | *Saudades da juventude*, Suite No I |
|           | Preludes for guitar |
| 1942 (55) | *Bachianas Brasilieras No 7*, for orchestra: Preludio, Giga, Tocata, Fuga |
|           | String Quartet No 7 |

1944 (57)    *Bachianas Brasilieras No 8*, for orchestra: Preludio, Aria, Tocata, Fuga

                String Quartet No 8

1945 (58)    *Bachianas Brasilieras No 5*, for voice and orchestra of cellos: Aria, Dansa (1938–45)

                *Bachianas Brasilieras No 9*, for vocal orchestra

                Piano Concerto No 1

                Fantasia for cello

Villa-Lobos also composed much chamber music and many songs.


## VIVALDI, Antonio Lucio

*b Venice, 4 March 1676*
*d Vienna, 28 July 1741, aged sixty-five*

Little is known of his early life; his father, a violinist, probably taught him. From the age of fifteen he trained for the priesthood, until 1703 when he was ordained. His greater interest, however, was in music, and he was casual in his priestly duties. In 1703 he began his long association with the Foundling Hospital – a girl's music school – in Venice. As *maestro di violino* there, and later as *maestro dei concerti*, he was able to extend himself musically. He spent all his time composing and travelling, playing for the Pope and having audiences with Charles VI. The 1730s show a gradual decline in his popularity; the Church and the Foundling Hospital disowned him; Charles VI, with whom he might have found employment, died in 1740. Vivaldi was buried in a pauper's grave.

1705 (*c*30)    *p Suonate da camera a tre*, Op 1
1709 (*c*34)    *p Sonate a violino e basso per il cambala*, Op 2
1712 (*c*37)    *p Twelve concerti, L'estro armonico*, Op 3
              *p Twelve concerti, La stravaganza*, Op 4 (*c*1712–13)
1713 (*c*38)    *fp Ottone in Villa*, opera
1714 (*c*39)    *fp Orlando finto pazzo*, opera
              *Moyses deus Pharaonis*, oratorio
1715 (*c*40)    *fp Nerone fatto Cesare*, opera
1716 (*c*41)    *fp Arsilda Regine di Ponto*, opera
              *Juditha triumphans*, oratorio
              *p* Six sonate: four for violin solo and bass, two for two violins and basso continuo, Op 5
              *p Sei concerti a cinque*, Op 6 (1716–*c*1717)
              *p Sette concerti a cinque*, Books I and II, Op 7 (1716–*c*1717)
1717 (*c*42)    *fp Tieteberga*, opera
1718 (*c*43)    *fp Scanderbeg*, opera
1720 (*c*45)    *fp La verità in cimento*, opera
1721 (*c*46)    *fp Silvia*, opera
1722 (*c*47)    *L'adorazione delli tre Re Magi*, oratorio
1724 (*c*49)    *fp Giustino*, opera
1725 (*c*50)    *p Il cimento dell'Armonia e dell'Inventione*, twelve concerti of which four are known as *The Four Seasons*, Op 8
1726 (*c*51)    *Cunegonda*, opera
1727 (*c*52)    *Ipermestra*, opera
1728 (*c*53)    *Rosilena ed Oronta*, opera
              *p Twelve concerti, La Cetra*, Op 9
1729–30 (*c*54–5) *p* Sei concerti a flauto traverso, due violini, alto (viola), organo e violoncello, Op 10
              *p Sei concerti a violino principale*, Op 11
              *p Sei concerti a violino principale*, Op 12
1732 (*c*57)    *fp La fida ninfa*, opera

1733 (*c*58)   *fp Motezuma*, opera
1734 (*c*59)   *fp L'Olimpiade*, opera
1735 (*c*60)   *fp Griselda*, opera
              *fp Aristide*, opera
1736 (*c*61)   *fp Ginevra, Principessa di Scozia*, opera
1737 (*c*62)   *fp Catone in Utica*, opera
              *p Il pastor fido*, sonates pour la musette, viele, flute, hautbois,
                 violon avec la Basso continuo, Op 13 (*c*1737)
1738 (*c*63)   *fp L'Oracolo in Messenia*, opera
1739 (*c*64)   *fp Feraspe*, opera
*c*1740 (*c*65)  *p* Six sonate a cello e basse, Op 14

Vivaldi's total output in the concerto genre numbers over four hundred, including two hundred and twenty solo concerti, some sixty concerti ripieni, forty-eight bassoon concerti, twenty-five cello concerti, plus many works for various instruments. There are about forty-six known operas of the hundred that Vivaldi claimed to have written.


**WAGNER, Richard**
*b Leipzig, 22 May 1813*
*d Venice, 13 February 1883, aged sixty-nine*

He was of Jewish ancestry, which made his later virulent anti-Semitism the more surprising. As a boy he was interested in music, theatre and literature. At eighteen he entered Leipzig University, more for a wild student life than for study. At twenty he was given the position of chorus-master at the theatre at Würtsburg, then of musical director of the Magdburg Opera Company. He fell in love with the actress Minna Planer, whom he married two years later. In constant flight from their creditors, the pair eventually arrived in Paris. Wagner met Meyerbeer, who introduced him to influential people; but there was little interest in his music, so he turned to journalism. After a year or so the couple were completely penniless, and Wagner spent some weeks in a debtor's prison. However, Dresden Opera accepted *Rienzi* and then, in 1843, produced *The Flying Dutchman*; Wagner's stock rose, and he was made *Kapellmeister* to the Saxon court. He lived wildly beyond his means, and joined a revolutionary movement in Dresden. A warrant was issued for his arrest, and he fled into political exile in Switzerland. In Zurich he concentrated on publishing essays of musical polemics and then began the 'Ring' cycle, writing his own libretti first, in the reverse chronological order. In 1859 the Wagners settled again in Paris; but shortly afterwards Minna left him. Wagner became emotionally involved with Liszt's illegitimate daughter Cosima, who was married to the conductor Hans von Bülow. Soon after that the eighteen-year-old homosexual Ludwig II of Bavaria asked Wagner to move in with him in Munich, but the scandal of this relationship forced Wagner to move again, to Lake Lucerne, where he eventually married Cosima. In 1876, with help from Ludwig, he built the Festival Theatre in Bayreuth, and a splendid villa nearby in which the Wagner family still lives. After the Bayreuth première of *Parsifal* in 1882 the Wagners went to Venice for the winter, and there Wagner succumbed to a heart attack.

1830 (17)   Overture
1831 (18)   Piano Sonata
1832 (19)   Symphony in C major
            *Die Hochzeit*, opera (unfinished)
1833 (20)   *Die Feen*, opera
1834 (21)   *Das Liebesverbot*, opera
1840 (27)   *Faust*, overture
1842 (29)   *fp Rienzi*, opera

| 1843 | (30) | *fp The Flying Dutchman*, opera |
| 1845 | (32) | *fp Tannhäuser*, opera |
| 1851 | (38) | *fp Lohengrin*, opera |
| 1857–8 | (44–5) | The *Wesendonck Lieder*, five songs with orchestra |
| 1865 | (52) | *fp Tristan und Isolde*, music drama |
| 1868 | (55) | *fp Die Meistersinger von Nürnberg*, opera |
| 1869 | (56) | *fp Das Rheingold* (No 1 of *Der Ring des Nibelungen*), music drama |
| 1870 | (57) | *fp Die Walküre* (No 2 of *Der Ring des Nibelungen*), music drama |
| | | *Siegfried Idyll*, for orchestra |
| 1876 | (63) | *fp Siegfried* (No 3 of *Der Ring des Nibelungen*), music drama |
| | | *fp Götterdämmerung* (No 4 of *Der Ring des Nibelungen*), music drama |
| 1882 | (69) | *fp Parsifal*, religious music drama |

## WALTON, (Sir) William
*b Oldham, 29 March 1902*
*d Ischia, 8 March 1983, aged eighty*

At the age of ten he won a place as a chorister at Christ Church, Oxford, but he had little formal musical training. At Oxford he made a number of influential friends, particularly Sacheverell Sitwell, with whose family he lived for the next ten years. This connection immensely broadened his horizons in literature and the visual arts; it brought him also the friendship of Bernard van Dieren, Peter Heseltine and, most important, Constant Lambert, who was perhaps the greatest single influence on his career. The music he wrote to *Façade*, some experimental poems written by Edith Sitwell and intended to be read as a drawing-room entertainment with musical backing, became Walton's most popular work to date, and established him before the public. In 1948 he married in Buenos Aires, and made his permanent home in Ischia, off the coast of Naples. He was knighted in 1951. He travelled to many parts of the world to conduct his own compositions.

| 1916 | (14) | Piano Quartet |
| 1922 | (20) | *fp* (privately) *Façade – An Entertainment*, for reciter and chamber ensemble |
| 1923 | (21) | String Quartet (withdrawn) |
| 1925 | (23) | *Portsmouth Point*, overture |
| 1926 | (24) | *Siesta*, for orchestra |
| 1927 | (25) | Viola Concerto (soloist at *fp* was Hindemith, *qv*) |
| | | Sinfonia Concertante for piano and orchestra |
| 1931 | (29) | *fp Belshazzar's Feast*, for baritone, chorus and orchestra |
| 1934 | (32) | *fp* Symphony No 1 (first three movements only, performed in full 1935) |
| | | *Escape Me Never*, ballet from the film |
| 1937 | (35) | *Crown Imperial*, coronation march for orchestra |
| | | *In Honour of the City*, for chorus and orchestra |
| 1939 | (37) | Violin Concerto |
| 1940 | (38) | *The Wise Virgins*, ballet (arranged from the music of J. S. Bach) |
| 1941 | (39) | *Scapino*, overture |
| 1942 | (40) | *Major Barbara*, film score |
| | | *The First of the Few*, film score, including 'Spitfire', prelude and fugue |
| 1943 | (41) | *Henry V*, incidental music for the film |
| | | *The Quest*, ballet |
| 1947 | (45) | *Hamlet*, incidental music for the film |
| | | String Quartet in A minor |
| 1949 | (47) | Violin Sonata |

| 1953 (51) | *Orb and Sceptre*, coronation march for orchestra |
| | *Coronation Te Deum* |
| 1954 (52) | *Troilus and Cressida*, opera |
| 1955 (53) | *Richard III*, incidental music for the film |
| | *Johannesburg Festival Overture* |
| 1956 (54) | Cello Concerto |
| 1957 (55) | Partita for orchestra |
| 1960 (58) | Symphony No 2 |
| | fp *Anon. in Love*, six songs for tenor and guitar |
| 1961 (59) | *Gloria*, for contralto, tenor and bass soli, mixed choir and orchestra |
| 1962 (60) | fp *A Song for the Lord Mayor's Table*, cycle of six songs for soprano and piano |
| 1963 (61) | *Variations on a Theme of Hindemith*, for orchestra (theme from Hindemith's *Nobilissima Visione*) |
| 1965 (63) | *The Twelve*, for choir and orchestra, or organ |
| 1966 (64) | *Missa Brevis* |
| 1967 (65) | *The Bear*, one-act opera for three solo voices and chamber orchestra |
| 1968 (66) | *Capriccio-burlesca*, for orchestra |
| 1970 (68) | *Improvisations on an Impromptu of Benjamin Britten*, for orchestra |
| 1972 (70) | *Jubilate Deo*, for double mixed chorus and organ |
| | Sonata for string orchestra, arranged from the String Quartet |
| | Five Bagatelles for guitar |
| 1974 (72) | *Cantico del Sole* |
| | *Magnificat* and *Nunc Dimittis* |
| 1982 (80) | *Prologo e Fantasia*, for orchestra |
| | *Passacaglia*, for solo cello |

Walton has also composed other incidental and film music.


## WARLOCK, Peter (Philip Heseltine)
*b London, 30 October 1894*
*d London, 17 December 1930, aged thirty-six*

He studied first at Eton, then privately. In 1920 he founded the periodical *The Sackbut*. He wrote books about Gesualdo and about his friend Delius, many of whose orchestral works he arranged for the piano. He committed suicide by gassing himself.

| 1917 (23) | *An Old Song*, for small orchestra |
| 1922 (28) | *Serenade for Frederick Delius*, for orchestra |
| 1923 (29) | *The Curlew*, song cycle for voice, flute, English horn and string quartet |
| 1926 (32) | *Capriol Suite*, for strings (also arranged for full orchestra) |


## WEBER, Carl Maria von
*b Eutin, near Lübeck, 18 November 1786*
*d London, 5 June 1826, aged thirty-nine*

His father was a *Kapellmeister*, and his mother a singer. His childhood was spent touring with his parents, to the detriment of his education; but he could sing and play piano by the age of four. He studied with Michael Haydn in Salzburg for a time, and soon after the age of eleven he began a career as a concert pianist, in spite of a congenital disease of the hip. From 1801 to 1816 he held such posts as *Kapellmeister* at Breslau, a music secretaryship in Stuttgart and directorship of the Prague Opera, while making concert tours and composing orchestral works. In 1817 he took up the directorship of the Dresden Court Opera and he held this position for the rest of his short life. He died of consumption.

| 1800 (14) | *Das Waldmädchen*, opera |
| 1801 (15) | *Peter Schmoll und seine Nachbarn*, opera |
| 1806–7 (20–1) | Symphony No 1 in C major |
| 1807 (21) | Symphony No 2 in C major |
| 1810 (24) | Piano Concerto No 1 in C major |
| 1811 (25) | *Abu Hassan*, opera |
| | Bassoon Concerto |
| | Clarinet Concerto No 1 in F minor |
| | Clarinet Concerto No 2 in E♭ major |
| | Concertino for clarinet in C minor and E♭ major |
| 1812 (26) | Piano Concerto No 2 in E♭ major |
| | Piano Sonata No 1 in C major |
| 1815 (29) | Concertino for horn and orchestra in E minor |
| | Quintet for clarinet and string quartet in E♭ major |
| 1816 (30) | Piano Sonata No 2 in A♭ major |
| | Piano Sonata No 3 in D minor |
| 1819 (33) | *Invitation to the Dance*, for piano (orchestrated by Berlioz, 1841) |
| 1821 (35) | *fp Der Freischütz*, opera |
| | *Konzertstücke*, for piano and orchestra, in E minor |
| 1822 (36) | Piano Sonata No 4 in E minor |
| 1823 (37) | *fp Euryanthe*, opera |
| 1826 (39) | *fp Oberon*, opera |

## WEBERN, Anton von
*b Vienna, 3 December 1883*
*d Mittersill, 15 September 1945, aged sixty-one*

He was born of an old aristocratic family. He attended the Gymnasium at Klagenfurt from 1894, and also had private lessons on violin and cello. From about 1901 he began to write songs; then he studied music at the University of Vienna, from which he took his doctorate. He showed some of his songs to Schoenberg, who accepted him as a pupil in 1904. In 1908 he became conductor at Bad Ischl, then returned to Vienna as an occasional conductor and chorus *répétiteur*. In 1910 he became assistant conductor at the Stadttheater in Danzig, but when Schoenberg moved to Berlin, Webern followed him. From 1913 to 1914 he lived in Vienna, and after World War I he held many posts in various towns, but never for long; he always came back to Vienna. In the 1920s his success slowly grew; he was asked to conduct his own works abroad, and he won the Vienna Music Prize in 1924. Political changes in 1934 ended his activities with the Workers' Symphony Orchestra, and he had to live by teaching. He died in a shooting accident; an American soldier came to arrest Webern's son-in-law because of black-market activities while Webern was staying with him and in a nervous moment fired at Webern by mistake.

| 1908 (25) | Passacaglia, for orchestra, Op 1 |
| | *Entflieht auf Leichten Kahnan*, for chorus, Op 2 |
| | Five Lieder, Op 3 |
| | Five Lieder, Op 4 (1908–9) |
| 1909 (26) | Five Movements for string quartet, Op 5 |
| 1910 (27) | Six Pieces for large orchestra, Op 6 |
| | Four Pieces for violin and piano, Op 7 (1910–15) |
| 1911–12 (28–9) | Two Lieder, Op 8 |
| | Five Pieces for orchestra, Op 10 (1911–13) |
| 1913 (30) | Six Bagatelles for string quartet, Op 9 |
| 1914 (31) | Three Little Pieces for cello and piano, Op 11 |
| 1914–18 (31–5) | Four Lieder, with thirteen instruments, Op 13 |

1915–17 (32–4) Four Lieder, Op 12
1917–21 (34–8) Six Lieder, with violin, clarinet, bass clarinet, viola and cello,
              Op 14
1917–22 (34–9) Five Geistliche Lieder, Op 15
1924 (41)    Five Canons for voice, clarinet and bass clarinet, Op 16
             Six Volkstexte, Op 17
1925 (42)    Three Lieder, Op 18
1926 (43)    Two Lieder, Op 19
1927 (44)    String Trio, Op 20
1928 (45)    Symphony for small orchestra, Op 21
1930 (47)    Quartet for violin, clarinet, saxophone and piano, Op 22
1934 (51)    Three Gesänge from *Viae invaie*, Op 23
             Concerto for flute, oboe, clarinet, horn, trumpet, trombone, violin,
                 viola and piano, Op 24
1935 (52)    Three Lieder, Op 25
             *Das Augenlicht*, for mixed chorus and orchestra, Op 26
1936 (53)    Variations for piano, Op 27
1938 (55)    String Quartet, Op 28
1939 (56)    Cantata No 1, *Jone*, Op 29
1940 (57)    Variations for orchestra, Op 30
1941–3 (58–60) Cantata No 2, *Jone*, Op 31


## WEELKES, Thomas
*b Sussex?, baptised 25 October 1576*
*d London, buried 1 December 1623, aged forty-seven*

The earliest known fact about him is the publication of his first volume of
madrigals in 1597. In 1598, for three or four years, he was organist at Winchester
College. In 1602 he joined the choir of Chichester Cathedral, and in that year
was awarded the BMus from New College, Oxford.

He wrote a vast number of madrigals, sacred works and services, and some
instrumental works.


## WEILL, Kurt
*b Dessau, 2 March 1900*
*d New York, 3 April 1950, aged fifty*

He was born of a Jewish family. His early music studies were with Bing and
Humperdinck; then he became coach and conductor for the opera companies in
Dessau and Lüdenscheid. In 1921 he settled in Berlin and studied with Busoni
for three years; then began his great collaboration with Bertolt Brecht. In 1933,
with Hitler in power, Weill and his wife escaped to Paris, and they were quite
penniless until he worked again with Brecht and received a commission to
write a symphony. Unfortunately, the symphony was poorly received; his
music was banned in Germany and copies of his scores were destroyed. After a
brief stay in London he went to the USA, where his success was assured. He
died of a heart attack.

1921 (21)    Symphony No 1
1923 (23)    *Fantasie, Passacaglia and Hymnus,* for orchestra
1924 (24)    *Quodlibet,* for string quartet
             *The Protagonist,* opera
1925 (25)    Concerto for violin and woodwinds
1927 (27)    *Lindbergh's Flight,* cantata
             *The New Orpheus,* cantata

                    *The Royal Palace*, opera
                    *Mahagonny*, opera
1928 (28)           *The Threepenny Opera*
1933 (33)           *The Silver Lake*, opera
                    Symphony No 2
1935 (35)           *A Kingdom for a Cow*, musical play
1936 (36)           *Johnny Johnson*, musical
1937 (37)           *The Eternal Road*, incidental music
1938 (38)           *Knickerbocker Holiday*, musical
1939 (39)           *The Ballad of the Magna Carta*, incidental music for radio drama
1941 (41)           *Lady in the Dark*, musical
1943 (43)           *One Touch of Venus*, musical
1947 (47)           *Street Scene*, opera
                    *Down in the Valley*, folk opera
1949 (49)           *Lost in the Stars*, opera
Weill also wrote many songs.


**WEINBERGER, Jaromir**
*b Prague, 8 January 1896*
*d St Petersburg, Florida, 8 August 1967, aged seventy-one*

He studied at the Prague Conservatory, and with Max Reger in Leipzig, then taught in Prague, Bratislava and Vienna. He lived in America from 1939 and became an American citizen in 1948.

1927 (31)           *Schwanda the Bagpiper*, opera
1929 (33)           *Christmas*, for orchestra
1930 (34)           *The Beloved Voice*, opera
                    Bohemian Songs and Dances for orchestra
1931 (35)           Passacaglia, for orchestra
1932 (36)           *The Outcasts of Poker Flat*, opera
1934 (38)           *A Bed of Roses*, opera
1937 (41)           *Wallenstein*, opera
1938 (42)           Variations on *Under the Spreading Chestnut Tree*, for orchestra
1940 (44)           *Song of the High Seas*, for orchestra
                    Saxophone Concerto
1941 (45)           *Lincoln Symphony*
                    *Czech Rhapsody*, for orchestra
                    *The Bird's Opera*, for orchestra
1957 (61)           *Préludes religieuses et profanes*, for organ
1960 (64)           *Aus Tirol*, for orchestra
1961 (65)           *Eine Walserouverture*
Weinberger also composed:
*Overture to a Puppet Show*, for orchestra
*Overture to a Cavalier's Play*, for orchestra
*The Legend of Sleepy Hollow*, for orchestra
*Mississippi Rhapsody*, for band
*Prelude to the Festival*, for band
*Homage to the Pioneers*, for band
Chamber music, choral works and songs

## WELLESZ, Egon
*b Vienna, 21 October 1885*
*d Oxford, 9 November 1974, aged eighty-nine*

He studied at Vienna University. He was greatly influenced by Mahler, Strauss and Schoenberg, and had a special interest in baroque and eighteenth-century opera and Byzantine music. He was largely instrumental in introducing contemporary British composers to the Continent. In 1933 he was elected a director of the International Musicological Society. He was made professor of musical history at Vienna University, and in 1932 was given an honorary doctorate by Oxford University. He settled in England after the Anschluss of 1938; was made a fellow of Lincoln College, Oxford, and appointed lecturer in musical history in 1943. He was made a member of the Royal Danish Academy in 1946, awarded a CBE in 1957 and won other honours. In 1972 he suffered a stroke from which he died two years later.

| | |
|---|---|
| 1905 (20) | *Sinfonischer Prolog*, for orchestra |
| 1911 (26) | *Vorfrühling*, for orchestra |
| 1914 (29) | Suite for orchestra |
| 1921 (36) | *Die Prinzessin Girnara*, opera (revised 1928) |
| 1924 (39) | *Das Wunder der Diana*, ballet |
| | *Persisches Ballett* |
| | *Alkestis*, opera |
| | *Die Nächtlichen*, ballet |
| 1926 (41) | *Achilles auf Skyros*, ballet |
| | *Der Opferung des Gefangenen*, opera |
| 1928 (43) | *Scherz, List und Rache*, opera |
| 1929 (44) | *Festlicher Marsch*, for orchestra |
| 1931 (46) | *Die Bakchantinnen*, opera |
| 1934 (49) | Piano Concerto |
| 1936–8 (51–3) | *Prosperos Beschwörungen*, for orchestra |
| 1945 (60) | Symphony No 1 |
| 1948 (63) | Symphony No 2 |
| 1951 (66) | Symphony No 3 |
| | *Incognita*, opera |
| 1952 (67) | Symphony No 4 |
| 1956 (71) | Symphony No 5 |
| 1961 (76) | Violin Concerto |
| 1964 (79) | Music for strings |
| 1965 (80) | Symphony No 6 |
| 1967–8 (82–3) | Symphony No 7 |
| 1969 (84) | Divertimento for chamber orchestra |
| | Symphonic Epilogue for orchestra |
| 1970 (85) | Symphony No 8 |
| 1971 (86) | Symphony No 9 |

Wellesz also wrote much choral and solo vocal music; chamber and instrumental works; and many books and essays on music.


## WIDOR, Charles-Marie-Jean-Albert
*b Lyons, 21 February 1844*
*d Paris, 12 March 1937, aged ninety-three*

His grandfather and father were organ-builders, and his father was also a good performer who gave his son his first lessons. At eleven he became organist at the Lycée in Lyons, and various other organ posts followed until 1870, when he took a one-year appointment at St Sulpice in Paris – which eventually was to last for sixty-four years. In 1890 he became professor of organ and composition at the Paris Conservatory, and he was elected to the Académie des Beaux Arts in 1910.

possibly 1870 (26) Symphony No 1
| | | |
|---|---|---|
| 1876 | (32) | Piano Concerto |
| 1880 | (36) | *La Korrigane*, ballet |
| 1882 | (38) | Violin Concerto |
| 1885 | (41) | *Conte d'avril*, incidental music |
| | | *Les Jacobites*, incidental music |
| 1886 | (42) | *Maîtres Ambros*, lyric drama |
| | | Symphony No 2 |
| 1887 | (43) | *La Nuit de Walpurgis*, symphonic poem with chorus |
| 1889 | (45) | *Fantasie*, for piano |
| 1890 | (46) | *Jeanne d'Arc*, ballet-pantomime |
| 1895 | (51) | Symphony No 2 |
| 1898 | (54) | *Ouverture Espagnole* |
| 1900 | (56) | Chorale and Variations for harp |
| 1905 | (61) | *Les pêcheurs de Saint-Jean*, lyric drama |
| 1906 | (62) | Piano Concerto |
| 1908 | (64) | *Sinfonia Sacra*, for organ and orchestra |
| 1911 | (67) | *Symphonie Antique*, for organ, chorus and orchestra |
| 1924 | (80) | *Nerto*, lyric drama |

Widor also composed a piano trio, a quartet and two quintets, other instrumental and chamber works, sacred and secular vocal works, ten organ symphonies, and eight sonatas and other pieces for organ.


## WIENIAWSKI, Henryk
*b Lublin, Poland, 10 July 1835*
*d Moscow, 31 March 1880, aged forty-four*

Born of a musical family, he showed exceptional talent for the violin at a very early age. He entered the Paris Conservatory in 1843; then, apart from periods of teaching – 1860 to 1872 in St Petersburg and 1875 to 1877 at Brussels Conservatory – he toured widely as a master performer, despite a severe heart condition which ultimately killed him.

| | | |
|---|---|---|
| 1853 | (18) | Polonaise No 1 for violin and orchestra |
| | | *Souvenir de Moscow*, for violin and orchestra |
| | | Violin Concerto No 1 |
| 1860 | (25) | *Légende*, for violin and orchestra |
| 1862 | (27) | Violin Concerto No 2 |

Wieniawski's large output of other compositions featured exclusively the violin.


## WILBYE, John
*b Diss, Norfolk, baptised 7 March 1574*
*d Colchester, September-November 1638, aged sixty-four*

He entered the service of the Kytsons of Hengrave Hall, a very musical establishment, and stayed there until it was dispersed in 1628. He spent his last ten years in Colchester with Lady Kytson's youngest daughter.

He left a large number of madrigals, and a few sacred works.

# WILLIAMSON, Malcolm
b Sydney, 21 November 1931

At the age of eleven he entered the Sydney Conservatory to study piano and horn, and composition under Goossens. In 1953 he went to London to continue composition studies under Lutyens and Stein. In both Australia and the USA, which he regularly visits, he holds university fellowships. In 1975 he was appointed Master of the Queen's Music.

| | |
|---|---|
| 1957 (26) | Piano Sonata No 1 |
| 1958 (27) | *Santiago de Espada*, overture |
| | Piano Concerto No 1 |
| 1961 (30) | Organ Concerto |
| 1963 (32) | *Our Man in Havana*, opra |
| | *Elevamini Symphony* |
| 1964 (33) | Sinfonia Concertante for piano, three trumpets and string orchestra |
| | Piano Concerto No 3 |
| | Variations for cello and piano |
| | *The Display*, a dance symphony in four movements |
| | *The Merry Wives of Windsor*, incidental music |
| | *Elegy JFK*, for organ |
| | Three Shakespeare Songs for high voice and guitar (or piano) |
| 1965 (34) | *The Happy Prince*, one-act opera |
| | Sinfonietta |
| | *Symphonic Variations*, for orchestra |
| | Concerto Grosso for orchestra |
| | Violin Concerto |
| | *Four North Country Songs*, for voice and orchestra |
| | Concerto for two pianos (eight hands) and wind quintet |
| 1966 (35) | *The Violins of St Jacques*, opera |
| | *Julius Caesar Jones*, opera |
| | *Sun Into Darkness*, ballet |
| | Five Preludes for piano |
| | Two Organ Epitaphs for Edith Sitwell |
| | Six English Lyrics for low voice and piano |
| 1967 (36) | *Dunstan and the Devil*, one-act opera |
| | *Pas de Quatre*, music to the ballet *Nonet*, for flute, oboe, clarinet, bassoon and piano |
| | *Spectrum*, ballet (music identical with the *Variations* for cello and piano, 1964) |
| | *The Moonrakers*, cassation for audience and orchestra |
| | Serenade for flute, piano, violin, viola and cello |
| | Sonata for two pianos |
| 1968 (37) | *The Growing Castle*, chamber opera for four singers |
| | *Knights in Shining Armour*, cassation for audience and piano |
| | *The Snow Wolf*, cassation for audience and piano |
| | Piano Quintet |
| | *From a Child's Garden*, settings of twelve poems, for high voice and piano |
| 1969 (38) | *Lucky-Peter's Journey*, a comedy with music |
| | Symphony No 2 |
| | *The Brilliant and the Dark*, choral-operatic sequence for women's voices |
| 1971 (40) | *Genesis*, cassation for audience and instruments |
| | *The Stone Wall*, cassation for audience and orchestra |
| | *Peace Pieces*, six organ pieces in two volumes |

Death of Cuchulain, for five male voices and percussion instruments

In Place of Belief, setting of ten poems by Per Lagerqvist for voices and piano duet

1972 (41)  The Red Sea, one-act children's opera

Symphony No 3, The Icy Mirror, for soprano, mezzo-soprano, two baritones, chorus and orchestra

Partita for viola on themes of Walton

The Musicians of Bremen, for six male voices

Love the Sentinel, for unaccompanied choir

1973 (42)  The Winter Star, cassation for audience and instruments

Concerto for two pianos and strings

Ode to Music, for chorus, echo chorus and orchestra

Pietà, four poems for soprano, oboe, bassoon and piano

Little Carols of the Saints, five organ pieces

The World at the Manger, Christmas cantata

Canticle of Fire, for chorus and organ

1974 (43)  The Glitter Gang, cassation for audience and orchestra

Perisynthyon, ballet

Hammarskjold Portrait, song cycle for soprano and string orchestra

1976 (45)  Piano Trio

1977 (46)  Symphony No 4

Mass of Christ the King, for chorus and orchestra

Les Olympiques, for mezzo and string orchestra

The Lion of Suffolk, for organ

1977–80 (46–9) Mass of St Margaret of Scotland

1980 (49)  Symphony No 5, Aquero

Lament in memory of Lord Mountbatten of Burma, for violin and string orchestra

Little Mass of St Bernadette, for voices and organ

Ode for Queen Elizabeth, for string orchestra

Choric Hymn, for mixed chorus

Konstanz Fanfare, for brass, percussion and organ

Richmond Fanfare, for brass, percussion and organ

1981 (50)  Josip Broz Tito, for baritone and orchestra

Fontainebleau Fanfare, for brass, percussion and organ

Mass of the People of God

Williamson has also written concert suites and music for the theatre, cinema and television.


## WOLF, Hugo
b Windischgraz (then Austria), 13 March 1860
d Vienna, 22 February 1903, aged forty-two

His father was a versatile instrumentalist, and Hugo learnt piano and violin at an early age. In 1875 he went to the Vienna Conservatory, but was expelled. All his life he wrecked his opportunities by impulsive or rude behaviour; as a teacher he lost his pupils, as a conductor he lost his jobs, and his work as a music critic made him many enemies. The tide turned in 1887, when his creative energy burst forth in an enormous output of work. After 1890 his inspiration began to dry up, his optimism gradually faded and by 1898 his mental collapse was complete. He died in a private asylum.

1877–8 (17–18) Lieder aus der Jugendzeit
1877–97 (17–37) Lieder nach verschiedenen Dichtern
1879–80 (19) String Quartet in D minor

1880–8 (20–8) *Eichendorff-Lieder*
1883–5 (23–5) *Penthesilea*, symphonic poem
1887 (27)     *Italian Serenade*, for string quartet (arranged for small orchestra in 1892)
                Violin Sonata
1888 (28)     *Mörike-Lieder*, fifty-three songs
                *Goethe-Lieder*, fifty-one songs (1888–9)
1890 (30)     *Spanish Song Book*, song settings of forty-four Spanish poems
1891 (31)     *Italian Song Book*, Book I, twenty-two songs
                *The Feast of Sulhaug*, incidental music
1896 (36)     *fp Der Corregidor*, opera
                *Italian Song Book*, Book II, twenty-four songs


## WOLF-FERRARI, Ermanno
*b Venice, 12 January 1876*
*d Venice, 21 January 1948, aged seventy-two*

Following the wish of his father, who was a painter, he attended the Accademia di Belle Arti in Rome from 1891 to 1892, while learning music in his spare time. He went to Munich to study music in 1893, returning to Venice in 1895. From 1902 to 1907 he was director of the Liceo Benedetto Marcello in Venice. He spent much of his time supervising the production of his own operas.

1895 (19)     Violin Sonata in G minor, Op 1
1901 (25)     *p* Piano Quintet in D♭ major, Op 6
                *p* Piano Trio in F♯ major, Op 7
1902 (26)     *p* Piano Trio in D major, Op 5
                *p* Violin Sonata in A minor, Op 10
1903 (27)     *p* Chamber Symphony in B♭ major, Op 8
                *fp Le donne curiose*, opera
                *La Vita nuova*, oratorio
1906 (30)     *fp School for Fathers*, opera
                *fp I quatro (sic) rusteghi*, comedy-opera
1909 (33)     *fp Susanna's Secret*, opera
1911 (35)     *fp The Jewels of the Madonna*, opera
1936 (60)     *fp Il campiello*, opera
1939 (63)     *fp Dama Boba*, opera


## WOOD, Hugh
*b Parbold, Lancashire, 27 June 1932*

His parents were musical. After reading Modern History at New College, Oxford, he went to London in 1954, studying composition under Lloyd Webber, Hamilton and Seiber. From 1958 to 1967 he gave evening classes at Morley College, and from 1962 to 1965 he taught harmony at the Royal Academy of Music. In 1966 he was appointed Cramb Research Fellow at Glasgow University. He has lectured at Liverpool University and, from 1976, at Churchill College, Cambridge.

1957 (25)     String Quartet in B♭
1958 (26)     Variations for viola and piano
1959 (27)     Logue Songs
                Trio for flute, viola and piano
1962 (30)     String Quartet No 1
1965 (33)     *Scenes from Comus*, for soli and orchestra

|          | Three Choruses |
|          | Capriccio for organ |
| 1967 (35) | Quintet for clarinet, horn, violin, cello and piano |
|          | *The Horses,* song cycle |
| 1968 (36) | *The Rider Victory,* song cycle |
| 1969 (37) | Cello Concerto |
| 1970 (38) | String Quartet No 2 |
| 1971 (39) | Chamber Concerto |
| 1972 (40) | Violin Concerto |
| 1973 (41) | *Song Cycle to Poems of Pablo Neruda* |
|          | *Two Choruses of Yeats,* for chorus |
|          | *Songs to Poems by Robert Graves,* for voice and piano |
| 1978 (46) | String Quartet No 3 |
| 1982 (50) | Symphony |
| 1984 (52) | Piano Trio |

## XENAKIS, Iannis
*b Braïla, Greece, 29 May 1922*

During the first ten years of his life he became familiar with the rich folk-music of the Danube, and was influenced by the Byzantine music of the Orthodox religious rites. It was during his secondary education from 1932 that he first came into contact with western romantic music. Musically largely self-taught, he did not emerge as a composer until after 1947. He entered Athens Polytechnic with the intention of becoming an engineer. In 1941 he became secretary to various resistance groups, and for five years played a part in the armed struggle for liberation. In 1945 he was wounded and lost the sight of one eye; later he was captured and condemned to death, but managed to escape. He arrived in Paris in 1947 and took French nationality. He met there not only Honegger, Milhaud and Messiaen, but also Le Corbusier the architect, for whom he did some outstanding construction designs.

| | |
|---|---|
| 1953–4 (31–2) | *Metastaseis,* for orchestra of sixty-one players |
| 1955–6 (33–4) | *Pithoprakta,* for orchestra of fifty players |
| 1956–7 (34–5) | *Achorripsis,* for twenty-one players |
| 1956–62 (34–40) | *ST/4,* for string quartet |
| | *ST/10-080262,* for ten players |
| | *Morsima-Amorsima,* for piano and strings |
| | *Atrées,* for ten players |
| | *ST/48,* for orchestra of forty-eight players |
| 1957 (35) | *Diamorphoses,* electroacoustic music |
| 1958 (36) | *Concret PH,* electroacoustic music |
| 1959 (37) | *Duel,* game for two orchestras |
| | *Syrmos,* for eighteen strings or a multiple |
| | *Analogiques A & B,* for nine strings and four-channel tape |
| 1959–62 (37–40) | *Stratégie,* game for two orchestras and two conductors |
| 1960 (38) | *Orient-Occident,* electroacoustic music |
| 1960–1 (38–9) | *Herma,* for solo piano |
| 1962 (40) | *Polla Ta Dhina,* for children's chorus and orchestra |
| | *Bohor,* electroacoustic music |
| 1963–4 (41–2) | *Eonta,* for piano and five brass instruments |
| 1964 (42) | *Hiketides,* stage music for voices and instruments |
| | *Idem,* instrumental suite for brass and strings |
| 1964–5 (42–3) | *Akrata,* for sixteen wind instruments |
| 1965–6 (43–4) | *Oresteia,* stage music for mixed chorus and chamber ensemble |
| | *Oresteia Suite,* concert version of *Oresteia* |

|           | *Terretektorh*, for orchestra of eighty-eight musicians scattered in the audience |
| 1966 (44) | *Nomos Alpha*, for violoncello |
| 1967 (45) | *Polytope de Montréal*, light and sound spectacle |
|           | *Nuits*, for twelve mixed voices a capella |
|           | *Medea*, stage music for male chorus and instrumental ensemble |
| 1967–8 (45–6) | *Nomos Gamma*, for orchestra of ninety-eight musicians scattered in the audience |
| 1968–9 (46–7) | *Kraanerg*, ballet music for four-channel tape and orchestra |
| 1969 (47) | *Anaktoria*, for octet |
|           | *Synaphai*, for piano and orchestra |
|           | *Persephassa*, for six percussionists placed surrounding the audience |
| 1969–70 (47–8) | *Hibiki-Hana-Ma*, twelve-channel electroacoustic music |
| 1971 (49) | *Charisma*, for clarinet and violoncello |
|           | *Aroura*, for twelve strings or a multiple |
|           | *Persepolis*, light and sound spectacle |
|           | *Antikhthon*, ballet music for orchestra |
| 1972 (50) | *Linaia-Agon*, for three brass instruments |
|           | *Mikka*, for solo violin |
|           | *Polytope de Cluny*, electroacoustic and converted music for four-channel tape |
| 1973 (51) | *Eridanos*, for orchestra |
|           | *Cendrées*, for mixed chorus and orchestra |
|           | *Evryali*, for solo piano |
| 1974 (52) | *Erikhthon*, for piano and orchestra |
|           | *Gmeeoorh*, for organ |
|           | *Noomena*, for orchestra |
| 1975 (53) | *Empreintes*, for orchestra |
|           | *Phlegra*, for eleven players |
|           | *Psappha*, for solo percussion |
|           | *N'shima*, for five instruments and two mezzo-sopranos |
| 1976 (54) | *Theraps*, for solo contrabass |
|           | *Khoaï*, for solo harpsichord |
|           | *Retours-Windungen*, for twelve cellists |
|           | *Dmaathen*, for oboe and percussion |
|           | *Epeï*, for six players |
| 1977 (55) | *Akanthos*, for nine players |
|           | *Kottos*, for solo cello |
|           | *Hélène*, for mezzo-soprano soloist, female chorus and two clarinets |
|           | *Diatope*, for four- or eight-track tapes |

## ZELENKA, Jan Dismas
*b Bohemia, 16 October 1679*
*d Dresden, 22 December 1745, aged sixty-six*

His father was an organist. He studied in Prague and in 1710 became a double-bass player in the royal orchestra at Dresden. He worked in Italy in 1715 and in Vienna from 1717 to 1719, then he was appointed *Kapellmeister* in Dresden, where he remained for the rest of his life. His lack of recognition as a composer caused him to spend his last years in loneliness and disappointment.

He wrote a large amount of sacred vocal music, some chamber and other instrumental works.

## ZEMLINSKY, Alexander von
*b Vienna, 14 October 1871*
*d Larchmont, New York, 15 March 1942, aged seventy*

He studied at the Vienna Conservatory, and became the teacher of Webern, and of Schoenberg, who married his sister Mathilde. He was *Kapellmeister* at the Carltheater in Vienna in 1899, at the Hofoper from 1906 to 1926 and at the Kroll Opera in Berlin from 1927 to 1930. He toured widely as a conductor. In 1938 he moved to Prague and then, with the outbreak of war, on to the USA.

| | |
|---|---|
| 1892 (21) | Symphony No 1 |
| 1895 (24) | String Quintet |
| | String Quartet No 1 |
| 1896 (25) | *Frühlingsglaube*, for voices and strings |
| | *Frühlingsbegräbnis*, for voices and orchestra |
| 1897 (26) | *Sarema*, opera |
| | *Es war einmal*, opera (1897–9) |
| | Symphony No 2 |
| 1900 (29) | *Das gläserne Hertz*, ballet |
| | *Psalm LXXXIII*, for voices and orchestra |
| 1903 (32) | Symphony No 3 |
| | *Die Seejungfrau*, orchestral fantasy |
| 1904 (33) | *Der Traumgörge*, opera |
| 1908 (37) | *Kleider machen Leute*, comic opera |
| 1910 (39) | *Psalm XXIII*, for voices and orchestra |
| 1914 (43) | *Cymbeline*, incidental music |
| | String Quartet No 2 |
| 1915 (44) | *Eine florentinische Tragödie*, opera |
| 1920 (49) | *Der Zwerge*, opera |
| 1923 (52) | *Lyrische Symphonie*, for soprano, baritone and orchestra |
| | String Quartet No 3 |
| 1932 (61) | *Der Kreidekreis*, opera |
| 1934 (63) | Sinfonietta for orchestra |
| 1935 (64) | *Psalm XIII*, for voices and orchestra |
| | *Der König Kandaules*, opera |
| 1936 (65) | String Quartet No 4 |

# PART TWO

This chronologically arranged survey of compositions begins with the first major composition of the first named composer and continues to the end of 1984.

Which composers were born, which died, and what music was written (or first performed or published) in any given year can be seen under the heading of that year. Within each year composers are listed chronologically, the oldest first. As in Part One, composers' ages are given beside each entry.

The entries in this section are sometimes condensed; for fuller details, cross-reference should be made to Part One.

**c1300**

MACHAUT was born

**1377**

MACHAUT died

**c1400**

DUFAY and JOSQUIN DESPREZ were born

**1474**

DUFAY died

**c1505**

TALLIS was born

**1510**

GABRIELI, A. was born

**1521**

JOSQUIN DESPREZ died

**c1525**

PALESTRINA was born

**1532**

LASSUS was born

**1543**

BYRD was born

**1548?**

VICTORIA was born

**1553**

MARENZIO was born

**1554**

PALESTRINA (c29)
p First Book of Masses

**1557**

MORLEY and GABRIELI, G. were born

**1560**

FARNABY and GESUALDO were born

**1562**

SWEELINCK was born
GABRIELI, A. (52)
p Sacrae cantiones, a 5 vv motets (1562–5)

**1563**

BULL and DOWLAND were born
PALESTRINA (c38)
p First Book of Motets

**1567**

MONTEVERDI and CAMPIAN were born
TALLIS (c62)
p Psalm Tunes printed in Archbishop
   Parker's Psalter
PALESTRINA (c42)
Missae Papae Marcelli

**1569**

PALESTRINA (c44)
p Second Book of Masses

**1570**

PALESTRINA (c45)
p Third Book of Masses
Missa Brevis

**1571**

PRAETORIUS was born

**1572**

TOMKINS was born

**c1573**

PUJOL was born

**1574**

WILBYE was born

**1575**

**BYRD** (32)
*pf* Seventeen Motets

**1576**

**WEELKES** was born
**GABRIELI, A.** (66)
*p Cantiones ecclesiasticae, a 4 vv* motets

**1578**

**GABRIELI, A.** (68)
*p Cantiones sacrae,* motets

**1583**

**FRESCOBALDI, JOHNSON** and
**GIBBONS** were born

**1584**

**PALESTRINA** (*c*59)
*p* Settings of *The Song of Solomon*
**MONTEVERDI** (17)
*p* Cantonettas for three voices

**1585**

**SCHÜTZ** was born; **TALLIS** died

**1586**

**GABRIELI, A.** died
**BYRD** (43)
*p A Printed Broadside,* for six voices

**1587**

**SCHEIDT** was born
**GABRIELI, G.** (30)
*p* Concerti for six to sixteen voices
*p Madrigali e ricercare*
**MONTEVERDI** (20)
*p* Madrigals for five voices, Book I

**1588**

**BYRD** (45)
*p* Psalmes, Songs and Sonnets

**1589**

**GABRIELI, A.** (posthumous)
*p Madrigali e ricercare, a 4*
**BYRD** (46)

*p Cantiones sacrae,* Book I, twenty-nine
motets for five voices
*p* Songs of sundrie natures

**1590**

**PALESTRINA** (*c*65)
*p Aeterne Christe Munera,* mass
*Stabat Mater* (*c*1590)
**MONTEVERDI** (23)
*p* Madrigals for five voices, Book II

**1591**

**BYRD** (48)
*p Cantiones sacrae,* Book II, thirty-two
motets

**1592**

**MONTEVERDI** (25)
*p* Madrigals for five voices, Book III
**SWEELINCK** (30)
*p Chansons françaises, in three parts* (1592–4)

**1593**

**MORLEY** (36)
*p* Canzonets, or Little Short Songs to Three
Voyces

**1594**

**PALESTRINA** and **LASSUS** died
**MORLEY** (37)
*p* Madrigalls to Foure Voyces
**GESUALDO** (34)
Madrigals, Books I–IV

**1595**

**MORLEY** (38)
*p* The First Booke of Ballets to Fiue Voyces
*p* The First Booke of Canzonets to Two
Voyces

**1597**

**MORLEY** (40)
*p* Two songs in 'Canzonets or Little Short
Songs to Foure Voyces'
*p* Canzonets or Little Short Aers to Fiue
and Sixe Voyces
*p* A Plaine and Easie Introduction to
Practicall Musicke
**GABRIELI, G.** (40)
*p Sacrae symphoniae,* Book I

DOWLAND (34)
*p* First Book of Songes or Ayres

## 1598

MORLEY (41)
*p Madrigalls to Fiue Voyces*
FARNABY (38)
*p* Canzonets to Foure Voyces

## 1599

MARENZIO died
MORLEY (42)
*p* The Firste Booke of Consort Lessons

## 1600

FARNABY died
MORLEY (43)
*p* The First Booke of Ayres or Little Short
  Songs to sing and play to the Lute with
  the Base Viole
DOWLAND (37)
*p* Second Book of Songes

## 1601

MORLEY (44)
*p* Two madrigals in *The Triumphs of Oriana*
CAMPIAN (39)
*p* A Book of Airs to be Sung to the Lute

## 1602

LAWES was born; CAVALLI died

## 1603

MORLEY died
DOWLAND (40)
*p* Third Book of Songes or Ayres
MONTEVERDI (36)
*p* Madrigals for Five Voices, Book IV

## 1604

DOWLAND (41)
*p Lachrymae*

## 1605

CARISSIMI born
GABRIELI, A. (posthumous)
*p Canzoni alla francese et ricercare Arlosi*
BYRD (62)

*p Gradualia*, Book I, sixty-three motets
MONTEVERDI (38)
*p* Madrigals for five voices, Book V

## 1607

BYRD (64)
*p Gradualia*, Book II, forty-five motets
CAMPIAN (45)
*p* Songs for a Masque to Celebrate the
  Marriage of Sir James Hay
MONTEVERDI (40)
Scherzi Musicali for three voices
*fp Orfeo*, opera

## 1608

GABRIELI, G. (51)
*p* Canzona (*La Spiritosa*)
MONTEVERDI (41)
*fp L'Arianna*, opera
*Il ballo delle ingrate*, ballet

## 1610

MONTEVERDI (43)
*p* Masses
*p* Vespers

## 1611

VICTORIA died
BYRD (68)
*p* Psalmes, Songs and Sonnets
GESUALDO (*c*51)
Madrigals, Books V and VI
SCHÜTZ (26)
*p* Italian Madrigals

## 1612

GABRIELI, G. died
SWEELINCK (50)
*p Rimes françaises et italiennes*
DOWLAND (49)
*p* Fourth Book of Songes, *A Pilgrimes Solace*
GIBBONS (29)
*p* Madrigals and Mottets of Five Parts: Apt
  for Viols and Voyces

## 1613

GESUALDO died
CAMPIAN (51)
*p* Songs for a Masque to Celebrate the
  Marriage of Princess Elizabeth

**BULL** (49)
*p* Anthem for the marriage of Princess
  Elizabeth

## 1614

**MONTEVERDI** (47)
*p* Madrigals for five voices, Book VI

## 1615

**GABRIELI, G.** (posthumous)
*p* Canzoni e sonate
*p* Sacrae symphoniae, Book II
**MONTEVERDI** (48)
*fp* Tirsi e Clori, ballet
**FRESCOBALDI** (32)
*p* Toccate d'involatura
*p* Ricercare e canzone francesi

## 1616

**FROBERGER** died

## 1617

**MONTEVERDI** (50)
*La Maddalena*, opera

## 1619

**SWEELINCK** (57)
*p* Cantiones sacrae
**MONTEVERDI** (52)
*p* Madrigals, Book VII
**SCHÜTZ** (34)
*p* Psalms and Motets
*p* Psalm Davids for choirs and
  instruments

## 1620

**CAMPIAN** died

## 1621

**LOCKE** was born; **SWEELINCK** and
**PRAETORIOUS** died
**SCHEIDT** (34)
*Ludi musici*, for instrumental ensemble

## 1623

**BYRD** and **WEELKES** died
**SCHÜTZ** (38)
*Resurrection Oratorio*
*Easter Oratorio*

*p* Historia der Auferstehung Jesu Christi, for
  voices and instruments

## 1624

**FRESCOBALDI** (41)
*p* Capricci sopra diversi soggetti
**SCHEIDT** (37)
*Tabulatura nova*, keyboard music

## 1625

**GIBBONS** died
**SCHÜTZ** (40)
*p* Cantiones sacrae, for four voices

## 1626

**COUPERIN, L.** was born; **DOWLAND**
and **PUJOL** died

## 1627

**MONTEVERDI** (60)
*Armida*, opera
**FRESCOBALDI** (44)
*p* Second Book of Toccate
**SCHÜTZ** (42)
*fp* Dafne, opera

## 1628

**BULL** died
**MONTEVERDI** (61)
*fp* Mercurio e Marte, opera
**FRESCOBALDI** (45)
*p* Libro delle canzoni

## 1629

**SCHÜTZ** (44)
*p* Symphoniae sacrae, Part I

## 1630

**FRESCOBALDI** (47)
*Arie musicali*

## 1632

**LULLY** was born
**MONTEVERDI** (65)
*p* Scherzi Musicali for one or two voices

## 1633

**JOHNSON** died

## 1635

**FRESCOBALDI** (52)
*p Fiori musicali*

## 1636

**SCHÜTZ** (51)
*Musicalische exequien* (Funeral music)
*Kleine Geistliche Concerte*, Book I

## 1637

**BUXTEHUDE** was born

## 1638

**WILBYE** died
**MONTEVERDI** (71)
*p Madrigali guerrieri e amorosi*, Book VIII
**SCHÜTZ** (53)
*fp Orpheus and Euridice*, ballet

## 1639

**SCHÜTZ** (54)
*Kleine Geistliche Concerte*, Book II

## 1640

**MONTEVERDI** (73)
*Selva morale e spirituale*

## 1641

**MONTEVERDI** (74)
*Il ritorno d'Ulisse in patria*, opera

## 1642

**MONTEVERDI** (75)
*L'incoronazione di Poppea*, opera

## 1643

**MONTEVERDI** and **FRESCOBALDI** died

## 1645

**CHARPENTIER, M. A.** was born (c1645);
**LAWES** died
**SCHÜTZ** (60)
*The Seven Words from the Cross*, choral work

## 1647

**SCHÜTZ** (62)
*p Symphoniae sacrae*, Part II

## 1648

**SCHÜTZ** (63)
*p Musicali ad chorum sacrum*

## 1649

**BLOW** was born

## 1650

**SCHÜTZ** (65)
*p Symphoniae sacrae*, Part III
**CAVALLI** (48)
*Magnificat*
**MONTEVERDI** (posthumous)
*p Masses for four voices, and psalms*

## 1651

**MONTEVERDI** (posthumous)
*p Madrigals and Canzonettes*, Book IX

## 1653

**CORELLI** and **PACHELBEL** were born

## 1654

**SCHEIDT** died

## 1656

**TOMKINS** died

## 1658

**TORELLI** was born
**LULLY** (26)
*fp Ballets d'Alcidiane*

## 1659

**PURCELL** was born
**LULLY** (27)
*fp Ballet de la raillerie*

## 1660

**SCARLATTI, A.** and **FUX** were born
**LULLY** (28)
*fp Ballet de Xerxes*

## 1661

**COUPERIN, L.** died
**LULLY** (29)
*fp Ballet de l'impatience*

*fp Ballet des saisons*
*fp Ballet de l'Ercole amante*

## 1663

**LULLY** (31)
*fp Ballet des arts*
*fp Ballet des noces de village*

## 1664

**SCHÜTZ** (79)
*Christmas Oratorio*
**LULLY** (32)
*fp Ballet des amours déguises*
*fp* Entr'actes for Corneille's *Oedipe*
*fp Miserere*, concert setting of 'Miserere
  mei Deus', psalm
*fp Le mariage forcé*, comedy ballet
*fp La Princesse d'Elide*, comedy ballet

## 1665

**SCHÜTZ** (80)
*Four Passions* (1665–6)
**LULLY** (33)
*fp L'amour médecin*, comedy ballet
*fp La Naissance de Venus*, ballet
*fp Ballet des gardes*

## 1666

**LULLY** (34)
*fp Le triomphe de Bacchus dans les Indes*,
  ballet
*fp Ballet des Muses*

## 1667

**FROBERGER** died
**LULLY** (35)
*fp Le Sicilien*, comedy ballet

## 1668

**COUPERIN** was born
**LULLY** (36)
*fp Georges Dandin*, comedy ballet
*fp Le Carnaval, ou Mascarade de Versailles*,
  ballet
*fp Plaude Laetare*, motet

## 1669

**LULLY** (37)
*fp Monsieur de Pourceaugnac*, comedy ballet
*fp Ballet de Flore*

## 1670

**LULLY** (38)
*fp Les amants magnifiques*, comedy ballet
*fp Le bourgeois gentilhomme*, comedy ballet

## 1671

**ALBINONI** was born
**SCHÜTZ** (86)
*Deutches Magnificat*
**LULLY** (39)
*fp Psyche*, tragi-comedy
*fp Ballet des ballets*
**BUXTEHUDE** (34)
**Wedding Arias**

## 1672

**SCHÜTZ** died

## 1673

**LULLY** (41)
*fp Cadmus et Hermione*, opera

## 1674

**CARISSIMI** died
**LULLY** (42)
*fp Alceste, ou Le triomphe d'Alcide*, opera

## 1675

**VIVALDI** was born (*c*1675)
**CAVALLI** (73)
*Vespers*
**LULLY** (43)
*fp Thésée*, opera

## 1676

**CAVALLI** died
**LULLY** (44)
*fp Atys*, opera

## 1677

**LOCKE** died
**LULLY** (45)
*fp Isis*, opera
*fp Te Deum*

**1678**

LULLY (46)
*fp Psyche*, opera
BUXTEHUDE (41)
Wedding Arias

**1679**

ZELENKA was born
LULLY (47)
*fp Bellérophon*, opera
SCARLATTI, A. (19)
*fp Gli equivoci nel sembiante*, opera

**1680**

GEMINIANI was born
LULLY (48)
*fp Proserpine*, opera
PURCELL (21)
Nine Fantasias of four parts

**1681**

TELEMANN was born
LULLY (49)
*fp Le triomphe de l'amour*, ballet
CORELLI (28)
*p* Sonatas in three parts (twelve sonatas da
   chiesa)

**1682**

LULLY (50)
*fp Persée*, opera
PURCELL (23)
'Hear My Prayer', anthem (*c*1682)

**1683**

RAMEAU was born
LULLY (51)
*fp Phaéton*, opera
*fp De profundis*
PURCELL (24)
Twelve Sonatas of three parts
SCARLATTI, A. (23)
*fp Pompeo*, opera
*fp Psiche*, opera

**1684**

LULLY (52)
*fp Amadis de Gaule*, opera
*fp* Motets for two choirs

**BLOW** (35)
*Venus and Adonis*, masque
Ode for St Cecilia's Day 'Begin the Song'

**1685**

BACH, J. S., HANDEL and
SCARLATTI, D. were born
LULLY (53)
*fp Roland*, opera
*fp Le temple de la paix*, ballet
CORELLI (32)
*p* Sonatas in three parts (twelve sonatas da
   camera)

**1686**

PORPORA was born
LULLY (54)
*fp Armide et Renaud*, opera
*fp Acis de Galathée*, opera

**1687**

LULLY died

**1688**

PURCELL (29)
*How Pleasant is this Flowery Plain*, secular
   cantata

**1689**

CORELLI (36)
*p* Sonatas in three parts (twelve sonatas da
   chiesa)
PURCELL (30)
*fp Dido and Aeneas*, opera
*Musick's Handmaid*, for harpsichord

**1690**

PURCELL (31)
*The Prophetess or The History of Dioclesian*,
   opera
SCARLATTI, A. (30)
*fp Gli equivoci in amore*, opera
COUPERIN (22)
Pièces d'orgue en deux messes:
   *Messe pour les couvents*, twenty-one
      organ pieces
   *Messe pour les paroisses*, twenty-one
      organ pieces
*Messe Solennelle*

**1691**

PURCELL (32)
*King Arthur* or *The British Worthy*, opera
*The Wives' Excuse*, incidental music

**1692**

TARTINI was born
BUXTEHUDE (55)
Sonata in D major for viola da gamba, cello
   and harpsichord
PURCELL (33)
*The Faery Queen*, opera
*The Libertine*, incidental music
*Oedipus*, incidental music
COUPERIN (24)
Trio Sonata, *La Steinkerque*

**1693**

PURCELL (34)
*Epsom Wells*, incidental music

**1694**

CORELLI (41)
*p* Sonatas in three parts (twelve sonatas da
   camera)
PURCELL (35)
*The Married Beau*, incidental music
SCARLATTI, A. (34)
*fp Pirro e Demetrio*, opera
ALBINONI (23)
*Zenobia, regina de Palmireni*, opera

**1695**

SAMMARTINI was born
PURCELL died
PURCELL (36)
*The Indian Queen*, opera
*The Tempest or The Enchanted Island*, opera
*Bonduca*, incidental music

**1696**

BUXTEHUDE (59)
Seven Trio Sonatas for violin, gamba and
   basso continuo, Op 1
Seven Trio Sonatas, for violin, gamba and
   basso continuo, Op 2
PURCELL (posthumous)
*p* A choice collection of Lessons for the
   Harpsichord or Spinet
*p* Harpsichord Suites 1–8

**1697**

LECLAIR was born
BLOW (48)
'My God, my God, look upon me', anthem

**1698**

SCARLATTI, A. (38)
*fp Flavio Cuniberto*, opera
*fp La donna ancore e' fedele*, opera

**1699**

SCARLATTI, A. (39)
Two sonatas for flute and continuo

**1700**

BLOW (51)
*p Amphion Anglicus*, collection of songs
   and vocal chamber music
CORELLI (47)
*p* Sonatas for violin and violone or
   harpsichord (six 'da chiesa': five
   'da camera': one variations on *La Folia*)

**1703**

SCARLATTI, D. (18)
*fp Ottavia ristituta al trono*, opera
*fp Giustina*, opera
c1703–07
BACH, J. S. (18–22)
Prelude and Fugue in C minor, for clavier
Toccata and Fugue in C major, for clavier
Sonata in D major, for clavier (*c*1704)

**1704**

CHARPENTIER, M-A. died
SCARLATTI, D. (19)
*fp Irene*, opera

**1705**

BUXTEHUDE (68)
Wedding Arias
VIVALDI (*c*30)
*p Suonate da camera a tre*, Op 1

**1706**

SCARLATTI, A. (46)
*Il sedecia, re di Gerusalemme*, oratorio
RAMEAU (23)
*p* Harpsichord Works, Book I

## pre 1707

**HANDEL**
Sonata for viola da gamba

## 1707

**BUXTEHUDE** died
**SCARLATTI, A.** (47)
*fp Il trionfo della libertà*, opera
*fp Mitridate eupatore*, opera
**ALBINONI** (36)
Sinfonie e Concerti a cinque
**HANDEL** (22)
'Laudate pueri Dominum', aria
*Rodrigo*, opera (*c1707*)

## 1708

**BLOW** died
**TELEMANN** (27)
Trio Sonata in E♭ major (1708–12)
**BACH, J. S.** (23)
Passacaglia and Fugue in C minor for
organ (*c1708–17*)
Most of the 'Great' Preludes and Fugues
(*c1708–17*)
The Toccatas (*c1708–17*)
**HANDEL** (23)
*La Resurrezione*, Easter oratorio
**PORPORA** (22)
*Agrippina*, opera

## 1709

**TORELLI** died
**COUPERIN** (41)
*Messe à l'usage des couvents*
**VIVALDI** (*c34*)
*p* Sonate a violino e basso per il cambala,
Op 2

## 1710

**ARNE, BACH, W. F., BOYCE,
PARADIES** and **PERGOLESI** were born
**SCARLATTI, A.** (*c50*)
*Est dies tropael*, motet (*c1710*)
*Informata vulnerate*, cantata (*c1710*)
**ALBINONI** (39)
Concerti a cinque
**SCARLATTI, D.** (25)
*fp La Sylvia*, opera

## 1711

**SCARLATTI, D.** (26)

*fp Tolomeo e Alessandro*, opera
*fp Orlando*, opera
**HANDEL** (26)
*Rinaldo*, opera
**PORPORA** (25)
*Flavio Anicio Olibrio*, opera
*Il martirio di S. Giovanni Nepomuceno*,
oratorio

## 1712

**VIVALDI** (*c37*)
*p* Twelve concerti, *L'estro armonico*, Op 3
*p La stravaganza*, Op 4, concertos (1712–13)
**SCARLATTI, D.** (27)
*fp Tetide in sciro*, opera
**HANDEL** (27)
*Il pastor Fido*, opera (first version)

## 1713

**CORELLI** died
**COUPERIN** (45)
Harpsichord Works, Book I
**VIVALDI** (*c38*)
*fp Ottone in Villa*, opera
**HANDEL** (28)
*Teseo*, opera
*Te Deum and Jubilate*, for the Peace of
Utrecht
**SCARLATTI, D.** (28)
*fp Ifigenia in Aulide*, opera
*fp Ifigenia in Tauride*, opera
**PORPORA** (27)
*Basilio, re d'Oriente*, opera

## 1714

**BACH, C. P. E.** and **GLUCK** were born
**CORELLI** (posthumous)
*p* Concerti Grossi
**VIVALDI** (*c39*)
*fp Orlando finto pazzo*, opera
*Moyses deus Pharaonis*, oratorio
**SCARLATTI, D.** (29)
*fp Amor d'un ombra*, opera
**PORPORA** (28)
*Arianna e Teseo*, opera
**TARTINI** (23)
Violin Sonata in G minor, 'Devil's Trill'

## 1715

**SCARLATTI, A.** (55)
*fp Tigrone*, opera
Twelve sinfonias
Four string quartets (without harpsichord)

COUPERIN (47)
*Leçons de ténèbres*, for one and two voices
VIVALDI (c40)
*fp Nerone fatto Cesare*, opera
TELEMANN (34)
Concerto in A major (1715–20)
Suite in D minor (1715–20)
HANDEL (30)
*Amadigi di Gaula*, opera
The *Water Music* (1715–17)
SCARLATTI, D. (30)
*fp Ambleto*, opera

### 1716

ALBINONI (45)
Twelve concerti a cinque (c1716)
VIVALDI (c41)
*fp Arsilda Regina di Ponto*, opera
*Juditha triumphans*, oratorio
*p* Six sonate, Op 5
*p* Six concerti a cinque, Op 6 (1716–c17)
*p* Seven concerti a cinque, Op 7 (1716–c17)
TELEMANN (35)
*Die Kleine Kammermusik*
Six Suites for violin, querflute and piano

### 1717

STAMITZ J. was born; PACHELBEL died
COUPERIN (49)
Harpsichord Works, Book II
VIVALDI (c42)
*fp Tieteberga*, opera
BACH, J. S. (32–38)
English Suites (c1717–23)
The Inventions, Little Preludes and
    Symphonies (c1717–23)
The *Brandenburg* Concerti (c1717–23)
The Suites (Overtures) for orchestra
    (c1717–23)
The Violin Concerti (c1717–23)
The Sonatas (Suites) for violin, flute, cello
    and viola da gamba (c1717–23)

### 1718

SCARLATTI, A. (58)
*fp Telemaco*, opera
VIVALDI (c43)
*fp Scanderbeg*, opera
TELEMANN (37)
Six Trios for two violins, cello and bass
    continuo
SCARLATTI, D. (33)
*fp Berenice*, opera

PORPORA (32)
*Temistocle*, opera

### 1719

SCARLATTI, A. (59)
*fp Marco Attilo Regolo*, opera
PORPORA (33)
*Faramondo*, opera

### 1720

SCARLATTI, A. (60)
*fp Tito o sempronio gracco*, opera
    (completed version for Rome
    production)
VIVALDI (c45)
*fp La verità in cimento*, opera
BACH, J. S. (35)
Chromatic Fantasia and Fugue, for clavier
    (1720–23)
HANDEL (35)
The *Chandos Anthems* (c1720)
*Huit suites de pièces*, for harpsichord (c1720)
*Acis and Galatea*, secular cantata (c1720)
*Radamisto*, opera (c1720)

### 1721

SCARLATTI, A. (61)
*fp Griselda*, opera
VIVALDI (c46)
*fp Silvia*, opera
HANDEL (36)
*Floridante*, opera
PORPORA (35)
*Il martirio di Santa Eugenia*, oratorio

### 1722

COUPERIN (54)
Harpsichord Works, Book III
Four *Concerts Royaux*
ALBINONI (51)
Twelve concerti a cinque (c1722)
VIVALDI (c47)
*L'adorazione delle tre Re Magi*, oratorio
BACH, J. S. (37)
*The Well-Tempered Clavier*, Book I
French Suites

### 1723

TELEMANN (42)
*Hamburger Ebb und Fluht*, overture in
    C major

BACH, J. S. (38)
St. John Passion
HANDEL (38)
*Ottone*, opera
PORPORA (37)
*Adelaide*, opera
LECLAIR (26)
*p* Sonatas for Violin Alone, with a Bass,
  Book I

## 1724

COUPERIN (56)
*Les goûts-réunis*, ten 'concerts' for various
  instruments
VIVALDI (*c*49)
*fp Giustino*, opera
HANDEL (39)
*Giulio Cesare*, opera
Fifteen Chamber Sonatas
PORPORA (38)
*Griselda*, opera

## 1725

SCARLATTI, A. died
VIVALDI (*c*50)
*p* Twelve Concerti, Op 8; four are known
  as *The Four Seasons*
TELEMANN (44)
*Pimpinone*, opera
HANDEL (40)
*Rodelinda*, opera
Trio Sonata in D minor

## 1726

VIVALDI (*c*51)
*Cunegonda*, opera
PORPORA (40)
*Imeneo in Atene*, opera

## 1727

VIVALDI (*c*52)
*Ipermestra*, opera
HANDEL (42)
*Zadok the Priest*, coronation anthem
*Admeto*, opera
PORPORA (41)
*Ezio*, opera

## 1728

VIVALDI (*c*53)
*Rosilena ed Oronta*, opera
*p* Twelve concerti, *La Cetra*, Op 9

TELEMANN (47)
*Der getreuer Musikmeister*, cantata
RAMEAU (45)
*p* Harpsichord Works, Book II
HANDEL (43)
*Tolomeo*, opera
LECLAIR (31)
*p* Sonatas for Violin Alone, with a Bass,
  Book II

## 1729

VIVALDI (*c*54)
Concerti, Op 10, 11 and 12 (1729–30)
BACH, J. S. (44)
St Matthew Passion
The Clavier Concerti (1729–36)
PORPORA (43)
*Semiramide riconosciuta*, opera

## 1730

COUPERIN (62)
*p* Harpsichord Works, Book IV
PORPORA (44)
*Mitridate*, opera

## 1731

BACH, J. S. (46)
St. Mark Passion
HANDEL (46)
Nine Sonatas for two violins and continuo
  (*c*1731)
PORPORA (45)
*Poro*, opera
PERGOLESI (21)
*Salustia*, opera
BACH, C. P. E. (17)
Trio in B minor

## 1732

HAYDN, J. was born
VIVALDI (*c*57)
*fp La fida ninfa*, opera
HANDEL (47)
*Ezio*, opera
*Sosarme*, opera
*Esther*, oratorio
PORPORA (46)
*Germanico in Germania*, opera
PERGOLESI (22)
*Lo frate innamorato*, opera
*La serva padrona*, opera

## 1733

**COUPERIN** died
**VIVALDI** (*c*58)
*fp Motezuma*, opera
**RAMEAU** (50)
*Hippolyte et Aricie*, opera
**BACH, J. S.** (48)
Mass in B minor
Christmas Oratorio
**HANDEL** (48)
*Orlando*, opera
*Huit Suites de pièces*, for harpsichord
**PORPORA** (47)
*Arianna in Nasso*, opera
**ARNE** (23)
*Dido and Aeneas*, opera
*The Opera of Operas*, opera
*Rosamund*, opera
**PERGOLESI** (23)
*Il prigionier superbo*, opera


## 1734

**VIVALDI** (*c*59)
*fp L'Olimpiade*, opera
**HANDEL** (49)
*Persichore*, ballet
*Arianna*, opera
*Il pastor fido*, opera (second and third
    versions)
*p* Six Concerti Grossi
**PORPORA** (48)
*Enea nel Lazio*, opera
*Davide e Bersabea*, oratorio
**LECLAIR** (37)
*p* Sonatas for Violin Alone, with a Bass,
    Book III
**PERGOLESI** (24)
*Adriano in Siria*, opera
*La contadina astuta*, opera


## 1735

**VIVALDI** (*c*60)
*fp Griselda*, opera
*fp Aristide*, opera
**RAMEAU** (52)
*Les Indes galantes*, opera-ballet
**BACH, J. S.** (50)
Italian Concerto
Partita in B minor, for clavier
Ascension Oratorio (1735–36)
**HANDEL** (50)
*Alcina*, opera
**PORPORA** (49)
*Ifigenia in Aulide*, opera

*Polifemo*, opera
**PERGOLESI** (25)
*L'Olimpiade*, opera
*Flamincio*, opera


## 1736

**VIVALDI** (*c*61)
*fp Ginevra, Principessa di Scozia*, opera
**BACH, J. S.** (51)
Easter Oratorio
**HANDEL** (51)
*Atalanta*, opera
*Alexander's Feast*, secular cantata
Six Fugues for harpsichord
**ARNE** (26)
*Zara*, incidental music
**PERGOLESI** (26)
*Stabat Mater*, for female voices


## 1737

**HOPKINSON** and **HAYDN, M.**
were born
**VIVALDI** (*c*62)
*fp Catone in Utica*, opera
*p Il pastor fido*, sonatas (*c*1737)
**RAMEAU** (54) *Castor et Pollux*,
    opera-ballet
**BACH, J. S.** (52)
Masses, in F: A: Gm and G major (1737–40)
**HANDEL** (52)
*Berenice*, opera
Concerto grosso in C major
**PORPORA** (51)
*Lucio Papirio*, opera
**LECLAIR** (40)
*p* Six Concertos for violin


## 1738

**VIVALDI** (*c*63)
*fp L'Oracolo in Messenia*, opera
**HANDEL** (53)
*Xerxes*, opera
Six Organ Concerti
**SCARLATTI, D.** (53)
*p Essercizi per Gravicembalo*
**PORPORA** (52)
*Carlo il Calvo*, opera
**ARNE** (28)
*Comus*, a masque
**PARADIES** (28)
*Allessandro in Persia*, opera


## 1739

**DITTERSDORF** was born

**VIVALDI** (*c*64)
*fp Feraspe*, opera
**RAMEAU** (56)
*Dardanus*, opera
*Les Fêtes d'Hebe*, ballet
**HANDEL** (54)
*Israel in Egypt*, oratorio
*Saul*, oratorio
Ode for St Cecilia's Day
Twelve Concerti Grossi
Seven Trio Sonatas
**SCARLATTI, D.** (54)
*p XLII Suites de pièces pour la clavecin*
**PORPORA** (53)
*Il Barone di Zampano*, opera

## 1740

**PAISELLO** was born
**VIVALDI** (*c*65)
*p Six sonate a cello e basse*, Op 14 (*c*1740)
**HANDEL** (55)
*p* Concerti for oboe and strings
*p* Six Organ Concerti
Three Double Concerti (1740–50)
**PORPORA** (54)
*Il trionfo di Camilla*, opera
**ARNE** (30)
*Alfred*, a masque
*The Judgement of Paris*, opera

## 1741

**VIVALDI** and **FUX** died
**RAMEAU** (58)
*p* Harpsichord Works, Book III
**BACH, J. S.** (56)
Six partitas for clavier
**HANDEL** (56)
*Messiah*, oratorio
Five Concerti Grossi
**GLUCK** (27)
*Artaserse*, opera

## 1742

**GRÉTRY** was born
**BACH, J. S.** (57)
The 'Goldberg' Variations for clavier
**HANDEL** (57)
*Forest Music*
**PORPORA** (56)
*Statira*, opera
**BACH, C. P. E.** (28)
'Prussian' Sonata
**GLUCK** (28)
*Demetrio*, opera

## 1743

**BOCCHERINI** was born
**HANDEL** (58)
*Samson*, oratorio
The *Dettingen Te Deum*
**ARNE** (33)
*Britannia*, a masque
*Eliza*, opera
**BACH, C. P. E.** (29)
Sonata for clavier, *Wurtemburgian*
**GLUCK** (29)
*Il Tigrane*, opera

## 1744

**BACH, J. S.** (59)
*The Well-Tempered Clavier*, Part II
**HANDEL** (59)
*Semele*, secular oratorio
**ARNE** (34)
*Abel*, oratorio
**BACH, W. F.** (34)
Clavier sonata No 2 in A major (*c*1744)

## 1745

**STAMITZ, K.** was born; **ZELENKA** died
**RAMEAU** (62)
*Platée*, ballet
**HANDEL** (60)
*Belshazzar*, oratorio
**GLUCK** (31)
*Ippolito*, opera

## 1746

**HANDEL** (61)
*Occasional Oratorio*
**LECLAIR** (49)
*Scylla et Glaucus*, opera
**GLUCK** (32)
*Artamene*, opera
*p* Six Sonatas for two violins and continu

## 1747

**BACH, J. S.** (62)
*A Musical Offering*, for flute, violin and
    clavier
**HANDEL** (62)
*Judas Maccabaeus*, oratorio
**PORPORA** (61)
*Filandro*, opera
**BACH, C. P. E.** (33)
Sonata in D major

**GLUCK** (33)
*Le nozze d'Ercole e d'Ebe*, opera

## 1748

**RAMEAU** (65)
*Pigmalion*, ballet
*Zais*, ballet
**HANDEL** (63)
*Joshua*, oratorio

## 1749

**CIMAROSA** was born
**BACH, J. S.** (64)
*The Art of Fugue*
**HANDEL** (64)
*Music for the Royal Fireworks*
*Solomon*, oratorio
*Susanna*, oratorio

## 1750

**BACH, J. S., SAMMARTINI** and
**ALBINONI** died
**HANDEL** (65)
*Theodora*, oratorio
**ARNE** (40)
*p* Seven trio-sonatas for two violins with
    figured bass
**BOYCE** (40)
*p* Eight Symphonies in Eight Parts . . .
    Opera seconda (*c*1750)
**GLUCK** (36)
*Ezio*, opera

## 1752

**CLEMENTI** was born
**HANDEL** (67)
*Jephtha*, oratorio
**GLUCK** (38)
*Issipile*, opera

## 1753

**GLUCK** (39)
Nine Symphonies

## 1754

**RAMEAU** (71)
*Zephyre*, ballet

## 1755

**GLUCK** (41)
*Les Amours champêtres*, opera

*Alessandro*, ballet
**HAYDN** (23)
String Quartets Nos 1–13

## 1756

**MOZART** was born
**GLUCK** (42)
*Antigono*, opera
*Le Chinois poli en France*, opera
**HAYDN** (24)
Organ Concerto No 1 in C major
Piano Concerto in C major

## 1757

**SCARLATTI, D.** and **STAMITZ, J.** died

## 1758

**BOYCE** (48)
Ode to the New Year
**GLUCK** (44)
*L'Isle de Merlin, ou le Monde renversé*, opera

## 1759

**HANDEL** died
**TELEMANN** (78)
*St Mark Passion*
**GLUCK** (45)
*L'Arbre enchanté*, opera
**HAYDN** (27)
Symphony No 1 in D major
**HOPKINSON** (22)
*My Days Have Been So Wondrous Free*, for
    voice and harpsichord

## 1760

**CHERUBINI** was born
**RAMEAU** (78)
*Les Paladins*, opera-ballet
**HANDEL** (posthumous)
*p* Six Organ Concerti
**HAYDN** (28)
Organ Concerto No 2 in C major
Symphony No 2 in C major (*c*1760)
**GOSSEC** (26)
Requiem Mass

## 1761

**GLUCK** (47)
*Le Cadi dupé*, opera
*Don Juan*, ballet

**HAYDN** (29)
Symphony No 3 in G major
Symphony No 4 in D major
Symphony No 5 in A major
Symphony No 6 in D major, *Le matin*
Symphony No 7 in C major, *Le midi*
Symphony No 8 in G major, *Le soir, ou la tempête*
Symphony No 19 in D major
**GOSSEC** (27)
*Le Tonnelier*, opera
**BACH, J. C.** (26)
*fp Artaserse*, opera
*fp Catone in Utica*, opera

## 1762

**GEMINIANI died**
**ARNE** (52)
*Artaxerxes*, opera
*Love in a Village*, pasticcio
**BACH, C. P. E.** (48)
Harp Sonata in B minor
**GLUCK** (48)
*Orfeo ed Euridice*, opera
**HAYDN** (30)
Symphony No 9 in C major
**BACH, J. C.** (27)
*fp Alessandro nell'Indie*, opera
**MOZART** (6)
Sonata in C major for violin and piano, K6 (1762–4)

## pre 1763

**HAYDN**
Symphony No 10 in D major
Symphony No 11 in Eb major
Piano Sonata No 3 in A major

## 1763

**HAYDN** (31)
Symphony No 12 in E major
Symphony No 13 in D major
**BACH, J. S.** (28)
*Orione*, opera
*Zanaida*, opera
**HOPKINSON** (26)
*Collection of Psalm Tunes*
**MOZART** (7)
Violin Sonata in D major, K7
Violin Sonata in Bb major, K8

## pre 1764

**HAYDN**
Symphonies Nos 14 and 15

## 1764

**RAMEAU** and **LECLAIR died**
**ARNE** (54)
*Judith*, oratorio (possibly 1761)
*L'Olimpiade*, opera
**GLUCK** (50)
*Poro*, opera
*La Rencontre imprévue*, opera
**HAYDN** (32)
Symphonies Nos 16–18 (*c*1764)
Symphony No 22 in Eb major, *Der Philosoph*
**MOZART** (8)
Symphony No 1 in Eb major, K16
Symphony No 4 in D major, K19
Seven Violin Sonatas, K9 in G; K10 in Bb; K11 in G; K12 in A; K13 in F; K14 in C; K15 in Bb

## 1765

**GLUCK** (51)
*Semiramide*, ballet
**HAYDN** (33)
Symphony No 26 in D minor, *Lamentation* (*c*1765)
Symphony No 30 in C major, *Alleluia*
Symphony No 31 in D major, *Horn Signal*
String Quartets Nos 14–19
**GOSSEC** (31)
*Le Faux Lord*, opera
**BACH, J. C.** (30)
*Adriano in Siria*, opera
**BOCCHERINI** (22)
*La confedarazione*, opera
**MOZART** (9)
Symphony No 5 in Bb major, K22
Piano Sonata in C major (four hands), K19d
Three Sonatas by J. C. Bach arranged as concertos with string orchestra, K107

## 1766

**GLUCK** (52)
*L'Orfano della China*, ballet
**HAYDN** (34)
Piano Sonatas Nos 4–7
Piano Sonatas Nos 8–12 (1766–7)
Mass No 4, *Great Organ*
**GOSSEC** (32)
*Les Pêcheurs*, opera
**MOZART** (10)
Six Violin Sonatas, K26 in Eb; K27 in G; K28 in C; K29 in D; K30 in F; K31 in Bb

## 1767

**GLUCK** (53)
*Alceste*, opera
**HAYDN** (35)
Piano Sonatas Nos 13–16 (c1767)
Piano Sonata No 17
**GOSSEC** (33)
*Le Double déguisement*, opera
*Toinon et Toinette*, opera
**BACH, J. C.** (32)
*Carattaco*, opera
**HOPKINSON** (30)
*The Psalms of David,* for voices and organ
**DITTERSDORF** (28)
*Amore in musica*, opera
**MOZART** (11)
Symphony No 6 in F major, K43
Symphony No 43 in F major, K76
Four Piano Concertos, K37 in F; K39 in
  B♭ ; K40 in D; K41 in G
Three Sonatas for organ and strings, K62 in
  E♭ ; K68 in B♭ ; K69 in D

## 1768

**PORPORA** died
**MOZART** (12)
*Bastien und Bastienne*, operetta
Symphony No 7 in D, K45
Symphony No 8 in D, K48

## pre 1769

**HAYDN**
Two Violin Concerti in C and G

## 1769

**TELEMANN** died
**BOYCE** (59)
Ode to the King's Birthday
**HAYDN** (37)
String Quartets Nos 20–25
**GRÉTRY** (27)
*Le tableau parlant*, opéra – comique
**MOZART** (13)
Symphony No 9 in C major, K73
Symphony No 42 in F major, K75
Mass in C major, K66

## pre 1770

**HAYDN**
Viola Concerto in D major

## 1770

**BEETHOVEN** was born: **TARTINI** died
**BACH, C. P. E.** (56)
*Passion Cantata*
Duo in E minor
Solfeggio in C minor
**GLUCK** (56)
*Paride ed Elena*, opera
**HAYDN** (38)
Mass No 5, *Little Organ*, or *St John*
  (1770–80)
**BACH, J. C.** (35)
*Gioas, Re di Giuda*, oratorio
**DITTERSDORF** (31)
*Il viaggatore americano*, opera
**MOZART** (14)
Five Symphonies, No 10 in G, K74; No 11
  in D, K80; No 45 in D, K95; No 47 in D,
  K97; No 12 in G, K110
String Quartet in G major, K80

## after 1770

**HAYDN**
Piano Concerto in G major

## pre 1771

**HAYDN**
Piano Concerto in F major
Violin Concerto in A major

## 1771

**HAYDN** (39)
Piano Sonata No 18 in C minor
String Quartets Nos 26–31
**DITTERSDORF** (32)
*L'amore disprezzato*, opera
**GRÉTRY** (29)
*Zémire et Azor*, opéra – comique
**MOZART** (15)
Five Symphonies, No 46 in C, K95; No 13
  in F, K112; No 14 in A, K114; No 50 in D,
  finale only, to the overture of *Asanio in
  Alba*, K120; Symphony in D, finale only,
  to the overture of *La finta giardinera*,
  K121

## pre 1772

**HAYDN**
Symphony No 43, *Mercury*
Symphony No 44, *Trauersymphonie*

## 1772

**BOYCE** (62)
Ode to the New Year
**HAYDN** (40)
Symphony No 45, *Farewell*
Symphony No 46
Symphony No 48, *Maria Teresa*
Symphony No 52 (1772–4)
Mass No 3, *St Cecilia*
String Quartets Nos 32–37. *Sun* or *Great*
  Quartets
**BACH, J. C.** (37)
*Endimione*, cantata
*Temistocle*, opera
**CIMAROSA** (23)
*Le stravaganze del conte*, opera
**MOZART** (16)
*Lucio Silla*, opera
Nine Symphonies, No 15 in G, K124; No 16
  in C, K128; No 17 in G, K129; No 19 in
  Eb , K132; No 20 in D, K133; No 21 in A,
  K134; Symphony in D, K161; No 22 in C,
  K162; No 51 in D, K163

## pre 1773

**HAYDN**
Symphony No 49, *The Passion*

## 1773

**BACH, C. P. E.** (59)
Fantasia in C minor
**HAYDN** (41)
Piano Sonatas Nos 19–24 (No 2–4 without
  violin, Piano Sonatas Nos 22–4)
**DITTERSDORF** (34)
*Il tutore e la pupilla*, opera
**MOZART** (17)
Four Symphonies; No 23 in D, K181; No 24
  in Bb , K182; No 25 in Gm, K183; No 26
  in Eb , K184
Piano Concerto in D major, K175
Concertone in C major for two violins,
  K190
Six String Quartets: K168 in F; K169 in A;
  K170 in C; K171 in Eb ; K172 in Bb ;
  K173 in Dm
String Quintet in Bb , K174

## pre 1774

**HAYDN**
Symphony No 53, *The Imperial*

## 1774

**SPONTINI** was born
**GLUCK** (60)
*Iphigénie en Aulide*, opera
**HAYDN** (42)
Symphony No 55, *The Schoolmaster*
**GOSSEC** (40)
*Sabinus*, opera
*La Nativité*, oratorio
**DITTERSDORF** (35)
*Il tribunale di Giove*, opera
**MOZART** (18)
Four Symphonies: No 27 in G, K199; No 2
  in C, K200; No 29 in A, K201; No 30 in D
  K202
Bassoon Concerto in Bb , K191
Six Piano Sonatas: K279 in C; K280 in F;
  K281 in Bb ; K282 in Eb ; K283 in G;
  K284 in D
Piano Sonata in Bb (four hands), K358

## 1775

**BOÏELDIEU** was born
**ARNE** (65)
*Caractacus*, incidental music
**BOYCE** (65)
Ode to the King's Birthday
**BACH, C. P. E.** (61)
*The Israelites in the Wilderness*, oratorio
**GOSSEC** (41)
*Alexis et Daphné*, opera
**DITTERSDORF** (36)
*Il finto pazzo per amore*, opera
*Il maniscalco*, opera
*Lo sposo burlato*, opera
**MOZART** (19)
*La finta giardiniera*, opera
*Il re pastore*, opera
Symphony No 49 in C, K102
Five Violin Concerti: K207 in Bb ; K211 in
  D; K216 in G; K218 in D; K219 in A
Sonata in Bb for organ and strings, K212

## pre 1776

**HAYDN**
Symphony No 59, *Feuersymphonie*

## 1776

**HAYDN** (44)
Symphony No 60 in C, *Il distratto*
Piano Sonatas Nos 25–30
**GOSSEC** (42)
*Hylas et Sylvie*, incidental music

**BACH, J. C.** (41)
*Lucio Silla*, opera
**DITTERSDORF** (37)
*La contadina felice*, opera
*La moda*, opera
*Il barone di Rocca Antica*, opera
**MOZART** (20)
Three Piano Concerti; K238 in B♭ ; K242 in
F, for three pianos; K246 in C
Piano Trio in B♭ , K254
Five Sonatas for organ and strings: K224 in
F; K225 in A; K241 in G; K244 in F; K245
in D
Mass in C major, K257
Adagio to K219, Violin Concerto, K261
Rondo Concertante to K207, Violin
Concerto K269

## 1777

**GLUCK** (63)
*Armide*, opera
**HAYDN** (45)
Symphony No 63, *La Roxolane*
Piano Sonatas Nos 31 and 32 (1777–8)
**DITTERSDORF** (38)
*L'Arcifanfano, re de' matti*, opera
**MOZART** (21)
Piano Concerto in E♭ , K271
Violin Concerto in D, K271a
Piano Sonata in C, K309
Sonata for organ and strings in G, K274

## 1778

**HUMMEL** and **SOR** were born; **ARNE**
died
**GOSSEC** (44)
*La Fête du Village*, opera
**GRÉTRY** (36)
*L'amant jaloux*, opéra – comique
**CIMAROSA** (29)
*L'Italiana in Londra*, opera
**MOZART** (22)
Symphony No 31 in D, *Paris*, K297
Concerto in C for flute and harp, K299
Two Flute Concerti: K313 in G; K314 in D
Andante in C major for flute, K315
Sinfonia Concertante for wind instru-
ments (app. K9)
Six Piano Sonatas: K310 in Am; K311 in D;
K330 in C; K331 in A; K332 in F; K333 in
B♭
Seven Violin Sonatas: K296 in C; K301 in
G; K302 in E♭ ; K303 in C; K304 in Em;
K305 in A; K306 in D
**CHERUBINI** (18)
*Demophon*, opera

## 1779

**BOYCE** died
**GLUCK** (65)
*Iphigénie en Tauride*, opera
**HAYDN** (47)
Symphony No 69, *Laudon*
Piano Sonatas Nos 33–37 (1779–80)
**GOSSEC** (45)
*Les Scythes enchaînés*, ballet
*Mirsa*, ballet
**BACH, J. C.** (44)
*Amadis des Gaules*, opera
**MOZART** (23)
Symphony No 32 in G, K318
Symphony No 33 in B♭ , K319
Sinfonia Concertante in E♭ for violin and
viola, K364
Sonata for organ and strings in C, K328
Mass in C major, K317

## 1780

**BACH, C. P. E.** (66)
Symphony in F major
**CIMAROSA** (31)
*Giuditta*, oratorio
**MOZART** (24)
Symphony No 34 in C major, K338
Six Variations for violin and piano on
*Hélas, j'ai perdu mon amant*, K360
Sonata for organ and strings in C, K336
**BEETHOVEN** (10)
Nine Variations on a March by Dressler

## 1781

**GIULIANI** was born
**HAYDN** (49)
Symphony No 73, *La Chasse*
Concerto No 2 for horn and strings
String Quartets Nos 38–43. *Russian* or
*Jungfern* Quartets
**GOSSEC** (47)
*L'Arche d'Alliance*, oratorio
**CIMAROSA** (32)
*Il convito*, opera
*Il pittore parigino*, opera
**MOZART** (25)
*Idomeneo*, opera
Rondo for violin and orchestra in C, K373
Concerto Rondo in E♭ for horn, K371
Twelve Variations on *La bergère Célimène*
for violin and piano, K359
Sonata for two pianos, K448
Five Violin Sonatas: K376 in F; K377 in F;
K378 in B♭ ; K379 in Gm and G; K380 in
E♭

BEETHOVEN (11)
'Schilderung eines Mädchen', song

## 1782

AUBER, FIELD and PAGANINI were born
GOSSEC (48)
*Thésée*, opera
CIMAROSA (33)
*La ballerina amante*, opera
*Absalon*, oratorio
MOZART (26)
Five Fugues for string quartet, K405
*Il Seraglio*, opera
Symphony No 35 in D, *Haffner*, K385
Three Piano Concerti: K413 in F; K414 in A; K415 in C
Horn Concerto, K412
Three unfinished violin sonatas, K402–4
String Quartet, K387
Two Concerti Rondo: K382 in Dm; K386 in A
BEETHOVEN (12–32)
Seven Bagatelles for piano (1782–1802)

## 1783

HAYDN (52)
Cello Concerto in D major
MOZART (27)
Symphony No 36 in C, *Linz*, K425
Two Horn Concerti: K417 in Eb ; K447 in Eb
Two String Quartets: K421 in Dm; K428 in Eb
Votive mass
BEETHOVEN (13)
*p* Three Piano Sonatas (composed very early)
Minuet in Eb for piano

## pre 1784

HAYDN
Piano Sonatas Nos 38–40

## 1784

SPOHR was born; BACH, W. F. died
HAYDN (52)
*Armida*, opera
String Quartets Nos 44–50 (1784–7)
GRÉTRY (42)
*L'Épreuve villageoise*, opéra – comique
*Richard Coeur-de-Lion*, opéra - comique
CIMAROSA (35)
*L'Olimpiade*, opera

*Artaserse*, opera
MOZART (28)
Six Piano Concerti: K449 in Eb ; K450 in Bb ; K451 in D; K453 in G; K456 in Bb ; K459 in F
Violin Sonata in Bb ,K454
Piano Sonata in Cm, K457
String Quartet in Bb , K458
BEETHOVEN (14)
*p* Rondo, allegretto in A major for piano
*p* 'An einem Säugling', song

## 1785

HAYDN (53)
Symphony No 87 in A major
Piano Sonata No 41 in Ab  (*c*1785)
Piano Sonata No 42 in G minor (1785–6)
Piano Sonata No 44 in Ab  (1785–6)
MOZART (29)
Three Piano Concerti: K466 in Dm; K467 in C; K482 in Eb
Two String Quartets: K464 in A; K465 in C
Piano Quartet in Gm, K478
Violin Sonata in Eb , K481
BEETHOVEN (15)
Piano Quartets Nos 1–3
Piano Trio No 9
Prelude in F minor for piano

## 1786

WEBER was born
HAYDN (54)
Symphony No 82, *The Bear*
Symphony No 83, *La Poule*
Symphony No 84
Symphony No 85, *La Reine* (*c*1786)
Symphony No 86, *The Miracle* (*c*1786)
GOSSEC (52)
*Rosine*, opera
DITTERSDORF (47)
*Doktor und Apotheker*, opera
*Betrug durch Aberglauben*, opera
BOCCHERINI (43)
*La Clementina*, opera
CIMAROSA (37)
*L'impresario in Angustie*, opera
MOZART (30)
*The Impresario*, opera
*Le nozze di Figaro*, opera
Symphony No 38 in D, *Prague*, K504
Three Piano Concerti: K488 in A; K491 in Cm; K503 in C
Horn Concerto in Eb , K495
Two Piano Sonatas (four hands), K357 in G; K497 in F

String Quartet in D, K499
Piano Quartet in E♭ , K493
Three Piano Trios; K496 in G; K498 in B♭ ,
  for clarinet, viola and piano; K502 in B♭
BEETHOVEN (16)
Trio in C major for piano, flute and
  bassoon

## 1787

GLUCK died
BACH, C. P. E. (73)
*The Resurrection and Ascension of Jesus*,
  oratorio
HAYDN (55)
Symphonies Nos 88 and 89
String Quartets Nos 51–57, *Seven Words*
Piano Sonata No 45 (1787–8)
DITTERSDORF (48)
*Die Liebe in Narrenhaus*, opera
*Democrito coretto*, opera
MOZART (31)
*Don Giovanni*, opera
*Eine Kleine Nachtmusik*, for strings
Three String Quintets, K406 in Cm; K515
  in C; K516 in Gm
Piano Sonata in C (four hands), K521
Violin Sonata in A, K526

## 1788

BACH, C. P. E. died
BACH, C. P. E. (74)
Concerto in E♭ for harpsichord, forte-
  piano and strings
Quartet in G major
HAYDN (56)
Symphonies Nos 90 and 91
Symphony No 92, *Oxford*
*Toy Symphony*
HOPKINSON (51)
Seven Songs
MOZART (32)
Symphony No 39 in E♭ major, K543
Symphony No 40 in G minor, K550
Symphony No 41 in C major, *Jupiter*, K551
Piano Concerto in D major, *Coronation*,
  K537
String Quartet in D minor, K546
Three piano trios: K542 in E; K548 in C;
  K564 in G
Piano Sonata in C (Sonatina), K545
Violin Sonata in F, K547
CHERUBINI (28)
*Ifigenia in Aulide*, opera

## 1789

HAYDN (57)
String Quartets Nos 58–59
Piano Sonata No 46
Piano Sonata No 47 (1789–90)
DITTERSDORF (50)
*Hieronimus Knicker*, opera
CIMAROSA (40)
*Cleopatra*, opera
MOZART (33)
String Quartet in D, K575
Two Piano Sonatas: K570 in B♭ ; K576 in D
BEETHOVEN (19)
Two Preludes through all twelve major
  keys, for piano or organ

## pre 1790

HAYDN
Violin Sonata No 1

## 1790

HAYDN (58)
Piano Sonata No 48 (c1790)
Seven Nocturnes for the King of Naples
DITTERSDORF (51)
*Das rote Käppchen*, opera
MOZART (34)
*Cosi fan tutti*, opera
String Quintet in D, K593
Two String Quartets: K589 in B♭ ; K590
  in F
BEETHOVEN (20)
'Musik zu einem Ritterballett', for
  orchestra
Twenty-four Variations on 'Venni Amore',
  for piano
Two Cantatas

## 1791

MEYERBEER and HÉROLD were born;
MOZART and HOPKINSON died
HAYDN (59)
Symphony No 93
Symphony No 94, *Surprise*
Symphony No 95
Symphony No 96, *Miracle*
DITTERSDORF (52)
*Hokus Pokus*, opera
MOZART (35)
*Die Zauberflöte*, opera
*La clemenza di Tito*, opera
Piano Concerto in B♭ , K595
Clarinet Concerto in A, K622

String Quintet in E♭, K614
Requiem in D Minor, unfinished,
    completed by Süssmeyer
**BEETHOVEN** (21)
Variations on 'Es wa einmal', for piano

## 1792

**ROSSINI** was born; **PARADIES** died
**HAYDN** (60)
Symphonies Nos 97 and 98
*The Storm*, oratorio
**CIMAROSA** (43)
*Il matrimonio segreto*, opera
**BEETHOVEN** (22)
Allegro and Menuetto in G major for two
    flutes

### pre 1793

**HAYDN**
String Quartets Nos 60–69

## 1793

**HAYDN** (61)
Symphony No 99
String Quartets Nos 70–75
**CIMAROSA** (44)
*I Traci amanti*, opera
Concerto for two flutes and orchestra
**BEETHOVEN** (23)
*p* Twelve Variations on 'Se vuol ballare',
    for violin and piano
**BOÏELDIEU** (18)
*La fille coupable*, opera

## 1794

**HAYDN** (62)
Symphony No 100, *Military*
Symphony No 101, *The Clock*
**DITTERSDORF** (55)
*Das Gespeust mit der Trommel*, opera
**CIMAROSA** (45)
*Penelope*, opera
**BEETHOVEN** (24)
Trio for two oboes and English horn
Rondo Allegro in G major for violin and
    piano
*p* Variations on a Waldstein theme for
    piano (four hands)

### pre 1795

**HAYDN**
Piano Sonata No 49

## 1795

**HAYDN** (63)
Symphony No 102
Symphony No 103, *Drum Roll*
Symphony No 104
**DITTERSDORF** (56)
*Don Quixote der Zweite*, opera
*Gott Mars*, opera
*Schach vom Schiras*, opera
**BEETHOVEN** (25)
Three Piano Trios
*p* Twelve *Deutsche Tänze*, for orchestra
Piano Concerto No 2
Six Allemandes for violin and piano
Six Minuets for piano
*p* Nine Variations on 'Quant' è più bello',
    for piano
Twelve Variations on Minuet from *Le
    Nozze Disturbate*, for piano
'Die Flamme lodert', opferlied
Four Songs
**BOÏELDIEU** (20)
Harp Concerto
**PAGANINI** (13)
Variations on 'La Carmagnole'

## 1796

**BERWALD** was born
**HAYDN** (64)
Trumpet Concerto
Mass No 9, *Heiligenmesse*
Mass No 10, *Paukenmesse*
**GOSSEC** (62)
*La Reprise de Toulon*, opera
**DITTERSDORF** (57)
*Der Durchmarsch*, opera
*Die Lustigen Weiber von Windsor*, opera
*Ugolino*, opera
**CIMAROSA** (47)
*Gli Orazi e Curiazi*, opera
**BEETHOVEN** (26)
Twelve Variations on a Russian Dance
    from Wianizky's 'Waldmachen'
'Ah, perfido', scena and aria for soprano
    and orchestra
*p* Six Variations on 'Nel cor più', for piano
'Farewell to Vienna's citizens', song

## 1797

**SCHUBERT** was born
**HAYDN** (65)
*The Creation*, oratorio (1797–8)
String Quartets Nos 76–81 (1797–8)

DITTERSDORF (58)
*Der Terno secco*, opera
*Der Mädchenmarkt*, opera
CHERUBINI (37)
*Médée*, opera
BEETHOVEN (27)
Symphony in C, *Jena* (authenticity
  doubtful)
Quintet for piano and wind
*p* String Quintet in E♭
*p* String Trio in E♭
*p* Serenade in D for string trio
*p* Piano Sonatas Nos 1–4
*p* Cello Sonatas Nos 1 and 2
*p* Twelve Variations on 'See, the
  conquering hero comes', for piano and
  cello
*p* Sonata in D for piano (four hands)
*p* Rondo for piano
War Song of the Austrians, for voices and
  piano
SOR (19)
*Telemaco*, opera
*Don Trastillo*, opera (lost)


## 1798

DONIZETTI was born
HAYDN (66)
Mass No 11, *Nelson*
*The Seasons*, oratorio (1798–1801)
Piano Sonata No 50
BEETHOVEN (28)
*p* Three String Trios
*p* Trio for clarinet (or violin), cello and
  piano
*p* Twelve Variations on 'Ein Mädchen', for
  piano and cello
*p* Six Variations on a Swiss Air, for piano
  or harp
*p* Piano Sonatas Nos 5–7
*p* Twelve minuets
*p* Eight variations on 'Une fièvre brûlante',
  for piano


## 1799

HALÉVY was born; DITTERSDORF died
HAYDN (67)
String Quartets Nos 82 and 83
Mass No 12, *Theresienmesse*
BEETHOVEN (29)
*p* Violin Sonatas Nos 1–3
*p* Piano Sonata No 8, *Pathétique*
*p* Piano Sonatas Nos 9 and 10
*p* Seven Ländler Dances for piano

*p* Seven Variations on 'Kind, willst du', for
  piano
Ten Variations on 'La stessa, la
  stessissima', for piano
Eight Variations on 'Tandeln und
  Scherzen'
'Der Wachtelschlag', song


## 1800

HAYDN (68)
*Te Deum*
CHERUBINI (40)
*Les Deux Journées*, opera
BEETHOVEN (30)
Symphony No 1 in C major
*Mount of Olives*, oratorio
 Piano Concerto No 3 in C minor
Septet for strings and wind
String Quartets Nos 1–6
Sonata for piano, violin and viola
Sonata for piano and horn (or violin)
Piano Sonata No 11
Air with Six Variations on 'Ich denke
  dein', for piano (four hands)
Six very easy variations on an original
  theme, for piano
BOÏELDIEU (25)
*Le calife de Bagdad*, opera
WEBER (14)
*Das Waldmädchen*, opera


## 1801

BELLINI was born; CIMAROSA and
STAMITZ, K. died
BOCCHERINI (58)
*Stabat Mater*
BEETHOVEN (31)
*fp The Creatures of Prometheus*, ballet
*p* Piano Concerto No 1 in C
String Quintet in C
*p* Violin Sonata No 5 in F, *Spring*
WEBER (15)
*Peter Schmoll und seine Nachbarn*, opera


## 1802

BEETHOVEN (32)
Symphony No 2 in D
*p* Serenade for flute, violin and viola
*p* Seven Variations on 'Bei Mannern', for
  cello and piano
*p* Piano Sonatas Nos 12 and 13
*p* Piano Sonata No 14, *Moonlight*
*p* Piano Sonata No 15, *Pastoral*
Piano Sonatas Nos 16–20

Violin Sonatas Nos 6–8
Violin Sonata No 9, *Kreutzer*
*p* Rondo for piano
Six Variations on an original theme for
　piano
Fifteen Variations and Fugue on a theme
　from 'Prometheus', for piano
Terzetto, *Tremate*, for soprano, tenor and
　bass
*p* Six Ländler Dances
Opferlied, songs

## 1803

**ADAM** and **BERLIOZ** were born
**HAYDN** (71)
String Quartet No 84
**GOSSEC** (69)
*Les Sabots et le Cerisier*, opera
**CHERUBINI** (43)
*Anacréon*, opera
**BEETHOVEN** (33)
*Fidelio*, opera begun (last revision 1814)
*p* Six Songs for soprano
Romance in G for violin and orchestra
*p* Twelve Kontretänze, for orchestra
*p* Three songs
Six songs (1803–10)
**BOÏELDIEU** (28)
*Ma Tante Aurore*, opera

## 1804

**GLINKA** and **STRAUSS, J. (Sr.)** were
born
**BEETHOVEN** (34)
Symphony No 3, *Eroica*
Triple Concerto in C major, for violin,
　cello, piano and orchestra
*p* Fourteen Variations in E♭ for violin,
　cello and piano
*p* Three Grand Marches, for piano (four
　hands)
Piano Sonata No 21, *Waldstein*
Piano Sonata No 23, *Appassionata*
Andante favori, for piano
*p* Seven Variations on 'God Save the King ,
　for piano
*p* Five Variations on 'Rule, Britannia', for
　piano

## 1805

**BOCCHERINI** died
**BEETHOVEN** (35)
Symphony No 5 in C minor
Piano Concerto No 4 in G

*p* Romance in F for violin and orchestra
*p* Nine songs

## 1806

**ARRIAGA** was born; **HAYDN, M.** died
**BEETHOVEN** (36)
Symphony No 4 in B♭
Violin Concerto in D major
*p* Piano Sonata No 22
Thirty-two Variations in C minor for piano
　(1806–7)
**WEBER** (20)
Symphony No 1 (1806–7)

## 1807

**BEETHOVEN** (37)
*Coriolanus*, overture
*Leonora No 1*, overture
String Quartets Nos 7–9, *Rassumovsky*
Mass in C major
'In questa tomba oscura', arietta
**SPONTINI** (33)
*La Vestale*, opera
**PAGANINI** (25)
Sonata, *Napoleone*
**WEBER** (21)
Symphony No 2

## 1808

**BALFE** was born
**BEETHOVEN** (38)
*p* 'Sehnsucht', songs with piano
**ROSSINI** (16)
Sonata for two violins, cello and double-
　bass

## 1809

**MENDELSSOHN** was born; **HAYDN, J.**
died
**BEETHOVEN** (39)
*p* Symphony No 6 in F, *Pastoral*
Piano Concerto No 5 in E♭ , *Emperor*
String Quartet No 10, *Harp*
*p* Trios Nos 4 and 5, for violin, cello and
　piano
*p* Cello Sonata No 3
Military March in F
Three songs
**SPONTINI** (35)
*Ferdinand Cortez*, opera
**ROSSINI** (17)
Variations for clarinet and orchestra

## 1810

**CHOPIN, NICOLAI** and **SCHUMANN**
were born
**BEETHOVEN** (40)
*Egmont*, incidental music
*p* Wind Sextet
*p* Sextet in E♭ for strings and horns
String Quartet No 11, *Quartett serioso*
*p* Piano Sonatas Nos 24 and 25
*p* Fantasy in G minor for piano
*p* Six Variations in D for piano
*p* Three Songs for soprano and piano
Four songs
**PAGANINI** (28)
*Polacca con Variazione*, for violin and
orchestra
**WEBER** (24)
Piano Concerto No 1
**ROSSINI** (18)
*La cambiale di matrimonio*, opera

## 1811

**LISZT** and **THOMAS** were born
**BEETHOVEN** (41)
*The Ruins of Athens*, overture and eight
numbers
*King Stephen*, overture and nine numbers
*p* Choral Fantasia for chorus, piano and
orchestra
Piano Trio No 6, *The Archduke*
*p* Piano Sonata No 26, *Les Adieux*
*p* Four Ariettas and Duet for soprano,
tenor and piano
Song
**WEBER** (25)
*Abu Hassan*, opera
Bassoon Concerto
Clarinet Concertos Nos 1 and 2
Concertino for clarinet
**SCHUBERT** (14)
Quintet-Overture

## 1812

**FLOTOW** and **WALLACE** were born
**BEETHOVEN** (42)
Symphonies Nos 7 and 8
Piano Trio No 10
Violin Sonata No 10
**BOÏELDIEU** (37)
*Jean de Paris*, opera
**WEBER** (26)
Piano Concerto No 2
Piano Sonata No 1

**HÉROLD** (21)
*Mlle de la Vallière*, cantata
**ROSSINI** (20)
*La Scala di seta (The Silken Ladder)*, opera
**SCHUBERT** (15)
Quartet-Overture
String Quartets Nos 1–3
*Eine Kleine Trauermusik*, nonet
Sonata movement for piano trio in B♭
major

## 1813

**ALKAN, DARGOMIZHSKY, VERDI** and
**WAGNER** were born; **GRÉTRY** died
**GOSSEC** (79)
*Dernière Messe des vivants*
**BEETHOVEN** (43)
*Wellington's Victory*, for orchestra
Triumphal March for orchestra
Song
**PAGANINI** (31)
*Le Streghe*, for violin and orchestra
**HÉROLD** (22)
*Hymne sur la Transfiguration*, for voices and
orchestra
**ROSSINI** (21)
*L'Italiana in Algeri*, opera
*Tancredi*, opera
**SCHUBERT** (16)
Minuet and Finale of a wind octet in
F major
*Des Teufels Lustschloss*, opera (1813–14)
Symphony No 1
String Quartets Nos 4–6
Three Sonatinas for violin and piano
Five Minuets
Five German Dances

## 1814

**CHERUBINI** (54)
String Quartet No 1
**BEETHOVEN** (44)
*Leonore Prohaska*, incidental music
*Der glorreiche Augenblick*, cantata
Overture in C, *Namensfeier*
Piano Sonata No 27
Polonaise in C for piano
*Merkenstein*, duet
*p* Three books of Irish songs
*p* 'Germania', bass solo
Elegiac song
**FIELD** (22)
Three Nocturnes for piano
**SCHUBERT** (17)
String Quartets Nos 7 and 8

Quartet for flute, guitar, viola and cello
'Gretchen am Spinnrade' (*Gretchen at the Spinning Wheel*), song

## 1815

**CHERUBINI** (55)
String Quartets Nos 2 and 3 (1815–29)
**BEETHOVEN** (45)
*Calm Sea and Prosperous Voyage*, for chorus and orchestra
Cello Sonatas Nos 4 and 5
Three Duos for clarinet and bassoon
Twenty-five Scotch songs
Twelve songs of varied nationality
Songs
**PAGANINI** (33)
Concerto for violin
**WEBER** (29)
Quintet for clarinet and string quartet
Concertino for horn and orchestra
**HÉROLD** (24)
*La Gioventù di Enrico Quinto*, opera
**ROSSINI** (23)
*Elisabetta, Regina d'Inghilterra*, opera
**SCHUBERT** (18)
Symphonies Nos 2 and 3
String Quartet No 9
Piano Sonatas Nos 1 and 2
'Der Erlkönig', song

## 1816

**PAISELLO** died
**BEETHOVEN** (46)
*An die ferne Geliebte*, song cycle
Military March
Three songs
**PAGANINI** (34)
Sonata, *Maria Luisa*
**WEBER** (30)
Piano Sonatas Nos 2 and 3
**HÉROLD** (25) *Charles de France*, opera
**ROSSINI** (24)
*Otello*, opera
*The Barber of Seville*, opera
**BERWALD** (20)
Theme and Variations for violin and orchestra
**SCHUBERT** (19)
Symphony No 4, *Tragic*
Symphony No 5
*Konzertstücke*, for violin and orchestra
Rondo for violin and orchestra
*Adagio and Rondo Concertante*, for piano quartet
String Trio

Piano Sonata No 3
**HALÉVY** (17)
*Les derniers moments du Tasso*, cantata

## 1817

**GADE** was born
**BEETHOVEN** (47)
Symphony No 9, *Choral* (1817–23)
String Quintet in C minor
p Piano Sonata No 28
Three songs
Fugue in D
p Twenty-six Welsh songs
**PAGANINI** (35)
Concerto No 1
**HÉROLD** (26)
*Les Rosières*, opera
*La Clochette*, opera
**ROSSINI** (25)
*La Cenerentola*, opera
*La Gazza ladra (The Thieving Magpie)*, opera
**BERWALD** (21)
Double Concerto for two violins and orchestra (lost)
Septet for violin, viola, cello, clarinet, bassoon, horn and double-bass
**SCHUBERT** (20)
String Quartets Nos 10 and 11
Piano Sonatas Nos 4–9
Violin Sonata in A major
'An die Musik', song
'Tod und das Mädchen', song
**HALÉVY** (18)
*La mort d'Adonis*, cantata
**ARRIAGA** (11)
Octet
**CHOPIN** (7)
Polonaises Nos 13 and 14

## 1818

**GOUNOD** and **LITOLFF** were born
**BEETHOVEN** (48)
Six Themes Varied for piano, flute or violin (1818–19)
Ten National Themes with Variations, for flute or violin and piano
Piano Sonata No 29. *Hammerklavier* (1818–19)
'Ziemlich Lebhaft', for piano
*Missa Solemnis* in D major
**HÉROLD** (27)
*Le Premier Venu*, opera
**ROSSINI** (26)
*Mosè*, opera

SCHUBERT (21)
Symphony No 6
Piano Sonatas Nos 10 and 11
ARRIAGA (12)
Two Overtures
Symphony in D

## 1819

OFFENBACH and SUPPÉ were born
SPONTINI (45)
*Olympie*, opera
PAGANINI (37)
*Inno all'armonia*, cantata (lost)
Introduction and Variations on 'Non più
    mesta', 'Di tanti palpiti' and 'Dal tuo
    stellato soglio'
WEBER (33)
*Invitation to the Dance*, for piano
HÉROLD (28)
*Les Troqueurs*, opera
*L'Amour Platonique*, opera
BERWALD (23)
Quartet for piano, clarinet, horn and
    bassoon
SCHUBERT (22)
Piano Quintet, *The Trout*
Piano Sonatas Nos 12 and 13
HALÉVY (20)
*Herminie*, cantata

## 1820

VIEUXTEMPS was born
BEETHOVEN (50)
Allegro con brio, for violin and orchestra
Piano Sonata No 30
Song
HÉROLD (29)
*L'Auteur Mort et Vivant*, opera
ROSSINI (28)
*Maometto II*, opera
Solemn Mass
BERWALD (24)
Symphony No 1
Violin Concerto
SCHUBERT (23)
*Die Zauberharfe*, melodrama
String Quartet No 12
HALÉVY (21)
*De Profundis*, for three voices and orchestra
ARRIAGA (14)
*Los esclavos felices*, opera
Theme and Variations for string quartet

## 1821

BEETHOVEN (51)
Piano Sonata No 31
*p* Bagatelles for piano
SPONTINI (47)
*Nurmahal*, opera
SOR (43)
*Le Foire de Smyrne*, ballet (lost)
*Le Seigneur Genereux*, ballet (lost)
WEBER (35)
*Konzertstücke*, for piano and orchestra
*fp Der Freischütz*, opera
SCHUBERT (24)
*Alfonso und Estrella*, opera (1821–2)
Symphony No 7 (sketched)
*Variation on a Theme by Diabelli*
MENDELSSOHN (12)
Piano Sonata No 2
CHOPIN (11)
Polonaise No 15

## 1822

FRANCK and RAFF were born
BEETHOVEN (52)
*Consecration of the House*, overture
'Bundeslied' (1822–3)
'The Kiss', arietta
SOR (44)
*Cendrillon*, ballet
WEBER (36)
Piano Sonata No 4
ROSSINI (30)
*Zelmira*, opera
SCHUBERT (25)
Symphony No 8, *Unfinished*
GLINKA (18)
*Variations on a Theme of Mozart*, for piano
ARRIAGA (16)
*La Húngara*, variations for string quartet
MENDELSSOHN (13)
Piano Quartet No 1, Op 1
CHOPIN (12)
Polonaise No 16

## 1823

LALO was born
BEETHOVEN (53)
Piano Sonata No 32
*p* Bagatelles for piano
Variations on a Waltz by Diabelli
'Minuet of Congratulations'
Cantata in E♭
SOR (45)
*L'Amant Peintre*, ballet

**WEBER** (37)
*fp Euryanthe*, opera
**HÉROLD** (32)
*Le Muletier*, opera
*Lasthénie*, opera
*Vendôme en Espagne*, opera
**ROSSINI** (31)
*Semiramide*, opera
**SCHUBERT** (26)
*Fierrebras*, opera
*Der häusliche Kreig*, opera
*Rosamunde*, incidental music
Piano Sonata No 14
*Die Schöne Mullerin*, song cycle
**MENDELSSOHN** (14)
Piano Quartet No 2
Violin Sonata

## 1824

**BRUCKNER** and **SMETANA** were born
**BEETHOVEN** (54)
String Quartet No 12
*p The Ruins of Athens*, march and chorus
*p* Variations on 'Ich bin der Schneider
 Kakadu'
**HÉROLD** (33)
*Le Roi René*, opera
**SCHUBERT** (27)
Octet in F major for strings and wind
String Quartet No 13
String Quartet no 14, *Death and the Maiden*
Introduction and Variations for flute and
 piano
Sonata for cello and piano, *Arpeggione*
**ARRIAGA** (18)
Three String Quartets
**MENDELSSOHN** (15)
Symphony No 1
Piano Quartet No 3

## 1825

**STRAUSS, J. (Jr.)** was born
**BEETHOVEN** (55)
Great Fugue in B♭, for strings
String Quartet No 13, *Scherzoso* (1825–6)
Rondo a capriccio, for piano (1825–6)
**BOÏELDIEU** (50)
*La dame blanche*, opera
**PAGANINI** (43)
Sonata, *Militaire*
**HÉROLD** (34)
*Le Lapin Blanc*, opera
**ROSSINI** (33)
*Il viaggio a Reims*, opera

**BERWALD** (29)
Serenade for tenor and six instruments
**SCHUBERT** (28)
Piano Sonatas Nos 15–17
**BELLINI** (24)
*Adelson e Salvina*, opera
*Bianca e Fernando*, opera
**MENDELSSOHN** (16)
*Wedding of the Camacho*, comic opera
*Trumpet Overture*, for orchestra
String Octet
Capriccio for piano
**CHOPIN** (15)
Polonaise No 8

## 1826

**WEBER** and **ARRIAGA** died
**BEETHOVEN** (56)
String Quartets Nos 14–16
Andante maestoso in C major, for piano
**SOR** (48)
*Hercule et Omphale*, ballet
**PAGANINI** (44)
Concertos Nos 2 and 3
**WEBER** (39)
*fp Oberon*, opera
**HÉROLD** (35)
*Marie*, opera
**ROSSINI** (34)
*Le Siège de Corinthe*, opera
**SCHUBERT** (29)
String Quartet No 15
Piano Trio
*Rondo Brillant*, for violin and piano
Piano Sonata No 18
**GLINKA** (22)
Memorial Cantata
*Pathétique*, trio for piano, clarinet and
 bassoon, or piano, violin and cello
**MENDELSSOHN** (17)
*A Midsummer Night's Dream*, overture
String Quintet
Piano Sonata No 1
Six songs (1826–7)
**CHOPIN** (16)
Polonaise No 11
Three Ecossaises
Introduction and Variations on *Der
 Schweizerbub*

## 1827

**BEETHOVEN** died
**SOR** (49)
*Le Sicilien*, ballet

**HÉROLD** (36)
*Astophe et Joconde*, ballet
*La Somnambule*, ballet
**ROSSINI** (35)
*Moïse*, opera (French version of *Mosè*)
**BERWALD** (31)
*Gustav Wasa*, opera
*Konzertstücke*, for bassoon and orchestra
**SCHUBERT** (30)
Piano Trio
*Phantasie*, for violin and piano
*Die Winterreise*, song cycle
**HALÉVY** (28)
*L'artisan*, opera
**BELLINI** (26)
*Il Pirata*, opera
**BERLIOZ** (24)
*Les frances–juges*, overture
*Waverley*, overture
*La Mort d'Orphée*, cantata
**MENDELSSOHN** (18)
String Quartet No 2
Fugue for string quartet
Piano Sonata No 3
*p* Seven Pieces for piano
**CHOPIN** (17)
Nocturne No 19


# 1828

**SCHUBERT** died
**SOR** (50)
*Hassan et le Calife*, ballet (lost)
**AUBER** (46)
*La muette de Portici*, opera
**PAGANINI** (46)
*È Pur Amabile*, canzonetta for voice and
    piano
*La Tempesta*, for chorus and orchestra
*Maestoso sonata sentimentale*
Sonata and Variations on 'Pria ch'io
    l'impegno'
*Le Couvent du St Bernard*, for male voices
    and orchestra
**HÉROLD** (37)
*Lydie*, ballet
*La Fille mal gardée*, ballet
**ROSSINI** (36)
*fp Comte Ory*, comedy-opera
**SCHUBERT** (31)
Symphony No 9 in C major, *The Great*
Symphony No 10 (unfinished, recently
    discovered)
String Quintet in C major
Piano Sonatas Nos 19–21
*Schwanengesang*, song cycle

**HALÉVY** (29)
*Le roi et le batelier*, opera
*Clari*, opera
**BERLIOZ** (25)
*Herminie*, cantata
**CHOPIN** (18)
*Krakowiak*, concerto rondo for orchestra
*Fantasia on Polish Airs*, for piano and
    orchestra
Rondo for two pianos
Piano Sonata No 1
Polonaises Nos 9 and 10


# 1829

**GOTTSCHALK** and **RUBINSTEIN** were
born; **GIULIANI** and **GOSSEC** died
**SPONTINI** (55)
*Agnes von Hohenstaufen*, opera
**PAGANINI** (47)
Variations on 'God Save the King'
Variations on 'O mamma, mamma cara'
Sonata, *Varsaria*
Sonata, *Appassionata*
**HÉROLD** (38)
*La Belle au bois dormant*, ballet
*L'Illusion*, opera
*Emmeline*, opera
**ROSSINI** (37)
*William Tell*, opera
**HALÉVY** (30)
*Le dilettante d'Avignon*, opera
**BELLINI** (28)
*La Straniera*, opera
*Zaira*, opera
**BERLIOZ** (26)
*Cléopâtre*, cantata
*Huit scènes de Faust*, cantata
*Irlande*, five songs with piano (1829–30)
**BALFE** (21)
*I rivali di se stesso*, opera
**CHOPIN** (19)
Piano Concerto No 2
Introduction and Polonaise for cello and piano
Twelve Grand Studies for piano (1829–32):
    No 5 'Black Keys', No 12 'Revolutionary'
Polonaise No 12
Waltzes Nos 10 and 13
*Variations on a Theme by Paganini*
**SCHUMANN** (19)
*Papillons*, twelve pieces for piano (1829–31)
**MENDELSSOHN** (20)
*Die Heimkehr aus der Fremde*, operetta
String Quartet No 1
*Variations concertantes*, for cello and piano
Three Fantasies for piano
Twelve Songs

## 1830

GOLDMARK was born
AUBER (48)
*Fra Diavolo*, opera
PAGANINI (48)
*Quel jours heureux*, for solo, chorus and
   piano
Concertos Nos 4 and 5
*Moto Perpetuo*, for violin and orchestra
HÉROLD (39)
*L'Auberge d'Aurey*, opera
DONIZETTI (33)
*Anna Bolena*, opera
HALÉVY (31)
*Manon Lescaut*, ballet
BELLINI (29)
*I Capuletti ed i Montecchi*, opera
BERLIOZ (27)
*Symphonie fantastique* (revised 1831)
*Sardanapale*, cantata
GLINKA (26)
String Quartet
BALFE (22)
*Un avvertimento ai gelosi*, opera
MENDELSSOHN (21)
*Hebrides*, concert overture
Symphony No 5, *Reformation*
Eighteen Songs
CHOPIN (20)
Piano Concerto No 1
Nine Mazurkas for piano (1830–1)
Nocturnes Nos 4–6 for piano (1830–1)
SCHUMANN (20)
*Theme and Variations on the name 'Abegg'*,
   for piano
LISZT (19–38)
Piano Concerto No 1 (1830–49)
WAGNER (17)
Overture

## 1831

PAGANINI (49)
Sonata amoroso galante
*Potpourri*
*St Patrick's Day*, variations on an Irish
   song
Sonatina e Polacchetta
Concertino for bassoon, horn and
   orchestra
MEYERBEER (40)
*Robert le diable*, opera
HÉROLD (40)
*Zampa*, opera
HALVYÉ (32)
*La langue musicale*, opera

BELLINI (30)
*La Sonnambula*, opera
*Norma*, opera
BERLIOZ (28)
*Le Corsaire*, overture (revised 1855)
*King Lear*, overture
MENDELSSOHN (22)
Piano Concerto No 1
*Die erste Walpurgisnacht*, for solo voices,
   chorus and orchestra
CHOPIN (21)
Waltzes Nos 1 and 3
*Andante Spianoto*, and *Grand Polonaise
   Brillant* (1831–4)
NICOLAI (21)
Symphony
LISZT (20)
*Harmonies poétiques et religieuses*, for piano
   and orchestra
WAGNER (18)
Piano Sonata

## 1832

CLEMENTI died
FIELD (50)
*fp* Piano Concerto No 1
HÉROLD (41)
*La Médicine sans Médicin*, opera
*Le Pré aux Clercs*, opera
ROSSINI (40)
Stabat Mater (1832–41)
DONIZETTI (35)
*L'Elisir d' Amore*, opera
HALÉVY (33)
*La tentation*, ballet-opera
ADAM (29)
*Faust*, ballet
BERLIOZ (29)
*Le Cinq Mai*, cantata (1830–2)
MENDELSSOHN (23)
*Meerstille* (*Calm Sea and Prosperous Voyage*)
   concert overture
*Capriccio Brillant*, for piano and orchestra
Six Preludes and Fugues for piano (1832–7)
CHOPIN (22)
Allegro de Concert
Scherzo No 1
NICOLAI (22)
Mass
SCHUMANN (22)
Six Concert Studies on Caprices by
   Paganini, Set 1
THOMAS (21)
*Hermann et Ketty*, cantata
ALKAN (19)
*Hermann et Ketty*, vocal work

Chamber Concerto No 1
**WAGNER** (19)
Symphony in C major
*Die Hochzeit*, opera (unfinished)

## 1833

**BORODIN** and **BRAHMS** were born;
**HÉROLD** died
**CHERUBINI** (73)
*Ali Baba*, opera
**HÉROLD** (41)
*Ludovic*, opera (completed by Halévy)
**DONIZETTI** (36)
*Lucrezia Borgia*, opera
**BELLINI** (32)
*Beatrice di Tenda*, opera
**HALÉVY** (34)
*Ludovic*, opera (completion of Hérold's
    work)
*Les souvenirs de Lafleur*, opera
**GLINKA** (29)
Sextet for piano and strings (1833–4)
**BALFE** (25)
*Enrico IV al Passo della Marna*, opera
**MENDELSSOHN** (24)
Symphony No 4, *Italian*
*Die schöne Melusine*, overture
Fantasy in F♯ minor for piano
Three Capriccios for piano (1833–4)
**CHOPIN** (23)
Bolero in C major
*Introduction and Variations on a Theme by
    Hérold*
**SCHUMANN** (23)
Six Concert Studies on Caprices by
    Paganini, Set II
**WAGNER** (20)
*Die Feen*, opera

## 1834

**PONCHIELLI** was born; **BOÏELDIEU**
died
**PAGANINI** (52)
Sonata for viola and orchestra
**DONIZETTI** (37)
*Rosmonda d'Inghilterra*, opera
**ADAM** (31)
*Le Châlet*, opera
**BERLIOZ** (31)
*Harold in Italy*, symphony with solo viola
*Les nuits d'été*, song cycle for soprano and
    orchestra
*Sara la baigneuse*, for choirs and orchestra
**MENDELSSOHN** (25)
*Rondo Brillant*, for piano and orchestra

Piano Sextet
*p Songs Without Words*, Book 1, for piano
Three Studies for piano (1834–7)
Seven Songs
**CHOPIN** (24)
Études Nos 13–24 (1834–6)
Fantaisie Impromptu in C♯ minor
Polonaises Nos 1–2 (1834–5)
Prelude No 26
**SCHUMANN** (24)
*Carnaval*, twenty-one pieces for piano
    (1834–5)
**WAGNER** (21)
*Das Liebesverbot*, opera
**ALKAN** (21)
Chamber Concerto No 2
*L'Entrée en Loge*, vocal

## 1835

**CUI, SAINT-SAËNS** and **WIENIAWSKI**
were born; **BELLINI** died
**CHERUBINI** (75)
String Quartets Nos 4–6
**AUBER** (53)
*The Bronze Horse*, opera (revised 1857)
**DONIZETTI** (38)
*Lucia di Lammermoor*, opera
**HALÉVY** (36)
*La juive*, opera
*L'éclair*, opera
**BELLINI** (34)
*I Puritani*, opera
**BALFE** (27)
*The Siege of Rochelle*, opera
**MENDELSSOHN** (26)
*p Songs Without Words*, Book II, for piano
Four Songs
**CHOPIN** (25)
Ballade
Nocturnes Nos 7 and 8
Waltzes Nos 2, 9 and 11
**NICOLAI** (25)
Symphony
*Funeral March* (for the death of Bellini)
**LISZT** (24)
*Années de pèlerinage*, for piano begun
    (completed 1883)

## 1836

**DELIBES** was born
**CHERUBINI** (76)
*Requiem Mass*
**MEYERBEER** (45)
*Les Huguenots*, opera

**ADAM** (33)
*Le Postillon de Longjumeau*, opera
**GLINKA** (32)
*A Life for the Tsar*, opera
*The Moldavian Gipsy*, incidental music
**BALFE** (28)
*The Maid of Artois*, opera
**MENDELSSOHN** (27)
*St Paul*, oratorio
Etude for piano
**CHOPIN** (26)
Ballade (1836–9)
Nocturnes Nos 9 and 10 (1836–7)
Twenty-four Preludes for piano (1836–9)
**SCHUMANN** (26)
*Phantasie*, for piano

## 1837

**BALAKIREV** and **WALDTEUFEL** were
born; **FIELD** and **HUMMEL** died
**CHERUBINI** (77)
String Quintet
**AUBER** (55)
*Le Domino noir*, opera
**BERLIOZ** (34)
*Grande messe des morts*, requiem
**BALFE** (29)
*Catherine Grey*, opera
*Joan of Arc*, opera
**MENDELSSOHN** (28)
Piano Concerto No 2
String Quartets Nos 3–5 (1837–8)
Three Organ Preludes and Fugues
Six Songs
Two Pieces for piano
**CHOPIN** (27)
Impromptu, Op 29
Nocturne in C minor, Op 20
Scherzo No 2
**SCHUMANN** (27)
*Davidsbündler-Tänze*, eighteen piano
    pieces (revised 1850)
p *Études symphoniques*, twelve symphonic
    studies for piano
*Fantasiestücke*, for piano, Books I and II
**THOMAS** (26)
*La double échelle*, opera
**GOUNOD** (19)
Scherzo for orchestra

## 1838

**BIZET** and **BRUCH** were born
**PAGANINI** (56)
Sonata, *La Primavera*
**HALÉVY** (39)

*Guido et Ginevra*, opera
**BERLIOZ** (35)
*Benvenuto Cellini*, opera (1834–8)
*Roméo and Juliet*, dramatic symphony
    (1838–9)
**BALFE** (30)
*Falstaff*, opera
*Diadeste*, opera
**MENDELSSOHN** (29)
Serenade and Allegro Gioioso, for piano
    and orchestra
Cello Sonata
Piano Trio No 1
**CHOPIN** (28)
Nocturnes Nos 11 and 12 (1838–9)
Polonaises Nos 3 and 4 (1838–9)
Waltz No 4
**NICOLAI** (28)
*Von Himmel Hoch*, overture
**SCHUMANN** (28)
*Kinderscenen*, thirteen short piano pieces
*Kreisleriana*, for piano
*Novelleten*, eight piano pieces
**THOMAS** (27)
*Le Perruquier de la Régence*, opera

## 1839

**MUSSORGSKY** was born; **SOR** died
**HALÉVY** (40)
*Les treize*, opera
*Le shérif*, opera
**ADAM** (36)
*La Jolie Fille de Gand*, ballet
**BERLIOZ** (36)
*Rêverie et Caprice*, for violin and orchestra
**GLINKA** (35)
*Valse-fantasie*, for orchestra
**MENDELSSOHN** (30)
*Ruy Blas*, overture
p *Songs Without Words*, Book III, for piano
Seven Songs
**CHOPIN** (29)
Études Nos 25–7
Impromptu, Op 36
Scherzo No 3
Piano Sonata No 2
**SCHUMANN** (29)
*Nachtstücke*, for piano
**NICOLAI** (29)
*Henry II*, opera
**LISZT** (28)
Piano Concerto No 2
**THOMAS** (28)
*Le panier fleuri*, opera
*La Gipsy*, ballet

VERDI (26)
*fp Oberto*, opera

## 1840

**TCHAIKOVSKY** and **STAINER** were born; **PAGANINI** died
**DONIZETTI** (43)
*La Favorita*, opera
*La Fille du Régiment*, opera
**HALÉVY** (41)
*Le drapier*, opera
**BERLIOZ** (37)
*Symphonie funèbre et triomphale*, for chorus, strings and military band
**GLINKA** (36)
*Farewell to Petersburg*, song cycle
**MENDELSSOHN** (31)
*Lobgesang (Hymn of Praise)*, symphony-cantata (Symphony No 2)
**CHOPIN** (30)
Ballade, Op 47 (1840–1)
Fantasia in F minor
Waltz No 5
**NICOLAI** (30)
*Gildippe ed Odoardo*, opera
*Il Templario*, opera
**SCHUMANN** (30)
*Dichterliebe*, song cycle
*Frauenliebe und Leben*, song cycle
*Liederkreiss*, nine songs (Heine)
**LISZT** (29)
*Malediction*, for piano and strings (c1840)
**THOMAS** (29)
*Carlino*, opera
**ALKAN** (27)
*Pas redoublé*, for wind band
*Grand duo concertante*, for violin and piano
**WAGNER** (27)
*Faust*, overture
**GADE** (23)
*Faedrelandets Muser*, ballet
*Echoes from Ossian*, overture
Piano Sonata
**GOUNOD** (22)
*Marche militaire suisse*, for orchestra
**FRANCK** (18)
Three Piano Trios, Op 1

## 1841

**CHABRIER** and **DVOŘÁK** were born
**AUBER** (59)
*Les Diamants de la couronne*, opera
**HALÉVY** (42)
*Le guitarrero*, opera
*La reine de Chypre*, opera

**ADAM** (38)
*Giselle*, ballet
**BALFE** (33)
*Keolanthe*, opera
**MENDELSSOHN** (32)
*Songs Without Words*, Books IV and VII, for piano
*Cornelius March*
Six Songs
Variations in Bb major, Eb major
*Variations sérieuses*
**CHOPIN** (31)
Nocturnes Nos 13 and 14
Polonaise No 5
Prelude No 25
Waltz No 12
**NICOLAI** (31)
*Il Proscritto*, opera
**SCHUMANN** (31)
Symphony No 1, *Spring*
Symphony No 4 (revised 1851)
*Overture, Scherzo and Finale*, for orchestra (*Finale* revised 1845)
Piano Concerto (1841–5)
**THOMAS** (30)
*Le Comte de Carmagnola*, opera
**ALKAN** (28)
Piano Trio
**GADE** (24)
Symphony No 1

## 1842

**BOITO, MASSENET** and **SULLIVAN** were born; **CHERUBINI** died
**BERWALD** (46)
Symphony No 2, *Sérieuse*
Symphony No 3
**DONIZETTI** (45)
*Linda de Chamounix*, opera
**GLINKA** (38)
*Russlan and Ludmilla*, opera
**MENDELSSOHN** (33)
Symphony No 3, *Scottish*
Cello Sonata (1842–3)
*Songs Without Words*, Book VIII, for piano (1842–5)
*Kinderstücke (Children's Pieces)*, for piano
**CHOPIN** (32)
Ballade, Op 52
Impromptu, Op 51
Polonaise No 6
Scherzo No 4
**SCHUMANN** (32)
Piano Quintet
Piano Quartet
Three String Quartets

Andante and Variations for two pianos,
two cellos and horn (1842?)
Four *Fantasiestücke*, for piano trio
*Liederkreis*, twelve songs (Eichendorf)
**THOMAS** (31)
*Le Guerillero*, opera
**VERDI** (29)
*fp Nabucco*, opera
**WAGNER** (29)
*fp Rienzi*, opera
**GADE** (25)
*Napoli*, ballet
Violin Sonata No 1
**FRANCK** (20)
Piano Trio No 4


## 1843

**GRIEG** was born
**DONIZETTI** (46)
*Maria de Rohan*, opera
*Don Pasquale*, opera
*Dom Sébastien*, opera
**HALÉVY** (44)
*Charles VI*, opera
**BALFE** (35)
*The Bohemian Girl*, opera
*Geraldine*, opera
**MENDELSSOHN** (34)
*Athalie*, incidental music
String Quartet Pieces, Op 81
*Songs Without Words*, Books V and VI, for
piano
**CHOPIN** (33)
Berceuse, Op 57
Nocturnes Nos 15 and 16
**SCHUMANN** (33)
*Das Paradies und die Peri*, cantata
**LISZT** (32)
*Valse Impromptu*, in A♭ major
**THOMAS** (32)
*Angélique et Médor*, opera
*Mina*, opera
**VERDI** (30)
*fp I Lombardi*, opera
**WAGNER** (30)
*fp The Flying Dutchman*, opera
**FRANCK** (21)
Andante quietoso for violin and piano

## 1844

**RIMSKY-KORSAKOV, SARASATE** and
**WIDOR** were born
**BERWALD** (48)
*A Country Wedding*, for organ (four hands)

**HALÉVY** (45)
*Le Lazzarone*, opera
**BERLIOZ** (41)
*Roman Carnival*, overture
**BALFE** (36)
*The Castle of Aymon*, opera
*The Daughter of St Mark*, opera
**MENDELSSOHN** (35)
Violin Concerto
*p* Six Organ Sonatas (1844-5)
**CHOPIN** (34)
Piano Sonata No 3
**NICOLAI** (34)
*Ein Feste Burg*, overture with chorus
**ALKAN** (31)
Symphony (lost)
**VERDI** (31)
*fp Ernani*, opera
*fp I due Foscari*, opera
**GADE** (27)
*In the Highlands*, overture


## 1845

**FAURÉ** was born
**BERWALD** (49)
Symphony No 5, *Singulière*
Symphony No 6
Five Piano Trios
**GLINKA** (41)
Spanish Overture No 1, *Jota Aragonesa*
**BALFE** (37)
*The Enchantress*, opera
**MENDELSSOHN** (36)
Piano Trio No 2
String Quintet
*Songs Without Words*, for cello and piano
**SCHUMANN** (35)
Symphony No 2 (1845-6)
**CHOPIN** (35)
Cello Sonata, Op 65
Barcarolle, Op 60
Polonaise No 7
**WALLACE** (33)
*fp Maritana*, opera
**VERDI** (32)
*fp Alzira*, opera
*fp Giovanna d'Arco*, opera
**WAGNER** (32)
*fp Tannhäuser*, opera
**ALKAN** (31)
*Romance du phare d'Eddystone*, vocal (lost)

## 1846

**AUBER** (74)
*fp Manon Lescaut*, opera

**HALÉVY** (47)
*Les mousquetaires de la reine*, opera
**BERLIOZ** (43)
*The Damnation of Faust*, dramatic cantata
**BALFE** (38)
*The Bondman*, opera
**MENDELSSOHN** (37)
*fp Elijah*, oratorio
String Quartet No 6
*Lauda Sion*, cantata
**CHOPIN** (36)
Nocturnes Nos 17 and 18
Waltzes Nos 6–8, Op 64 (1846–7)
**THOMAS** (35)
*Betty*, ballet
**VERDI** (33)
*fp Attila*, opera
**GADE** (29)
*p* String Quintet
**FRANCK** (24)
*Ruth*, cantata
*Ce qu'on entend sur la montagne*, symphonic
  poem (*c*1846)

## 1847

**MENDELSSOHN** died
**HALÉVY** (48)
*Les premier pas*, opera
**GLINKA** (43)
*Greeting to the Fatherland*, for piano
**BALFE** (39)
*The Maid of Honour*, opera
**MENDELSSOHN** (38)
*Lorely*, opera (unfinished)
**SCHUMANN** (37)
*Genoveva*, opera (1847–8)
Piano Trios Nos 1 and 2
**FLOTOW** (35)
*Martha*, opera
**DARGOMIZHSKY** (34)
*Esmeralda*, opera (possibly *c*1839)
**VERDI** (34)
*fp Macbeth*, opera
*fp I masnadieri*, opera
**ALKAN** (33)
*Etz chajjim Hi*, opera
**GADE** (30)
Symphony No 3
**LITOLFF** (29)
*Die Braut von Kynast*, vocal score (*c*1847)
**BORODIN** (14)
Flute Concerto (with piano)

## 1848

**PARRY** and **DUPARC** were born;

**DONIZETTI** died
**HALÉVY** (49)
*Le val d'Andorra*, opera
**BERLIOZ** (45)
*La Mort d'Ophelie*, two-part female chorus
  (also for voice and piano)
**GLINKA** (44)
*Wedding Song (Kamarinskaya)*, fantasia for
  orchestra
**RAFF** (26)
*Psalm CXXI*, for soli and chorus
*König Alfred*, opera (1848–50)
**SMETANA** (24)
*Festive Overture* (1848–9)

## 1849

**GODARD** was born; **STRAUSS, J. (Sr.)**,
**CHOPIN** and **NICOLAI** died
**MEYERBEER** (58)
*Le Prophète*, opera
**HALÉVY** (50)
*Le fée aux roses*, opera
*Prométhée Enchainé*, incidental music
*Italic*, cantata
**ADAM** (46)
*Le Toréador*, opera
**NICOLAI** (39)
*fp The Merry Wives of Windsor*, opera
**SCHUMANN** (39)
*Manfred*, dramatic poem
Three *Fantasiestücke*, for piano and clarinet
  with violin or cello
*Adagio and Allegro*, for piano and horn
**LISZT** (38)
*Héroïde funèbre*, for orchestra (1849–50)
**THOMAS** (38)
*Le Caïd*, opera
**VERDI** (36)
*fp Luisa Miller*, opera
**GADE** (32)
*p* String Octet
**BRUCKNER** (25)
Requiem in D minor

## 1850

**HALÉVY** (51)
*La tempesta*, opera
*La dame du Picque*, opera
**SCHUMANN** (40)
Symphony no 3, *Rhenish*
Cello Concerto in A minor
**LISZT** (39)
*Prometheus*, symphonic poem
*Consolations*, for piano
*Liebestraüme*, nocturnes for piano

THOMAS (39)
*Le songe d'une nuit d'été*, opera
GADE (33)
*Mariotta*, incidental music
Symphony No 4
p Violin Sonata No 2

## 1851

d'INDY was born; SPONTINI died
SCHUMANN (41)
Piano Trio No 3
Four *Marchenbilder*, for piano and viola (or
    violin)
Two Violin Sonatas
THOMAS (40)
*Raymond*, opera
VERDI (38)
fp *Rigoletto*, opera
WAGNER (38)
fp *Lohengrin*, opera
GOUNOD (33)
*Sapho*, opera
FRANCK (29)
*Le valet de ferme*, opera
BRAHMS (18)
Scherzo in E♭ minor
The first three sets of songs (1851–3)

## 1852

STANFORD and TARREGA were born
BERWALD (56)
Three Piano Trios (1852–4)
HALÉVY (53)
*Le juif errant*, opera
ADAM (49)
*Si j'étais roi*, opera
BALFE (44)
*The Devil's in It*, opera
*The Sicilian Bride*, opera
MENDELSSOHN (posthumous)
fp *Christus*, oratorio (unfinished)
LISZT (41)
*Hungarian Rhapsodies*, Nos 1–15
GADE (35)
Symphony No 5
*Spring Fantasy*, for voices and orchestra
GOUNOD (34)
*Faust*, opera (1852–9)
*La nonne sanglante*, opera (1852–4)
BRAHMS (19)
Piano Sonata No 1 (1852–3)
Piano Sonata No 2
BALAKIREV (15)
*Grande Fantaisie on Russian Folksongs*, for
    piano and orchestra
Septet for flute, clarinet, strings and piano

## 1853

MESSAGER was born
HALÉVY (54)
*Le nabab*, opera
SCHUMANN (43)
Violin Concerto
*Märchenerzählungen*, four pieces for piano,
    clarinet (or violin) and viola
*Introduction and Allegro*, for piano
*Fantasy*, for violin
THOMAS (42)
*la Tonelli*, opera
VERDI (40)
fp *La Traviata*, opera
fp *Il Trovatore*, opera
OFFENBACH (34)
*Le mariage aux lanternes*, operetta
RAFF (31)
*Te Deum*, for chorus and orchestra
*Samson*, opera (unperformed) (1853–7)
SMETANA (29)
*Festive Symphony* (1853–4)
RUBINSTEIN (24)
*Melody in F*
BRAHMS (20)
Piano Trio No 1 (1853–4)
Piano Sonata No 3
WIENIAWSKI (18)
*Polonaise No 1*, for violin and orchestra
*Souvenir de Moscow*, for violin and
    orchestra
Violin Concerto No 1

## 1854

CATALANI, HUMPERDINCK,
JANÁČEK and MOSKOWSKI were born
MEYERBEER (63)
*L'étoile du nord*, opera
BERLIOZ (51)
*L'Enfance du Christ*, oratorio (1850–4)
SCHUMANN (44)
p *Albumblätter*, twenty pieces for piano
LISZT (43)
*Hungaria*, symphonic poem
*Orpheus*, tone poem
*Les Préludes*, symphonic poem
RAFF (32)
Grosse Symphonie (lost)
Suite No 1 for orchestra
BRUCKNER (30)
Solemn Mass in B♭ major
BRAHMS (21)
Piano Concerto No 1 (1854–8)
Four Ballades for piano
Variations on a Theme by Schumann, for
    piano

BALAKIREV (17)
String Quartet, *Quatour original russe* (1854–5)
BIZET (16)
*La Prêtresse*, one-act opera

## 1855

CHAUSSON and LIADOV were born
BERWALD (59)
Piano Concerto
HALÉVY (56)
*Jaguarita l'Indienne*, opera
LISZT (44)
*Totentanz*, for piano and orchestra (c1855)
THOMAS (44)
*La cour de Célimène*, opera
VERDI (42)
*fp I Vespri Siciliani*, opera
GADE (38)
*p Novelleten*, for piano trio
GOUNOD (37)
Symphonies Nos 1 and 2
*Messe solennelle de St Cécile*
SUPPÉ (36)
Requiem
RAFF (33)
*Dornröschen*, for soli, chorus and orchestra
LALO (32)
String Quartet
SMETANA (31)
Piano Trio
BRAHMS (22)
Symphony No 1 begun (completed 1876)
Piano Quartet No 3 begun (completed 1875)
SAINT-SAËNS (20)
Symphony No 1
Piano Quintet with double-bass *ad lib*
BALAKIREV (18)
Piano Concerto No 1 (*c* 1855)
Octet for flute, oboe, horn, piano and strings (1855–6)
'Three Forgotten Songs'
BIZET (17)
Symphony in C major
DVOŘÁK (14)
'Forget-Me-Not Polka' (1855–56)

## 1856

SINDING was born; ADAM and SCHUMANN died
BERWALD (60)
Two piano quintets (1856–58, possibly 1853–54)
HALÉVY (57)
*Valentine d'Aubigny*, opera

ADAM (53)
*Le Corsaire*, ballet
BERLIOZ (53)
*The Trojans*, opera (1856–9)
LISZT (45)
*Die Hunnenschlacht*, symphonic poem
*Tasso*, symphonic poem
DARGOMIZHSKY (43)
*fp Russalka*, opera
GADE (39)
Symphony No 6 (c1856)
BRAHMS (23)
Variations on a Hungarian theme, for piano
Variations on an original theme, for piano
BRUCH (18)
String Quartet in C minor

## 1857

CHAMINADE and ELGAR were born; GLINKA died
BALFE (49)
*The Rose of Castille*, opera
LISZT (46)
*Dante Symphony* (possibly 1855–6)
*Faust Symphony* (possibly 1854–7)
*Mazeppa*, symphonic poem
THOMAS (46)
*Le carnaval de Venise*, opera
*Psyche*, opera
Messe Solennelle
VERDI (44)
*fp Araldo*, opera
*fp Simon Boccanegra*, opera
WAGNER (44)
*Wesendonck Lieder* (1857–8)
ALKAN (43)
*Sonate de concert*, for cello and piano
*Halelouyoh*, vocal
GOUNOD (39)
*Le médecin malgré lui*, opera
BRAHMS (24)
Serenade for orchestra in D major (1857–8)
Serenade for orchestra in A major (1857–60)
*German Requiem* (1857–68)
CUI (22)
Scherzo for orchestra, Nos 1 and 2
SAINT-SAËNS (22)
Organ Fantasia No 1
BIZET (19)
*Clovis et Clothilde*, cantata
*Le Docteur Miracle*, operetta
BRUCH (19)
Piano Trio in C minor

**MUSSORGSKY** (18)
*Souvenir d'enfance*, for piano
**DVOŘÁK** (16)
Mass in B♭ major (1857–9)


## 1858

**LEONCAVALLO, PUCCINI** and **SMYTH**
were born
**AUBER** (76)
p Piano Trio in D major, Op 1
**HALÉVY** (59)
*La magicienne*, opera
*Vanina d'Ornano*, opera (unfinished)
*Noé, or Le déluge*, opera (unfinished,
   completed by Bizet)
**OFFENBACH** (39)
*Orpheus in the Underworld*, operetta
**FRANCK** (36)
*Ave Maria*, motet
**RAFF** (36)
*Wachet auf!* for soli and orchestra
**SMETANA** (34)
*Richard III*, symphonic poem
*Wallenstein's Camp*, symphonic poem
   (1858–9)
**CUI** (23)
*The Caucasian Prisoner*, opera
**SAINT-SAËNS** (23)
Piano Concerto No 1
**BALAKIREV** (21)
Overture on Russian Themes
**BRUCH** (20)
*Scherz, List und Rache*, opera
**MUSSORGSKY** (19)
Scherzo for orchestra
*Edipo*, for mixed chorus (1858–60)


## 1859

**IPPOLITOV-IVANOV** was born; **SPOHR**
died
**MEYERBEER** (68)
*Dinorah*, opera
**BERWALD** (63)
p Cello sonata
**HALÉVY** (60)
*Les plages du Nil*, cantata
**LISZT** (48)
*Hamlet*, symphonic poem
*Die Ideale*, for orchestra
**VERDI** (46)
fp *Un ballo in maschera*, opera
**ALKAN** (45)
*Marcia Funèbre*, for piano
*Stances de Millevoye*, for piano

**RAFF** (37)
Symphony No 1
**BRAHMS** (26)
*Marienlieder*, for four-part mixed choir
String Quartets Nos 1 and 2 (1859–73)
**CUI** (24)
*The Mandarin's Son*, opera
*Tarantella*
**SAINT-SAËNS** (24)
Violin Concerto No 1
**BIZET** (21)
*Don Procopio*, opera
**MUSSORGSKY** (20)
*Marcia di Sciamie*, for soloist, choir and
   orchestra
*Impromptu passione*, for piano


## 1860

**ALBÉNIZ, CHARPENTIER, WOLF** and
**MAHLER** were born; **PADEREWSKI** was
born (or possibly in 1866)
**BALFE** (52)
*Bianca*, opera
**LISZT** (49)
*Fantasy on Hungarian Folk Tunes*, for piano
   and orchestra (c1860)
**THOMAS** (49)
*Le Roman d'Elvire*, opera
**GOUNOD** (42)
*Philémon et Baucis*, opera
**SMETANA** (36)
*Haakon Jarl*, symphonic poem (1860–1)
**BRAHMS** (27)
String Sextet No 1 in B♭ major
**WIENIAWSKI** (25)
*Légende*, for violin and orchestra
**BRUCH** (22)
String Quartet in E major
**CHABRIER** (19)
Impromptu for piano
**BOITO** (18)
*Il Quattro Giugno*, cantata


## 1861

**ARENSKY, LOEFFLER** and
**MACDOWELL** were born
**BALFE** (53)
*The Puritan's Daughter*, opera
**DARGOMIZHSKY** (48)
*Baba-Yaga*, fantasy for orchestra
**GADE** (44)
*Hamlet*, concert overture
*Michelangelo*, overture
**BRAHMS** (28)
Piano Quartets Nos 1 and 2

Variations and Fugue on a Theme by
  Handel, for piano
'Soldaten Lieder', five songs
Fifteen Romances from Magelone (1861–8)
**PONCHIELLI** (27)
*La Savoiarda*, opera
**BALAKIREV** (24)
Piano Concerto No 2 begun (resumed
  1909)
**MUSSORGSKY** (22)
*Alla marcia, notturna*, for orchestra
Scherzo and Finale for a symphony in
  D major
**DVOŘÁK** (20)
String Quintet
**BOITO** (18)
*Le Sorelle d'Italia*, opera
**RIMSKY-KORSAKOV** (17)
Symphony No 1 (1861–5)

## 1862

**BOËLLMANN, DEBUSSY, DELIUS** and
**GERMAN** were born; **HALÉVY** died
**BERWALD** (66)
*Estrella de Soria*, opera
**BERLIOZ** (59)
*Béatrice et Bénédict*, opera (1860–2)
**VERDI** (49)
fp *La Forza del destino*, opera
fp *Inno delle nazioni*, for chorus
**GOUNOD** (44)
*La Reine de Saba*, opera
**RAFF** (40)
*Deuschland Auferstchung*, for male voices
  and orchestra (1862–3)
**SMETANA** (38)
*On the Seashore*, for piano
**BORODIN** (29)
Symphony No 1 (1862–7)
**BRAHMS** (29)
Cello Sonata No 1 (1862–5)
Piano Studies (Variations on a Theme by
  Paganini), Books I and II (1862–3)
**WIENIAWSKI** (27)
Violin Concerto No 2
**DVOŘÁK** (21)
String Quartet No 1
**SULLIVAN** (20)
*The Tempest*, incidental music

## 1863

**MASCAGNI** and **PIERNÉ** were born
**ROSSINI** (71)
Petite Messe Solennelle

**BALFE** (55)
*The Armourer of Nantes*, opera
*Blanche de Nevers*, opera
**LISZT** (52)
Two Concert Studies for piano
**BRUCKNER** (39)
Symphony in F minor (unnumbered,
  known as No 00)
Overture in G minor
*Germanenzug*, for chorus and brass
**SMETANA** (39)
*The Brandenburgers in Bohemia*, opera
**BRAHMS** (30)
*Rinaldo*, cantata (1863–8)
**PONCHIELLI** (29)
*Roderico*, opera
**SAINT-SAËNS** (28)
Piano Trio No 1
**BIZET** (25)
*The Pearl Fishers*, opera
**BRUCH** (25)
*Die Lorely*, opera
**MASSENET** (21)
Ouverture de Concert
*David Rizzio*, cantata

## 1864

**d'ALBERT, STRAUSS, R.** and **ROPARTZ**
were born; **MEYERBEER** died
**BALFE** (56)
*The Sleeping Queen*, opera
**GADE** (47)
Symphonies Nos 2 and 7
p Piano Trio in F major
p *Fantasiestücke*, for cello and piano
Fantasies for clarinet
**GOUNOD** (46)
*Mireille*, opera
**OFFENBACH** (45)
*La Belle Hélène*, operetta
**BRUCKNER** (40)
Mass No 1 in D minor
Symphony in D minor (revised 1869,
  known as No 0)
*Um Mitternacht*, for male-voice chorus
**BRAHMS** (31)
String Sextet No 2 (1864–5)
Piano Quintet in F minor
**BRUCH** (26)
*Frithjof-Scenen*, for solo voices, chorus and
  orchestra (c1864)
**SULLIVAN** (22)
*L'île enchantée*, ballet music
*Kenilworth*, cantata
**GRIEG** (21)
Album Leaves, for piano (1864–78)

DUPARC (16)
*Six Rêveries*, for piano

## 1865

DUKAS, GLAZUNOV, SIBELIUS and
NIELSEN were born; WALLACE died
MEYERBEER (posthumous)
*fp L'Africaine*, opera
THOMAS (54)
*Marche religieuse*, for orchestra
WAGNER (52)
*fp Tristan und Isolde*, music drama
GADE (48)
*p* String Sextet
GOUNOD (47)
'Chant des compagnons'
FRANCK (43)
*The Tower of Babel*, oratorio
BRAHMS (32)
Trio for piano, violin and horn
BIZET (27)
*Ivan the Terrible*, opera
*Chasse fantastique*, for piano
STAINER (25)
*Gideon*, oratorio
DVOŘÁK (24)
Symphonies Nos 1 and 2
Cello Concerto in A major
*The Cypresses*, originally for string quartet,
    later for voice and piano
Clarinet Quintet
MASSENET (23)
Suite for orchestra No 1
GRIEG (22)
*In Autumn*, concert overture
Violin Sonata No 1

## 1866

SATIE, CILÈA and BUSONI were born
LISZT (55)
*Deux Légendes*, for piano
THOMAS (55)
*Mignon*, opera
DARGOMIZHSKY (53)
*The Stone Guest*, opera (unfinished)
OFFENBACH (47)
*Bluebeard*, operetta
*La vie parisienne*, operetta
BRUCKNER (42)
Symphony No 1 (revised 1891)
Mass No 2 in E minor
SMETANA (42)
*The Bartered Bride*, opera
SAINT-SAËNS (31)
Suite in D minor for piano and cello (or
    violin or viola)

DELIBES (30)
*La Source (Nalla)*, ballet
BALAKIREV (29)
Symphony No 1 begun (completed 1898)
BIZET (28)
*Trois esquisses musicales*, for piano
TCHAIKOVSKY (26)
Symphony No 1, *Winter Daydreams*
SULLIVAN (24)
*In Memoriam Overture*
*Irish Symphony*
Cello Concerto
RIMSKY-KORSAKOV (22)
Overture on Russian Themes
Symphony No 3 (1866–73)

## 1867

GIORDANO, BEACH, GRANADOS and
KOECHLIN were born
LISZT (56)
*Legend of St Elizabeth* (possibly 1857–62)
DARGOMIZHSKY (54)
*The Triumph of Bacchus*, opera-ballet
VERDI (54)
*fp Don Carlos*, opera
GOUNOD (49)
*Roméo et Juliette*, opera
OFFENBACH (48)
*La Grande Duchesse de Gérolstein*, operetta
RAFF (45)
*De Profundis*, for chorus and orchestra
STRAUSS, J. Jr. (42)
*Blue Danube Waltz*
BORODIN (34)
*The Bogatirs*, opera-farce
BALAKIREV (30)
Overture on Czech Themes
*Thamar*, symphonic poem (1867–82)
BIZET (29)
*The Fair Maid of Perth*, opera
MUSSORGSKY (28)
*St John's Night on the Bare Mountain*
*La disfatta di Sennacherib*, for chorus and
    orchestra, first version
Symphonic Intermezzo 'in modo classico'
SULLIVAN (25)
*Cox and Box*, operetta
GRIEG (24)
Violin Sonata No 2
Lyric Pieces for piano, Book I
RIMSKY-KORSAKOV (23)
*Fantasia on Serbian Themes*, for orchestra
*Sadko*, tone poem
DUPARC (19)
Sonata for piano and cello (destroyed)
*Feuilles Volantes*, for piano

## 1868

BANTOCK was born; ROSSINI and BERWALD died
THOMAS (57)
*Hamlet*, grand opera
WAGNER (55)
*fp Die Meistersinger von Nürnberg*, opera
OFFENBACH (49)
*La Périchole*, operetta
RAFF (46)
*Die Parole*, opera (unperformed)
BRUCKNER (44)
Mass No 3, *Grosse Messe* (revised 1871 and 1890)
SMETANA (44)
*fp Dalibor*, opera
Solemn Prelude for orchestra
STRAUSS, J. Jr (43)
*Tales from the Vienna Woods*, for orchestra
SAINT-SAËNS (33)
Piano Concerto No 2
BIZET (30)
Symphony in C major, *Roma*
*Marche funèbre*, for orchestra
*Marine*, for piano
*Variations chromatiques*, for piano
BRUCH (30)
Violin Concerto No 1
MUSSORGSKY (29)
*fp* (privately) *Zenitha (The Marriage)*, opera
*The Nursery*, song cycle (1868–72)
TCHAIKOVSKY (28)
*Fate*, symphonic poem
BOITO (26)
*Mefistofele*, opera
RIMSKY-KORSAKOV (24)
*The Maid of Pskov (Ivan the Terrible)*, opera (1868–72)

## 1869

ROUSSEL and DAVIES were born; BERLIOZ, DARGOMIZHSKY and GOTTSCHALK died
WAGNER (56)
*fp Das Rheingold*, music drama
RAFF (47)
*Dame Kobold*, comic opera
Symphony No 2
BRUCKNER (45)
'Locus iste', motet
BORODIN (36)
*Prince Igor*, opera begun (left unfinished)
Symphony No 2 begun (completed 1876)
BRAHMS (36)
*p* Piano Studies in five books, Books I and II

Eighteen *Liebeslieder Walzers*
CUI (34)
*William Ratcliffe*, opera
SAINT-SAËNS (34)
Piano Concerto No 3
BALAKIREV (32)
*fp Islamey*, piano fantasy
BIZET (31)
*Vasco da Gama*, symphonic ode with chorus
MUSSORGSKY (30)
*Boris Godunov*, opera (first version with piano)
TCHAIKOVSKY (29)
*Romeo and Juliet*, fantasy overture (final version 1880)
SULLIVAN (27)
*The Prodigal Son*, oratorio
RIMSKY-KORSAKOV (25)
*Antar*, symphonic suite
GRIEG (26)
Piano Concerto in A minor
DUPARC (21)
*Beaulieu*, for piano

## 1870

LEHÁR, NOVÁK and SCHMITT were born; BALFE died
WAGNER (57)
*fp Die Walküre*, music drama
*Siegfried Idyll*, for orchestra
BRAHMS (37)
*Alto Rhapsody*, for alto, chorus and orchestra
*Triumphlied*, for chorus and orchestra
SAINT-SAËNS (35)
*Introduction and Rondo Capriccioso*, for violin and orchestra
*Mélodies persanes*, six songs
DELIBES (34)
*Coppélia*, ballet
BRUCH (32)
Symphonies Nos 1 and 2
DVOŘÁK (29)
*Dramatic (Tragic) Overture*
Three String Quartets
*Notturno*, for strings
*Alfred*, opera
SULLIVAN (28)
*Overture di Ballo*, concert overture
WIDOR (26)
Symphony No 1
FAURÉ (25)
Two vocal duets

## 1871

ZEMLINSKY born
**VERDI** (58)
*fp Aida*, opera
**GADE** (54)
Symphony No 8
**GOUNOD** (53)
Saltarello for orchestra
**LITOLFF** (53)
*La Boîte de Pandora*, vocal score
**RAFF** (49)
Two Songs for chorus and orchestra
Symphony No 3
*Italian Suite*
**BRUCKNER** (47)
'Os uisti', motet
**STRAUSS, J. (II)** (46)
*Indigo und die vierzig Räuber*, operetta
**BRAHMS** (38)
*Schicksallied (Song of Destiny)*
**SAINT-SAËNS** (36)
*Marche héroïque*, for orchestra
*Omphale's Spinning-wheel*, symphonic
  poem
**BIZET** (33)
*Jeux d'enfants*, for piano duet
*Petite Suite d'Orchestre*
**TCHAIKOVSKY** (31)
String Quartet in D major
**DVOŘÁK** (30)
*King and Charcoal Burner*, opera (first
  version)
Overture in F major
Piano Trios Nos 1 and 2
Cello Sonata
*Rosmarine*, songs with piano
**MASSENET** (29)
Suite for orchestra No 2, *Scènes hongroises*


## 1872

ALFVÉN, SKRIABIN and VAUGHAN
WILLIAMS were born
**DARGOMIZHSKY** (posthumous)
*fp The Stone Guest*, opera
**LITOLFF** (54)
*Héloïse et Abelard*, vocal score
**FRANCK** (50)
*Panis Angelicus*, for voice and instruments
**RAFF** (50)
Symphony No 4
**LALO** (49)
*Deux Aubades*, for small orchestra
*Divertissement*, for small orchestra
Violin Concerto

**BRUCKNER** (48)
Symphony No 2 (revised 1891)
**PONCHIELLI** (38)
*I Promessi Sposi*, opera
**SAINT-SAËNS** (37)
*La Princesse jaune*, opera
**BIZET** (34)
*L'Arlésienne*, incidental music
*Djarmileh*, opera
**BRUCH** (34)
*Hermione*, opera
*Odysseus*, cantata
**MUSSORGSKY** (33)
*Khovantschina*, opera
**TCHAIKOVSKY** (32)
Symphony No 2, *Little Russian*
**DVOŘÁK** (31)
*May Night*, nocturne for orchestra
Piano Quintet in A major
**GRIEG** (29)
*Sigurd Jorsalfar*, incidental music


## 1873

RACHMANINOV, REGER and JONGEN
were born
**VERDI** (60)
String Quartet
**GOUNOD** (55)
*Funeral March of a Marionette*, for orchestra
**RAFF** (51)
Symphony No 5
*Morgenlied*, for chorus and orchestra
**LALO** (50)
*Symphonie espagnole*, for violin and
  orchestra
**BRUCKNER** (49)
Symphony No 3, *Wagner* (revised 1877 and
  1888)
**BRAHMS** (40)
Variations on a Theme by Haydn,
  *St Anthony*, for orchestra
**PONCHIELLI** (39)
*Il Parlatore Eterno*, opera
*Le Due Gemelle*, ballet
**SAINT-SAËNS** (38)
*Phaeton*, symphonic poem
Cello Concerto No 1
**BIZET** (35)
*Patrie*, overture
**DVOŘÁK** (32)
Symphony No 3
*Romance*, for violin and orchestra
Octet, *Serenade*
String Quartet in A minor
String Quartet in F minor
Violin Sonata

MASSENET (31)
*Phèdre*, concert overture
Suite for orchestra No 3, *Scènes dramatiques*
SULLIVAN (31)
*The Light of the World*, oratorio
FAURÉ (28)
*Cantique de Jean Racine*

DUPARC (26)
*Suite des Valses*, for orchestra
*Poème*, nocturne for orchestra (parts 2 and 3 lost)
d'INDY (23)
*Max et Thecla*, symphonic overture, Part 2 of *Wallenstein Trilogy*
*Jean Hunyade*, symphony (1874–5)

## 1874

HOLST, SCHMIDT, SCHOENBERG, IVES and SUK were born
THOMAS (63)
*Gille et Gillotin*, opera
VERDI (61)
Requiem Mass
GADE (57)
*Novelleten,* for string orchestra
LITOLFF (56)
*La Fiancée du Roi de Garbe*, vocal score
FRANCK (52)
*Redemption*, cantata with symphonic interlude
RAFF (52)
Symphony No 6
Suite No 2 for orchestra
BRUCKNER (50)
Symphony No 4, *Romantic* (revised 1880)
SMETANA (50)
*The Two Widows*, opera
*Má Vlast*, cycle of six symphonic poems (1874–9)
STRAUSS, J. (II) (49)
*Die Fledermaus*, operetta
PONCHIELLI (40)
*I Lituani*, opera, revised as *Aldona*
SAINT-SAËNS (39)
*Danse macabre*, symphonic poem
MUSSORGSKY (35)
*Sorochintsky Fair*, opera
*Night on the Bare Mountain*, arrangement by Rimsky-Korsakov of a passage in *Sorochintsky Fair*
*Jesus Navin*, for contralto, bass, chorus and piano
*Pictures from an Exhibition*, for piano
*Sunless*, song cycle
TCHAIKOVSKY (34)
Piano Concerto No 1 (1874–5)
String Quartet in F major
DVOŘÁK (33)
Symphony No 4
*Rhapsody for Orchestra*, in A minor
String Quartet in A minor
MASSENET (32)
Suite for orchestra No 4, *Scènes pittoresques*

## 1875

COLERIDGE-TAYLOR, GLIÈRE, HAHN and RAVEL were born; BIZET died
LALO (52)
*Allegro Symphonique*
GOLDMARK (45)
*The Queen of Sheba*, opera
BORODIN (42–46)
String Quartet No 1 (1875–9)
BRAHMS (42)
Fifteen *Neues Liebeslieder* for piano duet
String Quartet No 3
PONCHIELLI (41)
*A Gaetano Donizetti*, cantata
CUI (40)
*Angelo*, opera
SAINT-SAËNS (40)
Piano Concerto No 4
BIZET (37)
*fp Carmen*, opera
MUSSORGSKY (36–38)
*Songs and Dances of Death*, song cycle (1875–7)
TCHAIKOVSKY (35)
Symphony No 3, *Polish*
*Swan Lake*, ballet
String Quartet in E♭ minor
DVOŘÁK (34)
Symphony No 5
*Serenade for Strings*
String Quintet, with double-bass
Piano Quartet
Piano Trio
Moravian Duets for voices and piano
BOITO (33)
*La Notte Difonde*, for four voices and piano
MASSENET (33)
*Eve*, oratorio
SULLIVAN (33)
*Trial by Jury*, operetta
*The Zoo*, operetta
GRIEG (32)
*Peer Gynt*, incidental music
RIMSKY-KORSAKOV (31)
Quartet No 1
Three Pieces for piano
Six Fugues

FAURÉ (30)
*Allegro Symphonique*, for orchestra
Suite for orchestra
*Les Djinns*, for chorus and orchestra
DUPARC (27)
*Lénore*, symphonic poem
MESSAGER (22)
Symphony

## 1876

FALLA, WOLF-FERRARI, CARPENTER,
BRIAN and RUGGLES were born
WAGNER (63)
fp *Siegfried*, music drama
fp *Götterdämmerung*, music drama
GOUNOD (58)
*Cinq-Mars*, opera (1876–7)
FRANCK (54)
*Les Éolides*, symphonic poem
RAFF (54)
Symphony No 7
LALO (53)
Cello Concerto
SMETANA (52)
*The Kiss*, opera
String Quartet No 1, *From My Life*
GOLDMARK (46)
*Rustic Wedding*, symphony
BRAHMS (43)
Symphony No 1 (completed)
PONCHIELLI (42)
*La Giaconda*, opera
SAINT-SAËNS (41)
*The Deluge*, oratorio
DELIBES (40)
*Sylvia*, ballet
TCHAIKOVSKY (36)
*Slavonic March*, for orchestra
*Variations on a Rococo Theme*, for cello and
   orchestra
DVOŘÁK (35)
Piano Concerto in G minor
String Quartet in E major
Piano Trio
*Stabat Mater*
MASSENET (34)
Suite for orchestra No 5, *Scènes napolitaines*
RIMSKY-KORSAKOV (32)
Sextet for strings
Quintet for piano and wind
WIDOR (32)
Piano Concerto
FAURÉ (31)
Violin Sonata in A major
GODARD (27)
Violin Concerto No 2, *Concerto romantique*

d'INDY (25)
*Attendez-moi sous l'Orme*, opera (1876–8)
*Anthony and Cleopatra*, overture
STANFORD (24)
Symphony in B♭ major
LIADOV (21)
*Birulki*, for piano
WOLF (16–30)
*Nachgelassene Werke* (1876–90)
DEBUSSY (14–17)
Trio in G minor (1876–9)
STRAUSS, R. (12)
*Festmarch*, for orchestra, Op 1

## 1877

AUBERT, DOHNÁNYI and QUILTER
were born
RAFF (55)
Symphony No 8
*Thuringer Suite*, for orchestra
*Benedetto Marcello*, opera (unperformed)
   (1877–8)
*Die Tageszeiten*, for chorus, piano and
   orchestra (1877–8)
BRUCKNER (53)
Symphony No 5 (revised 1878)
BRAHMS (44)
Symphony No 2
SAINT-SAËNS (42)
*Samson and Delilah*, opera
Suite for orchestra
*La Jeunesse d'Hercule*, symphonic poem
TCHAIKOVSKY (37)
Symphony No 4
*Francesca da Rimini*, symphonic fantasy
*Waltz-Scherzo*, for violin and orchestra
CHABRIER (36)
*L'Etoile*, opera
DVOŘÁK (36)
*The Cunning Peasant*, opera
Symphonic Variations for orchestra
String Quartet in D minor
BOITO (35)
*Nerone*, operatic tragedy (1877–1915)
MASSENET (35)
*Le Roi de Lahore*, opera
*Narcisse*, cantata
SULLIVAN (35)
*The Sorcerer*, operetta
'The Lord Chord', song
STANFORD (25)
*Festival Overture*
MESSAGER (24)
*Don Juan et Haydée*, cantata
JANÁČEK (23)
Suite for strings

416

WOLF (17)
*Lieder aus der Jugendzeit* (1877–8)
*Lieder nach verschiedenen Dichtern*
  (1877–97)
BOËLLMANN (15)
Piano Quartet

## 1878

BOUGHTON, HOLBROOKE and
SCHREKER were born
GOUNOD (60)
*Marche Religieuse*, for orchestra
OFFENBACH (59)
*Madame Favart*, operetta
FRANCK (56)
Cantabile for organ
*Fantaisie*, for organ
*Pièce héroïque*, for organ
BRUCKNER (54)
*Abendzauber*, for baritone and male chorus
SMETANA (54)
*The Secret*, opera
*Czech Dances*
BRAHMS (45)
Piano Concerto No 2 (1878–81)
Violin Concerto
Violin Sonata No 1 (1878–9)
SAINT-SAËNS (43)
Symphony No 2
BRUCH (40)
Violin Concerto No 2
STAINER (38)
*The Daughter of Jairus*, cantata
TCHAIKOVSKY (38)
Violin Concerto
DVOŘÁK (37)
Serenade in D minor, for orchestra
*Slavonic Dances*, for orchestra, first series
*Slavonic Rhapsodies*, for orchestra
String Sextet
Bagatelles for two violins, cello and
  harmonium or piano
SULLIVAN (36)
*Henry VIII*, incidental music
*HMS Pinafore*, operetta
*The Martyr of Antioch*, oratorio
RIMSKY-KORSAKOV (34)
*May Night*, opera
*Variations on B.A.C.H.*, for piano
Four Pieces for piano
SARASATE (34)
*Zigeunerweisen*, orchestral fantasy
FAURÉ (33)
Violin Concerto
PARRY (30)
Piano Concerto
Symphony No 1 (1878–82)

GODARD (29)
*Les Bijoux de Jeanette*, opera
*La Tasse*, dramatic symphony for solo
  voices, chorus and orchestra
Piano Concerto
d'INDY (27)
*The Enchanted Forest*, ballad-symphony
Piano Quartet in A major (1878–88)
MESSAGER (25)
*Fleur d'Oranger*, ballet
ELGAR (21)
*Romance*, for violin and piano (or
  orchestra)
*Promenades*, for wind

## 1879

BRIDGE, SCOTT, COWELL,
CANTELOUPE, HARTY, IRELAND and
RESPIGHI were born
LISZT (68)
*Via Crucis*
GADE (62)
*En Sommertag paa Landet*, for orchestra
GOUNOD (61)
*The Redemption*, oratorio
FRANCK (57)
*Béatitudes*, cantata
Piano Quintet in F minor
RAFF (57)
Symphony No 9
*Weltende*, oratorio (1879–81)
BRUCKNER (55)
String Quartet
BRAHMS (46)
Rhapsody in G minor, for piano
Rhapsody in B minor, for piano
*p* Piano Studies, Books III–V
SAINT-SAËNS (44)
*Suite Algerienne*
Violin Concerto No 2
MUSSORGSKY (40)
'Song of the Flea', song
TCHAIKOVSKY (39)
*Eugene Onegin*, opera
*Capriccio Italien*, for orchestra
Piano Concerto No 2 (1879–80)
CHABRIER (38)
*Une Education manquée*, operetta
DVOŘÁK (38)
*Czech Suite*, for orchestra
Festival March
Polonaise in E♭ for orchestra
Mazurka for violin and orchestra
Violin Concerto in A minor (1879–80)
String Quartet in E♭ major

MASSENET (37)
Suite for Orchestra No 6 *Scènes de féerie*
RIMSKY-KORSAKOV (35)
*Legend,* for orchestra (1879–80)
*Sinfonietta on Russian Themes*
FAURÉ (34)
Piano Quartet No 1
DUPARC (31)
*La Roussalka,* opera (1879–95) (destroyed)
GODARD (30)
*Scènes poétiques*
d'INDY (28)
*Le Chant de la Cloche,* opera (1879–83)
LIADOV (24)
*Arabesque,* for piano
ELGAR (22)
*Harmony Music,* for wind instruments
*Intermezzos for Wind,* five pieces
WOLF (19)
String Quartet (1879–80)
MASCAGNI (16)
Symphony in C minor
STRAUSS, R. (15)
Overture in A minor

## 1880

BLOCH, MEDTNER, PIZZETTI were
born; OFFENBACH died
LISZT (69)
*Hungarian Rhapsodies* Nos 16–20 (*c*1880)
GADE (63)
Violin Concerto
FRANCK (58)
*L'Organiste,* fifty-five pieces for
   harmonium
RAFF (58)
*Die Sterne,* for chorus and orchestra
BORODIN (47)
*In the Steppes of Central Asia,* orchestral
   'picture'
BRAHMS (47)
*Academic Festival Overture*
*Tragic Overture* (1880–1)
Piano Trio No 2 (1830–2)
PONCHIELLI (46)
*Il Figliuol Prodigo,* opera
SAINT-SAËNS (45)
Violin Concerto No 3
MUSSORGSKY (41)
*Turkish March,* for orchestra
Piano Pieces
Five Popular Russian Songs for male
   chorus
TCHAIKOVSKY (40)
*Romeo and Juliet,* overture (final revision)
Serenade for strings

CHABRIER (39)
*Dix pièces pittoresques,* for piano
DVOŘÁK (39)
Symphony No 6
Violin Sonata in F major
Seven Gipsy Songs
MASSENET (38)
*La Vierge,* oratorio
SULLIVAN (38)
*The Pirates of Penzance,* operetta
GRIEG (37)
Two Elegiac Melodies
RIMSKY-KORSAKOV (36)
*The Snow Maiden,* opera (1880–1)
WIDOR (36)
*La Korrigane,* ballet
FAURÉ (35)
*Berceuse,* for violin and piano
GODARD (31)
Sym_hony
*Diane: poème dramatique*
d'INDY (29)
*Le Camp de Wallenstein,* symphonic
   overture, Part I of *Wallenstein Trilogy*
JANÁČEK (26)
*Dumka,* for violin and piano
HUMPERDINCK (26)
*Humoreske*
CHAUSSON (25)
*Les Caprices de Marianne,* opera
*Joan of Arc,* for chorus
SINDING (24)
*Carmen nuptiale,* for voices and orchestra
MAHLER (20)
*Klagende Lieder*
PADEREWSKI (20)
Violin Sonata
WOLF (20–28)
*Eichendorf-Lieder* (1880–8)
DEBUSSY (18)
Andante for piano
*Danse bohémienne,* for piano
'La belle au bois dormant', song (1880–3)
STRAUSS, R. (16)
Symphony in D minor
String Quartet
BUSONI (14)
String Quartet No 1 (1880–1)

## 1881

BARTÓK, ENESCO and MIASKOWSKI
were born; MUSSORGSKY,
VIEUXTEMPS and WIENIAWSKI died
LISZT (70)
*Mephisto Waltz*

GOUNOD (63)
*Le Tribut de Zamora*, opera
OFFENBACH (posthumous)
*fp The Tales of Hoffman*, operetta
FRANCK (59)
*Rebecca*, for soli, chorus and orchestra
RAFF (59)
*Die Eifersüchtigen*, opera (unperformed)
LALO (58)
*Rhapsodie norvégienne*
BRUCKNER (57)
Symphony No 6
SMETANA (57)
*fp Libuse*, opera
BORODIN (48)
String Quartet No 2
CUI (46)
*Marche solennelle*
BRUCH (43)
*p Kol Nidrei*, for cello and piano (or
   orchestra)
TCHAIKOVSKY (41)
*Joan of Arc*, opera
DVOŘÁK (40)
*Legends*, for orchestra
String Quartet in C major
MASSENET (39)
Suite for orchestra No 7, *Scènes alsaciennes*
*Hérodiade*, opera
SULLIVAN (39)
*Patience*, operetta
GRIEG (38)
Norwegian Dances
FAURÉ (36)
*Le Ruisseau*, for voices and piano
Ballade for piano and orchestra
STANFORD (29)
*The Veiled Prophet*, opera
DEBUSSY (19)
Fugue for piano
MASCAGNI (18)
Symphony in F major
*In Filanda*, for voices and orchestra
STRAUSS, R. (17)
Violin Concerto in D minor (1881–2)
GLAZUNOV (16)
*Overture on Greek Themes*, No 1 (1881–4)
Symphony No 1
NIELSEN (16)
Sonato No 1 in G for violin and piano
   (unpublished) (1881–2)
SIBELIUS (16)
Piano Quartet (1881–2)
Piano Trio (1881–2)

# 1882

GRAINGER, KODÁLY, MALIPIERO,
STRAVINSKY, PONCE and TURINA
were born; RAFF died
THOMAS (71)
*Françoise de Rimini*, opera
WAGNER (69)
*fp Parsifal*, music drama
FRANCK (60)
*Hulda*, opera (1882–5)
*Le chasseur maudit*, symphonic poem
RAFF (60)
Symphonies No 10 and No 11
LALO (59)
Ballet Suites Nos 1 and 2, *Namouna*
SMETANA (58)
String Quartet No 2
BRAHMS (49)
String Quintet No 1
PONCHIELLI (48)
*In Memoria di Garibaldi*, cantata
DELIBES (46)
*Le Roi s'amuse*, incidental music
TCHAIKOVSKY (42)
*1812*, overture
Piano Trio in A minor
DVOŘÁK (41)
*My Home*, overture
SULLIVAN (40)
*Iolanthe*, operetta
RIMSKY-KORSAKOV (38)
Piano Concerto (1882–3)
WIDOR (38)
Violin Concerto
FAURÉ (37)
*Romance*, for violin and orchestra
*La Naissance de Vénus*, for soli, chorus and
   orchestra
GODARD (33)
*Symphonie*, ballet
d'INDY (31)
*La Mort de Wallenstein*, symphonic
   overture, Part 3 of *Wallenstein Trilogy*
STANFORD (30)
Serenade in G for orchestra
*Elegiac Symphony*
CHAUSSON (27)
*Viviane*, symphonic poem
*Poème de l'amour et de la mer*, for voice and
   piano (1882–92)
Piano Trio
SINDING (26)
Piano Quintet (1882–4)
IPPOLITOV-IVANOV (23)
*Yar-Khmel*, for orchestra

**MAHLER** (22)
*Lieder und Gesänge aus der Jugendzeit*
**MACDOWELL** (21)
Piano Concerto No 1
**DEBUSSY** (20)
*Intermezzo*, for orchestra
*Printemps*, for women's choir and orchestra
*Triomphe de Bacchus*, for piano duet
Two Four-part Fugues for piano
**PIERNÉ** (19)
*Edith*, cantata
**STRAUSS, R.** (18)
Horn Concerto No 1 (1882–3)
**GLAZUNOV** (17)
*Overture on Greek Themes*, No 2 (1882–5)
String Quartet
**NIELSEN** (17)
Two Character Pieces for piano
  (unpublished)
String Quartet in Dm (unpublished)
*Duet in A*, for two violins (unpublished)
  (1882–3)
**BUSONI** (16)
*Spring, Summer, Autumn, Winter*, for male
  voice and orchestra
*Il Sabato del villagio*, for solo voices, chorus
  and orchestra
*Serenata*, for cello and piano


## 1883

**BAX, CASELLA, SZYMANOWSKI,
BERNERS, WEBERN** and **PARKER** were
born; **FLOTOW** and **WAGNER** died
**BRUCKNER** (59)
Symphony No 7
**SMETANA** (59)
*The Prague Carnival*
String Quartet No 2
**STRAUSS, J. (II)** (58)
*Eine Nacht in Venedig*, operetta
**BRAHMS** (50)
Symphony No 3
**DELIBES** (47)
*Lakmé*, opera
**CUI** (48)
*Suite Concertante*, for violin and orchestra
**CHABRIER** (42)
fp *España*, orchestral rhapsody
*Trois valses romantiques*, for piano duo
**DVOŘÁK** (42)
*Husitská*, overture
Scherzo Capriccioso for orchestra
Piano Trio in F minor
**GRIEG** (40)
Lyric Pieces for piano, Book II

**FAURÉ** (38)
*Élégie*, in C minor
**PARRY** (35)
Symphony No 2, *Cambridge*
*The Birds*, incidental music
**GODARD** (34)
*Symphonie Gothique*
**CATALANI** (29)
*Dejanire*, opera
**ELGAR** (26)
*Une Idyll*, for violin and piano (c1883)
Fugue for oboe and violin
**MAHLER** (23)
*Lieder eines fahrenden Gesellen*, song cycle
  for voice and orchestra
**WOLF** (23)
*Penthesilea*, symphonic poem (1883–5)
**MACDOWELL** (22)
*Modern Suite No 1*, for piano
**DEBUSSY** (21)
*Invocation*, for men's chorus and orchestra
*Le Gladiateur*, cantata
**PIERNÉ** (20)
*Le chemin de l'amour*, opera-comique
*Trois pièces formant suite de concert*, for
  orchestra.
**d'ALBERT** (19)
Suite for piano
**STRAUSS, R.** (19)
*Concert Overture*
Piano Quartet (1883–4)
**DUKAS** (18)
*King Lear*, overture
**GLAZUNOV** (18)
Serenade No 1
String Quartet
**NIELSEN** (18)
Piano Trio in G (unpublished)
**BUSONI** (17)
Piano Sonata in F minor


## 1884

**GRIFFES** and **GRUENBERG** were born;
**SMETANA** died
**GADE** (67)
*Holbergiana Suite*
**GOUNOD** (66)
fp *Mors et Vita*, oratorio
**FRANCK** (62)
*Les djinns*, symphonic poem for piano and
  orchestra
*Prélude, Chorale et Fugue*, for piano
'Nocturne', song
**LALO** (61)
Scherzo

BRUCKNER (60)
Symphony No 8, *Apocalyptic* (possibly
 1887, revised 1890)
*Te Deum*
BRAHMS (51)
Symphony No 4 (1884–5)
BALAKIREV (47)
*Russia*, symphonic poem
TCHAIKOVSKY (44)
*Mazeppa*, opera
*Concert-fantasy*, for piano and orchestra
MASSENET (42)
*Manon*, opera
SULLIVAN (42)
*Princess Ida*, operetta
GRIEG (41)
Lyric Pieces for piano, Book III
FAURÉ (39)
Symphony in D minor (unpublished)
GODARD (35)
*Pedro de Zalamea*, opera
*Symphonie Orientale*
d'INDY (33)
Lied for cello (or viola) and orchestra
*Saugefleure*, orchestral legend
STANFORD (32)
*Canterbury Pilgrims*, opera
*Savonarola*, opera
CHAUSSON (29)
*Hélène*, opera (1884–5)
PUCCINI (26)
*Le Villi*, opera
PADEREWSKI (24)
Polish Dances for piano, Books I and II
MACDOWELL (23)
*Forest Idylls*, for piano
DEBUSSY (22)
Suite for orchestra No 1
*Divertissement No 1*, for orchestra
*Diane au bois*, for chorus
*L'enfant prodigue*, cantata
PARKER (21)
Concert Overture
*Regulus*, overture héroïque
Venetian Overture
Scherzo for orchestra
d'ALBERT (20)
Piano Concerto in Bb
STRAUSS, R. (20)
Symphony in F minor
p Serenade for wind
p Cello Sonata
GLAZUNOV (19)
Serenade No 2
DUKAS (19)
*Götz von Berlichingen*, overture

# 1885

BERG, BUTTERWORTH, RIEGER,
WELLESZ, TAYLOR and VARÈSE born
FRANCK (63)
*Symphonic Variations*, for piano and
 orchestra
STRAUSS, J. (II) (60)
*Zigeunerbaron*, operetta
BORODIN (52)
*Petite Suite*, for piano
Scherzo in Ab for piano
PONCHIELLI (51)
*Marion Delorme*, opera
SAINT-SAËNS (50)
Violin Sonata No 1
TCHAIKOVSKY (45)
*Manfred Symphony*
CHABRIER (44)
*Habanèra*, for piano
DVOŘÁK (44)
Symphony No 7
*The Spectre's Bride*, cantata
MASSENET (43)
*Le Cid*, opera
SULLIVAN (43)
*The Mikado*, operetta
GRIEG (42)
*Holberg Suite*, for piano or strings
WIDOR (41)
*Conte d'avril*, incidental music
*Les Jacobites*, incidental music
PARRY (37)
*Guinevere*, opera (1885–6)
MESSAGER (32)
*La Béarnaise*, operetta
MACDOWELL (24)
p *Hamlet and Ophelia*, symphonic poem
DEBUSSY (23)
*Almanzor*, for chorus
PARKER (22)
Symphony
String Quartet
PIERNÉ (22)
Symphonic Overture
*Fantaisie-Ballet*, for piano and orchestra
GLAZUNOV (20)
*Stenka Razin*, tone poem
SIBELIUS (20)
String Quartet

# 1886

COATES, DUPRÉ and SCHOECK were
born; LISZT and PONCHIELLI died
LITOLFF (68)
*Les Templiers*, vocal score

FRANCK (64)
Violin Sonata in A major
LALO (63)
Symphony in G minor
GOLDMARK (56)
*Merlin*, opera
BORODIN (53)
*Serenata alla Spagnola* (Movement in string
quartet 'B-La-F')
BRAHMS (53)
Cello Sonata No 2
Violin Sonatas Nos 2 and 3
CUI (51)
*Deux Morceaux*, for cello and orchestra
SAINT-SAËNS (51)
*Le Carnaval des animaux*, for piano and
orchestra
Symphony No 3 with organ and two
pianos
CHABRIER (45)
*Gwendoline*, opera
DVOŘÁK (45)
*Slavonic Dances*, for orchestra, second
series
*St Ludmila*, oratorio
SULLIVAN (44)
*The Golden Legend*, cantata
RIMSKY-KORSAKOV (42)
*Fantasia Concertante on Russian Themes*, for
violin and orchestra
WIDOR (42)
*Maître Ambros*, lyric drama
Symphony No 2
FAURÉ (41)
Piano Quartet No 2
PARRY (38)
*Suite moderne*, for orchestra
GODARD (37)
*Symphony Légendaire*
d'INDY (35)
*Symphony on a French Mountain Air*
Suite in D for trumpet, two flutes and
string quartet
STANFORD (34)
*The Revenge*, choral-ballad
MESSAGER (33)
*Les deux pigeons*, ballet
CATALANI (32)
*Edmea*, opera
CHAUSSON (31)
*Hymne Védique*, for chorus and orchestra
*Solitude dans les bois*, for orchestra
ALBENIZ (26)
*Recuerdof de Viaje*, for piano
*Torre Bermeja*, for piano
DELIUS (24)
*Florida Suite*, for orchestra

GERMAN (24)
*The Rival Poets*, operetta
PIERNÉ (23)
*Don Luis*, opéra-comique
d'ALBERT (22)
Symphony in F
STRAUSS, R. (22)
*Aus Italien*, symphonic fantasia
*Macbeth*, symphonic poem (1886–90)
GLAZUNOV (21)
Symphony No 2
BUSONI (20)
String Quartet in C minor
Little Suite for cello and piano
CILÈA (20)
Piano Trio
SATIE (20)
*Ogives*, for piano
HOLBROOKE (18)
Piano Concerto (1886–90)

## 1887

TOCH and VILLA-LOBOS were born;
BORODIN died
VERDI (74)
*fp Otello*, opera
GADE (70)
*p* Violin Sonata No 3
FRANCK (65)
*Prélude, Chorale et Finale*, for piano
STRAUSS, J. (II) (62)
*Simplizius*, operetta
BRAHMS (54)
Double Concerto for violin, cello and
orchestra
*Zigeunerliede*
BRUCH (49)
Symphony No 3
STAINER (47)
*St Mary Magdalen*, cantata
*Jubilee*, cantata
*The Crucifixion*, oratorio
CHABRIER (46)
*Le Roi malgré lui*, opera
DVOŘÁK (46)
Piano Quintet in A major
Piano Quartet in Eb major
Terzetto for two violins and viola
MASSENET (45)
*Parade Militaire*
SULLIVAN (45)
*Ruddigore*, operetta
GRIEG (44)
Violin Sonata No 3
RIMSKY-KORSAKOV (43)
*Capriccio espagnol*, for orchestra

WIDOR (43)
*La Nuit de Walpurgis,* symphonic poem
   with chorus
FAURÉ (42)
*Pavane,* with chorus *ad lib*
*Requiem*
d'INDY (36)
*Serenade and Valse,* for small orchestra
Trio for clarinet, cello and piano
STANFORD (35)
*Irish Symphony*
Prelude *Oedipus Rex*
*Queen of the Seas,* overture
JANÁČEK (33)
*Sarka,* opera
CHAUSSON (32)
*Chant Nuptial*
LIADOV (32)
Scherzo for orchestra
SMYTH (29)
Violin Sonata
IPPOLITOV-IVANOV (28)
*Ruth,* opera
p Violin Sonata
ALBÉNIZ (27)
Piano Concerto
*Rhapsodia Española,* for orchestra
WOLF (27)
*Italian Serenade,* for string quartet, later
   for orchestra
p Violin Sonata
MACDOWELL (26)
Six Idylls after Goethe for piano
Six Poems after Heine for piano
DEBUSSY (25)
*The Blessed Damozel (La Damoiselle élue),*
   cantata (1887–8)
*Cinq Poèmes de Baudelaire,* songs (1887–9)
PIERNÉ (24)
Piano Concerto
d'ALBERT (23)
String Quartet No 1
ROPARTZ (23)
*La cloche des morts,* for orchestra
GLAZUNOV (22)
*Suite Caractéristique* (possibly 1884)
*Lyric Poem,* for orchestra
NIELSEN (22)
String Quartet in Gm
CILÈA (21)
Suite for orchestra
SATIE (21)
*Trois sarabandes,* for piano

## 1888

DARKE was born; ALKAN died

GADE (71–73)
*Ulysses,* march (1888–90)
GOUNOD (70)
Petite Symphonie for ten wind
   instruments
LITOLFF (70)
*L'escadron volant de la reine,* vocal score
FRANCK (66)
*Ghisele,* opera (1888–90)
Symphony in D minor (1886–8)
*Psyche,* symphonic poem
LALO (65)
*Le Roi d'Ys,* opera
CUI (53)
*Le Filibustier,* opera (1888–9)
TCHAIKOVSKY (48)
*The Sleeping Beauty,* ballet
*Hamlet,* overture
Symphony No 5
CHABRIER (47)
*Marche joyeuse,* for orchestra
SULLIVAN (46)
*The Yeoman of the Guard,* operetta
GRIEG (45)
Lyric Pieces for piano, Book IV
RIMSKY-KORSAKOV (44)
*Russian Easter Festival Overture*
*Schéhérezade,* symphonic suite
FAURÉ (43)
*Caligula,* incidental music
GODARD (39)
*Jocelyn,* opera
d'INDY (37)
*Fantasie,* for oboe and orchestra
STANFORD (36)
Symphony in F major
MESSAGER (35)
*Isoline,* opera
LIADOV (33)
Mazurka for orchestra
CHAMINADE (31)
*Callirhoe,* ballet
MAHLER (28)
Symphony No 1
*Lieder aus des Knaben Wunderhorn,* song
   cycle for voice and orchestra
PADEREWSKI (28)
Piano Concerto
WOLF (28)
*Mörike-Lieder,* fifty-three songs
*Goethe-Lieder,* fifty-one songs (1888–9)
MACDOWELL (27)
*Lancelot and Elaine,* symphonic poem
*Romance,* for cello
*Marionettes,* for piano
DEBUSSY (26)
*Petite Suite,* for piano duet

*Arabesques I* and *II*, for piano
*Ariettes oubliées*, songs
**DELIUS** (26)
*Marche caprice*, for orchestra
*Sleigh Ride*, for orchestra
**d'ALBERT** (24)
Overture to *Grillparzer*
**ROPARTZ** (24)
*Les Landes*, for orchestra
*Marche de fête*
**STRAUSS, R.** (24)
*Don Juan*, symphonic poem
*p* Violin Sonata
**DUKAS** (23)
*Velléda*, cantata
**NIELSEN** (23)
Little Suite in A minor, for strings
String Quintet in G
Symphonic Rhapsody (unpublished)
**SIBELIUS** (23)
Theme and Variations for quartet
**BUSONI** (22)
Symphonic Suite
*Konzert-Fantasie* (Symphonisches
    Tongedicht), for piano and orchestra
**SATIE** (22)
*Trois Gymnopédies*, for piano
**VAUGHAN WILLIAMS** (16)
Piano Trio
**SUK** (14)
Mass in B♭ major


## 1889

**THOMAS** (78)
*La tempête*, ballet
**VERDI** (76–85)
Four Sacred Pieces (1889–98)
**FRANCK** (67)
String Quartet in D major
**LALO** (66)
Piano Concerto
**DVOŘÁK** (48)
Symphony No 8
**SULLIVAN** (47)
*The Gondoliers*, operetta
**WIDOR** (45)
*Fantasie*, for piano
**FAURÉ** (44)
*Shylock*, incidental music
*Petite pièce*, for cello and piano
**PARRY** (41)
Symphony No 3, *English*
Symphony No 4
**JANÁČEK** (35)
Six Lach Dances

**SINDING** (33)
*Til molde*, for baritone, voices and piano
*Konzertouverture*, for orchestra
**PUCCINI** (31)
*Edgar*, opera
**ALBÉNIZ** (29)
*Suite Española*, for piano
**MACDOWELL** (28)
*Lamia*, symphonic poem
*Les Orientales*, for piano
**DEBUSSY** (27)
*Fantaisie*, for piano and orchestra (1889–90)
**GERMAN** (27)
*Richard III*, incidental music
**PIERNÉ** (26)
*Marche Solennelle*
*Pantomime*, for orchestra
**ROPARTZ** (25)
*Carnaval*, for orchestra
*Cinq pièces brèves*, for orchestra
**STRAUSS, R.** (25)
*Tod und Verklärung*, symphonic poem
**GLAZUNOV** (24)
*The Forest*, fantasia, (possibly 1887)
**NIELSEN** (24)
*Fantàsistykker*, for oboe and piano
**SIBELIUS** (24)
Piano Quintet
Suite for String Trio
String Quartet
Violin Sonata
**BUSONI** (23)
String Quartet No 2
**CILÈA** (23)
*Gina*, opera
**GIORDANO** (22)
*Marina*, opera
**SUK** (15)
*Fantasy*, for strings
Piano Trio (1889–90)


## 1890

**MARTINŮ, IBERT, GURNEY** and
**MARTIN** were born; **GADE** and
**FRANCK** died
**GADE** (73)
*p* String Quartet in D major
**LITOLFF** (72)
*König Lear*, vocal score (*c*1890)
**FRANCK** (68)
Chorales for organ
**BRAHMS** (57)
String Quintet No 2
**CUI** (55–68)
Three String Quartets in Cm: D: E♭ (1890–
    1913)

TCHAIKOVSKY (50)
*The Queen of Spades*, opera
DVOŘÁK (49)
Gavotte for three violins
*Dumka*, for piano trio (1890–1)
MASSENET (48)
*Visions*, symphonic poem
WIDOR (46)
*Jeanne d'Arc*, ballet-pantomime
FAURÉ (45)
*Cinq Mélodies de Verlaine*, songs
GODARD (41)
*Dante*, opera
d'INDY (39)
*Karadec*, incidental music
String Quartet No 1
MESSAGER (37)
*La Basoche*, operetta
CATALANI (36)
*Lorely*, opera
CHAUSSON (35)
Symphony in B♭ major
LIADOV (35)
*Dal tempo antico*, for piano
ELGAR (33)
*Froissart*, concert overture
SMYTH (32)
*Anthony and Cleopatra*, overture
Serenade in D for orchestra
IPPOLITOV-IVANOV (31)
*Asra*, opera
CHARPENTIER (30)
*Impressions d'Italie*, orchestral suite
WOLF (30)
*Spanish Song Book*
ARENSKY (29)
fp *A Dream on the Volga*, opera
MACDOWELL (29)
Piano Concerto No 2
Twelve Studies for Piano, Books I and II
DEBUSSY (28)
*Ballade*, for piano
*Rêverie*, for piano
*Suite Bergamasque*, for piano (1890–1905)
*Tarantelle Styrienne (Danse)*, for piano
*Valse romantique*, for piano
GERMAN (28)
Symphony No 1
MASCAGNI (27)
*Cavalleria Rusticana*, opera
PARKER (27)
*Count Robert of Paris*, overture
PIERNÉ (27)
*Scherzo Caprice*, for piano and orchestra
GLAZUNOV (25)
*The Sea*, fantasy for orchestra
*Wedding March*

*Une Fête Slav*, for orchestra
NIELSEN (25)
String Quartet in Fm
Five Pieces for piano
Symphony No 1 (1890–2)
SIBELIUS (25)
Two Overtures (1890–91)
BUSONI (24)
*Konzertstücke*, for piano
Violin Sonata No 1
SATIE (24)
*Trois Gnossiènnes*, for piano
RACHMANINOV (17)
Piano Concerto No 1 (1890–1)
Six songs (1890–3)

## 1891

BLISS, PROKOFIEV and GRANDJANY
were born; DELIBES and LITOLFF died
BRAHMS (58)
Clarinet Quintet
Piano Trio
BRUCH (53)
Violin Concerto No 3
DVOŘÁK (50)
*Nature, Life and Love*, cycle of overtures:
    'Amid Nature'; 'Carnaval'; 'Othello'
    (1891–2)
*Forest Calm*, for cello and orchestra
Rondo for cello and orchestra
SULLIVAN (49)
*Ivanhoe*, opera
GRIEG (48)
Lyric Pieces for piano, Book V
FAURÉ (46)
*La bonne chanson*, nine songs (1891–2)
d'INDY (41)
*Tableaux de voyage*, for orchestra
STANFORD (39)
*Eden*, oratorio
JANÁČEK (37)
*The Beginning of a Romance*, opera
*Rákos Rákóczy*, ballet
CHAUSSON (36)
Concerto for piano, violin and string
    quartet
ELGAR (34)
*La Capriceuse*, for violin and piano
SMYTH (33)
Suite for strings
WOLF (31)
*The Feast of Sulhaug*, incidental music
*Italian Song Book*, Book I
LOEFFLER (30)
*The Nights in the Ukraine*, for violin and
    orchestra

**MACDOWELL** (30)
Suite No 1 for orchestra
*The Lovely Alda*, symphonic poem
*The Saracens*, symphonic poem
**DEBUSSY** (29)
*Rodrigue et Chimène*, opera (1891–2, unfinished)
*Marche écossaise*
*Mazurka*, for piano
*Trois mélodies de Verlaine*, songs
*Deux Romances*, songs
**GERMAN** (29)
Funeral March
**MASCAGNI** (28)
Solemn Mass
*L'Amico Fritz*, opera
**PIERNÉ** (28)
*Le Collier de saphire*, ballet
**GLAZUNOV** (26)
*Oriental Rhapsody*
**SIBELIUS** (26)
*Scène de ballet*
Piano Quartet
**SATIE** (25)
*Trois Préludes* from *Les fils des étoiles*, for piano
**BEACH** (24)
Mass for chorus and orchestra
**RACHMANINOV** (18)
Scherzo for strings
**REGER** (18)
Piano Trio
Violin Sonata
**IVES** (17)
Variations on 'America', for organ
**SUK** (17)
*Dramatic Overture*
Piano Quartet

## 1892

**GROFÉ, HOWELLS, MILHAUD** and **HONEGGER** were born; **LALO** died
**BRAHMS** (59)
*Fantasien*, for piano
Thirteen piano pieces
**SAINT-SAËNS** (57)
Piano Trio No 2
**DVOŘÁK** (51)
*Te Deum*
**TCHAIKOVSKY** (52)
*Iolanthe*, opera
*Casse Noisette (The Nutcracker)*, ballet
p String sextet
**MASSENET** (50)
*Werther*, opera

**SULLIVAN** (50)
*Haddon Hall*, opera
**RIMSKY-KORSAKOV** (48)
fp *Mlada*, opera
**PARRY** (44)
*The Frogs*, incidental music
**CATALANI** (38)
*La Wally*, opera
**MOSZKOWSKY** (38)
*Boabdil*, opera
**LIADOV** (37)
*Kukalki*, for piano
**ELGAR** (35)
*Serenade for Strings*
*The Black Knight*, cantata
**DUPARC** (34)
*Danse lente*, for orchestra
**LEONCAVALLO** (34)
*I Pagliacci*, opera
**CHARPENTIER** (32)
*La vie du poète*, cantata
**DEBUSSY** (30)
*Fêtes galantes*, songs (first series)
**DELIUS** (30)
*Irmelin*, opera
**GERMAN** (30)
*Gipsy Suite*
*Henry VIII*, incidental music
**MASCAGNI** (29)
*I Rantzau*, opera
**PIERNÉ** (29)
*Les joyeuses commères de Paris*, ballet
**ROPARTZ** (28)
*Serenade*
**STRAUSS, R.** (28)
*Guntram*, opera (1892–3)
**DUKAS** (27)
*Polyeucte*, overture
**GLAZUNOV** (27)
Symphony No 3 (possibly 1890)
*The Kremlin*, symphonic picture (possibly 1890)
*Le Printemps*, tone poem
String Quintet
**SIBELIUS** (27)
*En Saga*, symphonic poem
*Kullervo*, symphonic poem
**CILÈA** (26)
*La Tilda*, opera
**SATIE** (26)
*Uspud*, ballet
*Sonneries de la Rose-Croix*, for piano
**BEACH** (25)
*Festival Jubilate*, for chorus and orchestra
**GIORDANO** (25)
*Mala Vita*, opera

**BANTOCK** (24)
*Aeygpt*, ballet
*Fire Worshippers*, for soli, chorus and
  orchestra
**NOVÁK** (22)
*Korzár*, overture
**ZEMLINSKY** (21)
Symphony No 1
**RACHMANINOV** (19)
*Prélude* and *Danse orientale*, for cello and
  piano
Five *Morceaux de Fantaisie*, for piano
*Intermezzo*
**REGER** (19)
Cello Sonata
**SUK** (18)
Serenade for strings
**HAHN** (17)
*Fin d'amour*, ballet-pantomime
**AUBERT** (15)
*Sous bois*, song


## 1893

BENJAMIN, ROGERS and MOORE were
born; GOUNOD, TCHAIKOVSKY and
CATALANI died
**VERDI** (80)
*fp Falstaff*, opera
**STAINER** (53)
*The Story of the Cross*, cantata
**TCHAIKOVSKY** (53)
Symphony No 6, *Pathétique*
Piano Concerto No 3
**DVOŘÁK** (52)
Symphony No 9, *From the New World*
String Quintet in E♭ major
String Quartet, *American*
**SULLIVAN** (51)
*Utopia, Ltd*, operetta
**GRIEG** (50)
Lyric pieces for piano, Book VI
**FAURÉ** (48)
*Dolly Suite*, for piano duet
**PARRY** (45)
*Hypatia*, incidental music
**MESSAGER** (40)
*Madame Chrysanthème*, operetta
**HUMPERDINCK** (39)
*Hänsel und Gretel*, opera
**LIADOV** (38)
*Une tabatière à musique*, for piano
**DUPARC** (35)
*Aux Etoiles*, nocturne
**PUCCINI** (35)
*Manon Lescaut*, opera

**SMYTH** (35)
Mass in D major
**ALBÉNIZ** (33)
*The Magic Opal*, opera
**PADEREWSKI** (33)
*Polish Fantasy on Original Themes*, for
  piano and orchestra
**MACDOWELL** (32)
Piano Sonata No 1, *Tragica*
**DEBUSSY** (31)
String Quartet in G minor
*Proses lyriques*, songs
**GERMAN** (31)
Symphony No 2
*Romeo and Juliet*, incidental music
*The Tempter*, incidental music
**PARKER** (30)
Suite for piano, violin and cello
**PIERNÉ** (30)
*Lizarda*, opéra-comique (1893–4)
*Bouton d'or*, ballet
*Le docteur blanc*, ballet
**d'ALBERT** (29)
Piano Concerto in E
Piano Sonata
String Quartet No 2
*Der Rubin*, opera
*Der Mensch und das Leben*, for chorus
**ROPARTZ** (29)
*Le diable couturier*, opera
*Dimanche breton*, for orchestra
String Quartet No 1
**GLAZUNOV** (28)
Symphony No 4
**NIELSEN** (28)
*Snefrid*, melodrama (unpublished)
**SIBELIUS** (28)
*Karelia*, overture and orchestral suite
*The Swan of Tuonela*, symphonic legend
**SATIE** (27)
*Danses gothiques*, for piano
*Quatre Préludes*, for piano
**JONGEN** (20)
Piano Trio in B minor (1893–1905)
Violin Sonata No 1 in D minor (1893–1905)
**RACHMANINOV** (20)
*Aleko*, opera
*The Rock*, fantasy for orchestra
*Trio élégiaque*
*Romance* and *Danse hongroise*, for violin
  and piano
Suite No 1, *Fantasy*, for two pianos
Six songs
**SUK** (19)
Piano Quintet
**RAVEL** (18)
*Sérénade grotesque*, for piano

## 1894

**MOERAN, PISTON, WARLOCK** were born; **RUBINSTEIN** and **CHABRIER** died
**BRUCKNER** (70)
Symphony No 9 (unfinished, *fp* 1903)
**BRAHMS** (61)
Two sonatas for clarinet or viola and piano
**SAINT-SAËNS** (59)
Preludes and Fugues for organ
**MASSENET** (52)
*La Navarraise*, opera
*Thaïs*, opera
**PARRY** (46)
*Lady Radnor's Suite*, for orchestra
**STANFORD** (42)
Symphony in D major, *L'Allegro ed il pensiero*
**MESSAGER** (41)
*Mirette*, operetta
**JANÁČEK** (40–49)
*Jenůfa*, opera (1894–1903)
**ELGAR** (37–39)
*King Olaf*, cantata (1894–6)
**LEONCAVALLO** (36)
*Serafita*, symphonic poem
**IPPOLITOV-IVANOV** (35)
*Armenian Rhapsody* (1894–5)
**ALBÉNIZ** (34)
*San Antonio de la Florida*, opera
**CHARPENTIER** (34)
*Poèmes chantées*, for voice and piano or orchestra
**MAHLER** (34)
Symphony No 2, *Resurrection*
**ARENSKY** (33)
*fp Raphael*, opera
**LOEFFLER** (33)
*Fantasy Concerto*, for cello and orchestra
**MACDOWELL** (33)
Twelve Virtuoso Studies for piano
**DEBUSSY** (32)
*Prélude à l'après-midi d'un faune*, for orchestra
**PARKER** (31)
String Quintet
Suite for piano and violin
**STRAUSS, R.** (30)
*Also sprach Zarathustra*, symphonic poem
**GLAZUNOV** (29)
*Carnival*, Overture
*Chopiniana*, Suite
String Quartet
**NIELSEN** (29)
Symphonic Suite for piano
*Humoreske-bagateller*, for piano (1894–7)
**SIBELIUS** (29)
*Spring Song*, symphonic poem

**CILÈA** (28)
Cello Sonata
**SATIE** (28)
*Prélude de la porte héroïque du ciel*, for piano
**GIORDANO** (27)
*Regina Diaz*, opera
**NOVÁK** (24)
Serenade in F for small orchestra (1894–5)
**SCHMITT** (24)
*En été*, for orchestra
**SKRIABIN** (22)
Piano Concerto
*Rêverie*, for orchestra
**JONGEN** (21)
*p* String Quartet No 1
**RACHMANINOV** (21)
*Caprice bohémien*, for orchestra
Six Piano Duets
Seven Piano Pieces
**AUBERT** (17)
'Vielle chanson Espagnole'

## 1895

**HINDEMITH, ORFF, JACOB, CASTELNUOVO-TEDESCO** and **SOWERBY** were born; **GODARD** and **SUPPÉ** died
**STRAUSS, J. (II)** (70)
*Waldmeister*, operetta
**SAINT-SAËNS** (60)
Piano Concerto No 5
**BALAKIREV** (58)
Ten songs (1895–6)
**DVOŘÁK** (54)
Suite for orchestra
Cello Concerto
Two String Quartets
**SULLIVAN** (53)
*The Chieftan*, operetta
**GRIEG** (52)
Lyric Pieces for piano, Book VII
**WIDOR** (51)
Symphony No 2
**RIMSKY-KORSAKOV** (51)
*Christmas Eve*, opera
**FAURÉ** (50)
*Romance*, for cello and piano
**STANFORD** (43)
Suite of Ancient Dances
Piano Concerto No 1
**HUMPERDINCK** (41)
*Die Sieben Geislein*, opera
**CHAUSSON** (40)
*Le Roi Arthus*, opera, *fp* 1903
**ELGAR** (38)
Organ Sonata in G major

IPPOLITOV-IVANOV (36)
*Caucasian Sketches*, orchestral suite
ALBÉNIZ (35)
*Enrico Clifford*, opera
CHARPENTIER (35)
*Impressions fausses*, for voice and orchestra
MAHLER (35)
Symphony No 3
LOEFFLER (34)
*Divertimento*, for violin and orchestra
MACDOWELL (34)
Piano Sonata No 2, *Eroica*
DELIUS (33)
*Over the Hills and Far Away*, tone poem
GERMAN (33)
Symphonic Suite in D minor
MASCAGNI (32)
*Guglielmo Ratcliff*, opera
*Silvano*, opera
PIERNÉ (32)
*La coupe enchantée*, opéra-comique
*Salome*, ballet
d'ALBERT (31)
*Chismonda*, opera
STRAUSS, R. (31)
*Till Eulenspiegel*, symphonic poem
GLAZUNOV (30)
*Cortège Solennelle* in D, for orchestra
Symphony No 5
NIELSEN (30)
Sonata in A for violin and piano
SIBELIUS (30)
Cassazione, for orchestra (unpublished)
*Lemminkäinen and the Maidens*, symphonic
    poem
*Lemminkäinen in Tuonela*, symphonic poem
*Lemminkäinen's Homecoming*, symphonic
    poem
BUSONI (29)
Suite for Orchestra No 2
SATIE (29)
*Messe des pauvres*
NOVÁK (25)
Piano Concerto
ZEMLINSKY (24)
String Quintet
String Quartet No 1
SKRIABIN (23)
Symphony No 1
RACHMANINOV (22)
Symphony No 1
HOLST (21)
*The Revoke*, opera
RAVEL (20)
*Menuet antique*
BRIAN (19)
*Requiem*, for baritone, chorus and

orchestra (discarded)
WOLF-FERRARI (19)
Violin Sonata
DOHNÁNYI (18)
*fp* Piano Quintet
SCHREKER (17)
*Love Song*, for strings and harp (lost)
IRELAND (16)
Two Pieces for piano
ENESCO (14)
*Ouverture tragica e ouverture trionfale*
Four *Sinfonie scolastiche* (1895–6)

## 1896

HANSON, THOMSON, WEINBERGER,
ROBERTSON, GERHARD and
SESSIONS were born; THOMAS and
BRUCKNER died
GOLDMARK (66)
*The Cricket on the Hearth*, opera
BRAHMS (63)
Four Serious Songs
SAINT-SAËNS (61)
Violin Sonata No 2
DVOŘÁK (55)
Four Symphonic Poems:
    'The Watersprite'
    'The Noonday Witch'
    'The Golden Spinning-wheel'
    'The Wood Dove'
SULLIVAN (54)
*The Grand Duke*, operetta
GRIEG (53)
Lyric Pieces for piano, Book VIII
d'INDY (45)
*Istar*, symphonic variations for orchestra
STANFORD (44)
*Shamus O'Brien*, opera
MESSAGER (43)
*Le Chevalier d'Harmenthal*, operetta
MOSZKOWSKY (42)
*Laurin*, ballet
CHAUSSON (41)
*Poème*, for violin and orchestra
ELGAR (39)
*The Light of Life (Lux Christi)*, oratorio
PUCCINI (38)
*La Bohème*, opera
ALBÉNIZ (36)
*Pepita Jiménez*, opera
*Cantos de España*, for piano
*España*, for piano
CHARPENTIER (36)
*Sérénade à Watteau*, for voice and orchestra
WOLF (36)
*fp Der Corregidor*, opera

*Italian Song Book*, Book II
**MACDOWELL** (35)
*Indian Suite* (Suite No 2) for orchestra
*Woodland Sketches*, for piano
**GERMAN** (34)
*As You Like It*, incidental music
**MASCAGNI** (33)
*Zanetto*, opera
**STRAUSS, R.** (32)
*Don Quixote*, fantasy variations for cello
   and orchestra
**DUKAS** (31)
Symphony in C major
**GLAZUNOV** (31)
Symphony No 6
**NIELSEN** (31)
*Hymnus amoris*, for baritone, bass, chorus
   and orchestra (1896–7)
**BUSONI** (30)
Violin Concerto (1896–7)
**BEACH** (29)
Symphony 'Gaelic'
Sonata for violin and piano
**GIORDANO** (29)
*Andrea Chénier*, opera
**ZELIMSKY** (25)
*Frühlingsglaube*, for voices and strings
*Frühlingsbegräbnis*, for voices and orchestra
**ALFVÉN** (24)
Sonata and Romance for violin and piano
**RACHMANINOV** (23)
Six *Moments musicaux*, for piano
Six songs for female or boys' voices
Twelve songs
**HOLST** (22)
*Fantasiestücke*, for oboe and string quartet
Quintet for wind and piano
Four songs
**IVES** (22)
Symphony No 1 (1896–8)
Quartet No 1, *Revival Service*
**SCHMIDT** (22)
Symphony No 1
**SUK** (22)
String Quartet No 1
**COLERIDGE-TAYLOR** (21)
Symphony in A minor
**RAVEL** (21)
'Sainte', song
**AUBERT** (19)
*Rimes tendres*, song cycle
**DOHNÁNYI** (19)
*Zrinyi*, overture

**1897**

TANSMAN and KORNGOLD were born
BRAHMS and BOËLLMANN died
**CUI** (62)
*p* Five Little Duets for flute and violin with
   piano
**SAINT-SAËNS** (62)
Seven Improvisations for grand organ
**DVOŘÁK** (56)
'Heroic Song'
**MASSENET** (55)
*Sappho*, lyric play
*Fantaisie*, for cello and orchestra
*Marche solennelle*
*Devant la Madone*, opera
**SULLIVAN** (55)
*Te Deum*
**RIMSKY-KORSAKOV** (53)
Three Song Cycles:
   *In Spring*
   *To the Poet*
   *By the Sea*
Piano Trio
**FAURÉ** (52)
Theme and Variations for piano
**PARRY** (49)
Symphonic Variations
**d'INDY** (46)
*Fervaal*, lyric drama
String Quartet No 2
**MESSAGER** (44)
*Les P'tites Michu*, operetta
**CHAUSSON** (42)
*Chant funèbre*
*Ballata*
Piano Quartet
**ELGAR** (40)
Imperial March
*The Banner of St George*, ballad for soprano
   chorus and orchestra
*Sea Pictures*, for contralto and orchestra
**LEONCAVALLO** (39)
*La Bohème*, opera
**IPPOLITOV-IVANOV** (38)
*p* String Quartet
**DEBUSSY** (35)
*Chansons de Bilitis*, songs
**GERMAN** (35)
*Hamlet*, symphonic poem
*In Commemoration*, fantasia
**PIERNÉ** (34)
*Vendée*, opera-comique
*L'an mil*, symphonique poem with chorus
**d'ALBERT** (33)
*Gernot*, opera
*Seejungfraulein*, for voice and orchestra

DUKAS (32)
*The Sorcerer's Apprentice*, symphonic poem
NIELSEN (32)
String Quartet in E♭
BUSONI (31)
*Comedy Overture*
CILÈA (31)
*L'Arlesiania*, opera
SATIE (31)
*Deux pièces froides*, for piano
SCHMITT (27)
*Musique de plein air*, for orchestra (1897–9)
ZEMLINSKY (26)
*Sarema*, opera
*Es war einmal*, opera (1897–9)
Symphony No 2
ALFVÉN (25)
Symphony No 1 in F minor
REGER (24)
Piano Quintet (1897–8)
Cello Sonata (1897–8)
Violin Sonata (1897–8)
HOLST (23)
*A Winter Idyll*, for orchestra
*Clear and Cool*, for chorus and orchestra
IVES (23–28)
Symphony No 2 (1897–1902)
HAHN (22)
*Nuit d'amour bergamasque*, symphonic
  poem
AUBERT (20)
*Les Noces d'Apollon et d'Urainie*, cantata
DOHNÁNYI (20)
Symphony No 1
ENESCO (16)
*Romanian Poem*
KODÁLY (15)
Overture for orchestra

**1898**

GERSHWIN and HARRIS were born
SAINT-SAËNS (63)
Preludes and Fugues for organ
SULLIVAN (56)
*The Beauty Stone*, opera
GRIEG (55)
*Symphonic Dances*, for orchestra
Lyric Pieces for piano, Book IX
RIMSKY-KORSAKOV (54)
*Mozart and Salieri*, opera
WIDOR (54)
*Overture Espagnole*
FAURÉ (53)
*Pelléas et Mélisande*, incidental music
*Papillon*, for cello and piano
*Sicilienne*, for cello and piano

*Fantaisie*, for flute and piano
Andante for violin and piano
d'INDY (47)
*L'Étranger*, lyric drama (1898–1901)
*Medée*, incidental music
*Chansons et danses*, for seven wind
  instruments
STANFORD (46)
*Te Deum*
MESSAGER (45)
*Véronique*, operetta
HUMPERDINCK (44)
*Moorish Rhapsody*, for orchestra
CHAUSSON (43)
*Soir de fête*, symphonic poem
ELGAR (41)
*Caractacus*, cantata
*Variations on an Original Theme*
  *('Enigma')* for orchestra (1898–9)
SMYTH (40)
*Fantastic*, opera
IPPOLITOV-IVANOV (39)
*p* Piano Quartet
MACDOWELL (37)
*Sea Pieces*, for piano
MASCAGNI (35)
*Iris*, opera
d'ALBERT (34)
*Die Abreise*, opera
STRAUSS, R. (34)
*Ein Heldenleben*, symphonic poem
SIBELIUS (33)
Symphony No 1 (1898–9)
*King Christian II*, incidental music
BUSONI (32)
Violin Sonata No 2
GIORDANO (31)
*Fedora*, opera
GRANADOS (31)
*Maria del Carmen*, opera
NOVÁK (28)
Two Ballads for chorus and piano duet
*Maryša*, dramatic overture
ALFVÉN (26)
Symphony No 2 in D major (1898–99)
*Elegy*, for horn and organ
JONGEN (25)
*Fantaisie*, for violin and orchestra
HOLST (24)
*Ornulf's Drapa*, for baritone and orchestra
IVES (24–33)
*Calcium Light Night*, for chamber orchestra
  (1898–1907)
*Central Park in the Dark*, for orchestra
  (1898–1907)
COLERIDGE-TAYLOR (23)
Ballade for orchestra

*Hiawatha's Wedding Feast*, cantata
**HAHN** (23)
*L'île du rêve*, opera
**ENESCO** (17)
*p* Violin Sonata No 1
**STRAVINSKY** (16)
Tarantella for piano


## 1899

**AURIC, CHÁVEZ, POULENC** and
**THOMPSON** were born; **STRAUSS, J. (II)**
and **CHAUSSON** died
**CUI** (64)
*The Saracen*, opera
**MASSENET** (57)
*Cendrillon*, opera
*Brumaire*, overture
**SULLIVAN** (57)
*The Rose of Persia*, operetta
**RIMSKY-KORSAKOV** (55)
*The Tsar's Bride*, opera
**PARRY** (51)
*A Repentance*, incidental music
**STANFORD** (47)
Evening Service in C major
**CHAUSSON** (44)
String Quartet (unfinished)
**LIADOV** (44)
*Slava*, for voices, harps and pianos
**ELGAR** (42)
*In the South (Alassio)*, concert overture
  (1899–1904)
*Sérénade Lyrique*, for orchestra
**ALBÉNIZ** (39)
*p Catalonia*, orchestral rhapsody
**ARENSKY** (38)
*Nal and Damayanti*, opera (completed)
**DELIUS** (37)
*Paris – The Song of a Great City*, nocturne
  for orchestra
**GERMAN** (37)
*The Seasons*, symphonic suite
**PARKER** (36)
*A Northern Ballad*, symphonic poem
**d'ALBERT** (35)
Cello Concerto
**GLAZUNOV** (34)
String Quartet
**SIBELIUS** (34)
*Scènes historiques*, Suite No 1
**SATIE** (33)
*Génévieve de Brabant*, puppet opera
*Jack-in-the-Box*, ballet
**BEACH** (32)
Piano Concerto

**BANTOCK** (31)
String Quartet in C minor
**JONGEN** (26)
Symphony
Violin Concerto
**HOLST** (25)
*Sita*, opera (1899–1906)
*Walt Whitman*, overture
**SCHOENBERG** (25)
*Verklärte Nacht*, for string sextet (arranged
  for string orchestra 1917)
**SUK** (25)
Symphony No 1 in E major
**COLERIDGE-TAYLOR** (24)
Solemn Prelude
*Death of Minnehaha*, cantata
**GLIÈRE** (24)
Symphony No 1 (1889–1900)
**RAVEL** (24)
*Pavane pour une Infante défunte*, for piano
**BRIAN** (23)
*Pantalon and Columbine*, romance for small
  orchestra
**AUBERT** (22)
*Fantaisie*, for piano and orchestra
**ENESCO** (18)
*Fantaisie Pastorale*


## 1900

**BUSH, A., KŘENEK, WEILL, COPLAND**
and **ANTHEIL** were born; **SULLIVAN**
died
**SAINT-SAËNS** (65)
String Quartet
**MASSENET** (58)
*La Terre promisée*, oratorio
**RIMSKY-KORSAKOV** (56)
*Legend of Tsar Sultan*, opera
**WIDOR** (56)
Chorale and Variations for harp
**FAURÉ** (55)
*Promethée*, lyric tragedy
**PARRY** (52)
*Agamemnon*, incidental music
**LIADOV** (45)
*Polonaise*, for orchestra
**SINDING** (44)
*Sange*, for female voices and piano
*Legende*, for violin and orchestra
**ELGAR** (43)
*The Dream of Gerontius*, oratorio
**LEONCAVALLO** (42)
*Zaza*, opera
**PUCCINI** (42)
*Tosca*, opera

432

IPPOLITOV-IVANOV (41)
*Assia*, lyric scenes
CHARPENTIER (40)
*Louise*, opera
MAHLER (40)
Symphony No 4
MACDOWELL (39)
Piano Sonata No 3, *Norse*
DEBUSSY (38)
*Nocturnes*, for orchestra and chorus
GERMAN (38)
*Nell Gwynne*, incidental music
PIERNÉ (37)
Violin Sonata
d'ALBERT (36)
*Kain*, opera
ROPARTZ (36)
Five Motets
GLAZUNOV (35)
*Ouverture Solonnelle*
NIELSEN (35)
*Fest – praeludium*, for piano
Cantata for the Lorens Frelich Festival
 (unpublished)
SIBELIUS (35)
*Finlandia*, symphonic poem
BANTOCK (32)
Tone Poem No 1, *Thalaba the Destroyer*
NOVÁK (30)
Two Ballads for chorus and piano duet
SCHMITT (30)
*Le palais hanté*, for orchestra (1900–4)
ZELIMSKY (29)
*Das gläserne Hertz*, ballet
*Psalm LXXXIII*, for voices and orchestra
VAUGHAN WILLIAMS (28)
*Bucolic Suite*, for orchestra
RACHMANINOV (27–33)
Twelve songs (1900–6)
REGER (27)
Two *Romances*, for solo instruments and
 orchestra
Two String Quartets
Two Clarinet Sonatas
HOLST (26)
*Cotswolds Symphony*
*Suite de Ballet*
*Ave Maria*, for eight-part female choir
SCHOENBERG (26–39)
*Gurre-Lieder*, for solo voices, chorus and
 orchestra (1900–13)
COLERIDGE-TAYLOR (25)
*Hiawatha's Departure*, cantata
GLIÈRE (25)
String Octet
String Sextet No 1
String Quartet No 1

BRIAN (24)
*Tragic Prelude*, for orchestra (discarded)
AUBERT (23)
*Suite Brève*, for two pianos
*Trois esquisses*, for piano
*La Lettre*, vocal work
HOLBROOKE (22)
*The Raven*, symphonic poem
Variations on 'Three Blind Mice', for
 orchestra
Variations on 'The Girl I Left Behind Me',
 for orchestra
SCHREKER (22)
*Flammen*, opera
*Psalm CXVI*, for three female voices, organ
 and orchestra
SCOTT (21)
Symphony No 1
BLOCH (20–49)
*Helvetia*, symphonic fresco for orchestra
 (1900–29)

# 1901

FINZI and RUBBRA were born; STAINER
and VERDI died
DVOŘÁK (60)
*fp Rusalka*, opera
GRIEG (58)
Lyric Pieces for piano, Book X
FAURÉ (56)
*La voile du bonheur*, incidental music
STANFORD (49)
*Much Ado About Nothing*, opera
*Irish Rhapsody* No 1
ELGAR (44)
*Cockaigne*, overture
*Introduction and Allegro for strings* (1901–5)
*Pomp and Circumstance Marches* Nos 1–4
 (1901–7)
Concerto Allegro for piano
SMYTH (43)
*The Forest*, opera
PADEREWSKI (41)
*Manru*, opera
LOEFFLER (40)
*Divertissement Espagnol*, for saxophone and
 orchestra
MACDOWELL (40)
Piano Sonata No 4, *Keltic*
DEBUSSY (39)
*Pour le piano* (possibly 1896)
GERMAN (39)/SULLIVAN (posthumous)
*The Emerald Isle*, operetta (completed by
 German after Sullivan's death)
MASCAGNI (38)
*Le Maschera*, opera

PIERNÉ (38)
*La Fille de Tabarin*, opéra-comique
*Poème symphonique*, for piano and
   orchestra
*Konzertstücke*, for harp
STRAUSS, R. (37)
*Feuersnot*, opera
DUKAS (36)
Piano Sonata in E♭ minor
GLAZUNOV (36)
*The Seasons*, ballet (possibly earlier)
NIELSEN (36)
Cantata for the Student's Association
Symphony No 2, *The Four Temperaments*
   (1901–2)
SIBELIUS (36)
Symphony No 2
*Cortège*, for orchestra (unpublished)
*Portraits*, for strings
BANTOCK (33)
Tone Poem No 2, *Dante*
Tone Poem No 3, *Fifine at the Fair*
NOVÁK (31)
Two Choruses, for female chorus and
   piano
SKRIABIN (29)
Symphony No 2
RACHMANINOV (28)
Piano Concerto No 2
Cello Sonata
Suite No 2 for two pianos
IVES (27–30)
Symphony No 3 (1901–4)
COLERIDGE-TAYLOR (26)
*The Blind Girl of Castel-Cuille*, cantata
*Toussaint l'ouverture*, concert overture
*Idyll*, for orchestra
RAVEL (26)
*Jeux d'eau*, for piano
*Myrrha*, cantata
WOLF-FERRARI (25)
*p* Piano Quintet
*p* Piano Trio
HOLBROOKE (23)
*Ode to Victory*, for chorus and orchestra
*Ulalume*, symphonic poem (1901–3)
SCHREKER (23)
*Der Ferne Klang*, opera
HARTY (22)
Trio
BLOCH (21)
Symphony in C♯ minor (1901–2)
ENESCO (20)
*Romanian Rhapsody No 1*
*Symphonie Concertante*, for cello and
   orchestra
*p* Violin Sonata No 2

KODÁLY (19)
Adagio for violin (or viola) and piano
CASELLA (18)
*Pavana*, for piano

# 1902

DURUFLÉ, RODRIGO and WALTON
were born
SAINT-SAËNS (67)
Coronation March
Cello Concerto No 2
MASSENET (61)
*Le Jongleur de Notre Dame*, opera
Piano Concerto
RIMSKY-KORSAKOV (58)
*fp Kaschey the Immortal*, opera
d'INDY (51)
Symphony No 2 (1902–3)
HUMPERDINCK (48)
*Dornröschen*, opera
*Cantata ved, abeljubilaeet* for soli, chorus
   and orchestra
ELGAR (45)
Coronation Ode
*Falstaff*, symphonic study (1902–13)
*Dream Children*, for piano or small
   orchestra
SMYTH (44)
String Quartet in E minor
MAHLER (42)
Symphony No 5
Five Rückert Songs
LOEFFLER (41)
*Poème*, for orchestra
MACDOWELL (41)
*Fireside Tales*, for piano
*New England Idylls*
DEBUSSY (40)
*Pelléas et Mélisande*, opera
DELIUS (40)
*Appalachia*, for orchestra and chorus
GERMAN (40)
*Merrie England*, operetta
PARKER (39)
Organ Concerto
PIERNÉ (39)
*The Children's Crusade*, oratorio
d'ALBERT (38)
*Der Improvisator*, opera
SIBELIUS (37)
*The Origin of Fire*, for voices and orchestra
GLAZUNOV (37)
Symphony No 7
*Ballade*
NIELSEN (37)
*Saul and David*, opera

CILÈA (36)
*Adriana Lecouvreur*, opera
BANTOCK (34)
Tone Poem No 4, *Hudibras*
Tone Poem No 5, *Witch of Atlas*
Tone Poem No 6, *Lalla Rookh*
*The Time Spirit*, for chorus and orchestra
ROUSSEL (33)
Piano Trio
NOVÁK (32)
*In The Tatra Mountains*, symphonic poem
JONGEN (29)
*Fantaisie sur deux Noëls wallons*, for
    orchestra
Piano Quartet
RACHMANINOV (29)
*The Spring*, cantata
REGER (29)
Piano Quintet
Violin Sonata
HOLST (28)
*The Youth's Choice*, opera
SCHMIDT (28)
*Notre Dame*, opera
IVES (28–36)
Violin Sonata No 2 (1902–10)
COLERIDGE-TAYLOR (27)
*Meg Blane*, rhapsody for mezzo and chorus
HAHN (27)
*La Carmélite*, opera-comique
GLIÈRE (27)
String Sextet No 2
RAVEL (27)
*Alcyone*, cantata
WOLF-FERRARI (26)
*p* Piano Trio
*p* Violin Sonata
AUBERT (25)
*La Légende du Sang*
HOLBROOKE (24)
*Queen Mab*, for chorus and orchestra
SCHREKER (24)
*Romantische Suite* (unpublished)
*Ekkehard*, symphonic overture
*Phantastiche Ouverture* (unpublished)
*Schwanengesang*, for chorus and orchestra
BRIDGE (23)
*Berceuse*, for violin and small orchestra
RESPIGHI (23)
Piano Concerto
BARTÓK (21)
Scherzo for orchestra
ENESCO (21)
*Romanian Rhapsody No 2*
STRAVINSKY (20)
*Storm Cloud*, for voice and piano
*Scherzo* for piano

## 1903

BERKELEY, L., BLACHER,
KHACHATURIAN and RAINIER were
born; WOLF died
CHAUSSON (posthumous)
*fp Le Roi Arthus*
CUI (68)
Mlle Fifi, opera
BALAKIREV (66)
Ten songs
RIMSKY-KORSAKOV (59–61)
*The Invisible City of Kitezh*, opera (1903–5)
*Serenade*, for cello and piano
*Souvenir de trois chants polonaises*, for
    violin and orchestra
d'INDY (52)
*Choral Varié*, for saxophone and orchestra
ELGAR (46)
Symphony No 2 (*c*1903–10)
*The Apostles*, oratorio
PADEREWSKI (42)
Symphony (1903–7)
DEBUSSY (41)
*Le Diable dans le beffroi*, libretto and
    musical sketches
*Rhapsody*, for saxophone, contralto and
    orchestra (1903–5)
*Danse sacré et danse profane*, for harp and
    strings
*D'un cahier d'esquisses*, for piano
*Estampes*, for piano
DELIUS (41)
*Sea Drift*, for baritone, chorus and
    orchestra
GERMAN (41)
*A Princess of Kensington*, operetta
PARKER (40)
*Vathek*, symphonic poem
*The Eternal Feminine*, incidental music
    (lost)
d'ALBERT (39)
*Tiefland*, music drama
*Wie Wir die Natur erleben*, for voice and
    orchestra
DUKAS (38)
*Variations, Interlude and Finale on a Theme
    by Rameau*, for piano
NIELSEN (38)
*Helios*, overture
*Sunen*, for chorus and orchestra (1903-4)
SIBELIUS (38)
Violin Concerto
*Romance*, for strings
BUSONI (37)
Piano Concerto, with male chorus
    (1903–4)

**SATIE** (37)
*Trois morceaux en forme de poire*, for piano
  duet
**BANTOCK** (35)
Serenade for four horns
**ROUSSEL** (34)
*Resurrection*, for orchestra
Violin Sonata
**NOVÁK** (33)
*Slovac Suite*, for small orchestra
*Eternal Longing*, for orchestra
**SCHMITT** (33)
*Scherzo vif*, for violin and orchestra
**ZEMLINSKY** (32)
Symphony No 3
*Die Seejungfrau*, orchestral fantasy
**SKRIABIN** (31)
Symphony No 3, *Divine Poem*
**VAUGHAN WILLIAMS** (31)
*The House of Life*, song cycle
**RACHMANINOV** (30)
*Variations on a Theme by Chopin*, for piano
Ten Preludes for piano
**REGER** (30)
*Gesang der Verklarten*, for voice and
  orchestra
**HOLST** (29)
*Indra*, symphonic poem
*King Estmere*, for chorus and orchestra
Quintet for wind
**IVES** (29–34)
*Three Places in New England*, for orchestra
  (1903–14)
Violin Sonata No 1 (1903–8)
**SCHOENBERG** (29)
*Pelleas und Melisande*, suite for orchestra
**SUK** (29)
*Fantasy*, for violin and orchestra
**COLERIDGE-TAYLOR** (28)
*The Atonement*, oratorio
**RAVEL** (28)
*Schéhérezade*, song cycle with orchestra
*Alyssa*, cantata
String Quartet in F major
**BRIAN** (27)
*Burlesque*, variations and overture on an
  original theme for orchestra
*Legende*, for orchestra (lost)
'Shall I Compare Thee . . .', part song
**WOLF-FERRARI** (27)
*fp Le donne curiose*, opera
*p* Chamber Symphony
*La Vita nuova*, oratorio
**AUBERT** (26)
*La Momie*, ballet
**DOHNÁNYI** (26)
*p* String Quartet

*p* Cello Sonata
**HOLBROOKE** (25)
*The New Renaissance*, overture
*The Bells*, for chorus and orchestra
**CANTALOUBE** (24)
*Colloque Sentimentale*, for voices and string
  quartet
**SCOTT** (24)
Symphony No 2 (three symphonic dances)
**BARTÓK** (22)
*Kossuth*, tone poem
Violin Sonata
**ENESCO** (22)
Suite for orchestra
**CASELLA** (20)
*Variations sur une chaconne*, for piano

# 1904

**DALLAPICCOLA, KABALEVSKY** and
**SKALKOTTAS** were born; **DVOŘÁK**
died
**FAURÉ** (59)
Impromptu for harp
**d'INDY** (53)
Violin Sonata
**STANFORD** (52)
Violin Concerto No 1
Evening Service in G major
**JANÁČEK** (50)
*Osud (Fate)*, opera
**LIADOV** (49)
*Baba Yaga*, symphonic poem
**SINDING** (48)
*Hannamaal*, for male voices and orchestra
**PUCCINI** (46)
*Madam Butterfly*, opera
**MAHLER** (44)
Symphony No 6
**DEBUSSY** (42)
*La Mer*, three symphonic sketches
*L'isle joyeuse*, for piano
*Masques*, for piano
*Fêtes galantes*, songs (second series)
*Trois Chansons de France*
**DELIUS** (42)
*Koanga*, opera
**GERMAN** (42)
*Welsh Rhapsody*, for orchestra
**d'ALBERT** (40)
Two Songs with orchestra
*Mittelalterliche Venushymne*, for tenor, male
  chorus and orchestra
*An den Genius von Deutschland*, for soli and
  chorus
**ROPARTZ** (40)
Cello Sonata No 1

STRAUSS, R. (40)
*Symphonia Domestica*
GLAZUNOV (39)
Violin Concerto
SIBELIUS (39)
Symphony No 3 (1904–7)
*Kuolema*, incidental music (includes 'Valse
    Triste')
GIORDANO (37)
*Siberia*, opera
DAVIES, H. W. (35)
*Everyman*, oratorio
ROUSSEL (35–37)
Symphony No 1, *La poème de la forêt*
    (1904–6)
ZEMLINSKY (33)
*Der Traumgörge*, opera
ALFVÉN (32)
Swedish Rhapsody No 1, *Midsommervaka*
VAUGHAN WILLIAMS (32)
*Songs of Travel*
JONGEN (31)
*Lalla Rookh*, symphonic poem
REGER (31)
String Quartet
*Serenade*, for flute, violin and viola
*Variations and Fugue on a Theme of
    Beethoven*, for two pianos
String Trio
Cello Sonata
Violin Sonata
HOLST (30)
*The Mystic Trumpeter*, for soprano and
    orchestra
IVES (30)
Orchestra Set No 1 (1904–11)
*Thanksgiving and/or Father's Day* (Part 4 of
    *Holidays Symphony*)
SUK (30)
Symphony No 2 in C minor, *Asrael*
    (1904–6)
*Prague*, symphonic poem
GLIÈRE (29)
String Sextet No 3
BRIAN (28)
*For Valour*, concert overture
*Hero and Leander*, symphonic poem (lost)
Psalm 23, for tenor, chorus and orchestra
    (1904–5)
CARPENTER (28)
Improving Songs for Anxious Children
AUBERT (27)
*The Blue Forest*, opera (1904–10)
*Chrysothemis*, ballet
DOHNÁNYI (27)
p Serenade for string trio

HOLBROOKE (26)
*The Vikings*, symphonic poem
BRIDGE (25)
*Novelleten*, for string quartet
Violin Sonata
CANTALOUBE (25)
*Dans la montagne*, suite for violin and
    piano
HARTY (25)
Piano Quartet
BLOCH (24)
*Hiver*, symphonic poem (1904–5)
*Printemps*, symphonic poem (1904–5)
MEDTNER (24)
Nine songs (Goethe)
PIZZETTI (24)
Three Symphonic Preludes to *Oedipus Rex*
BARTÓK (23)
*Rhapsody*, for piano and orchestra
*Burlesca*, for orchestra
Piano Quintet
STRAVINSKY (22)
Sonata in F♯ minor for piano
Cantata (lost)
*The Mushrooms going to War*, for bass and
    piano
CASELLA (21)
Toccata for piano
TOCH (17)
Scherzo for orchestra
Piano Concerto (lost)

## 1905

ALWYN, BLITZSTEIN, LAMBERT,
RAWSTHORNE, SIEBER and TIPPETT
were born
BALAKIREV (68)
Piano Sonata in B minor
BRUCH (67)
Suite on a popular Russian melody
RIMSKY-KORSAKOV (61)
*fp* Orchestral Variations on a Russian
    people's song
WIDOR (61)
*Les Pêcheurs de Saint-Jean*, lyric drama
PARRY (57)
*The Clouds*, incidental music
d'INDY (54)
*Jour d'été à la montagne*, symphonic
    triptych
HUMPERDINCK (51)
*Die Heirat wieder Willen*, comic opera
MAHLER (45)
Symphony No 7 in E minor
*Kindertotenlieder*, song cycle for voice and
    orchestra

LOEFFLER (44)
*La Mort de Tintagiles*, symphonic poem for two viola d'amore and orchestra
*La Villanelle du Diable*, symphonic fantasy for organ and orchestra
*A Pagan poem*, for piano, English horn and three trumpets
DEBUSSY (43)
*Images*, for piano, Book I
DELIUS (43)
*A Mass of Life*, for solo voices, chorus and orchestra
MASCAGNI (42)
*Amica*, opera
d'ALBERT (41)
*Flauto Solo*, musical comedy
STRAUSS, R. (41)
*Salome*, opera
GLAZUNOV (40)
Symphony No 8
*Scène Dansante*
NIELSEN (40)
*Drømmen om 'Glade Tul'*, for piano
SIBELIUS (40)
*Pelléas et Mélisande*, incidental music
*Not With Lamentations*, for mixed voices
SATIE (39)
*Pousse l'amour*, operetta
ROUSSEL (36)
*Divertissement*, for piano and wind quartet
LEHÁR (35)
*The Merry Widow*, operetta
NOVÁK (35)
Serenade in D for small orchestra
ALFVÉN (33)
Symphony No 3 in E major
*En Skargardssagen*, symphonic poem
REGER (32)
Sinfonietta for orchestra
*Suite in the Old Style*, for violin and piano
HOLST (31)
*Song of the Night*, for violin and orchestra
SCHOENBERG (31)
String Quartet No 1
COLERIDGE-TAYLOR (30)
Five Choral Ballads
GLIÈRE (30)
String Quartet No 2
RAVEL (30)
*Miroirs*, for piano
Sonatina, for piano
BRIAN (29)
Psalm 137, for baritone, chorus and orchestra
HOLBROOKE (27)
*Les Hommages*, for orchestra

BRIDGE (26)
Piano Quintet
*Phantasie Quartet*
*Norse Legend*, for violin and piano
IRELAND (26)
*Songs of a Wayfarer*
RESPIGHI (26)
*Re Enzo*, comic opera
*Notturno*, for orchestra
Suite in G major for string orchestra and organ
*Burlesca*
BARTÓK (24)
Suite No 1 for orchestra
Suite No 2 for orchestra (revised 1943)
ENESCO (24)
Symphony No 1
*p* String Octet
STRAVINSKY (23)
Symphony in E♭ major (1905–7)
CASELLA (22)
Symphony No 1 (1905–6)
SZYMANOWSKI (22)
*Concert Overture*
WEBERN (22)
Quartet
BERG (20–3)
Seven 'Frühe Lieder', for soprano and piano or orchestra (1905–8)
WELLESZ (20)
*Sinfonischer Prolog*, for orchestra

# 1906

FRANKEL, SHOSTAKOVITCH, COOKE and LUTYENS were born
GRIEG (63)
*Moods*, for piano
RIMSKY-KORSAKOV (62)
*Le coq d'or*, opera (1906–7)
WIDOR (62)
Piano Concerto
FAURÉ (61)
Piano Quintet
*La chanson d'Eve*, song cycle (1906–10)
d'INDY (55)
*Souvenirs*, tone poem
LIADOV (51)
*Eight Popular Russian Songs*, for orchestra
ELGAR (49)
*The Wand of Youth*, suites for orchestra (final versions, 1906–7)
*The Kingdom*, oratorio
SMYTH (48)
*The Wreckers*, opera
ALBÉNIZ (46)
*Merlin*, opera

*Ibéria*, piano cycle (1906–9)
**DELIUS** (44)
Piano Concerto
**PARKER** (43)
*The Prince of India*, incidental music
**STRAUSS, R.** (42)
*Elektra*, opera (1906–8)
**DUKAS** (41)
*Villanelle*, for horn and piano
**NIELSEN** (41)
fp *Maskarade*, opera
String Quartet in F
**SIBELIUS** (41)
*Pohjola's Daughter*, symphonic fantasy
*The Liberated Queen*, cantata
**SATIE** (40)
*Passacaille*, for piano
*Prélude en tapisserie*, for piano
**BANTOCK** (38)
*Omar Khayyam*, for soli, chorus and
  orchestra
**NOVÁK** (36)
*Toman and the Wood-nymph*, symphonic
  poem
Six Male Choruses
**SCHMITT** (36)
*Sélamik*, for orchestra
**VAUGHAN WILLIAMS** (34)
*Norfolk Rhapsodies* Nos 1–3
**RACHMANINOV** (33)
*Francesca da Rimini*, opera
*The Miserly Knight*, opera
Fifteen songs
**REGER** (33)
*Serenade*
**HOLST** (32)
*Songs of the West*, for orchestra
Two *Songs Without Words*
**SCHOENBERG** (32)
Chamber Symphonies Nos 1 and 2
**IVES** (32)
*The Pond*, for flute, harp, piano and string
  quartet
**COLERIDGE-TAYLOR** (31)
*Kubla Khan*, rhapsody for mezzo and
  chorus
**RAVEL** (31)
Introduction and Allegro for harp, flute,
  clarinet and string quartet
**BRIAN** (30)
*First English Suite*
*Carmilham*, for contralto, chorus and
  orchestra
Psalm 68, for soprano, double chorus and
  orchestra (1906–7)
**WOLF-FERRARI** (30)
fp *School for Fathers*, opera

fp *I quatro (sic) rusteghi*, comedy-opera
**QUILTER** (29)
*To Julia*, song cycle
**HOLBROOKE** (28)
*Byron*, for chorus and orchestra
Variations on 'Auld Lang Syne', for
  orchestra
**BRIDGE** (27)
Three Idylls for string orchestra
String Quartet in E minor
Nine Miniatures for cello and piano
**IRELAND** (27)
Piano Trio No 1, *Phantasy Trio*
**BLOCH** (26)
*Poèmes d'Automne*, for voice and orchestra
**PIZZETTI** (26)
String Quartet
**STRAVINSKY** (24)
*Conductor and Tarantula*, for voice and
  piano (lost)
**KODÁLY** (24)
*Summer Evening*, for orchestra
**MALIPIERO** (24)
*Sinfonia del Mare*
**BAX** (23)
Piano Trio in E major
**BERG** (21–3)
Piano Sonata (1906–8)
**SCHOECK** (20)
*Serenade*, for small orchestra (1906–7)


## 1907

**MACONCHY** was born; **GRIEG** died
**CUI** (72)
*Matteo Falcone*, opera
**BALAKIREV** (70)
Symphony No 2 (1907–8)
**STANFORD** (55)
*Stabat Mater*
**MESSAGER** (54)
*Fortuno*, operetta
**ELGAR** (50)
Symphony No 1 (1907–8)
**IPPOLITOV-IVANOV** (48)
Symphony
**MAHLER** (47)
Symphony No 8, *Symphony of a Thousand*
**DEBUSSY** (45)
*Images*, for piano, Book II
**DELIUS** (45)
*A Village Romeo and Juliet*, opera
*Brigg Fair*, orchestral rhapsody
*Songs of Sunset*
**GERMAN** (45)
*Tom Jones*, operetta

PIERNÉ (44)
*Canzonetta*, for clarinet
d'ALBERT (43)
*Tragaldabas* comic opera
ROPARTZ (43)
*Pastorale and Dance*, for oboe and orchestra
Violin Sonata No 1
DUKAS (42)
*Ariadne and Bluebeard*, opera
GLAZUNOV (42)
*Canto di destino*, overture
NIELSEN (42)
*Saga-drøm*, for orchestra (1907–8)
SIBELIUS (42)
*Belshazzar's Feast*, suite for orchestra
*Night-ride and Sunrise*, tone poem
BUSONI (41)
*Elégien*, for piano
CILÈA (41)
*Gloria*, opera
BEACH (40)
*The Chambered Nautilus*, for chorus and
   orchestra
GIORDANO (40)
*Marcella*, opera
NOVÁK (37)
*Lady Godiva*, overture
SCHMITT (37)
*La Tragédie de Salomé*, ballet
ALFVÉN (35)
Swedish Rhapsody No 2, *Uppsalarapsodi*
VAUGHAN WILLIAMS (35)
*Towards the Unknown Region*, song for
   chorus and orchestra
*In the Fen Country*, symphonic impression
JONGEN (34)
*Félyane*, opera (unfinished)
RACHMANINOV (34)
Symphony No 2
*The Isle of the Dead*, symphonic poem
Piano Sonata No 1
REGER (34)
*Variations and Fugue on a Theme of Hiller*
HOLST (33)
*Somerset Rhapsody*, for orchestra
Nine Hymns from the Rig-Veda (1907–8)
SCHOENBERG (33)
String Quartet No 2
*Friede auf Erden*, for choir
SUK (33)
*A Summer Tale*, symphonic poem
GLIÈRE (32)
Symphony No 2
RAVEL (32)
'Sur l'herbe', song
*Rhapsodie espagnole*, for orchestra
*Pièce en forme de Habanera*

*Cinq mélodies populaires greques*, for voice
   and piano
BRIAN (31)
*The Vision of Cleopatra*, for soli, chorus and
   orchestra
*Fantastic Symphony* (revised 1912)
DOHNÁNYI (30)
p String Quartet in D major
QUILTER (30)
*Serenade*, for orchestra
HOLBROOKE (29)
*Apollo and the Seaman*, for orchestra
Piano Concerto No 1
BRIDGE (28)
*Isabella*, symphonic poem
Trio No 1 *Phantasie*
HARTY (28)
*Comedy Overture*
*Ode to a Nightingale*, for soprano and
   orchestra
RESPIGHI (28)
*Fantasy*, for piano and orchestra
String Quartet in D major
String Quartet in D minor
MEDTNER (27)
Three Songs (Heine)
BARTÓK (26)
Hungarian Folksongs, for piano
MIASKOVSKY (26)
Sonata No 1 for piano
GRAINGER (25)
*Molly on the shore*, for strings
STRAVINSKY (25)
*Faun and Shepherdess*, for mezzo and
   orchestra
Pastorale for soprano and piano
Symphony in E♭
Two Songs (1907–8)
TURINA (25)
Piano Quintet
BAX (24)
*Fatherland*, for two sopranos, chorus and
   orchestra
CASELLA (24)
Cello Sonata No 1
SZYMANOWSKI (24)
Symphony No 1
PROKOFIEV (16)
Piano Sonata No 1 (1907–9)
Four Pieces for piano (1907–11)


# 1908

CARTER and MESSIAEN were born;
RIMSKY-KORSAKOV, SARASATE and
MACDOWELL, died

GOLDMARK (78)
*A Winter's Tale*, opera
WIDOR (64)
*Sinfonia Sacra*, for organ and orchestra
FAURÉ (63)
*Sérénade*, for cello and piano
JANÁČEK (54–63)
*Mr Brouček's Excursion to the Moon*, opera
   (1908–17)
ALBÉNIZ (48)
*Navarra*, for piano
MAHLER (48)
*Das Lied von der Erde* (The Song of the
   Earth), song cycle with orchestra
DEBUSSY (46)
*Ibéria*, from *Images* for orchestra
*The Fall of the House of Usher* (sketched,
   uncompleted 1908–10)
*Children's Corner*, for piano
*Trois chansons de Charles d'Orléans*, for
   unaccompanied choir
DELIUS (46)
Dance Rhapsody No 1 for orchestra
*In a Summer Garden*, for orchestra
PIERNÉ (45)
*The Children of Bethlehem*, oratorio
NIELSEN (43)
Cantata for the Anniversary of
   Copenhagen University
SIBELIUS (43)
String Quartet in five movements, *Voces
   Intimae*
BUSONI (42–45)
*The Bridal Choice*, for orchestra (1908–11)
SATIE (42)
*Aperçus désagréables*, for piano duet
BEACH (41)
Piano Quintet
DAVIES, H. W. (39)
*Solemn Melody*, for organ and strings
NOVÁK (38)
*The Storm*, for soli, chorus and orchestra
   (1908–10)
ZEMLINSKY (37)
*Kleider machen Leute*, comic opera
SKRIABIN (36)
*Poem of Ecstacy*, for orchestra
VAUGHAN WILLIAMS (36)
String Quartet in G minor
REGER (35)
*Symphonic Prologue to a Tragedy*
Violin Concerto
Piano Trio
Sonata for clarinet or viola and piano
IVES (34)
*The Unanswered Question*, for small
   orchestra

HOLST (34)
*Savitri*, opera
Choral Hymns from the Rig-Veda, Group I
SCHOENBERG (34)
*Buch der hängenden Gärten*, setting of
   fifteen poems for voice and piano
GLIÈRE (33)
*The Sirens*, symphonic poem
HAHN (33)
*Promethée triomphant*, for soli, chorus and
   orchestra
*La Pastorale de Noël*, a Christmas Mystery
RAVEL (33)
*Gaspard de la nuit*, for piano
*Ma mère l'oye*, for piano
FALLA (32)
*Pièces espagnoles*, for piano
AUBERT (31)
*Crépuscles d'Automne*, song cycle
QUILTER (31)
*Songs of Sorrow*
CANTALOUBE (30)
*Eglogue d'automne*, for voices and orchestra
HOLBROOKE (30)
Dramatic Choral Symphony
SCHREKER (30)
*Der Geburstag der Infantin*, a pantomime
*Der Wind*, for clarinet and piano quartet
   (unpublished)
*Rokoko*, ballet
BRIDGE (29)
*Dance Rhapsody*, for orchestra
Suite for strings
RESPIGHI (29)
*Concerto in the Old Style*, for violin and
   orchestra
MEDTNER (28)
Twelve songs (Goethe)
BARTÓK (27)
*Portraits*, for orchestra (1907–8)
Violin Concerto No 1
String Quartet No 1 in A minor
MIASKOVSKY (27)
Symphony No 1
GRAINGER (26)
*Country Gardens*, for piano
KODÁLY (26)
String Quartet No 1
MALIPIERO (26)
Cello Sonata
STRAVINSKY (26)
*Chant Funèbre*, for wind instruments
*Fireworks*, for orchestra
*Scherzo Fantastique*, for orchestra
*Lament on the Death of Rimsky-Korsakov*,
   for chorus and orchestra
Four Studies for piano

*Le Rossignol*, opera (1908–14)
**BAX** (25)
*Lyrical Interlude*, for string quintet
**CASELLA** (25)
Symphony No 2 (1908–9)
Sarabande for piano or harp
**WEBERN** (25)
Passacaglia, for orchestra
*Entflieht auf Leichten Kahnan*, for chorus
Ten Lieder
**BERG** (23)
*An Leukon*, for voice and piano
**VILLA-LOBOS** (21)
*Recouli*, for small orchestra
**PROKOFIEV** (17–21)
Four Pieces for piano (1908–12)


# 1909

**HOLMBOE** and **SEIGMEISTER** were born; **ALBÉNIZ** and **TARREGA** died
**LIADOV** (54)
*The Enchanted Lake*, symphonic poem
**SINDING** (53)
*Kantate ved hundreaarsften*, for soli, chorus and orchestra
**ELGAR** (52)
*Elegy*, for string orchestra
Violin Concerto (*c*1909-10)
**IPPOLITOV-IVANOV** (50)
*Treachery*, opera
**MAHLER** (49)
Symphony No 9
**DEBUSSY** (47)
*Rondes de Printemps*, from *Images* for orchestra
Rhapsody, for clarinet and orchestra (1909-10)
*Petite pièce*, for clarinet and piano, in B♭ major
Préludes for piano, Book I (1909-10)
*Homage à Haydn*, for piano
*La plus que lente*, for piano
*Trois ballades de François Villon*, songs (1909-10)
*Le Promenoir des deux amants*, songs (1904-10)
**GERMAN** (47)
*Fallen Fairies*, comic opera
**d'ALBERT** (45)
*Izeÿl*, music drama
**STRAUSS, R.** (45)
*Der Rosenkavalier*, opera (1909-10)
**DUKAS** (44)
*Prélude élégiaque*, for piano
Vocalise

**GLAZUNOV** (44)
Symphony No 9 begun
**NIELSEN** (44)
Cantata for a Commemoration (unpublished)
Cantata for the National Exhibition at Århus (unpublished)
**BUSONI** (43)
*Berceuse élégiaque*, for orchestra
**LEHÁR** (39)
*The Count of Luxemburg*, operetta
**SKRIABIN** (38)
*Poem of Fire – Prometheus*, for orchestra, piano and chorus (1909–10)
**VAUGHAN WILLIAMS** (37)
*A Sea Symphony* (Symphony No 1), for soloists, chorus and orchestra
*The Wasps*, incidental music
*On Wenlock Edge*, song cycle
**JONGEN** (36)
Violin Sonata No 2
**RACHMANINOV** (36)
Piano Concerto No 3
**REGER** (36)
*The 100th Psalm*, for voice and orchestra
*Die Nonnen*, for voice and orchestra
String Quartet
**HOLST** (35)
First Suite for Military Band
*A Vision of Dame Christian*, incidental music
Choral Hymns from the Rig-Veda, Group 2
**SCHOENBERG** (35)
Five Pieces for orchestra (revised 1949)
*Erwartung*, monodrama for voice and orchestra
**COLERIDGE-TAYLOR** (34)
*Bon-Bon*, suite
**GLIÈRE** (34–36)
Symphony No 3, *Ilya Murometz* (1909-11)
**HAHN** (34)
*Le Bal de Béatrice d'Este*, ballet
**RAVEL** (34)
*Menuet sur le nom d'Haydn*, for piano
**FALLA** (33–39)
*Nights in the gardens of Spain*, for piano and orchestra (1909–15)
*Trois mélodies*, songs
**WOLF-FERRARI** (33)
*Susanna's Secret*, opera
**QUILTER** (32)
Seven Elizabethan Lyrics
**HOLBROOKE** (31)
*Pierrot and Pierrette*, opera
**BRIDGE** (30)
*Dance Poem*, for orchestra
**HARTY** (30)
Violin Concerto

**IRELAND** (30)
Violin Sonata No 1
**RESPIGHI** (30)
*Chaconne*, for violin, strings and organ
**PIZZETTI** (29–32)
*Phaedra*, opera (1909–12)
**BARTÓK** (28)
*For Children*, for piano
**KODÁLY** (27)
Cello Sonata (1909–10)
**BAX** (26)
*Enchanted Summer*, for tenor, chorus and
    orchestra
Christmas Carol
**CASELLA** (26)
*Italia*, orchestral rhapsody
Orchestral Suite in C major
*Notturnino*, for piano or harp
*Berceuse triste*, for piano
**SZYMANOWSKI** (26)
Symphony No 2
**WEBERN** (26)
Five Movements for string quartet
**BERG** (24)
Four songs (1909–10)
**BUTTERWORTH** (24)
'I Fear Thy Kisses', song
**DUPRÉ** (23)
Sonata for violin and piano
**PROKOFIEV** (18)
Sinfonietta (1909-14)
Two Poems for female voices and orchestra
    (1909–10)
Four Études for piano

## 1910

**BARBER, SCHUMAN** and **STILL** were
born; **BALAKIREV** died
**BALAKIREV** (73)
Suite on pieces by Chopin
**MASSENET** (68)
*Don Quixote*, opera
**FAURÉ** (65)
Nine Préludes
**HUMPERDINCK** (56)
*Königskinder*, opera
**LIADOV** (55)
*Dance of the Amazons*, for orchestra
*Kikimora*, symphonic poem
**SINDING** (54)
*Romanze*, for violin and orchestra
**ELGAR** (53)
*Romance*, for bassoon and orchestra
**PUCCINI** (52)
*Girl of the Golden West*, opera

**MAHLER** (50)
Symphony No 10 begun (left unfinished)
**PARKER** (47)
*Mona*, opera
**GLAZUNOV** (45)
*Cortège Solonnelle* in B flat for orchestra
**NIELSEN** (45)
Symphony No 3 *Espansiva* (1910–11)
*At a Young Artist's Bier*, for string quartet
**GIORDANO** (43)
*Mese Mariano*, opera
**ROUSSEL** (41)
*Evocations*, for orchestra (1910–11)
**ZEMLINSKY** (39)
*Psalm XXIII*, for voices and orchestra
**VAUGHAN WILLIAMS** (38)
*Fantasia on a Theme by Thomas Tallis*, for
    strings
**RACHMANINOV** (37)
*The Bells*, choral symphony
Thirteen Piano Preludes
*Liturgy of St John Chrystosum*
**REGER** (37)
Piano Concerto
Piano Quartet
Cello Sonata
String Sextet
**HOLST** (36)
*Beni Mora*, oriental suite for orchestra
*The Cloud Messenger*, ode
Choral Hymns for the Rig-Veda, Group 3
**IVES** (36–42)
Symphony No 4 (1910–16)
**SCHOENBERG** (36–39)
*Die Glückliche Hand*, music drama
    (1910–13)
**SUK** (36)
String Quartet No 2 (1910–11)
**COLERIDGE-TAYLOR** (35)
*Endymion's Dream*, for chorus
**HAHN** (35)
*La fête chez Thérèse*, ballet
**DOHNÁNYI** (33)
*Der Schlier der Pierette*, ballet
*p* Piano Quintet
**QUILTER** (33)
Three English Dances
Four Songs
**CANTALOUBE** (31)
*Vers la princesse lointaine*, symphonic poem
    (1910–11)
*Le Mas*, opera (1910–13)
**HARTY** (31)
*With the Wild Geese*, tone poem
**RESPIGHI** (31)
*Semirama*, lyric tragedy

**BLOCH** (30)
*fp Macbeth*, opera
**MEDTNER** (30)
Three Songs (Nietsche)
Violin Sonata
**BARTÓK** (29)
*Four Dirges*, for piano
*Deux Images*, for orchestra
**MIASKOVSKY** (29)
*Silence*, symphonic poem
**MALIPIERO** (28)
*Sinfonia del Silenzio e della Morte*
*Impressioni dal vero, I* (1910–11)
**STRAVINSKY** (28)
*The Firebird*, ballet
*Two poems of Verlaine*, for voice and piano
**BAX** (27)
*In the Faery Hills*, symphonic poem
Violin Sonata No 1 (1910–15)
**CASELLA** (27)
*Barcarola*, for piano
**WEBERN** (27)
Six Pieces for large orchestra
Four Pieces for violin and piano (1910–15)
**BERG** (25)
String Quartet
**VILLA-LOBOS** (23)
*Suite dos canticos sertanejos*, for small
    orchestra
**PROKOFIEV** (19)
*Dreams*, symphonic poem
*Autumnal Sketch*, for orchestra (revised
    1934)
*Deux poèmes*, for voice and piano (1910–11)
**MILHAUD** (18–23)
*La brèbis égarée*, opera (1910–15)
**KORNGOLD** (13)
Piano Trio (1910–13)

# 1911

**MENOTTI, GILDER** and **PETTERSSON**
were born; **MAHLER** died
**CUI** (76)
*The Captain's Daughter*, opera
*p* Violin Sonata
**BRUCH** (73)
*Konzertstücke*, for violin
**WIDOR** (67)
*Symphonie Antique*, for organ, chorus and
    orchestra
**STANFORD** (59)
Symphony No 7
**HUMPERDINCK** (57)
*The Miracle*, a pantomime
**SMYTH** (53)
*March of the Women*, for orchestra

*Three Songs of Sunrise*, for unaccompanied
    chorus
**DEBUSSY** (49)
*The Martyrdom of St Sebastian*, incidental
    music
**GERMAN** (49)
Coronation March and Hymn
**MASCAGNI** (48)
*Isabeau*, opera
**PARKER** (48)
*Collegiate Overture*, with male chorus
**ROPARTZ** (47)
*Serenade*, for string quartet (1911–12)
String Quartet No 2
**GLAZUNOV** (46)
Piano Concerto
**NIELSEN** (46)
Violin Concerto
**SIBELIUS** (46)
Symphony No 4
*Rakastava Suite*, for orchestra
*Canzonetta*, for strings
*Valse romantique*, for orchestra
**SATIE** (45)
*En habit de cheval*, for orchestra
**NOVÁK** (41)
*On Native Soil*, for eight male choruses
**VAUGHAN WILLIAMS** (39)
*Five Mystical Songs*, for baritone, chorus
    and orchestra
**JONGEN** (38)
*S'Arka*, ballet
Cello Sonata (1911–12)
**RACHMANINOV** (38)
*Six Études-Tableaux*, for piano
**REGER** (38)
*Eine Lustspielouverture*
*Die Weihe der Nacht*, for chorus and
    orchestra
String Quartet
Violin Sonata
**HOLST** (37)
*Invocations*, for cello and orchestra
*Hecuba's Lament*, for chorus and orchestra
Second Suite for Military Band
*Oh England My Country*, for choir and
    orchestra
**IVES** (37)
*Browning Overture*
*The Gong on the Hook and Ladder*, for small
    orchestra
*Tone-Roads*, No 1 for chamber orchestra
    (1911–15)
*Hallowe'en*, for piano and strings
**SCHMIDT** (37)
Symphony No 2 (1911–13)

444

SCHOENBERG (37)
*Herzgewächse,* for soprano, celesta,
  harmonium and harp
COLERIDGE-TAYLOR (36)
*Bamboula,* rhapsodic dance
Violin Concerto
*A Tale of Old Japan,* cantata
RAVEL (36)
*L'heure espagnole,* opera
*Valses nobles et sentimentales,* for piano or
  orchestra
BRIAN (35)
*In Memoriam,* symphonic poem
*Doctor Merryheart,* comedy overture for
  orchestra
WOLF-FERRARI (35)
*fp The Jewels of the Madonna,* opera
AUBERT (34)
*Nuit Mauresque* (possibly 1907)
QUILTER (34)
*Where the Rainbow Ends,* incidental music
Three Songs of the Sea
BRIDGE (32)
*The Sea,* for orchestra
BARTÓK (30)
*Duke Bluebeard's Castle,* opera
*Allegro barbaro,* for piano
Three Burlesques for piano
ENESCO (30)
Symphony No 2
MIASKOVSKY (30)
Sonata for cello and piano
Sinfonietta for small orchestra
Symphony No 2
PONCE (29)
*Trio Romantico,* for piano trio
STRAVINSKY (29)
*Petrushka,* ballet
*Two Poems of Balmont,* for voice and piano
*Zvedoliki,* for male chorus and orchestra
  (1911–12)
TURINA (29)
Quartet
WEBERN (28)
Five Pieces for orchestra (1911–13)
Two lieder
BUTTERWORTH (26)
'Requiescat', song
Two English Idylls for small orchestra
Six Songs from Housman's *A Shropshire
  Lad*
WELLESZ (26)
*Vorfrühling,* for orchestra
COATES (25)
Miniature Suite for orchestra
SCHOECK (25)
Violin Concerto (1911–12)

*Dithyrambe,* for double chorus and
  orchestra
*Erwin und Elmire,* incidental music
  (1911–16)
PROKOFIEV (20)
*Magdalene,* opera (1911–13)
Piano Concerto No 1 (1911–12)
MILHAUD (19)
Violin Sonata


# 1912

CAGE, GILLIS, JONES and FRANÇAIX
were born; COLERIDGE-TAYLOR and
MASSENET died
PARRY (64)
*Prosperina,* incidental music
Symphonic Fantasia
SINDING (56)
*Der heilige Berg,* opera
ELGAR (55)
*The Music Makers,* for contralto, chorus and
  orchestra
IPPOLITOV-IVANOV (53)
*The Spy,* opera
DEBUSSY (50)
*Jeux,* poème dansé for orchestra
*Khamma,* ballet
*Gigues,* from *Images* for orchestra
*Syrinx,* for solo flute
DELIUS (50)
*On Hearing the First Cuckoo in Spring,* for
  orchestra
*Song of the High Hills,* for wordless chorus
  and orchestra
*Summer Night on the River,* for orchestra
d'ALBERT (48)
*Die verschenkte Frau,* comic opera
ROPARTZ (48)
*Le Pays,* opera
*À Marie endormie,* for orchestra
*La Chasse du Prince Arthur,* for orchestra
STRAUSS, R. (48)
*Ariadne auf Naxos,* opera (first version)
DUKAS (47)
*La Péri, poème dansé,* for orchestra
NIELSEN (47)
Sonata No 2 for violin and piano
Paraphrase on 'Nearer My God to Thee',
  for wind (unpublished)
SIBELIUS (47)
*Scènes historiques,* Suite No 2 for orchestra
Two Serenades for violin (1912–13)
BUSONI (46)
*Nocturne Symphonique,* for orchestra

445

**SATIE** (46)
*Choses vues à droit et à gauche (sans lunettes)*, for violin and piano
**ROUSSEL** (43)
*The Spider's Feast*, ballet
**NOVÁK** (42)
Four Poems for chorus
*The Wedding Shift*, for soli, chorus and orchestra
**SCHMITT** (42)
*Le petit elf ferme-l'oeil*, ballet (1912–13)
**ALFVÉN** (40)
*Sten Sture*, cantata for male voices
**VAUGHAN WILLIAMS** (40)
Fantasia on Christmas Carols
*Phantasy Quintet*, for strings
**JONGEN** (39)
*Deux rondes wallons*, for orchestra
**RACHMANINOV** (39)
Fourteen Songs
**REGER** (39)
*A Romantic Suite*
*Konzert im Alten Stil*
*Romischer Triumphgesang*, for voice and orchestra
**HOLST** (38)
Choral Hymns from the Rig-Veda, Group 4
**IVES** (38)
*Decoration Day* (Part 2 of *Holidays Symphony*)
*Lincoln, the Great Commoner*, for chorus and orchestra
**SCHOENBERG** (38)
*Pierrot Lunaire*, song cycle
**GLIÈRE** (37)
*Chrysis*, ballet
**HAHN** (37)
*Le Bois sacré*, ballet-pantomime
*Le Dieu bleu*, ballet
**RAVEL** (37)
*Daphnis et Chloé*, ballet with chorus
**BRIAN** (36)
'Three Herrick Songs'
*The Pilgrimage to Kevlaar* (lost)
**CARPENTER** (36)
Violin Sonata
**HOLBROOKE** (34)
*The Children of Don*, opera
**BRIDGE** (33)
String Sextet
**IRELAND** (33)
*Greater Love Hath No Man*, motet
**BLOCH** (32)
*Israel Symphony*, for voices and orchestra (1912–16)
Prelude and Two Psalms for high voice (1912–14)

**MEDTNER** (32)
Three Nocturnes for piano and violin
**BARTÓK** (31)
Four Pieces for Orchestra
**MIASKOVSKY** (31)
Sonata No 2 for piano
**PONCE** (30)
Piano Concerto
**TURINA** (30)
*La Procesion del Rocio*, symphonic poem
**BAX** (29)
*Christmas Eve on the Mountains*, for orchestra
*Nympholept*, for orchestra
**CASELLA** (29)
*Le Couvent sur l'eau*, ballet (1912–13)
**SZYMANOWSKI** (29)
*Hagith*, opera (1912–13)
**GRIFFES** (28)
*The Pleasure Dome of Kubla Khan*, symphonic poem (1912–16)
*Tone Images*, for mezzo-soprano and piano
**GRUENBERG** (28)
Sonata for violin and piano
*The Witch of Brocken*, children's opera
**BERG** (27)
Five Orchestral Songs
**BUTTERWORTH** (27)
*A Shropshire Lad*, rhapsody for orchestra
*On Christmas Night*, for chorus
*We Get Up in the Morn*, arranged for male chorus
*In the Highlands*, arranged for female voices and piano
*p 'Love Blows as the Wind Blows'*, for baritone and string quartet
Eleven Folk Songs from Sussex
'Bredon Hill' and other songs
**TAYLOR** (27)
*The Siren Song*, for orchestra
**DUPRÉ** (26)
*Fantaisie*, for piano and orchestra
**RUGGLES** (26)
*The Sunken Bell*, opera (destroyed), (c1912–23)
**VILLA-LOBOS** (25)
*Aglaia*, opera
**PROKOFIEV** (21)
Piano Concerto No 2
*Ballade*, for cello and piano
Piano Sonata No 2
*Sarcasms*, for piano (1912–14)
Toccata in C major for piano
**MILHAUD** (20)
String Quartet No 1

**1913**

BRITTEN, GOULD, LLOYD and
LUTOSLAWSKI were born
**SAINT-SAËNS (78)**
*fp The Promised Land*, oratorio
**FAURÉ (68)**
*Pénélope*, opera
**CHARPENTIER (53)**
*Julien*, opera
**DEBUSSY (51)**
*La Boîte à Joujoux*, ballet music for piano
Preludes for piano, Book 2
*Trois poèmes de Stephane Mallarmé*, songs
**MASCAGNI (50)**
*Parisina*, opera
**ROPARTZ (49)**
*Dans l'ombre de la montagne*, for orchestra
*Soir sur les Chaumes*, for orchestra
**STRAUSS, R. (49)**
*Alpine Symphony*
**NIELSEN (48)**
*Canto Serioso*, for horn and piano
**SIBELIUS (48)**
*Scaramouche*, pantomime
*Il Bardo*, symphonic poem
**BUSONI (47)**
*Indian Fantasy*, for piano and orchestra
**CILÈA (47)**
*Il Canto della vita*, for voice, chorus and
 orchestra
**SATIE (47)**
*Le piège de Medusa*, operetta
*Chapitres tournés en tous sens*, for piano
*Croques et agarceries d'un gros bonhomme en
 bois*, for piano
*Descriptions automatiques*, for piano
*Embryons desséchés*, for piano
*Enfantines*, children's piano pieces
**NOVÁK (43)**
*The Zvikov Imp*, comic opera
**SCHMITT (43)**
*Rêves*, for orchestra (1913–15)
**VAUGHAN WILLIAMS (41)**
*A London Symphony* (Symphony No 2)
**JONGEN (40)**
*Impressions d'Ardennes*, for orchestra
**RACHMANINOV (40)**
Piano Sonata No 2
**REGER (40)**
*Vier Tondichtunger nach A. Böcklin*
*Eine Ballettsuite*
**HOLST (39)**
*St Paul's Suite*, for strings
*Hymn to Dionysus*, for choir and orchestra
**IVES (39)**
*The Fourth of July* (Part 3 of *Holidays
 Symphony*)

*Washington's Birthday* (Part 1 of *Holidays
 Symphony*)
*Over the Pavements*, for chamber
 orchestra
**FALLA (38)**
*fp La Vida Brève*, opera
**CARPENTER (37)**
*Gitanjali*, song cycle
**AUBERT (36)**
*Sillages*, three pieces for piano
**DOHNÁNYI (36)**
*Tante Simone*, opera
*p* Violin Sonata
**SCHREKER (35)**
*Das Spielwerk und die Prinzessin*, opera
*Die Gezeichneten*, opera (1913–15)
**CANTALOUBE (35)**
*Au Printemps*, for voice and orchestra
**HARTY (34)**
*The Mystic Trumpeter*, cantata
**IRELAND (34)**
*The Forgotten Rite*, for orchestra
*Decorations*, for piano
*Three Dances for piano*
*Three Songs*
**RESPIGHI (34)**
*Carnival*, overture
**SCOTT (34)**
Nativity Hymn, for chorus and orchestra
**BLOCH (33)**
*Trois Poèmes Juifs*, for orchestra
**MIASKOVSKY (32)**
*Alastor*, symphonic poem
**STRAVINSKY (31)**
*The Rite of Spring*, ballet
*Three Little Songs*, for voice and piano
Scherzo for orchestra
Three Japanese Lyrics
**BAX (30)**
Scherzo for orchestra
**CASELLA (30)**
*Notte di Maggio*, for voice and orchestra
**WEBERN (30)**
Six Bagatelles for string quartet
**GRUENBERG (29)**
*The Bride of the Gods*, opera
**BERG (28)**
Three Orchestral Pieces (1913–14)
Four Pieces for clarinet and piano
**BUTTERWORTH (28)**
*Banks of Green Willow*, idyll for orchestra
**VILLA-LOBOS (26)**
*Suite da terra*, for small orchestra
Suite for piano
**TOCH (26)**
*From My Fatherland*, for orchestra
**HOWELLS (21)**
Piano Concerto No 1

MILHAUD (21)
Suite Symphonique No 1 (1913–14)

## 1914

FINE, MELLERS and PANUFIK were
born; LIADOV died
PARRY (66)
Symphonic Poem
*The Acharnions*, incidental music
STANFORD (62)
*Irish Rhapsody* No 4
MESSAGER (61)
*Béatrice*, operetta
HUMPERDINCK (60)
*Die Marketenderin*, light opera
LIADOV (59)
*Naenia Dirae*
SINDING (58)
*Jubilaeumskantate*, for soli, chorus, and
    orchestra
ELGAR (57)
*p Sospiri*, for orchestra
*Carillon*, recitation with orchestra
DEBUSSY (52)
*Berceuse héroïque*, for piano
DELIUS (52)
*North Country Sketches*, for orchestra
PARKER (51)
*Fairyland*, opera
STRAUSS, R. (50)
*Die Frau ohne Schatten*, opera (1914–17)
*Josephs-Legende*, ballet
NIELSEN (49)
*Serenato in vano*, for five instruments
Symphony No 4 *The Inextinguishable*
    (1914–16)
SIBELIUS (49)
Symphony No 5 (1914–15)
*Oceanides*, symphonic poem
BUSONI (48–50)
*Arlecchino*, opera (1914–16)
SATIE (48)
*Cinq grimaces pour le 'Songe d'une nuit
    d'été'*, for orchestra
*Heures séculaires et instantées*, for piano
*Les Pantins dansent*, for piano
*Sports et divertissements*, for piano
*Trois valses du précieux dégoûte*, for piano
*Vieux sequins et veilles cuirasses*, for piano
NOVÁK (44)
*Karlštejn*, opera (1914–15)
SCHMITT (44)
*Dionysiaques*, for band (1914–25)
ZEMLINSKY (43)
*Cymbeline*, incidental music
String Quartet No 2

REGER (41)
*Eine Vaterländische Ouverture*
Piano Quartet
Piano Sonata
*Variations and Fugue on a Theme of Mozart*,
    for piano
Cello Sonata
Three Canons, Duets and Fugues in
    Ancient style for two violins
HOLST (40)
*The Planets*, suite for orchestra (1914–16)
IVES (40)
*Protests*, piano sonata
SUK (40)
*Meditation on a Theme of an old Bohemian
    Chorale*, for string quartet
RAVEL (39)
*Two Hebrew Songs*, for soprano and
    orchestra
Piano Trio in A minor
BRIAN (38)
*Red May*, march for brass band (lost)
*English Rhapsody* (lost)
Children's Operetta (lost)
QUILTER (37)
*A Children's Overture*
Four Child Songs
HOLBROOKE (36)
*Dylan*, opera
BRIDGE (35)
*Summer*, tone poem
CANTALOUBE (35)
*Triptyque*, for voice and orchestra
RESPIGHI (35)
Suite for strings and organ
PIZZETTI (34)
*Sinfonia del Fuoco*
BARTÓK (33)
*The Wooden Prince*, ballet (1914–16)
Fifteen Hungarian Peasant Songs
    (1914–17)
MIASKOVSKY (33)
Symphony No 3
KODÁLY (32)
Duo for violin and cello
MALIPIERO (32)
*Impressioni dal vero, II* (1914–15)
PONCE (32)
*Balada Mexicana*, for piano and orchestra
STRAVINSKY (32)
*Pribaoutki*, for voice and instruments
*Valse des fleurs*, for two pianos
Three Easy Pieces, for piano duet (1914–15)
*Les Noces*, dance scenes (1914–23)
Three Pieces for string quartet
TURINA (32)
*Margot*, lyric comedy

**BAX** (31)
Piano Quintet in G minor (1914–15)
**CASELLA** (31–34)
*Siciliana* and *Burlesca*, for piano trio
  (1914–17)
**WEBERN** (31)
Three Little Pieces for cello and piano
Four Lieder (1914–18)
**GRUENBERG** (30)
Suite for violin and piano
*Puppet Suite*, for orchestra
Piano Concerto No 1
**TAYLOR** (29)
*The Chambered Nautilus*, for chorus and
  orchestra
*The Highwayman*, for baritone, women's
  voices and orchestra
**WELLESZ** (29)
Suite for orchestra
**DUPRÉ** (28)
*Psyché*, cantata
**VILLA-LOBOS** (27)
*Izaht*, opera
*Ibericarabé*, symphonic poem
*Dansas dos Indios Mesticos*, for orchestra
Suite for strings
*Suite popular Brasiliera*, for guitar
**PROKOFIEV** (23)
Violin Concerto No 1
*Scythian Suite*, for orchestra (1914–15)
*The Ugly Duckling*, for voice and piano
**HOWELLS** (22)
*The Tinker's Song*, for two voices and piano
Variations for eleven instruments
**MILHAUD** (22)
String Quartet No 2 (1914–15)
Sonata for two violins and piano
*Printemps*, for violin and piano
**COWELL** (17)
*Vestiges*, for orchestra (1914–20)


## 1915

**DIAMOND** was born; **GOLDMARK** and
**SKRIABIN** died
**SAINT-SAËNS** (80)
*La Cendre rouge*, ten songs
**FAURÉ** (70–73)
*Le jardin clos*, songs (1915–18)
**PARRY** (67)
*An English Suite*, for orchestra
**STANFORD** (63)
Piano Concerto No 2
**JANÁČEK** (61)
*Taras Bulba*, rhapsody for orchestra
  (1915–18)

**SINDING** (59)
*Abendstimmung*, for violin and orchestra
**ELGAR** (58)
*Polonia*, symphonic prelude
*Une voix dans le désert*, recitation with
  orchestra
**DEBUSSY** (53)
Cello Sonata
*En blanc et noir*, for two pianos
*Six épigraphes antiques*, for piano
*Douze études*, for piano
*Noël des enfants*, for chorus
**ROPARTZ** (51)
*Divertissement No 1*
**BUSONI** (49)
*Indian Diary*
**SATIE** (49)
*Avant-dernières pensées*, for piano
**GIORDANO** (48)
*Madame Sans-Géne*, opera
**BANTOCK** (47)
*Hebridean Symphony*
**ZEMLINSKY** (44)
*Eine Florentinische Tragödie*, opera
**JONGEN** (42)
*Suites en deux parties*, for viola and
  orchestra
**RACHMANINOV** (42)
Vesper Mass
**REGER** (42)
*Der Einsiedler*, for chorus and orchestra
*Serenade*, for flute, violin, viola, or two
  violins and viola
String Trio
**HOLST** (41)
*Japanese Suite*, for orchestra
**IVES** (41)
Orchestral Set No 2
*Tone-Roads*, No 3 for chamber orchestra
*Concord*, piano sonata (1909–15)
**GLIÈRE** (40)
*Trizna*, symphonic poem
**RAVEL** (40)
Three Songs for unaccompanied choir
**BRIAN** (39)
English Suite No 2 (lost)
*Legend*, for orchestra (lost)
**CARPENTER** (39)
*Adventures in a Perambulator*, for
  orchestra
Concertino for piano and orchestra
**FALLA** (39)
fp *El Amor Brujo*, ballet
**DOHNÁNYI** (38)
Violin Concerto No 1
**HOLBROOKE** (37)
*The Enchanter*, opera

**BRIDGE** (36)
*The Open Air* and *The Story of My Heart*, poems for orchestra
*Lament*, for strings
String Quartet in G minor
**IRELAND** (36)
Preludes for piano
**RESPIGHI** (36)
*Sinfonia drammatica*
**SCOTT** (36)
Piano Concerto No 1
**BLOCH** (35)
*Schelomo*, for cello and orchestra (1915–16)
**PIZZETTI** (35–41)
*Deborah and Jael*, opera (1915–21)
**BARTÓK** (34)
Twenty Roumanian Christmas Songs for Piano
Roumanian Folk Dances for Piano
String Quartet No 2 in A minor (1915–17)
**ENESCO** (34)
Suite for orchestra
**KODÁLY** (33)
Sonata for unaccompanied cello
**STRAVINSKY** (33)
*Souvenir d'une Marche Boche*, for piano
*Berceuses du chat*, for voice and clarinets (1915–16)
*Trois histories pour enfants*, for voice and piano (1915–17)
**TURINA** (33)
*Evangelio*, symphonic poem
**BAX** (32)
Violin Sonata No 2
*Légende*, for violin and piano
*The Maiden with the Daffodils*, for piano
*Winter Waters*, for piano
**SZYMANOWSKI** (32)
Symphony No 3, *Song of the Night* (1915–16)
**WEBERN** (32–34)
Four Lieder (1915–17)
**GRIFFES** (31)
*Fantasy Pieces*, for piano
*Three Tone Pictures*, for piano
**COATES** (29)
*From the Countryside*, suite for orchestra
**SCHOECK** (29)
*Trommelschlage*, for chorus and orchestra
**VILLA-LOBOS** (28)
String Quartets Nos 1 and 2
**BLISS** (24)
Piano Quartet (c1915)
String Quartet (c1915)
**PROKOFIEV** (24)
*Chout*, ballet, revised 1920
*The Gambler*, opera, revised 1928

*Cinq poésies*, for voice and piano
*Visions fugitives*, for piano (1915–17)
**HOWELLS** (23)
Three Dances for violin and orchestra
**CASTELNUOVO-TEDESCO** (20)
*Copias*, for guitar
**HANSON** (19)
Prelude and Double Fugue for two pianos

## 1916

**BABBITT** and **GINASTERA** were born;
**BUTTERWORTH** (killed in action),
**GRANADOS** (drowned when the 'Sussex'
was torpedoed); **REGER** died
**d'INDY** (65–7)
*Sinfonia brève de ballo Gallico*
**STANFORD** (64)
*The Critic*, opera
**SMYTH** (58)
*The Boatswain's Mate*, opera
**IPPOLITOV-IVANOV** (57)
*Ole the Norseman*, opera
**LOEFFLER** (55)
*Hora Mystica*, symphony with men's voices
**DEBUSSY** (54)
*Ode à la France*, for chorus (1916–17)
Sonata for flute, viola and harp
**DELIUS** (54)
Dance Rhapsody No 2 for orchestra
Violin Concerto
**PARKER** (53)
*Cupid and Psyche*, a masque
*An Allegory of War and Peace*, for chorus and band
**d'ALBERT** (52)
*Die toten Augen*, opera
**NIELSEN** (51)
*Chaconne*, for piano
**SIBELIUS** (51)
*Everyman*, incidental music
**BUSONI** (50–58)
*Doktor Faust*, opera (1916–24)
**SATIE** (50)
*Parade*, ballet
*Trois mélodies*, songs
**GRANADOS** (48)
*Goyescas*, opera
**NOVÁK** (46)
*Strength and Defiance*, for six male choruse
**JONGEN** (43)
String Quartet No 2
**RACHMANINOV** (43)
*Neuf Études-Tableaux*, for piano (1916–17)
Six Songs

REGER (43)
Quintet in A major
SCHMIDT (42)
*Fredigundis*, opera (1916–21)
BRIAN (40)
Three Comic Dances for Orchestra (lost)
*Razamoff*, symphonic drama (lost)
DOHNÁNYI (39)
*Variations on a Nursery Song*, for piano and
  orchestra
QUILTER (39)
Three songs of William Blake
SCHREKER (38)
Chamber Symphony
BRIDGE (37)
'A Prayer', for chorus
SCOTT (37)
*La Dame sans Merci*, for baritone, chorus
  and orchestra
BLOCH (36)
String Quartet No 1
MEDTNER (36–38)
Piano Concerto No 1 (1916–18)
BARTÓK (35)
Suite for piano
GRAINGER (34)
*In a Nutshell*, suite for piano and orchestra
KODÁLY (34)
String Quartet No 2 (1916–17)
STRAVINSKY (34)
*Rénard*, a burlesque
*Valse pour les enfants*, for piano (1916–17)
TURINA (34)
*Navidad*, incidental music
BAX (33)
*Elegy*, trio for flute, viola and harp
*Ballade*, for violin and piano
*Dream in Exile*, for piano
CASELLA (33)
*Elegia eroica*, for orchestra
*Pagine di Guerra*, for orchestra
*Pupazzetti*, for nine instruments
GRIFFES (32)
*The Kairn of Koridwen*, dance drama
*Roman Sketches*, for orchestra
*Two Sketches on Indian Themes*, for string
  quartet
DUPRÉ (30)
Four Motets for chorus
Six Preludes for piano
Three Pieces for cello and piano
VILLA-LOBOS (29)
Symphony No 1, *The Unforeseen*
Three Symphonic Poems:
  *Centauro de Ouro*
  *Miremis*
  *Naufragio de Kleonica*

*Sinfonietta on a Theme by Mozart*
*Marcha religiosa* No 1, for orchestra
Cello Concerto
String Quartet No 3
BLISS (25)
Two Pieces for clarinet and piano
PROKOFIEV (25)
Symphony No 1, *Classical* (1916–17)
*Cinq poésies d'Anna Akhmatova*, for voice
  and piano
HONEGGER (24)
String Quartet No 1 (1916–18)
Violin Sonata (1916–18)
HOWELLS (24)
Suite, 'The B's', for orchestra
*Lady Audrey's Suite*, for string quartet
Piano Quartet
MILHAUD (24)
String Quartet No 3
HINDEMITH (21)
Cello Concerto No 1 (unpublished)
SOWERBY (21)
Woodwind Quintet
HANSON (20)
Symphonic Prelude
Piano Quintet
KORNGOLD (19)
*Der Ring des Polykrates*, opéra bouffe
TANSMAN (19)
Symphony No 1
WALTON (14)
Piano Quartet


# 1917

ARNELL was born; CUI died
FAURÉ (72)
Violin Sonata No 2
ELGAR (60)
fp *The Spirit of England*, for voices and
  orchestra
*Le Drapeau Belge*, recitation with orchestra
*Fringes of the Fleet*, song cycle
PUCCINI (59)
*La Rondine*, opera
DEBUSSY (55)
Violin Sonata
DELIUS (55)
*Eventyr*, for chorus and orchestra
MASCAGNI (54)
*Lodoletta*, opera
*Satanic Rhapsody*
ROPARTZ (53)
*Musiques au jardin*, for orchestra
Violin Sonata No 2
NIELSEN (52)
Theme and Variations for piano

Cantata for the Centenary of the
Merchant's Committee
*Pan and Syrinx,* for orchestra (1917–18)
**SIBELIUS** (52)
*Humoresques,* for violin and orchestra
**BUSONI** (51)
*Turandot,* opera
*Die Brautwahl,* orchestral suite
**JONGEN** (44)
*Tableaux pittoresques,* for orchestra
**HOLST** (43)
*Hymn of Jesus,* for chorus and orchestra
*A Dream of Christmas,* for female chorus,
piano and strings
**SUK** (43)
*Harvestide,* symphonic poem
**RAVEL** (42)
*Le Tombeau de Couperin,* for piano
**BRIAN** (41)
Comic Opera (revised 1925)
**CARPENTER** (41)
Symphony No 1
**AUBERT** (40)
*Tu es Patrus,* for chorus and organ
*Six poèmes Arabes* (possibly 1907)
**HOLBROOKE** (39)
Violin Concerto
**BRIDGE** (38)
Cello Sonata
**IRELAND** (38)
Violin Sonata No 2
Piano Trio No 2
*The Cost,* songs
**RESPIGHI** (38)
*The Fountains of Rome,* symphonic poem
*Old Airs and Dances for Lute,* transcribed
for orchestra, Series I
Violin Sonata in B minor
**SCOTT** (38)
*The Alchemist,* opera
**KODÁLY** (35)
Seven Piano Pieces (1917–18)
**MALIPIERO** (35)
*Armenia,* for orchestra
*Ditirambo Tragico*
**STRAVINSKY** (35)
Etude for pianola
Berceuse for voice and piano
*Chant du Rossignol,* symphonic poem
Five Easy Pieces for piano duet
*Chant des bateliers du Volga,* for wind and
percussion
Canons for two horns
**TURINA** (35)
*La Adultera penitente,* incidental music
**BAX** (34)
*Between Dusk and Dawn,* ballet

Symphonic Variations for piano and
orchestra
*November Woods,* symphonic poem
*Moy Well (An Irish Tone Poem),* for two
pianos
*Tintagel,* symphonic poem
*An Irish Elegy,* for English horn, harp and
strings
**SZYMANOWSKI** (34)
Violin Concerto No 1
String Quartet
**WEBERN** (34)
Six Lieder with instruments (1917–21)
Five Lieder (1917–22)
**GRIFFES** (33)
*Sho-Jo,* pantomimic drama
**BERG** (32)
*Wozzeck,* opera (1917–21)
**DUPRÉ** (31)
*De Profundis,* for soli, chorus, organ and
orchestra
**SCHOECK** (31)
*Don Ranudo de Colibrados,* comic opera
(1917–18)
**VILLA-LOBOS** (30)
*Amazonas,* ballet for orchestra
*Uirapurú,* ballet
Symphony No 2, *The Ascension*
Five Symphonic Poems:
*Fantasia*
*Lobishome*
*Iara*
*Saci Perêrê*
*Tedio de alvorada*
*Sexteto mistico,* for flute, clarinet,
saxophone, harp, celesta and double-
bass
String Quartet No 4
**PROKOFIEV** (26)
Piano Concerto No 3 (1917–21)
Piano Sonatas Nos 3 and 4
*Seven, they are seven,* for voices and
orchestra
**HOWELLS** (25)
Elegy for viola and string quartet
*Rhapsodic Quintet,* for clarinet and
string quartet
Suite, for clarinet and piano
*Puck's Minuet & Merry-Eye,* for orchestra
(1917–20)
**MILHAUD** (25)
Symphony No 1 for small orchestra, *Le
Printemps*
**WARLOCK** (23)
*An Old Song,* for small orchestra
**HINDEMITH** (22)
Three Pieces for cello and piano

SOWERBY (22)
Piano Concerto No 1 (revised 1919)
Serenade, for string quartet
*Comes Autumn Time*, for organ
HANSON (21)
*Symphonic Legend*
Concerto da camera for piano and string
    quartet
POULENC (18)
*Rapsodie nègre*, for cello, piano, flute and
    string quartet

# 1918

BERNSTEIN and ROCHBERG were born;
BOITO, DEBUSSY and PARRY died
SAINT-SAËNS (83)
*Fantasia* No 3 for organ
FAURÉ (73)
Cello Sonata No 1
*Une Châtelaine et sa tour*, for harp
d'INDY (67)
*Sarabande et Minuet*, for piano and
    instruments
ELGAR (61)
Piano Quintet in A minor (1918–19)
String Quartet in E minor
Violin Sonata in E minor
PUCCINI (60)
*Il Trittico*, three one-act operas:
    *Suor Angelica*
    *Il Tabarro*
    *Gianni Schicchi*
DELIUS (56)
*A Song Before Sunrise*, for small orchestra
d'ALBERT (54)
*Der Stier von Olivera*, opera
ROPARTZ (54)
Piano Trio
Cello Sonata No 2 (1918–19)
NIELSEN (53)
Three Compositions for piano
SIBELIUS (53)
*Our Native Land*, cantata for mixed voices
    and orchestra
SATIE (52)
*Socrates*, symphonic drama for four
    sopranos and chamber orchestra
BANTOCK (50)
*Pibroch*, for cello and piano or harp
NOVÁK (48)
Three Czech Songs for male chorus and
    orchestra
SCHMITT (48)
*Légende*, for violin, viola, sax and orchestra
ALFVÉN (46)
Symphony No 4 in C minor (1918–19)

JONGEN (45)
*p Sérénade Tendre*, for string quartet
*p Sérénade Triste*, for string quartet
CARPENTER (42)
Four Negro Songs
RUGGLES (42)
*Mood*, for violin and piano
SCHREKER (40)
*Der Schatzgräber*, opera
CANTALOUBE (39)
*L'Arlade*, six songs with piano
IRELAND (39)
*Leaves from a Child's Sketchbook*, for piano
RESPIGHI (39)
*Il Tramonto*, for mezzo-soprano and string
    quartet
BLOCH (38)
Suite for Viola (1918–19)
Suite for Viola and Piano (1918–19)
PIZZETTI (38)
Violin Sonata
BARTÓK (37)
*The Miraculous Mandarin*, ballet (1918–19)
MIASKOWSKY (37)
Symphonies Nos 4 and 5
GRAINGER (36)
*Children's March*, for piano
MALIPIERO (36)
*Pantea*, ballet
*L'Orfeide*, opera (1918–21)
*Grottesco*, for small orchestra
STRAVINSKY (36)
*L'historie du soldat*, for speakers, dancer
    and ensemble
Three Pieces for clarinet solo
*Lied ohne Name*, for two bassoons
*Ragtime*, for eleven instruments
Four Russian Songs (1918–19)
TURINA (36)
*Poema en forma de canciones*, for voice and
    piano
BAX (35)
String Quartet No 1 in G major
*Folk Tale*, for cello and piano
GRIFFES (34)
*Poem*, for flute and orchestra
Piano Sonata
TAYLOR (33)
*Portrait of a Lady*, for eleven instruments
SCHOECK (32)
*Das Wandbild*, scene and pantomime
VILLA-LOBOS (31)
*Jesus*, opera
*Vidapura*, oratorio
*Marcha religiosa*, Nos 3 and 7
MARTINŮ (28)
*Czech Rhapsody*, for chorus

**BLISS** (27)
*Madame Noy*, for soprano and instruments
**MILHAUD** (26)
*L'homme et son désir*, ballet
Symphony No 2 for small orchestra,
    *Pastorale*
Sonata for flute, oboe, clarinet and piano
String Quartet No 4
**HOWELLS** (26)
*Sir Patrick Spens*, for chorus and orchestra
*Phantasy*, for string quartet
Three Carol-anthems (1918–20)
Three sonatas for violin and piano
    (1918–23)
**ROGERS** (25)
String Quartet No 1
Free Variations and Fugue for string
    quartet
**HINDEMITH** (23)
String Quartet No 1
Violin Sonatas Nos 1 and 2
**GERHARD** (22)
Piano Trio
*L'Infantament Meravellos de Shahrazade*, for
    voice and piano
**COWELL** (21)
Symphony No 1
**POULENC** (19)
*Trois mouvements perpetuelles*, for piano
Sonata for piano (four hands)
Sonata for two clarinets
*Toréador*, songs (1918–32)


## 1919

**LEONCAVALLO** and **PARKER** died
**FAURÉ** (74)
*Fantaisie*, for piano and orchestra
*Mirages*, four songs
**MESSAGER** (66)
*Monsieur Beaucaire*, operetta
**HUMPERDINCK** (65)
*Gaudeamus*, musical scenes
**JANÁČEK** (65)
*Katya Kabanova*, opera (1919–21)
*The Diary of a Young Man who Disappeared*,
    song cycle
**ELGAR** (62)
Cello Concerto
**DELIUS** (57)
*Fennimore and Gerda*, opera
**GERMAN** (57)
Theme and Six Variations for orchestra
**PIERNÉ** (56)
Piano Quintet
Cello Sonata

**MASCAGNI** (56)
*Si*, opera
**d'ALBERT** (55)
*Revolutionshochzeit*, opera
**NIELSEN** (54)
Suite, *Den Luciferiske*, for piano
**SIBELIUS** (54)
*Song of the Earth*, cantata for mixed voices
    and orchestra
*Scène Pastorale*, for orchestra
**BUSONI** (53)
Concertino for clarinet and small orchestr
**SATIE** (53)
*Quatre petites pièces montées*, for small
    orchestra
*Nocturnes*, for piano
**BANTOCK** (51)
*Colleen*, viola sonata in F major
**ROUSSEL** (50)
Symphony No 2 (1919–21)
Impromptu for harp
**NOVÁK** (49)
*Lucerna*, musical fairy-tale (1919–22)
**JONGEN** (46)
*Poème héroïque*, for violin and orchestra
**HOLST** (45)
*Ode to Death*
*Festival Te Deum*
**IVES** (45–53)
Orchestral Set No 3 (1919–27)
**SUK** (45)
*Legend of Dead Victors*, for orchestra
*Towards a New Life*, for orchestra
**GLIÈRE** (44)
*Imitation of Jezekiel*, symphonic poem for
    narrator and orchestra
**HAHN** (44)
*Fête triomphale*, opera
*Nausica*, opéra-comique
**BRIAN** (43)
English Suite No 3
*Tales of Olden Times*, for small orchestra,
    (lost)
Symphony No 1, *Gothic*
**CARPENTER** (43)
*Birthday of the Infanta*, ballet
**FALLA** (43)
fp *The Three-Cornered Hat*, ballet
*Fantasia bética*, piano solo
**AUBERT** (42)
*La Habanera*, symphonic poem
**DOHNÁNYI** (42)
Suite in F♯ minor
**SCHREKER** (41)
*Irrelohe*, opera
**BRIDGE** (40–50)
*The Christmas Rose*, opera (1919–29)

**IRELAND** (40)
*The Holy Boy*, prelude for piano, later
   orchestrated
*Summer Evening*, for piano
**RESPIGHI** (40)
*La boutique fantasque*, ballet
**ENESCO** (38)
Symphony No 3 with organ and chorus
**KODÁLY** (37)
*Serenade*, for two violins and viola
**MALIPIERO** (37–39)
*Tre Commedie Goldiane*, opera (1919–21)
**STRAVINSKY** (37)
Piano-Rag-Music, for piano
*La Marseillaise*, for solo violin
**BAX** (36)
Harp Quintet in F minor
Piano Sonatas Nos 1 and 2
*What the Minstrel Told Us*, for piano
**BERNERS** (36)
Three Pieces for orchestra
**GRIFFES** (35)
Nocturnes for orchestra
**GRUENBERG** (35)
Sonata for violin and piano
*The Hill of Dreams*, for orchestra
Symphony No 1
**RIEGGER** (34)
Piano Trio
**TAYLOR** (34)
*Through the Looking-glass*, suite for
   chamber orchestra
**COATES** (33)
*Summer Days*, suite
**SCHOECK** (33)
*Venus*, opera (1919–20)
**VILLA-LOBOS** (32)
*Zoé*, opera
Symphony No 3, *The War*
Symphony No 4, *The Victory*
*Dansa frenetica*, for orchestra
**GURNEY** (29)
*The Apple Orchard*, for violin and piano
Five Preludes for piano (1919–20)
Scherzo for violin and piano (1919–20)
**BLISS** (28)
*As You Like It*, incidental music
*Rhapsody*, for solo voices and instruments
Piano Quintet (lost)
**PROKOFIEV** (28)
*The Love of Three Oranges*, opera
*The Fiery Angel*, opera
*Overture on Hebrew Themes*, for piano,
   clarinet and string quartet
**HONEGGER** (27)
Violin Sonata No 2
*Dance of the Goat*, for flute

**MILHAUD** (27)
Suite symphonique No 2, *Protée*
*Machines agricoles*, songs
**MOERAN** (25)
Three Piano Pieces
**HINDEMITH** (24)
Cello Sonata
Viola Sonata
Sonata for solo viola
**SOWERBY** (24)
Trio for flute, viola and piano
**HANSON** (23)
Symphonic Rhapsody
**KORNGOLD** (22)
*Much Ado About Nothing*, incidental music
**GERSHWIN** (21)
*Lullabye*, for string quartet
*La La Lucille*, musical
*Morris Gest Midnight Whirl*, musical
**POULENC** (20)
*Valse*, for piano
*Le Bestaire*, song cycle
*Cocardes*, songs
**KŘENEK** (19)
Serenade for piano, violin, viola and cello
Piano Sonata No 1
**SHOSTAKOVICH** (13)
Scherzo for orchestra
Eight Preludes for piano


# 1920

**BUSH, G., FRICKER** and **SHAPERO**
were born; **BRUCH** and **GRIFFES** died
**FAURÉ** (75)
*Masques et Bergamasques*, suite for
   orchestra
**d'INDY** (69)
*Le Poème de Rivages* (1920–1), symphonic
   suite
*Légende de St Christophe*, opera
**JANÁČEK** (66)
*Ballad of Blanik*, symphonic poem
**SMYTH** (62)
*Dreamings*, for chorus
**DELIUS** (58)
*Hassan*, incidental music
**PIERNÉ** (57)
*Paysages franciscains*, for orchestra
**SIBELIUS** (55)
*Hymn of the Earth*, cantata for mixed voices
*Valse lyrique*, for orchestra
*Valse chevaleresque*, for orchestra
**BUSONI** (54)
Divertimento for flute and orchestra
Sonatina No 6 for piano

SATIE (54)
*La belle excentrique*, for orchestra
*Premier minuet*, for piano
*Trois petites mélodies*, songs
BEACH (53)
Variations for flute and string quartet
SCHMITT (50)
*Antoine et Cléopatre*, incidental music
ZEMLINSKY (49)
*Der Zwerge*, opera
VAUGHAN WILLIAMS (48)
*Shepherd of the Delectable Mountains*, opera
   (1920–1)
*The Lark Ascending*, for violin and orchestra
Three Preludes for organ
*Suite de Ballet*, for flute and piano
Mass in G minor (1920–1)
RAVEL (45)
*La Valse*, choreographic poem for orchestra
Sonata for violin and cello (1920–2)
BRIAN (44)
Five Symphonic Dances
*Legend*, for violin and piano
CARPENTER (44)
*A Pilgrim Vision*, for orchestra
RUGGLES (44)
*Men and Angels*, for orchestra
DOHNÁNYI (43)
*Hitvallas*, for tenor, chorus and orchestra
IRELAND (41)
Piano Sonata
*Three London Pieces*, for piano
RESPIGHI (41)
*Scherzo Veneziano*, choreographic comedy
*Dance of the Gnomes*, for orchestra
BLOCH (40)
Violin Sonata No 1
BARTÓK (39)
Eight Improvisations on Peasant Songs
MIASKOVSKY (39)
Sonata No 3 for piano
MALIPIERO (38)
*Oriente immaginario*
STRAVINSKY (38)
*Pulcinella*, ballet
Symphonies for wind instruments
Concertino for string quartet
TURINA (38)
*Sinfonia Sevillana*
*Danzas fantasticas*
BAX (37)
*The Truth About Russian Dancers*, ballet
*The Garden of Fand*, symphonic poem
*Summer Music*, for orchestra
*Phantasy*, for viola and orchestra
Four Pieces for piano

BERNERS (37)
*Fantaisie Espagnole*, for orchestra
CASELLA (37)
Five Pieces for string quartet
SZYMANOWSKI (37)
*King Roger*, opera
GRUENBERG (36)
*Vagabondia*, for orchestra
TOCH (33)
*Phantastische Nachtmusik*, for orchestra
VILLA-LOBOS (33)
Symphony No 5, *The Peace*
*Dansa diabolica*, for orchestra
*Chôros No 1*, for guitar
GURNEY (30)
*Five Western Watercolours*, for piano
BLISS (29)
*The Tempest*, overture and interludes
   (1920–1)
Two Studies for orchestra
Concerto for piano, tenor voice, strings
   and percussion (revised as Concerto for
   two pianos and orchestra, 1924)
*Conversations*, for chamber orchestra
*Rout*, for soprano and chamber orchestra
   (revised for full orchestra 1921)
PROKOFIEV (29)
*Five Songs Without Words*, for voice and
   piano
HONEGGER (28)
*Pastorale d'été*, for orchestra
Viola Sonata
Cello Sonata
MILHAUD (28)
*Le boeuf sur le toit*, ballet
*Ballade*, for piano and orchestra
Five Studies for piano and orchestra
*Sérénade* (1920–1)
String Quartet No 5
*Printemps*, six pieces for piano
BENJAMIN (27)
*Three Impressions*, for voice and string
   quartet
MOERAN (26)
Theme and Variations for piano
Piano Trio in E minor
*Ludlow Town*, song cycle
CASTELNUOVO-TEDESCO (25)
*La Mandragola*, opera (1920–3)
*Cipressi*, for guitar
SOWERBY (25)
Cello Sonata
*The Edge of Dreams*, song cycle
HANSON (24)
*Before the Dawn*, symphonic poem
*Exaltation*, symphonic poem

COWELL (23)
*Communication*, for orchestra
KORNGOLD (23)
*The Dead City*, opera
GERSHWIN (22)
*George White's Scandals of 1920*, musical
*Broadway Brevities of 1920*
AURIC (21)
*Les Mariés de la Tour Eiffel*, ballet
CHÁVEZ (21)
Symphony
Piano Sonata No 1
POULENC (21)
*Cinq impromptus*, for piano
*Suite in C major*, for piano
SHOSTAKOVICH (14)
Five Preludes for piano

## 1921

ARNOLD, SIMPSON and SHAPEY were
born; SAINT-SAËNS and
HUMPERDINCK died
FAURÉ (76)
Piano Quintet No 2
JANÁČEK (67)
Violin Sonata
MASCAGNI (58)
*Il Piccolo Marat*, opera
d'ALBERT (57)
*Sirocco*, opera
STRAUSS, R. (57)
*Schlagobers*, ballet
DUKAS (56)
*La Plainte, au loin, du faune*, for piano
NIELSEN (56)
*Springtime in Fyn*, for soprano, tenor, bass
  and orchestra
Symphony No 5 (1921–2)
SIBELIUS (56)
*Suite mignonne*, for flute and strings
*Suite champêtre*, for strings
BUSONI (55)
*Elegy*, for clarinet and piano
Romance and Scherzo for piano
GIORDANO (54)
*Giove a Pompeii*
VAUGHAN WILLIAMS (49)
*A Pastoral Symphony* (Symphony No 3)
HOLST (47)
*The Perfect Fool*, opera
*The Lure*, ballet
GLIÈRE (46)
*Cossacks of Zaporozh*, symphonic poem
HAHN (46)
*La Colombe de Bouddha*, conte lyrique

BRIAN (45)
English Suite No 4
CARPENTER (45)
*Krazy Kat*, ballet
FALLA (45)
*Homage pour le tombeau de Debussy*, for
  guitar
AUBERT (44)
*Dryade*, symphonic poem
QUILTER (44)
Three Pastoral Songs
Five Shakespeare Songs
IRELAND (42)
*Mai-Dun*, symphonic rhapsody
*Land of Lost Content*, song cycle
RESPIGHI (42)
*Adagio with Variations*, for cello and
  orchestra
BLOCH (41–43)
Piano Quintet (1921–3)
MEDTNER (41)
Sonata-Vocalise No 1
PIZZETTI (41)
Cello Sonata
BARTÓK (40)
Violin Sonata No 1 (Atonal)
ENESCO (40)
*Oedipus*, opera (begun *c*1921)
Violin Concerto
MALIPIERO (39)
*Impressioni dal vero, III* (1921–2)
STRAVINSKY (39)
Suite No 2 for chamber orchestra
*Les cinq doigts*, for piano
TURINA (39)
*Canto a Sevillana*, song cycle
BAX (38)
Symphony No 1 (1921–2)
*Of a Rose I Sing*, for small chorus, harp,
  cello and double-bass
Viola Sonata
*Mater Ora Filium*, for unaccompanied
  chorus
CASELLA (38)
*A Notte alta*, for orchestra
VARÈSE (36)
*Offrandes*, for soprano, chorus and
  orchestra
WELLESZ (36)
*Die Prinzessin Girnara*, opera
DUPRÉ (35)
Four Pieces for piano
VILLA-LOBOS (34)
*Malazarte*, opera
Quartet for harp, celesta, flute and
  saxophone, with women's voices

457

MARTINŮ (31)
*Istar*, ballet
BLISS (30)
*A Colour Symphony* (1921–2, revised 1932)
*Mêlée fantasque*, for orchestra (revised 1965)
PROKOFIEV (30)
Five Songs
HONEGGER (29)
*Horace Victorieux*, 'mimed symphony'
Sonatina for clarinet and piano (1921–2)
*King David*, oratorio
MILHAUD (29)
Symphony No 3 for small orchestra, *Sérénade*
Symphony No 4 for strings, *Ouverture, Chorale, Etude*
*Saudades de Brasil*, dance suite for orchestra
MOERAN (27)
*In the Mountain Country*, symphonic impression
*On a May Morning*, for piano
HINDEMITH (26)
*Chamber Music* No 1 (1921–2)
SOWERBY (26)
Symphony No 1
Violin Sonata No 1
CASTELNUOVO-TEDESCO (25)
Thirty-three Shakespeare Songs (1921–5)
HANSON (25)
Concerto for organ, strings and harp
GERSHWIN (23)
*A Dangerous Maid*, musical
*George White's Scandals of 1921*, musical
CHÁVEZ (22)
*El Fuego Neuvo*, ballet
String Quartet No 1
POULENC (22)
*La Baigneuse . . .*, for orchestra
KŘENEK (21)
Symphony No 1
String Quartets Nos 1 and 2
WEILL (21)
Symphony No 1
RUBBRA (20)
*The Secret Hymnody*, for chorus and orchestra
SHOSTAKOVICH (15)
Theme with Variations for orchestra

## 1922

FOSS, HAMILTON and XENAKIS born
FAURÉ (77)
Cello Sonata No 2
*L'horizon chimérique*, songs

d'INDY (71)
*Le Rêve de Cynias*, lyric comedy (1922–3)
DELIUS (60)
*A Pagan Requiem* (possibly 1914–16)
STRAUSS, R. (58)
*Intermezzo*, opera (1922–3)
NIELSEN (57)
*Hyldest til Holberg*, for solo voices, chorus and orchestra
Wind Quintet
SIBELIUS (57)
*Suite caractéristique*
BANTOCK (54)
*Song of Songs*, for soli, chorus and orchestra
NOVÁK (52)
*Grandfather's Legacy*, opera (1922–5)
JONGEN (49)
*Rhapsody*, for piano and instruments
HOLST (48)
Fugal Overture No 1
SCHMIDT (48)
Romance for piano
GLIÈRE (47)
*Comedians*, ballet (also in 1930)
RAVEL (47)
*Berceuse sur le nom Fauré*
FALLA (46)
*El Retablo de Maese Pedro*, opera
Seven Spanish Popular Songs
DOHNÁNYI (45)
*The Tower of the Voivod*, romantic opera
QUILTER (45)
*As You Like It*, incidental music
BRIDGE (43)
*Sir Roger de Coverley*, for string quartet or orchestra
Piano Sonata (1922–5)
RESPIGHI (43)
*The Sleeping Beauty*, musical fable
*Concerto Gregoriano*, for violin and orchestra
BLOCH (42)
*In the Night*, for piano
*Poems of the Sea*, for piano (1922–4)
PIZZETTI (42)
*Lo straniero*, opera
Requiem
BARTÓK (41)
Violin Sonata No 2
MIASKOVSKY (41)
*Fancies*, six pieces for piano
GRAINGER (40)
*Shepherd's Hey*, for orchestral solo piano/wind band
STRAVINSKY (40)
*Mavra*, opéra bouffe

BAX (39)
*The Happy Forest*, symphonic poem
GRUENBERG (38)
*Four Indiscretions*, for string quartet
*Four Bagatelles*, for cello and piano
*The Sleeping Beauty*, children's opera
COATES (36)
*Joyous Youth*, suite
*The Merrymakers*, overture
SCHOECK (36)
*Élégie*, song cycle (1922–3)
IBERT (32)
*Ballad of Reading Gaol*, ballet
*Ports of Call (Escales)*, orchestral suite
MARTINŮ (32)
Three Symphonic poems:
  *The Grove of Satyrs*
  *Shadows*
  *Vanishing Midnight*
HOWELLS (30)
*Sine Nomine*, for two voices, chorus and
  orchestra
*Procession*, for orchestra
MILHAUD (30)
*La création du monde*, ballet (1922–3)
Symphony No 5, for small wind orchestra
Three *Rag-Caprices*
String Quartet No 6
ROGERS (29)
*Diedre*, opera
MOERAN (28)
Rhapsody No 1
*Three Fancies*, for piano
WARLOCK (28)
*Serenade for Frederick Delius*, for orchestra
HINDEMITH (27)
String Quartets Nos 2 and 3
Suite for klavier
Sonata for solo viola
*Die Junge Magd*, song cycle
SOWERBY (27)
*Ballad of King Estmere*, for two pianos and
  orchestra
*From the Northlands*, for piano
GERHARD (26)
*Seven Haï-Ku*, for voice and five
  instruments
HANSON (26)
Symphony No 1, *Nordic*
COWELL (25)
*The Building of Banba*, ballet
TANSMAN (25)
*Sextuor*, ballet
GERSHWIN (24)
*George White's Scandals of 1922*, musical
*Blue Monday Blues* (also called *135th Street*),
  opera

*Our Nell*, musical
POULENC (23)
Sonata for clarinet and bassoon
Sonata for trumpet, horn and trombone
*Chanson à boire*, for a cappella male choir
THOMPSON, R. (23)
*Pierrot and Cathurnis*, orchestral prelude
ANTHEIL (22)
Symphony No 1
*Airplane Sonata*, for piano
*Sonata Sauvage*, for piano
KŘENEK (22)
*Die Zwingburg*, opera
Symphonic Music, for nine instruments
Symphonies Nos 2 and 3
WALTON (20)
*fp* (privately) *Façade*, for reciter and
  chamber ensemble
SHOSTAKOVICH (16)
*Two Fables of Krilov*, for mezzo-soprano
  and orchestra
Suite in F♯ minor for two pianos
*Three Fantastic Dances*, for piano

## 1923

LIGETI and MENNIN were born
FAURÉ (78)
Piano Trio
JANÁČEK (69)
String Quartet No 1
ELGAR (66)
*fp King Arthur*, incidental music
SMYTH (65)
*Fête galante*, opera
*Soul's Joy*, for unaccompanied chorus
IPPOLITOV-IVANOV (64)
*Mtzyry*, symphonic poem (1923–4)
LOEFFLER (62)
'Avant que tu ne t'en ailles', poem
PIERNÉ (60)
*Cydalise and the Satyr*, ballet
d'ALBERT (59)
*Mareika von Nymwegen*, opera
NIELSEN (58)
Prelude and Theme with Variations for
  violin
SIBELIUS (58)
Symphony No 6
SATIE (57)
*Ludions*, songs
BUSONI (56)
Ten Variations on a Chopin prelude
BANTOCK (55)
*Pagan Symphony*
SCHMITT (53)
*Kermesse*, waltz for orchestra (1923–4)

ZEMLINSKY (52)
*Lyrische Symphonie*, for soprano, baritone
  and orchestra
String Quartet No 3
ALFVÉN (51)
*Bergakungen*, pantomime drama
VAUGHAN WILLIAMS (51)
*Old King Cole*, ballet
HOLST (49)
Choral Symphony (1923–4)
Fugal Overture No 2
SCHMIDT (49)
Piano Concerto No 1
SCHOENBERG (49)
Serenade for septet and baritone
HAHN (48)
*Aboulette*, operetta
GLIÈRE (48–50)
*Shahk-Senem*, opera (1923–5)
FALLA (47–50)
Concerto for harpsichord, flute, oboe,
  clarinet, violin and cello (1923–6)
RUGGLES (47)
*Vox clamans in deserto*, for small orchestra
AUBERT (46)
*La Nuit ensorcelée*, ballet
IRELAND (44)
Cello Sonata
SCOTT (44)
*The Incompetent Apothecary*, ballet
RESPIGHI (44)
*Belfagor*, lyric comedy
*La Primavera*, lyric poem for soloists,
  chorus and orchestra
BLOCH (43)
*Baal Shem*, for violin and piano
*Melody*, for violin and piano
*Enfantines*, for piano
*Five Sketches in Sepia*, for piano
*Nirvana*, for piano
BARTÓK (42)
Dance Suite for Orchestra
MIASKOVSKY (42)
Symphonies Nos 6 and 7
KODÁLY (41)
*Psalmus Hungaricus*, for tenor, chorus and
  orchestra
PONCE (41)
*Estampas Nocturnas*, for orchestra
STRAVINSKY (41)
Octet for wind instruments
TURINA (41)
*Jardin d' Oriente*, opera
BAX (40)
*Romantic Overture*, for small orchestra
*Saga Fragment*, for piano, strings, trumpet
  and cymbals

Piano Quartet
Oboe Quintet in G
Cello Sonata in E minor
CASELLA (40)
Concerto for string quartet (1923–4)
BERG (38–40)
Chamber Concerto (1923–5)
TAYLOR (38)
*A Kiss in Xanadu*, pantomime for two
  pianos
VARÈSE (38)
*Hyperprism*, for small orchestra and
  percussion
*Octandre*, for small orchestra and
  percussion
*Intégrales*, for chamber orchestra and
  percussion
VILLA-LOBOS (36)
Suite for voice and viola
BLISS (32)
String Quartet (1923–4) (lost)
*Ballads of the Four Seasons*, song cycle
*The Women of Yueh*, song cycle
PROKOFIEV (32)
Piano Sonata No 5
HONEGGER (31)
*Chant de joie*
HOWELLS (31)
*Pastoral Rhapsody*, for orchestra
String Quartet, 'In Gloucestershire'
Six Choral Songs (1923–5)
MILHAUD (31)
Symphony No 6 for soprano, contralto,
  tenor and bass soli, oboe and cello
WARLOCK (29)
*The Curlew*, song cycle
HINDEMITH (28)
String Quartet No 4
*Kleine Sonata für Viola d'amore und
  Klavier*
Sonata for solo cello
HANSON (27)
*North and West*, symphonic poem
*Lux Aeterna*, symphonic poem with viola
  obbligato
String Quartet
ROBERTSON (27)
*Endicott Overture*
SESSIONS (27)
*The Black Maskers*, incidental music
THOMSON, V. (27)
*Two Sentimental Tangos*
GERSHWIN (25)
*The Rainbow*, musical
*George White's Scandals of 1923*, musical
AURIC (24)
*Les Fâcheux*, ballet

CHÁVEZ (24)
Piano Sonata No 2
POULENC (24)
*Les Biches*, ballet
ANTHEIL (23)
Violin Sonata No 1
*Ballet Mécanique* (1923–4, revised 1953)
BUSH, A. (23)
String Quartet
COPLAND (23)
*As It Fell Upon A Day*, for soprano, flute
    and clarinet
KŘENEK (23)
*Der Sprung über den Schatten*, opera
*Orpheus und Eurydike*, opera
Piano Concerto No 1
String Quartets Nos 3 and 4
WEILL (23)
*Fantasie, Passacaglia and Hymnus*, for
    orchestra
WALTON (21)
String Quartet (withdrawn)
SHOSTAKOVICH (17)
Piano Trio No 1


# 1924

BANKS and NONO were born;
BUSONI, FAURÉ, PUCCINI and
STANFORD died
WIDOR (80)
*Nerto*, lyric drama
FAURÉ (79)
String Quartet
d'INDY (73)
Piano Quintet
JANÁČEK (70)
*The Cunning Little Vixen*, opera
*The Makropoulos Affair*, opera (1924–6)
*Miade* (Youth), suite for wind
ELGAR (67)
*fp Pageant of Empire*, for chorus and
    orchestra
d'ALBERT (60)
*Aschenputtel*, orchestral suite
Symphonic Prelude to *Tiefland*
ROPARTZ (60)
String Quartet No 3 (1924–5)
STRAUSS, R. (60–63)
*The Egyptian Helen*, opera (1924–7)
DUKAS (59)
*Sonnet de Ronsard*, for voice and piano
NIELSEN (59)
Symphony No 6, *The Simple* (1924–5)
SIBELIUS (59)
Symphony No 7

SATIE (58)
*Mercure*, ballet
*Relâche*, ballet
GIORDANO (57)
*Le Cena delle Beffe*, opera
BANTOCK (56)
*The Seal-woman*, opera
SCHMITT (54)
*Fonctionnaire M.C.XII*, for orchestra
VAUGHAN WILLIAMS (52)
*Hugh the Drover*, opera
HOLST (50)
*At The Boar's Head*, opera
*Terzetto*, for flute, oboe and viola
SCHMIDT (50)
Fantasy and Fugue for organ
Toccata for organ
Prelude and Fugue for organ
SCHOENBERG (50)
Quintet for wind
GLIÈRE (49)
Two Poems for soprano and orchestra
*For the Festival of the Comintern*, fantasy for
    wind orchestra
*March of the Red Army*, for wind orchestra
RAVEL (49)
*Tzigane*, for violin and piano
RUGGLES (48)
*Men and Mountains*, for orchestra
SCHREKER (46)
*Christophorus*, opera
*Der Singende Teufel*, opera
HARTY (45)
*Irish Symphony*
RESPIGHI (45)
*Concerto in the Mixo-Lydian Mode*, for
    orchestra
*The Pines of Rome*, symphonic poem
*Old Airs and Dances for Lute*, Series II
String Quartet, *Doric*
BLOCH (44)
Concerto Grosso for strings with piano
    obbligato (1924–5)
*In The Mountains (Haute Savoie)*, for string
    quartet
*Night*, for string quartet
*Three Landscapes*, for string quartet
Three Nocturnes, for piano trio
Violin Sonata No 2, *Poème mystique*
*Exotic Night*, for violin and piano
*From Jewish Life*, for cello and piano
*Méditation Hébraïque*, for cello and piano
MEDTNER (44)
Violin Sonata
BARTÓK (43)
*Five Village Scenes*, for female voice and
    piano

STRAVINSKY (42)
Serenade in A for piano
Concerto for piano and wind
Piano Sonata
BAX (41)
Symphony No 2 (1924–5)
*Cortège*, for orchestra
String Quartet No 2 in E minor (1924–5)
BERNERS (41)
*Le Carrosse du St Sacrement*, opera
CASELLA (41)
*La Giara*, ballet
Partita, for piano (1924–5)
SZYMANOWSKI (41)
*Prince Potemkin*, incidental music
WEBERN (41)
Five Canons for voice, clarinet and
 bass-clarinet
Six Volkstexte
WELLESZ (39)
*Das Wunder der Diana*, ballet
*Persisches Ballett*
*Alkestis*, opera
*Die Nachtlichen*, ballet
DUPRÉ (38)
Variations for piano
SCHOECK (38)
*Penthesiles*, opera (1924–5)
VILLA-LOBOS (37)
*Choros* Nos 2 and 7
BLISS (33)
*Masks I–IV*, for piano
PROKOFIEV (33)
Symphony No 2 (1924–5)
Quintet for oboe, clarinet, violin, viola and
 double-bass
HONEGGER (32)
*Pacific 231*, Mouvement Symphonique
 No 1 for orchestra
HOWELLS (32)
Piano Concerto No 2
MILHAUD (32)
*Les malheurs d'Orphée*, opera
*Esther de Carpentras*, comic opera (1924–5)
*Le Train Bleu*, ballet
BENJAMIN (31)
*Pastoral Fantasy*, for string quartet
Sonatina for violin and piano
MOORE (31)
*The Pageant of P. T. Barnum*, suite for
 orchestra
MOERAN (30)
Rhapsody No 2
HINDEMITH (29)
Piano Concerto
*Chamber Music* No 2
Sonata for solo violin

*Das Marienleben*, song cycle
SOWERBY (29)
*Synconata*, for jazz orchestra
COWELL (27)
*Ensemble*, for chamber orchestra
TANSMAN (27)
Sinfonietta
GERSHWIN (26)
*Rhapsody in Blue* (arr Grofé), for piano
 and orchestra
*Sweet Little Devil*, musical
*George White's Scandals of 1924*, musical
*Primrose*, musical
*Lady, Be Good*, musical (including song
 'Fascinating Rhythm')
AURIC (25)
Chamber Suite
*Les Matelots*, ballet
CHÁVEZ (25)
Sonatina for violin and piano
Sonatina for cello and piano
POULENC (25)
*Promenade*, for piano
*Poèmes de Ronsard* (1924–5)
THOMPSON, R. (25)
*The Piper at the Gates of Dawn*, orchestral
 prelude
*The Wind in the Willows*, for string quartet
BUSH, A. (24)
Piano Quartet
Five Pieces for clarinet, horn and string
 quartet (1924–5)
COPLAND (24)
Symphony for organ and orchestra
KŘENEK (24)
Concerto Grosso
Concertino for flute, cembalon, violin and
 strings
Violin Concerto No 1
Seven Orchestral Pieces
Symphony for wind and percussion
Violin Sonata No 1
WEILL (24)
*Quodlibet*, for string quartet
*The Protagonist*, opera
FINZI (23)
*Severn Rhapsody*
RUBBRA (23)
Double Fugue for orchestra
SKALKOTTAS (20)
String Trio (lost)
String Quartet (lost)
SEIBER (19)
String Quartet No 1
*Sarabande and Gigue*, for cello and piano
*Missa Brevis*, for unaccompanied
 chorus

SHOSTAKOVICH (18)
Symphony No 1 (1924–5)
Scherzo for orchestra
Prelude and Scherzo for string octet
  (1924–5)

## 1925

BERIO, BOULEZ, SCHULLER and
THEODORAKIS were born;
MOSKOWSKI and SATIE died
d'INDY (74)
*Diptyque méditerranéen* (1925–6)
Cello Sonata
JANÁČEK (71)
*Sinfonietta* (1925–6)
Concertino for seven instruments
STANFORD (posthumous)
*fp The Travelling Companion*, opera
LOEFFLER (64)
*Memories of my Childhood*, for orchestra
DELIUS (63)
*Caprice and Elegy*, for cello and orchestra
SIBELIUS (60)
*Tapiola*, symphonic poem
BEACH (58)
*The Canticle of the Sun*, for chorus and
  orchestra
ROUSSEL (56)
*Pour une fête de printemps*, tone poem
*Sérénade*, for harp, flute, violin, viola and
  cello
*Joueurs de flûte*, for flute and piano
Violin Sonata
*Segovia*, for guitar
SCHMITT (55)
*Salammbô*, film score
*Danse d'Abisag*, for orchestra
VAUGHAN WILLIAMS (53)
*Concerto accademico*, for violin and string
  orchestra
*Flos Campi*, suite for viola, choir and small
  orchestra
*Sancta civitas*, oratorio
SCHMIDT (51)
Chaconne for organ
String Quartet in A
GLIÈRE (50)
*Cleopatra*, ballet
HAHN (50)
*Mozart*, musical comedy
RAVEL (50)
*L'enfant et les sortilèges*, opera
BRIAN (49)
Comic Opera (revised version)
CARPENTER (49)
*Skyscrapers*, ballet

RUGGLES (49)
*Portals*, for thirteen strings or string
  orchestra
AUBERT (48)
*Capriccio*, for violin and orchestra
QUILTER (48)
*The Rake*, ballet suite
Five Jacobean Lyrics
HOLBROOKE (47)
*The Birds of Rheannon*, symphonic poem
Symphony No 3 *Ships*
SCOTT (46)
*The Saint of the Mountain*, opera
*The Ballad of Fair Helen of Kirkconnel*, for
  baritone and orchestra
BLOCH (45)
*Prélude (Recueillement)*, for string quartet
PIZZETTI (45–47)
*Fra Gherado*, opera (1925–27)
MIASKOVSKY (44)
Symphony No 8
Sonata No 4 for piano
KODÁLY (43)
*Meditations on a Theme of Debussy*, for
  piano
MALIPIERO (43)
*Filomela e l'infatuato*, opera
*Merlino maestro d'organi*, opera (1925–8)
*Il Mistero di Venezia*, opera (1925–8)
STRAVINSKY (43)
Suite No 1 for small orchestra
BAX (42)
Piano Sonata No 3
WEBERN (42)
Three Lieder
GRUENBERG (41)
*Four Whimsicalities*, for string quartet
*Poem in the Form of a Sonata*, for cello and
  piano
*Jazz Suite*
BERG (40)
*Lyric Suite*, for string quartet (1925–6)
TAYLOR (40)
*Fantasy on Two Themes*, for orchestra
*Jurgen*, for orchestra
*Circus Days*, for jazz orchestra
COATES (39)
*The Selfish Giant*, fantasy
VILLA-LOBOS (38)
*Chôros* Nos 3, 8 and 10
IBERT (35)
Concerto for cello and wind instruments
*Scherzo féerique*
MARTINŮ (35)
*On tourne*, ballet
*Half-Time*, symphonic poem
Piano Concerto No 1

**PROKOFIEV** (34)
*Pas d'acier*, ballet (1925–6)
Divertimento for orchestra (1925–9)
**HONEGGER** (33)
*Judith*, opera
Concertino for piano and orchestra
**HOWELLS** (33)
*My Eyes for Beauty Pine*, for chorus and
    organ
*Paradise Rondel*, for orchestra
**MILHAUD** (33)
String Quartet No 7
*Deux Hymnes*
**BENJAMIN** (32)
*Three Mystical Songs*, for unaccompanied
    chorus
**ROGERS** (32)
String Quartet No 2
**MOERAN** (31)
*Summer Valley*, for piano
**HINDEMITH** (30)
Concerto for orchestra
*Chamber Music Nos 3 and 4*
**ORFF** (30)
Prelude for orchestra
**SOWERBY** (30)
*From the Northland*, for orchestra
*Monotony*, for jazz orchestra
*The Vision of Sir Launfal*, for chorus and
    orchestra
**CASTELNUOVO-TEDESCO** (29)
*Le danze del re David*, for piano
**HANSON** (29)
*The Lament of Beowulf*, for chorus
**TANSMAN** (28)
*La Nuit Kurde*, opera (1925–7)
Symphony No 2
**GERSHWIN** (27)
*Novelettes*, for violin and piano
Concerto in F for piano and orchestra
*Tell Me More*, musical
*Tip-toes*, musical
*Song of the Flame*, musical
*Oh, Kay!*, musical (including songs
    'Do, Do, Do' and 'Someone to Watch
    Over Me')
**AURIC** (26)
*Pastorale*, ballet
**CHÁVEZ** (26)
*Energia*, for nine instruments
**POULENC** (26)
*Napoli Suite*, for piano
**BUSH, A.** (25)
Two Songs for soprano, chorus and
    orchestra
**COPLAND** (25)
*Grogh*, ballet

*Dance Symphony* (1922–5)
*Music for the Theater*, suite for small
    orchestra
**KŘENEK** (25)
*Jonny spielt auf*, opera
*Mammon*, ballet
*Der vertauschte Cupido*, ballet
**WEILL** (25)
Concerto for violin and woodwind
**RUBBRA** (24)
*La belle dame sans merci*, for chorus and
    orchestra
Violin Sonata No 1
**WALTON** (23)
*Portsmouth Point*, overture
**BERKELEY, L.** (22) 'The Thresher', for
    voice and piano
**SKALKOTTAS** (21)
Violin Sonata
**LAMBERT** (20)
*Romeo and Juliet*, ballet (1925–6)
**SEIBER** (20)
*Serenade*, for six wind instruments
*Sonata da Camera*, for violin and cello

## 1926

**BROWN, FELDMAN, KURTÁG** and
**HENZE** were born
**PUCCINI** (posthumous)
*fp Turandot*, opera
**JANÁČEK** (72)
*Capriccio*, for piano and wind
*Festliche Messe*
**SMYTH** (68)
*Entente Cordiale*, opera
*Sleepless Dreams*, for chorus and orchestra
*A Spring Canticle*, for chorus and orchestra
**d'ALBERT** (62)
*Der Golem*, music drama
**ROPARTZ** (62)
Romance and Scherzino for violin and
    orchestra
**NIELSEN** (61)
Flute Concerto
**SIBELIUS** (61)
*The Tempest*, incidental music
**NOVÁK** (56)
*Signorina Gioventu*, ballet-pantomime
    (1926–8)
**SCHMITT** (56)
*Final*, for cello and orchestra
**HOLST** (52)
*The Golden Goose*, choral ballet
*Chrissemas Day in the Morning*, for piano
**SCHMIDT** (52)
Piano Quintet in G

GLIÈRE (51)
*Red Poppy*, ballet (1926–7)
HAHN (51)
*La Reine de Sheba*, scène lyrique
*Une Revue*
*Le Temps d'aimer*, musical comedy
RAVEL (51)
*Chansons madécasses*, for voice, flute, cello
   and piano
RUGGLES (50)
*Sun-treader*, for orchestra (1926–31)
BRIDGE (47)
String Quartet No 3
SCOTT (47)
*Karma*, ballet
BLOCH (46)
*America: An Epic Rhapsody*, for orchestra
Four Episodes for chamber orchestra
MEDTNER (46)
Piano Concerto No 2 (1926–7)
BARTÓK (45)
Piano Concerto No 1
*Three Village Scenes*, for chorus and
   orchestra
*Cantata Profana*, for tenor and baritone
   soli, chorus and orchestra
*Out of Doors*, suite for piano
*Mikrokosmos*, for piano (1926–37)
Nine Little Pieces for piano
Piano Sonata
KODÁLY (44)
*Háry János*, opera
MALIPIERO (44)
*L'Esilio dell' Eroe*, five symphonic
   impressions
STRAVINSKY (44)
*Pater Noster*, for chorus a capella
*Oedipus Rex*, opera-oratorio (1926–7)
TURINA (44)
*La oracion del torero*, for string quartet
Piano Trio
BERNERS (43)
*The Triumph of Neptune*, ballet
CASELLA (43)
*Introduction, Aria and Toccata*, for orchestra
*Concerto Romano*, for organ and orchestra
*Adieu à la vie*, for voice and orchestra
*Scarlattiana*, for small orchestra
SZYMANOWSKI (43)
*Harnasie*, ballet
*Stabat Mater*
WEBERN (43)
Two Lieder
GRUENBERG (42)
*Jazzettes*, for violin and piano
RIEGGER (41)
Rhapsody for orchestra

*Study in Sonority*, for ten instruments
TAYLOR (41)
*The King's Henchman*, opera
VARÈSE (41)
*Amériques*, for orchestra
WELLESZ (41)
*Archilles auf Skyros*, ballet
*Der Opferung des Gefangenen*, opera
COATES (40)
*The Three Bears*, fantasy
TOCH (39)
Piano Concerto
*Spiel*, for wind
VILLA-LOBOS (39)
*Chôros* Nos 4, 5, 6 and 6 *bis*
IBERT (36)
*Jeux*, for orchestra
MARTIN (36)
*Rythmes*, three symphonic movements
BLISS (35)
*Hymn to Apollo*, for orchestra (revised
   1965)
Introduction and Allegro for orchestra
   (revised 1937)
MILHAUD (34)
*Le pauvre matelot*, opera
ROGERS (33)
Symphony No 1, *Adonais*
MOERAN (32)
*Irish Love Song*, for piano
PISTON (32)
Three Pieces for flute, clarinet and bassoon
Piano Sonata
WARLOCK (32)
*Capriol Suite*, for strings
HINDEMITH (31)
*Cardillac*, opera
SOWERBY (31)
*Mediaeval Poem*, for organ and orchestra
HANSON (30)
*Pan and the Priest*, symphonic poem
Organ Concerto
THOMSON, V. (30)
*Sonata da Chiesa*, for five instruments
COWELL (29)
*Atlantis*, ballet
*Seven Paragraphs*, for chamber ensemble
TANSMAN (29)
Piano Concerto No 1
GERSHWIN (28)
Preludes for piano
HARRIS (28)
*Impressions of a rainy day*, for string quartet
CHÁVEZ (27)
*Los cuatro soles*, ballet
POULENC (27)
Trio for oboe, bassoon and piano

*Chansons gaillardes*
**ANTHEIL** (26)
*Jazz Symphonietta*, for twenty-two
 instruments
**COPLAND** (26)
Piano Concerto
**KŘENEK** (26)
*Der Diktator*, opera
*Drei Lustige Märsche*, for orchestra
*Das Geheime Königreich*, opera (1926–7)
**DURUFLÉ** (24)
Scherzo for organ
**WALTON** (24)
*Siesta*, for orchestra
**BLITZSTEIN** (21)
*Sarabande*, for orchestra
**LAMBERT** (21)
*Pomona*, ballet
*Poems by Li-Po*
**SIEBER** (21–23) Divertimento for clarinet
 and string quartet (1926–8)
**SHOSTAKOVICH** (20)
Piano Sonata No 1


## 1927

**JOSEPHS** and **JOUBERT** were born
**d'INDY** (76)
Concerto for piano, flute, cello and string
 quartet
*Suites en parties*, for harp, flute, viola and
 cello
**JANÁČEK** (73)
*From the House of the Dead*, opera (1927–8)
*Glagolitic Mass*
**SMYTH** (69)
Concerto for violin and horn
**PIERNÉ** (64)
*Sophie Arnould*, opéra-comique
**NIELSEN** (62)
*En Fantasirejse til Faerøerne*, rhapsodic
 overture
Prelude and Presto for violin (1927–8)
**ROUSSEL** (58)
Piano Concerto
**SCHMITT** (57)
*Ronde burlesque*, for orchestra
**VAUGHAN WILLIAMS** (55)
*Along the Field*, eight songs for voice and
 violin
**RACHMANINOV** (54)
Piano Concerto No 4
**HOLST** (53)
*The Morning of the Year*, choral ballet
*Egdon Heath*, symphonic poem
*The Coming of Christ*, mystery play

**SCHMIDT** (53)
Fugue in F for organ
**SCHOENBERG** (53)
String Quartet No 3
**HAHN** (52)
Violin Concerto
**AUBERT** (50)
p *Noël pastoral*, for piano and orchestra
p Violin Sonata in D minor and D major
**HOLBROOKE** (49)
*Columba*, for orchestra
**SHREKER** (49)
*Vom Ewigen Leben*, for voice and orchestra
**BRIDGE** (48)
*Enter Spring*, for orchestra
**IRELAND** (48)
Sonatina for piano
**RESPIGHI** (48)
*The Sunken Bell*, opera
*Church Windows*, symphonic impressions
*The Birds*, suite for small orchestra
*Three Botticelli Pictures*, for orchestra
*Brazilian Impressions*, for orchestra
**SCOTT** (48)
Violin Concerto
**BARTÓK** (46)
String Quartet No 3
**MIASKOVSKY** (46)
Symphonies 9 and 10
*Souvenirs*, six pieces for piano
**GRAINGER** (45)
*Shallow Brown*, for chorus and orchestra
*Irish Tune from County Derry*
**BAX** (44)
Violin Sonata No 3 in G minor
**CASELLA** (44)
Concerto for strings
Cello Sonata No 2
**WEBERN** (44)
String Trio
**VARÈSE** (42)
*Arcana*, for orchestra
**COATES** (41)
*Four Ways*, suite
**TOCH** (40)
*Die Prinzessin auf der Erbse*, opera
*Narziss*, for orchestra (lost)
*Gewitter*, for orchestra (lost)
*Komödie*, for orchestra
**IBERT** (37)
*Angélique*, opera
**MARTINŮ** (37)
*Le raid merveilleux*, ballet (1927–8)
*La revue de cuisine*, ballet
*La bagarre*, symphonic poem
**BLISS** (36)
Oboe Quintet

Four Songs for high voice and violin
**HONEGGER** (35)
*Antigone*, lyric drama
**MILHAUD** (35)
Violin Concerto No 1
*Carnival of Aix*, for piano and orchestra
**PISTON** (33)
Symphonic Piece
**CASTELNUOVO-TEDESCO** (32)
Piano Concerto No 1
**HINDEMITH** (32)
*Chamber Music* No 5
**ORFF** (32)
Concertino for wind
**HANSON** (31)
*Heroic Elegy*, for chorus and orchestra
**SESSIONS** (31)
Symphony No 1
**WEINBERGER** (31)
*Schwanda the Bagpiper*, opera
**COWELL** (30)
*Some Music*, for orchestra
Suite for violin and piano
**TANSMAN** (30)
Piano Concerto No 2
**GERSHWIN** (29)
*Strike Up The Band*, musical
*Funny Face*, musical (including songs
  'He Loves and She Loves' and
  'Swonderful')
**HARRIS** (29)
Concerto for clarinet, piano and string
  quartet
**AURIC** (28)
*Sous le Masque*, opera
**CHÁVEZ** (28)
*HP* (ie Horsepower) ballet
**POULENC** (28)
*Concert châmpetre*, for harpsichord and
  orchestra (1927–8)
*Deux novelettes*, for piano (1927–8)
*Airs chantés* (1927–8)
**BUSH, A.** (27)
*Symphonic Impressions*
Prelude and Fugue, for piano
**KŘENEK** (27)
*Schwergewicht*, opera
*Triumph der Empfindsamkeit*, orchestral
  suite
*Potpourri*, for orchestra
**WEILL** (27)
*Lindbergh's Flight*, cantata
*The New Orpheus*, cantata
*The Royal Palace*, opera
*Mahagonny*, opera
**DURUFLÉ** (25)
*Triptyque*, for piano

**WALTON** (25)
Viola Concerto
Sinfonia Concertante for piano and
  orchestra
**KHACHATURIAN** (24)
*Poème*, for piano
**SKALKOTTAS** (23)
Piano Sonatina
Fifteen Little Variations for piano
**ALWYN** (22)
Five Preludes for orchestra
**LAMBERT** (22)
Music for orchestra
*Elegiac Blues*
**SHOSTAKOVICH** (21)
*The Nose*, opera (1927–8)
*The Age of Gold*, ballet (1927–30)
Symphony No 2, *October*
*Aphorisms*, for piano
**HOLMBOE** (18)
Symphony in F


# 1928

**KORTE, MUSGRAVE** and
**STOCKHAUSEN** were born; **JANÁČEK**
died
**JANÁČEK** (74)
String Quartet No 2, *Intimate Pages*
**ELGAR** (71)
*fp Beau Brummell*, incidental music
**IPPOLITOV-IVANOV** (69)
*Episodes from Schubert's Life*, for orchestra
**LOEFFLER** (67)
*Clowns*, intermezzo
**d'ALBERT** (64)
*The Black Orchid*, burlesque opera
**ROPARTZ** (64)
*Rhapsody*, for cello and orchestra
**NIELSEN** (63)
Clarinet Concerto
*Bohmisk-dansk folketom*, for strings
Three Pieces for piano
**BANTOCK** (60)
*Pilgrim's Progress*, for soli, chorus and
  orchestra
**LEHÁR** (58)
*Frederica*, operetta
**SCHMITT** (58)
Symphonie Concertante for piano and
  orchestra
**ALFVÉN** (56)
*Manhem*, cantata for male voices
**VAUGHAN WILLIAMS** (56)
*Sir John in Love*, opera
*Te Deum*, in G major

JONGEN (55)
*Pièce symphonique,* for piano and orchestra
HOLST (54)
*Moorside Suite,* for brass band
SCHMIDT (54)
Symphony No 3
Four Little Preludes and Fugues for organ
SCHOENBERG (54)
Variations for orchestra
GLIÈRE (53)
String Quartet No 3
RAVEL (53)
*Bolero,* for orchestra
CARPENTER (52)
String Quartet
HOLBROOKE (50)
Piano Concerto No 2
SCHREKER (50)
Little Suite for chamber orchestra
BRIDGE (49)
*Rhapsody,* for two violins and viola
RESPIGHI (49)
*Toccata,* for piano and orchestra
MIASKOVSKY (48)
*The Yellowed Pages,* seven pieces for piano
PIZZETTI (48)
*Concerto dell' Estate*
BARTÓK (47)
*Rhapsodies* Nos 1 and 2, for violin and
  orchestra
*Rhapsody* No 1 for cello and piano
String Quartet No 4
GRAINGER (46)
Colonial Songs
*Over the Hills and Far Away,* for orchestra
TURINA (46)
*Ritmos,* choreographic fantasy
BAX (45)
Symphony No 3 (1928–9)
Sonata for two pianos
Sonata for viola and harp
BERNERS (45)
Fugue for orchestra
CASELLA (45)
*La Donna Serpente,* opera (1928–31)
Violin Concerto
WEBERN (45)
Symphony for small orchestra
BERG (43–9)
*Lulu,* opera (1928–34)
WELLESZ (43)
*Scherz, List und Rache,* opera
DUPRÉ (42)
Symphony with organ
SCHOECK (42–44)
*Vom Fischer und syner Fru,* dramatic cantata
  (1928–30)

TOCH (41)
*Fanal,* for organ and orchestra
*Bunte Suite*
VILLA-LOBOS (41)
*Chôros* Nos 11 and 14
MARTINŮ (38)
*Les Lames de Couteau,* opera
*The Soldier and the Dancer,* opera
*Echéc au roi,* ballet
Concertino for piano (left hand) and
  chamber orchestra
*Entr'acte,* for orchestra
*La Rapsodie*
BLISS (37)
*Pastoral: Lie Strewn the White Flocks,* for
  mezzo-soprano, chorus, flute, drums
  and string orchestra
PROKOFIEV (37)
*The Prodigal Son,* ballet
Symphony No 3
HONEGGER (36)
*Rugby,* Mouvement Symphonique No 2
MILHAUD (36)
*Christophe Columb,* opera (revised 1956)
*Cantate pour louer le Seigneur*
BENJAMIN (35)
Concerto quasi una fantasia, for piano and
  orchestra
MOORE (35)
*A Symphony of Autumn*
*Moby Dick,* for orchestra
ROGERS (35)
Symphony No 2
HINDEMITH (33)
Concerto for organ and chamber orchestra
*Chamber Music* No 6
ORFF (33)
*Entrata* (revised 1940)
SOWERBY (33)
Symphony No 2
GERHARD (32)
Wind Quintet
THOMSON, V. (32)
*Symphony on a Hymn Tune*
COWELL (31)
Sinfonietta for chamber orchestra
TANSMAN (31)
*Lumières,* ballet
GERSHWIN (30)
*An American In Paris,* for orchestra
*Rosalie,* musical
*Treasure Girl,* musical
HARRIS (30)
Piano Sonata
AURIC (29)
*Les Enchantements de la Fée Alcine,* ballet
*Rondeau,* ballet

POULENC (29)
*Trois pièces*, for piano
THOMSON, R. (29)
*Jazz Poem*, for piano and orchestra
ANTHEIL (28–9)
*Transatlantic*, opera (1928–29)
BUSH, A. (28)
*Relinquishment*, for piano
COPLAND (28)
Symphony No 1
KŘENEK (28)
Piano Sonata No 2
Little Symphony
*Leben des Orest*, opera (1928–9)
WEILL (28)
*The Threepenny Opera*
DURUFLÉ (26)
*Prélude, récitatif et variations*, for flute,
    viola and piano
SKALKOTTAS (24)
String Quartet No 1
Sonata No 1 for violin and piano (lost)
Symphonic Suite (lost)
BLITZSTEIN (23)
*Triple Sec*, opera-farce
LAMBERT (23)
Piano Sonata (1928–9)
SHOSTAKOVICH (22)
*Six Romances on Words by Japanese poets*,
    for tenor and orchestra (1928–32)
*New Babylon*, for orchestra, (film music)
MESSIAEN (20)
Fugue in D minor for orchestra
*Le Banquet céleste*, for organ
*Le Banquet eucharistique*, for orchestra
    (unpublished)
HOLMBOE (19)
Symphony in D
Quintet for viola and string quartet

## 1929

CRUMB, HODDINOTT, LEIGHTON and
PREVIN were born
d'INDY (78)
String Sextet
NIELSEN (64)
Cantata for the Centenary of the
    Polytechnic High School
*Hymne til kunsten*, for soprano, tenor,
    chorus and wind
Twenty-nine Little Preludes for organ
SIBELIUS (64)
Symphony No 8 (destroyed)
GIORDANO (62)
*Il re*, opera

ROUSSEL (60)
Symphony No 3 (1929–30)
LEHÁR (59)
*The Land of Smiles*, operetta
NOVÁK (59)
*Nikotina*, ballet-pantomime
SCHMITT (59)
*Cancunik*, for orchestra
VAUGHAN WILLIAMS (57)
*Benedicite*, for soprano, chorus and
    orchestra
JONGEN (56)
*Passacaille et Gigue*, for orchestra
Suite for viola and orchestra
HOLST (55)
*The Tale of the Wandering Scholar*, opera
Concerto for two violins
Twelve Songs
SCHMIDT (55)
String Quartet in G
SCHOENBERG (55)
*Von Heute auf Morgen*, opera
DOHNÁNYI (52)
*A Tenor*, opera
HOLBROOKE (51)
*Bronwen*, opera
Symphony No 4
SCHREKER (51)
*Der Schmied von Gent*, opera (1929–32)
BRIDGE (50)
Trio No 2
CANTALOUBE (50)
*Lauriers*, pieces for orchestra
IRELAND (50)
*Ballade*, for piano
RESPIGHI (50)
*The Festivals of Rome*, orchestral suite
BLOCH (49)
*Abodah*, for violin and piano
PIZZETTI (49)
*Rondo veneziano*, for orchestra
MIASKOVSKY (48)
Serenade for small orchestra
Sinfonietta for string orchestra
*Lyric Concerto*, for small orchestra
GRAINGER (47)
*English Dance*, for orchestra
MALIPIERO (47)
*Torneo notturno*, opera
PONCE (47)
Three *Bocetas Sinfónicos*, for orchestra
Sonata for cello and piano
Miniature string quartet
STRAVINSKY (47)
Capriccio for piano and orchestra
Quatre Études for orchestra

**TURINA** (47)
*Triptico*, songs
**BAX** (46)
Overture, Elegy and Rondo for orchestra
*Legend*, for viola and piano
**GRUENBERG** (45)
*Jack and the Beanstalk*, children's opera
*The Enchanted Isle*, symphonic poem
*Nine Moods*, for orchestra
*Music for an Imaginary Ballet*
**BERG** (44)
Three Pieces for Orchestra
*Der Wein*, concert aria (possibly 1920)
**RIEGGER** (44)
Suite for flute
**WELLESZ** (44)
*Festlicher Marsch*, for orchestra
**COATES** (43)
*Cinderella*, fantasy
**TOCH** (42)
*Kleine Ouvertüre zu Der Fächer*
**VILLA-LOBOS** (42)
*Introdução aos Chôros*, for orchestra
*Chôros* Nos 9, 12 and 13
*Suite sugestiva*, for voice and orchestra
Twelve Studies for guitar
**IBERT** (39)
*Persée et Andromédée*, opera
**MARTINŮ** (39)
*Journée de bonté*, opera
*The Butterfly that Stamped*, ballet
**BLISS** (38)
*Serenade*, for baritone and orchestra
**PROKOFIEV** (38)
Symphony No 4 (1929–30, revised 1947)
**MILHAUD** (37)
Viola Concerto
Concerto for percussion and small
  orchestra
**MOORE** (36)
Violin Sonata
**ROGERS** (36)
*The Raising of Lazarus*, for chorus and
  orchestra
**PISTON** (35)
Suite No 1 for orchestra
**SOWERBY** (34)
Cello Concerto (1929–34)
*Prairie*, symphonic poem
*Florida Suite*, for piano
**THOMSON, V.** (33)
*Five Portraits*, for four clarinets
**WEINBERGER** (33)
*Christmas*, for orchestra
**COWELL** (32)
*Irish Suite*, for chamber orchestra

**TANSMAN** (32)
*Le cercle éternel*, ballet
**GERSHWIN** (31)
*Show Girl*, musical
**HARRIS** (31)
*American Portraits*, for orchestra
**POULENC** (30)
*Aubade*, for piano and eighteen
  instruments
*Hommage à Roussel*, for piano
*Huit Nocturnes*, for piano (1929–38)
**THOMPSON, R.** (30)
Symphony No 1
**BUSH, A.** (29)
*Dialectic*, for string quartet
*Songs of the Doomed*, for tenor, female
  chorus and piano
**COPLAND** (29)
*Symphonic Ode* (revised 1955)
*Vitebsk*, for piano trio
**RUBBRA** (28)
Triple Fugue for orchestra
**DURUFLÉ** (27)
Prelude, Adagio and Chorale Variations,
  for organ
**BLACHER** (26)
*Habemeajaja*, chamber opera (lost)
Symphony (unpublished, destroyed)
**KABALEVSKY** (25)
Piano Concerto No 1
String Quartet in A minor
**SKALKOTTAS** (25)
Concerto for wind (lost)
Little Suite for violin and chamber
  orchestra (lost)
String Quartet No 2 (lost)
*Easy Music*, for string quartet (lost)
Sonatinas Nos 1 and 2 for violin and
  piano
Octet for flute, clarinet, bassoon, trumpet,
  trombone and piano trio
**BLITZSTEIN** (24)
*Parabola and Circula*, opera-ballet
**LAMBERT** (24)
*The Rio Grande*, for chorus, piano and
  orchestra
**SHOSTAKOVICH** (23)
Symphony No 3, *The First of May*
**MESSIAEN** (21)
*Préludes*, for piano
**HOLMBOE** (20)
Concerto for orchestra
**BARBER** (19)
Serenade for string orchestra or string
  quartet

# 1930

McCABE and TAKEMITSU were born;
WARLOCK died
**d'INDY** (79)
String Quartet No 4
Suite for flute obbligato, violin, viola, cello
   and harp
Piano Trio No 2 in the form of a suite
**ELGAR** (73)
*Pomp and Circumstance March*, No 5
*Severn Suite*, for brass band, or orchestra
**SMYTH** (72)
*The Prison*, for unaccompanied chorus
**DELIUS** (68)
*A Song of Summer*, for orchestra
**STRAUSS, R.** (66–8)
*Arabella*, opera (1930–2)
**NIELSEN** (65)
Cantata for the 50th Anniversary of the
   Young Merchants' Educational
   Association
Cantata for the 50th Anniversary of the
   Danish Cremation Union
Two Preludes for organ
*Klaviermusik for Smaa og Store*, two volumes
**VAUGHAN WILLIAMS** (58)
Prelude and Fugue for orchestra
*Job, a Masque for Dancing*, for orchestra
**JONGEN** (57)
*Sonata Eroica*
**RACHMANINOV** (57)
Three Russian Folk Songs for chorus and
   orchestra (possibly 1927)
**HOLST** (56)
Choral Fantasia
*Hammersmith*, prelude and scherzo for
   orchestra
**SCHMIDT** (56)
*Variationen über ein Husarenlied*, for
   orchestra (1930–1)
**BRIAN** (54)
Symphony No 2 (1930–1)
**AUBERT** (53)
*Feuilles d'images*, for orchestra
**DOHNÁNYI** (53)
*Szeged Mass*, for twelve voices, orchestra
   and organ
**SCHREKER** (52)
Four Little Pieces for orchestra
*Das Welb des Intaphernes*, for speaker and
   orchestra
**BRIDGE** (51)
*Oration 'Concert elegiaco'*, for cello and
   orchestra
**CANTALOUBE** (51)
*Vercingétorisc*, opera (1930–2)

**IRELAND** (51)
Piano Concerto
**RESPIGHI** (51)
*Metamorphosen modi XII*, theme and
   variations for orchestra
*Bach's Prelude and Fugue in D major*,
   transcribed for orchestra
**PIZZETTI** (50)
Piano Concerto
**BARTÓK** (49)
Piano Concerto No 2 (1930–1)
**GRAINGER** (48)
*Lord Peter's Stable-boy*, for chorus and
   orchestra
*Spoon River*, for piano duet
*To a Nordic Princess*, for orchestra
**KODÁLY** (48)
*Dances of Marosszek*, for piano
**MALIPIERO** (48)
*La bella e il mostro*, opera
**STRAVINSKY** (48)
*Symphony of Psalms*, for chorus and
   orchestra
**BAX** (47)
Symphony No 4 in E♭ (1930–1)
*Overture to a Picaresque Comedy*, for
   orchestra
*Winter Legends*, for piano and orchestra
**BERNERS** (47)
*Luna Park*, ballet
**CASELLA** (47)
Serenade for small orchestra
**WEBERN** (47)
Quartet for violin, clarinet, saxophone and
   piano
**GRUENBERG** (46)
*Four Diversions*, for string quartet
**RIEGGER** (45)
Fantasy and Fugue for organ and
   orchestra
**TAYLOR** (45)
*Peter Ibbetson*, opera
**TOCH** (43)
*Der Fächer*, opera
*Kleine Theater-suite*
**VILLA-LOBOS** (43)
*Bachianas Brasilieras* Nos 1 and 2
**IBERT** (40)
*Le Roi d'Yvetot*, opera
*Divertissement*, for chamber orchestra
**MARTINŮ** (40)
*Serenade*, for chamber orchestra
Violin Sonata No 1
**BLISS** (39)
*Morning Heroes*, symphony for orator,
   chorus and orchestra
*Fanfares for Heroes*, for ensemble

PROKOFIEV (39)
*Sur le Borysthène* (*On the Dnieper*), ballet
*Four Portraits*, symphonic suite (1930–1)
String Quartet No 1
HONEGGER (38)
*Les aventures du roi pausole*, light opera
Symphony No 1
MILHAUD (38)
*Maximilien*, opera
MOORE (37)
*Overture on an American Theme*
PISTON (36)
Flute Sonata
COWELL (35)
*Reel No 1*, for orchestra
Suite for woodwind quintet
*Polyphonica*, for twelve instruments
*Exultation*, for ten strings
HINDEMITH (35)
*Concert music*, for piano, brass and harps
ORFF (35)
*Catulli Carmina*, for chorus and orchestra
  (revised 1943)
SOWERBY (35)
Organ Symphony
HANSON (34)
Symphony No 2, *Romantic*
SESSIONS (34)
Piano Sonata No 1
THOMSON, V. (34)
Violin Sonata
WEINBERGER (34)
*The Beloved Voice*, opera
Bohemian Songs and Dances for orchestra
TANSMAN (33)
*Triptyque*, for string orchestra
GERSHWIN (32)
*Girl Crazy*, musical
HARRIS (32)
String Quartet No 1
CHÁVEZ (31)
Sonata for horns
POULENC (31)
*Épitaphe*, song
BUSH, A. (30)
Dance Overture (1930–5)
COPLAND (30)
Piano Variations
KŘENEK (30)
String Quartet No 5
*Karl V*, opera (1930–3)
DURUFLÉ (28)
Suite for organ
KABALEVSKY (26)
*Poem of Struggle*, for chorus and orchestra
SKALKOTTAS (26)
Concerto for piano, violin and chamber

orchestra (lost)
ALWYN (25)
Piano Concerto
BLITZSTEIN (25)
*Cain*, ballet
*Romantic Piece*, for orchestra
SHOSTAKOVICH (24)
*Lady Macbeth of the Mtsensk District*, opera
  (1930–2)
*The Bolt*, choreographic spectacle (1930–1)
*Alone*, film music (1930–1)
MACONCHY (23)
Concertino for piano and orchestra
*The Land*, for orchestra
MESSIAEN (22)
*Les Offrandes oubliées*, for orchestra
*Simple chant d'une âme*
*Diptyque*, for organ
HOLMBOE (21)
Three String Trios (1930–1)
BRITTEN (17)
'Hymn to the Virgin'

## 1931

WILLIAMSON was born; d'INDY and
NIELSEN died
ELGAR (74)
*p Nursery Suite*, for orchestra
PIERNÉ (68)
*Divertissement sur un thème pastoral*, for
  orchestra
*Fantasie basque*, for violin
NIELSEN (66)
*Commotio*, for organ
Allegretto in F for two recorders
CILEA (65)
Suite for orchestra
BEACH (64)
*Christ in the Universe*, for chorus and
  orchestra
ROUSSEL (62)
*Bacchus and Ariadne*, ballet
NOVÁK (61)
Twelve Lullabies for female chorus
*Autumn Symphony*, for mixed chorus and
  orchestra
VAUGHAN WILLIAMS (59)
Symphony No 4 (1931–4)
Piano Concerto
*In Windsor Forest*, cantata
SCHMIDT (57)
Chaconne for orchestra
SUK (57)
Mass in Bb major
HAHN (56)
Piano concerto

472

*Brummel*, operetta
**RAVEL** (56)
Piano Concerto in G major
Piano Concerto for the left hand
**BRIAN** (55)
Symphony No 3 (1931–2)
**BRIDGE** (52)
*Phantasm*, rhapsody for piano and
   orchestra
**IRELAND** (52)
*Songs Sacred and Profane*
**SCOTT** (52)
Cello Concerto
**PIZZETTI** (51–55)
*Oreseolo*, opera (1931–5)
**BARTÓK** (50)
Forty-four Duos for two violins
**GRAINGER** (49)
*The Nightingale and the Two Sisters*, for
   orchestra
**KODÁLY** (49)
*The Spinning Room*, lyric scenes (1931–2)
*Theater Overture*
*Pange lingua*, for chorus and organ
**MALIPIERO** (49)
Concerto for orchestra
**STRAVINSKY** (49)
Violin Concerto
**TURINA** (49)
*Rapsodia sinfonica*, for piano and strings
Piano Quartet
**BAX** (48)
Symphony No 5 in C♯ minor (1931–2)
*The Tale the Pine Trees Knew*, symphonic
   poem
Nonet for flute, oboe, clarinet, harp and
   strings
String Quintet
**CASELLA** (48–52)
*Introduction, corale e marcia*, for
   woodwind (1931–5)
**SZYMANOWSKI** (48)
Symphonie concertante for piano (1931–2)
**GRUENBERG** (47)
*The Emperor Jones*, opera
*The Dumb Wife*, opera
**RIEGGER** (46)
*Dichotomy*, for chamber orchestra
Canons for woodwind
**VARÈSE** (46)
*Ionisation*, for forty-one percussion and
   two sirens
**WELLESZ** (46)
*Die Bakchantinnen*, opera
**TOCH** (44)
*Tragische Musik*, for orchestra (lost)
*Zwei Kultische Stücke*, for orchestra (lost)

**VILLA-LOBOS** (44)
String Quartet No 5
**MARTIN** (41)
*Chaconne*, for cello and piano
Violin Sonata
**MARTINŮ** (41)
*Spaliček*, ballet
Partita (Suite No 1)
Cello Concerto
**BLISS** (40)
Clarinet Quintet
**PROKOFIEV** (40)
Piano Concerto No 4 for the left hand
**GROFÉ** (39)
*Grand Canyon Suite*, for orchestra
**HONEGGER** (39)
*Cries of the World*, for chorus and
   orchestra
*Amphion*, ballet-melodrama
**BENJAMIN** (38)
*The Devil Take Her*, comic opera
**ROGERS** (38)
*The Marriage of Aude*, opera
*The Exodus*, for chorus and orchestra
**PISTON** (37)
Suite for oboe and piano
**HINDEMITH** (36)
*The Unceasing*, oratorio
**SOWERBY** (36)
Passacaglia, Interlude and Fugue for
   orchestra
**THOMSON, V.** (35)
*Four Portraits*, for violin and piano
Serenade for flute and violin
Quartet No 1
*Stabat Mater*
**WEINBERGER** (35)
Passacaglia for orchestra
**COWELL** (34)
*Competitive Sport*, for chamber orchestra
*Synchrony*, for orchestra
*Steel and Stone*, for chamber orchestra
*Rhythmicana*, for orchestra
*Heroic Dance*, for chamber orchestra
*Havana Hornpipe*, for orchestra
**TANSMAN** (34)
Symphony No 3, *Symphony concertante*
   (1931–2)
*Concertino*, for piano
**GERSHWIN** (33)
*Of Thee I Sing*, musical
*2nd Rhapsody*, for piano and orchestra
*Delicious*, film score
**HARRIS** (33)
*Toccata*, for orchestra
**AURIC** (32)
*La Concurrence*, ballet

POULENC (32)
*Bagatelle*, for violin and piano
*Trois poèmes de Louise Lalanne*, songs
Nine songs
THOMPSON, R. (32)
Symphony No 2
ANTHEIL (31)
*Helen Retires*, opera
KŘENEK (31)
Theme and Thirteen Variations for
 orchestra
*A Little Wind-music*
RUBBRA (30)
Piano Concerto
Violin Sonata No 2
WALTON (29)
fp *Belshazzar's Feast*, for baritone, chorus
 and orchestra
BLACHER (28)
Concerto for two trumpets and strings
 (destroyed)
SKALKOTTAS (27)
Piano Concerto No 1
Octet for Woodwind quartet and string
 quartet
Thirty-six Greek Dances for orchestra
 (1931–6)
BLITZSTEIN (26)
*The Harpies*, opera
Piano Concerto
LAMBERT (26)
Concerto for piano and nine instruments
SHOSTAKOVICH (25)
*Hamlet*, incidental music
MESSIAEN (23)
*Le Tombeau resplendissant*, for orchestra
HOLMBOE (22)
Concerto for chamber orchestra
*Requiem*, for boys' voices and chamber
 orchestra
BARBER (21)
*School for Scandal*, overture
*Dover Beach*, for voice and string quartet
MENOTTI (20)
*Variations on a Theme of Schumann*, for
 piano
FRANÇAIX (19)
Eight Bagatelles for piano


## 1932

GOEHR, MEALE, SHCHEDRIN and
WOOD were born; d'ALBERT died
DELIUS (70)
*Prelude to Irmelin*
MASCAGNI (69)
*Pinotta*, opera

d'ALBERT (68)
*Mister Wu*, opera
BEACH (65)
*Cabildo*, opera
ROUSSEL (63)
Quartet
NOVÁK (62)
*From Life*, for twelve male choruses
ZEMLINSKY (61)
*Der Kreidekreis*, opera
ALFVÉN (60)
*Spamannen*, incidental music
*Vi*, incidental music
VAUGHAN WILLIAMS (60)
*Magnificat*
RACHMANINOV (59)
*Variations on a Theme by Corelli*, for piano
SCHMIDT (58)
Piano Quintet in B
SCHOENBERG (58)
*Moses und Aron*, opera
BRIAN (56)
Symphony No. 4
CARPENTER (56)
*Patterns*, for piano and orchestra
*Song of Faith*, for chorus and orchestra
IRELAND (53)
*A Downland Suite*, for brass band
RESPIGHI (53)
*Belkis, Queen of Sheba*, ballet
*Mary of Egypt*, mystery play
*Old Airs and Dances for Lute, Series III*
SCOTT (53)
*The Masque of the Red Death*, ballet
MIASKOVSKY (52)
Symphonies Nos 11 and 12
GRAINGER (50)
*Blithe Bells*, for orchestra
MALIPIERO (50)
Violin Concerto
*Sette Invenzione*, for orchestra
*Inni*, for orchestra
STRAVINSKY (50)
Duo concertante for viola and piano
*Suite Italienne*, from *Pulcinella*
BAX (49)
Cello Concerto in G minor
Sinfonietta
*A Northern Ballad*, for orchestra (1932–3)
Piano Sonata no 4 in G major
CASELLA (49)
*La Favola d'Orfeo*, opera
Sinfonia for clarinet, trumpet and piano
SZYMANOWSKI (49)
Violin Concerto No 2 (1932–3)
RIEGGER (47)
Scherzo for orchestra

VARÈSE (47)
*Metal* (unfinished or lost)
COATES (46)
*The Jester at the Wedding*, ballet
*From Meadow to Mayfair*, suite
DUPRÉ (46)
Concerto for organ and orchestra
SCHOECK (46)
*Praeludium*, for orchestra
VILLA-LOBOS (45)
*Caixinha de Bôas Festas*, ballet
IBERT (42)
*Donogoo*, for orchestra
*Paris*, symphonic suite
MARTINŮ (42)
Sinfonia for two orchestras
*Les Rondes*, for orchestra
Overture for the Sokol Festival
PROKOFIEV (41)
Piano Concerto No 5
Sonata for two violins
HONEGGER (40)
Mouvement symphonique No 3 (1932–3)
Sonatina for violin and cello
MILHAUD (40)
String Quartet No 8
BENJAMIN (39)
Violin Concerto
MOERAN (38)
*Farrago*, suite for orchestra
HINDEMITH (37)
*Philharmonic Concerto*
SOWERBY (37)
Piano Concerto No 2
THOMSON, V. (36)
Quartet No 2
WEINBERGER (36)
*The Outcasts of Poker Flat*, opera
COWELL (35)
*Jig*, for orchestra
*Reel No 2*, for orchestra
TANSMAN (35)
*La Grande Ville*, ballet
Two Symphonic Movements
GERSHWIN (34)
*Cuban Overture*, for orchestra
*George Gershwin Song-Book*, piano
   arrangement of eighteen songs
HARRIS (34)
Chorale for strings
Fantasy for piano and woodwind quintet
String Sextet
CHÁVEZ (33)
String Quartet No 2
POULENC (33)
Concerto for two pianos and orchestra
Sextet for piano and wind (1932–40)

*Intermezzo*, in D minor for piano
Improvisations for piano (1932–43)
*Le bal masqué*, cantata
KŘENEK (32)
*Cantata on the Transitoriness of Earthly
   Things*
BLACHER (29)
*Kleine Marschmusik*, orchestra
KHACHATURIAN (29)
Violin Sonata
String Quartet in C major
Trio in G minor, for clarinet, violin and
   piano
KABALEVSKY (28)
Symphonies Nos 1 and 2
March for wind band
BLITZSTEIN (27)
*The Condemned*, choral opera
SHOSTAKOVICH (26)
*From Karl Marx to Our Own Days*,
   symphonic poem with voices
Twenty-four Preludes for piano (1932–3)
*Encounter*, film music
MESSIAEN (24)
*Hymne au Saint Sacrement*, for orchestra
*Apparition de l'Eglise éternelle*, for organ
*Fantasie burlesque*, for piano
HOLMBOE (23)
Overture
Concerto for strings
Trio for oboe, bassoon and horn
Duets for flute and viola
Duo for flute and violin
Duo for flute and cello
SIEGMEISTER (23)
Theme and Variations for piano
BARBER (22)
Cello Sonata
FRANÇAIX (20)
Concertino for piano and orchestra
Scherzo for piano
BRITTEN (19)
Sinfonietta for chamber orchestra
Phantasy Quartet for oboe and strings
GOULD (19)
Chorale and Fugue in jazz


# 1933

CROSSE and PENDERECKI were born;
DUPARC died
IPPOLITOV-IVANOV (74)
*The Last Barricade*, opera (1933–4)
ROPARTZ (69)
*Sérénade champêtre*
GLAZUNOV (68)
*Epic Poem*

VAUGHAN WILLIAMS (61)
*The Running Set*, for orchestra
JONGEN (60)
*Symphonie Concertante*, for organ and
    orchestra
*La Légende de Saint-Nicholas*, for children's
    chorus and orchestra
HOLST (59)
*Brook Green Suite*, for strings
*Lyric Movement*, for viola and strings
SCHMIDT (59)
Symphony No 4
HAHN (58)
*O mon bel inconnu!* musical comedy
CARPENTER (57)
*Sea Drift*, symphonic poem
DOHNÁNYI (56)
*Symphonic Minutes*, for orchestra
IRELAND (54)
*Legend*, for piano and orchestra
SCOTT (54)
*Rima's Call to the Birds*, for soprano and
    orchestra
*Mystic Ode*, for chorus and orchestra
BLOCH (53)
*Avodath Hakodesh*, sacred service for
    baritone, chorus and orchestra
PIZZETTI (53)
Cello Concerto (1933–4)
MIASKOVSKY (52)
Symphonies 13 and 14
KODÁLY (51)
*Dances of Galantá*, for orchestra
MALIPIERO (51)
*La favola del figlio cambiato*, opera
PONCE (51)
*Canto y Danza de los Antiguos Mexicana*,
    *(Songs and Dances of Old Mexico)*, for
    orchestra
*Three Songs of Tagore*, for low voice and
    orchestra
Sonata for violin and piano
String Trio
STRAVINSKY (51)
*Persephone*, melodrama (1933–4)
TURINA (51)
Piano Trio
BAX (50)
Sonatina in D for cello and piano
CASELLA (50)
Concerto for violin, cello, piano and
    orchestra
RIEGGER (48)
*Divertissement*, for flute, harp and cello
COATES (47)
Two Symphonic Rhapsodies
*London Every Day*, suite

TOCH (46)
Symphony for piano and orchestra
*Variations on a Mozart Theme*, for orchestra
VILLA-LOBOS (46)
*Pedra Bonita*, ballet
MARTIN (43)
Four Short Pieces for guitar
MARTINŮ (43)
*The Miracle of Our Lady*, opera
BLISS (42)
Viola Sonata
PROKOFIEV (42)
Cello Concerto (1933–8)
*Chant symphonique*, for orchestra
HOWELLS (41)
*A Kent Yeoman's Wooing Song*, for soli,
    chorus and orchestra
MILHAUD (41)
Piano Concerto No 1
BENJAMIN (40)
*Prima Donna*, comic opera
MOORE (40)
String Quartet
PISTON (39)
Concerto for orchestra
String Quartet No 1
CASTELNUOVO-TEDESCO (38)
*Homage to Boccherini*, sonata for guitar
HANSON (37)
*The Merry Mount*, opera
COWELL (36)
*Four Casual Developments*, ballet
Scherzo for orchestra
*Four Continuations*, for chamber
    orchestra
String Quartet No 2, *Mosaic*
TANSMAN (36)
Partita for string orchestra
GERSHWIN (35)
*Pardon My English*, musical
*Let Them Eat Cake*, musical
Two waltzes for piano
HARRIS (35)
Symphony No 1
String Quartet No 2
AURIC (34)
*Les Imaginaires*, ballet
CHÁVEZ (34)
Symphony No 1, *Sinfonia di Antigona*
*Soli*, No 1 for oboe, clarinet, trumpet and
    bassoon
Cantos de Mexico
POULENC (34)
*Feuillets d'album*, for piano
*Villageoises*, for piano
COPLAND (33)
Symphony No 2, *Short Symphony*

KŘENEK (33)
*Cefalo e Procri*, opera
WEILL (33)
*The Silver Lake*, opera
Symphony No 2
FINZI (32)
*A Young Man's Exhortation*, song cycle
RUBBRA (32)
*Bee-Bee-Bei*, opera
BERKELEY, L. (30)
Violin Sonata No 2 (c1933)
BLACHER (30)
*Capriccio*, for orchestra
*Kurmusik*, for small orchestra
KHACHATURIAN (30)
Symphony No 1 (1933–4)
*Dance Suite*
KABALEVSKY (29)
Symphony No 3, *Requiem for Lenin*
BLITZSTEIN (28)
*Surf and Seaweed*, orchestral suite
SHOSTAKOVICH (27)
Piano Concerto No 1 for piano, string
    orchestra and trumpet
*The Human Comedy*, incidental music
    (1933–4)
MACONCHY (26)
String Quartet No 1
MESSIAEN (25)
*L'Ascension*, for organ
Mass for eight sopranos and four violins
HOLMBOE (24)
Wind Quintet
SIEGMEISTER (24)
*American Holiday*, for orchestra
*Strange Funeral in Braddock*, for orchestra
BARBER (23)
*Music for a Scene from Shelley*, for orchestra
CAGE (21)
Sonata for solo clarinet
FRANÇAIX (21)
*Scuola di Ballo*, ballet
*Divertissement*, for string trio, wind, harp
    and double-bass
*A trois*, for string trio
*A quatre*, for flute, oboe, clarinet and
    bassoon
BRITTEN (20)
*A Boy was Born*, for unaccompanied voices
*Friday Afternoons*, twelve children's songs
    with piano (1933–5)
Two Part-songs for chorus and piano
LLOYD (20)
Canon for orchestra
*Ieruin*, opera (1933–4)

**1934**

BIRTWISTLE, MAXWELL DAVIES,
DICKINSON, MATHIAS and
SCHNITTKE were born; DELIUS,
ELGAR, HOLST and SCHREKER died
IPPOLITOV-IVANOV (75)
*Catalan Suite*, for orchestra
DELIUS (72)
*Songs of Farewell*, for chorus and orchestra
PIERNÉ (71)
*Fragonard*, ballet
*Giration*, ballet
STRAUSS, R. (70)
Symphony for wind instruments
ROUSSEL (65)
Symphony No 4
Sinfonietta for strings
ZEMLINSKY (63)
Sinfonietta for orchestra
VAUGHAN WILLIAMS (62)
*Fantasia on Greensleeves*, orchestra
Suite for viola and small orchestra
RACHMANINOV (61)
*Rhapsody on a Theme by Paganini*, for piano
    and orchestra
SCHMIDT (60)
Piano Concerto No 2
Prelude and Fugue in A for organ
SCHOENBERG (60)
Suite in G for strings
BRIAN (58)
Violin Concerto No 1 (lost)
Violin Concerto No 2
CARPENTER (58)
Piano Quintet
FALLA (58)
Fanfare for wind and percussion
CANTALOUBE (55)
*Pièces Françaises*, for piano and orchestra
IRELAND (55)
*A Comedy Overture*, for brass band
RESPIGHI (55)
*La Fiamma*, melodrama
Concerto for oboe, horn, violin,
    double-bass, piano and string orchestra
*Passacaglia in C minor*
BLOCH (54–56)
*A Voice in the Wilderness*, symphonic poem
    for cello and orchestra (1934–6)
BARTÓK (53)
String Quartet No 5
MIASKOVSKY (53)
Symphony No 15
KODÁLY (52)
*Jesus and the Merchants*, for chorus and
    orchestra

MALIPIERO (52)
Symphony No 1
Piano Concerto No 1
STRAVINSKY (52)
Divertimento from *Le baiser de la fée*
BAX (51)
Symphony No 6 in C major
Concerto for flute, oboe, harp and string
    quartet
Octet for horn, strings and piano
Clarinet Sonata in D major
CASELLA (51)
Cello Concerto (1934–5)
*Notturno e Tarentella*, for cello
WEBERN (51)
Concerto for nine instruments
Three Gesänge (Songs)
GRUENBERG (50)
*Serenade to a Beauteous Lady*, for orchestra
WELLESZ (49)
Piano Concerto
TOCH (47)
*Big Ben*, for orchestra
IBERT (44)
*Diane de Poitiers*, ballet
*Concertino da camera*, for alto sax and small
    orchestra
MARTIN (44)
Piano Concerto No 1
MARTINŮ (44)
*Inventions*, for orchestra
BLISS (43)
*Things to Come*, suite for orchestra from
    music for the film
PROKOFIEV (43)
*Lieutenant Kijé*, symphonic suite with
    baritone *ad lib*
*Egyptian Night*, symphonic suite
HONEGGER (42)
*Sémiramis*, ballet
Cello Concerto
String Quartet No 2 (1934–6)
HOWELLS (42)
*Pageantry*, for brass band
MOERAN (40)
*Nocturne*, for baritone, chorus and
    orchestra
PISTON (40)
Prelude and Fugue for orchestra
HINDEMITH (39)
*Mathis der Maler*, opera, also symphony
ORFF (39)
*Bayerische Musik*
GERHARD (38)
*Ariel*, ballet
THOMSON, V. (38)
*Four Saints in Three Acts*, opera

WEINBERGER (38)
*A Bed of Roses*, opera
COWELL (37)
Movement for instruments
GERSHWIN (36)
*I Got Rhythm*, variations for piano and
    orchestra
HARRIS (36)
Symphony No 2
*When Johnny Comes Marching Home*,
    overture
*Songs for Occupations*, for chorus
Piano Trio
POULENC (35)
Two Intermezzi for piano
*Presto, Badinage and Humoresque*, for piano
*Huit chansons polonaises*
*Quatre chansons pour enfants* (1934–5)
COPLAND (34)
*Hear Ye! Hear Ye!*, ballet
*Statements*, for orchestra
KŘENEK (34)
Piano Sonata No 3
RUBBRA (33)
Sinfonia concertante for piano and
    orchestra
*Rhapsody*, for violin and orchestra
RODRIGO (32)
*Cantico de la Esposa*, for voice and piano
WALTON (32)
*Escape Me Never*, ballet from the film
fp Symphony No 1 (first three movements
    only)
BERKELEY, L. (31)
Three Pieces for two pianos (1934–8)
Polka for piano
BLITZSTEIN (29)
Variations for orchestra
SEIBER (29)
*Eva spielt mit Puppen*, opera
String Quartet No 2 (1934–5)
TIPPETT (29)
String Quartet No 1 (1934–5)
SHOSTAKOVICH (28)
*Bright Stream*, comedy ballet (1934–5)
Suite for jazz orchestra No 1
Cello Sonata
*Maxim's Youth*, film music
*Girl Companions*, film music (1934–5)
*Love and Hate*, film music
CARTER (25)
Flute Sonata (withdrawn)
*Tom and Lily*, oratorio (incomplete)
SCHUMAN (24)
*Choreographic Poem*, for seven instruments
CAGE (22)
Six Short Inventions for seven instruments

FRANÇAIX (22)
Suite for violin and orchestra
*Serenade*, for orchestra
*A cinq*, for flute, string trio and harp
*A deux*, sonatina for violin and piano
String Quartet
BRITTEN (21)
*Simple Symphony*, for string orchestra
Suite for violin and piano (1934–5)
*Holiday Diary*, suite for piano
*Te Deum* in C major
LUTOSLAWSKI (21)
Piano Sonata
PANUFNIK (20)
Piano Trio
GINASTERA (18)
*Panambi*, ballet

# 1935

MAW and SALLINEN were born; BERG,
DUKAS, IPPOLITOV-IVANOV,
LOEFFLER and SUK died
PIERNÉ (72)
*Images*, ballet
MASCAGNI (72)
*Nero*, opera
STRAUSS, R. (71)
*The Silent Woman*, opera
*Der Friedenstag*, opera (1935–6)
ZEMLINSKY (64)
*Psalm XIII*, for voices and orchestra
*Der König Kandaules*, opera
VAUGHAN WILLIAMS (63)
*Five Tudor Portraits*, choral suite
SCHMIDT (61)
Toccata and Fugue in A♭ for organ
*Das Buch mit sieben Siegeln*, oratorio
    (1935–7)
HAHN (60)
*Malvina*, operetta
*Le Marchand de Vénise*, opera
CARPENTER (59)
*Danza*, for orchestra
FALLA (59)
*Pour le tombeau de Paul Dukas*, for piano
DOHNÁNYI (58)
Sextet in C
SCOTT (56)
Concerto for two violins
*Let Us Now Praise Famous Men*, for chorus
    and orchestra
BLOCH (55)
Piano Sonata
PONCE (53)
*Elegiac Poem*, for chamber orchestra
*Suite en Estilo Antiguo, (Suite in Olden*

*Style)*, for orchestra
Sonata for violin and piano
STRAVINSKY (53)
Concerto for two pianos
TURINA (53)
Serenade for quartet
BAX (52)
*The Morning Watch*, for chorus and
    orchestra
*Overture to Adventure*, for orchestra
WEBERN (52)
*Das Augenlicht*, for chorus and orchestra
Three Lieder
BERG (50)
Violin Concerto
RIEGGER (50)
*New Dance*, for orchestra
COATES (49)
*The Three Men*, suite
TOCH (48)
*Pinocchio*, for orchestra
IBERT (45)
*Gonzaque*, opera
MARTIN (45)
Rhapsody for strings
MARTINŮ (45)
*The Suburban Theatre*, opera
*Le Jugement de Paris*, ballet
Concertino No 2, for piano
BLISS (44)
*Music for Strings*
PROKOFIEV (44)
*Romeo and Juliet*, ballet (1935–6)
Violin Concerto No 2
*Musiques d'enfants*, for piano
MILHAUD (43)
Cello Concerto No 1
String Quartet No 9
BENJAMIN (42)
*Heritage*, for orchestra
*Romantic Fantasy*, for violin, viola and
    orchestra
MOORE (42)
*White Wings*, opera (possibly 1948)
PISTON (41)
String Quartet No 2
Piano Trio No 1
HINDEMITH (40)
Concerto for orchestra
Viola Concerto, *Der Schwanendreher*
ORFF (40)
*Carmina Burana*, scenic cantata (1935–6)
HANSON (39)
*Drum Taps*, for baritone, chorus and
    orchestra
SESSIONS (39)
Violin Concerto

COWELL (38)
*Six Casual Developments*, for chamber
  orchestra
GERSHWIN (37)
*Porgy and Bess*, opera
CHÁVEZ (36)
Symphony No 2, *Sinfonia India*
*Obertura Republicana*
POULENC (36)
*Margot*, incidental music
*Suite française*, for chamber orchestra
*Cinq poèmes* (Eluard)
'A sa guitare', song (Ronsard)
ANTHEIL (35)
*Dreams*, ballet
KŘENEK (35)
*The Coronation of Poppea*, opera, after
  Monteverdi (1935–6)
WEILL (35)
*A Kingdom for a Cow*, musical play
FINZI (34)
*Introit*, for violin and orchestra (revised
  1945)
DURUFLÉ (33)
Three Dances for orchestra
BERKELEY, L. (32)
Overture for orchestra
*Jonah*, oratorio
String Quartet No 1
*Etude, Berceuse, Capriccio*, for piano
'How Love Came In', for voice and piano
BLACHER (32)
*Fest im Süden*, dance drama
*Divertimente*, Piano Concerto
  (unpublished, lost)
SKALKOTTAS (31)
Concertino for two pianos and orchestra
Symphonic Suite No 1
String Quartet No 3
String Trio
Sonatinas Nos 3 and 4 for violin and
  piano
BLITZSTEIN (30)
*Send for the Militia*, theatre sketch
RAWSTHORNE (30)
Viola Sonata (revised 1954)
SHOSTAKOVICH (29)
Symphony No 4 (1935–6)
Five Fragments for small orchestra
MESSIAEN (27)
*La nativité du Seigneur*, nine meditations
  for organ
HOLMBOE (26)
Suite No 1 for chamber orchestra
Overture
Symphony No 1 for chamber orchestra
Violin Sonata No 1

SIEGMEISTER (26)
String Quartet No 1
SCHUMAN (25)
Symphony No 1, for eighteen instruments
FRANÇAIX (23)
*Les Malheures de Sophie*, ballet
*Le Roi nu*, ballet
Quadruple Concerto for flute, oboe,
  clarinet and bassoon
Saxophone Quartet
DIAMOND (20)
Partita for oboe, bassoon and piano
BABBITT (19)
*Generatrix*, for orchestra


# 1936

BENNETT, BLAKE and REICH were
born; GERMAN, GLAZUNOV and
RESPIGHI died
STRAUSS, R. (72)
*Daphne*, opera (1936–7)
GLAZUNOV (71)
Saxophone Concerto
ROUSSEL (67)
*Rhapsodie flamande*
*Concertino for cello*
NOVÁK (66)
*South Bohemian Suite*
ZEMLINSKY (65)
String Quartet No 4
VAUGHAN WILLIAMS (64)
*Riders to the Sea*, one-act opera
*The Poisoned Kiss*, romantic extravaganza
  for voices and orchestra
*Dona nobis pacem*, cantata
JONGEN (63)
*Triptyque*, three suites for orchestra
RACHMANINOV (63)
Symphony No 3
SCHOENBERG (62)
Violin Concerto
HAHN (61)
*Beaucoup de bruit pour rien*, musical
  comedy
CARPENTER (60)
Violin Concerto
WOLF-FERRARI (60)
fp *Il campiello*, opera
QUILTER (59)
*Julia*, opera
HOLBROOKE (58)
Cello Concerto
*Aucassin et Nicolette*, ballet
IRELAND (57)
*London Overture*, for orchestra

**SCOTT** (57)
*Ode to Great Men*, for tenor and
    orchestra
**MEDTNER** (56)
Violin Sonata, *Sonata Epica*
**BARTÓK** (55)
*Music for Strings, Percussion and Celesta*
*Petite Suite*, for piano
**MIASKOVSKY** (55)
Symphony No 16
**KODÁLY** (54)
*Te Deum*
**MALIPIERO** (54)
*Julius Caesar*, opera
Symphony No 2, *Elegiaca*
**STRAVINSKY** (34)
*Jeu de cartes*, ballet
*Praeludium*, for jazz ensemble
**BAX** (53)
Concerto for bassoon or viola, harp and
    string sextet
String Quartet No 3 in F major
**BERNERS** (53)
*A Wedding Bouquet*, ballet
**WEBERN** (53)
Variations for piano
**GRUENBERG** (52)
*Helena of Troy*, opera
**RIEGGER** (51)
Music for voice and flute
**TAYLOR** (51)
*Lucrece*, for string quartet
**VARÈSE** (51)
*Density 21.5*, for flute solo
**WELLESZ** (51)
*Prosperos Beschwörungen*, for orchestra
    (1936–8)
**COATES** (50)
*London Again*, suite
**DUPRÉ** (50)
*Poème héroïque*, for organ and brass
**TOCH** (49)
*Musical Short Story*, for orchestra (lost)
*Orchids*, for orchestra (lost)
**VILLA-LOBOS** (49)
*Bachianas Brasilieras* No 4 for piano
    (1930–6)
**MARTIN** (46)
Symphony for full orchestra (1936–7)
*Danse de la peur*, for two pianos and small
    orchestra
String Trio
**MARTINŮ** (46)
*Julietta, or The Key to Dreams*, opera
    (1936–7)
**BLISS** (45)
*Kenilworth Suite*, for brass

**PROKOFIEV** (45)
*Peter and the Wolf*, for narrator and
    orchestra
*Russian Overture*
Cantata for the Twentieth Anniversary of
    the October Revolution (1936–7), for
    chorus, band and orchestra (1936–7)
**HONEGGER** (44)
Nocturne
String Quartet No 3
**MILHAUD** (44)
*Suite provençale*
**MOORE** (43)
*The Headless Horseman*, opera
**ROGERS** (43)
Symphony No 3, *On a Thanksgiving Song*
**CASTELNUOVO-TEDESCO** (41)
Concerto for two guitars and orchestra
Concertino for harp and chamber
    orchestra
Tarantella
**ORFF** (41)
*Olympischer Reigen*, for chorus and
    orchestra
**SOWERBY** (41)
Organ Concerto No 1
**SESSIONS** (40)
String Quartet No 1
**COWELL** (39)
String Quartet No 4, *United*
**TANSMAN** (39)
Viola Concerto
Two Intermezzi
**GERSHWIN** (38)
Three Preludes for piano
*Shall We Dance*, film score (1936–7)
**HARRIS** (38)
*Symphony for Voices*
*Time Suite*, for orchestra
Prelude and Fugue for string orchestra
Piano Quintet
**AURIC** (37)
Sonata in G, for violin and piano
**POULENC** (37)
*Litanies à la Vierge noire*, for voices and
    organ
*Petites voix*, for children's choir
*Sept chansons*, for a capella choir
*Les soirées de Nazelles*, for piano
**ANTHEIL** (36)
*Course*, dance score
**BUSH, A.** (36)
Concert Piece for cello and piano
**COPLAND** (36)
*El salón México*, for orchestra
**KŘENEK** (36)
Adagio and Fugue for string orchestra

String Quartet No 6
**WEILL** (36)
*Johnny Johnson*, musical
**FINZI** (35)
*Interlude*, for oboe and string quartet
*Earth, Air and Rain*, song cycle
**RUBBRA** (35)
Symphony No 1
**BERKELEY, L.** (33)
Five Short Pieces for piano
**BLACHER** (33)
Three Orchestral Studies (unpublished, destroyed)
*Divertimento*, for wind
*Geigenmusik*, for violin and orchestra
**KHACHATURIAN** (33)
Piano Concerto
**KABALEVSKY** (32)
Piano Concerto No 2
**SKALKOTTAS** (32)
Piano Trio
Piano Suite No 1
**ALWYN** (31)
*Marriage of Heaven and Hell*, choral work
**BLITZSTEIN** (31)
*The Cradle Will Rock*, play in music (1936–7)
**LAMBERT** (31)
*Summer's Last Will and Testament*, for chorus and orchestra
**RAWSTHORNE** (31)
Concerto for clarinet and string orchestra
**TIPPETT** (31)
Piano Sonata (1936–7, revised 1942)
**SHOSTAKOVICH** (30)
*Salute to Spain*, incidental music
*Four Romances on Verses of Pushkin*, for bass and piano
*Volochayevka Days*, film music
*Maxim's Return*, film music
**CARTER** (27)
Incidental music to *Sophocles* (unpublished)
*Mostellaria*, for tenor, baritone, male chorus and chamber orchestra (unpublished)
*Pocahontas*, ballet
**HOLMBOE** (27)
Suites Nos 2 and 3 for chamber orchestra
Serenade for clarinet and piano quartet
Quartet for flute and piano trio
Quintet for flute, oboe, clarinet, violin and viola
**BARBER** (26)
Symphony No 1, in one movement
*Adagio for Strings*, arranged from String Quartet No 1

String Quartet No 1
**SCHUMAN** (26)
String Quartet No 1
**MENOTTI** (25)
*Trio for a Housewarming Party*, for flute, cello and piano
**PETTERSSON** (25)
Four Improvisations for string trio
**FRANÇAIX** (24)
*Le jeu sentimental*, ballet
*La Lutherie enchantée*, ballet
*Au Musée Grévin*, for orchestra
Piano Concerto
*Cinq portraits de jeunes filles*, for piano
**GILLIS** (24)
*Four Moods in Three Keys*, for chamber orchestra
**BRITTEN** (23)
*Our Hunting Fathers*, song cycle
*Soirées musicales*, suite
**GOULD** (23)
Little Symphony
Symphonette No 2
**LLOYD** (23)
*The Serf*, opera
**DIAMOND** (21)
*TOM*, ballet
Violin Concerto No 1
*Psalm*, for orchestra
Concerto for string quartet
Cello Sonata
Sinfonietta
**BERIO** (11)
Pastorale

## 1937

**BEDFORD, GLASS** and **NILSSON** were born; **GERSHWIN, GURNEY, PIERNÉ, RAVEL, ROUSSEL, SZYMANOWSKI** and **WIDOR** died
**PIERNÉ** (74)
*Gulliver in Lilliput*, ballet
**ROPARTZ** (73)
*Requiem*, with orchestra
**BANTOCK** (69)
*King Solomon*, for narrator, chorus and orchestra
**ROUSSEL** (68)
String Trio
**ALFVÉN** (65)
Swedish Rhapsody No 3, *Dalarapsodi*
**VAUGHAN WILLIAMS** (65)
*Festival Te Deum*, in F major
**SCHMIDT** (63)
*Fuga Solemnis*, for organ
**SCHOENBERG** (63)
String Quartet No 4

**HAHN** (62)
*Aux bosquets d'Italie*, ballet
*Le oui des jeunes filles*, opera
**BRIAN** (61)
Symphony No 5, *Wine of Summer*
**AUBERT** (60)
*Les fêtes d'été*, for orchestra
**RESPIGHI** (posthumous)
*fp Lucrezia*, opera
**BRIDGE** (58)
String Quartet No 4
**CANTALOUBE** (58)
*Poème*, for violin and orchestra
**IRELAND** (58)
*These Things Shall Be*, for baritone, chorus
   and orchestra
*Green Ways*, for piano
**SCOTT** (58)
Harpsichord Concerto
**BLOCH** (57)
Violin Concerto (1937–8)
*Evocations*, symphonic suite
**ENESCO** (56)
*Suite Villageoise*, for orchestra
**MIASKOVSKY** (56)
Symphonies Nos 17 and 18
**MALIPIERO** (55)
Piano Concerto No 2
Cello Concerto
**BAX** (54)
Violin Concerto
*A London Pageant*, for orchestra
*Northern Ballad* No 2, for orchestra
**CASELLA** (54)
Concerto for orchestra
*Il deserto tentato*, oratorio
**GRUENBERG** (53)
*Green Mansions*, radio opera
Piano Quintet
**TAYLOR** (52)
*Ramuntcho*, opera
*Casanova*, ballet
**VARÈSE** (52)
*Espace*, for orchestra
**COATES** (51)
*Springtime*, suite
**SCHOECK** (51)
*Massimilla Doni*, opera
**VILLA-LOBOS** (50)
*Currupira*, ballet
*Sabastiao*, for three voices
*Descobrimento do Brasil*, four suites for
   chorus and orchestra
**IBERT** (47)
*L'Aiglon*, opera (with Honegger)
**MARTINŮ** (47)
*Alexandre bis*, opera

*Comedy on the Bridge*, opera
**BLISS** (46)
*Checkmate*, ballet
**HONEGGER** (45)
*L'Aiglon*, opera (with Ibert)
*1001 Nights*, a musical spectacle
**GROFÉ** (45)
*Broadway at Night*, for orchestra
*Symphony in Steel*
**MILHAUD** (45)
*Cantate de la paix*
**BENJAMIN** (44)
*Overture to an Italian Comedy*, for orchestra
*Nightingale Lane*, for two voices and piano
**MOERAN** (43)
Symphony in G minor
**PISTON** (43)
Symphony No 1
*Concertino*, for piano and chamber
   orchestra
**HINDEMITH** (42)
*Symphonic Dances*, for orchestra
Organ Sonatas Nos 1 and 2
**ORFF** (42)
*Der Mond*, opera (1937–8)
**THOMSON, V.** (41)
*Filling Station*, ballet
**WEINBERGER** (41)
*Wallenstein*, opera
**COWELL** (40)
*Immediate Tragedy*, ballet
*Deep Song*, ballet
*Old American Country Set*, for orchestra
*Sarabande*, for oboe, clarinet and
   percussion
*Chrysanthemums*, for soprano, two saxes
   and four strings
Three Ostinati with Chorales, for oboe,
   clarinet and piano
**TANSMAN** (40)
*Bric-à-Brac*, ballet
Fantasy for cello
Fantasy for violin
**GERSHWIN** (39)
*A Damsel in Distress*, film score
**HARRIS** (39)
Symphony No 3
String Quartet No 3
**AURIC** (38)
*La Seine au Matin*, for orchestra
**POULENC** (38)
*Deux marches et un intermède*, for chamber
   orchestra
Mass in G major
*Sécheresses*, cantata
*Bourée d'Auvergne*, for piano
*Tel jour telle nuit*, songs

**BUSH, A.** (37)
Piano Concerto for baritone, piano, chorus
and orchestra
**KŘENEK** (37)
Piano Concerto No 2
**WEILL** (37)
*The Eternal Road,* incidental music
**RUBBRA** (36)
Symphony No 2
String Quartet
**WALTON** (35)
*Crown Imperial,* coronation march
*In Honour of the City,* for chorus and
orchestra
**BERKELEY, L.** (34)
*Domini est terra,* for chorus and orchestra
*Mont Juic,* suite of Catalan dances for
orchestra (with Britten)
**BLACHER** (34)
*Lustspiel – Ouvertüre* (unpublished,
destroyed)
*Concertante Musiche,* for orchestra
**KHACHATURIAN** (34)
*Song of Stalin,* for chorus and orchestra
**RAINIER** (34)
*Three Greek Epigrams,* for soprano and
piano
**DALLAPICCOLA** (33)
*Volo di Notte,* opera (1937–8)
**KABALEVSKY** (33)
*The Testament,* for chorus and orchestra
**SKALKOTTAS** (33)
Piano Concerto No 2 (1937–8)
Violin Concerto (1937–8)
Five Pieces for violin and piano (1937–8)
Suite for cello and piano (lost) (1937–8)
**BLITZSTEIN** (32)
*I've Got a Tune,* radio song-play
*Plowed Under,* theatre sketch
**LAMBERT** (32)
*Horoscope,* ballet
**RAWSTHORNE** (32)
Theme and variations for two violins
**TIPPETT** (32)
*A Song of Liberty*
**SHOSTAKOVICH** (31)
Symphony No 5
**MACONCHY** (30)
String Quartet No 2
**MESSIAEN** (29)
*Poèmes pour mi,* for voice and orchestra
**CARTER** (28)
*The Ballroom Guide,* for orchestra
English Horn Concerto (incomplete)
*The Bridge,* oratorio (incomplete)
*Let's Go Gay,* for female voices and two
pianos (unpublished)

*Harvest Home,* for unaccompanied voices
(unpublished)
*To Music,* for unaccompanied voices
(unpublished)
**HOLMBOE** (28)
*Psalm LXII,* for boys' voices
**SIEGMEISTER** (28)
*Abraham Lincoln Walks at Midnight,* for
orchestra
**BARBER** (27)
*First Essay for Orchestra*
**SCHUMAN** (27)
Symphony No 2
String Quartet No 2
*Choral Étude*
**MENOTTI** (26)
*Amelia al Ballo,* opera
**FRANÇAIX** (25)
*Le diable boiteux,* chamber opera
*Musique de Cour,* for flute, violin and
orchestra
**GILLIS** (25)
*The Woolyworm,* symphonic satire
*The Crucifixion,* for solo voices, narrator,
chorus and orchestra
*The Panhandle,* suite for orchestra
*Thoughts Provoked on Becoming a
Prospective Papa,* suite for orchestra
**BRITTEN** (24)
*Mont Juic,* suite of Catalan dances for
orchestra (with Berkeley, L.)
*Variations on a Theme of Frank Bridge,* for
strings
*On This Island,* song cycle
**GOULD** (24)
Piano Concerto
Spirituals for orchestra
**DIAMOND** (22)
Variations for small orchestra
Quintet for flute, string trio and piano
**GINASTERA** (21)
*Danzas Argentinas,* for piano
**BERNSTEIN** (19)
Pianoforte Trio
Music for two pianos

## 1938

**STRAUSS, R.** (74–6)
*The Love of Danae,* opera (1938–40)
**BEACH** (71)
Piano Trio
**BANTOCK** (70)
*Aphrodite in Cyprus,* symphonic ode
**SCHMITT** (68)
*Oriane et le prince d'amour,* ballet
*Enfants,* for small orchestra

VAUGHAN WILLIAMS (66)
*The Bridal Day*, masque
*Serenade to Music*, for sixteen solo voices
  and orchestra
JONGEN (65)
*Hymne à la Meuse*, for chorus and orchestra
SCHMIDT (64)
Toccata for piano
Piano Quintet in A
GLIÈRE (63)
Harp Concerto
BRIAN (62)
*Prometheus Unbound*, cantata (1938–44)
IRELAND (59)
Piano Trio No 3
BLOCH (58)
Piece for string quartet
PIZZETTI (58–62)
*L'Oro*, opera (1938–42)
BARTÓK (57)
Violin Concerto No 2
Sonata for two pianos and percussion
*Contrasts*, trio for clarinet, violin and piano
MIASKOVSKY (57)
Children's Pieces for Piano, in three books
KODÁLY (56)
*Variations on a Hungarian Folksong*, for
  orchestra (1938–9)
MALIPIERO (56)
*Anthony and Cleopatra*, opera
Triple Concerto for violin, cello and piano
PONCE (56)
*Instantáneas Mexicanas*, for orchestra
STRAVINSKY (56)
*Dumbarton Oaks*, for chamber orchestra
WEBERN (55)
String Quartet
GRUENBERG (54)
String Quartet
Piano Concerto No 2
COATES (52)
*The Enchanted Garden*, ballet
DUPRÉ (52)
Variations for piano and organ
RIEGGER (52)
String Quartet No 1 (1938–9)
SCHOECK (52)
*Das Schloss Durande*, opera (1938–39)
TOCH (51)
*The Idle Stroller*, suite for orchestra
VILLA-LOBOS (51)
*Bachianas Brasilieras* Nos 3 and 6
String Quartet No 6
IBERT (48)
*La Famille Cardinal*, opera (with
  Honegger)
Capriccio for ten instruments

MARTIN (48)
*Le Vin herbe (Der Zaubertrank)* opera
  (1938–41)
*Ballade*, for saxophone, strings, piano and
  percussion
Sonata da chiesa, for viola d'amore and
  organ
MARTINŮ (48)
Concerto for two string orchestras, piano
  and timpani
Concerto Grosso for orchestra
*Tre ricercare*, for orchestra
Quartet No 5
Madrigals for women's voices
BLISS (47)
Piano Concerto
PROKOFIEV (47)
*Alexander Nevsky*, cantata (1938–9)
HONEGGER (46)
*La Famille Cardinal*, opera (with Ibert)
*La danse des morts*, for solo voices, chorus
  and orchestra
*Joan of Arc at the Stake*, incidental music
HOWELLS (46)
*Hymnus Paradisi*, for soli, chorus and
  orchestra
MILHAUD (46)
*Medée*, opera
BENJAMIN (45)
Two Jamaican pieces for orchestra,
  'Jamaican Song', 'Jamaican Rumba'
*Cotillon Suite*, for orchestra
Sonatina for cello and piano
MOORE (45)
*Dedication*, for chorus
PISTON (44)
*The Incredible Flutist*, ballet
CASTELNUOVO-TEDESCO (43)
*Aucassin et Nicolette*, for voice,
  instruments and marionettes
HINDEMITH (43)
*Nobilissima visione*, ballet
SOWERBY (43)
*Theme in Yellow*, for orchestra
Clarinet Sonata
HANSON (42)
Symphony No 3
ROBERTSON (42)
Piano Quintet
WEINBERGER (42)
Variations on *Under the Spreading Chestnut
  Tree*, for orchestra
SESSIONS (41)
*Scherzino and March*, for orchestra
TANSMAN (41)
*La toison d'or*, opera
Symphony No 4

**HARRIS** (40)
*Soliloquy and Dance,* for viola and piano
**AURIC** (39)
*Ouverture,* for Orchestra
Trio in D, for oboe, clarinet and bassoon
**CHÁVEZ** (39)
Concerto for four horns
**POULENC** (39)
Concerto for organ, strings and timpani
Four Penitential Motets (1938–9)
**COPLAND** (38)
*An Outdoor Overture*
*Billy the Kid,* ballet and orchestral suite
**WEILL** (38)
*Knickerbocker Holiday,* musical
**RUBBRA** (37)
*Prism,* ballet music
**BERKELEY, L.** (35)
*The Judgement of Paris,* ballet
Introduction and Allegro for two pianos
  and orchestra
**BLACHER** (35)
Symphony
**DALLAPICCOLA** (34)
*Canti di prigionia,* for chorus and
  instruments (1938–41)
**KABALEVSKY** (34)
*Colas Breugnon,* opera
*Vasilek,* ballet
*The Comedians,* suite for small orchestra
**SKALKOTTAS** (34)
Cello Concerto (lost)
*The Maiden and Death,* ballet
Duo for violin and viola
Eight Variations on a Greek Folksong,
  piano trio
Piano Concerto No 3 (1938–9)
**BLITZSTEIN** (33)
*No for an Answer,* opera (1938–40)
**RAWSTHORNE** (33)
Symphonic Studies for orchestra
**TIPPETT** (33)
Concerto for double string orchestra
  (1938–9)
**LUTYENS** (32)
String Quartets Nos 1 and 2
Partita for two violins
Sonata for solo viola
**SHOSTAKOVICH** (32)
Suite for jazz orchestra No 2
String Quartet No 1
Film music
**MACONCHY** (31)
String Quartet No 3
**CARTER** (29)
Prelude, Fanfare and Polka for small
  orchestra (unpublished)

*Heart Not So Heavy as Mine,* for
  unaccompanied voices (unpublished)
Musical Studies (withdrawn)
*Tell Me, Where is Fancy Bred?,* alto and
  guitar
**HOLMBOE** (29)
Violin Concerto
*Rapsodisk Interludium,* for clarinet, violin
  and piano
**CAGE** (26)
*Metamorphosis,* for piano
**FRANÇAIX** (26)
*Le jugement d'un fou,* ballet
*Verrières de Venise,* ballet
**GILLIS** (26)
*The Raven,* for narrator and orchestra
Symphony No 1, *An American Symphony*
  (1939–40)
**JONES** (26)
Symphonic Prologue
**BRITTEN** (25)
Piano Concerto No 1 in D major (revised
  1945)
**LUTOSLAWSKI** (25)
Symphonic Variations for orchestra
**DIAMOND** (23)
Cello Concerto
Music for double string orchestra, brass
  and timpani
*Heroic Piece,* for small orchestra
*Elegy in memory of Ravel,* for brass, harps
  and percussion
Piano Quartet
**GINASTERA** (22)
Two Songs with piano
*Songs of Tucumán,* for voice, flute, harp,
  violin and drums
*Psalm,* for clarinet, chorus, boys' chorus
  and orchestra
**BERNSTEIN** (20)
Piano Sonata
*Music for the Dance,* Nos 1 and 2
*The Birds,* incidental music
**SHAPERO** (18)
*Three Pieces for Three Pieces,* for woodwind
  trio
**FOSS** (16)
Four Two-part Inventions for piano
*Drei Goethe-Lieder*


## 1939

**SCHMIDT** died
**VAUGHAN WILLIAMS** (67)
*Five Variants of Dives and Lazarus,* for
  strings and harp

**JONGEN** (66)
*Ouverture-Fanfare*, for orchestra
**SCHOENBERG** (65)
*Kol Nidrei*, for speaker, chorus and
   orchestra
**WOLF-FERRARI** (63)
*Dama Boba*, opera
**DOHNÁNYI** (62)
*Cantus Vitae*, symphonic cantata
**HOLBROOKE** (61)
*Tamerlaine*, concerto for clarinet/
   saxophone, bassoon and orchestra
**IRELAND** (60)
*Concertino Pastorale*, for strings
**SCOTT** (60)
Symphony No 3, *The Muses*
**BARTÓK** (58)
Divertimento for Strings
String Quartet No 6
**MIASKOVSKY** (58)
Symphony No 19
**KODÁLY** (57)
Concerto for orchestra
*The Peacock Variations*, for orchestra
**MALIPIERO** (57)
*Ecuba*, opera
**BAX** (56)
Symphony No 7 in A♭
**BERNERS** (56)
*Cupid and Psyche*, ballet
**CASELLA** (56)
Sinfonia (1939–40)
**WEBERN** (56)
Cantata No 1, *Jone*
**VILLA-LOBOS** (52)
*New York Skyline*, for orchestra
**MARTIN** (49)
Three Ballades for instruments
**MARTINŮ** (49)
Field Mass
**PROKOFIEV** (48)
*Simeon Kotko*, opera
*Zdravitsa*, cantata
Piano Sonata No 6 (1939–40)
Piano Sonata No 7 (1939–42)
Piano Sonata No 8 (1939–44)
**HOWELLS** (47)
Concerto for strings
**MILHAUD** (47)
Symphony No 1 for full orchestra
*King René's Chimney*, for wind quartet
**MOORE** (46)
*The Devil and Daniel Webster*, opera
**PISTON** (45)
Violin Concerto No 1
Violin Sonata

**CASTELNUOVO-TEDESCO** (44)
Guitar Concerto
Violin Concerto No 2, *The Prophets*
**HINDEMITH** (44)
Violin Concerto
**SOWERBY** (44)
*Forsaken of Man*, cantata
**SESSIONS** (43)
*Pages from a Diary*, for piano
**COWELL** (42)
Symphony No 2, *Anthropos*
*Shipshape*, overture
*Symphonic Set*, for orchestra
*American Melting Pot*, for orchestra
*Celtic Set*, for orchestra
**KORNGOLD** (42)
*Die Kathrin*, opera
**HARRIS** (41)
Symphony No 4
String Quartet No 4
**CHÁVEZ** (40)
Four Nocturnes for voice and orchestra
**POULENC** (40)
*Fiançailles pour rire*, songs
**KŘENEK** (39)
*Eight Column Line*, ballet
Symphonic Pieces for string orchestra
Suite for cello
**WEILL** (39)
*The Ballad of the Magna Carta*, incidental
   music for radio drama
**RUBBRA** (38)
Symphony No 3
**RODRIGO** (37)
*Concierto de Aranjuez*, for guitar and
   orchestra
**WALTON** (37)
Violin Concerto
**BERKELEY, L.** (36)
Serenade for string orchestra
Five Songs (1939–40)
**BLACHER** (36)
*Harlekinade*, ballet
*Concerto da camera*
**KHACHATURIAN** (36)
*Happiness*, ballet
*Masquerade*, incidental music
**RAINIER** (36)
String Quartet
**KABALEVSKY** (35)
Symphony No 4, *Shchors*, for chorus and
   orchestra
**SKALKOTTAS** (35)
Three Pieces, for violin and piano
Concertino for oboe and piano
Concerto for violin, viola, wind and
   double-bass (1939–40)

Scherzo for piano quartet (1939–40)
**ALWYN** (34)
Violin Concerto
*Rhapsody*, for piano quartet
*Sonata-Impromptu*, for violin and viola
**RAWSTHORNE** (34)
String Quartet No 1, *Theme and Variations*
**TIPPETT** (34)
*Fantasia on a Theme by Handel*, for piano
   and orchestra (1939–41)
*A Child of Our Time*, oratorio (1939–41)
**FRANKEL** (33)
*Elégie Juivre*, for cello and piano
**LUTYENS** (33)
Three Pieces for orchestra
String Trio
**SHOSTAKOVICH** (33)
Symphony No 6
Film music
**MESSIAEN** (31)
*Les corps glorieux*, for organ
**CARTER** (30)
*Canonic Suite*, for four saxophones
**HOLMBOE** (30)
Symphony No 2
Concerto for piano and chamber orchestra
Violin Sonata No 2
**BARBER** (29)
Violin Concerto
**SCHUMAN** (29)
*American Festival Overture*
*Prelude for Voices*
String Quartet No 3
*Quartettino*, for four bassoons
**GILDER** (28)
*Seascape*, for piano and orchestra
**MENOTTI** (28)
*The Old Maid and the Thief*, opera
**CAGE** (27)
*Imaginary Landscape*, No 1
*First Construction (In Metal)*, for percussion
   sextet
**GILLIS** (27)
*An American Symphony* (Symphony No 1)
   (1939–40)
**JONES** (27)
Five Pieces for orchestra
**BRITTEN** (26)
Violin Concerto in D minor (revised 1958)
*Canadian Carnival*, for orchestra (1939–40)
*Ballad of Heroes*, for voices and orchestra
*Les Illuminations*, song cycle
**GOULD** (26)
Symphonette No 3
*Jericho*, for concert band
**BABBITT** (23)
String Trio

**ARNELL** (22)
String Quartet No 1
**BERNSTEIN** (21)
*Scenes from the City of Sin*, for piano (four
   hands)
**BUSH, G.** (19)
Sonata for two pianos
**SHAPERO** (19)
Trumpet Sonata


# 1940

**STRAUSS, R.** (76)
*Capriccio*, opera (1940–1)
**VAUGHAN WILLIAMS** (68)
*Six Choral Songs – to be sung in time of war*
*Valiant for Truth*, motet
**CARPENTER** (64)
Symphony No 2
**FALLA** (64)
*Homenajes*, for orchestra
**BRIDGE** (61)
*Rebus*, for orchestra
*Vignettes de danse*, for small orchestra
Divertimento for flute, oboe, clarinet and
   bassoon
**PIZZETTI** (60)
Symphony in A major
**MIASKOVSKY** (59)
Symphonies Nos 20 and 21
**MALIPIERO** (58)
*La vita e'sogno*, opera
**STRAVINSKY** (58)
Symphony in C
Tango for piano
**PONCE** (57)
*Ferial*, divertimento sinfónico
**WEBERN** (57)
Variations for orchestra
**VILLA-LOBOS** (53)
Preludes for guitar
*Saudades da juventude*, Suite No 1
**MARTINŮ** (50)
Military March
**BLISS** (49)
*Seven American Poems*, for low voice and
   piano
**PROKOFIEV** (49)
*The Duenna*, opera (1940–1)
*Cinderella*, ballet (1940–4)
**MILHAUD** (48)
String Quartet No 10, *Birthday Quartet*
**BENJAMIN** (47)
Sonatina for chamber orchestra
**ROGERS** (47)
Symphony No 4

PISTON (46)
Chromatic Study for organ
HINDEMITH (45)
Symphony in E♭ major
Cello Concerto No 2
Theme and Variations for piano and
  strings *The Four Temperaments*
Harp Sonata
SOWERBY (45)
Symphony No 3
GERHARD (44)
*Don Quixote*, ballet (1940–1)
ROBERTSON (44)
Prelude, Scherzo and Ricercare for
  orchestra
String Quartet
WEINBERGER (44)
Saxophone Concerto
*Song of the High Seas*, for orchestra
COWELL (43)
*Pastorale and Fiddler's Delight*, for orchestra
*Voxhumana*, for orchestra
*Ancient Desert Drone*, for orchestra
*Concerto Piccolo*, for piano and orchestra
KORNGOLD (43)
*Songs of the Clown*
Four Shakespeare Songs
HARRIS (42)
*Western Landscape*, ballet
*American Creed*, for orchestra
*Ode to Truth*, for orchestra
*Challenge*, for baritone, chorus and
  orchestra
*Evening Piece*, for orchestra
String Quintet
AURIC (41)
Five *Chansons Françaises*, for chorus
CHÁVEZ (41)
*Antigona*, ballet
Piano Concerto
*Xochipili-Macuilxochitl*, for Mexican
  orchestra
POULENC (41)
*Histoire de Babar le petit éléphant*, for piano
  and narrator (1940–5)
*Mélancolie*, for piano
Cello Sonata (1940–8)
*Banalities*, songs
THOMPSON, R. (41)
Suite for oboe, violin and viola
BUSH, A. (40)
Symphony No 1
COPLAND (40)
*Quiet City*, orchestral suite for trumpet,
  English horn and strings
KŘENEK (40)
*Tarquin*, opera

Little Concerto for organ, cembalo and
  chamber orchestra
FINZI (39)
*Dies natalis*, cantata
DURUFLÉ (38)
Andante and Scherzo for orchestra
WALTON (38)
*The Wise Virgins*, ballet
BLACHER (37)
*Fürstin Tarakanowa*, opera
*Hamlet*, symphonic poem
Concerto for strings
BERKELEY, L. (37)
Symphony No 1
Sonatina for recorder (flute) and piano
Four Concert Studies, Set I, for piano
Five Housman Songs for tenor and piano
KHACHATURIAN (37)
Violin Concerto
KABALEVSKY (36)
*The Golden Spikes*, ballet
*The Comedians*, suite for small orchestra
Suite for jazz
SKALKOTTAS (36)
Ten Musical Sketches for string quartet
Piano Suites Nos 2, 3 and 4
Sonata No 2 for violin and piano
String Quartet No 4
Thirty-two Piano Pieces, (1940–1)
Four Piano Studies
Two Quartets for oboe, bassoon, trumpet
  and piano (1940–2)
Concertino for trumpet and piano (1940–2)
ALWYN (35)
*Masquerade*, overture
Divertimento for solo flute
LAMBERT (35)
*Dirge*, for voices and strings
SEIBER (35)
*Besardo Suite* No 1
LUTYENS (34)
*Midas*, ballet for string quartet and piano
Chamber Concertos Nos 1 and 2 (1940–1)
SHOSTAKOVICH (34)
*King Lear*, incidental music
Piano Quintet in G minor
Three Pieces for solo violin
CARTER (31)
Pastorale for cor anglais, horn, viola, cello
  and piano
HOLMBOE (31)
Chamber Concerto No 2 for flute, violin
  and strings
Chamber Concerto No 3 for clarinet, two
  trumpets, two horns and strings
Concertino for violin, viola and strings
Concertino No 2 for violin and strings

The Devil, The Mayor, opera
Serenade for flute and piano trio
Notturno for wind quintet
**SIEGMEISTER** (31)
*Johnny Appleseed*, choral
**BARBER** (30)
*A Stop-watch and an Ordnance Map*, for
  male chorus and orchestra
**SCHUMAN** (30)
Secular Cantata No 1, 'This is our Time'
**FRANÇAIX** (28)
*L'Apostrophe*, opera
**GILLIS** (28)
Symphony No 2, *A Symphony of Faith*
Symphony No 3, *A Symphony of Free Men*
  (1940–1)
*Portrait of a Frontier Town*, suite for
  orchestra
**BRITTEN** (27)
*Paul Bunyan*, operetta (c1940–1, revised
  1974)
*Sinfonia da requiem*, for orchestra
*Diversions on a Theme*, for piano (left hand)
  and orchestra
*Seven Sonnets of Michelangelo*, for tenor
  and piano
**GOULD** (27)
Latin-American Symphonette
*A Foster Gallery*, for orchestra
**PANUFNIK** (26)
Five Polish Peasant Songs
**DIAMOND** (25)
Symphony No 1
Concerto for small orchestra
Quartet No 1
**GINASTERA** (24)
Three Pieces for piano
*Malambo*, for piano
**ARNELL** (23)
Violin Concerto
**BERNSTEIN** (22)
*The Peace*, incidental music
Sonata for violin and piano
Four studies for two clarinets, three
  bassoons and piano
**BUSH, G.** (20)
Rhapsody for clarinet and string quartet
**SHAPERO** (20)
String Quartet
**FOSS** (18)
Music for *The Tempest*
Two Symphonic Pieces
Four Preludes for flute, clarinet and
  bassoon

## 1941

**BRIDGE, DAVIES, HARTY, SINDING**
and **PADEREWSKI** died
**NOVÁK** (71)
*De Profundis*, symphonic poem
*St Wenceslas Triptych*, for organ and
  orchestra
*Home*, for six male choruses
**SCHMITT** (71)
*Janian*, for strings
**VAUGHAN WILLIAMS** (69)
*England, My England*, for baritone, chorus
  and orchestra
**JONGEN** (68)
*Ouverture de fête*, for orchestra
*La cigale et le fourmi*, for children's choir
  and orchestra
**RACHMANINOV** (68)
*Three Symphonic Dances*, for orchestra
**SCHOENBERG** (67)
Variations and Recitative for organ
**CARPENTER** (65)
*Song of Freedom*, for chorus and orchestra
**IRELAND** (62)
*Sarnia*, for piano
*Three Pastels*, for piano
'O Happy Land', song
**BARTÓK** (60)
Concerto for two pianos and percussion
  (also orchestra)
**MIASKOVSKY** (60)
Symphonies Nos 22 and 23
**MALIPIERO** (59)
*I Capriccio di Callot*, opera (1941–2)
**PONCE** (58)
*Conciérto del sur*, for guitar and orchestra
**WEBERN** (58–60)
Cantata No 2, *Jone* (1941–3)
**RIEGGER** (56)
Canon and Fugue for strings or orchestra
**TAYLOR** (56)
*Processional*, for orchestra
**MARTIN** (51)
Sonata da chiesa for flute and string
  orchestra
**BLISS** (50)
String Quartet
**PROKOFIEV** (50)
*War and Peace*, opera (1941–3)
Suite for orchestra, *1941*
*A Summer's Day*, suite for small
  orchestra
Symphonic March
String Quartet No 2
**HONEGGER** (49)
Symphony No 2 for strings and trumpet

HOWELLS (49)
Four Anthems
MILHAUD (49)
Clarinet Concerto
Piano Concerto No 2
Concerto for two pianos
Four Sketches
MOORE (48)
*Village Music*, suite for small orchestra
PISTON (47)
Sinfonietta for orchestra
ORFF (46)
*Die Kluge*, opera (1941–2)
SOWERBY (46)
*Poem*, for viola with organ and orchestra
GERHARD (45)
*Hommaje a Pedrell*, symphony
SESSIONS (45)
*Montezuma*, opera (1941–62)
THOMSON, V. (45)
Symphony No 2
WEINBERGER (45)
*Lincoln Symphony*
*Czech Rhapsody*, for orchestra
*The Bird's Opera*, for orchestra
COWELL (44)
*Schoonthree*, for orchestra
*Tales of our Countryside*, for orchestra
*Two Bits*, for flute and piano
*Grinnell Fanfare*, for organ and brass
KORNGOLD (44)
*Psalm*, for voices and orchestra
HARRIS (43)
*From this Earth*, ballet
*Acceleration*, for orchestra
Violin Sonata
POULENC (42)
*Les animaux modèles*, ballet
*La fille du jardinier*, incidental music
*Exultate Deo*, for choir
*Salve Regina*, for choir
THOMPSON, R. (42)
String Quartet No 1
BUSH, A. (41)
*Meditation on a German Song*, for violin,
    piano and strings
COPLAND (41)
Piano Sonata
KŘENEK (41)
*Lamentations of Jeremiah*, for chorus
WEILL (41)
*Lady in the Dark*, musical
RUBBRA (40)
Symphony No 4
*The Morning Watch*, for choir and orchestra
WALTON (39)
*Scapino*, overture

BLACHER (38)
*Das Zauberbuch von Erzeram*, ballet
KABALEVSKY (37)
*Youth Parade*, for children's chorus and
    orchestra
SKALKOTTAS (37)
*Largo*, for cello and piano
RAWSTHORNE (36)
*The Creel*, suite for piano duet
SEIBER (36)
*Besardo Suite No 2*, for strings
*Pastorale and Burlesque*, for flute and
    strings (1941–2)
*Transylvanian Rhapsody*
*Fantasy*, for cello and piano
TIPPETT (36)
String Quartet No 2 (1941–2)
COOKE (35)
Cello Sonata
LUTYENS (35)
Five Intermezzi for piano
SHOSTAKOVICH (35)
*The Gamblers*, opera
Symphony No 7, *Leningrad*
MESSIAEN (33)
*Quatuor pour la fin du temps*, for violin,
    clarinet, cello and piano
HOLMBOE (32)
Symphony No 3, *Sinfonia Rustica*
Symphony No 4, *Sinfonia Sacra*, for chorus
    and orchestra
Symphonic Overture
SCHUMAN (31)
Symphonies Nos 3 and 4
*Newsreel*, suite for orchestra
CAGE (29)
*Double Music*, for percussion
GILLIS (29)
*The Night Before Christmas*, for narrator
    and orchestra
BRITTEN (28)
*Scottish Ballad*, for two pianos and
    orchestra
*Matinées musicales*, for orchestra
String Quartet No 1
GOULD (28)
*Lincoln Legend*, for orchestra
LLOYD (28)
*Trinidad March*, for military band
*Charade*, suite for orchestra
LUTOSLAWSKI (28)
Symphony No 1 (1941–7)
*Variations on a Theme of Paganini*, for two
    pianos
DIAMOND (26)
*The Dream of Audubon*, ballet

BABBITT (25)
Composition for orchestra
*Music for the Mass I*, for chorus
GINASTERA (25)
*Estancia*, ballet
ARNELL (24)
String Quartet No 2
BERNSTEIN (23)
Symphony No 1, *Jeremiah* (1941–44)
Clarinet Sonata (1941–42)
BUSH, G. (21)
*The Spanish Rivals*, opera
*La belle dame sans merci*, choral
Piano Concerto
Sinfonietta Concertante for cello
FRICKER (21)
Three Preludes for piano (1941–4)
SHAPERO (21)
*Nine-minute Overture*
Piano Sonata (four hands)
FOSS (19)
*Allegro Concertante*, for orchestra
*Dance Sketch*, for orchestra
Duo for cello and piano

## 1942

ROPARTZ (78)
*De profundis*, with orchestra
STRAUSS, R. (78)
Horn Concerto No 2
NOVÁK (72)
Five mixed choruses
Ten children's choruses
ALFVÉN (70)
Symphony No 5 in A minor
VAUGHAN WILLIAMS (70)
*Coastal Command*, orchestral suite
SCHOENBERG (68)
Piano Concerto
GLIÈRE (67)
Concerto for coloratura soprano
CARPENTER (66)
Symphony No 3
DOHNÁNYI (65)
*Suite en Valse*, for orchestra (1942–3)
IRELAND (63)
*Epic March*
MEDTNER (62)
Piano Concerto No 3, *Ballade* (1942–3)
PIZZETTI (62)
Piano Sonata
MALIPIERO (60)
*Minnie la candida*, opera
STRAVINSKY (60)
*Danses concertantes*, for chamber orchestra
*Four Norwegian Moods*, for orchestra

*Circus Polka*, for orchestra
CASELLA (59)
*Paganiniana*, for orchestra
GRUENBERG (58)
Symphonies Nos 2 and 3
RIEGGER (57)
Passacaglia and Fugue, for band or
   orchestra
COATES (56)
*Four Centuries*, suite
VILLA-LOBOS (55)
*Bachianas Brasilieras* No 7 for orchestra
String Quartet No 7
PROKOFIEV (51)
Flute Sonata
*Ballad of an Unknown Boy*, cantata
*Ivan the Terrible*, film score
MARTIN (52)
*Die Weise von Liebe und Tod des Cornets*, for
   voice and orchestra (1942–3)
MARTINŮ (52)
Symphony No 1
MILHAUD (50)
String Quartet No 11
BENJAMIN (49)
Concerto for oboe and strings
MOORE (49)
Quintet for woodwinds and horn
ROGERS (49)
*The Passion*, oratorio
MOERAN (48)
Violin Concerto
PISTON (48)
*Fanfare for the Fighting French*
Flute Quintet
*Interlude*, for viola and piano
GERHARD (46)
Violin Concerto (1942–5)
SESSIONS (46)
Duo for violin and piano
THOMSON, V. (46)
*Canon for Dorothy Thomson*
*The Mayor La Guardia Waltzes*
COWELL (45)
Symphony No 3, *Gaelic*
*Trickster Coyote*, for flute and percussion
KORNGOLD (45)
*Prayer*, for tenor, chorus and orchestra
'Tomorrow', song
TANSMAN (45)
Symphony No 5
HARRIS (44)
*What so proudly we hail*, ballet
Symphony No 5
Piano Concerto with band
CHÁVEZ (43)
Toccata for percussion instruments

POULENC (43)
Violin Sonata **(1942–3)**
*Chansons villageoises*, songs
THOMPSON, R. (43)
*Solomon and Balkis*, opera
ANTHEIL (42)
Symphony No 4
BUSH, A. (42)
A Birthday Overture
COPLAND (42)
*Rodeo*, ballet
fp *A Lincoln Portrait*, for narrator and
   orchestra
*Danzon Cubano*
KŘENEK (42)
Viola Sonata
FINZI (41)
Prelude and Fugue for string trio
*Let us Garlands Bring*, five songs
DURUFLÉ (40)
*Prélude et fugue sur le nom Alain*, for organ
RODRIGO (40)
*Concierto Heroico*, for piano and orchestra
WALTON (40)
*Major Barbara*, film score
*The First of the Few*, film score, including
   'Spitfire' prelude and fugue
BERKELEY, L. (39)
String Quartet No 2
Sonatina for violin and piano
KHACHATURIAN (39)
*Gayane*, ballet
Symphony No 2
DALLAPICCOLA (38)
*Marsia*, ballet (1942–3)
*Cinque Frammente di Saffo*
KABALEVSKY (38)
*Before Moscow*, opera
*People's Avengers*, suite for chorus and
   orchestra
*Our Great Fatherland*, cantata
SKALKOTTAS (38)
Little Suite for strings
*The Return of Ulysses*, overture (1942–3)
Double-bass Concerto (1942–3)
ALWYN (37)
Concerto Grosso No 1
BLITZSTEIN (37)
*Labor for Victory*, radio series
LAMBERT (37)
*Aubade héroïque*, for orchestra
RAWSTHORNE (37)
Piano Concerto No 1
SEIBER (37)
*Balaton*, opera
*La Blanchisseuse*, ballet music

TIPPETT (37)
Two madrigals: *The Source* and *The*
   *Windhover*
FRANKEL (36)
*Youth Music*, for string orchestra
LUTYENS (36)
Three Symphonic Preludes
Nine Bagatelles for cello and piano
Two Songs (Auden) for voice and piano
SHOSTAKOVICH (36)
*Native Leningrad*, suite
Piano Sonata No 2
*Six Romances on Verses of English poets*, for
   bass and piano
CARTER (33)
Symphony No 1 (revised 1954)
*The Defense of Corinth*, for speaker, male
   voices and piano
HOLMBOE (33)
Chamber Concerto No 4 for violin, cello
   and orchestra
*Sonatina capricciosa*, for flute and piano
BARBER (32)
*Second Essay for Orchestra*
SCHUMAN (32)
Piano Concerto
*Requiescat*
Secular Cantata No 2, 'A Free Song'
MENOTTI (31)
*The Island God*, opera
CAGE (30)
*Wonderful Widow of 18 Springs*, for voice
   and closed piano
GILLIS (30)
Three Sketches for strings
BRITTEN (29)
*A Ceremony of Carols*, for treble voices and
   harp
Hymn to St Cecilia, for unaccompanied
   voices
FINE (28)
*Alice in Wonderland*, incidental music
PANUFNIK (28)
Tragic Overture
DIAMOND (27)
Symphony No 2
Concerto for two solo pianos
BABBITT (26)
*Music for the Mass II*, for chorus
ARNELL (25)
Symphony No 2
BERNSTEIN (24)
Sonata for clarinet and piano
Symphony No 1, *Jeremiah*
SHAPERO (22)
Violin Sonata

**FOSS** (20)
*The Prairie*, for soloists, chorus and
    orchestra
Clarinet Concerto (later arranged as Piano
    Concerto No 1)

## 1943
**FERNEYHOUGH, COWIE and
HOLLOWAY** were born;
**RACHMANINOV** died
**ROPARTZ** (79)
*Indiscret*, ballet
*Petit Symphonie*
**NOVÁK** (73)
*May Symphony*, for soli, chorus and
    orchestra
**SCHMITT** (73)
*Essais de locomotives*, film score
**VAUGHAN WILLIAMS** (71)
Symphony No 5 in D major
**JONGEN** (70)
Piano Concerto
**SCHOENBERG** (69)
*Ode to Napoleon*, for speaker, strings and
    piano
**CARPENTER** (67)
*The Anxious Bugler*, for orchestra
**DOHNÁNYI** (66)
Symphony No 2 in D minor
**IRELAND** (64)
*Fantasy Sonata*, for clarinet and piano
**MIASKOVSKY** (63)
Symphony No 24
**BARTÓK** (62)
*Concerto for Orchestra*
**MALIPIERO** (61)
*L'allegra brigata*, opera
**STRAVINSKY** (61)
*Ode: Elegiac Chant*, for orchestra
**BAX** (60)
*Work in Progress*, overture
**CASELLA** (60)
Concerto for strings, piano and percussion
Harp Sonata
**PONCE** (60)
Viola Concerto
**RIEGGER** (58)
Duos for three woodwind
**TAYLOR** (58)
*Christmas Overture*, for orchestra
**VARÈSE** (58)
*Ecuatorial*, for bass and orchestra
**IBERT** (53)
String Quartet in C
**MARTIN** (53)
*Sechs Monologe aus Jedermann*, for voice
    and piano

**MARTINŮ** (53)
Symphony No 2
*In Memory of Lidice*, for orchestra
Concerto for two pianos
Violin Concerto
**PROKOFIEV** (52)
Sonata for violin and piano
**BLISS** (52)
*Three Jubilant and Three Solemn Fanfares*,
    for wind or military band
**HONEGGER** (51)
*Jour de fête suisse*, suite
**HOWELLS** (51)
Sonata for oboe and piano
**MILHAUD** (51)
*Bolivar*, opera
**MOORE** (50)
*In Memoriam*, symphonic poem
**MOERAN** (49)
Rhapsody No 3 for piano and orchestra
**PISTON** (49)
Symphony No 2
Prelude and Allegro for organ and strings
Passacaglia for piano
**HINDEMITH** (48)
*Cupid and Psyche*, overture
*Symphonic Metamorphoses on a Theme by
    Weber*, for orchestra
*Ludus Tonalis*, for piano
**ORFF** (48)
*Catulli Carmina* (revised version)
**HANSON** (47)
Symphony No 4, *Requiem*
**THOMSON, V.** (47)
Flute Sonata
**COWELL** (46)
*American Pipers*, for orchestra
Little Concerto for piano and orchestra
*Action in Brass*, for horn, two trumpets and
    two trombones
*This is America*, for brass ensemble
*Improvisation on a Persian Mode*, for
    orchestra
**TANSMAN** (46)
Symphony No 6, *In Memoriam*
*Symphonic études*
**HARRIS** (45)
Cantata for chorus, organ and brass
Mass for male chorus and organ
**POULENC** (44)
*Figure humaine*, cantata
*Metamorphoses*, songs
*Deux poèmes*, songs
'Montparnasse', song
**BUSH, A.** (43)
*Esquisse: le 14 juillet*, for piano
*Britain's Part*, for speaker, choir,

percussion and piano
**COPLAND** (43)
Violin Sonata
**KŘENEK** (43)
String Quartet No 7
**WEILL** (43)
*One Touch of Venus*, musical
**RODRIGO** (41)
*Concierto de Estio*, for violin and orchestra
**WALTON** (41)
*The Quest*, ballet
*Henry V*, incidental music for the film
**BERKELEY, L.** (40)
Divertimento for orchestra
String Trio
**BLACHER** (40)
*Romeo und Julia* (chamber opera)
**RAINIER** (40)
Suite for clarinet and piano
**DALLAPICCOLA** (39)
*Sex carmina Alcaei*, for soprano and
    instruments
**SKALKOTTAS** (39)
Sonata Concertante for bassoon and piano
**ALWYN** (38)
*Pastoral Fantasia*, for viola and strings
**BLITZSTEIN** (38)
*Freedom Morning*, symphonic poem
**SEIBER** (38)
*Fantasia concertante*, for violin and strings
    (1943–4)
**TIPPETT** (38)
*Boyhood's End*, song cycle
*Plebs angelica*, motet for double chorus
**SHOSTAKOVICH** (37)
Symphony No 8
**MESSIAEN** (35)
*Visions de l'Amen*, for two pianos
*Rondeau*, for piano
**CARTER** (34)
*Three Poems of Robert Frost*, for voice and
    piano
*Warble for Lilac Time*, for voice and piano/
    small orchestra
*Voyage*, for mezzo/baritone and piano
**HOLMBOE** (34)
Chamber Concerto No 5 for viola and
    orchestra
Chamber Concerto No 6 for violin and
    orchestra
*Den Galsindede Tyk*, ballet
Four Songs
**SIEGMEISTER** (34)
*Ozark Set*, for orchestra
**SCHUMAN** (33)
Symphony No 5 for strings
*William Billings*, overture

*A Prayer in Time of War*, for orchestra
**PETTERSSON** (32)
*Barefoot Songs* (1943–5)
**CAGE** (31)
*She is Asleep*, for percussion, voice and
    prepared piano
*Amores*, for prepared piano and percussion
*Perilous Night*, suite for prepared piano
    (1943–4)
**GILLIS** (31)
Symphony No 4
*Prairie Poem*, for orchestra
**JONES** (31)
*Comedy Overture*
**BRITTEN** (30)
Prelude and Fugue for strings
*Rejoice in the Lamb*, a festival cantata
*Serenade*, song cycle
**GOULD** (30)
Symphonies Nos 1 and 2
Viola Concerto
*Interplay*, for piano and orchestra
Concertette for viola and orchestra
**DIAMOND** (28)
Quartet No 2
**GINASTERA** (27)
Overture to *Faust*
*Five Popular Argentine Songs*, for voice and
    piano
*Las Horas de una Estancia*, for voice and
    piano
**ARNELL** (26)
Symphony No 1
**BERNSTEIN** (25)
'I Hate Music', five songs for soprano
*Seven Anniversaries*, for piano
**BUSH, G.** (23)
Divertimento for strings
Sonatina for piano
Nocturne for strings
*The Rehearsal*, overture
**ARNOLD** (22)
*Beckus the Dandipratt*, overture
*Larch Trees*, symphonic poem
**FOSS** (21)
*Paradigm*, for percussion
**SCHULLER** (18)
Six Early Songs
**KURTÁG** (17)
Suite for piano

## 1944

**TAVENER** was born; **BEACH,
CHAMINADE** and **SMYTH** died
**VAUGHAN WILLIAMS** (72)
Symphony No 6 (1944–7)

Concerto for oboe and strings
*A Song of Thanksgiving*, for soprano, chorus and orchestra
String Quartet No 2
**JONGEN** (71)
*Bourrée*, for orchestra
**RUGGLES** (68)
*Organum*, for orchestra (1944–7)
**IRELAND** (65)
*A Maritime Overture*, for military band
**BLOCH** (64)
*Suite Symphonique*
**PIZZETTI** (64)
Violin Concerto
**BARTÓK** (63)
Sonata for unaccompanied violin
**MALIPIERO** (62)
Symphony No 3, *Delle campane*
**STRAVINSKY** (62)
Elegy for solo viola
Sonata for two pianos
*Babel*, cantata
*Scherzo à la Russe*, for jazz ensemble
*Scènes de ballet*, for orchestra
**CASELLA** (61)
*Missa Solemnis, Pro Pace*
**BAX** (61)
*Legend*, for orchestra
**GRUENBERG** (60)
Violin Concerto
**COATES** (58)
*The Three Elizabeths*, suite
**VILLA-LOBOS** (57)
*Bachianas Brasilieras* No 8, for orchestra
String Quartet No 8
**IBERT** (54)
*Suite Elisabethaine*, for orchestra
Trio for violin, cello and harp
**MARTIN** (54)
*Petite symphonie concertante* (1944–5)
Passacaglia for organ
*In terra pax*, oratorio
**MARTINŮ** (54)
Symphony No 3
Cello Concerto (1944–5)
**BLISS** (53)
*Miracle in the Gorbals*, ballet
*The Phoenix*, march
'Auvergnat', for voice and piano
**PROKOFIEV** (53)
Symphony No 5
**HOWELLS** (52)
*Collegium Regale*, canticles of chorus
Suite for strings
**MILHAUD** (52)
Symphony No 2 for full orchestra
*Suite française*
*Jeux de printemps*

**BENJAMIN** (51)
Symphony No 1 (1944–5)
**MOORE** (51)
*Down East Suite*, for violin and piano or orchestra
**ROGERS** (51)
*The Warrior*, opera
**MOERAN** (50)
*Overture for a Masque*
Sinfonietta
**PISTON** (50)
*Fugue on a Victory Tune*
Partita for violin, viola and organ
**HINDEMITH** (49)
*Hérodiade*, for speaker and chamber orchestra
**ORFF** (49)
*Die Bernauerin*, opera (1944–5)
**SOWERBY** (49)
*Classic Concerto*, for organ and strings
Violin Sonata No 2
*Canticle of the Sun*, cantata
**GERHARD** (48)
*Alegrias*, ballet suite
*Pandora*, ballet (1944–5)
**ROBERTSON** (48)
Rhapsody for piano and orchestra
*American Serenade*, for string quartet
**SESSIONS** (48)
Symphony No 2 (1944–6)
**THOMSON, V.** (48)
Suite No 1, *Portraits*
Suite No 2
**COWELL** (47)
*United Music*, for orchestra
*Animal Magic*, for wind band
**TANSMAN** (47)
Symphony No 7
Partita for piano and orchestra
*Le roi qui jouait le fou*, ballet
**HARRIS** (46)
Symphony No 6
**AURIC** (45)
*Quadrille*, ballet
**CHÁVEZ** (45)
*Hija de Colquide*, ballet
String Quartet No 3
**POULENC** (45)
*Les mamelles de Tiresias*, opera bouffe
*La nuit de la Saint-Jean*, incidental music
*Le Voyageur sans baggage*, incidental music
*Un soir de neige*, cantata
**BUSH, A.** (44)
*Lyric Interlude*, for violin and piano
**COPLAND** (44)
*Appalachian Spring*, ballet and orchestral suite

**KŘENEK** (44)
*Cantata for Wartime,* for female chorus and orchestra
Sonata for violin and piano (1944–5)
**RUBBRA** (43)
*Soliloquy,* for cello and orchestra
**BERKELEY, L.** (41)
'Lord, when the Sense of Thy sweet Grace', for mixed chorus and organ
**KHACHATURIAN** (41)
Concerto for violin and cello
*Masquerade Suite*
**DALLAPICCOLA** (40)
*Il Prigioniero,* opera (1944–8)
*Due liriche di Anacreonte,* for soprano and instruments (1944–5)
**KABALEVSKY** (40)
*The Family of Taras,* opera (c1944)
**SKALKOTTAS** (40)
Symphonic Suite No 2
Concerto for two violins (piano arrangement only) (1944–5)
**BLITZSTEIN** (39)
*The Airborne,* for voices and orchestra (1944–6)
**RAWSTHORNE** (39)
*Street Corner Overture*
**SEIBER** (39)
*Notturno,* for horn and strings
**TIPPETT** (39)
Symphony No 1 (1944–5)
*The Weeping Babe,* motet
**FRANKEL** (38)
String Trio No 1
Trio for clarinet, cello and piano
Sonata No 1 for solo violin
String Quartet No 1
**LUTYENS** (38)
*Suite Gauloise,* for small orchestra
**SHOSTAKOVICH** (38)
*Russian River,* suite
*Eight English and American Folksongs,* for low voice and orchestra
Piano Trio No 2
String Quartet No 2
*Children's Notebook,* for piano
Film music
**MESSIAEN** (36)
*Vingt regards sur l'enfant Jésus,* for piano
**CARTER** (35)
*Holiday Overture* (revised 1961)
*The Harmony of Morning,* for female voices and small orchestra
**HOLMBOE** (35)
Symphony No 5
Chamber Concerto No 7 for oboe and orchestra
*Jeg Ved En Urt,* for chorus

**SIEGMEISTER** (35)
*Sing Out, Sweet Land,* musical
*Prairie Legend,* for orchestra
*As I Was Going Along,* choral
**BARBER** (34)
Symphony No 2 (revised 1947)
*Capricorn Concerto,* for flute, oboe, trumpet and strings
*Excursions,* for piano
**SCHUMAN** (34)
*Circus Overture,* for orchestra
*Te Deum*
**MENOTTI** (33)
*Sebastian,* ballet
**CAGE** (32)
*A Book of Music,* for two prepared pianos
Three Dances for two amplified prepared pianos (1944–5)
**FRANÇAIX** (32)
*Mouvement Perpetuel,* for cello and piano
**GILLIS** (32)
Symphony No 5 (1944–5)
*A Short Overture to an Unwritten Opera,* for orchestra
*The Alamo,* symphonic poem
**JONES** (32)
*Cloud Messenger,* for orchestra
**BRITTEN** (31)
*Festival Te Deum,* for chorus and orchestra
**GOULD** (31)
Concerto for orchestra
**FINE** (30)
*The Choral New Yorker,* cantata
**DIAMOND** (29)
*The Tempest,* incidental music
*Rounds,* for string orchestra
**GINASTERA** (28)
*Twelve American Preludes,* for piano
**ARNELL** (27)
Symphony No 3
**BERNSTEIN** (26)
*Fancy Free,* ballet and suite
*On the Town,* musical comedy and dance episodes
**BUSH, G.** (24)
Sonata for trumpet and piano
**FRICKER** (24)
Piano Prelude
**SHAPERO** (24)
*Three Amateur Sonatas,* for piano
**ARNOLD** (23)
Horn Concerto
*Variations on a Ukranian Folksong,* for piano
**FOSS** (22)
*The Heart Remembers,* ballet
*Within These Walls,* ballet
Symphony
*Ode,* for orchestra (revised 1958)

SCHÜLLER (19)
Horn Concerto

## 1945

BARTÓK and MASCAGNI died,
WEBERN was accidentally shot dead
STRAUSS, R. (81)
*Metamorphoses*, for twenty-three solo
   instruments
Oboe Concerto
VAUGHAN WILLIAMS (73)
*Story of a Flemish Farm*, orchestral suite
SCHOENBERG (71)
Prelude to a *Genesis* suite
CARPENTER (69)
*The Seven Ages*, symphonic suite
DOHNÁNYI (68)
*Six Pieces*, for piano
BLOCH (65)
String Quartet No 2
BARTÓK (64)
Piano Concerto No 3
Viola Concerto
KODÁLY (63)
*Missa Brevis*
STRAVINSKY (63)
Symphony in three movements
*Ebony Concerto*, for clarinet and jazz
   ensemble
BAX (62)
*Legend-Sonata*, for cello and piano
GRUENBERG (61)
*American Suite*, for orchestra
*Volpone*, opera
*One Night of Cleopatra*, opera
*The Miracle of Flanders*, mystery play
TAYLOR (60)
*Elegy*, for orchestra
WELLESZ (60)
Symphony No 1
SCHOECK (59)
*Sommernacht*, for strings
Suite in A for strings
TOCH (58)
*The Covenant*, for orchestra (lost)
VILLA-LOBOS (58)
Piano Concerto No 1
*Bachianas Brasilieras* Nos 5 and 9
Fantasia for cello
MARTIN (55)
*Golgotha*, oratorio (1945–8)
MARTINŮ (55)
Symphony No 4
*Thunderbolt P-47*, for orchestra
BLISS (54)
*Baraza*, concert piece for piano and
   orchestra, with men's voices *ad lib*

PROKOFIEV (54)
Symphony No 6 (1945–7)
Piano Sonata No 9 (1945–7)
MILHAUD (53)
*The Bells*, ballet
Cello Concerto No 2
String Quartet No 12, *In Memory of Fauré*
BENJAMIN (52)
*From San Domingo*, for orchestra
*Red River Jig*, for orchestra
*Elegy, Waltz and Toccata*, for viola and
   orchestra
MOORE (52)
Symphony in A major
MOERAN (51)
Cello Concerto
PISTON (51)
Sonata for violin and harpsichord
HINDEMITH (50)
Piano Concerto
JACOB (50)
Symphony No 2
Clarinet Concerto
ORFF (50)
*Astutuli*, opera (1945–6)
SOWERBY (50)
Trumpet Sonata
GERHARD (49)
*The Duenna*, opera (1945–7)
HANSON (49)
Serenade for flute, strings, harp and
   orchestra
ROBERTSON (49)
*Punch and Judy Overture*
COWELL (48)
*Philippine Return*, for orchestra
*Big Sing*, for orchestra
*Fanfare*, for wind band
*Two Appositions*, for wind band
*Grandma's Rumba*, for wind band
*Triad*, for trumpet and piano
Violin Sonata No 1
*Hymn*, for string orchestra
KORNGOLD (48)
Violin Concerto
String Quartet No 3
TANSMAN (48)
Concertino for guitar and orchestra
HARRIS (47)
Piano Concerto No 1
CHÁVEZ (46)
*Piramide*, ballet
POULENC (46)
*Le soldat et la sorcière*, incidental music
*Chansons françaises*, for choir
BUSH, A. (45)
*Resolution Overture*
English Folk Songs for chorus

KŘENEK (45)
*Vertrauenssache,* opera
FINZI (44)
*Farewell to Arms,* for tenor and small
  orchestra
Five Bagatelles for clarinet and piano
BERKELEY, L. (42)
Piano Sonata
Violin Sonata
Six Preludes for piano
*Festival Anthem,* for mixed choir and organ
BLACHER (42)
*Partita,* for strings and percussion
KHACHATURIAN (42)
Solemn Overture, *To the End of the War*
RAINIER (42)
Sonata for viola and piano
DALLAPICCOLA (41)
*Ciaccona, Intermezzo e Adagio,* for cello
KABALEVSKY (41)
String Quartet No 2
SKALKOTTAS (41)
*Mikri Serenata,* for cello and piano
*Bolero,* for cello and piano
ALWYN (40)
Concerto for oboe, harp and strings
BLITZSTEIN (40)
*Galoopchik,* musical play
RAWSTHORNE (40)
*Cortèges,* fantasy overture
SEIBER (40)
*Phantasy,* for flute, horn and strings
TIPPETT (40)
String Quartet No 3 (1945–6)
FRANKEL (39)
String Quartet No 2
LUTYENS (39)
Chamber Concerto No 3
Five Little Pieces for clarinet and piano
SHOSTAKOVICH (39)
Symphony No 9
Two Songs
Film music
CARTER (36)
*Musicians Wrestle Everywhere,* for voices
  and strings
Piano Sonata (1945–6)
HOLMBOE (36)
Chamber Concerto No 8, (Sinfonia
  Concertante)
SIEGMEISTER (36)
*Western Suite,* for orchestra
*A Tooth for Paul Revere,* choral
BARBER (35)
Cello Concerto
SCHUMAN (35)
*Undertow,* ballet

GILDER (34)
*The Tide,* for soprano, baritone, chorus,
  organ and orchestra
MENOTTI (34)
Piano Concerto in A minor
FRANÇAIX (33)
*La main de gloire,* opera
GILLIS (33)
*To an Unknown Soldier,* symphonic poem
JONES (33)
Symphony No 1
BRITTEN (32)
*Peter Grimes,* opera
String Quartet No 2
*The Holy Sonnets of John Donne,* for voice
  and piano
GOULD (32)
*Harvest,* for vibraphone, harp and strings
Ballade for band
MELLERS (31)
String Trio
DIAMOND (30)
Symphonies Nos 3 and 4
GINASTERA (29)
Duo for flute and oboe
ARNELL (28)
String Quartet No 3
BERNSTEIN (27)
*Hashkivenu,* for voices and organ
*Afterthought,* for voice and piano
BUSH, G. (25)
Sonata for violin and piano
SHAPERO (25)
Serenade for string orchestra
FOSS (23)
*Song of Anguish,* for voice and piano or
  orchestra
MENNIN (22)
Concertino for flute, strings and
  percussion
SCHÜLLER (20)
*Vertige d'Eros,* for orchestra


# 1946

FINNESEY was born; FALLA died
VAUGHAN WILLIAMS (74)
Partita, for double string orchestra
  (1946–8)
Introduction and Fugue for two pianos
DOHNÁNYI (69)
Piano Concerto No 2
QUILTER (69)
*Tulips,* for chorus and orchestra
CANTALOUBE (67)
*Rustiques,* for oboe, clarinet and bassoon

IRELAND (67)
*fp Satyricon Overture*
SCOTT (67)
*Maureen O'Hara*, opera
Oboe Concerto
BLOCH (66–68)
*Concerto Symphonique*, for piano
MALIPIERO (64)
Symphony No 4. *In Memoriam*
STRAVINSKY (64)
Concerto in D for strings
BAX (63)
*Te Deum*, for chorus and organ
*Gloria*, for chorus and organ
BERNERS (63)
*Les Sirènes*, ballet
GRUENBERG (62)
*Dance Rhapsody*, for violin and orchestra
Symphony No 4
RIEGGER (61)
Symphony No 3 (1946–7)
DUPRÉ (60)
Sinfonia for piano and organ
MARTIN (56)
Overture to Racine's *Athalie*, for orchestra
MARTINŮ (56)
Symphony No 5
BLISS (55)
*Adam Zero*, ballet
HONEGGER (54)
Symphony No 3, *Liturgique*
Symphony No 4, *Deliciae basiliensis*
HOWELLS (54)
*Gloucester Canticles*, for chorus
MILHAUD (54)
Symphony No 3, *Hymnus Ambrosianus*
Piano Concerto No 3
Violin Concerto No 2
String Quartet No 13
BENJAMIN (53)
*Caribbean Dance*, for orchestra
MOORE (53)
Quintet for clarinet and strings
MOERAN (52)
*Fantasy Quartet*, for oboe and strings
PISTON (52)
Divertimento for nine instruments
HINDEMITH (51)
*When Lilacs in the Dooryard Bloomed*, requiem
SESSIONS (50)
Piano Sonata No 2
COWELL (49)
Symphony No 4, *Short Symphony*
Festival Overture for two orchestras
Saxophone Quartet

KORNGOLD (49)
*The Silent Serenade*, comedy with music
Cello Concerto
HARRIS (48)
Accordion Concerto
Concerto for two pianos
AURIC (47)
*La Fontaine de Jouvenance*, ballet
*Impromptu*, for oboe and piano
POULENC (47)
Two songs
BUSH, A. (46)
*The Press-gang*, childrens' opera
*Homage to William Sterndale Bennett*, for strings
*English Suite*, for strings
*Winter Journey*, for soprano, baritone, chorus, strings and harp
COPLAND (46)
Symphony No 3
KŘENEK (46)
*Symphonic Elegy*, for string orchestra
Piano Concerto No 3
RUBBRA (45)
*Missa cantuariensis*, for double choir
BERKELEY, L. (43)
Nocturne for orchestra
Introduction and Allegro for solo violin
Five songs
BLACHER (43)
Concerto for jazz orchestra (unpublished)
*Die Flut*, chamber opera
*Chiarina*, ballet
DALLAPICCOLA (42)
Two Pieces for orchestra (1946–7)
SKALKOTTAS (42)
Little Suite No 2 for violin and piano
ALWYN (41)
Suite of Scottish Dances
BLITZSTEIN (41)
*Show*, ballet
*Native Land*, orchestral suite
*Regina*, opera
RAWSTHORNE (41)
*Prisoner's March*, for orchestra
TIPPETT (41)
*Little Music*, for strings
FRANKEL (40)
*Novelette*, for violin and piano
*Pieces for Geraldine*, for piano
SHOSTAKOVICH (40)
String Quartet No 3
HOLMBOE (37)
Chamber Concerto No 9 for violin, viola and orchestra
Chamber Concerto No 10 for woodwind, brass and strings

Cantata No 5
*Lave og Jon*, opera
**SIEGMEISTER** (37)
*Lonesome Hollow*, for orchestra
*Lazy Afternoon*, choral
*Summer Day*, for band
**BARBER** (36)
*Medea: the Cave of the Heart*, ballet
**MENOTTI** (35)
*The Medium*, opera
**CAGE** (34)
Sonatas and Interludes for prepared
  pianos (1946–8)
**FRANÇAIX** (34)
*Rhapsodie*, for viola and wind
*Les bosquets de Cythère*, for orchestra
*La douce France*, for orchestra
**GILLIS** (34)
Symphony No 5½, (*A Symphony for Fun*)
  (1946–7)
**BRITTEN** (33)
*The Rape of Lucretia*, opera
*Variations and Fugue on a Theme of Purcell*
  (*A Young Person's Guide to the Orchestra*)
**GOULD** (33)
*Minstrel Show*, for orchestra
Symphony No 3
**FINE** (32)
*Fantasia*, for string trio
Violin Sonata
**MELLERS** (32)
Sonata for viola and piano
Serenade for oboe, clarinet and bassoon
**DIAMOND** (31)
Quartet No 3
Violin Sonata
**BABBITT** (30)
*Fabulous Voyage*, musical
**GINASTERA** (30)
*Lamentation of the Prophet Jeremiah*, for
  chorus
*Suite of Creole Dances*, for piano
**ARNELL** (29)
Piano Concerto
Piano Trio
**BERNSTEIN** (28)
*Facsimile*, ballet
**BUSH, G.** (26)
Four Pieces for piano
**FRICKER** (26)
Four Fughettas for two pianos
**ARNOLD** (25)
Symphony for strings
**SHAPEY** (25)
String Quartet No 1
Piano Sonata

**SIMPSON** (25)
Piano Sonata
**FOSS** (24)
*Song of Songs*, for voice and orchestra
*Composer's Holiday*, for violin and piano
**MENNIN** (23)
Symphony No 3
**BOULEZ** (21)
Piano Sonata No 1
Sonatina for flute and piano
*Le visage nuptial*, for voices and chamber
  orchestra
**BERIO** (21)
Four Popular Songs (1946–7)
**HENZE** (20)
Chamber Concerto for solo piano, solo
  flute and strings
Sonata for violin and piano


# 1947

**PATTERSON** was born; **CASELLA** and
**HAHN** died
**ROPARTZ** (83)
*Divertissement No 2*
**SCHOENBERG** (73)
*A Survivor from Warsaw*, cantata
**BRIAN** (71)
Symphony No 6, *Sinfonia Tragica* (1947–8)
**AUBERT** (70)
*Offrande*, for orchestra
**SCOTT** (68)
*Hymn of Unity*, for soli, chorus and
  orchestra
**KODÁLY** (65)
Viola Concerto
String Quartet
**MALIPIERO** (65)
Symphony No 5, *Concertante in eco*, with
  two pianos
Symphony No 6, *Degli archi*, for strings
**STRAVINSKY** (65)
*Orpheus*, ballet
*Petit Canon pour la fête de Nadia Boulanger*,
  for voices
**BAX** (64)
Two Fanfares for the wedding of Princess
  Elizabeth and Prince Philip
*Morning Song*, for piano and small
  orchestra
*Epithalamium*, for chorus and organ
**RIEGGER** (62)
Sonatina for violin and piano
**VARÈSE** (62)
*Étude pour espace*, for two pianos and
  percussion

SCHOECK (61)
Cello Concerto
TOCH (60)
*Hyperion*, for orchestra
MARTIN (57)
*Trois chants de Noël*, for voice, flute and
  piano
MARTINŮ (57)
Quartet No 7
PROKOFIEV (56)
*The Story of a Real Man*, opera (1947–8)
*Flourish, Mighty Homeland*, cantata
Sonata for violin
MILHAUD (55)
Symphony, *1848*
Concerto for marimba and vibraphone
BENJAMIN (54)
Ballade for strings
MOORE (54)
*Farm Journal*, suite for chamber
  orchestra
ROGERS (54)
*A Letter from Pete*, cantata
PISTON (53)
Symphony No 3
String Quartet No 3
HINDEMITH (52)
*Symphonia Serena* (possibly 1946)
Clarinet Concerto
ORFF (52)
*Antigone*, opera (1947–8)
SOWERBY (52)
Symphony No 4
ROBERTSON (51)
*Trilogy*, for orchestra
SESSIONS (51)
fp *The Trial of Lucullus*, opera
THOMSON, V. (51)
*The Seine at Night*, for orchestra
*The Mother of Us All*, opera
COWELL (50)
*Tune Takes a Trip*, for five clarinets
KORNGOLD (50)
*Symphonic Serenade*, for strings
Five Songs for middle voice
TANSMAN (50)
Music for orchestra
*Isaiah the Prophet*, for tenor, chorus and
  orchestra
HARRIS (49)
*Quest*, for orchestra
POULENC (48)
Flute Sonata
THOMPSON, R. (48)
Symphony No 3 (1947–9)
ANTHEIL (47)
Symphony No 5 (1947–8)

BUSH, A. (47)
*Piers Plowman's Day*, suite
Three Concert Studies for piano trio
KŘENEK (47)
Symphonies Nos 4 and 5 (1947–9)
WEILL (47)
*Street Scene*, opera
*Down in the Valley*, folk opera
FINZI (46)
*Ode for St Cecilia's Day* (possibly 1950)
RUBBRA (46)
*Festival Overture*
Symphony No 5 (1947–8)
Cello Sonata
DURUFLÉ (45)
*Requiem*, for soli, chorus, organ and
  orchestra
RODRIGO (45)
Four *Madrigales Amatorias*, for voice and
  piano
WALTON (45)
*Hamlet*, incidental music for the film
String Quartet in A minor
BERKELEY, L. (44)
Piano Concerto
*Four Poems of St Teresa of Avila*, for
  contralto and orchestra
*Stabat Mater*, for voices and twelve
  instruments
'The Lowlands of Holland', for voice and
  piano
BLACHER (44)
*Die Nachtschwalbe*, nocturne
Variations on a theme of Paganini, for
  orchestra
Piano Concerto No 1
KHACHATURIAN (44)
*Symphonie-Poème*
RAINIER (44)
*Sinfonia da Camera*
SKALKOTTAS (43)
*Four Parties*, for violin and cello
Classic Symphony
*Henry V*, incidental music (lost) (1947–8)
ALWYN (42)
*Manchester Suite*, for orchestra
Piano Sonata
Three songs (Louis MacNiece)
RAWSTHORNE (42)
Concerto for oboe and string orchestra
TIPPETT (42)
*The Midsummer Marriage*, opera (1947–52)
COOKE (41)
Symphony No 1
FRANKEL (41)
String Quartet No 3
*The Aftermath*, for tenor, trumpet, timpani

and strings
*Sonatina Leggiera*, for piano
**LUTYENS** (41)
*The Pit*, dramatic scene for voices and
orchestra
Viola Concerto
Chamber Concertos Nos 4 and 5
**SHOSTAKOVICH** (41)
Violin Concerto No 1 (1947–8)
*Poem of the Motherland*, cantata
Film music
**MESSIAEN** (39)
*Turangalîla*, symphony
**CARTER** (38)
*The Minotaur*, ballet
*Emblems*, for male voices and piano
**HOLMBOE** (38)
Symphony No 6
**SIEGMEISTER** (38)
*Summer Night*, for orchestra
Symphony No 1
**BARBER** (37)
*Knoxville: Summer of 1915*, ballet suite for
voice and orchestra
**SCHUMAN** (37)
*Night Journey*, ballet
Violin Concerto
**MENOTTI** (36)
*The Telephone*, opera
*Errand into the Maze*, ballet
**FRANÇAIX** (35)
*L'heure du Berger*, for orchestra
*Eloge de la danse*, for piano
*Divertissement*, for oboe, clarinet and
bassoon
**GILLIS** (35)
Symphony No 6
*Dude Ranch*, for orchestra
Three Short Pieces for strings
**JONES** (35)
*The Flute Player*, for orchestra
*Miscellany*, twenty pieces for small
orchestra
**BRITTEN** (34)
*Albert Herring*, opera
Canticle No 1, 'My Beloved is Mine'
Prelude and Fugue on a Theme of Vittoria
for organ
**GOULD** (34)
*Fall River Legend*, ballet
**MELLERS** (33)
*Prometheus*, incidental music
**PANUFNIK** (33)
Twelve Miniature Studies for piano
Nocturne for orchestra
Lullaby for strings and two harps
Divertimento for strings

**DIAMOND** (32)
*Romeo and Juliet*, incidental music
Violin Concerto No 2
Piano Sonata
**GINASTERA** (31)
*Pampeana No 1*, for violin and piano
*Ollantay*, three symphonic movements
Toccata, Villancico and Fugue for organ
*Rondo on Argentine Childrens' Songs*, for
piano
**ARNELL** (30)
*Punch and the Child*, ballet
Harpsichord Concerto
**BERNSTEIN** (29)
'La Bonne Cuisine', four recipes for voice
and piano
*Simchu na*, for chorus and orchestra/piano
*Reena*, for chorus and orchestra
**BUSH, G.** (27)
Christmas Cantata
**FRICKER** (27)
Wind Quintet
String Quartet in one movement
Sonata for organ
*Three Sonnets of Cecco Angiolieri*, for tenor
and seven instruments
Two Madrigals
**SHAPERO** (27)
Piano Sonata No 1
**ARNOLD** (26)
Violin Sonata No 1
Viola Sonata
*Children's Suite*, for piano
**SHAPEY** (26)
Piano Quintet
**FOSS** (25)
String Quartet
**MENNIN** (24)
Fantasia for string orchestra
**BERIO** (22)
*Petite Suite*, for piano
**BOULEZ** (22)
*Le soleil des eaux*, for voices and orchestra
(1947–8)
Piano Sonata No 2 (1947–8)
**SCHÜLLER** (22)
Symphonic Study (1947–8)
**HENZE** (21)
Symphony No 1 (first version)
Violin Concerto No 1
Concertino for piano and wind orchestra
with percussion
String Quartet No 1
Five Madrigals for small mixed choir and
eleven solo instruments

**1948**

BERKELEY, M. was born; GIORDANO, LEHÁR, PONCE and WOLF-FERRARI died
STRAUSS, R. (84)
Duet Concertino for clarinet, bassoon and strings
NOVÁK (78)
*Žižka*, incidental music
*Song of the Zlin Workers*, small cantata
BRIAN (72)
*The Tinker's Wedding*, comedy overture
Symphony No 7
CARPENTER (72)
*Carmel Concerto*
AUBERT (71)
*Le Tombeau de Chateaubriande*, for orchestra
QUILTER (71)
*The Sailor and His Lass*, for soloist, chorus and orchestra
KODÁLY (66)
*Czinka Panna*, opera
MALIPIERO (66)
*Mondi celeste e infernali*, opera (1948–9)
Symphony No 7, *Delle canzoni*
Piano Concerto No 3
STRAVINSKY (66)
Mass, for chorus and double wind quintet
*The Rake's Progress*, opera (1948–51)
GRUENBERG (64)
Variations for orchestra
RIEGGER (63)
String Quartet No 2
Music for brass choir
WELLESZ (63)
Symphony No 2
MARTIN (58)
*Ballade*, for cello and piano
Eight Piano Preludes
MARTINŮ (58)
Piano Concerto No 3
*The Strangler*, ballet
BLISS (57)
*The Olympians*, opera (1948–9)
PROKOFIEV (57)
*The Stone Flower*, ballet (1948–53)
MOORE (55)
*The Emperor's New Clothes*, opera for children
MOERAN (54)
Serenade in G major
PISTON (54)
Toccata, for orchestra
Suite No 2 for orchestra
HINDEMITH (53)
Concerto for trumpet, bassoon and strings

Septet for wind instruments
HANSON (52)
Piano Concerto
ROBERTSON (52)
Violin Concerto
THOMSON, V. (52)
*Wheatfield at Noon*, for orchestra
*Acadian Songs and Dances*
COWELL (51)
Symphony No 5
*Festive Occasion*, for orchestra
*Tall Tale*, for brass ensemble
*Saturday Night at the Firehouse*, for orchestra
TANSMAN (51)
Music for strings
HARRIS (50)
*Elegy and Paean*, for viola and orchestra
AURIC (49)
*Le Peintre et son Modèle*, ballet
CHÁVEZ (49–51)
Violin Concerto (1948–50, revised 1962)
POULENC (49)
*Quatre petites prières (St Francis)*, for choir
ANTHEIL (48)
*McKonkey's Ferry*, overture for orchestra
Symphony No 6
*Serenade*, for string orchestra
Piano Sonata No 4
*Songs of Experience* (Blake Poems), for voice and piano
BUSH, A. (48)
Violin Concerto
*Wat Tyler*, opera (1948–51)
COPLAND (48)
Concerto for clarinet and strings, with harp and piano
KŘENEK (48)
Violin Sonata No 2
Piano Sonata No 4
Sonata for viola and piano
FINZI (47)
*Love's Labours Lost*, incidental music
RUBBRA (47)
*The Buddha*, suite for flute, oboe, violin, viola and cello
RODRIGO (46)
*Ausencias de Dulcinea*, for bass, four sopranos and orchestra
BERKELEY, L. (45)
Concerto for two pianos and orchestra
BLACHER (45)
Violin Concerto
RAINIER (45)
*Dance of the Rain*, for tenor and guitar
*Ubunzima*, for high voice and guitar

DALLAPICCOLA (44)
*Quattro liriche di Antonio Machado*, for
soprano and piano
KABALEVSKY (44)
Violin Concerto
SKALKOTTAS (44)
Sinfonietta
Piano Concertino
Little Dance Suite for orchestra (1948–9)
ALWYN (43)
*Three Winter Poems*, for string quartet
BLITZSTEIN (43)
*The Guests*, ballet
RAWSTHORNE (43)
Violin Concerto No 1
Clarinet Quartet
SEIBER (43)
*Johnny Miner*, radio opera
String Quartet No 3, *Quartetto lyrico*
(1948–51)
TIPPETT (43)
Suite in D major
COOKE (42)
Oboe Quartet
FRANKEL (42)
*Early Morning Music*, for oboe, clarinet and
bassoon
String Quartet No 4
LUTYENS (42)
Chamber Concerto No 6
Three Improvisations for piano
*Aptote*, for solo violin
Nine Songs
SHOSTAKOVICH (42)
*From Jewish Folk Poetry*, song cycle
Film music
MACONCHY (41)
String Quartet No 5
CARTER (39)
Wind Quintet
Sonata for cello and piano
HOLMBOE (39)
Chamber Concerto No 11 for trumpet,
horns and strings
BARBER (38)
String Quartet No 2
Piano Sonata
SCHUMAN (38)
Symphony No 6
PETTERSSON (37)
Fugue for woodwind
FRANÇAIX (36)
*Les desmoiselles de la nuit*, ballet
*Symphonie d'archets*
Quintet for wind instruments
GILLIS (36)
Symphony No 7, *Saga of a Prairie School*

BRITTEN (35)
*St Nicholas*, for voices and instruments
*The Beggar's Opera*, by John Gay realised
from original airs
GOULD (35)
Serenade of carols
FINE (34)
*Toccata Concertante*, for orchestra
Partita for wind quintet
MELLERS (34)
*Lysistrata*, a play in music
PANUFNIK (34)
*Sinfonia Rustica*
DIAMOND (33)
*Chaconne*, for violin and piano
BABBITT (32)
Composition for flute, clarinet, violin and
cello
Composition for twelve instruments
String Quartet No 1
GINASTERA (32)
String Quartet No 1
ARNELL (31)
Symphony No 4
BERNSTEIN (30)
*Four Anniversaries*, for piano
Brass Music
BUSH, G. (28)
Concerto for oboe and strings
*A Summer Serenade*, choral
FRICKER (28)
Symphony No 1 (1948–9)
*Rondo Scherzoso*, for orchestra
SHAPERO (28)
Symphony for classical orchestra
*The Travellers*, for orchestra
ARNOLD (27)
Festival Overture
*The Smoke*, overture
Symphonic Suite
Sonatina for flute and piano
SIMPSON (27)
*Variations and Finale on a Theme of Haydn*,
for piano
FOSS (26)
Oboe Concerto
*Ricordare*, for orchestra
*Capriccio*, for cello and piano
HAMILTON (26)
Symphonic Variations for string orchestra
Quintet for clarinet and string quartet
HENZE (22)
*The Magic Theatre*, opera
*Chorus of the Captured Trojans*, for chorus
and orchestra
Chamber Sonata for piano, violin and cello
(revised 1963)

*Lullaby of the Blessed Virgin*, for boys' choir and instruments
*The Reproach*, concert aria for voice and instruments
*Whispers from Heavenly Death*, cantata
**KORTE** (20)
String Quartet No 1

## 1949

**NOVÁK, SKALKOTTAS, STRAUSS, R.**
and **TURINA** died
**NOVÁK** (79)
*Stars*, for female chorus and orchestra
**VAUGHAN WILLIAMS** (77)
*Fantasia (quasi variazione) on the Old 104th Psalm Tune*, for piano, chorus, organ and orchestra
*An Oxford Elegy*, for speaker, chorus and small orchestra
*Folk Songs of the Four Seasons*, cantata
**SCHOENBERG** (75)
*Fantasia*, for violin and piano
**BRIAN** (73)
Symphony No 8
**QUILTER** (72)
*Love at the Inn*, opera
**BLOCH** (69)
*Scherzo fantasque*, for piano
**PIZZETTI** (69)
*Vanna Lupa*, opera
**GRUENBERG** (65)
Cello Concerto
**IBERT** (59)
*Etude-Caprice, pour un tombeau de Chopin*, for solo cello
**MARTIN** (59)
Concerto for seven wind instruments
**MARTINŮ** (59)
Sinfonia Concertante
*Mazurka-Nokturne*, for string quartet
**PROKOFIEV** (58)
*Winter Bonfire*, suite for narrator, boys' chorus and orchestra (1949–50)
Sonata for cello and piano
**HONEGGER** (57)
Concerto da camera
**HOWELLS** (57)
*Music for a Prince*, suite for orchestra
Sonata for clarinet and piano
*A Maid Peerless*, for four voices, female chorus, strings and piano
Three Motets (1949–58)
**MILHAUD** (57)
Piano Concerto No 4
String Quartets Nos 14 and 15 (can be played together as octet)

**BENJAMIN** (56)
*The Tale of Two Cities*, opera (1949–50)
*Valses Caprices*, for clarinet (or viola) and piano
**PISTON** (55)
Piano Quintet
Duo for violin and cello
**HINDEMITH** (54)
Horn Concerto
Concerto for woodwind, harp and orchestra
Organ Sonata No 2
**SOWERBY** (54)
*Ballade*, for English horn and strings
**THOMSON, V.** (53)
Cello Concerto
**COWELL** (52)
*O'Higgins of Chile*, opera
*Four Declamations with Return*, for cello and piano
*The Sax-happy Quartet*
*Congratulations*, for strings
*A Curse and a Blessing*, for wind band
Overture for orchestra
**TANSMAN** (52)
*Ricercari*, for orchestra
*Tombeau de Chopin*, for strings
**HARRIS** (51)
*Kentucky Spring*, for orchestra
**AURIC** (50)
*Phèdre*, ballet
**POULENC** (50)
Piano Concerto
**BUSH, A.** (49)
Symphony No 2, 'Nottingham'
*Song of Fellowship*, for baritone, chorus and orchestra
**WEILL** (49)
*Lost in the Stars*, opera
**FINZI** (48)
Clarinet Concerto
*Before and After Summer*, song cycle
**RODRIGO** (47)
*Concierto Galante*, for cello and orchestra
**WALTON** (47)
Violin Sonata
**BERKELEY, L.** (46)
*Colonus' Praise*, for chorus and orchestra
Three Mazurkas for piano
Scherzo for piano
**BLACHER** (46)
*Preussisches Märchen*, ballet-opera
*Hamlet*, ballet
**RAINIER** (46)
*Barbaric Dance Suite*, for piano
**DALLAPICCOLA** (45)
*Job*, mystery play (1949–50)

*Tre poemi*, for soprano and chamber
  orchestra
**KABALEVSKY** (45)
Cello Concerto
**SKALKOTTAS** (45)
*Nocturne-Divertimento*, for xylophone and
  orchestra
*The Sea*, for orchestra
Sonatina for cello and piano
*Zarte Melodie*, for cello and piano
**ALWYN** (44)
Symphony No 1
**RAWSTHORNE** (44)
Concerto for string orchestra
Cello Sonata
**SEIBER** (44)
*Andantino and Pastorale*, for clarinet and
  piano
*Ulysses*, cantata (possibly 1946–7)
**FRANKEL** (43)
*May Day*, overture
**LUTYENS** (43)
String Quartet No 3
**SHOSTAKOVICH** (43)
Ballet Suite No 1, for orchestra
String Quartet No 4
*The Song of the Forests*, oratorio
Film music
**HOLMBOE** (40)
String Quartets Nos 1, 2 and 3
**SIEGMEISTER** (40)
*From My Window*, for orchestra
*The New Colossus*, choral
**SCHUMAN** (39)
*Judith*, ballet
**PETTERSSON** (38)
Concerto for violin and string quartet
**BRITTEN** (36)
*The Little Sweep (Let's Make an Opera)*
*Spring Symphony*, for voices and orchestra
A Wedding Anthem, for voices and organ
**LUTOSLAWSKI** (36)
Overture for strings
**FINE** (35)
*The Hour-glass*, choral cycle
**PANUFNIK** (35)
*Hommage à Chopin*, for soprano and piano
**DIAMOND** (34)
*Timon of Athens*, symphonic portrait
*L'âme de Debussy*, song cycle
**BABBITT** (33)
*Into the Good Ground*, film score
**BERNSTEIN** (31)
Symphony No 2, *The Age of Anxiety*, for
  piano and orchestra
*Prelude, Fugue and Riffs*, for clarinet and
  jazz ensemble

Two Love Songs
**ROCHBERG** (31)
Symphony No 1
*Night Music*, for chamber orchestra
**BUSH, G.** (29)
*Yorick*, overture
Four Songs of Herrick
**FRICKER** (29)
*Prelude, Elegy and Finale*, for string
  orchestra
Concerto for violin and small orchestra
  No 1 (1949–50)
**ARNOLD** (28)
Clarinet Concerto
**SHAPEY** (28)
String Quartet No 2
*Three Essays on Thomas Wolfe*, for piano
**FOSS** (27)
*The Jumping Frog of Calveras County*, opera
Piano Concerto No 2
**HAMILTON** (27)
Symphony No 1
String Quartet No 1
**MENNIN** (26)
Symphony No 4, *The Cycle*, for choir and
  orchestra
*The Christmas Story*, cantata
**BERIO** (24)
*Magnificat*, for two sopranos, mixed chorus
  and instruments
**BOULEZ** (24)
*Livre pour cordes*, for string orchestra
*Livre pour quatour*, for string quartet
**HENZE** (23)
*Ballet Variations*
*Jack Pudding*, ballet
Symphony No 2
Symphony No 3 (1949–50)
*Apollo et Hyazinthus*, for harpsichord,
  contralto and eight solo instruments
Variations for piano
Serenade, for solo cello
**KURTÁG** (23)
*Klárisok*, for chorus
**LEIGHTON** (20)
Symphony for strings
**PREVIN** (20)
*The Sun Comes Up*, film score


**1950**

**OLIVER** was born; **BERNERS, CILÈA,
KOECHLIN, MIASKOWSKI, MOERAN**
and **WEILL** died

STRAUSS, R. (posthumous)
Four Last Songs
SCHMITT (80)
*Scènes de la vie moyenne*, for orchestra
VAUGHAN WILLIAMS (78)
Concerto Grosso for string orchestra
*The Sons of Light*, cantata
*Sun, Moon, Stars and Man*, song cycle
BRIAN (74)
*Turandot*, opera (1950–1)
DOHNÁNYI (73)
Twelve studies for piano
BLOCH (70)
Concertino for viola, flute and strings
Piece for string quartet
PIZZETTI (70)
*Ifigenia*, opera
ENESCO (69)
*Vox Maris*, symphonic poem
MALIPIERO (68)
Symphony in one movement
Piano Concerto No 4
BAX (67)
Concertante for orchestra with piano (left
    hand)
TAYLOR (65)
*Restoration Suite*, for orchestra
TOCH (63)
Symphony No 1
MARTIN (60)
Violin Concerto (1950–1)
*Five Ariel Songs*, for chamber choir
MARTINŮ (60)
Double Violin Concerto No 2
*Intermezzo*, for orchestra
Sinfonietta, *La Jolla*, for piano and
    orchestra
Piano Trio No 2
BLISS (59)
String Quartet No 2
PROKOFIEV (59)
*Sinfonia concertante*, for cello and
    orchestra (reworking of the 1933–8 cello
    concerto)
*On Guard for Peace*, choral
MOORE (57)
*Giants in the Earth*, opera
ROGERS (57)
*The Veil*, opera
*The Prophet Isaiah*, cantata
PISTON (56)
Symphony No 4
HINDEMITH (55)
Sinfonietta
*Requiem for Those we Love* (possibly 1946)
JACOB (55)
Sinfonietta in D major

*A Goodly Heritage*, cantata
ORFF (55)
*Trionfo di Afrodite*, opera
SOWERBY (55)
*Christ Reborn*, cantata
GERHARD (54)
Impromptus for piano
TANSMAN (53)
*Phèdre*, ballet
POULENC (51)
*Stabat Mater*
ANTHEIL (50)
*Volpone*, opera
BUSH, A. (50)
*The Dream of Llewelyn ap Gruffydd*, for
    male chorus and piano
*Times of Day*, three children's pieces for
    piano
COPLAND (50)
Piano Quartet
*Twelve Poems of Emily Dickinson*, for voice
    and piano
KŘENEK (50)
*Dark Waters*, one-act opera
Piano Concerto No 4
Double Concerto for violin, piano and
    chamber orchestra
Piano Sonata No 5
FINZI (49)
*Intimations of Immortality*, for tenor, chorus
    and orchestra
BERKELEY, L. (47)
Sinfonietta for orchestra
Elegy for violin and piano
Toccata for violin and piano
Theme and Variations for solo violin
BLACHER (47)
*Lysistrata*, ballet
Concerto for clarinet, bassoon, horn and
    trumpet
*Dialogue*, for piano and strings
KHACHATURIAN (47)
Cello Concerto
RAINIER (47)
*Ballet Suite*, for orchestra
LAMBERT (45)
*Tiresias*, ballet
RAWSTHORNE (45)
Symphony No 1
TIPPETT (45)
*Heart's Assurance*, song cycle (1950–1)
COOKE (44)
String Trio
FRANKEL (44)
*Three Poems*, for cello and piano
LUTYENS (44)
*Concertante*, for five players

SHOSTAKOVICH (44)
*Two Romances on Verses by Mikhail Lermontov*, for voice and piano
Twenty-four Preludes and Fugues for piano
Film music
MESSIAEN (42)
*Le merle noir*, for piano and flute
*Messe de la Pentecôte*
CARTER (41)
Eight Études and a Fantasy for flute, oboe, clarinet and bassoon
String Quartet No 1 (1950–1)
*Eight Pieces for four timpani* (one player) (1950–6)
HOLMBOE (41)
Symphony No 7
Chamber Concerto No 12 for trombone and orchestra
*Isomeric*, for two violins and piano
SIEGMEISTER (41)
Symphony No 2
SCHUMAN (40)
String Quartet No 4
GILDER (39)
*Christmas Sounds*, for soli, chorus and orchestra
MENOTTI (39)
*The Consul*, opera
CAGE (38)
String Quartet in Four Parts
FRANÇAIX (38)
*Les camélias*, ballet
*Les zigues de Mars*, ballet
Two Pieces for guitar
*Variations de Concert*, for cello and strings
GILLIS (38)
Symphony No 8
*The Man Who Invented Music*, for narrator and orchestra
JONES (38)
Symphony No 2
BRITTEN (37)
*Lachrymae*, for viola and piano
*Five Flower Songs*, for unaccompanied chorus
GOULD (37)
*Family Album*, for orchestra
LUTOSLAWSKI (37)
Concerto for orchestra (1950–4)
MELLERS (36)
*The Tragicall History of Christopher Marlowe*, opera (1950–2)
PANUFNIK (36)
*Old Polish Suite*, for string orchestra
DIAMOND (35)
Piano Concerto

*Chorale*, for chorus
Quintet for two violas, two cellos and clarinet
BABBITT (34)
Composition for viola and piano
GINASTERA (34)
*Pampeana No 2*, for cello and piano
ARNELL (33)
Symphony No 5
String Quintet
BERNSTEIN (32)
*Peter Pan*, incidental music
*Yigdal*, for chorus and piano
*Trouble in Tahiti*, one-act opera
FRICKER (30)
Symphony No 2 (1950–1)
Concertante No 1 for English horn and strings
Violin Sonata
Four Impromptus (1950–2)
ARNOLD (29)
Symphony No 1
Serenade for small orchestra
Eight English Dances
String Quartet No 1 (possibly 1946)
SHAPEY (29)
Violin Sonata
HAMILTON (28)
Clarinet Concerto
MENNIN (27)
Symphony No 5
Violin Concerto
*Canto and Toccata*, for piano
Five Pieces for piano
NONO (26)
*Variazione di Schoenberg*, for chamber orchestra
BERIO (25)
Concertino for solo clarinet, solo violin, harp, celeste and strings
*Opus Number Zoo*, for woodwind quintet and narrator (revised 1970)
SCHÜLLER (25)
Symphony for brass and percussion
HENZE (24)
*Rosa Silber*, ballet
Piano Concerto No 1
*Symphonic Variations*, for piano and orchestra
KURTÁG (24)
Suite for piano duet
JOSEPHS (23)
*Machine Made*, for theatre orchestra
JOUBERT (23)
String Quartet No 1
Divertimento for piano duet

STOCKHAUSEN (22)
*Chöre für Doris*, for choir
*Choral*, for choir
Three Lieder for voice and chamber
  orchestra
LEIGHTON (21)
*Veris gratia*, for oboe, cello and strings

## 1951

LAMBERT, MEDTNER and
SCHOENBERG died
SCHMITT (81)
*Introit, récit et congé*, for cello and orchestra
  (1951–2)
VAUGHAN WILLIAMS (79)
*The Pilgrim's Progress*, for soloists, chorus
  and orchestra
*Romance* in D♭, for harmonica, strings
  and piano
SCHOENBERG (77)
*De Profundis*, for a cappella choir
BRIAN (75)
Symphony No 9
BLOCH (71)
*Cinq Pièces Hébraïques*, for viola and piano
String Quartet No 3 (1951–2)
MALIPIERO (69)
*Sinfonia del zodiaco*
STRAVINSKY (69)
*Mass*, for horns and orchestra
RIEGGER (66)
*In Certainty of Song*, cantata
Nonet for brass
Piano Quintet
WELLESZ (66)
Symphony No 3
*Incognita*, opera
SCHOECK (65)
Horn Concerto
*Festlichen Hymnus*
TOCH (64)
Symphony No 2
IBERT (61)
Sinfonia Concertante
MARTIN (61)
Concerto for cembalo and small orchestra
  (1951–2)
MARTINŮ (61)
Piano Trio No 3
*Stowe Pastorals*, for chamber ensemble
*Serenade*, for two clarinets and string trio
Symphony No 6, *Fantasies Symphoniques*
  (1951–3)
PROKOFIEV (60)
Symphony No 7 (1951–2)

HONEGGER (59)
Symphony No 5, *Di Tre Re*
*Monopartita*, for orchestra
HOWELLS (59)
Cello Concerto (unfinished)
MILHAUD (59)
*The Seven-branched Candelabra*, for piano
BENJAMIN (58)
*Orlando's Silver Wedding*, ballet
*North American Square Dance*, for orchestra
PISTON (57)
String Quartet No 4
HINDEMITH (56)
*Die Harmonie der Welt*, symphony
JACOB (56)
Concerto for flute
*Fantasia on Songs of the British Isles*
SOWERBY (56)
*Concert Piece*, for organ and orchestra
GERHARD (56)
Concerto for piano and strings
HANSON (55)
*Fantasia on a Theme of Youth*, for piano and
  strings
SESSIONS (55)
String Quartet No 2
THOMSON, V. (55)
*Five Songs of William Blake*, for baritone
  and orchestra
COWELL (54)
Symphony No 6
KORNGOLD (54)
Symphony in F♯ major
TANSMAN (54)
Symphony No 8
HARRIS (53)
*Cumberland Concerto*, for orchestra
Symphony No 7
AURIC (52)
*Chemin de Lumière*, ballet
CHÁVEZ (52)
Symphony No 3
ANTHEIL (51)
*Eight Fragments from Shelley*, for chorus
BUSH, A. (51)
*Trent's Broad Reaches*, for horn and piano
*Outdoors and Indoors*, for cello and piano
COPLAND (51)
*Pied Piper*, ballet
KŘENEK (51)
Concerto for harp and chamber orchestra
Concerto for two pianos and orchestra
Piano Sonata No 6
RUBBRA (50)
*Festival Te Deum*
String Quartet No 2

**BERKELEY, L.** (48)
*Gibbons Variations*, for voices, strings and organ
Three Greek Songs for voice and piano
**RAINIER** (48)
Five Pieces for keyboard
**DALLAPICCOLA** (47)
*Canti di Liberazione*, for chorus and orchestra (1951–5)
**ALWYN** (46)
Concerto Grosso No 2
Festival March
**RAWSTHORNE** (46)
Piano Concerto No 2
Concertante Pastorale for flute, horn and strings
**SEIBER** (46)
Concertino for clarinet and strings
*The Seasons*, for orchestra
**COOKE** (45)
Violin Sonata No 2
**FRANKEL** (45)
Concerto for violin and orchestra
*Mephistopheles' Serenade and Dance*, for orchestra
**LUTYENS** (45)
*Penelope*, music drama for voices and orchestra
*Requiem for the Living*
*Nativity*, for soprano and strings or organ
**SHOSTAKOVICH** (45)
Ballet Suite No 2, for orchestra
*Ten Poems on Texts by Revolutionary Poets*, for chorus
Film music
**HOLMBOE** (42)
Chamber Symphony No 1
*Primavera*, for flute and piano trio
Symphony No 8, *Sinfonia Boreale*
**SIEGMEISTER** (42)
*Pastoral*, for band
**MENOTTI** (40)
*Amahl and the Night Visitors*, opera
*Apocalypse*, for orchestra
**CAGE** (39)
Concerto for prepared piano and chamber orchestra
*Imaginary Landscape No 4*
*Music of Changes*, for piano
**JONES** (39)
Symphony No 3
Concert Overture
**BRITTEN** (38)
*Billy Budd*, opera
*Six Metamorphoses after Ovid*, for solo oboe
**GOULD** (38)
*The Battle Hymn of the Republic*

**LLOYD** (38)
*John Socman*, opera
**LUTOSLAWSKI** (38)
*Little Suite*, for orchestra
*Silesian Triptych*, for soprano and orchestra
**MELLERS** (37)
*Festival Galliard*, for orchestra
**PANUFNIK** (37)
Concerto in modo antico for trumpet and orchestra
**DIAMOND** (36)
Symphony No 6
Quartet No 4
Piano Trio
*Mizmor L'David*, for voices, organ and orchestra
*The Midnight Meditation*, song cycle
**ARNELL** (34)
*Harlequin in April*, ballet
String Quartet No 4
**BERNSTEIN** (33)
*Five Anniversaries*, for piano
*Silhouette (Galilee)*, for voice and piano
**BUSH, G.** (31)
*Twelfth Night, an entertainment*, choral
**FRICKER** (31)
*Canterbury Prologue*, ballet
Viola Concerto (1951–3)
Concertante No 2 for three pianos, strings and timpani
**SHAPERO** (31–38)
Concerto for orchestra (1951–8)
**ARNOLD** (30)
*Sussex*, overture
Concerto for piano duet and strings
Sonatina in three movements for clarinet and piano
Sonatina in three movements for oboe and piano
**SHAPEY** (30)
*Fantasy*, for orchestra
String Quartet No 3
Cantata
**SIMPSON** (30)
Symphony No 1
String Quartet No 1 (1951–2)
**HAMILTON** (29)
*Clerk Saunders*, ballet
Symphony No 2
Flute Quartet
Piano Sonata (revised 1971)
**BANKS** (28)
Divertimento for flute and string trio
Duo for violin and cello
**MENNIN** (28)
*Canzona*, for band

511

NONO (27)
Composizione No 1, for orchestra
*Polifonica-monodia-ritmica*, for
  instrumental ensemble
*Epitaph for Lorca*, for speaker, chorus and
  orchestra (1951–3)
BERIO (26)
Two Pieces for violin and piano
BOULEZ (26)
*fp Polyphonie X*, for eighteen instruments
Second version of *Le visage nuptial*, for
  soprano, alto, choir and orchestra
SCHÜLLER (26)
*Dramatic Overture*
FELDMAN (25)
*Intersections I*, for orchestra, piano and
  cello
*Projections 1* and 2, for flute, trumpet,
  violin and cello
HENZE (25)
*Boulevard Solitude*, lyric drama
*A Country Doctor*, radio opera
*Labyrinth*, choreographic fantasy
*The Sleeping Princess*, ballet
JOUBERT (24)
Overture for orchestra
Sonata for viola and piano
Five Songs for tenor and piano
STOCKHAUSEN (23)
*Formel*, for orchestra
*Kreuzspiel*, for instrumental ensemble
Sonatine for violin and piano
LEIGHTON (22)
*Primavera romana*, overture
Piano Concerto No 1
TAKEMITSU (21)
*The Joy to Live*, ballet
GOEHR (19)
Piano Sonata (1951–2)
*Songs of Babel*
SHCHEDRIN (19)
*The Story of a Real Man*, symphonic poem

## 1952

KNUSSEN was born
VAUGHAN WILLIAMS (80)
*Sinfonia Antarctica* (Symphony No 7)
AUBERT (76)
*Cinéma*, for orchestra
BRIAN (76)
*The Cenci*, opera
DOHNÁNYI (75)
Violin Concerto No 2
Harp Concerto
BLOCH (72)
*Sinfonia Brève*

Concerto Grosso for string quartet and
  string orchestra
MALIPIERO (70)
Violin Concerto
STRAVINSKY (70)
Cantata on old English texts
Concertino for twelve instruments
RIEGGER (67)
Woodwind Quintet
Concerto for piano and woodwind quintet
WELLESZ (67)
Symphony No 4
DUPRÉ (66)
Quartet for organ and string trio
*La France au Calvaire*, oratorio (1952–3)
SCHOECK (66)
*Befreite Sehnsucht*, song cycle
MARTIN (62)
*La Tempête*, opera (1952–5)
MARTINŮ (62)
*What Men Live By*, TV opera
*Rhapsodie*, for viola and orchestra
BLISS (61)
*The Enchantress*, scena for contralto and
  orchestra
Piano Sonata
PROKOFIEV (61)
Cello Concertino
HONEGGER (60)
*Suite archaïque*
BENJAMIN (59)
*Divertimento on Themes by Gluck*, for
  orchestra
MOORE (59)
*Cotillion*, suite for string orchestra
PISTON (58)
*Fantasy*, for English horn, harp and
  strings
HINDEMITH (57)
Symphony in B♭ for military band
Sonata for four horns
SOWERBY (57)
String Trio
GERHARD (56)
Symphony No 1 (1952–3)
THOMSON, V. (56)
*Sea Piece with Birds*, for orchestra
COWELL (55)
*Symphony No 7*
*Fiddler's Jig*, for violin and string orchestra
*Fantasie*, for wind band
*Four Trumpets for Alan*, for four trumpets
  and piano
KORNGOLD (55)
'Sonnet to Vienna', song
THOMPSON (54)
*A Trip to Nahant*, symphonic fantasy

AURIC (53)
*Ecossaise*, for orchestra
BUSH, A. (52)
Concert Suite for cello and orchestra
*Defender of Peace*, for orchestra
Three English Song Preludes for organ
Ten English Folk Songs for chorus
*Voices of the Prophets*, for voices and piano
KŘENEK (52)
Sinfonietta for string orchestra, *La Brasiliera*
*Pallas Athene weint*, opera
RUBBRA (51)
Viola Concerto
FINZI (51)
*Love's Labours Lost*, orchestral suite
RODRIGO (50)
Four *Villancicos*, for voice and piano
Four *Villancicos*, for chorus *Canciones de Navidad*
BERKELEY, L. (49)
Flute Concerto
Four Ronsard Sonnets, Set 1, for two tenors and piano
BLACHER (49)
Piano Concerto No 2
DALLAPICCOLA (48)
*Quaderno musicale di Annalibera*, for piano
Goethe-Lieder (1952–3)
KABALEVSKY (48)
Piano Concerto No 3
Cello Sonata
RAWSTHORNE (47)
*Canticle of Man*, chamber cantata
TIPPETT (47)
*Dance Clarion Air*, madrigal
LUTYENS (46)
String Quartets Nos 4–6
SHOSTAKOVICH (46)
Ballet Suite No 3, for orchestra
String Quartet No 5
*Four Monologues on Verses of Pushkin*, for bass and piano
*The Sun Shines Over Our Motherland*, cantata
CARTER (43)
Sonata for flute, oboe, cello and harpsichord
Elegy for strings
SIEGMEISTER (43)
*Darling Corrie*, opera
MENOTTI (41)
Violin Concerto
CAGE (40)
*Water Music*, for pianist with accessory instruments
*Williams Mix*, for tape

*4' 33"* *(tacet)*, for piano in four movements
FRANÇAIX (40)
*Le Roi Midas*, ballet
Sonatina for trumpet and piano
*Serenade BEA*, for strings
BRITTEN (39)
Canticle No 2, 'Abraham and Isaac', for contralto, tenor and piano
GOULD (39)
*Dance Variations*, for two pianos and orchestra
FINE (38)
String Quartet
*Mutability*, song cycle
MELLERS (38)
*Galliard*, for trombone and piano
PANUFNIK (38)
*Heroic Overture*
GINASTERA (36)
Piano Sonata No 1
ROCHBERG (34)
String Quartet No 1
Twelve Bagatelles for piano
BUSH, G. (32)
Trio for oboe, bassoon and piano
FRICKER (32)
Concerto for piano and small orchestra (1952–4)
String Quartet No 2 (1952–3)
ARNOLD (31)
*Curtain Up*, overture
Three Shanties for wind quintet
SHAPEY (31)
Symphony No 1
Quartet for oboe and string trio
Oboe Sonata
Suite for piano
FOSS (30)
*Parable of Death*, for narrator, tenor and orchestra
HAMILTON (30)
*Bartholomew Fair*, overture
Violin Concerto
MENNIN (29)
Concertato for orchestra, *Moby Dick*
Quartet No 2
BERIO (27)
*Allez Hop*, for voice, mime and dance
Five Variations for piano (1952–3)
BOULEZ (27)
*fp Structures*, Book 1, for two pianos
BROWN (26)
*Folio and Four Systems*, for piano and orchestra
Music for violin, cello and piano
HENZE (26)
*King Stag*, opera (1952–5)

The Idiot, ballet-pantomime
Quintet for wind instruments
String Quartet No 2
**JOUBERT** (25)
O Lorde, the Maker of Al Thing, for chorus
and organ
Torches, carols for chorus and organ or
orchestra
**STOCKHAUSEN** (24)
Spiel, for orchestra
Punkte, for orchestra (1952–3)
Kontrapunkte, for ten instruments (1952–3)
Schlagtrio, for piano and timpani
Klavierstücke I–IV (1952–3)
Étude, musique concrète
**LEIGHTON** (23)
Concerto for violin and small orchestra
Concerto for viola, harp, timpani and
strings
**SHCHEDRIN** (20)
Piano Quintet
**DAVIES, P. M.** (18)
Quartet Movement, for string quartet


# 1953

**MULDOWNEY** was born; **BAX,
JONGEN, PROKOFIEV** and **QUILTER**
died
**BRIAN** (77)
English Suite No 5
Symphony No 10 (1953–4)
**DOHNÁNYI** (76)
Stabat Mater
**BLOCH** (73)
String Quartets Nos 4 and 5
**PIZZETTI** (73)
Cagliostro, opera
**STRAVINSKY** (71)
Septet
Three Songs from William Shakespeare, for
mezzo and piano
**BAX** (70)
Coronation March
**RIEGGER** (68)
Variations for piano and orchestra
**VARÈSE** (68)
Déserts, for orchestra (1953–4)
**TOCH** (66)
Circus Overture
Notturno, for orchestra
**MARTINŮ** (63)
The Marriage, opera
Accusation against the Unknown, TV opera
Concerto for violin, piano and orchestra
Overture

Fresky Piero della Francesco, for orchestra
**BLISS** (62)
Processional, for orchestra and organ
**HONEGGER** (61)
Christmas Cantata
**MILHAUD** (61)
David, opera
**BENJAMIN** (60)
Three Fanfares
**MOORE** (60)
Piano Trio
**ROGERS** (60)
String Trio
**ROBERTSON** (57)
The Book of Mormon, oratorio
**SESSIONS** (57)
Sonata for solo violin
**COWELL** (56)
Symphonies Nos 8, 9, 10 and 11
Rondo for orchestra
Towards a Bright Day, for orchestra
Singing Band, for brass
**KORNGOLD** (56)
Straussiana, for orchestra
Theme and Variations for orchestra
**HARRIS** (55)
Piano Concerto No 2
Abraham Lincoln Walks at Midnight,
chamber cantata
**CHÁVEZ** (54)
Symphony No 4, Sinfonia Romantica
Symphony No 5, Symphony for Strings
**POULENC** (54)
Dialogues des Carmelites, opera (1953–6)
Sonata for two pianos
**ANTHEIL** (53)
Capital of the World, ballet
**BUSH, A.** (53)
The Spell Unbound, children's opera
Pavanne for the Castleton Queen, for brass
band
Northumbrian Impressions, for oboe and
piano
The Ballad of Freedom's Soldier, for tenor,
baritone, chorus and orchestra
**KŘENEK** (53)
Concerto for cello and orchestra
**WALTON** (51)
Coronation Te Deum
Orb and Sceptre, coronation march for
orchestra
**BERKELEY, L.** (50)
Suite for orchestra
**BLACHER** (50)
Abstrakte Oper No 1, opera
Orchester-Ornament Studie in Pianissimo,
for orchestra

RAINIER (50)
*Cycle for Declamation*, for solo soprano, tenor or baritone
ALWYN (48)
Symphony No 2
*The Magic Island*, symphonic prelude
SEIBER (48)
Three Pieces for cello and orchestra
TIPPETT (48)
Piano Concerto (1953–4)
Divertimento for chamber orchestra, *Sellinger's Round* (1953–5)
*Fantasia Concertante on a Theme by Corelli*, for strings
FRANKEL (47)
*Concertante Lirico*, for string orchestra
Piano Quartet
LUTYENS (47)
Three Songs and Incidental Music for Group Theater's *Homage to Dylan Thomas*
SHOSTAKOVICH (47)
Ballet Suite No 4
Symphony No 10
Concertino for two pianos
MACONCHY (46)
*Proud Thames*, overture
MESSIAEN (45)
*Reveil des oiseaux*, for piano and orchestra
HOLMBOE (44)
*Traet*, for four voices and chamber orchestra
SIEGMEISTER (44)
Divertimento for orchestra
BARBER (43)
*Souvenirs*, ballet suite
SCHUMAN (43)
*The Mighty Casey*, baseball opera
*Voyage*, for piano
GILDER (42)
*Nursery Suite*, for orchestra
CAGE (41)
*Music for Piano '4-84 for 1-84 Pianists'* (1953–6)
FRANÇAIX (41)
*Canon at the octave*, for horn and piano
*Divertimento*, for flute and keyboard
*L'insectarium*, for harpsichord
Symphony
BRITTEN (40)
*Gloriana*, opera
*Winter Words*, songs
GOULD (40)
Inventions for four pianos and orchestra
MELLERS (39)
Symphony

BABBITT (37)
Woodwind Quartet
GINASTERA (37)
Variations Concertante for chamber orchestra
ARNELL (36)
*The Great Detective*, ballet
*Lord Byron*, symphonic portrait
BERNSTEIN (35)
*Wonderful Town*, musical comedy
ROCHBERG (35)
Chamber Symphony for nine instruments
FRICKER (33)
Violin Concerto No 2, *Rapsodie concertante*
ARNOLD (32)
*Homage to the Queen*, ballet
Symphony No 2
Oboe Concerto
Violin Sonata No 2
Sonatina for recorder and piano
SHAPEY (32)
String Quartet No 4
Cello Sonata
SIMPSON (32)
String Quartets Nos 2 and 3 (1953–4)
XENAKIS (31)
*Metastaseis*, for orchestra
BANKS (30)
Sonata for violin and piano
Four Pieces for orchestra
LIGETI (30)
String Quartet
MENNIN (30)
Symphony No 6
NONO (29)
*Due Espressioni*, for orchestra
BERIO (28)
*Chamber Music*, for female voice, clarinet, cello and harp
SCHÜLLER (28)
Recitative and Rondo for violin and orchestra
BROWN (27)
*Twenty-five pages – from one to twenty-five pianos*
HENZE (27)
*The End of a World*, radio opera
*Ode to the Westwind*, for cello and orchestra
KURTÁG (27)
*Koreai Kantáta*
JOUBERT (26)
Miniature String Quartet
*The Burghers of Calais*, cantata
MUSGRAVE (25)
*A Tale for Thieves*, ballet
*A Suite of Bairnsangs*, for voice and piano

STOCKHAUSEN (25)
*Elektronische Studie* I, electronic music
HODDINOTT (24)
*fp Fugal Overture*, for orchestra
*fp Nocturne*, for orchestra
LEIGHTON (24)
Concerto for oboe and strings
*A Christmas Caroll*, for baritone, chorus,
   piano or organ and strings
SHCHEDRIN (21)
*The Twentyeight*, cantata


## 1954

IVES died
VAUGHAN WILLIAMS (82)
Concerto for bass tuba and orchestra
Violin Sonata in A minor
*This Day (Hodie)*, cantata
BRIAN (78)
Symphony No 11
*Elegy*, symphonic poem for orchestra
DOHNÁNYI (77)
*American Rhapsody*
SCOTT (75)
Sinfonietta for strings, organ and harp
KODÁLY (72)
*Spartacus*, ballet
STRAVINSKY (72)
*In Memoriam Dylan Thomas*, for voice,
   trombones and string quartet
Four Songs
*Two Poems of Balmont*, for orchestra
RIEGGER (69)
*Suite for Younger Orchestra*
TAYLOR (69)
*The Dragon*, opera
MARTINŮ (64)
*Mirandolina*, opera
*Hymn to Jacob*, for soli, chorus, horn,
   strings and organ
*Mount of Three Lights*, cantata
*The Epic of Gilgamesh*, oratorio (1954–5)
BLISS (63)
*A Song of Welcome*, for solo voices, chorus
   and orchestra
HOWELLS (62)
*Missa Sabrinensis*, for soli, chorus and
   orchestra
*St Paul's Canticles*, for chorus
MILHAUD (62)
Harp Concerto
ROGERS (61)
*The Nightingale*, opera
PISTON (60)
Symphony No 5

SOWERBY (59)
*All on a Summer's Day*, for orchestra
*Fantasy*, for trumpet and organ
SESSIONS (58)
*The Idyll of Theocritus*, for soprano and
   orchestra
THOMSON, V. (58)
Concerto for flute, strings and percussion
HARRIS (56)
Fantasy for piano and orchestra
AURIC (55)
*La Chambre*, ballet
POULENC (55)
*Bucolique*, for orchestra
*Matelote provençale*, for orchestra
BUSH, A. (54)
*Autumn Poem*, for horn and piano
*Men of Blackmoor*, opera (1954–5)
COPLAND (54)
*The Tender Land*, opera
KŘENEK (54)
Symphony, *Pallas Athene*
Violin Concerto No 2
*Elf Transparente*, for orchestra
FINZI (53)
*Grand Fantasia and Toccata*, for piano and
   orchestra
RUBBRA (53)
Symphony No 6
RODRIGO (52)
*Concert-Serenade*, for harp and orchestra
WALTON (52)
*Troilus and Cressida*, opera
BERKELEY, L. (51)
*A Dinner Engagement*, opera
*Nelson*, opera
Trio for violin, horn and piano
Sonatina for piano duet
BLACHER (51)
*Two Inventions*, for orchestra
Viola Concerto
KHACHATURIAN (51)
*Spartacus*, ballet
RAINIER (51)
Six Pieces for five woodwind instruments
DALLAPICCOLA (50)
*Piccola musica notturna*, for orchestra
ALWYN (49)
*Lyra Angelica*, for harp and strings
RAWSTHORNE (49)
*Practical Cats*, for speaker and orchestra
String Quartet No 2
SEIBER (49)
*Elegy*, for violin and small orchestra
*To Poetry*, song cycle
COOKE (48)
Oboe Concerto

LUTYENS (48)
*Infidelio*, seven scenes for voices and
   instruments
*Valediction*, for clarinet and piano
SHOSTAKOVICH (48)
*Festival Overture*
*Five Romances (Songs of Our Days)*, for bass
   and piano
Film music
CARTER (45)
Symphony No 1, revised version
Variations for orchestra
HOLMBOE (45)
Sinfonia in memoriam
String Quartet No 4
Piano Trio
BARBER (44)
*Prayers of Kierkegaard*, for soprano, chorus
   and orchestra
STILL (44)
*Oedipus*, opera (1954–6)
Symphony No 1 (1954–6)
GILDER (43)
*A Sea Suite*, for orchestra
MENOTTI (43)
*The Saint of Bleecker Street*, opera
CAGE (42)
*34' 46.776" for a pianist*, for prepared piano
FRANÇAIX (42)
*Paris à nous deux*, opera
Violin Concerto
JONES (42)
Symphony No 4
BRITTEN (41)
*The Turn of the Screw*, opera
Canticle No 3, 'Still Falls the Rain', for
   tenor, chorus and piano
LUTOSLAWSKI (41)
*Dance Preludes*, first version for clarinet
   and piano
DIAMOND (39)
Sinfonia concertante
Sonata for solo violin
BABBITT (38)
String Quartet No 2
GINASTERA (38)
*Pampeana No 3*, pastoral symphony
BERNSTEIN (36)
*Serenade*, for violin, strings and percussion
*On the Waterfront*, film score
ROCHBERG (36)
*David the Psalmist*, cantata
Three Psalms for chorus
BUSH, G. (34)
Symphony No 1
FRICKER (34)
*Dance Scene*, for orchestra

Nocturne and Scherzo for piano (four
   hands)
SHAPERO (34)
*Poems of Helavi*, cantata
ARNOLD (33)
Sinfonietta No 1 for two oboes, two horns
   and strings
Concerto for flute and strings
Harmonica Concerto
Concerto for organ and orchestra
*The Tempest*, incidental music
SHAPEY (33)
Concerto for clarinet with six instruments
*Sonata Variations*, for piano
HAMILTON (32)
String Octet
*Four Border Songs and the Fray of Suport*
*Songs of Summer*, for soprano and piano
BANKS (31)
Five North Country Folk Songs for
   soprano or tenor, piano and string
   orchestra
*Psalm LXX*, for soprano and chamber
   orchestra
NONO (30)
*The Red Mantle*, ballet
*Liebeslied*, for chorus and instruments
*La Victoire de Guernica*, for chorus and
   orchestra
*Canti per 13*, for thirteen instruments
   (1954–5)
BERIO (29)
*Nones*, for orchestra
Variations for chamber orchestra
*Mutations*, electronic music
BOULEZ (29)
*Le marteau sans maître*, for alto voice and
   six instruments
KURTÁG (28)
Viola Concerto
JOUBERT (27)
*Antigone*, a radio opera
Symphonic Prelude for orchestra
Concerto for violin
'There is no Rose', for unaccompanied
   chorus
MUSGRAVE (26)
*Cantata for a Summer's Day*
STOCKHAUSEN (26)
*Elektronische Studie* II, electronic music
*Klavierstücke* V–X
CRUMB (25)
String Quartet
LEIGHTON (25)
*The Birds*, for soli, chorus, piano and
   strings

Concerto for two pianos, timpani and
strings
**HODDINOTT** (23)
*fp* Concerto for clarinet and string
orchestra
**GOEHR** (22)
Fantasia for orchestra (revised 1958)
Fantasias for clarinet and piano
**SHCHEDRIN** (22)
Piano Concerto No 1
**BENNETT** (18)
Piano Sonata
Sonatina for flute

# 1955

**ENESCO, HONEGGER** and **ROPARTZ**
died
**VAUGHAN WILLIAMS** (83)
Symphony No 8
**BRIAN** (79)
*Faust*, opera
**STRAVINSKY** (73)
*Greeting Prelude*, for orchestra
*Canticum Sacrum ad Honorem Sancti Marci
Nominis*
**RIEGGER** (70)
*Dance Rhythms*, for orchestra
**VARÈSE** (70)
*Good Friday Procession in Verges*, electronic
composition for film (1955–6)
**COATES** (69)
*The Dam Busters*, film score
**TOCH** (68)
Symphony No 3
**MARTIN** (65)
*Études*, for string orchestra (1955–6)
**MARTINŮ** (65)
*Three frescoes*, for orchestra
Oboe Concerto
*The Opening of the Wells*, chamber cantata
Piano Concerto No 4, *Incantations* (1955–6)
**BLISS** (64)
Violin Concerto
*Meditations on a Theme of John Blow*, for
orchestra
*Elegiac Sonnet*, for tenor, string quartet and
piano
**MILHAUD** (63)
Symphonies Nos 5 and 6
**PISTON** (61)
Symphony No 6
**ORFF** (60)
*Der Sänger der Vorwelt*, opera
*Comoedia de Christi resurrectione*, for chorus
and orchestra

**GERHARD** (59)
Concerto for harpsichord, strings and
percussion (1955–6)
String Quartet No 1 (1955–6)
**HANSON** (59)
Symphony No 5, *Sinfonia sacrae*
**SESSIONS** (59)
Mass for unison male voices and organ
**COWELL** (58)
Ballad for strings
Symphony No 12 (1955–6)
*Set of Two*, for violin and piano (1955–6)
*Set of Four*, for harpsichord (1955–6)
*Set of Five*, for violin, piano and percussion
(1955–6)
String Quartet No 5 (1955–6)
Septet for five wordless voices, clarinet
and keyboard
**TANSMAN** (58)
Capriccio for orchestra
*Le Sermant*, opera
Concerto for orchestra
**ANTHEIL** (55)
*Cabezza de Vacca*, cantata (1955–6)
**COPLAND** (55)
*Symphonic Ode*
*A Canticle of Freedom*, for chorus and
orchestra (revised 1965)
**KŘENEK** (55)
Capriccio for cello and chamber orchestra
Harp Sonata
*The Bell-Tower*, one-act opera (1955–6)
*Spiritus Intelligentiae, Sanctus*, for voices
and electronics (1955–6)
**FINZI** (54)
Cello Concerto
**RUBBRA** (54)
Piano Concerto
**RODRIGO** (53)
*Fantasia para un gentilhombre*, for guitar
(c1955)
**WALTON** (53)
*Johannesburg Festival Overture*
*Richard III*, incidental music for the film
**BERKELEY, L.** (52)
Suite from *Nelson*, for orchestra
Concerto for flute, violin, cello and
harpsichord (or piano)
Sextet for clarinet, horn and string quartet
Concert Study in E♭ for piano
*Crux fidelis*, for tenor and mixed chorus
*Look up Sweet Babe*, for soprano and mixed
chorus
*Salve regina*, for voices and organ
**BLACHER** (52)
*Der Mohr von Venedig*, ballet
*Orchester-Fantasie*

KHACHATURIAN (52)
Three Suites for orchestra
RAINIER (52)
*Requiem,* for tenor and chorus
DALLAPICCOLA (51)
*An Mathilde,* cantata
KABALEVSKY (51)
*Nikita Vershinin,* opera
ALWYN (50)
*Autumn Legend,* for English horn and
  strings
BLITZSTEIN (50)
*Reuben, Reuben,* musical play
RAWSTHORNE (50)
*Madame Chrysanthème,* ballet
TIPPETT (50)
Sonata for four horns
COOKE (49)
Clarinet Concerto
LUTYENS (49)
Music for orchestra I
*Capriccii,* for two harps and percussion
*Nocturnes,* for violin, guitar and cello
Sinfonia for organ
SHOSTAKOVICH (49)
Film music
HOLMBOE (46)
String Quartet No 5
Chamber Concerto No 13 for oboe, viola
  and orchestra
SIEGMEISTER (46)
*Miranda and the Dark Young Man,* opera
*Hootenanny,* for band
SCHUMAN (45)
*Credendum,* for orchestra
CAGE (43)
*26' 1.499" for a string player*
FRANÇAIX (43)
*Fantaisie,* for cello and orchestra
BRITTEN (42)
Hymn to St Peter, for choir and organ
*Alpine Suite,* for recorder trio
GOULD (42)
*Jekyll and Hyde Variations,* for orchestra
*Derivations,* for clarinet and band
LUTOSLAWSKI (42)
*Dance Preludes,* second version for clarinet
  and instruments
FINE (41)
*Serious Song and Lament,* for string
  orchestra
ARNELL (38)
*Love in Transit,* opera
BERNSTEIN (37)
*The Lark,* French and Latin choruses
*Get Hep!,* marching song
*Salome,* incidental music

ROCHBERG (37)
Duo Concertante for violin and cello
BUSH, G. (35)
*In Praise of Mary,* choral
FRICKER (35)
*Litany,* for double string orchestra
*Musick's Empire,* for chorus and small
  orchestra
*The Tomb of St Eulalia,* elegy for counter-
  tenor, gamba and harpsichord
Horn Sonata
SHAPERO (35)
*Credo,* for orchestra
ARNOLD (34)
*Tam O'Shanter,* overture
Little Suite for Orchestra No 1
Serenade for guitar and strings
*John Clare,* cantata
FOSS (34)
*Griffelkin,* opera
*The Gift of the Magi,* ballet
SHAPEY (34)
*Challenge – the Family of Man,* for orchestra
Piano Trio
XENAKIS (33)
*Pithoprakta,* for orchestra (1955–6)
BANKS (32)
Three North Country Folk Songs for
  soprano or tenor and piano
Three Studies for cello and piano
NONO (31)
*Incontri,* for twenty-four instruments
*Il Canto Sospeso,* for soli, chorus and
  orchestra
BOULEZ (30)
*Symphonie mécanique,* music for the film
SCHÜLLER (30)
*Symphonic Tribute to Duke Ellington*
HENZE (29)
Symphony No 4
*Quattro Poemi,* for orchestra
Three Symphonic Studies (revised 1964)
JOSEPHS (28)
*The Ants,* comedy overture
Symphony No 1
*Siesta,* for violin and piano
JOUBERT (28)
*Great Lord of Lords,* for chorus and organ
*In the Drought,* one-act opera
Symphony No 1
KORTE (27)
*Concertato on a Choral Theme,* for orchestra
MUSGRAVE (27)
*The Abbot of Drimock,* chamber opera
Five Love Songs for soprano and guitar
STOCKHAUSEN (27)
*Gruppen,* for three orchestras (1955–7)

*Zeitmasze*, for oboe, flute, English horn, clarinet and bassoon
*Gesang de Jünglinge*, electronic music
**CRUMB** (26)
Sonatina for unaccompanied cello
**HODDINOTT** (26)
*fp* Symphony No 1
**TAKEMITSU** (25)
Chamber Concerto
**DAVIES, P. M.** (21)
*Stedman Doubles*, for clarinet and percussion (revised 1968)
Sonata for trumpet and piano

## 1956

**CHARPENTIER, GLIÈRE** and **FINZI** died
**VAUGHAN WILLIAMS** (84)
Symphony No 9 (revised 1958)
Two Organ Preludes, *Romanza* and *Toccata*
*Epithalamium*, cantata (1956–7)
*Ten Blake Songs*, for tenor and oboe
*A Vision of Aeroplanes*, motet
**RIEGGER** (71)
Variations for violin and viola
**WELLESZ** (71)
Symphony No 5
**TOCH** (69)
*Peter Pan*, for orchestra
**MARTIN** (66)
*Overture in Homage to Mozart*, for orchestra
**MARTINŮ** (66)
*Legend of the Smoke*, chamber cantata
*The Greek Passion*, opera (1956–9)
**BLISS** (65)
*Edinburgh Overture*
**HOWELLS** (64)
*An English Mass*, for chorus
**MILHAUD** (64)
Symphony No 7
**BENJAMIN** (63)
*Mañana*, opera
**MOORE** (63)
*The Ballad of Baby Doe*, opera
**PISTON** (62)
*Serenata*, for orchestra
Quintet for wind
**CASTELNUOVO-TEDESCO** (61)
*All's Well that Ends Well*, opera
**JACOB** (61)
Piano Concerto No 2
Sextet
Piano Trio
**ORFF** (61)
*Nanie und Dithyrambe*, with choir
**GERHARD** (60)
Nonet for eight winds and accordion

**HANSON** (60)
*Elegy in Memory of Serge Koussevitsky*, for orchestra
**SESSIONS** (60)
Piano Concerto
**COWELL** (59)
Variations for orchestra
*A Thanksgiving Psalm*, for male chorus
*Persian Set*, for orchestra (1956–7)
**HARRIS** (58)
*Folk Fantasy for Festivals*, for piano and choir
**AURIC** (57)
*Hommage à Marguerite Long*, for orchestra
**POULENC** (57)
*Le travail du peintre*, song cycle
*Deux mélodies*, songs
**KŘENEK** (56)
*Monologue*, for clarinet
Sonatina for oboe
**FINZI** (55)
*In Terra Pax*, for chorus and orchestra
*Eclogue*, for piano and string orchestra
**RUBBRA** (55)
Symphony No 7
**WALTON** (54)
Cello Concerto
**BERKELEY, L.** (53)
*Ruth*, opera
**BLACHER** (53)
*Hommage à Mozart*, for orchestra
**KHACHATURIAN** (53)
*Ode to Joy*, for voices and orchestra
**DALLAPICCOLA** (52)
*Concerto per la notte di natale dell'anno*, for soprano and chamber orchestra
*Cinque canti*, for baritone and eight instruments
**KABALEVSKY** (52)
Symphony No 5
*Song of the Party Membership Card*, for chorus and orchestra
*Romeo and Juliet*, symphonic suite
**ALWYN** (51)
Symphony No 3
**RAWSTHORNE** (51)
Violin Concerto No 2
**TIPPETT** (51)
Symphony No 2 (1956–7)
**LUTYENS** (50)
Chorale for Orchestra (*Hommage à Stravinsky*)
Three Duos (horn and piano; cello and piano; violin and piano) (1956–7)
*In the Temple of a Bird's Wing*, for baritone and piano (also 1965)

SHOSTAKOVICH (50)
*Katerina Ismailova*, opera
String Quartet No 6
*Spanish Songs*, for soprano and piano
Film music
MACONCHY (49)
*The Sofa*, one-act opera (1956–7)
MESSIAEN (48)
*Oiseaux exotiques*, for piano, wind and
  percussion
HOLMBOE (47)
*Epitaph*, symphonic metamorphoses
*Quartetto medico*, for flute, oboe, clarinet
  and percussion
SIEGMEISTER (47)
Clarinet Concerto
BARBER (46)
*Summer Music*, for woodwind quintet
SCHUMAN (46)
*New England Triptych*, for orchestra
STILL (46)
*Ballad of the Bladebone Inn*, overture
Symphony No 2
MENOTTI (45)
*The Unicorn, the Gorgon and the Manticore*,
  ballet
FRANÇAIX (44)
*Hymne Solonnelle*, for orchestra
JONES (44)
*Ievenctid*, overture
BRITTEN (43)
*The Prince of the Pagodas*, ballet
*Antiphon*, for choir and organ
GOULD (43)
*Santa Fé Saga*, for band
*Dialogue*, for piano and strings
MELLERS (42)
Sonatina for recorder and piano
PANUFNIK (42)
Rhapsody for orchestra
DIAMOND (41)
Sonata for solo cello
GINASTERA (40)
Harp Concerto
ARNELL (39)
*Landscape and Figures*, for orchestra
BERNSTEIN (38)
*Candide*, comic operetta and overture
ROCHBERG (38)
Sinfonia Fantasia
BUSH, G. (36)
*If The Cap Fits*, opera
FRICKER (36)
Suite for harpsichord
Cello Sonata
ARNOLD (35)
*The Dancing Master*, opera

*The Open Window*, opera
*Solitaire*, ballet suite
*A Grand Overture*, for orchestra
SHAPEY (35)
*Mutations* No 1, for piano
SIMPSON (35)
Symphony No 2
FOSS (34)
Psalms for chorus and orchestra
HAMILTON (34)
Scottish Dances
Sonata for chamber orchestra
XENAKIS (34)
*Achorripsis*, for orchestra (1956–7)
*ST/4*, for string quartet
*ST/10-080262*, for ten players
*Morsima-Amorsima*, for piano and strings
*Atrées*, for ten players
*ST/48*, for orchestra
BANKS (33)
*Pezzo Dramatico*, for piano
MENNIN (33)
Cello Concerto
Sonata Concertante for violin and piano
BERIO (31)
*Allelujah*, I and II, for orchestra
String Quartet
*Perspectives*, electronic music
HENZE (30)
*Maratona*, ballet
*Ondine*, ballet (1956–7)
*Concerto per il Marigny*, for piano and
  seven instruments
Five Neapolitan Songs for voice and
  chamber orchestra
JOUBERT (29)
Dance Suite for piano
*The God Pan*, for female voices and piano
*Incantation*, for unaccompanied chorus
STOCKHAUSEN (28)
*Klavierstücke XI*
HODDINOTT (27)
*fp Septet for wind, strings and piano*
LEIGHTON (27)
Cello Concerto
GOEHR (24)
String Quartet No 1 (1956–7)
SHCHEDRIN (24)
Symphony No 1 (1956–8)
*The Little Humpbacked Horse*, ballet
DAVIES, P. M. (22)
Clarinet Sonata (1956–7)
Five pieces for piano
MAW (21)
*Eight Chinese Lyrics*, for mezzo solo
*Requiem*, for soli, chorus and orchestra
  (1956–7)

NILSSON (19)
*Frequenzen*, for eight players (c1956)

## 1957

CANTELOUBE, COATES, KORNGOLD,
SCHOECK and SIBELIUS died
**BRIAN** (81)
Symphony No 12
*Agamemnon*, opera
**MALIPIERO** (75)
Quintet for piano and strings
**STRAVINSKY** (75)
*Agon*, ballet
*Threni (Lamentations of Jeremiah)*, for
soloists, chorus and orchestra
**RIEGGER** (72)
*Movement*, for two trumpets, trombone
and piano
Symphony No 3
*Festival Overture*
**VARÈSE** (72)
*Poème Electronique* (1957–8)
**TOCH** (70)
Symphony No 4
**MARTIN** (67)
*La Mystère de la Nativité*, oratorio (1957–9)
**MARTINŮ** (67)
Piano Concerto No 5, *Fantasia Concertante*
*The Parables*, for orchestra (1957–8)
**BLISS** (66)
*Discourse*, for orchestra (first version,
recomposed 1965)
**MILHAUD** (65)
Symphony No 8, *Rhodanienne*
Oboe Concerto
*Aspen Serenade*
**MOORE** (64)
*Gallantry*, a soap opera
**PISTON** (63)
Viola Concerto
**SOWERBY** (62)
*The Throne of God*, for chorus and orchestra
**GERHARD** (61)
*Don Quixote*, ballet suite
**SESSIONS** (61)
Symphony No 3
**THOMSON, V.** (61)
*The Lively Arts*, fugue
**WEINBERGER** (61)
*Préludes religieuses et profanes*, for organ
**COWELL** (60)
Music for orchestra
*Ongaku*, for orchestra
Symphony No 13, *Madras*
**POULENC** (58)
*Elegy*, for horn and piano

**BUSH, A.** (57)
Nocturne for piano
Melodies for viola and piano
*Two Ballads of the Sea*, for piano (1957–8)
**COPLAND** (57)
Orchestral Variations
Piano Fantasy
**KŘENEK** (57)
*Jest of Cards*, ballet
*Sestina*, for soprano and ensemble
Suite for guitar
*Missa Duodecim Tonorum*, for choir and
organ (1957–8)
**RUBBRA** (56)
*In Honorem Mariae matris Dei*, cantata
**WALTON** (55)
Partita for orchestra
**BERKELEY, L.** (54)
'Sweet was the Song', for voices and organ
Sonatina for guitar
**BLACHER** (54)
*Music for Cleveland*, for orchestra
**KHACHATURIAN** (54)
*Lermontov Suite*
**DALLAPICCOLA** (53)
*Requiescat*, for chorus and orchestra
(1957–8)
**KABALEVSKY** (53)
*Spring Sings*, operetta
*Songs of Morning, Spring and Peace*, cantata
for children's chorus and orchestra
(1957–8)
**ALWYN** (52)
*Elizabethan Dances*, for orchestra
**BLITZSTEIN** (52)
*This is the Garden*, for chorus and orchestra
*Juno*, musical play (1957–9)
**RAWSTHORNE** (52)
Violin Sonata
**COOKE** (51)
Oboe Sonata
Scherzo for piano
**LUTYENS** (51)
*Six Tempi for Ten Instruments*
Variations for solo flute
*De Amore*, cantata
**SHOSTAKOVICH** (51)
Symphony No 11, *The Year 1905*
Piano Concerto No 2
**HOLMBOE** (48)
Flute Sonata
Concertino for recorder and string trio
*Aspekte*, for wind quartet
*Kairos* (Sinfonias Nos 1 to 4), for strings
(1957–62)
**SIEGMEISTER** (48)
Symphony No 3

SCHUMAN (47)
*Prologues,* for chorus and orchestra
CAGE (45)
Concerto for piano and orchestra (1957–8)
*Winter Music,* for one to twenty pianists
FRANÇAIX (45)
*Eight Exotic Dances,* for two pianos
*Marche Solonnelle,* for organ
*Six Grandes Marches,* for orchestra
GILLES (45)
*Tulsa,* for orchestra
BRITTEN (44)
*Noye's Fludde,* mystery play
*Songs from the Chinese,* for high voice and
  guitar
GOULD (44)
*Declaration Suite*
LUTOSLAWSKI (44)
Five songs
PANUFNIK (43)
*Sinfonia Elegiaca*
DIAMOND (42)
*The World of Paul Klee,* for orchestra
BABBITT (41)
*All Set,* for ensemble
ARNELL (40)
*The Angels,* ballet
BERNSTEIN (39)
*West Side Story,* musical and symphonic
  dances
*Harvard Choruses*
BUSH, G. (37)
Symphony No 2, *The Guildford*
FRICKER (37)
Octet for flute, clarinet, bassoon, horn,
  violin, viola, cello and double-bass
  (1957–8)
Variations for piano (1957–8)
*The Vision of Judgment,* oratorio (1957–8)
ARNOLD (36)
Symphony No 3
*Toy Symphony*
*Four Scottish Dances,* for orchestra
SHAPEY (36)
String Quartet No 5 with female voices
  (1957–8)
*Rhapsodie,* for oboe and piano
Duo for viola and piano
SIMPSON (36)
Violin Concerto (1957–9)
FOSS (35)
*Behold! I build an House,* for chorus
HAMILTON (35)
Five Love Songs for tenor and orchestra
Cantata for tenor and piano
XENAKIS (35)
*Diamorphoses,* electroacoustic music

NONO (33)
*Virianti,* for violin, woodwind and strings
*La Terra e la Compagne,* for soli, chorus and
  instruments (1957–8)
BERIO (32)
Divertimento for Orchestra
*Serenata,* for flute and fourteen
  instruments
*El mar la mar,* for voices and instruments
*Momenti,* for electronic sound
BOULEZ (32)
*Doubles,* for orchestra
*Poésie pour pouvoir,* for reciter, orchestra
  and tape
*Deux improvisations sur Mallarmé,* for
  soprano and instrumental ensemble
Piano Sonata No 3
SCHÜLLER (32)
*Little Fantasy,* for orchestra
FELDMAN (31)
Pieces for four pianos
HENZE (31)
*Nocturnes and Arias,* for soprano and
  orchestra
*Sonata per archi* (1957–8)
JOSEPHS (30)
*Elegy,* for strings
*Wry Rumba,* for wind quintet
*Twelve Letters,* for speaker, clarinet, piano
  and string trio
JOUBERT (30)
Piano Concerto
*A North Country Overture*
Sonata No 1 in one movement for piano
*Two Invocations,* for tenor and piano
*Welcome Yule,* for unaccompanied chorus
HODDINOTT (28)
*fp Rondo Scherzoso,* for trumpet and piano
LEIGHTON (28)
Passacaglia, Chorale and Fugue for
  orchestra
*Burlesque,* for orchestra
TAKEMITSU (27)
Requiem for strings
WILLIAMSON (26)
Piano Sonata No 1
GOEHR (25)
*The Deluge,* cantata
Capriccio for piano
WOOD (25)
String Quartet in B♭
BIRTWISTLE (23)
*Refrains and Choruses,* for flute, oboe,
  clarinet, bassoon and horn
DAVIES, P. M. (23)
*St Michael,* sonata for seventeen wind
  instruments

*Alma redemptoris mater*, for six wind
   instruments
**MAW** (22)
Sonatina for flute and piano
Nocturne for mezzo-soprano and chamber
   orchestra (1957–8)
**BENNETT** (21)
Five Pieces for Orchestra
String Quartet No 3
Violin Sonata
Sonata for solo violin
Sonata for solo cello
*Four Improvisations*, for violin
**NILSSON** (20)
*Kreutzungen*, for instrumental ensemble
*Buch der Veränderungen*, for chamber
   orchestra
*Mädchentotenlieder* (1957–8)

## 1958

**HOLBROOKE, SCHMITT** and
**VAUGHAN WILLIAMS** died
**SCHMITT** (87)
Symphony No 2
**VAUGHAN WILLIAMS** (86)
*The First Nowell*, for soloist, chorus and
   orchestra
*Four Last Songs*, for voice and piano
*Thomas the Rhymer*, opera (uncompleted)
*Vocalises*, for soprano and clarinet
**SCOTT** (79)
Piano Concerto No 2
**PIZZETTI** (78)
*Murder in the Cathedral*, opera
**MARTIN** (68)
*Overture in Rondo*, for orchestra
*Pseaumes de Genève*, for mixed choir,
   children's voices, organ and orchestra
**MARTINŮ** (68)
*Ariadne*, opera
Three Estampes for orchestra
**BLISS** (67)
*The Lady of Shalott*, ballet
**HOWELLS** (66)
*St John's Canticles*, for chorus
*Missa Aedis Christi*, for chorus
**MILHAUD** (66)
Violin Concerto No 3, *Concerto royal*
**BENJAMIN** (65)
*Le Tombeau de Ravel*, for viola, cello and
   piano
**PISTON** (64)
*Psalm and Prayer of David*, for chorus and
   seven instruments
**CASTELNUOVO-TEDESCO** (63)
*The Merchant of Venice*, opera

*Saul*, oratorio
**HINDEMITH** (63)
Octet
**JACOB** (63)
*Diversions*, for woodwind and strings
*Old Wine in New Bottles*, for wind
   instruments
Suite for recorder and string quartet
Miniature String Quartet
**ORFF** (63)
*Oedipus, der Tyrann*, opera
**HANSON** (62)
*Mosaics*, for orchestra
**SESSIONS** (62)
Symphony No 4
String Quintet
**COWELL** (61)
*Antiphony*, for divided orchestra (1958–9)
**CHÁVEZ** (59)
*Inventions No 1*, for piano
**POULENC** (59)
*La voix humaine*, lyric tragedy (monodrama
   for soprano)
**BUSH, A.** (58)
*Ballad of Aldermaston*, for speaker, chorus
   and orchestra
*The World is His Song*, for baritone, chorus
   and orchestra
**RUBBRA** (57)
Oboe Sonata
*Pezzo Ostinato*, for solo harp
**BERKELEY, L.** (55)
Concerto for piano and double string
   orchestra
*Five Poems by W. H. Auden*, for voice and
   piano
**KHACHATURIAN** (55)
Sonatina for piano
**KABALEVSKY** (54)
*Leninists*, cantata
**BLITZSTEIN** (53)
*Lear*, orchestral study
**RAWSTHORNE** (53)
*Halle Overture*
**SEIBER** (53)
*Permutazione a cinque*, for flute, oboe,
   clarinet, horn and bassoon
*Portrait of the Artist as a Young Man*,
   chamber cantata
**TIPPETT** (53)
*King Priam*, opera (1958–61)
*Crown of the Year*, for chorus and
   orchestra
*Prelude, Recitative and Aria*, for flute,
   oboe and harpsichord
**COOKE** (52)
Violin Concerto

LUTYENS (52)
*Piano e Forte*, for solo piano
SHOSTAKOVICH (52)
*Moscow, Cheremushki*, musical comedy
MACONCHY (51)
*The Three Strangers*, one-act opera
SIEGMEISTER (49)
*The Mermaid in Lock No 7*, opera
BARBER (48)
*Vanessa*, opera
MENOTTI (47)
*Maria Golovin*, opera
CAGE (46)
*Fontana Mix*, for tape
*Variations I*
FRANÇAIX (46)
*La dame dans la lune*, ballet
Divertimento for horn and orchestra
JONES (46)
Symphony No 5
*The Country Beyond the Stars*, for chorus
  and orchestra
BRITTEN (45)
*Nocturne*, for tenor, seven obbligato
  instruments and strings
*Sechs Hölderlin-Fragmente*, song cycle
GOULD (45)
*Rhythm Gallery*, for narrator and
  orchestra
*St Lawrence Suite*, for band
LUTOSLAWSKI (45)
*Funeral Music*, for strings
Three Postludes for orchestra (1958–63)
DIAMOND (43)
Woodwind Quintet
GINASTERA (42)
String Quartet No 2
ARNELL (41)
*Moonflowers*, opera
BERNSTEIN (40)
*The Firstborn*, incidental music
ROCHBERG (40)
Symphony No 2
*Cheltenham Concerto*, for chamber
  orchestra
*Dialogues*, for clarinet and piano
FRICKER (38)
*Comedy Overture*, for orchestra
Toccata for piano and orchestra (1958–9)
SHAPERO (38)
*On Green Mountain*, for jazz combo
ARNOLD (37)
Sinfonietta No 2, for flutes, horns and
  strings
SHAPEY (37)
*Ontogeny*, for orchestra
*Walking Upright*, song cycle

SIMPSON (37)
Canzona for brass
FOSS (36)
*Symphony of Chorales*
HAMILTON (36)
*Overture 1912*
Concerto for jazz trumpet and orchestra
Sonata for solo cello
XENAKIS (36)
*Concret PH*, electroacoustic music
BANKS (35)
*Episode*, for chamber orchestra
LIGETI (35)
*Apparitions*, for orchestra (1958–9)
*Artikulation*, for tape
MENNIN (35)
Piano Concerto
NONO (34)
*Cori di Didone*, for chorus and percussion
Composizione No 2 for orchestra
BERIO (33)
*Tempi Concertati*, for flute, violin, two
  pianos and other instruments (1958–9)
*Differences*, for five instruments and tape
*Sequence I*, for flute
*Theme (Homage to Joyce)*, electronic music
SCHÜLLER (33)
*Contours*, for orchestra
*Spectra*, for orchestra
HENZE (32)
*Der Prinz von Homburg*, opera
*Three Dithyrambs*, for chamber orchestra
Chamber Music
*Three Tentos*, for guitar
JOUBERT (31)
String Trio
KORTE (30)
*The Story of the Flutes*, symphonic poem
MUSGRAVE (30)
*Obliques*, for orchestra
String Quartet
*A Song for Christmas*, for voice and piano
HODDINOTT (29)
fp Harp Concerto
fp Four Welsh Dances for orchestra
fp Concertino for viola and small
  orchestra
fp Serenade for string orchestra
LEIGHTON (29)
*The Light Invisible*, sinfonia sacra
TAKEMITSU (28)
*Solitude sonore*, for orchestra
*Black Painting*, for reciter and small
  orchestra
WILLIAMSON (27)
*Santiago de Espada*, overture
Piano Concerto No 1

GOEHR (26)
*La Belle Dame sans merci*, ballet
WOOD (26)
Variations for viola and piano
DICKINSON (25)
String Quartet No 1 (revised 1974)
PENDERECKI (25)
*Emanations*, for two string orchestras
*Epithaphiom on the death of Artur Malawski*,
 for string orchestra and timpani
*The Psalms of David*, for chorus and
 instruments
DAVIES, P. M. (24)
*Stedman Caters* (revised 1968)
Sextet
*Prolation*, for orchestra
MATHIAS (24)
Divertimento for string orchestra
MAW (23)
*Nocturne*, for mezzo and chamber
 orchestra
NILSSON (21)
*Stunde eines Blocks*, for soprano and six
 players
*Zwanzig Gruppen für Blaser*, for piccolo,
 oboe and clarinet (1958–9)
*Quantitaten*, for piano

## 1959

ANTHEIL, BLOCH, MARTINŮ and
VILLA LOBOS died
BRIAN (83)
Symphonies Nos 13 and 14
MALIPIERO (77)
*Sei poesie di Dylan Thomas*, for soprano and
 ten instruments
*Musica da Camera*, for wind quintet
STRAVINSKY (77)
Movements for piano and orchestra
Double Canon for string quartet
*Tres sacrae cantiones*, completion of
 Gesualdo
*Epitaphium*, for flute, clarinet and harp
GRUENBERG (75)
*A Song of Faith*, oratorio (1959–62)
RIEGGER (74)
Variations for violin and orchestra
*Quintuple Jazz*, for ensemble
Sinfonietta for orchestra
TOCH (72)
*Epilogue*, for orchestra
*Intermezzo*, for orchestra
MARTINŮ (69)
*Mikeš of the Mountains*, chamber cantata
*Festival of Birds*, for children's voices and
 trumpet

*The Prophecy of Isaiah*, for voices and
 ensemble
*The Burden of Moab*, for male voices and
 piano
Chamber Music for clarinet, harp and
 piano quartet
Nonet for wind quintet, string trio and
 double-bass
BENJAMIN (66)
String Quartet No 2
*Tartuffe*, opera (1959–60)
ROGERS (66)
Symphony No 5, *Africa*
PISTON (65)
Concerto for two pianos and orchestra
*Three New England Sketches*, for
 orchestra
SOWERBY (64)
*Ark of the Covenant*, cantata
GERHARD (63)
Symphony No 2
HANSON (63)
*Summer Seascapes*, for orchestra
THOMSON, V. (63)
*Collected Poems*, for soprano, baritone and
 orchestra
*Fugues and Cantilenas*, for orchestra
COWELL (62)
Concerto for percussion
*Mela Fair*, for orchestra
*Characters*, for orchestra
*Homage to Iran*, for violin and piano
HARRIS (61)
*Give Me the Splendid Silent Sun*, cantata
POULENC (60)
*Gloria*, for voices and orchestra
BUSH, A. (59)
*Dorian Passacaglia and Fugue*
*Byron Symphony*, for baritone, chorus and
 orchestra (1959–60)
COPLAND (59)
*Dance Panels*, ballet
KŘENEK (59)
Six Motets from Kafka
RUBBRA (58)
Violin Concerto
BERKELEY, L. (56)
Overture for light orchestra
Sonatina for two pianos
'So Sweet Love Seemed', for voice and
 piano
BLACHER (56)
*Musica Giocosa*, for orchestra
RAINIER (56)
Trio-suite for violin, cello and piano
DALLAPICCOLA (55)
*Dialoghi*, for cello and orchestra

ALWYN (54)
Symphony No 4
BLITZSTEIN (54)
*Sacco and Vanzetti*, opera (1959–64)
RAWSTHORNE (54)
Symphony No 2, *A Pastoral Symphony*
SEIBER (54)
*Improvisation for Jazz Band and Symphony Orchestra*
COOKE (53)
Five Part-songs for unaccompanied chorus
FRANKEL (53)
Bagatelles for eleven instruments
Eight Songs for medium voice and piano
LUTYENS (53)
*Quincunx*, for solo voices and orchestra (1959–60)
SHOSTAKOVICH (53)
Cello Concerto No 1
CARTER (50)
String Quartet No 2
HOLMBOE (50)
*The Knife*, chamber opera (1959–60)
SIEGMEISTER (50)
*They Came to Cordura*, film score
BARBER (49)
*A Hand of Bridge*, opera for four solo voices and chamber orchestra
SCHUMAN (49)
*Three Moods*, for piano
FRANÇAIX (47)
*Danse des trois Arlequins*, for piano
*L'horloge de Flore*, for oboe and orchestra
Concerto for harpsichord, flute and strings
BRITTEN (46)
*Cantata Academica, Carmen Basiliense*, for solo voices, chorus and orchestra
*Missa Brevis*
LUTOSLAWSKI (46)
*Dance Preludes*, third version for instruments
PANUFNIK (45)
*Polonia*, for orchestra
DIAMOND (44)
Symphony No 7
ARNELL (42)
*Paralyzed Princess*, operetta
ROCHBERG (41)
*La bocca della verita*, for oboe and piano
String Quartet No 2
BUSH, G. (39)
*Songs of Wonder*
FRICKER (39)
Serenade No 1 for flute, clarinet, bass-clarinet, viola, cello and harp
Serenade No 2 for flute, oboe and piano

ARNOLD (38)
Guitar Concerto
Oboe Quartet
*Five Songs of William Blake*, for voices and strings
SHAPEY (38)
Violin Concerto
*Rituals*, for orchestra
*Soliloquy*, for narrator, string quartet and percussion
*Evocation*, for violin, piano and percussion
*Form*, for piano
SIMPSON (38)
Variations and Fugue for recorder and string quartet
FOSS (37)
*Introductions and Goodbyes*, opera
HAMILTON (37)
Sinfonia for two orchestras
*Ecossaise*, for orchestra
XENAKIS (37)
*Duel*, game for two orchestras
*Syrmos*, for eighteen strings
*Analogiques A and B*, for nine strings and 4-channel tape
*Stratégie*, game for two orchestras and two conductors (1959–62)
BERIO (34)
*Quaderni I, II and III*, from 'Epifanie' for orchestra (1959–63)
BOULEZ (34)
fp *Tombeau*, for orchestra
SCHÜLLER (34)
Concertino for jazz quartet
*Seven Studies on Themes of Paul Klee*, for orchestra
FELDMAN (33)
*Atlantis*, for chamber orchestra
HENZE (33)
*Elegy for Young Lovers*, opera (1959–61)
*The Emperor's Nightingale*, ballet
Piano Sonata
JOSEPHS (32)
*Little Venice Serenade*, for small orchestra
*Pièces pour ma belle-mère*, for piano
*Concerto a Dodici*, for wind ensemble
KORTE (31)
*For a Young Audience*, for orchestra
*Fantasy*, for violin and piano
MUSGRAVE (31)
*Triptych*, for tenor and orchestra
STOCKHAUSEN (31)
*Carré*, for four orchestras and four choirs (1959–60)
*Refrain*, for piano, celesta and percussion
*Zyklus*, for one percussionist
*Kontakte*, for electronic sound (1959–60)

CRUMB (30)
*Variazioni,* for orchestra
HODDINOTT (30)
*fp Nocturne and Dance,* for harp and
  orchestra
*fp* Piano Sonata No 1
GOEHR (27)
*Hecuba's Lament,* for orchestra (1959–61)
Variations for flute and piano
Four Songs from the Japanese
*Sutter's Gold,* cantata (1959–60)
WOOD (27)
String Quartet in B♭
Logue Songs
Trio for flute, viola and piano
String Quartet No 2
Three Piano Pieces
DICKINSON (26)
*Three Juillard Dances,* for instrumental
  ensemble
*Variations,* ballet
*Vitalitas,* ballet
Monologue for strings
PENDERECKI (26)
*Strophes,* for soprano, narrator and ten
  instruments
BIRTWISTLE (25)
*Monody for Corpus Christi,* for soprano,
  flute, horn and violin
*Précis,* for piano
DAVIES, P. M. (25)
*Ricercare and doubles on 'To many a well'*
*William Byrd: Three Dances,* arranged for
  school or amateur orchestra
Five motets, for soloists, double choir and
  instrumental ensemble
*Five Klee Pictures,* for school, amateur or
  professional orchestra (revised 1976)
MATHIAS (25)
Improvisations for solo harp
MAW (24)
*Six Chinese Songs,* for contralto and piano
BENNETT (23)
*The Approaches of Sleep,* for soli, chorus
  and orchestra
NILSSON (22)
*Und Die Zieger seiner Augen wurden
  langsam zurückgedreht,* for solo voices,
  chorus and mixed media
*Ein irrender Sohn,* for voice and
  instruments
McCABE (20)
Violin Concerto No 1

# 1960

ALFVÉN, BENJAMIN, DOHNÁNYI,
SEIBER and BOUGHTON died
BRIAN (84)
Symphonies Nos 15, 16 and 17
KODÁLY (78)
Symphony in C major
MALIPIERO (78)
String Quartet No 3
STRAVINSKY (78)
*Monumentum pro Gesualdo,* for orchestra
RIEGGER (75)
Introduction and Fugue for cello and wind
Duo for piano and orchestra
DUPRÉ (74)
Trio for organ, violin and cello
MARTIN (70)
*Drey Minnelieder,* for soprano and piano
BLISS (69)
*Tobias and the Angel,* opera
HOWELLS (68)
*Triptych,* for brass band
MILHAUD (68)
Symphony No 10
Symphony No 11 (possibly 1960)
PISTON (66)
Symphony No 7
Violin Concerto No 2
ORFF (65)
*Ludus de nato Infante mirificus,* opera
GERHARD (64)
Symphony No 3, *Collages,* for tape and
  orchestra
String Quartet No 2 (1960–2)
SESSIONS (64)
Divertimento for orchestra
THOMSON, V. (64)
Requiem Mass
Mass for solo voice and piano (with
  orchestra 1962)
WEINBERGER (64)
*Aus Tirol,* for orchestra
COWELL (63)
Symphony No 14
*Concerto Brevis,* for accordion and
  orchestra
*Thesis,* for orchestra
*Variations on Thirds,* for orchestra
Introduction and Allegro for viola and
  harpsichord
Prelude and Allegro for violin and
  harpsichord
AURIC (61)
*Le Bal de Voleurs,* ballet
CHÁVEZ (61)
*Love Propitiated,* opera

POULENC (61)
*Elegy*, for two pianos
BUSH, A. (60)
Suite for harpsichord or piano
COPLAND (60)
Nonet for strings
DURUFLÉ (58)
Four Motets on Gregorian themes for choir
a cappella
WALTON (58)
Symphony No 2
*fp Anon in Love*, six songs for tenor and
guitar
BERKELEY, L. (57)
*A Winter's Tale*, suite for orchestra
Prelude and Fugue for clavichord
*Improvisation on a Theme of Falla*, for
piano
*Missa brevis*, for mixed choir and organ
'Thou hast made me', for mixed choir and
organ
BLACHER (57)
*Rosamunde Floris*, opera
KHACHATURIAN (57)
Rhapsody for violin and orchestra
*Ballade*, for bass with orchestra
RAINIER (57)
*Pastoral Tryptych*, for solo oboe
*Phala-Phala*, dance concerto for orchestra
(1960–1)
DALLAPICCOLA (56)
*Ulisse*, opera (1960–8)
KABALEVSKY (56)
*Overture Pathétique*, for orchestra
*The Spring*, symphonic poem
*Gasts in the Kitchen-garden*, play for
children
Major-minor études for cello
*Camp of Friendship*, six children's songs
Three Dancing Songs for children
SEIBER (55)
*Invitation*, ballet
*A Three-cornered Fanfare*
FRANKEL (54)
*Messa Stromentale*, orchestral mass without
words
LUTYENS (54)
Wind Quintet
SHOSTAKOVICH (54)
*Novorossiysk Chimes (The Fire of Eternal
Glory)*, for orchestra
String Quartets Nos 7 and 8
*Satires (Pictures of the Past)*, for soprano
and piano
Film music
MACONCHY (53)
*The Departure*, one-act opera

MESSIAEN (52)
*Chronochromie*, for orchestra
HOLMBOE (51)
*Monolith*, symphonic metamorphoses
*The Forest*, for soli, chorus and orchestra
*Solhymne*, for chorus
*Tropos*, for viola and string quartet
SIEGMEISTER (51)
Flute Concerto
*Theater Set*, for orchestra
String Quartet No 2
BARBER (50)
*Toccata Festiva*, for organ and orchestra
SCHUMAN (50)
Symphony No 7
STILL (50)
Symphony No 3
CAGE (48)
*Cartridge Music*
*Theater Piece*, for one to eight
performers
FRANÇAIX (48)
Piano Sonata
*Le Dialogue des Carmélites*, suite for
orchestra
JONES (48)
*O Lord, have Thou Respect*, anthem for
chorus
BRITTEN (47)
*A Midsummer Night's Dream*, opera
FINE (46)
*Diversion*, for orchestra
MELLERS (46)
*Eclogue*, for recorder, harpsichord,
percussion, violin and cello
DIAMOND (45)
Symphony No 8
Quartet No 5
GINASTERA (44)
*Cantata Drammatico No 1*
ROCHBERG (42)
*Time-Span*, for orchestra
BUSH, G. (40)
*Dialogue*, for oboe and piano
FRICKER (40)
Symphony No 3
SHAPERO (40)
Partita for piano and orchestra
ARNOLD (39)
*Rinaldo and Armida*, ballet
Symphony No 4
*Song of Simeon*, nativity play, with chorus,
brass, harp, percussion, celesta and
strings
SHAPEY (39)
*Dimensions*, for soprano and twenty-three
instruments

*De Profundis*, for solo double-bass and
   instruments
*Movements*, for woodwind quartet
*Five*, for violin and piano
*This Day*, for voice and piano
**FOSS** (38)
*Time Cycle*, four songs with orchestra
**HAMILTON** (38)
Piano Concerto
**XENAKIS** (38)
*Orient-Occident*, electroacoustic music
*Herma*, for piano (1960–1)
**LIGETI** (37)
*Atmospheres*, for orchestra
**NONO** (36)
*Homage to Emilio Vedova*, for tape
*Ha Venido*, for female voices
*Sara Dolce Tacere*, for eight solo voices
**BERIO** (35)
*Circles*, for voice, harp and two percussion
**BOULEZ** (35)
*fp Pli selon pli*, for soprano and orchestra
**SCHÜLLER** (35)
Capriccio for tuba and orchestra
*Contrasts*, for wind quintet and orchestra
*Variants*, for jazz quartet and orchestra
*Meditations*, for voices
**FELDMAN** (34)
*Durations I and II*, for various
   combinations
**HENZE** (34)
*Antifone*, for orchestra
**JOSEPHS** (33)
Concerto da camera for violin, harpsichord
   and strings
**JOUBERT** (33)
*Pro Pace*, three unaccompanied choral
   motets
**KORTE** (32)
Quintet for oboe and strings
**MUSGRAVE** (32)
Trio for flute, oboe and piano
*Colloquy*, for violin and piano
*Monologue*, for piano
**HODDINOTT** (31)
*fp* Concerto No 1 for piano, wind and
   percussion
Sextet for flute, clarinet, bassoon, violin,
   viola and cello
**LEIGHTON** (31)
*fp* Piano Concerto No 2
**PREVIN** (31)
*Overture to a Comedy*, for orchestra
**PENDERECKI** (27)
*Anaklasis*, for strings and percussion
   groups
String Quartet No 1

**BIRTWISTLE** (26)
*The World is Discovered*, for instrumental
   ensemble
**DAVIES, P. M.** (26)
*O Magnum Mysterium*, for chorus,
   instruments and organ
Five Voluntaries, arranged for school or
   amateur orchestra
Organ Fantasia from *O Magnum Mysterium*
**MAW** (25)
*Five Epigrams*, for unaccompanied chorus
**BENNETT** (24)
*Journal*, for orchestra
*Calendar*, for chamber ensemble
*Winter Music*, for flute and piano (or
   orchestra)
**NILSSON** (23)
*Szene 1*, for chamber orchestra
*Reaktionen*, for four percussionists
**McCABE** (21)
Partita for string quartet


# 1961

**GRAINGER** and **RIEGGER** died
**BRIAN** (85)
Symphonies Nos 18 & 19
**STRAVINSKY** (79)
*A Sermon, a Narrative and a Prayer*, cantata
**VARÈSE** (76)
*Nocturnal*, for soprano and orchestra
**WELLESZ** (76)
Violin Concerto
**TOCH** (74)
*Short Story*, for orchestra
**MARTIN** (71)
*Monsieur de Pourceaugnac*, opera (1961–2)
**HOWELLS** (69)
*A Hymn for St Cecilia*, for chorus and
   orchestra
*A Sequence for St Michael*, for chorus
**MOORE** (68)
*Wings of the Dove*, opera
**PISTON** (67)
Symphonic Prelude
**JACOB** (66)
Trombone Concerto
*Fantasia on Scottish Tunes*
*Improvisations on a Scottish Tune*, for
   orchestra
**HANSON** (65)
*Bold Island Suite*, for orchestra
**THOMSON, V.** (65)
*A Solemn Music*, for orchestra
**WEINBERGER** (65)
*Eine Walserouverture*

530

COWELL (64)
*Chiaroscuro*, for orchestra
TANSMAN (64)
*Psalms*, for tenor, chorus and orchestra
HARRIS (63)
*Canticle to the Sun*, cantata
CHÁVEZ (62)
Symphony No 6
*Soli No 2*, for wind quintet
POULENC (62)
*La dame de Monte Carlo*, monologue for
    soprano and orchestra
THOMPSON, R. (62)
*The Nativity*, church opera
BUSH, A. (61)
*The Ferryman's Daughter*, children's opera
*Three Raga Melodies*, for violin
*The Tide That Will Never Turn*, for two
    speakers, baritone, chorus and orchestra
KŘENEK (61)
*Ausgerechnet und Verspielt*, opera
RUBBRA (60)
*Cantata da Camera (Crucifixus pro nobis)*
WALTON (59)
*Gloria*, for soli, chorus and orchestra
BERKELEY, L. (58)
Concerto for violin and chamber orchestra
Five Pieces for violin and orchestra
BLACHER (58)
Variations on a theme
KHACHATURIAN (58)
Piano Sonata
RAINIER (58)
*Quanta*, for oboe and string trio (1961–2)
KABALEVSKY (57)
Rondo for violin and piano
RAWSTHORNE (56)
Concerto for ten instruments
*Improvisations on a Theme by Constant
    Lambert*, for orchestra
TIPPETT (56)
*Magnificat* and *Nunc Dimittis*
*Three Songs for Achilles*, for voice and
    guitar
COOKE (55)
*O Sing unto the Lord*, for chorus and organ
FRANKEL (55)
*Serenata Concertante*, for piano trio and
    orchestra
LUTYENS (55)
Symphonies for solo piano, wind, harps
    and percussion
*Catena*, cantata
SHOSTAKOVICH (55)
Symphony No 12, *1917*
CARTER (52)
*Holiday Overture*, revised version

Double concerto for harpsichord and
    piano
HOLMBOE (52)
String Quartet No 6
*Epilogue*, symphonic metamorphoses
    (1961–2)
Quintet for two trumpets, horn, trombone
    and tuba (1961–2)
BARBER (51)
*Dies Natalis*, choral preludes
CAGE (49)
*Atlas eclipticalis*, for orchestra (1961–2)
*Variations II*
*Music for Carillon No 4*
JONES (49)
*The Knife*, opera
BRITTEN (48)
Cello Sonata in C major
*War Requiem*, for voices and organ
LUTOSLAWSKI (48)
*Jeux Vénitiens*, for chamber orchestra
FINE (47)
*Romanza*, for wind quintet
MELLERS (47)
Cello Sonata
*Alba in Nine Metamorphoses*, for flute and
    orchestra
DIAMOND (46)
Nonet for three violins, three violas and
    three cellos
GINASTERA (45)
Piano Concerto No 1
ARNELL (44)
Brass Quintet
BERNSTEIN (43)
*Fanfares*, for orchestral ensemble
ROCHBERG (43)
*Songs of Innocence and Experience*, for
    soprano and chamber orchestra
BUSH, G. (41)
*Whydah Variations*, for two pianos
*A Lover's Progress*, songs
FRICKER (41)
Twelve Studies for piano
Cantata for tenor and chamber ensemble
    (1961–2)
ARNOLD (40)
Symphony No 5
Divertimento No 2, for full orchestra
SHAPEY (40)
*Incantations*, for soprano and ten
    instruments
*Discourse*, for flute, clarinet, violin and
    piano
FOSS (39)
*Echoi*, for clarinet, cello, piano and
    percussion (1961–3)

**BANKS** (38)
*Sonata da camera*, for ensemble
**LIGETI** (38)
*Fragment*, for eleven instruments
*Volumina*, for organ (1961–2)
**NONO** (37)
*Intolleranza 1960*, scenic action
**BERIO** (36)
*Visage*, electronic music with voice
**BOULEZ** (36)
*Structures, Book II*, for two pianos
**BROWN** (35)
*Available Forms II*
**FELDMAN** (35)
*Directions III and V*, for various
    combinations
**HENZE** (35)
*Six absences pour le clavecin*, for
    harpsichord
**JOSEPHS** (34)
*The Magical Being*, ballet
*Meditatio de Beornmundo*, for viola, two
    oboes, two horns and strings
*Aeolian Dances*, for orchestra
*Monkchester Dances*, for orchestra
*An Old English Suite*, for clarinet sextet
String Quintet, incorporated in
    Requiem
**JOUBERT** (34)
*Silas Marner*, opera
Octet for clarinet, bassoon, horn, string
    quartet and double bass
Passacaglia and Fugue for organ
*Christ Is Risen*, for chorus and organ
*Missa Beata Ioannis*, for chorus and
    orchestra
**KORTE** (33)
Symphony No 2
*Four Blake Songs*, for voices and piano
**MUSGRAVE** (33)
Serenade for five instruments
*Sir Patrick Spens*, for tenor and guitar
**HODDINOTT** (32)
*fp* Concerto No 2 for piano and orchestra
*fp* Violin Concerto
**LEIGHTON** (32)
Concerto for strings
*Crucifixus pro nobis*, for tenor, chorus and
    organ
**TAKEMITSU** (31)
*Tree Music*, for orchestra
*Arc*, for piano and orchestra (1961–6)
**WILLIAMSON** (30)
Organ Concerto
**GOEHR** (29)
Violin Concerto (1961–2)
Suite for six instruments

**MEALE** (29)
Songs for Sheridan Plays
**SHCHEDRIN** (29)
*Not Love Alone*, opera
Chamber Suite
**PENDERECKI** (28)
*Fluorescences*, for orchestra
*Dimensions of Time and Silence*, for choir
    and orchestra
*Polymorphia*, for forty-eight strings
*Threnody*, for fifty-two stringed
    instruments
*Kanon*, for strings and tape
**DAVIES, P. M.** (27)
String Quartet
*Ave Maria, Hail Blessed Flower*, carol for
    SATB
*Te Lucis Ante Terminum*, for choir and
    instrumental ensemble
**MATHIAS** (27)
Piano Concerto No 2
Music for strings
**MAW** (26)
*Essay*, for organ (revised 1963)
*Our Lady's Song*, carol for unaccompanied
    voices
**BENNETT** (25)
*The Ledges*, opera
*Suite Française*, for small orchestra
Oboe Sonata
**BLAKE** (25)
String Quartet No 1 (1961–2)
**NILSSON** (24)
*Szene II*, for chamber orchestra
**McCABE** (22)
Sinfonia for organ


## 1962

**IBERT** and **IRELAND** died
**BRIAN** (86)
*The Jolly Miller*, comedy overture
Symphony No 20
**SCOTT** (83)
Sinfonietta for strings
**STRAVINSKY** (80)
*The Flood*, musical play
Anthem 'The Dove descending breaks the
    air'
Eight Instrumental Miniatures, for fifteen
    players
**TOCH** (75)
*The Last Tale*, opera
**BLISS** (71)
*The Beatitudes*, cantata
**MILHAUD** (70)
Symphony No 12

532

MOORE (69)
*The Greenfield Christmas Tree*, a Christmas
  entertainment
ROGERS (69)
Sonata for violin and piano
PISTON (68)
*Lincoln Center*, festival overture
String Quartet No 5
JACOB (67)
*News from Newtown*, cantata
ORFF (67)
*Ein Sommernachtstraum*, opera
GERHARD (66)
*Concert for Eight*, for instruments
THOMSON, V. (66)
*A Joyful Fugue*, to follow *A Solemn Music*
*Pange lingua*, for organ
COWELL (65)
Symphony No 15, *Thesis*
Quartet for flute, oboe, cello and harp
TANSMAN (65)
*Resurrection*, for orchestra
Six Symphonic Studies for orchestra
HARRIS (64)
Symphonies Nos 8 and 9
POULENC (63)
*Sept répons des ténèbres*, for soprano,
  chorus and orchestra
Clarinet Sonata
Oboe Sonata
BUSH, A. (62)
*The Sugar Reapers*, opera
*Variations, Nocturne and Finale on an
  English Sea Song*, for piano and
  orchestra
COPLAND (62)
*Connotations*, for orchestra
*Down a Country Lane*, for orchestra
KŘENEK (62)
*5+1*, ballet
*Alpbach Quintet*, for wind
WALTON (60)
fp *A Song for the Lord Mayor's Table*, song
  cycle
BERKELEY, L. (59)
*Batter My Heart*, for soprano, chorus, organ
  and chamber orchestra
Sonatina for oboe and piano
'Autumn's Legacy', for voice and piano
KHACHATURIAN (59)
Cello Sonata
DALLAPICCOLA (58)
*Preghiere*, for baritone and chamber
  orchestra
KABALEVSKY (58)
Cello Sonata
*Requiem* (1962–3)

RAWSTHORNE (57)
*Medieval Diptych*, for baritone and
  orchestra
Divertimento for chamber orchestra
Quintet for piano and wind
Piano Trio
SEIBER (posthumous)
p Violin Sonata
TIPPETT (57)
Concerto for orchestra (1962–3)
*Praeludium*, for brass, bells and percussion
Piano Sonata No 2
*Songs for Ariel*
FRANKEL (56)
Symphony No 2
Sonata No 2 for solo violin
LUTYENS (56)
*Music for Orchestra II*
Five Bagatelles for piano
SHOSTAKOVICH (56)
Symphony No 13, *Babi-Yar*
HOLMBOE (53)
Double-bass Sonata
*Hevjid i homrum*, for four voices (1962–4)
BARBER (52)
Piano Concerto
*Andromache's Farewell*, for soprano and
  orchestra
SCHUMAN (52)
*Song of Orpheus*, fantasy for cello and
  orchestra
FRANÇAIX (50)
Suite for flute
JONES (50)
*St Peter*, oratorio
LUTOSLAWSKI (49)
*Trois poèmes d'Henri Michaux*, for chorus
  and orchestra (1962–3)
FINE (48)
Symphony No 2
MELLERS (48)
Trio for flute, cello and piano
*Cantilena e ciacone*, for viola
*Noctambule and Sun-Dance*, for wind band
PANUFNIK (48)
Piano Concerto
*Landscape*, for string orchestra
*Autumn Music*, for orchestra
DIAMOND (47)
*This Sacred Ground*, for baritone, chorus
  and orchestra
Quartet No 6
ARNELL (45)
Concerto for two violins and strings
SHAPEY (41)
*Convocation*, for chamber group
*Chamber Symphony*, for ten solo players

533

*Piece*, for violin and instruments
*Birthday Piece*, for piano
**SIMPSON** (41)
Symphony No 3
**HAMILTON** (40)
Arias for small orchestra
Sextet
**XENAKIS** (40)
*Polla Ta Dhina*, for children's chorus and
    orchestra
*Bohor*, electroacoustic music
**BANKS** (39)
Trio for horn, violin and piano
**LIGETI** (39)
*Poème symphonique*, for one hundred
    metronomes
*Aventures*, for three singers and seven
    instruments
*Nouvelles aventures*, for three singers and
    seven instruments (1962–5)
**NONO** (38)
*Canti di Hiroshima*, for orchestra
*Canciones a Guiomar*, for six female voices
    and instruments
**BERIO** (37)
*Passaggio*, messa in scena for soprano, two
    choirs and instruments
**SCHÜLLER** (37)
*Journey to the Stars*, film score
*Journey into Jazz*, for narrator, jazz quintet
    and orchestra
*Movements*, for flute and strings
Piano Concerto
Six Renaissance Lyrics for tenor and seven
    instruments
**BROWN** (36)
*Novara*, for instrumental ensemble
**FELDMAN** (36)
*The Swallows of Salangan*, for chorus and
    instruments
*Last Pieces*, for piano
*Durations IV*, for various combinations
**HENZE** (36)
*In re cervo*, opera
*Les Caprices de Marianne*, incidental music
Symphony No 5
*Novae de infinito laudes*, cantata
**JOSEPHS** (35)
*The Nottingham Captain*, music-theatre
Cello Concerto
*Five Fictitious Folk Songs*, for woodwind
    quartet
*King of the Coast*, musical for children
    (1962–8)
**JOUBERT** (35)
'Sweet Content', for unaccompanied
    chorus

Sinfonietta for orchestra
*In Memoriam 1820*, for orchestra
**KORTE** (34)
*Ceremonial Prelude and Passacaglia*, for
    band
Nocturne and March for band
**MUSGRAVE** (34)
Chamber Concerto No 1
*The Phoenix and the Turtle*, for small chorus
    and orchestra
**STOCKHAUSEN** (34)
*Momente*, for voices and instruments
    (1962–4)
**CRUMB** (33)
Five Pieces for piano
**HODDINOTT** (33)
fp Symphony No 2
fp Variations for flute, clarinet, harp and
    string quartet
fp *Rebecca*, for unaccompanied voices
**LEIGHTON** (33)
*Festive Overture*
*Missa Sancti Thomae*, for chorus and organ
**PREVIN** (33)
Symphony for strings
**TAKEMITSU** (32)
*Coral Island*, for soprano and orchestra
**GOEHR** (30)
*A Little Cantata of Proverbs*
Two Choruses for mixed choir a cappella
**MEALE** (30)
*Homage to Garcia Lorca*, for two string
    orchestras (1962–3)
**WOOD** (30)
String Quartet No 1
**PENDERECKI** (29)
*Stabat Mater*, for choir
**BIRTWISTLE** (28)
Chorales for orchestra (1962–3)
**DAVIES, P. M.** (28)
First fantasia on *In Nomine* of John
    Taverner, for orchestra
Sinfonia for chamber orchestra
*The Lord's Prayer*, for SATB
    unaccompanied
*Leopardi Fragments*, for voices and
    instruments
Four Carols, for SATB unaccompanied
**MATHIAS** (28)
Sonata for violin and piano
Dance Overture
Invocation and Dance for orchestra
Serenade for small orchestra
Partita for organ
*All Thy Works Shall Praise Thee*, for mixed
    voices and organ
Variations on a hymn tune for organ

MAW (27)
Chamber Music for five instruments
Scenes and Arias for voices and
  instruments
SALLINEN (27)
*Mauermusik*, for orchestra
BENNETT (26)
*London Pastoral Fantasy*, for tenor and
  chamber orchestra
Sonata No 2 for solo violin
*Fantasy*, for piano
*Three Elegies*, for chorus
NILSSON (25)
*Entrée*, for orchestra and tape
*Szene III*, for chamber orchestra
CROSSE (24)
*Concerto da Camera*, for violin, wind and
  percussion
*Changes*, for soli, chorus and orchestra
McCABE (23)
*Concerto Funèbre*, for viola and chamber
  orchestra
HOLLOWAY (19)
*Garden Music*, for eight players
TAVENER (18)
Piano Concerto (1962–3)
*Three Holy Sonnets*, for voice and orchestra

## 1963

HINDEMITH and POULENC died
BRIAN (87)
Symphony No 21
STRAVINSKY (81)
*Abraham and Isaac*, for baritone and
  chamber orchestra
TOCH (76)
*Jephta*, rhapsodic poem (Symphony No 5)
Capriccio for orchestra
*Puppetshow*, for orchestra
Symphony No 6
*The Enamoured Harlequin*, for orchestra
MARTIN (73)
*Les quatre éléments*, symphonic studies
  (1963–4)
BLISS (72)
*Belmont Variations*, for brass band
*A Knot of Riddles*, for baritone and eleven
  instruments
*Mary of Magdala*, cantata
HOWELLS (71)
*Stabat Mater*, cantata
MILHAUD (71)
*Pacem in terris*, for choir and orchestra
PISTON (69)
*Variations on a theme by Edward
  Burlinghame Hill*, for orchestra

*Capriccio*, for harp and string orchestra
CASTELNUOVO-TEDESCO (68)
*Songs of Songs*
JACOB (68)
Suite for brass band
GERHARD (67)
*The Plague*, for speaker, chorus and
  orchestra (1963–4)
*Hymnody*, for eleven players
HANSON (67)
*For the First Time*, for orchestra
SESSIONS (67)
*Psalm 140*, for soprano and organ/orchestra
COWELL (66)
Symphonies Nos 16, 17 and 18
TANSMAN (66)
Six Movements for string orchestra
HARRIS (65)
*Epilogue to Profiles in Courage: J.F.K.*, for
  orchestra
*Salute to Death*, for voices and orchestra
BUSH, A. (63)
Prelude, Air and Dance for violin, string
  quartet and percussion (1963–4)
KŘENEK (63)
*Der Goldene Bock*, opera
*San Fernando Sequence*, for electronics
WALTON (61)
*Variations on a Theme of Hindemith*, for
  orchestra
BERKELEY, L. (60)
*Four Ronsard Sonnets*, for tenor and
  orchestra
*Justorum Animae*, for mixed choir
'Counting the Beats', for voice and piano
'Automne', for voice and piano
BLACHER (60)
*Demeter*, ballet
*Konzertstücke*, for wind quintet and strings
RAINIER (60)
Cello Suite (1963–5)
KABALEVSKY (59)
Three Songs of Revolutionary Cuba
Three Songs
Five Songs (1963–4)
BLITZSTEIN (58)
*The Magic Barrel*, opera
*Idiots First*, opera
RAWSTHORNE (58)
*Carmen Vitale*, for soprano, chorus and
  orchestra
COOKE (57)
*The Lord at First did Adam Make*, for chorus
LUTYENS (57)
*Music for Orchestra III*
*Encomion*, for chorus, brass and percussion
String Quintet

*Fantasie Trio*, for flute, clarinet and piano
Wind Trio
*Présages*, for solo oboe
*The Country of the Stars*, motet
**SHOSTAKOVICH** (57)
Overture on Russian and Kirghiz folk
   themes
Film music
**MACONCHY** (56)
Serenata Concertante for violin and
   orchestra
*Samson and the Gates of Gaza*, cantata
   (1963–4)
**MESSIAEN** (55)
*Sept Hai-Kai*, for orchestra
**HOLMBOE** (54)
Sonata for violin and viola
*Requiem for Nietzsche*, for soli, chorus and
   orchestra (1963–4)
**SIEGMEISTER** (54)
*The Plough and the Stars*, opera (1963–9)
**SCHUMAN** (53)
Symphony No 8
**STILL** (53)
*Elegie*, for baritone, voices and small
   orchestra
**MENOTTI** (52)
*Labyrinth*, opera
*The Last Savage*, opera
*Death of the Bishop of Brindisi*, cantata
**CAGE** (51)
*Variations III and IV*
**FRANÇAIX** (51)
Six Preludes for strings
**BRITTEN** (50)
Symphony for cello and orchestra
*Cantata misericordium*, for tenor, baritone,
   string quartet, string orchestra, piano,
   harp and timpani
*Nocturnal*, after John Dowland, for guitar
**PANUFNIK** (49)
Two Lyric Pieces for young players
*Sinfonia Sacra*
**DIAMOND** (48)
Quartet No 7
**GINASTERA** (47)
Piano Quintet
Violin Concerto
*Don Rodrigo*, opera (1963–4)
**ARNELL** (46)
*Musica Pacifica*, for orchestra
**BERNSTEIN** (45)
Symphony No 3, *Kaddish*
**ROCHBERG** (45)
Piano Trio
**BUSH, G.** (43)
Wind Quintet

**FRICKER** (43)
*O longs désirs*, five songs for soprano and
   orchestra
**ARNOLD** (42)
Little Suite for Orchestra No 2
**SHAPEY** (42)
Brass Quintet
String Quartet No 6
*Seven*, for piano (four hands)
**HAMILTON** (41)
*Sonatas and Variants*, for ten wind
   instruments
*Nocturnes with Cadenza*, for piano
**XENAKIS** (41)
*Eonta*, for piano and five brass instrument
   (1963–4)
**BANKS** (40)
*Equation I*, for jazz group and ensemble
**LIGETI** (40)
*Requiem* (1963–5)
**MENNIN** (40)
Symphony No 7 (1963–4)
*Canto*, for orchestra
**BERIO** (38)
*Sincronie*, for string quartet (1963–4)
*Sequence II*, for harp
**SCHÜLLER** (38)
*Yesterday in Fact*, film score for jazz quintet
   and five instruments
*Composition in Three Parts*, for orchestra
*Diptych*, for brass quintet and band
*Meditation*, for band
*Threnos*, for oboe and orchestra
**BROWN** (37)
*Times Five*, for instruments and tape
*From Here*, for chorus and orchestra
**FELDMAN** (37)
*Christian Wolff in Cambridge*, for chorus
**HENZE** (37)
*Adagio*, for clarinet, horn, bassoon and
   string quintet
*Ariosi*, for soprano, violin and orchestra
*Los Caprichos*, fantasia for orchestra
*Lucy Escott Variations*, for piano/
   harpsichord
*Being Beauteous*, cantata
*Cantata della fiaba estrema*
**JOSEPHS** (36)
*Pathelin*, opera-entertainment
Chacony for violin and piano
Piano Sonata
*Requiem*, for baritone, double chorus,
   string quintet and orchestra
*Four Chinese Lyrics*, for two voices and
   piano or guitar
**JOUBERT** (36)
*Sonata a Cinque*, for flute, two violins, cello

and harpsichord
*Leaves of Life*, ballad cantata for soli,
chorus and piano
*Urbs Beata*, cantata for soli, chorus and
orchestra
*O Lord Our Lord*, for chorus and organ
**KORTE** (35)
*Southwest*, a dance overture
*Prairie Song*, for trumpet and band
*Introductions*, for brass quintet
*Mass for Youth*, with orchestra or keyboard
**MUSGRAVE** (35)
*The Five Ages of Man*, for chorus and
orchestra
**STOCKHAUSEN** (35)
*Plus Minus*, 'for Working out'
**CRUMB** (34)
*Night Music I*, for soprano, celeste, piano
and percussion
*Night Music II*, for violin and piano
**HODDINOTT** (34)
*fp* Sinfonia for string orchestra
*fp* Divertimento for oboe, clarinet, horn
and bassoon
**WILLIAMSON** (32)
*Our Man in Havana*, opera
*Elevamini Symphony*
**GOEHR** (31)
*Little Symphony*
*Little Music for Strings*
*Virtutes*, cycle of songs and melodramas for
chorus, piano duet and percussion
**SHCHEDRIN** (31)
Concerto for orchestra No 1
*Bureaucratadia*, cantata
**DICKINSON** (30)
Motets
**PENDERECKI** (30)
Violin Concerto
**DAVIES, P. M.** (29)
*Veni Sancte Spiritus*, for soli, chorus and
small orchestra
**MATHIAS** (29)
Quintet for flute, oboe, clarinet, horn and
bassoon
**MAW** (28)
Round for children's choir, mixed choir
and piano
*The Angel Gabriel*, for unaccompanied
voices
**REICH** (27)
*The Plastic Haircut*, film music
**BEDFORD** (26)
*Piece for Mo*, for instrumental ensemble
*Two Poems*, for chorus
**NILSSON** (26)
*Versuchungen*, for orchestra

**CROSSE** (25)
*Meet My Folk*, for children's chorus and
instruments
*Ceremony*, for cello and orchestra
Violin Concerto
**McCABE** (24)
Variations for Piano
Three Folk Songs for high voice and
piano
**FERNEYHOUGH** (20)
Sonatina for three clarinets and bassoon
**TAVENER** (19)
*Three Sections*, from T. S. Eliot's *The Four
Quartets*, for tenor and piano (1963–4)
**FINNISSY** (17)
*Song 5*, for piano (1963–5)
*Song 8*, for piano (1963–7)
*Le Dormeur du Val*, for mezzo and
ensemble (1963–8)

# 1964

**BLITZSTEIN, GRUENBERG and TOCH**
died
**BRIAN** (88)
Cello Concerto
Concerto for Orchestra
Symphony No 22, *Symphonia Brevis*
**MALIPIERO** (82)
Symphony No 8
*In Time of Daffodils*, for solo voices and
instruments
**STRAVINSKY** (82)
*Elegy for JFK*, for baritone or mezzo and
three clarinets
*Fanfare for a New Theater*, for two trumpets
Variations for orchestra
**WELLESZ** (79)
Music for strings
**TOCH** (76)
Symphony No 7
Sinfonietta for strings
Theme and Variations for orchestra
**MARTIN** (74)
*Pilate*, cantata
**BLISS** (73)
*Homage to a Great Man (Winston Churchill)*,
march for orchestra
*The Golden Cantata*, for tenor, mixed
chorus and orchestra
**GROFÉ** (72)
*World's Fair Suite*
**HOWELLS** (72)
*Motet on the Death of President Kennedy*, for
chorus
**MILHAUD** (72)
*La mère coupable*, opera (1964–5)

String Septet
Harpsichord Concerto
**ROGERS** (71)
*The Light of Man*, for chorus and orchestra
**PISTON** (70)
Sextet for stringed instruments
Piano Quartet
**SOWERBY** (69)
Symphony No 5
Piano Sonata
**SESSIONS** (68)
Symphony No 5
**THOMSON, V.** (68)
*Autumn Concertino*, for harp, strings and
    percussion
*The Feast of Love*, for baritone and
    orchestra
**COWELL** (67)
Concerto for koto and orchestra
**TANSMAN** (67)
*Il usignolo di Boboli*, opera
**HARRIS** (66)
*Horn of Plenty*, for orchestra
Duo for cello and piano
**CHÁVEZ** (65)
*Resonancias*, for orchestra
*Tambuco*, for six percussion
**COPLAND** (64)
*Emblems for a Symphonic Band*
*Music for a Great City*, for orchestra
**KŘENEK** (64)
*O Holy Ghost*, choral
**RUBBRA** (63)
String Quartet No 3
Improvisation for solo cello
**BERKELEY, L.** (61)
*Diversions*, for eight instruments
'Songs of the Half-light', for high voice
    and guitar
Mass for five voices
**BLACHER** (61)
Cello Concerto
**RAINIER** (61)
Concerto for cello and orchestra
**DALLAPICCOLA** (60)
*Quattro liriche di Antonio Machado*, version
    for soprano and orchestra
*Parole di San Paolo*, for voice and
    instruments
**KABALEVSKY** (60)
Cello Concerto No 2
Rhapsody for piano and orchestra, *School
    Years*
**ALWYN** (59)
Concerto Grosso No 3
**RAWSTHORNE** (59)
Symphony No 3

*Elegiac Rhapsody*, for strings
**FRANKEL** (58)
Symphony No 3
*Pezzi Pianissimi*, for clarinet, cello and
    piano
**LUTYENS** (58)
Music for piano and orchestra
Music for wind
*Scena*, for violin, cello and percussion
**SHOSTAKOVICH** (58)
String Quartets Nos 9 and 10
*The Execution of Stepan Razin*, cantata
**MACONCHY** (57)
*Three Settings of Poems by Gerald Manley
    Hopkins*, for high voice and chamber
    orchestra (1964–70)
**MESSIAEN** (56)
*Couleurs de la cité céleste*, for orchestra
**CARTER** (55)
Piano Concerto
**HOLMBOE** (55)
String Quartet No 7
**SCHUMAN** (54)
Symphony No 9
String Trio
**STILL** (54)
Concerto for strings
Symphony No 4
**MENOTTI** (53)
*Martin's Lie*, opera
**JONES** (52)
Symphony No 6
**BRITTEN** (51)
Cello Suite No 1
*Curlew River*, parable for church
    performance
**GOULD** (51)
*World War I: Revolutionary Prelude,
    Prologue* (1964–5)
*Marches: Formations*, for band
*Festive Music*, for off-stage trumpet and
    orchestra
**LUTOSLAWSKI** (51)
String Quartet
**MELLERS** (50)
*Laus Amoris*, for strings
**PANUFNIK** (50)
'Song to the Virgin Mary'
**DIAMOND** (49)
Quartet No 8
*We Two*, song cycle
**GINASTERA** (48)
*Cantata Drammatico No 2, Bomarzo*
**BUSH, G.** (44)
Greek Love Songs
**FRICKER** (44)
Symphony No 4 (1964–6)

ARNOLD (43)
Sinfonietta No 3 for strings and wind
*Water Music*
FOSS (42)
*Elytres*, for orchestra
HAMILTON (42)
Organ Concerto
*Cantos*, for orchestra
*Jubilee*, for orchestra
XENAKIS (42)
*Hiketides*, stage music for voices and
    instruments
*Idem*, suite for brass and strings
*Akrata*, for sixteen wind instruments
    (1964–5)
BANKS (41)
*Three Episodes*, for flute and piano
*Divisions*, for orchestra
NONO (40)
*La Fabbrica Illuminata*, for voice and tape
BOULEZ (39)
*fp Figures – Doubles – Prismes*,
    for orchestra
*Eclat*, for fifteen instruments
SCHÜLLER (39)
Five Bagatelles for orchestra
Shakespearean Songs for baritone and
    orchestra
BROWN (38)
*Corroborree*, for two or three pianos
HENZE (38)
*The Young Lord*, comic opera
*Tancredi*, ballet
Divertimenti for two pianos
Choral Fantasy
JOSEPHS (37)
Symphony No 2
Octet for clarinet, bassoon, horn, string
    quartet and double-bass
*Protégez-moi*, children's chorus and
    instruments
*La Répétition de Phèdre*, ballet (1964–5)
JOUBERT (37)
*The Holy Mountain*, canticle for chorus and
    two pianos
*The Beatitudes*, for unaccompanied chorus
*The Quarry*, one-act opera
Communion Service in D for chorus and
    organ
KORTE (36)
*Diablerie*, for woodwind quintet
MUSGRAVE (36)
*The Decision*, opera (1964–5)
STOCKHAUSEN (36)
*Mikrophonie* I, for mixed media
*Mixtur*, for five orchestral groups and
    electronics

CRUMB (35)
Four Nocturnes for violin and piano
HODDINOTT (35)
*fp Jack Straw*, overture
*fp Harp Sonata*
*fp Intrada*, for organ
*fp Sarum Fanfare*, for organ
*fp Toccata all Giga*, for organ
*fp Danegeld*, for unaccompanied voices
LEIGHTON (35)
Symphony
Mass for chorus and organ
WILLIAMSON (33)
*The Display*, dance symphony
*The Merry Wives of Windsor*, incidental
    music
Piano Concerto No 3
Sinfonia Concertante for piano, trumpets
    and orchestra
Variations for cello and piano
*Elegy J.F.K.*, for organ
Three Shakespeare Songs for voice and
    guitar (or piano)
GOEHR (32)
*Five Poems and an Epigram of William
    Blake*, for chorus
Three Pieces for piano
PENDERECKI (31)
Sonata for cello and orchestra
BIRTWISTLE (30)
Three Movements with Fanfares, for
    orchestra
*Entr'actes and Sappho Fragments*, for
    soprano and instruments
*Description of the Passing of a Year*,
    narration for mixed choir a cappella
DAVIES (30)
Seven *In Nomine*, for instrumental
    ensemble (1964–5)
Second Fantasia on John Taverner's *In
    Nomine*, for orchestra
*Shakespeare Music*, for instrumental
    ensemble
*Ave, Plena Gracia*, for SATB with optional
    organ
MATHIAS (30)
Piano Sonata
Divertimento for flute, oboe and piano
Prelude, Aria and Finale for strings
*Make a Joyful Noise Unto the Lord*, for
    mixed voices and organ
SCHNITTKE (30)
Music for piano and chamber orchestra
MAW (29)
*One Man Show*, comic opera
*Corpus Christi Carol*
*Balulalow*, carol for unaccompanied voices

**SALLINEN** (29)
*Elegy for Sebastian Knight,* for solo cello
**BENNETT** (28)
*The Mines of Sulphur,* opera
*Jazz Calendar,* ballet
*Aubade,* for orchestra
String Quartet No 4
*Nocturnes,* for piano
**BLAKE** (28)
*Three Choruses to poems by Robert Frost,* for
   chorus
**REICH** (28)
Music for three or more pianos or piano
   and tape
**BEDFORD** (27)
*A Dream of the Seven Lost Stars,* for mixed
   chorus and chamber ensemble (1964-5)
**NILSSON** (27)
*La Bran,* for choir and orchestra
**CROSSE** (26)
Symphonies Nos 1 and 2
**McCABE** (25)
*Variations on a Theme of Hartman,* for
   orchestra
Symphony for ten wind instruments
*Musica Notturna,* for vïolin, viola and
   piano
Three Pieces for clarinet and piano
Movement for clarinet, violin and cello
   (revised 1966)
Five Bagatelles for piano
Prelude for organ
*Johannis-Partita,* for organ
*Mary Laid Her Child,* for unaccompanied
   chorus
**HOLLOWAY** (21)
Concertino No 1 for small orchestra
   (1964–5)
*Three Poems of William Empson,* for mezzo
   and ensemble
**TAVENER** (20)
*The Cappemakers,* for narrators, soli, chorus
   and instruments
**FINNISSY** (18)
*Song 6,* for ensemble (1964–5)

## 1965

**COWELL** and **VARÈSE** died
**BRIAN** (89)
Symphonies Nos 23, 24 and 25
**KODÁLY** (83)
Variations for piano
**MALIPIERO** (83)
*Costellazione,* for piano
**STRAVINSKY** (83)
*Introitus,* for male voices and ensemble

Canon for concert introduction or encore
**WELLESZ** (80)
Symphony No 6
**MARTIN** (75)
Cello Concerto (1965–6)
**MILHAUD** (73)
*Music for Boston,* for orchestra
*Music for Prague,* for orchestra
*Elégie pour Pierre,* for viola and percussion
*Cantate de Job,* for chorus and organ
**PISTON** (71)
Symphony No 8
*Pine Tree Fantasy,* for orchestra
*Ricercare,* for orchestra
**JACOB** (70)
*Festival Te Deum,* for chorus and orchestra
**SOWERBY** (70)
*Solomon's Garden,* for chorus and orchestra
**GERHARD** (69)
Concerto for orchestra
**SESSIONS** (69)
Piano Sonata No 3
**COWELL** (68)
Symphony No 19
**HARRIS** (67)
Symphony No 10
*Rhythm and spaces,* for string orchestra
**CHÁVEZ** (66)
Violin Concerto No 2
*Soli No 3,* for bassoon, trumpet, viola,
   timpani and orchestra
*Inventions No 2,* for violin, viola and cello
**BUSH, A.** (65)
Partita Concertante
Two Dances for cimbalon
**RUBBRA** (64)
*Inscape,* suite for chorus, strings and harp
**RODRIGO** (63)
*Sonata Pimpante,* for violin and piano
   (1965–6)
**WALTON** (63)
*The Twelve,* for chorus and orchestra
**BERKELEY, L.** (62)
Partita for chamber orchestra
Three Songs for four male voices
**BLACHER** (62)
*Tristan,* ballet
**KHACHATURIAN** (62)
*Concerto-Rhapsody,* for cello and
   orchestra
**RAINIER** (62)
String Trio (1965–6)
**KABALEVSKY** (61)
Spring Plays and Dances for piano
*Symphonic Prelude . . .*
Rondo for cello and piano
Twenty Easy Pieces for violin and piano

**RAWSTHORNE** (60)

*Tankas of the Four Seasons*, for tenor and chamber ensemble

Concertante for violin and piano

**TIPPETT** (60)

*Vision of St Augustine*, for baritone, chorus and orchestra

*The Shires Suite*, for choir and orchestra (1965–70)

**FRANKEL** (59)

String Quartet No 5

*Catalogue of Incidents from 'Romeo and Juliet'*, for orchestra

**LUTYENS** (59)

*The Numbered*, opera (1965–7)

*The Valley of Hatsu-Se*, for solo voice and instruments

*Magnificat* and *Nunc Dimittis*, for unaccompanied chorus

*The Hymn of Man*, motet for unaccompanied male chorus

**SHOSTAKOVICH** (59)

*Five Romances on Texts from 'Krokodil' magazine*, for bass and piano

**MACONCHY** (58)

Variazione Concertante for orchestra

Notebook for Harpsichord (1965–6)

**MESSIAEN** (57)

*La Transfiguration de notre Seigneur Jésus-Christ*, for chorus and orchestra (1965–9)

*Méditations sur le mystère de la Sainte Trinité*, for organ

**HOLMBOE** (56)

String Quartet No 8

Violin Sonata No 3

**SIEGMEISTER** (56)

*In Our Time*, choral

Sextet for brass and percussion

**CAGE** (53)

*Variations V*

**FRANÇAIX** (53)

*Bis*, for piano

*La Princesse de Clèves*, opera

*Double Piano Concerto*

**JONES** (53)

Capriccio for flute, harp and strings

**BRITTEN** (52)

*Gemini Variations*, for flute, violin and piano (four hands)

*Songs and Proverbs of William Blake*, for voice and piano

*The Poet's Echo*, for voice and piano

*Voices for Today*, anthem for chorus

**LUTOSLAWSKI** (52)

*Paroles tissées*, for voice and instruments

**MELLERS** (51)

*Cat Charms*, nine pieces for piano

**BABBITT** (49)

*Relata I*, for orchestra

**GINASTERA** (49)

Concerto for strings

**BERNSTEIN** (47)

*Chichester Psalms*, for chorus and orchestra

**ROCHBERG** (47)

*Music for the Magic Theater*

*Zodiac*, for orchestra

*Black Sounds*, for winds and percussion

*Contra mortem et tempus*, for violin, flute, clarinet and piano

*La bocca della verita*, for violin and piano

**FRICKER** (45)

Four *Dialogues*, for oboe and piano

Ricercare for organ

Four songs for soprano and piano (or orchestra)

**ARNOLD** (44)

Five *Fantasies*, for bassoon, clarinet, flute, horn and oboe

**SHAPEY** (44)

String Trio

*Configurations*, for flute and piano

**FOSS** (43)

*Fragments of Archilochos*, for chorus, speaker, soloists and chamber ensemble

**HAMILTON** (43)

String Quartet No 2

*Dialogues*, for soprano and five instruments

*Aubade*, for solo organ

**XENAKIS** (43)

*Oresteia*, stage music and suite (1965–6)

*Terretektorh*, for orchestra (1965–6)

**BANKS** (42)

Horn Concerto

**NONO** (41)

*Die Ermittlung*, incidental music on tape

**BERIO** (40)

*Laborintus II*, for voices, instruments and tape

*Rounds*, for cembalo

*Sequence III*, for solo voice

**SCHÜLLER** (40)

*American Triptych*, for orchestra

Symphony

Concerto for orchestra, *Gala Music* (1965–6)

**BROWN** (39)

String Quartet

*Nine Rarebits*, for one or two harpsichords

**FELDMAN** (39)

*De Kooning*, for piano trio, horn and percussion

*Journey to the End of Night*, for soprano and

four wind instruments
*Four Instruments*
**HENZE** (39)
*The Bassarids*, opera
*In Memoriam: The White Rose*, for chamber orchestra
**JOSEPHS** (38)
Piano Concerto No 1
*Canzonas on a Theme of Rameau*, for strings
Sonata for violin and piano
*So She Went into the Garden*, for chorus and piano
*Four Japanese Lyrics*, for voice, clarinet and piano
**KORTE** (37)
String Quartet No 2
*Aspects of Love*, songs
**MUSGRAVE** (37)
*Festival Overture*, for orchestra
*Excursions*, for piano (four hands)
**STOCKHAUSEN** (37)
*Stop*, for orchestra
*Mikrophonie* II, for choir, organ and electronics
*Solo*, for a melody instrument and tape (1965–6)
**CRUMB** (36)
*Madrigals, Books I and II*, for soprano, vibraphone and double-bass
**HODDINOTT** (36)
fp Concerto Grosso No 1
fp *Aubade and Scherzo*, for horn and strings
fp *Dives and Lazarus*, cantata
**LEIGHTON** (36)
*Communion Service*, for chorus and organ
**WILLIAMSON** (34)
*The Happy Prince*, opera
Violin Concerto
Concerto Grosso for orchestra
Sinfonietta
*Symphonic Variations*, for orchestra
Concerto for two pianos (eight hands) and wind quintet
*Four North Country Songs*, for voice and orchestra
**GOEHR** (33)
*Pastorals*, for orchestra
**MEALE** (33)
*The Maids*, incidental music
*Images*, for orchestra
Nocturnes for orchestra (1965–7)
**SHCHEDRIN** (33)
*Solfeggi*, song cycle
Symphony No 2
**WOOD** (33)
*Scenes from Comus*, for soli and orchestra
Three Choruses

Capriccio for organ
**DICKINSON** (32)
*The Judas Tree*, for actors, singers and ensemble
**PENDERECKI** (32)
Capriccio for oboe and strings
**BIRTWISTLE** (31)
*Tragoedia*, for instrumental ensemble
*Ring a Dumb Carillon*, for soprano, clarinet and percussion
*Carmen Paschale*, motet for mixed chorus and organ
**DAVIES, P. M.** (31)
*Revelation and Fall*, for soprano and sixteen instruments
*The Shepherd's Calendar*, for singer and instruments
*Shall I die for mannes sake*, carol for soprano alto and piano
*Ecce manus tradentis*, for mixed choir and instruments
**MATHIAS** (31)
*Festival Te Deum*, for mixed voices and organ
*Wassail Carol*, for mixed voices and organ/ orchestra
*O Sing Unto The Lord*, for mixed voices and organ
**SCHNITTKE** (31)
*Dialog*, for cello and seven instruments
**MAW** (30)
String Quartet
**SALLINEN** (30)
*Cadenze*, for solo violin
**BENNETT** (29)
Symphony No 1
Trio for flute, oboe and clarinet
*Diversions*, for piano
**REICH** (29)
*Oh Dem Watermelons*, film music
*It's Gonna Rain*, for tape
**BEDFORD** (28)
*This One for You*, for orchestra
*Music for Albion Moonlight*, for soprano and instruments
'O Now the Drenched Land Awakes', for baritone and piano duet
**NILSSON** (28)
*Litanei über das verlorene Schlagzeug*
**McCABE** (26)
Chamber Concerto for viola, cello and orchestra
Concertante for harpsichord and chamber ensemble
Symphony No 1, *Elegy*
String Trio
Fantasy for brass quartet

Bagatelles for two clarinets
Elegy for organ
**FERNEYHOUGH** (22)
*Four Minatures,* for flute and piano
**HOLLOWAY** (22)
Music for Eliot's *Sweeney Agonistes*
*In Chymick Art,* cantata for soprano,
  baritone and nine players (1965–6)
Concerto for organ and wind
*Four Housman Fragments,* for soprano and
  piano
**TAVENER** (21)
Chamber Concerto (revised 1968)
*The Whale,* for chorus and orchestra
  (1965–6)
*Cain and Abel,* cantata
**FINNISSY** (19)
*From the Revelations of St John the Divine,*
  for soprano and ensemble (1965–70)
*Song 7,* for piano (1965–6)


# 1966

**TAYLOR** died
**BRIAN** (90)
Symphony No 26
**MALIPIERO** (84)
Symphony No 9
**STRAVINSKY** (84)
*Requiem Canticles,* for solo voices,
  chorus and orchestra
*The Owl and the Pussycat,* for voice and
  piano
**BLISS** (75)
*Fanfare Prelude,* for orchestra
**MILHAUD** (74)
*Jerusalem à Carpentras,* incidental music
*Music for Indiana,* for orchestra
*Music for Lisbon,* for orchestra
*Music for New Orleans,* for orchestra
Piano Quintet
**MOORE** (73)
*Carry Nation,* opera
**PISTON** (72)
Variations for cello and orchestra
Piano Trio No 2
**CASTELNUOVO-TEDESCO** (71)
Sonata for cello and harp
**JACOB** (71)
Oboe Sonata
*Variations on a Theme of Schubert*
**SOWERBY** (71)
*Symphonia brevis,* for organ
**GERHARD** (70)
*Epithalamium,* for orchestra
*Gemini,* for violin and piano

**HANSON** (70)
*Summer Seascape*
**ROBERTSON** (70)
Piano Concerto
**SESSIONS** (70)
Symphony No 6
Six Pieces for cello
**THOMSON, V.** (70)
*Lord Byron,* opera (1966–8)
*Fantasy in Homage to an Earlier England,*
  for orchestra
*The Nativity,* for soloists, chorus and
  orchestra (1966–7)
*Étude,* for cello and piano
**TANSMAN** (69)
*Concertino,* for oboe and chamber
  orchestra
**CHÁVEZ** (67)
*Soli No 4,* for brass trio
**BUSH, A.** (66)
*Joe Hill: The Man Who Never Died,* opera
  (1966–8)
**KRENEK** (66)
*Glauben und wissen,* choral
*Proprium Missae,* choral
*Der Zauberspiel,* TV opera
**RUBBRA** (65)
Eight Preludes for piano
**WALTON** (64)
*Missa Brevis*
**BERKELEY, L.** (63)
Three Pieces for organ
**KHACHATURIAN** (63)
Suite for Orchestra No 4
**BLACHER** (63)
*Virtuose Musik,* for violin, ten wind
  instruments, timpani, percussion and
  harp
*Plus Minus One,* for string quartet and jazz
  ensemble (unpublished)
**RAINIER** (63)
*Aequora Lunae,* for orchestra (1966–7)
**KABALEVSKY** (62)
*The Motherland,* cantata
**ALWYN** (61)
*Derby Day,* overture
**RAWSTHORNE** (61)
Cello Concerto
Sonatine for flute, oboe and piano
String Quartet No 3
**TIPPETT** (61)
*The Knot Garden,* opera (1966–70)
**COOKE** (60)
*Song on May Morning,* for unaccompanied
  chorus
**FRANKEL** (60)
Symphony No 4

LUTYENS (60)
*The Fall of the Leafe*, for oboe and string
  quartet
*Music for Three*, for flute, oboe and piano
*Akapotik Rose*, for soprano and
  instruments
*And Suddenly It's Evening*, for tenor and
  instruments
SHOSTAKOVICH (60)
Cello Concerto No 2
String Quartet No 11
*Preface . . .*, for bass and piano
HOLMBOE (57)
String Quartet No 9
Quartet for flute and string trio
Sonatina for oboe and piano
Three 'Jaeger-sänge' (1966–8)
SIEGMEISTER (57)
*Dick Whittington and his Cat*, for orchestra
BARBER (56)
*Antony and Cleopatra*, opera
JONES (55)
Violin Concerto
CAGE (54)
*Variations VI*
GILLES (54)
Piano Concerto No 2
BRITTEN (53)
*The Burning Fiery Furnace*, parable for
  church performance
*The Golden Vanity*, for boys and piano
GOULD (53)
*Columbia*, for orchestra
*Venice*, audiograph for two orchestras
PANUFNIK (52)
*Jagiellonian Triptych*, for string orchestra
DIAMOND (51)
Quartets Nos 9 and 10
BABBITT (50)
Sextets for violin and piano
GINASTERA (50)
*Bomarzo*, opera
ARNELL (49)
*Robert Flaherty*, a symphonic portrait
FRICKER (46)
*Three Scenes*, for orchestra
*The Day and the Spirits*, for soprano and
  harp (1966–7)
Fantasy for viola and piano
SHAPEY (45)
Partita for violin and thirteen players
*Poème*, for violin and piano
*Mutations No 2*, for piano
Partita for solo violin
FOSS (44)
*Discrepancy*, for twenty-four wind
  instruments

HAMILTON (44)
*Five Scenes*, for trumpet and piano
Flute Sonata
*Threnos*, for organ
XENAKIS (44)
*Nomos Alpha*, for violincello
BANKS (43)
*Assemblies*, for orchestra
*Settings from Roget*, for jazz singer and
  ensemble
LIGETI (43)
Cello Concerto
*Lux aeterna*
NONO (42)
*Ricorda cosa ti hanno fatto in Auschwitz*, for
  tape
BERIO (41)
*Il cambattimento di Tancredi e Clorinda*, for
  voices, violins and continuo
*Sequence IV*, for piano
*Sequence V*, for trombone
SCHÜLLER (41)
*The Visitation*, opera
*Study in Textures*, for band
Five Etudes for orchestra
Sacred Cantata
BROWN (40)
*Modules 1 and 2*, for orchestra
FELDMAN (40)
*First Principles*, for chamber orchestra
  (1966–7)
HENZE (40)
Double concerto for oboe, harp and
  strings
Fantasia for strings
*Muses of Sicily*, concerto for choir, pianos,
  wind instruments and timpani
JOSEPHS (39)
Concerto for light orchestra
Trio for flute, violin and piano
Fourteen Studies for piano
String Trio
*This is the Key to the Kingdom*, for children's
  chorus
*Two Cat Songs*, for chorus
JOUBERT (39)
*Te Deum*, for chorus and organ
MUSGRAVE (38)
Nocturnes and Arias for orchestra
Chamber Concertos Nos 2 and 3
STOCKHAUSEN (38)
*Adieu*, for wind quintet
*Hymnen*, for mixed media
*Telemusik*, electronic music
CRUMB (37)
*Eleven Echoes of Autumn*, for violin, flute,
  clarinet and piano

**HODDINOTT** (37)
*fp Pantomime*, overture
*fp* Concerto No 3 for piano and orchestra
*fp Variants*, for orchestra
*fp* Concerto Grosso No 2
*fp* String Quartet No 1
*fp* Piano Sonata No 4
**TAKEMITSU** (36)
*Dorian Horizon*, for strings
**WILLIAMSON** (35)
*Julius Caesar Jones*, opera
*The Violins of St Jacques*, opera
*Sun Into Darkness*, ballet
Five Preludes for piano
Two Organ Epitaphs for Edith Sitwell
Six English Lyrics for voice and piano
**GOEHR** (34)
*Arden muss sterben (Arden Must Die)*,
 opera
**SHCHEDRIN** (34)
Piano Concerto No 2
**DICKINSON** (33)
*Martin of Tours*, for soli, chorus and organ
*Elegy*, for counter-tenor, harpsichord and
 cellos
**BIRTWISTLE** (32)
*Punch and Judy*, opera (1966–7)
*Verses*, for clarinet and piano
**DAVIES, P. M.** (32)
*Notre dame des fleurs*, for solo voices and
 instruments
Five carols, for SA unaccompanied
*Solita*, for flute with musical box
**MATHIAS** (32)
Concerto for orchestra
Symphony No 1
*Three Medieval Lyrics*, for chorus and
 instruments
**SCHNITTKE** (32)
String Quartet
**MAW** (31)
Sinfonia for small orchestra
*The Voice of Love*, song cycle
*Six Interiors*, for tenor and guitar
**SALLINEN** (31)
*Notturno*, for piano
**BENNETT** (30)
*Epithalamion*, for voices and orchestra
*Childe Rolande*, for voice and piano
**BLAKE** (30)
*Beata L'Alma*, for soprano and piano
Chamber Symphony
**REICH** (30)
*Come Out*, for tape
*Melodica*, for tape
*Reed Phase*, for soprano saxophone and
 tape

**BEDFORD** (29)
*That White and Radiant Legend*, for soprano,
 speaker and instruments
*Piano Piece I*
**CROSSE** (28)
*Purgatory*, opera
**McCABE** (27)
Piano Concerto No 1
Concerto for chamber orchestra (revised
 1968)
Partita for solo cello
*Nocturnal*, for piano and string quartet
Miniconcerto for organ, percussion and
 audience
*Rain Songs*, for soli, cello and harpsichord
*Great Lord of Lords*, for chorus and organ
*A Hymne to God the Father*, for
 unaccompanied chorus
*Canticles for Salisbury*, for chorus and
 organ
**FERNEYHOUGH** (23)
*Coloratura*, for oboe and piano
*Epigrams*, for piano
Sonata for two pianos
Three Pieces for piano
**HOLLOWAY** (23)
Concerto for orchestra
**FINNISSY** (20)
*Song 1*, for soprano
*Afar*, for ensemble (1966–7)
*Horrorzone*, for soprano and ensemble
 (1966–7)
*As When upon a Tranced Summer Night*, for
 ensemble (1966–8)
**KNUSSEN** (14)
Symphony No 1 (1966–7)

## 1967

**AUBERT** and **KODÁLY** died
**BRIAN** (91)
Symphonies Nos 27 to 31
Fanfare for orchestral brass
**KODÁLY** (85)
*Laudes Organi*, for chorus and organ
**MALIPIERO** (85)
Symphony No 10
*Carnet de Notes*, for chamber orchestra
*Cassazione*, for string sextet
**WELLESZ** (82)
Symphony No 7 (1967–8)
**MARTIN** (77)
String Quartet
**BLISS** (76)
*River Music*, for unaccompanied choir
**MILHAUD** (75)
Promenade Concert for orchestra

PISTON (73)
Clarinet Concerto
*Ricercare*, for orchestra
JACOB (72)
Concerto for band
Six Miniatures
*Animal Magic*, cantata
SOWERBY (72)
Organ Concerto No 2
*Dialogue*, for organ and piano
*Organ Passacaglia*
GERHARD (71)
Symphony No 4, *New York*
HANSON (71)
*Dies Natalis*, for orchestra
SESSIONS (71)
Symphony No 7
THOMSON, V. (71)
*Shipwreck and Love Scene*, from 'Don Juan',
  for tenor and orchestra
HARRIS (69)
Symphony No 11
CHÁVEZ (68)
*Inventions No 3*, for harp
THOMPSON, R. (68)
String Quartet No 2
BUSH, A. (67)
Suite for two pianos
COPLAND (67)
*Inscape*, for orchestra
KŘENEK (67)
Five Pieces for trombone and piano
*Exercises of a Late Hour*, for small orchestra
  and tape
*Horizons Circled*, for orchestra
*Perspectives*, for orchestra
*Sardakai*, opera (1967–9)
DURUFLÉ (65)
*Cum Jubilo*, mass for baritone, choir,
  organ and orchestra
RODRIGO (65)
*Concierto Andaluz*, for four guitars and
  orchestra
WALTON (65)
*The Bear*, opera
BERKELEY, L. (64)
*Castaway*, opera
Oboe Quartet
Nocturne for harp
*Signs in the Dark*, for mixed choir and
  strings
KABALEVSKY (63)
*Recitative and Rondo*, for piano
RAWSTHORNE (62)
*Overture for Farnham*
Theme, Variations and Finale for orchestra
*Scena rustica*, for soprano and harp

*The God in the Cave*, cantata
FRANKEL (61)
Concerto for viola and orchestra
Symphony No 5
LUTYENS (61)
*Time Off? Not the Ghost of a Chance*, a
  charade
*Novenaria*, for orchestra
*Scroll for Li-Ho*, for violin and piano
*Helix*, for piano (four hands)
SHOSTAKOVICH (61)
Violin Concerto No 2
*Funeral-Triumphal Prelude*, for orchestra
*October*, symphonic poem
*Seven Romances on Poems of Alexander Blok*,
  for soprano and piano trio
*Spring, Spring*, for bass and piano
Film music
HOLMBOE (58)
Symphony No 9
SIEGMEISTER (58)
*I have a Dream*, cantata
Symphony No 4 (1967-70)
JONES (56)
*Orestes*, opera
MENOTTI (56)
*Canti della lontananza*, song cycle
CAGE (55)
*HPSCHD*, for harpsichords and tape
  (1967–9)
FRANÇAIX (55)
Flute Concerto
BRITTEN (54)
*The Building of the House*, overture with or
  without chorus
Cello Suite No 2
GOULD (54)
*Vivaldi Gallery*, for string quartet and
  divided orchestra
LUTOSLAWSKI (54)
Symphony No 2
PANUFNIK (53)
*Katyń Epitaph*, for orchestra
DIAMOND (52)
*To Music*, choral symphony
Violin Concerto No 3
*Hebrew Melodies*, song cycle
GINASTERA (51)
Symphonic Studies for orchestra
ARNELL (50)
*Sections*, for piano and orchestra
BUSH, G. (47)
*The Equation*, opera
Music for orchestra
FRICKER (47)
Seven Counterpoints for orchestra
*Episodes I*, for piano (1967–8)

*Ave Maris Stella*, for male voices and piano
*Cantilena and Cabaletta*, for solo soprano
 (1967-8)
**ARNOLD** (46)
Symphony No 6
*Peterloo*, for orchestra
*Concert Piece*, for piano and percussion
*Trevelyan Suite*, for wind band
**SHAPEY** (46)
*Partita-Fantasy*, for cello and sixteen
 players
*Reyem*, for flute, violin and piano
*Deux*, for two pianos
*For Solo Trumpet*
*Songs of Ecstasy*, for soprano, tape and
 instruments
**SIMPSON** (46)
Piano Concerto
Trio for clarinet, cello and piano
**FOSS** (45)
Cello Concerto
*Baroque Variations*, for orchestra
*Phorion*, for orchestra, electronic organ,
 harpischord and guitar
**HAMILTON** (45)
*Agamemnon*, opera (1967–9)
*The Royal Hunt of the Sun*, opera (1967–9)
**XENAKIS** (45)
*Polytope de Montréal*, light and sound
 spectacle
*Nuits*, for twelve mixed voices a capella
*Medea*, stage music
*Nomos Gamma*, for orchestra (1967–8)
**BANKS** (44)
*Sequence*, for cello
**LIGETI** (44)
*Lontana*, for orchestra
Two Studies for organ (1967–9)
**MENNIN** (44)
Piano Sonata
**NONO** (43)
*A Floresta*, for speaker, instruments and
 tape
*Per Bastiana Tai-Yang Cheng*, for orchestra
 and tape
*Contrappunto Dialettico*, for tape (1967–8)
**BERIO** (42)
*Rounds*, for piano
*Sequence VI*, for viola
*O King*, for voice and five players
**SCHULLER** (42)
*The Five Senses*, TV ballet
*Triplum*, for orchestra
**BROWN** (41)
*Event – Synergy II*, for instrumental
 ensemble (1967–8)

**FELDMAN** (41)
*Chorus and Instruments*
*In Search of an Orchestration*, for orchestra
**HENZE** (41)
Piano Concerto No 2
*Telemanniana*, for orchestra
*Moralities*, three scenic cantatas
**JOSEPHS** (40)
*Adam and Eve*, for speaker and ensemble
*Polemic*, for strings
*Rail*, symphonic picture
Concerto for oboe, percussion and small
 orchestra
Symphony No 3, *Philadelphia*, for chamber
 orchestra
*Mortales*, for soli, chorus, children's chorus
 and orchestra (1966–7)
**MUSGRAVE** (39)
Concerto for orchestra
Music for horn and piano
Impromptu for flute and oboe
**STOCKHAUSEN** (39)
*Prozession*, for mixed media
**CRUMB** (38)
*Echoes of Time and the River*, for orchestra
**HODDINOTT** (38)
fp Organ Concerto
fp *Night Music*, for orchestra
fp Clarinet Sonata
fp Suite for harp
**LEIGHTON** (38)
*Missa brevis*, for chorus
**TAKEMITSU** (37)
*November Steps*, double concerto for
 Japanese instruments
**WILLIAMSON** (36)
*Dunstan and the Devil*, opera
*Pas de Quatre*, ballet
*The Moonrakers*, cassation
Serenade for instruments
Sonata for two pianos
*Spectrum*, ballet
**GOEHR** (35)
String Quartet No 2
*Warngedichte*, for voice and piano
**SHCHEDRIN** (35)
Concerto for orchestra No 2
**WOOD** (35)
Quintet for clarinet, horn, violin, cello and
 piano
*The Horses*, song cycle
**DICKINSON** (34)
*The Dry Heart*, for chorus
*Fanfares and Elegies*, for six brass and organ
*Paraphrase I*, for organ
*Paraphrase II*, for piano

PENDERECKI (34)
*Pittsburgh Overture*, for wind and percussion
*Capriccio*, for violin and orchestra
*Dies Irae*, oratorio
DAVIES, P. M. (33)
*Antechrist*, for chamber ensemble
Five Little Pieces for piano
*Hymnos*, for clarinet and piano
MATHIAS (33)
Sinfonietta for orchestra
Invocations for organ
Toccata Giocosa for organ
Communion Service in C
*Litanies*, concertante music for orchestra
MAW (32)
*Severn Bridge Variations*, for orchestra
Sonata for strings and two horns
*The Rising of the Moon*, opera (1967–70)
*Double Canon for Igor Stravinsky*, for various instruments
BENNETT (31)
*A Penny for a Song*, opera
Symphony No 2
Wind Quintet
*The Music That Her Echo Is*, song cycle
BLAKE (31)
*What is the Cause?* – for six unaccompanied voices
*Sequence*, for two flutes
REICH (31)
*Piano Phase*, for two pianos or two marimbas
*Slow Motion Sound*, for tape
*My Name Is*, for three or more tape recorders, performers and audience
*Violin Phase*, for violin and pre-recorded tape or four violins
BEDFORD (30)
*Trona for Twelve*, for instrumental ensemble
*Five*, for five strings
*18 Bricks Left on April 21st*, for two electric guitars
NILSSON (30)
*Revue*, for orchestra
CROSSE (29)
*The Grace of Todd*, opera
McCABE (28)
Dance Movements for horn, violin and piano
Rounds for brass quintet
*Fantasy on a Theme of Liszt*, for piano
*Aspects of Whiteness*, for chorus and piano (revised 1969)
FERNEYHOUGH (24)
*Prometheus*, for woodwind ensemble

HOLLOWAY (24)
*Melodrama*, for speaker, male chorus and ensemble
Concertino No 2 for small orchestra
TAVENER (23)
*Grandma's Footsteps*, for chamber orchestra (1967–8)
Three Surrealist Songs for mezzo-soprano, tape and piano doubling bongoes (1967–8)
FINISSY (21)
*Song 2 and Song 4*, for ensemble
*Untitled Piece to honour Igor Stravinsky*, for flute
*Jeanne d'Arc*, for soprano and ensemble (1967–71)
PATTERSON (20)
Wind Quintet

## 1968

CASTELNUOVO-TEDESCO, ROGERS and SOWERBY died
BRIAN (92)
*Legend – ave atque vale*, for orchestra
Symphony No 32
MALIPIERO (86)
*Gli eroi di Bonaventura*, for orchestra
Flute Concerto
STRAVINSKY (85)
Two Sacred Songs arranged from Hugo Wolf
MARTIN (78)
Piano Concerto No 2
*Maria-Triptychon*, for soprano, solo violin and orchestra
HOWELLS (76)
*The Coventry Mass*, for chorus and organ
*Sarum Canticles*, for chorus
*Winchester Canticles*, for chorus
MILHAUD (76)
*Tobie et Sarah*, incidental music
*Musique pour l'univers Claudélien*, for orchestra
Piano Trio
*Music for Graz*, for orchestra (1968–9)
JACOB (73)
Divertimento in E♭
Suite for bassoon and string quartet
GERHARD (72)
*Libra*, for flute, clarinet, violin, guitar, piano and percussion
HANSON (72)
Symphony No 6
*Psalm CXXI*, for chorus and orchestra
SESSIONS (72)
Symphony No 8

TANSMAN (71)
Four Movements for orchestra
HARRIS (70)
Concerto for amplified piano, brass and
  percussion
Piano Sextet
AURIC (69)
*Imaginées I*, for flute and piano
BUSH, A. (68)
*The Alps and Andes of the Living World*, for
  speaker, tenor, chorus and orchestra
*Five Songs of the Asian Struggle*, for chorus
  and piano (1968–9)
*Time Remembered*, for chamber orchestra
  (1968–9)
KŘENEK (68)
*German Mass*
*Six Profiles*, for orchestra
RUBBRA (67)
Symphony No 8
Violin Sonata No 3
*Advent Cantata*, for baritone, chorus and
  small orchestra
RODRIGO (66)
*Concieto Madrigal*, for two guitars and
  orchestra
WALTON (66)
*Capriccio burlesca*, for orchestra
BERKELEY, L. (65)
Theme and Variations for piano duet
'The Windhover', for mixed choir
BLACHER (64)
*Collage*, for orchestra
KABALEVSKY (64)
*Sisters*, opera (1968–9)
*Colas Breugnon*, revised version
*Music for the Memorial in Bryansk*, for
  orchestra
RAWSTHORNE (63)
Concerto for two pianos and orchestra
Trio for flute, viola and harp
FRANKEL (62)
*Konzert für Jungendpublikum*, for orchestra
LUTYENS (62)
*Essence of Our Happiness*, for voices and
  orchestra
*A Phoenix*, for soprano and instruments
*Horai*, for violin, horn and piano
*Epithalamium*, for organ (soprano solo
  optional)
*The Egocentric*, for voice and piano
*The Tyme Doth Flete*, for unaccompanied
  voices
SHOSTAKOVICH (62)
String Quartet No 12
Sonata for violin and grand piano

MACONCHY (61)
String Quartet No 9 (1968–9)
HOLMBOE (59)
Chamber Symphony No 2
Trio for flute, cello and piano
SIEGMEISTER (59)
Ballad for brass
MENOTTI (57)
*Help, Help, the Globolinks*, children's opera
FRANÇAIX (56)
Clarinet Concerto
*Divertissement*, for bassoon and strings
BRITTEN (55)
*The Childrens' Crusade*, for children's
  voices and orchestra
*The Prodigal Son*, parable for church
  performance
GOULD (55)
*Troubador Music*, for four guitars and
  orchestra
LUTOSLAWSKI (55)
*Livre pour orchestre*
MELLERS (54)
*Natalis Invicta Solis*, for piano
PANUFNIK (54)
*Reflections*, for piano
*Universal Prayer*
BABBITT (52)
*Relata II*, for orchestra
GINASTERA (52)
Cello Concerto No 1
ARNELL (51)
*The Food of Love*, overture
*Nocturne: Prague 1968*, for mixed media
BERNSTEIN (50)
*So Pretty*, for voice and piano
ROCHBERG (50)
Symphony No 3, *A Twentieth-century
  Passion*, for voices and orchestra
*Tableaux*, for soprano and eleven players
FRICKER (48)
Concertante No 4, for flute, oboe, violin
  and strings
*Refrains*, for solo oboe
*Gladius Domini*, toccata for organ
Six Pieces for organ
*Magnificat*, for soli, choir and orchestra
*Some Serious Nonsense*, for tenor and
  instruments
SHAPERO (48)
Three Improvisations for piano and
  synthesizer
SIMPSON (47)
Clarinet Quintet
HAMILTON (46)
*Pharsalia*, opera

**XENAKIS** (46)
*Kraanerg*, ballet music (1968–9)
**BANKS** (45)
Violin Concerto
*Tirade*, for mezzo or baritone, piano, harp and three percussion instruments
*Findings Keepings*, for chorus, drums and double-bass
**LIGETI** (45)
*Ramifications*, for string orchestra (1968-9)
Ten Pieces for wind quintet
String Quartet No 2
*Continuum*, for harpsichord
**MENNIN** (45)
*Cantata de virtute*, for chorus and orchestra (1968–9)
**NONO** (44)
*Musica-manifesto No 1*, for tape
**BERIO** (43)
Sinfonia
*Questo vuol dire che*, for three female voices, small choir and tape
**BOULEZ** (43)
fp *Domaines*, for clarinet and twenty-one instruments
**SCHÜLLER** (43)
*Colloquy*, for two pianos and orchestra
Double-bass Concerto
*Fanfare for St Louis*, for orchestra
**FELDMAN** (42)
*False Relationships and the Extended Ending*, for two chamber groups
*Vertical Thoughts 2*, for orchestra
**HENZE** (42)
*Essay on Pigs*, for voice and orchestra
*The Raft of the 'Medusa'*, oratorio
**JOSEPHS** (41)
*The Appointment*, TV opera
Serenade for small orchestra
Toccata for guitar
*Three Medieval Lyrics*, for chorus and wind quintet
**JOUBERT** (41)
*The Choir Invisible*, choral symphony
'Let There Be Light', unaccompanied choral motet
Three Songs for chorus and organ
*Under Western Eyes*, opera
*Six Poems of Emily Brontë*, for soprano and piano
*Magnificat and Nunc Dimittis*, for chorus and organ
**KORTE** (40)
Symphony No 3
*Matrix*, for instruments
*May the Sun Bless Us*, for male voices, brass and percussion

**MUSGRAVE** (40)
*Beauty and the Beast*, ballet (1968–9)
Clarinet Concerto
**STOCKHAUSEN** (40)
*Aus den Sieben Tagen*, fifteen compositions for ensemble
*Für Kommende Zeiten*, for ensemble
*Kurzwellen*, for piano and amplified instruments
*Spiral*, for mixed media
*Stimmung*, for six vocalists
**CRUMB** (39)
*Songs, Drones and Refrains of Death*, for baritone and instruments
**HODDINOTT** (39)
fp Symphony No 3
fp Sinfonietta No 1
fp *Fioriture*, for orchestra
fp Divertimenti for eight instruments
fp *Nocturnes and Cadenzas*, for clarinet, violin and piano
fp Piano Sonata No 5
fp *Roman Dream*, for soprano and instruments
fp *An Apple Tree and a Pig*, for unaccompanied voices
**LEIGHTON** (39)
Dance Suite for orchestra
*An Easter Sequence*, for female voices, organ and trumpet
**PREVIN** (39)
Cello Concerto
**TAKEMITSU** (38)
*Asterism*, for piano and orchestra
**WILLIAMSON** (37)
*The Growing Castle*, opera
*Knights in Shining Armour*, cassation
*The Snow Wolf*, cassation
Piano Quintet
*From a Child's Garden*, twelve poems for voice and piano
**GOEHR** (36)
*Naboth's Vineyard*, a dramatic madrigal
*Romanza*, for cello and orchestra
**MEALE** (36)
*King Lear*, incidental music
*Very High Kings*, for orchestra
**SHCHEDRIN** (36)
*Carmen*, ballet
*Poetoria*, for soli, chorus and orchestra
**WOOD** (36)
*The Rider Victory*, song cycle
**DICKINSON** (35)
*Outcry*, for alto, chorus and strings
**PENDERECKI** (35)
*The Devils of Loudon*, opera (1968–9)
String Quartet No 2

*Capriccio for Siegfried Palm*, for solo cello
**BIRTWISTLE** (34)
*Nomos*, for four amplified wind
　instruments and orchestra
*Linoi*, for clarinet and piano
**DAVIES, P. M.** (34)
*Missa Super L'Homme Armé*, for speaker or
　singer and instrumental ensemble
*Stedman Caters*, for instrumental ensemble
*Purcell: Fantasia on a Ground and two
　Pavans*, realisation for instrumental
　ensemble
**MATHIAS** (34)
String Quartet
Piano Concerto No 3
*Lift Up Your Heads O Ye Gates*, for mixed
　voices and organ
**SCHNITTKE** (34)
*. . . Pianissimo . . .*, for large orchestra
Concerto for oboe, harp and string
　orchestra
Serenade for clarinet, violin, double-bass,
　percussion and piano
*Quasi una Sonata*, for violin and piano
**SALLINEN** (33)
Violin Concerto
**BENNETT** (32)
*All The King's Men*, children's opera
Piano Concerto
*Crazy Jane*, for soprano and instruments
**BLAKE** (32)
*The Almanack*, for mixed chorus
**REICH** (32)
*Pendulum Music*, for three or more
　microphones, amplifiers and
　loud-speakers
**BEDFORD** (31)
*Gastrula*, for orchestra
*Pentomino*, for wind quintet
*Piano Piece II*
'Come in Here, Child', for soprano and
　amplified piano
**GLASS** (31)
*1 plus 1*, for solo and table-top
**McCABE** (29)
*The Morning Watch*, for chorus and organ
Concertino for piano duet and orchestra
Concertante Music for orchestra
*Metamorphoses*, for harpsichord and
　orchestra
*Canto* for guitar
*Intermezzi*, for piano
*The Lion, the Witch and the Wardrobe*,
　children's opera
Oboe Quartet
**FERNEYHOUGH** (25)
Sonatas for string quartet

*Epicycle*, for twenty strings
**HOLLOWAY** (25)
Divertimento No 1 for amateur orchestra
*Four Poems of Stevie Smith*, for
　unaccompanied soprano (1968–9)
**TAVENER** (24)
*In Alium*, for soprano and orchestra
**FINNISSY** (22)
*Song 10*, for ensemble
*Song 9*, for piano
*World*, for soli, chorus and orchestra
　(1968–74)
*Transformations of the Vampire*, for
　ensemble (1968–71)
*Autumnal*, for piano (1968–71)
**PATTERSON** (21)
Wind Trio
**KNUSSEN** (16)
Concerto for Orchestra, revised 1976
*Pantomime*, for wind quintet and string
　quartet, revised 1978

# 1969

**MOORE** died
**WELLESZ** (84)
Divertimento for chamber orchestra
Symphonic Epilogue for orchestra
**MARTIN** (79)
*Erasmi Monumentum*, for orchestra and organ
*Poèmes de la mort*, for solo male voices and
　three electronic guitars (1969–71)
**BLISS** (78)
*The World is Charged with the Grandeur of
　God*, for chorus and wind
Miniature Scherzo for piano
*Angels of the Mind*, song cycle
**MILHAUD** (77)
Suite in G for orchestra
*Music for Ars Nova*, for orchestra
*Stanford Serenade*, for chamber orchestra
**PISTON** (75)
*Ceremonial Fanfare*, for wind
**JACOB** (74)
*Redbridge Variations*
Piano Quartet
**ORFF** (74)
*De Temporum fine comoedia*, cantata
　(1969–71)
**GERHARD** (73)
*Leo*, chamber symphony
**HANSON** (73)
*Streams in the Desert*, for chorus and
　orchestra
**TANSMAN** (72)
*Hommage à Erasme de Rotherdam*, for
　orchestra

*Concertino*, for flute and chamber orchestra
*Diptyque*, for orchestra
*Hommage à Chopin*, for guitar
**HARRIS** (71)
Symphony No 12
Symphony No 13 (possibly 1969)
**AURIC** (70)
*Imaginées II*, for cello and piano
**CHÁVEZ** (70)
*Clio*, symphonic ode
Variations for violin and piano
*Discovery*, for orchestra
*Fuego Olimpico*, suite for orchestra
**BUSH, A.** (69)
Scherzo for wind and percussion
Serenade for string quartet
*The Freight of Harvest*, for tenor and piano
Sonata for piano (1969–70)
**COPLAND** (69)
*Inaugural Fanfare*, for wind
*An Evening Air*, for piano
**KŘENEK** (69)
*Fivefold Enfoldment*, for orchestra
**RUBBRA** (68)
*Missa brevis*, for voices and organ
**RODRIGO** (67)
*Sonate a la Espagñola*, for guitar
**BERKELEY, L.** (66)
Symphony No 3
*Windsor Variations*, for piano duet
**BLACHER** (66)
*Zweihunderttausend Taler*, opera
**RAINIER** (66)
Trios and Triads for ten trios and
    percussion (1969–73)
**RAWSTHORNE** (64)
*Triptych*, for orchestra
**FRANKEL** (63)
Symphonies Nos 6 and 7
**LUTYENS** (63)
*Isis and Osiris*, lyric drama (1969–70)
String Trio
*Trois pièces brêves*, for chamber organ
*The Tides of Time*, for double-bass and
    piano
*The Dying of the Sun*, for guitar
*Temenos*, for organ
**SHOSTAKOVICH** (63)
Symphony No 14
**MACONCHY** (62)
*And Death Shall Have No Dominion*,
    choral
**CARTER** (60)
Concerto for orchestra
**HOLMBOE** (60)
String Quartet No 10
Cello Sonata

**BARBER** (59)
*Despite and Still*, song cycle
**SCHUMAN** (59)
*In Praise of Shahn*, canticle for orchestra
**STILL** (59)
Violin Concerto
**JONES** (58)
Investiture Processional Music
*The Three Hermits*, for chorus and organ
*The Ballad of the Standard Bearer*, for tenor
    and piano
*Triptych*, for chorus and piano
**CAGE** (57)
*Cheap Imitation*, for piano
**BRITTEN** (56)
Suite for harp
'Who are these children?', for tenor and
    piano
**GOULD** (56)
*Soundings*, for orchestra
**LUTOSLAWSKI** (56)
Cello Concerto (1969–70)
**MELLERS** (55)
*Opus Alchymicum*, for organ
**PANUFNIK** (55)
*Thames Pageant*, for young singers and
    players
**DIAMOND** (54)
Music for chamber orchestra
**BABBITT** (53)
String Quartet No 3
Four Canons for female chorus
**BERNSTEIN** (51)
*Shivaree*, for double brass ensemble and
    percussion
**FRICKER** (49)
Saxophone Quartet
Praeludium for organ
**SHAPERO** (49)
Three Studies for piano and synthesizer
**FOSS** (47)
*Geod*, for orchestra with optional voices
**HAMILTON** (47)
*Circus*, for two trumpets and orchestra
**XENAKIS** (47)
*Anaktoria*, for octet
*Synaphai*, for piano and orchestra
*Persephassa*, for six percussion
*Hibiki-Hana-Ma*, 12-channel
    electroacoustic music (1969-70)
**BANKS** (46)
*Dramatic Music*, for youth orchestra
*Fanfare*, for orchestra
*Intersections*, for orchestra and tape
*Equation II*, for jazz group and ensemble
**LIGETI** (46)
Chamber Concertante for thirteen

instruments (1969–70)
**NONO** (45)
*Musiche per Manzù*, for tape
*Y Entonces Comprendió*, for six female
  voices, chorus, tape and electronics
  (1969–70)
**BERIO** (44)
*Opera*
*Modification* (Hornpipe), for five
  instruments
*Sequence VII*, for oboe
**SCHÜLLER** (44)
*Shapes and Designs*, for orchestra
**FELDMAN** (43)
*On Time and the Instrumental Factor*, for
  orchestra
**HENZE** (43)
Symphony no 6
*Compases*, for viola and twenty-two
  players (1969–70)
*El Cimarrón*, recital for four musicians
  (1969–70)
**BROWN** (42)
*Modules 3*, for orchestra
**JOSEPHS** (42)
*Variations on a Theme of Beethoven*, for
  orchestra
Concerto for two violins and chamber
  orchestra
Twenty-nine Preludes for piano
Symphony No 4 for alto, baritone and
  orchestra (1969–70)
**JOUBERT** (42)
*The Martyrdom of St Alban*, cantata
Three Sacred Songs for chorus
**KORTE** (41)
*Facets*, for saxophone quartet
*Dialogues*, for saxophone and tape
**MUSGRAVE** (41)
*Memento vitae*, for orchestra (1969–70)
*Night Music*, for chamber orchestra
*Soliloquy*, for guitar and tape
**STOCKHAUSEN** (41)
*Fresco*, for four orchestral groups
*For Dr K*, for instruments
*Pole für 2* (1969–70)
*Expo für 3* (1969–70)
**CRUMB** (40)
*Night of the Four Moons*, for ensemble
*Madrigals, Books III* and *IV*
**HODDINOTT** (40)
fp Symphony No 4
fp Divertimento for orchestra
fp Sinfonietta 2
fp Horn Concerto
fp *Nocturnes and Cadenzas*, for cello and
  orchestra

fp *Investiture Dances*, for orchestra
fp *Black Bart*, for voices and orchestra
fp Violin Sonata No 1
**LEIGHTON** (40)
Piano Concerto No 3, *Estivo*
**PREVIN** (40)
*Coco*, film score
**TAKEMITSU** (39)
*Stanza I*, for ensemble
*Crossing*, for orchestra
**WILLIAMSON** (38)
*Lucky Peter's Journey*, comedy with
  music
*The Brilliant and the Dark*, choral-operatic
  sequence
Symphony No 2
**GOEHR** (37)
*Konzertstücke*, for piano and small
  orchestra
*Nonomiya*, for piano
Paraphrase on a Monteverdi madrigal, for
  solo clarinet
**MEALE** (37)
*Clouds Now and Then*, for orchestra
*Soon It Will Die*, for orchestra
Variations for orchestra
**WOOD** (37)
Cello Concerto
**DICKINSON** (36)
*Five Diversions*, for orchestra
**PENDERECKI** (36)
*Utrenja*, for solo voices, choirs, and
  orchestra (1969–71)
**BIRTWISTLE** (35)
*Down by the Greenwood Side*, dramatic
  pastoral
*Verses for Ensemble*, for instrumental
  ensemble
*Medusa*, for instrumental ensemble
  (1969–70)
*Ut Heremita Solus*, arrangement of
  instrumental motet
*Hoquetus David (Double Hoquet)*,
  arrangement of instrumental motet
*Cantata*, for soprano and instrumental
  ensemble
**DAVIES, P. M.** (35)
*St Thomas Wake*, foxtrot for orchestra on a
  pavan by John Bull
*Worldes Bliss*, for orchestra
*Eight Songs for a Mad King*, for male singer
  and chamber ensemble
*Vesalii icones*, for dancer, solo cello and
  ensemble
*Eram quasi Agnus*, instrumental motet
*Gabrielli: Canzona*, realisation for chamber
  ensemble

MATHIAS (35)
*Ave Rex*, for chorus and organ or orchestra
*Psalm 150*, for chorus, organ and orchestra
MAW (34)
*The Rising of the Moon*, opera (1969–70)
SALLINEN (34)
String Quartet No 3
BENNETT (33)
*A Garland for Marjory Fleming*, for soprano and piano
REICH (33)
*Pulse Music*, for phase-shifting pulse gate
*Four Log Drums*, for phase-shifting pulse gate and log drums
BEDFORD (32)
*The Tentacles of the Dark Nebula*, for tenor and instruments
GLASS (32)
*Two Pages*
*Music in 5ths*
*Music in Similar Motion*
McCABE (30)
Sonata for clarinet, cello and piano
Concerto for piano and wind quintet
*The Greensleeves Round*, for harpsichord
Two Studies for piano
*To Us In Bethlem City*, for unaccompanied chorus
*This Town's a Corporation Full of Crooked Streets*, an entertainment
COWIE (26)
Concerto for bass clarinet and tape
FERNEYHOUGH (26)
*Missa brevis*, for twelve solo voices
*Firecycle Beta*, for orchestra (1969–71)
*Funérailles*, for string ensemble and harp (1969–74)
HOLLOWAY (26)
*Scenes from Schumann*, for orchestra (1969–70)
TAVENER (25)
*Celtic Requiem*, for voices and orchestra
FINNISSY (23)
*n*, for ensemble (1969–70)
*Folk-song Set*, for voice and ensemble (1969–70)
*Song 11*, for soprano and clarinet (1969–71)
PATTERSON (22)
Trumpet Concerto
OLIVER (19)
*Slippery Souls*, a Christmas Drama, for chorus and instruments
KNUSSEN (17)
*Masks*, for flute
*Fire*, capriccio for flute and string trio

# 1970

GERHARD and SCOTT died
MALIPIERO (88)
Symphony No 11
WELLESZ (85)
Symphony No 8
MARTIN (80)
Three Dances for oboe, harp, string quintet and string orchestra
BLISS (79)
Cello Concerto
MILHAUD (78)
*St Louis, roi de France*, opera
PISTON (76)
*Fantasia*, for violin and orchestra
JACOB (75)
*A York Symphony*, for orchestra
*A Joyful Noise*, for brass band
*The Pride of Youth*, for brass band
HANSON (74)
*The Mystic Trumpeter*, for narrator, chorus and orchestra
SESSIONS (74)
*Rhapsody*, for orchestra
*When Lilacs Last in the Dooryard Bloom'd*, cantata
KŘENEK (70)
*Gib uns dem Frieden*, choral mass
Duo for flute and double-bass
RUBBRA (69)
Piano Trio No 2
Four Studies for piano
RODRIGO (68)
*Con Antonio Machado*, for voice and piano
WALTON (68)
*Improvisations on an Impromptu of Benjamin Britten*, for orchestra
BERKELEY, L. (67)
*Dialogues*, for cello and chamber orchestra
String Quartet No 3
Theme and Variations for guitar
BLACHER (67)
Concerto for high trumpet and strings
*Trigal*, for small orchestra
RAINIER (67)
*The Bee Oracles*, for tenor or baritone and ensemble
DALLAPICCOLA (66)
*Sicut umbra*, for mezzo-soprano and twelve instruments
*Tempus aedificandi*, for chorus
ALWYN (65)
Sinfonietta for strings
RAWSTHORNE (65)
Oboe Quartet

TIPPETT (65)
Symphony No 3 (1970–2)
*Songs for Dov*, for voice and orchestra
FRANKEL (64)
*Overture to a Ceremony*, for orchestra
LUTYENS (64)
*Anerca*, for narrator, guitars and
  percussion
*Vision of Youth*, for soprano and
  instruments
*In the Direction of the Beginning*, for voice
  and piano
*Oda a la Tormenta*, for mezzo and piano
*Verses of Love*, for unaccompanied voices
SHOSTAKOVICH (64)
*March of the Soviet Militia*, for wind
  orchestra
String Quartet No 13
*Loyalty*, for male chorus
Film music
MACONCHY (63)
*Ariadne*, for soprano and orchestra
*The Jesse Tree*, opera
MESSIAEN (62)
*Des canyons aux étoiles*, for piano, horn and
  orchestra (1970–4)
HOLMBOE (61)
Chamber Symphony No 3, *Frise*
Symphony No 10 (1970–1)
STILL (60)
Piano Concerto
MENOTTI (59)
*The Leper*, drama
*Triplo concerto a tre*, symphonic piece
CAGE (58)
*Song Books*
FRANÇAIX (58)
Violin Concerto
*Jeu poétique*, for harp and orchestra
GILLES (58)
*The Nazarene*, opera
BRITTEN (57)
*Owen Wingrave*, opera
MELLERS (56)
*The Ancient Wound*, monodrama
BABBITT (54)
String Quartet No 4
BERNSTEIN (52)
*Warm-up*, a round for mixed chorus
ROCHBERG (52)
*Mizmor L'Piyus*, for bass-baritone and
  small orchestra
*Songs of Krishna*, for soprano and piano
FRICKER (50)
*Paseo*, for guitar
*The Roofs*, for soprano and percussion

HAMILTON (48)
*Alastor*, for orchestra
*Voyage*, for horn and chamber orchestra
*Epitaph for This World and Time*, for three
  choruses and three organs
BANKS (47)
*Meeting Place*, for jazz group, ensemble
  and electronics
NONO (46)
*Voci . . .*, for soli, speakers, chorus and
  orchestra
BERIO (45)
*Memory*, for electric piano and electric
  cembalo
BOULEZ (45)
*Multiples*, for orchestra
*fp Cummings ist der Dichter*, for voices and
  instruments
SCHÜLLER (45)
*The Fisherman and his Wife*, children's opera
*Consequents*, for orchestra
*Museum Piece*, for ensemble
FELDMAN (44)
*Madam Press died last week at 90*, for
  instrumental ensemble
*The Viola in My Life, I, II and III*
BROWN (43)
*Syntagm III*, for instrumental ensemble
JOSEPHS (43)
Sonata for cello and piano
*Nightmusic*, for alto and orchestra
*Death of a Young Man*, for baritone and
  orchestra
JOUBERT (43)
Symphony No 2
*Dialogue*, for solo voices, cello and
  harpsichord
Duo for violin and cello
*African Sketchbook*, for vocal quartet and
  wind quintet
*Kontakion*, for cello and piano
KORTE (42)
*Gestures*, for electric brass, percussion,
  piano and band
*Psalm XIII*, for chorus and tape
MUSGRAVE (42)
*Elegy*, for viola and cello
*From One to Another*, for viola and tape
Impromptu No 2 for flute, oboe and
  clarinet
STOCKHAUSEN (42)
*Mantra*, for two pianists
*Sternklang*, for five groups
*Trans*, for orchestra
CRUMB (41)
*Ancient Voices of Children*, for soprano, boy

soprano and seven instruments
*Black Angels*, for electric string quartet
**HODDINOTT** (41)
fp *The Sun, the Great Luminary of the
    Universe*, for orchestra
fp Sinfonietta No 3
fp Violin Sonata No 2
fp Cello Sonata
fp Fantasy for harp
**LEIGHTON** (41)
Concerto for organ, timpani and strings
Dance Suite No 2
**GOEHR** (38)
Symphony in one movement
Concerto for eleven instruments
*Sonata about Jerusalem*
*Shadowplay-2*, music theater for tenor and
    instruments
**WOOD** (38)
String Quartet No 2
**DICKINSON** (37)
*Transformations*, for orchestra
**PENDERECKI** (37)
*Kosmogonia*, for soli, chorus and orchestra
**BIRTWISTLE** (36)
*Four Interludes from a Tragedy*, for clarinet
    and tape
*Nenia on the Death of Orpheus*, for soprano
    and instruments
*Prologue*, for tenor and instruments
**DAVIES, P. M.** (36)
*Taverner*, opera in two acts
Points and Dances from *Taverner*
*Sub tuam protectionem*, for piano
*Ut re mi*, for piano
**MATHIAS** (36)
*Festival Overture*
Capriccio for flute and piano
Concerto for harp
*O Salutaris Hostia*, for unaccompanied
    male voices
*Bless the Lord*, for mixed voices and organ
*Gloria*, for male voices and organ
**SALLINEN** (35)
Chorali for orchestra
Chaconne for organ
*Four Études*, for violin and piano
**BENNETT** (34)
Guitar Concerto
**REICH** (34)
*Four Organs*, for four electric organs and
    maracas
*Phase Patterns*, for four electric organs
**BEDFORD** (33)
*The Garden of Love*, for instrumental
    ensemble
*The Sword of Orion*, for instrumental
    ensemble

**GLASS** (33)
*Music with Changing Parts*
**NILSSON** (33)
*Attraktionen*, for string quartet
*Exit*, for orchestra
*Om Kanalerna pa Mars*, for mezzo, tenor
    and eight instruments
**McCABE** (31)
*Notturni ed Alba*, for soprano and orchestra
Piano Concerto No 2, *Sinfonia Concertante*
*Concertante Variations on a Theme of
    Nicholas Maw*, for strings
Canzona for wind and percussion
Studies Nos 3 and 4, for piano
*Basse Danse*, for two pianos
*Norwich Canticles*, for unaccompanied
    chorus
**CROSSE** (32)
*The Story of Vasco*, opera
**COWIE** (27)
*Dungeness Choruses*
**HOLLOWAY** (27)
*The Wind Shifts*, for high voices and
    strings
**TAVENER** (26)
*Nomine Jesu*, for voices and orchestra
*Coplas*, for voices and tape
**FINNISSY** (24)
*Alice I, II* and *III* (1970–5)
**PATTERSON** (23)
Concertante for orchestra
Partita for orchestra
Monologue for solo oboe
**KNUSSEN** (18)
*Little Fantasies*, for wind quintet (revised
    1976)
Symphony No 2 for soprano and chamber
    orchestra (1970–1)
*Choral*, for wind orchestra (1970–2)
**MULDOWNEY** (18)
*Bitter Lemons*, for unaccompanied female
    chorus

## 1971

**DUPRÉ, RAWSTHORNE, ROBERTSON,
    RUGGLES** and **STRAVINSKY** died
**WELLESZ** (86)
Symphony No 9
**MARTIN** (81)
*Requiem* (1971–2)
**BLISS** (80)
Two Ballads for women's chorus and small
    orchestra
*Triptych*, for piano
**MILHAUD** (79)
*Music for San Francisco*, for orchestra

Hommage à Stravinsky
Harp Sonata
*Promesse de Dieu*, for unaccompanied
  chorus (1971–2)
**PISTON** (77)
Flute Concerto
**JACOB** (76)
Rhapsody for Three Hands, for piano
**SESSIONS** (75)
Three Choruses on Biblical Texts (1971–2)
Concerto for viola and cello
**AURIC** (73)
*Imaginées III*, for clarinet and piano
**THOMPSON, R.** (72)
*Wedding Music*, for string quartet
**BUSH, A.** (71)
*Africa*, symphonic movement for piano
  and orchestra (1971–2)
**COPLAND** (71)
Duo for flute and piano
**KŘENEK** (71)
*Orga-nastro*, for organ and tape
*Kitharaulos*, for oboe, harp and small
  orchestra (1971–72)
**RUBBRA** (70)
*Sinfonia Sacra*, for soli, chorus and
  orchestra
**BERKELEY, L.** (68)
*Palm Court Waltz*, for orchestra or piano
  duet
*In Memoriam Igor Stravinsky*, for string
  quartet
Duo for cello and piano
Introduction and Allegro for double-bass
  and piano
'Chinese Songs', for voice and piano
**BLACHER** (68)
Concerto for clarinet and chamber
  orchestra
Sonata for two cellos, and eleven
  instruments *ad lib*
**RAINIER** (68)
*Quinque*, for harpsichord
**DALLAPICCOLA** (67)
*Tempus destruendi*, for chorus
**RAWSTHORNE** (66)
Quintet for piano, clarinet, horn, violin
  and cello
**LUTYENS** (65)
*Dirge for the Proud World*, for soprano,
  counter-tenor, harpsichord and cello
*Driving Out the Death*, for oboe and string
  trio
*Islands*, for narrator, solo voices and
  instrumental ensemble
*Requiescat (Igor Stravinsky 1971)*, for
  soprano and string trio

*The Tears of Night*, for voices and
  instruments
**SHOSTAKOVICH** (65)
Symphony No 15
**MACONCHY** (64)
String Quartet No 10
**MESSIAEN** (63)
*Le Tombeau de Jean-Pierre Guézec*, for horn
  and tape
**CARTER** (62)
String Quartet No 3
Canon for Three
**HOLMBOE** (62)
*Tempo Variabile*, for orchestra
**SIEGMEISTER** (62)
Symphony No 5, *Visions of Time*
*On This Ground*, for piano
**BARBER** (61)
*The Lovers*, for baritone, chorus and
  orchestra
**JONES** (60)
*The Witnesses*, for male chorus and
  orchestra
*Môr*, for chorus and piano
**MENOTTI** (60)
fp *The Most Important Man in the World*,
  opera
**CAGE** (59)
*Les Chants de Maldoror*
*62 Mesostics*, for amplified voice
*WGBH-TV*, for composer and technicians
**FRANÇAIX** (59)
Theme and Variations for orchestra
Quartet for cor anglais and string trio
**BRITTEN** (58)
Cello Suite No 3
Canticle No IV, 'Journey of the Magi'
**GOULD** (58)
Suite for tuba and three horns
**PANUFNIK** (57)
Violin Concerto
**GINASTERA** (55)
*Cantata Drammatico No 3, Milena*
*Beatrix Cenci*, opera
**ARNELL** (54)
*I Think of All Soft Limbs*, for mixed media
**BERNSTEIN** (53)
*Mass*, a theatre piece for singers, players
  and dancers
*Two Meditations from Mass*, for violin, cello
  and piano
**BUSH, G.** (51)
*A Nice Derangement of Epitaphs*, choral
**FRICKER** (51)
*Sarabande in memoriam Igor Stravinsky*
Nocturne, for chamber orchestra

Concertante No 5 for piano and string
  quartet
*A Bourrée for Sir Arthur Bliss*, for cello
Intrada for organ
**SHAPEY** (50)
*Praise*, for baritone, double chorus and
  ensemble
**SIMPSON** (50)
*Energy*, symphonic study for brass band
Symphony No 4 (1971–2)
**HAMILTON** (49)
Violin Concerto No 2, *Amphion*
**XENAKIS** (49)
*Charisma*, for clarinet and violoncello
*Aroura*, for twelve strings
*Persepolis*, light and sound spectacle
*Antikhthon*, ballet music for orchestra
**BANKS** (48)
Three Short Songs, for voice and jazz
  quartet
*Limbo*, for three solo voices, eight
  instruments and tape
Music for wind band
*Nexus*, for orchestra and jazz band
Four Pieces for string quartet
**LIGETI** (48)
*Melodien*, for orchestra
*Horizont*, for recorder
**MENNIN** (48)
Sinfonia for orchestra
**NONO** (47)
*Ein Gespenst*, for soprano, chorus and
  orchestra
*Como una ola de fuerza y luz*, for piano,
  orchestra and tape (1971–2)
**BERIO** (46)
*Bewegung I*, for orchestra
*Bewegung II*, for baritone and orchestra
*Ora*, for voices and orchestra
*Autre fois*, for flute, clarinet and harp
*Agnus*, for two sopranos and three clarinets
*Amores*, for voices and instruments
**SCHÜLLER** (46)
*The Power Within Us*, oratorio
**FELDMAN** (45)
*Chorus and Orchestra I*
*The Viola in My Life IV*, for viola and
  orchestra
*Three clarinets, cello and piano*
*Rothko Chapel*, for solo viola, soprano, alto,
  chorus, percussion and celeste
*I Met Heine . . .*, for voice and chamber
  ensemble
**HENZE** (44)
Violin Concerto No 2
*Heliogabalus imperator*, for orchestra
  (1971–2)

*Der langwierige Weg in die Wohnung*, for
  orchestra
**JOSEPHS** (44)
Symphony No 5, *Pastoral*
Piano Concerto No 2 with chamber
  orchestra
*The Last Post*, for orchestra
Horn Trio for horn, violin and piano
String Quartet
*Happytaphs*, for children's chorus and
  piano
*A Child of the Universe*, music-theatre
**JOUBERT** (44)
*The Raising of Lazarus*, oratorio with
  orchestra
*Behold, the Tabernacles of God*, for chorus
  and organ
**KORTE** (43)
*I Think You Would Have Understood*, for
  mixed media
*Remembrances*, for flute and tape
**MUSGRAVE** (43)
Horn Concerto
*Primavera*, for soprano and flute
**STOCKHAUSEN** (43)
*Sternlang*, for five groups
*Trans*, for orchestra
**CRUMB** (42)
*Voice of the Whale*, for flute, cello and piano
**HODDINOTT** (42)
fp *The Tree of Life*, for soli, chorus, organ
  and orchestra
fp Concertino for trumpet, horn and
  orchestra
fp Concerto for oboe and strings
fp Horn Sonata
fp Violin Sonata No 3
fp *Out of the Deep*, motet
**LEIGHTON** (42)
*Dance Overture*
*Laudes animantium*, for soli and chorus
*The Second Service*, for chorus and organ
**PREVIN** (42)
Guitar Concerto
**TAKEMITSU** (41)
*Cassiopea*, for percussion and orchestra
**WILLIAMSON** (40)
*Genesis*, cassation
*The Stone Wall*, cassation
*Death of Cuchulain*, for five male voices and
  percussion
*Peace Pieces*, for organ
*In Place of Belief*, settings of ten poems for
  voices and piano duet
**MEALE** (39)
*Incredible Floridas*, for chamber
  ensemble

558

**WOOD** (39)
Chamber Concerto
**DICKINSON** (38)
*Winter Afternoon*, for six soloists and
  double-bass
Organ Concerto
Concerto for strings, percussion and
  electric organ
*Translations*, for recorder, viola da gamba
  and harpsichord
**PENDERICKI** (38)
*Actions*, for jazz ensemble
*De Natura Sonoris II*, for winds, percussion
  and strings
*Prélude (1971)*, for wind, percussion and
  contrabasses
**BIRTWISTLE** (37)
*An Imaginary Landscape*, for orchestra
*The Fields of Sorrow*, for voices and
  instruments
*Meridian*, for voices and instruments
*Chronometer*, for eight-track electronic tape
**DAVIES, P. M.** (37)
*From Stone to Thorn*, for mezzo and
  instruments
*Bell Tower*, for percussion
*Buxtehude: Also hat Gott die Welt geliebet*,
  cantata
Suite from *The Devils*, for soprano and
  instrumental ensemble
Suite from *The Boyfriend*, for small
  orchestra
**MATHIAS** (37)
*Holiday Overture*
Concerto for harpsichord, strings and
  percussion
**MAW** (36)
*Epitaph – Canon in Memory of Igor
  Stravinsky*, for flute, clarinet and harp
**SALLINEN** (36)
String Quartet No 4
Solo Cello Sonata
*Suita Grammaticale*, for children's choir
  and orchestra
Symphony No 1
**BLAKE** (35)
*Metamorphoses*, for orchestra
Nonet for wind
**REICH** (35)
*Drumming*, for drums, marimbas,
  glockenspiels, metallophone, voices and
  electronic organ
**BEDFORD** (34)
*Nurse's Song with Elephants*, for singer and
  ten acoustic guitars
*Star Clusters, Nebulae and Places in Devon*,
  for mixed double chorus and brass

*With 100 Kazoos*, for instrumental
  ensemble and kazoos
'Some Stars Above Magnitude 2.9', for
  soprano and piano
**GLASS** (34–7)
*Music in 12 Parts*
**McCABE** (32)
Symphony No 2
Dance-Prelude for oboe d'amore and
  piano
*Requiem Sequence*, for soprano and piano
**FERNEYHOUGH** (28)
*Cassandra's Dream Song*, for flute
*Sieben Sterne*, for organ
*Time and Motion Study I*, for bass clarinet
  (1971–7)
**HOLLOWAY** (28)
*Banal Sojourn*, for high voice and piano
*Fantasy-Pieces*, for thirteen players
**TAVENER** (27)
*In Memoriam Igor Stravinsky*, for two alto
  flutes, organ and bells
*Responsorium*, for voices and flutes
**FINNISSY** (25)
*Babylon*, for mezzo and ensemble
*Untitled Piece to honour Igor Stravinsky II*,
  for flute, viola and harp
*Tsuru-Kame*, for voices, dancers and
  instruments (1971–3)
**PATTERSON** (24)
Horn Concerto
Piccola Sinfonia
Symphonic Study
**KNUSSEN** (19)
*Turba*, for double-bass
**MULDOWNEY** (19)
*A Heavyweight Dirge*, for soli and
  ensemble


## 1972

**BRIAN** and **GROFÉ** died
**MARTIN** (82)
*Ballade*, for viola, wind orchestra, cembalo,
  harp and timpani
**BLISS** (81)
*Metamorphic Variations*, for orchestra
Three Songs for voice and piano
**MILHAUD** (80)
*Ode pour Jerusalem*, for orchestra
*Les Momies d'Egypte*, for unaccompanied
  chorus
*Ani Maamin*, for chorus and orchestra
**JACOB** (77)
Double-bass Concerto
*Tuba Suite*, for orchestra or piano
Psalm 103 for chorus

SESSIONS (76)
Concertino for chamber orchestra
TANSMAN (75)
*Stèle (in memoriam Stravinsky)*, for voice and instruments
*Variations on a Theme of Skriabin*, for guitar
BUSH, A. (72)
*The Liverpool Overture*
*Corenty ne Kwe-Kwe*, for piano
*Song for Angela Davis*, for chorus and piano
COPLAND (72)
Three Latin-American Sketches
*Threnody I*, for flute and string trio
*Night Thoughts*, for piano
*Vocalise*, for flute and piano
KŘENEK (72)
*Statisch und Ekstatisch*, for orchestra
WALTON (70)
Sonata for string orchestra
*Jubilate Deo*, for double chorus and organ
Five Bagatelles for guitar
BERKELEY, L. (69)
*Four Concert Studies, Set II*, for piano
'Hymn for Shakespeare's Birthday', for mixed choir and organ
Three Latin Motets, for five-part choir
BLACHER (69)
*Yvonne, Prinzessin von Burgund*, opera
*Stars and Strings*, for jazz ensemble and strings
RAINIER (69)
*Organ Gloriana*, for organ
TIPPETT (67)
Piano Sonata No 3 (1972–3)
FRANKEL (66)
Symphony No 8
*Pezzi Melodici*, for orchestra
*Marching Song*, opera (1972–3)
LUTYENS (66)
*The Linnet from the Leaf*, for voices and instrumental groups
*Voice of Quiet Waters*, for chorus and orchestra
*Counting Your Steps*, for chorus, flutes and percussion
*Chimes and Cantos*, for voice and instruments
*Dialogo*, for tenor and lute
*Plenum I*, for piano
SHOSTAKOVICH (66)
String Quartet No 14 (1972–3)
MESSIAEN (64)
*La fauvette des jardins*, for piano
HOLMBOE (63)
*A Lyk Wake Dirge*, for four voices
*The Wee Wee Man*, for four voices
String Quartet No 11

JONES (61)
Sinfonietta
Symphony No 7
Symphony No 8
CAGE (60)
*Bird Cage*, for twelve tapes
FRANÇAIX (60)
Trio for flute, cello and harp
*A Huit*, for clarinet, bassoon, horn and string quartet
LUTOSLAWSKI (59)
Preludes and Fugue for thirteen solo strings
PANUFNIK (58)
*Triangles*, for three flutes and three cellos
*Winter Solstice*, for soli, chorus and instruments
*Invocation for Peace*, for treble voices, two trumpets and two trombones
GINASTERA (56)
Piano Concerto No 2
ROCHBERG (54)
String Quartet No 3
*Electrikaleidoscope*, for violin, cello, flute, clarinet and electric piano
*Ricordanza*, for cello and piano
BUSH, G. (52)
*Lord Arthur Saville's Crime*, opera
FRICKER (52)
*Introitus*, for orchestra
*Ballade*, for flute and piano
*Fanfare for Europe*, for trumpet
*Come Sleep*, for contralto, alto flute and bass-clarinet
Seven Little Songs for Chorus
SHAPEY (51)
Violin Sonata
SIMPSON (51)
Symphony No 5
FOSS (50)
*Ni Bruit, ni vitesse*, for pianos and percussion
*Cave of the Winds*, for wind quintet
HAMILTON (50)
*Commedia*, concerto for orchestra
*Palinodes*, for solo piano
*Descent of the Celestial City*, for chorus and organ
XENAKIS (50)
*Linaia-Agon*, for three brass instruments
*Mikka*, for solo violin
*Polytope de Cluny*, electroacoustic music
BANKS (49)
*Walkabout*, for children's voices and instruments
*Equation III*, for jazz group, ensemble and electronics

String Quartet
*Shadows of Space*, for four-track tape
**LIGETI** (49)
*Kylwyria*, opera
Double Concerto for flute, oboe and
   orchestra
*Clocks and Clouds*, for twelve female voices
   and orchestra
**NONO** (48)
*Al gran sole carico d'amore*, scenic action
   (1972–5)
**BERIO** (47)
Concerto for two pianos and orchestra
   (1972–3)
*E Vó*, for soprano and instruments
*Recital I (for Cathy)*, for mezzo and
   instruments
**BOULEZ** (47)
*. . . Explosante-fixe . . .*, for ensemble and
   live electronics (1972–4)
**SCHÜLLER** (47)
*Poems of Time and Eternity*, for chorus and
   nine instruments
*Capriccio Stravagante*, for orchestra
**FELDMAN** (46)
*Cello and Orchestra*
*Chorus and Orchestra II*
*Voice and Instruments*
*Voices and Instruments*
*Piano and Voices I and II*
**BROWN** (45)
*Time Spans*, for orchestra
*New Piece: Loops*, for chorus and/or
   orchestra
*Sign Sounds*, for instrumental ensemble
**JOSEPHS** (45)
*Saratoga Concerto*, for guitar, harp and
   harpsichord and chamber orchestra
*Encore on a Theme of Scott Joplin*, for guitar,
   harp and harpsichord
*Songs of Innocence*, for chorus and
   orchestra
Symphony No 6 for soli, chorus and
   orchestra (1972–4)
**JOUBERT** (45)
*Three Hymns to St Oswald*, for chorus and
   organ
'Four Stations on the Road to Freedom', for
   unaccompanied chorus
Piano Sonata No 2
**MUSGRAVE** (44)
*The Voice of Ariadne*, chamber opera
   (1972–3)
**STOCKHAUSEN** (44)
*Alphabet für Liège*, for soloists and duos
*Am Himmel Wander Ich . . .*, Indianerlieder
*Ylem*, for nineteen players/singers

**HODDINOTT** (43)
fp *Aubade*, for small orchestra
fp Piano Sonata No 6
fp *The Hawk is Set Free*, for orchestra
**LEIGHTON** (43)
*Elizabethan Lyrics*, for female voices
*Sarum Mass*, for soli, chorus and organ
**TAKEMITSU** (42)
*Gémeaux*, for oboe, trombone and two
   orchestras
**WILLIAMSON** (41)
*The Red Sea*, opera
Symphony No 3, *The Icy Mirror*, for solo
   voices, chorus and orchestra
Partita for viola on themes of Walton
*The Musicians of Bremen*, for six male
   voices
*Love the Sentinel*, for unaccompanied
   voices
**GOEHR** (40)
Concerto for piano and orchestra
**MEALE** (40)
*Evocation*, for oboe, violin and chamber
   orchestra
**SHCHEDRIN** (40)
*Anna Karenina*, ballet
*Lenin Lives*, cantata
**WOOD** (40)
Violin Concerto
**DICKINSON** (39)
*Suite for the Centenary of Lord Berners*, for
   clavicord (1972–83)
**PENDERECKI** (39)
*Partita*, concerto for harpsichord, five solo
   instruments (amplified) and orchestra
Cello Concerto
*Canticum Canticorum Salomonis (Song of
   Songs)*, for sixteen-voice chorus,
   chamber orchestra and dance pair
**BIRTWISTLE** (38)
*The Triumph of Time*, for orchestra
*Tombeau – in memoriam Igor Stravinsky*, for
   flute, clarinet, harp and string quartet
*Dinah and Nick's Love Song*, for
   instruments
*La Plage*, for soprano and instruments
*Epilogue – Full Fathom Five*, for baritone
   and instruments
**DAVIES, P. M.** (38)
*Blind Man's Buff*, a masque
*Canon in memoriam Igor Stravinsky*, for
   instrumental ensemble
*Fool's Fanfare*, for speaker and instruments
*Hymn to St Magnus*, for mezzo-soprano
   and chamber ensemble
*Tenebrae super Gesualdo*, for mezzo, guitar
   and chamber ensemble

*Lullabye for Ilian Rainbow*, for guitar
*J. S. Bach: Prelude and Fugue in C♯ minor*,
realisation for instrumental ensemble
*Dunstable: Veni sancte spiritus – veni creator
spiritus*, realisation for instrumental
ensemble
**MATHIAS** (38)
*Elegy for a Prince*, for baritone and
orchestra
*Alleluya Psallat*, for mixed voices and
organ
*Celtic Dances*, for orchestra
*'A Vision of Time and Eternity'*, for
contralto and piano
*The Law for the Lord*, for unaccompanied
mixed voices
**MAW** (37)
Concert Music for orchestra
*Five Irish Songs*, for chorus
Serenade for small orchestra
*Life Studies*, for fifteen solo strings
*Personae*, for piano
**SALLINEN** (37)
*Four Dream Songs*, for soprano and piano
or orchestra
Symphony No 2, *Symphonic Dialogue*
**BENNETT** (36)
*Commedia II*, for flute, cello and piano
**BLAKE** (36)
*Scenes*, for solo cello
*The Bones of Chuang Tzu*, for baritone and
piano
**REICH** (36)
*Clapping Music*, for two performers
**BEDFORD** (35)
*An Easy Decision*, for soprano and piano
*Holy Thursday with Squeakers*, for soprano
and instruments
*Spillihpnerak*, for viola
*When I Heard the Learned Astronomer*, for
tenor and instruments
**McCABE** (33)
Oboe d'amore Concerto
String Quartet No 2
*Voyage*, for soli, chorus and orchestra
**COWIE** (29)
*Shinkokinshu*, for high voice and ensemble
**FERNEYHOUGH** (29)
*Transit*, for six solo voices, chamber
orchestra and electronics
**HOLLOWAY** (29)
*Evening with Angels*, for sixteen players
Divertimento No 2 for wind nonet
*Cantata on the Death of God* (1972–3)
Georgian Songs for baritone and piano
*Five Little Songs about Death*, for
unaccompanied soprano (1972–3)

**TAVENER** (28)
*Variations on 'Three Blind Mice'*, for
orchestra
*Ultimos ritos*, for voices and orchestra
with amplified instruments
*Ma fin est mon commencement*, for voices
and instruments
*Canciones espanolas*, for voices and
instruments
*Little Requiem for Father Malachy Lynch*, for
voices and instruments
**FINNISSY** (26)
*Snowdrift*, for piano
*Songs 3 and 12*, for soprano and ensemble
(1972–3)
*Mysteries*, music-theatre
**PATTERSON** (25)
*Fiesta Sinfonica*
*Comedy for Five Winds*
*Kyrie*, for chorus and piano
**OLIVER** (22)
*Music for the Wreck of the Deutschland*, for
piano quintet
*Sirens*, song-cycle for baritone and piano
*Overheard on a Saltmarsh*, for six male
voices
*The Three Wise Monkeys*, one-act opera for
children
**KNUSSEN** (20)
*Rosary Songs*
*Océan de Terre*, for ensemble (1972–3)
*Puzzle Music*, for ensemble (1972–3)
**MULDOWNEY** (20)
*Driftwood to the Flow*, for eighteen solo
strings

## 1973

**FRANKEL** and **MALIPIERO** died
**MARTIN** (83)
*Polyptyque*, for violin and two small string
orchestras
*Fantasy on Flamenco Rhythms*, for piano
**PISTON** (79)
Duo for cello and piano
**JACOB** (78)
Saxophone Quartet
**ORFF** (78)
*Rota*, for chorus and instruments
**THOMSON, V.** (77)
*Cantata based on Nonsense Rhymes*
**AURIC** (74)
*Imaginées IV*, for viola and piano
**BUSH, A.** (73)
*Festival March of British Youth*, for brass
band
Four Songs for mezzo and piano

COPLAND (73)
*Threnody II*, for string trio
KŘENEK (73)
*Choralvorspiel*, for organ
*Flaschenpost vom Paradies*, for electronics
BERKELEY, L. (70)
*Antiphon*, for string orchestra
*Voices of the Night*, for orchestra
Sinfonia Concertante for oboe and
    orchestra
RAINIER (70)
*Duo-Vision and Prayer*, for tenor and piano
*Ploërmel*, for winds and percussion
ALWYN (68)
Symphony No 5, *Hydriotaphia*
TIPPETT (68)
*The Ice Break*, opera (1973–6)
LUTYENS (67)
*One and the Same*, scene for soprano,
    speaker, two female mimes, male mime
    and instrumental ensemble
*The Waiting Game*, three scenes for mezzo,
    baritone and small orchestra
*Rape of the Moone*, for wind octet
*Laudi*, for soprano and instruments
*Roads*, for two sopranos, counter-tenor,
    baritone and bass
*Plenum II*, for solo oboe
*Plenum III*, for string quartet
*Tre*, for solo clarinet
SHOSTAKOVICH (67)
*Six Poems of Maria Tsvetaeva*, suite for
    contralto and piano
CARTER (64)
Duo for violin and piano
HOLMBOE (64)
String Quartet No 12
*Diafora*, for strings
Sextet for flute, clarinet, bassoon and
    string trio
*Ondata*, for six percussion
SIEGMEISTER (64)
String Quartet No 3
BARBER (63)
*fp* String Quartet
SCHUMAN (63)
*Concerto on Old English Rounds*, for solo
    viola, women's chorus and orchestra
*To Thy Love*, choral fantasy
MENOTTI (62)
*fp* Suite for two cellos and piano
*Tamu-Tamu*, opera
PETTERSSON (62)
Symphonic Movement
CAGE (61)
*Etcetera*, for small orchestra and tape

FRANÇAIX (61)
*La ville mystérieuse*, for orchestra
*Cassazione*, for three orchestras
*Neuf pièces caractéristiques*, for ensemble
GILLES (61)
*Behold the Man*, opera
*Let Us Pray*, choral
BRITTEN (60)
*Death in Venice*, opera
MELLERS (59)
*A Blue Epiphany*, for guitar
PANUFNIK (59)
Sinfonia Concertante for flute, harp and
    strings
BABBITT (57)
*Arie da Capo*, for flute, clarinet, piano,
    violin and cello
GINASTERA (57)
String Quartet No 3
*Puneña No 1*, for flute
Toccata for piano
Serenata for baritone, cello and nine
    instruments
ARNELL (56)
*Astronaut One*, for mixed media
BERNSTEIN (55)
*A Little Norton Lecture*, for male chorus
FRICKER (53)
Gigue for cello
*The Groves of Dodona*, for six flutes
ARNOLD (52)
Symphony No 7
SHAPEY (52)
Thirty-one variations for piano
SIMPSON (52)
String Quartet No 4
FOSS (51)
*MAP*, a musical game
XENAKIS (51)
*Eridanos*, for orchestra
*Cendrées*, for mixed chorus and orchestra
*Evryali*, for piano
BANKS (50)
*Prospects*, for orchestra
LIGETI (50)
*San Francisco Polyphony*, for orchestra
MENNIN (50)
*fp* Symphony No 8
NONO (49)
*Siamo la Gioventù del Vietnam*, for unison
    voices
BERIO (48)
*Eindrücke*, for orchestra (1973–4)
*Still*, for orchestra
*. . . Points on the Curve to Find . . .*, for piano
    and twenty-two instruments

*Linea,* for two pianos, vibraphone and marimbaphone
**SCHÜLLER** (48)
Three Nocturnes for orchestra
**FELDMAN** (47)
*String Quartet and Orchestra*
*Voices and Cello*
*For Frank O'Hara,* for instrumental ensemble
**HENZE** (47)
*La Cubana,* a vaudeville
*Voices,* for two voices and instruments
*Tristan,* preludes for piano and orchestra
**BROWN** (46)
*Centering,* for solo violin and ten instruments
**JOSEPHS** (46)
Five Pieces for unaccompanied voices
Solo Oboe Pieces
**JOUBERT** (46)
*The Prisoner,* opera
Concerto for bassoon and chamber orchestra
*Coverdale's Carol,* for unaccompanied chorus
*Threnos,* for harpsichord and twelve solo strings
**MUSGRAVE** (45)
Viola Concerto
**STOCKHAUSEN** (45)
*Inori,* for soloist and orchestra (1973–4)
**CRUMB** (44)
*Makrokosmos I,* for piano
**HODDINOTT** (44)
*fp* Symphony No 5
*fp The Floore of Heav'n,* for orchestra
**LEIGHTON** (44)
*Laudate pueri,* for three choirs
**TAKEMITSU** (43)
*Autumn,* for two Japanese instruments and orchestra
**WILLIAMSON** (42)
*The Winter Star,* cassation
Concerto for two pianos and strings
*Ode to Music,* for chorus, echo chorus and orchestra
*Pietà,* for soprano, oboe, bassoon and piano
*Canticle of Fire,* for chorus and organ
*Little Carols of the Saints,* five organ pieces
*The World at the Manger,* cantata
**GOEHR** (41)
*Metamorphosis,* dance for orchestra
**SHCHEDRIN** (41)
Symphonic Fanfares
**WOOD** (41)
*Song Cycle to Poems of Pablo Neruda*

*Two Choruses of Yeats,* for chorus
*Songs to Poems by Robert Graves,* for voice and piano
**DICKINSON** (40)
*Hymns, Blues and Improvisations,* for piano quintet and tape
**PENDERECKI** (40)
Symphony No 1
**BIRTWISTLE** (39)
*Grimethorpe Aria,* for brass band
Five Choral Preludes arranged from Bach, for soprano and instrumental ensemble
*Chanson de geste,* for solo sustaining instrument and tape
**DAVIES, P. M.** (39)
*Fiddlers at the Wedding,* for mezzo and chamber orchestra (1973–4)
*Stone Litany,* for mezzo and orchestra
Renaissance Scottish Dances, for instrumental ensemble
*Si quis diligit me,* motet for instrumental ensemble
*Purcell: Fantasia on One Note,* realisation for instrumental ensemble
**MATHIAS** (39)
*Magnificat* and *Nunc Dimittis,* for mixed voices and organ
*Missa Brevis,* for mixed voices
Intrada for orchestra
Laudi for orchestra
*Ceremony after a Fire Raid,* for mixed voices, piano and percussion
**MAW** (38)
*Serenade,* for chamber orchestra
*Life Studies,* for fifteen solo strings
*Personae,* for piano
**BENNETT** (37)
Concerto for Orchestra
Viola Concerto
*Commedia III* and *IV*
*Scena I,* for piano
*Scena II,* for cello
**BLAKE** (37)
String Quartet No 2
*In Praise of Krishna,* for soprano and nine players
**REICH** (37)
*Six Pianos,* for six pianos
*Music for Mallet Instruments, Voices and Organ,* for marimbas, glockenspiels, metallophone, voices and organ
*Music for Pieces of Wood,* for five pairs of tuned claves
**BEDFORD** (36)
*A Horse, His Name was Hunry Fencewaver Walkins,* for instrumental ensemble
*Jack of Shadows,* for solo viola and

instruments
*Pancakes . . .*, for wind quintet
*Variations on a Rhythm by Mike Oldfield*, for percussion
**NILSSON** (36)
*Nazm*, for soli, chorus and orchestra
*Tesbih*, for orchestra
*Déjà-connu*, for wind quintet
**McCABE** (34)
*Maze Dances*, for solo violin
Madrigal for chamber orchestra
*The Castle of Arianrhod*, for horn and piano
*Das Letzte Gerichte*, for voice, guitar and percussion
*Time Remembered*, for soprano and ensemble
*Upon the High Midnight*, three carols for chorus
*The Teachings of Don Juan*, ballet
*Arabesque*, for ensemble
*The Goddess Trilogy*, for horn and piano (1973–5)
**COWIE** (30)
String Quartet No 1
*Endymion Nocturnes*, for tenor and string quartet
*Somnus el inductus*, for four trombones
**FERNEYHOUGH** (30)
*Time and Motion Study II*, for cello, tape and electronics (1973–6)
**HOLLOWAY** (30)
Five Madrigals for unaccompanied mixed voices
*Domination of Black*, symphonic poem (1973–4)
**TAVENER** (29)
*Thérèse*, opera (1973–6)
*Requiem for Father Malachy*, for choir and instruments
**FINNISSY** (27)
*Song 13*, for violin
*Circle, Chorus and Formal Act*, music-theatre
*Commedia*, music-theatre (1973–5)
*Medea*, music-theatre (1973–6)
**PATTERSON** (26)
*Sonors*, for orchestra
*Intersections*, for instrumental ensemble
*Gloria*, for chorus and piano
*Time-Piece*, for six male voices
*The Abode of the Dead*, for voices and ensemble
*You'll Never Be Alone*, for voices and ensemble
*Fluorescence*, for organ
**OLIVER** (23)
Ricercare for clarinet, violin, cello and

piano
*A Fur Coat for Summer*, one-act opera
*Sufficient Beauty*, for baritone, actor and orchestra
*The Donkey*, children's opera
*Perseverance*, religious opera (1973–4)
**KNUSSEN** (21)
Symphony No 3 (1973–9)
**MULDOWNEY** (21)
String Quartet No 1

# 1974

**MARTIN, MILHAUD** and **WELLESZ** died
**MARTIN** (84)
*Et la vie l'emporta*, chamber cantata
**BLISS** (83)
*Lancaster*, orchestral prelude
**HOWELLS** (82)
*Exultate Deo*, for chorus and organ
**JACOB** (79)
Sinfonia Brevis
*Havant Suite*, for chamber orchestra
Quartet for clarinets
**TANSMAN** (77)
*Georges Dandin*, comic opera
**CHÁVEZ** (75)
*Estudio a Rubinstein*, for piano
**BUSH, A.** (74)
Two Songs for baritone and piano
*Letter Galliard*, for piano
**KŘENEK** (74)
*Von Vorn Herein*, for small orchestra, piano and cello
*Feierstag*, cantata (1974–5)
**BERKELEY, L.** (71)
Guitar Concerto
Suite for strings
'Herrick Songs', for voices and harp
**BLACHER** (71)
*Poème*, for orchestra
*Pentagramm*, for strings
**WALTON** (72)
*Cantico del Sole*
*Magnificat* and *Nunc Dimittis*
**RAINIER** (71)
*Primordial Canticles*, for organ
*Prayers from the Ark*, for harp (1974–5)
Violin Concerto (1974–7)
**KABALEVSKY** (70)
*To The Heroes of the 1905 Revolution*, for wind band
**ALWYN** (69)
*Mirages*, song cycle
**COOKE** (68)
Cello Concerto

**LUTYENS** (68)
*The Winter of the World,* for orchestras
*Kareniana,* for instrumental ensemble
*Sloth, One of the Seven Deadly Sins,* for
  male voices
**SHOSTAKOVICH** (68)
String Quartet No 15
*Four Verses of Captain Lebjadkin,* for bass
  and piano
*Suite on Verses of Michelangelo Buonarroti,*
  for bass and piano
**MACONCHY** (67)
Three Songs for tenor and harp
*Siren's Song,* for chorus
*King of the Golden River,* opera (1974–5)
**MESSIAEN** (66)
*Saint François d'Assise,* opera (1974–83)
**CARTER** (65)
Brass Quintet
*Fantasy on Purcell's Fantasy on One Note,*
  for brass quintet
**HOLMBOE** (65)
Violin Concerto
Recorder Concerto
*Fanfare,* for three trumpets and timpani
**SIEGMEISTER** (65)
Piano Concerto
*A Cycle of Cities,* for soli, chorus, orchestra
  and dancers
*Night of the Moonspell,* opera (1974–6)
**SCHUMAN** (64)
*Prelude for a Great Occasion,* for brass and
  percussion
**JONES** (63)
Symphony No 9
**CAGE** (62)
*Score and twenty-three parts*
Two Pieces for piano
*Etudes Austale,* thirty-two pieces for piano
  (1974–5)
**FRANÇAIX** (62)
Double-bass Concerto
**BRITTEN** (61)
Suite on English Folk Tunes, for orchestra
Canticle No V, 'The Death of St Narcissus',
  for tenor and harp
*A Birthday Hansel,* for voice and harp
**DIAMOND** (59)
*fp* Quartet No 10
**GINASTERA** (58)
*Turbai ad Passionem Gregorianum,* for soli,
  chorus and orchestra
**BERNSTEIN** (56)
*Dybbuk,* ballet and suites
**ROCHBERG** (56)
*Imago mundi,* for orchestra

**BUSH, G.** (54)
*The Cat Who Went to Heaven,* opera
*Dafydd in Love,* choral
**FRICKER** (54)
*Spirit Puck,* for clarinet and percussion
Trio Sonata for organ
Two Petrarch Madrigals
**ARNOLD** (53)
Clarinet Concerto
Fantasy for brass band
**SIMPSON** (53)
String Quartet No 5
**FOSS** (52)
*fp Orpheus,* for viola, cello or guitar and
  orchestra
**HAMILTON** (52)
*The Cataline Conspiracy,* opera
Piano Sonata No 2
**XENAKIS** (52)
*Erikhthon,* for piano and orchestra
*Gmeeoorh,* for organ
*Noomena,* for orchestra
**NONO** (50)
*Für Paul Dessau,* for tape
*Notturni-Albe,* for piano and tape
**BERIO** (49)
*Per la dolce memoria di quel giorno,* ballet
*Après visage,* for orchestra and tape
*Calmo,* for soprano and instruments
*Chorus,* for voices and instruments
**BOULEZ** (49)
*Rituel, in memoriam Maderna,* for
  orchestra in eight groups
**FELDMAN** (48)
*Instruments I*
*Voice and Instruments II*
**HENZE** (48)
*We Come to a River,* for chorus and
  orchestra (1974–6)
**JOSEPHS** (47)
*The Four Horsemen of the Apocalypse,*
  overture
Concerto for brass band
Concerto for school orchestra
*A Trio of Trios,* for piano and violins
Sonata for two trumpets, horn, trombone
  and tuba
**JOUBERT** (47)
*The Magus,* for soli, chorus and
  orchestra
*Sleep Canticle,* for unaccompanied chorus
*Crabbed Age and Youth,* for counter-tenor,
  recorder, viola da gamba and
  harpsichord
**KORTE** (46)
*Libera me,* four songs

**MUSGRAVE** (46)
*Space Play*, concerto for nine instruments
**STOCKHAUSEN** (46)
*Atmen gibt das Leben . . .*, for mixed choir
*Herbstmusik*, for four players
*Vortrag über Hu*, for solo voice
**CRUMB** (45)
*Makrokosmos II*, for amplified piano
**HODDINOTT** (45)
fp *The Beach of Falesa*, opera
fp *Ritornelli*, for solo trombone, winds and
    percussion
**LEIGHTON** (45)
Symphony No 2, *Sinfonia mistica*
**PREVIN** (45)
*The Good Companions*, film score
*Four Outings*, for brass quintet
**WILLIAMSON** (43)
*The Glitter Gang*, cassation
*Perisynthyon*, ballet
*Hammarskjold Portrait*, song cycle
**GOEHR** (42)
Chaconne for wind
Lyric Pieces
**MEALE** (42)
*Juliet's Memoirs*, opera (1974–5)
**DICKINSON** (41)
*Lust*, for six solo voices
**PENDERECKI** (41)
*The Dream of Jacob*, for orchestra
**BIRTWISTLE** (40)
*Chorales from a Toyshop*, for variable
    orchestration
**DAVIES, P. M.** (40)
*Miss Donnithorne's Maggot*, for mezzo and
    chamber orchestra
*Dark Angels*, for voice and guitar
*All Sons of Adam*, motet for instrumental
    ensemble
*Psalm 124*, motet for instrumental
    ensemble
**MATHIAS** (40)
Concertino in F, for oboe, bassoon and
    piano
*This Worldes Joie*, for chorus and orchestra
**SALLINEN** (39)
*Metamorfora*, for cello and piano
**BENNETT** (38)
*Spells*, for soprano, chorus and orchestra
*Love Spells*, for soprano and orchestra
*Four-piece Suite*, divertimento for two
    pianos
*Sonnet Sequence*, for tenor and strings
*Time's Whiter Series*, for counter-tenor and
    lute
**BLAKE** (38)
*Toussaint*, opera (1974–6)

**BEDFORD** (37)
*Star's End*, for rock instruments and
    orchestra
*Twelve Hours of Sunset*, for mixed choir
    and orchestra
*The Golden Wine is Drunk*, for sixteen solo
    voices
*Because He Liked to be at Home*, for tenor
    (doubling recorder) and harp
**GLASS** (37)
*Another Look at Harmony*, for ensemble
**NILSSON** (37)
*Taqsim-Caprice-Maqam*, for ensemble
**McCABE** (35)
*The Chagall Windows*, for windows
*The Play of Mother Courage*, chamber opera
*Sam*, for orchestra
**COWIE** (31–2)
*Leighton Moss*, cantata for chorus
    and chamber orchestra
**FERNEYHOUGH** (31)
*Time and Motion Study III*, for sixteen
    solo voices, chamber orchestra and
    electronics
**HOLLOWAY** (31)
*Lights Out*, for baritone and piano
*In the Thirtieth Year*, for tenor and piano
*Author of Light*, for contralto and piano
*The Leaves Cry*, for soprano and piano
*Sea Surface Full of Clouds*, cantata (1974–5)
**FINNISSY** (28)
*Orfeo*, music-theatre (1974–5)
*Wild Flowers*, for two pianos
*Evening*, for ensemble
*Cipriano*, for ten solo voices
*Ives*, for voices
**PATTERSON** (27)
*Fusions*, for orchestra
*Floating Music*, for ensemble
*Conversations*, for clarinet and piano
*Chromascope*, for brass band
**OLIVER** (24)
*Past Tense*, for voices and instruments
*Cademus Observed*, for baritone solo
*The Boy and the Dolphin*, for orchestra
*Tom Jones*, opera (1974–5)
**MULDOWNEY** (22)
*Music at Chartres*, for orchestra
*Solo/Ensemble*, for orchestra

## 1975

**BLACHER, BLISS, DALLAPICCOLA,
GRANDJANY** and **SHOSTAKOVICH**
died
**BLISS** (83)
*Shield of Faith*, cantata

JACOB (80)
Concerto for organ, strings and percussion
*Rhapsody*, for piano
*Fantasy Sonata*, for organ
SESSIONS (79)
Five Pieces for chamber orchestra
HARRIS (77)
Symphony No 14
CHÁVEZ (76)
Five Caprichos for piano
BUSH, A. (75)
*Suite of Six*, for string quartet
Sonatina for recorders and piano
KŘENEK (75)
*Dream Sequence*, for wind band
BERKELEY, L. (73)
Quintet for piano and wind
*The Lord is My Shepherd*, choral
*The Hill of the Graces*, choral
KABALEVSKY (71)
*Prague Concerto*, for piano and string
   orchestra
BLACHER (72)
*Das Geheimnis des entwendeten Briefs*,
   chamber opera
LUTYENS (69)
*Eos*, for small orchestra
*Fanfare for a Festival*, for three trumpets
   and three trombones
*Pietá*, for harpsichord
*Ring of Bone*, for solo piano
SHOSTAKOVICH (69)
*The Dreamers*, ballet
Sonata for viola and grand piano
MACONCHY (68)
*Two Epitaphs*, for female chorus
*Epyllion*, for solo cello and fifteen strings
Sinfonietta for orchestra (1975–6)
CARTER (66)
*A Mirror on which to Dwell*, for soprano
   and ensemble
HOLMBOE (66)
String Quartets Nos 13 and 14
Flute Concerto
*Triade*, for trumpet and organ
SIEGMEISTER (66)
*Shadows and Light*, for orchestra
String Quartet No 4
*Fables from the Dark Wood*, ballet (1975–6)
GILDER (64)
*A Processional Overture*
CAGE (63)
*Child of Tree*, for percussion and amplifiers
*Lecture on the Weather*
FRANÇAIX (63)
*Quasi Improvisando*, for eleven wind
   instruments

BRITTEN (62)
*Phaedra*, dramatic cantata for mezzo-
   soprano and small orchestra
String Quartet No 3
*Sacred and Profane*, eight medieval lyrics
   for unaccompanied voices
LUTOSLAWSKI (62)
*Les espaces du sommeil*, for baritone and
   orchestra
*Sacher Variations*, for cello
MELLERS (61)
*Threnody*, for eleven strings
PANUFNIK (61)
*Sinfonia di Sfere*
BABBITT (59)
*Kräfte*, opera
GINASTERA (59)
*Popol Vuh*, for orchestra
ARNELL (58)
*Jennifer + Robert = Wedding*, for piano
   (four hands)
BERNSTEIN (57)
*By Bernstein*, a revue
ROCHBERG (57)
Violin Concerto
Piano Quintet
FRICKER (55)
Symphony No 5
String Quartet No 3
ARNOLD (54)
*Fantasy on a Theme of John Field*, for
   orchestra
String Quartet No 2
Fantasy for harp
SHAPEY (54)
*Songs of Eros*, for soprano and orchestra
*Oh Jerusalem*, for soprano and flute
SIMPSON (54)
String Quartet No 6
*Media Morte . . .*, motet for voices, brass
   and timpani
HAMILTON (53)
*Sea Music*, for chorus and string
   quartet
Violin Sonata No 1
Cello Sonata No 2
*Te deum*
*Aurora*, for orchestra
*A Vision of Canopus*, for organ
*To Columbus*, for chorus, brass and
   percussion
XENAKIS (53)
*Empreintes*, for orchestra
*Phlegra*, for eleven players
*Psappha*, for solo percussion
*N'shima*, for two mezzos and five
   instruments

BERIO (50)
*Il malato immaginario*, incidental music
*La ritirata notturna di Madrid*, for orchestra
*Sequence VIII*, for percussion
*Sequence IX*, for violin
SCHÜLLER (50)
*Four Soundscapes*, for orchestra
*Triplum II*, for orchestra
Violin Concerto (1975–6)
FELDMAN (49)
*Piano and Orchestra*
*Instruments II*
*Four Instruments II*, for piano, violin, viola
 and cello
HENZE (49)
*Katharina Blum*, film score
*Ragtimes and Habaneras*, for brass band
*Royal Winter Music*, for guitar (1975–6)
String Quartet No 3 (1975–6)
JOSEPHS (48)
Concerto for clarinet and chamber
 orchestra
Sonata No 2 for violin and piano
Waltz and Song for harp and strings
MUSGRAVE (47)
*Orfeo I* and *II*, for flute, strings and tape
STOCKHAUSEN (47)
*Musik im Bauch*, for six percussionists
*Tierkreis (Zodiac)*, for various vocal and
 instrumental combinations
HODDINOTT (46)
*fp Landscapes*, for orchestra
*The Magicians*, one-act opera
*Five Landscapes*, for tenor and piano
LEIGHTON (46)
*Laudes montium*, for baritone, chorus and
 orchestra
GOEHR (43)
String Quartet No 3
TAKEMITSU (45)
*Gitimalya*, for orchestra
*Quatraine*, for clarinet, violin, cello, piano
 and orchestra
DICKINSON (42)
*Late Afternoon in November*, for sixteen solo
 voices
String Quartet No 2, with tape and piano
DAVIES, P. M. (41)
*Ave maris Stella*, for instrumental ensemble
*The Door of the Sun*, for viola
*The Kestrel Paced round the Sun*, for flute
*The Seven Brightnesses*, for clarinet
Three Studies for percussion
*My Lady Lothian's Lilte*, for mezzo and
 ensemble
*Stevie's Ferry to Hoy*, for piano

MATHIAS (41)
*Vistas*, for orchestra
Clarinet Concerto
*Jubilate*, for organ
*Zodiac Trio*, for flute, viola and harp
MAW (40)
*Te Deum*, for treble, tenor, chorus and
 organ
*Reverdie*, five songs for male voices
SALLINEN (40)
*Canto e Ritornello*, for violin solo
Symphony No 3
*Chamber Music I*, for string orchestra
BENNETT (39)
Violin Concerto
Oboe Quartet
*Travel Notes, Book I*, for string quartet
GLASS (38)
*Einstein on the Beach*, opera
NILSSON (38)
*Szene IV*, for jazz saxophone and chorus
McCABE (36)
*Behold the Silly Tender Babe*, for chorus and
 organ
*Mary Queen of Scots*, ballet
COWIE (32)
*Leviathan*, symphony poem for orchestra
Clarinet Concerto No 2
FERNEYHOUGH (32)
*Unity Capsule*, for flute
HOLLOWAY (32)
Concertino No 3, *Homage to Weill*, for
 eleven players
*Clarissa*, opera
FINNISSY (29)
Piano Concertos Nos 1 and 2 (1975–6)
*Bouffe*, music-theatre
*Ru Tchou – The Ascent of the Sun*, for
 drummer
*Offshore*, for orchestra (1975–6)
*Tom Fool's Wooing*, music-theatre (1975–8)
PATTERSON (28)
*The Circular Ruins*, for orchestra
*Strange Meeting*, for orchestra
*Count Down*, for brass band
*Cataclysm*, for brass band
*Requiem*, for chorus and orchestra
*Shadows*, for clarinet and tape
BERKELEY, M. (27)
*Meditations*, for string orchestra
OLIVER (25)
*Luv*, for orchestra
*Bad Times*, for baritone and string quartet
KNUSSEN (23)
*Trumpets*, for violin and three clarinets
*Ophelia Dances*, for ensemble

MULDOWNEY (23)
*Perspectives*, for orchestra
Cantata for soli, chorus, two cellos and
    percussion
*Da Capo al Fine*, tape for ballet

## 1976

**BRITTEN, DARKE** and **PISTON** died
HOWELLS (84)
*The Fear of the Lord*, for chorus and organ
*Let All the World*, antiphon for chorus
*Come My Soul*, anthem for chorus
*Sweetest of Sweetes*, anthem for chorus
PISTON (82)
Concerto for string quartet, woodwind
    and percussion
HANSON (80)
*New Land, New Covenant*, oratorio
TANSMAN (79)
*Elégie in memory of Darius Milhaud*, for
    orchestra
BUSH, A. (76)
*Compass Points*, for pipes
BERKELEY, L. (73)
Fantaisie for organ
ALWYN (71)
Six Nocturnes, for baritone and orchestra
String Quartet No 2, *Spring Waters*
*Moto Perpetuo*, for recorders
TIPPETT (71)
Symphony No 4 (1976–7)
LUTYENS (70)
*Mare et Minutiae*, for string quartet
*Constants*, for cello and piano
MACONCHY (69)
Three Pieces for harp
String Quartet No 11
*Hopkins Motets*
CARTER (67)
A Symphony of Three Orchestras (1976–7)
HOLMBOE (67)
Tuba Concerto
*Nuigen*, for piano trio
*Firefir*, for four flutes
SIEGMEISTER (67)
*An Entertainment*, for violin, piano and
    orchestra
SCHUMAN (66)
Symphony No 10
*Casey at the Bak*, cantata
*The Young Dead Soldiers*, for soprano and
    ensemble
MENOTTI (65)
*The hero*, comic opera
*The Egg*, church opera
*Landscapes and Remembrances*, cantata

Symphony, *The Halcyon*
CAGE (64)
*Apartment House*, mixed media event
*Branches*
Quartet for twelve amplified voices and
    concert band
Quartets Nos 1 to 8
*Renga*, for seventy-eight instruments and
    voices
FRANÇAIX (64)
Concerto Grosso for wind quintet, string
    quintet and orchestra
BRITTEN (63)
Eight Folk Song Arrangements with harp
    and piano
*Welcome Ode*, for young people's chorus
    and orchestra
GOULD (63)
American Ballads
Symphony of Spirituals
LUTOSLAWSKI (63)
*Mi-parti*, for orchestra
PANUFNIK (62)
String Quartet No 1
GINASTERA (60)
*Puneña No 2*, for cello
*On a Theme of Pau Casals*, for string
    quintet and strings
Guitar Sonata
BERNSTEIN (58)
*600 Pennsylvania Avenue*, musical
BUSH, G. (56)
*Magnificat and Nunc Dimittis*, choral
*A Little Love-Music*, songs
Concertino No 2 for piano and orchestra
FRICKER (56)
String Quartet No 4
*Seachant*, for flute and double-bass
*Invention and Little Toccata*, for organ
*Sinfonia*, for seventeen wind instruments
    (1976–7)
SIMPSON (55)
Symphony No 6
Quartet for horn and piano trio
ARNOLD (55)
Philharmonic Concerto
*The Return of Odysseus*, for chorus and
    orchestra (1976–7)
HAMILTON (54)
*Tamburlaine*, lyric drama
*The Alexandrian Sequence*, for chamber
    orchestra
XENAKIS (54)
*Therapos*, for solo double-bass
*Khoaï*, for harpsichord
*Retours-Windungen*, for twelve cellos
*Dmaathen*, for oboe and percussion
*Epeï*, for six players

LIGETI (53)
*Monument, Self-Portrait,* for two pianos
*Three Objects,* for two pianos
MENNIN (53)
*Voices,* for violin, piano, harp, harpsichord
   and percussion
NONO (52)
*Safferte onde Serene,* for piano and tape
BERIO (51)
*Il Retorno degli Snovidenia,* for cello and
   orchestra (1976–7)
FELDMAN (50)
*Orchestra*
*Oboe and Orchestra*
*Routine Investigations,* for instrumental
   ensemble
*Voice, Violin and Piano*
HENZE (50)
*Don Chisciotte,* opera
*Jephte,* oratorio
*Violin Sonata*
*String Quartets Nos 4 and 5 (1976–7)*
*Amicizia,* for clarinet, trombone, cello,
   piano and percussion
JOSEPHS (49)
Symphony No 7 for small orchestra
STOCKHAUSEN (48)
*Amour,* five pieces for clarinet
*Tierkreis,* for instruments
HODDINOTT (47)
Violin Sonata No 4
*A Contemplation upon Flowers,* for soprano
   and orchestra
LEIGHTON (47)
*Hymn to Matter,* for baritone, chorus,
   strings and percussion
TAKEMITSU (47)
*Marginalia,* for orchestra
*Mar concerto Green,* for harp, cello and
   strings
WILLIAMSON (45)
Piano Trio
GOEHR (44)
*Psalm IV,* for soloist, female chorus and
   organ
*Fugue on the Notes of Psalm IV,* for string
   orchestra
DICKINSON (43)
Solo, for baryton, tape and viola da gamba
*Surrealist Landscape,* for mezzo
BIRTWISTLE (42)
*Melencolia I,* for orchestra
DAVIES, P. M. (42)
Three Organ Voluntaries
*Kinloche His Fantassie,* for instrumental
   ensemble
*Anakreontika,* Greek songs for mezzo and

instruments
*The Blind Fiddler,* for soprano and
   instruments
Symphony No 1
*The Martyrdom of St Magnus,* chamber
   opera
MATHIAS (42)
*Carmen Paschale,* chorus
*Communion,* for voices and organ
MAW (41)
*Annes!* for mixed chorus
*Nonsense Rhymes for Children,* twenty
   songs with piano
*Life Study No 2*
SALLINEN (41)
*Chamber Music II,* for alto flute and strings
Cello Concerto
*The Red Line,* opera (1976–8)
BENNETT (40)
*Zodiac,* for orchestra
*Serenade,* for orchestra
*The Little Ghost who Died for Love,* for
   soprano and piano
*Travel Notes, Book II,* for wind ensemble
BLAKE (40)
Violin Concerto
REICH (40)
*Music for Eighteen Musicians*
BEDFORD (39)
*Alleluia Timpanis,* for orchestra
*The Odyssey,* for chorus and orchestra
*Circe Variations,* for instrumental ensemble
*The Ones Who Walked Away from Omelas,*
   for instrumental ensemble
GLASS (39)
*Paris,* opéra-comique
NILSSON (39)
*Flöten aus der Einsamkeit,* for soprano and
   nine players
McCABE (37)
Sonata on a motet for string orchestra
Piano Concerto No 3, *Dialogues*
*Couples,* theme music for piano
*Stabat Mater,* for soprano, chorus and
   orchestra
Five Folk Songs for high voice, horn and
   piano
COWIE (33)
*Gesangbuch,* for twenty-four voices and
   twelve instruments
FERNEYHOUGH (33)
*La Terre est un homme* (1976–9)
Piano Variations
Piano Concerto (1976–7)
*Commedia,* opera (1976–8)
HOLLOWAY (33)
*Romanza,* for violin and small orchestra

**TAVENER** (32)
*A Gentle Spirit*, for soprano, tenor and
ensemble
*Canticle of the Mother of God*, for soprano
and chorus
**FINNISSY** (30)
*Jazz*, for piano
*Songs 16, 17 and 18*
*Pathways of Sun and Stars*, orchestra
*Mr Punch*, music-theatre (1976–7)
**PATTERSON** (29)
Clarinet Concerto
*Wildfire*, for orchestra
*Diversions*, for saxophone ensemble
**OLIVER** (26)
Symphony
*O No*, comedy for brass band
*Many Happy Returns*, for brass band
*Magnificat* and *Nunc Dimittis*, for boys'
voices, recorders and organ
*The Elixir*, for soloists and chorus
*The Waiter's Revenge*, for six voices
*Three Instant Operas*, for children
*The Great McPorridge Disaster*, for voices
and instruments
**KNUSSEN** (24)
*Autumnal*, for violin and piano
**MULDOWNEY** (24)
Three-part Motet, for eleven instruments
Twelve Shorter Chorale Preludes of Bach,
for eight wind-players
Ten Longer Chorale Preludes of Bach, for
eight wind-players
*One From Arcady*, for unaccompanied
violin
*Three From Arcady*, for cor anglais, viola
and cello
*The Earl of Essex's Galliard*, for actors,
dancers and seven players
*Changes*, ballet (1976–9)

**1977**

**HANSON** (81)
Symphony No 7, *Sea*, with chorus
**TANSMAN** (80)
*Musique à six*, for clarinet, string quartet
and piano
**BUSH, A.** (77)
Twenty-four Preludes for Piano
**RAINIER** (74)
Concertante Duo for oboe, clarinet and
small orchestra
**ALWYN** (72)
*Miss Julie*, opera
*What Shall We Do With a Drunken Sailor*,
vocal

**TIPPETT** (72)
String quartet No 4 (1977–8)
**LUTYENS** (71)
*Rondel*, for chamber ensemble
**MACONCHY** (70)
*Héloïse and Abelard*, choral
**SIEGMEISTER** (68)
Violin Concerto
**CAGE** (65)
*Freeman Etudes*, for violin
*Telephones and Birds*, for three performers
*Lulets*, for four performers with conch
shells
*49 Waltzes for Five Boroughs*
**FRANÇAIX** (65)
Quintet for clarinet and string quartet
**PANUFNIK** (63)
*Dreamscape*, for mezzo and piano
*Sinfonia Mistica*
**GINASTERA** (61)
*Barabbas*, opera
**ARNELL** (60)
*Ring Bells*, electronic church bells and
chorus
**BERNSTEIN** (59)
*Three Meditations from Mass*, for violoncello
and orchestra
*Songfest*, cycle for six singers and orchestra
*Slava!*, overture for orchestra/band
CBS Music
**FRICKER** (57)
*A Wish for a Party*, for male voices
*Anniversary*, for organ
Two Songs for baritone and piano
**ARNOLD** (56)
Sonata for flute and piano
**SIMPSON** (56)
String Quartet No 7
Symphony No 7
**HAMILTON** (55)
*Cleopatra*, dramatic scene for soprano and
orchestra
*Hyperion*, for clarinet, horn, violin, cello
and piano
*Spirits of the Air*, for solo bass trombone
**XENAKIS** (55)
*Akanthos*, for nine players
*Kottos*, for solo cello
*Hélène*, for mezzo, female chorus and two
clarinets
*Diatope*, for tapes
**SCHÜLLER** (52)
Horn Concerto
Symphony No 7
String Quartet No 7
**FELDMAN** (51)
*Neither*, one-act opera

*Instruments III*, for flute, oboe and
    percussion
*Piano*
*Only*, for solo voice
*Flute and Orchestra* (1977–8)
**HENZE** (51)
*Aria de la Folia Española*, for chamber
    orchestra
*Il Vitalino Raddoppiato*, for violin and
    chamber orchestra
**JOSEPHS** (50)
Symphony No 8 for wind instruments
Piano Quintet
Sonata Duo for piano (four hands)
Sonata for flute and piano
**JOUBERT** (50)
'Lines from the Youth of Man', for a capella
    choir
**MUSGRAVE** (49)
*Mary, Queen of Scots*, opera
**STOCKHAUSEN** )49)
*Tierkreis*, for chamber orchestra
*Jubiläum*, for orchestra
*In Freundschaft*, for six instruments
*Der Jahreslauf*, for dancers and orchestra
**HODDINOTT** (48)
*What The Old Man Does is Always Right*,
    one-act opera
*French Suite*, for orchestra
*Passaggio*, for orchestra
*Sinfonia Fidei*, for soprano, tenor, chorus
    and orchestra
*Italian Suite*, for recorder and guitar
Cello Sonata No 2
**PREVIN** (48)
*E,G,B,D,F*, for piano
**TAKEMITSU** (47)
*A Flock Descends into the Pentagonal
    Garden*, for orchestra
**WILLIAMSON** (46)
Symphony No 4
*Mass of Christ the King*, for chorus and
    orchestra
*Les Olympiques*, for mezzo and string
    orchestra
*The Lion of Suffolk*, for organ
*Mass of St Margaret of Scotland* (1977–80)
**GOEHR** (45)
*Romanza on the notes of Psalm IV*, for string
    orchestra
**DICKINSON** (44)
Aria for horn, oboe, clarinet and bassoon
*Four Auden Songs*, for soprano/tenor and
    piano
*A Memory of David Munrow*, for two
    counter-tenors, two recorders, viola da
    gamba and harpsichord

*Schubert in Blue*, for mezzo and piano
**BIRTWISTLE** (43)
*Silbury Air*, for orchestra
*For O, for O, the Hobby Horse is Forgot*, for
    instrumental ensemble
*Bow Down*, improvised music-theatre
*Frames, Pulse and Interruptions*, ballet
*Carmen Arcadiae Mechanicae Perpetuum*, for
    orchestra (1977–8)
**DAVIES, P. M.** (43)
*Westerlings*, for unaccompanied choir
*Runes from a Holy Island*, for chamber
    ensemble
*A Mirror of Whitening Light*, for chamber
    orchestra
*Our Father Whiche in Heaven Art*, motet for
    instrumental ensemble
*Norn pater noster*, prayer for SATB and
    organ
*Ave iex angelorum*, for SATB
    unaccompanied or organ
**MATHIAS** (43)
Dance Variations for orchestra
*Vivat Regina*, for brass
*Helios*, for orchestra
*Requiescat*, for orchestra
*Melos*, for flute, harp, strings and
    percussion
*A Royal Garland*, for chorus and orchestra
*The Fields of Praise*, for tenor and piano
**BENNETT** (41)
*Actaeon (Metamorphosis I)*, for horn and
    orchestra
Music for Strings
*Kandinsky Variations*, for two pianos
*Scena III*, for solo clarinet
*Eustace and Hilda*, for piano and TV
    incidental music
*The Christians*, TV incidental music
**BEDFORD** (40)
*The Song of the White Horse*, for chorus and
    orchestra
*On the Beach at Night*, for voices and
    instruments
*The Way of Truth*, for chorus and
    electronics (1977–8)
**NILSSON** (40)
*Mez*, for ensemble
**McCABE** (38)
*Jubilee Suite*, for orchestra
Clarinet Concerto
*Reflections of a Summer Night*, for chorus
    and orchestra
*A Lute-book Lullaby*, for SSA and flute
**COWIE** (34)
*L'or de la trompette d'été*, for eighteen
    strings

*Cathedral Music*, sonata for symphonic brass
String Quartet No 2
**HOLLOWAY** (34)
*This Is Just To Say*, for tenor and piano
*Divertimento No 3, Nursery Rhymes*, for soprano and wind quintet
*The Rivers of Hell*, for chamber ensemble
*The Blue Doom of Summer*, cantata for voice and harp
*Willow Cycle*, for tenor and harp
*Hymn for Voices*, for unaccompanied chorus
*From High Windows*, for baritone and piano
*The Consolation of Music*, for chorus
**TAVENER** (33)
*Kyklike Kinesis*, for soprano, chorus, cello and orchestra
*Lamentation, Lost Prayer and Exaltation*, for soprano with handbells/piano
*Palin*, for piano
*Palintropos*, for piano and orchestra
*The Last Prayer of Mary Queen of Scots*, for soprano and handbells
**FINNISSY** (31)
*Mine Eyes Awake*, for soprano and piano interior
*English Country Tunes*, for piano
*all.fall.down*, for piano
*All the Trees they are so High*, for violin
*Lost Lands*
*Long Distance*, for piano and ensemble (1977–8)
**PATTERSON** (30)
*Spare Parts*, for six male voices
*Games*, for organ
**BERKELEY, M.** (29)
Concerto for oboe
**OLIVER** (27)
*Kyoto*, organ duet
*The Garden*, for voices and instruments
*The Duchess of Malfi*, opera
*A Stable Home*, dramatic cantata
**KNUSSEN** (25)
*Cantata*, for oboe and string trio
*Sonya's Lullaby*, for piano (1977–8)
*Where the Wild Things Are*, fantasy in two acts (1977–8)
**MULDOWNEY** (25)
*Four from Arcady*, for four oboes
*Variations on Mein Junges Leben*, for eight players
*Double Helix*, for eight players
*Entr'acte*, for eight players
*Procurans Odium*, for soprano and eight players

## 1978

**CHÁVEZ, GILLES** and **KHATCHATURIAN** died
**JACOB** (83)
Sonata for viola and piano
**KŘENEK** (78)
*The Dissembler*, for orchestra
**TIPPETT** (73)
Triple Concerto for violin, viola, cello and orchestra (1978–9)
**LUTYENS** (72)
*Doubles*, for string quartet
Seven Preludes for piano
*Elegy of the Flowers*, for three instrumental groups
*Footfalls*, for flute and piano
**MACONCHY** (71)
*Sun, Moon and Stars*, for soprano and piano
*Contemplation*, for cello and piano
**CARTER** (69)
*Syringa*, for mezzo/baritone and eleven instruments
**MENOTTI** (67)
*The Trial of the Gypsy*, for voices and piano
**CAGE** (66)
*A Dip in the Lake*
Chorals for Violin
**LUTOSLAWSKI** (65)
*Novelette*, for orchestra (1978–9)
**PANUFNIK** (64)
*Metasinfonia*, for organ, strings and timpani
**HAMILTON** (56)
*Anna Karenina*, opera
Piano Sonata No 3
**LIGETI** (55)
*Le Grand Macabre*, music-theatre
**BERIO** (53)
*Encore*, for orchestra
**SCHÜLLER** (53)
*Deai*, for two orchestras
**FELDMAN** (52)
*Why Patterns*, for flute, alto flute, piano and percussion
*Spring of Chosroes*, for violin and piano
**JOUBERT** (51)
*Déploration*, for harp, percussion and strings
**MUSGRAVE** (50)
*O Caro m'e il Sonno*, for unaccompanied chorus
**STOCKHAUSEN** (50)
*Michaels Reise um die Erde*, for trumpet and orchestra
**HODDINOTT** (49)
*Dulciu Iuventutis*, for chorus and piano duet

Sonata for guitar
**LEIGHTON** (49)
*Columba ea*, for soli, strings, celeste and
  harpsichord
**MEALE** (46)
*Viridian*, for string orchestra
**WOOD** (46)
String Quartet No 3
**PENDERECKI** (45)
*Paradise Lost*, opera
**DICKINSON** (45)
Four Duos for flute/oboe and cello
*Reminiscences*, for mezzo, sax and piano
**DAVIES, P. M.** (44)
*The Two Fiddlers*, children's opera
*Le Jongleur de Notre Dame*, a masque
*Salome*, ballet
*Four Lessons*, for two clavichords
Dances from *The Two Fiddlers*, for
  instrumental ensemble
**MATHIAS** (44)
*Shine, for Your Light Has Come*, for chorus
  and organ
*Nativity Carol*, for chorus
*A May Magnificat*, for chorus and organ
Eight Shakespeare Songs, for chorus and
  piano
*Fantasy*, for organ
**SCHNITTKE** (44)
Violin Concerto No 3
Sonata for cello and piano
**SALLINEN** (43)
*Dies Irae*, for soli, male chorus and
  orchestra
**BENNETT** (42)
Double-bass Concerto
Horn Sonata, with piano
Violin Sonata, with piano
**BLAKE** (42)
*Sonata à la Marcia*, for chamber orchestra
*Arias*, for solo clarinet
*From the Mattress Grave*, for high voice
  and eleven players
*Nine Poems of Heine*, for high voice and
  orchestra
**REICH** (42)
*Music for a Large Ensemble*
**BEDFORD** (41)
*The Rime of the Ancient Mariner*, school
  opera
**McCABE** (39)
*Images*, for brass band
Symphony No 3, *Hommages*
*Star Preludes*, for violin and piano
String quartet No 3
**HOLLOWAY** (35)
*He-She-Together*, for chorus

*Killing Time*, for unaccompanied soprano
*Three Slithy Toves*, for two clarinets
*The Noon's Repose*, for tenor and harp
  (1978–9)
Second Concerto for Orchestra (1978–9)
**TAVENER** (34)
Six Russian Folk Songs for soprano and
  ensemble
*The Immurement of Antigone*, for soprano
  and orchestra
**FINNISSY** (32)
*Sir Tristram*, for soprano and ensemble
*Coro*, for tenor and ensemble
Piano Concerto No 3
*Runnin' Wild*, for saxophone
*Mountainfall*, for mezzo
*Ohi! Ohi! Ohi!* for solo voice
Piano Concerto No 4 (1978–9)
*Fast Dances, Slow Dances*, for piano
  (1978–9)
Piano Studies (1978–9)
**PATTERSON** (31)
*Brain Storm*, for four voices and live
  electronics
**BERKELEY, M.** (30)
Fantasia Concertante
*The Wild Winds*, for soprano and small
  orchestra
String Trio
*Strange Meeting*, for piano
**OLIVER** (28)
Sonata for guitar
*Exchange*, for three male voices and piano
*Canzonet*, for five male voices
*The Girl and the Unicorn*, opera
**KNUSSEN** (26)
*Coursing*, for chamber orchestra
**MULDOWNEY** (26)
*Warrior Queen*, for eight saxes and
  percussion
Five Melodies for four saxophones
*A Garland of Chansons*, for six oboes and
  three bassoons
*Two from Arcady*, for basset-horn and tuba
*Three Hymns to Agape*, for oboe
*A First Show*, for percussion and tape


## 1979

**HARRIS** died
**JACOB** (84)
Viola Concerto No 2
**KŘENEK** (79)
Concerto for organ and strings
*Die Vierwinde*, for organ
*Opus 231*, for violin and organ

ALWYN (74)
*Green Hills*, piano solo
LUTYENS (73)
*Echoi*, for mezzo and orchestra
*Cantata*, for soprano and ensemble
'She Tells Her Love While Half Asleep',
  for unaccompanied voice
*The Great Seas*, for piano
*Prelude*, for solo violin
Cantata for soprano, alto, baritone and
  ensemble
Trio for clarinet, cello and piano
*The Roots of the World*, for chorus and cello
*That Sun*, for contralto and piano
MACONCHY (72)
*Romanza*, for viola and piano
GILDER (68)
Sonata, for violin and piano
PETTERSSEN (68)
Violin Concerto
LUTOSLAWSKI (66)
*Epitaph*, for oboe and piano
PANUFNIK (65)
*Concerto Festivo*, for orchestra
SIMPSON (58)
String Quartet No 8
ARNOLD (58)
Symphony No 8
BERIO (54)
*Un Re in Ascolto*, opera (1979–83)
FELDMAN (53)
*Violin and Orchestra*
String Quartet
JOUBERT (52)
*Herefordshire Canticles*, for soli, chorus and
  orchestra
*The Turning Wheel*, for soprano and piano
MUSGRAVE (51)
*A Christmas Carol*, opera
STOCKHAUSEN (51)
*Michaels Heimkehr*, for dancers, chorus and
  orchestra
HODDINOTT (50)
*The Rajah's Diamond*, one-act opera
Sonatina for two pianos
*Scena*, for string quartet
Ritornelli for brass
LEIGHTON (50)
Mass for treble voices and organ
DICKINSON (46)
*A Birthday Surprise*, for orchestra
PENDERECKI (46)
*Ubu Roi*, opera
*Te Deum*, for soli, chorus and orchestra
BIRTWISTLE (45)
*agm*, choral

*Some Petals from the Garland*, instrum piano
  ensemble
DAVIES, P. M. (45)
*Black Pentecost*, for voices and orchest
*Solstice of Light*, for tenor, chorus and
  organ                                    rom
*Kirkwall Shopping Songs*, for children's
  voices, recorders, percussion and pia*he*
Nocturne for alto flute
*The Lighthouse*, chamber opera
MATHIAS (45)
*Songs of William Blake*, for mezzo, cello,
  harp, piano and strings
SCHNITTKE (45)
Symphony, *St Florian*
*Passacaglia*, for orchestra (1979–80)
MAW (44)
*La Vita Nuova*, for soprano and chamber
  ensemble
SALLINEN (44)
Symphony No 4
BENNETT (43)
*Sonnets to Orpheus*, for cello and orchestra
*Just Friends in Print*, for voice and piano
*Nonsense*, for youth choir and orchestra
BLAKE (43)
*Cassation*, for wind octet
Clarinet Quintet
REICH (43)
*Octet*, for two pianos, string quartet and
  woodwinds
*Variations for Winds, Strings and Keyboards*,
  for orchestra
BEDFORD (42)
*The Death of Baldur*, school opera
*Of Beares, Foxes, and Many, Many Wonders*,
  for chorus and orchestra
McCABE (40)
*The Shadow of Light*, for orchestra
Motet for chorus
*Les Soirs Bleus*, for soprano, recorder, cello
  and harpsichord
COWIE (36)
*Columbine*, for soprano and chamber
  orchestra
*Brighella's World*, for baritone and piano
HOLLOWAY (36)
Serenade in C
Conundrums, for soprano and wind
  quintet
Idyll for small orchestra (1979–80)
Sonata for horn and orchestra (1979–80)
Adagio and Rondo for horn and orchestra
  (1979–80)
Aria for chamber orchestra (1979–80)
TAVENER (35)
*Akhmatova: Requiem*, for soprano and

576

baritone soli, brass, percussion and strings
*Greek Interlude*, for flute and piano
Six Abbasid Songs for four flutes and percussion
**FINNISSY** (33)
*Talawva*, for mezzo and ensemble
*. . . fairest noonday . . .*, for tenor and piano
*Alongside*, for ensemble
*Kagami-Jishi*, for flute and harp
*Grainger*, for piano
*Sikangnuga*, for flute
*Hinomi*, for percussion
*Sea and Sky*, orchestra (1979–80)
**PATTERSON** (32)
*Voices of Sleep*, for soprano, chorus and orchestra
**BERKELEY, M.** (31)
*Etude des fleurs*, for cello and piano
Sonata for violin and piano
*Rain*, for tenor, violin and cello
Organ Sonata
*Primavera*, for orchestra
*Fanfare and National Anthem*, for chorus and orchestra
**OLIVER** (29)
Study for piano
*A Dialogue Between Mary and Her Child*, for soprano, baritone and chorus
*Ballad of the Breadman*, carol for unison voices and piano/guitar
*The Dreaming of the Bones*, one-act opera
**KNUSSEN** (27)
*Coursing*, for chamber orchestra
Symphony No 3
*Songs and a Sea Interlude*, for soprano and orchestra (1979–80)
*Where the Wild Things Are*, opera (1979–80)
**MULDOWNEY** (27)
*Macbeth*, ballet music for orchestra
*Six Psalms*, for soli, chorus, ensemble and tape
*. . . In a Hall of Mirrors . . .*, for alto sax and piano
*A Little Piano Book*, twenty-four pieces

## 1980

**BANKS** and **PETTERSSON** died
**RUBBRA** (79)
*How Shall My Tongue Express?*, for unaccompanied chorus
Duo for cor anglais and piano
*Mass in Honour of Ste Teresa of Avila*, for unaccompanied chorus
Canzona for Brass in honour of Ste Cecilia

**ALWYN** (75)
*Leave Taking*, song cycle
Rhapsody for piano, violin, viola and cello
String Quartet No 3
**TIPPETT** (75)
*Wolf Trap Fanfare*, for brass ensemble
*The Mask of Time*, for soli, chorus and orchestra (1980–3)
**SIEGMEISTER** (71)
*Julietta*, opera
**CAGE** (68)
*Litany for the Whale*, vocal work
**LLOYD** (67)
*The Vigil of Venus*, for voices and orchestra
**PANUFNIK** (66)
Concertino for timpani, percussion and strings
String quartet No 2, *Messages*
*Iubilum, Celebracion Sinfonica*, for orchestra
Fanfare for four trumpets
**GINASTERA** (64)
Variations and Toccata on *Aurora lucis mitilat*, for organ
Cello Concerto No 2 (1980–1)
**BERNSTEIN** (62)
Divertimento for orchestra
*A Musical Toast*, for orchestra
*Touches*, for piano
**ROCHBERG** (62)
*Octet, A Grand Fantasia*
*Trio*, for clarinet, horn and piano
**SHAPEY** (59)
*Song of Songs II*, for baritone, ensemble and tape
*Song of Songs III*, for soprano, baritone, ensemble and tape
Four Etudes for violin
**FOSS** (58)
*Measure for Measure*, for tenor and chamber orchestra
*Curriculum Vitae With Time Bomb*, for accordion and percussion
*Night Music for John Lennon*, for brass quintet and orchestra
**HAMILTON** (58)
*Mass in A*, for chorus a capella
*Vespers*, for mixed chorus, two pianos, harp and percussion
*Dick Whittington*, lyric comedy (1980–1)
**NONO** (56)
*Fragmente-Stille*, for string quartet
**BERIO** (55)
*Entrata*, for orchestra
*Sequence IXa*, for clarinet
**FELDMAN** (54)
*Repertoire*, for violin, cello and piano

*The Turfan Fragments,* for orchestra
*Trio,* for violin, cello and piano
*Principal Sound for Organ*
**HENZE** (54)
*Pollicino,* opera for children
*El Rey de Harlem, Imaginary Theatre I,* for
  solo voice and eight instruments
*Barcarola,* for orchestra
*The Return of Ulysses,* after Monteverdi
**JOSEPHS** (53)
Consort Music for brass
Double-bass Concerto
Double-bass Sonata
*Tombeaux,* for organ
*Equus,* ballet
**MUSGRAVE** (52)
*The Last Twilight,* for chorus, brass and
  percussion
*From One to Another,* for viola and fifteen
  strings
**LEIGHTON** (51)
Fantasy on a Chorale for violin and organ
*Missa de Gloria,* organ solo
*Columba,* opera
*Animal Heaven,* for soprano, recorder, cello
  and harpsichord
*Missa Cornelia,* for treble voices and organ
**PREVIN** (51)
*Principals,* for orchestra
*Reflections,* for orchestra
**TAKEMITSU** (50)
*Far Calls Coming Far,* for violin and
  orchestra
**WILLIAMSON** (49)
Symphony No 5, *Aquero*
*Lament in memory of Lord Mountbatten of
  Burma,* for violin and string orchestra
*Little Mass of St Bernadette,* for voices and
  organ
*Ode for Queen Elizabeth,* for string
  orchestra
*Choric Hymn,* for mixed chorus
*Konstanz Fanfare,* for brass, percussion
  and organ
*Richmond Fanfare,* for brass, percussion
  and organ
**GOEHR** (48)
*Sinfonia,* for orchestra
**MEALE** (48)
String Quartet
**PENDERECKI** (47)
Symphony No 2
**BIRTWISTLE** (46)
*On the Sheer Threshold of the Night,*
  choral
**DAVIES, P. M.** (46)
*Cinderella,* children's opera

*The Yellow Cake Revue,* for voice and
*A Welcome to Orkney,* for chamber
  ensemble
*Little Quartet,* for string quartet
Symphony No 2
*Farewell to Stromness,* piano interlude
  *The Yellow Cake Revue*
*Yesnaby Ground,* piano interlude from *T
  Yellow Cake Revue*
**SCHNITTKE** (46)
*Minnesang,* for chorus (1980–1)
Symphony No 2 *St Florian*
**MAW** (45)
*The Ruin,* for SATB and solo horn
**SALLINEN** (45)
*Song Around a Song,* for children's choir
**BENNETT** (44)
Harpsichord Concerto
*Metamorphoses,* octet
*Puer Nobis,* for chorus
**BLAKE** (44)
*Capriccio,* for seven players
**REICH** (44)
*My Name Is – Ensemble Portrait (Octet),* for
  tape
**BEDFORD** (43)
*Fridiof's Saga,* school opera
*Requiem,* for soprano solo, chorus and
  orchestra
*Fridiof Kennings,* for saxophone quartet
**CROSSE** (43)
*A Year and a Day,* for solo clarinet
String Quartet
*Harvest Songs,* for choir and orchestra
*Voice from the Tomb,* for medium voice
  and piano
**McCABE** (41)
*Siberia,* for unaccompanied chorus
Violin Concerto No 2
*Portraits,* for flute and piano
Dances for trumpet and piano
*Mosaic (Study No 6),* for piano
**COWIE** (37)
*Harlequin,* for solo harp
*The Falls of Clyde,* for two pianos
*Commedia Lazzis,* for guitar
Concerto for orchestra
*Madrigals,* for twelve voices
*Leonardo,* for chamber orchestra
Symphony No 1 ('The American')
*Kelly,* opera
*Kelly – Nolan – Kelly,* for clarinet in A
*Kelly Variations,* for piano
**FERNEYHOUGH** (37)
*Funérailles Version II,* for harp and
  strings
String Quartet No 2

HOLLOWAY (37)
Ode for four winds and strings
*Wherever We May Be*, five songs for
  soprano and piano (1980–1)
TAVENER (36)
*Risen!* for chorus and orchestra
*Sappho: Lyrical Fragments*, for two
  sopranos and strings
FINNISSY (34)
*Lord Melbourne*, for soprano, clarinet and
  piano
*Green Bushes*, for contralto and piano
Piano Concerto No 5
*Boogie–Woogie*, for piano
*Nancarrow*, for piano
*Moon's Goin' Down*, for solo voice or
  instrument
Piano Concerto No 6 (1980–1)
*Nobody's Jig*, for string quartet
*Whitman*, for voice and instruments
  (1980–3)
PATTERSON (33)
*Sing Praises!*, for chorus and orchestra
*At the Still Point of the Turning World*, for
  ensemble
*Deception Pass*, for brass ensemble
BERKELEY, M. (32)
*American Suite*, for flute, recorder and
  cello/bassoon
Chamber Symphony
*Uprising*, symphony in one movement
OLIVER (30)
*The Key to the Zoo*, for narrator and
  instruments
*The Child from the Sea*, for solo, chorus and
  orchestra
*Wedding Anthem*, for treble voices and
  organ
*A String of Beads*, for chorus and orchestra
*Jacko's Play*, children's operetta
*A Man of Feeling*, for soprano, baritone and
  piano
MULDOWNEY (28)
Piano Trio
*Five Theatre Poems*, for baritone and piano
String Quartet No 2
*From 'Little Gidding'*, for baritone, treble
  and piano
*Theatre Poems*, for mezzo and ensemble


## 1981

THOMSON, V. (85)
Nineteen Piano Portraits
BERKELEY, L. (78)
Bagatelles for two pianos

RAINIER (78)
*Concertante for Two Winds*, for oboe,
  clarinet and orchestra
MACONCHY (74)
*Piccola Musica*, for violin, viola and cello
*Trittico*, for two oboes, bassoon and
  harpsichord
*Little Symphony*
CARTER (73)
*In Sleep, In Thunder*, for tenor and fourteen
  instruments
GILDER (70)
*Three Pastorals*, for orchestra
LUTOSLAWSKI (68)
*Grave*, for cello and piano
PANUFNIK (67)
*Sinfonia Votura*
GINASTERA (65)
Piano Sonata No 2
BERNSTEIN (63)
*Halil*, for flute and orchestra
SHAPEY (60)
Fanfare for brass quintet
FOSS (59)
*Solo*, for piano solo
*Solo Observed*, for piano and three
  instruments or for orchestra
HAMILTON (59)
Symphony No 3, *Spring*
Symphony No 4
*La Ricordanza*, for tenor and orchestra
*The Morning Watch*, for mixed chorus and
  ten wind instruments
NONO (57)
*Das Atmende Klarsein*, for bass flute and
  small chorus
*Fragment from Prometheus*, for three
  sopranos, chorus, bass flute, bass
  clarinet and tape
BERIO (56)
*La Vera Storia*, suite for orchestra
*Accordo*, for four groups of musicians
*Chorale on Sequence VIII*, for ensemble
*Sequence IXb*, for alto saxophone
BOULEZ (56)
*Répons*, for soloists, tape and ensemble
FELDMAN (55)
*Bass Clarinet and Percussion*
JOSEPHS (54)
*The Brontés*, overture
*Eight Aphorisms*, for trombone octet
Quartet Prelude in honour of Joseph
  Haydn
String Quartet No 4
*Testimony*, toccata for organ
*Blessings*, for chorus and organ
*Spring Songs*, for chorus

**MUSGRAVE** (53)
*Preipeteia*, for orchestra
*An Occurrence at Owl Creek Bridge*, radio
  opera
**LEIGHTON** (52)
*Household Pets*, for piano
*These are Thy Wonders*, for high voice and
  organ
**TAKEMITSU** (51)
*Rain Tree*, for three keyboards
*Towards the Sea*, for alto flute and guitar
*A Way Alone*, for string quartet
**WILLIAMSON** (50)
*Josip Broz Tito*, for baritone and orchestra
*Fontainbleau Fanfare*, for brass, percussion
  and organ
*Mass of the People of God*
**GOEHR** (49)
*Deux Etudes*, for orchestra
*Behold the Sun*, for soprano, vibraphone
  and chamber ensemble
**SHCHEDRIN** (49)
*Supplice de Pougatchev*, for choir a cappella
*Stanzas from Eugene Onegin*, for choir a
  capella
*The Frescoes of Dionysys*, for nine
  instruments
*Notebook for Youth*, fifteen pieces for piano
**BIRTWISTLE** (47)
*Pulse Sampler*, for oboe and claves
**DAVIES, P. M.** (47)
*The Medium*, monodrama for
  mezzo-soprano
Piano Sonata
*The Rainbow*, music-theatre for children
*Hill Runes*, for guitar
*The Bairns of Brugh*, for chamber ensemble
Tenor arias from *The Martyrdom of St
  Magnus*
*Salome*, reduction of ballet score for theatre
  orchestra
*Little Quartet No 2*, for string quartet
*Lullabye for Lucy*, for mixed chorus
Brass Quintet
*Seven Songs Home*, for children's voices
**MATHIAS** (47)
*Rex Gloriae*, for unaccompanied voices
**SCHNITTKE** (47)
*Two Little Pieces for Organ*
String Quartet
Violin Concerto No 4 (1981–2)
**MAW** (46)
Flute Quartet
*Summer Dances*, for youth orchestra
**BENNETT** (45)
*Six Tunes for the Instruction of Singing-birds*,
  flute solo

Music for string quartet
Impromptu on the name of Haydn, for
  piano
Sonatina for clarinet solo
*Noctuary*, ballet, for piano
*Vocalise*, for soprano and piano
*Isadora*, ballet
**REICH** (45)
*Tehillim*, for voices and ensemble
**BEDFORD** (44)
*Alleluia Timpanis* (revised)
*Prelude for a Maritime Nation*, for
  orchestra
*Ocean Star a Dreaming Song*, for youth
  orchestra
Symphony for twelve musicians
Wind Sextet
String Quartet
Vocoder Sextet
*Elegy and Caprice*, for oboe and piano
Toccata for piano
*Sonata in One Movement*, for piano
**CROSSE** (44)
*Elegy and Scherzo Alla Marcia*, for string
  orchestra
*Wildboy*, ballet score
*Fear No More*, for oboe, oboe d'amore and
  cor anglais
*Peace for Brass*
*Dreascanon I*, for choir, piano and
  percussion
**McCABE** (42)
*Desert I: Lizard*, for woodwind and
  percussion
*Desert II: Horizon*, for ten brass
  instruments
*Afternoons and Afterwards*, for piano
*Music's Empire*, for soli, chorus and
  orchestra
**COWIE** (38)
*Kelly Choruses*, for voices and harp
*Choral Symphony (Symphonies of Rain, Sea
  and Speed)* (1981–2)
**FERNEYHOUGH** (38)
*Lemma – Icon – Epigram*, for piano
*Superscripto*, for solo piccolo
**HOLLOWAY** (38)
*Clarissa Symphony*, for soprano, tenor and
  orchestra
Sonata for Violin Solo
*Brand*, dramatic ballad for soli, chorus,
  organ and orchestra
*The Lovers' Well*, for bass-baritone and
  piano
*From Hills and Valleys*, for brass band
  (1981–2)
*Men Marching*, for brass band (1981–2)

TAVENER (37)
*Prayer for the World*, for sixteen solo voices
*Funeral Ikos*, for chorus
*Mandelion*, for organ
*Trisagion*, for brass quintet
*The Great Canon of the Ode to Saint Andrew of Crete*, for chorus
FINNISSEY (35)
Piano Concerto No 7
*Kelir*, for six voices
*Tree Setting*, for piano
*Jiseï*, for ensemble
*Reels*, for piano
*White Rain*, for piano or clavichord
*Duru-duru*, for mezzo, flute, percussion and piano
*Stomp*, for accordion
*An-dimironnai*, for solo cello
*Keroiylu*, for oboe, bassoon and piano
*Yalli*, for solo cello
*Terekkeme*, for solo cembalo
*Rushes*, for piano
PATTERSON (34)
*The Canterbury Psalms*, for chorus and orchestra
Concerto for orchestra
BERKELEY, M. (33)
String Quartet No 1
String Quartet No 2
*Wessex Graves*, for voice and harp
*Flames*, for orchestra (1981–2)
OLIVER (31)
Wind Octet
Mass for unaccompanied chorus
MULDOWNEY (29)
*In Dark Times*, for soli and ensemble
*Sports et Divertissements*, for reciter and ensemble

## 1982

ORFF died
JACOB (87)
Flute Concerto No 2, for flute and strings
SESSIONS (86)
Concerto for orchestra
THOMSON, V. (86)
Ten Etudes for piano
COPLAND (82)
*Midday Thoughts*, for piano
*Proclamation*, for piano
WALTON (80)
*Passacaglia*, for solo cello
*Prologo e Fantasia*, for orchestra
BERKELEY, L. (79)
Mazurka for piano

Sonnet for high voice and piano
*Faldon Park*, opera
MACONCHY (75)
*My Dark Heart*, for soprano and ensemble
Wind Quintet
LUTOSLAWSKI (69)
*Mini Overture*
PANUFNIK (68)
*A Procession for Peace*, for orchestra
GINASTERA (66)
Piano Sonata No 3
BERNSTEIN (64)
*A Quiet Place and Trouble in Tahiti*, opera (1982–4)
ROCHBERG (64)
String Quartet
*The Confidence Man*, opera
ARNOLD (61)
Trumpet Concerto
HAMILTON (60)
*Love is Life's Spring*, for soprano and piano
*The Passion According to St Mark*, for soli and chorus
*Lancelot*, opera (1982–3)
LIGETI (59)
Trio for violin, horn and piano
*Three Fantasies*, for choir a capella
*Magyar Studies*, for choir a capella
NONO (58)
*Donde Estas Hermano?*, for female voices
*Quando Stanno Morendo*, for female vocal quartet, flute, cello and electronics
FELDMAN (56)
*For John Cage*, for violin and piano
*Three Voices*, for sopranos and tape
JOSEPHS (55)
*High Spirits*, overture
Percussion Concerto, with brass
Two Flute Studies
*The Montgolfiers' Famous Flying Globe*, operetta for schools
Viola Concerto
MUSGRAVE (54)
*Fanfare*, for brass quintet
LEIGHTON (53)
Fantasy-Octet, *Homage to Percy Grainger*
TAKEMITSU (52)
*Grass*, for male chorus
*Rain Tree Sketch*, for piano
*Rain Spell*, for flute, clarinet, harp, piano and vibraphone
*Rain Coming*, for chamber orchestra
GOEHR (50)
*Behold the Sun*, opera (1982–4)
SHCHEDRIN (50)
Solemn Overture
Concertino for chorus a cappella

581

**WOOD** (50)
Symphony
**DICKINSON** (49)
*The Unicorns*, for soprano and brass band
**DAVIES, P. M.** (48)
*Songs of Hoy*, masque for children's voices
*Sea Eagle*, for horn
*Image, Reflection, Shadow*, for ensemble
Sinfonia Concertante for chamber
  orchestra
Organ Sonata
*Tallis: Four Voluntaries*, for brass quintet or
  band
*Gesualdo: Two Motets*, for brass quintet or
  band
*March – The Pole Star*, for brass quintet
  or band
**MATHIAS** (48)
*Lux Aeterna*, for soli, chorus, organ and
  orchestra
*Salvator Mundi*, for female choir, piano
  duet, percussion and strings
*Antiphonies*, for organ
**SCHNITTKE** (48)
Septet
*Seid Nüchtern und Wachet . . .*, cantata
**MAW** (47)
*Night Thoughts*, for solo flute
*Spring Music*, for orchestra (1982–3)
String Quartet No 2
**SALLINEN** (47)
*Shadows*, prelude for orchestra
**BENNETT** (46)
*Anniversaries*, for ensemble
*Freda's Fandango*, for ensemble
*After Syrinx*, for oboe and piano
*Summer Music*, for flute and piano
**BLAKE** (46)
String Quartet No 3
*Change is Going to Come*, for mezzo,
  baritone, chorus and four players
**REICH** (46)
*Vermont Counterpoint*, for ensemble and
  tape
**BEDFORD** (45)
*The Juniper Tree*, for soprano, recorder and
  harpsichord
**CROSSE** (45)
*A Wake*, for flute, clarinet, cello and piano
*Trio: Rhymes and Reasons*, for clarinet, cello
  and piano
**McCABE** (43)
Concerto for Orchestra
*Desert III: Landscape*, for violin, cello and
  piano
String Quartet No 4
*Lamentation Rag*, for piano

**COWIE** (39)
*Kelly Ballet*
Harp Concerto
*Kate Kelly's Roadshow*, music-theatre
Symphony No 2 ('The Australian')
**FERNEYHOUGH** (39)
*Carceri d' Invenzione*, for chamber orchestra
**HOLLOWAY** (39)
*From Hills and Valleys*, for brass band
Suite for saxophone
*Anthem*, for unaccompanied chorus
*Women in War*, review for four female
  soloists and piano
*Serenata Notturna*, for four horns and small
  orchestra
*Showpiece* (Concertino No 4) for fourteen
  players (1982–3)
**TAVENER** (38)
*Towards the Son: Ritual Procession*, for
  chamber orchestra
*Doxa*, for chorus
*Lord's Prayer*, for chorus
*Mandoodles*, for a young pianist
*The Lamb*, for unaccompanied chorus
**FINNISSEY** (36)
*Warara*, for tenor, flute, clarinet and two
  percussion
*Aijal*, for flute, oboe and percussion
*Banumbirr*, for ensemble
*Tya*, for ensemble
*Mississippi Hornpipe*, for violin and piano
*Dilok*, for oboe and percussion
*Gerhana*, for solo percussion
*Anninnia*, for soprano and piano
*Ouraa*, for ensemble (1982–3)
*Lyrics and Limericks*, for voice and piano
  (1982–4)
**PATTERSON** (35)
Sinfonia for strings
**BERKELEY, M.** (34)
Nocturne for flute, harp, violin, viola and
  cello
Piano Trio
*Sonata in One Movement*, for guitar
*Gregorian Variations*, for orchestra
*The Romance of the Rose*, for orchestra
*Easter*, anthem for choir, organ and brass
*The Crocodile and Father William*, for girls'
  choir

# 1983

**GINASTERA, HOWELLS, LUTYENS** and
**WALTON** died
**RAINIER** (80)
*Grand Duo*, for cello and piano

**TIPPETT** (78)
*Festal Brass with Blues,* for brass ensemble
**MACONCHY** (76)
*Tribute,* for violin and woodwinds
*L'Horloge,* for soprano, clarinet and piano
Music for strings
**CARTER** (74)
*Triple Duo*
*Changes,* for guitar
**LUTOSLAWSKI** (70)
fp Symphony No 3
*Chain I,* for small orchestra
**PANUFNIK** (69)
*Arbor Cosmica,* for twelve solo strings
**ROCHBERG** (65)
Oboe Concerto
**NONO** (59)
*Guai Ai Gelidi Mostri,* for two contraltos,
  ensemble and electronics
*Homage to Gyorgy Kürtag,* for contralto,
  bass tuba, flute and electronics
**BERIO** (58)
*Song,* for clarinet solo
**FELDMAN** (57)
*Crippled Symmetry,* for flute, piano and
  percussion
*Clarinet and String Quartet*
String Quartet No 2
**HENZE** (57)
*Three Auden Songs,* for tenor and piano
**TAKEMITSU** (53)
*From far beyond Chrysanthemums and
  November fog,* for violin and piano
*Rocking Mirror Daybreak,* for violin duo
*Star Isle,* for orchestra
*Orion,* for cello and orchestra
*Towards the edge of dream,* for guitar and
  orchestra (1983–4)
**MEALE** (51)
Aria from *Voss,* for soprano, baritone and
  orchestra
**PENDERECKI** (50)
*Requiem,* for soli, chorus and orchestra
**BIRTWISTLE** (49)
*Deowa,* for soprano and clarinet
*Duets for Storab,* for two flutes
**DAVIES, P. M.** (49)
*Birthday Music for John,* trio for flute, viola
  and cello
*Into the Labyrinth,* cantata
*Sinfonietta Accademica,* for chamber
  orchestra
**MATHIAS** (49)
Symphony No 2
*Tantum Ergo,* for choir and organ
*Angelus,* for women's voices
*Alleluja! Christ is risen!,* anthem

Horn Concerto
*Missa brevis*
*Let Us Now Praise Famous Men,* for chorus
  and orchestra
Organ Concerto
Violin Sonata No 2
**SCHNITTKE** (49)
*Schall und Hall,* for trombone and organ
**SALLINEN** (48)
*The Iron Age,* suite for soprano, choir and
  orchestra
*The King Goes Forth to France,* opera
**BENNETT** (47)
*Memento,* for flute and string orchestra
Concerto for wind quintet
Guitar Sonata
*Letters to Lindbergh,* for female voices and
  piano duet
*Seachange,* for unaccompanied chorus
**BLAKE** (47)
*Rise, Dove,* for baritone and orchestra
**REICH** (47)
*Eight Lines,* arrangement of Octet for
  chamber orchestra
*The Desert Music,* for chorus and orchestra
**BEDFORD** (46)
*The Valley Sleeper, the Children, the Snakes
  and the Giant,* for orchestra
*Five Diversions,* for two flutes
**CROSSE** (46)
*Wave Songs,* for cello and piano
**COWIE** (40)
*Missa Brevis* (Mass for Peace)
*Ancient Voices,* for four voices
String Quartet No 3 ('Creative Arts
  Quartet')
String Quartet No 4 ('Australia II')
**FERNEYHOUGH** (40)
*Adagissimo,* for string quartet
**HOLLOWAY** (40)
Second Idyll for small orchestra
Viola Concerto (1983–4)
Serenade in E♭ for wind quintet and
  string quintet (1983–4)
**TAVENER** (39)
*He Hath Entered the Heven,* for
  unaccompanied trebles
*To a Child Dancing in the Wind,* for soprano,
  flute, harp and viola
**FINNISSEY** (37)
*Vaudeville,* for mezzo, baritone and
  ensemble
*Australian Sea Shanties,* for voices,
  recorders and piano
*Soda Fountain,* for voices and cymbals
*Ngano,* for soli, chorus, flute and
  percussion (1983–4)

PATTERSON (36)
*Mass of the Sea,* for soli, chorus and
  orchestra
BERKELEY, M. (35)
Cello Concerto
*Or Shall We Die?* oratorio
MULDOWNEY (31)
Piano Concerto
*The Duration of Exile,* for mezzo and
  ensemble
*A Second Show,* for contralto and ensemble


## 1984

JACOB died
CARTER (75)
*Canon For 4,* 'Homage to William', for flute,
  bass clarinet, violin and cello
*Riconoscenza,* for solo violin
TAKEMITSU (54)
*Vers l'arc en ciel, Palma,* for guitar, oboe
  d'amore and orchestra
WOOD (52)
Piano Trio
DICKINSON (51)
Piano Concerto
DAVIES, P. M. (50)
*Agnus Dei,* for two sopranos, viola and
  cello
Sonatine for violin and cimbalom
*Unbroken Circle,* for ensemble
*The Number 11 Bus,* music theatre
Guitar Sonata
*One Star, At Last,* carol for chorus
Symphony No 3

BENNETT (48)
*After Syrinx II,* for marimba
*Nonsense,* for chorus and piano duet
*Five Sonnets of Louise Labé,* for soprano and
  eleven players
*Lullay Mine Liking,* for unaccompanied
  chorus
BEDFORD (47)
♩=120, for bass clarinet and tape
HOLLOWAY (41)
*Moments of Vision,* cycle for speaker and
  four players
Romanza for oboe and strings
*On Hope,* cantata for soprano, mezzo and
  string quartet
TAVENER (40)
*Sixteen Haiku of Seferis,* for soprano, tenor
  and ensemble
*Ikon of Light,* for chorus and string trio
*Little Missenden Calm,* for oboe, clarinet,
  bassoon and horn
*Vigil Service,* for a capella choir, four
  violins and organ
*Chant,* for solo guitar
*Mini Song Cycle for Gina,* for voice and
  piano
FINNISSEY (38)
*Câtana,* for ensemble
*Delal,* for trumpet and piano
BERKELEY, M. (36)
*Funerals and Fandangos,* for solo violin
*Music from Chaucer,* for brass quintet
Horn Concerto
KNUSSEN (32)
*Higglety Pigglety Pop!,* opera
MULDOWNEY (32)
Saxophone Concerto

584

# PART THREE

This timeline enables the reader to see at a glance when each composer was born and died, as well as who was contemporary with whom. Horizontal lines begin with the year of the composer's birth, and end with that of his death. At the end of each line the composer's age at death is also given.

Composers are listed chronologically according to their dates of birth. At the top of each new page there is in small print the name at the end of the preceding page, to show continuity.

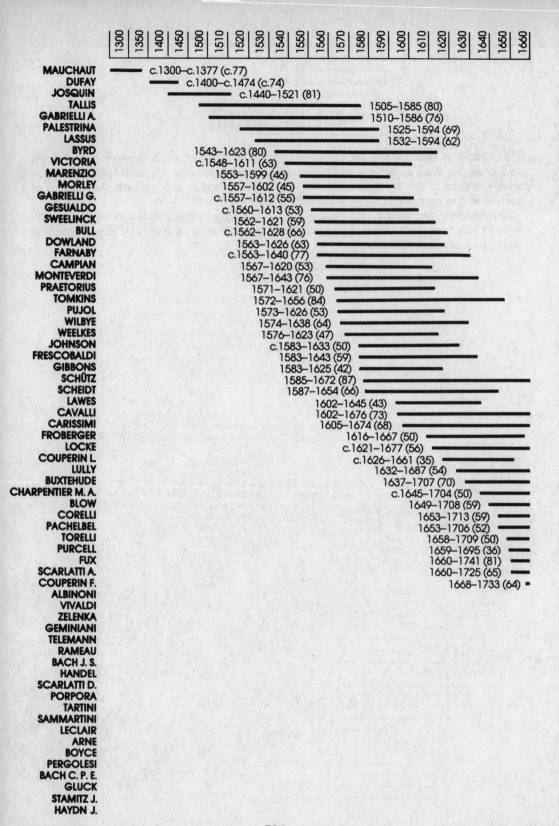

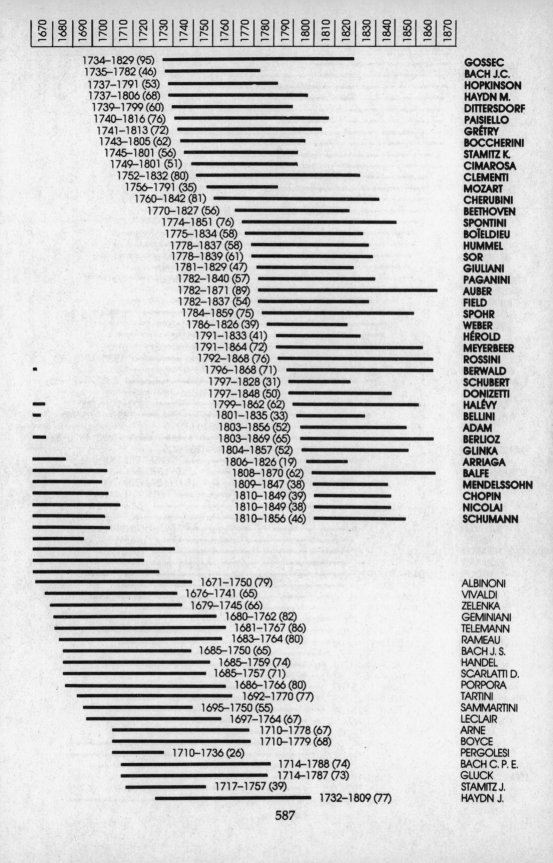

| 1670 | 1680 | 1690 | 1700 | 1710 | 1720 | 1730 | 1740 | 1750 | 1760 | 1770 | 1780 | 1790 | 1800 | 1810 | 1820 | 1830 | 1840 | 1850 | 1860 | 1870 |

1734–1829 (95) **GOSSEC**
1735–1782 (46) **BACH J.C.**
1737–1791 (53) **HOPKINSON**
1737–1806 (68) **HAYDN M.**
1739–1799 (60) **DITTERSDORF**
1740–1816 (76) **PAISIELLO**
1741–1813 (72) **GRÉTRY**
1743–1805 (62) **BOCCHERINI**
1745–1801 (56) **STAMITZ K.**
1749–1801 (51) **CIMAROSA**
1752–1832 (80) **CLEMENTI**
1756–1791 (35) **MOZART**
1760–1842 (81) **CHERUBINI**
1770–1827 (56) **BEETHOVEN**
1774–1851 (76) **SPONTINI**
1775–1834 (58) **BOÏELDIEU**
1778–1837 (58) **HUMMEL**
1778–1839 (61) **SOR**
1781–1829 (47) **GIULIANI**
1782–1840 (57) **PAGANINI**
1782–1871 (89) **AUBER**
1782–1837 (54) **FIELD**
1784–1859 (75) **SPOHR**
1786–1826 (39) **WEBER**
1791–1833 (41) **HÉROLD**
1791–1864 (72) **MEYERBEER**
1792–1868 (76) **ROSSINI**
1796–1868 (71) **BERWALD**
1797–1828 (31) **SCHUBERT**
1797–1848 (50) **DONIZETTI**
1799–1862 (62) **HALÉVY**
1801–1835 (33) **BELLINI**
1803–1856 (52) **ADAM**
1803–1869 (65) **BERLIOZ**
1804–1857 (52) **GLINKA**
1806–1826 (19) **ARRIAGA**
1808–1870 (62) **BALFE**
1809–1847 (38) **MENDELSSOHN**
1810–1849 (39) **CHOPIN**
1810–1849 (38) **NICOLAI**
1810–1856 (46) **SCHUMANN**

1671–1750 (79) **ALBINONI**
1676–1741 (65) **VIVALDI**
1679–1745 (66) **ZELENKA**
1680–1762 (82) **GEMINIANI**
1681–1767 (86) **TELEMANN**
1683–1764 (80) **RAMEAU**
1685–1750 (65) **BACH J. S.**
1685–1759 (74) **HANDEL**
1685–1757 (71) **SCARLATTI D.**
1686–1766 (80) **PORPORA**
1692–1770 (77) **TARTINI**
1695–1750 (55) **SAMMARTINI**
1697–1764 (67) **LECLAIR**
1710–1778 (67) **ARNE**
1710–1779 (68) **BOYCE**
1710–1736 (26) **PERGOLESI**
1714–1788 (74) **BACH C. P. E.**
1714–1787 (73) **GLUCK**
1717–1757 (39) **STAMITZ J.**
1732–1809 (77) **HAYDN J.**

(Schumann) ████████████████████ 1810–1856 (46)
LISZT ████████████████████████████ 1811–1886 (74)
THOMAS ██████████████████████████████ 1811–1896 (84)
FLOTOW ██████████████████████████ 1812–1883 (70)
ALKAN ████████████████████████████ 1813–1888 (74)
DARGOMIZHSKY ██████████████████ 1813–1869 (55)
VERDI ████████████████████████████████ 1813–1901 (87)
WAGNER ██████████████████████████ 1813–1883 (69)
GADE ████████████████████████████ 1817–1890 (73)
GOUNOD ██████████████████████████████ 1818–1893 (75)
LITOLFF ████████████████████████████ 1818–1891 (73)
OFFENBACH ██████████████████████ 1819–1880 (61)
SUPPÉ ████████████████████████████ 1819–1895 (76)
VIEUXTEMPS ██████████████████████ 1820–1881 (61)
RAFF ████████████████████████ 1822–1882 (60)
FRANCK ██████████████████████████ 1822–1890 (67)
LALO ██████████████████████████ 1823–1892 (69)
BRUCKNER ████████████████████████████ 1824–1896 (72)
SMETANA ████████████████████████ 1824–1884 (60)
STRAUSS J. jun. ██████████████████████████ 1825–1899 (73)
GOTTSCHALK ████████████████ 1829–1869 (40)
RUBINSTEIN ██████████████████████ 1829–1894 (64)
GOLDMARK ██████████████████████████████ 1830–1915 (84)
BORODIN ████████████████████ 1833–1887 (53)
BRAHMS ████████████████████████ 1833–1897 (63)
PONCHIELLI ████████████████████ 1834–1886 (51)
CUI ██████████████████████████████ 1835–1918 (83)
WIENIAWSKI ████████████████ 1835–1880 (44)
SAINT-SAËNS ████████████████████████████████ 1835–1921 (86)
DELIBES ████████████████████ 1836–1891 (54)
BALAKIREV ██████████████████████████ 1837–1910 (73)
WALDTEUFEL ████████████████████████████ 1837–1915 (78)
BIZET ██████████████ 1838–1875 (36)
BRUCH ██████████████████████████████ 1838–1920 (82)
MUSSORGSKY ████████████████ 1839–1881 (42)
STAINER ██████████████████████ 1840–1901 (60)
TCHAIKOWSKY ████████████████████ 1840–1893 (53)
CHABRIER ████████████████████ 1841–1894 (53)
DVOŘÁK ██████████████████████ 1841–1904 (62)
MASSENET ████████████████████████ 1842–1912 (70)
BOITO ██████████████████████████ 1842–1918 (76)
SULLIVAN ████████████████████ 1842–1900 (58)
GRIEG ██████████████████████ 1843–1907 (64)
RIMSKY-KORSAKOV ██████████████████████ 1844–1908 (64)
SARASATE ██████████████████████ 1844–1908 (64)
WIDOR ████████████████████████████████ 1844–1937 (93)
FAURÉ ██████████████████████████ 1845–1924 (79)
DUPARC ██████████████████████████████ 1848–1933 (85)
PARRY ████████████████████████ 1848–1918 (70)
GODARD ████████████████ 1849–1895 (45)
d'INDY ████████████████████████████ 1851–1931 (80)
STANFORD ████████████████████████ 1852–1924 (71)
TARREGA ████████████████████ 1852–1909 (57)
MESSAGER ██████████████████████████ 1853–1929 (76)
CATALANI ██████████████ 1854–1893 (39)
MOSKOWSKI ████████████████████████ 1854–1925 (70)
HUMPERDINCK ███████████████████████ 1854–1921 (67)
JANÁČEK ██████████████████████████ 1854–1928 (74)
CHAUSSON ████████████████ 1855–1899 (44)
LIADOV ██████████████████ 1855–1914 (59)
SINDING ████████████████████████████ 1856–1941 (85)
CHAMINADE ██████████████████████████████ 1857–1944 (86)
ELGAR ██████████████████████████ 1857–1934 (76)
LEONCAVALLO ██████████████████████ 1858–1919 (61)
PUCCINI ██████████████████████ 1858–1924 (65)
SMYTH ██████████████████████████████ 1858–1944 (86)

1858–1944 (86) (Smyth)
1859–1935 (75) IPPOLITOV-IVANOV
1860–1909 (48) ALBÉNIZ
1860–1956 (95) CHARPENTIER G.
1860–1908 (47) MACDOWELL
1860–1903 (42) WOLF
1860–1941 (80) PADEREWSKI
1860–1911 (51) MAHLER
1861–1906 (44) ARENSKY
1861–1935 (74) LOEFFLER
1862–1897 (35) BOËLLMANN
1862–1918 (55) DEBUSSY
1862–1934 (72) DELIUS
1862–1936 (74) GERMAN
1863–1945 (81) MASCAGNI
1863–1919 (56) PARKER
1863–1937 (73) PIERNÉ
1864–1932 (67) d'ALBERT
1864–1949 (85) STRAUSS R.
1864–1955 (91) ROPARTZ
1865–1935 (69) DUKAS
1865–1936 (70) GLAZUNOV
1865–1957 (91) SIBELIUS
1865–1931 (66) NIELSON
1866–1925 (59) SATIE
1866–1950 (84) CILÈA
1866–1924 (58) BUSONI
1867–1944 (77) BEACH
1867–1948 (81) GIORDANO
1867–1916 (48) GRANADOS
1867–1950 (83) KOECHLIN
1868–1946 (78) BANTOCK
1869–1941 (71) DAVIES W.
1869–1937 (68) ROUSSEL
1870–1948 (78) LEHÁR
1870–1958 (87) SCHMITT
1870–1949 (78) NOVÁK
1871–1942 (70) ZEMLINSKY
1872–1960 (88) ALFVÉN
1872–1915 (43) SKRIABIN
1872–1958 (85) VAUGHAN WILLIAMS
1873–1943 (69) RACHMANINOV
1873–1916 (43) REGER
1873–1953 (79) JONGEN
1874–1934 (59) HOLST
1874–1951 (76) SCHOENBERG
1874–1939 (64) SCHMIDT
1874–1935 (61) SUK
1874–1954 (79) IVES
1875–1912 (37) COLERIDGE-TAYLOR
1875–1937 (62) RAVEL
1875–1956 (81) GLIÈRE
1875–1947 (71) HAHN
1876–1972 (96) BRIAN
1876–1971 (95) RUGGLES
1876–1946 (69) FALLA
1876–1948 (72) WOLF-FERRARI
1876–1951 (75) CARPENTER
1877–1969 (92) AUBERT
1877–1960 (82) DOHNÁNYI
1877–1953 (75) QUILTER
1878–1960 (82) BOUGHTON
1878–1934 (55) SCHREKER
1878–1958 (80) HOLBROOKE
1879–1970 (91) SCOTT
1879–1962 (82) IRELAND

| Name | Dates |
|---|---|
| (Ireland) | 1879–1962 (82) |
| RESPIGHI | 1879–1936 (56) |
| BRIDGE | 1879–1941 (61) |
| CANTELOUPE | 1879–1957 (78) |
| HARTY | 1879–1941 (61) |
| BLOCH | 1880–1959 (78) |
| MEDTNER | 1880–1951 (71) |
| PIZZETTI | 1880–1968 (87) |
| BARTÓK | 1881–1945 (64) |
| ENESCO | 1881–1955 (73) |
| MIASKOWSKI | 1881–1950 (69) |
| GRAINGER | 1882–1961 (78) |
| KODÁLY | 1882–1967 (84) |
| MALIPIERO | 1882–1973 (91) |
| PONCÉ | 1882–1948 (65) |
| STRAVINSKY | 1882–1971 (88) |
| TURINA | 1882–1949 (66) |
| BAX | 1883–1953 (69) |
| CASELLA | 1883–1947 (63) |
| BERNERS | 1883–1950 (66) |
| PARKER | 1883–1919 (36) |
| SZYMANOWSKI | 1883–1937 (54) |
| WEBERN | 1883–1945 (61) |
| GRIFFES | 1884–1920 (35) |
| GRUENBERG | 1884–1964 (79) |
| BERG | 1885–1935 (50) |
| BUTTERWORTH | 1885–1916 (31) |
| RIEGGER | 1885–1961 (75) |
| TAYLOR | 1885–1966 (80) |
| WELLESZ | 1885–1974 (89) |
| VARÈSE | 1885–1965 (79) |
| COATES | 1886–1957 (71) |
| SCHOECK | 1886–1957 (70) |
| DUPRÉ | 1886–1971 (85) |
| TOCH | 1887–1964 (76) |
| VILLA-LOBOS | 1887–1959 (72) |
| DARKE | 1888–1976 (88) |
| MARTIN | 1890–1974 (84) |
| MARTINŮ | 1890–1959 (69) |
| IBERT | 1890–1962 (71) |
| GURNEY | 1890–1937 (47) |
| BLISS | 1891–1975 (83) |
| PROKOFIEV | 1891–1953 (61) |
| GRANDJANY | 1891–1975 (83) |
| GROFÉ | 1892–1972 (80) |
| HOWELLS | 1892–1983 (90) |
| MILHAUD | 1892–1974 (81) |
| HONEGGER | 1892–1955 (63) |
| BENJAMIN | 1893–1960 (66) |
| MOORE | 1893–1969 (75) |
| ROGERS | 1893–1968 (75) |
| MOERAN | 1894–1950 (55) |
| PISTON | 1894–1976 (82) |
| WARLOCK | 1894–1930 (36) |
| HINDEMITH | 1895–1963 (68) |
| ORFF | 1895–1982 (87) |
| JACOB | 1895–1984 (88) |
| CASTELNUOVO-TEDESCO | 1895–1963 (68) |
| SOWERBY | 1895–1968 (73) |
| WEINBERGER | 1896–1967 (71) |
| GERHARD | 1896–1970 (73) |
| ROBERTSON | 1896–1971 (74) |
| HANSON | 1896 |
| THOMSON | 1896 |
| SESSIONS | 1896 |
| COWELL | 1897–1965 (68) |
| KORNGOLD | 1897–1957 (60) |

| Dates | Composer |
|---|---|
| 1897–1957 (60) | (Korngold) |
| 1897 | TANSMAN |
| 1898–1937 (38) | GERSHWIN |
| 1898–1979 (81) | HARRIS |
| 1899–1963 (64) | POULENC |
| 1899–1978 (79) | CHÁVEZ |
| 1899 | AURIC |
| 1899–1984 (85) | THOMPSON |
| 1900–1950 (50) | WEILL |
| 1900–1959 (58) | ANTHEIL |
| 1900 | BUSH A. |
| 1900 | COPLAND |
| 1900 | KRENEK |
| 1901–1956 (55) | FINZI |
| 1901 | RUBBRA |
| 1902 | DURUFLÉ |
| 1902 | RODRIGO |
| 1902–1983 (80) | WALTON |
| 1903–1978 (74) | KHACHATURIAN |
| 1903 | BERKELEY L. |
| 1903 | RAINIER |
| 1903–1975 (72) | BLACHER |
| 1904–1949 (45) | SKALKOTIAS |
| 1904–1975 (71) | DALLAPICCOLA |
| 1904 | KABALEVSKY |
| 1905–1964 (58) | BLITZSTEIN |
| 1905–1951 (45) | LAMBERT |
| 1905–1960 (55) | SEIBER |
| 1905–1971 (66) | RAWSTHORNE |
| 1905 | ALWYN |
| 1905 | TIPPETT |
| 1906–1973 (67) | FRANKEL |
| 1906–1975 (68) | SHOSTAKOVITCH |
| 1906 | COOKE |
| 1906–1983 (76) | LUTYENS |
| 1907 | MACONCHY |
| 1908 | CARTER |
| 1908 | MESSIAEN |
| 1909 | SEIGMEISTER |
| 1909 | HOLMBOE |
| 1910–1971 (60) | STILL |
| 1910 | BARBER |
| 1910 | SCHUMAN |
| 1911–1980 (68) | PETTERSSON |
| 1911 | MENOTTI |
| 1911 | GILDER |
| 1912–1978 (65) | GILLIS |
| 1912 | CAGE |
| 1912 | FRANCAIX |
| 1912 | JONES |
| 1913–1976 (63) | BRITTEN |
| 1913 | LUTOSLAWSKI |
| 1913 | GOULD |
| 1913 | LLOYD |
| 1914–1962 (48) | FINE |
| 1914 | MELLERS |
| 1914 | PANUFNIK |
| 1915 | DIAMOND |
| 1916 | BABBITT |
| 1916–1983 (67) | GINASTERA |
| 1917 | ARNELL |
| 1918 | BERNSTEIN |
| 1918 | ROCHBERG |
| 1920 | FRICKER |
| 1920 | BUSH G. |
| 1920 | SHAPERO |

591

| | 1920 | 1930 | 1940 | 1950 | 1960 | 1970 | 1980 |
|---|---|---|---|---|---|---|---|

| Name | Year | |
|---|---|---|
| (Shapero) | 1920 | ——————————————— |
| ARNOLD | 1921 | ——————————————— |
| SHAPEY | 1921 | ——————————————— |
| SIMPSON | 1921 | ——————————————— |
| FOSS | 1922 | ——————————————— |
| HAMILTON | 1922 | ——————————————— |
| XENAKIS | 1922 | ——————————————— |
| LIGETI | 1923 | ——————————————— |
| MENNIN | 1923 | ——————————————— |
| BANKS | | 1923–1980 (56) |
| DODGSON | 1924 | ——————————————— |
| NONO | 1924 | ——————————————— |
| BOULEZ | 1925 | ——————————————— |
| BERIO | 1925 | ——————————————— |
| SCHÜLLER | 1925 | ——————————————— |
| THEODORAKIS | 1925 | ——————————————— |
| BROWN | 1926 | ——————————————— |
| FELDMAN | 1926 | ——————————————— |
| HENZE | 1926 | ——————————————— |
| KURTÁG | 1926 | ——————————————— |
| JOSEPHS | 1927 | ——————————————— |
| JOUBERT | 1927 | ——————————————— |
| MUSGRAVE | 1928 | ——————————————— |
| KORTE | 1928 | ——————————————— |
| STOCKHAUSEN | 1928 | ——————————————— |
| CRUMB | 1929 | ——————————————— |
| PREVIN | 1929 | ——————————————— |
| HODDINOTT | 1929 | ——————————————— |
| LEIGHTON | 1929 | ——————————————— |
| McCABE | 1930 | ——————————————— |
| TAKEMITSU | 1930 | ——————————————— |
| WILLIAMSON | 1931 | ——————————————— |
| GOEHR | 1932 | ——————————————— |
| SHCHREDIN | 1932 | ——————————————— |
| WOOD | 1932 | ——————————————— |
| MEALE | 1932 | ——————————————— |
| CROSSE | 1933 | ——————————————— |
| PENDERECKI | 1933 | ——————————————— |
| BIRTWISTLE | 1934 | ——————————————— |
| DAVIES P. M. | 1934 | ——————————————— |
| DICKINSON | 1934 | ——————————————— |
| MATHIAS | 1934 | ——————————————— |
| SCHNITTKE | 1934 | ——————————————— |
| MAW | 1935 | ——————————————— |
| SALLINEN | 1935 | ——————————————— |
| BENNETT | 1936 | ——————————————— |
| BLAKE | 1936 | ——————————————— |
| REICH | 1936 | ——————————————— |
| BEDFORD | 1937 | ——————————————— |
| CROSSE | 1937 | ——————————————— |
| NILSSON | 1937 | ——————————————— |
| GLASS | 1937 | ——————————————— |
| FERNEYHOUGH | 1943 | ————————————— |
| HOLLOWAY | 1943 | ————————————— |
| COWIE | 1943 | ————————————— |
| TAVENER | 1944 | ————————————— |
| FINNISEY | 1946 | ———————————— |
| PATTERSON | 1947 | ———————————— |
| BERKELEY M. | 1948 | ———————————— |
| OLIVER | 1950 | ——————————— |
| KNUSSEN | 1952 | ——————————— |
| MULDOWNEY | 1952 | ——————————— |